"This book will be of great benefit to the entire Exponential-e engineering team."
— CHRIS CHRISTOU
    Engineering Manager
    Exponential-e

"An extremely valuable tool for anyone involved in the design, operation, and maintenance of MPLS-based networks. The reader will walk away with a clear and practical understanding of all aspects of the complexities associated with MPLS network operations. I highly recommend that this text be part of any MPLS network engineer's library."
— GARY HORN
    DIRECTOR, Enterprise Architecture and Network Security
    Advocate Health Care

"A thorough and solid publication that reflects Alcatel-Lucent's industry-leading and innovative approaches to Layer 2 Services. An invaluable asset for any network designer/architect."
— RAY MILLER, Jr.
    Senior Network Engineer
    Sting Communications

T0219363

Designing and Implementing IP/MPLS-Based Ethernet Layer 2 VPN Services

An Advanced Guide for VPLS and VLL

Zhuo (Frank) Xu

Alcatel-Lucent SRA No. 1

WILEY

Wiley Publishing, Inc.

Alcatel·Lucent

Designing and Implementing IP/MPLS-Based Ethernet Layer 2 VPN Services: An Advanced Guide for VPLS and VLL

Published by
Wiley Publishing, Inc.
10475 Crosspoint Boulevard
Indianapolis, IN 46256
www.wiley.com

Copyright © 2010 Alcatel-Lucent

Published by Wiley Publishing, Inc., Indianapolis, Indiana

Published simultaneously in Canada

ISBN: 978-0-470-45656-9

For general information on our other products and services please contact our Customer Care Department within the United States at (877) 762-2974, outside the United States at (317) 572-3993 or fax (317) 572-4002.

Wiley also publishes its books in a variety of electronic formats. Some content that appears in print may not be available in electronic books.

Library of Congress Control Number: 2009937280

To my grandfather, GuangXiao Xu, and to my parents, Yin and WeiMin. You have given me so much love and set perfect examples for me to be passionate, disciplined, and dedicated to my career and my life.

— Zhuo (Frank) Xu

About the Author

Zhuo (Frank) Xu is a seasoned telecom professional with 16 years experience working for Alcatel-Lucent and other telecommunication service providers. He is a recognized MPLS/VPLS service routing expert. Zhuo holds several industry IP certifications, including the distinction of being the world's first Alcatel-Lucent Service Routing Architect (SRA), and is accredited with a patent associated with the MPLS FRR protocol. Educated in Beijing at the Beijing Polytechnic University, P.R. China, Zhuo holds a Bachelor's degree in Electronics Engineering.

Credits

Acknowledgments

First, I thank members of the Alcatel-Lucent senior management team — Basil Alwan, Ravi Parmasad, James Watts, and Barry Denroche — for helping to make this book happen. Your constant support made this book possible. It is an honor for me to work with such an excellent product and with such an outstanding team. Ravi: Special thanks for your encouragement and help as a leader and a friend.

Thanks to Mac Virdy, Jim Tam, and George Carroll for providing the resources that helped me deliver the content of this book. Your strong support and encouragement made the job of writing this book much easier. Mac: You and the network design engineering team provided a friendly and helpful environment that helped to make this book's development much easier. George: Thanks for your consistent attention and help since day one, when I started working on this book.

This publication is the result of the efforts of many individuals who all contributed in different capacities to bringing this book to market.

I express my gratitude to Karyn Lennon for all of her efforts in securing the team who contributed to this book and in managing the many diverse activities needed to publish the book. Without your enthusiasm, passion, and hard work, there was no way I could have finished this book. You did an amazing job organizing the project and coordinating all the parties (editors, artists, technical reviewers, illustrators, publishing authorities, marketing departments, and our customers) who contributed to this book. Your efficiency and patience made it possible for me to keep focused on content delivery. Karyn, it would have been impossible for me to stay focused on completing the content of the book without you taking care of everything else.

This book has benefited enormously from the technical reviewer team of Mustapha Aissaoui, Florin Balus, Footer (Richard) Foote, Prashanth Ishwar, Sivaramakrishna Kuditipudi, Anthony Peres, Jorge Rabadan, and Ray Qiu. Thank you all for the detailed input and technical discussions, and for spending significant amounts of time contributing to the book. I appreciate all of your insight, the thoroughness of your input, and for juggling this activity with everything else that you needed to do. Special thanks to Mustapha for the tens of hours of technical discussion sessions we had on the topics covered by the book. Thanks to Vach Kompella; it's my pleasure to have you write the forward for this book. Also, I thank James Zhang and Chris Fang from the IPD support team for helping me with the research of many technical questions.

To the editorial team — Mary Buchanan and Karen Sayer — thank you for helping to ensure that the accurate message and wording came through.

To the illustration team of Blair Buchanan, Alex Cedzynski, and Peter Wayne, thank you for transforming my images into sleek illustrations that will truly contribute to the educational value of this publication. Peter: Thank you for your creativity in setting the illustration style and leading this team to complete all of these illustrations in a short period of time.

I also thank the many Alcatel-Lucent customers that I have worked with over the years. It has always been my pleasure to work with you — you have all helped me understand how the technology is used in the industry. Our discussions and experiences led to the case studies and real-life network deployment scenarios of this publication. Special thanks to Gary Horn, Ray Miller, and Chris Christou — as industry experts and our customers, your input to this book was invaluable.

And to the Wiley team, led by Sara Shlaer, thanks for your guidance and patience with me during my first publishing endeavor.

Contents at a Glance

Contents

Foreword

If we have learned one thing from the plethora of wireline connectivity technologies, it is that they change constantly. Over the years, while Ethernet was taking over enterprise networks, Frame-Relay, ATM, and SONET/SDH ruled the service provider domain. Attempts were made to unify these technologies, but in the end, the result was independently operated networks, with some interoperability at the edges.

Consequently, the infrastructure of the service providers was expensive and lacked consistency, and a massive transformation was long overdue. IP/MPLS, the emerging technology of the 1990s, provided an abstraction that enabled service providers to interconnect their disparate networks, while endowing that same network with a uniform set of characteristics that was independent of the underlying carrier technology: QoS awareness, traffic-engineering, and fast recovery times in the face of outages. However, MPLS wasn't multi-protocol enough, and needed a killer app to make it universally applicable.

Enter pseudowire technology: Virtual Leased Lines (VLL) and Virtual Private LAN Service (VPLS). Based on the MPLS architecture, pseudowires allowed a service provider to abstract out the idiosyncrasies of wired technologies. This allowed them to continue to support various connectivity technologies at the edge of their networks to customers while migrating to a modern architecture in the core. Customers with both IP and non-IP traffic could now be connected across a multi-service, multi-protocol network.

MPLS absorbed the best of the Layer 2 capabilities of the network infrastructure, but the story didn't stop there. While VLL addressed the problems of a transition to a modern networking architecture, VPLS typified the best of the connectivity models. Ethernet, as a Layer 2 technology, was just another technology like Frame-Relay or ATM. Ethernet, as a network model, delivered the ease-of-use that has made it the choice for enterprises.

VPLS is not simply an Ethernet emulation — it is a connectivity model that abstracts a LAN. It can be used as a VPN service, connecting multiple customer sites together, providing them the ease-of-use and consistent feel of a single Ethernet network. But it can just as well be used as an infrastructure technology, providing the service provider with a highly reliable LAN service spanning a larger geographic area than has been covered by customary Ethernet networks.

I hope that as you read this book, you will appreciate the opportunities IP/MPLS VPNs present to address the connectivity and architectural requirements of customers.

Vach Kompella
Director, MPLS Development
Alcatel-Lucent

Introduction

Internet Protocol/Multi Protocol Label Switching (IP/MPLS) Virtual Private Network (VPN) technology has been widely adopted by service providers for use in their backbone networks. It has significant advantages compared to legacy ATM, Frame-Relay, Ethernet, or IP networks. With IP/MPLS VPN technology, service providers can now build service-oriented networks with multiple services in a single converged network with high availability, reliability, and performance.

The IP/MPLS VPN network uses an evolutionary service-oriented network architecture, which brings the concepts of service entity and service router into the network. The service-oriented network de-couples the roles of Provider Edge (PE) routers and Provider (P) backbone routers. Service instances are created at the edge of the network in the customer-facing PE routers, and MPLS pseudowires are used to connect multiple service instances residing on different PE routers belonging to the same service. P routers connect to PE routers in the network to carry traffic across the backbone network, providing high bandwidth throughput, traffic engineering capability, and fast convergence.

One of the biggest challenges for service providers who migrate from legacy networks to modern IP/MPLS VPN networks is to acquire the knowledge of IP/MPLS VPN, especially for the newly developed pseudowire-based Layer 2 VPN (L2VPN) technologies such as Virtual Private Wire Service (VPWS) and Virtual Private LAN Service (VPLS). In modern IP/MPLS VPN service routing networks, both the network architecture and the protocols underneath are changed significantly:

- The service architecture introduces many new concepts, such as Service Access Points (SAPs), Service Distribution Paths (SDPs), service instances, and pseudowires (PWs).
- IP routing protocols are improved with the Traffic Engineering (TE) extension, and the TE-based Constrained Shortest Path First (CSPF) is introduced to perform more optimal path calculation.
- MPLS is improved with Resource Reservation Protocol Traffic Engineering (RSVP-TE) as the Label Switched Path (LSP) signaling protocol. New resiliency features such as secondary LSP, Fast Reroute, and make-before-break (MBB) are introduced to improve convergence performance. Targeted LDP (T-LDP) is used to signal MPLS pseudowires to connect the service instances in different PE routers.

- New pseudowire-based VPN services such as VLL and VPLS are used to provide multiple services in the IP/MPLS backbone network. Service resiliency features such as pseudowire switching and pseudowire redundancy are introduced to provide more reliable service deployment.

The ease of deployment and the high bandwidth throughput of modern Ethernet technology make it more attractive for both service providers and customers as a Layer 2 transport technology. Ethernet VPN has also become more popular as it enables service providers to offload the IP routing peering responsibilities to their customers, and focuses instead on optimal traffic forwarding. Customers would like to have total control of IP routing without being obligated to follow the providers' routing policies. Virtual Private LAN Service (VPLS) is capable of connecting multiple geographically separated customer sites with a Virtual Bridge. The customer sites connected by the VPLS service appear to be in the signal LAN segment, with spanning tree interoperability. In the backbone network, VPLS service instances are connected by MPLS pseudowire through MPLS or IP transport tunnels.

With all these innovations in the service providers' networks, networking professionals need to update their knowledge of IP/MPLS VPN and obtain an in-depth understanding of the service routing architecture. This book is written to provide readers with a thorough understanding of the new IP/MPLS Layer 2 VPN technology.

How This Book Is Organized

Many readers may have some experience with the newly evolved IP/MPLS VPN technologies. They may have some experience with legacy IP routing and/or Ethernet bridging networks and may find that some of the terminologies sound familiar: IGP, BGP, spanning tree, LSP, RSVP, and so on. However, they may find that these terminologies have different meanings and the protocols' behaviors are altered in IP/MPLS VPN networks. Furthermore, there are many new concepts such as SAP, SDP, pseudowire, LSP, detour LSP, and more.

This book is organized in a hierarchical manner in four parts to help readers obtain a solid understanding of a service routing network.

- Part I presents a high-level overview of the limitation of the traditional service providers' networks, and the challenge for service providers to provide more types of services to customers (Chapter 1). It also introduces the evolution of IP/MPLS VPN multi-service networks and the requirements for building a service-oriented IP/MPLS VPN network infrastructure (Chapter 2).

- Part II discusses the protocols supporting the IP/MPLS VPN networks in detail. The discussion includes enhanced MPLS switching with different types of LSPs (Chapter 3), traffic engineering extensions for IGP and CSPF (Chapter 4), the RSVP-TE protocol for MPLS LSP signaling (Chapter 5), secondary LSP (Chapter 6), RSVP-TE MPLS LSP Fast Reroute (Chapter 7), and the use of the Label Distribution Protocol (LDP) for MPLS transport tunnels and VPN pseudowire signaling (Chapter 8). Part II is the foundation of the in-depth understanding of the IP/MPLS VPN network. These protocol details are mandatory for advanced network design and troubleshooting in service routing networks.

- Part III discusses the IP/MPLS service routing architecture and the multiple services provided by the IP/MPLS VPN service networks. It starts with the "big picture" of IP/MPLS VPN pseudowire-based service routing architecture (Chapter 9), followed by the introduction of the different types of Virtual Leased Line (Chapter 10). Then, the in-depth discussion of the Virtual Private LAN Services (VPLS) architecture is presented (Chapter 11). The scalable hierarchical extension of VPLS (H-VPLS) is also introduced (Chapter 12) followed by the high availability of the service network (Chapter 13). VLL resiliency (Chapter 14) and VPLS resiliency (Chapter 15) follow.

- Part IV presents advanced VPLS services topics including the use of BGP autodiscovery in VPLS to improve the configuration efficiency (Chapter 16); the adoption of Provider Backbone Bridging (PBB, 802.1ah) to the VPLS implementation to further improve the VPLS solution's scalability (Chapter 17); and finally, the Operation, Administration, and Maintenance (OAM) tools in the VPLS service (Chapter 18).

Some material is presented in the format of Notes, Warnings, or other sidebars. Notes are used to clarify the critical concepts and some commonly misunderstood technical terms, or as quick reference reminders while designing the service routing network. Warnings are notices regarding potential service-impacting configurations and operations.

Many acronyms are used throughout the book. Each acronym is fully spelled out when it's mentioned for the first time in each chapter, followed by its abbreviation. The Glossary at the end of the book presents the full list of acronyms with brief explanations.

Conventions Used in This Book

Alcatel-Lucent provides a modular approach for configuring the individual entities of Alcatel-Lucent Service Router Portfolio (ALSRP) nodes. ALSRP nodes can be provisioned and managed either directly using the command-line interface (CLI) of individual nodes or through a service-aware network management system (Alcatel-Lucent 5620 SAM). Alcatel-Lucent 5620 Service Awareness Manager (SAM) provides different types of interfaces, including a graphical user interface (GUI), for provisioning the nodes of a network. In this book, only the command-line configuration option for configuration and managing ALSRP nodes is presented.

CLI commands are entered at the command-line prompt. Entering a command makes navigation possible from one command context (or level) to another. When you initially enter a CLI session, you are in the root context. At the root context, the prompt indicates the active central processor module slot and the name of the node. Navigate to another level by entering the name of successively lower contexts. As you change through the levels, the prompt also changes to indicate the context you are in. Figure 1 shows an example CLI navigation and prompt change according to the context.

Figure 1   Navigation and Prompt Change

```
A:PE-1#
A:PE-1# show
A:PE-1>show#
```

The root prompt shown in Figure 1 indicates that the active CPM slot of the node is A and the name of the node is configured as PE-1. Upon entering the command show, the prompt changes to indicate the show context. As you can see in this paragraph, when CLI codes are used inline along with the main text, they are indicated by the use of monofont text.

To get contextual help at a given prompt, simply enter a question mark (?). In a given CLI context, you can enter commands at that context level by simply entering the text. It is also possible to enter a command in a lower context as long as the command is formatted in the proper command and parameter syntax. Figures 2 and 3 show the two methods to navigate to the show service context.

Figure 2 Navigation by Entering Context-Level Commands

```
A:PE-1# show
A:PE-1>show# service
A:PE-1>show>service#
```

Figure 3 Navigation by Entering Lower Context-Level Commands

```
A:PE-1# show service
A:PE-1>show>service#
```

Figure 4 shows the command options for the oam vccv-ping command. This code is presented here to explain the syntax of CLI command options. The purpose of the command in Figure 4 is explained in Chapter 18.

Figure 4 An Example of CLI Command Options

```
A:PE-1#oam vccv-ping
  - vccv-ping <sdp-id:vc-id> [src-ip-address <ip-addr> dst-ip-address
    <ip-addr> pw-id <pw-id>][reply-mode {ip-routed|control-channel}][fc
    <fc-name> [profile {in|out}]] [size <octets>] [count<send-count>]
    [timeout <timeout>] [interval <interval>][ttl <vc-label-ttl>]

 <sdp-id:vc-id>          : sdp-id - [1..17407]
                           vc-id  - [1..4294967295]
 <ip-routed|control*>  : keywords - specify reply mode
                           Default: control-channel
 <fc-name>               : be|l2|af|l1|h2|ef|h1|nc - Default: be
 <in|out>                : keywords - Default: out
 <octets>                : [88..9198] octets - Default: 88
 <send-count>            : [1..100] - Default: 1
 <timeout>               : [1..10] seconds - Default: 5
 <interval>              : [1..10] seconds - Default 1
 <ip-addr>               : a.b.c.d
 <vc-label-ttl>          : [1..255]
 <pw-id>                 : [1..4294967295]
```

In the command syntax, square brackets indicate optional parameters of a command; angle brackets indicate that a substitution is required for the placeholder; and a pipe (|) indicates an either/or relationship between the parameters on either side of the pipe. To shorten some of the code presentation, later in the book, part of some listings' outputs is stripped and replaced with ellipses (...) to indicate the stripping.

For further information regarding the use of the command-line interface, refer to the *System Basics Guide*, which is part of the ALSRP product manuals. This book is one of the series of technical books to be published related to Alcatel-Lucent service routers. This book provides reference to the Alcatel-Lucent manuals that come with the Alcatel-Lucent 7750 Service Router, the Alcatel-Lucent 7450 Ethernet Service Switch, or the Alcatel-Lucent 7710 Service Router platforms. If you are an Alcatel-Lucent customer and you don't have access to the Alcatel-Lucent's Service product manuals, contact your Alcatel-Lucent account manager. If you are not a customer of Alcatel-Lucent, visit the "Contact Us" area at `www.alcatel-lucent.com`.

A standard set of icons is used in the diagrams throughout this book. A representation of these icons and their meanings is listed under the section "Standard Icons" at the end of the Introduction.

Audience

The target audience of this book includes network design, maintenance, or support professionals working for telecommunication service providers or equipment vendors who want to acquire expert-level, in-depth knowledge on the latest IP/MPLS VPN technology. It is highly recommended that readers have a solid understanding of legacy IP and Ethernet switched networks and related protocols; some hands-on networking experience is also recommended.

Alcatel-Lucent Service Routing Certification Program

For those who feel they need more IP Service Routing training and hands-on experience, I encourage you to review the offerings from the Alcatel-Lucent Service Routing Certification Program. Visit `www.alcatel-lucent.com/src` for a complete overview of the four certifications in this industry-leading program.

Feedback Is Welcome

It would be my pleasure to hear back from you. Please forward your comments and suggestions for improvements to the following email address:

`sr.publications@alcatel-lucent.com`

With that, I welcome you to explore the exciting world of IP/MPLS VPN service routing networks.

— *Zhuo (Frank) Xu*

Standard Icons

Enterprise

Residence

Internet

Cell Site &
Base Service

Service Access Point

Pseudowire

Forwarding Database

Broadband Service Router

Service Router

Network
Management

Satellite Transmission

Failure

Customer Equipment

Provider Equipment

Broadband Remote
Access Server

Radio Network Controllers
and Base Station Controllers

Broadband Service Aggregator

Microwave Connection

Data

Network

IP/MPLS VPN Service Network Overview

I

Telecommunication operators must constantly evolve their networks to meet the needs of their customers. Building a converged, high performance, highly available, and highly flexible network to provide multiple services in a cost efficient way is the goal for today's providers. The new generation of IP/MPLS VPN service-oriented networks has become the operators' best choice to reach this goal.

Building Converged Service Networks with IP/MPLS VPN Technology

1

Multi Protocol Label Switching (MPLS) and Virtual Private Network (VPN) technologies provide features that help service providers meet the evolving needs of their customers. These technologies are essential for building the converged service networks required in today's market.

Chapter Objectives

- Identify the new trends and demands for a service provider's backbone network

- Review the evolution of MPLS technology

- Describe the innovation of multi-service VPN

This chapter briefly reviews traditional networks with legacy technologies and their limitations, and shows how the innovations of MPLS and VPN technologies overcome these limitations. It also presents the benefits of using an IP/MPLS VPN service architecture.

1.1 The Increasing Demands on Service Provider Networks

Service provider networks must evolve to keep pace with the changing times. Service providers are often classified by how much of the regional access infrastructure they own, versus how much they must contract from other providers:

- **Tier 1 operators** — The top one or two providers in a country who typically own the access infrastructure (copper or fiber) within their serving region. Tier 1 service providers are usually the first to establish infrastructures within the region — the incumbent operators.

- **Tier 2 or Tier 3 operators** — Providers that may either use the Tier 1 operator's access infrastructure or build its own infrastructure in some service areas. Tier 2 providers use a mix of their own infrastructure and some infrastructure from Tier 1 providers, while Tier 3 providers rely entirely on agreements to use infrastructure from other providers. These providers typically emerge as competitors to the already established Tier 1 providers, and are thus at a disadvantage in competing with the incumbent providers for market control.

Service providers may also be classified according to the types of services they offer to their end-customers:

- **Telco** — Traditionally offering voice services as well as business services
- **Internet Service Provider (ISP)** — Offering Internet access for residential and business customers
- **VPN Service Provider/Ethernet Service Provider** — Offering business VPN services
- **Cable Multi-System Operator (MSO)** — Offering residential and business services

An operator may offer some or all of these services to their end-customers.

Both residential (consumer) and enterprise (business) customers of service providers constantly demand new services and innovations from their service providers. Traditional Leased Line, Frame-Relay (FR), and Asynchronous Transfer Mode (ATM) based services are characteristic of organizations that manage their own enterprise networks (with their own IT teams), but those enterprises must purchase the connectivity infrastructure (typically point-to-point leased lines or FR/ATM Permanent Virtual Connections) from a service provider. Driven by enterprise business goals and geared toward focusing on core competencies and cost reduction, enterprises have begun looking to service providers for managed connectivity solutions.

Enterprises have also been demanding more in terms of bandwidth speeds for connectivity. The old "80/20 rule" (80% of the traffic stays within the local site, and 20% of the traffic is between remote sites) is no longer valid. Because many enterprises have consolidated their data centers to a few sites, the need for higher-speed remote connectivity has become extremely important to enterprise IT managers. In addition, enterprises are now in the process of implementing bandwidth-intensive applications like video conferencing, web conferencing, and electronic image sharing across a wide area, thus prompting a need for additional bandwidth in their Wide Area Networks (WANs).

Residential services are also evolving from dial-up Internet connectivity to broadband connectivity. Services for residential customers are evolving to include triple- or quad-play services that include voice, Video on Demand (VoD), broadcast television, and Internet access.

Traditionally a service provider has separate networks for offering voice and data services. Within a data network, a traditional service provider would typically have separate networks for offering Leased Line-, FR-, and ATM-based services for business customers and a separate network offering Internet-based services (Internet access and Internet-based secure connectivity) for residential and business customers. In residential areas, TV content for consumers is most often delivered by MSOs, who have their own dedicated infrastructure (mostly cable plants). Enterprises usually use Ethernet switches and IP routers to build their LANs and purchase Leased Line services from operators to connect their remote locations.

Given the ever-changing landscape of customer demands, service provider networks must keep pace by staying competitive while increasing profitability. It is evident that the approach of building separate networks is not cost-effective when a service provider must offer multiple services. The ideal way to approach network design is a solution wherein multiple services can be converged on a single network infrastructure. This is why MPLS as a technology for service provider networks has gained rapid momentum in the marketplace.

The most obvious trend is the fast growth of IP and Ethernet traffic in the network. Because of the boom of the Internet, and the invention of Gigabit Ethernet, IP/Ethernet traffic is now dominant in telecommunication networks. Residential customers require faster Internet access services and better IP service quality to support Voice over IP (VoIP). Enterprise customers are conducting more and more of their business electronically across geographically separated locations. Many bandwidth-intensive and time-sensitive IP-based applications are widely used for business-critical missions. IP data is growing in strategic importance in wireless networks. Mobile users are keen for rich IP-based multimedia services. Service providers also want to deliver television content over IPTV applications, which require a network throughput with very high bandwidth and low latency. It's clear that building a network optimal for IP/Ethernet traffic delivery is crucial to service providers.

Because enterprises are now starting to use more and more IP/Ethernet-based applications, they require their IT infrastructures to have high throughput, and to be reliable, secure, and cost-efficient. This generates a great demand for the service providers to provide VPN. VPN allows the service provider to deliver services to different customers using the same service delivery backbone network, while isolating each customer using virtual service instances to ensure privacy and security. During the past two decades, there were already many enterprises using the routed RFC2547bis VPN to achieve intranet connectivity. Now, with the fast growth of Ethernet technology, more and more business customers require bridged Layer 2 Ethernet VPN service. Layer 2 VPN gives the customers full control of their routing domains and fewer peering complications with service providers.

Service providers also look for network solutions that consolidate voice, data, and video services into one network infrastructure and allow them to serve residential and business customers from the same network. The network must be cost-efficient and robust. The network must also be capable of providing different Quality of Service (QoS) on the service provided to conform to different Service Level Agreements (SLAs).

With these new trends and demands, service providers intend to transition their networks to IP/MPLS core networks, providing various VPN services to their customers.

1.2 MPLS Overview

Multi Protocol Label Switching is a label-switching mechanism used by MPLS-capable routers or switches to exchange traffic. In the control plane, the MPLS-capable devices assign labels to be used for certain types of traffic and distribute labels through certain label distribution protocols. Each device distributes locally assigned labels to other MPLS devices and receives label distribution information from other devices. Each device builds a Label Information Base (LIB) that stores the label information. In the data plane, each device performs MPLS encapsulation on data traffic before sending it to other MPLS devices. When an MPLS device receives MPLS-encapsulated traffic, the device makes forwarding decisions based on the MPLS label value in the MPLS encapsulation header. In MPLS data encapsulation, the MPLS header (32 bits long, containing a 20-bit numerical value used as the label value) is inserted between the Layer 2 header and the Layer 3 header of the data to be encapsulated. Therefore, MPLS is sometimes referred as a *Layer 2.5 protocol*, and the MPLS header is sometimes referred to as the *shim header*.

Before MPLS devices can forward MPLS-encapsulated traffic to each other, MPLS label distribution in the control plane must be completed. When exchanging label information, each MPLS device stores the label, as well as the label mapping information for the type of traffic that uses each label. All traffic that uses the same label is referred to as a *Forwarding Equivalent Class* (FEC). The label distribution process distributes the FEC–Label mapping information among MPLS devices. Therefore, MPLS devices form a Label Switched Path (LSP) for each FEC. The LSP is an end-to-end *connection* for traffic belonging to the same FEC to be forwarded. MPLS builds a connection-oriented path in a connectionless network.

MPLS was first introduced to improve Layer 3 routing performance of regular IP routers. For an MPLS-capable router or Layer 3 switch, MPLS label swapping is less expensive than routing IP packets. In a routed IP network, the IP packets are routed from their source to their destination hop-by-hop. When each router routes an IP packet, the router removes the Layer 2 header (usually an Ethernet header), then checks the IP header for the destination IP address. The router then must perform a lookup in its routing table to find the IP address of the next-hop interface and the egress interface's Layer 2 encapsulation information. After the next-hop lookup is completed, the router rewrites the packet by adding the new Layer 2 encapsulation header to the packet and then forwards the packet to the next-hop interface. This procedure is performed for every IP packet at every hop. With the introduction of MPLS, the routers can build MPLS LSPs for each FEC. All traffic belonging to the same FEC is MPLS-label–switched to its destination rather than routed. When a Label Switched Router (LSR) performs MPLS switching on an MPLS-encapsulated packet, the MPLS label-swapping operation is much simpler. Therefore, the IP destination lookup process is replaced by the relatively cheaper label-swapping process. Using MPLS switching to replace IP routing is sometime referred to as a *routing shortcut*.

Furthermore, Border Gateway Protocol (BGP) can be removed from the core of the network because the LSR routers in the core of the network do not have to route these packets. As long as the MPLS label distribution process builds the LSP for each router in the core to reach all edge routers that have BGP peerings with routers outside the Autonomous System (AS), traffic across the core network can be MPLS-switched rather than IP-routed. The core router uses the MPLS label to switch the traffic to the correct edge router. BGP full mesh within the AS can be removed. Only the edge routers need to have BGP peering among each other. Using MPLS switching to remove BGP full mesh from the core network to route Internet traffic is sometimes referred to as a *BGP shortcut*. The label distribution process used by traditional MPLS-capable devices is in most cases the Label Distribution Protocol (LDP).

1.3 The MPLS Value Proposition

MPLS has evolved substantially since its early days of deployment. The reasons for using MPLS in a network have also changed. MPLS is no longer used to provide an IP routing shortcut. The two biggest changes in the MPLS technology are:

- Resource Reservation Protocol (RSVP) is extended to support MPLS label distribution — RSVP-TE. RSVP-TE (the *TE* stands for traffic engineering) brings many traffic engineering features and resiliency features to MPLS tunneling technology.
- Pseudowire (PW)-based MPLS L2VPN is implemented in many vendors' MPLS-capable routers and switches.

With these evolutions in MPLS technology, MPLS is now widely deployed in the backbone networks of service providers to provide VPN services to their customers.

The introduction of RSVP-TE into MPLS label distribution gives MPLS outstanding flexibility and reliability that the traditional routed or switched network cannot have:

- MPLS provides traffic engineering capabilities to control the data forwarding path in the network. Using RSVP-TE, MPLS routers can signal an explicitly routed LSP. The operator can manually specify the path and the hops along the path for the LSP to travel end-to-end. Therefore, operators can manipulate the data traffic paths in the network, as follows:
    - In an IP-only network, packets traveling from source nodes to destination nodes use a path that is determined by routing information

computed by IP routers. An IP-only network offers little flexibility for providing alternate paths for traffic flow. An MPLS-based network supports traffic engineering whereby an MPLS path (logical connection) can be defined to use network links that are different from the normal path taken by IP packets. This helps to better utilize links within an enterprise network.

- With the help of the traffic engineering extensions of Open Shortest Path First (OSPF) and IS-IS, RSVP-TE allows the use of Constraint Shortest Path First (CSPF)-based MPLS tunnel path calculation. When performing path calculation, CSPF can consider criteria other than the Interior Gateway Protocols (IGP) routing metric, such as the link's bandwidth reservation and the administrative group membership (link-coloring).

- MPLS provides outstanding reroute performance. Network infrastructures based on FR/ATM or legacy Ethernet cannot offer quick convergence during failover.MPLS provides outstanding reroute performance using mechanisms such as Secondary (backup) LSP and Fast Reroute (FRR) that can deliver reroute times in the millisecond range:

  - **Secondary LSP** — RSVP-TE supports the concept of *LSP and LSP-Path*. It allows several (up to eight) LSP-Paths to be provisioned within the same LSP. In normal circumstances, the primary LSP-Path actively forwards traffic; if the primary LSP-Path fails, one of the secondary LSP-Paths takes over the traffic. When a hot-standby secondary LSP-Path is provisioned, the failover performance is in the tens of milliseconds range.

  - **FRR** — When using RSVP-TE to signal LSP, all routers can be aware of the entire path the LSP traverses. Therefore, each router can signal a protection LSP to take a path away from the potential failure point. If network failure happens, the MPLS router closest to the failure uses the pre-signaled protection path to protect the LSP. This is called *MPLS FRR*. FRR can provide tens of milliseconds failover time after a failure is detected.

- The pseudowire-based IP/MPLS VPN implementation makes it possible to take full advantage of the flexibility provided by MPLS. The new VPN model decouples native service processing from VPN encapsulation and allows services with different characteristics to share the same IP/MPLS backbone. The customer service-specific service access entities are in charge of providing native format traffic to meet the customer's requirements, and the VPN service network entities are in charge of performing VPN encapsulation and de-encapsulation to transport the service across the network backbone.

Resiliency features such as pseudowire switching and pseudowire redundancy ensure end-to-end service delivery with the desired quality.

With the MPLS enhancement and the new pseudowire-based VPN service, the service provider can now deploy different types of services for many customers in a single converged backbone network using IP/MPLS technology. The IP/MPLS VPN network has the following advantages:

- **Cost Efficiency** — It eliminates the requirement for service providers to build separate networks for different types of services. All services are shared in the same backbone infrastructure. Using an IP/MPLS network with Gigabit Ethernet or 10 Gigabit Ethernet Layer 2 infrastructure significantly reduces the cost compared to the legacy technologies like ATM and FR.

- **Flexibility** — All MPLS pseudowire-based VPN services use a common service architecture, differing only in the customer-facing attachment circuit. When a new type of service is implemented, it can be smoothly deployed into the existing IP/MPLS backbone by simply adding the new type of access interface in the provider edge (PE) service router. The TE capability provided by IGP-TE and CSPF allows the operator to easily control the service traffic's forwarding paths in the core network.

- **Reliability** — The pseudowires used by VPN PE routers and the MPLS transport tunnel LSP support both redundancy and quick failover. The service architecture allows the operator to multi-home services to more than one PE router, to achieve service-peering redundancy. With the addition of the MPLS resiliency features that have quick failover, the service network can be built with high availability.

- **Scalability** — IP/MPLS VPN service is highly scalable. The IP/MPLS VPN service architecture allows the core routers (P routers) to perform MPLS switching for service traffic without being aware of each service instance. Only the PE routers in the edge of the backbone network are aware of each service instance. Only the PE routers with customer circuits attached are involved in service provisioning. All service instances sharing the same PE router are isolated by VPN encapsulation.

LDP is one of the protocols MPLS uses to signal LSP. With LDP, the MPLS router distributes labels and establishes LSPs automatically. LDP distributes labels mapped with IP prefixes; therefore, its convergence performance is dependent on the underlying routing protocol. The introduction of RSVP-TE into MPLS LSP signaling brings significant improvement to the flexibility, reliability, and performance of the IP/MPLS network's service transport mechanism. With an RSVP-TE–signaled LSP transport tunnel, an IP network can now provide carrier-level convergence performance by using resiliency features such as FRR and Secondary LSP.

The newly enhanced MPLS technology allows the operator to deliver traffic flows for many customers using many different types of services in a single converged network. It is now the new WAN backbone technology.

1.4 MPLS Enables Converged Multi-Service Networks

For decades, computer networks have been generally categorized as LAN, MAN, and WAN. Each type of network has its own architecture and traffic delivery mechanism. Their speeds, costs, and reliability differ too. Different types of service providers use different types of networks to provide the services for these networks. With the technology innovation and the growth of the customer demands, the requirements for networking are also changing constantly:

- The wide deployment of cost-efficient and high-throughput Ethernet switches and small IP routers brought the first wave of networking evolution. Many computers can be connected by these LAN-oriented networking devices and gain great speed to run time-sensitive applications or traffic-intense applications.

- The invention of the Internet brought the second wave of networking evolution. Computer networks all over the world can be connected by the shared public Internet backbone. This wave brought the demand for a high-performance and highly reliable backbone Internet router.

- Now, the third wave of networking evolution has arrived. With the invention of VoIP, IPTV, and other IP-based multimedia applications, ISPs not only provide access to the Internet, but they also want to provide these services with additional profit over their backbone infrastructure. These services require bandwidth and global reachability, as well as a guaranteed end-to-end QoS. To achieve this, the concept of *service router* is used. *Service routers* allocate their resources according to the requirements of different services and deliver the services with the required quality.

Therefore, a converged multi-service network is desired by service providers to meet the new requirements. Figure 1.1 illustrates such a converged network with multiple services.

Figure 1.1   Converged Multi-Service Network

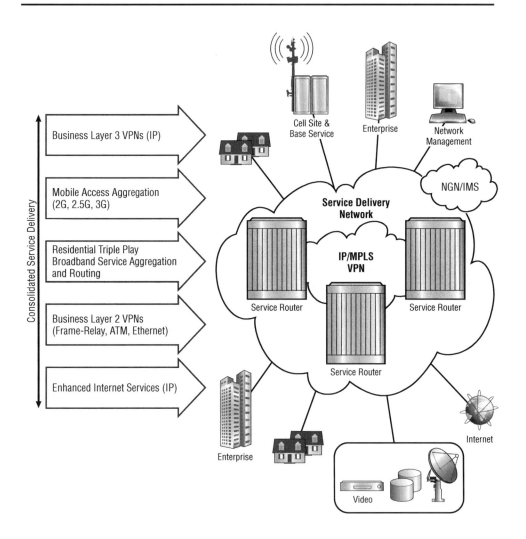

In Figure 1.1, the service delivery network provides multiple services in a single backbone network that contains service routers. The service delivery network provides various services to many enterprises and residential customers. Such a network is based on the new evolved IP/MPLS VPN service technology.

1.5 MPLS-Enabled Business VPN Services

Nowadays, more new applications running in residential and enterprise networks generate new demands for the telecommunications backbone networks:

- **Complex L3 VPN** — Many enterprise customers require VPN services with *complex* connectivity. Simply connecting all customer routers is not adequate. Layer 3 VPN is also referred to as *Virtual Private Routed Network* (VPRN). Customers require different VPN topologies such as:

    - **Extranet** — Some enterprises want to share part of their networks with partners to improve productivity while isolating other parts of their networks.

    - **Hub-Spoke VPN** — Many customers require their branch offices to be connected with their headquarters and want the traffic to be forced through the headquarters' firewall.

    - **Overlay VPN** — Customers may want to have Internet access through some of their sites while isolating the rest of their network from the Internet.

- **L2 VPN: Virtual Private LAN Service (VPLS) and Virtual Leased Line (VLL)** — Many customers want to take advantage of the simplicity of Layer 2 peering with the service provider. They want to purchase Layer 2 connectivity services (point-to-point or point-to-multipoint) from the service provider, while handling their own Layer 3 routing. Service providers also like the fact that they do not need to deal with Layer 3 routing peering and isolation with different customers, and can focus only on providing Layer 2 reachability. With the introduction of Gigabit Ethernet and 10G Ethernet in customer networks and backbone networks, VPLS and Ethernet VLL services have become very popular. VLL is also referred to as Virtual Private Wire Service (VPWS).

- **MPLS-Enabled IPTV Infrastructure** — With the new generation of IPTV solutions, delivering television content (regular definition and high definition) over IP networks has become possible and profitable. Many service providers want to use their IP backbone network to deliver TV content to compete with traditional cable service providers. Delivering IPTV content requires the backbone network to have large bandwidth and promising service quality.

- **MPLS-Enabled Mobile Infrastructure and Mobile Backhauling** — The new generation of the mobile networks provides both voice and high-bandwidth data service through cellular services. Mobile service providers are looking for a cost-efficient and optimal solution of using a converged network to deliver both voice and data services in backbone networks.

- **Improved Access Technologies** — The significant growth of access technologies provides more bandwidth to the end subscribers. Today's Digital Subscriber Line (DSL) technology and Passive Optical Network (PON) technology can give the end-user 10-Mbps, 100-Mbps, or even higher throughput. Bandwidth-intensive applications such as IPTV, Personal TV, faster download, and online gaming can be deployed end-to-end across a backbone network.

All the above changes and new demands challenge service providers to build a high-throughput, highly reliable, and cost-efficient converged backbone network to meet the requirements of different customers. Also, service providers are looking for more revenue-generating services to sell to the customers rather than selling the *big fat pipe*. The boundary between carriers and content providers has become ambiguous. Cable TV providers are now providing Internet access and VoIP telephony services. ISPs are now providing TV content to their customers through IPTV and are using DSL and PON technology to provide Internet and voice services. Cellular providers are also providing mobile data services and delivering TV content to cellular phones thorough 2G or 3G technologies along with the mobile voice services.

The evolution of IP/MPLS VPN technology provides a solution for all of these types of service providers. With IP/MPLS VPN technology, all types of services can be provided in a single converged MPLS service backbone network, as follows:

- The high-throughput backbone (usually connected with Gigabit Ethernet or 10 Gigabit Ethernet) provides enough bandwidth to deliver bandwidth-demanding applications such as IPTV.

- The flexible IP/MPLS VPN technology allows multiple services such as voice, data, broadcast TV, mobile backhauling, and ATM/FR circuits to be provisioned in a single network.

- The advanced QoS functions allow differentiation among different types of services and customers and treat the different types of traffic flows in their network based on their unique characteristics. Delivering guaranteed service quality to fulfill SLAs while using available resources in the network to serve statistically multiplexed subscribers can be achieved simultaneously.

- The highly reliable service routing engine provides hot redundancy in the control plane. MPLS resiliency provides carrier-level convergence performance to protect services from network failures. Service outages can be minimized.

Figure 1.2 illustrates an IP/MPLS VPN service network.

Figure 1.2   An IP/MPLS VPN Service Network

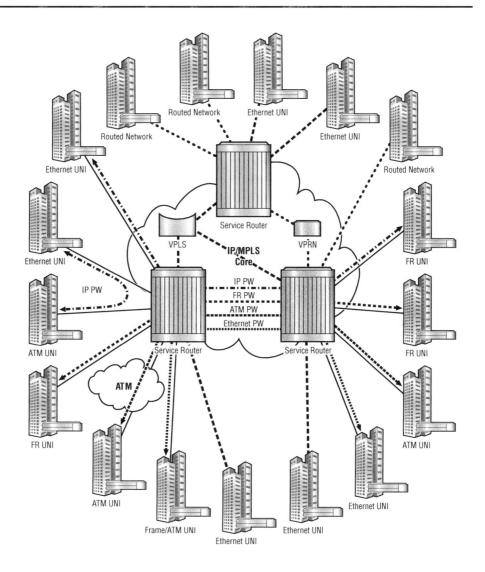

The invention and implementation of the pseudowire-based IP/MPLS VPN solution gives service providers a scalable and secure approach to providing services to multiple customers using the same backbone network while efficiently isolating customer traffic.

- The pseudowire-based VPN model decouples the role of the customer-facing edge routers (Provider Edge, or PE, routers) and the role of backbone-transiting routers (Provider, or P, routers). MPLS pseudowires connect PE routers to customer-facing service instances. The MPLS backbone network only transits pseudowire-encapsulated VPN traffic end-to-end, hiding the details of the core network topology from the service. Therefore, the service-aware PE router can be focused on providing access to customer devices, multiplexing and de-multiplexing traffic from multiple services, and making VPN forwarding decisions. The P routers are in charge of providing highly available, high-throughput *forwarding pipes* with guaranteed QoS.

- The pseudowire-based IP/MPLS VPN model provides different types of services using the same IP/MPLS backbone. These services include:

  - **VLL** — A highly scalable point-to-point piping service that carries customer traffic between two customer sites. VLL services support many legacy access technologies, such as ATM, FR, Ethernet, and Circuit Emulation Service (CES).

  - **VPLS** — A multipoint-to-multipoint Ethernet bridging service that bridges customer Ethernet traffic among geographically separated locations.

  - **VPRN** — A multipoint-to-multipoint IP routing service that routes customer IP traffic among different sites and exchanges customer routes among these sites. VPRN services can provide various service topologies such as Intranet, Extranet, Overlay VPN, or Hub-Spoke VPN.

- The pseudowire-based VPN model unifies the service deployment architecture in the network. Different types of VPN services for different customers use the same VPN infrastructure: Service instances in each customer-facing PE router are connected by the end-to-end pseudowire(s), and PE routers are connected to each other by Service Distribution Paths (SDPs) using Generic Routing Encapsulation (GRE) or MPLS tunneling. Different types of services share the same MPLS backbone with a similar core-facing configuration. Services differ only in Service Access Point (SAP) configuration in the service instances of local PE routers. This unified service deployment module makes the backbone network easier to maintain and expand.

- The pseudowire-based IP/MPLS VPN services are standardized and supported by multiple vendors, and therefore multi-vendor interoperability can be achieved.

Summary

Traditional telecommunications service providers build different network infrastructures to provide different types of services to different customers. These separate network infrastructures create high operational expenses and capital expenses. Different types of networks are incompatible with each other, and the resources cannot be shared.

New applications such as IPTV and the fast growth of Internet applications such as voice, video, and gaming demand more bandwidth and service quality from the service provider. Service providers want to provide multiple services to maximize their revenue. Converged networks with multi-service capability, high performance, high availability and cost efficiency are required to achieve these goals.

The innovation of pseudowire-based IP/MPLS VPN technology provides a solution to the service providers. By implementing an IP/MPLS VPN service routing backbone network, service providers can deploy different types of services (e.g., L2VPN, L3VPN, Internet Routing, Triple Play, and VoIP) over a converged IP/MPLS backbone network.

- IP/MPLS service routing with high-throughput Ethernet connections provides a cost-efficient solution for the deployment of a scaled network.
- IP/MPLS VPN service architecture makes it possible to deliver multiple services in a single backbone network, and the uniform service architecture reduces the operation and management overhead of the network.
- MPLS resiliency features ensure that the network has outstanding convergence performance. Minimum service outages during network failures are guaranteed.

These innovations allow service providers to meet the evolving needs of their customers by providing multiple services using a single converged network.

IP/MPLS VPN Multi-Service Network Overview

2

An IP/MPLS VPN multi-service network provides the capability of building a converged reliable network supporting many different types of services to many different customers. The network uses MPLS pseudowires to connect Virtual Private Network (VPN) member routers in the core network.

Chapter Objectives

- Identify the performance characteristics required for a service-oriented network.

- Explain the Layer 2 VPN services.

- Describe the building blocks of an IP/MPLS VPN Service Routing network.

- Discuss the architectures and services that are enabled by IP/MPLS VPN technology.

- Introduce the IP/MPLS VPN-based Triple Play and Mobile Backhauling solutions.

This chapter provides an overview of the building blocks that enable the convergence of multiple services into an IP/MPLS multi-service network. Multi Protocol Label Switching (MPLS) pseudowire-based VPN technology is a key building block for enabling MPLS-based services. Along with the advanced per-service Quality of Service (QoS) deployment, service providers can deliver scaled services to large numbers of customers while meeting various requirements.

Service providers can now deploy IP/MPLS VPN-based service solutions to provide different types of services to different customers using a single converged IP/MPLS network. The Triple Play and Mobile Backhauling solutions are also discussed in brief at the end of the chapter.

2.1 IP/MPLS Layer 2 VPN Requirements

As discussed in Chapter 1, new demands from customers and the upsurge of new bandwidth-intensive IP-based services and applications require that service providers take a different networking approach to be successful in today's market. MPLS-based VPNs offer a solution to meet service provider goals. This chapter introduces the IP/MPLS VPN technology building blocks that enable the solution for service providers.

To meet the requirements of service providers, the new-generation multi-service network must have the following characteristics:

- **Multi-Service with Cost Efficiency** — The backbone network must provide various types of services to meet the requirements of enterprise and residential customers. The requirements of enterprise customers include providing Time Division Multiplex (TDM), FR, and ATM connectivity as well as business VPN services with high throughput. The requirements of residential customers include voice service, High-Speed Internet (HSI) service, and more recently video-based services like Broadcast Television (BTV), Video on Demand (VoD), remote health care and distance learning. These services should be provided by a single converged backbone network to maintain cost efficiency. The network should also be flexible and adaptive to new technologies and be able to provide new types of services.

- **High Availability (HA)** — The backbone network must be highly available. The infrastructure should allow multiple levels of resiliency to protect the service traffic. With proper design, the network must be able to provide 99.999 percent service availability. This requires that the underlying technology have rich resiliency features.

- **Quality of Service (QoS)** — The network must be capable of assigning application-specific QoS treatment to the traffic flows of different services.

Providing granular QoS to the network can improve service availability and performance and also help with cost efficiency. The QoS capability should allow the limited resources to be used in the most optimal manner, giving critical services higher priority, while allowing non-critical services to use the available resources as much as possible. Therefore, the system can provide services with different Service Level Agreements (SLAs).

- **Scalability** — The service delivery infrastructure must be scalable to allow a large number of residential and enterprise customers to share the same network. With so many customers and services sharing the same network infrastructure, the system must be able to maintain the desired level of performance. The network and the devices must be able to support thousands or more services without sacrificing performance or manageability.

- **Service Management** — The network must be capable of provisioning and managing a large variety of QoS policies, security policies, and accounting policies for each service. The system must be able to deploy all policies at per-service granularity. The multi-service network solution must also provide network management support from which the network infrastructure and services can be provisioned, modified, and monitored from a centralized location. The network management solution must have *service awareness*: It must understand the end-to-end service and associate all related components in the service view. It also must be able to provide management services for each service.

- **Service Assurance** — The system must contain rich Operation, Administration, and Maintenance (OAM) features to test and monitor every perspective of service and network health. Traffic mirroring to a local or remote centralized location must be supported for troubleshooting and security purposes. The system must also provide granular, accurate, and real-time service and system statistics.

The IP/MPLS VPN-based multi-service network fulfills all the requirements above, and therefore many service providers and enterprises worldwide select it as the networking technology of choice.

2.2 IP/MPLS Layer 2 VPN Services

The previous chapter introduced the challenge for service providers to provide multiple types of services to customers with a converged high-performance and cost-efficient network. IP/MPLS pseudowire-based VPN provides a solution for these service providers.

A service provider can offer two choices for VPN services: the Layer 2 approach or the Layer 3 approach. This section explains the Layer 2 approach and provides two examples of Layer 2 VPN.

> **Note:** Layer 3 VPN consists of routed IP VPN services (RFC 4364, formally RFC 2547bis), referred to as *Virtual Private Routed Network* (VPRN). Layer 3 VPN services are typically offered as a managed service and are ideal for customers who prefer their network connectivity to be managed by a service provider. Layer 3 VPN services are beyond the scope of this book.

The Layer 2 approach is commonly referred to as Layer 2 VPN (L2VPN). The Layer 2 VPN service may be either:

- **Point-to-Point Virtual Leased Line (VLL) Service** — This is also referred to as *Virtual Private Wire Service* (VPWS).
- **Multipoint-to-Multipoint Ethernet Bridging Service** — Virtual Private LAN Service (VPLS). VPLS is also referred to as *Metro-Ethernet service*.

Layer 2 services are typically offered to customers who want to manage their own networks. Layer 2 VPN provides the simplicity for a service provider to leave the management of routing (Layer 3) protocols to the customer while the service provider focuses on providing high-throughput Layer 2 connections.

The following sections outline the use of VLL and VPLS for Layer 2 VPN.

Virtual Leased Line

A Virtual Leased Line (VLL) is an example of a Layer 2 VPN. A VLL is analogous to a private line within the MPLS enterprise infrastructure. It offers a point-to-point connection between any two end-users, applications, or devices. Figure 2.1 illustrates several VLL connections. A VLL can be used for applications that require dedicated point-to-point connectivity. A VLL can be deployed within an enterprise network for point-to-point connectivity within a campus or point-to-point connectivity between WAN sites.

Figure 2.1 illustrates five VLL services sharing two service routers in the IP/MPLS core network. In each VLL, two customer sites are connected by the VLL service provided by the two service routers. Each service router has a VLL service instance provisioned on it. The two service instances belonging to the same VLL service at the two service routers are connected by a pseudowire (PW) over the IP/MPLS core network. The pseudowire is a logical point-to-point MPLS connection between two service routers participating in the same service. In an IP/MPLS network, service transport tunnels transport the VLL service traffic across the core network.

Figure 2.1 Layer 2 Point-to-Point VPN — Virtual Leased Line

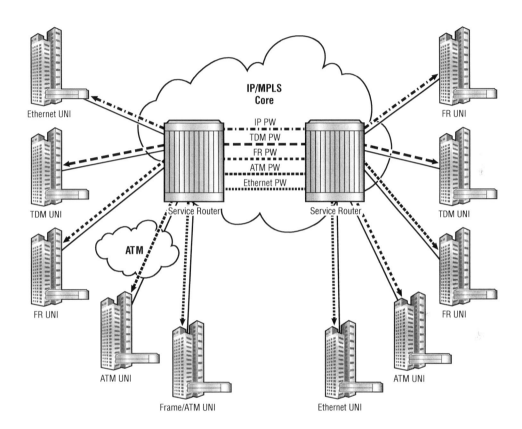

The VLL is the simplest type of VPN to deploy with least resource consumption; therefore, it is a preferred solution for any point-to-point connectivity requirements. The VLL is completely transparent to the end-user data and application protocol. From the customer's perspective, the service provider's network that provides the VLL service acts like a wire (hence the term *pseudowire*) and connects the two sites. Therefore, VLL is also referred to as Virtual Private Wire Service (VPWS). The VLL service accepts native format traffic from one customer site and sends it to the other customer site. The endpoints of the VLL can be configured with the traffic parameters such as required bandwidth and priority of traffic relative to other traffic in the network. MPLS provides a quick recovery time for the VLL in the event of any transit router or link failure within the network.

Point-to-point wire-like connectivity services supporting legacy networking technologies can be deployed in the IP/MPLS VPN network. Customers want point-to-point ATM, FR, or TDM circuits to be served by the VLL services. For ATM customers, the ATM VLL is provisioned to switch traffic from one ATM Virtual Circuit (VC), trunking all VCs belonging to some or all Virtual Paths (VPs), or to simply switch all ATM cells from one site to another site (port mode ATM). Both Cell Mode and AAL5 SDU Frame Mode circuits are available for customers.

Customers can also use the legacy ATM OAM to monitor the health of the circuit and test its connectivity. ATM FR interworking with point-to-point connections is also supported. For customers with TDM interfaces, the Circuit Emulation Service (CES) VLL services can connect two TDM interfaces from two sites. The CES VLL supports both structured and unstructured interfaces.

With the VLL service provisioned in the backbone network, the provider's network behaves to the customer like an ATM or FR switch. The implementation details of the IP/MPLS VPN are invisible to customers. All VLL services are isolated by the service instances created in the customer-facing PE routers in the backbone network. The core router MPLS switches the MPLS VPN-encapsulated traffic from one PE router to another PE router. Details regarding VLL service are discussed in Chapter 10.

VLL services are frequently used by enterprise customers that require a point-to-point connection between two geographically separated locations. Many mobile operators deploy VLL services in their IP/MPLS backbone networks to backhaul the mobile traffic while implementing new IP-based data applications to provide more types of services to their subscribers.

Virtual Private LAN Service (VPLS)

VPLS is another example of a Layer 2 VPN. VPLS enables multipoint connectivity at Layer 2 within an enterprise infrastructure.

Figure 2.2 illustrates a VPLS service within a network where three service routers participate in the same VPLS service. Each service router has a VPLS service instance (also referred as a *Virtual Switching Instance*, or *VSI*). Each VSI performs MAC address learning and constructs a table that maps MAC addresses to the corresponding MPLS paths (pseudowires) or the customer access ports. The VPLS concept is similar to a logical LAN connection — for example, all end devices connected to the same VPLS service appear as if they are within the same LAN segment (broadcast domain).

Figure 2.2 Layer 2 Multipoint VPN — Virtual Private LAN Service

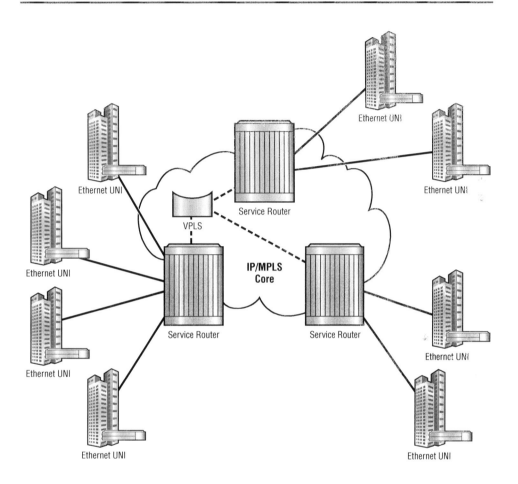

VPLS can be deployed within an enterprise network for multipoint connectivity within a campus or multipoint connectivity between WAN sites. VPLS provides transparent bridging services to geographically separated customer sites. By using VPLS services, customers can significantly expand the coverage of their private LAN while keeping the routing control to themselves.

VPLS is a bridged Layer 2 multipoint VPN. A VPLS service is dedicated to each VPLS customer. In an IP/MPLS backbone network, member service routers that participate in the same VPLS service are connected by pseudowires. Each VPLS service is a single LAN segment. All sites connected to the same VPLS service are in the same broadcast domain. VPLS is a Layer 2 VPN; therefore, it is transparent to routing protocols. The service provider provides only bridging services to customers, leaving the routing topology design to the customers. It is an ideal solution for non-IP protocols (e.g., Interwork Packet Exchange, IPX) within a campus. The customer also likes the simplicity of the VPLS service because peering with the service provider in Layer 2 requires fewer restrictions than peering with the service provider in Layer 3.

Ethernet has been the most widely deployed Layer 2 technology for enterprise customers. Service providers are now also adopting Ethernet in their backbone networks to take advantage of its high throughput and low maintenance costs. Ethernet technology is mature and widely used, and therefore widely understood. An IP/MPLS VPN network allows multipoint Ethernet bridging services to be provisioned for Ethernet customers. VPLS service instances are provisioned in the customer-facing service routers involved in the service, and multiple services in the same router are isolated by the service instances and do not exchange traffic. The service provider's network behaves similarly to an Ethernet bridge or switch to the customers it services. Therefore, the VPLS service instance in a service router is referred to as a virtual bridge (VB).

As an important part of any Ethernet bridged network, VPLS supports VLAN trunking, double tagging (Q-in-Q), and VLAN translation. Variations of Spanning Tree Protocol (STP) can be transparently passed by the VB, or the VB can participate in STP with the customer switches it serves. This book focuses on VPLS services because VPLS contains many facets and network design options. Chapters 11 through 18 discuss these facets in detail.

2.3 Meeting the Service Network Requirements Using IP/MPLS VPN Architecture

To provide the services discussed previously (VLL, VPLS, etc.), the service provider must build a network backbone capable of delivering such services. This section discusses the requirements for service providers to build such a multi-service network.

An IP/MPLS VPN network is an MPLS switching-enabled, service-oriented, IP-routed VPN network. The evolution of MPLS technology is the foundation of the IP/MPLS VPN network. The equipment to build such a network must:

- Support IP routing protocols, including scalable Interior Gateway Protocol (IGP) and BGP. The equipment must support traffic engineering capability if advanced MPLS resiliency is desired.

- Be capable of MPLS switching in the data plane and MPLS label signaling in the control plane. To take advantage of the advanced MPLS resiliency, the equipment must support RSVP-TE as the label distributed protocol. To implement VLL and VPLS services, the equipment must support Target LDP (T-LDP) to signal the pseudowires used by these services.

- Support the deployment of service-based QoS, accounting, and security policies. The QoS implementation must be service-oriented. For services sharing the same physical equipment, the QoS must provide granularity for per-service management.

- Be designed to provide high availability. Redundant control plane and data plane design is required to achieve carrier-level performance and reliability.

- Provide strong scalability to support thousands of service instances without compromising performance.

- Support advanced MPLS and VPN resiliency features to take advantage of its scalability, resiliency, and stability.

- Support a network management solution so that the service providers can deploy, modify, and monitor all services in real time. The network management solution must also be intelligent so that the manual interferences can be reduced to minimal.

The IP/MPLS VPN network is a routed IP network. For MPLS to work properly, all network devices must be able to support scalable routing protocols. OSPF or IS-IS should be used as the Interior Gateway Protocol (IGP) in the provider networks because of the requirement for scalability and reliability. In the backbone network, IGP communicates the internal topology of the network and the location of all Provider Edge (PE) and Provider (P) routers to the network elements.

Also, to support advanced IP/MPLS routing/switching, the traffic engineering (TE) extensions of IGP (OSPF-TE and ISIS-TE) are highly desirable. These TE extensions of the routing protocols carry TE-related information in the routing updates to allow each router in the network to build a Traffic Engineering Database (TED). The use of TE and Constraint Shortest Path First (CSPF) allows the system to take more factors (e.g., resources booked by the system and administrative policies) into account when routing traffic. With the support of TE, operators can route traffic through a path other than the IGP best route. Furthermore, with the help of TE and CSPF, RSVP-TE brings resiliency features such as Fast Reroute and secondary LSP into the MPLS LSPs. This makes the service transport tunnel more reliable and significantly improves the convergence performance of the IP/MPLS backbone.

Figure 2.3 illustrates the overall architecture of an IP/MPLS VPN multi-service network.

Figure 2.3   Overview of IP/MPLS VPN Service Network Architecture

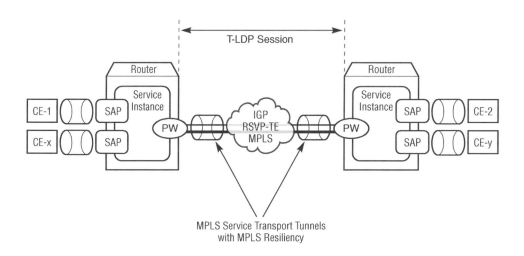

MPLS Service Transport Tunnels
with MPLS Resiliency

In Figure 2.3, two service routers connected to the IP/MPLS backbone network have VPN service instances defined. The service instances that belong to the same VPN service are connected by pseudowires. Each service instance contains Service Access Points (SAPs) to provide customer access. The service instances are virtual software entities residing in the service router.

For networks sharing multiple services, service-related policies must be deployed with per-service granularity. In a shared backbone network, service providers need to deploy QoS policies for different traffic flows in the same service, and for different traffic flows that belong to different services. These QoS policies ensure that the different type of services being purchased by different types of customers are delivered as promised by the SLA. Accounting policies provide service-related statistics, and security policies must provide the protection required by the customers. To fulfill these requirements, policy deployment in an IP/MPLS VPN network must be service-oriented. The policies must be able to be applied to each individual logical service entity, but not to hardware (e.g., ports). This is a key differentiator between a service-oriented network and a hardware-oriented network. Figure 2.4 illustrates the differences between a service-oriented network and a hardware-oriented network.

Figure 2.4 Service-Oriented Networks versus Hardware-Oriented Networks

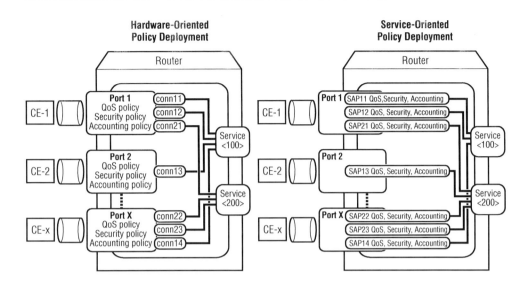

In Figure 2.4, in the hardware-oriented policy deployment (left), the policies (QoS, security, and accounting) are deployed on a per-port basis. The connections that belong to different services sharing the same port must share the same policy. The router does not have a view of the services; it only knows that several connections are associated with each other. The service provider cannot specify a policy for an individual SAP or service. In the service-oriented policy deployment (right), each service is the actual software entity in the service router. Each service uses a SAP to connect to the customer, and each SAP has its own QoS, security, and accounting policies.

MPLS switches and routers must support High Availability (HA) features. HA requires a holistic approach and cannot be an afterthought. HA attributes must include distributed forwarding planes, redundant equipment for control/fabric, modular line card designs, Layer 2 and Layer 3 protocol redundancy, and equipment port and line card failover protection. From an MPLS services standpoint, Non-Stop Routing (NSR) capability is a key prerequisite because one of the primary goals of the service provider is to have minimum interruption for its services, especially during software upgrades.

NSR provides the system with the ability to support Non-Stop Service (NSS). An IP/MPLS-based VPN network is service-oriented. When the underlying routing protocols and traffic forwarding tunnels are robust, the services using the infrastructure are also robust. Redundancy in the design of the control and data planes guarantees the maximum service availability to achieve the highest level of SLAs. With NSS, each component belonging to a service instance has its state maintained in the event of failover. In many conditions, an In Service System Upgrade (ISSU) can be performed to eliminate a service outage during a router upgrade. HA aspects, including NSR and NSS, are covered in detail in Chapter 13.

Service provider networks need to support thousands of customer VPNs concurrently. Therefore, it is important that the MPLS equipment deployed must simultaneously support thousands of service instances for IP/MPLS VPN, as well as Triple Play and Mobile Backhauling services, in order to meet established performance criteria.

2.4 IP/MPLS VPN-Enabled Applications

IP/MPLS-based VPN networks help enable a variety of applications and services:

- **Business (Enterprise) VPN Services** — These may include Layer 2 and/or Layer 3 VPN services.

- **Internet Enhanced Services (IES) with Advanced QoS, Accounting, and Security Policies** — The IES service is a routed IP service, and Layer 2 VPN may be used as the mechanism to backhaul traffic for an Ethernet, FR, or ATM access circuit.

- **Triple Play Services** — BTV, VoD, VoIP, and Internet access. All services are differentiated by an advanced QoS policy to ensure quality of service delivery and the effective use of free bandwidth.

- **Mobile Backhauling Services** — Using VLL or VPLS to enable connectivity between the base stations and the mobile core

By introducing the IP/MPLS Layer 2 VPN solution to the service provider's network, many new applications are made available to service providers. Service providers can build a converged network serving a wide variety of customers with different service requirements. Two new and upcoming solutions are the Triple Play solution and the Mobile Backhauling solution, introduced in the following sections.

Note: Detailed coverage of the Triple Play solution and the Mobile Backhauling solutions is beyond the scope of this book. The following sections introduce these solutions simply as illustrations of IP/MPLS VPN–enabled applications.

The Triple Play Solution

With many available services provided and its strong QoS implementation, the Alcatel-Lucent Service Routing Portfolio (ALSRP) allows a scaled Triple Play solution to be deployed. A Triple Play network provides IPTV, VoIP, Internet access, and other IP-based applications for subscribers. Intensive QoS, accounting, and security policies can be deployed for each subscriber to ensure service quality and security. The Triple Play solution is a new way for service providers to provide combined voice, data, and video applications to a large quantity of customers. Figure 2.5 illustrates an overview of the Triple Play solution.

Figure 2.5   Overview of the Triple Play Solution

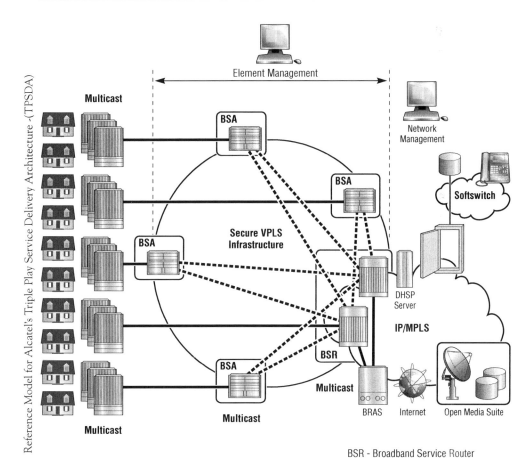

BSR - Broadband Service Router
BSA - Broadband Service Aggregator
BRAS - Broadband Remote Access Server

Triple Play architecture is based on two major network elements, optimized for their respective roles — the broadband service aggregator (BSA) and broadband service router (BSR). An important characteristic of BSAs and BSRs is that they effectively form a distributed *virtual node*, with BSAs performing subscriber-specific functions where the various functions can be scaled, and BSRs providing the routing intelligence where it is most cost-effective.

BSAs are Layer 2 devices that forward traffic using Layer 2 mechanisms but have the QoS and filtering intelligence to enforce higher-layer policies. BSAs terminate Layer 2 access traffic and route traffic over IP/MPLS, with support for a full set of MPLS and IP routing protocols. The BSR supports hundreds of GE and SONET uplink ports (for large-scale deployments) and sophisticated QoS for per-service and per-content/source differentiation.

A Layer 2 forwarding model using a secure and resilient VPLS infrastructure provides connectivity between BSAs and BSRs. The BSA-BSR interconnections form a multipoint Ethernet network with security extensions to prevent unauthorized communication, denial of service, and theft of service. This approach supports all modes of operation, including multiple home gateway models, single or multiple network IP edges, and single or multiple circuits in the last mile.

As described above, MPLS enables delivery of business and residential services and hence is a suitable choice for deploying converged multi-service network infrastructures.

The Mobile Backhauling Solution

Today, mobile customers want more than wireless voice and messaging services from mobile service providers. The introduction of third-generation (3G) mobile network deployment and many IP-based mobile applications has significantly increased the demand to transport data over mobile networks. Mobile service providers have to find the balance between consumer attraction and satisfaction, and the profitability of their networks. To reduce transportation costs, mobile service providers have started to deploy an IP/MPLS VPN-based mobile backhauling solution by building an IP/MPLS multi-service core.

The mobile backhauling solution enables cost-efficient, integrated mobile backhauling of GSM and UMTS networks today, including High Speed Packet Access (HSPA) and HSPA+ technologies, with a strong, investment-protected path to Long-Term Evolution (LTE). This gives service providers the flexibility to deploy different backhaul media options simultaneously (including fiber, copper, and wireless transport), in the most appropriate configuration to best address the network requirements. Figure 2.6 illustrates an overview of a mobile backhauling solution.

Figure 2.6 Mobile Backhauling Solution Example

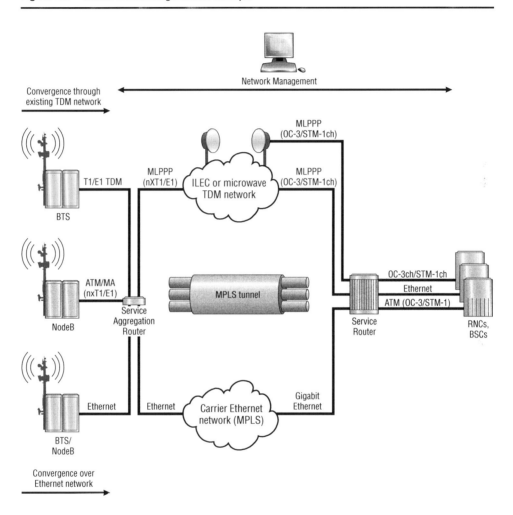

The mobile backhauling solution set offers flexible backhaul evolution by supporting all transport technologies — from TDM, ATM, DSL, and microwave to all IP, MPLS, and pseudowires. By providing stringent and guaranteed QoS for all mobile services, the mobile backhauling solution set efficiently allocates scarce backhaul network resources, offering the following benefits:

- Provides a scalable and efficient mobile Radio Access Network (RAN) that is able to reduce the transport cost per Mbps (megabits per second).

- Enables increased average revenue per user (ARPU) by supporting voice, video, multimedia, and new broadband data services with guaranteed, end-to-end QoS.

- Leverages IP/MPLS and pseudowire technology to support the evolution of the RAN interfaces and the 3GPP2 and 3GPP/LTE standards.

- Delivers a field-proven product set that is carrier-grade, highly available, and scalable with available independent test results.

- Supports a complete suite of service-aware management and tools, with seamless integration to third-party OSS/BSS for improved operational performance monitoring and management.

Summary

The IP/MPLS VPN service network can provide multiple services for different types of customers over a single converged network. It can also provide:

- Point-to-point wire-like services for legacy technologies such as ATM, FR, and TDM through VLL

- Point-to-point and multipoint Ethernet bridging services through Ethernet VLL and VPLS

  The routed IP VPN service is also provided by the VPRN service.

  To build an IP/MPLS VPN multi-service network, the network must be capable of IP routing in the backbone. TE capability is also highly desired, with IP routing protocols to provide optimal traffic forwarding control. The IP/MPLS VPN service architecture requires support for RSVP-TE to signal LSP. RSVP-TE–signaled LSP provides more flexible control of the LSP's path through TE and CSPF, and it has rich resiliency features such as secondary LSP and MPLS FRR to minimize service outages during network failure. Target LDP is required to signal the pseudowires used by the IP/MPLS VPN.

  To provide different service qualities to fulfill different customer requirements in a service-oriented network, providers must be able to deploy QoS, accounting, and security policies with per-service granularity. These polices should be deployed based on the logical service entity, not on the hardware.

With the evolving IP/MPLS VPN technology, service providers can extend their range and category of services to their customers while maintaining reasonable costs. Many operators have deployed the Triple Play service to provide combined voice, data, and video services to a large number of subscribers. Mobile service providers have started to build IP/MPLS VPN multi-service networks to backhaul the mobile traffic.

IP/MPLS VPN
Protocol Fundamentals

II

The new generation of service-oriented networks requires enhancement of IP/MPLS protocols. This section discusses all the protocols required to build an IP/MPLS VPN network, and the enhancements made to these protocols to improve the IP/MPLS VPN network's reliability, performance, and flexibility.

Using MPLS Label Switched Paths as Service Transport Tunnels

3

In an IP/MPLS VPN network, MPLS Label Switched Paths (LSPs) are widely used as transport tunnels for VPN service traffic. Understanding the different signaling protocols used to establish the LSPs and the different types of LSPs is a prerequisite for understanding the MPLS tunneling mechanism.

Chapter Objectives

- Review the basic MPLS concepts, such as MPLS header, label, and MPLS label operations

- Identify the different types of LSP (static-LSP, LDP-LSP, and RSVP-TE LSP)

- Introduce the interface LDP (iLDP) and auto-created LDP-LSP

- Explain the different subtypes of RSVP-TE LSP and their characters and relationships

- Describe configuration of RSVP-TE LSP

This chapter discusses the new, enhanced Multi Protocol Label Switching (MPLS) used by the IP/MPLS Virtual Private Network (VPN) service network to transport service traffic. These enhancements make MPLS more suitable for service delivery, rather than its earlier use as an IP routing shortcut. In the new MPLS architecture, RSVP-TE is introduced as a new label distribution protocol to signal LSPs.

RSVP-TE–signaled LSPs can be used as service transport tunnels. RSVP-TE brings enhanced features such as make-before-break (MBB), Fast Reroute (FRR), and traffic engineering (TE) capacity into MPLS tunneling. This makes the service delivery more robust and optimal. The LDP protocol can still be used as a service transport tunnel signaling protocol to build MPLS tunnels.

3.1 Basic MPLS Concepts Review

MPLS routers distribute labels to each other to forward MPLS encapsulated traffic. These labels form *Label Switched Paths* (LSPs). An LSP can be loosely defined as a series of labels logically connected together so traffic can be encapsulated using these labels and be switched from point A to point B in the network. An IP/MPLS VPN service network uses the LSP differently than the traditional IP routed network that uses MPLS LSPs as routing shortcuts. However, the basic concepts of the MPLS and LSP remain the same. This section reviews these basic concepts. Readers familiar with basic MPLS concepts such as MPLS header, LER/LSR, and label distribution may choose to skip this section and proceed to the section, "Label Switch Path Types."

The benefits of MPLS switching over regular IP routing are its TE capability and its rich resilience features. With RSVP-TE, MPLS LSPs can be manually provisioned from one router to reach another router. In addition, the path the LSP traverses can be engineered, rather than following the core routing table's *best path*. Therefore, the operators have more control over the service traffic forwarding path in their networks. Also, with RSVP-TE, the LSPs can have multiple protection mechanisms enabled, so the failover time is shortened significantly.

MPLS Tunnel and MPLS Label Stack

The MPLS tunnel is the key concept to understanding MPLS architecture. *Tunnel* refers to a forwarding path from one router to another router. When a tunnel is established, the forwarding path from the source to the destination is defined prior to the arrival of the traffic. The traffic being forwarded enters the tunnel from the tunnel's source router and exits the tunnel from the tunnel's destination router. All the routers along the forwarding path of the tunnel simply pass the traffic to the next-hop MPLS router, until it reaches the end of the tunnel. The MPLS tunnel is also generally referred to as a *Label Switched Path*.

Each time a packet is forwarded through an MPLS tunnel, an MPLS header (which contains the actual MPLS label) is inserted into the packet used by the MPLS routers to forward the traffic. Therefore, the packet in the MPLS tunnel is MPLS-encapsulated.

Every MPLS header has a fixed length of 32 bits. The actual MPLS label is the first 20 bits of the MPLS header. The MPLS header is stackable — one of the most desirable features of MPLS. A service payload can be put into an MPLS tunnel by pushing an MPLS header into its encapsulation header. The MPLS-encapsulated packet can then be put into another MPLS tunnel by pushing another MPLS header into the packet's header. This process continues, and creates label stacks. Therefore, packets currently in an MPLS tunnel can be tunneled again. Most vendors' implementations for MPLS routers support a label stack of at least four to five MPLS headers. Figure 3.1 illustrates an MPLS-encapsulated data packet with an MPLS label stack.

Figure 3.1 MPLS Label Stack

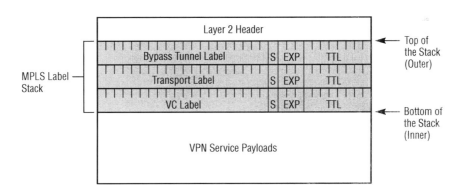

In Figure 3.1, the packet has a label stack with a depth of three labels. Each label is used for a different tunnel:

- **Bypass Tunnel Label** — The bypass tunnel label on the top of the label stack is used by MPLS FRR to route the traffic in the protection tunnel.

- **Transport Tunnel Label** — The transport tunnel label in the middle of the label stack is used by the service transport tunnel to carry service traffic across the service backbone networks.
- **VC Label** — The VC label on the bottom of the label stack is used for IP/MPLS VPN pseudowires to encapsulate traffic for different services. The VC-label is also generally referred to as the *service-label*.

These tunnels and their uses are introduced in later chapters. This example is used to demonstrate that by stacking MPLS labels, a packet can be put into one tunnel, and then be tunneled again. Every time the packet needs to be tunneled, another MPLS label is pushed on the top of the label stack. Every time a router needs to extract the packet out of a tunnel, it pops out (removes) the top label from the label stack. Each MPLS router only processes the labels it requires, ignoring the rest of the label stack.

MPLS Headers and MPLS Labels

Each MPLS header in the MPLS label stack includes the following four fields:

- **Label (20 bits)** — The most significant 20 bits in the MPLS header is the label, with values ranging from 0 to 1,048,575. This label is assigned by the MPLS router to identify traffic.
- **EXP bits (3 bits)** — The next 3 bits are the experimental bits used for Quality of Service (QoS) marking. The three EXP bits can have eight different values for the MPLS router to use to provide service differentiation. QoS is beyond the scope of this book.
- **S bit (1 bit)** — The S bit is the *bottom-of-stack* indicator. The most inner label in the label stack has this bit set to a value of one to indicate the end of the MPLS label stack.
- **TTL bits (8 bits)** — The last 8 bits are time to live (TTL) bits. TTL is used primarily for loop prevention. Each time an MPLS packet travels through an LSR, the TTL bits of the most outer MPLS header in the label stack are reduced by 1. The default value, 255, is set to the TTL bits. When an MPLS router receives an MPLS packet, it subtracts the TTL bits. If the value is zero, the packet is discarded.

Figure 3.2 illustrates the format of the MPLS encapsulation header in MPLS-encapsulated traffic. The example presents an MPLS-encapsulated packet with a single-label MPLS label stack.

Figure 3.2 MPLS Header Format

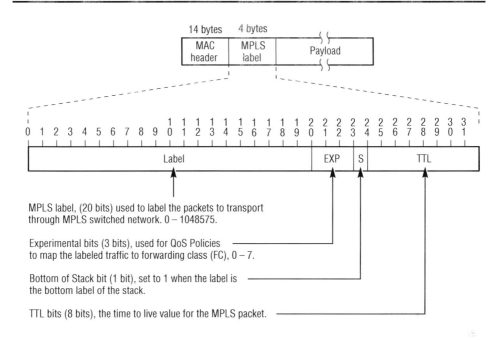

The MPLS label is the first 20 bits of the MPLS header. MPLS labels are used by MPLS routers to identify the traffic and perform actions accordingly. Before an MPLS label can be used to perform MPLS encapsulation, the MPLS routers must agree on the label's meaning. This is performed by the label distribution process, or static label mapping configuration. Before MPLS routers forward traffic through the MPLS tunnel, the traffic destination MPLS router allocates a label from its label space. Then, the traffic destination router distributes this label to the traffic source MPLS router to use when sending the traffic. Upon receiving the label, the traffic source router uses it as an egress label to perform traffic MPLS encapsulation before sending the traffic to the receiver router. The traffic destination router uses the same label as an ingress label to de-encapsulate the traffic from the traffic source. The MPLS label's value range is 0–1,048,575. There are several values reserved by the Internet Assigned Number Authority (IANA) for common uses. Table 3.1 lists all the reserved MPLS label values.

Table 3.1 MPLS Reserved Label Values

MPLS Reserved Label Values	Label Meaning	Restrictions
0	**IPv4 Explicit Null** — The last hop (tail) node of the LSP distributes this label to its previous hop. When it receives an MPLS packet with top label value 0, the switch will not perform label lookup, but will pop the label out directly. Used to speed up switching performance.	Must be at bottom of the stack
1	**Router Alert** — When an MPLS switch receives a packet with top label value 1, it sends the packet to the control plane for further processing. OAM functions use this label to indicate that it is a special-purpose packet, and that it requires control plane inspection.	Must not be at bottom of the stack
2	**Ipv6 Explicit Null** — Similar function to label value 0 for Ipv6 MPLS packets	Must be at bottom of the stack
3	**Implicit Null** — Used by the last hop (tail) node of the LSP to signal the Penultimate Hop Popping (PHP) behavior. When the LSP's penultimate hop (second to last hop) receives a label mapping of 3, it will *not* put the label value into the MPSL packets to send to the tail node. Instead, the penultimate hop router pops up the label for the tail node. An MPLS data packet ingress to a node with label value 3 should never exist.	Must be at bottom of the stack
4–15	Reserved for future use	

The PHP and Implicit Null (3) Label

When MPLS was first implemented, the hardware resources on the MPLS switches were limited. Label operations were using a great deal of CPU and memory resources, so many performance optimization techniques, including Penultimate Hop Popping (PHP), were created to make label switching more efficient and less resource-consuming.

PHP allows the second to last hop MPLS switch to assume some of the label lookup tasks from the last hop router of the LSP; it does this by removing or popping out the label before sending the MPLS packet to the last hop MPLS switch. If PHP is desired, the last hop switch sends an implicit null (3) label mapping to the previous hop switch. When the penultimate hop router receives the explicit null label mapping, it performs label popping instead of label swapping for related traffic. This eliminates the null label lookup that was performed by the last hop switch and saves resources. However, the horsepower of today's MPLS switches makes the resource saving of PHP invisible and unnecessary. Most modern switches retain PHP only for backward compatibility.

The drawback of the PHP operation is that it may break the end-to-end QoS design in the MPLS backbone. This is especially true where the MPLS EXP bits are used for QoS marking. When performing PHP, the second to last hop switch removes the label for LSP, and the QoS marking on the label is lost. If the last hop switch is configured to perform QoS forwarding based on the MPLS EXP bits, it cannot receive the required information. Therefore, the traffic is forwarded to the Best Effort (BE) class by default.

The Alcatel Lucent Service Routing Portfolio (ALSRP) service routers support PHP as a penultimate hop router. As an LSR, if the router receives an implicit null (3) label from the last hop LER, it understands the request and performs PHP on certain traffic accordingly. However, as a last hop LER, the router will not distribute an implicit null (3) label to the previous hop LSR. The hardware capacity of service routers can achieve full line-rate forwarding — there is no need to require the previous hop's LSR to perform PHP to save processing power.

Forwarding Equivalent Class

The traditional MPLS label mapping and distribution is based on Forwarding Equivalent Class (FEC)-to-Label Value mapping distributed by LDP. When the router is running LDP, it advertises and receives FEC-Label bindings. The LDP label distribution contains two pieces of information: the label and who should use the label. Because the traditional MPLS is used to forward IP traffic, an FEC is always an IP-prefix from the router's IP routing table, which indicates the router that has an MPLS tunnel to forward the traffic.

When LDP is used in an MPLS/VPN network, the FEC is a system-IP address (router-id) of the MPLS router. The LDP distributes information on how to reach a specific router with a certain label. By distributing the router-id to label binding information using LDP, all the MPLS routers know how to send traffic to other MPLS routers through MPLS tunnels. In an MPLS service network, the LDP-signaled LSPs are used to carry the VPN service traffic. The LDP FEC-Label advertising mechanism is only used to build MPLS tunnels for carrying the VPN service traffic.

In contrast, when RSVP-TE is used to signal LSPs, it only distributes labels and not the FEC information. RSVP-TE uses a mechanism different from LDP to signal LSPs. It only signals an LSP from one MPLS router to another MPLS router; it does not specify what types of traffic should use the LSP. In an IP/MPLS VPN network, the MPLS label-distributing protocols only handle the setup of the LSP. The Service Distribution Path (SDP) in the MPLS router decides which service's traffic flow should be forwarded though the LSP by answering the question of who should use the label to pass the traffic. Details regarding the SDP and the VPN service architecture are introduced in Chapter 9.

Control Plane: Label Distribution

The process of multiple MPLS routers agreeing on the meaning of certain labels is referred to as *MPLS label distribution*. For any MPLS router, there are two types of MPLS labels:

- **Ingress Label** — The label that a router expects to see on the MPLS encapsulated traffic it receives. In a router's Label Information Base (LIB), the ingress labels are the labels assigned locally and distributed to other routers. When a router wants other routers to use certain label values to encapsulate the traffic before sending traffic to it, the router assigns a label from its own label space and distributes the label to other routers. This label is the ingress label for the MPLS router which distributes it.

- **Egress Label** — The label that a router uses to perform MPLS encapsulation before sending the traffic out. In a router's LIB, the egress labels are the labels received from other router(s). When a router wants to send traffic to another router, it checks its LIB to find the correct egress label (distributed by the traffic destination router) and uses that label to egress traffic.

When a router wants to send MPLS traffic to another router, the traffic destination router must first distribute a label to the traffic source router. This label is used as an egress label for the sender router to send traffic. The same label is used as an ingress label for the traffic destination router to receive traffic. This label is the agreement between the traffic source and the traffic destination routers.

The direction of label distribution is always the opposite of the direction of traffic flow. Label distribution flows from traffic destination to traffic source, and the traffic flows from traffic source to traffic destination. In this book, the directions always refer to the dataflow direction. The traffic source is *upstream*, and the traffic destination is *downstream*. Labels are always distributed from a downstream router to an upstream router; the traffic always flows from an upstream router to a downstream router.

Label distribution can be performed by protocols, or through manual static label mapping configuration. In a Layer 2 VPN service network, there are two protocols used to distribute labels:

- **Link Distribution Protocol (LDP)** — An MPLS router can use LDP to distribute FEC-Label mappings to its LDP neighbors. LDP distributes labels and builds LDP-LSPs automatically. There are two types of LDP used in the MPLS service network:
    - **Link-LDP (also known as interface LDP or iLDP)** — iLDP is used to distribute labels for LDP-LSPs used as transport tunnels.
    - **Target LDP (T-LDP)** — T-LDP is used to distribute vc-labels for L2VPN pseudowires.
- **RSVP-TE (RFC3209)** — RSVP-TE is used to signal an explicit routed LSP. RSVP-TE LSP has more configuration granularity and resilience features than LDP-LSP.

LDP and RSVP-TE are discussed in detail in later sections. Explicit routed LSP is discussed in Chapter 4.

Data Plane: MPLS Label Operations

In the data plane, the MPLS router must perform label operations on the network traffic. There are three types of label operations:

- **PUSH** — The PUSH operation appends the MPLS header onto the traffic. PUSH is also called *MPLS encapsulation*. When the traffic enters the MPLS domain, the MPLS router pushes a label onto it. If the traffic is currently MPLS-encapsulated, the PUSH operation stacks another MPLS header on the top of the MPLS stack.
- **SWAP** — The SWAP operation replaces the MPLS header in the traffic with another MPLS header. SWAP operations happen within the MPLS domain. If the traffic has more than one MPLS header in the MPLS stack, the SWAP operation is only performed on the top MPLS header of the stack.
- **POP** — The POP operation removes the MPLS header in the traffic. POP is also called *MPLS de-encapsulation*. When the traffic leaves the MPLS domain, the

MPLS pops the label out from the traffic. If the traffic has more than one MPLS header in the MPLS stack, the POP operation only removes the top MPLS header. Then, the router will process the exposed MPLS stack accordingly.

Roles and Actions for MPLS Routers

An MPLS router in an MPLS network can have the following roles:

- **Label Edge Router (LER)** — The LER MPLS router resides in the MPLS domain boundary. Traffic enters and exits the MPLS domain through the LER. There are two types of LERs:

  - **Ingress LER (iLER)** — Non-MPLS traffic enters the MPLS domain through the iLER. iLER *pushes* an egress label to the non-MPSL traffic (MPLS encapsulation) before sending the traffic into the MPLS domain.

  - **Egress LER (eLER)** — MPLS traffic exits the MPLS domain through the eLER. eLER *pops* the ingress label from the MPLS traffic (MPLS de-encapsulation) before sending the traffic out of the MPLS domain.

- **Label Switched Router (LSR)** — The LSR in MPLS resides within the MPLS domain. The LSR connects the iLER and eLER to form the MPLS backbone network. A Label Switched Path (LSP) always starts from an iLER and ends at an eLER. The LSP may go through multiple LSRs. An LSR has both ingress labels (distributed to the previous-hop router) and egress labels (received from the next-hop router). When an LSP receives the MPLS traffic, it replaces the ingress label in the traffic with the egress label and sends the traffic out to the next-hop router. This is done without inspecting the MPLS-encapsulated traffic's payload.

These roles are logical concepts that are relevant to the LSP being discussed. A physical router capable of MPLS switching may have multiple roles for different LSPs being discussed. For example, the router can be an iLER for one LSP, but an eLER for another LSP.

In an end-to-end IP/MPLS VPN solution, the service provider's backbone network is actually the MPLS domain. Customer networks are the non-MPLS domain. Customer traffic enters and exits the MPLS domain through a Provider Edge (PE) router; PE routers are the LERs. Provider (P) routers remain in the middle of the MPLS service VPN network to connect PE routers; Provider routers are LSRs. The architecture of the IP/MPLS VPN solution and the concept of P and PE routers are discussed in Chapter 9.

Figure 3.3 illustrates an example of MPLS routers in the MPLS domain performing label distribution and traffic forwarding. The numbered events are detailed in the following list.

Before the MPLS routers in the MPLS domain can forward any traffic, the MPLS protocol configuration is required, as well as the control plane label distribution. The sequence of the events is:

1. If RSVP-TE LSP or static-LSP is used, the LSP must first be configured and administratively enabled. If LDP is used, explicit LSP configuration is not required.

2. The labels must be distributed from the downstream eLER to the upstream iLER. If static LSP is used, label distribution is not required. Label mapping is manually configured in each router statically.

3. After all routers in the LSP have their required labels, the traffic can be forwarded into the MPLS domain. The iLER performs a PUSH with an egress label 103, which was received from the next-hop LSR router.

4. The LSRs along the LSP path SWAP labels on the traffic, hop-by-hop toward the eLER router.

5. When traffic arrives at the eLER router, the router performs a POP to remove the label. The eLER then forwards the traffic outside the MPLS domain.

Figure 3.3 MPLS Domain Example

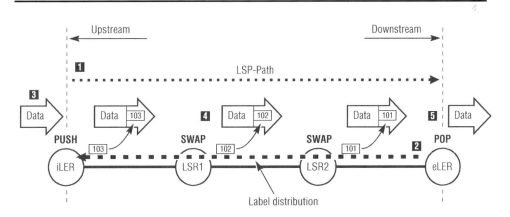

Label Distribution and Storage (Retention) Modes

The MPLS routers distribute labels to each other to establish the LSPs. The MPLS routers also receive label distribution information from other adjacent MPLS routers. Any time an MPLS router must establish LSPs, it must decide how to distribute labels to other routers and how to store the labels received from other routers. There are three modes of label handling in the MPLS router's control plane:

- **Label Distribution Mode** — Downstream Unsolicited (DU) versus Downstream on Demand (DoD). When the router uses DU mode, the router distributes a label to the adjacent MPLS routers without being requested. If the router considers that a label needs to be distributed, it distributes the label to other routers regardless of whether the recipient needs the label. When the router uses DoD mode, it does not distribute a label to another router until it receives an explicit request for a label from that router.

- **Distribution Control Mode** — Ordered Control versus Independent Control. When a router is in Ordered Control label distribution mode, it does not distribute a label to the upstream router until it receives a valid label from the downstream router. In Ordered Control mode, the label is distributed from the eLER router upstream toward the iLER router in an ordered fashion. When a router is in Independent Control mode, it distributes labels to other adjacent routers regardless of whether it has received a label from the downstream router.

- **Label Retention Mode** — Liberal versus Conservative. In Liberal label retention mode, a router stores all the labels it receives from other routers in the LIB. In Conservative label retention mode, a router validates the labels received from other routers and only stores the valid labels into the LIB. The router discards the invalid labels.

In theory, any combination of these three modes is possible. In reality, only certain mode combinations make sense.

In the Alcatel-Lucent Service Router Portfolio (ALSRP), when using LDP as the label distribution protocol, the label distribution mode is Downstream Unsolicited, Independent Control, with Liberal Retention. The LDP protocol distributes the FEC-Label mapping. When LDP is enabled, the router distributes the labels for certain address prefixes (in the IP/MPLS VPN network that is the router's system-id) in the routing table to adjacent LDP routers. The LDP router automatically distributes the FEC-Label mapping to all its neighbor routers regardless of whether the neighbor routers need it or not; this is the Downstream Unsolicited mode. The LDP router distributes FEC-Label mapping regardless of whether it received a label for the FEC from the downstream router; this is the Independent Control mode. The LDP router stores all the FEC-Label mappings received in its LIB; this is the Liberal Retention mode.

When using RSVP-TE as the label distribution protocol, the label distribution is Downstream on Demand, Ordered Control with Conservative Retention. The RSVP-TE router distributes labels to establish an explicitly routed LSP. To establish an RSVP-TE LSP, the label is distributed in the upstream direction, from the LSP's eLER router toward the iLER router. The RSVP-TE router only distributes a label when there is a request from the upstream router; this is the *Downstream on Demand* mode. The RSVP-TE router only distributes a label to an upstream router when it has received a label from the downstream router; this is the Ordered Control mode. The RSVP-TE router validates the labels received, stores the labels that pass validation, and discards invalid labels; this is the Conservative Retention mode.

Details regarding the LDP label distribution and LSP establishment are introduced in Section 3.3. Details regarding to the RSVP-TE label distribution and LSP establishment are introduced in Section 3.4.

3.2 Label Switch Path Types

In traditional routed IP networks, tunnels are not used frequently. Packets are forwarded based on routing tables. The routing decision is made on a hop-by-hop basis on each router. When the data packets arrive, the router uses the data headers to find the next-hop router and forwards the data packet accordingly.

In contrast, in MPLS, tunneling is a fundamental mechanism, especially in the case of the RSVP-TE–signaled LSPs. An MPLS LSP or tunnel is an end-to-end, unidirectional path that can carry traffic from Router A to Router B. Tunnels are established prior to the arrival of data packets. Using label negotiation and distribution, MPLS routers build the tunnels with commonly agreed label values. The path of the tunnel is also decided during the tunnel establishment. When data packets arrive, it is not necessary to perform Layer 3 routing. The routers in the middle of the tunnel use pre-negotiated labels to switch the traffic without any routing table lookups; the data is forwarded through the tunnel and reaches the far-end router. In MPLS, the series of labels used to switch traffic from one router to a far-end router forms an LSP.

To form an LSP between two routers, the routers must decide the path of the LSP. After the path is decided, there must be agreements with all routers along the path (LSR) for the labels used. This is the LSP *signaling process*. LSPs built by different types of signaling protocols have different characteristics. There are three types of LSPs used in the MPLS service network:

- **Static-LSP** — Static-LSPs are manually configured at each router in the MPLS network. In each hop, the label map is manually defined. There is no signaling protocol required to signal the static-LSP.

- **LDP-LSP** — LDP-LSP is established by iLDP automatically. After iLDP is enabled in the corresponding interfaces, the FEC-Label mapping is distributed automatically. The LDP-LSP is established for every FEC.

- **RSVP-TE LSP** — RSVP-TE can be used to signal an explicit hop LSP. The RSVP-TE LSP must be configured in the Head-End (HE) router (the iLER). After the configuration, the HE router calculates the path the LSP must travel and then signals the resource reservation and label distribution.

The static-LSP and LDP-LSP are straightforward. When the configuration for the static-LSP (label maps in each hop) is done, the LSP configuration is complete. If all the interfaces along the path are operationally **up** and the label maps are configured correctly, the static-LSP is ready to forward traffic. For LDP-LSP, if the iLDP adjacencies are established, the FEC-Label bindings are distributed automatically. Thus, the LDP-LSPs to all FECs are built automatically. The case of the RSVP-TE LSP is more complicated. The relatively simple details of static-LSP are addressed in the following subsection, and the next two sections introduce LDP-LSP and RSVP TE-LSP in greater detail.

Static-LSP

As with the static routing in the routed IP networks, in some cases, manual configuration of static-LSP is required. Static-LSP requires the following manual end-to-end configuration in the network:

- The ingress router (iLER) must define the egress label value, the next-hop router IP address, the PUSH action, and the IP address of the terminating router (eLER).

- All intermediate transiting routers (LSRs) must define the ingress label value, the SWAP action, and the egress label value.

- The egress router (eLER) must define the ingress label value and the POP action.

  Because all label switching actions along the static LSP's path are manually defined, it is not necessary to involve label distribution or signaling protocols.

Therefore, the control overhead for static LSP is very low. The router only needs to keep track of the manually defined label values and corresponding actions in the database. There is no end-to-end view from the transiting and terminating routers with respect to the location of the LSP's Head-End and Tail. The originating router has the terminating router's IP address defined in the to x.x.x.x field, but there is no reachability check. If the outgoing interface (next-hop) is up, the static LSP is considered operationally up. The static-LSP does not recognize the concept of state either; if the interfaces in the label map are operationally up, that portion of the LSP is considered functional. Figure 3.4 presents a CLI configuration example of a static-LSP from Router PE-164 to Router PE-165 (traveling through Router PE-163).

Figure 3.4 Static-LSP Configuration Example

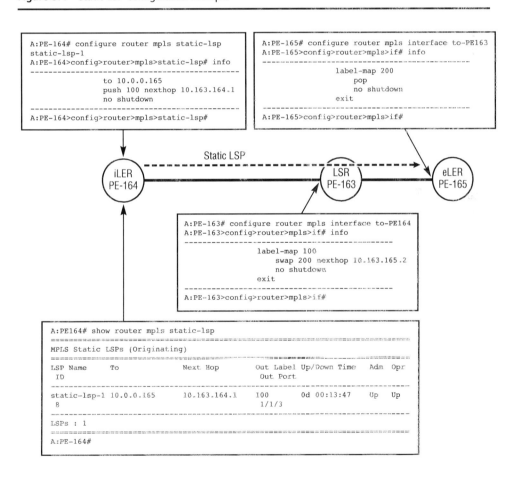

Static-LSP requires intense manual configuration on all involved routers. Once there is a network failure, the operator must perform manual configuration changes to reroute the static-LSP around the failure. In a large-scale network, it is nearly impossible to keep track of the configurations on each hop router to ensure the correctness and consistency of large numbers of static-LSP label mappings. Operators should only use static-LSP in occasional cases for testing purposes or temporary work-arounds.

3.3 LDP-LSP — LDP Label Distribution

LDP label distribution has been used in the traditional MPLS switching world for many years. In the traditional IP routing networks, the IP router can be MPLS-switching-capable. In this case, it may have been desirable to use MPLS switching to carry IP traffic to its destination, instead of using IP routing. This was because of the lower resource consumption of MPLS switching, compared to IP routing in the legacy software-based IP routers. Today, this is not the case because the hardware-based service routers can perform all tasks at line-rate speed. For all the IP prefixes using label-switching, the operator can use LDP to distribute the FEC-Label mapping.

Note: LDP label distribution details for switching IP traffic in a routed network are beyond the scope of this book. The LDP label distribution process is described in RFC 3036/5036 as well as many publications on legacy MPLS switching for IP packets.

This section discusses the LDP used for IP/MPLS VPN backbone transport tunnel signaling. The procedure is similar to the traditional LDP label distribution, with several enhancements, modifications, and limiting criteria.

An Overview of P Routers, PE Routers, and Transport Tunnels

In the IP/MPLS VPN service routing solution, LDP is only used to distribute labels for the VPN services' transport tunnels. The *transport tunnel* is an MPLS or GRE tunnel that can encapsulate the traffic and then send it from one PE router to another PE router across the backbone. Details regarding transport tunnels or SDP, P routers, and PE routers are presented in Chapter 9.

The transport tunnel hides the detailed topology of a provider's backbone network. The IP/MPLS VPN backbone network contains many routers with one or both of the following roles:

- **Provider Edge (PE) Routers** — PE routers are service-aware. VPN services are provisioned only in PE routers. PE routers accept customer traffic into the service and perform VPN and transport tunnel encapsulation. The PE routers then send the traffic to the remote peering PE router(s) that are participating in the same service. The PE router is the iLER and the eLER for the VPN-encapsulated traffic.

- **Provider (P) Routers** — P routers are not service-aware. P routers are used to connect PE routers in the service network, to provide bandwidth and path diversity. The P router is the LSR for the VPN-encapsulated customer traffic. It only swaps transport labels (outer labels) for customer traffic.

The roles of P and PE routers are *logical*. Each physical router in the service network can have one or both roles. The transport tunnel is used to provide a logical connection between PE routers to hide the actual path that the traffic must traverse (links and P routers). Thus, when deploying services, the PE router only needs to consider which remote PE router it needs to send traffic to. The method of arriving at that PE router is handled by transport tunnels. There are three types of transport tunnels:

- **GRE Tunnel** — Uses IP encapsulation to build end-to-end tunnels to reach the remote PE router. GRE tunnels follow the IGP path in the backbone.

- **LDP Tunnel** — Uses LDP-signaled LDP-LSPs with MPLS encapsulation to reach the remote PE router. LDP tunnels follow the IGP path in the backbone.

- **RSVP-TE Tunnel** — Uses RSVP-TE-signaled LSP with MPLS encapsulation to reach the remote PE router. The RSVP-TE tunnel can follow the IGP path, the traffic engineering (TE) path, or a manually defined path.

The RSVP-TE tunnels are introduced in Chapter 5. The LDP tunnel and GRE tunnel are discussed in this chapter.

> **Note:** *Transport tunnel* is a more general term for the tunnel used from one router to another. If MPLS is used, a transport tunnel is an LSP (signaled by LDP or RSVP-TE). If GRE is used, a transport tunnel is an IP-over-IP tunnel.
>
> A *Service Distribution Path* (SDP) contains one or more transport tunnels. SDPs use transport tunnels to carry the VPN traffic. SDP is discussed in Chapter 9.

LDP Label Generation and Distribution for Service Transport Tunnel

The LDP in a service network only signals the transport tunnel. The transport tunnels are used by the PE router to reach the remote PE router(s). In a service network, all routers (P, PE, or P/PE) are identified by advertising their system-IP addresses into the backbone's routing protocol. Therefore, the LDP only builds tunnels to reach each router's system-IP address.

The legacy LDP for IP routing assigns (generates) labels for all prefixes in the routing table with a valid next hop and distributes these labels to all LDP peers. This task is unnecessary with a service routing network. The LDP in the service network is used only for tunnel label generation, to reach the remote PE's system-IP. By default, *the LDP in the service network routers only allocates (generates) and distributes labels for the system-IP address.* Therefore, fewer labels require generation and distribution — the label distribution is more efficient. In LDP label distribution for LDP-LSP that is used for transport tunnels (SDPs), the FEC is always a /32 IP address — a router's system IP address. The following rules for ALSRP LDP label generation apply:

- The LDP router generates FEC-Label mapping for its own system-IP address and distributes it to LDP peers.
- The LDP router may also distribute FEC-Label mapping for system-IP addresses received from other routers. It can do this if it currently has an egress label bound to the system-IP address received from the next-hop router.

LDP relies on IGP to provide reachability information. The example in Figure 3.5 assumes that IGP has been deployed and is functioning properly. When there is a network failure, the convergence of LDP relies on the underlying IGP. LDP activates a stored label for traffic encapsulation only when the label is received from the router that is the next-hop router of the IP-prefix the label is bound to. The next-hop router information is collected from the IGP routing table. Therefore, if there is a network failure, the LDP does not converge to use a different label until the IGP converges and changes the routing table content. Any mechanisms that speed up the IGP convergence will benefit the LDP convergence. This includes mechanisms such as:

- **Bi-directional Forwarding Detection (BFD)** — A lightweight Hello protocol with a higher heartbeat rate that can detect remote failure faster than a regular routing protocol. BFD detects failures and notifies the upper-layer protocols such as OSPF, RSVP-TE.

- **EFM OAM (802.3ah)** — An Ethernet-link OAM protocol that detects Ethernet-link failures in subseconds. When it detects a failure, the port is disabled so these upper-layer protocols can converge.
- **Tuning the IGP** — Tunes the IGP protocol timers to detect failures faster, for example, to shorten the OSPF Hello timer and dead timer.

Figure 3.5 illustrates a provider backbone network with P and PE routers. In this network, LDP builds LDP-LSPs for other routers to reach PE-1 (10.0.0.1/32).

Figure 3.5 Building LDP-LSP Using LDP Automatic Label Distribution

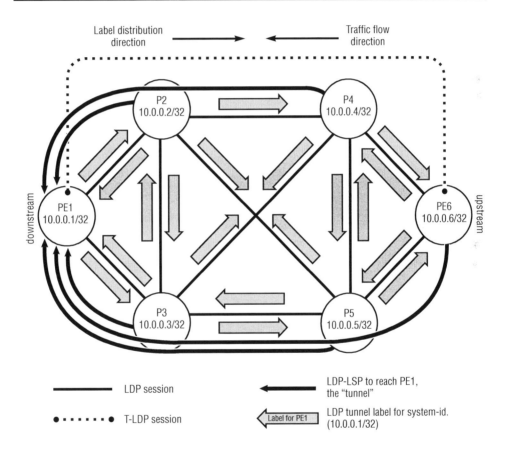

Figure 3.5 illustrates the LDP label distribution to build transport tunnels used by all other P/PE routers to reach PE1 (PE1 has a system-IP address of 10.0.0.1/32). The entire network has four P routers in the core and two PE routers in the edge. The T-LDP sessions are only required between PE routers; they are not involved in

the LDP tunnel establishment but are used for service pseudowire establishment. (Pseudowires are discussed in Chapter 9.) As shown in Figure 3.5, the label distribution is in the upstream direction. The label being distributed is bound with the system-IP of the router. The label is used as an egress label by the router receiving the label. It uses this label to encapsulate the traffic and send the traffic destined for the system-IP address that is bound with that specific label value. The LDP router also distributes the labels of any received system-IP address with a label bound to it.

The label is distributed with an LDP `Label Mapping` message. This message has an FEC type-length value (TLV) that indicates the IP prefix that the label reaches, and a General Label TLV with the label value. The label distribution to the peer tells the receiver: "If you want to reach `<IP-address>` from me, use the label value `<X>`." In any LDP router, the label generation process is as follows:

1. For every IP-prefix that requires label distribution, the LDP router allocates a label value from the available label value range. Then, the LDP installs this label into the LIB as the ingress label for the IP-prefix. This is referred to as *label generation*.

2. The LDP router distributes the label to all peering LDP routers. For each IP-prefix that requires label distribution, the LDP router generates one label and distributes it to all peering routers.

3. When an LDP router receives any label from its peering routers, it stores the label (with the IP-prefix association) in the LIB.

The LDP label distribution for a transport tunnel in a service routing network uses the following rules:

*   **Downstream Unsolicited (DU) Distribution** — A router distributes labels to all LDP peers with active LDP sessions. Labels are distributed to all the LDP peers regardless of whether the peer is downstream from the IP-prefix bound with the label. The router respects the split-horizon rule, which states that a router will not distribute a label associated with an IP-prefix to the next-hop router of that same IP-prefix.

*   **Ordered Control** — An LDP router will not generate and distribute a label for an IP-prefix to its LDP peers unless:

    *   The label is for its own system-IP address. Each router generates a label for its own system-IP address and distributes the label to all its LDP peers.

- The IP-prefix in the routing table is a system-IP (/32) address, and the router currently has an egress label received from the next-hop router.

- **Liberal Retention** — The router keeps all the labels it has received for all IP prefixes. If a label received for a system-IP is not from the next-hop router, it is still stored in the LIB in the control plane. However, this label will not be used as the active label for traffic destined to that system-IP. Therefore, this label will not be put into the Label Forwarding Information Base (LFIB) in the data plane. Liberal Retention speeds up the failure convergence because these databases store all labels for the same IP-prefix. When a failure occurs, the IP-prefix's next-hop router may change. In this scenario, the router simply retrieves the label value distributed by the new next-hop router for the label database, installs it to the LFIB, and uses it to forward traffic — it does not wait for the new next-hop router to distribute the label.

Although the transport tunnel is only required between PE routers, when LDP is used to build transport tunnels, all P and PE routers have transport tunnels created automatically between them. The LDP signaling of LDP-LSPs is automatic. All PE and P routers generate and distribute their system-IP addresses. All P and PE routers have LDP tunnels between them, regardless of whether the tunnel is required. In the example shown in Figure 3.5, LDP distributes the label bound with IP address 10.0.0.1/32. Five unidirectional LSPs were established to reach PE-1, one for each P or PE router.

LSPs Generated by LDP

In theory, an LSP represents a forwarding path composed of a series of labels in each router along the path — a path that carries traffic from one end of the network to the other end. RSVP-TE and LDP use different approaches to build LSPs.

The RSVP-TE Approach

For example, consider the scenario in which an LSP transport tunnel from PE1 to PE2 is required over the MPLS backbone network. When using RSVP-TE, the LSP is explicitly defined in the Head-End (HE) router, PE1. In the LSP configuration, the operator specifies the far-end (or Tail) router PE2, as well as some path-related LSP information. The HE router PE1 has an entry in the LSP database for this LSP. The RSVP-TE LSP is an actual entity that can be configured, administratively enabled or disabled, modified, or deleted. When using this LSP to carry traffic for SDP, the operator must enter the name of the LSP in the SDP configuration. RSVP-TE LSP has an end-to-end view in the HE router where it is defined. For a network that requires an LSP full mesh using RSVP-TE, the operator must create each LSP individually in the HE router. To test an RSVP-TE LSP using LSP-ping, the operator must enter the name of the LSP.

The LDP Approach

The LSPs created by LDP differ from those created by RSVP-TE. In a service routing network with LDP enabled in all P and PE routers, the LDP performs automatic label generation and distribution for all routers' system-IP addresses. When the LDP label generation and distribution is complete, an LDP-LSP full mesh (one LSP between any two routers) is created among all LDP routers. However, there is no end-to-end view of the LSP. The label distribution process automatically builds LDP-LSP in a hop-by-hop manner. Note that LDP-LSP is a virtual concept; in every router, there is no explicit creation of an LDP-LSP. When using LDP-LSP in an SDP, the operator enters **ldp** in the SDP configuration. The SDP then uses the LDP-LSP, automatically created by the LDP, to carry the traffic to its far-end router. To reach a PE router, that router's system-IP address must be used as the traffic destination address. To test an LDP-LSP using LSP-ping, the IP-prefix (system-IP) of the far-end router represents the LSP; there is no name for the LDP-LSP.

Active Label

The LDP uses downstream unsolicited label distribution with Liberal Retention mode. This means that when a PE router generates a label for an IP-prefix (either its own system-IP or a /32 address it has an egress label for), it distributes this label to all its LDP peers. Therefore, one PE router may receive more than one label for the same IP-prefix from different LDP peers. In this case, all the received labels for the same IP-prefix are stored in the LIB. However, only the label received from the current next-hop router (indicated by the IGP routing table) is *active* and is used to forward the traffic. Only that active label is provided to the LFIB in the data plane. Figure 3.6 illustrates an example of an LIB with labels received and distributed from an LDP router as well as the active labels installed from the LIB to the LFIB.

Figure 3.6 shows the router's label databases. The top of the graphic illustrates the LIB, which stores all the labels that are generated and received. The bottom of Figure 3.6 shows the LFIB, which contains only those active labels that are actually being used.

Figure 3.6 Label Information Base and Label Forwarding Information Base: Installing Active Labels

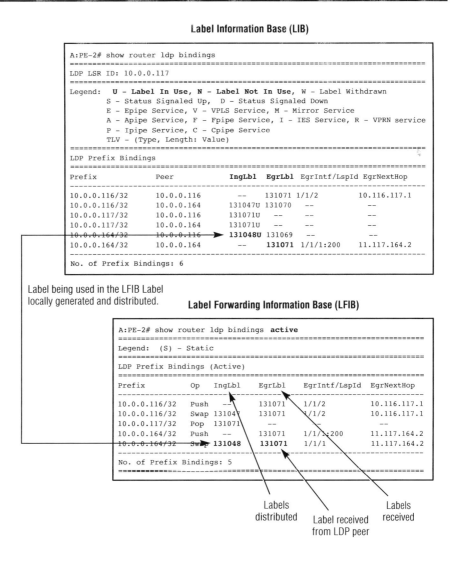

Label being used in the LFIB Label locally generated and distributed.

Labels distributed

Label received from LDP peer

Labels received

Equal Cost Multi-Path in LDP

In a network with multiple forwarding paths, it may be desirable to balance traffic among them. The Equal Cost Multi-Path (ECMP) is used by IGP to route traffic to the same destination through different paths. By default, the service router's Routing Table Manager (RTM) selects a single next hop for every IP-prefix to install to the routing table. With ECMP enabled, the RTM allows more than one next hop used for one IP-prefix. An ECMP prerequisite is that these routes must be learned from the same routing protocol and have the same cost value.

LDP is closely linked with IGP. LDP consults the IGP routing table to select the label to use (active label) from a group of labels received for the same IP-prefix. When ECMP is enabled, the routing table may have more than one entry for one IP-prefix. Each entry has a different next-hop router. The LDP then will also use more than one label to forward traffic to that IP-prefix destination. LDP uses all the labels received from the router that is considered by the routing table as the next hop for that IP-prefix. Figure 3.7 illustrates the LFIB content change before and after enabling ECMP.

In Figure 3.7, for the same destination IP prefix, the routing table has two entries with different next-hop IP addresses. Therefore, the LDP has two sets of active label bindings for the same destination. Figure 3.8 demonstrates the multiple LDP-LSPs after the ECMP has been enabled.

Figure 3.8 illustrates the effect of ECMP in the service network used as an example in this chapter. Without ECMP, every P and PE router uses one LDP-LSP to reach the PE1 (10.0.0.1/32) because of LDP label generation and distribution. We assume that the entire network uses the same physical links (e.g., Gigabit Ethernet). In studying the LSPs to reach PE1, you see that Routers P4, P5, and PE6 have equal paths. When the ECMP is enabled on all routers, LDP in each of these routers creates two LDP-LSPs to PE1, using the two labels from both next-hop routers.

Figure 3.7 LFIB Content before and after Enabling ECMP

```
A:PE-2# show router route-table                              Before ECMP
===============================================================================
Route Table (Router: Base)
===============================================================================
Dest Prefix                          Type    Proto   Age        Pref
       Next Hop[Interface Name]                          Metric
-------------------------------------------------------------------------------
10.0.0.116/32                        Remote  OSPF    00h45m35s  10
       10.116.117.1                                         1000
10.0.0.117/32                        Local   Local   22h54m34s  0
       system                                               0
10.0.0.164/32                        Remote  OSPF    01h01m52s  10
       11.117.164.2                                         1000
=== output omitted ===
A:PE-2# configure router ecmp 2
A:PE-2# show router route-table
===============================================================================
Route Table (Router: Base)                                   After ECMP
===============================================================================
Dest Prefix                          Type    Proto   Age        Pref
       Next Hop[Interface Name]                          Metric
-------------------------------------------------------------------------------
10.0.0.116/32                        Remote  OSPF    00h45m43s  10
       10.116.117.1                                         1000
10.0.0.117/32                        Local   Local   22h54m42s  0
       system                                               0
10.0.0.164/32                        Remote  OSPF    00h00m00s  10
       10.117.164.2                                         1000
10.0.0.164/32                        Remote  OSPF    00h00m00s  10
       11.117.164.2                                         1000
=== output omitted ===
```

```
A:PE-2# show router ldp bindings active                      Before ECMP
===============================================================================
Legend:  (S) - Static
===============================================================================
LDP Prefix Bindings (Active)
===============================================================================
Prefix         Op   IngLbl   EgrLbl   EgrIntf/LspId  EgrNextHop
-------------------------------------------------------------------------------
10.0.0.116/32  Push  --      131071   1/1/2          10.116.117.1
10.0.0.116/32  Swap 131047   131071   1/1/2          10.116.117.1
10.0.0.117/32  Pop  131071   --       --             --
10.0.0.164/32  Push  --      131071   1/1/1:200      11.117.164.2
10.0.0.164/32  Swap 131048   131071   1/1/1          11.117.164.2
-------------------------------------------------------------------------------
No. of Prefix Bindings: 5
===============================================================================
A:PE-2# configure router ecmp 2
A:PE-2# show router ldp bindings    active                   After ECMP
===============================================================================
Legend:  (S) - Static
===============================================================================
LDP Prefix Bindings (Active)
===============================================================================
Prefix         Op   IngLbl   EgrLbl   EgrIntf/LspId  EgrNextHop
-------------------------------------------------------------------------------
10.0.0.116/32  Push  --      131071   1/1/2          10.116.117.1
10.0.0.116/32  Swap 131047   131071   1/1/2          10.116.117.1
10.0.0.117/32  Pop  131071   --       --             --
10.0.0.164/32  Push  --      131071   1/1/1:100      10.117.164.2
10.0.0.164/32  Swap 131048   131071   1/1/1          10.117.164.2
10.0.0.164/32  Push  --      131071   1/1/1:200      11.117.164.2
10.0.0.164/32  Swap 131048   131071   1/1/1          11.117.164.2
-------------------------------------------------------------------------------
No. of Prefix Bindings: 7
===============================================================================
```

Figure 3.8 Link LDP ECMP Transport Tunnel Establishment

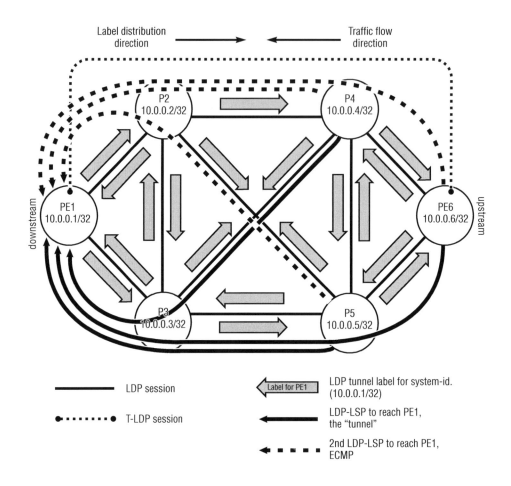

3.4 RSVP-TE LSPs

RSVP-TE is widely used in large-scale MPLS service VPN networks because of its TE capability and resiliency features. RSVP-TE LSPs are used as transport tunnels to carry IP/MPLS VPN-encapsulated service traffic. The RSVP-TE-signaled LSP has the following characteristics:

- **Predetermined Path** — RSVP-TE-signaled LSPs are explicit hop LSPs. RSVP-TE allows the operator to predetermine the path that the LSPs must travel.

- **Explicit LSP Configuration and Signaling Process to Establish the LSP** — RSVP-TE LSP must be explicitly defined in the HE router. After configuration, the LSP must be administratively enabled. At that point, the HE router starts the LSP establishment signaling process by sending a PATH message.

- **Resource Reservation and Control Plane Connection Admission Control (CAC)** — RSVP-TE-signaled LSP uses a reservation (RESV) message to distribute labels and reserve resources to the LSP. When signaling an RSVP-TE LSP, the routers along the path (including the HE, LSR, and TE router) perform a resource availability check. If there is no available resource to fulfill the LSP's requirement, the signaling process is terminated. This prevents overbooking of the network resources in the control plane.

- **Rich Resiliency Features** — RSVP-TE LSPs can be protected by secondary LSP or Fast Reroute (FRR). With these features enabled, the LSP can quickly converge from a network failure. Also, RSVP-TE LSP supports the make-before-break (MBB) manner of LSP modification. When the LSP must be altered (e.g., because of increasing bandwidth), the RSVP-TE does not tear down the existing LSP until the new LSP is established. Traffic is not lost when the LSP's parameters are modified.

RSVP-TE LSP in a Service Network: LSP, LSP-Path, RSVP Session, Label, and Path

When the protocol RSVP-TE is used as a label distribution protocol to signal LSP in MPLS switching, it introduces a hierarchical label distribution mechanism. This mechanism is different from the traditional LDP downstream unsolicited label distribution mechanism previously introduced. RSVP-TE protocol performs DoD label distribution with Ordered Control and Conservative Retention. It requires explicit provisioning of the LSP in the HE router and uses RSVP-TE messages to signal the LSP.

A clear definition of the terms used in discussing RSVP-TE MPLS LSP is crucial for these discussions. This section defines the principal terms used for the RSVP-TE LSP discussions throughout the entire book.

RSVP-TE LSPs have four basic entities defined in a hierarchical manner:

- **LSP** — LSP is a logical entity that only exists in the HE router of an LSP. LSP represents the MPLS reachability from one router (HE router) to another router (TE router). One LSP can contain more than one LSP-Path.

Note: In some publications, the *LSP* is also referred to as an *LSP-Tunnel*. *LSP* and *LSP-Tunnel* are equivalent and exchangeable terms, however, for the ease of discussion and consistency, LSP is used throughout this book.

- **LSP-Path** — An LSP-Path is a logical entity defined in the HE router to represent an MPLS label connection that can reach the LSP's TE router. Once established, the LSP-Path is formed by a series of RSVP sessions in all the routers along the LSP-Path. In reality, when an MPLS FRR one-to-one detour LSP is used, one LSP-Path can have two sets of RSVP sessions.

  From the data plane's perspective, an LSP-Path is a series of labels associated together for the HE router to use to encapsulate MPLS traffic and send it to the TE router.

Note: In some publications, the term *LSP* is used to describe the series of labels sent from the iLER to the eLER. In this book, the term *LSP* is used to describe the LSP-Tunnel. The end-to-end MPLS forwarding path formed by the label is referred to as the *LSP-Path*.

In addition, the LDP-LSP that is established is equivalent to the LSP-Path established by RSVP-TE.

- **RSVP Session** — An RSVP session is an MPLS label cross-connect. It is the physical implementation of the LSP-Path on every router along the actual path of the LSP-Path. In each MPLS router, one RSVP session associates one ingress label and one egress label of the same LSP-Path. RSVP sessions must be refreshed frequently to maintain the session state.

- **Label** — An MPLS label is a 20-bit value that resides in the MPLS header and is used by the MPLS router to encapsulate traffic. Two MPLS routers agree on the meaning of the label via protocol exchange or static configuration. Label mappings in all routers along the LSP form the data path of the LSP-Path.

- **Path** — The path is a logical entity containing a list of IP hops. When an LSP is associated with a path, the path regulates the LSP as to which route it must take. A path can be associated with any LSPs to control their routes.

Figure 3.9 presents all these entities and their relationships.

In Figure 3.9, SDP is also presented in the figure as a reference only. SDP uses one or more LSPs to carry service traffic for itself. The LSP is at the top of the RSVP-TE LSP hierarchy. One LSP can have one or more LSP-Paths in it. One LSP-Path is formed by a series of RSVP sessions in each router along the path of the LSP-Path.

Figure 3.9 SDP, LSP, LSP-Path, RSVP Session and Labels

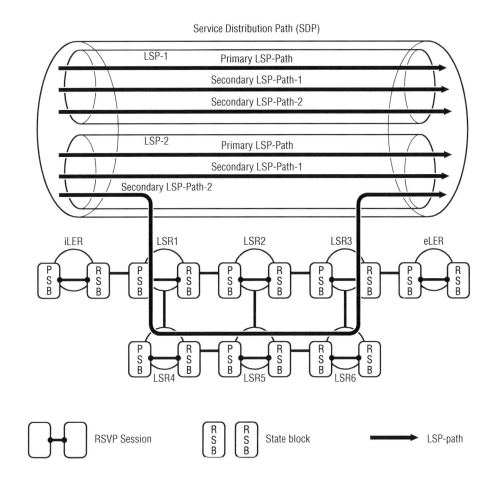

When configuring RSVP-TE LSP in the HE router, the operator must define the LSP first. An LSP uses one or more MPLS LSP-Paths to reach the far-end router. In the router configuration, the LSP is identified by lsp-name. In the RSVP signaling, the LSP is identified by the tunnel-id and the ext-tunnel-id in the

SESSION objects in all RSVP messages. All LSP-Paths that belong to the same LSP have the same SESSION object — therefore, they all have the same tunnel-id. (This is why the LSP is sometimes referred to as an *LSP-Tunnel*.) An LSP must have at least one primary LSP-Path and up to seven secondary LSP-Paths defined in it. But at any one time, only a single LSP-Path can be used to carry the traffic for the LSP. This single LSP-Path is called the *active LSP-Path* or *active path* of the LSP. LSP-Paths have a primary/backup relationship. The primary LSP-Path is the most preferred path. The secondary LSP-Paths are used as protection or backup paths. When the primary LSP-Path fails, the first available secondary LSP-Path assumes the traffic-forwarding task. If there is more than one secondary LSP-Path available when the primary LSP-Path fails, the router chooses one secondary LSP-Path to forward the traffic. The actual active LSP-Path selection criteria are introduced in later sections.

The LSP-Path is an MPLS forwarding path established from the HE router to the TE router via a series of labels distributed in each hop. A router can use an LSP-Path to send traffic to a far-end router. The LSP is a logical representation of the MPLS tunnel used to reach the far-end router; the LSP-Path is the entity that actually carries the traffic using MPLS label switching. In RSVP-TE, one LSP-Path must belong to an LSP. Two objects are required for LSP identification:

- **Tunnel-id** — Tunnel-id is shared by all LSPs belonging to the same LSP. Tunnel-id is located in the SESSION object.
- **LSP-id** — Each individual LSP-Path has its own LSP-id. The LSP-id is located in the SENDER_TEMPLATE object.

All RSVP-TE sessions belonging to the same LSP-Path have the same SESSION and SENDER_TEMPLATE objects. Therefore, these sessions all have the same tunnel id and LSP-id. The LSP-Path is configured in the HE router under the LSP configuration.

When the LSP-Path is signaled and established, its RSVP sessions are visible on every router. The RSVP-TE protocol is used to signal the LSP-Path. The RSVP session is the actual entity that resides on every router involved in the same LSP-Path. When RSVP-TE signals the LSP-Path, it actually forms the LSP-Path by building a series of RSVP sessions on all the routers along the path from the HE router to the Tail router. These RSVP sessions all have the same SESSION and SENDER_TEMPLATE objects.

The RSVP session must belong to an LSP-Path, and an LSP-Path must belong to an LSP. Therefore, to identify an RSVP session, three identifications are required:

- **Tunnel-id** — Tunnel-id is shared by all LSP-Paths belonging to the same LSP. Tunnel-id is located in the SESSION object.
- **LSP-id** — Each individual LSP-Path has its own LSP-id. The LSP-id is located in the SENDER_TEMPLATE object.
- **Session Name** — In every router, each RSVP session has its own name that is stored in the SESSION_ATTRIBUTE object, along with the flag fields.

If the LSP-Path uses MPLS FRR one-to-one backup, two sets of RSVP sessions belong to the same LSP-Path. One set belongs to the original protected LSP-Path. The other set belongs to the detour LSP-Path. Both RSVP sessions share the same tunnel-id and the same LSP-id but use different session names in their SESSION_ATTRIBUTE objects. MPLS FRR is introduced in Chapter 5.

An RSVP session includes the following objects:

- **A Path State Block (PSB)** — Maintains the PATH state of the session and stores the PATH message.
- **A Reservation State Block (RSB)** — Maintains the RESV state of the session and stores the RESV message.
- **MPLS Labels** — Are stored/reserved for the session to use to ingress/egress traffic.

The *path* is a concept beyond the LSP, and it is defined separately from LSP or LSP-Paths. The *path* is a list of hops with which the LSP-Path associated with it must travel. A path only contains a list of loose hops or strict hops for the LSP-Path to traverse. When creating an LSP-Path, the LSP-Path must be associated with a path to find its route to the far-end router. Note that the path is associated only with the LSP-Path, not the LSP. An LSP can have more than one LSP-Path, and each LSP-Path can be associated with a different path.

RSVP-TE–signaled LSP-Paths are *explicit route* LSP-Paths. Before the RSVP-TE starts the signaling process to build an LSP-Path, it must build an *explicit routing object* (ERO) that contains all the interface IP addresses that the LSP-Path must pass through to reach its destination. When signaling the LSP-Path, the RSVP-TE PATH message follows the route specified by the ERO. The path configuration lists the hops the operator requires the LSP-Path to travel through. The path is not the ERO; the path is one of the constraints used by the HE router to calculate the ERO.

A path can have a hop list containing any type of IP address: interface, loopback, or system. The path describes the traffic's desired route by listing all hops in the route and their relationships. The ERO contains IP addresses belonging to the physical or logical interfaces on routers. The path can be strictly or loosely defined; the ERO is calculated based on the hops contained in the path's hop list. If there is no specific path requirement, an empty path can be defined and associated with the LSP-Path.

The *label* is the tag that the MPLS routers use to encapsulate and de-encapsulate traffic. The routers along the route of the LSP agree on the label to use for the LSP-Path to pass traffic. They arrive at this agreement by either using a static label mapping configuration or exchanging information through label distribution protocols (LDP, RSVP-TE). When using RSVP-TE to signal the LSP-Path, the HE router sends a PATH message with a LABEL_REQUEST object requesting labels from the Tail router. The Tail router sends an RESV message containing a LABEL object to distribute the label toward the HE router.

An LSP-Path includes a series of label mappings on all the routers along its route. Each RSVP session contains two labels for the LSP-Path it belongs to: an ingress label (for an LSR) or PUSH operation (for the HE router) and an egress label (for an LSR) or POP operation (for the Tail router). The two labels are bound together to form a cross-connect in the LSR.

The RSVP-TE MPLS LSP has the following hierarchical architecture:

- A path that includes a list of hops used as a constraint when the RSVP-TE calculates the ERO for the LSP

- Two labels (or one label with a PUSH or POP operation) that belong to one RSVP session

- Up to two sets of RVPS sessions among all the involved routers that can belong to one LSP

- Up to eight LSP-Paths (one primary/seven secondary) can belong to one LSP.

- Up to 16 LSPs can be bound to a Service Distribution Path (SDP).

SDP is mentioned here only to complete this discussion and provide the bigger picture. Services use SDP to pass traffic among PE routers. SDP is introduced in detail in Chapter 9.

Determining the LSP-Path's Path

A *path* is a list of the abstract nodes that the operator wants the LSP-Path to traverse through the network. Different paths can be defined in the HE router. When creating an LSP-Path under the LSP, the desired path is associated with the LSP-Path. After the path association, the router must calculate the actual path that the LSP-Path should take and program it into the ERO. The ERO is then inserted into the PATH message for the HE router to signal the LSP-Path. Figure 3.10 illustrates an example of this process of LSP-Path configuration.

In this example, the hop list in the path configuration is a rough description of how the operator wants the LSP-Path to traverse the network. When the operator defines a path to specify a desired route, there are two types of hops that can be specified:

- **Strict Hop** — Specifies the immediate next-hop LSR routers that the LSP-Path must traverse.
- **Loose Hop** — Specifies the downstream LSR routers that the LSP-Path must traverse. These routers are not necessarily adjacent to each other.

Alternatively, a path can also be empty. An empty path indicates that the operation has no preference for the path that the LSP-Path takes. When creating an LSP-Path in the LSP, the name of the path is a mandatory parameter. If the operator does not want to control the path, the operator must create and administratively enable at least one path with empty content. This path can be associated with any LSP-Path belonging to any LSP.

It is important to fully understand the concepts of *strict hop* and *loose hop* in the path definition, the relationship between them, IGP or CSPF types of LSP-Paths, and their impact on the ERO. If the hop list in the path is not correct, all LSP-Paths associated with the path cannot come up. The following section discusses the concepts of path and hop in detail.

Hop: Strict versus Loose

A path contains a list of abstract nodes that the LSP-Path must traverse. Each of these abstract nodes is a hop. A *hop* is an IP address (system or interface IP address) of an LSR in the path. Therefore, the *path* is the list of the LSRs that an LSP-Path must travel through. The actual index number in the hop configuration is irrelevant — the LSP-Path must follow the order of the hops.

In addition, a hop in the list can have a *strict* or *loose* character. *Strict* or *loose* describes the relationship between the current hop's IP address being defined and the previous hop's IP address in the hop list of the path definition. If the hop is the first one defined in the path list, the strict or loose character specifies the relationship between this hop and the HE router.

Figure 3.10 Configuration Example: Path, LSP, and LSP-Path

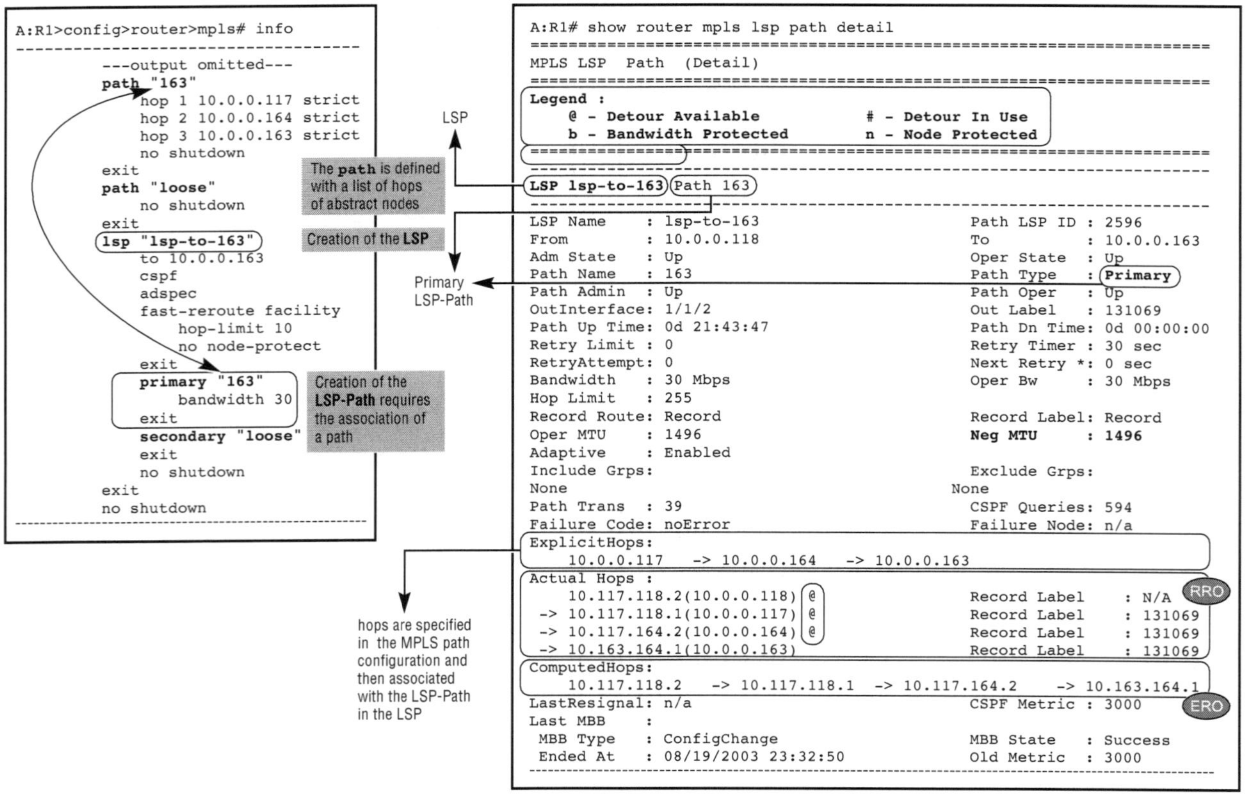

```
A:R1>config>router>mpls# info
---output omitted---
    path "163"
        hop 1 10.0.0.117 strict
        hop 2 10.0.0.164 strict
        hop 3 10.0.0.163 strict
        no shutdown
    exit
    path "loose"
        no shutdown
    exit
    lsp "lsp-to-163"
        to 10.0.0.163
        cspf
        adspec
        fast-reroute facility
            hop-limit 10
            no node-protect
        exit
        primary "163"
            bandwidth 30
        exit
        secondary "loose"
        exit
        no shutdown
    exit
no shutdown
```

The **path** is defined with a list of hops of abstract nodes

Creation of the **LSP**

Creation of the **LSP-Path** requires the association of a path

LSP
Primary LSP-Path

```
A:R1# show router mpls lsp path detail

MPLS LSP Path (Detail)
===============================================================
Legend :  @ - Detour Available       # - Detour In Use
          b - Bandwidth Protected    n - Node Protected
===============================================================
LSP lsp-to-163  Path 163
---------------------------------------------------------------
LSP Name    : lsp-to-163           Path LSP ID : 2596
From        : 10.0.0.118           To          : 10.0.0.163
Adm State   : Up                   Oper State  : Up
Path Name   : 163                  Path Type   : Primary
Path Admin  : Up                   Path Oper   : Up
OutInterface: 1/1/2                 Out Label   : 131069
Path Up Time: 0d 21:43:47          Path Dn Time: 0d 00:00:00
Retry Limit : 0                    Retry Timer : 30 sec
RetryAttempt: 0                    Next Retry *: 0 sec
Bandwidth   : 30 Mbps              Oper Bw     : 30 Mbps
Hop Limit   : 255
Record Route: Record               Record Label: Record
Oper MTU    : 1496                  Neg MTU     : 1496
Adaptive    : Enabled
Include Grps:                      Exclude Grps:
None                              None
Path Trans  : 39                   CSPF Queries: 594
Failure Code: noError              Failure Node: n/a
ExplicitHops:
    10.0.0.117    -> 10.0.0.164    -> 10.0.0.163
Actual Hops :
    10.117.118.2(10.0.0.118) @        Record Label    : N/A       (RRO)
 -> 10.117.118.1(10.0.0.117) @        Record Label    : 131069
 -> 10.117.164.2(10.0.0.164) @        Record Label    : 131069
 -> 10.163.164.1(10.0.0.163)          Record Label    : 131069
ComputedHops:
    10.117.118.2  -> 10.117.118.1  -> 10.117.164.2  -> 10.163.164.1   (ERO)
LastResignal: n/a                     CSPF Metric : 3000
Last MBB :
  MBB Type   : ConfigChange           MBB State   : Success
  Ended At   : 08/19/2003 23:32:50     Old Metric  : 3000
```

hops are specified in the MPLS path configuration and then associated with the LSP-Path in the LSP

A *strict hop* specifies an *immediate next-hop* relationship with the hop listed before it (previous hop) in the path definition. If the path contains the strict-hop IP address of an LSR, that LSR must have a direct Layer 3 connection to the router specified by the IP address listed in the previous hop. Strict hops define the order in which an LSP travels through a series of routers. For example, a path specifies that an LSP should travel through Router A and then through Node B and then through Node C. If two routers are not directly connected to each other and the second router is listed as a strict hop following the first router, the path is not a valid functioning path. Note that the system allows such a path to be created. However, when an LSP-Path is associated with this invalid path, it cannot become operationally up. An *adjacent strict hop* indicates that the two hops are listed beside each other in the path definition. Note that their hop-index numbers do not need to be sequentially incremental (e.g., n and n + 1). The hop-index value range is 1 to 1,024.

A *loose hop* specifies a *downstream location* relationship with the hop listed before it (previous hop) in the path definition. Although this can be an immediate next hop, it does not necessarily have to be one. Loose hops specify that the LSP-Path must go through a set of routers, but still allows the LSP-Path to traverse other routers along its path.

Strict hops and loose hops can be used together in one path definition. When combining strict hops and loose hops in the same path, the following rules must be observed to make a valid path so that LSP-Paths associated with this path can come up operationally:

1. In the path, the HE and Tail router are implicitly listed as hops. *The HE router can be treated as a strict hop 0, and the Tail router can be treated as a loose hop 1,025*. It is not necessary to include the HE and Tail routers' IP addresses in the path hop list unless the operator desires a path involving the interface address rather than the system address of the HE or Tail router to be included.

2. The router with IP addresses listed as strict hops must have a direct IP connection to the router with an IP address specified in the previous hop. If the router is the first hop in the list, it must be immediately adjacent to the HE router.

3. If any hop is followed by a loose hop, the two hops do not need to be directly connected.

4. If any hop is followed by a strict hop, the two hops must be directly connected.

Figure 3.11 presents a sample network with some LSR routers. It includes several examples showing path definitions for various scenarios.

Figure 3.11 Path Configuration Example: Loose Hop versus Strict Hop

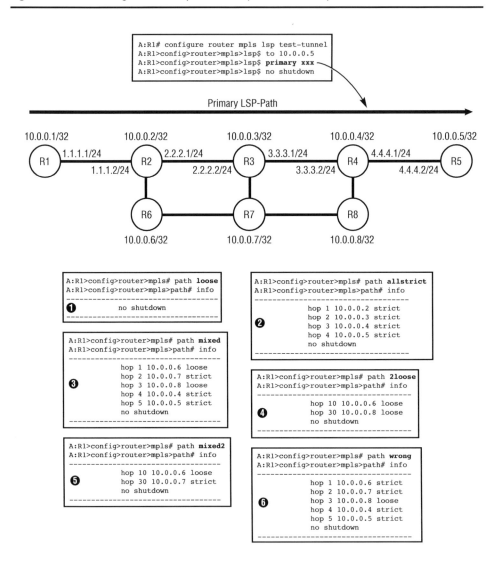

In Figure 3.11, six path examples are illustrated. The LSP from R1 to R5 uses one of these paths as its primary LSP-Path. In this example, the LSP configuration (at the top of the diagram) does not have CSPF enabled explicitly in the LSP

configuration. Therefore, IGP is used to calculate the actual path. The following list describes the numbered steps in the figure.

1. This `loose` path has an empty hop list. This path is used when there is no hop regulation. Therefore, there is no constraint on the path calculation for any LSP-Path associated with it.

2. This `allstrict` path contains only strict hops, so the LSP-Path associated with this path takes the specified path exactly (R1→R2→R3→R4→R5). If this path is not available (e.g., if there is a link failure in the middle of the path), the LSP-Path associated with this path cannot be established.

3. This `mixed` path contains three strict hops and two loose hops. Therefore, the LSP-Path specified with this path is:

   1. Take any route to R6 (decided by the IGP routing table).
   2. The immediate-next hop is R7.
   3. Take any route to R8 (decided by the IGP routing table).
   4. The immediate-next hop is R4.
   5. The immediate-next hop is R5 (Tail).

   The last hop is optional — if there are no alternative routes between R4 and R5, hop 5 can be omitted. However, adding hop 5 ensures that the LSP-Path goes through R4 immediately to R5. This route is ensured even if other routes are added into the network later.

4. This `2loose` path requires the LSP-Path to go through R6 first and then through R8. Beyond this restriction, the LSP-Path can take any route (as decided by IGP or CSPF).

5. This `mixed2` path requires the LSP-Path to go to R6 first and then immediately to R7. Beyond this restriction, the LSP-Path can take any route (as decided by IGP or CSPF).

6. This `wrong` path requires the LSP-Path associated with it to follow the path of:

   1. From the HE router go directly to Router R6 (the first strict hop must be immediately adjacent to the HE router).
   2. The immediate-next hop is R7.
   3. Then take any route to R8.
   4. The immediate-next hop is R4.
   5. The immediate-next hop is R5.

The path wrong is defined in Router R1. In the example topology, there is no direct connection between R1 and R6. Therefore, the path wrong is invalid. If any LSP-Path is associated with this path, the LSP-Path will never become operationally up since a direct route cannot be found between R1 and R6 by the path calculation. However, if the same path is configured in Router R2, the path is valid, because there is a direct link between R2 and R6. If an LSP-Path is associated with the path in R2, the LSP-Path can come up operationally.

The examples above explain how to specify the route that the operator wants the LSP-Path to follow using the defined path. This may not be enough for the actual RSVP-TE signaling to establish the LSP-Path. The router may need to calculate a more specific path and insert that result into the ERO object of the PATH message. This depends on the route calculation method of the LSP-Path. All LSP-Paths belonging to the same LSP must use the same calculation method. Therefore, the operator must configure the path calculation method (cspf or no cspf) under the LSP and apply it to all LSP-Paths belonging to the LSP.

RSVP-TE LSP-Path Path Computation: IGP-Directed versus CSPF-Directed

When RSVP-TE signals the LSP-Path, it must form an ERO for the PATH message. When the HE router generates the PATH message, each LSR processes and regenerates the PATH message toward the TE router. In this PATH message propagation process, the routers use the ERO's list of hops to route the PATH message. The associated path definition's hop list is used as an input to decide the route that the PATH message must travel — and the future established LSP-Path as well. At this stage, the router consults its routing database to determine the actual routes. This is achieved using one of the following route determination methods:

- **Regular IGP** — If CSPF is disabled (no cspf, the default value), a regular IGP routing table is consulted.
- **Constraint Shortest Path First (CSPF) with Traffic Engineering Database (TED)** — If CSPF is enabled, the LSP-Path is calculated using TED with CSPF.

The route determination method is defined in the LSP configuration.

If the LSP is configured with CSPF, the HE router uses the CSPF algorithm to consult the TED and calculates the routes using the associated path for the ERO. With CSPF, the PATH message and the LSP-Path are *source routed*, meaning that the HE router with the CSPF calculation determines the entire path of the LSP-Path. The ERO is composed in the HE router by the CSPF. Regardless of whether the path contains an empty list or a loose-hops, strict-hops, or mixed-hop list, an ERO is created by the CSPF in the HE router. In the CSPF-created ERO, the path list has the following characteristics:

- All hops are strict hops, and all the IP addresses are interface IP addresses.
- No IP address belongs to the HE router. All hops are the LSRs that the LSP and PATH message must travel through plus the Tail router.
- The hops begin at the ingress interface's IP address of the HE router's next-hop (NHop) LSR. This address is followed by the next-next-hop (NNHop) router's ingress interface IP address and then the NNHop router's next-hop router. The last hop is the Tail router's ingress interface IP address.

After the path calculation and the formation of the ERO, the HE router sends the PATH message to the next-hop router in the ERO's list. The PATH message is regenerated and forwarded by each hop router and follows the hops listed in ERO. Each LSR removes its own ingress interface IP address from the top of the ERO's hop list. At that point, the LSR regenerates a PATH message containing the shortened ERO and sends it to the next-hop router. Therefore, the PATH message with the CSPF-generated ERO in the HE router is source-routed to the Tail router. The ERO contains the entire list of hops that the PATH message and the LSP-Path will follow.

In the HE router, the CSPF must generate the full explicit strict hop that contains the entire route of the LSP. If the path associated with the LSP-Path is invalid (containing an incorrect hop list), the CSPF calculation will fail to calculate an ERO. In this case, the LSP-Path is put into an operationally down state with an error code of noCspfRouteToDestination, and the HE router does not send out a PATH message.

When checking the LSP-Path's status using the show router mpls lsp <name> path detail command, if the LSP-Path is CSPF-directed, there is a computed hops field in the CLI output below the actual hops field. The actual hops field contains the actual path that the LSP-Path traverses, recorded by the record route object (RRO) in the RSVP messages. The computed hops field contains the hop list calculated by the CSPF for the ERO. In an IGP-directed LSP, the computed hops field does not exist in the display because IGP does not calculate a complete path list for the LSP-Path.

If the LSP is configured with no cspf (default configuration), the HE router uses IGP to calculate ERO. This LSP is called an *IGP-directed LSP*. With regular IGP, the HE router only calculates the immediate next-hop router of the LSP-Path. At that point, it sends the PATH message to that immediate next-hop router. The next-hop router determines its immediate next hop by consulting its IGP routing table, and it then regenerates the PATH message. This process continues until the PATH message reaches the Tail router. Therefore, with IGP route calculation, the PATH message and the LSP-Path are routed hop-by-hop. The ERO calculation during this process is as follows:

- If the path's hop list is empty, there is no ERO in the PATH message. The HE router searches the IGP routing table to find the next hop to the Tail router and then sends the PATH message to this next-hop router. The next-hop router and the sequential downstream routers toward the Tail router each regenerates the PATH message to the IGP next-hop router. This behavior is repeated by all LSRs, hop-by-hop, until the PATH message reaches the Tail router.

- If the path contains any explicit list of hops, there will be an ERO composed for the PATH message. In an ERO, there is an explicit list of all the hops that the LSP-Path must go through. For every router, the following action is performed:

Note: Note that Step 1 applies to the HE router only. Steps 2–7 are applicable for all routers including the HE router.

1. For an HE router only: This step is performed only if the first hop in the path's hop list is not the IP address of the HE router's immediate-next hop. In that case, the HE router adds the Tail router's address at the bottom of the ERO list as a loose hop.

2. Consult the ERO hop list.
   - If one of the router's own IP addresses is in the top of the ERO's hop list, the address is removed.
   - If the router's own IP address is not in the ERO's hop list, this step is skipped.

3. In the ERO, if the top hop is a loose hop, the PATH message's next-hop router's ingress IP address is determined by consulting the IGP routing table.
   - If a route cannot be found, a `PathErr` message is sent backwards toward the HE router with an `ERROR` object. The error code is `routing error`, and the error value is `bad node`. The LSP set-up process is terminated.
   - If a next hop is found, the process skips to Step 5.

4. If the newly exposed top hop is a strict hop, the router verifies if that strict hop is directly connected to itself with an L3 interface by consulting its IGP routing table.

   - If the strict hop is not a directly connected neighbor router (e.g., the hop listed is actually two hops away), a `PathErr` message is sent backwards with an `ERROR` object. The error code is `routing error`, and the error value is `bad node`. The LSP set-up process is terminated.

   - If the strict hop is a directly connected neighbor router, this step is skipped, and the process goes to Step 6.

5. Insert the next-hop router's ingress IP address on the top of the ERO's hop list as a loose hop.

6. Use the newly composed ERO (Steps 2–5) to regenerate the PATH message and send it to the next-hop router.

7. Upon receiving the PATH message from the previous hop router, each router repeats Steps 2–6 until the PATH message reaches the TE router or the LSP set-up process is terminated because of a routing problem.

In the case of IGP-directed LSP, each router uses the following rules to calculate hops for the ERO:

1. Remove the router's IP address from ERO if it exists.

2. If the top of the hop list contains the IP address of the router's immediate next hop, send the PATH message over to the immediate next hop.

3. If the top of the hop list is not a directly connected neighbor router, do the following:

   a. Search the routing table to find the immediate-next hop's IP address at the top of the ERO hop list.

   b. Add the next-hop interface IP address to ERO.

   c. Send the PATH message over to the immediate next hop.

ERO is used to direct the PATH message from the HE router toward the Tail router. RRO is used to record the route that the PATH message actually travels from the HE router to the Tail route. The recording of the PATH message's actual route by the RRO is not affected by the difference between the path calculation based on hop type and the calculation based on a routing algorithm (IGP or CSPF). If the LSP has `record route` enabled (by default), every router records its egress interface IP address into the RRO. In addition, the HOP object in the PATH message is set to the egress interface's IP address at each router.

Hop Type and Path Calculation Impact on Fast Reroute Protection Availability

Both IGP and CSFP generate the hop list for the ERO of the PATH message in the HE router according to the hop list of the path that the LSP-Path is associated with. However, the hop-list contents generated by IGP and CSPF are different. IGP and CSPF also have different impacts on the LSP-Path's ability to allow FRR. (FRR is described in detail in Chapter 7.) The overall principle is that FRR cannot be enabled in an LSP if that LSP is associated with a path with any loose, explicit hops and is using IGP instead of CSPF to direct the LSP. In order to use FRR in an IGP-directed LSP-Path, the LSP-Path must be associated with a path having a complete and explicit strict hop list. In the ALSRP, if an IGP-directed LSP-Path is associated with a path containing any loose hops, when FRR is enabled, the LSP-Path is placed into an operationally **down** state with the error code of `looseHopsInFRRLsp`.

This happens because FRR requires that each router have a complete view of the path on which the LSP-Path must travel. With this complete information, the router can calculate the alternative path to avoid the link or node to be protected. When FRR is enabled in an LSP-Path, the HE router is the first assumed Point of Local Repair (PLR). An IGP-directed LSP-Path is routed hop-by-hop. If there are any loose hops in the LSP's associated path, the HE router does not make the complete decision of how to reach the loose hop in its ERO calculation. The HE router only calculates the immediate-next hop router. Therefore, unlike CSPF-directed LSP, the calculated ERO does not perform a full path calculation for the LSP-Path. If there are any loose hops in the path's hop list, the HE router does not know the exact path that the LSP-Path will travel. As mentioned previously, an IGP-directed LSP-Path is routed hop-by-hop. Therefore, the FRR calculation cannot be completed.

A CSPF-directed LSP-Path does not have this problem. Regardless of the information contained in the hop list of the path associated with the LSP-Path (loose, strict, empty, or mixed), the CSPF calculates the full path and generates the ERO with a complete list of strict hops containing interface addresses. Therefore, the FRR calculation in the HE router and all LSRs can be completed.

FRR always uses CSPF to perform path calculations and generate ERO for the protection tunnel (detour LSP or bypass tunnel), regardless of whether the protected LSP-Path is IGP-directed or CSPF-directed.

Note: If CSPF is not used in the LSP-Path's path calculation, can the system still reserve bandwidth to the LSP-Path? As long as RSVP-TE is used as the LSP signaling protocol, the LSP signaling process will reserve bandwidth. However, because IGP cannot access the bandwidth availability information in the TED, it may attempt to set up the LSP over a link without the required resources. In this case, the LSP setup is more likely to be rejected (CAC failure) by the routers along the path. It may receive ResvErr or PathErr messages. Setting bandwidth requirement in IGP-directed LSP may result in more LSP signaling failures.

3.5 Configuring RSVP-TE LSP

This section introduces the configuration and verification of RSVP-TE LSP and LSP-Paths. The focus here is the configuration procedure and the verification of different RSVP-TE LSP related entities: path, LSP, and LSP-Paths. For detailed information regarding the command grammar, configuration options, or range values, please refer to the ALSRP Service Routing manuals.

RSVP-TE LSP requires the explicit configuration of LSP in the HE router. This configuration includes defining the path that the LSP-Paths must travel, creating the LSP, and creating at least one primary LSP-Path. Also, the characteristics of the LSP and LSP-Paths are defined in the configuration options. Table 3.2 lists the available options for the LSP configuration.

Table 3.2 LSP Configuration Options and Descriptions

LSP	Description
LSP name	The name of the LSP. The LSP name is not present in the PATH messages. Instead, a system assigned tunnel-id is used for LSP-Path signaling (starting from 1). The tunnel name must be entered when creating the LSP.
To	The To field is the termination point (Tail) router's IP address. Usually, the Tail router's system IP address is used (/32). However, any other IP address can be used.
From	The From field is the HE router's IP address. If this address is absent, the HE router's system IP address is used.
Primary	Creates the primary LSP-Path. The predefined path is used as the parameter. This command associates the pre-defined path to the primary LSP-Path in the LSP. The configuration options are introduced in a later chapter.

(continued)

Table 3.2 *(continued)*

LSP	Description
Secondary	Creates the secondary LSP-Path. The predefined path is used as the parameter. The configuration options are introduced in Chapter 6.
Cspf	Enables the CSPF ERO calculation for the LSP-Path. With this option enabled, the system uses CSPF to calculate the ERO (with the path indicated by the LSP configuration) and calculates a series of interface IP addresses in the ERO. When CSPF is not enabled, the IGP determines the route of the LSP-Path when the actual hops (interface IP addresses) are not specified in the path definition used by the LSP-Path. CSPF is disabled by default (using IGP).
Metric	Configures the metric of the LSP. There is no default metric value. If no metric is configured, the CSPF or IGP metric is used.
Hop-limit	The maximum number of hops for all LSP-Paths belonging to the same LSP. This option is also available in LSP-Path configuration. The LSP-Path level configuration is more specific and overrides the LSP level configuration.
Include | exclude	The color (admin group) of the links the LSP-Paths belonging to this LSP should take (include) or avoid (exclude). This option is also available in LSP-Path configuration. The LSP-Path level configuration is more specific and overrides the LSP level configuration. The admin group(s) included or excluded must be defined previously in the MPLS configuration. There is no default admin group configuration. Link-coloring is discussed in more detail in Chapter 4.
Adaptive	This enables the MBB behavior. The MBB is enabled by default. This option is also available in LSP-Path configuration. The LSP-Path level configuration is more specific and overrides the LSP level configuration.
Adspec	This option adds the ADSPEC optional object into the PATH message to provide more LSP information signaling (e.g., the MTU of the interface). This option is disabled by default.
Rsvp-reservation-style	The reservation style [Shared Explicit (SE) or Fixed Filter (FF)] of the LSP-Paths belongs to this LSP. The default reservation style is SE.
Fastreroute	Enables the FRR protection. The FRR configuration is effective only on the primary LSP-Path. FRR is disabled by default.
Retry-timer	When an LSP-Path setup fails or there is an FRR in-use event, the router performs CSPF calculation to retry the establishment of the LSP-Path. This timer decides the delay time before each retry. The default value is 30 seconds.

LSP	Description
Retry-limit	When an LSP-Path setup fails or there is an FRR in-use event, the router will perform a CSPF calculation to retry the establishment of the LSP. This limit is the number of retries allowed. The default value is 0 (retry indefinitely).
Shutdown	Administratively disables the LSP. LSP is administratively disabled by default.

In most cases, the default values work properly. The mandatory required configuration entries are the LSP name, the Tail router address (To), and a primary path. After the creation of the LSP, the LSP-Path must be created. Table 3.3 lists the options for the LSP-Path creation.

Table 3.3 LSP-Path Configuration Options

LSP-Path	Description
Adaptive	This enables the MBB behavior. The MBB is enabled by default.
Include | exclude	The color (admin group) of the links that the LSP-Paths belonging to this LSP should take (include) or avoid (exclude).
Hop-limit	The maximum number of hops the LSP-Path can travel
Bandwidth	The bandwidth reservation required for the LSP-Path
Record	Records each hop the LSP-Path travels to the RRO object. This option is enabled by default and is required for FRR to work.
Record label	Records each hop's assigned label value for the LSP-Path traveling into the RRO object. This option is enabled by default and is required for FRR to work.
Shutdown	Administratively disables the LSP-Path. The LSP-Path is administratively enabled by default.

Configuring the RSVP-TE LSP

When using RSVP-TE LSP to establish LSP-Paths, the related MPLS and RSVP configuration must be deployed first. If CSPF is used to route the LSP, traffic engineering must be enabled in the IGP as well. RSVP-TE is part of the MPLS backbone infrastructure for VPN services. The recommendation is to deploy RSVP-TE LSP as a service tunnel in the following order:

1. Ensure that the network ports facing the backbone network are functioning properly.

2. Ensure that the IGP is running properly, and, if necessary, enable traffic engineering.

3. Enable the MPLS router in the router configuration.

4. Configure the RSVP routing instance in the router configuration.

5. In the MPLS configuration, define the path to be used for LSPs.

6. Configure the LSP and define the necessary parameters.

7. Configure LSP-Paths in the LSP.

8. Check the status of the LSP, the LSP-Path, and FRR.

When these steps are completed, the MPLS infrastructure is built. The operator can now configure the service infrastructure (SDP, service instances). The service infrastructure is introduced in Chapter 9. The IGP-TE and CSPF are introduced in Chapter 4.

LSP Configuration Procedure

The configuration of LSP, LSP-Path, and related components are required only in the HE router. Figure 3.12 illustrates a sample network showing configuration of an LSP with two LSP-Paths.

In this sample network, an LSP with multiple protections, including FRR and Secondary LSP, is defined as in the following list:

1. The CSPF is required because the operator wants to use loose hop in the path definition, and requires FRR. Therefore, traffic engineering is enabled in the OSPF configuration in all routers.

2. RSVP-TE LSP is required. Therefore, the MPLS routing instance must be configured with the desired MPLS interfaces listed in the MPLS configuration. When the `router mpls` is configured, the RSVP routing instance is automatically enabled with the interfaces listed in the MPLS configuration. RSVP protocol parameters can be enabled in the `configure router rsvp` context (not shown in this example). The operator must enable MPLS and RSVP in the entire MPLS backbone network.

3. The LSP is configured in the HE router. The path containing the explicit hop list must be configured prior to the creation of LSP. There are two paths defined in this example: `loose` and `goR6R8`. The `loose` path does not contain any hops, so CSPF will calculate the best path with no restrictions. The `goR6R8` path specifies that the LSP-Path associated with it must travel

through R6 and R8 but can take any route to get there. The paths must be administratively enabled by executing no shutdown.

Figure 3.12 LSP and LSP-Path Configuration Example

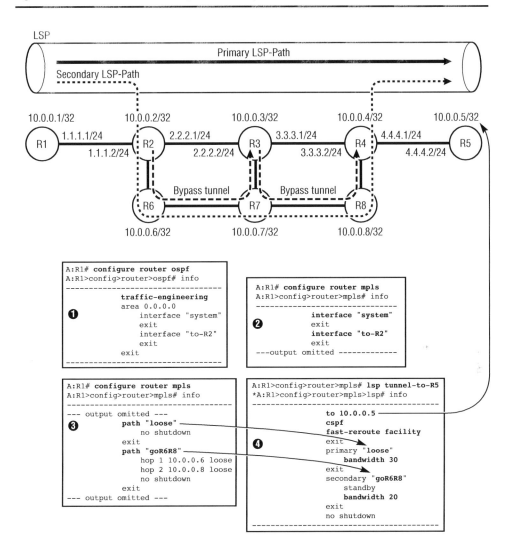

4. After the path is created and enabled, the LSP is created with a given name. At that point, the Tail router must be specified using the To command. In Figure 3.12, the primary LSP-Path is created in the LSP using the command `primary "loose"`. The LSP-Path is created by referencing a pre-created path in the `primary` command in the LSP configuration. The secondary LSP-Path is created by the command `secondary "goR6R8"`. In Figure 3.12, the LSP is configured with the following parameters:

- The primary LSP-Path in the LSP requires 30 Mbps of bandwidth.

- FRR facility protection is enabled for the primary LSP-Path.

- A pre-signaled (standby) secondary LSP-Path is also used to protect the primary LSP-Path. Because it is used only for backup purposes, only 20 Mbps of bandwidth is reserved. To provide path diversity, the path forces the secondary LSP-Path to take the longer route traveling through R6 and R8.

This is a brief example of the LSP configuration procedure. The details regarding FRR and secondary LSP-Paths are provided in Chapters 6 and 7.

Verifying RSVP-TE LSP Components: LSP, LSP-Path, and Path

There are several RSVP-TE LSP components that can be displayed with various commands. Table 3.4 lists the commands that display the status of these components.

Table 3.4 Commands for Verifying RSVP-TE LSP Components

Components	Commands	Description
Path	`Show router mpls path [name] [lsp-binding]`	Displays the path definition that contains an explicit hop list. The option of LSP-binding shows which LSP-Paths are using the listed path.
LSP	`Show router mpls lsp [name] [detail]`	Displays the LSP. The `detail` option displays the LSP-Paths belonging to the LSP.
LSP's active LSP-Path	`Show router mpls lsp [name] activepath`	Displays the current traffic carrying the active LSP-Path for the LSP.
LSP-Path	`Show router mpls lsp [name] path [name] [detail]`	Displays a particular LSP-Path's status. The LSP-Path is identified by the LSP-name and path name. The `detail` option displays the FRR detail.
RSVP session	`Show router rsvp session [detail]`	Displays all the RSVP sessions residing on a router.

Components	Commands	Description
FRR detour LSP	Show router rsvp session detour [detail]	Displays the RSVP sessions created for FRR one-to-one protection. The detour option displays the originated sessions. detour-transit filters the display by only showing transiting FRR detour LSPs. detour-terminate filters the display by only showing terminated FRR detour LSPs.
Bypass tunnel	Show router rsvp session bypass-tunnel [detail]	Displays the RSVP sessions created for FRR facility bypass tunnels.
RSVP-TE labels	Show router mpls label 32 131071 in-use	Displays the label used by RSVP-TE LSP-Paths within a certain range. The default range (32–131,071) can be changed to any <start> <finish> values.

GRE Transport Tunnel Overview

Generic Routing Encapsulation (GRE) is an IP encapsulation tunneling technique that can also be used in the IP/MPLS VPN network. GRE is a common tunnel encapsulation method supported by many vendors. After the SDP uses GRE tunneling to perform the tunnel encapsulation, the traffic appears as pure IP traffic. Therefore, the traffic can also traverse the networks with legacy routers that are not compatible with MPLS switching.

Similar to the LDP-LSP, the GRE tunnel is also automatically created by the system without explicit tunnel configuration. In fact, the creation of the GRE tunnel is simpler — no extra configuration is required. If IGP is working in the backbone, the GRE tunnel mesh is established and ready for use. As mentioned previously, an MPLS tunnel is a method of transporting traffic from one PE router to another PE router using MPLS encapsulation. To establish an MPLS tunnel (LDP-LSP or RSVP-TE LSP), the MPLS labels must be distributed. With GRE, if the two PE routers are reachable from each other's routing table, the tunnel exists. The only configuration required is to set the SDP to use GRE encapsulation.

Similar to the LDP-LSP, the GRE's failover during failure is dependent on the IGP failover. The GRE tunnel uses the IP routing table of the network backbone. If there is a network failure, when the IGP converges, the GRE uses the new routing table to route the traffic. Any techniques that benefit the IGP convergence also benefit GRE tunneling.

GRE Encapsulation Format

GRE uses IP encapsulation to build end-to-end tunnels to reach the remote PE router. In a pure IP routing network, GRE is used to tunnel IP traffic. Therefore, GRE is also called *IP over IP* because it uses an IP header to encapsulate the IP traffic. In the IP/MPLS VPN network, GRE is used to tunnel pseudowire-encapsulated L2VPN traffic. This type of tunneling is actually MPLS over IP tunneling. The VPN traffic must still be VPN-encapsulated on the pseudowire before it is GRE-encapsulated by an SDP using GRE encapsulation.

There are two types of GRE headers used for GRE encapsulation: RFC 2784 and RFC 1701. RFC 1701 adds extra options (keys and sequence number) in the GRE header. However, these options do not provide much benefit to the IP/MPLS VPN type of traffic. As of the time of writing, the RFC 2784 format is used for ALSRP Service Routers to perform GRE encapsulation on L2VPN traffic. Figure 3.13 illustrates the GRE header format defined by RFC 2784 and RFC 1701.

GRE encapsulation imposes 24 bytes of encapsulation overhead. The IP header used by GRE is 20 bytes long, and the GRE header itself is 4 bytes long. All L2VPN traffic requires a 4-byte vc-label VPN encapsulation before it is sent into the SDP. Therefore, the overall encapsulation overhead is 28 bytes. To support customer traffic with a maximum transfer unit (MTU) of 1,514 bytes (the basic requirement for Ethernet) over a GRE tunnel, the core link must support a minimum SDP-MTU of 1,542 bytes. MTU is discussed in detail in Chapter 9. Although the GRE-encapsulated traffic is IP traffic, the IP header used by GRE has the Do Not Fragment bit set to 1 (true). This means that GRE-encapsulated VPN traffic cannot be fragmented. The protocol type in the IP header used by GRE encapsulation is set to 0x8847 (MPLS unicast) or 0x8848 (MPLS multicast).

Figure 3.13 GRE Header Defined by RFC 2784 and RFC 1701

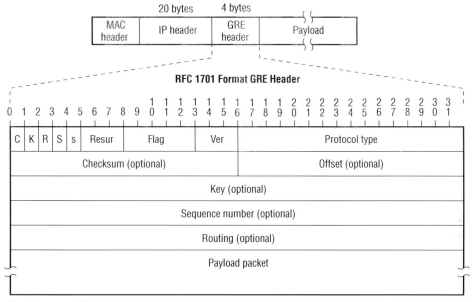

C - checksum present (bit 0): 0 - no checksum, 1 - checksum present
R - routing present (bit 1): 0 - no routing information, 1 - routing information present
K - key present (bit 2): 0 - no key, 1 - key present
S - sequence number present (bit 3): 0 - no sequence number, 1 - sequence number present
s - strict source route (bit 4): 0 - no strict source route, 1 - strict source route present
Notes:
1. If either C or R bits are set to 1, BOTH checksum and routing information are present in the GRE packet.
2. Currently, bits 5-12 (Resur and Flag) should be set to all ZEROs (0).

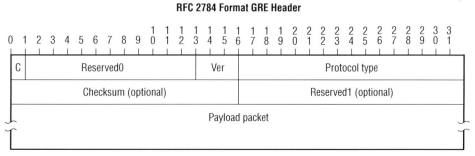

C - checksum present (bit 0): 0 - no checksum, 1 - checksum present
Reserved0: unless implemented RFC 1701, a router MUST discard a packet with a non-zero value in bits1-5;
6-12 for future use, SHOULD be set to zero and ignored.
Ver - version number (bits13-15) MUST be set to zero.
Checksum and Reserved1 fields are only present when the C bit is set to 1; Reserved1 field MUST be transmitted as all zeros.

Summary

MPLS was originally introduced as a routing shortcut to speed up the routing process for IP traffic. MPLS labels are distributed between MPLS routers and are inserted into the packet header. MPLS-encapsulated packets are switched by MPLS-capable switches/routers.

Now, MPLS is enhanced as a backbone technology in multi-service networks to forward VPN traffic using the following features:

- RSVP-TE is used to signal explicit routed LSP so that the operators can control the LSPs to traverse paths other than the best IGP path.

- MPLS resiliency features such as MBB, FRR, and Secondary LSP significantly improve the reliability and the availability of the network.

- The MPLS pseudowire-based VPN technology makes it possible to build a single converged MPLS backbone network that supports multiple types of services.

RSVP-TE can be used to signal MPLS LSPs and has the following hierarchical LSP architecture:

- The LSP is the top level object. Each LSP has one or more LSP-Paths. The SDP uses the LSP to carry the IP/MPLS VPN traffic.

- Within each LSP, there must be one primary LSP-Path. However, there can be up to seven secondary LSP-Paths. At any time, only one LSP-Path will be the active path and forward traffic for the LSP.

- Each LSP-Path is a collection of RSVP sessions along its path. The RSVP sessions must be refreshed to maintain the session state for the LSP-Path to be operationally up.

With the introduction of various types of MPLS LSPs into the service network, the operator has more choices of service transport tunnels to fulfill the requirement of different services.

Routing Protocol Traffic Engineering and CSPF

4

Traffic engineering is the ability to route traffic along a path other than the best path specified by the routing table. Constrained Shortest Path First (CSPF) is the algorithm enhanced from the SPF to take TE information into account when calculating a path. TE and CSPF are used to calculate the path for the MPLS RSVP-TE LSP.

Chapter Objectives

- Provide an overview of traffic engineering
- Briefly review OSPF and provide an introduction to OSPF-TE
- Review IS-IS and introduce IS-IS TE
- Explain the CSPF algorithm and the Traffic Engineering Database (TED)
- Discuss the use of administrative groups and Shared Link Risk Groups (SRLG) to control LSP's paths

This chapter discusses routing protocol enhancements for the IP/MPLS VPN solution. For readers who are already familiar with Interior Gateway Protocol (IGP) routing protocols in legacy IP routing networks, this chapter is still required reading because it includes a study of the traffic engineering (TE) enhancements made to these protocols to support RSVP-TE LSP path calculation.

4.1 Introducing Traffic Engineering

This section introduces traffic engineering (TE) and explains how to deploy it with MPLS.

What Is Traffic Engineering?

Network bandwidth is an expensive and limited resource. Congestion arises when there is a higher volume of traffic over the network than the bandwidth in the network can carry. Operators frequently use statistical multiplexing (overbooking of resources) in their network design to optimize the cost and performance (throughput) of a network. Optimization is required to achieve a balance between the amount of traffic and the amount of bandwidth in the network. The goal is to use network bandwidth in the most efficient way to carry as much traffic as possible. There are two common methods to optimize these two factors: traffic management and traffic engineering.

Traffic management (TM) places the bandwidth where the traffic is. With TM, network designers must:

- Predict the network traffic utilization rate and design the network to give more bandwidth to the locations with higher bandwidth requirements.
- Use Quality of Service (QoS) mechanisms to police or shape the traffic flow after traffic arrives at a device, or before the traffic is sent out from the port, and also to assign the bandwidth and the priority to more important traffic.

To perform traffic management, the network designers must fully understand the network traffic patterns and provide proper traffic predictions. Designers must then determine the bandwidth requirement of each network section and deploy the transportation circuit accordingly. The transport circuits may be very expensive. Therefore, more accurate predictions will provide a more cost-efficient network design. After the network is put into production, the operator must continue to monitor the traffic utilization rate on all circuits to decide if the link bandwidth design suits the customer traffic needs. Often, adjustments are required, meaning the purchase of more bandwidth, which incurs cost and time. Overall network bandwidth planning is a *strategic* task. Operators must monitor the traffic utilization rate constantly and decide if network expansion is required. Figure 4.1 illustrates traffic management by adding bandwidth to handle traffic in a network. If there is traffic congestion, the devices may drop or buffer certain types of traffic to reduce the congestion in various ways.

Figure 4.1 Traffic Management: Place the Bandwidth Where the Traffic Is

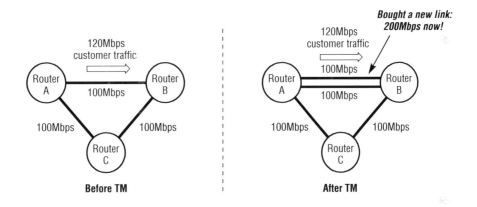

Traffic engineering (TE) places the traffic where the bandwidth is. TE decides where the traffic should be sent by collecting bandwidth booking information and considering certain constraints, such as bandwidth availability and links or nodes to avoid. TE resolves the conflict between the traffic requirement and the existing network bandwidth by manipulating the traffic flow to make use of less utilized links. Thus, the overall network bandwidth utilization rate is higher and more throughput is achieved within the same network without the cost of buying more bandwidth.

A typical scenario in which traffic engineering can reduce the traffic congestion is the case of *hyperaggregation*. Hyperaggregation occurs when all traffic goes through one congested link while leaving other links unutilized. Figure 4.2 illustrates a network scenario before and after traffic engineering.

Figure 4.2   Traffic Engineering: Place the Traffic Where the Bandwidth Is

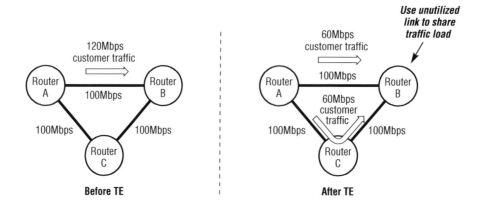

Figure 4.2 shows that without traffic engineering, all customer traffic from Router A to Router B takes the *IGP shortest path* of the AB link. This may cause congestion because there is only 100 Mbps of bandwidth. Meanwhile, there is unused bandwidth in links AC and CB. Placing some traffic over the longer but less utilized path A–C–B reduces or removes the congestion in the network.

This traffic engineering solution is *tactical*, and perhaps temporary. If the entire network must handle more traffic than it was originally designed to, traffic engineering may reduce the network congestion by improving the link bandwidth utilization, but it may not solve the root cause of the problem. The service provider may still need to buy more bandwidth.

Why Use Traffic Engineering?

Traffic engineering allows the network operator to direct traffic to follow a path other than the *best IGP path*, thus overriding the IGP routing decision. When deciding the traffic's route, the system can consider aspects other than the IGP cost. These other aspects considered by traffic engineering are called *constraints*. With traffic engineering, if there is unutilized bandwidth in the network, the operator can build *TE tunnels* to direct the traffic around the congestion and over the less-used links. With TE tunnels, the network operator also has better control of the traffic flow.

Another typical application of traffic engineering is to split different types of traffic over different paths, to provide different service quality. For example, an operator may want to put all business customer traffic (corporate VPN, web hosting, and database services) over its high bandwidth links, to provide *premium* service. At the same time, the operator may put the overbooked Internet residential subscribers in the same network over a lower-rated link to provide *Best Effort* service.

Before the use of Multi Protocol Label Switching (MPLS) in the service provider core network, traffic engineering was achieved in the routed IP network by *policy-based routing*. In this case, the operator creates a *routing policy* that defines the next-hop IP address of the traffic flow, rather than letting the routers consult the IGP routing table to determine the next hop of the traffic. Deploying a routing policy in the router forces certain traffic flows to go to the next-hop router rather than the router with the best cost. The routing policy can selectively re-direct some of the traffic to other routes to avoid link congestion. However, a policy-based routing solution is not scalable and is very complicated to deploy. Having too many manually configured routing policies in a large network makes the network unmanageable. It is almost impossible to track all routing policies in a large network and to ensure a well-functioning solution (e.g., one with loop-free traffic). If there is a network failure, the operator must manually change the routing policies affected by the failure to reroute the traffic around the failure. Another big challenge in a network with hundreds or more routers is the deployment of hop-by-hop routing policies consistently in all routers in the network.

When using MPLS, TE deployment over an RSVP-TE signaled LSP is more convenient and practical. This is one of the major reasons that operators prefer using IP/MPLS VPN services rather than plain IP routing to service their customers. When MPLS uses RSVP-TE to signal the LSP and uses CSPF with TE to calculate the path of the LSP, more than just the IGP path cost is considered when deciding where to establish the LSP. RSVP-TE LSPs are configured end-to-end, which means that intermediate routers do not need extra configuration to support TE tunnels as long as the RSVP-TE and IGP-TE protocol is supported. In addition, TE tunnels using MPLS/LSP can also take advantage of other MPLS benefits such as Fast Reroute (FRR), make-before-break (MBB), and secondary LSP. These features allow much quicker convergence during a network failover.

What Is the Relationship between TE and QoS?

TE is used by the control plane of the router to negotiate the service tunnels. With TE, the traffic can be directed away from the IGP best path if necessary. TE introduces the concepts of *bandwidth booking* and *Connection Admission Control* (CAC) into the service tunnel establishment. With TE, the system routes traffic to the service tunnel based on the TE information advertised by the routing protocol and the constraints requested by the tunnel configuration. TE's bandwidth advertisement and reservation are on the control plane only. TE only considers the control plane *reservation* information, and not the data plane's actual bandwidth *utilization* information.

In contrast, Quality of Service (QoS) is used by the data plane to ensure that the actual traffic flow conforms to the traffic policy. In most cases, the QoS policies are defined by the services sold to the customers.

Network design should include the correct bandwidth booking information (from the traffic engineering parameter configuration) and the correct QoS policy to ensure that traffic flow matches the desired traffic parameters. A good network design should have consistent TE configuration and QoS policy.

When RSVP-TE uses CSPF to calculate the path for LSP, the bandwidth consideration is based on the control plane booking information. This bandwidth booking information does not reflect the actual physical link's traffic utilization rate. The reservation, the request, and the CAC are all based on control plane information.

For example, if a service uses an LSP with a configured bandwidth of 50 Mbps, the 50 Mbps is signaled and reserved in all routers along the LSP-Path. However, this reservation is on the control plane only. The service can still send 500 Mbps of traffic over the LSP and congest the link. If an LSP is established, it can send any amount of traffic, and the 50 Mbps reservation does not affect the traffic volume. The best way to ensure that the booking reflects reality is to use QoS to enforce the traffic to conform to the booking value. In the same example, the operator can deploy a QoS policy in the service's SAP to police or shape the ingress traffic from the customer to 50 Mbps. Thus, this policy ensures that the service can only send 50 Mbps of traffic to the LSP.

Deploying Traffic Engineering with MPLS

To implement traffic engineering with MPLS, the router must meet the following entrance criteria:

- The router must support MPLS switching and RSVP-TE signaling so it can signal bandwidth reservation and other constraints to the MPLS LSP.

- The router's IGP protocols must be able to exchange the traffic engineering information among each other. This is implemented by the traffic engineering extensions of the IGP: OSPF-TE and IS-IS TE.

- The router must be able to consider the received traffic engineering metric when deciding where to establish the LSP. This requirement is implemented by enhancing the route calculation algorithm [Dijkstra Shortest Path First (SPF) algorithm] to support the Constrained Shortest Path First (CSPF).

Enhancement of the legacy IGP routing protocols with TE capability allows the advertisement of bandwidth-reservation-related information through the service providers' core networks. Each router can share the same view of the entire network's resource allocation and availability. This means that more than just IGP metrics are considered when establishing the MPLS tunnel negotiation. To store the bandwidth information, the routers running IGP enhancement (IS-IS TE or OSPF-TE) maintain separate databases containing the traffic engineering information. This stored information is generally referred as the *Traffic Engineering Database* (TED). The CSPF calculation is based on the TE link state information stored in the TED. Regular IP routing and LDP still use the information stored in the regular IGP database. Although these two databases may contain similar routing information, they are totally separate, and changes in one database do not affect the other.

With the introduction of TE enhancement of IGP and the use of the RSVP-TE protocol, operators can set up service tunnels with TE parameters and direct traffic away from the best IGP path.

4.2 Introducing OSPF-TE

This section introduces the traffic engineering extension for OSPF: OSPF-TE (defined in RFC 3630). OSPF-TE works in exactly the same manner as the legacy

OSPF except that OSPF-TE uses the Opaque-LSA Type 10 to advertise traffic engineering information to the network. This section briefly reviews the OSPF adjacency establishment and discusses the traffic engineering extension in more depth.

Legacy OSPF in Routed IP Networks

Open Shortest Path First (OSPF) is the most popular IP routing protocol, and its protocol behavior has become common knowledge. This section provides a brief review of OSPF adjacency establishment and a configuration example of enabling OSPF in the ALSRP service routers. The following sections then address the TE extension of OSPF. If you are familiar with OSPF, you may choose to skip this section.

OSPF is a link state routing protocol. Routers run OSPF to exchange Link State Advertisements (LSAs) to announce their reachability information. Each OSPF router must establish OSPF adjacencies with other OSPF routers before announcing its reachability. The OSPF adjacencies can only be built with a directly connected neighbor's IP interfaces. After the adjacency is established, the OSPF router generates LSAs to announce its own reachability information. When a router receives an LSA, it stores it in the LSA database and floods the LSA to all its OSPF neighbors. In this manner, LSAs are flooded to the entire network running OSPF. Each router collects the LSAs generated and flooded by other routers, and in this way, acquires a complete view of the entire network. The collected LSAs are placed into the OSPF database. The router then runs the Shortest Path First (SPF) algorithm against the OSPF database to calculate all possible routes to all possible destinations. The calculated routes will then be offered to the router's Routing Table Manager (RTM). OSPF may not be the only active routing protocol in the router. If other routing protocols are also active in the router, they may also offer the same routes to the RTM. Based on protocol preference, the RTM chooses one *best route* for all reachable destinations among these protocols.

Routers running OSPF have three databases to maintain and update:

- **Adjacency Database (Adjacency Table)** — The adjacency database contains a complete list of the router's OSPF neighbors. The OSPF adjacencies are tracked and maintained by constantly exchanging OSPF Hello packets between each peering router pair.
- **LSA Database** — The LSA database contains all the LSAs received from other OSPF routers. OSPF executes the SFP algorithm against the LSA database to

calculate the routes. Every LSA has a lifetime (age) of 30 minutes. If the LSA is not refreshed within the lifetime, it is removed from the LSA database (aged-out or expired). OSPF then executes the SPF algorithm against the database again and offers the new result to the RTM. In a single OSPF area (the area concept is introduced later), after the networks converge, the LSA databases of all the OSPF routers should be synchronized and contain the same information. This is a characteristic of link state protocols: *Every router has its own view of the entire network (LSA database) and calculates the routes itself by running the SPF algorithm against the LSA database.* Networks with unsynchronized OSPF databases cause routing problems.

- **Routing Database (Routing Table)** — The routing database is owned by the RTM. Each protocol offers its view of the network (routes) to the RTM. The RTM selects the routes and builds the routing table. For ease of discussion in this context, we assume that OSPF is the only routing protocol offering routes to the RTM. Therefore, OSPF generates the routing table.

Establishing OSPF Adjacency

For OSPF to function, it requires established OSPF adjacencies among the OSPF participating routers. To establish OSPF adjacencies, the OSPF routing instance must be created and administratively enabled, and then the interfaces participating in OSPF must be specified by the operator. At this point, if it is necessary, the operator can tune the adjacency parameters. Figure 4.3 presents an example of routers R1 and R2 establishing OSPF adjacency.

When the OSPF adjacencies are successfully established, a Full state is indicated in the adjacency table. At this point, the two routers execute the SPF algorithm to calculate the routes in the LSAs received during the adjacency establishment. Once the adjacency is established, the OSPF routers can exchange LSAs with other routers.

OSPF Area, OSPF Routers, and LSAs

To improve scalability, OSPF supports hierarchical area network design. The entire OSPF domain can be divided into multiple areas and connected by Area 0 — the backbone area.

Figure 4.3 OSPF Adjacency Establishment Process

```
A:R1# show router ospf neighbor
===============================================================
OSPF Neighbors
===============================================================
Interface-Name            Rtr Id        State   Pri RetxQ  TTL
---------------------------------------------------------------
to-117                    10.0.0.117    Full     1    0     38
to-116                    10.0.0.116    Full     1    0     32
---------------------------------------------------------------
No. of Neighbors: 2
===============================================================
```

1	Router 1 sends hello packets to router 2 to start the adjacency negotiation.	State: Init
2	Router 1 receives hello message from router 2.	State: 2-way
3	Router 1 sends DB-Descriptor to router 2 to begin exchanging adjacency parameters.	State: EX-Start
4	Router 1 receives DB-Descriptor from router 2, replies with DB-Summary.	State: Exchange
5	Router 1 receives DB-Summary, two routers exchange LSAs.	State: Loading
6	Routers finished exchanging LSAs. Routers' LSDBs synchronized. Adjacency formed.	State: Full

```
A:R1# configure router ospf
A:R1>config>router>ospf# info
------------------------------------
        traffic-engineering
        area 0.0.0.0
            interface "system"
            exit
            interface "to-117"
            exit
            interface "to-116"
            exit
        exit
------------------------------------
```

```
A:R2# configure router ospf
A:R2>config>router>ospf# info
------------------------------------
        traffic-engineering
        area 0.0.0.0
            interface "system"
            exit
            interface "to-118"
            exit
            interface "to-117"
            exit
        exit
------------------------------------
```

An Area Border Router (ABR) connects the different areas. All areas must be connected to Area 0, the backbone area. When performing route aggregation in the ABR, the number of LSAs for routers within an area can be significantly reduced before advertising the area's routes to the other area, thus increasing scalability. The OSPF area boundary is actually within the ABR connecting the two areas — the ABR contains links belonging to different areas. For an OSPF adjacency to come operationally up, both sides of the participating OSPF link must belong to the same area.

There are four types of OSPF areas:

- **Backbone Area 0** — An OSPF domain must have only one backbone Area 0. All areas can exchange LSAs through an ABR only to Area 0, the backbone. The ABR must have at least one link to Area 0. The backbone Area 0 can also connect outside the OSPF domain through the Autonomous System Border Router (ASBR).

- **Non-Backbone Regular Area** — A regular non-backbone area has a non-zero area-id. A non-backbone area accepts all routes advertised by an ABR connected to the backbone Area 0. The ABR converts LSAs from the non-backbone area to the backbone area. Non-backbone areas can also have an ASBR.

- **Stub Area** — A *stub area* is an area without any external reachability except via the ABR connected to the backbone area. Therefore, a stub area only needs a default route generated from the ABR for all traffic that goes outside the area. A stub area cannot have an ASBR. Thus, routers in the stub area only need to store LSAs within the area. In addition, they need a default-route LSA.

- **Not-So-Stubby-Area (NSSA)** — An NSSA is a stub area with connectivity outside the OSPF domain. An NSSA has ASBRs that advertise external routes into the NSSA using LSA Type 7. An ABR converts these LSAs to Type 5 (Table 4.1 describes the OSPF LSA types). An NSSA does not contain any LSAs from other areas within the OSPF domain except a default-route LSA.

> **Note:** Originally, the OSPF area was used to reduce the number of LSAs stored by each router in the network. This was sometimes necessary for low-end legacy routers in which the system resources (CPU and memory) were a concern. Today, most of the routers are powerful enough to handle tens of thousands of OSPF LSAs. Therefore, in many cases, it is not necessary to use areas with ABR aggregation to reduce the number of routes per router.
>
> Also, service providers now use IP/MPLS VPN to carry customer traffic; the routing protocol in the backbone network is only used for advertising the links and system-IP address for the P and PE routers. Thus, in most cases, the use of OSPF areas can be avoided.

Figure 4.4 illustrates an OSPF domain divided into several areas.

Figure 4.4   Multiple OSPF Areas and Different OSPF Router Types

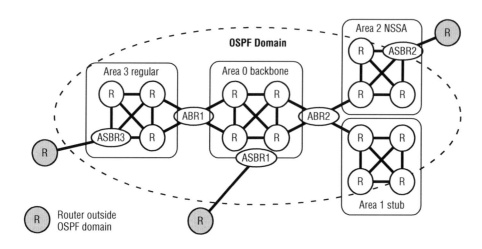

In Figure 4.4, three areas are connected by backbone Area 0. Area 1 is a stub area, with no outside connectivity. Therefore, ABR2 needs to advertise only a default route through the OSPF LSA to Area 1. Area 2 is an NSSA, and Area 3 is a non-backbone area. All areas are connected to Area 0. Routers outside the OSPF domain are connected by ASBRs. Figure 4.4 shows the following types of OSPF routers:

- **Regular OSPF Router** — All the regular OSPF routers with interfaces that participate in OSPF belong to one area. Regular routers can only generate LSA Type 1 if the interface is not the Designated Router (DR), and LSA Type 2 if the interface is the DR.

- **Area Border Router (ABR)** — The ABR is an OSPF router with OSPF-participating interfaces belonging to more than one area. The ABR is the router that connects these different areas. The ABR can be configured to aggregate the routes before using the LSAs to advertise the routes from one area to another area.

- **Autonomous System Border Router (ASBR)** — The ASBR is the router that connects the OSPF domain with the routers outside the domain. The ASBR exports routes from outside into the OSPF domain. Note that a stub area cannot contain any ASBRs.

Different types of areas generate and accept different types of LSAs. The LSA is the OSPF router's announcement for its reachability. OSPF routers only generate

LSAs for locally attached interfaces and routes that are exported from other protocols to OSPF. The OSPF router must be configured as an ASBR before the router
can export routes to OSPF. There are 11 types of LSAs that can be generated by an
OSPF router under different conditions. Table 4.1 lists all the OSPF LSA types with
brief descriptions.

Table 4.1 OSPF LSA Types

Type	Name	Originator	Description
1	Router LSA	All OSPF router	All interfaces participating in OSPF in the same LAN segment generate a router LSA to 224.0.0.6 (an OSPF-DR interface) to advertise locally attached links.
2	Network LSA	OSPF DR	The elected DR in a LAN segment sends the network LSA to 224.0.0.5 (for all OSPF speakers).
3	Summary LSA	ABR	ABR generates a summary LSA to advertise LSAs from one area to another area.
4	ASBR summary LSA	ASBR	ASBR generates the ASBR summary LSA into the OSPF domain to announce the location of ASBR.
5	AS-External LSA	ASBR	ASBR generates the External LSA into the OSPF domain to announce its reachability outside the OSPF domain.
6	Group member-ship LSA	MOSPF routers	Used for Multicast OSPF (MOSPF). MOSPF is beyond the scope of this book.
7	NSSA-External LSA	ASBR in NSSA areas	ASBR generates the NSSAS LSA into the OSPF NSSA area to announce its reachability outside the OSPF domain. The ABR converts them to Type 5 (AS-External LSA) and floods them into the backbone.
8	External-attributes LSA	IPv6 router	Used for IPv6 advertisement. IPv6 is beyond the scope of this book.
9	Opaque LSA (link local)	Not used	LSA Type 9 is not used.
10	Opaque LSA (area local)	OSPF-TE	The traffic engineering extension of OSPF uses LSA Type 10 to advertise TE information.
11	Opaque LSA (AS)	Not used	LSA Type 11 is not used.

Traffic Engineering in OSPF

The OSPF-TE (RFC 3630) defines the intra-area traffic engineering enhancement. Opaque LSA Type 10 (area scope) is used to carry the TE-related information and uses the standard OSPF LSA flooding mechanism. Routers store Type 10 LSAs in a separate database — the TED. The ALSRP service router refers to TED as an `Opaque-database` in the command-line interface (CLI).

All LSAs contain an LSA header and LSA payload. The LSA payload contains type-length values (TLV), which contain routing or TE information. There are two types of TLVs:

- **Router Address TLV** — Used to advertise the router-id of an OSPF router.
- **Link TLV** — Used to advertise the locally attached router links. In the case of OSPF-TE, the link TLV contains TE-related information. For an LSA Type 10, one LSA can only contain one link TLV with information for a single link.

Figure 4.5 shows an example of the Opaque-LSA used for OSPF-TE. As shown in Figure 4.5, in the `LINK INFO TLV`, there are 10 types of sub-TLVs containing TE information:

- **Sub-TLV 1** — Link type (1 octet)
- **Sub-TLV 2** — Link ID (4 octets)
- **Sub-TLV 3** — Local interface IP address (4 octets)
- **Sub-TLV 4** — Remote interface IP address (4 octets)
- **Sub-TLV 5** — Traffic Engineering metric (4 octets)
- **Sub-TLV 6** — Maximum bandwidth (4 octets)
- **Sub-TLV 7** — Maximum reservable bandwidth (4 octets)
- **Sub-TLV 8** — Unreserved bandwidth (32 octets)
- **Sub-TLV 9** — Administrative group (4 octets)
- **Sub-TLV 16** — Shared Risk Link Group (SRLG) (length variable)

In the TE Opaque-LSA, the link's color, SRLG membership, and the bandwidth information are used as constraints for the TE-capable LSP-Path calculation. By default, TE in OSPF is disabled. It must be explicitly enabled in the OSPF routing instance configuration. Figure 4.6 illustrates the configuration example of enabling OSPF-TE.

Enabling traffic engineering in OSPF is straightforward. Operators simply use the `traffic-engineering` command under the OSPF routing instance configuration.

Figure 4.5   OSPF-TE Opaque LSA Type 10

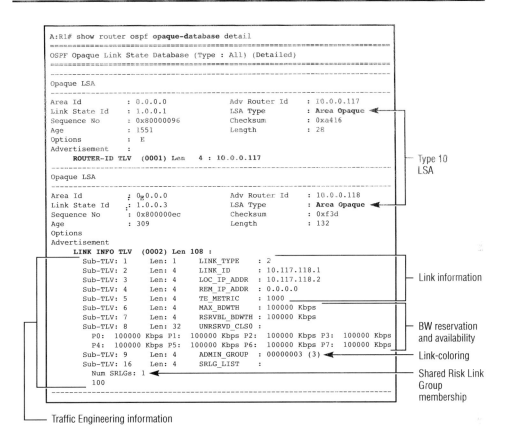

```
A:R1# show router ospf opaque-database detail
=================================================================================
OSPF Opaque Link State Database (Type : All) (Detailed)
=================================================================================
---------------------------------------------------------------------------------
Opaque LSA
---------------------------------------------------------------------------------
Area Id          : 0.0.0.0          Adv Router Id    : 10.0.0.117
Link State Id    : 1.0.0.1          LSA Type         : Area Opaque
Sequence No      : 0x80000096       Checksum         : 0xa416
Age              : 1551             Length           : 28
Options          : E
Advertisement    :
    ROUTER-ID TLV  (0001) Len   4 : 10.0.0.117
---------------------------------------------------------------------------------
Opaque LSA
---------------------------------------------------------------------------------
Area Id          : 0.0.0.0          Adv Router Id    : 10.0.0.118
Link State Id    : 1.0.0.3          LSA Type         : Area Opaque
Sequence No      : 0x800000ec       Checksum         : 0xf3d
Age              : 309              Length           : 132
Options          :
Advertisement    :
    LINK INFO TLV  (0002) Len 108 :
        Sub-TLV: 1    Len: 1    LINK_TYPE     : 2
        Sub-TLV: 2    Len: 4    LINK_ID       : 10.117.118.1
        Sub-TLV: 3    Len: 4    LOC_IP_ADDR   : 10.117.118.2
        Sub-TLV: 4    Len: 4    REM_IP_ADDR   : 0.0.0.0
        Sub-TLV: 5    Len: 4    TE_METRIC     : 1000
        Sub-TLV: 6    Len: 4    MAX_BDWTH     : 100000 Kbps
        Sub-TLV: 7    Len: 4    RSRVBL_BDWTH  : 100000 Kbps
        Sub-TLV: 8    Len: 32   UNRSRVD_CLS0  :
        P0:  100000 Kbps P1:  100000 Kbps P2:  100000 Kbps P3:  100000 Kbps
        P4:  100000 Kbps P5:  100000 Kbps P6:  100000 Kbps P7:  100000 Kbps
        Sub-TLV: 9    Len: 4    ADMIN_GROUP   : 00000003 (3)
        Sub-TLV: 16   Len: 4    SRLG_LIST     :
            Num SRLGs: 1
            100
---------------------------------------------------------------------------------
```

Type 10 LSA

Link information

BW reservation and availability

Link-coloring

Shared Risk Link Group membership

Traffic Engineering information

Figure 4.6   Enabling TE in OSPF

```
A:R1# configure router ospf
A:R1>config>router>ospf# info
------------------------------------------------
        traffic-engineering
        area 0.0.0.0
            interface "system"
            exit
            interface "to-117"
            exit
            interface "to-116"
            exit
        exit
------------------------------------------------
```

The IGP Database versus the Traffic Engineering Database (TED)

In an OSPF router, when the OSPF-TE is enabled, the TED is composed from all the stored LSAs and the local links running OSPF. The OSPF-TE TED has a different view of the network topology from the regular OSPF LSA database. The TED contains more information that can be used by the path calculation algorithm to apply route constraints. The TED and the regular OSPF database are decoupled and have no correlation with each other.

Because the OSPF-TE TED is used for RSVP-TE LSP-Path calculation, OSPF routers do not generate Opaque-LSAs for the OSPF interfaces that do not also participate in RSVP. Another difference is that the regular IGP database contains prefixes that other protocols export to OSPF, as well as prefixes generated by the ABR router to announce its reachability outside the local area. TED does not contain these two types of prefixes; TED only contains links (prefixes) that are local to the area and that have RSVP enabled.

Figure 4.7 presents the contrasting views of the same network from the regular IGP database's perspective and from the TE database's perspective.

You can see in Figure 4.7 that in contrast to the regular OSPF database, the TED has more TE information for traffic engineering. The TE information regarding an OSFP link in the LSA contains:

- **TE Metric** — The metric used by CSPF to calculate paths. If there is no explicit configuration, the TE metric is equal to the value of the regular OSPF metric (which, by default, is the OSPF auto-deduced bandwidth metric). The TE metric of a link can be configured to use a different value in an MPLS interface configuration.

- **Bandwidth Information** — This information consists of maximum bandwidth, reservable bandwidth, and unreserved bandwidth. The unreserved bandwidth is used to track RSVP-TE LSP bandwidth reservation. Because LSPs have eight different priorities (see the following note) and may be preemptive, the unreserved bandwidth sub-TLV has one bandwidth value for each priority.

- **Administrative Group** — A 32-bit field used to color or tag a link. LSPs set up using CSPF can be configured to include or exclude links with certain colors.

- **Shared Risk Link Group (SRLG)** — A link group membership value used to allow the automatic disjoint of a backup LSP (secondary LSP or FRR LSP) from a primary LSP in the LSP setup.

Figure 4.7 IGP Database View and TED View of Network Topology

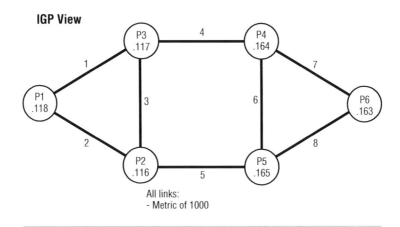

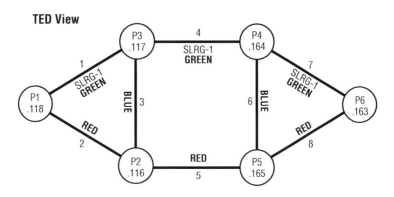

Note: RSVP-TE LSP supports preemptive LSP priority settings. In LSP priority, 0 is the highest priority, and 7 is the lowest priority. An LSP has two priorities: setup priority and holding priority. *Setup priority* defines the preference level when establishing the LSP. *Holding priority* defines the likelihood of the established LSP being bumped by new LSPs. As an example, consider an LSP with a setup priority of 7 and a holding priority of 0. This means that the LSP has the lowest priority to be established. Conversely, if the LSP is established, no other LSP can bump it either (holding priority 0).

When a link has a state change (e.g., failure or recovery), both the regular OSPF LSA and Opaque-TE LSA are flooded to the network to reflect the change in the IGP database and the TED. Furthermore, because the OSPF-TE Opaque LSAs contain bandwidth reservation information, any time there is a reservation change in a link, an LSA is flooded to update the link's resource information. The following examples demonstrate this update:

- An LSP is established over the link with bandwidth reservation. The unreserved bandwidth values on the link are updated.

- An LSP reserved bandwidth on that link took another path. Therefore, the RSVP session on that link is torn down, and a previously reserved bandwidth is released. The unreserved bandwidth value on the link is updated.

- A TE metric is changed in a link's OSPF-TE configuration.

- A subscription percentage is changed in a link. The `subscription percentage` is a change in the booking factor of the link. For example, if the link speed is 100 Mbps, by default, the booking factor is 100 percent. In this case, the LSA for that link advertises `reservable BW` and `unreserved BW` based on the 100 Mbps total bandwidth. If the booking factor changes to 300 percent, an LSA is sent out to update these two fields with a new calculation result based on the 300 Mbps total bandwidth.

- An administrative group or SRLG group is assigned to a link. The link's color group or SRLG membership is updated by flooding new LSAs.

- An RSVP interface status is changed on the link. If a link's RSVP interface state goes **down**, the router sends a Type 10 LSA with LS `Age = 3600` to age-out that link's state. When the link's RSVP state comes back up, the router sends another Type 10 LSA with LS `Age = 1` to re-advertise the link to the TED.

This is necessary because TE is used to calculate the path for the RSVP-TE signaled LSP. If an interface's RSVP state is down, the interface cannot be used by RSVP-TE to establish any LSP.

The IGP only contains the metric value associated with each link that indicates the distance or cost of a link. When the metric is set for a link (manually by the operator or automatically by the system), it will not change. The cost to a certain destination is calculated by the SPF algorithm using the accumulated cost of each link.

In OSPF-TE, for each link, the TED contains more information than the regular OSPF database. For example, the TED contains the bandwidth information (reservable, reserved) changes when there is a resource being booked. If there is an RSVP-TE LSP established over several links, the TED is updated to reflect the resource reservation. Figure 4.8 illustrates an LSP created with 50 Mbps bandwidth reservation and shows how the view of the TED changes to reflect the link reservation.

In Figure 4.8, an LSP is created from P1 to P6 with 50 Mbps reserved bandwidth. After the LSP is set up, OSPF-TE updates the TED with the bandwidth booking information. The process is detailed in the following steps (the step numbers correspond to the circled numbers in Figure 4.8).

1. The LSP with a primary LSP-Path 163 is established with a 50 Mbps bandwidth requirement. CSPF decides that the LSP-Path should take the path P1→P3→P4→P6.

2. After the LSP comes up, the link P1→P3 in the TED has only 50 Mbps of unreserved bandwidth.

3. A CSPF calculation exercise is performed in P1 to find a CSPF path to P6 with the requirement of 30 Mbps bandwidth. Because the path P1→P3→P4→P6 still has 50 Mbps of unreserved bandwidth, CSPF still chooses the same path as the LSP. Note that the triggered calculation exercise does not actually reserve bandwidth. (CSPF calculation exercise is introduced in a later section.)

4. A second CSPF calculation exercise is performed in P1 to find a CSPF path to P6 with the requirement of 60 Mbps bandwidth. Because the path P1→P3→P4→P6 only has 50 Mbps unreserved bandwidth, CSPF chooses a new path of P1→P2→P5→P6.

5. A third CSPF calculation exercise is performed in P1 to find a CSPF path to P6 with 200 Mbps bandwidth. The calculation fails because no link in this network can provide that amount of bandwidth.

Figure 4.8 TED Update after 50 Mbps LSP Is Established

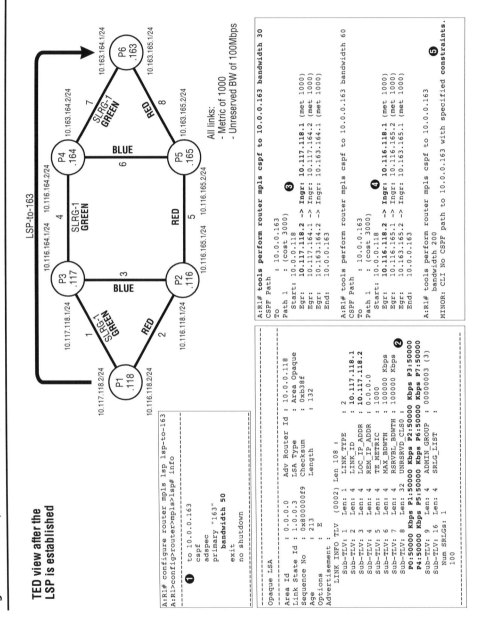

**TED view after the
LSP is established**

```
A:R1# configure router mpls lsp lsp-to-163
A:R1>config>router>mpls>lsp# info
----------------------------------------------------------
❶   to 10.0.0.163
    cspf
    adspec
    primary "163"
        bandwidth 50
    exit
    no shutdown
```

```
Opaque LSA

Area Id        : 0.0.0.0          Adv Router Id  : 10.0.0.118
Link State Id  : 1.0.0.3          LSA Type       : Area Opaque
Sequence No    : 0x800000f9       Checksum       : 0xb38f
Age            : 213              Length         : 132
Options        : E
Advertisement  :
  LINK INFO TLV (0002) Len 108 :
  Sub-TLV: 1   Len: 1   LINK_TYPE      : 2
  Sub-TLV: 2   Len: 4   LINK_ID        : 10.117.118.1
  Sub-TLV: 3   Len: 4   LOC_IP_ADDR    : 10.117.118.2
  Sub-TLV: 4   Len: 4   REM_IP_ADDR    : 0.0.0.0
  Sub-TLV: 5   Len: 4   TE_METRIC      : 1000
  Sub-TLV: 6   Len: 4   MAX_BDWTH      : 100000 Kbps
  Sub-TLV: 7   Len: 4   RSRVBL_BDWTH   : 100000 Kbps
  Sub-TLV: 8   Len: 32  UNRSRVD_CLS0   :
      P0:50000 Kbps P1:50000 Kbps P2:50000 Kbps P3:50000
      P4:50000 Kbps P5:50000 Kbps P6:50000 Kbps P7:50000   ❷
  Sub-TLV: 9   Len: 4   ADMIN_GROUP    : 00000003 (3)
  Sub-TLV: 16  Len: 4   SRLG_LIST      :
    Num SRLGs: 1
      100
```

```
A:R1# tools perform router mpls cspf to 10.0.0.163 bandwidth 30
CSPF Path
To        : 10.0.0.163
Path 1    : (cost 3000)
  Start: 10.0.0.118
  Egr: 10.117.118.2 ->  Ingr: 10.117.118.1 (met 1000)
  Egr: 10.117.164.1 ->  Ingr: 10.117.164.2 (met 1000)
  Egr: 10.163.164.2 ->  Ingr: 10.163.164.1 (met 1000)
  End: 10.0.0.163                                        ❸

A:R1# tools perform router mpls cspf to 10.0.0.163 bandwidth 60
CSPF Path
To        : 10.0.0.163
Path 1    : (cost 3000)
  Start: 10.0.0.118
  Egr: 10.116.118.2 ->  Ingr: 10.116.118.1 (met 1000)
  Egr: 10.116.165.1 ->  Ingr: 10.116.165.2 (met 1000)
  Egr: 10.163.165.2 ->  Ingr: 10.163.165.1 (met 1000)
  End: 10.0.0.163                                        ❹

A:R1# tools perform router mpls cspf to 10.0.0.163 with specified constraints.
      bandwidth 200
MINOR: CLI No CSPF path to 10.0.0.163                    ❺
```

LSP-to-163

All links:
- Metric of 1000
- Unreserved BW of 100Mbps

TE Parameters in the MPLS Interface

When operators enable OSPF-TE or IS-IS TE in a router, the default parameters are efficient and optimal for most scenarios. However, there are cases in which the IGP-TE or CSPF parameters need to be modified. Figure 4.9 presents a configuration example of these tunable parameters.

There are three OSPF-TE optional parameters:

- `te-metric` — The link metric for traffic engineering can be manually specified to override the system default behavior. When the TE metric is not enabled, the OSPF-TE or IS-IS TE uses the default IGP's link metric as the link's `te-metric` value. The TE-metric configuration is performed on a per-interface basis in the MPLS Interface Configuration context of the CLI.

- `subscription` — The booking factor of a TE-capable interface. The default value of 100 percent means that the link can only reserve up to 100 percent of its bandwidth. If the value is set to 200 percent with explicit configuration, a 200 percent overbooking is allowed. The booking factor configuration is performed on a per-interface basis in the RSVP Configuration context of the CLI. The system advertises and uses the maximum available bandwidth for reservation. For a 100 Mbps link, if `subscription 200` is configured, RSVP can book up to 200 Mbps of bandwidth on that link for LSP.

- `use-te-metric` — When CSPF is used to calculate the LSP's path, it must consider the metric (or cost) of the links to find the most optimal path. By default, CSPF calculates the path using the IGP metric value for the link. If `use-te-metric` is enabled in an LSP, the CSPF uses the TE-metric value for the link to calculate the path. The `use-te-metric` configuration is performed on a per-LSP basis in the MPLS LSP Configuration context of the CLI. The CSPF path calculation for LSP-Paths that belong to the same LSP must use same type of metric.

> **Note:** More detail on LSP can be found in Chapter 3. RSVP-TE is covered in Chapter 5. CSPF is covered in the section "The CSPF Algorithm" later in this chapter.

The link's TE configuration and the LSP's CSPF configuration are required regardless of the TE routing protocol used. Both OSPF-TE and IS-IS TE are only used for advertising the TE information across the network.

Figure 4.9   Tunable Traffic Engineering Parameters

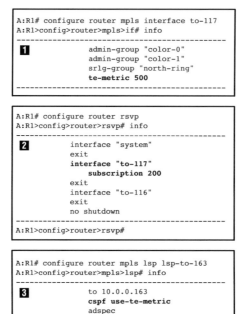

4.3 Introducing IS-IS TE

This section introduces the traffic engineering extension for IS-IS: IS-IS TE (defined in RFC 3784). We briefly review the IS-IS adjacency establishment and then discuss the traffic engineering extension. Because IS-IS is a widely deployed routing protocol and has been well documented by many publications, this section does not discuss the IS-IS protocol at a detailed level.

Legacy IS-IS in Routed IP Networks

Defined by RFC 1195, IS-IS is an Interior Gateway Protocol (IGP) capable of routing IP protocols and has been widely deployed in service providers' networks. Similar to OSPF, IS-IS is also a link state routing protocol. Because of its true hierarchical design, the scalability of IS-IS is higher than OSPF's. However, IS-IS is less popular than OSPF in the enterprise world because of its complexity: Fewer people understand IS-IS. Despite this, IS-IS's scalability, reliability, and clean hierarchical design make it more advantageous in the carriers' networks.

Unlike OSPF, IS-IS was originally designed to provide routing information for a protocol other than TCP/IP — the Connectionless Networking Protocol (CLNP). IS-IS uses CLNP's addressing and Layer 3 addressing, and the IS-IS packets are CLNP packets.

IS-IS Areas and IS-IS Adjacency

IS-IS supports a two-layer hierarchical network design similar to that of OSPF. However, in an OSPF router, each interface participating in OSPF can belong to a different area (at least one interface must belong to Area 0). With OSPF, an ABR resides in the boundary of the areas and exchanges routes among areas. In IS-IS, a router can reside in only one area. The area boundary is at the links between routers in different areas.

The communication among routers in the same local area is called *Level 1 (L1) communication*. The communication among routers in different areas is called *Level 2 (L2) communication*. Adjacent routers in different areas form a Level 2 adjacency between directly connected links, and they exchange only Level 2 routes between their areas. In IS-IS, the backbone area is a Level 2 area, and all non-backbone areas are Level 1 areas. The Level 2 backbone area must be *consistent* (reachable by other L2 or L1/L2 routers), and all non-backbone Level-1 areas must connect to the backbone area.

In IS-IS, all routers sharing the same area-id belong to the same area. There can be many areas in the same autonomous system using IS-IS. An IS-IS router can function as a:

- **Level 1 Only Router** — An L1 router has routing visibility only within the local area. An L1 router forms L1 adjacencies only with other routers participating in IS-IS. For an L1 router to reach another L1 router in a different area, its traffic must go through an L2 router or L1/L2 router within the local area to reach the other area, and then reach the target L1 router.

- **Level 2 Only Router** — An L2 router forms L2 adjacencies only with other L2 or L1/L2 routers. An L2 router transits traffic from one area to another area.
- **Level 1/Level 2 Router** — An L1/L2 router has both L1 adjacencies with local L1 routers and L2 adjacencies with L2 routers in other areas. In an IS-IS area, the L1/L2 router is the gateway for all L1 router traffic in the local area to reach other areas.

Figure 4.10 illustrates a sample IS-IS network with a two-level hierarchy. In the IS-IS two-level routing hierarchy, two Level 1 routers in different areas must communicate through a Level 2 or Level 1/Level 2 router. As indicated in the dotted lines in Figure 4.10, if Routers R11 and R3 want to communicate with each other, these routers must find the closest L2 or L1/L2 router in the local area first. Then, the local L2 or L1/L2 router traffic will reach the other area through other L2 or L1/L2 router(s). The target area's L2 or L1/L2 router traffic can then reach the target L1 router within its local area. To achieve full reachability in a network running IS-IS as the routing protocol, the IS-IS Level 2 backbone area must be consistent. This means that all L2 or L1/L2 routers must be able to reach each other through Level 2 communications. Otherwise, the IS-IS network will be partitioned, and full reachability cannot be provided.

IS-IS routers use a four-way handshake to form IS-IS adjacency. When an IS-IS interface comes up, it starts sending L1, L2, or L1/L2 Hello packets according to the interface's IS-IS configuration. When an IS-IS router receives the Hello packets with the correct level and sees the adjacent router's router-id in the Hello packets, it adds the adjacent router's router-id to the Hello packets. When both routers see their own router-id and the adjacent router's router-id in the Hello packets, the IS-IS adjacency is formed. After the adjacency is formed, the two routers exchange Complete Sequence Number Packet (CSNP) packets and then Link State packets. The Link State packets form the link state database (LSDB), which is used for route calculation. Figure 4.11 illustrates the IS-IS adjacency establishment between two routers and the sample IS-IS configuration on both routers.

Figure 4.10 IS-IS Two-level Routing Hierarchy

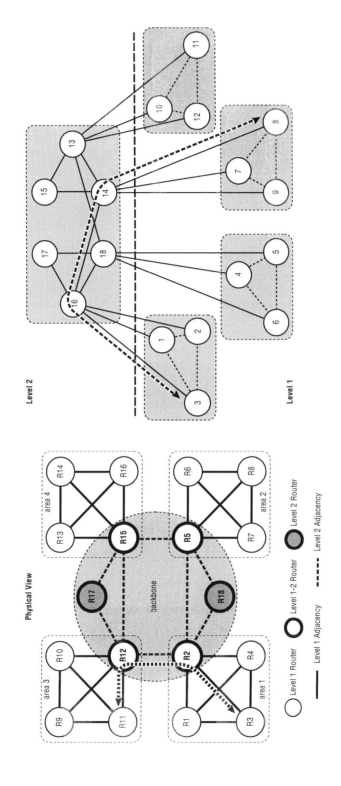

Figure 4.11 IS-IS Adjacency Establishment and Sample Configuration

```
A:R1# show router isis interface
===============================================================================
ISIS Interfaces
===============================================================================
Interface                    Level CircID  Oper State   L1/L2 Metric
-------------------------------------------------------------------------------
to-116                         L1    3       Up          10/-
-------------------------------------------------------------------------------
Interfaces : 1
===============================================================================
A:R1# show router isis adjacency
===============================================================================
ISIS Adjacency
===============================================================================
System ID                Usage State Hold Interface                MT Enab
-------------------------------------------------------------------------------
R2                         L1   Up    25   to-116                   No
-------------------------------------------------------------------------------
Adjacencies : 1
===============================================================================
```

R1 .118 ——————— R2 .116

1 Router 1 sends Hello packets to router 2 to start the adjacency negotiation with its own router-id.

2 Router 1 receives Hello packets from router 2 with the proper level and sees 2's router-id in the hello packet.

3 Router 1 sends Hello packets with its own router-id and router 2's router-id. The ISIS adjacency is therefore formed.

4 Router 1 and 2 exchange CSNPs.

5 Router 1 and 2 exchange LSPs based on the CSNPs exchanged.

```
A:R1# configure router isis
A:R1>config>router>isis# info
-------------------------------------
        area-id 49.0001
        traffic-engineering
        interface "to-116"
            level-capability level-1
        exit
-------------------------------------
```

```
A:R2# configure router isis
A:R2>config>router>isis# info
-------------------------------------
        area-id 49.0001
        traffic-engineering
        interface "to-118"
            level-capability level-1
        exit
-------------------------------------
```

IS-IS Routing Updates

IS-IS packets are CLNP packets. In a network with Ethernet connectivity, IS-IS packets are Ethernet-encapsulated. There are three types of IS-IS packets:

- **Hello Packets** — Hello packets are used by IS-IS routers to discover other IS-IS participating interfaces and to establish/maintain the adjacencies.

- **Link State Packets** — Link State packets contain actual routing information (link state information) for IS-IS. IS-IS Link State packets are similar to OSPF LSAs.
- **Sequence Number Packets (SNP)** — SNPs are similar to the Database Summary OSPF packets. They contain the sequence numbers of the LSPs in the IS-IS routers database. There are two types of SNPs:
    - **CSNP** (Complete SNP) — Contains all sequence numbers of the IS-IS router's database.
    - **PSNP** (Partial SNP) — Contains sequence numbers of only part of the IS-IS router's database.

Table 4.2 lists all IS-IS packets and their Protocol Data Unit (PDU) types.

Table 4.2 IS-IS Packet Types and PDU Types

Packet Type	PDU Type	Name
Hello packets	15	LAN Level 1 Hello packets
	16	LAN Level 2 Hello packets
	17	Point-to-point Hello packets
LSP	18	Level 1 LSP
	20	Level 2 LSP
SNP	24	Level 1 CSNP
	25	Level 2 CSNP
	26	Level 1 PSNP
	27	Level 2 PSNP

Traffic Engineering in IS-IS

The IS-IS TE (RFC 3784) defines the intra-area traffic engineering enhancements. There are four TE TLVs used by IS-IS TE:

- **Traffic Engineering Router ID TLV (Type 134)** — Contains a 4-octet router-id used for IS-IS TE.
- **Extended IP Reachability TLV (Type 135)** — Contains a 4-octet IP prefix (not used in IS-IS TE).
- **Extended IS Reachability TLV (Type 22)** — Used to carry the TE-related information (bandwidth, color). This TLV contains seven types of sub-TLVs in the LINK INFO TLV that contains TE information:
    - **Sub-TLV** 3 — Administrative group (4 octets)

- **Sub-TLV 6** — IPv4 interfaces address (4 octets)
- **Sub-TLV 8** — IPv4 neighbor address (4 octets)
- **Sub-TLV 9** — Maximum bandwidth (4 octets)
- **Sub-TLV 10** — Maximum reservable bandwidth (4 octets)
- **Sub-TLV 11** — Unreserved bandwidth (32 octets)
- **Sub-TLV 18** — Traffic Engineering metric (4 octets)

- **Shared Risk Link Group (SRLG) TLV (Type 138)** — This TLV is used to carry SRLG membership information.

By default, traffic engineering is disabled in IS-IS. It must be explicitly enabled from the IS-IS routing instance configuration. Figure 4.12 presents an IS-IS TE configuration example, an MPLS interface TE configuration example, and a section of the show router isis database detail containing TE information.

Figure 4.12   IS-IS TE Information in TLV

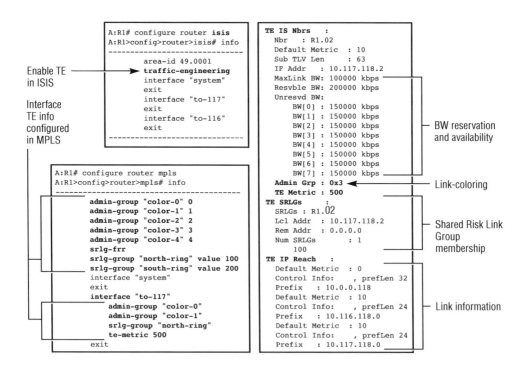

4.4 The CSPF Algorithm

Constrained Shortest Path First (CSPF) is an enhanced SPF algorithm used in an IP/MPLS VPN network for RSVP-TE LSP path calculation. CSPF in an RSVP-TE LSP-Path calculation is a two-step procedure:

1. Use the constraints to prune all the links from the TED that do not meet the requirements.

2. Use the SPF algorithm to calculate the LSP path from the TED.

   If there are multiple equal cost paths, CSPF picks only one as the path.

   The constraints used by CSPF to perform route selection include:

- **Bandwidth Information** — The amount of bandwidth the connection requests and the amount of bandwidth on the link that is available for reservation.

- **Administrative Groups** — The color of the links. The operator can configure certain links to belong to different administrative groups and request certain connections to avoid certain administrative groups.

- **Shared Risk Link Group (SRLG)** — The SRLG membership of the links. The operator can configure certain links to belong to different SRLGs and request certain connections to avoid certain SRLGs.

- **Explicit Route** — When TE is used to decide the LSP-Path's actual path in the network, the operator can provide a list of hops for the LSP-Path to go through or avoid. TE considers the hop list as a constraint when calculating the path for the LSP-Path.

- **Hop Limit** — When TE is used to decide the LSP-Path's actual path in the network, the operator can set up a limit of hops the LSP-Path can go through.

- **Resiliency Request** — When using TE to set up an LSP-Path, the LSP-Path can be configured with certain requests for protection. These resiliency requests can also be considered by the TE when deciding the LSP-Path's actual path in the network.

There are two types of RSVP-TE LSPs that use CSPF instead of regular SPF to calculate their paths and compose the explicit routing object (ERO):

- **CSPF-Directed LSP** — When an LSP has an explicit configuration of cspf, all LSP-Paths (primary and secondary) use CSPF to perform path calculation.

- **MPLS Fast Reroute (FRR) Protection Tunnels** — All FRR LSPs use CSPF to perform path calculation when they are detouring LSP for a one-to-one backup and to bypass tunnels for facility backup. FRR is introduced in Chapter 7.

Recall that when CSPF performs path calculation, if it succeeds, it composes an ERO that contains a complete list of strict hops with interface IP addresses only. Therefore, the CSPF-directed LSPs are source-routed. The Head-End (HE) router (source) defines the exact end-to-end path the LSP-Path travels.

CSPF can use the following constraints to prune links from the TED:

- **Bandwidth Requirement** — The CSPF-directed LSP's bandwidth requirement is considered as a constraint. All links whose *unreservable bandwidth* has less value than the required bandwidth are pruned from this calculation.

- **Administrative Group (Color of the Link)** — The CSPF-directed LSP may have an `include` or `exclude` list of link colors. CSPF prunes links with colors not desired before calculating the path.

- **SRLG Membership** — The CSPF prunes the links that are members of the same SRLG that contains the links used by the primary LSP for:

    - Secondary LSP(s) configured to protect the primary LSP

    - FRR detour LSP(s) or bypass tunnel(s) to protect the primary LSP, when SRLG is enabled for FRR

- **CSPF Use of TED** — Links that do not participate in RSVP are not considered by CSPF in the path calculation.

Figure 4.13 illustrates an example of the CSPF pruning process.

The network in Figure 4.13 has TE enabled with one LSP established between P1 and P6 reserving 50 Mbps of bandwidth. Some links in the network are colored, and some links are members of SRLG groups. Assume that CSPF is used to signal another LSP with two requirements:

- The LSP requires 60 Mbps of reserved bandwidth.
- The LSP wants to avoid any links colored green.

When the LSP is configured and administratively enabled, CSPF starts the path calculation process by pruning the links in the TED that do not meet the two constraints specified by the LSP. In Figure 4.13, the CSPF prunes links that do not fulfill the TE requirement.

Figure 4.13 CSPF Uses Constraints to Prune Links in TED.

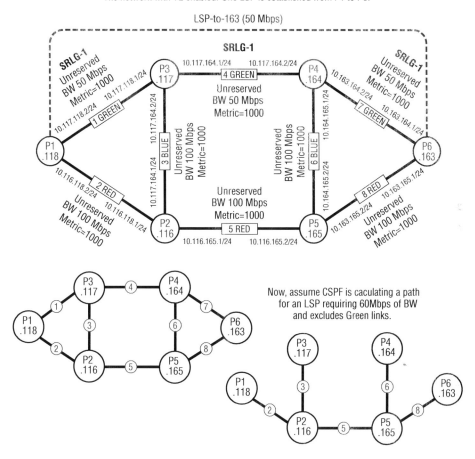

CSPF Path Calculation for RSVP-TE LSP

After CSPF prunes the links that do not meet the TE constraints, it performs the path calculation. In the path calculation, the following are considered by the CSPF:

- The list of strict or loose hops in the path associated to the LSP using CSPF
- The metric of each remaining link after the pruning process

The *hop list* in the associated path in the LSP is a series of manually configured loose or strict hops. Operators can use a hop list to control the desired direction of the hop. In most cases, the hop list set by the operator contains an *abstract node* — a logical representation of a router in the network.

An abstract node can also use Autonomous System (AS) numbers. In this case, the abstract node represents an AS as a single hop.

Note that in Figure 4.13, the two smaller diagrams at the bottom of the figure are the logical topology representations of the node. An abstract node is used to hide these topology details so the operator can control the route of LSPs more precisely. In most cases, the operator wants to control the LSP at a relatively high level, such as "I want this LSP to go through routers P1 and P3," rather than specifying, "I want this LSP to go through P1 then link P1–P4 then router P4 then link P4–P3 then router P3." Use of an abstract node in the hop list allows the operator to state the requirement in high-level terms and let the path calculation algorithm (SPF or CSPF) handle the details.

When CSPF finishes the pruning process for an LSP, it starts the path calculation using the hop list as input. There are two types of hops in the hop list:

- **Strict Hop** — Specifies an immediate-next hop router to the previous hop in the list.

- **Loose Hop** — Specifies a downstream router of the previous hop in the list.

When processing the hop list for all strict hops in the list, the CSPF needs to check only if it is a correct immediate next hop of the previous abstract node. If this is the case, the CSPF finds the direct link with the lowest metric to the strict hop, places the ingress interface IP address as a strict hop in the ERO, and continues its calculations. If the CSPF cannot find a directly connected IP interface to that hop, the CSPF fails the path calculation with error code noCspfRouteToDestination and stops the calculation process, and the LSP is not signaled. For all loose hops in the list, the CSPF consults the TED to find the lowest metric path to that hop. CSPF inserts the IP addresses of the intermediate routers' ingress interface into the ERO as strict hops. After the entire hop list is processed, CSPF builds an ERO with all strict hops. All IP addresses in the ERO are those of the intermediate routers' ingress interfaces.

CSPF can choose from many multiple routes to find one route to a hop using the metric as the selection criteria. There are two types of metrics:

- **IGP Metric** — Provided by IGP without the traffic engineering. If OSPF is used, the IGP metric is the metric contained in the regular LSAs (for example, Type 1, 2, or 3).

- **TE Metric** — Value used in Type 10 opaque LSAs for TE advertisement. By default, the TE metric is numerically equal to the IGP metric. The operator can manually override the TE metric by setting a different value in each interface in the MPLS Interface Configuration context of the command-line interface (CLI).

If the operator wants to use a TE metric to calculate the path of the LSP, two configurations are required:

- The TE metric of the links must be configured in the link's MPLS Interface Configuration context.
- The LSP must specify the `cspf use-te-metric` in the LSP configuration. CSPF calculation using the TE metric is configured on a per-LSP basis. When `use-te-metric` is enabled, all LSP-Paths belonging to the same LSP (primary, secondary, FRR) are calculated by CSPF using the TE metric.

Using CSPF to Check TE Availability

During network deployment, operators may wish to test the configuration by finding a path from Router A to Router B. In a routed IP network, `ping` and `trace-route` can be used for reachability testing purposes. In the case of an IP/MPLS VPN network, it can be useful to test the link constraint information. An operator may want to know the answer to questions like "Can I reserve 50 Mbps bandwidth between Route P1 and P6 for an LSP? If so, what is the path for the LSP?" The operator can create an LSP with certain constraints and test the network by trying to establish the LSP. However, this procedure is not efficient and may cause an accidental service outage. For example, establishment of a test LSP may bump some LSPs carrying live traffic in the production network.

It is necessary to test the TE deployment when an operator wants to deploy complex TE overlays on a network with administrative groups and SRLGs, or to set a different TE metric to the links. CSPF provides a test function in which the path calculation to a certain destination can be performed. With this function, the operator can easily test the constraint settings and path availability. The operator can perform a CSPF check from the router to test the network configuration. The CSPF check performs a CSPF path calculation with several optional constraints and returns the list of hops if it succeeds. Figure 4.14 presents the commands for a CSPF path check using the `tools perform router mpls cspf` command.

When performing a CSPF path check, if the bandwidth requirement is used, the router does not book the bandwidth. Therefore, no bandwidth resource is consumed by the CSPF path check. Figure 4.15 shows the output of a CSPF path check.

Figure 4.14 CSPF Path Check

```
A:R1# tools perform router mpls cspf
 - cspf to <ip-addr> [from <ip-addr>] [bandwidth <bandwidth>] [include-bitmap <bitmap>]
   [exclude-bitmap <bitmap>] [hop-limit <limit>] [exclude-address <excl-addr>
   [<excl-addr>...(upto 8 max)]] [use-te-metric] [strict-srlg] [srlg-group <grp-id>...(up to 8 max)]

<ip-addr>            : a.b.c.d
<ip-address>         : ip-address
<bandwidth>          : [1..100000] in Mbps
<bitmap>             : [0..4294967295] - accepted in decimal, hex(0x) or binary(0b)
<bitmap>             : bitmap
<limit>              : [1..255]
<excl-addr>          : a.b.c.d (system or egress ip-address)
<use-te-metric>      : keyword
<strict-srlg>        : keyword
<grp-id>             : [0..4294967295]
```

Figure 4.15 CSPF Path Check Examples

```
A:R1# tools perform router mpls cspf to 10.0.0.163                        ❶
CSPF Path
To        : 10.0.0.163
Path 1    : (cost 3000)
    Start: 10.0.0.118
    Egr:  10.117.118.2    -> Ingr:  10.117.118.1    (met 1000)
    Egr:  10.117.164.1    -> Ingr:  10.117.164.2    (met 1000)
    Egr:  10.163.164.2    -> Ingr:  10.163.164.1    (met 1000)
    End:  10.0.0.163

A:R1# tools perform router mpls cspf to 10.0.0.163 include-bitmap 00000001 ❷
MINOR: CLI No CSPF path to "10.0.0.163" with specified constraints.
A:R1# tools perform router mpls cspf to 10.0.0.163 exclude-bitmap 00000010
CSPF Path
To        : 10.0.0.163
Path 1    : (cost 3000)                                                   ❸
    Start: 10.0.0.118
    Egr:  10.116.118.2    -> Ingr:  10.116.118.1    (met 1000)
    Egr:  10.116.165.1    -> Ingr:  10.116.165.2    (met 1000)
    Egr:  10.163.165.2    -> Ingr:  10.163.165.1    (met 1000)
    End:  10.0.0.163

A:R1# tools perform router mpls cspf to 10.0.0.163 bandwidth 30           ❹
CSPF Path
To        : 10.0.0.163
Path 1    : (cost 3000)
    Start: 10.0.0.118
    Egr:  10.117.118.2    -> Ingr:  10.117.118.1    (met 1000)
    Egr:  10.117.164.1    -> Ingr:  10.117.164.2    (met 1000)
    Egr:  10.163.164.2    -> Ingr:  10.163.164.1    (met 1000)
    End:  10.0.0.163

A:R1# tools perform router mpls cspf to 10.0.0.163 bandwidth 60           ❺
CSPF Path
To        : 10.0.0.163
Path 1    : (cost 3000)
    Start: 10.0.0.118
    Egr:  10.116.118.2    -> Ingr:  10.116.118.1    (met 1000)
    Egr:  10.116.165.1    -> Ingr:  10.116.165.2    (met 1000)
    Egr:  10.163.165.2    -> Ingr:  10.163.165.1    (met 1000)
    End:  10.0.0.163

*A:R1# tools perform router mpls cspf to 10.0.0.163 bandwidth 110         ❻
MINOR: CLI No CSPF path to "10.0.0.163" with specified constraints.
```

The following types of CSPF path checks can be performed (numbers correspond to circled numbers in Figure 4.15):

1.   A CSPF path check to Router 10.0.0.163 with no constraint. The CSPF path calculation succeeds and returns the lowest-cost path.

2.   A CSPF path check to Router 10.0.0.163 with a constraint to use links with color (0x00000001). The CSPF path calculation fails and returns no path. The administrative groups are represented in bitmap format in the CSPF path check.

3.   A CSPF path check to Router 10.0.0.163 with a constraint to exclude links with color (0x00000010). The CSPF path calculation succeeds and returns the lowest-cost path.

4.   A CSPF path check to Router 10.0.0.163 with a constraint to reserve 30 Mbps of bandwidth. The CSPF path calculation succeeds and returns the lowest-cost path.

5.   A CSPF path check to Router 10.0.0.163 with constraint to reserve 60 Mbps of bandwidth. The CSPF path calculation succeeds and returns the lowest-cost path. The path returned is a different path from the previous result because the previous path cannot provide enough bandwidth.

6.   A CSPF path check to Router 10.0.0.163 with a constraint to reserve 110 Mbps of bandwidth. The CSPF path calculation fails and returns no CSPF path. All links in the network are 100 Mbps links.

4.5 RSVP-TE LSP Policy Control: Administrative Groups and SRLG Groups

This section introduces two LSP-Path control techniques: administrative groups (link-coloring) and Shared Risk Link Groups (SRLGs). Using these techniques, the path of the LSP-Path can be dynamically calculated to travel through or avoid certain topologies. Primary and backup LSP-Paths can be disjointed from each other to provide maximum resiliency without intensive configuration of the explicit hop list.

Note that the discussion of administrative groups and SRLGs includes scenarios with MPLS LSP resiliency using secondary LSP and FRR. These MPLS resiliency features are discussed in Chapters 6 and 7.

Administrative Groups and Link-Coloring Overview

As mentioned previously, an advantage of using traffic engineering is the ability to use link-coloring to direct LSPs. A CSPF-directed LSP can be configured to only travel through links with a certain color (include) or avoid links with a certain color (exclude). This inclusion or exclusion of the links is achieved by marking different colors on each set of links through the network. The operator can then configure an LSP to use or avoid links with certain colors.

In many cases, LSP topology redundancy is desired. In this scenario, the operator wants to create one LSP with two LSP-Paths and ensure that the LSP-Paths are physically separated from each other as much as possible. This maximizes the redundancy of the LSP. One way to achieve this redundancy is to create multiple paths with a different set of hops specified in each path and ensure that these paths take different routes. The operator then associates the different paths to different LSP-Paths. This ensures that the two LSP-Paths follow different path lists and travel separately. The explicit definition of hops in the LSP-Path's associated path gives the operator the strongest level of control. If desired, the operator can define the exact path the LSP-Path is allowed to travel. However, this approach leads to the following disadvantages, especially in a scaled network:

- **Scalability** — The explicit hop definition may introduce a big operational overhead in a scaled network. If all strict hops are used, a huge number of paths and hops may be listed in the path. Without careful network design, if loose hops are mixed with strict hops, the LSP-Path may not be well controlled.

- **Flexibility** — Hop listing in the path definition is sensitive to network topology changes. Adding or removing routers may make the path list invalid and require path re-definition. The path definition may not be able to absorb the network topology change without extra management or configuration costs.

- **Manageability** — As the LSPs and their paths increase with network size, it is difficult to track them in a scaled network. The LSP-Paths' directions may be uncontrollable.

There is another way of directing the LSPs to different routes — via the use of administrative groups (link-coloring). With administrative groups, the operator creates a set of links in the network with a tag or color and advertises the links' colors to the network through TE advertisement. When defining the LSP's path, the operator simply specifies the desired or unwanted link colors. When CSPF performs the LSP ERO calculation, these color requirements are considered, and the LSP is routed accordingly.

Figure 4.16 illustrates a *ring* topology, in which the operator needs to configure several LSPs with maximum protection. The best way to protect an LSP in a ring topology is to establish two LSP-Paths; the primary LSP travels on one side of the ring, and the secondary LSP travels on the other side.

Figure 4.16 Link-Coloring Example Topology

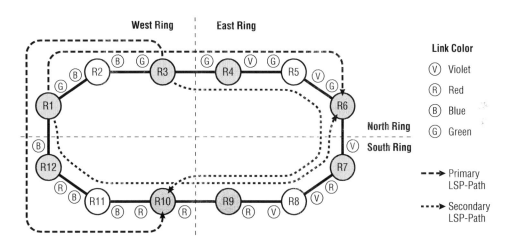

In this example, there are four LSPs required:

- **LSP from R1 to R6** — The primary LSP should take the North ring, and the secondary LSP should take the South ring.
- **LSP from R12 to R7** — The primary LSP should take the South ring, and the secondary LSP should take the North ring.
- **LSP from R3 to R10** — The primary LSP should take the West ring, and the secondary LSP should take the East ring.
- **LSP from R4 to R9** — The primary LSP should take the East ring, and the secondary LSP should take the West ring.

Note that Figure 4.16 only shows LSP-Paths R1–R6 and R3–R10. The requirement in this example is to use secondary LSPs in the opposite direction to protect the primary LSP.

If the explicit path hop-list approach is used, the mid-hops of each LSP must be listed in the paths. Also, if other nodes join the network later, the hop lists of many paths may need to be changed.

However, if an operator uses the administrative group approach to direct LSP paths, this protection policy can be implemented in an easier way:

- Mark the links in the North ring with the color green. Configure the LSP R1–R6's primary LSP to include green links. Configure the LSP's secondary LSP to exclude green links.

- Mark the links in the South ring with the color red. Configure the LSP R12–R7's primary LSP to include red links. Configure the LSP's secondary LSP to exclude red links (not shown in the diagram).

- Mark the links in the West ring with the color blue. Configure the LSP R4–R10's primary LSP to include blue links. Configure the LSP's secondary LSP to exclude blue links.

- Mark the links in the East ring with the color violet. Configure the LSP R4–R9's primary LSP to include violet links. Configure the LSP's secondary LSP to exclude violet links (not shown in the diagram).

If more nodes join the ring later, the operator only has to color their links correctly. LSP configuration is not required, and an empty loose path can be used by all LSPs all the time.

Note that there are other ways of coloring this network to achieve the same result. This is an example of how to use the coloring; it is not a network design guideline.

Coloring Links and Advertising in TE Routing

OSPF-TE uses link TLV in its advertisement to describe links. In the link TLV, the administrative group is a 4-octet sub-TLV (Type 0x9). There are 32 bits in the administrative group; each bit represents a group. The least significant bit is called Group 0, and the most significant bit is called Group 31. When a link is added to a group, the corresponding bit is set in the administrative group's sub-TLV. Every link's administrative group information is stored in the TED as one of the link's characters. Therefore, the CSPF calculation takes the group information into consideration when calculating the ERO for RSVP-TE LSP. There is no IGP-TE configuration required in the router; all the `admin-group` definition is done on a per-interface basis in the MPLS Interface Configuration context in the CLI.

Note that IS-IS TE also supports administrative groups. The configuration procedure is the same as when OSPF-TE is used as the routing protocol. However, we use OSPF-TE in this discussion because of its popularity.

Configuring Link-Coloring

To configure and use administrative groups to direct LSPs, there are three steps:

1. **Define Administrative Groups** — In the `configure router mpls` context, define the admin-group by associating a name and the group number (0–31).

2. **Apply the Admin-Group to the Links** — In the MPLS Interface Configuration context, the admin-groups can be associated with the interface. One interface can be associated with one or many admin-groups (up to all 32 groups).

3. **Configure the Include or Exclude Lists in the LSP** — The CSPF uses these conditions as filtering criteria when performing ERO calculations for these paths. Note that `cspf` must be explicitly enabled in the LSP for the LSP routing to be color-aware.

Figure 4.17 presents an example of administrative group configuration in the HE router. It illustrates the LSP configuration required to allow the LSP-Paths in the LSP to use the administrative groups to direct the paths.

Although FRR relies on CSPF to calculate the protection tunnel, it is not color-aware. The automatic detour LSP (one-to-one backup) or bypass tunnel (facility backup) creation does not take or avoid any link with colors. Operators can force the FRR protection to choose a manually specified path via a manual bypass tunnel in facility backup. (FRR is addressed in detail in Chapter 7.)

Warning: In a scaled network, the link-coloring exercise must start with careful planning and accurate documentation. The network design that uses link-coloring must include all possible failure scenarios and topology expansions. Incorrect link-coloring configuration may cause service outage.

Figure 4.17 Configuring Administrative Groups

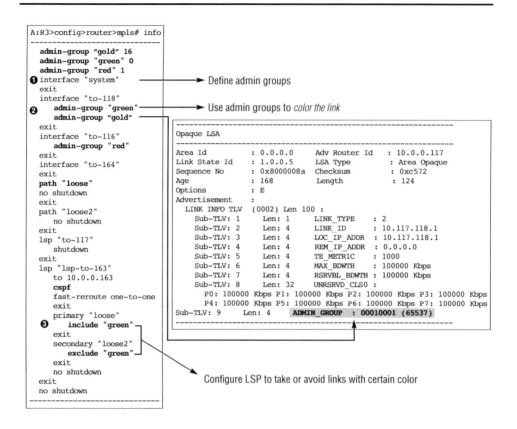

Shared Risk Link Groups

The use of administrative groups allows the operators to split the paths of primary LSP-Paths and secondary LSP-Paths serving the same LSP and thus achieve maximum topology redundancy. This avoids manual configuration of explicit hops for the LSP-Path's path. However, operators must still manually assign and set the administrative group(s) for all links in the network. Shared Risk Link Groups (SRLGs) take the controlled redundant path establishment one step further. SRLG allows the operators to create automatic secondary LSPs or FRR protection tunnels that are disjointed from the protected primary LSP. When SRLG is defined, links belonging to the same SRLG present the possibility of a shared common risk (e.g., the same physical fiber, transmission facility, or same router). The backup LSP (secondary LSPs or FRR LSPs) automatically avoids using links belonging to the same SRLG of the protected LSP. The risk is logical rather than physical, and any link can be defined as a member of any SRLG for any reason. Although FRR is not link-color–aware, it is aware of a link's SRLG membership. With the definition of SRLG, the protection configuration of the LSP is even easier. Less manual configuration is required. Figure 4.18 demonstrates the use of the SRLG in a sample network to direct the FRR bypass tunnel path.

Figure 4.18   SRLG Example: FRR Bypass Tunnel Deployment

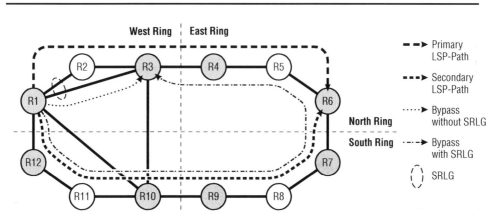

Figure 4.18 presents the same network as in Figure 4.16. In this network example, the FRR facility backup is desired, and there is an extra link between R1 and R3. Note that FRR is not aware of link colors. As the HE router, R1 will establish the bypass tunnel through the R1–R3 link.

In this example, SRLG is configured in the R1 router. Both links R1–R2 and R1–R3 are configured as members of the same SRLG. The primary LSP is configured to use link R1 R2 toward the R6 router (TE). When FRR and the secondary LSP are both configured to use the SRLG constraint for route calculation, they do not use any link belonging to the same SRLG as the link used by the SRLG. They are routed by CSPF through the South ring. In this configuration, the primary LSP and its backup LSPs are disjointed to allow maximum resiliency.

SRLG Membership Advertisement

The SRLG is advertised over the IGP's traffic engineering extension. The following new SRLG sub-TLV types are defined to contain the SRLG membership:

- **OSPF-TE** — type 0x10
- **IS-IS TE** — type 0x8A

There is no IGP-TE configuration required in the router; all SRLG definition is done in the MPLS Configuration context.

SRLG with Secondary LSPs

CSPF must be used in the LSP configuration, if the secondary LSPs need to use the predefined SRLG as the path calculation constraint. If the SRLG constraint is enabled in the secondary LSP but CSPF is not enabled in the LSP containing the secondary LSP, the secondary LSP is put operationally **down** by the cause code of srlgPrimaryCspfDisabled.

The SRLG regulation is configured on a per-secondary LSP basis. In the same LSP, it is possible to only have a subset of secondary LSPs enabled. Nevertheless, as long as one secondary LSP requires the SRLG constraint, the LSP must have CSPF enabled. When more than one secondary LSP has SRLG enabled, the route calculation will only disjoint all these secondary LSPs from the primary LSP. There is no SRLG consideration among secondary LSPs, so they may still use links from the same SRLG. This is because the purpose of all secondary LSPs is to protect the single primary LSP. If the operator wants these secondary LSPs to be disjointed, administrative groups (coloring) can be used among these secondary LSPs.

SRLG with Fast Reroute

All routers have the SRLG information because SRLG is advertised by IGP-TE through the entire network. When FRR is configured to support SRLG, each assumed FRR Point of Local Repair (PLR) starts adding the SRLG constraint into the CSPF calculation for protection tunnels.

When using SRLG in FRR, there are two modes of operation configurable in the srlg-frr [strict] command under the MPLS Interface Configuration context in the CLI:

- **Strict** — With the strict option, CSPF will not establish any detour LSP or bypass tunnel if there is no path that meets the SRLG constraint.

- **Non-Strict** — With the `non-strict` (default) option, if the CSPF cannot find a path for the detour LSP or bypass tunnel, it still tries to establish the protection tunnel over links that are not compliant to the SRLG constraint but that meet other constraints. Although the CSPF prefers to use the SRLG constraint, it is not mandatory.

> **Warning:** Enabling or disabling SRLG for FRR is a system-wide configuration and requires the MPLS routing instance to be manually set to `shutdown` and then to `no shutdown` to activate the change. This may cause service outage. It is recommended that the operator incorporates the SRLG into the initial network design and implementation to minimize the traffic loss.

SRLG Configuration Example

To configure and use SRLG to direct FRR and secondary LSP, the following steps are required:

1.   **Define SRLG Groups** — In the `configure router mpls` context, define the SRLG group by associating a name and a value (0–4,294,967,295) with the group.

2.   **Apply the SRLG-Group Membership to the Links** — In the MPLS Interface Configuration context, the SRLG membership can be associated with the interface. One interface can be associated with one or many SRLG groups.

3.   **Enable the SRLG Constraint `cspf` Calculation on a Per-Secondary LSP Basis** — The CSPF uses the SRLG constraint when performing the ERO calculation for these secondary LSPs. Note that `cspf` must be explicitly enabled in the LSP for the LSP routing to be SRLG-aware.

4.   **Enable SRLG Constraint `cspf` Calculation for FRR if Desired** — Use the command `srlg-frr [strict]` in the MPLS Interface Configuration context. Note that this is a per-router configuration and requires a manual `shutdown` and then `no shutdown` on the MPLS routing instance for the configuration to be effective.

Figure 4.19 illustrates an example of SRLG definition and using SRLG to direct FRR and secondary LSPs for the LSP `lsp-to-163`.

Figure 4.19   SRLG Configuration Example: Using SRLG to Direct FRR and Secondary LSP

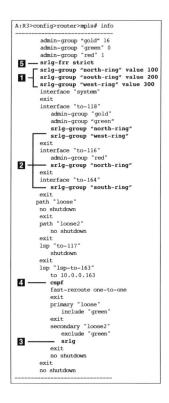

```
A:R3>config>router>mpls# info
----------------------------------
        admin-group "gold" 16
        admin-group "green" 0
        admin-group "red" 1
5 ─── srlg-frr strict
      ┌ srlg-group "north-ring" value 100
1 ─┤   srlg-group "south-ring" value 200
      └ srlg-group "west-ring" value 300
        interface "system"
        exit
        interface "to-118"
            admin-group "gold"
            admin-group "green"
            srlg-group "north-ring"
            srlg-group "west-ring"
        exit
        interface "to-116"
            admin-group "red"
2 ─────── srlg-group "north-ring"
        exit
        interface "to-164"
            srlg-group "south-ring"
        exit
        path "loose"
        no shutdown
        exit
        path "loose2"
            no shutdown
        exit
        lsp "to-117"
            shutdown
        exit
        lsp "lsp-to-163"
            to 10.0.0.163
4 ─────── cspf
            fast-reroute one-to-one
            exit
            primary "loose"
                include "green"
            exit
            secondary "loose2"
                exclude "green"
3 ─────────── srlg
            exit
            no shutdown
        exit
        no shutdown
----------------------------------
```

1 Define `srlg-group` in MPLS configuration.

2 Assign the SRLG group to MPLS interfaces.

3 Enable SRLG awareness in secondary LSP CSPF calculation.

4 `cspf` must be explicitly enabled if secondary LSP(s) desires to use SRLG constraint.

5 Enable SRLG awareness in FRR protection tunnel establishment.

```
-----------------------------------------------------------------
Opaque LSA
-----------------------------------------------------------------
Area Id          : 0.0.0.0      Adv Router Id   : 10.0.0.118
Link State Id    : 1.0.0.3      LSA Type        : Area Opaque
Sequence No      : 0x8000009c   Checksum        : 0xafec
Age              : 837          Length          : 132
Options          : E
Advertisement    :
  LINK INFO TLV  (0002) Len 108 :
    Sub-TLV: 1    Len: 1    LINK_TYPE    : 2
    Sub-TLV: 2    Len: 4    LINK_ID      : 10.117.118.1
    Sub-TLV: 3    Len: 4    LOC_IP_ADDR  : 10.117.118.2
    Sub-TLV: 4    Len: 4    REM_IP_ADDR  : 0.0.0.0
    Sub-TLV: 5    Len: 4    TE_METRIC    : 1000
    Sub-TLV: 6    Len: 4    MAX_BDWTH    : 100000 Kbps
    Sub-TLV: 7    Len: 4    RSRVBL_BDWTH : 100000 Kbps
    Sub-TLV: 8    Len: 32   UNRSRVD_CLS0 :
      P0: 100000 Kbps P1: 100000 Kbps P2: 100000 Kbps P3: 100000 Kbps
      P4: 100000 Kbps P5: 100000 Kbps P6: 100000 Kbps P7: 100000 Kbps
    Sub-TLV: 9    Len: 4    ADMIN_GROUP  : 00010001 (65537)
    Sub-TLV: 16   Len: 4    SRLG_LIST    :
      Num SRLGs: 1
      100
-----------------------------------------------------------------
```

> **Warning:**   The use of SRLG in a network requires careful planning, especially if there is any strict hop used in the LSP's path. If the strict hop is in the SRLG group, the CSPF calculation of backup LSP with SRLG constraint may result in no path found.

Using Administrative Groups and SRLG Together

Administrative groups and SRLG can be used together. Both are advertised in the corresponding sub-TLV of the link TLV. All routers can use the SRLG constraint defined in the network if CSPF is enabled in the LSP.

Summary

TE is a mechanism to establish a traffic forwarding path with a route other than the IGP shortest path. To establish this route, the routing protocols (OSPF, IS-IS) must have a TE extension (OSPF-TE, IS-IS TE) to pass extra information so the path calculation is performed using information such as bandwidth or color rather than the IGP metric.

When the IGP-TE protocol is enabled, the TE-related information is carried separately from the regular IGP routing information. OSPF-TE uses the opaque LSP Type 10 to carry TE information; IS-IS TE uses the TLV Type 22 to carry TE information in its LSPs. The service router stores the TE-related routing updates on a separate TED. The TED tracks TE-related information on the links in the network including:

- Administrative group membership (link colors)
- SRLG membership
- RSVP bandwidth reservation information.

When the RSVP-TE–signaled MPLS LSP needs to be established, the CSPF algorithm can be used to consult the TED to calculate the path of the LSP. The CSPF considers all the requirements of the LSP (administrative groups, SRLG, BW requirement) and prunes all links from the TED that do not meet the requirement and then calculates a path for the LSP. Therefore, the path calculation may calculate a different path other than the lowest metric IGP path.

Administrative group memberships can be associated with each link in the network. The operator can explicitly specify an LSP to traverse or avoid certain colors. An SRLG is another link tagging method. The MPLS resiliency features (FRR, secondary LSP) can use SRLG marking to route the protection tunnels. Therefore, the protection tunnels do not use the link of the same SRLG group that contains links used by the protected LSP. This results in maximized protection for the LSP.

RSVP-TE Protocol

5

In the IP/MPLS VPN network, the Resource Reservation Protocol–Traffic Engineering (RSVP-TE) is used to signal Multi Protocol Label Switching (MPLS) Label Switched Paths (LSPs). This chapter introduces the RSVP-TE protocol in detail and the signaling process used to signal the MPLS LSPs.

Chapter Objectives

- Provide an overview of the RSVP and RSVP-TE protocols
- Explain using RSVP-TE to signal explicitly routed MPLS LSP
- Introduce the RSVP-TE message used for MPLS LSP signaling
- Discuss the RSVP-TE make-before-break (MBB) style of MPLS LSP establishment
- Provide an overview of the RSVP-TE Hello protocol
- Explain RSVP-TE refresh overhead reduction

The Resource Reservation Protocol (RSVP) was originally designed to serve the IntServ Quality of Service (QoS) model. It was used to signal traffic characteristics and requirements of the traffic flows and to establish sessions. Later, it was extended to signal MPLS LSP. This chapter explains how RSVP-TE works as an MPLS label distribution protocol and how it signals LSPs. RSVP-TE supports the use of traffic engineering (TE) and MPLS resiliency features such as secondary LSP and/or Fast Reroute (FRR).

5.1 RSVP and RSVP-TE

Unlike OSPF or BGP, the Resource Reservation Protocol (RSVP) is not a routing protocol. It is a protocol used between routers to signal resource reservations. It was originally designed as a signaling protocol used by network elements to exchange resource information to help implement QoS solutions.

An IP host may use RSVP to negotiate resource requirements with routers for particular applications. Routers may use RSVP to exchange QoS requirements to set up sessions and implement Connection Admission Control (CAC) prior to the transmission of the data stream.

Note: Routing protocols can be loosely defined as protocols used among network elements to exchange network reachability information. The information exchanged by routing protocols includes network prefixes (network number, subnet mask), location of the network (next-hop), and the route attributes (metrics). OSPF, IS-IS, and BGP are examples of routing protocols.

Signaling protocols can be loosely defined as protocols used by network elements to set up connections or sessions and to maintain their states. The information exchanged by signaling protocols includes circuit-id (Labels, LSP-id, PW-id, etc.), resource requirements (bandwidth, priority, protection), and sometimes maintenance timers. RSVP and PIM are examples of signaling protocols.

RSVP-TE (RFC 3209)

MPLS architecture requires protocols within the control plane to distribute label information. The RSVP protocol was extended as RSVP-TE to be used as a label distribution protocol. Major benefits of using RSVP-TE to signal LSPs include:

- The ability to associate more than one LSP-Path into an LSP in a primary/backup manner (secondary LSP-Path feature). This setup provides more connection resiliency.

- The ability to signal explicitly routed LSPs (independent of routing protocols), where the routes of the LSP can be controlled (engineered) by the operator. This allows operators to deploy policies to control the traffic forwarding path.

- The ability to take resource reservation information into account during the LSP establishment process. This ensures that the LSP only traverses routers with sufficient resources available. Using CAC allows the MPLS router to prevent resource overbooking.

- The ability to provide detailed path information for the LSP-Path and signal the desired protections. RSVP-TE uses explicit routing objects (ERO) and record route objects (RRO) in the signaling messages to specify and track the LSP's path information.

- RSVP-TE signaling allows the LSP-Path to request FRR protection and routers to report the protection availability and usage for an LSP-Path. FRR can quickly re-direct traffic around network failures to minimize traffic loss.

    Note that in this book, the LSP created by LDP is referred to as *LDP-LSP*, and the LSP created by RSVP-TE is referred to as *RSVP-TE LSP*.

Introduction to RSVP Session

In the original RSVP protocol (RFC 2205), a *session* is defined as a dataflow with a particular destination IP address, IP protocol ID, and optionally, the destination port-id. The RSVP protocol with traffic engineering capability (RSVP-TE, RFC 3209) is used to signal end-to-end MPLS LSPs. The concept of an *RSVP session* therefore becomes more general. In an MPLS router running RSVP-TE, an *RSVP session* is a connection containing the mapping of an ingress label and an egress label belonging to the same LSP-Path. This connection is similar to the *cross-connect* of an ATM PVC. As a soft-state protocol, RSVP-TE requires periodically refreshing the RSVP sessions with signaling messages to maintain their states. An RSVP session is torn down when its refresh timer expires. An RSVP session for an LSP has the following content:

- **A Pair of Labels** — An ingress label distributed to the upstream router and an egress label received from the downstream router. A router receives traffic encapsulated with the ingress label and sends traffic encapsulated with the egress label.

- **A Pair of State Blocks** — The Path State Block (PSB) maintains a relationship with the upstream router by constantly receiving PATH messages refreshing the session. The RESV State Block (RSB) maintains a relationship with the downstream router by constantly receiving reservation (RESV) messages refreshing the session.

- **A Pair of Messages** — The original PATH and RESV messages used to establish the RSVP sessions are stored in the router to validate the subsequent *refreshing* of PATH and RESV messages.

Note: A *soft-state protocol* requires that the states of the protocol adjacency between two peering routers maintained by periodical exchanging of messages. Once the exchanging of the message stops, the protocol adjacency times out.

An *RSVP-TE-signaled LSP-Path* is a series of RSVP-TE sessions between the adjacent Label Switch Routers (LSRs) or Label Edge Routers (LERs) along the path with the same tunnel-id and LSP-id.

Tunnel-id versus LSP-id

The definitions of tunnel-id and LSP-id of an RSVP-TE-signaled LSP-Path can be confusing. Understanding the difference between the two terms is crucial to understanding the concept of *session* in RSVP. The tunnel-id, together with the destination IP address (Tail) of the LSP and the source IP address (interface of the Head-End router) of the LSP, uniquely define an LSP. These three values are encoded in the SESSION object of the RSVP-TE messages. The LSP-id value is encoded in the SENDER_TEMPLATE object and uniquely identifies a series of RSVP session instances within an LSP-Path. Under certain circumstances, one LSP can have multiple LSP-Paths; they all share the same SESSION object, but with different SENDER_TEMPLATE and SESSION_ATTRIBUTE objects in their PATH messages.

LSP, LSP-Path, and RSVP Session

An *LSP* is a logical MPLS tunnel. The source of the tunnel is the LSP's Head-End (HE) router, and the destination is the LSP's Tail router. An LSP represents the logical connection between two routers that can carry MPLS-encapsulated traffic. An LSP is uniquely defined by the three pieces of information (source-IP, destination-IP, tunnel-id) that are encoded in the SESSION object of the PATH message when setting up an LSP-Path. Note that one LSP contains one or more LSP-Paths.

An *LSP-Path* is the actual MPLS *connection* from the HE router to the Tail router. The LSP-Path is signaled through RSVP signaling by distributing labels from each hop. An LSP-Path is composed of a series of RSVP sessions on each hop along the path. It identifies itself using its unique LSP-id. Each LSP-Path can only belong to one LSP, while one LSP may have more than one LSP-Path serving it. The LSP-Path is an end-to-end representation of all the RSVP sessions along each hop.

The LSP-Path is formed by RSVP sessions at each hop of the MPLS router. For a successful resource reservation, each router receives a label from the downstream router to use as an egress label. Then, the router assigns a label to use as an ingress label and distributes it to the upstream router. Therefore, an MPLS *cross-connect* is built into the router to pass the MPLS traffic. The relationship between the LSP-Path and the RSVP session is similar to the cross-connect for an ATM PVC: An ATM PVC is composed of cross-connects from each hop ATM switch. RSVP sessions require a periodic refresh of PATH and RESV messages to maintain the session's operational state.

5.2 RSVP-TE Signaling Procedure

This section introduces the signaling procedures used to establish, maintain, and tear down the MPLS LSP. The RSVP-TE messages and objects are discussed in detail in a later section.

RSVP-TE is used as a label distribution protocol to signal LSP-Paths. This signaling process is similar to the flow of the original RSVP protocol signaling process — PATH and RESV messages signal the RSVP sessions on each router,

`PathErr` and `ResvErr` messages report the signaling errors, and then `PathTear` and `ResvTear` messages clear the sessions.

Setting Up an LSP-Path

RSVP-TE uses the Downstream on Demand (DoD) label distribution mode with Ordered Control. The demand (request) for labels is generated in the PATH message by the HE router and sent towards the Tail router in the downstream direction. Note that the directions of *downstream* and *upstream* refer to the traffic flow's directions. Before each router sends the PATH message to the next-hop router toward the Tail router, the router performs a CAC calculation. If the CAC grants the LSP-Path's resource requirement, the router propagates the PATH message to the next-hop router. The PATH message with the label and resource request is propagated downstream hop-by-hop until it reaches the Tail router. The Tail router then allocates a label and distributes it to the upstream router in the RESV message. Since the LSP-Path is unidirectional, the Tail router does not need to reserve any resources. All non-Tail routers along the path of the LSP-Path perform resource reservation on their outgoing interfaces. The resource reservation and label distribution starts from the previous hop router to the Tail router and goes upstream hop-by-hop toward the HE router. Each LSR along the path does not start resource reservation and label distribution toward the HE router until it receives a label from the downstream router (Ordered Control). This process is performed by the LSR in every hop of the LSP toward the HE router. After the entire process finishes, the HE router has an egress label for this LSP-Path. Each LSR router along the route has one ingress label and one egress label in the RSVP session. The Tail router has one ingress label. All required resources (for example, bandwidth) are reserved along the path.

Consider the scenario in which one router needs to set up an LSP to pass traffic to another router. In this scenario, the traffic source router is the HE router of the LSP, and the traffic destination router is the Tail router of the LSP. The HE router requires a label to use as an egress label to perform MPLS encapsulation and send the traffic. The HE router uses the `LABEL_REQUEST` object in the PATH messages to request the label. The Tail router uses the `LABEL` object in the RESV messages to distribute the label.

Forwarding Equivalent Class (FEC) Information in RSVP-TE Label Distribution

The LDP distributes FEC-Label binding, a label with an FEC indicating the label's use. In RSVP-TE label distribution, there is no information regarding which traffic flow(s) will use this label. RSVP decouples the LSP from the IP meaning. The only FEC information is the IP type of the tunnel. RSVP offers IPv4 FEC and IPv6 FEC. An IPV4 RSVP tunnel only carries IPV4 traffic. This is required because each intermediate node gets an Ether-type value as in the Layer 2 VPN traffic. In order to send the Layer 2 VPN traffic over the IPv4 RSVP tunnel, an extra label must be inserted because only the two tunnel endpoints that exchanged this label know that there is Layer 2 VPN traffic underneath it. Thus, the FEC information is present based implicitly on whether the IPv4/IPv6 tunnel is signaled.

Figure 5.1 illustrates LSP establishment using RSVP-TE. In this figure, an LSP is configured between the HE router (P1) and the far-end Tail router (P6).

RSVP-TE requires explicit configuration of the LSP and the LSP-Path in the HE router. After the LSP is configured and administratively enabled, the HE router sends out an RSVP-TE PATH message to the Tail router to signal the LSP. If resources are available, the Tail router responds with an RESV message to distribute the label and reserve the resources. The sequence of the events is:

1. The LSP is configured in the HE router. The RSVP-TE LSP definition has two steps:

    a. Define the *path* the LSP wants to travel. The RSVP-TE-signaled LSP-Path is an explicit hop LSP-Path, which means that the operator can control the hop(s) the LSP must travel through or avoid. This explicit hop list is used by the IGP or CSPF as a constraint when calculating the actual path for the LSP-Path. The hop-list configuration is optional. If cspf is configured in an LSP, the HE router uses CSPF to calculate the entire path of the LSP-Path; otherwise, the LSP-Path is set up using the route lookups on each router.

    b. Define the LSP and the LSP-Path. The Tail router's IP address must be specified with at least one LSP-Path defined. Then, the LSP must be administratively enabled.

Figure 5.1 RSVP-TE Signals MPLS LSP-Path

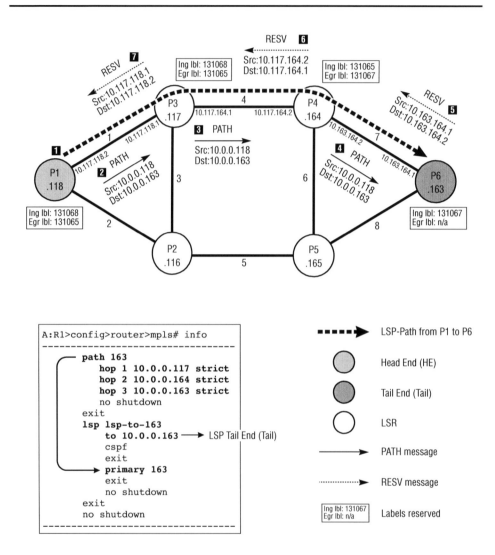

2. After the LSP-Path is configured and administratively enabled, the HE router calculates the LSP-Path's route and forms an ERO. If CSPF is involved, the ERO contains the actual list of all the hops the PATH message must follow. The HE router also performs CAC on the LSP-Path's resource request. If the CAC grants the resource, the HE router then sends the PATH message to the next-hop router.

3. The LSR (P3) receives the PATH message. The arrival of a PATH message generates a Path State Block (PSB). The original PATH message is stored in the router associated with the PSB. The LSR then performs a sanity check and CAC to validate if the router is capable of setting up such an LSP-Path. If the sanity check is successful, the router *regenerates* a new PATH message with a content update and sends it to the next-hop router. During this step, the source and destination IP addresses of the PATH message is *not changed*. The message's source IP address is still the HE router's system IP address, and its destination IP address is still the Tail router's system IP address. It appears that the PATH message is forwarded end-to-end from the HE router to the Tail router via the intermediate hops. In reality, the message is regenerated at every hop, and each LSR changes the message's content.

4. The next LSR (P4) processes the PATH message and then regenerates the new PATH message and sends it to the Tail router.

5. The Tail router (P6) receives the PATH message and recognizes that it is the termination point (Tail) of the LSP being established. The PSB is created, and the PATH message is stored. The Tail router then assigns a label and distributes the label to the previous-hop router by sending the RESV message upstream toward the HE router.

   The IP address in the HOP object in the stored PATH message is used as the RESV message's destination IP address. (The HOP object is introduced in later sections.) The RESV message is always generated hop-by-hop. Its source IP address is always the sending router's egress interface IP address, and its destination IP address is always the receiving router's ingress interface IP address.

6. The LSR (P4) receives the RESV message. The arrival of the RESV message generates a RESV State Block (RSB). The RESV message is stored in the router. Then, the LSR performs resource checking, resource reservation, and label distribution in the same manner as the Tail router. An RESV message with a label is sent to the upstream LSR.

7. The LSR (P3) performs the same actions as P4 — it creates the RSB and stores the RESV message. The LSR then reserves the resources and sends an RESV message to the HE router.

8. (Not shown in the diagram.) When the HE router receives the RESV message with the label request, it performs resource checking and resource reservation. At this point, the LSP-Path establishment process is completed.

The LSP is put into an operationally **up** state and is ready to forward traffic for SDP. From this point forward, the PATH and RESV messages are sent periodically to *refresh* the LSP-Path to maintain its operational state in all routers along the path of the LSP.

When the LSP establishment process is complete, every router along the LSP-Path has the following content that forms an RSVP session, created for the LSP:

- A PSB that is maintained by the constant receipt of valid PATH messages for this LSP-Path.

- An RSB that is maintained by the constant receipt of valid RESV messages for this LSP-Path.

- An ingress/egress label pair for the LSP-Path. The HE router has only the egress label, and a *push* action. The Tail router has only the ingress label, and a *pop* action.

The RSVP session's PSB and RSB are in the control plane. The label pair is in both the control plane (LIB) and the data plane (LFIB). The object values of SESSION and SENDER_TEMPLATE (or FILTER_SPEC) stored in the PSB uniquely identify the LSP-Path ownership of an RSVP session. An end-to-end RSVP-TE-signaled LSP-Path is formed by these RSVP sessions.

Maintaining the LSP-Path

After the LSP-Path has been established, it must be refreshed to maintain its operational state. As a soft-state protocol, RSVP requires a constant refresh of all the RSVP sessions by the PATH and RESV messages in order to maintain the LSP-Path operational state. If certain refresh messages are not received as expected, the RSVP sessions expire and are cleared to release the occupied resources.

The RSVP state is refreshed at every hop by the PATH and RESV messages generated between the adjacent routers. For each router, in every PATH state, the router generates a PATH message to the next-hop downstream router at every *refresh interval*. For each router, every time a PATH message is received for a certain session, the PSB is refreshed, and the expiration timer is reset to zero. In the upstream direction, the RESV message is generated to refresh the RSB of the RSVP session in the same manner. The contents of these refreshed PATH and RESV messages are consistent with the contents of the original PATH and RESV messages used to establish the LSP-Path.

A very important perspective of RSVP session refresh is commonly misunderstood: The RSVP session refresh does not work in a *Hello–Acknowledgement* handshake manner. The generation of a message is *not* in response to a received message. When a PATH message is received, it is not acknowledged with an RESV message. By default, if either side fails to receive more than three PATH or RESV messages consecutively, the RSVP session times out. The next section explains how the RSVP refreshment mechanism works.

RSVP Refresh Mechanism: R, L, and K Values

For most routing or signaling protocols (e.g., IS-IS, OSPF, LDP, or BGP), the increase in traffic caused by *Keep-Alive* or *Hello* messaging is insignificant. This is because each router only peers with a limited number of neighbors and therefore needs to maintain only a limited number of adjacencies.

In the case of RSVP-TE, there may be tens of thousands of RSVP sessions to be maintained. This is especially true in the case of the core routers, through which most of the LSP-Paths travel. The volume of RSVP session refreshing traffic can be significant. If all RSVP sessions require a refresh at the same time, the message refresh traffic may compete with customer data traffic. If the refresh messages get lost, the RSVP session may time out, and the LSP-Path may be torn down. Therefore, special care must be taken to ensure that RSVP sessions are not all refreshed during the same short time period (burst) — *refresh synchronization must be avoided*. RSVP-TE uses the following timers to control the refresh interval to prevent refresh synchronization and to avoid unnecessary session time-out:

- **R (Refresh Timer)** — A locally configurable value (default is 30 seconds). R is passed to the adjacent router in the TIME_VALUE object in the PATH and RESV messages.

- **L (Lifetime Timer)** — The lifetime of the RSVP session states. When the L timer expires, the related PATH or RESV state expires and the RSVP session is cleared. Note that in the ALSRP, the L and K timers share the same value.

- **K (Keep-Alive Multiplexer)** — The number of consecutive refresh messages that may be skipped before the RSVP session times out. The keep-alive multiplexer is shared by the RSVP state refresh and the RSVP Hello protocol. (The RSVP Hello protocol is discussed in a later section.)

In each PATH and RESV message, the desired R value is sent to the adjacent node through the TIME_VALUE object. This value is used by the receiving router to decide the lifetime (L value) of the message, which determines how long a PATH message can maintain the PATH or RESV state of an RSVP session. It also determines when the receiving router should expect the next PATH or RESV refresh. If the router cannot receive the next refresh within K*R seconds, the state expires. Hence, each router has its own global configuration of an R timer and passes the information to the adjacent routers through the refresh message. The R value in different routers can be configured differently, and the refresh scheme will still work successfully. Therefore, the RSVP refreshing mechanism can be asymmetric. Figure 5.2 illustrates the RSVP-TE LSP session refresh process.

Figure 5.2   RSVP Session Refresh Mechanism

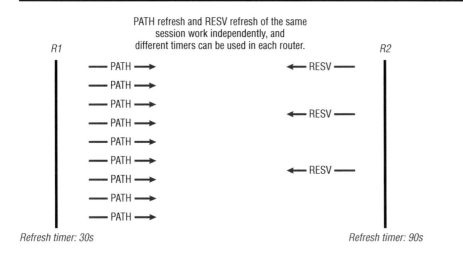

For each RSVP session in an MPLS router (LER and/or LSR), there is one associated PATH state and one associated Reservation (RESV) state. The routers provide the information required to send the refresh PATH message. The Reservation state stores information for the resource being reserved. Missing PATH refresh messages from an upstream router causes the Path state of the RSVP session to time out. This timeout clears the entire LSP-Path with a PathTear message. Missing RESV messages from a downstream router causes the Reservation state of the RSVP session to time out, and the router uses a ResvTear message to clear the LSP-Path.

The PATH state and RESV state refreshments between two adjacent routers with the same LSP-Path's RSVP sessions are independent from each other. The router generates a PATH message to the next-hop downstream neighbor for every refresh interval. Independently, the router expects an RESV message from the downstream router for the same session. This is a proactive way to prevent failure.

Every LSP-Path's RSVP session requires a periodic refresh. In a scaled network, this may consume too great a portion of the system's resources. To reduce the pressure of processing large numbers of RSVP messages, *RSVP message pacing* and *RSVP refresh reduction* can be used in reaction to a failure. RSVP message pacing and RSVP refresh reduction are discussed in detail in later sections.

Tearing Down an LSP-Path

LSP-Path teardown can be proactive or reactive. When the LSP-Path is no longer required, the HE router sends a PathTear message to clear the RSVP sessions along the LSP to release the resources.

Alternatively, if the RSVP session(s) belonging to the LSP-Path times out, the LSP-Path should be torn down, and all related RSVP sessions will be cleared in all hops to release the resources. In this case, the router with the RSVP session maintenance time-out may send messages to clear the LSP-Path.

Two RSVP messages can be used to tear down an LSP-Path:

- PathTear messages travel downstream from the HE router toward the Tail router.
- ResvTear messages travel upstream from the Tail router toward the HE router.

An LSR sends only one type of tear message for an LSP-Path. If the RESV state times out, then only a ResvTear is sent upstream, and similarly if the PATH state times out, the LSR sends a PathTear downstream.

If the LSP-Path is no longer required, it should be removed from the network to release the resources. The LSP-Path can be manually torn down by administratively disabling it in the HE router. Figure 5.3 illustrates the RSVP-TE signaling process for tearing down an LSP-Path.

The process of tearing down an LSP-Path is much simpler than setting up the LSP. This process does not require a resource availability check or state block creation. Upon receiving a legitimate PathTear or ResvTear message, the router clears the corresponding RSVP session and the related state blocks, releases all resources occupied by the RSVP session, and sends out the corresponding PathTear or ResvTear messages to the next-hop router(s).

Figure 5.3   Tearing Down an RSVP-TE-Signaled LSP-Path

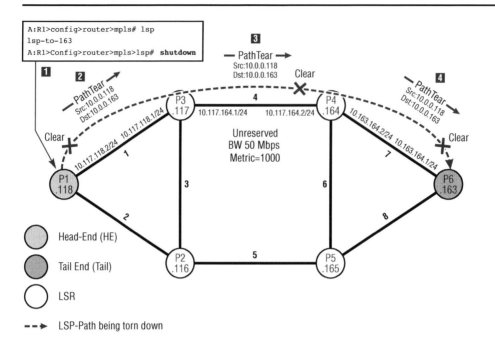

5.3 RSVP-TE Messages and Objects

Unlike routing protocols such as OSPF or ISIS, the RSVP-TE protocol has no concept of *adjacency* or *neighbor relationships*. When an interface is configured to participate in RSVP-TE, providing the interface is operational, RSVP-TE can use that interface to establish LSPs. When two routers have a link with RSVP-TE enabled on both sides, they can establish an RSVP-TE LSP over that link. The purpose of RSVP-TE is to establish, maintain, and tear down the LSPs. RSVP-TE is used to negotiate the RSVP sessions hop-by-hop to build the end-to-end LSP. RSVP-TE must maintain every RSVP session individually.

RSVP-TE Message Format and Type Overview

The RSVP-TE protocol uses *RSVP-TE messages* to exchange information. RSVP-TE messages are IP packets with a protocol ID of 0x2E (RSVP, decimal value 46). Figure 5.4 presents the common format for RSVP messages.

Figure 5.4 RSVP Message Format

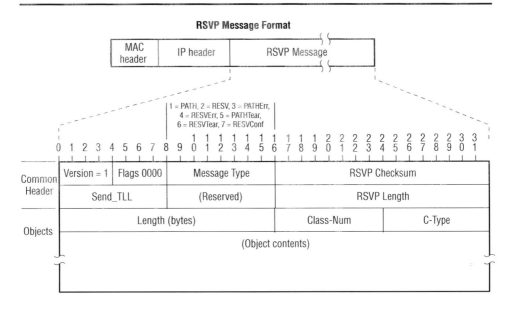

The RSVP-TE message's structure starts with the RSVP header and is followed by many objects. Objects are the basic elements of the RSVP messages. Each type of message includes different types of objects. Each object contains the object-id and object content. Table 5.1 lists the types of RSVP messages. Table 5.2 (shown later) lists the types of objects used for LSP signaling. In Table 5.1, "Type" represents the type of the message, and "RA-bit" represents whether the router-alert bit in the message is set or not.

Table 5.1 RSVP Message Types

Message	Direction	Packet IP	Type	RA-bit	Description
PATH	Downstream	End-to-end	1	Yes	Used to signal the request to set up an LSP and maintain the LSP's PSB
RESV	Upstream	Hop-by-hop	2	No	Used to distribute labels and reserve resources for the LSP. It creates and maintains the RSB.

(continued)

Table 5.1 RSVP Message Types   *(continued)*

Message	Direction	Packet IP	Type	RA-bit	Description
PATH Error	Upstream	Hop-by-hop	3	No	Used for LSR to report errors for a received PATH message. The PathErr message is propagated upstream to the HE router.
RESV Error	Downstream	Hop-by-hop	4	No	Used for LSR to report errors for a received RESV message. The ResvErr message is propagated downstream to the Tail router.
PATH Tear	Downstream	End-to-end	5	Yes	Used for the router to clear the LSP in the downstream direction toward the Tail router
RESV Tear	Upstream	Hop-by-hop	6	No	Used for the router to clear the LSP in the upstream direction toward the HE router
Hello	Both ways	Hop-by-hop	20	No	Used by the RSVP Hello protocol as a *heartbeat* to ensure that the RSVP adjacent interfaces are alive. When an RSVP interface misses a certain number of Hello packets from the peering interface, it considers the interface down and clears all RSVP sessions on that interface.
Bundle	Both ways	Depends on the message	12	No	Used to aggregate the PATH or RESV refresh to reduce the RSVP refresh overhead
ACK	Both ways	Hop-by-hop	13	No	Used to acknowledge initial LSP establishing PATH and RESV messages

Message	Direction	Packet IP	Type	RA-bit	Description
Summary-refresh	Both ways	Hop-by-hop	15	No	Used to replace the LSP refreshing PATH/ RESV messages to reduce the RSVP refresh overhead

Note that in this table, *end-to-end* packet IP addressing means that the message's source IP address is the HE router's IP address, and the destination IP address is the Tail router's IP address. Every intermediate RSVP-capable router intercepts the message and regenerates the same message. The regenerated packet always uses the IP source and destination address from the received RSVP message. This is why all messages with end-to-end IP addressing have their RA-bits set: the next-hop router may not be the packets' destination (from an IP address perspective), but must still process them. The RA-bit set in the message forces the receiving router to process the message. In this table, *hop-by-hop* packet IP addressing means that the message uses the local egress interface's IP address as the packet source IP address, and the next-hop router's ingress interface's IP address as the packet destination IP address.

In Table 5.1, the three message types (Bundle, ACK, and Summary-refresh) are used for RSVP-TE refresh reduction to reduce the signaling traffic when maintaining large numbers of RSVP sessions. Refresh reduction is introduced in a later section.

PATH Messages

PATH messages are used by the HE router to establish an LSP-Path to the Tail router. This message could optionally request the reservation of resources (such as bandwidth) on this LSP-Path. The success of this message causes the resources to be reserved during the RESV message (which is a response to the PATH message). This RESV message from the intermediate downstream router also contains the downstream label used to send data along this established LSP-Path.

For any router, the arrival of a *new* PATH message creates a PSB. Alternatively, the router may already have a PSB for the PATH message (identified with the same SESSION, SESSION_ATTRIB and SENDER_TEMPLATE object values). In this case, the PSB is refreshed after the arrival of each sequential PATH message. Figure 5.5 presents an example of the PSB content display for an RSVP-TE LSP-Path in a router.

Figure 5.5   Path State Block and Reservation State Block Contents

```
A:R4# tools dump router rsvp psb detail
-------------------------------------------------------------------------------
PSB:
 EndPt 10.0.0.163  Tid 22  XTid  10.0.0.164  Sndr 10.0.0.164  LspId 43520  PHop
0.0.0.0

PSB Curr State : PRIMARYS_CONNECTED  Prev State : PRIMARYS_INIT  Flags : 0x0
 localLabel 0 outLabel 131070
 Incoming IfIndex: Interface: Local API(-1)
 Refresh interval 30, Send Path refresh in 15 secs,  Path Refresh timeout 0 secs
 PrevHop: Addr -> 0.0.0.0  LIH 2
 DnStream Nbr: Addr-> 10.163.164.1  IfIndex to-163(2)
 UpStream Neighbor is NULLP
 Session Attribute:
   Session Name :to-163::loose Hold Prio :0 Setup Prio :7
   IncludeGroup :0x0 IncludeAllGroup :0x0 ExcludeGroup :0x0
 TSpec :Flags 0x8000 QOSC 1, PDR (infinity), PBS 80.000 Mbps, CDR (80.000 Mbps)
MTU: 0
 PSB RRO : ->
  (0) * Flags : 0x0 :
  (0) * IPv4 -> 10.163.164.2
 PSB SENT RRO : ->
  (0) * Flags : 0x0 :
  (0) * IPv4 -> 10.163.164.2
 PSB FILTERSPEC RRO : ->
  (0) * Flags : 0x0 :
  (0) * IPv4 -> 10.163.164.1
  (1) * Flags : 0x1 : LP_AVAIL
  (1) * Label : 131070
 SendTempl : Sender:10.0.0.164_43520
 AdSpec not present

Num Paths Received   :0
 Num Paths Transmitted:929
 Num Resvs Received   :951
 Num Resvs Transmitted:0

Num Summmary Paths Received   :0
 Num Summmary Paths Transmitted:0
 Num Summmary Resvs Received   :0
 Num Summmary Resvs Transmitted:0
-------------------------------------------------------------------------------

Total PSB Count   : 1
```

The PSB is cleared by one of the following two scenarios:

- Arrival of the `PathTear` message for the same LSP-Path (identified by the same object values of `SESSION` and `SENDER_TEMPLATE`)

- Arrival of the `ResvTear` message for the same LSP-Path to clear its RSB. The related PSB is also removed from the router.

Figure 5.6 illustrates the example of HE router R1 establishing an LSP-Path to R5 by generating the PATH message toward R5. It also shows that every next-hop router changes the content of the HOP, ERO, and RRO objects.

Figure 5.6 PATH Messages with ERO, RRO, and LABEL_REQUEST Objects

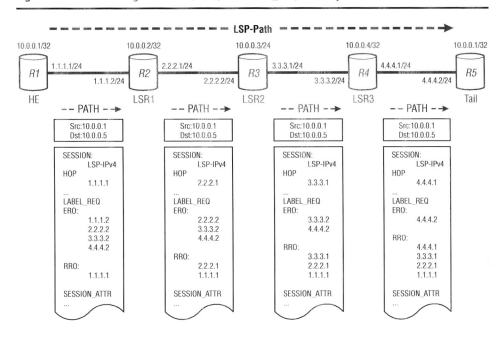

After the LSP-Path is configured in the HE router and administratively enabled, the HE router starts the LSP-Path set-up sequence; it calculates the nodes through which the LSP-Path should travel from the PATH HE router to the Tail router. If CSPF is specified in the LSP configuration, the path this LSP-Path takes is predetermined in the HE router by the CSPF calculation result. CSPF generates a complete list of strict hops as content of the ERO. The HE router then sends the PATH message to the next-hop LSR, according to the hop list of the ERO. The PATH message always travels along the path indicated in ERO (if an ERO message does exist). When configuring a path that can be shared by many LSP-Paths, a router's system IP address or any interface IP address can be used to indicate the path the LSP should travel. However, when the CSPF calculation is performed to calculate the actual path (list of hops) for the ERO, only interface addresses are placed in the ERO. Thus, there is no ambiguity or inaccuracy with respect to the actual path the PATH message will travel.

In the PATH message, a SESSION object describes the type of session this PATH message is trying to set up. For RSVP-TE-signaled LSP-Paths, the session type is either LSP-IPv4 or LSP-IPv6. A LABEL_REQUEST object is always present in the PATH message because the HE node requests the labels from a downstream LSR. The ERO contains the predefined routes that the PATH message and the LSP-Path being established should traverse. The RRO contains the actual routes that the PATH message travels. There are also other objects in the PATH message to carry required information for the LSP-Path establishment. Figure 5.7 illustrates the objects used by PATH and RESV messages to establish the LSP.

Figure 5.7 Objects Used to Set Up an LSP-Path with PATH and RESV Messages

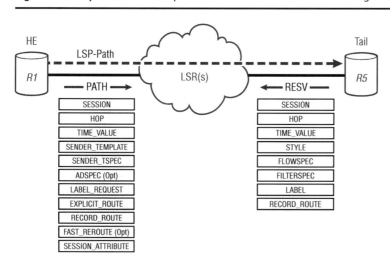

Upon receiving the PATH message, the router creates a PSB. The PSB's LSP-Path ownership is defined by the SESSION and SENDER_TEMPLATE objects. Also stored in the PSB are other objects such as ERO, RRO, and SENDER_TSPEC. The router then performs the resource availability check by comparing the bandwidth required in the SESSION_ATTRIBUTE object with the available bandwidth in its egress interface listed in the ERO. If the resource is not available, a PathErr message is sent upstream to terminate the LSP set-up effort. If resources are available, the router regenerates a PATH message and sends it to the next-hop downstream router. When a router regenerates the PATH message and sends it to the next-hop router, the source and destination IP addresses of the PATH message are not changed. It appears that the PATH message is forwarded end-to-end from the HE router to the Tail router by the intermediate hops. However, the PATH message is actually *regenerated* for every hop, and each LSR changes the message content as shown in the following steps:

1.   The LSR removes the IP subobject indicating an IP address of its own from the ERO.

2.   The LSR appends the egress interface's IP address into the RRO as an IP subobject.

3.   The LSP places its own egress interface's IP address into the HOP to replace the existing IP subobject.

The LSP-Path is always unidirectional. The LSP-Path in Figure 5.6 only transports traffic from R1 to R5. If traffic in the opposite direction is also desired, a separate LSP-Path must be established from R5 to R1. This separate LSP-Path is totally distinct from the LSP-Path from R1 to R5.

The RSVP ERROR messages are used to report LSP-Path set-up failures such as no resource information or a network failure making the route unavailable. There are two ERROR message types: `PathErr` (path error), and `ResvErr` (reservation error). A `PathErr` message always travels in an upstream direction (from Tail to HE direction), and a `ResvErr` message always travels in a downstream direction (from HE to Tail direction). When there is an error in the LSP establishment or a failure in the established LSPs, `PathErr` or `ResvErr` messages are sent. The routers respond with `PathTear` or `ResvTear` messages. Therefore, all reservations in the network for that LSP are cleared. Note that in the FRR scenario, the `PathErr` message is also used by the Point of Local Repair (PLR) router to report the FRR in-use event. The detailed behavior of FRR is introduced in Chapter 7.

RESV Messages

The RESV message is used by MPLS routers to distribute labels and reserve resources. After a successful reservation of required resources, the Tail router sends RESV messages to the upstream next-hop router to distribute the label desired for the LSP-Path.

For any router, the arrival of a *new* RESV message creates an RSB. However, a router may currently have an RSB for the RESV message received for an LSP-Path (identified by the same `SESSION`, and `FILTER_SPEC` object values). In this case, the RSB is refreshed after the arrival of each sequential RESV message. The RESV message may contain new `FILTER_SPEC` objects, in which case the RSB is also updated. Figure 5.8 illustrates an example of RSB content display.

Bandwidth Reservation and CAC for RSVP-TE LSP Are Only in the Control Plane

A common misunderstanding is that the use of RSVP-TE to signal LSP enables the control of the actual network traffic. RSVP-TE LSP signaling and the CAC for resources reside only in the control plane. The bandwidth requirement, the CAC, and the CSPF calculation for available resources on the link are all logical. The actual link utilization rate is not monitored and considered in calculations by CSPF. A customer can book 100-Mbps bandwidth in the link for the LSP and actually send 200-Mbps traffic over the LSP; RSVP-TE cannot prevent this. To control the data traffic volume on a link, QoS must be used. QoS is beyond the scope of this book.

The best network design relies on a combination of the following:

- A good understanding of the traffic requirement from customers and an expectation of the traffic pattern

- A well-designed physical overlay with the correct bandwidth information configuration

- A consistent and accurate bandwidth booking mechanism for IGP-TE and RSVP-TE

- Use of RSVP-TE to perform resource booking and CAC in the control plane

- Use of QoS in the data plane to enforce the traffic volume to adhere to planned bandwidth in the control plane

Figure 5.8   CLI Output for Reservation State Block

```
A:R4# tools dump router rsvp rsb detail
--------------------------------------------------------------------------------
RSB:
 EndPt 10.0.0.163  Tid 22  XTid 10.0.0.164  Sndr 0.0.0.0  LspId 0  NHop 10.163.164.1
 Style SE, refresh in 0 secs
 RSVP Hop 10.163.164.1  LIH 2
 Reservation Info: Bw 80000
 FlowSpec :Flags 0x8000 QOSC 1, PDR (infinity), PBS 80.000 Mbps, CDR (80.000 Mbps)
          CBS 0, EBS 0, RSpecR 0, RSpecS 0 MTU 1500 MPU 20
 FwdFlowspec :Flags 0x8000 QOSC 1, PDR (infinity), PBS 80.000 Mbps, CDR (80.000 Mbps)
            CBS 0, EBS 0, RSpecR 0, RSpecS 0 MPU 20
 FilterSpec:
 Timeout in : 133 secs, LocLabel: 0  Sender: 10.0.0.164 lspId: 43520 OutIfId: 0
 RRO :
  (0) * Flags : 0x0 :
  (0) * IPv4 -> 10.163.164.1
  (1) * Flags : 0x1 : LP_AVAIL
  (1) * Label : 131070
--------------------------------------------------------------------------------

Total RSB Count   : 1
```

The RSB from the router is cleared by one of the following two scenarios:

- Arrival of the `ResvTear` message for the same LSP-Path (identified by the same object values of `SESSION` and `FLOW_SPEC`). If there are multiple `FILTER_SPEC` objects in the RSB, the RSB is torn down only when all `FILTER_SPEC` objects are torn down. This is the case in the Shared Explicit (SE) style because many `FILTER_SPEC` objects may map to the same RSB. (The SE reservation style is discussed in a later section.)

- Arrival of the `PathTear` message for the same LSP-Path to destroy an RSVP session. The related RSB is then removed from the router.

Figure 5.9 illustrates the same network as Figure 5.6 with the same LSP-Path being signaled. In this figure, the Tail router responds with an RESV message to establish the RSVP session along the path for the LSP. This figure shows every next-hop router generating the content of the LABEL, HOP, and RRO objects.

Figure 5.9 RESV Messages with LABEL and RRO Objects

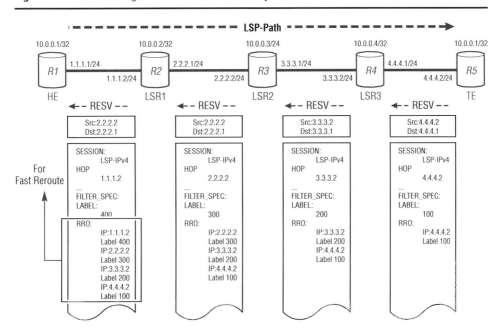

When the Tail router receives the PATH message, it assigns a label for the upstream router to use and sends an RESV message back toward the HE router to establish the RSVP session. A LABEL object distributes the label to the upstream LSR. The RESV message also contains the RRO object so the receiving HE router is aware of the entire route the PATH message actually travels. The RESV message is sent to the IP address specified in the HOP object of the previously received and stored PATH message for the same LSP.

When each LSR router receives a RESV message from the downstream router, it places the received label value in its own LIB as an egress label. The RSB is created, and the RESV message with all its objects is stored. The LSR router then assigns a label for its upstream router, generates a RESV message, and sends the message to the upstream router. When generating the RESV message for the next hop, the LSR router modifies the following in the RESV message:

- Places the label value allocated for the upstream router into the LABEL object.
- Appends the egress interface's IP address into the RRO as an IP subobject and the label value as a Label subobject.
- Places its own egress interface's IP address into the HOP to replace the existing IP subobject.

This behavior is repeated, hop-by-hop, in the upstream direction and eventually reaches the HE router. At this stage, all routers have their RSVP sessions established, and the LSP-Path is established. After the signaling process is finished, each router along the path has an entry in its LIB that stores the ingress and/or egress labels for the LSP.

For example, in Figure 5.6 in the LSP from R1 to R5:

- Router R1 receives an egress label value of 400 from the next-hop downstream Router R2, and as the ingress LER (iLER), it does not need to assign an ingress label and distribute traffic because there is no upstream router.
- Router R2's LIB has an entry for this LSP with an ingress label of 400 (that it assigned and distributed to R1) for incoming traffic from upstream, and an egress label of 300 (received from downstream Router R3).
- Router R3 has an ingress label value of 300 and an egress value of 200.
- R4 has an ingress label of 200 and an egress label of 100.
- The Tail router (egress LER, eLER) has only an ingress label of 100, which it assigned and distributed to R2.

> ## End-to-End PATH Message versus Hop-by-Hop RESV Message
>
> The PATH message always uses end-to-end IP addressing. The packet's source IP address is the IP address of the HE router, and its destination IP address is the IP address of the Tail router. Although at each hop the LSR actually changes the content of some objects and regenerates the PATH message, it never changes the packet source/destination IP addresses. For the same reason, the RA-bit in the packet is always set, so every router with its RSVP enabled must process the packet, although the packet is not destined to the router. Like the PATH message, the PathTear message has end-to-end IP addressing with the RA-bit set.
>
> RESV messages are addressed to the immediate upstream router's interface IP address. The RESV message is always hop-by-hop addressed. The message's source IP address is the sender's egress interface IP address, where the PATH message is received. The message's destination IP address is the previous hop (upstream) router's IP interface in the received PATH message. The RA-bit is not set in the RESV message. The ResvTear message is also addressed hop-by-hop without setting the RA-bit.

The RROs in the PATH messages contain IPv4 subobjects. The subobject contains the router's local egress interface IP addresses. The RROs in the RESV messages contain both the IPv4 subobject and the LABEL subobject. The IPv4 subobject contains the router's local egress interface IP address for the message. The LABEL subobject also contains the label generated and distributed by the local router. RRO information is used to calculate MPLS FRR paths. FRR is introduced in Chapter 7.

PathTear and ResvTear Messages

The PathTear and ResvTear messages are used by MPLS routers to tear down the LSP-Path. As mentioned previously, LSP-Path teardown can be caused by manually disabling the LSP or by failures that prevent the routers from maintaining the RSVP session (these failures are reported by PathErr or ResvErr messages). When any router along the LSP wants to remove the LSP-Path, it sends a PathTear message downstream toward the Tail router and sends an ResvTear message upstream to the HE router.

The PathTear message uses the same end-to-end IP addressing scheme as the PATH message regardless of which router generates the PathTear message. The PathTear message's source IP address is the HE router's IP address, and the message destination IP address is the Tail router's IP address of the LSP. A PathTear message travels downstream in the same way as a PATH message. A `PathTear` message has its RA-bit set. When a router receives a `PathTear` message, the router uses the values of `SESSION` and `SENDER_TEMPLATE` to identify the corresponding PSB:

- If a corresponding RSVP session (PSB, RSB, and labels) currently exists, the entire RSVP session is cleared. The router (if it is not a Tail router) generates a `PathTear` message to the downstream next-hop router.

- If only a PSB exists, it means that the LSP is currently being established so the PSB is removed and the LSP set-up process is terminated. The router (if it is not the one reporting the error) may send a `PathTear` message to the downstream next-hop router.

The `ResvTear` message uses the same hop-by-hop IP addressing scheme as the RESV message. The `ResvTear` message travels upstream in the same manner as the RESV message. The `ResvTear` message does not have an RA-bit set. When a router receives a `ResvTear` message, the router uses the values of `SESSION` and `FILTER_SPEC` to identify the corresponding RSB. In the corresponding RSVP session (PSB, RSB, and labels), the entire RSVP session is cleared. If there are multiple `FILTER_SPEC` objects in the RSB, the RSB is torn down only when all `FILTER_SPEC` objects are torn down. This is the case in the Shared Explicit (SE) reservation style because many `FILTER_SPEC` objects may map to the same RSB. The router (if it is not an HE router) then generates an `ResvTear` message upstream.

Figure 5.3 presented an example of an HE router proactively tearing down an LSP by administratively disabling the LSP. The `PathTear` message was propagated by each LSR downstream to clear all the RSVP sessions belonging to the LSP. Alternatively, Figure 5.10 presents two examples of tearing down an LSP because of a session timeout (a failure). In these examples, we assume that the links connecting all routers are still capable of sending and receiving RSVP messages and that all routers can still process and generate RSVP messages. Figure 5.10 illustrates a case of LSP teardown due to an RSVP session timeout.

In the scenario shown in Figure 5.10, the RSVP session between LSR P3 and P4 has timed out in the P4 router. The P4 router clears the RSVP session and sends two messages to tear down the LSP in both directions:

- `PathTear` message to the downstream router
- `ResvTear` message to the upstream router

The router in every hop clears the RSVP session and releases the resources reserved for the LSP. The router upstream then generates a `ResvTear` message and sends it to the upstream router. When the HE router receives the **ResvTear** message, the LSP-Path is put into an operationally **down** state.

Figure 5.11 illustrates the objects used by the **PathTear** and **ResvTear** messages to tear down the LSP-Path.

Figure 5.10 Tearing Down an LSP-Path because of Session Timeout

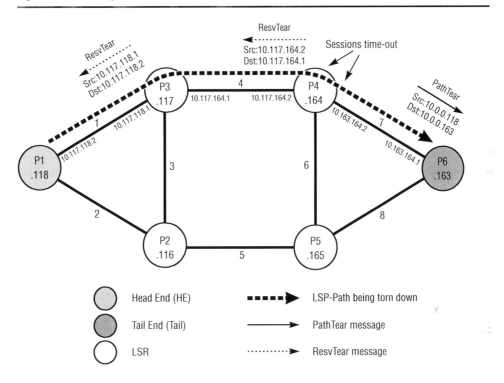

Figure 5.11 PathTear and ResvTear Messages

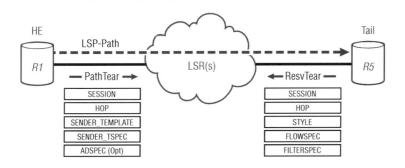

For details regarding the format of these messages and their objects, please refer to RFC 3209.

Path Error and RESV Error Messages

Path Error (`PathErr`) and RESV Error (`ResvErr`) messages are used for RSVP-capable routers to report errors to the HE or Tail routers during the LSP-Path set-up process or to report errors when the LSP-Path is established. The messages contain the `ERROR` object with an *error code* and an *error value* indicating the problem. Upon receiving the error messages, the HE or Tail router clears the RSVP session or stops the LSP-Path set-up effort by sending out `PathTear` or `ResvTear` messages.

`PathErr` is a failure response to the PATH message and may be generated by an LSR in the middle of the LSP-Path. The `PathErr` message is propagated upstream until the HE router receives it. The `PathErr` message uses the same hop-by-hop IP addressing scheme as the RESV message. The `PathErr` message does not have the RA-bit set. When the HE router receives the `PathErr` message, it puts the LSP into an operationally **down** state and sends out a `PathTear` message. The `PathTear` message clears the LSP-Path or the PSB created by the LSP set-up effort along the path.

`ResvErr` is a failure response to the RESV message and may be generated by an LSR in the middle of the LSP path. The `ResvErr` message is propagated downstream until the Tail router receives it. It uses the same hop-by-hop IP addressing scheme as the RESV message. The `ResvErr` message does not have the RA-bit set. When the Tail router receives the `ResvErr` message, it sends a `ResvTear` message upstream to the HE router. The `ResvTear` message clears the LSP or the PSB created by the LSP set-up effort along the path. When the HE router receives the `ResvTear` message, the LSP is put into an operationally **down** state.

Figure 5.12 illustrates an example of LSP set-up failure. `PathErr` messages are used to signal the error to the HE router. The HE router then uses the `PathTear` message to stop the LSP set-up effort.

In Figure 5.12, the Router P1 tries to set up an LSP to P6 requesting a certain amount of bandwidth. The method that the HE router uses to determine that the route P1 → P3 → P4 → P6 is suitable is irrelevant to this error signaling discussion. There is not enough bandwidth in Link 7 between P4 and P6. Figure 5.12 illustrates the following sequence of events:

1. The HE router sends a PATH message with certain bandwidth requirements toward the LSP Tail router.

2. The downstream next-hop router (P3) receives the PATH message, creates the path state, then regenerates the PATH message to the next-hop router (P4).

Figure 5.12 PathErr during the LSP-Path Setup

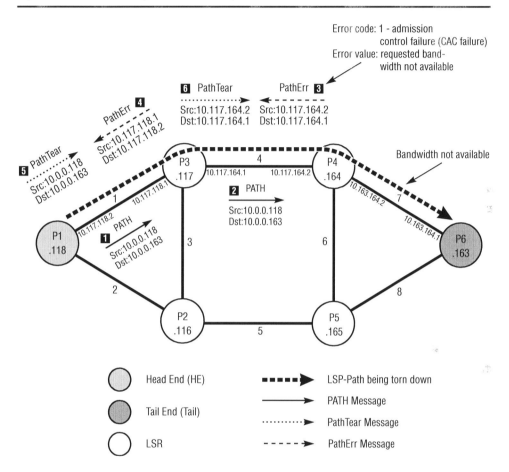

3. Router P4 receives the PATH message. P4 determines that there is not enough bandwidth in the local Link 7. This is a CAC failure. P4 decides that there is no available resource to support this LSP-Path. P4 then generates a PathErr message with the proper error code and error value (as shown in the top-right of the diagram). The PathErr message is sent to the upstream next-hop router where the PATH message of the failed LSP-Path set-up effort is received.

4. When router P3 receives the `PathErr` message from P4, it generates another `PathErr` message and sends it upstream to the HE router.

5. The HE router receives the `PathErr` message from P3. The HE router puts the LSP-Path into an operationally **down** state via the error code received in the `PathErr` message. The HE router then sends the `PathTear` message to downstream routers to clear the PATH state created by the initial PATH message.

6. In router P3, the arrival of the `PathTear` message clears the PSB. P3 then regenerates a `PathTear` message and sends it to the downstream next-hop router P4 to clear the path state.

7. (Not shown in the diagram). Router P4 receives the `PathTear` message and clears the path state.

Figure 5.13 illustrates the objects used by `PathErr` and `ResvErr` messages to report an error for the LSP.

Figure 5.13 PathErr and ResvErr Messages

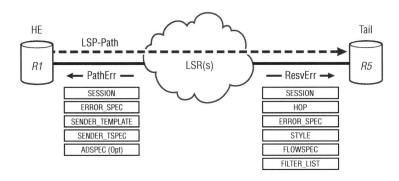

For details regarding the format of the messages and their objects, please refer to RFC 3209.

RSVP-TE Objects Used for MPLS LSP Signaling

Table 5.2 provides a list of RSVP-TE objects used for MPLS LSP-Path signaling. For more information on the detailed format of RSVP-TE messages and objects, please refer to RFC 2205, RFC 3209, and RFC 4090.

Table 5.2 RSVP-TE Messages and Their Objects for MPLS LSP Signaling

Message	Object Name	Class	Description
PATH	SESSION	1	Contains the destination IP of the LSP, the tunnel-id, and the extended-tunnel-id. The SESSION object uniquely identifies an LSP. All LSP-Paths belonging to the same LSP have the same SESSION object.
	HOP	3	Contains the IP address of the egress interface from which the message is sent out to the next-hop router.
	TIME_VALUE	5	Contains the refresh interval of the RSVP session. The router expects a refresh on every session within every refresh interval.
	SENDER_TEMPLATE	11	Contains the information regarding the originator of the LSP: the sender system IP address and the LSP-id. The SESSION object and the SENDER_TEMPLATE object together uniquely identify an LSP. All RSVP sessions belonging to the same LSP have the same SESSION object and SENDER_TEMPLATE object in the PATH and RESV messages. The LSP ID identifies the LSP-Path within the LSP.
	SENDER_TSPEC	12	Contains the parameters available for the traffic flow, such as the MTU of the LSP, and the bandwidth required for the LSP.
	ADSPEC (opt)	13	Contains additional information regarding the LSP being established. Used for MTU negotiation.
	LABEL_REQUEST	19	Requests distribution of a label to establish the LSP.
	EXPLICIT_ROUTE (ERO)	20	Contains a series of loose or strict hops (abstract node) that the LSP must traverse.
	RECORD_ROUTE (RRO)	21	Contains a series of hops indicating the route the PATH message actually traveled.
	FAST_REROUTE (opt)	205	Used by the LSP requesting MPLS FRR reduction. Contains the desired backup method (facility or one-to-one), the bandwidth required for the protection, and the link-coloring requirement.

(continued)

Table 5.2 RSVP-TE Messages and Their Objects for MPLS LSP Signaling *(continued)*

Message	Object Name	Class	Description
	SESSION_ATTRIBUTE	207	Contains the attribute of the LSP being established, including the LSP's name, setup, and holding priority, and flags regarding the FRR requirement.
	DETOUR (opt)	63	Used to establish the detour LSP for one-to-one backup FRR
RESV	SESSION	1	Contains the destination IP of the LSP, the tunnel-id, and the extended-tunnel-id. The SESSION object uniquely identifies an LSP. All LSP-Paths belonging to the same LSP have the same SESSION object.
	HOP	3	Contains the IP address of the egress interface from which the message is sent out to the next-hop router.
	TIME_VALUE	5	Contains the refresh interval of the RSVP session. The router expects a refresh on every session within every refresh interval.
	STYLE	8	Indicates the RSVP reservation style for the LSP. Can be Shared Explicit (SE) or Fixed Filter (FF).
	FLOW_SPEC	9	The response to the SENDER_TSPEC in the PATH message. It contains the parameters of the reservation for the LSP, including the MTU of the LSP, and the bandwidth required for the LSP.
	FILTER_SPEC	10	The response to the SENDER_ATTRIBUTE in the PATH message. It contains the sender's system IP address and the LSP-id.
	LABEL	16	Contains the label value distributed to the upstream next-hop router.
	RECORD ROUTE (RRO)	21	Contains a series of hops indicating the route the PATH message actually traveled. The RRO in the RESV message also records the label distributed by each hop if the record label is enabled on the LSP.
PathTear	SESSION	1	Contains the destination IP of the LSP, the tunnel-id, and the extended-tunnel-id. The SESSION object uniquely identifies an LSP. All LSP-Paths belonging to the same LSP have the same SESSION object.

Message	Object Name	Class	Description
	HOP	3	Contains the IP address of the egress interface from which the message is sent out to the next-hop router.
	SENDER_TEMPLATE	11	Contains the information regarding the originator of the LSP: the sender system IP address and the LSP-id. The SESSION object and SENDER_TEMPLATE object together uniquely identify an LSP. All RSVP sessions belonging to the same LSP have the same SESSION object and SENDER_ TEMPLATE object in the PATH and RESV messages. The LSP ID identifies the LSP-Path within the LSP.
	SENDER_TSPEC	12	Contains the parameters available for the flow, such as the MTU of the LSP, and the bandwidth required for the LSP.
	ADSPEC (opt)	13	Contains additional information regarding the LSP being established. Used for MTU negotiation.
ResvTear	SESSION	1	Contains the destination IP of the LSP, the tunnel-id, and the extended-tunnel-id. The SESSION object uniquely identifies an LSP. All LSP-Paths belonging to the same LSP have the same SESSION object.
	HOP	3	Contains the IP address of the egress interface from which the message is sent out to the next-hop router.
	STYLE	8	Indicates the RSVP reservation style for the LSP. Can be Shared Explicit (SE) or Fixed Filter (FF).
	FLOW_SPEC	9	The response to the SENDER_TSPEC in the PATH message. It contains the parameters of the reservation for the LSP, such as the MTU of the LSP, and the bandwidth required for the LSP.
	FILTER_SPEC	10	The response to the SENDER_ATTRIBUTE in the PATH message. It contains the sender's system IP address and the LSP-id.

(continued)

Table 5.2 RSVP-TE Messages and Their Objects for MPLS LSP Signaling *(continued)*

Message	Object Name	Class	Description
PathErr	SESSION	1	Contains the destination IP of the LSP, the tunnel-id, and the extended-tunnel-id. The SESSION object uniquely identifies an LSP. All LSP-Paths belonging to the same LSP have the same SESSION object.
	ERROR_SPEC	6	Contains the IP address of the generating router, error code, and error value indicating the reason for LSP establishment failure.
	SENDER_TEMPLATE	11	Contains the information regarding the originator of the LSP: the sender system IP address and the LSP-id. The SESSION object and SENDER_TEMPLATE object together uniquely identify an LSP. All RSVP sessions belonging to the same LSP have the same SESSION object and SENDER_ TEMPLATE object in the PATH and RESV messages. The LSP-id identifies the LSP-Path within the LSP.
	SENDER_TSPEC	12	Contains the parameters available for the flow, such as the MTU of the LSP, and the bandwidth required for the LSP.
	ADSEPC (opt)	13	Contains additional information regarding the LSP being established. Used for MTU negotiation.
ResvErr	SESSION	1	Contains the destination IP of the LSP, the tunnel-id, and the extended-tunnel-id. The SESSION object uniquely identifies an LSP. All LSP-Paths belonging to the same LSP have the same SESSION object.
	HOP	3	Contains the IP address of the egress interface from which the message is sent out to the next-hop router.
	ERROR_SPEC	6	Contains the IP address of the generating router, the error code, and error value indicating the reason for LSP establishment failure.
	STYLE	8	Indicates the RSVP reservation style for the LSP. Can be Shared Explicit (SE) or Fixed Filter (FF).

Message	Object Name	Class	Description
	FLOW_SPEC	9	The response to the SENDER_TSPEC in the PATH message. It contains the parameters of the reservation for the LSP, including the MTU of the LSP, and the bandwidth required for the LSP.
	FILTER_LIST	10	Contains the list of senders that the reservation error is referring to.

Figure 5.14 illustrates an operating LSP's status output. This is an example of an RSVP-TE-signaled LSP. The screen capture is from the HE router, where the end-to-end RSVP-TE LSP is defined and monitored. The terms in the diagram were explained in Chapter 3.

Figure 5.14   An RSVP-TE-Signaled LSP-Path

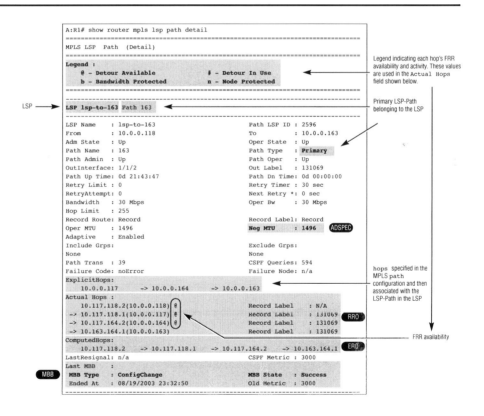

RSVP-TE LSP Bandwidth Reservation

When an LSP-Path with bandwidth requirement is established from its HE router to its Tail router, the bandwidth is reserved in all routers along the path. When the LSP-Path is established for the first time or modified for the first time, the PATH message simply performs CAC on the outgoing (dataflow) interface to check for available resources and validates the message on all the routers that the LSP-Path traverses (except the Tail router). When the Tail router of the LSP-Path receives the PATH message, the validation of the PATH message of the LSP-Path succeeds (for example, all objects in the PATH message are validated). The Tail router sends the RESV message upstream toward the upstream next-hop router. *The receipt of a new valid RESV message triggers the resource reservation in an MPLS router.* When an HE router or any LSR-Path receives an RESV message containing the information for a new LSP-Path (not a refresh of an existing LSP-Path), the HE and LSR routers reserve the corresponding bandwidth in their egress RSVP interfaces. If the router is an LSR, it generates the RESV message and sends it to the upstream next-hop router. If the router is the HE router of the LSP, it first performs a CAC and reserves the resources. If the resources are successfully reserved, the LSP-Path is put into an operationally up state and is ready to forward traffic.

The bandwidth reservation process on each router (HE, Tail, and LSRs involved) includes the following actions:

- Reserve bandwidth on the correct interface. The bandwidth should be reserved in the link toward the Tail router.
- Send an IGP-TE Link State Update (LSU) to notify all routers in the network of the link's unused bandwidth change. For example, if OSPF-TE is used, a Type 10 Opaque LSA is flooded to all OSPF routers with the new unreserved bandwidth field in the LSU.
- After the reservation is completed, the router (if it is not the HE router) sends an RESV message to the next-hop upstream router.

Figure 5.15 illustrates the bandwidth reservation process in an LSR router establishing an LSP.

In Figure 5.15, the entire network is connected with 100-Mbps Fast Ethernet links. One LSP-Path is being established from P1 to P6 with 40 Mbps of bandwidth. Figure 5.15 illustrates the following sequence of events:

1. HE Router P1 sends the PATH message along the path P1 → P3 → P4 → P6 to Tail Router P6.

Figure 5.15 RSVP-TE LSP Establishment and Bandwidth Reservation

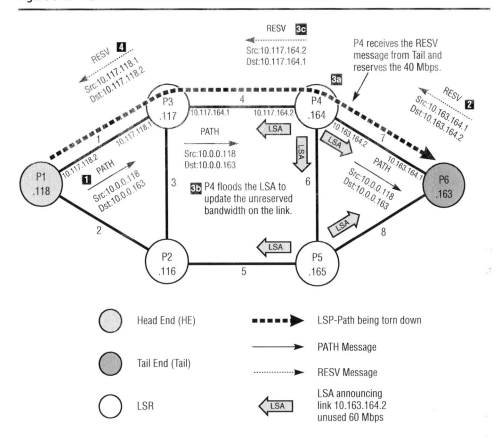

2. When P6 grants the request from the received PATH message, it sends the RESV message to Router P4.

3a. P4 reserves the 50-Mbps bandwidth requested for the LSP on the links P4–P6.

3b. P4 floods an OSPF LSU to all its OSPF neighbors to change the *unreserved bandwidth* on the link P4–P6. The LSU is then flooded to all OSFP routers in the network.

3c. P4 sends an RESV message to Router P3.

4. P3 performs the same bandwidth reservation procedure and sends an RESV message to Router P1.

RSVP-TE LSP Reservation Style

Reservation style refers to the way resources are reserved for an RSVP session on each hop of the LSP-Path in an RSVP-enabled interface. When multiple LSP-Paths belonging to the same LSP reserve bandwidth over a common link in a router, reservation style decides how these LSPs reserve the bandwidth. There are two reservation styles used for RSVP-TE MPLS LSP signaling:

- **Fixed Filter (FF)** — With the FF reservation style, the resource being reserved is dedicated to each sender. Every individual LSP-Path (sender) defined by the RSVP session and the LSP-id has its own exclusive bandwidth reservation. The total bandwidth reservation is the summary of the RSVP sessions reserved on all the LSP-Paths on that link.

- **Shared Explicit (SE)** — With the SE reservation style, LSP-Paths belong to the same LSP, but different LSP-ids can share the reserved resource. The SE LSP-Paths of the same LSP traversing the common link can share the bandwidth on that link. For these LSP-Paths, the total bandwidth reservation on the link equals the maximum reservation made by the LSP-Path with the biggest BW requirement.

In RSVP-TE LSP, the sender is defined by the SESSION and SENDER_TEMPLATE objects. These are the same two objects in a PATH message that uniquely identify an RSVP session in each router. When discussing the reservation style of an RSVP-TE LSP, the discussion centers around whether the reservation along the path should be shared if there is more than one session belonging to the same LSP (tunnel-id, end-point, extended-tunnel-id) but having different LSP-ids, or, alternatively, should each LSP-Path have its own reservation. This important factor affects the MBB feature of the LSP. (MBB is introduced in the next section.)

Figure 5.16 illustrates several scenarios in a sample topology where multiple LSPs with bandwidth reservations intersect in the network. Case 1 illustrates one LSP with two LSP-Paths (one primary and one hot-standby secondary) that both require bandwidth.

Note that the secondary LSP-Path is discussed in detail in Chapter 6. For the current discussion, you only need to know that, as with the primary LSP-Path, a hot-standby secondary LSP-Path is signaled as soon as the LSP has been administratively enabled.

Figure 5.16 RSVP-TE LSP Reservation Styles: FF versus SE

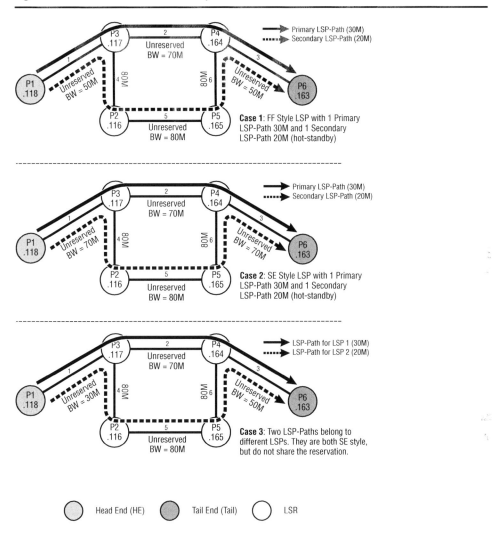

In Case 1, because the reservation style is configured as FF, the primary and secondary LSP-Paths do not share bandwidth reservation on the common path (Links 1 and 3), even though they belong to the same LSP. These links each have their own reservations, so the available bandwidth in these two links decreases to 50 Mbps after both LSPs are established. For the non-common paths (Links 2, 4, 5, and 6), each link only reserves bandwidth for one LSP-Path accordingly.

In Case 2, the same LSP has been modified to use the SE reservation style. After both LSP-Paths are established, Links 1 and 3 still have 70-Mbps bandwidth available. This is because in the SE reservation style, the two LSP-Paths belong to the same LSP and share the bandwidth reservation on all common paths. The 20 Mbps required for the secondary LSP-Path is shared with the 30 Mbps reserved for the primary LSP-Path.

Case 3 shows two LSP-Paths belonging to two different LSPs. Although they have common paths and both of the LSPs are configured to use the SE reservation style (default reservation style), they *do not* share bandwidth reservation. Two LSP-Paths with different LSPs (tunnel-ids, endpoint, and extended-tunnel-id) never share bandwidth reservation.

For RSVP-TE MPLS LSPs, the HE router sets the desired reservation style into flags within the SESSION_ATTRIBUTE object in the PATH message. The Tail router receives the reservation style of the LSP and sets it in the STYLE object. Furthermore, when the LSP is configured with the FF style, it cannot use the FRR facility backup method. MPLS FRR is discussed in Chapter 7. Table 5.3 compares the two RSVP-TE reservation styles.

Table 5.3 Types of RSVP Reservation Styles

Reservation Style	Description
Fixed Filter	Reserves exclusive resources for each sender. Total reservation is the sum of the reservations from all senders. There is one label for each sender, and P2P LSP between each sender/receiver pair.
Shared Explicit	Reserves shared resources for senders with the same LSP. One label for one reservation is shared by the listed members. One LSP is shared per group (one separate LSP per ERO).

In RSVP-TE signaling for MPLS, the reservation style is indicated in the STYLE object in RESV, via ResvTear and ResvErr messages.

5.4 Make-Before-Break (MBB)

As mentioned earlier, one of the advantages of using RSVP-TE to signal MPLS LSP is the improvement of the MPLS LSP's performance and reliability. This chapter introduces one of the RSVP-TE resiliency features, make-before-break (MBB). With MBB, live LSP parameters can be modified with minimum traffic loss.

When modifying the parameters of an LSP-Path that is already established and passing traffic, operators wish to minimize the traffic loss. In the case of an RSVP-TE-signaled LSP-Path, this is achieved using MBB. When re-establishing an LSP-Path using MBB, the existing LSP (series of RSVP sessions) keeps carrying traffic while the new LSP-Path is signaled. The LSP-Path will not be torn down until the new LSP-Path is established successfully and the traffic is switched over to the new LSP-Path. After the new LSP-Path comes **up** operationally, the traffic is switched to the new path before the old LSP-Path is destroyed. Therefore, the traffic interruption during the re-establishment of the LSP-Path is minimized, and in most cases is zero.

Furthermore, with MBB, if a new LSP-Path cannot be made, the existing LSP will not be broken. For example, if the LSP-Path's new requirement (more bandwidth) cannot be fulfilled, the original LSP-Path stays operationally **up** and continues to pass traffic. The router keeps trying to set up the new LSP-Path without affecting the traffic on the existing LSP. This guarantees that the new LSP-Path set-up effort (retries) does not cause traffic loss on the existing LSP.

In ALSRP service routers, the MBB manner of LSP-Path establishment is applicable for the following scenarios:

- Applying LSP-Path configuration modifications "on-the-fly" (e.g., changing bandwidth)
- HE router reverting traffic back from the FRR protection mode
- Automatically resignaling the existing LSP-Path for optimization, or the manual resignaling of the LSP-Path by executing the command:

```
tools perform router mpls re-signal lsp <lsp-name> path <path-name>
```

Figure 5.17 illustrates an example of desired MBB behavior. In this example, an LSP-Path originally reserved 60 Mbps of bandwidth. The configuration change on the LSP-Path requires 80 Mbps of bandwidth. With MBB, the new LSP-Path is established before the old LSP-Path is torn down.

In Figure 5.17, the original LSP-Path (represented by the dashed line) uses 60 Mbps of bandwidth. The links among the routers are all 100-Mbps links.

In this example, the operator wants to add another 20 Mbps to the LSP-Path, to make a total reservation of 80 Mbps. After the configuration is modified in the HE router for the LSP-Path's bandwidth, the HE router tries to set up the LSP-Path with new bandwidth. To reduce the traffic loss, the new LSP-Path should be established before the old LSP-Path is torn down. However, the link capacity is not enough to support a 60-Mbps LSP-Path and an 80-Mbps LSP-Path at the same time. This is true even if the operator wants to reduce the LSP-Path bandwidth to 50 Mbps — a 50-Mbps LSP-Path and a 60-Mbps LSP cannot coexist on the same 100-Mbps link. With MBB, all routers along the path understand that the new LSP-Path and the old LSP-Path are used for the same purpose and therefore can share the bandwidth. Thus, every router books only the extra 20-Mbps bandwidth and allows establishment of the 80-Mbps LSP-Path. At that point, the HE router tears down the old 60-Mbps LSP-Path.

Figure 5.17 Make-Before-Break Example

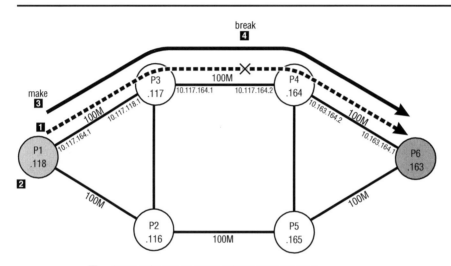

1   Existing LSP-Path P1-P6 has 60M bandwidth reserved.

2   Configuration of LSP-Path P1-P6 is modified in HE router and now requires 80M of bandwidth.

3   With make-before-break, the system understands the new LSP-Path is replacing the old LSP-Path, and now allows the 80M LSP-Path to be established. This is true even if the link has only 100-60=40M available bandwidth.

4   After the new LSP-Path comes up, the old LSP-Path is torn down. Therefore, the bandwidth modification does not cause any traffic loss, since the make (3) happens before the break (4).

Head End (HE)   →   New LSP-Path 80M BW

Tail End (Tail)   ▪▪▪▶   LSP-Path 60M BW

LSR

Implementation of MBB behavior on an RSVP-TE LSP-Path requires the following:

- The LSP-Path must support multiple RSVP sessions belonging to the same LSP. The resources used to carry traffic in the old LSP-Path must not be released until the new LSP-Path has been successfully established.

- If the LSP uses the SE reservation style, the old LSP-Path and the new LSP-Path will not compete for bandwidth over the link they intersect. In the case of increasing LSP-Path bandwidth, only the incremental portion (delta) should be counted during CAC. Multiple sessions (old and new) belonging to the same LSP (same SESSION object) should be treated the same as the explicit list of senders sharing the resources.

- If the LSP uses the FF reservation style, the old and new LSP-Paths cannot share the same resource in the common link as the SE-style LSP. In this case, the HE router can still follow MBB behavior, set up the new LSP with dedicated resources, and not tear down the original one until the new LSP-Path has been established. However, there is a short period of time when both LSP-Paths coexist in the network. The resources consumed on the common path of the two LSP-Paths are the sum of both.

- For an LSP using either SE or FF reservation styles, if the setup of the new LSP-Path fails (e.g., not enough resources), the original LSP-Path still stays up operationally and carries traffic. The new parameters (e.g., new value of bandwidth) are not applied to the LSP-Path until a manual shutdown and no shutdown are performed on the LSP-Path.

    As a side effect, when the signaling of a new LSP-Path with modified parameters fails, the configuration of the LSP in the HE router is not consistent with the actual characters of the LSP-Path and the RSVP session. When the LSP is manually resignaled and uses the new parameters, there may be cases in which the resource reservation will still fail, and the LSP is then operationally down. An example of this scenario is presented later in this section.

MBB requires two LSP-Paths (two sets of RSVP sessions) to serve the same LSP in a very short time period. The old LSP-Path is not torn down until the new LSP-Path is established. All nodes (iLER, LSR, eLER) must understand that both RSVP sessions are serving the same LSP: The two sessions have different LSP-ids but share the same tunnel-id and the same sender IP address. When a bandwidth change requirement is configured and activated in the HE node of the tunnel, two things happen:

- The existing LSP-Path is refreshed using the existing PATH message.
- A new PATH message is sent to the far-end destination router, with the following objects:

  - The original SESSION object, which is the same as the old LSP-Path's SESSION object. This object identifies the new LSP-Path belonging to the same LSP. An LSP is uniquely identified by the three values in the SESSION object: destination IP address (the Tail router system-IP address), tunnel-id, and extended-tunnel-id (which is the HE router's own system IP address).

  - A new SENDER_TEMPLATE, in which a new LSP-id is used to indentify that this is a new LSP-Path being established

  - A new ERO that specifies where the PATH message should travel to reach the destination node

Because this new PATH message contains the same SESSION object as the old LSP-Path, all routers receiving it understand that this PATH message is setting up a new LSP-Path for the same LSP in an MBB manner. There is a short time period when two sets of sessions are established for the same LSP-Path. When the actual resource reservation begins, the Tail router sends an RESV message back toward the HE router, with two sets of object, one for each LSP-Path. Each set contains the following parameters:

- FLOWSPEC — Which specifies the different bandwidth (rate) value
- FILTERSPEC — In which the LSP-id value is different between each LSP-Path
- LABEL — Where a different label value is distributed for each LSP-Path
- RRO — Where each RRO records the path (hop list) through which the PATH message traverses

The Tail router and every other router perform resource reservation and send the RESV message to the upstream next-hop router. After the reservation from each hop has successfully completed, the HE router switches the traffic to the new LSP-Path and then uses a PathTear message to tear down the original LSP-Path. The new LSP-Path now carries the data traffic. Therefore, there is no traffic loss during the entire MBB LSP-Path set-up period.

Figure 5.18 illustrates an RSVP-TE signaling example of using MBB to change the bandwidth of an LSP-Path.

Figure 5.18 MBB RSVP-TE Signaling Example

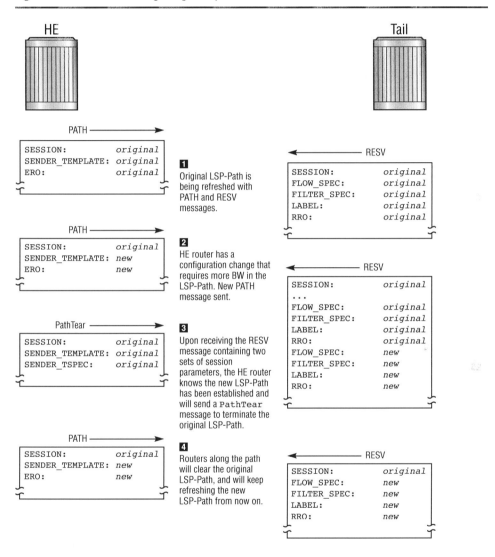

What Behavior Is Not Make-Before-Break?

There is often confusion about LSP resiliency and MBB. MBB is a behavior or mechanism used by the router to minimize traffic loss when establishing a new LSP-Path to replace an old LSP-Path. The MBB mechanism is *not* used to switch traffic between two established LSP-Paths. Thus, when FRR is operational during a link/node failure, it is not MBB behavior, because the PLR node is switching traffic from one LSP-Path (protected LSP-Path) to a different LSP-Path (the bypass/detour tunnel). Also, it is not MBB behavior when the HE router switches traffic from the primary LSP-Path of an LSP to a secondary LSP-Path, or among secondary LSP-Paths owing to a network failure.

The next part of this section presents some examples of MBB, including successful and failed ones.

Example 1 — Shared Explicit Style LSP-Path's MBB: A Success Case

Figure 5.19 illustrates a successful example of the use of MBB in an SE reservation style LSP-Path. The configuration of the LSP-Path is presented in Figure 5.19's CLI output. The change in the LSP-Path is highlighted in Figure 5.20's CLI output. The before and after displays of the RSVP session status at the HE router are presented in Figure 5.21.

Figure 5.19 illustrates the configuration of the original LSP-Path configured from router PE-165 to router PE-163. This LSP-Path belongs to the LSP named `lsp-165.163`, with a reserved bandwidth of 30 Mbps.

Figure 5.19 CLI Session: Original LSP and LSP-Path Configuration

```
*A:PE-165# configure router mpls lsp lsp-165-163
*A:PE-165>config>router>mpls>lsp# info
----------------------------------------------
                to 10.0.0.163
                cspf
                adspec
                fast-reroute one-to-one
                exit
                primary "loose"
                        bandwidth 30
                exit
                no shutdown
----------------------------------------------
*A:PE-165>config>router>mpls>lsp#
```

In this example, the configuration shows lsp-165-163's LSP-Path, loose, and uses the default SE reservation style. Note, in the ALSRP CLI, this default value is not shown in the info list of the configuration. To check the configured values including the default, the operator must use the info detail command. The network interface from node PE-165 toward node PE-163 is a 100-Mbps Fast Ethernet link. The original LSP-Path reserves 30 Mbps of bandwidth, and the new reservation is 85 Mbps.

During the modification of the LSP-Path bandwidth reservation, there are two RSVP sessions. The original session has a reservation of 30 Mbps. The new session has a reservation of 85 Mbps. As mentioned previously, the two sessions share a common 30-Mbps reservation. Only the delta bandwidth change of 55 Mbps is newly reserved for the LSP; not the sum of 115 Mbps. Thus, the old and new sessions can coexist, and the LSP-Path modification is performed in an MBB manner without traffic loss. Figure 5.20 illustrates that the 100-Mbps Fast Ethernet link from PE-165 toward the Tail router PE-163 has 30 Mbps of bandwidth reserved for the LSP-Path.

Figure 5.20   CLI Session Monitoring Using MBB

```
A:PE-165# show router rsvp session
===================================================================
RSVP Sessions
===================================================================
From           To          Tunnel LSP    Name                State
                           ID     ID
-------------------------------------------------------------------
10.0.0.165     10.0.0.163   1      30272 lsp-165-163::loose   Up
-------------------------------------------------------------------
Sessions : 1
===================================================================
A:PE-165# show router rsvp interface to-PE164
===================================================================
RSVP Interface : to-PE164
===================================================================
Interface           Total   Active    Total BW  Resv BW  Adm Opr
                    Sessions Sessions  (Mbps)    (Mbps)
-------------------------------------------------------------------
to-PE164            2        2         100       30       Up  Up
===================================================================
A:PE-165#
```

Before the LSP-Path's bandwidth change, the CLI command show router rsvp session displays one RSVP session belonging to Tunnel 1 in router PE-165 (this means that the RSVP session belongs to an LSP that has a tunnel-id of 1). After the bandwidth of the LSP-Path from CLI changes, the same command displays *two* sessions; one with LSP-id 30272, (the original session) and one with LSP-id 30274 (the new session). Both these sessions have the same tunnel-id. This means that, at this moment, the two sessions coexist for the same LSP. When the `show router rsvp session` command is repeated, only the new session is left, because the HE router cleared the old session upon receipt of the successful RESV message in the new session.

This is a clear demonstration of MBB behavior. The original session is not torn down until the new session is established. In addition, there is no traffic loss on that tunnel. The detailed RSVP interface display confirms that there are 85 Mbps reserved for the LSP after the MBB resignals the new LSP-Path. Figure 5.21 illustrates the LSP-Path status after the change has been made using MBB.

Figure 5.21   CLI Session: MBB after Configuration Changes

```
A:PE-165# configure router mpls lsp lsp-165-163 primary loose bandwidth 85
A:PE-165# show router rsvp session
===============================================================================
RSVP Sessions
===============================================================================
From            To             Tunnel LSP   Name                         State
                               ID     ID
-------------------------------------------------------------------------------
10.0.0.165      10.0.0.163     1      30272 lsp-165-163::loose           Up
10.0.0.165      10.0.0.163     1      30274 lsp-165-163::loose           Up
-------------------------------------------------------------------------------
Sessions : 2
===============================================================================
A:PE-165# show router rsvp session
===============================================================================
RSVP Sessions
===============================================================================
From            To             Tunnel LSP   Name                         State
                               ID     ID
-------------------------------------------------------------------------------
10.0.0.165      10.0.0.163     1      30274 lsp-165-163::loose           Up
-------------------------------------------------------------------------------
Sessions : 1
===============================================================================
A:PE-165# show router rsvp interface to-PE164
===============================================================================
RSVP Interface : to-PE164
===============================================================================
Interface               Total     Active    Total BW   Resv BW   Adm Opr
                        Sessions  Sessions  (Mbps)     (Mbps)
-------------------------------------------------------------------------------
to-PE164                2         2         100        85        Up  Up
===============================================================================
A:PE-165#
```

Example 2 — Fixed Filter Style LSP-Path's MBB: A Failure Case

When the LSP uses the FF reservation style, an exclusive reservation is required for every session. In this case, the HE router still tries to perform the LSP modification in an MBB manner. However, the new LSP session cannot share resources with the original session in any common link because of the FF reservation requirement. The MBB has a higher chance of failure owing to insufficient bandwidth.

In this example, if the sum of the resources required by both sessions from a common link is higher than the link capacity, the reservation of the new session fails. The configuration change cannot be implemented on the LSP-Path until the LSP-Path is administratively disabled and re-enabled by manually executing the `shutdown` and `no shutdown` commands. Figure 5.22 illustrates the CLI output of the LSP configuration and the session status for this scenario.

Figure 5.22 CLI Session: Original LSP Configuration and Tunnel Status

```
A:PE-165# configure router mpls lsp lsp-165-163
A:PE-165>config>router>mpls>lsp# info
-----------------------------------------------
                to 10.0.0.163
                    rsvp-resv-style ff
                cspf
                adspec
                fast-reroute one-to-one
                exit
                primary "loose"
                        bandwidth 45
                exit
                no shutdown
-----------------------------------------------
A:PE-165>config>router>mpls>lsp#exit all
A:PE-165# show router rsvp session
===============================================================
RSVP Sessions
===============================================================
From          To          Tunnel LSP   Name                     State
              ID     ID
---------------------------------------------------------------
10.0.0.165    10.0.0.163    1     30318 lsp-165-163::loose         Up
---------------------------------------------------------------
Sessions : 1
===============================================================
A:PE-165# show router rsvp interface to-PE164
===============================================================
RSVP Interface : to-PE164
===============================================================
Interface           Total   Active    Total BW  Resv BW  Adm Opr
                    Sessions Sessions  (Mbps)    (Mbps)
---------------------------------------------------------------
to-PE164              2       2        100       45       Up  Up
===============================================================
A:PE-165#
```

In this example, the LSP-Path's bandwidth is changed from 45 Mbps to 60 Mbps. In this case, because the reservation style of the tunnel is FF, the new session must be established using separate resource reservations. The only interface from PE-165 toward the PE-163 node has only 55 Mbps of unused bandwidth, which is not enough. Therefore, the HE router cannot perform the MBB modification of the bandwidth. Although the configuration has been changed in the LSP-Path, the original RSVP session — which uses 45 Mbps of bandwidth — is still operationally up and carrying traffic. Therefore, the configuration change is *not* propagated to the LSP-Path. Figure 5.23 shows that the RSVP session does not change after the configuration change, adhering to the *If cannot make, do not break* rule. The system retries the setup of the new LSP-Path, according to the retry counter configuration.

Figure 5.23 CLI Session: After the Configuration Changes — No RSVP Session Change

```
A:PE-165# configure router mpls lsp lsp-165-163 primary loose bandwidth 60
A:PE-165# show router rsvp session
===============================================================================
RSVP Sessions
===============================================================================
From            To              Tunnel LSP   Name                       State
                                ID     ID
-------------------------------------------------------------------------------
10.0.0.165      10.0.0.163      1      30318 lsp-165-163::loose          Up

Sessions : 1
===============================================================================
*A:PE-165# show router rsvp interface to-PE164
===============================================================================
RSVP Interface : to-PE164
===============================================================================
Interface               Total    Active   Total BW  Resv BW  Adm Opr
                        Sessions Sessions (Mbps)    (Mbps)
-------------------------------------------------------------------------------
to-PE164                2        2        100       45       Up  Up
===============================================================================
A:PE-165# configure router mpls lsp lsp-165-163
A:PE-165>config>router>mpls>lsp# info
----------------------------------------------
              to 10.0.0.163
              rsvp-resv-style ff
              cspf
              adspec
              fast-reroute one-to-one
              exit
              primary "loose"
                  bandwidth 60
              exit
              no shutdown
----------------------------------------------
A:PE-165>config>router>mpls>lsp#
```

In this case, as MBB is not possible because of insufficient bandwidth, an administrative disable/enable of the LSP is required (with traffic outage) to deploy the change to the LSP-Path. After the manual **shutdown** and **no shutdown**, the new RSVP session is established with the reservation of 60 Mbps as configured. Figure 5.24 illustrates that the new LSP is established after a manual **shutdown/no shutdown**.

In any circumstance, if the MBB resignal fails, the system maintains the original RSVP session for the LSP-Path. At this point, one of the following two conditions is required to make the LSP-Path change effective:

- More resources are made available in the network to make the reservation possible, and the MBB succeeds in later retries.

- A manual **shutdown** removes the old LSP-Path and clears the original session. This is followed by a manual **no shutdown**, which establishes the new LSP-Path using the modified parameters (assuming that the released resources from the old LSP-Path are sufficient to set up the new one).

Figure 5.24 CLI Session: After a Manual Disable/Enable of the LSP

```
*A:PE-165# configure router mpls lsp lsp-165-163 shutdown
*A:PE-165# configure router mpls lsp lsp-165-163 no shutdown
*A:PE-165# show router rsvp session
===============================================================================
RSVP Sessions
===============================================================================
From           To           Tunnel LSP   Name                          State
                            ID     ID
-------------------------------------------------------------------------------
10.0.0.165     10.0.0.163   1      30322 lsp-165-163::loose             Up
-------------------------------------------------------------------------------
Sessions : 1
===============================================================================
*A:PE-165# show router rsvp interface to-PE164
===============================================================================
RSVP Interface : to-PE164
===============================================================================
Interface              Total    Active    Total BW  Resv BW  Adm Opr
                       Sessions Sessions  (Mbps)    (Mbps)
-------------------------------------------------------------------------------
to-PE164               2        2         100       60       Up  Up
===============================================================================
*A:PE-165#
```

FF Style: Increasing Bandwidth versus Decreasing Bandwidth

In the case of the FF style of reserving LSPs, MBB fails if the new target bandwidth (sum of the old bandwidth and the new bandwidth for the LSP-Path on common links) is higher than the available bandwidth of the RSVP-TE link. This occurs regardless of whether the requirement increases or decreases the bandwidth. Consider the scenario where the original LSP-Path uses 80 Mbps of bandwidth from the 100-Mbps link and the operator wishes to reduce the bandwidth to 30 Mbps. If the LSP-Path's reservation style is FF, the change will not be applied to the path in an MBB manner. This is because MBB requires a new session using 30 Mbps of bandwidth. However, it cannot share the 80 Mbps with the older LSP-Path because the link only has $100 - 80 = 20$ Mbps of available bandwidth. This request fails, as does the request to set up a new LSP-Path of 30 Mbps over a link with only 20 Mbps of available bandwidth. A manual shutdown must first be performed to release the bandwidth, and then a no shutdown can establish the new 30-Mbps LSP-Path for the LSP.

Example 3 — What Happens after a Make-Before-Break Failure?

From the LSP-Path's signaling perspective, the modification of an LSP-Path using the MBB method is the same as setting up a new LSP-Path. The only difference is that the new LSP-Path shares the SESSION object with the original LSP-Path. Therefore, the two LSP-Paths belong to the same LSP. If the signaling process fails, the HE router tries to resignal the new LSP-Path based on the retry-timer and retry-limit configuration of the LSP. By default, the system retries the LSP-Path establishment every 30 seconds indefinitely, until either the new LSP-Path is set up successfully, or other changes have been made to the LSP-Path. Meanwhile, the existing LSP-Path is refreshed periodically as usual, thus maintaining its state and passing traffic.

In the following example, there is a single 100-Mbps link from PE-165 to PE-163. The network has two LSPs: The LSP with tunnel-id 1 uses 20 Mbps of BW, and the LSP with tunnel-id 108 uses 50 Mbps of BW. Both LSPs are from PE-165 to PE-163. lsp-165-163 is configured to use the reservation style FF with MBB enabled by default. In this example, the operator wants to change the bandwidth of the LSP-Path of lsp-165-163 from the current 20 Mbps to 40 Mbps. Because there is only 30 Mbps of unused bandwidth in the link (100 − 20 − 50 = 30 Mbps), the FF reservation styled MBB session will not succeed owing to the lack of bandwidth to set up a 40-Mbps session separately. Because the LSP is using the default retry configuration, every 30 seconds it tries to deploy the bandwidth change using MBB for its LSP-Path. Figure 5.25 illustrates the retry effort of the MBB.

In this example, after 2 minutes, the second LSP, lsp2-165-163, is removed. This frees up 50 Mbps more bandwidth in the link. Therefore, the next retry of MBB in the first LSP will succeed. The new RSVP session with 40 Mbps reservation is established and replaces the original session. The retry behavior in MBB is consistent regardless of the reservation style of the LSP (SE or FF). Only the configured retry parameters (timer and limit) for the LSP are relevant.

Figure 5.26 illustrates the CLI output of a MBB retry while the original LSP-Path is not affected. In this example, the system tries to change the LSP-Path's bandwidth from 20 Mbps to 150 Mbps. Because the link between PE-165 and PE-163 only has 100 Mbps of bandwidth, this request is not achievable.

Figure 5.26 presents the command output of the show router mpls lsp path detail command. This command displays the LSP-Path status. Several facts about MBB can be concluded from the CLI output:

- Oper Bandwi*: 20 Mbps means that the current LSP is reserving 20 Mbps of bandwidth.

Figure 5.25 CLI Session: Make-Before-Break Retry

```
A:PE-165# show router rsvp session
===================================================================
RSVP Sessions
===================================================================
From         To           Tunnel LSP   Name                  State
             ID     ID
-------------------------------------------------------------------
10.0.0.165   10.0.0.163   1      30324 lsp-165-163::loose     Up
10.0.0.165   10.0.0.163   108    7168  lsp2-165-163::loose    Up
-------------------------------------------------------------------
Sessions : 2
===================================================================
*A:PE-165# show router rsvp interface to-PE164
===================================================================
RSVP Interface : to-PE164
===================================================================
Interface          Total    Active   Total BW  Resv BW  Adm Opr
                   Sessions Sessions (Mbps)    (Mbps)
-------------------------------------------------------------------
to-PE164           2        2        100       70       Up   Up
A:PE-165# configure router mpls lsp lsp2-165-163       shutdown
!!! removing the second LSP which uses 50 Mb bandwidth
A:PE-165# show router rsvp session
===================================================================
RSVP Sessions
===================================================================
From         To           Tunnel LSP   Name                  State
             ID     ID
-------------------------------------------------------------------
10.0.0.165   10.0.0.163   1      30324 lsp-165-163::loose     Up
-------------------------------------------------------------------
Sessions : 1
===================================================================
A:PE-165# show router rsvp session
===================================================================
RSVP Sessions
===================================================================
From         To           Tunnel LSP   Name                  State
             ID     ID
-------------------------------------------------------------------
10.0.0.165   10.0.0.163   1      30324 lsp-165-163::loose     Up
10.0.0.165   10.0.0.163   1      30326 lsp-165-163::loose     Up
-------------------------------------------------------------------
Sessions : 2
===================================================================
A:PE-165# show router rsvp session
===================================================================
RSVP Sessions
===================================================================
From         To           Tunnel LSP   Name                  State
             ID     ID
-------------------------------------------------------------------
10.0.0.165   10.0.0.163   1      30326 lsp-165-163::loose     Up
-------------------------------------------------------------------
Sessions : 1
===================================================================
A:PE-165# show router rsvp interface to-sim164 detail
===================================================================
A:PE-165# show router rsvp interface to-PE164
===================================================================
RSVP Interface : to-PE164
===================================================================
Interface          Total    Active   Total BW  Resv BW  Adm Opr
                   Sessions Sessions (Mbps)    (Mbps)
-------------------------------------------------------------------
to-PE164           2        2        100       40       Up   Up
===================================================================
A:PE-165#
```

- Bandwidth: 150 Mbps indicates that the new administratively configured bandwidth (which the system is trying to set up using MBB) is 150 Mbps.
- MBB state: In Progress with the RetryAttempt 4 and Next Retry *: 7 sec shows that MBB failed four times and will try again in 7 seconds.

- Most importantly, the `Path Dn Time: 0d 00:00:00` shows that there is *no* service interruption. The `Oper State: Up` from the LSP-Path status output confirms that this LSP-Path is constantly **up**. Although the MBB manner of changing bandwidth is constantly failing at every retry, the original LSP-Path and all possible services using that LSP-Path to pass traffic are not affected.

Figure 5.26 Example of Failed MBB Resignal and Retry Effort

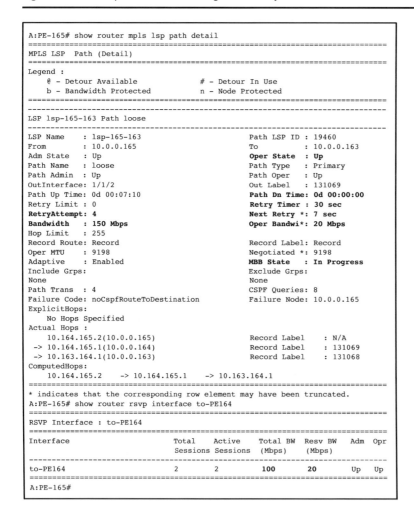

```
A:PE-165# show router mpls lsp path detail
===============================================================================
MPLS LSP  Path (Detail)
===============================================================================
Legend :
     @ - Detour Available            # - Detour In Use
     b - Bandwidth Protected         n - Node Protected
===============================================================================
-------------------------------------------------------------------------------
LSP lsp-165-163 Path loose
-------------------------------------------------------------------------------
LSP Name      : lsp-165-163          Path LSP ID : 19460
From          : 10.0.0.165           To          : 10.0.0.163
Adm State     : Up                   Oper State  : Up
Path Name     : loose                Path Type   : Primary
Path Admin    : Up                   Path Oper   : Up
OutInterface: 1/1/2                  Out Label   : 131069
Path Up Time: 0d 00:07:10            Path Dn Time: 0d 00:00:00
Retry Limit : 0                      Retry Timer : 30 sec
RetryAttempt: 4                      Next Retry *: 7 sec
Bandwidth   : 150 Mbps               Oper Bandwi*: 20 Mbps
Hop Limit   : 255
Record Route: Record                 Record Label: Record
Oper MTU    : 9198                    Negotiated *: 9198
Adaptive    : Enabled                MBB State   : In Progress
Include Grps:                        Exclude Grps:
None                                 None
Path Trans  : 4                      CSPF Queries: 8
Failure Code: noCspfRouteToDestination  Failure Node: 10.0.0.165
ExplicitHops:
    No Hops Specified
Actual Hops :
    10.164.165.2(10.0.0.165)         Record Label    : N/A
 -> 10.164.165.1(10.0.0.164)         Record Label    : 131069
 -> 10.163.164.1(10.0.0.163)         Record Label    : 131068
ComputedHops:
    10.164.165.2    -> 10.164.165.1    -> 10.163.164.1
===============================================================================
* indicates that the corresponding row element may have been truncated.
A:PE-165# show router rsvp interface to-PE164
===============================================================================
RSVP Interface : to-PE164
===============================================================================
Interface            Total    Active   Total BW  Resv BW  Adm  Opr
                     Sessions Sessions (Mbps)    (Mbps)
-------------------------------------------------------------------------------
to-PE164             2        2        100       20       Up   Up
===============================================================================
A:PE-165#
```

> ### Can I Turn Off Make-Before-Break?
>
> Yes. MBB is enabled by default and can be disabled on a per-LSP basis. If the MBB behavior is not desired, it can be disabled under that particular LSP's configuration. Using the keyword no `adaptive` disables MBB for this LSP on the primary and all secondary paths. When MBB is disabled in an LSP, the changes or resignaling occur in the following order: Tear down the existing LSP-Path, and set up the new LSP-Path. This is a *break first*, and *then make* process.

Make-Before-Break in Fast Reroute

The MBB behavior is also applicable for the Fast Reroute traffic revert scenario. Reversion occurs when network failure is restored, and the LSP-Path being protected reverts back to the original LSP-Path from the detour/bypass tunnel. FRR reversion is discussed in detail in Chapter 7.

> ### How Can I Maintain the MBB in the Case of Interoperations with Multiple Vendors' MPLS Routers/Switches?
>
> MBB is a feature that is required only in the HE router of the LSP. From the perspective of all other routers (LSR or Tail), it is simply another LSP-Path set-up request; those routers are not required to have support for MBB. During MBB, there are two LSP-Paths established. They share the same tunnel-ID and have the same sender and destination router. At one point, one LSP-Path (the original one) is torn down. The HE router is the only router required to support MBB. Provided the HE router uses MBB behavior to change the LSP-Path's parameters, there is seamless interoperation with any other MPLS routers/switches.

5.5 The RSVP-TE Hello Protocol

As mentioned earlier, RSVP is a *soft-state* protocol. All RSVP sessions require constant refreshment with PATH and RESV messages to maintain their session states. By default, if a session has a contiguous loss of PATH or RESV messages (by default, three times the *refresh-interval*), the session expires and is cleared. If there is a failure, the refresh message cannot be sent, and the failure is detected by a timeout of the refresh timer. The resources occupied by the session are then released. Therefore, the refresh-interval determines the elapsed time before the failure can be detected. After the refresh timer expires, the system either re-establishes the LSP-Path or puts the LSP-Path in an operationally **down** state. If a quicker reaction time is desired when the network fails, the refresh timer must be set to a smaller value so that the refreshing PATH and RESV messages are sent out more frequently. However, frequent sending and processing of refresh messages consume a large amount of system resources. In a large network, there may be many LSP-Paths requiring periodic state maintenance. The operator must choose between shortening the refresh timer to speed up the convergence or reducing the control plane overhead by specifying a longer refresh timer, which leads to longer convergence time.

To solve this problem, the Hello extension is introduced to the RSVP-TE protocol to detect neighboring router failures. This is a new mechanism borrowed from routing protocols such as OSPF. The Hello extension introduces the concept of *RSVP adjacency*. Prior to the introduction of the RSVP Hello protocol, the RSVP adjacency concept did not exist. The routers were only aware of the status of the interfaces running the RSVP protocol (operationally **up** or **down**) and the state of the LSP-Path (or, more accurately, the state of the RSVP sessions). Therefore, there was no need to maintain a neighbor relationship. Providing that the interface running the RSVP protocol is operationally **up**, the RSVP is considered to be functioning. The failure of peer nodes running RSVP is detected by the timeout of each individual LSP (or RSVP session).

With the introduction of the Hello protocol, the RSVP behaves more like other Layer 2 or Layer 1 failure detection protocols such as Bidirectional Forwarding Detection (BFD). It detects neighbor failures by constantly sending HELLO messages with a REQUEST object and expecting the reception of an ACKNOWLEDGEMENT object. When several Hello requests are not answered correctly, the neighbor is declared operationally **down**, and all RSVP sessions related to that neighbor are cleared. Since there is only one Hello adjacency at a link between two RSVP-TE peering routers, a faster messaging rate on the Hello protocol does not exhaust the system resources like shortening the RSVP refresh timer does. In comparison, the RSVP refresh timer default value is 30 seconds, while the RSVP Hello timer default value is 3 seconds.

The RSVP Hello protocol is significantly different from the Hello mechanisms of other protocols such as OSPF or IS-IS. Although they have the same purpose (detecting failed neighbors), the RSVP-TE Hello protocol can be unidirectional. Because it is based on a Hello–Acknowledge scheme, one router can be configured to use the Hello protocol to detect the existence of its neighbor. However, its neighbors do not have to perform the same action. As long as a neighbor answers the `Hello-request` (with the correct `instance` value) in the Hello–Acknowledge message, the adjacency is maintained.

The RSVP-TE Hello extension is configured on a per-interface adjacency basis. When there is more than one IP routing interface between two directly connected routers, each link needs a separate Hello adjacency. Figure 5.27 illustrates a case of two routers with three IP interfaces connected to each other, with three RSVP Hello adjacencies.

Figure 5.27 RSVP-TE Hello Adjacency

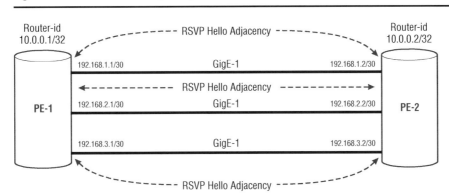

The RSVP HELLO Message

All RSVP packets are IP packets. The RSVP HELLO message is also an IP packet. The RSVP HELLO message has an IP time to live (TTL) value of 1, because it is used to communicate with Layer 3 directly-attached neighbors. The source IP address of the HELLO message is the egress IP interface's IP address of the sending router. The destination IP address is the ingress IP interface's IP address of the receiving router. Figure 5.28 illustrates the format of the RSVP `Hello Request` and `Hello Acknowledgement` objects.

The RSVP Hello protocol uses a 4-byte instance value to track the neighbor relationship. This instance value acts as a confirmation code of the RSVP adjacency status. Once the value is set, it will not change providing that the router's RSVP process is healthy. However, if the instance value changes, this means something has happened to the router (a system reload, or a protocol shutdown).

When a router generates a HELLO message, regardless if it is a request or an acknowledgement, it locally generates its own instance value and provides it to the

HELLO message. The destination instance value in both types of HELLO messages (REQUEST, ACK) are filled by the *source instance* value received in the HELLO message from the adjacent router running RSVP. If the router has not received a HELLO message before, 0x0 is used.

Figure 5.28 RSVP Hello REQUEST/ACK Object

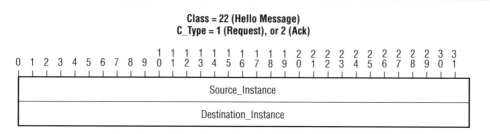

The Hello process starts when an interface of a router participating in the RSVP protocol with the Hello protocol enabled comes up, and at least one LSP-Path attempts a setup with a neighbor or a neighbor sends a Hello request. The router generates one instance value for each adjacency. The router encodes the instance value into the first HELLO message via the HELLO_REQUEST object. It sets the destination instance value to 0x0. The HELLO message is then sent to the adjacent RSVP neighbor. The neighbor router responds to the HELLO message with the HELLO_ACK object. In the HELLO_ACK object, the source instance is locally generated by the peering router and represents the adjacency from its neighbor router's perspective. The neighbor router uses the value of the source instance from the received HELLO_REQUEST object as the value of its HELLO_ACK object's destination instance. This is a *one-way* handshake process. If the neighbor router also has the Hello protocol configured in that interface, the same process is repeated in the other direction.

RFC 3209 states that the Hello protocol may be implemented unidirectionally with one side configured to run the Hello protocol while the far-end node does not. However, the adjacent router must be capable of supporting the Hello protocol. If an RSVP interface does not have Hello protocol capability, it will not respond to the HELLO_REQUEST with a HELLO_ACK. The two Hello adjacencies (from Router R1 to R2 and from Router R2 to R1) work *independently*. Each adjacency only cares about sending its own HELLO_REQUEST and receiving and verifying the HELLO_ACK from its peer.

The purpose of the RSVP Hello protocol is to detect the RSVP process failure of a directly connected RSVP-enabled neighbor router. The mechanism uses their instance values as matching criteria. Every router stores two instance values. The locally generated instance value is regenerated every time the RSVP process or RSVP interface restarts on a per-neighbor adjacency basis. The remote instance value is generated by the neighbor RSVP router and received via the HELLO_ACK messages. To keep the RSVP Hello adjacency, the node must constantly receive the HELLO_ACK from its neighbor before the Hello timer expires. In addition, the values of the two instances must match the locally stored instances. Conversely, when the neighbor router receives a HELLO_REQUEST, the destination instance value is matched in the same manner. If the messages are received constantly in a timely fashion with matched values, the RSVP adjacency is considered to be functioning well, and no further action is required. If the HELLO messages are not received before the Hello timer expires or the value match fails, the router considers that the RSVP adjacency is invalid and performs the following two actions:

- Clears all RSVP sessions on that RSVP interface. If the router is the HE router of the LSP-Path, it then resignals the LSP-Path. If the router is an LSR or eLER, the RSVP session is simply removed from the interface.

- Providing that the RSVP interface is physically up, the router sends a new HELLO message to its RSVP neighbor to form the relationship again. In the new HELLO message, the HELLO_REQUEST uses 0x0 as the value of the destination instance and a newly generated 4-byte value as the source instance.

What Is the Difference between the Hello and Keep-Alive Protocols?

Many routing or signaling protocols use *heartbeat* protocols to maintain a certain *state* of adjacency, or a *continuity* of a connection. In general, there are two types of heartbeats: Hello and Keep-Alive. They perform a similar function of detecting silent failures by constantly checking the peer's reachability. However, the Hello protocol in most cases is used to maintain a state over a *physical link* and usually uses broadcast packets to perform the check. This means that it is used to detect failure over immediately adjacent nodes. If there are multiple links, usually a per-Hello instance per link is required.

Alternatively, the Keep-Alive protocol is used primarily to reach a session between two routers, regardless of how many hops the two endpoints are apart. Keep-Alive messages are unicast packets with the remote peer's IP address being the packet's destination. A typical example of the use of Keep-Alive is the BGP session's Keep-Alive message. Between two routers, there is one Keep-Alive adjacency, regardless of how many links or routes connect them.

Figure 5.29 illustrates a CLI alarm log display of the RSVP interface with a Hello timeout event.

Figure 5.29   RSVP Neighbor helloTimedOut

```
A:PE-165# show log log-id 99 application RSVP
===============================================================================
Event Log 99
===============================================================================
Description : Default System Log
Memory Log contents  [size=500   next event=355  (not wrapped)]

338 2008/01/25 15:43:39.95 UTC WARNING: RSVP #2003 Base VR 1:
"Neighbor 10.164.165.1 on interface to-sim164 changed to active state"

325 2008/01/25 15:43:33.27 UTC WARNING: RSVP #2004 Base VR 1:
"Neighbor 10.164.165.1 on interface to-sim164 changed to inactive state because helloTimedOut"
A:PE-165#
```

5.6 Reducing RSVP Refresh Overhead

As mentioned previously, RSVP is a soft-state protocol that requires constant PATH and RESV refreshes on every single LSP-Path. This may cause scalability issues when there are many RSVP sessions in a router. The router must handle thousands or more PATH and RESV messages, especially during a network failure or reoptimization. Too many incoming messages may cause a system message queue overflow. Delay or loss of messages may cause the LSP-Path to go **down** operationally and interrupt the traffic. In other cases, the loss of PathTear or ResvTear messages may cause the router to hold resources for unused sessions for a relatively long time before other legitimate LSP-Paths can reuse them. The routers' CPU and memory resources may also be exhausted because of the processing of large numbers of messages and generating responses from them. Hence, more efficient state-refresh message generation and delivery mechanisms are desired. This is also recommended in RFC 2961, "RSVP Refresh Overhead Reduction Extensions."

RFC 2961 describes some RSVP-TE extensions that reduce the RSVP messaging overhead while maintaining the states of all LSP-Paths and the ability to quickly detect message loss or network failures. Table 5.4 summarizes these extensions, which are introduced later in this section.

Will Tuning the RSVP Refresh Timers Help Reduce the Signaling Overhead?

Yes and no. There are always pros and cons regarding the tuning of system timers. In most cases, the default values of the timers are the most efficient ones. The refresh-time timer basically controls how often refresh messages are sent from the system. The keep-multiplier timer decides the number of refresh messages that can be missed for a session before the session is cleared. To reduce the messages used to maintain session states, both timers can be increased. Therefore, less message packet processing is required in the control plane. However, the drawback is a slower reaction to network failure and longer convergence time. Also, the resources may be seized by the failed sessions for longer because of the long timeout process. To speed up the convergence against failure, the refresh-interval timer and the message loss counter should be decreased. However, this will generate more state-refresh messages. Operators must balance both performance and resources for these scenarios.

Table 5.4 RSVP-TE Extensions for Refresh Overhead Reduction

Extension	Description
RSVP message bundling	A new BUNDLE message that can contain one or more sub-BUNDLE messages is introduced to reduce the number of messages the router must send, receive, and process.
Reliable message delivery	Three new objects are defined to allow more efficient processing of unchanged refresh messages, MESSAGE_ID, MESSAGE_ID_ACK, and MESSAGE_ID_NACK. The reliable message delivery mechanism is done on a per-hop basis.
Summary-refresh	A new Summary-refresh message is introduced to allow partial transmission of the refresh message by encapsulating a list of message identifiers with the same values as the ones in the MESSAGE_ID object of the refresh messages.
Refresh-Reduction-Capable bit	In the common RSVP header, a flag indicating the capability of Refresh-Reduction is defined. Both peers must agree on the capability before the Refresh-Reduction feature can be used.

All the mechanisms described in Table 5.4 are intended to reduce the signaling transmission and processing overhead. However, they cannot reduce the number of PATH and RESV state blocks each router must maintain. The number of PATH and RESV state blocks a router must maintain depends solely on the number of RSVP sessions on that router.

BUNDLE Messages

The RSVP-TE BUNDLE message is a new type of RSVP message. It is used by the RSVP router to aggregate messages to the same neighbor into a single RSVP message, rather than sending messages individually. It uses the same RSVP common header with message Type 12 (binary 00001100 in the message type byte). A BUNDLE message contains one or more sub-BUNDLE message(s), which can be any RSVP message type except Type 12 (BUNDLE message). At the time of writing, ALSRP service router's RSVP-TE implementation only supports receiving the BUNDLE messages, but not BUNDLE message generation. Figure 5.30 presents the format of an RSVP BUNDLE message.

Figure 5.30 RSVP BUNDLE Message

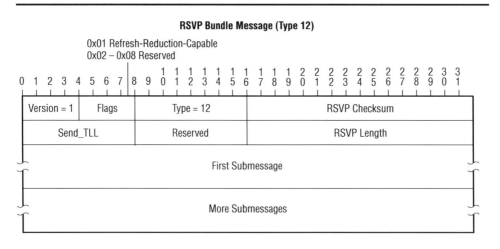

Similar to other RSVP messages (such as PATH or RESV), the BUNDLE message is an IP data packet with protocol number 46. The source IP address of the message should be a local IP of the originating router (system loopback or interfaces IP). The destination IP address should be the IP address of the receiving RSVP router. In the

BUNDLE message, the RA-bit is not set because the BUNDLE message is sent only between directly adjacent routers. Any message that is handled by the same RSVP neighbor can be aggregated to the same BUNDLE message. BUNDLE messages should only be sent to neighbor routers whose Refresh-Reduction-Capable bits are set.

When an RSVP router receives a BUNDLE message destined to itself, it simply de-encapsulates the message and handles the submessages individually as if they were received separately from the sender. The BUNDLE message offers a more efficient transmission mechanism.

Reliable Message Delivery

Originally, the RSVP message delivery mechanism did not contain procedures to ensure that the messages were delivered successfully. Upon LSP-Path creation or modification, the RSVP router simply sent initial PATH/RESV messages (also referred to as *trigger messages*). The router then sent sequential PATH/RESV messages (also referred to as *refresh messages*) at every refresh-interval.

Currently, the reliable message delivery extension has an additional scheme of acknowledging the messages with either an ACK message or an RSVP message using the MESSAGE_ID_ACK object. When both sides of the RSVP peers support message reliable delivery, the MESSAGE_ID object is added to *all* RSVP messages sent between the peers. The only exception to this is the BUNDLE message, in which the MESSAGE_ID only exists in the submessages, the ACK messages, and the HELLO messages. Figure 5.31 illustrates the format of the MESSAGE_ID object.

Figure 5.31 MESSAGE_ID Object

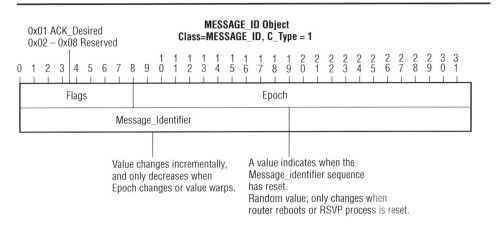

Figure 5.32 illustrates a PATH message packet capture with MESSAGE_ID present.

Figure 5.32   PATH message with MESSAGE_ID Object

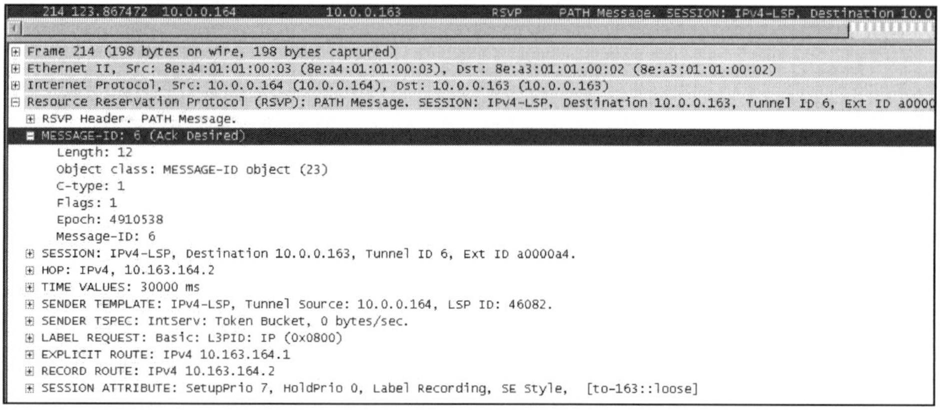

```
   214 123.867472  10.0.0.164              10.0.0.163          RSVP     PATH Message. SESSION: IPv4-LSP, Destination 10.0

⊞ Frame 214 (198 bytes on wire, 198 bytes captured)
⊞ Ethernet II, Src: 8e:a4:01:01:00:03 (8e:a4:01:01:00:03), Dst: 8e:a3:01:01:00:02 (8e:a3:01:01:00:02)
⊞ Internet Protocol, Src: 10.0.0.164 (10.0.0.164), Dst: 10.0.0.163 (10.0.0.163)
⊟ Resource Reservation Protocol (RSVP): PATH Message. SESSION: IPv4-LSP, Destination 10.0.0.163, Tunnel ID 6, Ext ID a0000
   ⊞ RSVP Header. PATH Message.
   ■ MESSAGE-ID: 6 (Ack Desired)
       Length: 12
       Object class: MESSAGE-ID object (23)
       C-type: 1
       Flags: 1
       Epoch: 4910538
       Message-ID: 6
   ⊞ SESSION: IPv4-LSP, Destination 10.0.0.163, Tunnel ID 6, Ext ID a0000a4.
   ⊞ HOP: IPv4, 10.163.164.2
   ⊞ TIME VALUES: 30000 ms
   ⊞ SENDER TEMPLATE: IPv4-LSP, Tunnel Source: 10.0.0.164, LSP ID: 46082.
   ⊞ SENDER TSPEC: IntServ: Token Bucket, 0 bytes/sec.
   ⊞ LABEL REQUEST: Basic: L3PID: IP (0x0800)
   ⊞ EXPLICIT ROUTE: IPv4 10.163.164.1
   ⊞ RECORD ROUTE: IPv4 10.163.164.2
   ⊞ SESSION ATTRIBUTE: SetupPrio 7, HoldPrio 0, Label Recording, SE Style,  [to-163::loose]
```

There are two main benefits for adding the MESSAGE_ID object into the RSVP messages:

1. The router can set the ACK_Desired flag in the MESSAGE_ID object to require an acknowledgement from the receiving router. This allows the router to confirm that the message is delivered successfully. Upon receiving the RSVP message with a MESSAGE_ID object containing the ACK_Desired flag, the receiver responds by either adding a MESSAGE_ID_ACK object piggybacked on any message that is sent toward the neighbor that requested the ACK, or by sending an ACK message. This mechanism of verifying the successful transmission of RSVP messages provides a more reliable signaling process.

   If the message with the MESSAGE_ID_ACK object or the ACK message is not received, the sending router resends the unacknowledged message within a certain time frame for a certain number of times (depending on the configuration of rapid-retransmit-timer and rapid-retry-limit). These two parameters are configured on a per-RSVP router basis, as shown in Figure 5.33.

2. The value of the message_identifier field in the MESSAGE_ID object is used by the ACK message and/or the Summary-refresh message as a key to validate the state of the LSP-Path. The value of the message_identifier field in the MESSAGE_ID object, along with the source IP address of the RSVP message, uniquely defines an LSP state. Note that Summary-refresh messages are explained in detail later in this chapter.

Figure 5.33 Configurable RSVP Timers for Reliable Message Delivery

```
A:PE-164# configure router rsvp
  - no rsvp
  - rsvp

[no] interface      + Configure RSVP on an IP interface
[no] keep-multiplier - Keep-multiplier used to declare a reservation or neighbor as down
[no] msg-pacing     + Enable/disable RSVP message pacing
[no] rapid-retransm* - Configure rapid retransmission interval for reliable delivery of RSVP messages
[no] rapid-retry-li* - Configure rapid retry limit for reliable delivery of RSVP messages
[no] refresh-time    - Interval between successive Path refresh Resv refresh and Srefresh messages
[no] shutdown        - Administratively enable/disable the RSVP instance
```

Trigger Message versus Refresh Message

In many RSVP messaging documents, the term *trigger message* is used frequently. *Trigger message* refers to the first PATH message that a router sends to establish an LSP-Path, and the first RESV message received by the router to confirm the reservation. These messages trigger the building of RSVP sessions and their related state blocks. Also, *trigger message* is used in another context; it is a message sent to update any change in the session parameter, such as protection availability. Such changes cause a trigger message for the LSP-Path being changed, and the router sends an actual PATH/RESV with new message IDs so that the neighbor router can update its session parameters accordingly.

The sequential PATH and RESV messages for the same LSP-Path are only used to keep the Path and RESV states refreshed; hence, they are called *refresh messages*. Summary-refresh messages are only used to suppress the refresh messages; trigger messages can never be suppressed.

The acknowledgment in the MESSAGE_ID object depends on the system implementation. In most cases, trigger messages should require an acknowledgement, and the refresh messages may or may not require acknowledgement.

Reliable Message Delivery versus Message Pacing

RSVP Message Pacing is a rate-limiting function that controls the burst of RSVP messages. The Reliable Message Delivery and Message Pacing features cannot coexist. When Reliable Message Delivery is enabled in any of the RSVP interfaces, Message Pacing cannot be enabled under the RSVP router configuration, and vice versa. Figure 5.34 illustrates the configuration example of Message Pacing.

Figure 5.34 Configuring RSVP Message Pacing

```
A:R1>config>router>rsvp# info
-----------------------------------------------
            msg-pacing
                period 1000
                max-burst 1000
            exit
            interface "system"
            exit
            interface "to-117"
            exit
            interface "to-116"
            exit
            no shutdown
-----------------------------------------------
```

The `max-burst` parameter defines the number of messages allowed to be sent out per interval. The `period` parameter defines that interval in milliseconds. This sample configuration sets the RSVP message rate at 1,000 messages per second. If the router generates more than 1,000 RSVP messages per second, the message flow is policed to 1,000 messages per second.

Summary-Refresh Message

The biggest contributor to the RSVP signaling message traffic load is the use of PATH and RESV messages to refresh the established LSPs. This may be a problem for a router with a large number of originating, transiting, or terminating LSPs. A Summary-refresh extension eliminates these refresh messages while refreshing all LSPs using the new, more efficient Summary-refresh messages. The Summary-refresh message uses only the `message_identifier` value received from the RSVP messages with the `MESSAGE_ID` object. This significantly reduces the signaling cost compared to the traditional method of using the same PATH/RESV messages for the LSP establishment to refresh the LSP. The `message_identifier` is only 4 bytes, compared to the PATH message, which is usually a few hundred bytes for each LSP-Path. Figure 5.35 illustrates a Summary-refresh message.

A Summary-refresh message contains one or more `MESSAGE_ID_LIST` objects. The `MESSAGE_ID_LIST` contains a `message_identifier` received from the peering router's `MESSAGE_ID` object. One `MESSAGE_ID_LIST` can contain many `message_identifier` values and can refresh many LSP states at the same time.

Upon receiving the Summary-refresh message, the router will refresh all states with matching ID values. The IDs are matched based on the source IP address of the message, the object type, and the `message_identifier` value. If there is no matching value in the LSP database, the receiver sends the RSVP messages back to the sender with `MESSAGE_ID_NACK` to indicate that no matching entries were found in the state database. When the Summary-refresh message sender receives the `MESSAGE_IN_NACK` object from the receiver, it performs a local check of the state database against the listed `message_identifier` values. If there are any matching entries, a regular PATH and/or RESV refresh message with the corresponding message ID value is sent to refresh the state again.

Figure 5.35 Summary-Refresh Message

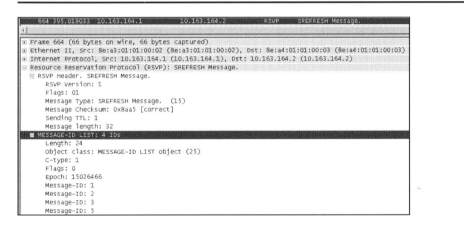

Summary-refresh relies on the `message_identifier` value to refresh the LSP-Paths' states. It requires that the router is capable of sending RSVP messages containing the `MESSAGE_ID` object. Only LSP-Paths with PATH messages containing `MESSAGE_ID` objects can be refreshed by the Summary-refresh message. If the peering router is not Refresh-Reduction-Capable, the Summary-refresh feature cannot be used. To ensure that Summary-refresh does not cause any LSP time-out, the Summary-refresh interval should not be longer than the RSVP refresh interval. By default, the router always uses the refresh interval time to send out Summary-refresh messages, similar to using PATH and RESV to refresh the path. When a router sends Summary-refresh messages to refresh LSP-Paths, the corresponding refreshing PATH and RESV messages are suppressed.

Refresh-Reduction Capability Negotiation

The three functions BUNDLE Message, Reliable Message Delivery, and Summary-refresh Message are referred to together as *RSVP refresh overhead reduction extensions*. The RSVP refresh overhead reduction extension features are configured on a *per-RSVP interface basis* and require the agreement of both peers to support it. When one RSVP interface of a router has the refresh-reduction enabled, it sets the `Refresh-Reduction-Capable` flag bit in the common RSVP header for all the RSVP messages it sends out. When the router receives the RSVP messages with the same flag set, it recognizes that its peering relationship with the neighbor supports Refresh-reduction and the router starts sending Summary-refresh messages. When the flag is cleared from the receiving RSVP messages originating from the peering router, the router stops sending Summary-refresh messages. Figure 5.36 illustrates the flags for the RSVP adjacency. The flags show the negotiated RSVP capabilities.

Figure 5.36   RSVP Adjacency with Capability Flags

```
A:PE-164# show router rsvp neighbor
===============================================================================
RSVP Neighbors
===============================================================================
Legend :
    LR - Local Refresh Reduction       RR - Remote Refresh Reduction
    LD - Local Reliable Delivery       RM - Remote Node supports Message ID
===============================================================================
Neighbor        Interface             Hello  Last Oper      Flags
                                      Change
===============================================================================
10.163.164.1    to-PE163              Up   1d 06:55:37      LR LD RR  RM
-------------------------------------------------------------------------------
Neighbors : 1
===============================================================================
A:PE-164#
```

When `Reliable-delivery` is enabled inside the refresh-reduction configuration, the router starts sending RSVP messages with a `MESSAGE_ID` object. If the remote PE router does not support such a feature or has the feature disabled, the `MESSAGE_ID` is ignored. Then the local router stops adding `MESSAGE_ID` into the outgoing RSVP messages. Figure 5.37 illustrates the RSVP Refresh-reduction capability negotiation result.

Figure 5.37 shows a peering relationship between two RSVP routers, PE-163 and PE-164. These routers have agreed to support refresh-reduction, and they both have Reliable Message Delivery enabled locally.

Figure 5.38 illustrates the RSVP signaling sequence between the two routers with Refresh-reduction enabled and also shows the `MESSAGE_ID` object in the PATH message.

Figure 5.37 RSVP Refresh-Reduction Capability

```
A:PE-164# show router rsvp interface to-PE163 detail
===============================================================================
RSVP Interface
(Detailed) : to-PE163
===============================================================================
-------------------------------------------------------------------------------
Interface : to-sim163
-------------------------------------------------------------------------------
Interface      : to-PE163          Port ID         : 1/1/3
Admin State    : Up                Oper State      : Up
Active Sessions: 1                 Active Resvs    : 0
Total Sessions : 1
Subscription   : 100 %             Port Speed      : 100 Mbps
Unreserved BW  : 100 Mbps          Reserved BW     : 0 Mbps
Total BW       : 100 Mbps          Aggregate       : Dsabl
Hello Interval : 3000 ms           Hello Timeouts  : 0
Authentication : Disabled
Auth Rx Seq Num: n/a               Auth Key Id     : n/a
Auth Tx Seq Num: n/a               Auth Win Size   : n/a
Refresh Reduc. : Enabled           Reliable Deli.  : Enabled
Bfd Enabled    : No
Neighbors      : 10.163.164.1
===============================================================================
A:PE-164#
```

Figure 5.38 RSVP Message Monitoring after Refresh-Reduction Is Enabled

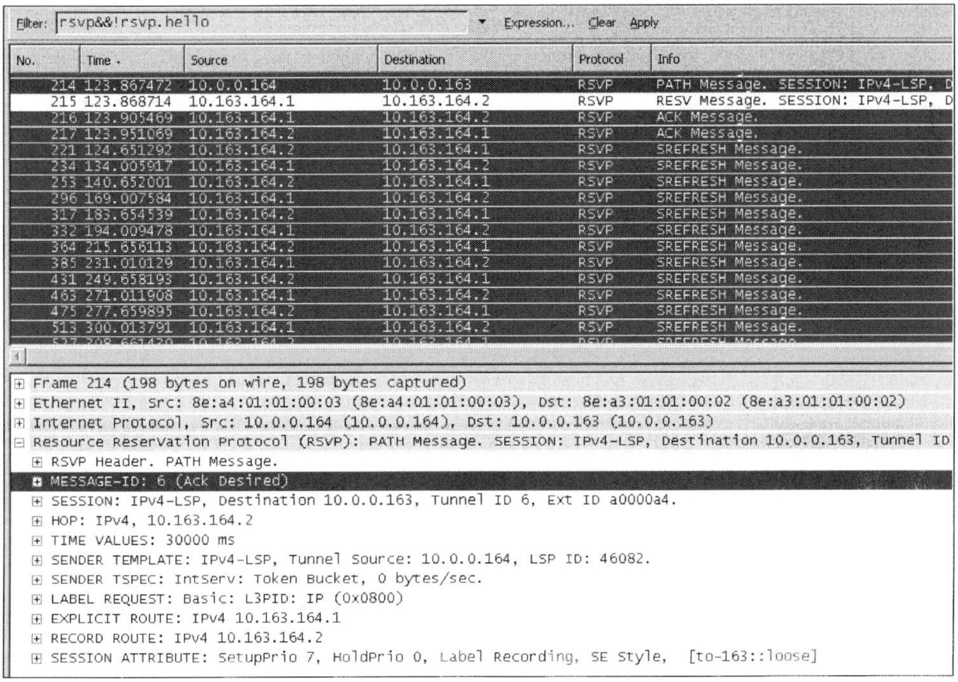

After the first PATH and RESV messages establish to PE-163's primary LSP-Path, these messages are acknowledged by the two ACK messages. At that point, there are no future PATH and RESV messages to refresh to PE-163's LSP-Path. All the refresh messages are replaced by the Summary-refresh message sent periodically (every refresh interval) by the two routers. Figure 5.38 illustrates that after the Summary-refresh is enabled, the PATH and RESV messages to refresh the LSPs are replaced by the Summary-refresh (SREFRESH) messages.

5.7 RSVP MD5 Authentication

As mentioned previously, without the RSVP-TE Hello protocol, the concept of RSVP-TE adjacency does not exist. Enabling RSVP-TE in a router interface enables the interface to use RSVP-TE messages to signal LSPs. RSVP security may be desired, with or without the RSVP-TE Hello protocol. In RSVP-TE, the signaling security can be enabled on a per-interface basis and uses message digest 5 (MD5) encrypted passwords. When RSVP security is enabled in an interface, all RSVP messages generated from that interface (for example, Hello packets and LSP signaling messages) include one INTEGRITY object. The RSVP-TE interface with security enabled also validates the received RSVP messages by expecting the INTEGRITY object and comparing its hashed password. RFC 2747, "RSVP Cryptographic Authentication," defines the standard for RSVP security. Figure 5.39 illustrates an RSVP message captured with an INTEGRITY object.

Figure 5.39   RSVP INTEGRITY Object

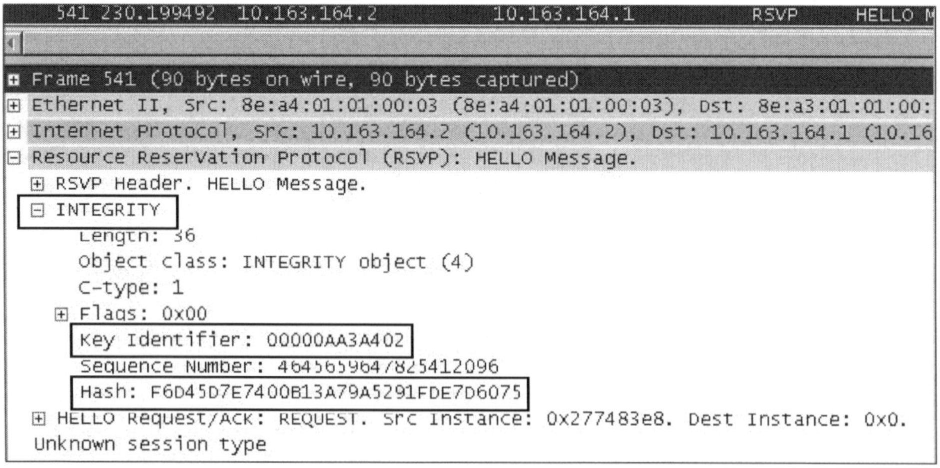

Figure 5.40 illustrates a configuration example of enabling MD5 authentication in the RSVP interface. It also shows the RSVP interface status including the details regarding the authentication.

Figure 5.40 RSVP MD5 Authentication Configuration Example

```
A:PE2# configure router rsvp
A:PE2>config>router>rsvp# info
-------------------------------------------------------------------------
            interface "system"
            exit
            interface "to-163"
              authentication-key "xWa.PPxuqA2ROtFODberXmcyeP5YTMRV" hash2
            exit
            interface "to-117"
            exit
            interface "to-165"
            exit
            no shutdown
-------------------------------------------------------------------------
```

```
A:PE2# show router rsvp interface to-163 detail
===============================================================================
RSVP Interface (Detailed) : to-163
===============================================================================
-------------------------------------------------------------------------------
Interface : to-163
-------------------------------------------------------------------------------
Interface       : to-163            Port ID        : 1/1/3
Admin State     : Up                Oper State     : Up
Active Sessions: 0                  Active Resvs   : 0
Total Sessions : 1
Subscription    : 100 %             Port Speed     : 100 Mbps
Unreserved BW   : 100 Mbps          Reserved BW    : 0 Mbps
Total BW        : 100 Mbps          Aggregate      : Dsabl
Hello Interval  : 3000 ms           Hello Timeouts : 0
Authentication : Enabled
Auth Rx Seq Num: 0x0000000000000000 Auth Key Id    : 178496514
Auth Tx Seq Num: 0x4078bd6e00000000 Auth Win Size  : 16
Refresh Reduc. : Disabled           Reliable Deli. : Disabled
Bfd Enabled     : No
Neighbors       : 10.163.164.1
===============================================================================
```

Enabling or disabling RSVP MD5 authentication security on an RSVP-TE interface may cause service outage if both sides of a link are not configured with the same mode (enable authentication or disable authentication) or the same password. An RSVP-TE authentication configuration mismatch may cause LSP-Paths to time out because the refreshing PATH and/or RESV messages cannot be authenticated, or the RSVP-TE Hello protocol has timed out.

Summary

The RSVP-TE protocol is the extension of the RSVP protocol and is used to signal explicitly routed MPLS LSPs. As an LSP signaling protocol, RSVP-TE provides an explicit definition of the path of the LSP and the resources reservation. RSVP-TE's predetermined path and end-to-end view of the LSP provides rich resiliency features such as MBB, FRR, and secondary LSP. Use of an RSVP-TE-signaled LSP as a service transport tunnel can significantly reduce the failover outage time.

RSVP-TE uses PATH messages to request labels and resource reservations, and uses RESV messages to distribute labels and reserve resources. The label distribution in RSVP-TE uses Downstream on Demand mode with Ordered Control. When establishing an RSVP-TE LSP-Path, each router along the LSP-Path's path builds the RSVP session with label mapping and state blocks. Each RSVP-TE LSP is a series of RSVP sessions on the RSVP routers along each hop. RSVP sessions must be constantly refreshed by the PATH or RESV messages.

The RSVP-TE-signaled LSP-Path supports the MBB path parameter modification. When modifying an established LSP-Path, the original LSP-Path is not torn down until the LSP-Path with new parameters is established and traffic is switched to the new LSP-Path. If the new LSP-Path set-up effort fails, the original LSP-Path remains unchanged. Therefore, the LSP-Path modification does not cause any traffic loss.

To improve failure detection and resource efficiency, the RSVP-TE Hello protocol is introduced to monitor the health of the RSVP interface. The RSVP-TE Hello protocol uses Hello packets to constantly check the RSVP adjacency over the RSVP interface. If the Hello protocol times out in an RSVP interface, all RSVP sessions residing on that interface are cleared, and the corresponding LSP is rerouted or torn down. With the RSVP-TE Hello protocol, the RSVP sessions can have longer refresh intervals and rely on the Hello protocol to detect RSVP adjacency failures.

In a network with many RSVP-TE-signaled LSPs, it is challenging to refresh every single RSVP session with regular PATH or RESV messages. To reduce the RSVP session refresh overhead, several techniques are involved:

- RSVP message bundling
- RSVP message reliable delivery
- RSVP Summary-refresh

The capability of the RSVP refresh overhead reduction is negotiated between each RSVP peering interface and is used only if both sides support the feature.

RSVP supports MD5 authentication. When RSVP authentication is enabled in an RSVP interface, the interface adds INTEGRITY objects into all RSVP messages it sends out. The interface also expects all incoming RSVP messages to have the same objects and rejects the messages without these objects.

MPLS Resiliency — Secondary LSP

6

RSVP-TE signaled LSP supports having multiple LSP-Paths within one LSP to improve tunnel robustness. The LSP-Paths used to protect the LSP are referred to as secondary LSPs. Secondary LSPs can rapidly protect the traffic when there is a failure along the path of the primary LSP.

Chapter Objectives

- An introduction to MPLS LSP resiliency

- An overview of the secondary LSP-Path within an LSP

- Identify the factors affecting convergence performance during network failures

- Understand the active forwarding path selection when there are multiple secondary LSPs available for the same LSP

Multi Protocol Label Switching (MPLS) technology provides a network with traffic engineering tunnel capability and the flexibility to carry any type of service traffic. In addition, it provides resiliency features that protect the tunnels against network failures. There are two types of protection for RSVP-TE signaled Label Switched Paths (LSPs): secondary LSPs and Fast Reroute (FRR). This chapter describes the use of secondary LSP-Paths to protect an LSP. FRR is introduced in Chapter 7.

6.1 Ensuring Reliability with MPLS Resiliency

One of the biggest advantages of using MPLS as the service transportation technology is its superior resiliency performance. Network reliability is a major concern to any network operator. Possible network failures include physical link failures, power failures for any network element, and software or hardware failures in the network equipment. One of the key concerns when selecting the correct networking technology is the reaction time to network failures and the quick restoration of services by rerouting the traffic around the network failure point. Quick detection of network failures and short convergence times are crucial to upholding Service Level Agreements (SLAs) to a service provider's customers.

Traditionally, failure detection and convergence time have been weak points in *packet switched networks* (PSNs). The Layer 2 Ethernet network relies on the Spanning Tree Protocol (STP) to maintain a loop-free forwarding environment and detect network failures. The reaction time of this switched Ethernet network is typically from several seconds to several minutes, depending on the specific STP flavor. The traditional Layer 3 IP network relies on dynamic routing protocols to optimize traffic forwarding paths. Routing protocols also handle the detection of network failures and propagate the failure information through the entire network. The service convergence time in a routed IP network is usually in seconds when link state routing protocols such as OSPF or IS-IS are used.

The packet switched network's convergence time of several seconds cannot compete with the convergence time in a circuit switched network (CSN), such as SONET or TDM. The Automatic Protection System (APS) feature in the SONET network can provide tens of milliseconds convergence time against link failure, but at a much higher cost. Because APS requires two links working in a primary/backup manner, which means that the number of links in the network could double if APS is deployed end-to-end.

PSNs are now able to provide similar convergence performance with the introduction of MPLS to the Ethernet/IP network. With the support of RSVP-TE and the Constraint Shortest Path First (CSPF) algorithm, MPLS LSPs with secondary LSP or FRR can now also provide subsecond convergence performance; the traffic loss is now minimal during a failure. MPLS resiliency delivers a failover performance similar to that of APS, without requiring physical layer redundancy of all network links. In an IP/MPLS VPN network, physical redundancies are deployed only in a few carefully chosen locations. Many carriers have decided to convert their core network from a plain Ethernet/IP to an IP/MPLS VPN service network. This chapter provides a detailed description of one MPLS resilience mechanism — the *secondary LSP*.

6.2 An Overview of Primary and Secondary LSPs

To protect the LSP against network failures, the operator can allow the LSP to have backup LSP-Paths. Each RSVP-TE LSP can have up to eight LSP-Paths. One of them is the *primary* LSP-Path; the rest are *secondary* LSP-Paths used to protect the primary LSP-Path. If the primary LSP-Path has a failed network resource along the path, the available secondary LSP-Path(s) can forward traffic for the LSP.

As mentioned in Chapter 3, the RSVP-TE signals explicitly routed LSPs. The Head-End (HE) router decides which nodes the LSP should traverse to reach its destination. One of the benefits of RSVP-TE LSP is that the operator can manipulate the LSP-Path's route calculation by describing a path for an LSP, which is represented by listed loose or strict hops.

The Head-End router makes this decision by calculating the path of the LSP-Path through consultation with the Interior Gateway Protocol (IGP) database, or by using CSPF with the Traffic Engineering Database (TED), while considering the requirements provided by the path configuration. The calculation result is used to set the value of the explicit routing object (ERO) of the PATH message used by the router to signal the LSP-Path. In an ordinary RSVP-TE LSP-Path, there is only one path decided by the router's calculation. If there is a network element failure along that path, the LSP-Path goes **down** operationally. The Head-End router must recalculate the new path and then resignal the LSP-Path. The LSP will become operationally **up** again if the resignal is successful.

The LSP and Secondary LSP-Paths

As mentioned in Chapter 3, the RSVP-TE LSP provides the HE router with an end-to-end view of the LSP. The LSP is identified by the **tunnel-id** and **extended-tunnel-id** in the **SESSION** object of the RSVP-TE messages. One LSP can contain one or more LSP-Paths. The LSP-Path is the actual entity being signaled by RSVP-TE that forms the MPLS end-to-end connection. When you configure an LSP, you actually define an RSVP-TE LSP (also referred to as an *LSP-Tunnel*). When you configure the path (**primary** or **secondary**) inside the LSP (not the **path** definition for hops in MPLS configuration), you define one LSP-Path that belongs to the LSP. Figure 6.1 illustrates an LSP with a primary LSP-Path and a hot-standby secondary LSP-Path.

Figure 6.1 Primary LSP and Secondary LSP

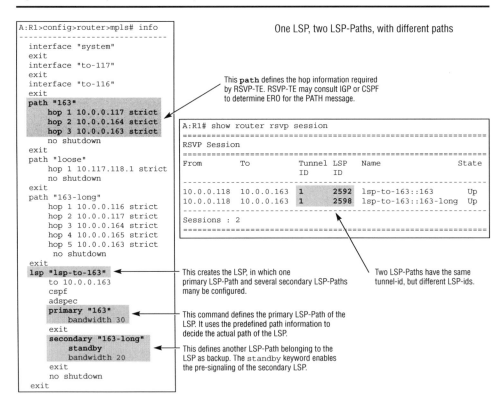

In summary, one RSVP-TE LSP can have more than one LSP-Path, although only one LSP-Path is used to forward traffic for the LSP at any time. (The LSP-Path that forwards traffic for the LSP is referred to as the *active path* of the LSP.) Hence, the RSVP-TE LSP can have *LSP redundancy*. The redundant LSP-Paths belong to the same LSP as the secondary LSP-Paths.

Secondary LSPs

When there is no network failure, the LSP uses the primary LSP-Path to forward traffic. When there is a network failure in a primary LSP-Path that is protected by secondary LSP-Paths, the system uses one of the secondary LSP-Paths to forward traffic. When the network failure is resolved, the router reverts the traffic from the active secondary LSP-Path back to the primary LSP-Path. Figure 6.2 shows an example of one primary LSP with two secondary *hot-standby* ("always ready") LSP-Paths. The LSP from Router P1 to Router P6 has three options to reach its destination:

- **The primary LSP-Path** — P1 → P3 → P4 → P6
- **The first secondary LSP-Path** — P1 → P2 → P5 → P6
- **The second secondary LSP-Path** — P1 → P3 → P4 → P5 → P6

Figure 6.2   Primary LSP with Multiple Hot-Standby Secondary LSPs

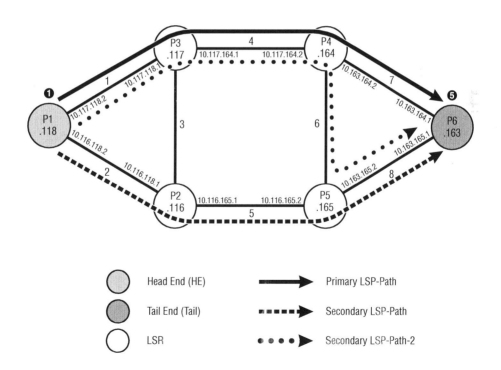

When the LSP is administratively enabled, the router always initially tries to establish the primary LSP-Path and all standby secondary LSP-Paths simultaneously. If the primary LSP-Path cannot be established before the LSP-Path signaling timer expires, the router tries to establish the non-standby secondary LSP-Path. At the same time, the router continues to try to establish the primary LSP-Path. Under these circumstances, the first available secondary LSP-Path is chosen to carry the traffic for the LSP. Providing that there is one LSP-Path operationally up, the LSP is operationally up. In this case, the LSP tries to establish the primary LSP-Path whenever the retry timer expires (by default, the timer is set to 30 seconds). The LSP-Path signaling retry effort can be limited by the `retry-timer` and `retry-limits` on a per LSP basis. When the primary LSP-Path is established, the LSP switches back to using the primary LSP-Path as the active LSP-Path to carry the traffic. The rules for choosing an LSP-Path as the active path and the switchover to secondary LSP-Paths are introduced later in this chapter.

> **Note:** When a router needs to switch traffic from the primary LSP-Path to the secondary LSP-Path (or vice versa) or to switch traffic from one secondary LSP-Path to another secondary LSP-Path, the action is not performed in a make-before-break (MBB) manner. MBB is only used when the router wants to signal an LSP-Path to replace an existing LSP-Path. MBB is discussed in Chapter 5.

Standby Secondary LSPs

When more than one LSP-Path is configured in the same RSVP-TE LSP, the primary LSP-Path is always signaled as soon as the LSP is administratively enabled. The secondary LSP-Path may or may not be signaled immediately after the LSP is enabled, depending on the configuration. Two options can be specified by the operator:

- **Standby** — When the standby option is explicitly enabled on a secondary LSP-Path, the secondary LSP-Path is signaled as soon as the LSP is administratively enabled. With this option, the secondary LSP-Path is pre-established and ready to provide hot-standby backup for the primary LSP-Path.

- **Non-Standby** — When the standby option is not specified on a secondary LSP (the default configuration), the system does not establish the secondary LSP-

Path as long as the primary LSP-Path is operationally **up**. This is a *cold-standby* mode. With this option, the system establishes the secondary LSP-Paths to provide protection only after the primary LSP-Path goes **down**.

Hot-standby using the secondary LSP-Path is pre-established before the failure on the primary LSP-Path. The hot-standby secondary LSP is always ready to carry the traffic for the LSP. When the primary LSP-Path fails, the HE router of the LSP can immediately switch the traffic to the secondary LSP; therefore the failover is very quick. The system needs only to switch traffic to the secondary LSP-Path because the secondary LSP-Path was already established before the failure occurred. In contrast, the cold-standby secondary LSP-Path is signaled *after* the primary LSP-Path fails. When the primary LSP-Path fails, the HE router must establish the secondary LSP-Path before it can switch the traffic to the secondary LSP-Path. Therefore, it takes longer for the non-standby secondary LSP-Path to take over the traffic. Note that the LSP with a hot-standby secondary LSP-Path reserves more resources because it always has more than one LSP-Path established in the network for the same LSP.

The concept of secondary LSP-Path and primary LSP-Path is only meaningful in the Head-End router of the LSP. When one LSP is configured with multiple LSP-Paths (one primary and several secondary), only the HE router can decide which LSP-Path will forward the traffic. Other routers are aware of the relationship among these multiple LSP-Paths because they all share the same tunnel-id and extended tunnel-id. However, the primary LSP-Path and the secondary LSP-Paths are separate LSP-Paths. The fact that all these LSP-Paths have the same tunnel-id is irrelevant in non-HE routers. Non-HE routers simply treat every LSP-Path independently and individually.

Characteristics of Secondary LSPs

The secondary LSP-Path is defined within the LSP configuration context by associating a pre-created path as a secondary LSP-Path. It shares the same tunnel-id as the primary LSP-Path belonging to the same LSP. Because the secondary and primary LSP-Paths belong to the same LSP, they all inherit the LSP-related configurations. Meanwhile, because the secondary and primary LSP-Paths are individual LSP-Paths, they each have their own LSP-Path-related characteristics. Table 6.1 shows the LSP and LSP-Path's configuration parameters. If the same parameter is configured under both the LSP level and the LSP-Path level, the LSP-Path level configuration overrides the LSP level configuration because the LSP-Path level configuration is more specific.

Table 6.1 LSP and LSP-Path Configuration Parameters

	Parameters	LSP Level	LSP-Path Level	
			Primary LSP	Secondary LSP
Tunnel-related	ADSPEC object	Yes	Yes	Yes
	CSPF or IGP	Yes	No	No
	FRR	Yes	Yes	No
	Metric	Yes	No	No
	Retry limit & timer	Yes	No	No
	Reservation style	Yes	No	No
Path-related	Make-before-break	Yes	Yes	Yes
	Hop-limit	Yes	Yes	Yes
	Bandwidth	Yes	Yes	Yes
	Admin Group	Yes	Yes	Yes
	Standby	No	n/a	Yes
	Record route	Yes	Yes	Yes
	Record label	Yes	Yes	Yes
	SRLG	Yes	Yes	Yes

In Table 6.1, the secondary LSP-Path can have its LSP-Path-level parameters set differently than those of the primary LSP-Path. There are a few parameters that are only meaningful for a certain path type:

- FRR is only available for primary LSP-Paths.
- Standby is only used when defining secondary LSP-Paths.

Other than the FRR and Standby parameters, each secondary LSP can be configured individually the same way as a primary LSP. For example, the operator can define different administration groups for each LSP-Path (primary and secondary) in the same LSP. This forces the LSP-Paths to traverse different paths in the network. Therefore, a network failure will only affect a subset of LSP-Paths in the same LSP — the topology protection is maximized.

When configuring FRR bypass tunnel/detour LSPs, the only configurable parameters are bandwidth and hop-limit. However, the secondary LSP has a greater number of configurable parameters, which allows the service provider to fine-tune resiliency deployment (protection). The service provider may prefer to use secondary LSP protection in the following scenarios:

- Protection must meet a specific criterion (such as traverse or avoid admin groups or SRLG groups).

- Several different alternative protections (more than one protection)
- More control is desired for the protection (control the exact path of a protection LSP-Path).

Secondary LSP-Paths can be used together with FRR (on a primary LSP-Path only) to provide more protection for the same LSP. The behavior during the failure of an LSP with both types of protection is discussed in Chapter 7.

6.3 What Affects Convergence Performance?

As mentioned previously, quick resolution of network failures is crucial to the service providers. A short convergence time is a major criterion when building a highly available network. In an MPLS-switched network with RSVP-TE-signaled LSPs, the secondary LSP can provide high convergence performance against network element failures. This significantly reduces the traffic loss in a network failure, compared to traditionally routed or switched IP/Ethernet networks.

In a large network, there may be many different types of network failures. The network can be designed and implemented with maximum redundancy and maximum reliability (e.g., backup power, backup links, backup routing instances, and multi-homing). However, these elements only reduce the number of outages in the network. They do not make a network unbreakable. Also, building such a network significantly raises the cost for the service provider. Other important aspects of network design are the way the network reacts to a failure and whether it can recover from the failure within the required time frame.

A network's reaction against a network failure can be summarized in four sequential phases:

1. **Failure Detection** — Identify and locate the failure.

2. **Failure Propagation** — Notify other nodes regarding the failure by spreading the failure information across the network.

3. **Service Recovery** — Re-direct the traffic to alternative path if possible, and restore the services.

4. **Optimization or Reversion** — When the failure is removed, it may be desirable to restore the traffic to the original path(s).

In each phase, there are different network elements involved, with different operations. Each of these network elements may have an impact on the convergence performance. In general, the network equipment must detect the failure first (*failure detection*). The equipment should pass the information to the element that can react to the failure

(*failure propagation*). The router receives this information and tries rerouting the service traffic to an alternative path (*service recovery*). After the failure has been removed, it may be necessary for the router to put the traffic back to the original path (*reversion*) to achieve optimal routing or more efficient bandwidth utilization. Service providers often desire the *sub-50ms failure recovery performance*, or *five-nines service availability*. To achieve this, rapid failure detection and quick convergence is critical.

Failure Detection

The network failure must be detected before any reaction can be taken to protect the services. Different network types have varying mechanisms to detect the different types of failures.

- Legacy Layer 2 Ethernet switched networks use the Spanning Tree Protocol (STP) to prevent forwarding loops and to detect network failures. STP messages (also referred to as *bridged protocol data units* — BPDUs) are used as *Hello packets* to monitor the link aliveness. When a switch port cannot receive a BPDU from its adjacent neighbor after a certain time, it considers the peer to be failed. The BPDU time-out detection may take several seconds or longer, depending on the flavor of STP that is configured.

- In a Layer 3 IP routed network, dynamic IP routing protocols such as OSPF or IS-IS use their *adjacency Hello packets* to monitor the adjacent neighbor activity. When the routing protocol stops receiving the Hello packets for a certain length of time, it considers the adjacency to be broken. The routing protocol sends routing updates to notify its neighbor routers of the route change. To reduce the CPU utilization rate, the routing protocol's *Hello interval* is usually several seconds or longer. Several Hello packets must be missed before a router considers the peer to be in a **down** state. Therefore, the failure detection time may be tens of seconds. If MPLS is used, the RSVP-TE Hello protocol can also be used to detect RSVP neighbor router failures. However, it still takes several seconds or longer to detect the router failure. Some lightweight Hello protocols such as Bidirectional Forwarding Detection (BFD) can be used to speed up the failure detection.

  This failure detection time is the key to the convergency performance. Although subsecond convergence time can be easily witnessed in the labs, achieving similar performance is challenging in a real network deployment. This is mainly because of the failure detection process. In the lab, service recovery testing is performed by directly pulling network cables out of the routers/switches' ports under test. In these tests, the failure is *local to the router's or switch's port*. Therefore, the equipment under test discovers the link failure immediately and goes into a **port** **down** state. No time is wasted on determining if there is a failure.

In real networks, especially larger networks owned by service providers, the routers/switches' ports are not directly connected by cables. There may be several switches and repeaters connecting these ports. When a failure happens in-between the transmission equipment, the router's local port is still operationally **up**. The physical port status may still be operationally **up**, because the *failure is not local to the router/switch*.

Figure 6.3 presents the failure detection, propagation, and convergence operation in a network.

Figure 6.3 Failure Detection, Propagation, and Service Recovery

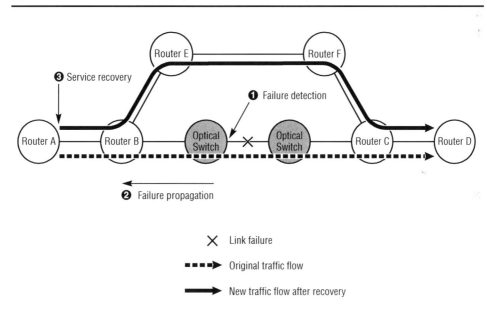

As shown in Figure 6.3, if the link between the two optical switches fails, the ports connecting Router B and Router C will still be operationally **up**, although no traffic can pass through these routers. In this case, it takes time for Router B to determine that the connection to Router C is not functioning. If OSPF with default timers is used in this network, it will take approximately 30 seconds before Router B begins to detect that the adjacency to Router C is **down**. Therefore, the traffic loss will be significant.

Remote failure detection can be the most time-consuming task in the failure recovery process. Techniques such as MPLS FRR or secondary LSP may speed up the service recovery significantly, but do not help speed up the detection of remote failures. The sub-50ms convergence time estimate does not include the time consumed by failure detection. In an IP/MPLS network, the best solution to speed up remote failure detection is via BFD or Ethernet for the First Mile (EFM) OAM (802.3ah) with routing protocols or RSVP-TE. Quicker failure detection can be achieved without significantly compromising the CPU performance. For details on using BFD or EFM OAM to help other protocols improve failure detection time, refer to Chapter 13.

Failure Propagation

Network failures may happen in any location in the network. The node that detects the failure may not be the node making the decision on how to handle the failure. Therefore, after the network failure is detected by a node, the information may need to be relayed to the node where the service recovery action happens. This relay of failure notification information is referred to as *failure propagation*. As an example, in a bridged Ethernet network, the STP requires any non-root switch to only propagate the topology change notification (TCN) toward the root bridge. Only the root bridge can build a new forwarding path for the traffic affected by the failure. As another example, if RSVP-TE LSP is provisioned in an MPLS network, only the Head-End router of the LSP can reroute the LSP to a new path. RSVP-TE LSP is HE-routed (the path is decided by the HE router). Therefore, the failure must be propagated to the Head-End router before the LSP can take a new path.

It takes time for information to pass from the failure detection node to the decision-making node. In general, failure propagation consumes less time than failure detection because most routing/signaling protocols used today are *event-triggered*. The routers forward the necessary information to the decision-making router as soon as they receive the message, rather than waiting an *update period* of time. As mentioned in Chapter 5, RSVP-TE uses both event-triggered (e.g., RSVP messages trigger LSP-Path status change) and the update-period (e.g., RSVP Hello protocol and the RSVP-TE LSP-Path state refresh) methods to detect and propagate failures.

One of the major differences between secondary LSP-Path and FRR is the location of the protection decision. When using the secondary LSP-Path, only the HE router of the LSP can switch the LSP's traffic between the primary LSP-Path and second-ary LSP-Paths. When a network failure happens along the LSP-Path's path, the failure must be propagated to the HE router. The HE router then switches the traffic to the secondary LSP-Path. In contrast, FRR protection is performed in the node local to the failure, this is referred to as the *Point of Local Repair* (PLR). Any router along the LSP-Path's path will reroute the LSP-Path as soon as it detects a network failure locally. Then, it notifies the HE router of the *local repair in use*. Also, if the secondary LSP-Path is not hot-standby, the router signals the secondary LSP-Path before it switches traffic into the network, which also consumes more time. In contrast, FRR bypass tunnels or detour LSPs are always pre-signaled. FRR eliminates the failure propagation time, which therefore makes the overall failure convergence faster and provides shorter service outage during a failure, compared to a secondary LSP-Path. However, a second-ary LSP-Path may be more desirable where a higher-level control of the LSP-Path's path is required. A comparison of these two mechanisms is provided in Chapter 7.

Service Recovery

When a router receives network topology change information (for example, network failure), it performs a routing calculation to update the routing table. Pure IP traffic is routed around the failed element by the routing protocol. However, in an RSVP-TE LSP with a non-standby secondary LSP-Path, path calculation and RSVP-TE signal-ing are required prior to the reroute of the traffic. If the secondary LSP is standby, the convergence is faster. Because FRR bypass tunnels or detour LSPs are always pre-signaled, there is no signaling process required when a router uses FRR to protect an LSP at the moment of failure. In addition, because FRR repair is always performed by the node that is local to the failure, the failure propagation is eliminated, and the FRR LSP convergence is usually faster than with IGP.

In IP/MPLS VPN service networks, the service itself also has protection mecha-nisms to help the service recovery. At the service level, resiliency is provided by pseudowire redundancy, which is discussed in Chapter 13.

Reversion after Failure Is Resolved

In most cases, a network failure causes a network topology change that leads to sub-optimal routing. When the failure is removed from the network, the traffic should be restored to its original path. This action is called *reversion*. In a legacy IP network, the reversion process is simply a routing table update. In the MPLS network, the reversion includes re-establishing the LSP-Path to the original path (optimization) and switching traffic back to the LSP-Path afterward.

In summary, convergence performance against network failure is a summary of four phases — failure detection, failure propagation, service recovery, and reversion. The first three phases are most significant, and are often timed to provide performance quotes. Different networking technologies (e.g., Ethernet bridging, IP routing, or MPLS switching) and different implementation and features may have an impact on the recovery process. Service providers must consider all network aspects (failover performance, OAM complexity, requirement of a new skill set, resource requirement on the technology, and equipment/support cost) to find the correct balance to build a high-performance, highly reliable, and cost-effective network.

6.4 Rules for Selecting Secondary LSPs

When the primary LSP-Path is operationally **up** in an LSP, the secondary LSP-Paths are not used to carry any data traffic. If the secondary LSP-Path is not standby, it is not even signaled. When a network failure along the primary LSP brings the primary LSP-Path **down**, the traffic is switched to one of the secondary LSP-Paths that is **up** and running. If there are no available standby secondary LSP-Paths, the HE router tries to establish a non-standby secondary LSP-Path to use if there are any configured in the LSP.

The standby secondary LSP-Paths share the same tunnel-id as the primary LSP-Path, but use a different LSP-id. Note that both IDs are carried in the PATH and RESV messages. The tunnel-id is in the SESSION object of both messages. The LSP-id is in the SENDER_TEMPLATE object in the PATH messages, and in the FILTERSPEC object in the RESV messages. When a standby secondary LSP-Path is created in an LSP, two or more LSP-Paths (RSVP sessions) simultaneously reserve resources for the same LSP. Figure 6.4 illustrates the LSP status for the primary and secondary LSP-Paths belonging to the same LSP.

Figure 6.4 illustrates that there is only one LSP that can be used as a service transport tunnel. However, there are actually three RSVP sessions reserved for that LSP: one primary LSP-Path and two secondary hot-standby LSP-Paths.

Figure 6.4 Primary and Hot-Standby Secondary LSP

```
A:PE-118# show router mpls lsp
===============================================================================
MPLS LSPs
(Originating)
===============================================================================
LSP Name                              To                Fastfail   Adm  Opr
                                                        Config
-------------------------------------------------------------------------------
to-116                                10.0.0.116        No         Up   Up
-------------------------------------------------------------------------------
LSPs : 1
===============================================================================
A:PE-118# show router rsvp session
===============================================================================
RSVP Sessions
===============================================================================
From         To           Tunnel LSP    Name                          State
ID      ID
-------------------------------------------------------------------------------
10.0.0.118   10.0.0.116      23   9728   to-116::primary-116           Up
10.0.0.118   10.0.0.116      23   9730   to-116::secondary-116         Up
10.0.0.118   10.0.0.116      23   9742   to-116::secondary-long        Up
-------------------------------------------------------------------------------
Sessions : 3
===============================================================================
A:PE-118#
```

Secondary LSP Selection Criteria

As discussed, within one LSP there can be up to eight LSP-Paths. There can be no more than one primary LSP-Path. (It is possible to define an LSP with eight secondary LSP-Paths without a primary LSP-Path, although this is not a recommended network design.) The secondary LSPs can be a combination of hot-standby or regular (non-standby) secondary LSPs. To fully understand the behavior of LSP with secondary LSP-Paths, the LSP-Path selection rules must be understood.

When there are multiple available LSP-Paths for the same LSP, only one LSP-Path forwards the traffic for the LSP at any time. The HE router must choose which one should be used to carry the traffic. If secondary LSP-Paths (non-standby) need to be established first, the HE router must choose which path to bring operationally up first as the active path. Figure 6.5 illustrates an LSP with one primary LSP-Path and seven hot-standby secondary LSP-Paths. In any scenario, there is only one *active forwarding path*.

Figure 6.5 Active LSP-Path in the LSP

```
A:R2# configure router mpls lsp to-117
A:R2>config>router>mpls>lsp# info
----------------------------------------------
                to 10.0.0.117
                    primary "loose"
                exit
                secondary "1"
                    standby
                exit
                secondary "2"
                    standby
                exit
                secondary "3"
                    standby
                exit
                secondary "4"
                    standby
                exit
                secondary "5"
                    standby
                exit
                secondary "6"
                    standby
                exit
                secondary "7"
                    standby
                exit
                no shutdown
----------------------------------------------
```

```
A:R2# show router mpls lsp to-117 path
===============================================================================
MPLS LSP to-117 Path
===============================================================================
-------------------------------------------------------------------------------
LSP Name     : to-117                    To           : 10.0.0.117
Adm State    : Up                        Oper State   : Up
-------------------------------------------------------------------------------
Path Name              Next Hop          Type      Out I/F   Adm   Opr
-------------------------------------------------------------------------------
1                      10.116.117.2      Standby   1/1/2     Up    Up
2                      10.116.117.2      Standby   1/1/2     Up    Up
3                      10.116.117.2      Standby   1/1/2     Up    Up
4                      10.116.117.2      Standby   1/1/2     Up    Up
5                      10.116.117.2      Standby   1/1/2     Up    Up
6                      10.116.117.2      Standby   1/1/2     Up    Up
7                      10.116.117.2      Standby   1/1/2     Up    Up
loose                  10.116.117.2      Primary   1/1/2     Up    Up
===============================================================================
A:R2# show router mpls lsp to-117 activepath
===============================================================================
MPLS LSP: to-117 (active paths)
===============================================================================
LSP Name      : to-117              LSP Id       : 27152
Path Name     : loose               Active Path  : Primary
To            : 10.0.0.117
===============================================================================
```

Figure 6.5 shows an LSP with all of the LSP-Paths operationally **up**. However, there is only one LSP-Path carrying the traffic for the LSP. In this LSP, because the primary LSP-Path is operationally **up**, this LSP-Path is the active LSP-Path and is displayed as the **active path** in the ALSRP service router's CLI output.

The following five rules are used by the router to decide which LSP-Path will be the active LSP-Path to carry the traffic for the LSP:

1. The primary LSP-Path is always preferred.

    Provided the primary LSP-Path is available, the router uses the primary LSP-Path to carry the data traffic. The router also will not signal any non-standby secondary LSP-Paths. Furthermore, when the network failure that causes the primary LSP-Path to be **down** is removed from the network, the router will always bring the primary LSP-Path **up** and revert the traffic back over to the primary LSP-Path.

2. When the primary LSP-Path goes **down**, if there is any hot-standby secondary LSP-Path operationally **up**, a non-standby secondary LSP-Path will not be signaled.

    An LSP can have both standby secondary LSP-Paths and non-standby secondary LSP-Paths configured to protect the primary LSP-Path. If there is any standby secondary LSP-Path that stays operationally **up** when the network failure happens, the router uses it to protect the primary LSP-Path. It will not signal a non-standby secondary LSP-Path even if this would result in a shorter path. The system uses the first available secondary LSP-Path.

3. When selecting a secondary LSP-Path, the secondary LSP-Paths that meet the Shared Risk Link Group (SRLG) requirement are preferred. Next, the first available LSP-Path is selected. Details regarding the use of SRLG are discussed in Chapter 4.

    When the primary LSP-Path goes operationally **down**, the system may need to choose one secondary LSP-Path to protect the traffic for a group of secondary LSPs. First, the router picks the operational secondary LSP-Path with the SRLG group configured. Because the use of the SRLG group disjoints the secondary LSP-Path from the primary LSP-Path, better resiliency is achieved. If there is more than one SRLG secondary LSP-Path available, or all available secondary LSP-Paths are not SRLG-enabled, the router uses the most stable LSP-Path from the available (operationally **up**) hot-standby secondary LSP-Paths. The most stable LSP-Path is the one that remains in an operationally **up** state for the longest time. If there is no available hot-standby secondary LSP-Path, the router tries signaling the first (in the order of configuration) non-standby secondary LSP-Path. If this fails, the router tries signaling the next secondary LSP-Path. The router will not stop until a secondary LSP-Path is established or all of them fail.

4. When the primary LSP-Path goes operationally **down**, if the current traffic carrying secondary LSP-Path goes **down** as well, the next first available choice of secondary LSP-Paths carries the traffic.

The secondary LSP-Path is not only used to protect the primary LSP-Path, but is also used to protect other secondary LSP-Paths. For example, if one network failure causes the primary LSP-Path to go **down**, the first available secondary LSP-Path is used to forward the traffic. If, then, another failure causes the current secondary LSP-Path to go **down**, another available secondary LSP-Path may be used to take over the traffic from the *current* secondary LSP-Path. The secondary LSP-Path selection still obeys the rule: *Use the first established secondary LSP-Path initially. If this is not available, signal the first non-standby secondary LSP-Path until no secondary LSP-Paths are available.*

5. No switching back among secondary LSP-Paths.

If the network failure causing the primary LSP-Path to go operationally **down** is removed, the router switches the traffic back to the primary LSP-Path as soon as the LSP-Path comes **up** operationally (reversion). The system does not revert or optimize among secondary LSP-Paths because the router considers all secondary LSPs to be equal. The system does not switch traffic from its current secondary LSP to another secondary LSP as long as the traffic bearing secondary LSP is operationally **up**.

6.5 Case Study: Using Administrative Groups in Secondary LSPs

Figure 6.6 shows an example of a network design that uses secondary LSP-Paths to protect the LSP. Link-coloring (administrative groups) is used to ensure that the primary and secondary LSP-Paths traverse different paths, so as to achieve maximum protection. Figure 6.6 illustrates how the secondary LSP-Paths traverse links with different colors from those of the links that the primary LSP-Path traverses.

In Figure 6.6, PE1 requires an LSP to PE7, and PE2 requires an LSP to PE8. Both LSPs require protection against network failures as follows:

- When there is no failure, the LSP should take the shortest path to ensure the link efficiency.
- The failover should be as quick as possible, and the protection path should be routed as far apart as possible from the LSP-Path being protected.
- Only in the worst case should the traffic take the longest path to reach the far-end PE router.
- Configuration overhead should be minimal and manageable.

Figure 6.6   Using Secondary LSP with Link-Coloring

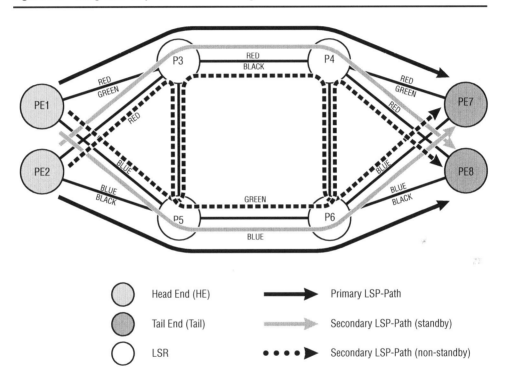

In Figure 6.6, the network design implements these requirements by choosing the secondary LSP-Path with link-coloring. The LSPs are designed with the following rules:

- The primary LSP-Path should take the shortest path.
- The standby secondary LSP-Path is used to protect the primary LSP-Path and should take a different path.

- Another non-standby secondary LSP-Path is used to protect the LSP-Path against the worst-case scenario. The non-standby secondary LSP-Path takes the longest path.

The most efficient way to control the direction of many connections and reduce control overhead is via admin groups (link-coloring), rather than explicitly specifying the hops that each LSP-Path must traverse. After the link-coloring is deployed as illustrated in Figure 6.6, the LSPs can be configured as listed in Table 6.2. Table 6.2 lists the color assignment for the primary and secondary LSP-Paths.

Table 6.2 LSP Design with Secondary LSP-Path and Admin Groups

LSP-Path	LSP: PE1–PE7	LSP: PE2–PE8
Primary	The LSP-Path will only take links with red color.	The LSP-Path will only take links with blue color.
Secondary (standby)	The LSP-Path will only take links with blue color.	The LSP-Path will only take links with red color.
Secondary (non-standby)	The LSP-Path will not take links with green color.	The LSP-Path will not take links with black color.

The configuration of link-coloring and LSP are introduced in Chapter 4. This example refers only to using link-coloring for secondary LSP-Paths and is not a network design recommendation.

Summary

The RSVP-TE-signaled LSP allows many LSP-Paths to service the same LSP. These LSP-Paths are associated with the same LSP in a primary/backup arrangement, consisting of one primary LSP-Path and up to seven secondary LSP-Paths. These secondary LSP-Paths protect the primary LSP-Path when it fails. The secondary LSP-Paths can be pre-signaled (hot-standby) or be signaled when the primary LSP-Path fails (non-standby).

When a network fails and the protection kicks in, there are four phases:

1. **Failure Detection** — Identify and locate the failure.

2. **Failure Propagation** — Notify peers regarding the failure, and spread the failure information across the network.

3. **Service Recovery** — Re-direct the traffic to alternative equipment, and, if possible, restore the services.

4.   **Optimization or Reversion** — When the failure is removed, it may be desirable to restore the traffic to the original path.

There can be multiple secondary LSP-Paths protecting the primary LSP-Path in the same LSP. When the primary LSP-Path fails, one secondary LSP-Path is selected as the active forwarding path and forwards traffic for the LSP. When there are multiple secondary LSP-Paths, the rules for selecting secondary LSP-Paths are:

1.   The primary LSP-Path is always preferred as long as it is operationally up.

2.   When the primary LSP-Path fails, if there are any pre-signaled secondary hot-standby LSP-Paths, any non-standby secondary LSP-Paths are not signaled.

3.   All secondary LSP-Paths are equal. The first one available (having been operationally up the longest) is chosen when the primary LSP-Path fails.

4.   If the current secondary LSP-Path selected as the active forwarding path also fails, the next available secondary LSP-Path takes over the traffic.

Secondary LSP and FRR are not mutually exclusive. To achieve maximum LSP resiliency with RSVP-TE, the operator can turn both features on. The use of secondary LSP and FRR makes the RSVP-TE LSP the most preferred tunneling technology for the carriers.

MPLS Resiliency — RSVP-TE LSP Fast Reroute

7

RSVP-TE LSP is capable of establishing protection prior to a failure happening; therefore it can switch the traffic to the protected route rapidly during the failure. This feature is referred to as Fast Reroute (FRR). With FRR, the MPLS tunnel's convergence performance is improved significantly.

Chapter Objectives

- Provide an overview of RSVP-TE LSP resiliency features and a comparison between secondary LSP and MPLS FRR

- Introduce MPLS FRR and the RSVP-TE extension to support MPLS FRR

- Describe the architecture of the MPLS FRR mechanism

- Explain FRR node protection versus link protection and FRR facility backup versus one-to-one backup

Operators want strong resilience in their networks. They expect the networks to be robust and converge quickly when there is a failure. To meet these requirements, RSVP-TE has been enhanced to support automatic establishment of protections for its LSPs. One of the enhancements is secondary LSP, covered in Chapter 6. Another enhancement is MPLS Fast Reroute (FRR). With MPLS FRR, when there is a failure along the path of the LSP-Path, the traffic is quickly switched to the pre-signaled protection paths so the outage is minimized.

This chapter introduces MPLS FRR and the RSVP-TE protocol enhancements to support FRR.

7.1 RSVP-TE LSP Resiliency

Chapter 6 introduced one MPLS resiliency feature — secondary LSP. This chapter introduces a second RSVP-TE LSP resiliency feature — MPLS Fast Reroute (FRR). MPLS FRR uses automatically created detour LSPs or bypass tunnels to protect the LSP. When using FRR, the LSP being configured needs to specify only the method and type of desired protection. With the help of the RSVP-TE protocol and the CSPF algorithm, the protections are automatically established without further manual configuration. Table 7.1 compares the two MPLS resiliency technologies: Secondary LSP and FRR.

Table 7.1 MPLS Resiliency Secondary LSP versus Fast Reroute

Functionality	Secondary LSP	Fast Reroute
LSP creation	Requires manual configuration of primary and secondary paths. Requires manual association of the secondary LSP-Path(s) to the LSP being protected.	Only needs to specify the desired method and type of protection in the LSP configuration. The establishment of protection tunnels is automatic.
Signaling requirement	No RSVP-TE enhancement for FRR required. CSPF and IGP-TE are optional.	Requires traffic engineering (TE) extension on IGP, and CSPF. RSVP-TE implementation must include the enhancement indicated by RFC 4090.

Functionality	Secondary LSP	Fast Reroute
Number of LSP-Paths required to achieve the required protection	Up to seven secondary LSP-Paths can be used to protect the primary LSP-Path. (If no primary, there can be eight secondary LSP-Paths.) Secondary LSP-Paths can be pre-signaled as *hot-standby*. Secondary LSP-Paths cannot be shared by many LSPs. Each LSP has its own set of LSP-Paths, including one primary, and optionally 0–8 secondary LSP-Paths with no primary LSP-Path.	Every hop (except the Tail node) creates one protection tunnel (LSP-Path) to protect the protected LSP-Path. The number of protection tunnels used to protect one LSP-Path depends on the number of hops and the topology of the network. When facility backup is used, multiple LSPs can be protected by the same set of protection tunnels.
Manual control level	Manual control on all paths. LSP-Path can be decided by a list of hops or using administration groups. All manual control options for primary LSP-Paths are applicable for secondary LSP-Paths as well.	FRR protection tunnels (detour LSP or bypass tunnel) are automatically created by the routers along the path of the LSP-Path. No manual control is allowed. The paths of the protection tunnels are decided by CSPF calculation and the active LSP-Path. Alternatively, a manual facility bypass tunnel can be configured if both FRR and manual control of the protection path are desired.
Location of protection	Only the Head-End (HE) router is aware of the secondary paths. When failure happens, the failure must be propagated to the HE router of the LSP for the HE router to use the secondary LSP protection.	When FRR is desired by an LSP, every node along the path will try to signal the protection tunnel. When a failure happens, the router closest to the failure provides protection.

(continued)

Table 7.1 MPLS Resiliency Secondary LSP versus Fast Reroute *(continued)*

Functionality	Secondary LSP	Fast Reroute
Signaling complexity	Low. Secondary LSP-Path is considered just another LSP-Path. Only the source of the LSP (HE) is aware of the secondary LSPs. For an LSR, the secondary LSP-Path is just another LSP-Path traversing the LSR. There is no extra signaling protocol enhancement or LSP maintenance required to support the secondary LSP-Path.	High. FRR requires the enhancement of the RSVP-TE protocol (RFC 4090) to support the signaling requirement. The MPLS router supporting FRR must also handle complex jobs such as maintaining the protected LSP's state in the failure, merging the traffic back, and reverting the traffic to the protected LSP when it is re-signaled. Every MPLS router along the LSP-Path requires these enhancements and coordination to support FRR.

MPLS FRR has less configuration overhead in comparison to secondary LSP-Path. When the RSVP-TE LSP is configured with the desired FRR, all the MPLS routers (except the Tail router of the LSP) along the LSP-Path automatically try to provide protection. Each router is aware of the original path with the help of the RRO received in the RESV message. Using this information with the help of CSPF, each router can calculate a path for the protecting tunnel to avoid a potential failure point. Compared to secondary LSP, FRR has several advantages:

- The automatic protection path calculation and signaling significantly reduce the manual configuration overhead.

- With FRR, when network failures occur, the MPLS router closest to the failure detours the traffic away from the point of failure. Therefore, the failure propagation time is shortened, and the failover time is shorter.

- FRR allows the use of one protection tunnel to protect more than one protected LSP (many-to-one relationship), providing their paths intersect. In a scaled network, this helps to reduce the number of LSP-Paths in the network.

Note that FRR and secondary LSPs can coexist to protect the same LSP. FRR is configured on a per-LSP-Path basis and only protects the primary LSP-Path.

Secondary LSP-Paths cannot have FRR enabled on them. It is possible to configure an LSP with both FRR and secondary LSP enabled for maximum protection. When there is a network failure, both FRR and secondary LSPs may be used to protect the primary LSP-Path and therefore maximize the LSP's robustness.

7.2 Fast Reroute Overview

Fast reaction against network failure (node failure and/or link failure) and to protect customer traffic has always been a challenge for service providers. It is also a crucial factor for operators when selecting technologies to deploy in their networks.

Traditional networks use equipment redundancy to achieve traffic protection. However, most of the fast convergence techniques have corresponding high costs, and there is not always a good balance between the performance and the cost. With an increase in redundant devices deployed comes a more robust network at a high cost. For example, the SONET/SDH network uses Automatic Protecting Switch (APS) to switch traffic to a protected link when the primary link fails. APS (both 1:1 and 1:N models) requires an over-provisioning of physical connections. In addition, the backup link's bandwidth is not used for transporting traffic when there is no network failure. An APS switch can provide a convergence time that is comparable to or exceeds the convergence time of APS, but its fast switch-over requires customers and service providers to deploy more hardware in the network.

However, even when redundant devices are deployed, the failover performance can also be a problem. Bridged Ethernet networks can have redundant links (trunks) and use STP to prevent loops, but even the fastest STP implementation cannot produce subsecond convergence time. Routers rely on routing protocols to detect failures, and routing updates provide the alternative next-hop information to route packets around the failure. The most popular routing protocols selected by service providers are OSPF and IS-IS. Both these protocols usually reroute traffic 5–10 seconds after the failures are detected in the network.

When service providers use the new generation of MPLS-capable service-aware routers to build their network backbone, new resiliency options are available. The RSVP-TE signaling protocol is extended to support automatic signaling of protection tunnels using FRR. It provides network failure protection by pre-establishing the alternative *protection path* and re-directing traffic around the network failure within tens of milliseconds after the failure is detected. With FRR protection, an IP/MPLS VPN network can match or exceed the convergence performance of a legacy APS-protected SONET/SDH network with a much lower cost, and include the flexibility of supporting multiple services over a common infrastructure.

With FRR, the MPLS routers signal the protection tunnels shortly after the LSP-Path establishment. Therefore, protections are already in place before the network failure happens. During the network failure, the MPLS router closest to the failure reacts by rerouting the traffic to the pre-established protection tunnel to reduce possible traffic loss caused by the failure. Then, the Head-End router of the LSP-Path tries to find a better path for the LSP-Path. With FRR, the protection tunnel signaling, the rerouting of the traffic, and the failure recovery are all automatic. Therefore minimal manual configuration is required.

To deploy FRR, the traffic engineering (TE) extension for Interior Gateway Protocols (IGP) and CSPF is required. The RSVP-TE protocol is used to signal the MPLS LSP service transport tunnels. FRR is designed to provide quick convergence (tens of milliseconds recovery time) to protect traffic over an LSP. When a failure happens, the traffic is detoured to the *protecting* LSP-Path from the MPLS router that is local to the failure. When the traffic is rerouted, the original LSP-Path's state is still maintained by the router providing the detour, via the notification of the `local-protect-in-use` flag to the source (HE) of the LSP-Path being protected.

FRR Protection Methods and Types

There are two methods of FRR protection, and each LSP can use only one method. One of the following desired protection methods is specified in the protected LSP's configuration:

- **One-to-One Backup** — Each LSP-Path desiring one-to-one backup has a protection LSP signaled that is dedicated to protect that LSP-Path. The one-to-one backup that is signaled is called the *detour LSP*.

- **Facility Backup** — Facility backup creates a common *bypass tunnel* to protect all LSP-Paths traversing a common facility path. Any LSP-Paths desiring FRR protection share the common protection tunnel when their paths intersect. This is a many-to-one protection relationship. The facility backup protection signaled is called the *bypass tunnel*.

Figure 7.1 illustrates each method of protection for three protected LSPs. The router roles in the illustration (MP, PLR, MP, Tail) are discussed later in this chapter.

Figure 7.1   FRR Protection Methods: One-to-One Backup versus Facility Backup

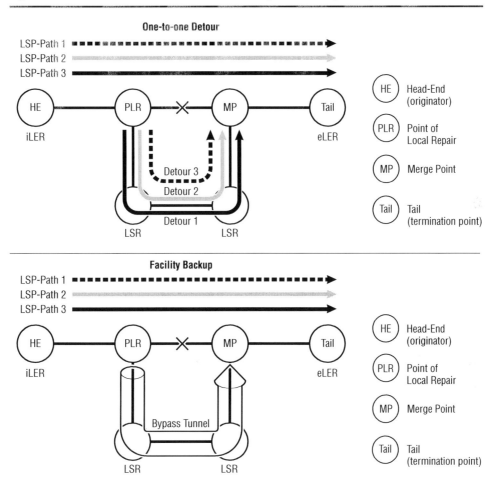

Topology-wise, both one-to-one and facility backup can protect different network elements as follows:

- **Link Protection** — Link protection protects the link between two routers. The protecting path (bypass tunnel or detour LSP) is created between two directly adjacent routers to protect a link between them.

- **Node Protection** — Node protection protects a Label Switch Router (LSR) in between two routers. The protection path (bypass tunnel or detour LSP) is created to route the traffic around an LSR in the original path of the LSP(s) being protected. There may be cases in which node protection is desired by an LSP; a router can only provide link protection. In this case, the router still establishes the link protection to provide as much protection as possible.

Figure 7.2 illustrates the topology view of MPLS FRR providing link protection and node protection.

Figure 7.2 FRR Protection Types: Link Protection versus Node Protection

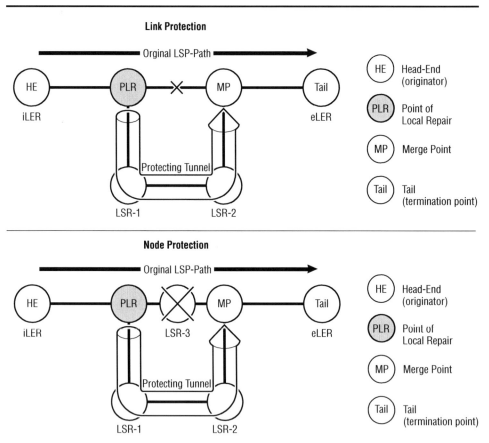

Both the protection types (link, node) and the protection methods (one-to-one, facility) must be specified for an LSP desiring protection. Therefore, there are four types of FRR for an LSP desiring protection:

- One-to-one link protection
- One-to-one node protection
- Facility link protection
- Facility node protection

The operator specifies the LSP-Path's type of protection in the LSP configuration. This protection type is signaled in the RSVP-TE messages. When a router receives an RSVP-TE message to establish the LSP-Path that desires protection, it tries to signal a protection to fulfill the requirement. If the effort is successful, the router reports the protection availability back to the Head-End (HE) router. For clarification of this discussion, Table 7.2 lists the terminology of the protections signaled by the FRR.

Table 7.2 FRR Protection Terminologies

Terminology	Description
Protected LSP	The LSP-Path being protected by FRR. This LSP-Path is the original LSP-Path that requires protection. Only the primary LSP-Path in an LSP can be protected by FRR.
Protection LSP	The LSP-Path established by FRR to provide protection. The term *protection LSP-Path* can refer to either a one-to-one detour LSP or a facility backup bypass tunnel.
Detour LSP	The LSP-Path established by FRR to provide one-to-one backup to certain LSP-Paths desiring protection
Bypass tunnel	The LSP-Path established by FRR to provide facility protection to certain LSP-Paths that traverse the same common facility

FRR Implementation Requirements

The FRR architecture provides a mechanism whereby the protection can be signaled automatically, and the failover is rapid. To speed up the convergence or failover around a network failure, MPLS FRR considers the following facts:

- When a network failure happens, the LSP-Path should be repaired as close as possible to the failure location. The router local to the failure should provide the repair. Therefore, little or no time is wasted by the failure propagation. The router providing FRR protection is called the *Point of Local Repair* (PLR). In

MPLS FRR, it is always the upstream router (the router closer to the HE router) closest to the failure that acts as the PLR and reroutes the traffic to the protection path. The PLR is the HE router of the protection LSP in use.

- During the failure, the router providing traffic protection (the PLR) should notify the protected LSP's HE router regarding the failure event. This is done by sending a `PathErr` message to the HE router with information that such an event has occurred. The PLR should also notify the HE router that the protection is currently in use. Thus, the HE router may look for another path to route the traffic on (for example, a hot-standby secondary LSP-Path). In MPLS FRR, when a PLR reroutes the traffic around the failure, it sets the `local-protection-in-use` flag in the RESV message sent back to the HE router.

- When rerouting traffic around the failure, the traffic should be merged back to the original path as soon as possible. The *Merge Point* (MP) router is the router where the rerouted traffic merges back to the original path. The MP router is also the termination (Tail) router of the protection tunnel.

- The HE router should also try to *revert* traffic back to the original path as soon as the network failure is fixed, or it should find a better path for the protected LSP and re-establish the protected LSP. The decision to re-signal the original LSP and bring traffic back can be made by either the HE router or the PLR router. In MPLS FRR, the choice of routers (the HE or the PLR) to re-signal the LSP-Path in failures is called the FRR's revertive mode. There are two revertive modes: local revertive mode or global revertive mode. In the ALSRP, the HE router is always in charge of re-signaling the new LSP-Path and reverting traffic back. This is referred to as *global revertive mode*. Revertive mode is explained in detail in a later section.

- Every router (except the Tail router) along the protected LSP should consider itself a potential PLR. Also, every router (except the HE router) of the protected LSP should consider itself to be an MP. Therefore, every PLR tries to signal the desired protection path when the protected LSP is established, and thus, all possible failure points along the path are protected. When MPLS FRR is used, every router (except the Tail router) along the path of the LSP *assumes the PLR role* and tries to signal the protection path. Also, every node (except the HE router) *assumes the MP role* and is ready to merge traffic back. All possible protection paths are signaled prior to any possible failures.

Note: Regardless of what protection method the MPLS FRR uses (one-to-one or facility), the routers only start to signal the protection tunnel(s) after the primary LSP-Path is signaled and established successfully. If the protected LSP cannot initially come up operationally, the protection LSP is not established and does not protect the LSP. An LSP-Path cannot be brought up operationally by FRR unless the LSP-Path has been successfully established over its original path at least once.

In the case of facility backup, many LSP-Paths may share the same protection LSP (bypass tunnel). The router only associates the LSP-Path to the existing eligible bypass tunnel or signals a new bypass tunnel for the LSP-Path if the protected LSP-Path itself has been successfully established once.

When the LSP-Path desiring FRR protection is being established, the router will not try to signal any FRR protection or associate any protection with the LSP-Path (facility backup) until the router receives the second RESV message (used for refreshing the session).

Furthermore, to reduce the number of detour/bypass tunnels in the system and make FRR more resource-efficient, the following optimizations are implemented in most vendors' FRR implementations:

- For facility backup, the traffic being protected should be merged back to the original path as soon as possible. Therefore, the immediate next hop of the failure location should merge the traffic back. This is the next-hop (NHop) router in the case of a link failure, or the next-next-hop (NNHop) in the case of a node failure. It is the MP router that merges traffic back to its original path.

- For one-to-one backup, if multiple detour LSPs intersect in a router, they are merged from that point, and only one detour LSP is signaled further along the path of the protected LSP-Path. The router merging the detour LSP is called the *Detour Merge Point* (DMP).

Note: FRR significantly reduces the traffic outage time after the network failure is detected. The detection of the network failure is not the task of the FRR. If the network failure is not local to the MPLS-capable router, the *time cost* of failure detection is much more crucial for overall service convergence. This scenario is quite common in a service provider's backbone network, where there are Layer 1 or Layer 2 hops between the MPLS switches. Features such as Bidirectional Forwarding Detection (BFD) or Ethernet for the First Mile (EFM) OAM (802.3ah) can improve the failure detection and propagation speed significantly. BFD is introduced in Chapter 13 and EFM OAM is introduced in Chapter 18.

RSVP-TE Enhancement for FRR as Defined in RFC 4090

FRR protection is only available for RSVP-TE-signaled explicitly routed LSPs; LDP-signaled LSPs are not protected by FRR. The LDP-signaled LSPs' convergence time against network failure depends on the core routing protocol's convergence. In order to have enough information to signal the FRR requirement and indicate the availability of the protection, the RSVP-TE protocol is enhanced to support FRR. RSVP-TE is introduced in Chapter 5. RFC 4090 defines these RSVP-TE enhancements and the basic behaviors of FRR. These enhancements include:

- **The New** FAST_REROUTE **Object (FRR Object) (Object Class 205)** — A new object is added in the PATH message to indicate the characters of the desired protection. The FRR object contains the following information:

  - The FRR protection tunnel LSP's set-up priority, holding priority, hop-limit, and bandwidth (bytes per second)

  - Protection method: one-to-one (0x1) or facility (0x2)

  - Administrative group (link-coloring) information such as include-any, exclude-any, and include-all subobjects. Each of these subobjects is a 32-bit masking, mapping to the 32-bit admin group bits.

Figure 7.3 presents the format of the FAST_REROUTE object.

Figure 7.3 FAST_REROUTE Object

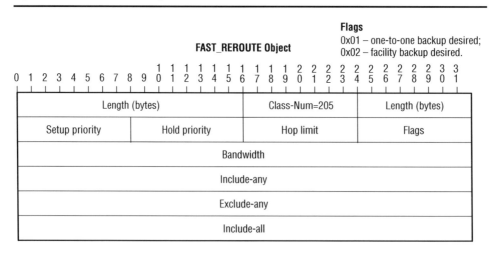

The signaling of MPLS FRR is optional, with not all vendors supporting PATH messages with the FRR object present. For multi-vendor compatibility, the ALSRP contains a *knob* to disable/enable addition of the FRR object. Figure 7.4 illustrates such a knob. The default configuration is to include (enable) the FRR object in the PATH message when FRR is required on the LSP.

Figure 7.4   Disable/Enable Adding FAST_REROUTE Object in the PATH Messages

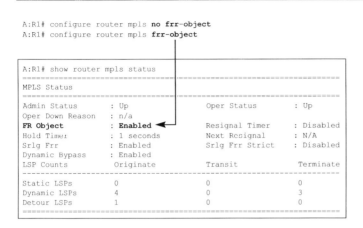

```
A:R1# configure router mpls no frr-object
A:R1# configure router mpls frr-object

A:R1# show router mpls status
===================================================================
MPLS Status
===================================================================
Admin Status         : Up              Oper Status         : Up
Oper Down Reason     : n/a
FR Object            : Enabled    ◄──   Resignal Timer      : Disabled
Hold Timer           : 1 seconds       Next Resignal       : N/A
Srlg Frr             : Enabled         Srlg Frr Strict     : Disabled
Dynamic Bypass       : Enabled
LSP Counts           Originate        Transit             Terminate
-------------------------------------------------------------------
Static LSPs          0                0                   0
Dynamic LSPs         4                0                   3
Detour LSPs          1                0                   0
===================================================================
```

- **New DETOUR Object (Object Class 63)** — This object is used in the PATH messages for one-to-one backup only. It contains a list of possible PLRs and the node each PLR should avoid.

  Figure 7.5 illustrates the format of the DETOUR object.

Figure 7.5   DETOUR Object

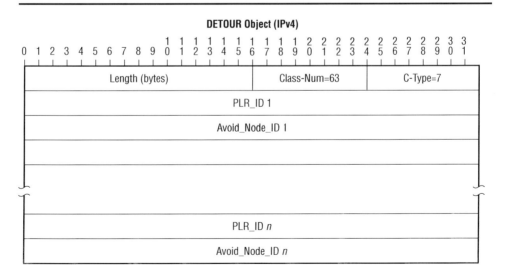

DETOUR Object (IPv4)

Length (bytes)		Class-Num=63	C-Type=7
PLR_ID 1			
Avoid_Node_ID 1			
PLR_ID n			
Avoid_Node_ID n			

- **FRR-Related Flags Defined in the** SESSION_ATTRIBUTE **Object** — In the PATH message, the SESSON_ATTRIBUTE object has an 8-bit flag field. In the RSVP-TE for MPLS LSP signaling (RFC 3209), the first three *least significant bits* are defined: local-protection-desired (0x1), label-recording-desired (0x2), and SE-style-desired (0x4). RFC 4090 uses the next two bits for FRR: bandwidth-protection-desired (0x8) and node-protection-desired (0x10). These two bits allow the HE router to indicate the desire for node protection and the reservation of bandwidth for the FRR protection tunnels.

- **FRR-Related Flags Defined in the RRO Object** — In the PATH and RESV messages, the RRO object has an 8-bit flag field in each IPv4 subobject. In the RSVP-TE for MPLS LSP signaling (RFC 3209), the first two least significant bits are used: local-protection-available (0x1) and local-protection-in-use (0x2). RFC 4090 uses the next two bits for FRR: bandwidth-protection-available (0x8) and node-protection-available (0x10). These two bits allow the Tail router to indicate the availability of node protection and reservation of bandwidth for the FRR protection tunnels.

7.3 Fast Reroute Architecture

This section introduces the network elements involved in FRR. This section also discusses each *role* of a router in FRR and its overall behavior, including the HE router, Tail router, PLR, MP, and DMP.

Requirement for MPLS Fast Reroute

As previously mentioned, FRR requires each router other than the Tail router to assume the PLR role and calculate an alternative path to protect the protected LSP-Path when the link to the next-hop router or the next-hop router itself has failed. To enable each router along the LSP-Path to provide FRR protection, the router must know the actual hops that the protected LSP is traversing and the entire topology of the network. With this information, the router can then calculate the alternative path *around* the actual path of the LSP-Path that desires protection. Figure 7.6 revisits the examples of link protection and node protection shown earlier.

Figure 7.6 Link Protection and Node Protection

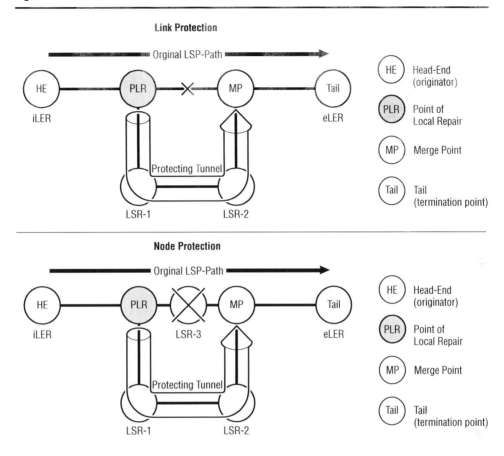

In Figure 7.6, the HE router signals the protected LSP-Path with FRR desired. When a router receives this requirement, it must have the following information before it can establish the protection tunnels:

- From this router's perspective, which link/node must be protected for this LSP-Path?
- Based on the protection type (link/node), which is this router's next-hop router (MP) to terminate the protecting tunnel and merge the traffic to the original path?
- Is there an alternate path to set up a tunnel to provide the protection for this LSP? This tunnel must originate from this router, terminate in the next-hop router (MP), and cannot intersect with the protected LSP-Path.

The first two items are addressed by the RSVP-TE message's record route object (RRO) that is added to the RSVP-TE. When establishing the protected LSP, the actual path travelled by the protected LSP-Path's PATH message and RESV message is recorded in the RRO. With RRO, each router along the path of the LSP-Path knows exactly what every hop of the LSP-Path is. The last item is addressed by using CSPF to consult the IGP-TE's TED.

> **Note:** Regardless of the configuration, FRR cannot protect against an HE router failure or a Tail router failure. FRR can only provide protection on failures in the Label Switch Routers or on the links between all routers along the LSP-Path. Also, for an LSP with secondary LSPs configured, FRR can only be enabled in the primary LSP, not the secondary LSPs.

Network Elements and Their Roles in FRR

The MPLS FRR is performed by the interaction of multiple routers in the network. The router where the protected LSP originates is the HE router. The router where the LSP terminates is the Tail router. Customer traffic enters the MPLS domain from the HE router and exits the MPLS domain at the Tail router. A HE router is also referred to as an *ingress LER* (iLER), and a Tail router is also referred to as an *egress LER* (eLER). The routers in between the LSP-Path only perform label swapping according to the label map, regardless of the labeled packet content. These routers are referred to as *LSRs*.

As discussed previously, when a failure happens in the network, the PLR router is the router that is local to the failure and the one that should perform the traffic protection. The MP router is the router that is the next hop to the failure point that merges protected traffic back to the rest of the original path.

As implied earlier, one router in the MPLS domain can have multiple roles during FRR. For example, the HE router may also be the PLR router if the failure is local to the HE router. A Tail router may also be the MP router if the failure is located immediately before the Tail router. Table 7.3 lists the different *roles* of the network elements in an MPLS FRR scenario.

Table 7.3 MPLS FRR Roles of Network Elements

Node Role	Node Function
Head-End (HE)	The source router of the protected LSP, also called the *iLER* (ingress Label Edge Router) of the LSP. The HE router's responsibility is to *push* the label for the ingress traffic before the packet enters the MPLS domain and then switch the packet out to the next-hop LSR. An HE router performs the following tasks: • During the original protected LSP setup, the requirement of FRR protection is specified by setting the `local-protection-required` flag in the PATH message. Optionally, the router may set the `node-protection-required` flag if node protection is required. • During network failure, when the FRR notification is received from the PLR router (through the `PathErr` and RSEV messages) in global revertive mode, the HE tries to search for another LSP to avoid the failure. If a secondary LSP is configured, the HE router tries to swap the traffic to the secondary LSP. The behavior of secondary LSPs and the interaction between the secondary LSP and FRR tunnels, and the rules of their actions are explained in detail in later sections.
Point of Local Repair (PLR)	The router that currently provides the FRR protection against the failure in the network. The PLR is responsible for the following tasks: • During the original protected LSP-Path setup, if the original LSP-Path requires FRR protection, the PLR sets up the traffic-protecting tunnel (either one-on-one detour LSP or facility bypass tunnel LSP). • After the protecting tunnel is established, the PLR notifies the HE router of the FRR's availability by setting the `Local-protection-available` flag in the RESV message. The PLR also continues to refresh the protecting tunnel's RSVP sessions. The PLR router is the HE router of the protecting tunnel. • When a local network failure is detected, the PLR routes the traffic to the protecting tunnel. • The PLR notifies the HE router that the traffic is being protected by setting the `local-repair-in-use` flag in the refresh RESV message and by sending the `PathErr` message to the HE router. • In local revertive mode, when a network failure is repaired, the PLR re-signals the original LSP back to the original path. • In global revertive mode, when a network failure is repaired, the PLR waits for the HE router to re-signal the LSP and switch traffic back.

(continued)

Table 7.3 MPLS FRR Roles of Network Elements *(continued)*

Node Role	Node Function
Merge Point (MP)	The router where the protected LSP and the protecting tunnel meet. During FRR, the MP merges the traffic from the protecting tunnel back to the original LSP-Path. In the case of link protection, the MP is the NHop of the PLR router. In case of node protection, the MP is the NNHop of the PLR router. With node protection, label negotiation may be required. Node protection is discussed in later sections.
Detour Merge Point (DMP)	In the case of a one-to-one backup, two or more detour LSP-Paths may intersect in the same router. This router will then merge several detours and only signal one detour after this point. In this scenario, the router is referred to as a DMP.
Tail-End (Tail or Termination)	The Tail of the protected LSP is also called the *eLER* of the LSP. The Tail router's responsibility is to *pop* the label out and forward the packet outside to the MPLS domain.

Figure 7.7 illustrates an example of an LSP requesting link protection on LSRs in the LSP's path.

Figure 7.7   FRR Example: Link Failure Protection

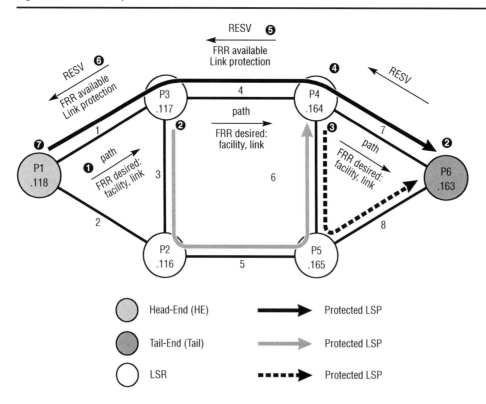

For MPLS FRR protection of an LSP-Path, you must configure the LSP with the desired protection type. When provisioning an RSVP-TE LSP on the HE router, the following FRR options can be specified if FRR is desired:

- Indicate that the LSP requires protection by FRR
- Methods of FRR required: one-to-one or facility
- Types of FRR required: link protection or node protection
- Other requirements, such as the hop limit of the protection path

In the example in Figure 7.7, the operator wants the LSP to use FRR facility backup with link protection. The following steps describe the process:

1. If protection is desired in an LSP, the RSVP-TE signals the LSP with a request for protection. Each router along the path of the LSP records the route and label for the HE router.

2. After the PATH message reaches the Tail router P6, P6 establishes the LSP-Path by sending an RESV message back. The FRR is established only after the protected LSP-Path comes up operationally. Therefore, at this moment, each router does not start the signaling or protection tunnels. The RESV message from P6 for the initial LSP path establishment does not report whether the local protection is available yet.

3. After the initial RESV reaches the P1 router, the protected LSP is established. Then, the CSPF in each router starts calculating the detour LSP or bypass tunnel based on the network topology stored in the TED, and the original path of the LSP recorded in the RRO object by each hop.

4. Each potential PLR router signals the detour LSP or bypass tunnel based on the CSPF calculation. If the detour LSP or bypass tunnel is established, the router then announces the protection availability to the HE router.

5. At this point, the HE router of the protected LSP has a view of what types of protection are available from which router.

    When a failure happens, the PLR immediately uses the pre-signaled protection to reroute the traffic around the failure and notifies the HE router via the `PathErr` message and the RESV message.

Note that when the protected LSP is established and routers are trying to signal the protection tunnels for FRR, the network failure has not happened yet. With FRR, all routers along the path of the protected LSP-Path pre-signal the protection tunnels after the protected LSP-Path is established. Every router (except the Tail) *assumes* the

PLR role and tries to find an alternative path and signal the protection tunnel to provide link/node protection. Therefore, when there is actually a failure, the routers closest to the failure are ready, and they immediately reroute traffic around the failure. In this manner, FRR can significantly improve a network's failover performance.

A router's role in FRR differs on a per-LSP-Path basis. One router can be the HE router of one LSP-Path, the MP router of another LSP-Path, and the PLR for several LSP-Paths when there is a local link failure. For the same protected LSP-Path, a router may be the PLR for the next-hop (downstream) failure and the MP for the previous-hop (upstream) failure. This applies to both one-to-one and facility backup.

Details regarding the protection establishment, rerouting the traffic when failure happens, or reverting back when failure is removed are discussed in later sections. The following section discusses the overall behavior of routers with different roles.

Head-End Router Behavior

The HE router of the protected LSP-Path is the origination point of the LSP-Path. The protected LSP-Path is defined in the HE router with the desired protection type: one-to-one or facility backup. The HE router sets the desired FRR type in the PATH message's `SESSION_ATTRIBUTE` objects.

The HE router tracks the FRR availability by examining the received RESV message's RRO objects for an LSP-Path. The HE router has a complete view of the LSP and each LSP-Path that belongs to the LSP. When the protected LSP-Path is signaled, the PATH message with certain FRR flags set in the `SESSION_ATTRIBUTE` is propagated from the HE router to the Tail router. When each hop (except the Tail router) sees the FRR flags, it assumes the PLR role and later tries to establish the protection tunnel. Every hop reports its FRR availability back to the HE router with RRO flags in the RESV message. Thus, the HE router is aware of the FRR availability for every hop.

The HE router is also aware of the network failure and the FRR protection that is in use. When a network failure occurs and the PLR uses FRR to reroute the traffic around the failure, the PLR notifies the HE router concurrently in two ways:

- The PLR sets the corresponding FRR `local-protection-in-use` flag in the RRO object of the RESV message.

- The PLR sends a `PathErr` message with an `ERROR` object. The error code is 25 (`0x19`) — `RSVP Notify Error`. The error value is 3 (`0x03`) — `tunnel locally repaired`.

At this point, the HE router updates the LSP-Path status to indicate the protection-in-use flag as well as the PLR location. The HE router reacts to the FRR event in the following manner:

- If there is an available hot-standby secondary LSP in the LSP, the HE router switches the traffic to the secondary LSP.
- In the absence of standby secondary LSP-Paths, any non-standby secondary LSP-Paths that are configured and dormant are initiated. These secondary LSP-Paths then try to set up their respective paths.
- The HE router re-signals the LSP-Path in a make-before-break (MBB) manner to find a better path for the LSP-Path. If this is successful, a new LSP-Path is established, and the traffic is switched back to the new protected LSP-Path.

When a network failure happens and FRR takes effect to protect the LSP, the HE router is notified immediately by the `PathErr` message notification from the PLR, and the RESV messages with the `local-protection-in-use` flag set in the RRO. When the HE router becomes aware that FRR is in use, it starts the *retry-timer* (the default value is 30 seconds). When the HE router detects a failure, it immediately starts an MBB process for the protected LSP-Path that had a failure. The HE router also switches traffic to any standby secondary LSP-Paths that are operationally **up**. If no standby secondary LSP-Paths are present, the HE router starts up any secondary LSP-Paths that were configured. If secondary LSP-Paths are successfully signaled, the HE switches traffic to the first secondary LSP-Path that was successful. The HE continues with the MBB process for the primary LSP-Path until it succeeds. Note that the MBB process is started immediately, but it actually tries to set up the LSP only after the retry-timer expiry. When the MBB process succeeds, the HE switches traffic to the successful protected LSP-Path that replaces the original protected LSP-Path. The MBB process may succeed because the cause of the fault is removed, in which case, the new MBB path for the LSP-Path follows the old path. Alternatively, the MBB process may have found another path for the LSP-Path that routed traffic around the failure point and satisfied the same constraints the primary LSP-Path required.

Point-of-Local-Repair (PLR) Router Behavior

The PLR router of the protected LSP is also the origination point (HE router) of the protection tunnel (detour LSP or bypass tunnel). When FRR is configured, all the routers (except the Tail router) along the path of the protected LSP assume the PLR role. They all pre-signal the protection tunnels (detour LSPs or bypass tunnels), so they are prepared to fix the failure local to each router. When FRR is configured, the HE router assumes the PLR role too. The other routers along the path receive a PATH message with the SESSION_ATTRIBUTE object's FRR flag(s) set and containing the optional FRR object. These routers also assume the PLR role. After the protected LSP is established, all routers start signaling the desired FRR protection tunnel. In the case of facility backup, if a bypass tunnel already fulfills the requirement, the router does not signal another tunnel.

When a network failure happens, the upstream router local to the failure assumes the actual PLR role and provides active protection for the protected LSP-Path. During the network failure, the PLR has the following responsibilities:

- The PLR starts to use the protection tunnel (detour LSP or bypass tunnel) to forward the traffic for the protected LSP-Path. The egress label that the PLR uses differs depending on the protection method:

    - In the case of one-to-one backup, the one-to-one detour is just another LSP-Path. The PLR simply uses the label that was distributed by the immediate downstream router on the detour LSP (the *detour label*) to detour the traffic arriving from the upstream router of the protected LSP-Path. The label arriving from the immediate upstream router of the protected LSP-Path is swapped with the detour label, and the traffic is sent through the detour LSP-Path.

    - In the case of facility backup, the data from the protected LSP-Path is tunneled through the bypass tunnel. Therefore, the outer label of the tunneled packet is the label distributed by the immediate downstream router of the bypass tunnel. The PLR also needs to know what label was expected by the router where this tunneled traffic merges (MP). The record label option makes this information available from the RRO. This is the inner label that must be in the tunneled packet. Thus, the PLR swaps the incoming label from the immediate upstream router in the protected path with these two labels and sends the path through the bypass tunnel.

    Details regarding both of these scenarios are discussed in later sections.

- The PLR notifies the HE router that there is a network failure by:

    - Setting the corresponding FRR in-use flag in the RRO object of the RESV message it generated toward the HE router.

- Sending a PathErr message with an ERROR object. The error code is 25 (0x19) – RSVP notify error. The error value is 3 (0x03) – tunnel locally repaired.

- The PLR also maintains the state of the protected LSP-Path by continuing to send the original PATH message to the MP router to refresh the protected LSP-Path. It acts like a refresh agent during the failure by refreshing the protected LSP-Path. The refresh mechanisms used by one-to-one detour and facility backup are different. Both of them are discussed in greater detail in later sections.

The HE router continues to attempt to set up a new LSP-Path to the Tail router. The success of this attempt may be due either to the removal of the failure or the HE router meeting the constraints using another path around the failure point. The PLR maintains the original LSP-Path. This LSP-Path is then torn down when the HE router switches traffic to the newly established protected LSP-Path that replaces the original LSP-Path. The LSP-Path teardown causes the PLR to clear its session and remove any detours. Bypass tunnels are removed if no LSP-Path is using the bypass tunnels for protection. The routers along the path of the new protected LSP-Path again attempt to create protections as assumed PLRs.

When the failure is removed, the PLR router becomes the assumed PLR again and is ready to protect the LSP-Path against future network failures.

Merge Point (MP) Router Behavior

The MP router is the point where the protection tunnel (detour LSP or bypass tunnel) and the protected LSP meet. The MP router is the termination point (Tail router) of the protection tunnel. Similar to the role of PLR, before the failure actually happens, every router (except the HE router) assumes the role of an MP router that can terminate the protection tunnel signaled by the assumed PLR upstream. When a failure happens, one of the downstream routers becomes the actual MP router and merges traffic back to the protected LSP-Path. When the failure is removed, the MP router becomes the assumed MP again, since there is no longer a failure.

The MP router's location, function, and behavior have variations depending on the protection type (link or node), protection method (one-to-one or facility backup), and implementation of FRR. The detailed behavior of MP routers is discussed with respect to each protection method in later sections. However, regardless of the implementation variations, the MP routers perform the following general functions:

- **Merge Traffic Back to the Protected LSP-Path** — When the protected traffic arrives at the MP, the MP router merges the traffic to the protected LSP-Path. The MP router must understand the meaning of the outer label in the traffic being rerouted around the failure.

  In one-to-one backup, the mapping of labels for the detour LSP and the protected LSP-Path is straightforward. There is one ingress label (detour LSP) and one egress label (protected LSP). The MP performs a *swap* operation.

  In facility protection, the traffic arrives with an extra (bypass tunnel) label. Initially, the MP *pops* out the bypass tunnel label to expose the original MPLS label-stack of the traffic. This label is the same label that was distributed to the immediate upstream router on the protected tunnel. Therefore, this label is already programmed to be swapped with the downstream label of the protected label. Additional details are provided in later sections.

- **Maintain the Protection Tunnel's State** — As the Tail router of the protection tunnel, the MP sends RESV messages upstream to refresh the protection tunnel.

- **Maintain the Protected LSP-Path's State** — As mentioned previously, the PLR refreshes the protected LSP by sending its original PATH message to the MP router. The MP router must understand the refresh messages and send the original RESV message back to refresh the protected LSP-Path as well. Thus, the protected LSP-Path does not time out because of the network failure.

Tail Router Behavior

If the Tail router of the protected LSP-Path is not also the MP router, there is no extra action required from the Tail router during the failure. The Tail router is not aware of the failure or of the FRR activity. After the failure is removed, the Tail router identifies an MBB re-signal to the LSP and reacts accordingly:

1. The Tail router receives a new PATH message arriving with a different LSP-id in the SENDER_TEMPLATE object.

2. The Tail router builds the Path State Block (PSB). The Tail router then builds the RESV State Block (RSB) and sends a new RESV message, with a new label, upstream to start the reservation process.

3. When the HE router confirms the establishment of the new LSP-Path for the protected LSP-Path, it sends the PathTear message to tear down the old

protected LSP-Path. After the Tail router receives the `PathTear` message, it removes the old PSB and RSB for the original protected LSP-Path.

4. If the HE router has a standby secondary LSP-Path active during the FRR, the HE switches the traffic to the secondary LSP-Path. The Tail router sees the traffic arriving with a different outer label.

Choosing the MP for the Protection Tunnel

The location of the PLR router is decided by the location of the failure. All routers assume the PLR role to establish their protections. When a failure occurs in the network, the upstream router that is local to the failure becomes the *actual* PLR. The location of the PLR cannot be chosen. The assumed PLR, which becomes the actual PLR and reroutes the traffic to the protection tunnel, depends on the location of the network failure. However, the location of the MP depends on the FRR implementation. There are two common options for the MP location where the protection tunnel terminates:

-   **Far-MP Approach** — The protection tunnel terminates *as close as possible to the Tail router of the protected LSP*. This allows the traffic to stay in the protected tunnel (alternative path) as long as possible.

-   **Near-MP Approach** — The protection tunnel terminates *as close as possible to the PLR router*. The MP is the PLR's NHop router (for link protection) or NNHop router (for node protection). Thus, the traffic is merged back to the original path of the protected LSP as soon as possible.

    The terms *far* and *near* refer to the relative distance between the MP and the PLR. Each approach has its advantages and disadvantages.

Far-MP Approach

The Far-MP approach provides more optimal traffic forwarding. When the PLR calculates the path for the protection tunnel using the Far-MP approach, the strategy is to avoid the link or node it protects and find the best path to send the traffic to the protected LSP-Path's original destination. Hence, the CSPF always chooses the shortest path to forward the traffic to the Tail router of the protected LSP-Path. The disadvantage is that the location of the protected LSP's Tail router determines the path of the protection tunnel. Consider the case in which the same PLR routers of different LSPs all have the same next-hop router with a common link. The link protection of these three protection tunnels protects the same link, but the MP is different if the Tail routers of the three protection tunnels are different. Therefore, in this scenario using the Far-MP approach, three different protection tunnels are created to protect the failure of the same network element, even if facility backup is used. This is because the three protected LSP-Paths have different Tail router locations. The top diagram in Figure 7.8 illustrates this example.

Figure 7.8 Merge Point (MP) Location Options Example I

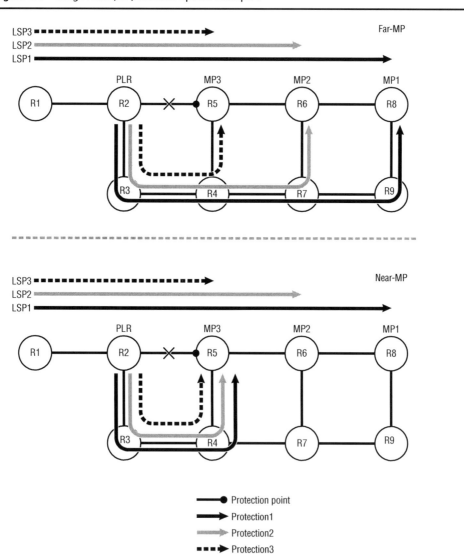

PART II ■ IP/MPLS VPN PROTOCOL FUNDAMENTALS

Near-MP Approach

The Near-MP approach is more topology-efficient. The bottom diagram in Figure 7.8 illustrates the protection tunnels using the Near-MP approach. All protection tunnels have the same path because they share a common topology. The three LSPs have different Tail routers, but for the link protection between R2 and R5, they all use the same PLR and MP router. Because this example requires link protection, the protected tunnel to protect link R2–R5 failure uses R2 as PLR, and R5 (R2's NHop router) as the MP. Obviously, this is a better solution for facility backup because these protected LSPs can share the same bypass tunnel of R2 → R3 → R4 → R5 to protect the link between R2 and R5. The drawback of the Near-MP approach is that its forwarding path may not be optimal; this is true especially if the NHop router or NNHop router is not in the best path to the Tail router. Figure 7.9 illustrates such an example.

Figure 7.9 Merge Point (MP) Location Options Example II — Ring Topology

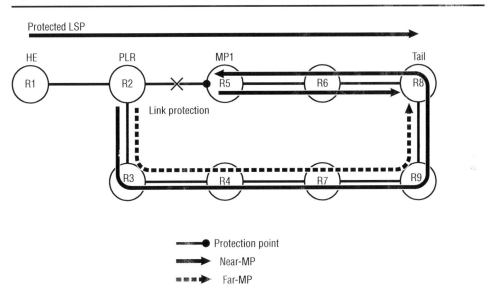

When using the Near-MP approach in the network shown in Figure 7.9, the protected traffic takes a longer path during the failure. The traffic must turn around at the Tail router and travel back to the MP in the protection tunnel and then travel back toward the Tail router again. If a Far-MP approach is used, the traffic takes the *shortest path from the PLR to the Tail Router.* The MP router is in the path between the PLR and the Tail, or in some cases, the MP is the Tail router.

The ALSRP implements both approaches in the most optimal way:

- The one-to-one backup detour LSP uses the Far-MP approach. The PLR chooses the best path to the Tail router, avoiding the link or node to be protected. Thus, the protected traffic reaches the Tail router in the most optimal path. In a one-to-one backup, the detour LSP is not shared by multiple LSPs; therefore, topology efficiency is not a concern.

- The facility backup bypass tunnel uses the Near-MP approach. The MP is the NHop router of the PLR providing link protection. The MP is the NNHop router of the PLR providing node protection. Thus, the link protection bypass tunnel is shared by all LSPs with two common hops connected by the same link. All LSPs with three common hops can share the same node protection bypass tunnel. In facility backup, topology efficiency is the major concern. Therefore, the most efficient solution is to allow as many protected LSP-Paths as possible to share the same protection.

For a router to assume the PLR role and signal a protection tunnel, the router requires detailed information regarding the original path of the protected LSP-Path. If this information cannot be provided, the FRR cannot be signaled successfully. The following information is required:

- The *complete* and *exact* original path information of the protected LSP, including every hop router it traverses. This information is acquired from the RRO object in the RESV messages.

- The labels that were distributed by each router to its upstream router. This information is needed for facility backup. The information is gained from the RRO of the RESV message.

- The network topology in order to calculate a possible alternative path to detour around the next-hop link/node. This information is acquired from the routing protocol and its traffic engineering extension.

- The CSPF algorithm to calculate the path for the protection tunnel.

Therefore, CSPF and traffic engineering are required to enable FRR in the network. For any router to calculate the protection tunnel for a protected LSP, it must know the complete and exact path information. The complete and exact path information is acquired from the RRO of the RESV message for the protected LSP-Path. RRO must be available (enabled by default) for FRR to work. FRR cannot be used to protect an IGP-directed LSP-Path with an empty hop list, because there is no ERO or RRO.

For more details regarding the IGP and CSPF-directed LSP-Path and strict/loose hops, refer to Chapter 3.

7.4 One-to-One Backup

In the method of one-to-one backup, each LSP-Path has its own set of pre-signaled detour LSPs. For LSP-Paths with different characters, operators may want to configure different types of protection. In one-to-one backup, each LSP can have its own detour LSPs with different hop limits and protection types (link or node). One-to-one backup has better *granularity* than facility backup but consumes more resources (more protecting LSPs are required). When a failure happens, each protected LSP uses its own detour LSP to protect the traffic.

When an HE router has an LSP configured with one-to-one backup, it sends the PATH message indicating the type of FRR desired in the following manner:

1. It adds the FAST_REROUTE object having the one-to-one backup desired flag set (0x10).

2. If node protection is desired, the SESSION_ATTRIBUTE object's flag also has the node-protection-desired bit set (=0x01). This is because the FAST_REROUTE object does not have a flag indicating node protection.

3. In a one-to-one backup for both link protection and node protection, the local-repair-desired flag bit in the SESSION object is not set (=0x01). This indicates that local revert mechanisms are not to be performed on this LSP-Path.

After the protected LSP-Path is successfully established, all routers (except the Tail router of the protected LSP) assume the PLR role and start signaling the detour LSPs. The PATH messages generated by each router (when they assume the PLR role to signal the detour LSPs) have the following content:

- They all use the same SESSION object and SENDER_TEMPLATE object as the protected LSP. Thus, the detour LSP has the same LSP-id, tunnel-id, ext-tunnel-id value, and sender address.

- They all have a DETOUR object containing the PLR router's IP address and the IP address that the detour LSP is trying to avoid.

- The ERO contains a path (list of link IP addresses) to reach the Tail router of the protected LSP that avoids the IP address being protected (the avoid node id field in the DETOUR object).

- The RRO of the DETOUR object inherits the RRO in the PATH message of the protected LSP-Path. Then, the local egress interface's IP address is appended into the RRO.
- The router's egress interface's IP address is also inserted into the HOP object.
- The name of the detour LSP set in the SESSION_ATTRIBUTE object. All detour LSPs have their name in the format of {Protected LSP name}::{Protect LSP path name}_detour. As an example, the name lsp-to-163::163_detour means that this detour is protecting the lsp with name *lsp-to-163* and path name *163*.

All one-to-one detour LSPs use the same LSP-id and tunnel-id as the protected LSPs. Figure 7.10 illustrates the LSP P1 → P3 → P4 → P6 with detour LSPs providing one-to-one backup with link protection.

Figure 7.10   One-to-One Link Protection Example

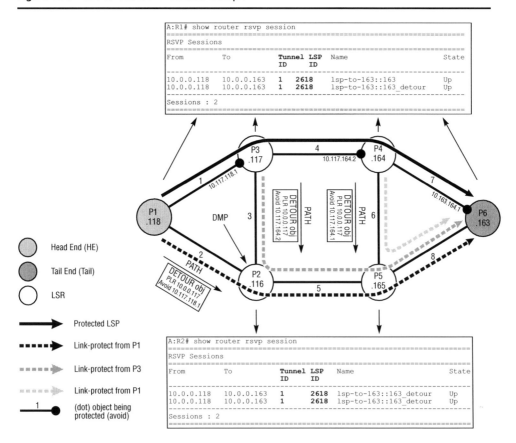

Figure 7.10   *(continued)*

```
A:R1# show router mpls lsp path detail
=======================================================================
MPLS LSP  Path  (Detail)
=======================================================================
Legend :      @ - Detour Available           # - Detour In Use
              b - Bandwidth Protected         n - Node Protected
=== output omitted ===
ExplicitHops:
10.0.0.117     -> 10.0.0.164    -> 10.0.0.163
Actual Hops :
   10.117.118.2(10.0.0.118) @       Record Label    : N/A
-> 10.117.118.1(10.0.0.117) @       Record Label    : 131070
-> 10.117.164.2(10.0.0.164) @       Record Label    : 131070
-> 10.163.164.1(10.0.0.163)         Record Label    : 131070
ComputedHops:
   10.117.118.2  -> 10.117.118.1  -> 10.117.164.2  -> 10.163.164.1
LastResignal: n/a                   CSPF Metric : 3000

Detour Stat*: Standby               Detour Type : Originate
Detour Avoi*: 10.117.118.1          Detour Orig*: 10.0.0.118
Detour Acti*: n/a                   Detour Up T*: 0d 00:00:15
In Interface: n/a                   In Label    : n/a
Out Interfa*: 1/1/1                 Out Label   : 131069
Next Hop    : 10.116.118.1
Explicit Ho*:
   10.116.118.2  -> 10.116.118.1  -> 10.116.165.2  -> 10.163.165.1
=======================================================================
* indicates that the corresponding row element may have been truncated.
```

In the network topology shown in Figure 7.10, all routers (except the Tail router) along the path of the protected LSP have detour LSPs signaled. In the link protection, for each PLR, the network element to be protected is the ingress interface of the NHop router. If the local router can no longer see this IP address in its routing table, the router switches the traffic to the detour LSP. In node protection, the NHop router is the network element to be protected.

The PLR router switches the traffic to the detour LSP when PLR sees a link failure, Hello time-out, or Hello instance mismatch on the outgoing link on the protected LSP-Path, or when it sees a `ResvTear` message or RESV state time-out on the protected LSP-Path.

As mentioned previously, if an operator wants an LSP-Path to have FRR protection, all routers along the path of the LSP-Path (except the Tail router) try to signal a protection tunnel. If the topology allows an LSP to contain n hops in the network, there should be $n - 1$ detour LSPs signaled, one for each router along the path. All the detour LSPs are signaled automatically, so there is no extra configuration overhead. However, in a scaled network with many LSPs requiring FRR protection, one-to-one backups may significantly increase the number of LSPs in the network.

Maintaining the State of the Protected LSP-Path during a Failure

As mentioned, during a failure the PLR notifies the HE router by setting the local-repair-in-use flag. The PLR does not refresh the PATH message of the protected LSP-Path toward the MP. The MP does not refresh RESV messages toward PLR. The PLR and MP maintain the state of the protected LSP-Path when there is a detour to protect the LSP-Path.

Data Plane: Forwarding Protected Traffic over Detour LSPs

When a failure happens, a router upstream of the failure becomes the PLR and switches the traffic to the detour LSP. For node protection, it is not necessarily the immediate upstream router that switches traffic to the detour LSP. Any upstream router that detects a failure on the protected LSP-Path can switch the traffic to the detour LSP. This typically happens in the case where the immediate upstream router cannot set up a detour LSP. Figure 7.11 illustrates the PLR's data plane forwarding behavior during a node failure. The behavior of the link protection detour LSP is similar.

The router tries to establish the node protection, one-to-one detour with three attempts. If the node protection detour cannot be set up, the router then switches to link protection. In this case, if the link protection cannot be established either, the PLR will keep retrying the node protection setup. Consider the case in Figure 7.11 where node protection is desired, and the third-hop LSR (router marked with X) tries a node protection setup. In this scenario, it will not be able to establish the node protection detour LSP. When the LSR *falls back* to set up link protection instead, it will find a path from itself to the second-hop LSR (router marked *PLR*) and then travel though the two routers in the bottom of the topology in Figure 7.11, and then to the MP router. At this stage, there would be a detour merge at the second-hop router (*detour merge* is discussed later). However, if link protection is desired, the second-hop LSR will find the path on the first attempt.

Protected traffic is rerouted into the detour LSP to travel around the node failure in the following sequence:

1. The Tail router distributes the labels for the protected LSP-Path (the 10x labels) toward the HE router when signaling the protected LSP.

2. After the protected LSP-Path is established, because one-to-one link protection is desired, the PLR signals the detour LSP to the MP router. The MP distributes the labels (the 20x labels) toward the PLR. It also programs a swap entry in the data plane to swap label 200 to label 100 of the protected

LSP-Path. Note that all routers along the protected LSP try to signal the protection, but in this topology, only the second-hop router from the HE has a path that can provide the node protection to the LSP-Path. The third-hop LSR (the LSR in the center of the figure) will find a link protection for the LSP-Path and merge traffic to the second-hop router (router marked *PLR*).

Figure 7.11 Label Used in One-to-One Backup Node Protection

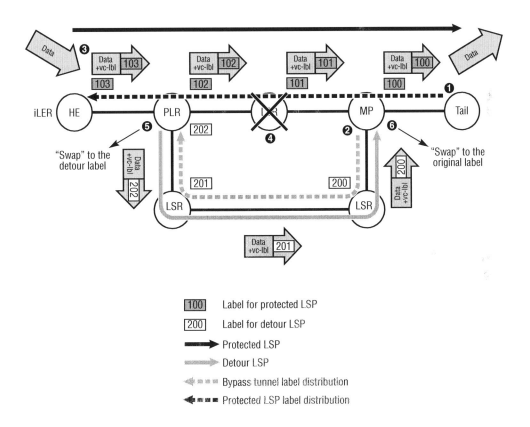

3. Before there is any network failure, traffic travels through the protected LSP-Path.

4. The LSR router between the PLR and the MP fails.

5. The PLR reroutes the traffic from the protected LSP-Path through the detour LSP. This is done by programming the swap on the PLR router of the *egress*

label of the protected LSP-Path to the *egress label of the detour LSP*. Label 103 is swapped to label 202 during the failure, instead of label 102.

6. When the MP router receives the traffic, it automatically swaps the label 200 with the egress label for the protected LSP (label 100). Thus, the traffic is merged back to the protected LSP and travels toward the Tail router.

Detour Merge Point (DMP)

In some cases, depending on network topology, there may be occasions in which multiple detour tunnels protecting the same LSP traverse the same path. In such a scenario with a one-to-one detour, the multiple detours protecting the same LSP are merged into one detour downstream router. The DMP is the router where multiple detour LSPs intersect and are merged. Merging overlapped one-to-one detour tunnels reduces the number of LSPs in the entire network. This moderates the scaling challenge caused by the $n-1$ detour LSP requirement for one-to-one backup. Figure 7.12 demonstrates one scenario in which two one-to-one detour LSPs merge at the DMP (R2).

Figure 7.12 Detour Merge Point

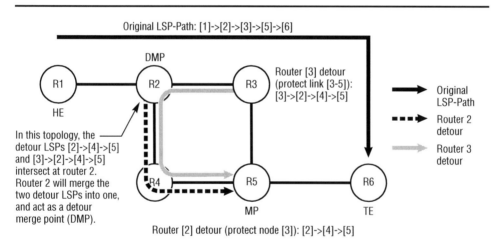

One-to-One Backup versus Secondary LSP

Frequently, one-to-one backup and secondary LSP are compared as possible alternatives when choosing an MPLS resiliency mechanism for a core network solution. They both provide LSP protection on a per-LSP-Path basis using a dedicated protection tunnel, rather than a shared bypass tunnel. However, they use different techniques to provide protection for the LSP, and their convergence performances are different. Table 7.4 compares the supported features on secondary LSP and FRR.

Table 7.4 Secondary LSP versus Fast Reroute

Features	Secondary LSP	FRR One-to-One	Facility
Color aware	Yes	No	No
SRLG aware	Yes	Yes	Yes
Number of protection tunnels per LSP	1–8 (configuration)	Up to $n-1$ for n-hop LSP-Path	Up to $n-1$ for n-hop LSP-Paths (shared)
Manual control of path	Yes	No	Optional (with manual bypass tunnel configuration)
RFC 4090 enhancement for RSVP-TE	No	Yes	Yes
Protection of Fixed Filter (FF) style LSP	Yes	Yes	No
Scalability	Medium	Medium	High

One-to-one backup detour LSPs are automatically signaled as soon as the protected LSP-Path is configured and established. Detour LSPs use the same tunnel-id and LSP-id as the protected LSP. If there is no DMP, for each n-hop LSP-Path, there can be up to $n-1$ detour LSPs signaled if every router can find an alternative path in the topology to provide protection. Each detour only protects the link or node failure immediately downstream from the PLR router. The failover to a one-to-one backup detour LSP can be within tens of milliseconds after the failure is detected by the PLR. The detour LSP's actual hop is determined via the protected LSP-Path's RRO when the CSPF consults the TED. The FRR is not link-color-aware; it cannot use administrative groups as constraints when calculating the detour LSP. Shared Risk Link Group (SRLG) can be used to control the path of the detour LSP. Chapter 4 presents an example of SRLG controlling FRR protection tunnel paths.

The secondary LSP is a manually configured secondary LSP-Path for the same LSP. Only the HE router is aware of the relationship between the primary LSP-Path and the secondary LSP-Paths. The secondary LSP-Path may or may not be presignaled before the network failure happens; this depends on whether *hot-standby* is configured. The HE router recognizes the protection provided by the secondary

LSP-Path. When a network failure occurs in the primary LSP-Path, the failure must be propagated to the HE router before it can switch the traffic over from the primary LSP-Path to the secondary LSP-Path. If hot-standby is not enabled, it takes some time for the HE router to establish the secondary LSP-Path. Therefore, the secondary LSP protection reaction time is slightly slower than an FRR detour LSP if the failure is not local to the HE router. Because the secondary LSP is also an explicitly configured LSP-Path, it is possible to copy or change most of the configurations of the protected primary LSP-Path. Secondary LSPs are aware of administration groups (link-coloring) and can be SRLG-disjointed from the primary LSP-Path. Each LSP can have up to seven secondary LSP-Paths to protect its primary LSP-Path. The number of LSPs in the network protecting the primary LSP-Path depends on the configuration. Only explicitly configured secondary LSP-Paths with the *standby* option enabled will coexist with the primary LSP-Path. Thus, it is easier to control the number of LSPs in the network with secondary LSPs compared to using FRR one-to-one detour LSPs (unless the manual bypass tunnel is used).

The one-to-one backup detour LSP and secondary LSP can coexist to protect the same LSP. The behavior of this combined protection during network failure is described in detail in later sections.

One-to-One Backup Configuration Example

By default, FRR is disabled in the LSP configuration. To enable FRR, the configuration must be explicitly specified in the LSP configuration context. As discussed in Chapter 3, when using RSVP-TE for LSP signaling, the LSP is manually created in the HE router first. There can be more than one LSP-Path in the same LSP: one primary LSP-Path and up to seven secondary LSP-Paths. Although the MPLS FRR is enabled in the LSP level, only the primary LSP-Path can be protected by the FRR. Figure 7.13 illustrates a one-to-one backup configuration example.

Figure 7.10 contains the CLI output of the protected LSP's status and one of the established detour LSPs. In the `show router rsvp session` command, filters can be added to show only the detour LSPs. There are three filters available as command options:

- `detour` — Show all originated detour LSPs that are one-to-one backups for the protected LSP-Paths, where the local router is the HE of the detour LSP (assumes the role of PLR).

- `detour-transit` — Show all detour LSPs not locally originated and not locally terminated.

- detour-terminate — Show all detour LSPs terminated locally, in which the local router is the Tail router of the detour LSP.

Figure 7.13 FRR One-to-One Backup Configuration Example

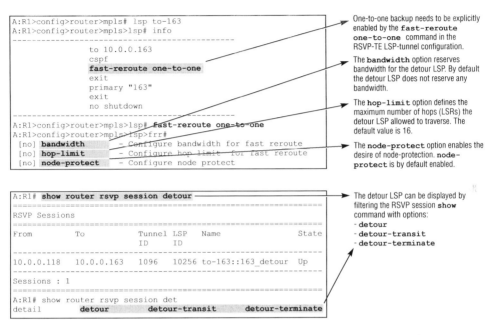

```
A:R1>config>router>mpls# lsp to-163
A:R1>config>router>mpls>lsp# info
-----------------------------------------
                to 10.0.0.163
                cspf
                fast-reroute one-to-one
                exit
                primary "163"
                exit
                no shutdown
-----------------------------------------
A:R1>config>router>mpls>lsp# fast-reroute one-to-one
A:R1>config>router>mpls>lsp>frr#
[no] bandwidth        - Configure bandwidth for fast reroute
[no] hop-limit        - Configure hop limit for fast reroute
[no] node-protect     - Configure node protect
```

One-to-one backup needs to be explicitly enabled by the **fast-reroute one-to-one** command in the RSVP-TE LSP-tunnel configuration.

The **bandwidth** option reserves bandwidth for the detour LSP. By default the detour LSP does not reserve any bandwidth.

The **hop-limit** option defines the maximum number of hops (LSRs) the detour LSP allowed to traverse. The default value is 16.

The **node-protect** option enables the desire of node-protection. **node-protect** is by default enabled.

```
A:R1# show router rsvp session detour
===============================================================
RSVP Sessions
===============================================================
From          To           Tunnel  LSP    Name              State
                           ID      ID
---------------------------------------------------------------
10.0.0.118   10.0.0.163    1096    10256  to-163::163_detour  Up
---------------------------------------------------------------
Sessions : 1
===============================================================
A:R1# show router rsvp session det
detail       detour       detour-transit     detour-terminate
```

The detour LSP can be displayed by filtering the RSVP session **show** command with options:
- **detour**
- **detour-transit**
- **detour-terminate**

7.5 Facility Backup

In a facility backup configuration, all protected LSPs with common network segments share the same bypass tunnel. One bypass tunnel between a pair of PLRs and MPs provides the FRR protection for all LSP-Paths that desire protection and that are traversing the link/node that the PLR-MP pair can protect. Compared to one-to-one backup, facility backup reduces the number of protection tunnels required to provide FRR. Facility backup bypass tunnels can be automatically signaled by MPLS routers assuming a PLR role. Manual FRR bypass tunnels can also be configured in the system to provide more control of the bypass tunnel's path. The manual bypass tunnel is introduced in the next section.

When multiple protected LSPs are protected against failure in the common path via the same bypass tunnel, they compete for bandwidth. Thus, it is not the best practice to use facility bypass tunnels to protect LSPs that require strict exclusive resource reservation. As of the date of publication, ALSRP service router's FRR implementation does not allow facility backup in LSPs enabled with a reservation style of Fixed Filter (FF). Only LSPs with Shared Explicit (SE) reservation style can have the FRR facility backup enabled. Details regarding reservation styles are discussed in Chapter 5.

Because facility backup uses a many-to-one protection mechanism, traffic from multiple protected LSPs share the same bypass tunnel. When a network failure happens, traffic flows from multiple protected LSPs are rerouted by the PLR through the single bypass tunnel. When these traffic flows reach the MP router, the MP router must merge the traffic flow back to different protected LSP-Paths. In order to do this, the MP router must identify which protected LSP-Path each traffic flow belongs to. The MP router requires information to merge the traffic back to the correct protected LSP-Paths. Therefore, the facility backup method uses a different traffic encapsulation mechanism compared to the one-to-one backup method. Facility backup takes advantage of the MPLS label stacking capability and uses a third label to encapsulate the protected traffic and carry it through the bypass tunnel. Note that the traffic encapsulation mechanism used is different from the encapsulation used for one-to-one backup. With facility backup, the PLR and MP routers use the following mechanisms to encapsulate the protected traffic:

- When the PLR reroutes the traffic away from the local failure, it keeps both labels in the protected traffic's MPLS label stack. It pushes the third *bypass tunnel label* to re-encapsulate the protected traffic and then sends the traffic over the bypass tunnel. The protected traffic now has one more label in the MPLS label stack, the bypass tunnel label on the top.

- All routers along the bypass tunnel swap only the top bypass tunnel label to switch the traffic toward the termination point of the tunnel. The protected traffic is *tunneled* from the PLR to the MP router; this is why the protection tunnel used by FRR facility backup is called the *bypass tunnel*.

- At the termination point of the bypass tunnel, the MP router first pops the bypass tunnel label to expose the original traffic. Then, the MP identifies the original LSP-Path by examining the outer labels (MPLS transport label) and merges the traffic back to the correct protected LSPs.

Recall that a one-to-one detour LSP uses the same SESSION and SESSION_ TEMPLATE objects as the protected LSP-Path. The facility bypass tunnel does not use these objects. The facility bypass tunnel is shared by many protected LSP-Paths, but it is an individual LSP-Path by itself, with its own LSP-id and Tunnel-id. Therefore, it uses its own SESSION and SESSION_TEMPLATE objects in the PATH messages. The bypass tunnel's tunnel source is the PLR, and its tunnel destination is the MP. The facility bypass uses the Near-MP approach:

- For link protection, the bypass tunnel originates at the PLR and terminates at the PLR's NHop router. The MP is always the NHop router of the PLR.

- For node protection, the bypass tunnel originates at the PLR and terminates at the PLR's NNHop router. The MP is always the NNHop router of the PLR.

Thus, LSP-Paths can share the bypass tunnel providing their paths go through same PLR and MP.

When an HE router has an LSP configured with facility backup desired, the HE router sends a PATH message indicating this by:

- Adding the FAST_REROUTE object having the `facility backup desired` flag set (0x02)

- Setting the SESSION_ATTRIBUTE object's flag of `local-protection-desired` bit to 1. If node protection is desired, it will also set the `node-protection-desired` bit to 1. The FAST_REROUTE object does not have a flag indicating node protection.

- Setting the `label-recording-desired` flag (=0x02) in the SESSION_ATTRIBUTE object

All routers (except the Tail router of the protected LSP) then assume the PLR role and start signaling the bypass tunnels. The PATH messages generated by each router (when they assume the PLR role to signal the bypass tunnel) have the following content:

- They all have a FASTREROUTE object, containing the PLR router's IP address and the IP address that the detour LSP is trying to avoid.

- In the SESSION_ATTRIBUTE object, the name of the bypass tunnel is set to the format of `bypass-{link|node}{IP address of the protected object}`. As an example, the bypass tunnel name of *bypass-link10.117.118.1* means that this tunnel is providing a link protection for the link with one side's IP address

`10.117.118.1`. All LSPs desiring link protection on that link, by that particular IP address, can share this tunnel.

These routers may recognize that there is already a suitable bypass tunnel present. This tunnel may be signaled by other protected LSP-Paths demanding the same protection and traveling the same path. Alternatively, the bypass tunnel may already have been configured manually (the manual bypass tunnel is discussed in a later section). In these cases, the router associates the protected LSP-Paths to the existing bypass tunnel instead of building a new one and sets the corresponding FRR available flags. The router uses the following criteria to determine if the bypass tunnel is suitable:

- The tunnel has the same PLR and MP and protects the target network element (link or node).
- The tunnel fulfills protection requirements such as hop limits or SRLG.

If there is not an existing bypass tunnel available, then every assumed PLR signals the bypass tunnel after the protected LSP is established. This signaling process builds new LSP-Paths with no correlation to any other LSPs. The router generates a new PATH message with new content. Once established, the bypass tunnel is a common protection facility and can be used by many LSP-Paths requiring the same protection; hence, the name *facility backup*. Figure 7.14 illustrates an example of facility backup.

Figure 7.14 Facility Backup Bypass Tunnels

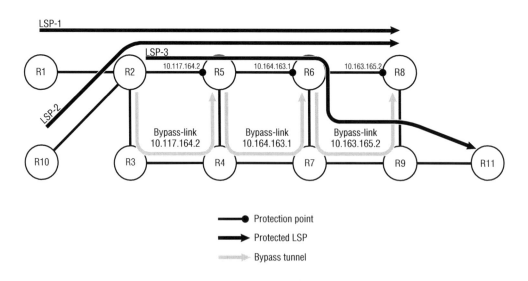

In Figure 7.14, LSP1 is configured from R1 to R8 with facility backup link protection desired. When R1 establishes LSP1 from R1 to R8, routers R2, R5, and R6 each build a bypass tunnel to protect the egress interface (link). After LSP1 and all the bypass tunnels are established, LSP2 is configured in router R10. R10 signals LSP2 to R8, and R2 signals LSP3 to R11. Both LSP2 and LSP3 request facility backup with link protection as well. In this case, R2 recognizes that there is already a bypass tunnel providing the link protection. R2 does not signal another bypass tunnel for LSP2 but uses the existing bypass tunnel as LSP2's FRR protection. This same scenario happens with R5 and R6 for LSP2; R2 and R5 use the existing bypass tunnels to protect LSP3.

With LSP3 there are two new bypass tunnels established to provide full FRR protection (not shown in Figure 7.14):

- R6 establishes bypass tunnel R6 → R8 → R9 → R7 to protect the direct link between R6 and R7.
- R7 establishes bypass tunnel R7 → R6 → R8 → R9 to protect the direct link between R7 and R9.

Maintaining the State of the Protected LSP during Failure — Refresh through the Bypass Tunnel

As mentioned, during the failure the PLR notifies the HE router using a RESV message with the `local-repair-in-use` flag set. The PLR also must send PATH messages in order for the protected LSP-Path to keep refreshing the PSB of the MP router for the protected LSP-Path. This prevents the protected LSP-Path from a refresh time-out. In the case of a facility bypass tunnel, the PLR sends the PATH message for the protected LSP-Path toward the MP router (NHop or NNHop router) through the bypass tunnel in the following manner:

- The PATH message is sent through the bypass tunnel encapsulated with the bypass tunnel label (like the traffic being protected).
- In the PATH message, the PLR must modify the first IPv4 subobject of the ERO. This is because the original ERO on the egress PATH message (for the protected LSP before the failure) contains the IP address of the failed interface. If the PLR does not replace that IP address with an active IP address of its own,

the MP may reject the refresh because the MP router considers the IP address in the failed interface as invalid. The MP router sends a `PathErr` message back to the PLR indicating `bad sub-object` TLV. Therefore, the PLR must modify the ERO before sending out the refresh PATH message.

- The MP router also sends the RESV message to the previous hop of the PATH message using hop-by-hop routing.

This process ensures that during the failure there is no time-out by the RSB in PLR and the PSB in MP for the protected LSP-Path.

Data Plane: Forwarding Protected Traffic over Bypass Tunnel

The facility backup mechanism uses a shared bypass tunnel to protect multiple LSPs sharing a *common facility*. When rerouting the traffic around the failure using facility backup, the PLR must push a label into the top of the traffic's MPLS label stack. The traffic being protected is already double-labeled; it has a top transport label and a bottom service label.

Note that in the IP/MPLS VPN network, LSPs are used to transport VPN service traffic. VPN services are always double-tagged with an inner vc-label and an outer transport label. Chapter 9 introduces the IP/MPLS VPN architecture and the VPN encapsulation of the service traffic.

After the PLR reroutes the traffic into the bypass tunnel, it has three labels in the stack: the top bypass tunnel label, the middle transport label, and the bottom service label.

In certain circumstances, the PLR may need to *swap* the transport label before it reroutes traffic into a facility bypass tunnel (the push operation). This is required if the facility bypass provides node protection. Figures 7.15, 7.16, and 7.17 illustrate the case of link protection and node protection with the PLR's use of labels when rerouting the traffic.

Figure 7.15 illustrates the label distribution and usage when using the facility backup bypass tunnel to provide link protection.

Figure 7.15 Label Usage on Facility Backup Link Protection

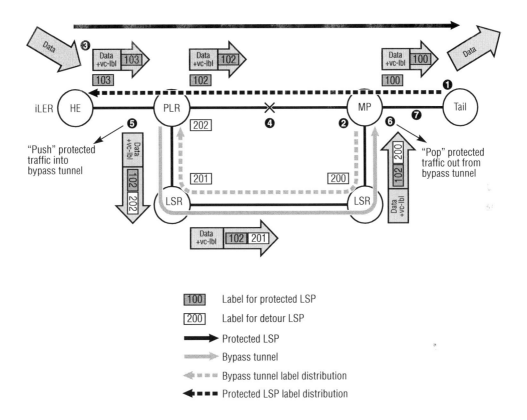

Facility link protection

[100]	Label for protected LSP
[200]	Label for detour LSP
→	Protected LSP
⇒	Bypass tunnel
◄----	Bypass tunnel label distribution
◄■■■■	Protected LSP label distribution

In Figure 7.15, the protected LSP-Path is established before the failure, and the following scenario begins:

1. The Tail router distributes the labels for the protected LSP-Path (10x labels) toward the HE router.

2. Because facility link protection is desired, the PLR signals the bypass tunnel to the MP. The MP distributes the labels (20x labels) toward the PLR.

3. Traffic travels through the protected LSP-Path.

4. The link between the PLR and the MP fails.

5. The PLR reroutes the traffic from the protected LSP-Path through the bypass tunnel as follows:

   a. The PLR performs a *swap* operation to replace label value 103 with value 102 as if there is no failure along the protected LSP.

   b. The PLR then performs a *push* operation with label 202 on top of the label stack. This label is used for traffic travel over the bypass tunnel. The triple-labeled traffic then travels through the bypass tunnel to reach the MP router.

6. When the MP router receives the traffic, it first *pops* the bypass tunnel label because the MP is the Tail router of the bypass tunnel. The MP then sees the original double-labeled traffic with the top label 102. The MP router understands the label value 102 because it distributes this label to the PLR for the PLR to use as an egress label for traffic over the protected LSP. This occurs because, in link protection, the MP is the PLR's NHop router and every router receives a label from the NHop router.

7. The MP router merges the traffic back by performing a swap operation: Replace label 102 with label 100 as if it received the traffic from the PLR over the protected LSP-Path. Traffic will then reach the Tail router over the protected LSP-Path.

This mechanism works perfectly in the case of link protection. From the MP's perspective, packets are constantly ingressing with the transport label 102. When FRR protects traffic, the PLR pushes an extra bypass tunnel label on top of the traffic's label stack, and the MP pops out the extra bypass tunnel label and exposes the original traffic's label stack.

However, in the facility backup node protection scenario, this mechanism may cause problems. Consider a scenario where the PLR performs the same actions of swapping the transport label then pushing the bypass tunnel label and sending traffic. When the MP router receives the traffic, it has trouble identifying which LSP-Path the traffic belongs to because the MP router is the NNHop router of the PLR, and the MP router does not understand the meaning of the exposed outer label in the traffic's original label stack. Figure 7.16 illustrates a network using a facility backup bypass tunnel to provide node protection.

Facility node protection (1)

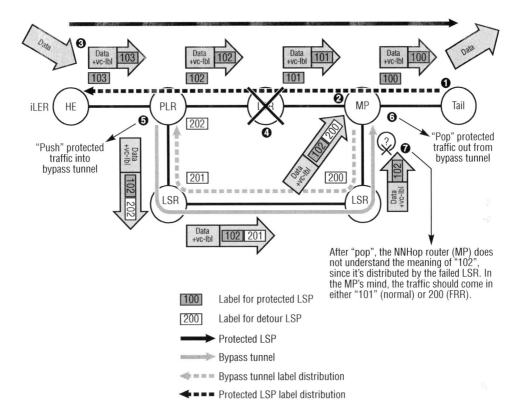

100   Label for protected LSP

200   Label for detour LSP

➡   Protected LSP

⇒   Bypass tunnel

◀ = = =   Bypass tunnel label distribution

◀ ■ ■ ■   Protected LSP label distribution

After "pop", the NNHop router (MP) does not understand the meaning of "102", since it's distributed by the failed LSR. In the MP's mind, the traffic should come in either "101" (normal) or 200 (FRR).

Protection cannot be achieved if the PLR behaves the same way as in the link protection scenario. In Figure 7.16, the protected LSP-Path was established before the failure, and the following scenario begins:

Note that the following events are *not* the way the FRR facility bypass tunnel handles traffic. This scenario is based on an unreal assumption and is presented to explain why the facility backup node protection cannot use the same mechanism as the link protection to forward the protected traffic. This scenario explains what *could* happen if it could use the same mechanism.

1.   The Tail router distributes the labels for the protected LSP (10x labels) toward the HE router.

2.   Because facility node protection is desired, the PLR signals the bypass tunnel to the MP. The MP distributes the labels (20x labels) toward the PLR.

3. Traffic travels through the protected LSP-Path.

4. The LSR router between the PLR and the MP fails.

5. The PLR reroutes the traffic from the protected LSP-Path through the bypass tunnel as follows:

    a. The PLR performs a *swap* operation to replace label 103 with label 102, as if there is no failure along the protected LSP. Note that we are assuming that the PLR behaves in the same manner as in the link protection case. (This is not true in reality, and this example is simply used to show the behavior that should *not* happen.)

    b. The PLR performs a *push* operation with label 202 on top of the label stack. This label is required for traffic to travel over the bypass tunnel. The triple-labeled traffic then travels through the bypass tunnel to reach the MP router.

6. When the MP router receives the traffic, it *pops* the bypass tunnel label because it is the Tail router of the bypass tunnel. The MP then sees the original double-labeled traffic with top label 102.

7. It is at this stage that there is a problem in this scenario. *The MP router does not understand the meaning of label value 102.* This is because the MP router does not have an ingress label mapping for value 102. In node protection, the MP and PLR are two hops away along the path of the protected LSP-Path. The MP is the PLR's NNHop router. In the establishment of the protected LSP-Path, the MP did not distribute the label to the PLR. It distributed the label (101) to the LSR between itself and the PLR. That LSR then distributed label 102 to the PLR. Therefore, the MP does not have an entry in the Label Information Base (LIB) for label 102. The MP discards MPLS traffic with unrecognized labels. Therefore, the protected traffic is then discarded. There may be a possibility that the MP has an entry of label value 102 in the LIB that is reserved for another LSP-Path. In this case, the traffic is handled as if it belonged to that LSP-Path and *cross-talk* between LSP-Path happens. This is a waste of bandwidth and a breach of security.

To solve this problem, the PLR must not use the label distributed by the currently failed NHop router when rerouting the traffic to the facility bypass tunnel providing node protection. During the failure, the PLR sends traffic to the NNHop router over the bypass tunnel and must use the label distributed by the NNHop router to perform the swap operation before pushing the bypass tunnel label.

How Does the PLR Know What Label Value Is Distributed by an NNHop Router?

The label distributed by the NNHop router is contained in the RRO object in the RESV message of the protected LSP-Path. The RRO object records both the system-ID of each hop and the label distributed by each hop. The RRO is stored in the RSB for the protected LSP-Path. Using the RRO, the PLR knows what label it should use, and the problem is solved. By default, the MPLS LSP is configured to record the labels in the RRO. If label recording is disabled in an LSP, the FRR facility backup for node protection cannot be configured on that LSP.

Figure 7.17 illustrates the actual PLR behavior during the FRR facility backup node protection.

Figure 7.17   PLR Swaps the Label for the MP before Pushing the Traffic to the Bypass Tunnel

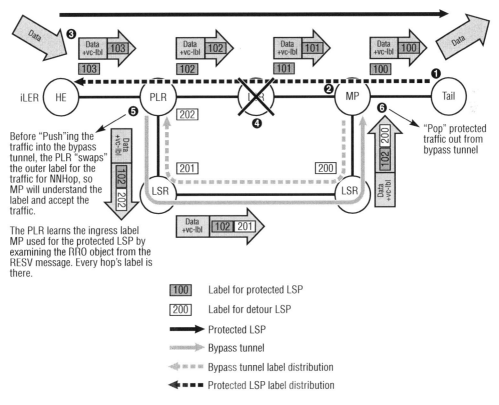

Facility node protection (2)

Before "Push"ing the traffic into the bypass tunnel, the PLR "swaps" the outer label for the traffic for NNHop, so MP will understand the label and accept the traffic.

The PLR learns the ingress label MP used for the protected LSP by examining the RRO object from the RESV message. Every hop's label is there.

"Pop" protected traffic out from bypass tunnel

100	Label for protected LSP
200	Label for detour LSP
➡	Protected LSP
➡	Bypass tunnel
◀===	Bypass tunnel label distribution
◀■■■	Protected LSP label distribution

In Figure 7.17, the protected LSP-Path is established before the failure, and the following scenario for FRR facility bypass protection of a node failure begins:

1. The Tail router distributes the labels for the protected LSP (10x labels) toward the HE router.

2. Because facility node protection is desired, the PLR signals the bypass tunnel to the MP. The MP distributes the labels (20x labels) toward the PLR.

3. Traffic travels through the protected LSP-Path.

4. The LSR router between the PLR and the MP fails.

5. The PLR reroutes the traffic from the protected LSP through the bypass tunnel as follows:

    a. The PLR performs the *swap* operation to change the transport label. Because PLR is currently providing node protection on the traffic over the bypass tunnel, it knows that the traffic will reach the NNHop router (MP) instead of the NHop router (failed LSR). Therefore, the PLR *swaps* out label 103 using the label distributed by the NNHop router to the NHop router (101), instead of the NHop router label of 102.

    b. The PLR performs a *push* operation with label 202 on top of the label stack. This label is used to encapsulate traffic that will travel over the bypass tunnel. The triple-labeled traffic then goes through the bypass tunnel to reach the MP router.

6. When the MP router receives the traffic, it *pops* the bypass tunnel label since it is the Tail router of the bypass tunnel. The MP router sees the original double-labeled traffic with the top label 101. The MP router recognizes the value 101 because it distributes this label to the failed LSR for use as an egress label for traffic over the protected LSP-Path.

7. The MP router merges the traffic back by performing a *swap* operation: Replace label 101 with label 100 as if it received the traffic from PLR over the protected LSP. Traffic will then reach the Tail router over the protected LSP.

Figure 7.18 presents an example of the HE router's view of FRR using a facility bypass tunnel to protect the LSP-Path. The figure presents the view from the HE router before and after a node failure along the LSP-Path (10.117.164.2/24). The following list compares the LSP-Path status output before (left) and after (right) the node failure:

1. Before the failure, the LSP has available FRR protection from all hops except the Tail router.

    a. The Tail router cannot provide FRR because it is the termination point and has no alternative path.

    b. The @ character indicates that FRR protection is available (`local-repair-available`) in a hop.

    c. The letter n indicates that node protection is desired and is available in the HE and second-hop router.

    d. The second-last-hop router always provides only link protection since it can only protect the link to the Tail router, not the Tail router itself.

    e. The output does not contain `Detour LSP` information, which implies that the FRR uses facility backup, not a one-to-one detour.

2. The LSP-Path's `up time` and `down time` indicate that there is no outage (0 down time) in this LSP-Path at this point.

3. After the link failure, the LSP-Path still indicates a zero (0) down time. Fast Reroute protects the LSP-Path and keeps the session operationally up.

4. The HE router recognizes the failure and the FRR protecting event:

    a. The `Failure code` indicates there is an FRR event (`tunnelLocallyRepaired`).

    b. The `Failure node` indicates the PLR (`10.0.0.117`) is currently protecting the LSP.

    c. The # sign indicates the location of the PLR in the LSP-Path.

5. Global revert MBB is immediately started upon receipt of the `PathError` message with `tunnelLocallyRepaired` flagged. However, the MBB LSP-Path setup is tried only after the retry-timer expires (by default, in 30 seconds). Upon expiry of the timer, the HE router starts retrying the CSPF

calculation to find a new path for the LSP-Path in the MBB manner. In this example, there are no other available paths so the CSPF calculation will fail and retry. The difference in CSPF queries values (Figure 7.18, middle of both outputs) is 5. This matches the output value of the RetryAttempt (bottom right). This demonstrates that all new CSPF queries after the failure are LSP-Path reverting retries using MBB. Because the new LSP-Path cannot be established, the old LSP-Path is maintained.

Figure 7.18 Facility Backup FRR in Use Example

```
A:R1# show router mpls lsp lsp-to-163 path detail
===============================================================================
MPLS LSP lsp-to-163 Path  (Detail)
===============================================================================
Legend :
     @ - Detour Available             # - Detour In Use
     b - Bandwidth Protected          n - Node Protected
===============================================================================
-------------------------------------------------------------------------------
LSP lsp-to-163 Path 163
-------------------------------------------------------------------------------
LSP Name     : lsp-to-163             Path LSP ID : 2596
From         : 10.0.0.118             To          : 10.0.0.163
Adm State    : Up                     Oper State  : Up
Path Name    : 163                    Path Type   : Primary
Path Admin   : Up                     Path Oper   : Up
OutInterface: 1/1/2                    Out Label   : 131069
Path Up Time: 0d 22:50:52 ❷          Path Dn Time: 0d 00:00:00
Retry Limit  : 0                      Retry Timer : 30 sec
RetryAttempt: 0                       Next Retry *: 0 sec
Bandwidth    : 30 Mbps                Oper Bw     : 30 Mbps
Hop Limit    : 255
Record Route: Record                  Record Label: Record
Oper MTU     : 1496                    Neg MTU     : 1496
Adaptive     : Enabled
Include Grps:                         Exclude Grps:
None                                  None
Path Trans  : 39                      CSPF Queries: 594
Failure Code: noError                 Failure Node: n/a
ExplicitHops:
     10.0.0.117      -> 10.0.0.164     -> 10.0.0.163
Actual Hops :
     10.117.118.2(10.0.0.118) @ n     Record Label    : N/A
  -> 10.117.118.1(10.0.0.117) @ n ❶  Record Label    : 131069
  -> 10.117.164.2(10.0.0.164) @       Record Label    : 131069
  -> 10.163.164.1(10.0.0.163)         Record Label    : 131069
ComputedHops:
     10.117.118.2     -> 10.117.118.1     -> 10.117.164.2     -> 10.163.164.1
LastResignal: n/a                     CSPF Metric : 3000
Last MBB     :
 MBB Type    : ConfigChange           MBB State   : Success
 Ended At    : 08/19/2003 23:32:50    Old Metric  : 3000
===============================================================================
* indicates that the corresponding row element may have been truncated.
```

Figure 7.18 *(continued)*

After the link failure

```
A:R1# show router mpls lsp lsp-to-163 path detail
===============================================================================
MPLS LSP lsp-to-163 Path  (Detail)
===============================================================================
Legend :
    @ - Detour Available             # - Detour In Use
    b - Bandwidth Protected          n - Node
Protected
===============================================================================
-------------------------------------------------------------------------------
LSP lsp-to-163 Path 163
-------------------------------------------------------------------------------
LSP Name    : lsp-to-163            Path LSP ID : 2596
From        : 10.0.0.118            To          : 10.0.0.163
Adm State   : Up                    Oper State  : Up
Path Name   : 163                   Path Type   : Primary
Path Admin  : Up                    Path Oper   : Up
OutInterface: 1/1/2                 Out Label   : 131069
Path Up Time: 0d 22:54:42 ❸        Path Dn Time: 0d 00:00:00
Retry Limit : 0                     Retry Timer : 30 sec
RetryAttempt: 0                     Next Retry *: 0 sec
Bandwidth   : 30 Mbps               Oper Bw     : 30 Mbps
Hop Limit   : 255
Record Route: Record                Record Label: Record
Oper MTU    : 1496                  Neg MTU     : 1496
Adaptive    : Enabled
Include Grps:                       Exclude Grps:
None                                None
Path Trans  : 39                    CSPF Queries: 599
Failure Code: tunnelLocallyRepaired Failure Node: 10.0.0.117
ExplicitHops:
    10.0.0.117     -> 10.0.0.164      -> 10.0.0.163
Actual Hops :
    10.117.118.2(10.0.0.118) @ n     Record Label    : N/A
 -> 10.117.118.1(10.0.0.117) @ # n ◄— ❹   Record Label  : 131069
 -> 10.163.165.1(10.0.0.163)         Record Label    : 131069
ComputedHops:
    10.117.118.2    -> 10.117.118.1    -> 10.117.164.2    -> 10.163.164.1
LastResignal: n/a                   CSPF Metric : 3000
Last MBB    :
  MBB Type  : ConfigChange           MBB State   : Success
  Ended At  : 08/19/2003 23:32:50    Old Metric  : 3000
In Prog MBB :
  MBB Type    : GlobalRevert          NextRetryIn : 11 sec
  Started At  : 08/20/2003 00:57:35 ❺ RetryAttempt: 5
  FailureCode : noCspfRouteToDestination  Failure Node: 10.0.0.118
===============================================================================
* indicates that the corresponding row element may have been truncated.
```

Moving Traffic Away from the Protection LSP-Path

In a protection switchover, the HE router of the protected LSP tries to find a path to move the traffic away from the FRR protection in the following manner:

- If the protected LSP-Path has a standby secondary LSP-Path that is operationally up, the HE router switches the traffic to the standby secondary LSP-Path.

- If the protected LSP-Path has secondary LSP-Paths but they are not pre-established *standby* LSP-Paths, the HE router will *not* try to bring up any secondary LSP-Paths to carry the traffic.

- With or without secondary LSP-Paths, the HE router will start the effort of re-signaling a new LSP (primary LSP). If the effort succeeds, the HE router switches the traffic to the newly established protected LSP in an MBB manner. If the effort fails, the HE router will try again every time the retry-timer expires.

Global revertive mode refers to this behavior of the protected LSP-Path's HE router to re-set-up the new LSP-Path and switch traffic. The mode of *local revertive* also exists, wherein the PLR tries to establish a new LSP and switches traffic to it. Most vendors' implementations support the global revertive mode. The ALSRP implements MPLS FRR in a global revertive mode.

Facility Backup Configuration Example

By default, MPLS FRR is disabled on the LSP configuration. To enable MPLS FRR, the configuration must be explicitly specified in the LSP configuration context. As introduced in Chapter 5, the LSP is first created when RSVP-TE is used for LSP signaling. There can be more than one LSP-Path in the same LSP, and one of them can be a primary LSP-Path. Although the MPLS FRR is enabled in the LSP level using the CLI, only the primary LSP-Path can be protected by FRR. Figure 7.19 presents a facility backup configuration example.

Figure 7.19 contains the CLI output of the protected LSP-Path's status and one of the established detour LSPs. Note that in the show router rsvp session command, the bypass tunnel option filters all other sessions but only displays locally originated facility backup bypass tunnels (the router is the HE of the bypass tunnel). If there are any transiting or terminating bypass tunnels, their RSVP sessions in the router will also be removed from the show command by the bypass tunnel filter.

Figure 7.19   FRR Facility Backup Configuration Example

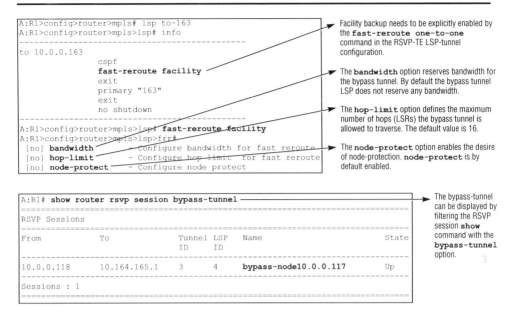

```
A:R1>config>router>mpls# lsp to-163
A:R1>config>router>mpls>lsp# info
-----------------------------------------------
to 10.0.0.163
                cspf
                fast-reroute facility
                exit
                primary "163"
                exit
                no shutdown
-----------------------------------------------
A:R1>config>router>mpls>lsp# fast-reroute facility
A:R1>config>router>mpls>lsp>frr#
  [no] bandwidth        - Configure bandwidth for fast reroute
  [no] hop-limit        - Configure hop limit for fast reroute
  [no] node-protect     - Configure node protect
```

Facility backup needs to be explicitly enabled by the **fast-reroute one-to-one** command in the RSVP-TE LSP-tunnel configuration.

The **bandwidth** option reserves bandwidth for the bypass tunnel. By default the bypass tunnel LSP does not reserve any bandwidth.

The **hop-limit** option defines the maximum number of hops (LSRs) the bypass tunnel is allowed to traverse. The default value is 16.

The **node-protect** option enables the desire of node-protection. **node-protect** is by default enabled.

```
A:R1# show router rsvp session bypass-tunnel
===============================================================
RSVP Sessions
===============================================================
From          To            Tunnel LSP   Name                    State
              ID     ID
---------------------------------------------------------------
10.0.0.118    10.164.165.1  3      4     bypass-node10.0.0.117   Up
---------------------------------------------------------------
Sessions : 1
===============================================================
```

The bypass-tunnel can be displayed by filtering the RSVP session **show** command with the **bypass-tunnel** option.

7.6 Manual Bypass Tunnel

RFC 4090 describes the automatic establishment of the bypass tunnel and the one-to-one detour through the RSVP-TE signaling. When an LSP-Path originates from an HE router or traverses though an LSR, if the local-protection desired flag in the SESSION_ATTRIBUTE object of the PATH message is set, all routers (except the Tail router) assume the role of PLR and try to signal the bypass/detour LSP as requested. When the protected LSP-Path is torn down, all signaled one-to-one detour LSPs for that LSP-Path are cleared as well. In the case of facility backup, if the last protected LSP-Path on the common network segment requesting facility backup is torn down, the bypass tunnel protection for that segment is removed as well.

In a service provider's core network, there are times when controlled actions are preferable to automatic activities. It may be desirable to use manual configuration to override automatic configuration as well as to disable automatic configuration while retaining controlled FRR protection. To achieve this, the MPLS router/switch must be capable of allowing manual configuration on the bypass tunnel, without receiving the request through the establishment of the protected LSP-Path. The manual bypass tunnel solves this problem.

This does not conflict with the automatic signal of protection that is presented by RFC 4090. When an LSP requests protection from a router (HE or LSR), the router first verifies whether there is a configured manual bypass tunnel that fulfills the requirement. If a preconfigured manual bypass tunnel exists, it is used as the protection; if it does not exist, the node signals a new bypass tunnel to protect the LSP as stated in RFC 4090. Before the preconfigured manual bypass tunnel can be selected to protect a certain LSP, it must match the following criteria:

- The manual bypass tunnel must merge back to the original path of the LSP-Path it will protect.
- The manual bypass tunnel must fulfill the requirement in the FRR object for the protected LSP.

Note: As per RFC 4090, when signaling dynamic facility bypass tunnels for FRR node protection, the bypass tunnel launched from the PLR node should merge back to the NNHop router, to protect the failure against the next-hop router of the PLR. If the PLR chooses a manual bypass tunnel to provide node protection on certain LSPs, this rule is no longer applicable. Providing the manual bypass tunnel can allow traffic to avoid the next-hop router and merge back to the original path along the LSP-Path, it is considered a suitable alternative and is used to protect the LSP. This is true even if the manual bypass tunnel is less optimal for the topology (as it contains a lot more hops in the path).

Figure 7.20 illustrates the use of a manual bypass tunnel that is not merged back to an NNHop router for node protection of the LSP.

In all the cases, manual bypass tunnels are always preferred over dynamic signaled tunnels, provided they can provide the desired protection. When manual bypass tunnels are not available, the routers will try to signal the dynamic bypass tunnels to provide FRR protection.

Figure 7.20 Using a Manual Bypass Tunnel That Does Not Merge Back to the NNHop Router

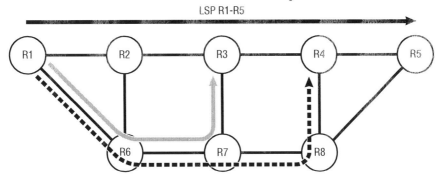

1 LSP R1-R5 follows path R1-R2-R3-R4-R5, requesting facility backup with node protection.

2 If dynamic bypass tunnel signaling is used, router R1 as PLR will signal the bypass tunnel LSP R1-R6-R7-R3 to protect LSP R1-R5 against node failure of R2.

LSP R1-R5

3 If there is already a manual bypass tunnel LSP configured in router R1, R1-R6-R7-R8-R4 it will protect the node failure of R2; even if this manual bypass tunnel is not merged back to the next-next-hop router, router R1 will still consider this bypass tunnel suitable to provide node failure protection (against R2) for LSP R1-R5, and hence will use it as protection, and will not signal a new dynamic bypass tunnel anymore.

Original LSP

Dynamic bypass

Manual bypass

Rules of Engagement: Selecting Bypass Tunnels

There are two types of bypass tunnels for the protected LSP: manual bypass tunnels preconfigured by the operator and dynamic bypass tunnels configured by the router when the LSP-Path is signaled. Therefore, it is necessary to clearly indicate when a manual bypass tunnel is associated with the protected LSP, and when the system will use a dynamic signaled bypass tunnel to protect the LSP. The basic rules for choosing bypass tunnels for the LSP being protected are as follows:

- Always select an eligible manual bypass tunnel over a dynamic bypass tunnel. Use manual bypass tunnels for a newly created LSP if there is currently a manually created bypass tunnel in the PLR suitable for the protection requirement. Use a dynamic single bypass tunnel only when there is no suitable manual bypass tunnel at any hop.

- If there are many manual bypass tunnels in the same PLR that fulfill the protection requirement of the protected LSP, select the tunnel with the lowest path cost to provide protection to the LSP. If two bypass tunnels have the same path cost, select the first available manual bypass tunnel.

- When the dynamic bypass tunnel function is disabled, the manually configured bypass tunnel is automatically associated with all suitable LSP-Paths traversing that node. The PLR protects these LSP-Paths using the manual bypass tunnel. If the manual bypass tunnel is created after the normal LSP-Paths are established, the tunnel protects the existing suitable LSP-Paths starting from the moment of the next RESV refresh.

- When the dynamic bypass tunnel function is enabled (default behavior), if a manual bypass tunnel is created, the existing LSPs with a dynamic bypass tunnel will *not* switch to the manual bypass tunnel. This is true even if the manual bypass tunnel is more optimal (has lower path cost). In this case, if the operator wants to switch from the dynamic bypass tunnel to a suitable manual bypass tunnel, it requires a *re-signal* (using MBB) of the existing protected LSP.

- The manual bypass tunnel takes precedence over the dynamic signaled bypass tunnel. Consider the scenario of an existing LSP requiring FRR protection that currently has a dynamic bypass tunnel signaled when the manual bypass tunnel comes up (assume that the bypass tunnel is suitable for the LSP being protected). In this case, any re-signal or administrative `shut` and `no shut` of the protected LSP-Path with a dynamic bypass tunnel causes the LSP-Path to use the manual bypass tunnel, providing it is suitable. This occurs regardless of whether the manual bypass tunnel is optimal or not. Furthermore, the dynamic bypass tunnel is torn down if this is the last LSP-Path it is protecting.

  Note that a bypass tunnel (both dynamically or manually created) can be shared by many LSP-Paths. If one LSP-Path being protected is re-signaled and then decides to use the newly created manual bypass tunnel, the dynamic bypass tunnels are not cleared providing there are still other LSP-Paths using them.

A manual bypass tunnel allows the operator to control the numbers and paths of the bypass tunnels. The preceding rules indicate that the manual bypass tunnel is preferred over the dynamic signaling of the bypass tunnel, as long as the manual bypass tunnel fulfills the protection needs of the LSP-Path. Even if the manual bypass tunnel is not in the optimal path, if it can provide the required protection if it is used by the

PLR to protect the suitable LSP, instead of signaling a more optimal dynamic one. Figure 7.21 presents the CLI output of both manual and dynamic bypass tunnels.

Figure 7.21   Manual and Dynamic Bypass Tunnels

```
A:PE-118# show router mpls bypass-tunnel
===============================================================================
MPLS Bypass Tunnels
===============================================================================
Legend :  m - Manual              d - Dynamic
===============================================================================
To              State  Out I/F      Out Label    Reserved   Protected  Type
                                                 BW (Kbps)  LSP Count
-------------------------------------------------------------------------------
10.164.165.2    Up     1/1/2        131065       0          1          d

10.0.0.163      Up     1/1/1        131068       0          1          m

10.0.0.117      Up     1/1/1        131066       0          1          m
-------------------------------------------------------------------------------
Bypass Tunnels : 3
===============================================================================
```

Another advantage of the manual bypass tunnel is its support of the use of administrative groups. Because the manual bypass tunnel is configured in the same manner as a regular LSP, the include and/or exclude list of administrative groups can be set in the LSP parameters. As discussed previously, the dynamic bypass tunnel signaled by the PLR is not aware of link-coloring and administrative groups. LSP-Paths using manual bypass tunnel configuration can also take advantage of administrative groups, which gives the operator more control of where to establish the bypass tunnel.

Figure 7.22 illustrates the re-signaling of an existing LSP-Path that requests a switch in protection from the dynamic bypass tunnel to the preconfigured manual bypass tunnel.

What If the Manual Bypass Tunnel Fails?

The PLR checks the protection status of all LSPs requesting protection every time it receives a RESV message for an LSP. If the manual bypass tunnel is no longer available, the PLR searches for other manual bypass tunnels to protect the LSP. If there is no available suitable manual bypass tunnel, dynamic bypass tunnels are established to protect the LSP.

Figure 7.22   Manual Bypass Tunnel Interaction with Dynamic Bypass Tunnel

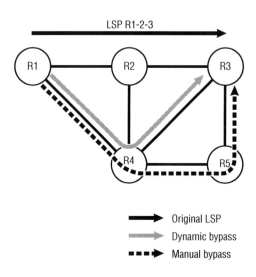

❶ LSP R1-2-3 originated from R1, going through R2 and reaching router R3, requesting node protection.

❷ When there is no suitable manual bypass tunnel, router R1 as PLR signals a bypass tunnel of R1-R4-R3 to protect failure against router R2.

❸ Operator manually creates a bypass tunnel LSP in router R1, going through path R1-R4-R5-R3. which can provide node protection against router R2 for any LSP traversing path R1-R2-R3.

❹ Because the dynamic bypass tunnel is already established when the operator creates the manual bypass tunnel, the original LSP will still use the dynamic bypass tunnel.

❺ When the original LSP is re-signaled, the router R1 as PLR found the manual bypass tunnel which is suitable for the node protection request of the LSP (even if it traverses more hops than the path the dynamic bypass tunnel would have taken), so the manual bypass tunnel will be used, and the previously dynamic signaled bypass tunnel will be cleared since there is no other LSP being protected by it.

LSP R1-2-3

➡ Original LSP

➡ Dynamic bypass

■■■➡ Manual bypass

Summary

The RSVP-TE-signaled MPLS LSPs support two major resiliency features: secondary LSPs and FRR. Secondary LSPs require a manual configuration of redundant LSP-Paths to protect the primary LSP in the same LSP. The HE router of the LSP switches traffic to the secondary LSP-Path when the primary LSP-Path is down. With FRR, each router along the LSP being protected pre-signals the protection and routes the traffic around the local failure. In many cases, MPLS FRR has a faster convergence time than secondary LSP because the failures are protected by the router local to the failure.

MPLS FRR (defined by RFC 4090) requires all routers along the protected LSPs to be involved in the failure protection. Every hop router assumes the role of PLR so when failures occur, the router closest to the failure will react. MPLS FRR provides two methods of protection:

- **One-to-One Backup** — Each protected LSP-Path has its own set of detour LSPs signaled by all routers involved. The protection is dedicated to the LSP-Path being protected.
- **Facility Backup** — All LSP-Paths share a common section of network using the same bypass tunnel. An extra label is used by the bypass tunnel to route the traffic around the failure. Using facility backup significantly reduces the number of LSPs that the network must maintain.

From a topology perspective, FRR can protect the failure over a link (link protection) or over a node (node protection). The desired method (one-to-one or facility) and topology (link or node) are configurable in the LSP and signaled through RSVP-TE PATH messages.

When a network failure happens, the router closest to the failure (PLR) reroutes the traffic over the pre-signaled detour LSP or bypass tunnel. The PLR uses RSVP-TE messages to notify the HE router of the failure and the protection in use. The HE router then tries to find a new path for the LSP being protected and re-signals the protected LSP in an MBB manner if there is an alternative path for the LSP.

Alternatively, the facility backup bypass tunnel can also be manually created in the network. This allows the operator to control the path of the bypass tunnel. When an LSP-Path that requires protection by the FRR facility backup is established, if any manual bypass tunnels are available and meet the protection requirement, the manual bypass tunnel is used, and the corresponding router will not signal another bypass tunnel dynamically.

Label Distribution Protocol

8

This chapter introduces the Label Distribution Protocol (LDP). LDP is one of the MPLS signaling protocols. It automatically builds LSPs that follow the Interior Gateway Protocol (IGP) path calculated from the IGP routing table. Targeted LDP (T-LDP) is used to signal pseudowires for Layer 2 VPN services (VLL and VPLS).

Chapter Objectives

- Provide an overview of LDP

- Explain the difference between link LDP and Targeted LDP

- Review the session establishment procedures of link LDP and Targeted LDP

- Review the LDP message types, formats, and their type–length values (TLVs)

- Explain LDP over RSVP (LDPoRSVP) tunneling

This chapter discusses the basic operational process of LDP. The detailed signaling procedures and message contents for the Layer 2 VPN pseudowire signaling are discussed separately for each service.

8.1 LDP Overview

Defined by RFC 3036 (later updated by RFC 5036), the *Label Distribution Protocol* is a signaling protocol used to distribute Multi Protocol Label Switching (MPLS) labels. Routers speaking LDP form LDP sessions among themselves and then generate MPLS labels and distribute them over LDP sessions. When LDP is used to distribute labels, two pieces of information are included:

- **Label Value** — The value of the MPLS label used by the receiver to encapsulate the traffic and send it out (egress label).
- **Forwarding Equivalent Class (FEC)** — The FEC defines the purpose of the label being distributed.

  Thus, the label distribution information is often referred to as *FEC-Label binding*.

  Traditionally, LDP is used in MPLS-capable IP routers to distribute labels for IPv4 addresses. Hence, the FECs signaled in LDP messages are IPv4 prefixes. When using LDP in service-oriented IP/MPLS VPN networks, two types of labels can be signaled through LDP:

- Transport labels are signaled through link LDP.
- Service-labels (vc-labels) are signaled through Targeted LDP.

  Both types of LDP sessions are described in the following section.

8.2 LDP Session Establishment and Management

LDP is a session-based protocol, similar to the Border Gateway Protocol (BGP). Two routers must establish *adjacency* before the actual label distribution can proceed. LDP sessions are Transmission Control Protocol (TCP) sessions maintained by the LDP keep-alive messages. There are two types of LDP peering relationships:

- **Link-LDP Sessions** — Also known as interface-LDP, link-LDP sessions can only be established between directly adjacent LDP routers. Two routers must have at least one directly connected IP interface; the two Layer 3 interfaces directly connecting the two routers have their IP addresses in the same IP subnet. There is only one link LDP session between two LDP routers, even if the two routers have more than one directly connected IP interface. Link-LDP sessions distribute the system address of the P/PE routers with MPLS label bindings to allow for carrying traffic across the P/PE backbone. This forms a full mesh of LDP-LSPs among all P/PE routers. Both Provider (P) routers and Provider Edge (PE) routers in the IP/MPLS VPN backbone network require link-LDP sessions to neighbors if LDP-LSP must be signaled. Different types of LSPs are discussed in detail in Chapter 3.

- **Targeted-LDP Sessions (T-LDP)** — T-LDP sessions can be established between any two LDP routers in the network provided their system-IP addresses are reachable. T-LDP sessions signal pseudowires and distribute vc-labels for the system to perform VPN encapsulation for VPN traffic sent over the pseudowires. PE routers require T-LDP sessions among themselves. P routers are not VPN-aware; therefore, they may not need T-LDP sessions. However, in the case of LDP over RSVP (LDPoRSVP, discussed in later sections in this chapter), T-LDP sessions may be added in P/PE routers to distribute prefix labels.

The two types of LDP sessions have no correlation. Link-LDP sessions are only required if LDP-signaled LSPs are required as transport tunnels. In an IP/MPLS VPN network, T-LDP sessions are always required between all PE routers because they are used for signaling the pseudowires used by VPN services.

The general LDP operation involves the following processes:

- **Peer Discovery** — Routers use LDP Hello messages to automatically discover the peers that also participate in LDP.

- **Session Establishment and Management** — LDP sessions are TCP sessions between peering routers. Session establishment and management includes setting up the LDP session between routers and maintaining the sessions using keep-alive messages.

- **Label Management** — LDP uses messages to distribute and withdraw FEC/Label mappings.

- **Notification** — LDP uses notification messages to notify errors to peering routers.

Link-LDP Adjacency Establishment

Link-LDP sessions are used to signal LDP-LSP. The automatically created LDP-LSP overlay shares the same topology as the IGP routing table. Therefore, in order to build the LDP-LSP for the entire network, every P or PE router in the entire VPN provider backbone network must have link-LDP sessions for all directly adjacent neighbors. Link-LDP adjacency can only be established between two directly connected Layer 3 interfaces. When there are multiple Layer 3 links between two adjacent routers, only one link-LDP session is established. The mechanism used by link-LDP to set up sessions is referred to as the *basic discovery mechanism*. The basic discovery mechanism requires four steps:

1. **Hello Adjacency Establishment** — The LDP router starts the neighbor *discovery process* by sending out link-LDP Hello messages in every LDP-enabled interface. The link-LDP session communicates only over directly connected interfaces in the same IP subnet. Therefore, the link-LDP Hello packet is a User Datagram Protocol (UDP) packet (port = 646) destined for the multicast IP address of 224.0.0.0 (all routers in the network). The LDP LSR-id with label space is announced in the Hello packet. After the discovery process, the LDP Hello adjacency is established.

2. **TCP Transport Connection Establishment** — Two routers must establish TCP sessions for the LDP Hello adjacency. When they attempt to open a new TCP connection, they must determine which router takes the active role and which takes the passive role. In a TCP session for LDP, the active role is the *client* using a random TCP source port number, and the passive role is the *server* using the well-known LDP port of 646. The active/passive role of the two routers is decided by comparing the *transport addresses* (contained in the Hello packets). The router with the numerically higher trasnport address wins the active role; the other router takes the passive role.

3. **LDP Session Initialization and Establishment** — The session establishment starts with exchanging an LDP *initialization message*, a TCP packet destined for the peering router's LDP LSR-id. The initialization message contains the protocol version, keep-alive timer, and other information.

4. **Label Binding Exchange** — The link-LDP session is now established. The link-LDP session is maintained by the constant reception of keep-alive messages from the peering router. LDP routers start to exchange label bindings through the LDP sessions.

After the link-LDP session is established between the two directly connected routers, both Hello messages and keep-alive messages are constantly exchanged between the neighboring routers. The Hello message is used as the heartbeat of each individual LDP-speaking Layer 3 link. The keep-alive message is used as the heartbeat for the single link-LDP session between the two peering routers. Figure 8.1 illustrates the link-LDP session establishment process between two directly connected LDP routers. In the illustration, only LDP messages are presented; the TCP transport connection establishment is not included in the diagram.

Figure 8.1   Link-LDP (link LDP) Session Establishment

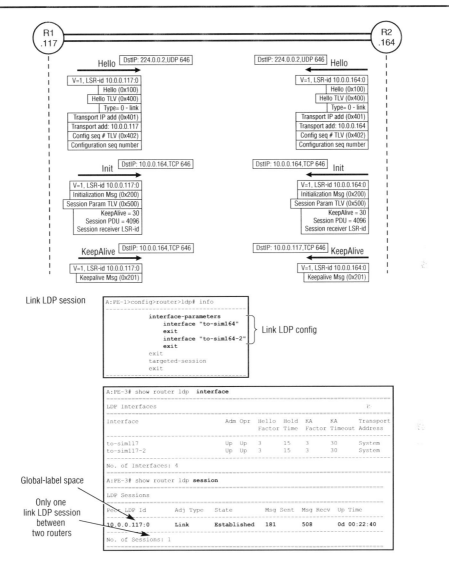

To enable link-LDP sessions between two routers, the IP interfaces must be specified in the LDP routing configuration. If desired, the following link-LDP session parameters can be configured to override the default values:

- **Hello Parameters** — Interval between sent Hello messages, and the Hello timer.
- **Keep-Alive Parameters** — Interval between sent keep-alive messages and the keep-alive timer.

- **Transport Address** — Address used specifically by the TCP transport connection establishment to set up the TCP session for LDP. By default, the transport address is the Hello packet's source address. In most cases, this address is also the system IP address. This behavior can be overridden by explicitly specifying the `transport address` to use in the link-LDP configuration.

  The session parameter configuration can be specified in two different levels:

- **Interface-Parameter Level** — If the non-default session parameters are applicable for all link-LDP interfaces, they can be specified in the `interface-parameter` level so all listed interfaces inherit the parameters.

- **Link-LDP Interface Level** — If the non-default session parameters are required for one or a subset of the link-LDP interfaces, they can be specified under particular LDP `interface` configurations.

When non-default session parameters are configured in both levels, the more specific configuration overrides the more general configuration. This means that the interface-level configuration is applied to the link-LDP interface, if there is one.

After the link-LDP session is established, the label distribution process starts. The Alcatel-Lucent Service Router Portfolio (ALSRP) service routers use link-LDP for Virtual Private Network (VPN) service transport tunnel establishment. Hence, each LDP router only distributes a label for one type of IP address — the router's system IP address. This /32 IP address uniquely identifies a router in the network. ALSRP service routers use global label space. Therefore, their LDP LSR-ids will always end with [:0]. When all the routers (P and PE) in the entire backbone network have their link-LDP adjacency established and have finished distributing the labels for the system IP address, the LDP-LSP transport tunnel overlay on the entire network is created and is ready to carry VPN traffic. The details regarding LDP-LSP are introduced later in this chapter.

Targeted LDP Session Establishment

Targeted LDP (T-LDP) sessions are used among PE routers to signal pseudowires and exchange vc-labels in VPN services. The mechanism used by T-LDP is referred to as the *extended discovery mechanism*. The T-LDP session establishment Hello packets (also referred to as the *targeted Hello messages*) are unicast to the T-LDP peering router and use the loopback IP address of the peering router as the packet's destination IP address. Most commonly, the system IP addresses are used as the LSR-id when establishing T-LDP sessions. Routers do not require being directly adjacent to establish T-LDP sessions. Other than this difference, the T-LDP peering routers use the same procedure as link LDP to establish the adjacency.

After the T-LDP session is established between the two peering routers, both Hello messages and keep-alive messages are constantly exchanged between the routers in the same fashion as with the link LDP. Figure 8.2 shows the T-LDP session establishment process. In the illustration, only LDP messages are presented; the TCP transport connection establishment is not included in the diagram.

Figure 8.2 Targeted LDP (T-LDP) Session Establishment

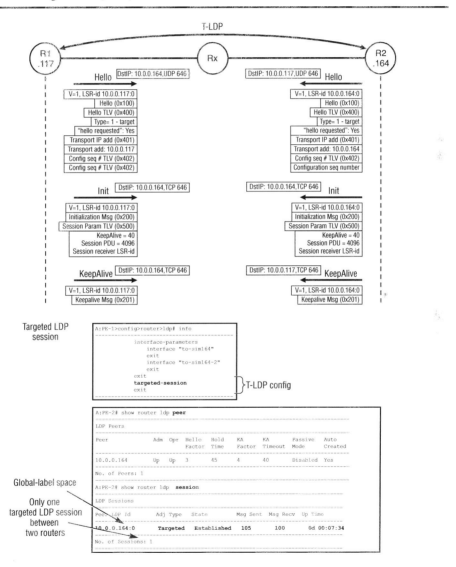

Similar to the link-LDP configuration, the non-default T-LDP session parameters can also be configured under the targeted-session context. The session parameters can also be specified on two levels:

- `Targeted-session` level affecting all T-LDP peers
- `Targeted-session peer` level, whose configuration is only applied to particular peer(s)

The rule of a more specific configuration overriding a more general configuration applies to a T-LDP session configuration as well.

If two routers are directly adjacent (connected directly by a Layer 3 interface) and have both link LDP and T-LDP enabled, two separate Hello adjacencies are established, but only a single TCP session and a single LDP session are formed and shared by link LDP and T-LDP.

T-LDP Session Auto-Creation for VPN Services

In link LDP, the LDP peers do not need to be explicitly configured in a router's LDP configuration. This is because the link-LDP sessions are always between directly adjacent LDP routers. Provided the IP interface is listed in the LDP router context, the LDP router will use the multicast Hello message to discover all peers attached to that interface. At that point, the link-LDP sessions are established to the adjacent LDP router(s).

T-LDP sessions are established over LDP routers that may not be directly adjacent. T-LDP sessions use IP unicast Hello messages to discover neighbor routers using the target peer's system IP address as the packet destination IP address. The auto-discovery process used for link LDP is not applicable for T-LDP. In theory, each T-LDP peer must be explicitly specified in the LDP router's `targeted-session` configuration. However, in a provider backbone IP/MPLS VPN network, a T-LDP session must be fully meshed among all PE routers. This may lead to greater configuration overhead. In ALSRP service routers, the T-LDP session configuration is improved to suit the service-oriented network architecture in the following ways:

- Provided the T-LDP is enabled in an LDP router, the T-LDP peers do not need to be listed explicitly in the configuration. (Listing the peers is allowed, but no longer necessary.)
- When an SDP (discussed in detail in Chapter 9) is created with a far-end PE router's system IP address, and if the SDP's signaling method is configured as LDP (by default), the same system IP address is automatically placed into the list of T-LDP peers. The router then tries to establish the T-LDP session between the local PE and the far-end PE router using default LDP parameters.

- The provider may want to explicitly list the peer with the required parameter settings in the targeted-session configuration only when a particular T-LDP peer needs its session parameters modified from the default values.

- In certain cases, peering with some routers is not desired. Explicitly listing the undesired peer(s) in the `targeted-session peer <peer-ip> shutdown` configuration disables the T-LDP session to that peer.

8.3 Using T-LDP to Signal Pseudowires for Layer 2 VPN Services

The most significant use of T-LDP in the IP/MPLS VPN network is to signal pseudowires for Layer 2 VPN services. Distributed Layer 2 VPN services require pseudowires to connect the service instances between PE routers. RFC 4447 specifies the use of T-LDP to signal VPN pseudowires. T-LDP is used to signal the pseudowires and pass control information between PE routers to manage the pseudowires. The particular process and behavior of VPN pseudowire signaling are introduced within each service's chapter. This section describes the basic T-LDP infrastructure and common Layer 2 VPN pseudowire signaling behavior from T-LDP's perspective.

T-LDP is used to signal pseudowires for Layer 2 VPN, including:

- **Virtual Leased Line (VLL) Service** — Point-to-point Layer 2 VPN services connecting two Customer Edge (CE) devices with native format attachment circuit (AC). The VLL PE routers use MPLS LSPs to carry the traffic between them. VLLs are also called *pipe* services because they behave like a point-to-point pipe. The following are examples of several VLL services:

  - **Apipe** — ATM point-to-point VPN service

  - **Cpipe** — Circuit Emulation Service (CES) VPN connections, also called *TDM leased line*

  - **Fpipe** — Frame-Relay point-to-point VPN service

  - **Epipe** — Ethernet point-to-point VPN service

  - **Ipipe** — Layer 3 IP point-to-point VPN service

- **Virtual Private LAN Service (VPLS)** — Multipoint-to-multipoint Ethernet bridging services connecting multiple customer sites. All customer sites connected by one VPLS service appear in the same LAN segment. VPLS member

PE routers have their service instances connected by mesh-pseudowires signaled by the T-LDP. With hierarchical VPLS, the service instances may also be connected by spoke-pseudowires signaled by T-LDP. VPLS and H-VPLS are discussed in Chapters 11 and 12.

- **VLL Service Using Spoke-Pseudowire Connecting to VPLS** — VPLS services have the ability to connect to point-to-point services using spoke-pseudowires. T-LDP is used to signal the spoke-pseudowires.

- **VLL Service Using Spoke-Pseudowire Connecting to Layer 3 Services** — T-LDP is used to signal the spoke-pseudowires:

  - Epipe spoke-pseudowire termination to VPLS service.

  - IES/VPRN (Internet Enhanced Service) service spoke-pseudowire termination with VPLS service. IES service is beyond the scope of this book.

In Layer 2 VPN pseudowire signaling, T-LDP is used to perform the following major tasks:

- vc-label distribution of the parameters of the pseudowires (control word, VCCV capability, interface parameters, etc.)

- Signaling the status of the pseudowires and of the attachment circuit

- In VPLS services, signaling the MAC-flush (the message to trigger VPLS service instance to flush its forwarding database) during a topology change. MAC-flush is explained in detail in Chapter 15.

Signaling vc-label for Pseudowires

Layer 2 VPN services use pseudowires to connect the member PE routers' service instances. The pseudowire is actually a label agreement made by two PE routers for the meaning of an MPLS label (vc-label) — the agreement includes the binding on the vc-label and the vc-id, vc-type, and the target interface parameters. The vc-id, vc-type, and the interface parameters uniquely identify a service FEC. With this agreement, the local PE router uses the received label from the binding to perform VPN encapsulation for the traffic of a service instance before sending the VPN traffic to the remote PE. When the remote PE router receives the traffic with this label value, it uses the label to identify the service instance to which the traffic belongs. Therefore, it uses this label value as a de-multiplexer by the PE router receiving VPN encapsulated traffic to identify the traffic from many ingress traffic flows for different services. The VPN encapsulation is then removed by the remote PE router, and traffic is forwarded to the correct service instance. Pseudowires are bidirectional; at least one pseudowire is required for two service instances on two PE routers to exchange VPN traffic.

The LDP messages used for pseudowire signaling are:

- **Label Mapping Message** — The PE router uses Label Mapping messages to advertise the FEC-label binding during pseudowire establishment. One Label Mapping message is sent from the local PE to the remote PE. The remote PE also sends a Label Mapping message to the local PE router.

- **Label Withdraw Message** — The PE router uses Label Withdraw messages to withdraw the FEC-label binding for a pseudowire previously established. This is the termination process of the pseudowire when a Label Withdraw message is sent from the local PE to the remote PE.

- **Label Release Message** — The PE router uses a Label Release message to confirm the withdraw of the FEC-label binding. This is a confirmation of the pseudowire termination when a Label Release message is sent from the local PE to the remote PE.

- **Notification Message** — The PE router uses a Notification message to report errors and pseudowire status changes to the T-LDP peer router.

- **Address Withdraw Message** — The VPLS PE router uses the Address Withdraw message to tell the remote member PE router's service instance to flush its forwarding database (FDB). The use of this message in the VPLS network is referred to as *MAC-flush*. MAC-flush is discussed in detail in Chapter 15.

After the service instance is created in a PE router, the pseudowire should be provisioned and administratively enabled. The PE router generates a local vc-label and then announces the FEC-Label binding by sending a Label Mapping message to every remote PE router participating in the same VPLS, or to a single remote PE router in the case of a VLL service. When a router receives such a Label binding, it uses the label as an egress label to encapsulate traffic before sending the traffic over that pseudowire. The Label Mapping message contains an FEC TLV and a Generic Label TLV. The FEC TLV contains an FEC element and a sub-TLV with virtual circuit information such as:

- The pseudowire's vc-type
- The pseudowire's vc-id
- Interface parameters, such as vc-MTU value

The Generic Label TLV contains the label value used for that pseudowire. For different types of services, the FEC TLV may contain different elements. The pseudowire is established when both sides of the PE router send their Label Mapping messages to each other. For the pseudowire to be established, the values in the received Label Mapping message including the vc-type, vc-id, and the vc-MTU values in the interface parameter TLV must match the local configuration of the pseudowire in the receiving PE router. Each PE router has received an egress vc-label to encapsulate its egress traffic and advertised an ingress vc-label to de-encapsulate its ingress traffic.

When a PE router tears down the pseudowire, a Label Withdraw message is sent to the remote PE router. The Label Withdraw message contains the same FEC TLV and Generic Label TLV used to establish the pseudowire. Upon receiving the Label Withdraw message, the remote PE router removes the vc-label binding from its label database and sends out a Label Release message to the local PE router to confirm the teardown. The Label Release message also contains the same FEC TLV and General Label TLV. However, the interface parameter field in the FEC TLV is not present when the FEC TLV is used in the Label Withdraw and Label Release messages.

Signaling Pseudowire Status

The T-LDP protocol is enhanced with several new TLV types to better support the Layer 2 VPN pseudowire signaling. However, the types of LDP messages used remain the same. One significant improvement is the use of LDP Notification messages with the new Pseudowire-Status TLV (0x96A) to signal the status of the pseudowires. The Pseudowire-Status TLV can be put either in the Label Mapping message or the Notification message to signal the pseudowire's status to the far-end PE router. The operation details and Pseudowire-Status TLV content are introduced in each service's chapter.

Signaling MAC-Flush for VPLS Topology Change

In VPLS services, the VPLS core is composed of many member PE routers connected by pseudowires. Where there is a topology change in the VPLS core, the router may want to generate an LDP Address Withdraw message (also referred to as a MAC-*flush* message) over the pseudowires to the peering member PE routers. A MAC-flush message notifies the receiving PE router that there is a forwarding infrastructure change. Thus, the receiver may remove some MAC entries in the corresponding service instance's FDB to speed up the convergence.

Two types of MAC-flush messages are used under different conditions in the VPLS network. Both MAC-flush messages are signaled using LDP Address Withdraw messages with a MAC-List TLV.

Configuring T-LDP Sessions in a Service Network

Unlike link LDP, in the ALSRP, T-LDP sessions can be either manually provisioned or explicitly created by the system. In most cases, the explicit T-LDP peering configuration is not required for the service network to be functional. As mentioned previously, T-LDP sessions are required for SDPs to signal pseudowires. Every time a PE router creates the first SDP connected to a specific far-end PE router, if the SDP's signaling method is T-LDP (by default), the system automatically tries to establish a T-LDP session to the SDP's far-end PE router, if there isn't one already established.

There are cases in which explicit T-LDP peering configurations are required. One case is when the operator wants to configure the session parameters away from the default values. The other scenario is the use of LDP over RSVP (LDPoRSVP), where explicit configuration of LDP peering between PE routers and inter-Area Border Routers (ABRs) is required. Details regarding LDPoRSVP are discussed later in this chapter. Figure 8.3 demonstrates the T-LDP explicit configuration in the CLI.

Figure 8.3   T-LDP Explicit Configuration Examples

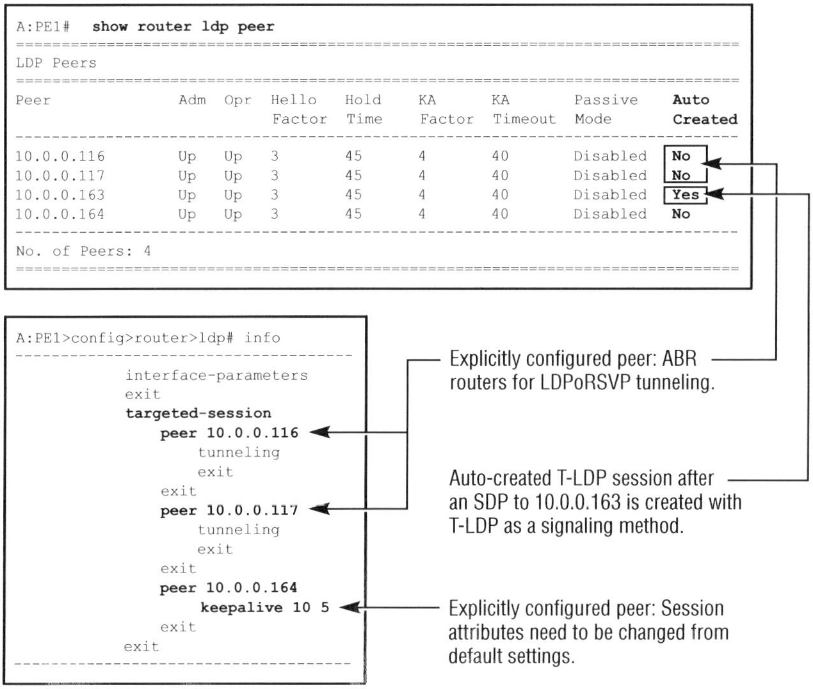

```
A:PE1#  show router ldp peer
===============================================================================
LDP Peers
===============================================================================
Peer          Adm  Opr  Hello   Hold   KA      KA       Passive    Auto
                         Factor  Time   Factor  Timeout  Mode       Created
-------------------------------------------------------------------------------
10.0.0.116    Up   Up   3       45     4       40       Disabled   No
10.0.0.117    Up   Up   3       45     4       40       Disabled   No
10.0.0.163    Up   Up   3       45     4       40       Disabled   Yes
10.0.0.164    Up   Up   3       45     4       40       Disabled   No
-------------------------------------------------------------------------------
No. of Peers: 4
===============================================================================
```

```
A:PE1>config>router>ldp# info
--------------------------------------
          interface-parameters
          exit
          targeted-session
              peer 10.0.0.116         ◄──── Explicitly configured peer: ABR
                  tunneling                  routers for LDPoRSVP tunneling.
                  exit
              exit
              peer 10.0.0.117         ◄──── Auto-created T-LDP session after
                  tunneling                  an SDP to 10.0.0.163 is created with
                  exit                       T-LDP as a signaling method.
              exit
              peer 10.0.0.164
                  keepalive 10 5      ◄──── Explicitly configured peer: Session
                  exit                       attributes need to be changed from
              exit                           default settings.
--------------------------------------
```

In Figure 8.3, the router PE1 has four T-LDP peers. The T-LDP peer to the PE router 10.0.0.163 is auto-created by the system after the first SDP is created and enabled to the PE router requesting T-LDP signaling. The peers to 10.0.0.116 and 10.0.0.117 are explicitly created for LDPoRSVP tunneling. Both peering routers (10.0.0.116 and 10.0.0.117) are ABRs with no service instances (P routers). Therefore, there is no SDP created that is connected to these routers, and there will not be an auto-created SDP from these routers to router PE1. Peer 10.0.0.164 is also a PE router. However, the T-LDP session to that PE router has a different keep-alive timer setting, and thus the explicit configuration is provisioned to override the default timers. The **show** command at the top of Figure 8.3 lists all peers and indicates if they are auto-created or configured explicitly.

8.4 LDP Messages and TLVs

LDP routers exchange information with each other by sending LDP messages. *LDP messages* are IP packets with UDP or TCP encapsulation. All LDP messages share the common format of LDP Header + Message Header + Message TLV. The message header is also a TLV variation. Different messages contain different TLVs. Figure 8.4 presents the basic LDP message format.

> **Note:** For a complete list of the message and TLV types, refer to RFC 5036. This section covers only the messages and TLVs used for Layer 2 VPN pseudowire signaling.

All Layer 2 VPN (VLL and VPLS) service signaling is performed through T-LDPs. For an IP/MPLS VPN backbone, a common best practice is to provision a full T-LDP mesh among all PE routers as one of the backbone infrastructures. Thus, when deploying VPN services in the backbone network, all signaling channels are operational.

Figure 8.4 LDP Message Format: LDP Header + Message Header + Message TLV

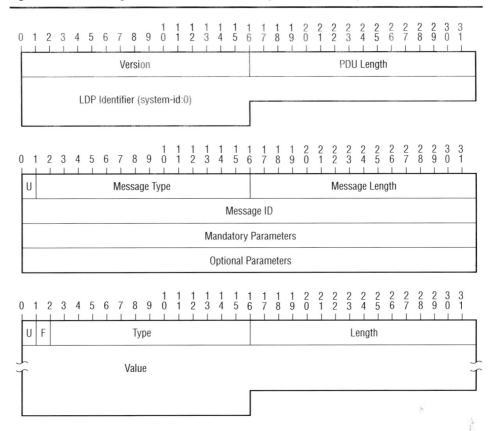

U Unknown TLV bit: When set to *0* (clear), upon receiving unknown TLV, the message needs to be returned to the originator. When set to *1* (set), the unknown TLV will be "silently ignored".

F Forward unknown bit: Only used when *U-bit* is set (2) and receives a message with unknown TLV needing to be forwarded. When set to *0* (clear), the message is not forwarded. When set to 1 (set), the message is forwarded.

LDP Messages

LDP routers use LDP messages to communicate with each other to establish adjacency, distribute and withdraw labels, and communicate status and errors. Table 8.1 lists the LDP messages used by LDP.

Table 8.1 T-LDP Messages

Type	LDP Message	Description
0x0001	Notification	Signal errors and other significant events. In Layer 2 VPN, Notification messages can be used to signal the pseudowire status by adding the Pseudowire Status TLV (0x096A).
0x0100	Hello	Used by a LDP router to announce itself as a router speaking LDP during the discovery process. Two LDPs peering with each other start the communication by sending a Hello message out. Hello messages are sent periodically and allow the peers to monitor the LDP router's reachability.
0x0200	Initialization	Used to establish LDP sessions (link LDP and/or T-LDP session). Session parameters exchanged in this message are Hello timers and keep-alive timers.
0x0201	KeepAlive	Used to monitor the health of the LDP session. Keep-alive messages are constantly exchanged between peering routers over the LDP session.
0x0300	Address	An LDP router sends address messages to advertise its interface addresses to the peer routers. Layer 2 VPN pseudowire signaling does not use address messages. Not used in VPWS.
0x0301	Address Withdraw	An LDP router sends an Address Withdraw message to withdraw the previously advertised interface addresses. In VPLS, the Address Withdraw message with MAC address-TLV is used to announce the topology change of the VPLS core and to request that the peering PE routers perform MAC-flush in the service instance's forwarding database (FDB).
0x0400	Label Mapping	An LDP router sends Label Mapping messages to advertise FEC-Label binding. In Layer 2 VPN PW signaling, the FEC is a VPN representing vc-id, and the label is the vc-label.
0x0401	Label Request	An LDP router sends Label Request messages to request an FEC-Label binding for a certain FEC. A Label Request message is used only in Downstream on Demand label distribution mode. Layer 2 VPN PW signaling does not use Label Request messages because Downstream Unsolicited mode is used for Layer 2 VPN pseudowire label distribution.
0x0402	Label Withdraw	Used to request that the LDP peer stop using the FEC-Label binding previously announced by the Label Mapping message. Layer 2 VPN PW signaling uses Label Withdraw messages to withdraw vc-labels.

Type	LDP Message	Description
0x0403	Label Release	Used to notify the peer that this router is not using the FEC-Label binding previously announced by the Label Mapping message from that router. This frees up the label value of the peer router. Layer 2 VPN PW signaling uses Label Release messages as confirmation of the withdraw of the vc-label binding.
0x0404	Label Abort Request	Used to withdraw an outstanding Label Request message. A Label Request message is used only in Downstream on Demand label distribution mode. Layer 2 VPN pseudowire signaling does not use Label Abort Request messages because Downstream Unsolicited mode is used for Layer 2 VPN pseudowire label distribution.
0x3E00 - 0x3EFF	Vendor Private	Reserved for vendor's proprietary LDP messaging implementation. Layer 2 VPN PW signaling does not use the Vendor Private message.
0x3F00 - 0x3FFF	Experimental	Reserved for experimental purposes. Layer 2 pseudowire signaling does not use the Experimental message.

The details regarding the T-LDP messages used to signal the pseudowires for different types of the Layer 2 VPN services are introduced in later chapters for each service type.

8.5 LDP over RSVP-TE Tunneling

Chapters 3 and 5 introduced the use of RSVP-TE as an MPLS label distribution and LSP establishment protocol. This chapter introduces the use of link-LDP as a label distribution protocol and the LDP-LSP. This section discusses a new type of end-to-end MPLS tunnel — the LDP over RSVP-TE tunnel (LDPoRSVP). LDPoRSVP allows the use of RSVP-TE LSP in a network in which end-to-end RSVP-TE LSP tunnels are not desirable or applicable.

Recommended Reading: Chapter 9

It is highly recommended that readers understand the IP/MPLS VPN service architecture, especially IP/MPLS VPN, before proceeding with this section. To fully understand LDPoRSVP, we recommend that you first read Chapter 9 to understand service entities and how regular IP/MPLS VPN traffic is encapsulated and tunneled through the service network. The discussion in this section refers to service-related entities such as SDP, service instances, service transport tunnels, and SAP, which are described in Chapter 9.

Service providers want to maximize their network's resiliency and use the optimal forwarding path for data traffic. Therefore, they usually seek to use RSVP-TE LSP tunneling with Constrained Shortest Path First (CSPF) path calculation to transport the VPN traffic. CSPF RSVP-TE LSPs can be explicitly routed, and therefore, the Head-End (HE) router can determine the entire path of the LSP before signaling it. RSVP-TE LSP supports secondary LSP and Fast Reroute (FRR). The CSPF algorithm takes factors other than IGP metrics into consideration when performing LSP path calculation — factors such as link-coloring (administrative group), Shared Risk Link Group (SRLG), and bandwidth reservation.

However, CSPF relies on the traffic engineering (TE) extension of the IGP protocols. The IGP protocol's TE advertisement capability is limited within a single network area. There are several cases in which end-to-end TE cannot be achieved because the network is divided into multiple areas:

- **OSPF or IS-IS Hierarchy Used in Networks with Many Routers** — TE and CSPF can be used to route RSVP-TE LSP only within each individual area.

- **Network with More Than One Routing Protocol Instance** — TE and CSPF can be used to route RSVP-TE LSP only within each of the network parts of a single instance.

- **Traffic Engineering Only Partially Enabled in the Network** — Other portions of the network do not support traffic engineering.

In these cases, end-to-end TE with CSPF path calculation for LSP-Paths cannot be deployed. There is one way to achieve TE end-to-end, which is to use the ABR as the router expanding the ERO in the second area. The ABR has the visibility of two different areas and has the TE database of both areas. Therefore, the ABR can calculate the hops with TE constraints on a per-area basis. However, this method is not fully optimal. With the help of LDPoRSVP, LDP can stitch together the RSVP-TE LSP within each network area or zones where TE is enabled and thus form an end-to-end MPLS tunnel. The SDP can use such a tunnel to carry VPN traffic.

Also, when RSVP-TE LSP is used in a network, the network requires a full mesh of LSPs among all PE routers to achieve full service reachability. For a network with N PE routers, $N * (N - 1)$ RSVP-TE LSPs are required to achieve full service reachability. In a scaled network, the operator may not be willing to manage a large number of RSVP-TE LSPs. In addition, all transiting routers in the backbone (core) must maintain the states of all LSPs, which may occupy significant amounts of resources on the core routers. Deploying LDPoRSVP changes the LSP layout from a flat topology to a hierarchical topology. This significantly reduces the number of LSPs required in the network, especially in the core of the network. The full service reachability required by all PE routers is still maintained.

LDPoRSVP is also referred to as *tunnel-in-tunnel* and can be viewed from two different perspectives:

- LDPoRSVP is a method of using LDP to stitch together RSVP-TE LSP tunnels in different areas to form an end-to-end, across-area MPLS tunnel. This allows RSVP-TE LSP to be expanded outside the local area.

- From a different perspective, LDPoRSVP is also a technique of using RSVP-TE in each area to tunnel LDP-LSP's traffic. This adds TE capability and tunnel resiliency to LDP-LSP tunnels.

From either perspective, the VPN traffic which is tunneled by the LDP-LSP across multiple areas in the service network is encapsulated (tunneled) again into an RSVP-TE LSP tunnel within each area.

Any IP/MPLS VPN service can take advantage of LDPoRSVP. The SDP between PE routers specifies which tunneling technique is used to carry the services' VPN traffic. The tunneling method can be GRE, LDP-LSP, or RSVP-TE LSP. When LDPoRSVP is used, the SDP still uses an LDP-LSP, although it uses RSVP-TE LSP to tunnel the traffic underneath each area. The tunneling details are transparent to the SDP using it; as far as the SDP is concerned, LDP-LSP is still used as the transport tunnel.

LDPoRSVP Applications: When to Use LDPoRSVP

As discussed later in this chapter, IGP hierarchical design with multiple areas is frequently used in a scaled network. In a network with multiple areas, the TE information cannot be passed across areas. Therefore, end-to-end TE cannot be achieved in a network with more than one IGP area using regular RSVP-TE LSP with IGP-TE and CSPF.

The LDPoRSVP tunnel is used in a network where the IGP hierarchical design is used in multiple areas when end-to-end TE capability and CSPF are still desired. In each area, the RSVP-TE LSP tunnel can be created with CSPF path calculation, and the ABR will use LDP to build end-to-end LSPs.

LDPoRSVP Scenario 1: End-to-End CSPF and TE in a Hierarchical IGP Network Design

In a routed IP network, IGP is used to provide reachability information within the network. Every router runs the IGP routing protocol and exchanges routing information with other routers to form the routing table. In most cases, one or both of the link state routing protocols (OSPF or IS-IS) is chosen in the network as the IGP. In a scaled network with a large number of routes, a flat IGP network design is often replaced by a hierarchical IGP design to reduce the routing table size but keep the full reachability. In a hierarchical IGP design, the network is divided into multiple areas. Routers within an area exchange routing information only with other routers in the same area. Routing information exchanged among areas is handled by ABRs. The ABRs can pass routing information from one area to another area, and often perform routing aggregation or summarization at the same time. Thus, a router within an area needs to keep only the intra-area routing information and the summarized routing information beyond its own area. This reduces the routing table size in intra-area routers.

Chapter 4 briefly introduced the area design of OSPF and ISIS. Figure 8.5 presents an example of a hierarchical IGP network.

Figure 8.5　Hierarchical IGP Design Example

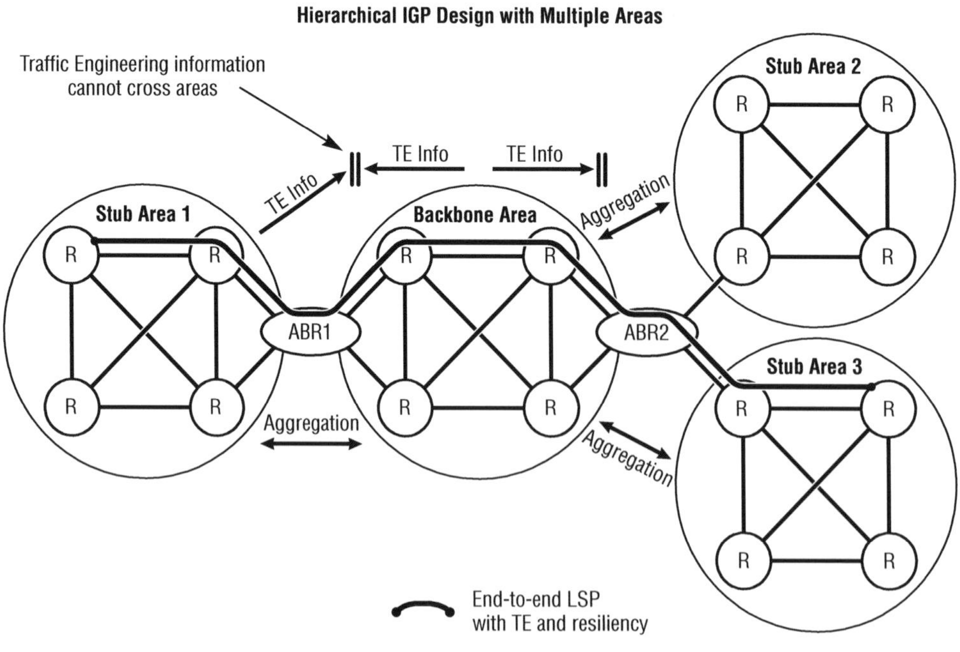

In Figure 8.5, the entire network is divided into four areas. Routes within one area are aggregated (summarized) by the ABRs before being passed to another area. This is a common IGP design in a scaled network. If the operator requires MPLS pseudowire-based VPN in this network, MPLS LSP tunnels (LDP or RSVP-TE) may need to be provisioned as service transport tunnels.

A problem with the IGP hierarchical network design is that the TE information cannot be sent across areas (as shown in Figure 8.5). Therefore, the TE database in each area has visibility of only its local area. In this network, the operator cannot establish an RSVP-TE-signaled LSP from Area 1 to Area 3 with bandwidth reservation and using CSPF to establish the LSP. This is because the TED of routers in Area 1 does not contain any TE information from Area 3, and the CSPF calculation cannot be completed. When cross-area LSP is desired, only IGP can be used to calculate the path. LDP-LSP- or IGP-directed RSVP-TE LSPs must be created to establish the end-to-end LSP.

Figure 8.6 demonstrates a network with multiple IGP areas. The LSP with CSPF path calculation cannot establish the path end-to-end, while the IGP-directed LSP can be established.

Figure 8.6 End-to-End CSPF Calculation Failed in a Multi-Area Network

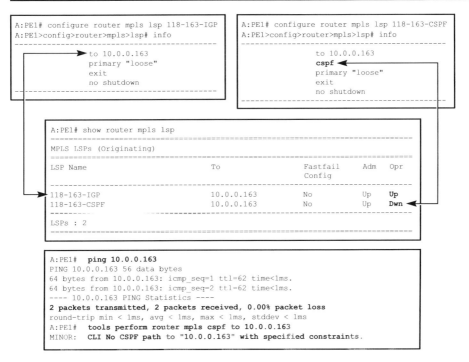

In Figure 8.6, two RSVP-TE LSPs are defined to the same Tail router. One LSP is IGP-directed; the other is CSPF-directed. Because the routers PE1 (10.0.0.118) and PE2 (10.0.0.163) are not in the same OSPF area, the CSPF-directed LSP cannot find a path and therefore has an operationally **down** status. The bottom section of Figure 8.6 shows the reachability test through a regular SPF in IGP (the successful `ping <dest-ip>` command) and through CSPF with TE (the failed `tools perform router mpls cspf to <dest-ip>` command).

> **Note:** In a network with an IGP hierarchical design, an RSVP-TE LSP can still be created and established end-to-end. However, it must use IGP SPF instead of CSPF to calculate the actual LSP hop-by-hop. Without the help of CSPF, the LSP can follow the IGP metric. Also, without the help of CSPF, the MPLS FRR can be deployed only in IGP-directed LSPs with all strict hops. This means that to use FRR, the operator must manually specify each individual hop for the LSP explicitly in the LSP configuration for all LSPs. In a network large enough to deploy an IGP hierarchy, strict hop LSPs are not the best option.

LDPoRSVP Scenario 2: Reducing the Number of LSPs in a Scaled Network

RSVP-TE LSP tunnels are unidirectional and end-to-end. This means that when any two PE routers want to establish the transport tunnel to carry traffic between them, a pair of LSPs is required, one for each direction. In a network with N PE routers, if each PE router requires a transport tunnel to all other PE routers (full mesh), then $N * (N - 1)$ LSPs are required. If RSVP-TE LSP resiliency is desired, more LSPs may be established in the network: secondary LSPs, FRR one-to-one detour LSPs, or FRR facility bypass tunnels. In addition, for every LSP, all routers along the path (LSRs) must maintain the state of the LSP by refreshing the RSVP sessions. The core routers must maintain significantly more sessions than the routers in the edge.

Figure 8.7 shows an example of a scaled network with 400 PE routers and a hierarchical design. There are several hundred routers in this network, and most of them are PE routers with services provided to the attached customers. Naturally, a network of this size should use a hierarchical IGP design. In this network, 20 PE routers are grouped into a stub area, and four ABRs are used to connect these stub areas into the backbone area. This network diagram is used for discussion of MPLS LSP scaling and is not a design recommendation. For ease of discussion, ABR redundancy is ignored, and ABRs and core routers do not have services provisioned locally.

Figure 8.7 Scaled Service Network with Hierarchical IGP Design

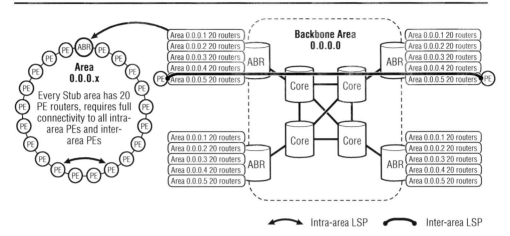

← → Intra-area LSP	⌒ Inter-area LSP

As mentioned previously, CSPF-directed RSVP-TE LSP cannot be used in a network with multiple areas. If RSVP-TE LSP is desired, the IGP-directed LSP should be used in this network. However, a network with 400 PE routers that require full service reachability also requires a large number of LSPs:

- Within each area, every PE router requires 38 (2 * 19) intra-area LSPs to connect to all PE routers with its area (intra-area LSPs can still be CSPF-directed).

- Every PE router requires 760 (2 * 380) inter-area LSPs to connect to all PE routers outside the area. 600 of these LSPs are traveling through the backbone of the network using different ABRs to reach the inter-area routers.

- In this example, ABRs are transit routers. Each ABR needs to carry all the inter-area LSPs for the PE routers in the non-backbone areas attached to that ABR. In this topology, there are 20 PE routers per non-backbone area. Therefore, every ABR needs to carry 15,200 (20 * 760) inter-area LSPs.

- The core routers are used to connect ABRs. In normal circumstances, each core router will carry 12,000 (20 * 600) inter-area LSPs for the ABR closest to it. In a network failure, more LSPs may be rerouted to a core router.

Maintaining a large number of LSPs (RSVP sessions) in a router is a burden to both the control plane and the data plane of MPLS routers. This can be especially important to the ABRs and core routers through which all inter-area LSPs are traveling. Constantly refreshing tens of thousands of LSPs consumes many resources: bandwidth, CPU, and memory in the router. Even if the hardware and software of the service router have the capability of handling such a configuration, managing a large number of connections is not desired by service providers.

The number of LSPs in the network can be significantly reduced with a hierarchal IGP network design and the use of LDPoRSVP tunneling. Figure 8.8 presents the network with LDPoRSVP implemented.

Figure 8.8   Using LDPoRSVP to Reduce the Number of LSPs in the Network

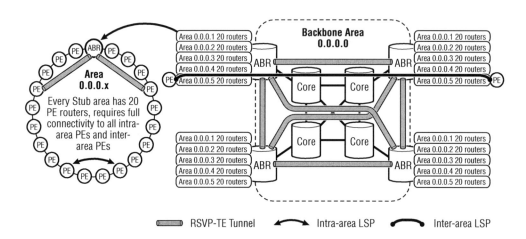

Within each area, every PE router has an RSVP-TE LSP created to the ABR. LDP is enabled in all the PE's router interfaces and the ABR's router interfaces. With LDPoRSVP in the network, PE routers in different areas (PE1 and PE2 at the right in Figure 8.8) use three RSVP-TE LSPs to carry traffic end-to-end:

- Intra-area RSVP-TE LSP in PE1's area
- RSVP-TE LSP in the backbone area between two ABRs
- Intra-area RSVP-TE LSP in PE2's area

These three RSVP-TE LSPs are stitched together by the LDPoRSVP and form an end-to-end LDP-LSP.

With such an LDPoRSVP implementation, the overall number of RSVP-TE LSPs in the entire network drops significantly:

- Within each area, every PE router still requires 38 (2 * 19) intra-area LSPs to connect to all PE routers in its area. Every PE router also requires one pair of LSPs connected to the ABR. LSP is unidirectional; two routers require two LSPs, one at each direction to pass traffic between them.

- For all PE routers, the inter-area tunneling is handled by LDPoRSVP, and therefore inter-area RSVP-TE LSPs are not required.

- For every ABR, there is one pair of LSPs with every router in the area it is attached to, and one pair of LSPs with each ABR. Therefore, there are 206 LSPs in every ABR.

- The core routers do not need to originate/terminate any LSP. These routers only need to carry the LSPs between the ABRs. In this example, every core router maintains four LSPs.

LDPoRSVP Scenario 3: End-to-End LSP with TE Partially Enabled in the Network

Similar to Scenario 1, in some cases, end-to-end deployment of TE is not desired by the operator, such as when a network has different routing protocols in different portions of the network, or if part of the network does not support traffic engineering in its routing protocols. Therefore, CSPF cannot perform path calculation end-to-end, and RSVP-TE LSPs with CSPF path calculation cannot be deployed as service transport tunnels in the entire network.

LDPoRSVP allows end-to-end service transporting tunnels to be built while taking advantage of the TE-capable portions of the network. One network may have different portions running different routing protocols, while some portions may or may not have TE capability. With LDPoRSVP, the operator can use RSVP-TE LSP in different portions of the network and use LDP-LSP to stitch them together to form end-to-end LDP tunnels.

LDPoRSVP Tunneling Architecture

As previously mentioned, LDPoRSVP is used in a network with hierarchical IGP design and uses an LDP-LSP to stitch RSVP-TE LSPs together in different areas. The building blocks of LDPoRSVP include:

- IGP hierarchical network design, wherein the different areas or zones are connected through ABRs or Autonomous System Boundary Routers (ASBRs)

- Intra-area RSVP-TE LSP tunnels between all PE routers and the ABRs or ASBRs. These RSVP-TE LSP tunnels are used to tunnel the LDP MPLS encapsulation.

- T-LDP sessions established between PE routers and ABRs to distribute LDP labels for their system IP addresses (router-id) to form end-to-end LDP-LSP tunnels

- Provisioning of tunnel-in-tunnel in PE and ABRs to enable LDPoRSVP

Figure 8.9 presents an example network in which LDPoRSVP TE is deployed to make end-to-end LDP tunnels for services while taking advantage of the resiliency and TE capability in each area. The VPLS service instances and the pseudowire between PE1 and PE2 show the end-to-end service taking advantage of the LDPoRSVP deployment. In Figure 8.9, the solid line with square ends represents the end-to-end LDP-LSP tunnel using three RSVP-TE tunnels in different areas to carry its traffic.

Figure 8.9   LDPoRSVP Network Example: Fully Meshed RSVP-TE Tunnels in Each Area

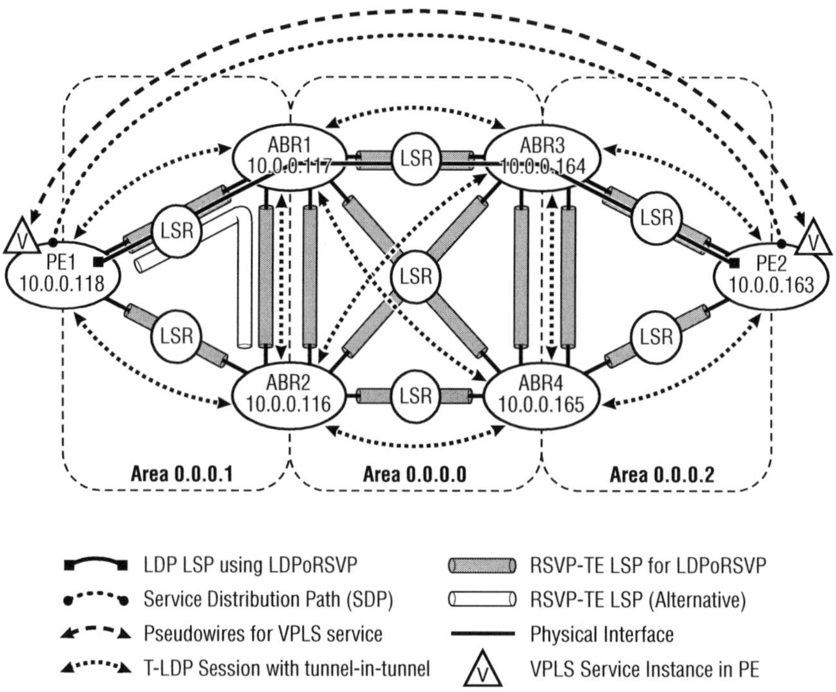

IGP Hierarchy

The IGP in the network must be hierarchical when LDPoRSVP is deployed and ABRs use the tunnel-in-tunnel technique to stitch RSVP-TE LSPs from two different areas together using LDP-LSP. Normally, when IGP hierarchy is deployed, the ABRs summarize/aggregate routes within each area before advertising the routes into other areas. This is to reduce the number of routes an intra-area router must carry. When using LDPoRSVP tunneling, the system IP addresses of all ABRs and

PE routers must *not* be aggregated. This is because all the PE routers must be aware of the IGP route to the far-end PE router(s) to form the LDP-LSP service tunnel. In a network requiring full PE router connectivity, every PE router should have routes to all other PE routers in the same network, regardless of the area or zone locations of the PE routers. IGP-TE should be deployed in every area whenever possible to support CSPF and RSVP-TE LSP resiliency and optimal routing.

LDP

In LDPoRSVP tunneling, the LDP-LSP is used to stitch the RSVP-TE LSP tunnels together. As mentioned previously, the LDP-LSP is built when the routers use LDP to distribute labels (FEC-Label mapping) between each other. In a network with LDPoRSVP, only the PE routers and the ABRs use LDP-LSP to form LDP-LSP between PE routers; the LSR routers within the core (intra-area) only need to establish RSVP-TE LSP tunnels. Therefore, only PE routers and ABRs need to use LDP to distribute label information. Since ABRs and PE routers may not be adjacent, T-LDP sessions must be established between the ABRs and the PE routers. The T-LDP session is used to distribute the system-IP addresses of the PE routers and ABRs and the corresponding labels to form the end-to-end LDP-LSP.

For the purpose of building an LDPoRSVP tunnel, only T-LDP sessions among PE routers and the ABRs within the same area are required. However, to provide forwarding redundancy, link LDP can be enabled in all router interfaces within the area. This establishes a full LDP-LSP mesh for all /32 system-IP addresses within the area, including all routers (PE, ABR, LSR) in the area. Therefore, in each area, there are not only RSVP-TE LSPs available among the ABRs and PE routers, but there are also LDP-LSPs. If the RSVP-TE cannot carry the traffic within the area from the PE router to the ABRs or vice versa, the intra-area LDP-LSP tunnels can assume the traffic.

In Figure 8.9, T-LDP sessions are established within each area among PE routers and ABRs:

- In the backbone area, four ABRs have fully meshed T-LDP sessions.
- In Area 1, all PE routers (PE1) must have T-LDP sessions to ABR(s). PE1 has a T-LDP session to both ABR1 and ABR2 (for redundancy purposes).
- In Area 2, all PE routers (PE2) must have T-LDP sessions to ABR(s).

  These T-LDP sessions will distribute the /32 system IP address for all ABRs and PE routers.

RSVP-TE LSP

RSVP-TE LSPs are used within each area to carry the LDP-LSP-encapsulated VPN traffic. Since RSVP-TE LSPs are intra-area LSPs, they can take full advantage of TE, CSPF path calculation, and RSVP-TE LSP resiliency (secondary LSP and/or FRR). If desired, link-coloring (administrative groups) or SRLGs can be used within each area to impact the CSPF path calculation result for all LSPs (primary LSPs, secondary LSPs, FRR protection tunnels). In the LDPoRSVP solution, the RSVP-TE LSP's job is to transport traffic for the LDP-LSP tunnels. The RSVP-TE LSPs among PE routers and ABRs, and among ABRs in a core area are required. As indicated in Figure 8.9, Area 1 and Area 2 have two PE-ABR LSPs; in Area 0, the ABRs have fully meshed RSVP-TE LSP among themselves.

Note that in Figure 8.9, the RSVP-TE LSP between ABR-1 and ABR-2 in Areas 0 and 1 and the RSVP-TE LSP between ABR-3 and ABR-4 in Areas 0 and 2 are not required if the ABRs will never have service deployed locally. Tunneling redundancy is provided by fully meshed RSVP-TE LSPs among ABRs in the backbone area and by RSVP-TE LSPs from one PE router to more than one ABR within an area. When one ABR is not reachable, RSVP-TE LSP to other ABRs can be used for tunneling the LDP-LSP's traffic. The LDPoRSVP solution requires the MPLS instance **router mpls** and the RSVP instance **router rsvp** to be enabled with all router interfaces involved.

> **Note:** Within each area, RSVP-TE LSP can also be used to transport VPN traffic directly (without LDPoRSVP). The use of RSVP-TE LSP to tunnel VPN traffic and the use of RSVP-TE LSP to tunnel LDPoRSVP traffic are not mutually exclusive.

LDPoRSVP Tunnel-in-Tunnel

The LDPoRSVP (also referred to as tunnel-in-tunnel) can be deployed in ABRs and PE routers after the hierarchical IGP is deployed with TE in each area, and all RSVP-TE LSP tunnels are provisioned within each area. In a service router, the SDP between PE routers carries the VPN traffic from one PE router to another. When using LDPoRSVP TE as a transport tunneling technique, the SDP still considers that the LDP-LSP is transporting the VPN traffic. The use of RSVP-TE LSP within each area to tunnel the LDP-LSP traffic is transparent to the SDP.

In a network with LDPoRSVP tunneling, two types (or roles) of routers are aware of the LDPoRSVP tunneling and are explicitly configured with LDPoRSVP: PE routers and ABRs.

- **PE Routers** — The SDPs are established between PE routers end-to-end across the multiple-area backbone network to transport the IP/MPLS VPN traffic. PE routers participating in the same service establish pseudowires over the SDP to send VPN traffic to the correct destination. PE routers in one area with LDPoRSVP enabled establish RSVP-TE LSPs to ABR(s) within the area and use them to tunnel the LDP-LSP-encapsulated traffic to the ABR(s).
- **ABRs** — The ABRs are located between areas. ABRs have RSVP-TE LSPs within each area they reside in. They relay the traffic between RSVP-TE LSP tunnels used by the same end-to-end LDP-LSP tunnel.

All other routers in the network (P routers acting as LSRs) are not aware of either the services or the LDPoRSVP tunneling. These routers are transiting routers with RSVP-TE LSP tunnels established through them and only perform label swapping on the outermost label to transit traffic between PE routers and/or ABRs.

Using LDPoRSVP to Transport VPN Service Traffic

In a network with end-to-end service deployment and LDPoRSVP tunneling enabled in each area, an extra level of MPLS encapsulation is involved to carry the IP/MPLS VPN traffic. Recall that Figure 8.9 presented an example of a multi-area network with LDPoRSVP enabled within each area. From the control plane's perspective, routers with different roles in an LDPoRSVP-enabled network distribute different types of labels for different purposes:

- In the entire network, the PE routers (PE1 and PE2 in Figure 8.9) use T-LDP sessions between each other to distribute vc-labels to establish the pseudowire. The pseudowire connects two PE routers' service instances to encapsulate VPN traffic end-to-end. Only PE routers understand the meaning of the vc-labels and process them accordingly.
- The PE routers and the ABRs use T-LDP to distribute LDP transport labels to establish end-to-end LDP-LSP transport tunnel. The LDP-LSP is used by the SDP as an MPLS transport tunnel to carry IP/MPLS VPN traffic across the backbone. The T-LDP session distributes the FEC-Label binding between session

peers, and the FECs being distributed are the /32 system-IP addresses of all ABRs and PE routers.

- Within each area, PE routers, the local ABRs (or the ABRs in the backbone area) and other intra-area LSRs use RSVP-TE to signal LSPs among them. These LSPs carry the LDP-LSP traffic between PE routers and ABRs within each area. If the ABR router is also a PE router, the same T-LDP session on that ABR/PE router is used to distribute both service FECs (vc-label binding) and tunnel LSP FECs (LDP transport label binding).

Note: The non-ABR routers can be used to stitch the RSVP-TE LSPs to form end-to-end LDPoRSVP LSP. The configuration of the non-ABR routers for LDPoRSVP is the same as the configuration of ABR routers.

When using LDPoRSVP, the customer packets are encapsulated in a three-label MPLS label stack before the ingress PE router sends the traffic to the MPLS backbone network. Figure 8.10 presents the LDPoRSVP label stack used to encapsulate the VPN service traffic.

Figure 8.10 LDPoRSVP MPLS Label Stack

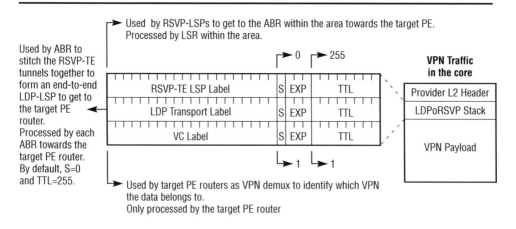

Table 8.2 compares these three labels used to encapsulate the VPN traffic.

Table 8.2 LDPoRSVP Label Stack

Label	S/TTL Value	Distributor	Operation	Location
RSVP-TE Tunnel LSP Label	0/255	Distributed hop-by-hop between all MPLS routers along the path: PE, LSR, ABR. RSVP-TE is used to distribute the label.	Processed by all MPLS routers along the path within each area	The top label
LDP-LSP Transport Label	0/255	Distributed between PE routers/ABRs or among ABRs. Each area is one hop. T-LDP or interface LDP (i-LDP) sessions between PE/ABR distribute the label.	Processed by two PE routers and the ABRs between the two PE routers	The middle label
vc-label	1/255	Distributed between PE routers, end-to-end. T-LDP sessions between the PE routers distribute the label.	Processed by PE routers only. Used as VPN demux for traffic receiving PE routers to identify which service owns the traffic.	The bottom label

When the router with LDPoRSVP enabled sends VPN traffic to the remote PE router through SDP using an LDP-LSP tunnel, the router first consults the Routing Table Manager (RTM) to find the LDP next-hop router in the direction toward the PE router. In this scenario, assume that PE1 must send traffic to PE2. PE1 determines that the LDP next hop to PE2 is ABR1. Then, because LDPoRSVP is enabled and the LDP peering to ABR1 is explicitly configured to use tunneling, the router uses the Tunnel Table Manager (TTM) to determine if there is any RSVP-TE LSP available to reach ABR1. One best-available RSVP-TE LSP is selected to carry the traffic to ABR2. Figure 8.11 presents a frame walk-through of a VPLS customer's Ethernet frame traveling through the provider's IP/MPLS VPN service network with LDPoRSVP. In this example, the link LDP is also enabled in all routers to add resiliency.

Figure 8.11 VPN Traffic Walk-Through in LDPoRSVP Network

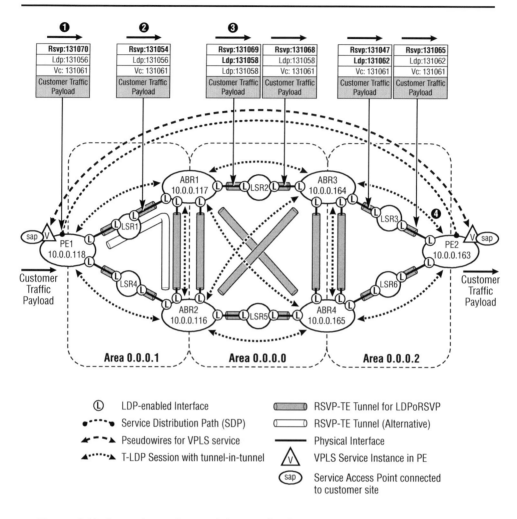

Rsvp:131070	**Rsvp:131054**	**Rsvp:131069**
Ldp:131056	Ldp:131056	**Ldp:131058**
Vc: 131061	Vc: 131061	Ldp:131058
Customer Traffic Payload	Customer Traffic Payload	Customer Traffic Payload

Legend:

- Ⓛ LDP-enabled Interface
- •·····• Service Distribution Path (SDP)
- ◄- ➤ Pseudowires for VPLS service
- ◄······➤ T-LDP Session with tunnel-in-tunnel
- ▭▭▭ RSVP-TE Tunnel for LDPoRSVP
- ▭▭▭ RSVP-TE Tunnel (Alternative)
- ——— Physical Interface
- △ⱽ VPLS Service Instance in PE
- (sap) Service Access Point connected to customer site

Figure 8.11 shows the end-to-end data path of a VPLS service across three areas using an LDPoRSVP transport tunnel. The customer Ethernet frame enters the provider's MPLS network from PE1's VPLS SAP. It travels through the backbone network and then leaves the provider's network at PE2's VPLS SAP. With the use of LDPoRSVP, the frame is encapsulated with a three-label MPLS label stack. When the traffic travels through the core network, routers with different roles (ABRs, PE and LSR routers) perform different actions on the frame. In this scenario, the following sequence of events occurs:

1. The *ingress PE router* (PE1) receives the native Ethernet traffic from the customer site through the VPLS SAP. After PE1 validates the traffic and makes a forwarding decision, it sends the traffic toward PE2 over the pseudowire (1) in the following sequence:

a. The vc-label (131061) is pushed into the MPLS stack for PE2 to use as a VPN de-multiplexer (demux). This label is distributed by PE2 over the T-LDP session for the VPLS pseudowire.

b. The LDP transport label (131056) assigned by ABR1 as the first hop of the LDP from PE1 to PE2 is pushed into the label stack.

c. Because the LDPoRSVP is used, the RSVP-TE LSP label (131070) assigned by LSR1 is pushed onto the top of the label stack. This label is used for traffic traversing LSP PE1-ABR1.

The customer frame with a three-label MPLS label stack is then sent over the wire to the P/LSR router.

2. The *intra-area LSR* LSR1 receives the encapsulated frame. Because the LSR is an intra-area LSR in the LDPoRSVP network, it is aware only of the RSVP-TE LSP used to tunnel the traffic between the PE routers and the ABRs. Therefore, it simply swaps the top RSVP-TE LSP label (131070) to another label (131054) distributed by the ABR1 for LSP PE1-ABR1 and sends the traffic toward ABR1 (2). The intra-area LSR does not care about the LDP transport label and the vc-label underneath.

3. The area border router ABR1 receives the traffic from the LSR. The ABR in LDPoRSVP network is the router in charge of stitching two RSVP-TE LSPs in the two areas together into one LDP tunnel. Therefore, as the Tail router of the LSP PE1-ABR1, ABR1 pops the top RSVP-TE LSP label (131054) and exposes the LDP transport label (131056) in the frame. Then, ABR1 swaps the LDP transport label to another LDP transport label (131058) distributed by ABR3. The ABR then pushes the RSVP-TE LSP label (131069) and sends the traffic to LSR2.

   - LSR2 performs a similar operation to that of LSR1. It swaps the top RSVP-TE label to a new value (131068) and sends the traffic to ABR3.

   - ABR3 performs a similar operation to that of ABR2. It pops the top RSVP-TE label, swaps the LDP transport label to a new value (131062) distributed by PE2, and then pushes the new RSVP-TE label (131047) for LSP ABR3-PE2. The traffic is sent to LSR3.

   - LSR3 performs a similar operation to that of LSR2. It swaps the top RSVP-TE label to a new value (131065) and sends the traffic to PE2.

4. The PE2 is the *egress PE router* of the VPN packet. When it receives the traffic, it pops the entire MPLS label stack in the following sequence:

   a. As the Tail router of RSVP-TE LSP ABR3-PE2, it first pops the LSP label (131065).

   b. As the termination point SDP using the LDP-LSP, it pops the LDP transport label (131062).

   c. As the egress PE router, it pops the vc-label, validates the traffic, and sends it to the traffic customer site.

   Note that the LDP label's TTL value is only subtracted by 1 when the VPN packet travels from PE1 to PE2. This is because the LDPoRSVP forms an end-to-end LDP-LSP, which is only one hop (from PE1 to PE2) from the LDP-LSP's perspective.

In the preceding example, the link LDP is also enabled in all routers in the network (indicated by the "L" circles on all interfaces in Figure 8.11) to add an extra layer of MPLS tunneling resiliency. For example, in Area 1, if all the RSVP-TE LSP tunnels between the PE and ABRs are not available, PE1 can still send traffic to ABR1 or ABR2 using normal LDP-LSPs established by the link-LDP label distribution.

Configuring LDPoRSVP

The LDPoRSVP is enabled by the following two-step configuration:

1. Configure the LDP routing instances to enable the use of LDPoRSVP tunneling.

2. Specify the FEC (target router) that uses the RSVP-TE LSP tunnel to tunnel the LDP traffic. The target router can be an ABR or a PE router within the same area.

Figure 8.12 presents a PE router's LDPoRSVP configuration. The IGP-TE configuration and the RSVP-TE LSPs to the ABRs are required but are not shown in the figure because the provisioning details of IGP-TE and RSVP-TE have been discussed previously. The configuration in the PE1 router's LDPoRSVP deployment includes the following commands:

1. Enable the LDPoRSVP in the router using the `prefer-tunnel-in-tunnel` command. This command is optional. If it is *not* configured, the system will prefer to use regular LDP-LSP tunnels and only use LDPoRSVP when LDP-

LSP tunnels are not available. If it is configured, the system will prefer to use LDPoRSVP tunneling for VPN traffic. When LDPoRSVP is enabled, for certain traffic, the router will use RTM to find the next-hop LDP router and then consult TTM to determine if there is an RSVP-TE LSP to further tunnel the LDP traffic.

Figure 8.12   Enable LDPoRSVP in LDP Routing Instance

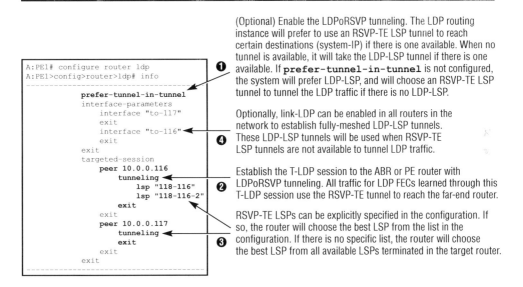

❶ (Optional) Enable the LDPoRSVP tunneling. The LDP routing instance will prefer to use an RSVP-TE LSP tunnel to reach certain destinations (system-IP) if there is one available. When no tunnel is available, it will take the LDP-LSP tunnel if there is one available. If **prefer-tunnel-in-tunnel** is not configured, the system will prefer LDP-LSP, and will choose an RSVP-TE LSP tunnel to tunnel the LDP traffic if there is no LDP-LSP.

❹ Optionally, link-LDP can be enabled in all routers in the network to establish fully-meshed LDP-LSP tunnels. These LDP-LSP tunnels will be used when RSVP-TE LSP tunnels are not available to tunnel LDP traffic.

❷ Establish the T-LDP session to the ABR or PE router with LDPoRSVP tunneling. All traffic for LDP FECs learned through this T-LDP session use the RSVP-TE tunnel to reach the far-end router.

❸ RSVP-TE LSPs can be explicitly specified in the configuration. If so, the router will choose the best LSP from the list in the configuration. If there is no specific list, the router will choose the best LSP from all available LSPs terminated in the target router.

2. Specify the ABR(s) as T-LDP peer(s) that use RSVP-TE LSP to tunnel LDP-LSP traffic if available. This is done by explicitly configuring `tunneling` in the targeted LDP peer configuration. In the ALSRP, the explicit creation of T-LDP peering is not required among PE routers. This is because when an SDP with T-LDP signaling is created in a router, the router automatically establishes the T-LDP peering session with the SDP's far-end router. These details are discussed in Chapter 9. The T-LDP configuration required in this example explicitly specifies two ABRs (not PE routers), with the tunneling option enabled. This is required for LDPoRSVP.

3. Optionally, list the RSVP-TE tunnels allowed to be used to tunnel LDP traffic. The operator can provision an explicit list of RSVP-TE LSP for a certain target router by using the `lsp <lsp-name>` command under the T-LDP peer tunneling configuration. When this list is present, the TTM will only choose RSVP-TE LSP from the list. If the list is absent under the tunneling

configuration, the TTM will choose any available RSVP-TE LSP terminated in the same target router as the LDPoRSVP tunnel.

4. Optionally, enable link LDP as the backup transport tunnel in case all RSVP-TE tunnels are not available. Note that even if the link LDP is enabled in all routers' network interfaces, the T-LDP is still mandatory for LDPoRSVP. In this case, the T-LDP is not used to distribute /32 system prefixes, but is used to specify the peer router to which the LDPoRSVP tunneling sends traffic.

The ABRs and the PE router have a similar configuration with respect to LDPoRSVP. The preferred-tunneling must be enabled in the LDP routing instance, and the T-LDP peering requires that RSVP tunneling be specified in the `targeted-session` context. Optionally, RSVP-TE LSP can be specified for each peer, and link LDP can be enabled on all network interfaces to establish LDP-LSP as the backbone if all RSVP-TE LSP tunnels fail. The other routers in the network (P routers as LSRs) do not require any explicit configuration to support LDPoRSVP. They only require that IGP-TE, RSVP, and MPLS are enabled to support RSVP-TE LSP signaling and that TE information is available for the CSPF calculation of the LSP-Path's actual path. Table 8.3 compares the configuration required on routers with different roles for LDPoRSVP implementation in a network.

Table 8.3 LDPoRSVP Configuration Roles of Routers in the Network

Roles	LDPoRSVP Mandatory Configuration	Optional Configuration	Comments
PE	`prefer-tunnel-in-tunnel` (optional) in LDP configuration, explicit list of ABRs as T-LDP target peer with tunneling enabled	Uses link LDP on all routing interfaces to build LDP-LSPs as backup. Explicit list of RSVP-TE LSP tunnels for each T-LDP peer using LDPoRSVP.	PE only runs LDPoRSVP tunneling in the local area, from itself to the ABR.
ABR/ ASBR	`prefer-tunnel-in-tunnel` (optional) in LDP configuration, explicit list of intra-area ABRs and PE routers as T-LDP target peer with tunneling enabled	Uses link LDP on all routing interfaces to build LDP-LSPs as backup. Explicit list of RSVP-TE LSP tunnels for each T-LDP peer using LDPoRSVP.	ABR runs LDPoRSVP across different areas. All peering ABRs and PE routers will use LDPoRSVP tunnel.

Roles	LDPoRSVP Mandatory Configuration	Optional Configuration	Comments
P (LSR)	No mandatory configuration required	Uses link LDP on all routing interfaces to build LDP-LSPs as backup.	P/LSR routers are not aware of LDPoRSVP. They only see RSVP-TE LSP within the area.

In the ALSRP, the MPLS LSP are used to carry VPN service traffic. When LDPoRSVP is deployed in a network, the SDPs can use these end-to-end LDP-LSPs to carry VPN traffic from the local PE router to the remote PE router. To use LDPoRSVP tunneling, the SDP must be configured as an MPLS encapsulation type and to use LDP distributed LSPs. Details regarding SDP types and configuration are in Chapter 9.

Figure 8.13 presents a configuration example in router PE1 in which the SDP uses LDP-LSP to take advantage of LDPoRSVP tunneling. In this network, there are two PE routers located in two different areas. The SDP configuration is end-to-end from PE1 to PE2. When established, it will carry all VPN traffic from PE1 to PE2. From the SDP's perspective, it uses the LDP-LSP tunnel as an MPLS transport tunnel. The SDP is not aware that the underlying RSVP-TE LSPs are tunneling the LDP-LSP traffic. Therefore, there is no specific configuration required for the SDP to use LDPoRSVP. When LDPoRSVP is deployed in the network, the traffic on that SDP is tunneled by LDPoRSVP automatically in the PE router when the SDP matches the following criteria (the parenthetical numbers match the circled numbers in Figure 8.13):

- The SDP must be an MPLS type SDP (1) using an LDP (2) created LSP as the transport tunnel.
- The SDP's far-end address has an associated LDP egress label distributed by the next-hop ABR (3).
- The LDP next-hop router to the far-end PE is an ABR within the area. Recall that T-LDP sessions are created between PE2–ABR2, ABR2–ABR1, and ABR1–PE1. Therefore, PE2's system IP address 10.0.0.163 has an FEC-Label mapping distributed by T-LDP.
- There is one RSVP-TE LSP available between the local PE router and the ABR.

Figure 8.13 Service Distribution Path (SDP) Using LDPoRSVP

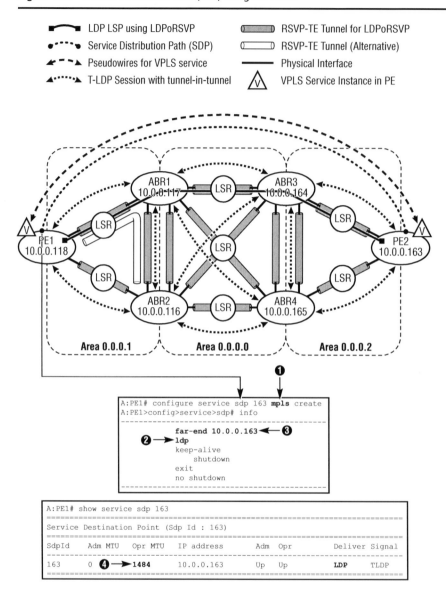

When the system decides to use LDPoRSVP tunneling for a certain SDP, the extra encapsulation introduced by LDPoRSVP is automatically taken into consideration by the SDP's operational maximum transfer unit (MTU). In this example, the SDP's operational MTU is 1,484 bytes (4). The network port used by the SDP has an MTU of 1,514 bytes. In such a port, for an MPLS SDP using RSVP-TE LSP tunneling or LDP tunneling without LDPoRSVP, the SDP MTU is set to 1,492. This is because the network port's Layer 2 encapsulation (14 byte Ethernet header) and the IP/MPLS VPN encapsulation (8 byte MPLS stack) are subtracted from the network port MTU: 1,514 − 22 = 1,492 bytes. In the case of an LDP SDP using LDPoRSVP, 4 more bytes of LDPoRSVP label are subtracted, so the SDP's operational MTU should be 1,488 bytes. In addition, in Figure 8.13's example, the RSVP-TE LSP used to tunnel the LDP traffic has FRR facility backup enabled. The system subtracts another 4 bytes from the SDP MTU because FRR facility backup introduces another MPLS label during the LSP protection process and therefore further reduces the SDP MTU. Finally, the SDP's operational MTU is calculated as 1,484 bytes.

Details regarding MPLS FRR are provided in Chapter 7. Details regarding MTU calculation are provided in Chapter 9.

LDPoRSVP Tunnel Selecting Criteria

When LDPoRSVP is enabled in a PE's or ABR's LDP router configuration, the SDP must be configured using the LDP-LSP type, so that the system can send IP/MPLS VPN traffic over the LDPoRSVP tunnel. As mentioned previously, if prefer-tunnel-in-tunnel is explicitly configured in the LDP configuration, the system will prefer to use the RSVP-TE LSP to tunnel LDP traffic. Otherwise, the system will prefer to use the LDP-LSP tunnel to carry traffic and only use LDPoRSVP tunneling when LDP-LSP tunnels are not available.

The SDP's selection of the LDP-LSP or LDPoRSVP tunnels happens after the PE router receives a T-LDP service-FEC binding. When the PE router receives a service-FEC binding from the remote PE router over the T-LDP session, it needs to perform LDP FEC resolution to find the forwarding path for the service-FEC. The PE router performs the FEC lookup in the RTM, and the lookup returns the next hop to the remote PE router and the advertising router (ABR, or the remote PE router itself). In a network with IGP areas and LDPoRSVP, the ABR should be the advertising router for the system IP address of the remote PE. Therefore, the next-hop router should be one of the T-LDP peers (ABR1 or ABR2 in the example). If the least-cost next-hop advertising router is the ABR and the tunneling option is enabled, the system performs a *tunnel lookup* in the TTM to choose the best RSVP-TE LSP to the closest ABR. When performing the tunnel lookup, the tunnel selection criteria are:

- If the tunneling configuration on that T-LDP peer has an explicit list of RSVP-TE LSPs, the system can only choose a tunnel from the list to tunnel the LDP traffic.

- If the tunneling configuration on that T-LDP peer does not have an RSVP-TE LSP list, the system can choose any RSVP-TE LSP originating from the local router and terminating at the ABR.

- When performing tunnel selection, the system only chooses from the RSVP-TE LSPs that are operationally **up**.

- If there is more than one RSVP-TE LSP available, the system chooses the one with the best (numerically lowest) LSP metric.

- If all RSVP-TE LSPs have equal LSP metrics, the system chooses the one with the longest **up** time (also referred to as the first-available or most-stable LSP).

- If there is neither a RSVP-TE LSP nor a LDP-LSP available, the system will fail the tunnel selection process and put the SDP into an operationally **down** state.

Figure 8.14 presents the configuration of the RSVP-TE LSP tunnel metric value. By default, all RSVP-TE LSP tunnels have metric value 1 (the best). Configuring the metric value manually allows operators to control the LSP selection if desired.

The RSVP-TE LSP tunnel selection on LDPoRSVP TE is preemptive and revertive. At any time, if an eligible RSVP-TE LSP becomes operative with a better metric (numerical lowest value), the LDPoRSVP will immediately switch to the current best tunnel. This behavior is applicable when a new RSVP-TE LSP with lower metric than the currently selected LSP is configured and signaled, and also when an RSVP-TE LSP with better metric was previously failed and becomes operational again.

Figure 8.14 RSVP-TE LSP Tunnel Metric Configuration

```
A:PE1# configure router mpls lsp 118-116
A:PE1>config>router>mpls>lsp# info
----------------------------------------
                to 10.0.0.116
                cspf
                fast-reroute facility
                exit
                metric 100
                primary "loose"
                exit
                no shutdown
----------------------------------------
```

```
A:PE1# show router tunnel-table
================================================================================
Tunnel Table (Router: Base)
================================================================================
Destination        Owner Encap TunnelId  Pref    Nexthop       Metric

--------------------------------------------------------------------------------
10.0.0.116/32      sdp   MPLS  116       5       10.0.0.116    0
10.0.0.116/32      rsvp  MPLS  7         7       10.116.118.1  100
10.0.0.116/32      rsvp  MPLS  10        7       10.117.118.1  1
10.0.0.116/32      rsvp  MPLS  15        7       10.116.118.1  1
10.0.0.116/32      ldp   MPLS  -         9       10.0.0.116    1
--- Output Omitted ---
```

Encapsulation Overhead and MTU Consideration with LDPoRSVP

When using LDPoRSVP, an extra label — the RSVP-TE LSP tunnel label — is appended to the top of the label stack for the encapsulated VPN traffic. This adds another 4 bytes of encapsulation overhead and makes the total MPLS label stack size increase to 12 bytes. When more encapsulation overhead is added, the overall frame size grows. Furthermore, the RSVP-TE LSP tunnel used to tunnel the LDP traffic may use FRR facility backup to provide protection on the LSP. During the network failure, the facility backup bypass tunnel protects the traffic and adds another label into the stack — the facility bypass tunnel label.

Figure 8.15 presents an IP/MPLS VPN-encapsulated OAM frame with a five-label MPLS label stack and LDPoRSVP tunneling. The frame was captured during a network failure when FRR facility backup was used to protect the RSVP-TE LSP tunnel.

In this example, a VPLS OAM frame is captured. The OAM frame has an extra Router Alert (RA) label with a value of 1 in the bottom of the label stack. Regular VPLS traffic has two labels in the label stack, and the service-label (in our example, value = 131061, TTL = 1) is at the bottom of the stack.

When more encapsulation overhead is used, the actual encapsulated frame size grows. In any network, a physical link can only transport certain sized data frames. The maximum size of the data frame is referred to as the *maximum transfer unit* (MTU). The various types of MTUs have been discussed previously in detail. The previous content only describes the particular case regarding the overhead caused by LDPoRSVP.

Figure 8-15 LDPoRSVP Encapsulation Example: MPLS Label Stack

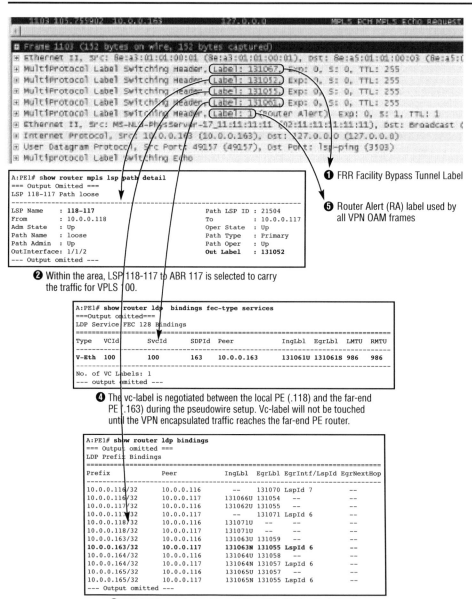

LDPoRSVP Resiliency

Network resiliency with quick failover is always desired. With the help of LDPoRSVP TE, a network divided into areas (hierarchical IGP) can use MPLS FRR and secondary LSP within each area. Recall that there are three types of routers in a network with LDPoRSVP: PE routers, ABRs, and intra-area LSRs. The protection provided for different types of routers in the network are different. Figure 8.16 presents the example network for the discussion of LDPoRSVP network resiliency.

The network resiliency is implemented on different levels on different types of routers to provide the end-to-end tunnel between PE1 and PE2:

- The RSVP-TE LSPs used to tunnel the LDP traffic can be protected by MPLS secondary LSP-Paths and/or MPLS FRR within each area. Multiple LSP-Paths can be provisioned in the RSVP-TE LSP tunnel. The primary LSP-Path can also have FRR enabled (one-to-one or facility backup). When any link fails or the intra-area LSR fails, secondary LSP and/or FRR will protect the RSVP-TE LSP within the area. However, because PE routers and ABRs are always the HE or Tail routers for the RSVP-TE LSP, the failures on these routers cannot be protected by the secondary LSP-Path and/or FRR.

- The LDPoRSVP tunnel can have more than one RSVP-TE LSP for the same destination PE router/ABR. Therefore, if one RSVP-TE LSP fails, the system can also choose an alternative RSVP-TE LSP to tunnel the LDP traffic. If there is no alternative RSVP-TE LSP available to the ABR/PE router, optionally, link LDP can be configured to build LDP-LSP tunnels to carry the traffic.

- ABR redundancy can also be configured. Between each area and the backbone area in Figure 8.16, there are two ABRs. PE routers are configured to peer with both ABRs in the same area as the RSVP-TE LSP and LDPoRSVP. If ABR1 fails, the system finds another T-LDP peer, ABR2 in our example, to carry the VPN traffic using LDPoRSVP tunneling for PE1.

This three-layer configuration maximizes the network resiliency and minimizes the failover time, and therefore achieves the best service availability.

Figure 8.16 LDPoRSVP Network Example

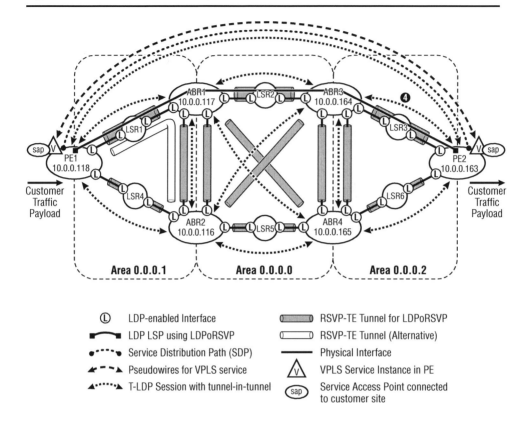

Summary

LDP is a session-based protocol used by MPLS-capable routers to distribute labels. Two routers must establish an LDP session before they can start exchanging label mapping information. LDP routers use LDP messages to exchange label distribution information. The FEC-Label mapping information is exchanged by LDP. LDP contains a label value for the receiver to use and specifies the traffic type (FEC). The router uses the label received from LDP peers to perform MPLS encapsulation.

There are two types of LDP sessions:

- **Link LDP** (also called *interface LDP*) — A link-LDP relationship can only be established between two directly connected IP interfaces of two routers. Link LDP is used to distribute IP-prefix Label Mapping for MPLS routers to create

LDP-LSPs. In the ALSRP, the LDP-LSP is one type of transport tunnel used by SDP to transport VPN traffic.

- **Targeted LDP (T-LDP)** — T-LDP is used to signal IP/MPLS VPN pseudowires. T-LDP sessions can be established over non-adjacent LDP routers. T-LDP messages are used to establish, tear down, and notify routers of the state of the pseudowires used by IP/MPLS VPN services.

LDPoRSVP tunneling allows the use of RSVP-TE LSPs and CSPF in each area of the network. It uses LDP-LSPs to stitch these intra-area RSVP-TE LSPs together to form an end-to-end LDP tunnel. LDPoRSVP can be used to solve two problem scenarios:

- When CSPF and RSVP-TE LSP is desired in a network with an IGP hierarchical design.
- A scaled network where the number of RSVP-TE LSP tunnels must be reduced. LDPoRSVP can segment and aggregate the LSPs and reduce the number of LSPs required in the core.

Ethernet VPN Services

III

A service-oriented network has its own architecture. This section starts with an introduction to the new IP/MPLS VPN service architecture, followed by a discussion of the two major forms of Ethernet Layer 2 VPN services: Virtual Leased Line (VLL) and Virtual Private LAN Service (VPLS). The high availability and service resiliency of VLL and VPLS are also presented.

IP/MPLS VPN Service Routing Architecture

The IP/MPLS VPN service network introduces a new service-oriented network architecture. In such an architecture, the backbone network used to tunnel the service traffic is decoupled from the services themselves. Multiple services share a single converged network.

9

Chapter Objectives

- Provide an overview of the IP/MPLS VPN network infrastructure and the roles of MPLS service network elements

- Explain the ALSRP service architecture and the different types of services it offers

- Discuss the Service Access Point (SAP), Service Distribution Path (SDP), transport tunnels, and pseudowires (PWs)

- Understand the maximum transfer unit (MTU) in a service network

This chapter builds on the concepts introduced in Chapter 2 to discuss the architecture of Internet Protocol Multi Protocol Label Switching (IP/MPLS)–based Virtual Private Network (VPN) services. An IP/MPLS VPN network can support various services within a single converged network by taking advantage of advanced MPLS capabilities. MPLS is widely deployed in service provider networks because of its flexibility, reliability, cost efficiency, and because it permits various types of services to share the provider's network infrastructure through the pseudowire-based VPN architecture. We begin with a description of the overall IP/MPLS VPN network architecture, followed by an in-depth discussion of service components such as Service Access Points (SAPs), Service Distribution Paths (SDPs), and pseudowires (PWs). This chapter provides readers with a thorough understanding of IP/MPLS VPN service networks and, specifically, the Alcatel-Lucent Service Routing Portfolio (ALSRP) service architecture.

9.1 IP/MPLS VPN Service Network Infrastructure

Traditionally, service providers built different types of backbone networks with dedicated hardware to provide diverse services to their customers. This service implementation model is called a *dedicated services model*. For example, a carrier may need to build separate networks to provide the following services to its customers:

- An ATM network with many ATM switches to provide ATM VP/VC switching for ATM customers

- A PSTN/GSM network to provide telephony services to land-line and mobile customers

- A SONET/SDH network to provide high-availability, high-bandwidth transport services to TDM customers

- An IP routed network to provide dedicated or public (Internet) network services to IP customers

A dedicated services model, in which each type of service is supported by its own network infrastructure, is not cost-efficient for service providers and customers. Providers must build multiple network infrastructures to support different networking technologies. As a result, service providers look for new technologies to provide a converged solution using a single network backbone that serves each customer's specific requirements. An MPLS-based multi-service VPN network provides this solution.

To appreciate the benefits of VPN, two important concepts must be understood: *virtual* and *private*. From the service provider's perspective, all customer services are supported over a common, shared backbone network. In the provider's network within the service routers, these individual services are isolated by assigning each one to a *virtual* service instance. Only service instances belonging to the same end-to-end service can communicate with each other. Service instances serving different customers do not exchange control information or data, although they may share the same hardware (the same service router, or the same physical access port). One customer is not aware of the existence of any other customer although they share the same service provider network. From a customer's perspective, the network resources are exclusively assigned to them. Each customer thinks the service provider's network is a part of its own *private* network.

Customer networks connect to the service provider's Provider Edge (PE) routers through attachment circuits. The attachment circuits transport native format packets, frames, or streams between customer networks and the PE routers where the VPNs are provisioned. Inside the service provider's core network, the PE routers connect to each other by MPLS PW over the IP or MPLS service transport tunnels and transport the VPN customer traffic over the provider network backbone.

> **Note:** For Layer 3 services, this model is called the *PE-based VPN approach.* All VPN intelligence resides in the service provider's PE node. Another approach is the *Customer Edge (CE)–based VPN approach.* In the CE-based VPN model, the service provider network is unaware that it is shared by multiple CE devices. Customers with different internal networks can use Generic Routing Encapsulation (GRE) to share the service provider network to carry all traffic. The service provider has no knowledge of the number of customer VPNs sharing its network. In the CE-based VPN model, the VPN intelligence resides in the CE router. The CE-based VPN is beyond the scope of this book.

All the intelligence behind the delivery of multiple services through a shared network backbone resides in the service provider's network. Consequently, no changes are required to the customer's network configurations when they move from a dedicated provider network to a shared IP/MPLS VPN provider network, unless they are migrating to a new type of service. Ultimately, it is the service provider's responsibility to deliver services to its diverse customer base.

The Service Concept and the Roles and Capabilities of a Service Router

Now that the key benefits of a VPN have been identified, it is important to understand the concept of a *service* and the role of a *service router*. The meaning of *service* has evolved alongside the changes in network architecture.

"Service" in a Legacy Network

In the legacy multiple dedicated networks solution, the routers are not *service-aware*. In the provider's network, there are ports or interfaces assigned to customers, and there are series of connections that connect these ports or interfaces. In such a network, a *service* to one customer refers to the collection of the ports/interfaces, connections among them and the related configuration, rather than to an end-to-end connectivity for a customer. The provisioning of these services is done by configuring the ports and connections on each device involved. The end-to-end services and the correlation with customers are not visible to the networking devices. There may be network management software that can help the provider to deploy end-to-end services by automatically configuring the series of connections in the nodes involved. But an individual device is not aware that a cross-connect belongs to a specific customer's service.

In a legacy network service, end-to-end features such as OAM, QoS, Security, and Accounting are deployed based on hardware such as a port or a cross-connect. If several services or customers share the same port, they must share the same QoS, OAM, Security, and Accounting policies. For example, two services sharing the same port cannot receive different QoS treatments because the QoS policy applies to the port or the cross-connect, not to each individual service. There is no deployment granularity to distinguish different services sharing the same hardware and applying these policies to individual services. The legacy network uses a *port-based* or *connection-based* service implementation.

"Service" in an MPLS-Based Multi-Service VPN Network

In an MPLS-based multi-service VPN network, any connectivity a service provider offers its customers is called a *service*. Examples of services or connectivity are:

- T1/E1 line connecting a PBX to a PSTN
- ATM PVC or Frame-Relay virtual circuit that connect routers' Frame-Relay interfaces
- Ethernet bridging connections that connect LANs from several locations
- A BGP circuit to provide Internet access

The Alcatel-Lucent Service Router Portfolio (ALSRP) provides a service-oriented solution. In the ALSRP, the service is implemented as a service instance in each service router. *Service instances* are software entities residing on the service routers. Therefore, the service routers are aware of the existence of services. Service-related functions (OAM, Security, or Accounting) are deployed in each service instance sub-entity (SAP, pseudowire), rather than in hardware (ports, connections, etc.).

In the ALSRP, a service is defined as:

> ... *a globally unique entity that refers to a type of connectivity service for either Internet or VPN connectivity. Each service is uniquely identified by a service ID within a service area. The ALSRP service model uses logical service entities to construct a service. In the service model logical service entities provide a uniform, service-centric configuration, management, and billing model for service provisioning.*

A service not only provides connectivity; but it also contains a full suite of functions to support customers, such as:

- Billing and statistics (accounting)
- Security
- Quality of Service (QoS)
- Operation, Administration, and Maintenance (OAM)
- Troubleshooting
- Management (provisioning, modification, monitoring)
- Filtering and Deep Packet Inspection (DPI)

From the service provider's perspective, many types of services are provided through a common network backbone infrastructure. Multiple services that reside in the same service router may also share the same hardware (e.g., the same access port). With the ALSRP, services are distinguished from one another because each service in the involved PE router has its own service instance. In addition, every function of a service is differentiated from any other service function.

A *service router* has a service database; each service instance and its related components are all tracked by the service database. Service router functions (for example, QoS and OAM) are deployed around a *logical* entity such as a service; they are not deployed around the *physical* hardware (port or interface). The service router has the granularity to deploy multiple types of policies (e.g., QoS, Security, and Accounting) to every service instance individually, regardless of whether they share the same hardware. From an OAM perspective, each service instance in a service router is monitored and managed individually without affecting any other service.

From the customer's perspective, a service is not several ports in different locations used to connect devices together. A service is a seamless end-to-end solution, which should include:

- Reliable connections with redundant forwarding paths and control plane components
- Accurate statistics and billing information for every service the customer has purchased
- Security features provided on a per-service basis
- Dedicated QoS for each service
- SLA conformance supported by detailed usage statistics
- OAM and troubleshooting functions provided on a per-service basis
- The service provider's internal network infrastructure and the existence of other services or customers are transparent to the customer.
- A service provider network that isolates services belonging to different customers

Services Offered by Service Router: Internet Service and VPN Service

In this section, we take a look at the types of services provided by the IP/MPLS VPN service network. There are two main categories of services offered by the ALSRP:

- **Internet Enhanced Service (IES)** — IES provides Internet access from the router's global routing table with enhanced QoS, Security, and Accounting functionality. In contrast to the Internet services provided by traditional IP networks, the IES service has much stronger QoS, Security, and Accounting functions and offers more connectivity variations (for example, local service access through IES Service Access Points (SAPs) or via VPN service through pseudowires).
- **Virtual Private Network (VPN) Services** — The services for different customers are isolated within this scope. L2VPN is implemented via Virtual Leased Line (VLL) Services, which are point-to-point virtual connections, and Virtual Private LAN Service (VPLS), which provides multipoint-to-multipoint Ethernet bridging. L3VPN is implemented via Virtual Private Routed Network (VPRN) as described in RFC 4364, formerly RFC 2547bis.

Note: An L2VPN service such as VPLS can access IES services in a remote PE router through pseudowires. This is known as *IES spoke-termination*. The IES service and the spoke-termination to the IES service are beyond the scope of this book. Internet services can also be offered through a VPRN service. VPRN service is beyond the scope of this book.

L2VPN services switch (or bridge) customer traffic based on the physical address (e.g., Ethernet MAC, ATM vpi/vci, TDM channel-id, or Frame-Relay DLCI). L3VPN services route customer traffic based on the logical address (IP address). For debugging or security purposes, mirroring services can also be provided for the customer or service provider to replicate the exact traffic on the wire from any point of the service network to any location in the service network. These services can be deployed locally in one service router or involve multiple service routers across the backbone network. Table 9.1 provides a brief description of the services types available in the ALSRP.

Note: ALSRP service routers also provide subscriber management (SM) and enhanced subscriber management (ESM) services as a key part of Alcatel-Lucent Triple Play Service Delivery Architecture (TPSDA). SM, ESM, and TPSDA are beyond the scope of this book.

Table 9.1 Service Types Offered by ALSRP

Service Types	Connectivity	Service Description
Internet Enhanced Service (IES)	L3	IES is a routed connectivity service in which the subscriber communicates with an IP router interface to send and receive Internet traffic. An IES has one or more logical IP routing interfaces, each with an SAP that acts as the access point to the subscriber's network. IES allows customer-facing IP interfaces to participate in the same routing instance used for service network core routing connectivity. IES service is beyond the scope of this book.

(continued)

Table 9.1 Service Types Offered by ALSRP *(continued)*

Service Types	Connectivity	Service Description
Virtual Private Routed Network (VPRN)	L3, multipoint	VPRN (RFC 4364, formally RFC 2547bis) provides a Layer 3 VPN service to end-customers. Each VPRN instance consists of a set of customer sites connected to one or more PE routers. Each associated PE router maintains a separate IP routing table for each VPRN instance. Additionally, the PE routers exchange the routing information via MP-BGP. The PE routers exchange routes with VPRN customers using PE-CE routing protocols, or statically configured routes. The VPRN service is beyond the scope of this book.
IP VLL (Ipipe)	L2, point-to-point	Ipipe provides IPv4 connectivity between any Layer 2 attachment circuits: Both sites connected to the Ipipe SAPs appear on the same IP subnet. This service enables service interworking between different link layer technologies and exchange IP packets.
Virtual Private LAN Service (VPLS)	L2, multipoint	VPLS allows the connection of multiple sites in a single bridged domain using a provider-managed MPLS network. The customer sites in a VPLS instance appear to be on the same LAN, regardless of their geographical location.
Ethernet VLL (Epipe)	L2, point-to-point	An Epipe service is a Layer 2 point-to-point bridging service in which the customer Ethernet frames are transported across a service provider's IP, MPLS, or Provider Backbone Bridge (PBB) VPLS network.[a] An Epipe service is completely transparent to the subscriber's data and protocols.
ATM VLL (Apipe)	L2, point-to-point	Apipe provides a point-to-point ATM switching service between users connected to service routers on an MPLS network. An ATM PVC [e.g., a cross-connect such as a Virtual Path (VP)] is configured on the service router's Apipe service instance. VPI/VCI translation is supported in the Apipe.
Frame-Relay VLL (Fpipe)	L2, point-to-point	The Fpipe provides a point-to-point Frame-Relay service between users connected to the service routers in the MPLS network. Users are connected to the service router using Frame-Relay DLCIs.

Service Types	Connectivity	Service Description
Circuit Emulation VLL (Cpipe)	L2, point-to-point	The Cpipe provides a point-to-point TDM service between users over the MPLS network. Two modes of circuit emulation are supported: Unstructured (SAToP as per RFC 4053) and Structured (CESoPSN, as per RFC 5086). The Unstructured mode is supported for DS1 and E1 channels. The Structured mode is supported for n*64 kbps circuits. In addition, DS1, E1, and n*64 kbps circuits are supported (per MEF8).
Service mirroring	n/a	Service mirroring is a traffic monitoring and diagnostic tool. It can mirror on an n-to-1 unidirectional service basis. The service mirroring can be either local or remote. Local service mirroring, when configured on a router, mirrors any traffic on any port or SAP local to that router. Remote mirroring allows tunneling of the mirrored data through the core network to another location, using either GRE or MPLS tunneling.

^aThe PBB VPLS is explained in Chapter 17.

With the ALSRP, a service provider can build a single converged network backbone to provide any or all of these services to its customers using IP/MPLS VPN technology to deliver these services.

9.2 Alcatel-Lucent Service Routing Architecture

In contrast to service-specific, hardware-dedicated networks based on traditional routers, multi-service networks based on the ALSRP have a unique and specific architecture. This architecture is fully compliant with the IP/MPLS pseudowire-based VPN architecture. This section introduces the basic infrastructure of a multi-service network based on IP/MPLS VPN and the Alcatel-Lucent service routing architecture. The roles of each network element in the multi-service network are also explained.

Network Elements in a Multi-Services IP/MPLS VPN Network

An IP/MPLS VPN-based multi-service network contains different types of network elements. Figure 9.1 illustrates a logical view of two customer sites connected by a service routing network. Both the customer and service provider have their own networks. The service provider creates service(s) in its network (represented by the dotted lines) to connect customer sites. Understanding the role of each network element is essential to understanding the network architecture.

The service provider network backbone contains Provider (P) routers, Provider Edge (PE) routers, and, optionally, Multi-Tenant Unit (MTU) devices. The customer network contains Customer Edge (CE) devices and Customer (C) devices. Table 9.2 describes the roles of each network element.

Figure 9.1 A Logical Representation of the Customer and Service Provider Networks

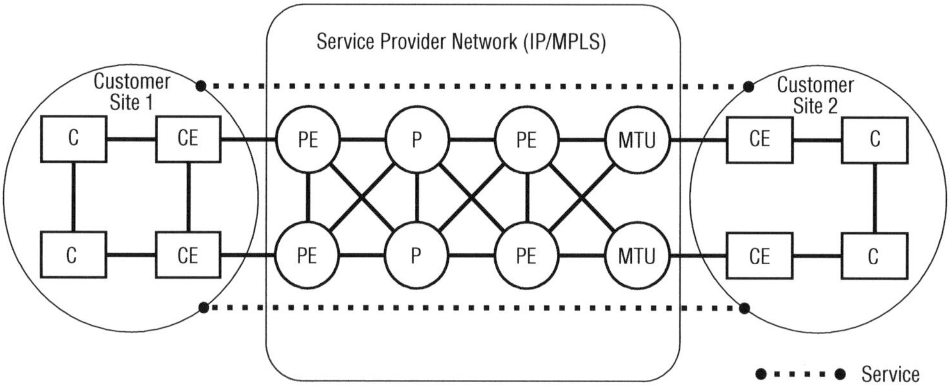

Table 9.2 Roles of Network Components

Router's Role	Location	Network Element Role Definition
Provider Edge (PE)	Provider Network	PE routers contain all the intelligence of VPN services. Service instances are provisioned in the PE router. The PE router receives native traffic from CE devices, performs VPN encapsulation, and sends the traffic to its peering PE routers through the pseudowires. PE routers may also peer with CE devices using control plane protocols, such as STP, OSPF, and BGP. The PE router resides in the edge of the MPLS domain, performing ingress Label Edge Router (iLER) and egress Label Edge Router (eLER) functions.

Router's Role	Location	Network Element Role Definition
Provider (P)	Provider Network	The P router resides in the backbone (core) of the service provider's network. P routers connect PE routers and transport traffic among them. If MPLS is used in the core network, the P router is a Label Switch Router (LSR). The P router is not aware of any VPN services. There is no service instance in the P router.
Multi-Tenant Unit (MTU)	Provider Network	The MTU device may be physically located at the customer sites. However, it is an extension of the provider's network. The MTU device has service instance(s) provisioned and performs VPN encapsulation and de-encapsulation for customer traffic. In most cases, MTU is a reduced version of the PE device, extending the VPN functionality outside to the customer's wiring closet with lower cost. As with the PE router, the MTU devices reside within the edge of the MPLS domain, performing iLER and eLER functions in the VPN.
Customer Edge (CE)	Customer Network	The term *CE* refers to any device in the customer network that has a direct connection to the service provider's network. The CE devices exchange traffic with the provider's network in native format.
Customer (C)	Customer Network	The term *C* refers to any device in the customer's network that has no direct connectivity to the service provider network. The C device has no visibility of the service provided by the provider.

These roles are logical concepts, and a service router can assume one or more of these roles depending on the service it supports. For example, a service router in the service provider network may terminate one service but transport traffic for another service. Where the service is originated and/or terminated by the router, the router is a PE router; for the service whose traffic is tunneled through, the router is a P router.

The ALSRP Service Model

In most cases, the ALSRP service routers are deployed in the service provider's network as PE routers and/or P routers to provide IP/MPLS VPN services. The IP/MPLS VPN architecture decouples the roles of the PE router and the P router. PE routers use service instances to make multiple customers to share the provider network.

PE routers also perform VPN encapsulation and VPN de-encapsulation to separate customer traffic into their own VPNs. Service instances in each PE router are connected to one another by MPLS pseudowires that ride over the network backbone through the service transport tunnels. Meshed or partially meshed IP or MPLS service transport tunnels are established among all PE routers through P routers in the provider's backbone. The PE and P routers use resiliency features to provide robust connections with high throughput to connect PE routers.

In the service provider's network backbone, the PE routers have *service intelligence*, which means that they can distinguish the various customer VPNs. An end-to-end service offered by the service provider may involve more than one PE router. Every PE router involved or participating in the same service has a service instance configured for the service. A PE router participating in a VPN service is sometimes referred to as a *member PE* of that service. The PE routers connect multiple customer devices to the service provider's network backbone and isolate these devices by creating different service instances for each customer. In every service instance, the PE router receives native format customer traffic from the attachment circuit — the circuit connecting the customer equipment to the PE. The PE router performs the VPN encapsulation on the traffic and forwards it to the provider network backbone. The PE router also receives VPN-encapsulated traffic from the remote PE router over the provider network backbone. It identifies the service instance that owns the traffic, and then performs de-encapsulation, and passes the traffic to the customer network in native format over the attachment circuit. All routers in the network backbone use interior routing protocols (e.g., OSPF or ISIS) to identify every P/PE router's location. In many network deployments, MPLS is used in the core network as a service tunneling technique to make the service delivery more efficient and reliable. PE routers establish the end-to-end service by using pseudowires to connect their service instances to each other. Figure 9.2 illustrates the logical view of the ALSRP service model.

From the service provider's perspective, a service is either *local* or *distributed*. A *local service* has only one member PE router with one service instance residing on it. The single service instance contains SAPs connected to CE devices. All customer traffic enters and leaves a single PE router via these SAPs. Pseudowires are not required for a local service because all customer traffic is locally switched or routed within the single PE router to CE devices.

A *distributed service* requires more than one PE router's participation. Service traffic must travel through the provider network from one PE to another. In the provider network, the service traffic is VPN encapsulated and transported among PE routers over pseudowires. Figure 9.3 illustrates a logical view of local and distributed services.

Figure 9.2 ALSRP Service Model in an IP/MPLS VPN Network

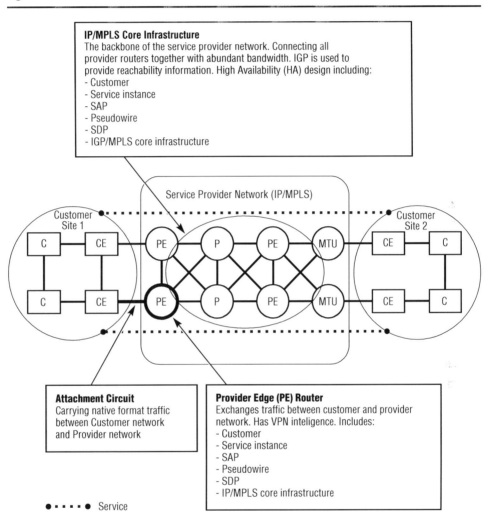

IP/MPLS Core Infrastructure
The backbone of the service provider network. Connecting all provider routers together with abundant bandwidth. IGP is used to provide reachability information. High Availability (HA) design including:
- Customer
- Service instance
- SAP
- Pseudowire
- SDP
- IGP/MPLS core infrastructure

Service Provider Network (IP/MPLS)

Customer Site 1

Customer Site 2

Attachment Circuit
Carrying native format traffic between Customer network and Provider network

Provider Edge (PE) Router
Exchanges traffic between customer and provider network. Has VPN inteligence. Includes:
- Customer
- Service instance
- SAP
- Pseudowire
- SDP
- IP/MPLS core infrastructure

●・・・・● Service

For a distributed service, customer sites are connected to more than one PE router. The distributed service has more than one PE member involved. Every PE router participating in the same service must have a service instance defined on it. The MPLS pseudowires connect the service instances in different PE routers belonging to the same service. The VPN traffic must travel though the provider's network backbone from one PE router to another. The service provider's network is a single network backbone shared by all VPN services for all customers.

Figure 9.3 Local Service versus Distributed Service

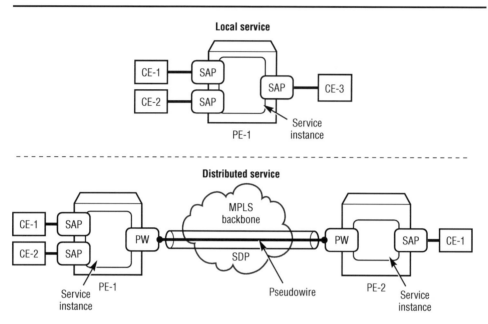

When multiple service instances reside in the same PE router, the traffic flows belonging to multiple services must travel through the service provider network backbone. The PE router must perform the traffic isolation and identification to ensure that the correct service instance is receiving the correct traffic. In an IP/MPLS VPN solution, this is done by creating pseudowires between two PE routers. For each service, any two member PE routers exchange MPLS labels with each other to encapsulate traffic for that service. The labels are referred to as a vc-label or service-label, and the two labels form a pseudowire between the two PE routers. The vc-label is used as a de-multiplexer to distinguish the flows at the receiving end of the tunnel. Figure 9.4 illustrates the PWE3 IP/MPLS VPN reference model, a commonly used service model for such services. This model is also referred to as the *Pseudowire Edge-to-Edge Emulation* (PWE3) reference model. It defines the basic architecture of using MPLS pseudowires to provide service emulation.

This is the single most important model for IP/MPLS VPN services. Understanding this model is key to understanding the delivery of L2VPN services over the MPLS backbone.

The following objects and relationships are described in this model:

- The emulated service is an end-to-end service passing traffic in native format between customer sites.
- The CE device connects the service provider network through an attachment circuit (AC).

Figure 9.4 PWE3 Reference Model (from RFC 4447)

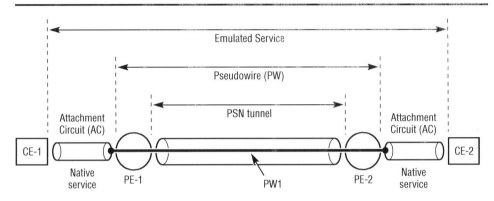

- There are several objects in the model involved in encapsulating and forwarding VPN service traffic between the two PE routers:
    - Packet Switching Network (PSN) tunnels such as MPLS or General Rouging Encapsulation (GRE; also known as *IP-in-IP*) tunnels that transport traffic to the far-end PE router. PSN tunnels belong to the service provider's network infrastructure and can be shared by multiple services.
    - Pseudowires established over the PSN tunnel between two PE routers to carry the traffic for that service. Pseudowires for different services can share the same PSN tunnel. The service's vc-label (service label) is used as an identifier (or a de-multiplexer) that allows the receiving PE to distinguish which traffic belongs to the different pseudowires over the same PSN tunnel.
    - Locally destined VPN traffic egresses to the customer site in native format over an attachment circuit.

The PWE3 model demonstrates the case of a point-to-point service, in which two CE devices and two PE routers are involved. The same architecture applies to multipoint services such as VPLS. In the case of multipoint services, additional PE and CE devices are involved and additional PSN tunnels, pseudowires, and SAPs are configured. The relationships among these objects remain the same. Multipoint services require each PE router to decide which far-end PE router should receive the traffic. This forwarding decision with its related signaling and learning processes of VPLS is discussed in Chapters 11 and 12.

The ALSRP service router's service model is fully compliant with the PWE3 service model. Figure 9.5 illustrates the comparison between ALSRP service router *service entities* and PWE3 objects.

Figure 9.5 ALSRP Service Model versus PWE3 Reference Model

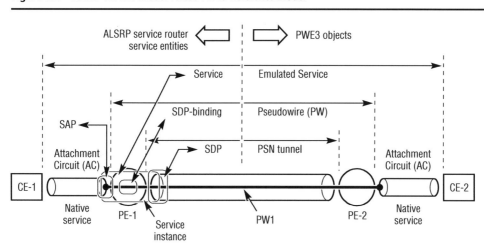

Service entities are the logical constructs of a service in a PE router, and the building blocks of a service. In an ALSRP network, there are six service entities, described in Table 9.3.

Table 9.3 Service Entities in ALSRP

Service Entity	Network Element Role Definition
Customer	Customer is the logical representation of a customer. The customer definition includes a mandatory customer-id and optional contact, description, and phone information. When creating a service instance in a service router, only one customer-id can be associated with it.
Service Instance	A service instance is the logical representation of a service in a PE router. Each service instance in the PE router has a service-id, which is associated with a customer-id. All service-related components are defined under the service instance. When performing troubleshooting, a service-id must be provided.[a]

Service Entity	Network Element Role Definition
Service Access Point (SAP)	An SAP is the logical representation of the attachment circuit, where a customer is attached to the service provider's network. An SAP exchanges native format traffic with customer devices over the attachment circuit.
Service Distribution Path (SDP)	An SDP is the logical representation of service reachability from one PE router to another PE router. SDP contains one or more service transport tunnels between two PE routers. Transport tunnels used by SDP carry VPN-encapsulated traffic from one PE router to another across the provider network backbone. When a distributed service transports traffic between PE routers, SDPs carry the encapsulated VPN traffic. The SDP configuration identifies the actual transport tunnel as well as its signaling method and other tunnel characteristics. SDPs are point-to-point and unidirectional.
Pseudowire (PW)	A PW is a bidirectional connection between the service instances in two PE routers. Only distributed services require the use of a PW to connect service instances in different member PE routers. In L2VPN services, a PW is established by using T-LDP signaling to distribute the vc-labels between PE routers.
Multi-Service Site	A multi-service site is a logical grouping of one or more customer-facing SAPs. The PE router may have more than one SAP servicing the same customer in the same service instance. The customer may desire a common QoS control over these SAPs in the same service instance (e.g., rate-limit the traffic for several attachment circuits). This goal is achieved by configuring multiple SAPs as a multi-service site with a common QoS policy.[b]

[a]For readers familiar with L3VPN, a VPRN service instance in a PE router is equivalent to a Virtual Routing Forwarder (VRF). Similarly, a VPLS service instance in a PE router is a Virtual Bridge (VB).

[b]Multi-service site is a logical collection used by Quality of Service (QoS). QoS is beyond the scope of this book. See *Advanced QoS for Multi-Service IP/MPLS Networks* by Ram Balakrishnan (Wiley, 2008) for more information.

Figure 9.6 illustrates an example of two distributed services and the logical relationship among the service entities in the PE routers. The two services (100 and 300) belong to two different customers (shown as Customer 1 and Customer 25). The two PE routers are connected by a pair of SDPs, each containing a unidirectional transport tunnel. Two SDPs are required to connect the two PE routers together, one for each direction. The lines with arrows represent the traffic flow for Customer 1 between CE-A and CE-B.

Figure 9.6 Service Entities in a Distributed Service Involving Two PE Routers

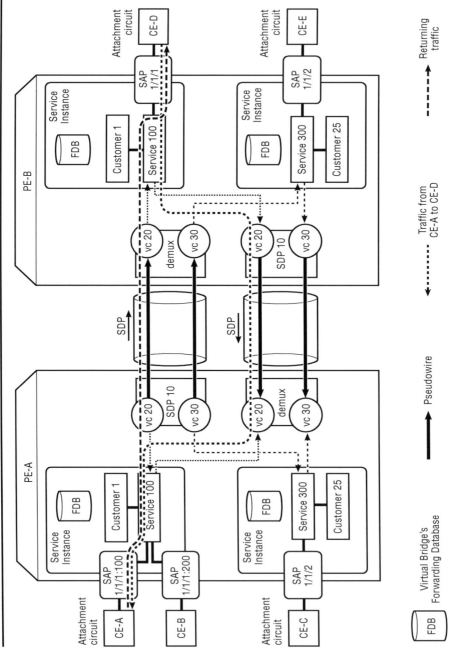

An overview of the VPN traffic flow between PE routers is described below. All of the involved entities, the signaling process, and the forwarding decision are discussed in greater detail in subsequent sections.

Traffic from CE-A enters the service provider network through the attachment circuit in SAP 1/1/1:100 in PE-A. PE-A's service instance, Service 100, determines that the traffic should be forwarded to PE-B. PE-A uses SDP 10 as the transport tunnel to reach PE-B, then uses the pseudowire, represented by VC (Virtual Circuit) ID 20, to forward the traffic. PE-A uses a vc-label (value not shown in the diagram) to encapsulate the traffic. The encapsulated VPN traffic is then sent to PE-B through SDP 10. SDP 10 performs the transport tunnel encapsulation on the VPN-encapsulated traffic and then sends the traffic toward PE-B. When PE-B receives the encapsulated VPN traffic from SDP, it first removes the SDP tunnel encapsulation from the traffic. Then, it uses the vc-label (as a service de-multiplexer) to identify the traffic ownership of VC 20. At that point, PE-B de-encapsulates the traffic and forwards it to CE-B through SAP 1/1/1. The return traffic from CE-B to CE-A travels through PE-B and PE-A using the same process in the reverse direction. Figure 9.6 illustrates the logical service entities and their relations in two PE routers with distributed service configured.

Each entity in a service instance must have an identification value (ID). Some of the entities' IDs are used by the VPN signaling process, and each ID has a scope of significance (the scope in which the ID value must be unique). The service instance ID distinguishes different services for the same or different customers. The service instance id is used by the PE router to isolate different services for different customers to protect the customer privacy. Within each PE router, different service instances are completely isolated and assigned their own set of entities. The forwarding database (FDB) for each service instance is independent, and traffic forwarding between service instances in the same PE router is prohibited. Every service instance uses SAPs to connect to its associated customer, and dedicated pseudowires to connect to the service instances in the remote PE routers that are participating in the same service. In a PE router, the pseudowires of multiple service instances may share the same SDP to carry traffic to the same remote PE router. The traffic flows belonging to different services use different vc-labels (or vpn-labels, in the case of L3VPN) to perform VPN encapsulation. The receiving PE router uses these labels as service de-multiplexers to ensure that the traffic flows are sent to the correct service instances. The privacy on the VPN traffic is also ensured across the network backbone, although the traffic may share the same SDP.

Table 9.4 describes the various ID types and their scopes.

Table 9.4 Identification Types of Service Entities and Their Scopes

Identification	Description	Scope
customer-id	Identifies a customer. The value range is (1–2,147,483,647). All services must belong to only one customer.	Locally significant. If the Alcatel-Lucent 5620 SAM is used, global significance is required.[a] The best practice is to keep it globally unique.
service-id	Identifies a service instance. The value range is (1–2,147,483,647).	Locally significant. If the Alcatel-Lucent 5620 SAM is used, global significance is required. The best practice is to keep the service-id globally unique. Unlike vc-id, service-id is not exchanged during vc-label signaling.
vc-id	Identifies the pseudowire (circuit) used between two PE routers in pseudowire signaling. The value range is (1–4,294,967,295). In the ALSRP, a combination of vc-id and sdp-id uniquely identifies a pseudowire, although the sdp-id is not used in pseudowire negotiation.	Point-to-point significant. The pair of PE routers on both sides of the pseudowire must use the same vc-id value to configure the pseudowire. And the same vc-id cannot be used for the two PE routers for other pseudowires.
sdp-id	Identifies an SDP, or transport tunnel. The value range is (1–17,407).	Locally significant to a PE node. sdp-id is used when provisioning a pseudowire, but not in pseudowire signaling.
sap-id	Identifies a customer service attachment point. Composed of port/channel-id with encapsulation type, and encapsulation-id. Can only be assigned to an access port. For a VLAN tag, use value (0–4,096).	Locally significant. Tags (for example, vlan-id) may be used to multiplex different streams of customer traffic over the same physical port.

Identification	Description	Scope
encapsulation-id	Used in SAP encapsulation to distinguish traffic from different customers at ingress to the same SAP. Values include vlan-id, ATM VPI/VCI, and Frame-Relay DLCI.	Port significant. Different ports in the same node can use the same encapsulation-id (for example, two ports can use the same vlan-id as encapsulation-id for different SAPs for the same or a different service).

[a]Alcatel-Lucent 5620 Service Awareness Manager (SAM). SAM is a network service management tool with a graphical user interface (GUI) and management database. SAM helps operators to provision, modify, and monitor services in the entire service network. SAM is beyond the scope of this book.

Each ID uniquely identifies a service entity within a specific scope. The *significance* of each entity-id is very important for the correct service deployment:

- **Port Significant** — The entity-id must be unique in a single port of the PE router.
- **Locally Significant** — The entity-id must be unique in a single PE router.
- **Point-to-Point Significant** — The entity-id must be equal on both sides of a pseudowire — significant within a pair of PE routers.
- **Globally Significant** — The entity-id must be unique in the entire service provider's network.

Understanding the meaning of the entity-id and its scope is crucial for correct deployment of the service. In a scaled network, it is important to have a consistent entity-id naming convention and to follow best practices on ID scoping. These measures significantly reduce management overhead and configuration errors. For example, suppose a service provider must deploy a VPLS service for a customer that involves three member PE routers. Since the service-id is locally significant to the PE router, the service provider can randomly assign service-id 100 to the VPLS service instance on PE1, service-id 200 in PE2, and service-id 305 in PE3. Provisioning the pseudowire correctly (vc-id set correctly), the service will certainly pass traffic for the VPLS customer. However, this random service-id assignment makes the provider's network harder to manage, especially if the network is large. When the service provider has many services for multiple customers in many PE routers, it is difficult to map the service instances (identified by service-id in each PE router) to the corresponding customer services. Therefore, as a best common practice (BCP), it is beneficial to maintain the global uniqueness of the service-id for the same end-to-end service. Also, by default, all service instances will be associated with the default customer-id 1. Having multiple customers created and associated with different services can be beneficial from a network management perspective.

Figure 9.7 illustrates an example of service configuration with entity-ids.

Figure 9.7   Service Entity Identifications

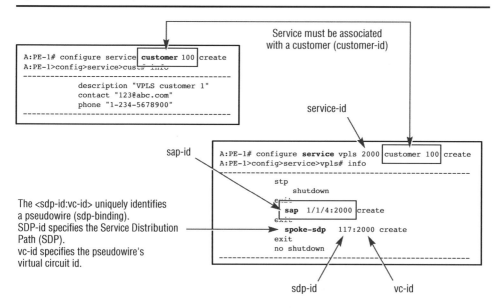

Warning: The entity-id is defined when the entity is created in the PE router. Once the entity is created, the entity-id cannot be modified. Changing the entity-id requires deletion of the original entity and creation of a new entity with a new entity-id. This is service-impacting. Plan the entity-id carefully before deploying services.

9.3 Service Access Point and SAP Components

A Service Access Point (SAP) is the logical representation of the attachment circuit where a customer attaches to the service provider's network and is configured under a service instance. CE devices connect to access ports on the PE using attachment circuits. These access ports can be Ethernet ports, SONET/SDH ports or channels, TDM ports or channels, Ethernet Link Aggregation Groups, or other media interface/bundle types supported. Different types of services use different types of physical ports or channels in their SAPs. Figure 9.8 illustrates examples of configuring ports and SAPs.

Note: Please refer to the ALSRP product manuals for details regarding the complete list of supported media types.

Figure 9.8 Physical Port and SAP Configuration for a Service

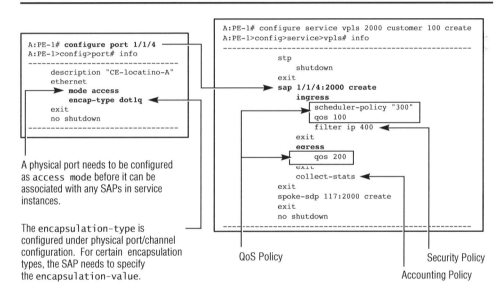

When provisioning a service instance for a customer, the SAP is configured under the service instance. The physical ports or channels connected to the customer are then associated with the SAP. All service-related policies (QoS, Accounting, and Security) are configured under the SAP, rather than the physical ports. A service instance can have more than one SAP, but an SAP can only have one port or channel. A multiplexing method may be used on a port (e.g., a vlan-id for an Ethernet port) to permit multiple SAPs to share the port. Thus, the shared port is associated with more than one SAP, under more than one service instance. Each SAP uses a different encapsulation-id to differentiate the traffic flows. As an example, consider a case in which two customers require VPLS services from the provider. They share the same physical port on the same Customer Premises Equipment (CPE). The provider will create two different VPLS services, one for each customer. The two VPLS service instances in the PE router will share the same access port: VPLS 100 and VPLS 101. The VPLS service 100 has an SAP associated with port 1/1/4 using vlan-id 2000. Consider another customer who is also connected to port 1/1/4, using vlan-id 2001. Another service instance is configured for the second customer as VPLS 101. The SAP for the second service is associated with the same port, but using vlan-id 2001. The two SAPs can have different QoS, Accounting, and Security Policies associated with them.

An SAP sends and receives traffic to customer devices over an attachment circuit. From the customer's perspective, the services from the provider's networks are a logical extension of their own networks. The traffic to and from the provider's network should be unaltered by the provider's network. Different services require different traffic formats. SAPs in certain types of services will allow membership of a port/channel/group with a compatible encapsulation format. (The different types of SAPs and their encapsulation formats are discussed in the corresponding chapters for each service.)

An SAP has two directions, ingress and egress. SAP ingress receives the service traffic from the access port and forwards it to the service router's switching fabric. SAP egress receives packets from the switching fabric and forwards it to the access port. The QoS Policy, Accounting Policy, and the Security or Filtering Policy are independently configured for each direction.

The six SAP components are described in Table 9.5 with their associated descriptions and values.

Table 9.5 SAP Components

Components	Description	Types of Values Used
sap-id	Port number, followed by encapsulation-id. There is no default value. The sap-id must be explicitly specified upon the configuration of an SAP.	LAG group number APS group number
encapsulation-type	Defined in the port/channel being used. The value must be set according to requirements. There is a default value for encapsulation-type. In the case of Ethernet access port, the default encapsulation type is null.	Ethernet value: null, dot1q, or QinQ

Components	Description	Types of Values Used
encapsulation-value	IDs used as a de-multiplexer (demux) value for certain encapsulation. There is no default value. When required, encapsulation value must be provided upon the configuration of an SAP.	Depends on the encapsulation type (e.g., vlan-id, ATM VPI/VCI).
Ingress/egress filter policy id	The traffic filtering policy is individually applied to an SAP for both ingress and egress. There is no default value. If no filter is applied, all traffic is accepted.	Filter-id. Filters must be configured prior to the association with the SAP.
Ingress/egress QoS policy id	Scheduler policies are deployed in both the ingress and egress directions. SAP-ingress and SAP-egress have separate QoS policy definitions. If not specified, both directions use their default policy 1, which is *best effort*.	Policy-id. Policies must be configured prior to the association with the SAP.
Accounting policy id	Statistics are enabled on a per-SAP basis to collect accounting information.	The collect-stats command enables statistics in the SAP. The policy must be configured before it can be associated to a SAP beforehand.

Note: In the ALSRP, each SAP is independent for any types of service. This means that different types of SAPs can coexist in a service as long as the SAP type is supported by that service. Different types of SAPs can be provisioned together within a service instance and within the end-to-end service involving more than one PE router and more than one service instance. As an example, in the same VPLS service instance, there can be an Ethernet dot1q SAP, an ATM bridged Ethernet SAP, and a Frame-Relay–bridged Ethernet SAP. The VPLS service exchanges traffic among these SAPs.

Some vendor's IP/MPLS VPN implementations require that one service instance contain only one type of SAP with one type of attachment circuit.

Operational Modes of Physical Ports: Network Mode versus Access Mode

IP/MPLS VPN service networks are asymmetrical. As shown in Figure 9.1, the routers in the service provider's network can have two roles: PE and P. The PE routers connect the customer's network with the provider's network. The P routers transport the traffic among the PE routers over the provider's network backbone. When a router is placed at the edge of the provider's network as a PE router, it connects the customers through attachment circuits, and it also connects the other P or PE routers inside the provider's network through core links. Both connections consist of physical links with ports. These two types of connections have different requirements for their ports:

- **Customer-Facing Access Ports** — When a port is customer-facing, it may be used to connect more than one customer. In a service-based router, every service is distinguished and treated differently, even if they share the same access port. Therefore, the access port must be service-aware and allow for *service granularity* to handle micro-flows. That is, it must support services with many SAPs, with each SAP having its own QoS, Security, and Accounting Policies.

- **Backbone-Facing Network Ports** — When a port is facing the backbone network, the port aggregates traffic from many customers' services and transports the aggregate over the network backbone. Since the traffic is aggregated, the network port facing the backbone does not need the service awareness to distinguish the traffic flows from different services. The service resources required for individual services do not need to be allocated with micro-flow granularity for a network-facing port.

An access port must perform deep processing of service packets and differentiate among services, while the network port must only forward packets and provide resilience to the aggregate flows. Therefore, the service router's architecture is *asymmetric*. A typical example concerns QoS. A service-based router must provide per-service QoS. As a result, an access port shared by many customers requires many QoS resources (buffers, schedulers) to provide dedicated QoS treatment for each customer. Because the network ports carry aggregated traffic, they need fewer QoS resources.

To suit the needs of a service-oriented network, a physical port in the ALSRP works in one of two operational modes: network mode or access mode. *Access mode ports* can be associated with SAPs and face the customer networks. *Network mode ports* can be associated with routed IP interfaces facing the core network and used by SDPs and transport tunnels (discussed in detail in the following section). The ALSRP requires specification of the port's operational mode. The operational mode is configured during the port configuration. In the ALSRP, all ports are network ports by default. Figure 9.9 illustrates example configurations of access and network ports.

Figure 9.9 Configuration Examples of Access and Network Ports

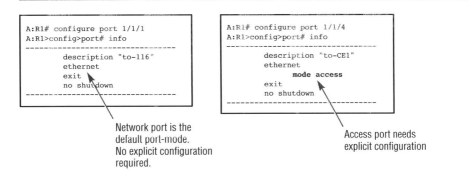

Network port is the default port-mode. No explicit configuration required.

Access port needs explicit configuration

Note that in this example, the default configurations are not displayed by the info command. Port 1/1/1 does not have explicit mode configuration because it is a network port by default and port 1/1/4 is explicitly configured as an access port.

> **Warning:** Changing the port operational mode requires a manual port shutdown. All SAPs associated wit that port must be removed before an access port can be reconfigured to a network port. These operations are service-impacting. Plan the roles of ports carefully to avoid changing the port mode configuration after the network is in production.

9.4 Service Distribution Paths and Transport Tunnels

A Service Distribution Path (SDP) is a logical representation of service reachability from one PE router to another. The SDP is used to carry VPN-encapsulated traffic between PE routers only. An SDP is not service-aware. An SDP is used solely for tunneling traffic to the destination. Also, an SDP is an end-to-end tunnel from one PE router to another router. There may be intermediate P router hops in the middle of the SDP, and the transport tunnel path may change owing to network failures. These hops and changes are not visible to the service instance, which is hidden within the shared transport tunnel. In one PE router, multiple services reaching the same far-end PE router can share the same SDP.

An SDP encapsulates the details concerning its transport tunnels. An SDP provides configuration *simplicity* because it hides the details of transport tunnels from the service instance. When a service instance must send traffic to a far-end PE router, it only needs to specify which SDP it wants to use. This is accomplished through either explicit configuration (**spoke/mesh-sdp <sdp-id>:<vc-id>** command) or automatic binding (for L3 VPRN services and beyond the scope of this book). The details regarding the particular tunneling technique (GRE, MPLS-LDP, or MPLS-RSVP-TE LSP), the number of tunnels to be used, and other tunnel-specific configurations (LDP over RSVP, CoS LSP Forwarding) are transparent to any service instances and are handled by the SDP configuration. An SDP is universal to all services. When traffic must reach the same far-end PE router, one SDP can be shared by many service instances in a PE router regardless of the service type. The service instances' pseudowires determine the required VPN encapsulation (vc-labels for l2vpn, vpn-labels for l3vpn). The SDP determines the required transport encapsulation (tunnel-label if MPLS-SDP, GRE-header if GRE-SDP).

The SDP also offers network design *flexibility*. Multiple SDPs using different types of transport tunnels can be configured to reach the remote PE routers and be available for any service to use. One service can use different types of SDPs to bind pseudowire and transport traffic; alternatively, one SDP can be used by multiple pseudowires belonging to different services. Within an SDP, multiple transport tunnels can be configured to perform load-balanced forwarding or Class-of-Service (CoS)–based forwarding. SDP load balancing and CoS-based forwarding are discussed in the next section.

Note: A *transport tunnel* is the tunnel (GRE or MPLS) that transports the service traffic across the backbone of the service network. An SDP may use one or more service tunnels to carry traffic.

An SDP is identified in a PE router by its numerical sdp-id. The sdp-id is locally significant to the PE router. Multiple services can share the same SDP by binding their vc-id to an sdp-id their pseudowire configurations. An SDP is shared by all services bound with it. All operations applied to the SDP (such as changing signaling method, path-MTU, or shutdown/no shutdown) will affect *all* services' pseudowires bound to it. As a result, an SDP is viewed as a virtual circuit multiplexer (vc-mux). Traffic flows from multiple service instances are multiplexed using the vc-label and then travel through the SDP to reach the far-end router. The receiving router uses the vc-label as a virtual circuit de-multiplexer (vc-demux) to distinguish the flows and send them to the correct service instances. This is illustrated in Figure 9.6 in the SDP peering with an entity called *demux*.

The SDP is a service-oriented logical path representation between two PE routers. The actual tunnel type used by an SDP can vary (GRE, LDP-LSP, or RSVP-TE LSP). When creating an SDP, the actual tunnel type must be specified. Multiple services may have different requirements for the traffic transport and therefore may require different tunnel types. Multiple SDPs can be configured to provide the required flexibility needed to transport different and multiple service types. There are three transport tunnel types, which are profiled in Table 9.6.

Table 9.6 Tunnel Types Used by SDP

Type	Description
GRE	Also called IP over IP. The GRE tunnel encapsulates the VPN traffic into IP packets and use the new IP header to route the encapsulated traffic to the far-end PE router. The GRE tunnel can send the traffic over a non-MPLS-capable network backbone. GRE tunnels rely on the IGP in the core network to automatically decide the path to the far-end router. GRE tunnels can auto-bind with VPRN services.[a] A GRE tunnel's failure convergence relies on the IGP to find an alternate route.
LDP-LSP	Tunnels based on an LDP-signaled Label Switched Path (LSP). The tunnels use tunnel-label (outer label) to encapsulate the VPN-encapsulated traffic and then send it to the far-end PE router. LDP (more specifically, link LDP) sends labels to the far-end PE router according to automatically determined IGP routes. An LDP-LSP can auto-bind to VPRN. The LDP-LSP's failure convergence relies on the IGP to find an alternate route.
RSVP-TE LSP	Tunnels based on RSVP-TE signaled LSPs. The tunnels use the tunnel-label (outer label) to encapsulate the VNP-encapsulated traffic and send it to the far-end PE router. RSVP-TE LSP must be provisioned and signaled before the tunnel can forward traffic. RSVP-TE LSPs must be explicitly specified in the SDP configuration. RSVP-TE tunnels take full advantage of RSVP-TE's resilience features. Fast reroute and/or secondary LSPs can protect the tunnel and improve the failure convergence significantly.

[a]When provisioning VPRN services, the pseudowires connecting remote PE routers are configured to auto-bind with GRE or LDP tunnels and follow the path decided by the core IGP. When auto-binding is enabled in VPRN, explicit pseudowire configuration is not required. VPRN service is beyond the scope of this book.

An SDP is unidirectional. When creating an SDP from one PE router to another PE router, the far-end PE router's system IP address is specified in the SDP configuration. An SDP transports traffic from one PE router to another PE router. For two PE routers to be able to transport traffic between each other, two SDPs are required, one for each direction. An SDP is point-to-point. When deploying service in a network with many PE routers, if the services require all PE routers to transport traffic between each other, a mesh of SDPs must be built. Similar to a BGP mesh, for a network with n PE routers, each router has $(n - 1)$ SDPs configured, one for each peering PE router. An SDP can be shared by many services that want to transport traffic to the same far-end PE router. When deploying a network with L2VPN services, SDPs are part of the service backbone infrastructure.

Note: In the ALSRP, when a service instance requires a pseudowire over an SDP to a remote PE router, it can use any type of SDP. One service can use different types of SDPs to create pseudowires to the same (when pseudowire redundancy is used) or different far-end PE routers, including the static-pseudowire type. This means that different types of SDPs can coexist in a service for the pseudowire's use. As an example, a PE router with one VPLS service can connect the service to one peering PE router with a GRE SDP, to another peering PE router using MPLS SDP with an LDP-LSP, and to a third PE router using MPLS SDP with an RSVP-TE LSP. This is applicable for all types of services (e.g., vc-switching services, VPLS, VPWS) and for pseudowire redundancy deployment. Some vendors' service implementations require one service instance to use only one type of SDP to connect all peering PE routers.

Pseudowire Signaling Method in SDP

An SDP provides a path for service traffic to travel from one PE router to another. However, having the SDPs between two PE routers is not enough for the service instance to pass traffic. For L2VPN services, the service instance must still build the *pseudowire* to the far-end PE router in order to pass traffic over the SDP.

Pseudowire establishment requires a label signaling protocol to signal the vc-label between the two PE routers' service instances for the same service. Different types of services require different signaling methods for vc-label signaling. Within the SDP configuration, the pseudowire signaling method is specified. The signaling method for the pseudowire is defined within the SDP configuration. When a pseudowire is bound to the SDP, that pseudowire is signaled using the signaling method specified by the SDP that it binds to. Service instances that want to use a certain SDP and its transport tunnel(s) must use the SDP with a compatible signaling method, so that its pseudowire(s) can be established. Table 9.7 compares the configuration of the SDP signaling method with T-LDP enabled or off.

Table 9.7 Configuration of SDP Signaling Method

Signaling Method	Description
T-LDP	When the SDP is created to serve L2VPN, the signaling method of the SDP must be configured as T-LDP because L2VPN (VPWS, VPLS) services require T-LDP to establish the pseudowires. By default, the SDP signaling method is configured as T-LDP.
off	When the SDP is used to serve L3VPN only (VPRN), the T-LDP signaling method is not required. Because VPRN does not use pseudowires, there is no need to use T-LDP signaling. However, SDP with T-LDP enabled has no problem carrying VPRN traffic. As a best practice, T-LDP should be enabled so the SDP can be shared by L2VPN and L3VPN services. L3VPN is beyond the scope of this book.

When an SDP with T-LDP signaling enabled is created from one PE router to anther PE router, a T-LDP session is automatically created by the PE router in which the SDP is created to the SDP's far-end PE router, if there isn't one already. The T-LDP session is used for the PE router to signal L2VPN pseudowires over that SDP. If there are only SDPs from a local PE router to a far-end PE router but there isn't any returning SDP created from that far-end PE router to the local PE router, the SDP stays down. This is because without the reverse direction SDP, the T-LDP session from the far-end PE router is not created. In such a case, the SDP stays down because the far-end PE router does not request a T-LDP session to the local PE router. When the SDP is configured on both routers, each router tries to establish a T-LDP session to its remote peer. Then, the T-LDP session is established between the two routers, and both SDPs (one for each direction) become operationally up.

SDP requires T-LDP as the method for services associated with it to signal pseudowires. Alternatively, the service instances can use a static pseudowire (static-vc) to carry traffic between them over the SDP. If all services using an SDP are using static-vc pseudowires, the signaling of that SDP can be turned off. When creating an SDP with the signaling method configured to be off, the system does not try to establish a T-LDP session to the SDP's far-end router. However, because SDPs can be shared by multiple types of services to transport the traffic, leaving the T-LDP signaling option on in the SDP configuration is the best practice.

> **Note:** To summarize, the best practice is always to enable T-LDP signaling in case it is needed for pseudowire signaling. Even if it is not required, it won't impact any services using the SDP without requiring T-LDP signaling.

SDP Metric

In the ALSRP, the service instance must manually specify the SDP to be used during the creation of the pseudowire. The only exception is if VPLS is deployed with BGP-AD (auto-discovery). When VPLS with BGP-AD is enabled, the system automatically chooses one SDP to each far-end member PE router among the available options. An *SDP metric* is used as one criterion to compare the preference of SDPs. In a case in which multiple SDPs are available, the metric can be used by the SDP selection process to choose one SDP for the service instance to use. The details regarding the SDP metric and SDP selection process are introduced in Chapter 16, "VPLS BGP Auto-Discovery."

Figure 9.10 shows the configuration of an SDP. The SDP in the example uses an RSVP-TE LSP as the tunnel to carry traffic. The LSP must have been previously configured and should be operationally up. When creating an SDP using any MPLS tunnel (LDP-LSP, or RSVP-TE LSP), the keyword mpls must be present in the configuration command the first time the SDP is created. If it is not present, the SDP uses the GRE tunnel. The far-end IP address indicates the destination of this SDP. In most cases, the system IP address (or router-id) of the remote PE router is used to identify the destination. An SDP is point-to-point, so there can only be one far-end IP address for every SDP. By default, the SDP is in shutdown state after being created. An explicit no shutdown command must be entered in the SDP configuration to enable the SDP.

Figure 9.10 SDP Configuration Example of an MPLS SDP Using RSVP-TE LSP

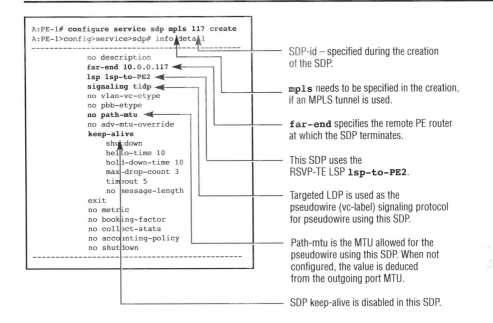

```
A:PE-1# configure service sdp mpls 117 create
A:PE-1>config>service>sdp# info detail
----------------------------------------------
        no description
        far-end 10.0.0.117
        lsp lsp-to-PE2
        signaling tldp
        no vlan-vc-etype
        no pbb-etype
        no path-mtu
        no adv-mtu-override
        keep-alive
            shutdown
            hello-time 10
            hold-down-time 10
            max-drop-count 3
            timeout 5
            no message-length
        exit
        no metric
        no booking-factor
        no collect-stats
        no accounting-policy
        no shutdown
----------------------------------------------
```

SDP-id – specified during the creation of the SDP.

mpls needs to be specified in the creation, if an MPLS tunnel is used.

far-end specifies the remote PE router at which the SDP terminates.

This SDP uses the RSVP-TE LSP **lsp-to-PE2**.

Targeted LDP is used as the pseudowire (vc-label) signaling protocol for pseudowire using this SDP.

Path-mtu is the MTU allowed for the pseudowire using this SDP. When not configured, the value is deduced from the outgoing port MTU.

SDP keep-alive is disabled in this SDP.

SDP Keep-Alive

An SDP carries VPN traffic flows for many service instances. When an SDP has a failure and becomes nonresponsive, all services using this SDP experience an outage. Monitoring the health of an SDP is critical. An SDP keep-alive function is designed for this purpose. When the SDP keep-alive function is enabled, the corresponding state machine is created. From then on, the operational state of SDP is associated with its keep-alive state. When an SDP with keep-alive enabled becomes operational, the system begins to send the SDP Echo Request message to the far-end PE router. Figure 9.11 illustrates a configuration example with a state display for SDP keep-alive.

The SDP keep-alive is unidirectional. To monitor the connectivity for one SDP from one PE to another, it is not required to enable SDP keep-alive in the reverse direction's SDP. The keep-alive sends SDP Echo Request messages and expects the SDP Echo Reply messages to monitor SDP connectivity. The SDP with keep-alive enabled sends a SDP Echo Request at every hello-time defined in the configuration.

The sdp-id is encoded in the SDP Echo Request message. For every message sent, the SDP expects to receive an SDP Echo Request with its own sdp-id in it. The response message should also indicate the nonError state.

Figure 9.11 SDP Keep-alive Configuration and State Monitoring

```
A:PE-3# configure service sdp 117
A:PE-3>config>service>sdp# keep-alive
A:PE-3>config>service>sdp>keep-alive# info detail
----------------------------------------------------
                hello-time 1
                hold-down-time 10
                max-drop-count 3
                timeout 5
                message-length 1200
                no shutdown
----------------------------------------------------
```

```
A:PE-3#  show service sdp 117 detail
===============================================================================
Service Destination Point (Sdp Id : 117) Details
===============================================================================
-------------------------------------------------------------------------------
 Sdp Id 117  -(10.0.0.117)
-------------------------------------------------------------------------------
SDP Id                : 117            SDP Source        : manual
Admin Path MTU        : 0              Oper Path MTU     : 9190
Far End               : 10.0.0.117     Delivery          : MPLS
Admin State           : Up             Oper State        : Up
Signaling             : TLDP           Metric            : 0
--- output omitted ---
KeepAlive Information :
Admin State           : Enabled        Oper State        : Alive
Hello Time            : 1              Hello Msg Len     : 1200
Hello Timeout         : 5              Unmatched Replies : 0
Max Drop Count        : 3              Hold Down Time    : 10
Tx Hello Msgs         : 11             Rx Hello Msgs     : 11
Associated LSP LIST :
Lsp Name              : to-117
Admin State           : Up             Oper State        : Up
Time Since Last Tran*: 02d03h46m
--- output omitted ---
```

The SDP keep-alive considers that a failure has occurred for each of the following conditions:

- SDP does not get any SDP Echo Reply message for the time specified in time-out.
- SDP receives an SDP Echo Response message indicating an error condition that exceeds the number of times specified in maximum-drop-count.

When one of these conditions occurs, the SDP is immediately brought down. When the failure is cleared, the system waits until the hold-down-time timer expires, then it reinitializes the SDP.

The format of the SDP Echo Request message depends on the SDP type. The Echo messages employ the same type of encapsulation as the VPN traffic using the SDP. For example, if the SDP is a GRE tunnel, the SDP Echo Request is GRE-encapsulated; if the SDP is an MPLS tunnel, the SDP Echo Request is MPLS-encapsulated. The keep-alive function tests the encapsulated data path for the customer traffic. In both cases, an MPLS label 1 (Router Alert) is used to indicate that this is an Operation, Administration, and Maintenance (OAM) packet so it should be sent to the control plane. After the far-end router removes the tunnel encapsulation, the Router Alert label is exposed. This causes the receiver to send the packet to the control plane for processing. The `originating-sdp-id` is encoded in the message data. The SDP Echo Reply is double-encapsulated; the outer encapsulation is GRE and the inner encapsulation is an MPLS Router Alert label (1). The SDP Echo Reply message must contain the `originator-sdp-id` and the status code of `noError` in the message body. Otherwise, the system will consider that there is a failure in the SDP and will bring the SDP down. The SDP Echo Request message and SDP Echo Reply messages are Ethernet frames with Ether-type `0x0a00`.

Pseudowire (PW)

A pseudowire is a bidirectional point-to-point logical connection between two service instances serving the same end-to-end service. A pseudowire is always bound to one SDP and signaled over the T-LDP session to the far-end PE router. One physical network port can serve more than one SDP, and one SDP can carry more than one pseudowire. Pseudowires serving different service instances (regardless of the type of service) can share the same SDP as long as these pseudowires are directed to the same far-end router. Figure 9.12 illustrates the relationship between a physical network port, an SDP, and a pseudowire. In the ALSRP, the pseudowire is configured within the service instance by binding the SDP with the vc-id. Therefore, pseudowire is also referred to as "SDP binding."

The pseudowire is the most important logical entity in the L2VPN service. It connects all of the PE routers that participate in the same end-to-end service. An SDP (transport tunnel) logically connects two PE routers together. A pseudowire logically connects two service instances to two PE routers. Many pseudowires between two PE routers, serving different service instance pairs, can share the same SDP. The pseudowire is point-to-point, but unlike SDP, it is bidirectional. The pseudowire can only be operational if both sides of the PE routers have the pseudowire configured correctly and administratively enabled.

Figure 9.12 Physical Link, Transport Tunnel (SDP), and Pseudowire

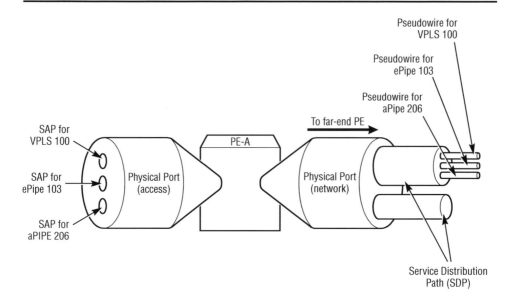

As previously mentioned, the SDP represents the service reachability to a remote-PE node over certain transport tunnels. The service instance must create pseudowires to carry its traffic to the far-end PE over the SDP. The action of creating a pseudowire and associating it to an SDP is called *binding*. During the binding process, the vc-labels used for service multiplexing are exchanged by the signaling process using T-LDP.

A pseudowire is an agreement between two PE routers. The agreement specifies the vc-label values to be used in the VPN encapsulation for customer data traffic. (The T-LDP signaling process of establishing pseudowires was introduced in Chapter 8.) A pseudowire is sometimes referred to as *VPN-LSP* because it uses the vpn-label (vc-label) to encapsulate traffic. In this sense, the VPN-LSP resides within the SDP, and it is one hop. The service ingress PE router (iLER) pushes the vc-label into the customer traffic. The service egress PE router (eLER) pops the vc-label out of the customer traffic. The transport tunnel encapsulation, forwarding of encapsulated traffic, and transport tunnel de-encapsulation are handled by the SDP, and are therefore transparent to this VPN-LSP.

Figure 9.13 illustrates the VPN encapsulation process while the customer traffic passes through the IP/MPLS VPN network backbone.

Figure 9.13 Data Plane: IP/MPLS VPN Traffic Encapsulation

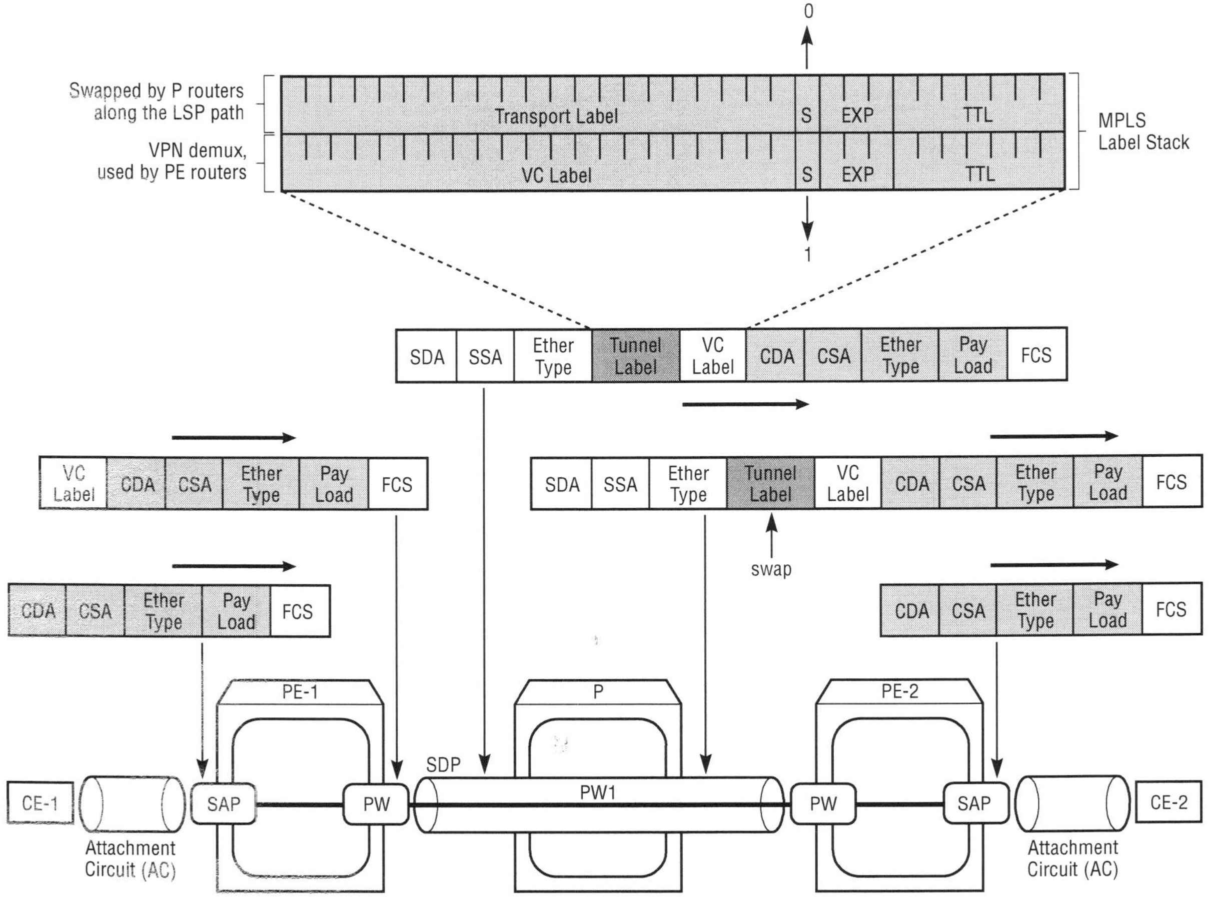

Figure 9.13 presents a customer frame walk-through in the service provider's network. This demonstrates the VPN encapsulation/de-encapsulation process and the transport tunnel encapsulation/de-encapsulation process. The customer packet from CE1 travels from left to the right through the service provider and reaches CE2. The diagram shows that the vc-label has been pushed into the MPLS label stack by Router PE1's pseudowire. The transport label is pushed into the MPLS label stack by Router PE1's SDP. The top illustration illustrates the double-encapsulated packet format. When the VPN-encapsulated packet travels through the P router along the path, only the transport label is swapped by the P router. The receiving PE router PE2 removes both MPLS labels and sends the de-encapsulated traffic to CE2 through the SAP.

Figure 9.14 illustrates the pseudowire signaling process (Events 1–3 in the following list) in the control plane and the VPN traffic encapsulation/de-encapsulation process in the data plane (Events 4–7). PE-B signals a vc-label <x> to PE-A. PE-A uses the pseudowire to send traffic to PE-B with VPN encapsulation using label <x>. Service 100 presents the traffic direction from CE-A to CE-B. The process for the reverse direction is the same. In Figure 9.14, PE-A and PE-B have service instance 100 configured, and the pseudowires are established for service 200 to pass traffic. In the traffic flow from CE-A to CE-B (the heavy dashed line), the following events occur:

1. **Control Plane** — PE-B assigns a label value <x> (VPN ingress label for vc-20) and stores the label in its local LIB (Label Information Base).

2. **Control Plane** — PE-B signals to PE-A over a T-LDP session with a label-mapping message. In the message, the vc-id of 20 and the vc-label <x> are both present.

3. **Control Plane** — PE-A receives the label mapping and stores the vc-label in the LIB as the VPN egress label for vc-20.

4. **Data Plane** — Data traffic from CE-A arrives at PE-A through the SAP. The service instance in PE-A for service 200 decides that the traffic is destined for PE-B and sends the traffic to vc-20. vc-20 encapsulates the traffic with vc-label <x> and sends the traffic over the SDP to reach the remote PE router. The SDP then selects one transport tunnel to carry the traffic over the backbone.

5. **Data Plane** — The transport tunnel performs tunnel encapsulation on the traffic with tunnel-label <y> and then sends the traffic to PE-B. The traffic on the wire is now double-encapsulated.

6. **Data Plane** — When PE-B receives the double-encapsulated traffic, it removes the tunnel-label <y> exposing the VPN-encapsulated traffic.

Figure 9.14 Pseudowire and the vc-label Distribution

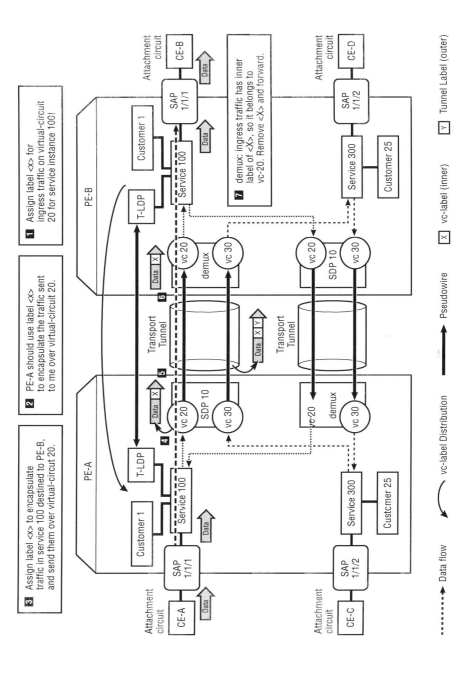

1 Assign label <x> for ingress traffic on virtual-circuit 20 for service instance 100!

2 PE-A should use label <x> to encapsulate the traffic sent to me over virtual-circuit 20.

3 Assign label <x> to encapsulate traffic in service 100 destined to PE-B, and send them over virtual-circuit 20.

7 demux: ingress traffic has inner label of <X>, so it belongs to vc-20. Remove <X> and forward.

Attachment circuit

CE-B

Customer 1

PE-B

T-LDP

SAP 1/1/1

Service 100

Data

vc 20

vc 30

demux

vc 20

vc 30

SDP 10

Service 300

Customer 25

SAP 1/1/2

CE-D

Attachment circuit

Transport Tunnel

Data X

Transport Tunnel

Data X Y

PE-A

Customer 1

T-LDP

Service 100

Data

vc 20

SDP 10

vc 30

Data X

vc 20

demux

vc 30

Service 300

Customer 25

SAP 1/1/1

CE-A

Data

Attachment circuit

SAP 1/1/2

CE-C

Attachment circuit

Pseudowire

Data flow

vc-label Distribution

X vc-label (inner)

Y Tunnel Label (outer)

7. **Data Plane** — The PE-B's vc-demux recognizes that the label <**x**> is used for traffic destined to service instance 100, vc-20. It removes the vc-label <**x**> and sends the traffic to service instance 100. Service instance 100 forwards the de-encapsulated traffic to its destination, CE-B.

> **Note:** vc-id is not the vc-label used for traffic encapsulation. vc-id is an identifier used to identify which pseudowire a system is signaling. A pseudowire is bidirectional; PE routers on both sides of the pseudowire must use the same vc-id to bind the pseudowire to the SDP. A pseudowire uses vc-id to identify itself in the control plane and to signal the vc-label. A pseudowire uses vc-label to encapsulate traffic in the data plane to send traffic to the far-end PE router.

One pseudowire is enough for a point-to-point VPN service that involves only two member PE routers. When the VPN service is multipoint, multiple pseudowires connecting each member PE routers' service instances are required. For a regular VPLS service, one pseudowire can only forward traffic between two PE routers. As a prerequisite, a full mesh of SDPs is required among all PE routers. The details regarding SDP and pseudowire configuration are introduced in subsequent chapters of this book.

9.5 Multiple Forwarding Paths in the Same SDP

As discussed in the previous section, one SDP can contain one or more transport tunnels toward the far-end PE router. An SDP using RSVP-TE LSPs can have one or more LSPs defined in its configuration. An SDP using an LDP-LSP may have more than one egress LDP label for the same far-end PE router ("/32" FEC) if Equal Cost Multiple Path (ECMP) is enabled and the local PE router has two or more equal-cost next-hop LDP peers. Alternatively, an SDP using a GRE tunnel may have more than one IP tunnel to the far-end PE router if ECMP is enabled for IP routing.

In a PE router, multiple services may share the same SDP if they have traffic flows to send to the same remote PE router. If an SDP has more than one forwarding path, it must make a traffic forwarding decision. The decision takes into consideration whether traffic flows belonging to different services should be distributed among these forwarding paths and which forwarding path the service should use. In the ALSRP, there are two options:

- The SDP can use load-balancing hashing algorithms to distribute traffic flows to all available (operational) forwarding paths. Using this method, all forwarding paths are treated equally and share a fair distribution of traffic flows decided by the load-balancing algorithms, which use a hashing technique. This option is the default behavior.

- The SDP can use multiple RSVP-TE LSPs and perform Class of Service (CoS)–based packet forwarding. The SDP maps traffic flows with different CoS requirements to different RSVP-TE LSPs.

Note: Load balancing uses one of two techniques: packet-based load balancing or flow-based load balancing. The ALSRP, and most other vendor offerings, use flow-based load balancing to prevent packets in the same flow from arriving out of sequence.

All SDP types and the CoS-based LSP forwarding and their behavior are examined in the remainder of this section.

Load Balancing on SDP Using RSVP-TE LSP

As discussed earlier, the SDP establishes service reachability from one PE router to another. The SDP configuration defines the remote PE router, the tunnel to be used (GRE, LDP-LSP, or RSVP-TE LSP), and the pseudowire signaling method used by service instances. An SDP using an RSVP-TE LSP can contain up to 16 LSPs. When there is more than one LSP defined in a single SDP, the SDP tries to use all available LSP. An available LSP is one that is operational with one active forwarding path. ECMP is used to load-balance traffic across the available LSPs.

Within a single SDP, *all defined LSPs are treated equally regardless of the number of hops they travel or the LSP metric defined.* The SDP tries to load-balance all traffic across all operational LSPs defined in it. In a local PE router, one SDP may be shared by the traffic flows from more than one service instance destined for the same remote PE router. Furthermore, within one service instance, there may be more than one traffic flow directed to the same remote PE router. If there is more than one operational LSP in the SDP, the SDP performs ECMP load balancing. Figure 9.15 illustrates an SDP performing ECMP among LSPs.

As discussed, customer traffic enters the service instance in the PE router from the SAP ingress. The service instance determines the destination PE router for the traffic and performs VPN encapsulation on the traffic using the vc-label negotiated during the establishment of the pseudowire. After the VPN encapsulation, the traffic is sent over the corresponding SDP to the remote PE router. If there are two or more available LSPs on the service traffic, ECMP load balancing is performed after the VPN encapsulation and during the transport tunnel encapsulation.

Figure 9.15: SDP ECMP on Multiple LSPs for VPN Service Traffic

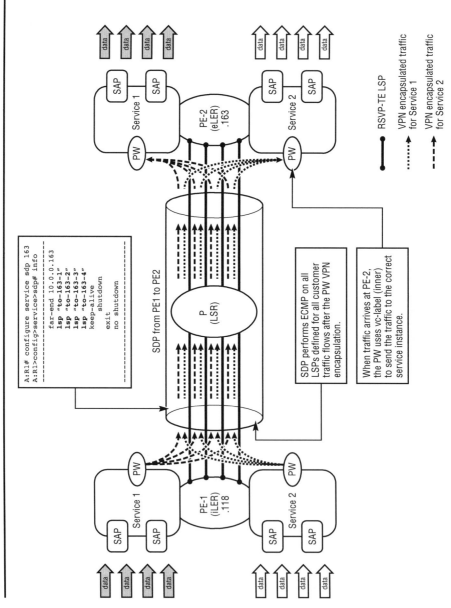

```
A:R1# configure service sdp 163
A:R1>config>service>sdp# info
--------------------------------------
        far-end 10.0.0.163
        lsp "to-163-1"
        lsp "to-163-2"
        lsp "to-163-3"
        lsp "to-163-4"
        keep-alive
                shutdown
            exit
        no shutdown
--------------------------------------
```

SDP from PE1 to PE2

SDP performs ECMP on all
LSPs defined for all customer
traffic flows after the PW VPN
encapsulation.

When traffic arrives at PE-2,
the PW uses vc-label (inner)
to send the traffic to the correct
service instance.

RSVP-TE LSP

VPN encapsulated traffic
for Service 1

VPN encapsulated traffic
for Service 2

When the PE router performs ECMP, it uses a hashing algorithm to assign traffic flows to LSPs. Within the SDP, each operational LSP has one active forwarding path, which is an operational RSVP-TE LSP. Each LSP-Path has its own label reservation; the label is used as the outer egress label (transport label) for the traffic using its assigned SDP. The SDP ECMP hashing output decides which transport label the traffic uses. Since the PE router is service-aware, it can inspect the customer traffic header information and use it in the hashing algorithm as follows:

- If the customer traffic is IP packets from Epipe, VPLS, or VPRN services, the customer traffic IP headers (source and destination IP address pairs) are used as hashing input for ECMP.

- If the customer traffic is non-IP Ethernet frames from Epipe or VPLS services, the customer traffic Ethernet headers (source and destination MAC address pairs) are used as hashing input for ECMP.

Multiple traffic flows (from the same service, or different services) have different transport tunnel label (outer label) values. Different LSPs assigned to the same SDP can have the same or different paths across the network. The SDP treats all tunnels equally and tries to distribute traffic among them.

One typical application for using ECMP across multiple LSPs is to allow the LSR routers in the transit path to perform more efficient load balancing over Ethernet Link Aggregation Groups (LAGs). LSR LAG load balancing is discussed in Chapter 13.

Load Balancing on SDP Using LDP-LSP or GRE Tunnels

SDP can use LDP-LSP as a transport tunnel. LDP-LSPs are established automatically by the system when LDP is enabled on every router interface in the network backbone. iLDP creates LSPs by distributing FEC/Label mappings according to the routing table. When there are multiple routes to the same destination in the routing table and ECMP is configured, the LDP creates one LSP per next-hop router. (The configuration of LDP and ECMP in the context of LDP is discussed in Chapter 8.) An SDP may have more than one LDP-LSP, but it cannot specifically choose which tunnel to use in the SDP configuration. When ldp is configured in the SDP, all ECMP LDP-LSPs reaching the far-end router are used by the SDP. Where there are multiple services sharing the SDP, the SDP uses a hashing algorithm to distribute traffic across different LDP-LSPs.

SDP can also use GRE as the transport tunnel. VPN traffic tunneled by GRE is encapsulated in IP packets and is routed using the IGP forwarding tables in the network backbone. When there are multiple paths to the same destination and ECMP is configured, there is more than one route (next hop) in the routing table for the same destination. As in the case of multiple LDP-LSPs, the SDP cannot specify which GRE tunnel to use in the configuration. When there are multiple routes to the same PE router, an SDP using GRE tunneling uses a hashing algorithm to distribute traffic flows from different services to different next-hop routers.

There is a significant difference between RSVP-TE LSP tunneling and LDP-LSP or GRE tunneling where multiple tunnels are concerned. RSVP-TE LSP tunneling is end-to-end from the Head-End (HE) router to the tail-end (Tail) router. When two RSVP-TE LSPs are signaled between two routers, every router in the path has two sets of RSVP sessions and two different labels. The two RSVP-TE LSPs are explicitly configured and signaled separately, and exist on every router as two different entities. Consequently, there are two end-to-end LSPs. Recall in Figure 9.15 there were four explicitly configured RSVP-TE LSPs between the PE routers. These LSPs were four distinct end-to-end entities. SDP can assign different traffic flows to different LSPs. Along the entire path between the two PE routers, these flows will have different transport labels.

Both GRE and LDP-LSP tunneling use the IGP routing table to make forwarding decisions on a hop-by-hop basis, in contrast to RSVP-TE LSP's end-to-end source routing. Because LDP-LSP and GRE tunnels are not end-to-end, they can only distinguish multiple paths in the hop where there are multiple next hops for the same destination. The end-to-end LDP-LSP or GRE tunnel is a virtual concept. The HE router, where the SDP is defined, does not have the visibility of the multiple paths in the middle if it does not have multiple routes to the far end of the SDP. The HE must see multiple forwarding paths in order to perform load balancing. Otherwise, the HE will put all traffic flows, belonging to one service or multiple services, to the single next-hop router. Only the P routers that actually see multiple next hops can perform ECMP at that hop. But since P routers are not service-aware, the load-balancing result may not be optimal.

ECMP Load Balancing: LER Hashing versus LSR Hashing

Whenever there are multiple equal-cost forwarding paths available for load balancing, traffic distribution decisions must be made by the system. Some typical scenarios include:

- An Ethernet Link Aggregation Group (LAG) containing multiple Ethernet links is used to carry traffic between two routers.

- ECMP LDP is enabled in a router, and there are multiple available IP routes or egress labels pointing to the next-hop router.
- SDP contains multiple transport tunnels (GRE or MPLS) to the far-end PE router.

Figure 9.16 illustrates the forwarding behavior of Label Edge Router (LER) and Label Switch Router (LSR) load balancing with LDP-LSP tunneling and GRE tunneling. In the diagram, the dashed arrows represent one traffic flow, and the dotted arrows represent another traffic flow.

Figure 9.16 LER and LSR Load Balancing on LDP-LSP and GRE Tunneling

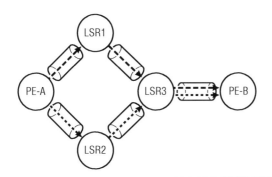

Scenario 1: LER Hashing: LDP & GRE

The PE router sees multiple next-hops and load balances the traffic based on service-id and traffic flows within the services to distribute the traffic among different forwarding paths. Per-service per-flow load balancing is achieved.

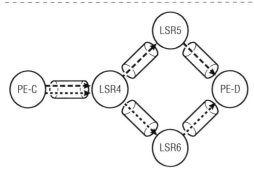

Scenario 2: LSR Hashing: LDP

The LSR router sees multiple next-hops and load balances the traffic based on the MPLS label stack (include vc-label) to distribute the traffic among different forwarding paths. Per-service load balancing is achieved.

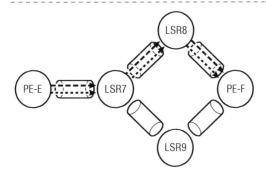

Scenario 3: LSR Hashing: GRE

When using GRE tunneling, LSR cannot perform load-balancing. This is because the GRE encapsulated traffic is viewed as regular IP packets by the LSR (P routers). IP router load balances the traffic on a per Src-IP/Dst-IP pair basis. All traffic between two PE routers with GRE encapsulation uses the same src-IP/Dst-IP pair. Therefore, they all travel through one link.

CoS-Based LSP Forwarding

Class of Service (CoS) based LSP forwarding is a mechanism that allows the SDP to distribute the service traffic to multiple LSPs based on the forwarding classes, rather than using ECMP. A discussion of CoS LSP forwarding requires an understanding of the basic concept of Quality of Service.

A Brief Overview of Quality of Service

Because the description of CoS-based LSP forward requires some basic knowledge of Quality of Service (QoS), this section provides a brief review of QoS and related ALSRP terminology. While this section provides an overview of QoS capabilities, you can find a more detailed discussion in a separate Alcatel-Lucent publication, *Advanced QoS for Multi-Service IP/MPLS Networks by* Ram Balakrishnan (Wiley, 2008).

The IP/MPLS VPN service network can provide multiple types of services on a single converged network. Different types of services have varying requirements for service delivery. For example, the ATM or TDM VLL services require low forwarding delay, low jitter, and are not tolerant of packet loss, while Internet Enhanced Services (IES) are less sensitive to delay and packet loss. Customers may also have specific service requirements. For example, business customers may be willing to pay higher rates for higher bandwidth with relatively low delay, while residential customers, not requiring such high bandwidth, can pay lower rates. To serve customers with different types of services, QoS is required to differentiate the traffic flows and treat each flow according to its own service needs. With QoS, traffic flows that require higher service quality (low delay, low loss) are served with higher priority than other flows. The service provider can honor the specific customer Service Level Agreements (SLAs) while making more efficient use of network resources.

Service Quality is represented by the following traffic characteristics:

- **Delay** — The measurement of the time for traffic to travel through the network from its ingress to egress
- **Jitter** — The variation in arrival time of packets in the same traffic flow (also called *delay variation*)
- **Packet Loss** — A measurement of packets dropped in transit
- **Throughput (Bandwidth)** — The rate of the traffic flow

By default, QoS is not used in the system, and all traffic flows are treated in the network in the same way, with *best effort*. All traffic flows treated with best effort may suffer losses during periods of traffic congestion. With QoS, services can be assigned different QoS policies, and their traffic treated according to these policies using the following steps:

1. The system *classifies* the traffic flows using certain criteria such as DSCP/IPP marking, CoS marking, and MPLS label EXP bits. Once classified, traffic flows can be treated differently.

2. The system then *differentiates* the traffic flows by mapping them into separate queues. Traffic is differentiated by policy or by the size of the queue. Each queue represents a different Forwarding Class (FC). There are eight forwarding classes and 56 subforwarding classes supported in the ALSRP. Traffic flows mapped to different FCs will then be handled differently (shape, police, schedule, etc.).

3. At egress, the system *marks* the traffic, so that the next-hop system can use the marking information to maintain a consistent classification and treatment for the traffic flows.

End-to-end QoS is achieved by applying consistent design and implementation of QoS policies throughout the entire network.

In the ALSRP, QoS is implemented through QoS Policies. There are five types of QoS policies, each applicable to different objects as listed here:

*   SAP-ingress policy
*   SAP-egress policy
*   Network Ingress policy
*   Network Egress policy
*   Network-Queue policy

Figure 9.17 illustrates QoS policies and their applicable objects on a service network. In Figure 9.17, the PE router has a customer-facing access port and a backbone-facing network port. As discussed earlier, the customer-facing SAPs are defined on the access port and receive customer traffic. The network port faces other P and PE routers in the MPLS network backbone and receives VPN-encapsulated traffic. The SAP-ingress and SAP-egress QoS policies are defined on the SAPs of a service instance. The Network Ingress and Network Egress QoS policies and the Network-Queue policy are defined on the network port. Table 9.8 describes the functions of these policies that are relevant to CoS LSP forwarding. The SAP QoS policies handle per-service traffic flows (micro-flows), while the Network QoS policies handle aggregated traffic flows (macro-flows) from many services sharing the same network port.

Figure 9.17 QoS Policies in a Service Router

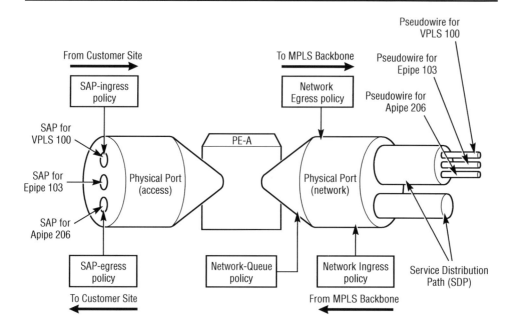

Table 9.8 QoS Policies in the ALSRP Service Routers

QoS Policy	Location	Functions
SAP-ingress	Defined in the service SAP-ingress configuration	For packets received at the SAP ingress, it performs classifying, shaping, policing, and queuing operations and maps the traffic to different forwarding classes.
SAP-egress	Defined in the service SAP-egress configuration	For traffic sent to the SAP egress, it performs shaping, policing, and marking operations.
Network Ingress, Network Egress	Defined in the L3 router interface configuration	For VPN-encapsulated service packets received at the network ingress, it performs shaping and policing operations and maps the traffic to different forwarding classes. For VPN-encapsulated service packets sent to the network egress, it performs shaping, policing, and marking operations.

QoS Policy	Location	Functions
Network-Queue	Defined in the network port/MDA configuration	Controls the network buffer on queuing macro-flows for different forwarding classes.

As discussed, customers' services may require different treatment for their traffic flows. Some traffic flows are considered higher in priority than others. Additional QoS techniques can be applied to ensure that higher-priority traffic flows are given special treatment. This can be accomplished in the network backbone using a different transport tunnel for each level of priority. For example, the tunnels serving more important traffic flows are provided more bandwidth reservation, a higher scheduling priority, and more failure protection. CoS-based LSP forwarding supports this capability.

SDP Using RSVP-TE LSPs with CoS-Based LSP Forwarding

The SDPs using RSVP-TE LSPs as transport tunnels can be configured to use CoS-based LSP forwarding. Inside the SDP, multiple RSVP-TE LSPs are created to forward traffic flows belonging to different Forwarding Classes (FCs). When the SDP has more than one available LSP, it may perform ECMP load balancing. With CoS-based LSP forwarding, the SDP decides which LSP to use based on the traffic's FC. Each FC is dedicated to a different LSP, with one default LSP for all FCs that do not have a dedicated LSP or for which the specified LSP is down. When the SDP forwards traffic to the far-end PE through a CoS-based LSP SDP, traffic flows with different FCs are treated differently depending on their LSP configuration.

CoS-based LSP forwarding must be coordinated with QoS policies. Service traffic enters the service network from the SAP ingress of a PE router's service instance. The SAP-ingress QoS policy configured on the SAP performs traffic classification and maps the traffic to certain FCs before sending the traffic to the switching fabric. This traffic's FC mapping is used to decide which SDP receives the traffic for transit across the network backbone. QoS polices are the principal tool for performing service differentiation, and CoS-based LSP forwarding enhances the transport tunnel selection in the SDP to provide better QoS performance.

As an example, if a service provider distinguishes two types of traffic flows in the network backbone and wants to treat them differently, there are two available forwarding classes:

- **Expedited Forwarding (EF)** — Traffic categorized as EF requires guaranteed bandwidth, minimal delay and jitter, and no packet loss.

- **Best Effort (BE)** — Traffic categorized as BE does not require minimal delay and loss but should use as much available bandwidth as possible, providing it is not competing with EF traffic.

When traffic enters a PE router's SAP, the SAP-ingress QoS policy classifies the packets into different FCs according to the policy's criteria. The SDP with CoS-based forwarding forwards the traffic over different LSPs toward the far-end PE router. Figure 9.18 illustrates CoS-based LSP forwarding.

Figure 9.18 shows one SDP from PE-A to PE-B. There are two VPLS services: vpls-100 and vpls-200. Both services share the same SDP and want to send traffic from PE-A to PE-B. When the traffic enters PE-A from the two SAP ingress points, the SAP-ingress QoS policies map the traffic to two internal forwarding classes: EF and BE. When the system needs to send these packets to the far-end PE router, it uses the SDP for PE-B. The SDP is configured with two LSPs, and CoS-based LSP forwarding is enabled. There are two RSVP-TE LSPs in the SDP:

- The EF-LSP is dedicated to the EF traffic class. Since EF traffic requires higher service priority with minimal traffic loss, both the secondary LSP and the Fast Reroute (FRR) one-to-one backup (not shown) are provisioned to protect the LSP. The EF-LSP, using control plane bandwidth reservation, takes the direct path from PE-A to PE-B to achieve optimal traffic forwarding.
- The BE-LSP is used for the BE traffic class. The BE traffic flows are served in a best effort manner. The LSP is configured to take the longer forwarding path, PE-A to P to PE-B, so it does not compete with the EF class traffic. Only FRR facility backup protection is required to protect the BE-LSP.

This example shows that from the transport tunnel's perspective, the CoS-based LSP forwarding takes advantage of the TE and resiliency capabilities of RSVP-TE LSPs. It places different classes of traffic into LSPs with different resource reservation, forwarding paths, and protection.

Note: The CoS-based LSP forwarding for SDP is an SDP universal configuration, and it will be effective on all services that share the same SDP. However, for multiple VLL services to take advantage of CoS-based LSP forwarding, they must use shared queuing in the SAP-ingress QoS policy. If shared queuing is not used, the CoS-based LSP forwarding will not be effective. The system will hash the traffic flows from multiple VLL services based on the service-id and distribute the traffic to all available LSPs regardless of the forwarding class mapping of the LSPs.

Figure 9.18 SDP Using CoS-Based LSP Forwarding

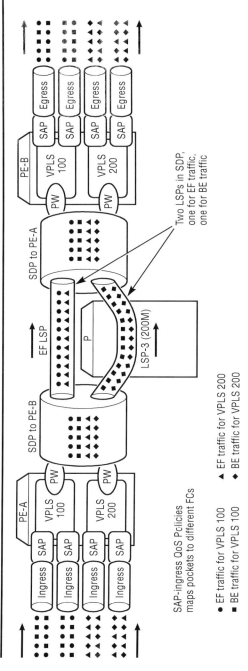

Configuring SDP with CoS-Based LSP Forwarding

Before deploying CoS-based LSP forwarding in an SDP, the RSVP-TE LSPs for different forwarding classes must be provisioned. From the RSVP-TE LSP configuration's perspective, there is no CoS-related configuration. Only the LSPs serving different forwarding classes may be configured with different resource reservations and resiliency features. When designing a network, ensure that higher-priority traffic takes a more optimal forwarding path with more failure protection.

For the CoS-based LSP forwarding to be effective on a service, the service instance must have a corresponding SAP-ingress QoS policy configured to map the traffic into an FC. Since there is no mandatory co-relation between SAP-ingress policy and the CoS-based forwarding, it is possible, and sometime intentional, for the SAP-ingress policy to map traffic to a set of FCs, while the LSPs in the SDP are configured to forward traffic to another set of FCs. If the SDP finds traffic flow belonging to an FC without a dedicated LSP, the traffic flow belonging to the uncorrelated FC is forwarded to the default LSP. Any SDP with CoS-based LSP forwarding must have a default LSP to accept any traffic for an FC without a dedicated LSP. The RSVP-TE LSP configuration is discussed in Chapter 5. The QoS configuration is beyond the scope of this book, and its configuration is not illustrated or discussed here. Figure 9.19 illustrates a CoS-based LSP forwarding configuration.

In the example, two LSPs are configured. The LSP 118-116 requires 100 MB bandwidth reservation with both a one-to-one FRR protection and hot-standby secondary LSP protection. This tunnel is used by SDP 116 to carry EF class traffic and uses the optimal forwarding path with high resiliency. The LSP 118-116-2 has no bandwidth reservation and is used to forward BE class traffic. It is also specified as the default LSP for all traffic classes not having a dedicated LSP specified in the SDP. By default, the class-forwarding configuration is administratively disabled, and an explicit no shutdown must be configured for it to be effective.

After an SDP is configured to use CoS-based LSP forwarding, all traffic for a specific FC is forwarded through its dedicated configured LSP. If there is no configured LSP, the default LSP forwards FC traffic. Since SDP is shared by multiple services, any traffic flows from any services may use the same LSP providing they are mapped to the same FC to which the tunnel is dedicated. This holds true regardless of which service the traffic belongs to, and no matter which SAP-ingress QoS policy the SAP uses to map the traffic. Traffic from many SAPs for many services are aggregated to use the same LSP providing they are mapped to that tunnel's FC and use the same SDP.

Figure 9.19 SDP Configuration for CoS-Based LSP Forwarding

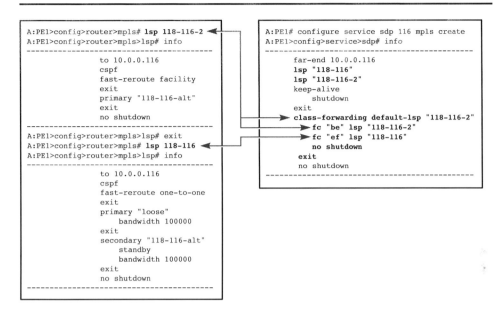

Note: The SDP's CoS-based LSP forwarding is an enhancement of QoS design. It may improve the service quality by adding more resiliency and forwarding path optimization for different FCs from the MPLS transport tunnel's perspective. It allows tunneling traffic of different FCs. To achieve end-to-end QoS, a QoS design with QoS policies deployed on SAP and the network side is still required. In addition, to achieve the maximum effect, the QoS design should be co-related to CoS-based LSP forwarding.

9.6 Maximum Transmission Unit in a Service Network

The *maximum transmission unit* (MTU) defines the maximum frame size (in bytes) that is permitted over a certain link or service. From the customer's perspective, the Ethernet service (Epipe or VPLS) must support an end-to-end, Layer 3 MTU of 1,500 bytes at a minimum. From the service provider's perspective, the IP/MPLS VPN services will not become operationally **up** if there is a service MTU mismatch between the peering PEs of the pseudowire. The correct MTU values for each entity must be defined in the IP/MPLS VPN service network. Sending oversized frames to a router may cause packet drop and retransmission, or packet fragmentation.

> **Note:** Fragmentation is an expensive operation. L2VPN customer traffic (VPN, Epipe) and MPLS-encapsulated traffic is dropped without fragmentation. Ordinary IP traffic is fragmented by the router before being forwarded.

The frame size allowed for a physical port is defined by two parameters:

- **Maximum Transmission Unit (MTU)** — The maximum frame size allowed for transmission on a port. When a system must transmit a packet or frame, the port MTU configuration is checked. If the frame size is greater than the MTU, the system discards the frame (L2) or fragments the packet (L3) before transmitting it.
- **Maximum Receiving Unit (MRU)** — The maximum frame size allowed for a port to accept an ingress frame or packet. When a port receives a frame greater than the configured MTU, it discards the frame.

In the ALSRP, and most other vendors' products, the MTU and MRU values are equal. The balance of the discussion in this section will refer to the MTU. The reader should assume that the discussion also applies to the MRU.

Types of MTUs in a Service Network

In an IP/MPLS VPN service network, there are two types of MTU:

- **Port MTU** — The MTU of a physical port (access port and network port). The port MTU value represents the maximum frame size a port can send to the link attached to it. The port MTU is manually configured in the service router. It is important to configure the correct physical port MTU value to match the link and the capabilities of the transmission equipment in between.
- **Service Entity MTU** — The MTU of a service entity such as a service instance, SDP, pseudowire, or LSP. The service entity MTU represents the maximum frame size that is accepted by the service entity. MTU values are derived from the port MTU minus the encapsulation overhead. Services are end-to-end; therefore, the MTU support should also be end-to-end. All

involved routers must have consistent MTU configurations on related service entities. A path through the network backbone may have different types of physical links and associated MTU values. The end-to-end MTU value is determined by the link with the *smallest* MTU value.

In an IP/MPLS VPN service network, there are many entities that require MTU definition. When the MTU is configured incorrectly, either the service will be operationally down or the traffic in the service is dropped. The MTU can either be manually specified or automatically negotiated. Configuring MTU values is sometimes confusing; however, in most cases, the default values are sufficient. Figure 9.20 illustrates several different MTU values in a service network.

As shown in Figure 9.20, there are several types of MTU in a service network. There is an MTU for the access port, the network port, the LSP-Path, the SDP-Path, the service, and the vc. Table 9.9 summarizes these MTU values. Because the focus of this book is MPLS L2VPNs in a typical Ethernet environment, the examples used to support the discussion of MTU use Ethernet.

Table 9.9 Types of MTU in a Service Network

MTU Type	Description	Value
Access Port MTU	The physical port MTU on the access port. It defines the maximum frame size that is supported on the PE-CE attachment circuit. All SAPs defined on an access port share the same MTU.	Configurable in the port configuration. The default value depends on port type and encapsulation type. Port MTUs are local to the router and require manual configuration.
Network Port MTU	The physical port MTU on the network port. It defines the maximum frame size that is supported on a backbone link between a PE and a P/PE router. The network port MTU will affect the MTUs of LSPs or SDPs using it.	Configurable in the port configuration. The default value depends on port type and encapsulation type. Port MTUs are local to the router and require manual configuration.

(continued)

Table 9.9 Types of MTU in a Service Network *(continued)*

MTU Type	Description	Value
LSP-Path MTU	The MTU of an RSVP-TE LSP. LSP-Path MTU signaling is optional and is disabled by default.	LSP-Path MTUs are not configurable. Each hop derives the MTU from the egress port MTU and signals it using the ADSPEC object. LSP-Path MTUs are end-to-end, and all hops accept the smallest MTU value along the path.
SDP-Path MTU	The SDP MTU defines the maximum end-to-end frame size of encapsulated traffic in an IP/MPLS VPN.	Configurable in the SDP configuration. By default, the value is derived from the LSP-Path MTU.
Service MTU	The Service MTU defines the maximum end-to-end frame size supported in an L2VPN service. This MTU is visible to the customer.	Configurable in the service configuration. The default value varies with the type of service.
Virtual Circuit (VC) MTU	The VC-MTU is used when signaling the pseudowires used by the services. Two sides of the pseudowire must have a matching VC-MTU value for the pseudowire to initialize.	Not configurable. It is derived from the Service MTU using the pseudowire.
OSPF MTU	The OSPF MTU defines the maximum size of the OSPF packet. It affects the number of LSAs contained in the OSPF update.	Configurable in the OSPF interfaces configuration. By default, it is derived from the MTU of the physical port used by the OSPF interface. The OSPF interfaces must have matching MTUs for the adjacency to come up.
IP MTU[a]	The Service MTU of Layer 3 VPN services (IES or VPRN). It is the maximum IP packet size the L3VPN customers can send in an IP packet across the provider's network.	Configurable in the Layer 3 VPN routing interfaces

[a]L3VPN services are beyond the scope of this book, so the IP MTU is not further discussed here.

Figure 9.20 Types of MTUs in the Service Network for L2VPN Services

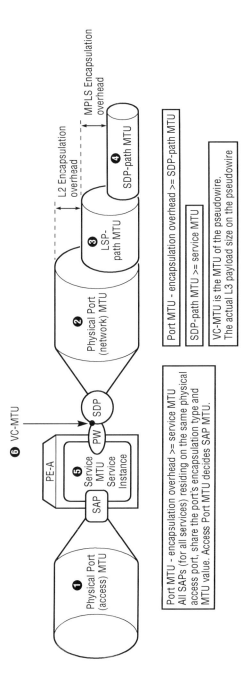

❶ Physical Port (access) MTU

PE-A

SAP

❺ Service MTU Service Instance

PW

SDP

❻ VC-MTU

❷ Physical Port (network) MTU

❸ LSP-path MTU

L2 Encapsulation overhead

❹ SDP-path MTU

MPLS Encapsulation overhead

Port MTU - encapsulation overhead >= service MTU
All SAPs (for all services) residing on the same physical
access port, share the port's encapsulation type and
MTU value. Access Port MTU decides SAP MTU.

Port MTU - encapsulation overhead >= SDP-path MTU

SDP-path MTU >= service MTU

VC-MTU is the MTU of the pseudowire.
The actual L3 payload size on the pseudowire.

Physical Access Port MTU

The access port MTU represents the maximum frame size that is supported over a link to a customer device. In a service router, an SAP is associated with an access port, and the MTU is one of the port characteristics. All SAPs exchange traffic with customer devices over their associated access ports. The access port MTU defines the maximum frame size of the native customer traffic for all SAPs defined on it.

In the ALSRP, the operational mode of the port must be defined. When a port is configured for access mode, the port is used for connecting customer-facing attachment circuits. The default MTU value of the access port depends on the encapsulation type of the port. For example, the Gigabit Ethernet port in access mode has the following encapsulation options:

- **Null Encapsulation Type** — Default MTU is 1,514 bytes. This provides 1,500 bytes of packet payload size and 14 bytes of Ethernet frame header exclusive of VLAN tagging.

- **dot1q Encapsulation Type** — Default MTU is 1,518 bytes. This provides 1,500 bytes of packet payload size and 14 bytes of Ethernet frame header, with a single VLAN tag of 4 bytes.

- **QinQ Encapsulation Type** — Default MTU is 1,522 bytes. This provides 1,500 bytes of Layer 3 payload size and 14 bytes of Ethernet L2 header, with two VLAN tags totaling 8 bytes.

Access port MTU values are configurable in the port configuration. However, the default access port MTU configuration is sufficient for most scenarios.

Figure 9.21 illustrates the configuration of the access port MTU. The value used in the diagram is for command-line interface (CLI) command reference only and is not a design recommendation.

Figure 9.21   Configure Access Port MTU

```
A:PE1# configure port 1/1/10
A:PE1>config>port# info
-------------------------------------------------
        ethernet
                mode access
                mtu 1600
        exit
        no shutdown
-------------------------------------------------
```

When SAPs are defined on an access port, the frame size of the native customer traffic through that SAP is limited by the port MTU. A change in the access port MTU value affects all SAPs associated with it. The access port MTU value must be large enough to accommodate a customer-requested MTU. In the case of the Ethernet L2VPN service (Epipe or VPLS), an IP payload of 1,500 bytes is commonly requested. The frame MTU value should be 1,514 (null), 1,518 (dot1q), or 1,522 (QinQ) including Ethernet frame headers. These values represent the default Ethernet port access mode MTU values.

> **Warning:** When changing the access port MTU, remember that all SAPs on the same port are affected. In this situation, check the service MTU of the service owning the SAP. If the SAP uses a port with a larger MTU than the SAP's service can provide, the customer may send oversized frames to the service, and the service may drop the traffic (L2VPN) or fragment the traffic (L3VPN).

Physical Network Port MTU

The network port MTU represents the maximum frame size that is supported between neighboring P or PE routers. Network ports are the ports facing the network backbone connecting P and PE routers. The physical network port MTU represents the biggest frame size that is supported on the wire in the core network. A network port carries IP/MPLS VPN-encapsulated traffic for many services, and many different SDPs may use it. Therefore, its MTU value limits all the MTU values of the associated SDPs.

Since a network port in the backbone carries various types of traffic, it may be desirable to configure as large a network port MTU as possible so it can carry many services requesting various MTUs. In the ALSRP, the Gigabit Ethernet port in network mode has a default MTU of 9,212 (compared to the access mode default of 1,514). This value is sufficient for all IP/MPLS VPN services' traffic flows.

The port MTU may be limited by the transmission equipment that connects the network ports together. In a service provider network, the P and PE routers are typically separated geographically. Transmission equipment must provide the physical connectivity to link the routers, optical plants, microwave, or radio networks. This equipment may impose limitations on the MTU that is used between two P/PE routers and therefore limit the end-to-end network MTU that is configured on the routers. For example, some radio equipment hardware supports a maximum Ethernet frame size of only 1,536 bytes. Therefore, if two network ports are connected over such a radio link, the network port MTU can only be set to 1,536, although the service router can support a larger value. In this case, all SDPs on the network must use a smaller SDP-Path MTU and only carry VPN traffic for services with a smaller MTU. Figure 9.22 illustrates this scenario.

Figure 9.22 Transmission Equipment Affecting Port MTU Configuration: Weakest Link

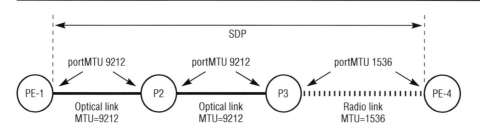

In Figure 9.22, the SDP is deployed end-to-end from PE1 to PE4. The physical path travels from PE1 to PE4 through P2 and P3. The radio equipment connecting P3 and PE4 has a hardware-limited MTU size of 1,536 bytes. Therefore, the ports between P3 and PE4 must be configured to use 1,536 as the network port MTU. Recall that the default MTU for the network Gigabit Ethernet port is 9,212 bytes. This value must be reconfigured to reflect the fact that the link between P3 and PE4 can carry frames no greater than 1,536 bytes. The new MTU value prevents the radio equipment from dropping oversized frames. The SDP's end-to-end Path MTU should be configured accordingly.

> **Warning:** Configuring the correct network port MTU value is very important. The configuration should reflect the physical link capacity. Service-related MTUs are derived from the network port MTU. If the network port MTU values in the backbone are configured incorrectly, VPN traffic may be silently discarded in the network backbone, or the services or pseudowires may not become operational.

LSP-Path MTU

The LSP-Path MTU represents the maximum frame size (including the MPLS header) that is supported over an LSP. Because of its fast convergence and traffic engineering capability, RSVP-TE LSPs are preferred as IP/MPLS VPN transport tunnels. RSVP-TE supports the signaling of the LSP-Path MTU in the LSP signaling messages using the ADSPEC object. Figure 9.23 illustrates the configuration of the ADSPEC object and the negotiation of the LSP-Path MTU in the PATH/RESV messages for LSP signaling.

The LSP-Path MTU negotiation is optional and, by default, is disabled in the RSVP-TE LSP configuration. It can be enabled in the LSP configuration context using the `adspec` command in the Head-End (HE) router of the LSP. When an LSP has the ADSPEC object enabled, the MTU of the LSP is negotiated by each hop. For every hop along the LSP, the router sets the LSP-Path MTU value using the following formula:

LSP-Path MTU = (Egress network port MTU) – (L2 overhead).

The following two examples illustrate the use of this formula:

- If the network port is Ethernet with its port MTU set to 9,212 and the encapsulation type is `null`, the LSP-Path MTU is calculated as 9,212 – 14 = 9,198. The frame overhead is the MAC header of 14 bytes.
- If the network port is Ethernet with its port MTU set to 9,212 and the encapsulation type is `dot1q`, the LSP-Path MTU is calculated as 9,212 – 18 = 9,194. The frame overhead is the MAC header of 14 bytes plus the 4-byte VLAN tag.

In an LSP, the MTU negotiation concludes on the *smallest* MTU value among all hops in the LSP-Path. The LSP-Path MTU is as large as the link with the smallest capacity in the path.

If the LDP-LSP is used as a transport tunnel, there is no MTU negotiation, and the MTU is not a characteristic of an LDP-LSP.

SDP-Path MTU

The SDP-Path MTU defines the maximum frame size of the service payload, excluding the MPLS encapsulation overhead in the SDP. IP/MPLS VPN services use SDPs to carry VPN-encapsulated traffic. The SDP-Path MTU determines the maximum frame size for customer traffic carried over the backbone links. All services using the same SDP are limited by the same SDP-Path MTU value. Services are associated with a specific SDP by configuring a pseudowire on it using the `sdp-binding` command in the service configuration. The SDP-Path MTU must be equal to or greater than the MTU of the service using it. Otherwise, the service's pseudowires remain operationally down with the error code `PathMtuTooSmall`.

Figure 9.23 LSP-Path MTU Negotiation Using ADSPEC Object

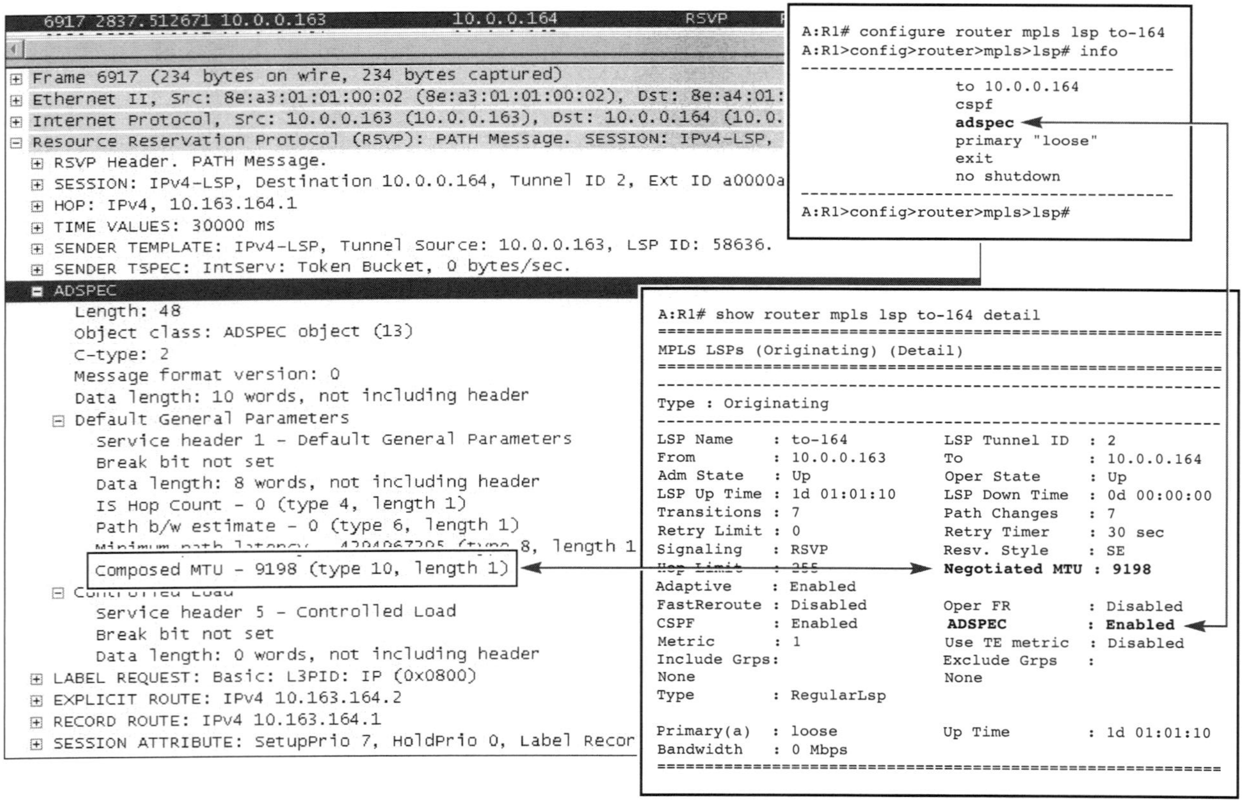

The SDP-Path MTU value can be manually configured or derived automatically by the system. By default, the SDP-Path MTU is derived from one of two values, as follows:

- If the SDP uses RSVP-TE LSP tunneling and the LSP has LSP-Path MTU negotiation enabled, the SDP calculates the MTU by subtracting 8 bytes (representing the inner and outer labels) from the LSP-Path. For example, if the LSP-Path MTU is 9,198 bytes, the SDP using this LSP calculates an SDP-Path MTU of 9,190 bytes.

- If the SDP uses MPLS tunneling with either LSP with no MTU negotiation or LDP-LSP, the SDP-Path MTU is calculated by subtracting the frame header and the 8-byte MPLS header from the Network Port MTU.

- If the SDP uses GRE tunneling, the SDP-Path MTU is calculated by subtracting the frame header and the 28-byte GRE header from the Network Port MTU. The GRE header includes the 4-byte inner vc-label, the 4-byte GRE header, and the 20-byte IP header.

The SDP-Path MTU value can also be manually configured under the SDP configuration context using the `path-mtu <value>` command. The explicit configuration value for the SDP-Path MTU is also called the *administrative* MTU. When there is an administrative MTU defined for the SDP, the system uses this value as the SDP-Path MTU. Figure 9.24 illustrates the various SDP MTU settings.

In Figure 9.24, the output from the `show service sdp` command displays the MTU-related fields `Adm MTU` and `Opr MTU`. The `Adm MTU` field displays the administrative, or configured, SDP-Path MTU value. If a value has not been configured, the field displays 0. `Opr MTU` displays the operational MTU currently used by the system. If there is an explicit configuration of the SDP-Path MTU, the `Opr MTU` is the same as `Adm MTU`. If there is no explicit configuration, `Opr MTU` is calculated using one of the methods described previously.

SDPs are unidirectional. It takes two SDPs (one in each direction) to establish an end-to-end connection between two PE routers. To be operational, the SDP-Path MTU values on these connections do not need to match, and MTU is not signaled in the SDP establishing process. However, in practice, these connections should have the same SDP-Path MTU value unless there are specific reasons not to.

Figure 9.24 SDP-Path MTU Configuration Example: Administrative MTU versus Operational MTU

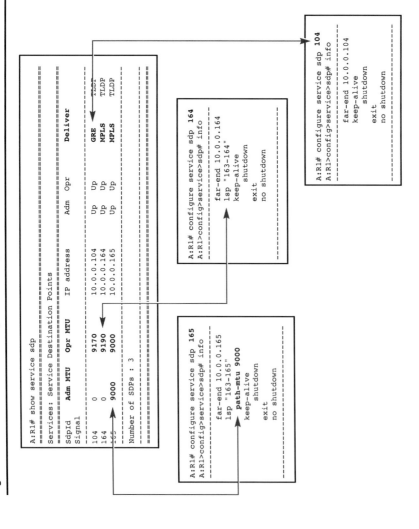

```
A:R1# show service sdp

Services: Service Destination Points
===============================================================================
SdpId    Adm MTU   Opr MTU   IP address    Adm  Opr   Deliver
Signal
===============================================================================
104      0         9170      10.0.0.104    Up   Up    GRE     TLDP
164      0         9190      10.0.0.164    Up   Up    MPLS    TLDP
165      9000      9000      10.0.0.165    Up   Up    MPLS    TLDP
-------------------------------------------------------------------------------
Number of SDPs : 3
===============================================================================
```

```
A:R1# configure service sdp 165
A:R1>config>service>sdp# info
----------------------------------------
            far-end 10.0.0.165
            lsp "163-165"
            path-mtu 9000
            keep-alive
                shutdown
            exit
            no shutdown
----------------------------------------
```

```
A:R1# configure service sdp 164
A:R1>config>service>sdp# info
----------------------------------------
            far-end 10.0.0.164
            lsp "163-164"
            keep-alive
                shutdown
            exit
            no shutdown
----------------------------------------
```

```
A:R1# configure service sdp 104
A:R1>config>service>sdp# info
----------------------------------------
            far-end 10.0.0.104
            keep-alive
                shutdown
            exit
            no shutdown
----------------------------------------
```

For SDPs using RSVP-TE LSP tunneling with the FRR facility *bypass tunnel* enabled, the SDP-Path MTU calculation takes the bypass tunnel overhead into consideration. For example, if a network port has an MTU of 9,212, the SDP MTU is 9,190 (9,212 – 22). If the SDP uses FRR facility *backup* enabled, the SDP derives a Path MTU of 9,186. Four more bytes are subtracted because FRR adds another MPLS label in the top of the label stack when protecting the traffic from a network failure.

For SDPs using LDP-LSP tunneling with LDPoRSVP, the SDP-Path MTU calculation takes the tunnel overhead into consideration. On a network with an MTU of 9,212, the SDP-Path MTU is 9,190. With LDPoRSVP, the SDP-Path MTU is 9,186 because LDPoRSVP adds a third 4-byte label on top of the MPLS label stack. If the RSVP-TE tunnel used to tunnel the LDP tunnel also has FRR facility backup enabled, the SDP-Path MTU is reduced to 9,182 to accommodate the 4-byte FRR facility bypass tunnel label.

Service MTU for the L2VPN Service

In the ALSRP, the *Service MTU* refers to L2VPN services including the VPLS and VPWS. The Service MTU defines the maximum frame size (VPN payload size) that the service can support. This is the MTU that a service instance uses to send traffic to the remote service instance. The default Service MTU size is 1,514 bytes for Ethernet-related VPN services (Epipe or VPLS). The Service MTU does not include the IP/MPLS VPN encapsulation overhead (vc-label, MPLS or GRE transport overhead, frame overhead). In most cases, for Ethernet L2VPN services such as VPLS and Epipe, the default Service MTU of 1,514 bytes is sufficient. The Ethernet VPN service removes the service-delimiting VLAN before sending the traffic to the pseudowire as untagged Ethernet frames. However, there are cases in which the VLAN tag is not service-limiting and remains in the frames sent to the pseudowire. In such cases, the Service MTU and SAP access port MTU need to be increased. These cases are discussed in greater detail in Chapter 11.

Note: The MTU of the L3VPN services (VPRN and IES) is called *IP-MTU* in the ALSRP. IP-MTU is beyond the scope of this book.

The default Service MTU value of 1,514 can be overridden by using the `service-mtu <value>` command to explicitly configure the value in the service instance configuration context. Figure 9.25 illustrates an example of the Service MTU configured to a non-default value of 1,000 (this value is used to demonstrate the CLI configuration; it is not a design recommendation).

Figure 9.25 Configuring Service MTU for VPLS Service

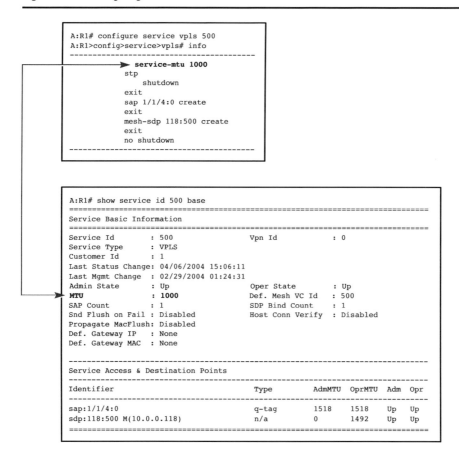

```
A:R1# configure service vpls 500
A:R1>config>service>vpls# info
-----------------------------------------
            service-mtu 1000
        stp
            shutdown
        exit
        sap 1/1/4:0 create
        exit
        mesh-sdp 118:500 create
        exit
        no shutdown
-----------------------------------------
```

```
A:R1# show service id 500 base
=======================================================================
Service Basic Information
=======================================================================
Service Id        : 500              Vpn Id          : 0
Service Type      : VPLS
Customer Id       : 1
Last Status Change: 04/06/2004 15:06:11
Last Mgmt Change  : 02/29/2004 01:24:31
Admin State       : Up               Oper State      : Up
MTU               : 1000             Def. Mesh VC Id : 500
SAP Count         : 1                SDP Bind Count  : 1
Snd Flush on Fail : Disabled         Host Conn Verify : Disabled
Propagate MacFlush: Disabled
Def. Gateway IP   : None
Def. Gateway MAC  : None


-----------------------------------------------------------------------
Service Access & Destination Points
-----------------------------------------------------------------------
Identifier                          Type     AdmMTU  OprMTU  Adm  Opr
-----------------------------------------------------------------------
sap:1/1/4:0                         q-tag    1518    1518    Up   Up
sdp:118:500 M(10.0.0.118)           n/a      0       1492    Up   Up
=======================================================================
```

For one end-to-end service, all member PE routers (two for VPWS services, or more for VPLS services) must have the same Service MTU. Otherwise, the pseudowire connecting the two PE routers for the service is not operational. This is because the pseudowire signaling among PE routers requires that both sides of the pseudowire have the same VC-MTU value. This value is calculated by subtracting 14 bytes from the Service MTU.

Virtual Circuit MTU (VC-MTU)

The VC-MTU defines the maximum packet payload size supported on a pseudowire. VC-MTU is not a configurable value. For any L2 service, the pseudowire VC-MTU is equal to the value of the Service MTU minus 14 bytes. The VC-MTU value is used for pseudowire signaling in IP/MPLS VPN services. The T-LDP Label Mapping message contains the Interface Parameter sub-TLV in the FEC TLV (0x128) with the VC-MTU value defined. Both ends of the pseudowire must have matching VC-MTU values for the pseudowire to be operational. When a pseudowire is signaled for a service, the VC-MTU is automatically calculated by subtracting 14 from the Service MTU. This value is carried in the T-LDP signaling message. Figure 9.26 illustrates the Label Mapping message and the output of the show router ldp bindings command.

Figure 9.26 VC-MTU in Service Pseudowire Signaling and CLI Display

```
A:R1#  show router ldp bindings
================================================================================
LDP LSR ID: 10.0.0.163
=== Output Omitted ===
LDP Service FEC 128 Bindings
================================================================================
Type    VCId   SvcId   SDPId   Peer          IngLbl    EgrLbl    LMTU   RMTU
--------------------------------------------------------------------------------
E-Eth   100    100     163     10.0.0.163    131062U   131067D   986    986
V-Eth   150    150     116     10.0.0.116    131052U   131071D   1500   1500
V-Eth   220    220     163     10.0.0.163    131057U   131065D   986    986
V-Eth   220    220     164     10.0.0.164    131064U   131063D   986    86
V-Eth   250    250     163     10.0.0.163    131056U   131064D   986    986
V-Eth   250    250     164     10.0.0.164    131063U   131060S   986    986
V-Eth   260    260     117     10.0.0.117    131069U   --        886    0
V-Eth   262    262     117     10.0.0.117    131066U   --        786    0
--- Output Omitted ---
--------------------------------------------------------------------------------
```

```
 4910 183.336847  10.0.0.118              10.0.0.163        LDP    Label
◄
 Generic Lay L or ser transmission control protocol, DST port 50041 (50041),
⊞ Internet Protocol, Src: 10.0.0.118 (10.0.0.118), Dst: 10.0.0.163 (10.0.0.163)
⊞ Transmission Control Protocol, Src Port: ldp (646), Dst Port: 50041 (50041),
⊟ Label Distribution Protocol
     Version: 1
     PDU Length: 54
     LSR ID: 10.0.0.118 (10.0.0.118)
     Label Space ID: 0
  ⊟ Label Mapping Message
        0... .... = U bit: unknown bit not set
        Message Type: Label Mapping Message (0x400)
        Message Length: 44
        Message ID: 0x0001949b
     ⊟ Forwarding Equivalence Classes TLV
        00.. .... = TLV Unknown bits: Known TLV, do not Forward (0x00)
        TLV Type: Forwarding Equivalence Classes TLV (0x100)
        TLV Length: 20
       ⊟ FEC Elements
         ⊟ FEC Element 1 VCID: 100
              FEC Element Type: Virtual Circuit FEC (128)
              0... .... = C-bit: Control Word NOT Present
              .000 0000 0000 0101 = VC Type: Ethernet (0x0005)
              VC Info Length: 12
              Group ID: 0
              VC ID: 100
            ⊟ Interface Parameter: MTU 986
                 ID: MTU (0x01)
                 Length: 4
                 MTU: 986  ◄───────────────── VC-MTU: MTU of
            ⊟ Interface Parameter: VCCV                    the pseudowire.
                 ID: VCCV (0x0c)                            In L2 VPN, VC-MTU =
                 Length: 4                                  service-MTU – 14 bytes
               ⊞ CC Type
               ⊞ CV Type
     ⊟ Generic Label TLV
        00.. .... = TLV Unknown bits: Known TLV, do not Forward (0x00)
        TLV Type: Generic Label TLV (0x200)
        TLV Length: 4
        Generic Label: 131070
     ⊟ Unknown TLV type (0x096A)
        10.. .... = TLV Unknown bits: Unknown TLV, do not Forward (0x02)
        TLV Type: Unknown TLV type (0x96A)
        TLV Length: 4
        TLV Value: 00000006
```

Use the CLI display commands to verify the VC-MTU pseudowire settings. In the ALSRP, the pseudowire VC-MTU is displayed by executing the command `show router ldp bindings`.

MTU Calculation and the Relationships among Different Types of MTUs

The previous section described six types of MTUs in a service network. For correct functioning of an IP/MPLS VPN service network, these MTUs must have the correct values assigned. Figure 9.27 illustrates the relationships that must be maintained between these MTU types.

Figure 9.27 illustrates several rules for configuring MTU values to ensure that all required service components operate properly. In the following rules, a Gigabit Ethernet port with null encapsulation is used as an example:

- The Network Port MTU must be configured to reflect the hardware limit of the link. Providing the value does not exceed the hardware limit, the best practice is to configure the Network Port MTU as large as possible to allow more services to share the same network port. The default MTU for Gigabit Ethernet is 9,212.

- When enabled, the LSP-Path MTU is derived from the network port MTU. In Figure 9.27, the value is 9,198.

- If manual configuration is desired, the SDP-Path MTU must be no greater than the network port MTU minus the frame overhead. By default, the SDP derives the Path MTU from the network port MTU. In Figure 9.27, the value is 9,190 $(9,212 - 14 - 8)$.

- For L2 services, the default Service MTU is 1,514. The VC-MTU is the Service MTU minus 14 bytes; therefore, the default VC-MTU is 1,500 bytes. In order to bind the pseudowire to it, the service can only use SDPs with a Path MTU no less than the value of its own Service MTU. In the example, the SDP-Path MTU of 9,190 can support the Service MTU of 1,514.

- The physical access port MTU must be no less than the Service MTU plus the customer encapsulation overhead. In this example, the Service MTU has the default value of 1,514. Assuming that the access port with SAPs for this service is a dot1q-encapsulated Ethernet port, the access port MTU should be no less than 1,518.

Figure 9.27 MTU Calculations and Their Relationships

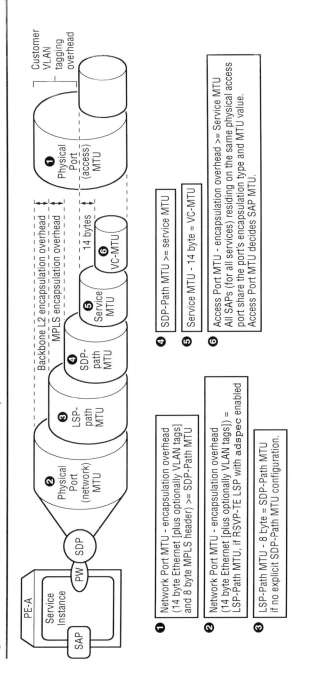

❶ Network Port MTU - encapsulation overhead (14 byte Ethernet [plus optionally VLAN tags] and 8 byte MPLS header) >= SDP-Path MTU

❷ Network Port MTU - encapsulation overhead (14 byte Ethernet [plus optionally VLAN tags]) = LSP-Path MTU, if RSVP-TE LSP with adspec enabled

❸ LSP-Path MTU - 8 byte = SDP-Path MTU if no explicit SDP-Path MTU configuration.

❹ SDP-Path MTU >= service MTU

❺ Service MTU - 14 byte = VC-MTU

❻ Access Port MTU - encapsulation overhead >= Service MTU All SAPs (for all services) residing on the same physical access port share the port's encapsulation type and MTU value. Access Port MTU decides SAP MTU.

From the service provider's perspective, there are two rules for calculating MTU:

1. The physical port MTU (access and network ports) must be configured correctly to reflect the capability of the physical link. The hardware may constrain a port MTU to a certain value. The physical perspective of the hardware must be respected.

2. The end-to-end service must provide a Service MTU value to support the value desired by the customer.

The first rule establishes a cap on the maximum MTUs that can be defined on a port. The second rule sets limits on the provider network to satisfy service customers. These rules also govern the setting of other MTU values. Table 9.10 illustrates the calculation of the minimum network port MTU required to support a 1,514-byte L2VPN Service MTU.

Table 9.10 Minimum Network Port MTU Value to Support a 1,514-Byte L2 Service MTU

Tunneling Techniques	POS Network Interface	Ethernet Network Interface
MPLS-encapsulated service tunnel	1,514 + 4 + 4 + 2 = 1,524 Encap-overhead = 10	1,514 + 4 + 4 + 14 = 1,536 Encap-overhead = 22
GRE-encapsulated service tunnel	1,514 + 4 + 4 + 20 + 2 = 1,544 Encap-overhead = 30	1,514 + 4 + 4 + 20 + 14 = 1,556 Encap-overhead = 42

MTUs must be calculated carefully when deploying a service. If there is a mismatch of MTUs, the service instance or the service entities will not be operational. Table 9.11 identifies possible MTU errors and how to address them.

Table 9.11 MTU Errors and Corrective Actions

MTU Error	Definition	Action
Service MTU mismatch	The two PE end nodes of the PW have mismatched Service MTUs.	Configure the same MTU on both ends of the PW.
Path MTU too small	The SDP-Path MTU is less than the Service MTU of the service. SDP binding will not become active, and if it is the only binding, the service will not activate.	Either increase the SDP-Path MTU or reduce the Service MTU.

MTU Error	Definition	Action
Port MTU too small	The SAP port MTU is less than the Service MTU. This will put the SAP in operationally down status.	Either increase the SAP access port MTU or reduce the Service MTU.

Figure 9.28 shows an example of MTU mismatch causing a SAP failure.

Figure 9.28   MTU Error Example: SAP Port's MTUs Are Too Small

Port MTU - encapsulation overhead >= service MTU
Example: Service-MTU is 1514 and the SAP uses a port with *dot1q*
Ethernet encapsulation. The access port's MTU must be at least 1518
(4 tag vlan-id overhead). Otherwise, the SAP won't become operationally up.

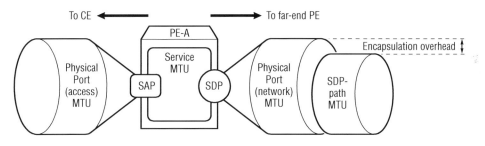

Port MTU - encapsulation overhead >= Service MTU
SDP-Path MTU >= Service MTU

```
A:PE-1# show service id 3000 sap 1/1/4:3000
===============================================================
Service Access Points (SAP)
===============================================================
Service Id          : 3000
SAP                 : 1/1/4:3000        Encap      : q-tag
Admin State         : UP                Oper State : Down
Flags               : PortMTUTooSmall
Multi Svc Site      : None
Last Status Change  : 08/05/2003 00:50:34
Last Mgmt Change    : 08/05/2003 00:50:27
===============================================================
```

```
A:PE-1# show service id 1000 sdp detail
-----------------------------------------------------------------
Sdp Id 117:1000  -(10.0.0.117)
-----------------------------------------------------------------
--- output omitted ---

Admin State        : UP                Oper State    : Down
--- output omitted ---
Endpoint           : N/A               Precedence    : 4
Class Fwding State : Down
Flags              : PathMTUTooSmall
Time to RetryReset : never             Retries Left  : 1406800
--- output omitted ---
```

Note: The default values used in these calculations are specific to the ALSRP. Other vendors may have their own default MTU values. For multi-vendor IP/MPLS VPN solutions, consult the related product manuals to ensure that the MTU values are consistent across the entire service. Alcatel-Lucent recommends setting the network port MTU and the SDP-Path MTU to a value greater than 9,000, or at least not less than 4,470 if it's allowed by the hardware.

The recommendation to configure the MTU as large as possible is only applicable in the network backbone-facing entities (for example, network port MTU, LSP MTU, or SDP MTU). For customer-facing SAPs, access ports, and Service MTUs, the configuration of MTU values should suit the customer's network characteristics. If customer sites have legacy equipment that only supports MTUs up to 1,514, the services (VPLS, Epipe) belonging to that customer should match the Service MTU and access port MTU values. Simply configuring large Service MTUs will not benefit the customer. Because SDPs are shared by multiple services, configuring the Path MTU as large as possible makes the SDP available to more services. Services will work on only the SDP that matches or exceed its MTU requirement. Using the minimum Service MTU (no less than the customer's requirement) provides more flexible choices.

Case Study: MTU Configuration

A network may contain several different types of physical connectivity, as illustrated earlier in Figure 9.22. In such a network, accepting the default values for all MTU configurations may result in service traffic being dropped. This case study examines the proper MTU settings in a network of mixed connectivity. Figure 9.29 illustrates the network topology containing a mix of Ethernet and radio links in the network backbone. Assume that all the Gigabit Ethernet ports are configured as network ports with null encapsulation. The SDP uses MPLS encapsulation and RSVP-TE LSP tunneling.

Figure 9.29 Case Study: Configuring Correct MTU Values

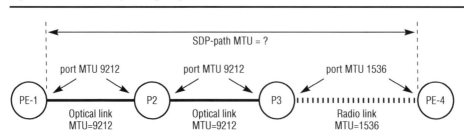

In this network, all network ports have a default port MTU of 9,212. Also, by default, the SDPs (one for each direction) between PE1 and PE4 have an SDP-Path MTU of 9,190 derived from the port MTU minus the frame and MPLS overhead. However, as shown in the dotted lines, the radio link between P3 and PE4 allows a maximum frame size of 1,536 bytes. This is less than the default port MTUs configured in the PE and P routers. If all MTUs remain set to their default values, the radio link may receive oversized frames and drop them. Properly configured MTUs will solve this potential problem.

The first step is to manually configure the MTUs of the Radio link facing network ports on P3 and PE4 to 1,536 to reflect the fact that the link allows a frame size of 1,536 bytes. As discussed earlier, the port MTU (access and network) should reflect the link's physical capacity.

With the new MTU settings on the network ports connected to the Radio link, the SDP from PE4 to PE1 adjusts the SDP-Path MTU to 1,514 bytes (1,536 – 22). However, the SDP from PE1 to PE4 still holds an MTU value of 9,212, based on the default Gigabit Ethernet MTU on PE1. Both SDPs are operational; however, different Path MTUs on SDP pairs is a suboptimal network design. To achieve proper design, the SDP in PE1 to PE4 must be configured with a Path MTU of 1,514.

Alternatively, since both SDPs use RSVP-TE LSPs, the LSPs can be configured to signal the LSP-Path MTU. Then, both SDPs will derive their Path MTU from their LSPs. Since the port MTUs in P3 and PE4 are configured to 1,536, the auto-negotiation of LSP-Path MTU calculates the value of 1,522 (1,536 – 14), using the lowest available MTU. Both SDPs now derive the same SDP-Path MTU value of 1,514 by subtracting 8 bytes from the LSP-Path MTU (1,522). The SDP-Path MTUs are adjusted automatically.

SDP MTU Discovery

In a large-scale network, it is time-consuming to manually configure port MTUs. The ALSRP provides a tool to automatically discover the proper SDP-Path MTU value after the SDPs are configured. By executing the oam sdp-mtu <sdp-id> size-inc <start-value> <end-value> step <setp> command, the system finds the proper MTU value for the SDP by testing the MTU values in the range. Figure 9.30 illustrates the SDP MTU discovery process.

Figure 9.30 SDP MTU Discovery

```
A:R1# oam sdp-mtu
  - sdp-mtu <orig-sdp-id> size-inc <start-octets> <end-octets>
[step <step-size>] [timeout <timeout>] [interval <interval>]

 <orig-sdp-id>        : [1..17407]
 <octets>             : start-octets [40..9198]
                        end-octets [40..9198]
 <step-size>          : [1..512]
 <timeout>            : [1..10] seconds
 <interval>           : [1..10] seconds

A:R1# oam sdp-mtu 164 size-inc 996 1002 step 2
Size    Sent    Response
--------------------------
996     .       Success
998     .       Success
1000    .       Success
1002    ...     Request Timeout
Maximum Response Size: 1000
A:R1#
```

In Figure 9.30, the CLI output shows that the maximum response frame size is 1,000 bytes. Based on this result, the maximum SDP-Path MTU for SDP 164 in Router R1 is 1,000.

9.7 IP/MPLS VPN Service Implementation Overview

The task of deploying an IP/MPLS VPN-based network is a complex one. An IP/MPLS VPN network contains many layers or building blocks, and each one requires provisioning and testing. The sequence of network provisioning and troubleshooting is also very important. Table 9.12 describes a recommended procedure for building a complex network.

Table 9.12 IP/MPLS VPN Service Implementation Steps

Step	Task	Note
1	Network design[a]	A good network design with proper documentation is mandatory for building a large network. In this book, we only discuss service deployment. The following considerations are also important:
		• Number and type of required services, as well as their characteristics (convergence, bandwidth, QoS, billing)
		• Network topology (ring, mesh, partial mesh)
		• Service topology (flat, redundant, hierarchical)
		• Service technology (MPLS, APS, LAG)

Step	Task	Note
2	Physical infrastructure	Configure the basic hardware and physical ports, links, and LAG groups. Ensure that all ports are operationally stable. All L1/L2 protocols (TDM, LAG, APS) should be in their correct states. Ensure that all ports are in the correct mode (network or access). Deploy L1/L2 features such as BFD or EFM OAM in this stage if possible.
3	IP routing infrastructure	Configure the IP addressing and routing for the network backbone. The IGP establishes the reachability of the P and PE routers across the backbone. Enable traffic engineering when necessary. If BGP is required, configure it at this stage. A complete and stable core IGP is a prerequisite for deploying MPLS.
4	MPLS infrastructure	If MPLS is desired, configure the necessary protocols such as LDP and RSVP-TE. If RSVP-TE LSP is desired, the LSPs must be configured manually. Enable features such as FRR and secondary LSP. Ensure that the LSPs are operational and the desired protection is set.
5	Service infrastructure	The service infrastructure includes the configuration of SDPs between PE routers and the establishment of T-LDP sessions. If there are VPRN services required, configure the MP-BGP configuration.
6	Deploy service	Once the service infrastructure is established and tested, the service can be provisioned as follows: • Configure all necessary customers, subscribers, or customer sites. • Configure all service instances in the PE routers that participate in the same service. • Configure all necessary SAPs and pseudowires. • Configure all necessary service entity policies (QoS, security, accounting).
7	OAM, troubleshooting	After deploying the service, the network is ready to serve customers. OAM and troubleshooting tools may be used to monitor and troubleshoot the services.

[a]Network design is a complex process. This section provides only basic insight and is not a complete design guideline.

Summary

IP/MPLS VPN networks are flexible, reliable, and cost-efficient and are used by service providers to provide various types of services to many customers through a single converged backbone infrastructure. The ALSRP implements an IP/MPLS VPN service solution and offers various types of services including IES, L2VPN (VPLS and VPWS), and VPRN. In the ALSRP service architecture, there are six types of service entities: customer, service instance, SAP, pseudowire, SDP and multi-service site.

A service network is composed of routers in the roles of Provider Edge (PE) and Provider (P). The SAP is the PE router's customer-facing service entity. It connects customers though the attachment circuit and handles native customer traffic. The SDP contains transport tunnel(s) connecting PE routers through the provider's network backbone. The use of tunneling technology hides the detailed backbone topology and reduces the service deployment complexity. Service instances in the member PE routers participating in the same service are connected by pseudowires over the SDPs.

Because the IP/MPLS VPN uses MPLS technology to encapsulate customer traffic before carrying the traffic through the network backbone, the MTU in each network segment (SAP, SDP) must be calculated and configured properly.

Deploying an IP/MPLS VPN is a complex task that requires network design prior to service implementation. It is important to adhere to proper procedures and to develop accurate documentation in order to successfully deploy an IP/MPLS VPN service.

Virtual Leased Line Services

10

This chapter discusses the point-to-point Layer 2 Virtual Private Network (VPN) services based on Internet Protocol/Multi Protocol Label Switching VPN (IP/MPLS VPN) Service Routing architecture — the Virtual Leased Line (VLL) services.

Chapter Objectives

- Introduce the VLL services and the use of various types of pseudowire-based services in VLL

- Explain the architecture of VLL services including the components of VLL services, the signaling process to establish these services, and the Pseudowire Status Notification used to maintain the pseudowires

- Discuss the use of pseudowire switching to relay VLL traffic from one terminating PE (T-PE) router to another

- Introduce the Ethernet VLL and other point-to-point VLL services: Epipe, Apipe, Fpipe, and Ipipe

VLL forwards customer traffic between two Service Access Points (SAPs) of the service. Because the service requires point-to-point forwarding, address learning and forwarding decision-making are not required. The service behaves like a *wire* between the two customer sites. Therefore, the VLL service is also referred to as *Virtual Private Wire Service* (VPWS). The VLL service can be local, where two SAPs reside on the same PE router, or distributed, which involves two service instances in two PE routers, connected by an MPLS pseudowire.

10.1 VLL Services Overview

This section introduces the Virtual Leased Line services provided by the ALSRP based on the IP/MPLS VPN architecture. The overall VLL common infrastructure and various types of VLL services are presented.

VLL Common Infrastructure

VLL services are point-to-point services providing connections using IP/MPLS VPN tunnels between two customer sites across the provider's IP/MPLS VPN backbone. VLL services use pseudowires to connect two PE router's service instances together, to provide customers with point-to-point VPN services. Customers use *native* format (original traffic type) attachment circuits to connect to the provider's PE routers. Regardless of the type of VLL services, from the customer's perspective, the service provider's network acts as a wire connecting two customer sites.

All VLL services share a common IP/MPLS VPN infrastructure. This common infrastructure is the *PWE3 reference model* (RFC 4447), introduced in Chapter 9. Various types of services differ only in the access technology they provide at the SAPs connecting the customers (for example, ATM, Ethernet, Frame-Relay, TDM), and the way the native service packets are adapted into the common pseudowire encapsulation.

Every VLL service is *point-to-point*; it uses two Service Access Points (SAPs) to connect the customer sites. A SAP is also referred to as an *attachment circuit* (AC). As discussed in Chapter 9, a VPN service can be either *local* or *distributed*. This also applies to the VLL service. Figure 10.1 illustrates the local VLL and distributed VLL services.

Figure 10.1 Local VLL Service versus Distributed VLL Service

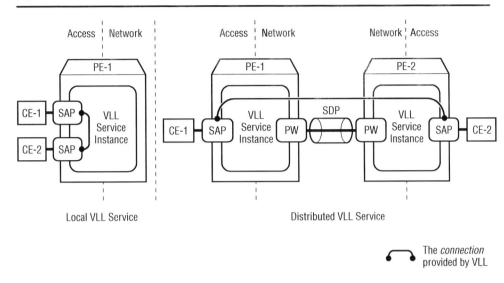

Local VLL Service   Distributed VLL Service

The *connection* provided by VLL

In a local VLL service, both customer attachment circuits are connected to one PE router in the provider's network. Therefore, all that is required to provide the service is one *service instance* in a single PE router containing two SAPs. In local VLL services, the traffic between two SAPs is locally switched. Traffic arriving from one SAP is sent to another SAP locally in the same PE router. Therefore, there is no MPLS pseudowire involved. The traffic comes into the PE router from SAP1-ingress; the PE router forwards it to the switching fabric and then to the other customer site through SAP2-egress.The returning traffic follows the opposite path back. Since pseudowire is not required, IP/MPLS VPN infrastructure such as IGP routing protocols and MPLS signaling protocols are not required.

In a distributed VLL service, the two SAPs connecting the two customer sites are located in different PE routers. Therefore, two PE routers participate in this service. Each PE router must have a service instance with one SAP connected to the locally attached customer site. The two PE routers also need a pseudowire to connect to each other to encapsulate the native service packets over the IP/MPLS infrastructure. The customer traffic ingress to one SAP is VPN-encapsulated and sends the pre-established pseudowire (PW) to the remote PE router. Then the remote PE router performs de-encapsulation on the VPN traffic and sends the traffic via its SAP-egress to the locally attached customer site.

Because the distributed VLL service requires traffic delivery through the backbone network, the IP/MPLS VPN infrastructure must be in place before the VLL service can be deployed. This infrastructure has the following requirements:

- P and PE routers in the provider's network must be connected through stable links (physical infrastructure).

- IGP should be functioning in the backbone network so that all the PE routers and all the P routers in the backbone network can reach each other. Alternatively, static routes can be configured to ensure Layer 3 reachability.

- If an MPLS transport tunnel is required, the MPLS label distribution protocol and signaling protocol must be provisioned and functioning (for example, LDP, RSVP-TE).

- The service architecture must be built and operationally up. PE routers need operational SDPs connecting the required remote PE routers.

- VPN signaling infrastructure must be established and functioning. T-LDP sessions must be established among all the PE routers involved in distributed VLL services. Alternatively, a static vc-label can be configured in each PE router to establish VPN traffic encapsulation.

When these prerequisites are met, VLL services can be configured in the PE routers and can pass customer traffic.

Point-to-Point versus Multipoint-to-Multipoint VPN Services

A significant difference between the point-to-point VPN services (VLL) and multipoint-to-multipoint services (VPLS or VPRN) occurs with respect to the *forwarding decision*. The forwarding decision in point-to-point VPN services is very simple and straightforward. With only two SAPs in the service, when the traffic arrives from one SAP, the forwarding decision is simple: *If the traffic is legitimate, forward it to another SAP; if the traffic is not legitimate, discard it.* Whether the traffic is legitimate is decided by examining the traffic's encapsulation type/value against the SAP encapsulation configuration, and applying filters to the traffic if there is any. If the traffic passes the examination and is allowed to the filter, the traffic is considered as legitimate and is forwarded; otherwise, the traffic is discarded. It is not necessary to specify the destination or whether the service should *flood* the traffic to multiple destinations or *forward* the traffic to a single destination. There is only one destination. Because there is no choice of destination, it is not necessary to build a forwarding database (FDB) for each possible destination to help make the forwarding decision, and the process of learning addresses is not required.

In general, VLL services consume fewer resources (for example, memory and CPU horsepower) in the PE router than multipoint services like VPLS and VPRN. Because fewer resources are required, more services can be configured. Thus, VLL service has a higher scaling limit per PE router. On the other hand, if a customer requires that multiple sites (destinations) be connected, using VLL to provide the service may require more service instances to be deployed to achieve the connectivity required.

Epipe is a point-to-point Ethernet service that bridges traffic between two customer sites, whereas *VPLS* is a multipoint-to-multipoint Ethernet service bridging traffic between two or more customer sites. Both VPLS and Epipe are Ethernet Layer 2 VPN services. Because Epipe contains only two Ethernet SAPs, it carries traffic only between the two SAPs. The traffic validation and classification is performed by comparing the SAP encapsulation type/value with the ingress traffic's tagging (this concept is introduced later in this chapter). If the Epipe service is used to connect two sites with 10,000 Ethernet flows between them, the Epipe service simply forwards traffic between the two sites.

Alternatively, a VPLS service with two SAPs can be created for this connectivity requirement.

Note: VPLS is introduced in Chapters 11 and 12. VPLS can also forward the traffic between the two customer sites. However, VPLS performs FDB learning and makes forwarding decisions based on the MAC entries in its FDB. If there are 10,000 Ethernet flows between two customer sites, VPLS must build an FDB with 10,000 entries of source MAC/bridge port mappings on both PE routers involved (this assumes that the service is distributed). In this case, VPLS service meets the same connectivity requirement as the Epipe, but consumes a much greater amount of system resources.

VLL Services Types

VLL services can be categorized with respect to service types. These service types are based on the type of native traffic formats the services provide to customers. Table 10.1 lists the VLL service types.

Table 10.1 VLL Service Types

Service Types	Service Description
IP VLL (Ipipe)	IP pseudowire service (Ipipe) provides IP connectivity between a host attached to a point-to-point access circuit (FR, ATM, PPP) with routed PDU IPv4 encapsulation, and a host attached to an Ethernet interface. It can provide point-to-point connectivity between any of the SAP types. Both hosts appear on the same LAN segment. This feature enables service interworking between different link layer technologies.
Ethernet VLL (Epipe)	An Ethernet VLL (Epipe) service is a Layer 2 point-to-point service wherein the customer data is encapsulated and transported across a service provider's IP, MPLS, or PBB VPLS network. An Epipe service is completely transparent to the subscriber's data and protocols.
ATM VLL (Apipe)	ATM VLL (Apipe) provides a point-to-point ATM (cell-based and/or AAL-5 based) service between users connected to service routers on an IP/MPLS network. An ATM PVC [for example, a Virtual Channel (VC) or a Virtual Path (VP)] is configured on the service router. VPI/VCI translation is supported in the ATM VLL.
Frame Relay VLL (Fpipe)	Frame-Relay VLL (Fpipe) provides a point-to-point Frame-Relay service between users connected to service router (SR) nodes on the IP/MPLS network. Users are connected to the service router using Frame-Relay PVCs.
Circuit Emulation VLL (Cpipe)	The Circuit Emulation Service (Cpipe) provides a point-to-point TDM service between users over the IP/MPLS network. Two modes of circuit emulation are supported, unstructured (SAToP, RFC 4053) and structured (CESoPSN, RFC 5086). The unstructured mode is supported for DS1 and E1 channels. The structured mode is supported for $n * 64$-kbps circuits. In addition, CES over Ethernet, DS1, E1, and $n * 64$-kbps circuits are supported (as per MEF8).

All of these service types use the same IP/MPLS VPN architecture — one pseudowire to connect two PE routers and each PE router having a service instance with a local SAP. This common architecture is discussed in the following section. The characteristics of different service types and their SAPs are introduced in later sections.

10.2 VLL Services Architecture

This section introduces the common architecture of all VLL services. Ethernet VLL (Epipe) is used as the study example. The topics discussed in this section include:

- VLL service components

- VLL service pseudowire establishment
- Signaling pseudowire status in VLL services using T-LDP

The various types of SAPs used are introduced in later sections.

VLL Service Components

In VLL service deployment, the required components include:

- A common IP/MPLS VPN service infrastructure in the backbone that is shared by all services
- Two PE routers, each with a service instance created for the VLL, including:
  - Common service instance parameters such as service-id, vc-id, and service-MTU
  - A SAP connected to the local customer site through the attachment circuit
  - A pseudowire connected to the remote member PE router's service instance and belonging to the same end-to-end VLL service

In a distributed VLL service, the IP/MPLS VPN infrastructure must be built with the following requirements before any configuration takes place:

- The PE and P routers should be fully reachable via the core IGP. If desired, deploy resiliency features such as Bidirectional Forwarding Detection (BFD) on specific IP interfaces and Ethernet for the First Mile (EFM) Operation, Administration, and Maintenance (OAM) on specific links. If RSVP-TE LSP is used, configure the MPLS and RSVP with the IGP traffic engineering (TE) extensions.
- Build the MPLS LSPs among PE routers. If desired, deploy MPLS resiliency features such as Fast Reroute (FRR) or secondary LSP on the MPLS LSPs.
- Deploy SDPs among PE routers with appropriate tunneling technology (LDP-LSP, RSVP-TE LSP, or GRE). Enable the appropriate signaling method and corresponding parameters' settings.
- Build the T-LDP sessions among the PE routers for the pseudowire signaling (T-LDP sessions are automatically created whenever SDPs are built, as discussed in Chapter 9).

Once the IP/MPLS VPN infrastructure is built, you can configure the two PE routers' service instances with related components. Figure 10.2 presents a network with two PE routers connected through a core of P routers, providing an Epipe service to the customer. In this example network, RSVP-TE LSP with Fast Reroute is used for traffic tunneling in the backbone.

Figure 10.2 VLL Service Configuration Example

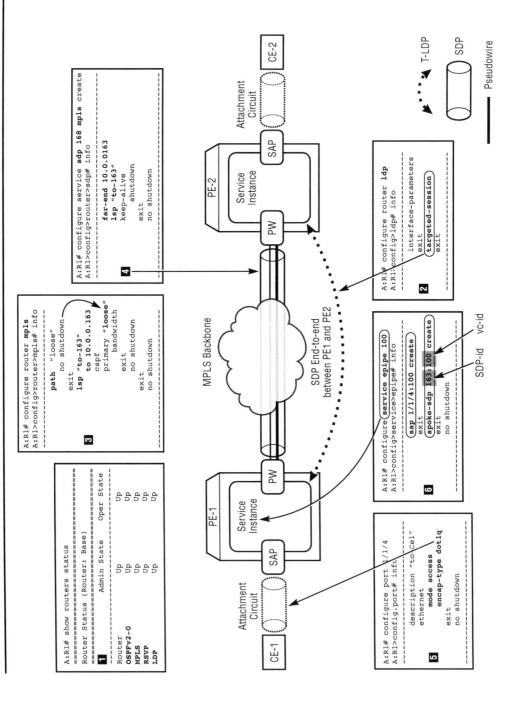

In this example, routers PE-1 and PE-2 have Epipe 100 configured to connect Customers CE-1 and CE-2 (see Step 6 in Figure 10.2). Figure 10.2 illustrates the following service components:

1. The PE and P routers have OSPF, MPLS, and RSVP routing instances configured with all interfaces using these protocols.

2. T-LDP session is established between the two PE routers for VLL pseudowire signaling.

3. An RSVP-TE LSP is created from PE-1 to PE-2 (an LSP from PE-2 to PE-1 is also created but not shown in Figure 10.2).

4. The SDP to reach PE-2 is created in PE-1 using the LSP previously created in Step 3. (Note that PE-2 also has an SDP created to PE-1 but this is not shown in the figure.)

5. The ports connected to the CE equipments should be configured as `access` mode.

6. The Epipe service 100 is created with one SAP containing the attachment circuit, and a pseudowire bound to the previously created SDP. Both PE routers have the service instances configured. However, only PE-1's configuration is shown in Figure 10.2.

> **Note:** In this example configuration, by default, the service uses service-id 100; therefore, the pseudowire is created using the command `spoke-sdp 163:100 create`. This command binds the pseudowire to a specific SDP (in this example, sdp-id 163). The action of binding a pseudowire to an SDP has two perspectives:
>
> - From the control plane's perspective, the vc-label used by the pseudowire is signaled through the T-LDP session to the far-end address of the SDP to which it binds.
>
> - From the data plane's perspective, the pseudowire uses the SDP it binds to as a service transport tunnel to carry the traffic for the service.

There are two different ways of binding a pseudowire to an SDP: spoke-binding or mesh-binding. The terms *spoke* or *mesh* refer to whether the service instance allows its multiple pseudowires to exchange traffic among them. For VLL services, only spoke-binding of a pseudowire to an SDP is allowed. The VPLS service instance allows binding to pseudowires via mesh-binding using the command `mesh-sdp <sdp-id>:<vc-id>`. The difference between mesh-pseudowire and spoke-pseudowire is explained in Chapter 12.

In Figure 10.2's example, the vc-id is the unique identifier of the pseudowire between PE-1 and PE-2 (see Item 6 in Figure 10.2). As explained in Chapter 9, the vc-id must be the same (numerically equal in value) on both sides of the pseudowire. To ensure that the pseudowire becomes operational, the two PE routers must use the same vc-id value in the spoke-sdp <sdp-id>:<vc-id> command.

Pseudowire Establishment Using T-LDP Messages

After the two service instances are configured and administratively enabled on both PE routers, the pseudowire establishment process begins. The two PE routers use the T-LDP session to negotiate the pseudowire for the service. Both routers send *LDP Label Mapping* messages to establish the pseudowire. In LDP pseudowire messaging, the pseudowire is called a *Virtual Circuit* (VC). The Label Mapping message contains the following information:

- An FEC TLV (0x100) with FEC-element sub-TLV (0x128) specifies the type of service-instance-related information. The FEC TLV is a mandatory TLV required for pseudowire establishment. If an operator changes any of the parameters in this TLV, the pseudowire has to be torn down and re-established. The FEC TLV contains the following elements:

  - vc-type — The type of the pseudowire. Each VLL service type requires different pseudowire types, which are specified in the vc-type field. The vc-type defined on both PE routers' pseudowire configurations must match for the pseudowire to come operationally **up**. The pseudowire types are listed in Table 10.2.

  - vc-id — The pseudowire identifier. The vc-id defined on both PE routers' pseudowire configurations must match for the pseudowire to come operationally **up**.

  - Interface Parameter — The interfaces-related parameters. The content of the interface parameter TLV differs based on the type of the pseudowire. One important parameter is the vc-MTU (maximum transfer unit) — the pseudowire's MTU. The vc-MTUs defined on both PE routers' pseudowire configuration must match for the pseudowire to come operationally up. The vc-mtu's value represents the service-mtu configured in the service minus the Layer 2 overhead. The earlier example of Epipe used the default service-mtu of 1,514 bytes and its Ethernet service. The vc-MTU was 1,514 – 14 = 1,500. The Ethernet header (Layer 2 overhead) was subtracted from the service-mtu.

- A Generic Label TLV (0x200) distributes the vc-label to the remote PE router. The local PE router uses this label as an *ingress label* to perform VPN de-encapsulation on received packets. The remote PE router uses this label as an *egress label* to perform VPN encapsulation on the forwarded pseudowire packets.

- An optional Pseudowire Status TLV (0x96A). The PW-Status TLV has two purposes:

  - Performs PW-Status capability negotiation. This concept is introduced in a later section.

  - Indicates the current status of the pseudowire and the attachment circuit.

Table 10.2   Pseudowire Type (vc-type) for T-LDP Signaling (from RFC 4446)

PW Type Value	PW Type	Description
0x0002	Apipe, ATM-sdu	ATM AAL5 SDU VCC transport
0x0003	Apipe, ATM-cell	ATM transparent cell transport
0x0004	Epipe, Ether-type VC	Ethernet Tagged Mode (VC type: VLAN)
0x0005	Epipe, Ether-type Ether	Ethernet Raw Mode (VC type: Ethernet)
0x0009	Apipe, ATM-vcc	ATM n-to-one VCC cell transport
0x000a	Apipe, ATM-vpc	ATM n-to-one VPC cell transport
0x000B	Ipipe	IP Layer 2 Transport
0x0011	Cpipe, satop-e1	Structure-agnostic E1 over Packet (SAToP)
0x0012	Cpipe, satop-t1	Structure-agnostic T1 (DS1) over Packet (SAToP)
0x0015	Cpipe, cesopsn	CESoPSN basic mode
0x0017	Cpipe, cesopsn-cas	CESoPSN TDM with CAS
0x0019	Fpipe	Frame-Relay DLCI

Figure 10.3 illustrates the process to establish a pseudowire using T-LDP signaling. The service instances in both PE routers are operationally up, and their SAPs are operationally up. When the pseudowire is established between the two service instances, after both the pseudowire and the SAPs become operationally up, the service will come up and is ready to forward traffic.

Figure 10.3   Pseudowire Establishment between Two PE Routers

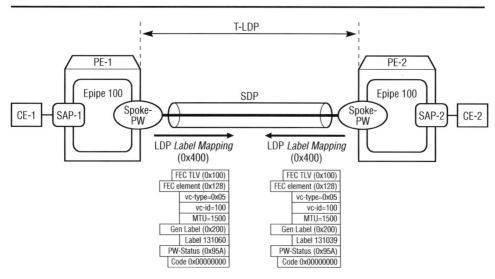

❶ IN PE-1, the Epipe 100 is first configured and enabled. Then, the spoke-pseudowire is configured. PE-1 assigns a vc-label (131060) and distributes it to PE-2. The PW-Status TLV has code (0x00000000).

❷ IN PE-2, the Epipe 100 is first configured and enabled. Then, the spoke-pseudowire is configured. PE-2 assigns a vc-label (131039) and distributes it to PE-1. The PW-Status TLV has code (0x00000000).

After the service Epipe 100 is configured and administratively enabled on both PE routers and the pseudowire signaling process is completed, the service status can be checked using the show service id <service-id> base command. Figure 10.4

illustrates the CLI output of the service status display at this stage. The service instance in PE-1 is operationally **up**, and the SAP and the service's pseudowire are also operationally **up**.

Figure 10.4   Service Status Display

```
A:R1#  show service id 100 base
================================================================================
Service Basic Information
================================================================================
Service Id          : 100             Vpn Id        : 0
Service Type        : Epipe
Customer Id         : 1
Last Status Change: 08/17/2003 01:16:12
Last Mgmt Change  : 08/29/2003 01:55:26
Admin State         : Up              Oper State    : Up
MTU                 : 1500
Vc Switching        : False
SAP Count           : 1               SDP Bind Count   : 1
--------------------------------------------------------------------------------
Service Access & Destination Points
--------------------------------------------------------------------------------
Identifier                           Type      AdmMTU  OprMTU  Adm Opr
--------------------------------------------------------------------------------
sap:1/1/4:100                        q-tag     1518    1518    Up  Up
sdp:163:100 S(10.0.0.163)            n/a       0       1492    Up  Up
================================================================================
```

Pseudowire Status Signaling

In distributed VLL services, two PE routers are involved, each with one service instance created for the VLL service. Each service instance contains one SAP and one pseudowire. The SAP is connected to the customer site and the pseudowire is connected to the remote PE router. For the VLL service to function end-to-end, both routers and all the components in their service instances must be operationally **up**. If any component fails, the VLL cannot forward traffic for customers.

Figure 10.5 illustrates a local SAP failure in PE-1. In this example, if there is a local failure on the SAP-1 in PE-1's Epipe100 service, the service instance and the pseudowire are still **up** and functioning. If router PE-2 continues sending traffic received from CE-2 to PE-1 over the pseudowire, PE-1 will drop the traffic in the service instance because its local SAP is not operationally **up**. In this scenario, the bandwidth between PE-1 and PE-2 is wasted because CE-2 is not made aware of the failure.

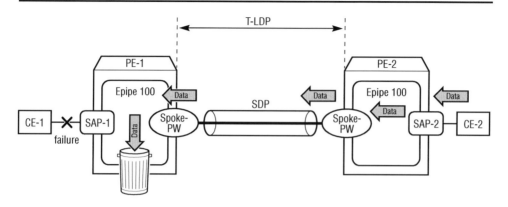

Therefore, when a PE router has any local failure on the attachment circuit or the pseudowire of a VLL service instance, it should notify the remote router that is participating in the same VLL service. The remote PE router can then translate the notification into an OAM message and propagate it to the remote CE device. The remote CE device (CE-2) will therefore stop sending the traffic to the remote PE (PE-2). When the failure is fixed, the local PE router should notify the remote router to restore the traffic flow. The failure triggers a notification to the service instance that there is an SAP failure, pseudowire failure, or an internal service instance failure. This notification is called *pseudowire status notification*. T-LDP is used to set up pseudowires for the service instances of two connected PE routers; T-LDP is also used for pseudowire status notification.

There are two methods to stop the remote router's traffic when there is a local failure in the local PE router:

- The PE router can send an LDP *Label Withdraw* message to the remote PE router notifying it to tear down the pseudowire. This method tears down the pseudowire when there is a failure, and it requires a pseudowire re-establishment when the local failure is removed. The label is withdrawn for the direction affected by the fault. It is possible that only one label is withdrawn. However, the PE that lost its egress label will drop packets received from the SAP. If the fault is repaired, only one label needs to be sent, not both labels of the pseudowire. After the pseudowire label has been withdrawn, the PE router stops sending the traffic to the backbone network. This is less efficient and is only used when the remote PE router does not support the pseudowire status notification method.

- The PE router can send an LDP *Notification* message to the remote PE router to report the failure. This method requires the use of a new LDP messaging TLV PW-Status TLV (0x96A), which indicates the failure to the remote PE router via a *status code*. The purpose of the Pseudowire Status Notification is to have the fault reported all the way to the remote CE so that it can stop forwarding traffic without having to cause the churn of withdrawing and resignaling the pseudowire labels.

When the local router sends the Label Mapping message to the remote PE to set up the pseudowire for the VLL service, the PW-Status TLV (0x096A) is appended at the end of message. The PW-Status TLV's I bit (Ignore) is set to 1. This indicates that if the receiver does not support this TLV, it should silently ignore the TLV. If the remote PE router supports the PW-Status TLV, it will also append the TLV to its Label Mapping message when setting up the reverse-direction pseudowire. In this manner, the two routers agree to use PW-Status TLV in this pseudowire. The status of the pseudowire is initially decided by the PW-Status TLV in the Label Mapping message and is updated later in the LDP Notification message through the PW-Status TLV. Figure 10.6 illustrates a Notification message with PW-Status TLV.

Figure 10.6 LDP Notification Messages Used for PW-Status Notification and PW-Status TLV

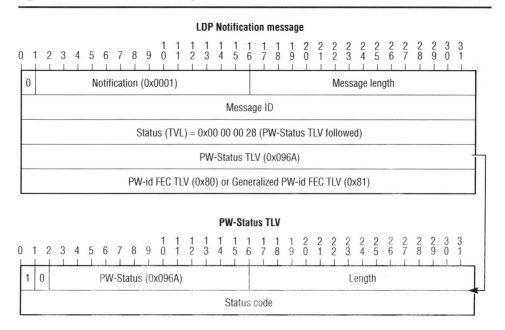

When the LDP Notification message is used for PW-Status signaling, the PW-Status TLV must be followed by an FEC TLV with either a PW-id (regular VPLS pseudowire), or a G-PW-id (BGP-AD-created pseudowire). The PW-Status indicates the status of the pseudowire or the attachment circuit, while the FEC TLV indicates the specific service.

If one of the PE routers does not support the PW-Status TLV, the router ignores the TLV in the receiving Label Mapping message and uses a Label Mapping message without the PW-Status TLV. Two PE routers signal the pseudowire independently. The peering PE router recognizes that the far-end PE router does not support this method and reverts back to the legacy Label Withdraw method.

If both PE routers in the VLL service recognize the PW-Status TLV in the Label Mapping messages received from each other, the LDP Notification message with the PW-Status TLV is used to notify each PE router of the status change of the pseudowire and service. Each time a PE router receives a PW-Status TLV in either the Label Mapping message or the Notification message, it stores the status code as Peer PW Bits in the local database.

A significant benefit of using PW-Status Notification instead of Label Withdraw messages to tear down the pseudowire is increased signaling efficiency. The pseudowire and corresponding vc-label are constantly available. When the fault entity recovers, the PE router must only send status notification to the remote PE router to clear the Peer PW bits so that CE-2 will exit the alarm state and restore the traffic. This is not a large signaling burden if there are only one or two services. However, when many VLLs share the same physical port and the port has a failure, all services will have SAP failures. The signaling burden is significant if all service instances must tear down the pseudowires and then set up the pseudowires again after the failure is removed from the port. Therefore, it is more efficient to use PW-Status Notification instead of Label Withdraw messages to tear down the pseudowire.

In the ALSRP, when spoke-pseudowires are used, the routers always try to negotiate the PW-Status Notification capability with the peering PE routers. All VLL services use spoke-pseudowires exclusively. This is a system default behavior and cannot be overridden. VPLS and its use of mesh-pseudowire are introduced in Chapter 11.

Figure 10.7 illustrates the Status Notification process on a previously active VLL service showing the Epipe service established between PE-1 and PE-2.

Figure 10.7 SAP Failure with Pseudowire Status Notification

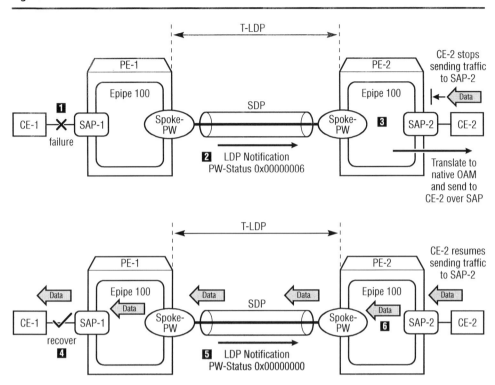

During the pseudowire set-up process, both routers see the PW-Status TLV in the received Label Mapping message; both routers recognize that the remote PE has the PW-Status Notification capability. When there is any failure in the service instance, the local PE notifies the remote PE by sending the Notification message. The pseudowire status notification in Figure 10.7 proceeds as follows (the list numbers refer to the numbered steps in the figure):

1. PE-1 detects a failure in SAP-1 and the SAP is operationally down.

2. PE-1 sends the LDP Notification message containing the PW-Status TLV with the error code (0x00000006). This contains both the SAP-ingress fault (0x00000002) and the SAP-egress fault (0x00000004).

3. When PE-2 receives the Notification message, it sets the Peer PW bits flag on the pseudowire. PE-2 translates this pseudowire status TLV Notification to CE-2 using the native service OAM if supported. CE-2 therefore stops sending traffic to PE-2 through the attachment circuit.

4. PE-1's SAP failure is removed and the SAP is operationally up.

5. PE-1 sends another LDP notification containing PW-Status TLV with the error code (0x000000000). This indicates that all errors are cleared and the pseudowire is forwarding traffic.

6. When PE-2 receives the message with an all-zero error code, it clears the peer PW bits flag and stops the fault notification to the CE-2 over the attachment circuits. CE-2 then exits the fault alarm and starts forwarding traffic to PE-2 again.

Figure 10.8 illustrates another example of a manual shutdown of service instance Epipe 100, but with the failure and recovery occurring within PE-1 instead of outside. An LDP Notification message is sent with a status code of 0x00000016.This code is the summary of the following error codes:

- 0x00000002 — SAP-ingress failure
- 0x00000004 — SAP-egress failure
- 0x00000010 — Pseudowire (egress) transmit fault

The failure and failure-cleared Notifications use the same process as the previous example.

The status code in the PW-Status TLV indicates the status of the pseudowire and the corresponding attachment circuit. During the pseudowire establishment, the PW-Status is signaled in the Label Mapping message. After the pseudowire is established, each time there is a status change in the SAP, pseudowire, or service instance, the PE router sends a notification with certain status codes. The receiving PE router stores these status codes as Peer PW bits. Table 10.3 provides a description for each PW-Status code.

Table 10.3 Pseudowire Status Codes for PW-Status Signaling

Value	Description
0x00000000	Pseudowire forwarding (All faults are cleared; PW operates normally.)
0x00000001	Pseudowire not forwarding (MTU issue, block-mesh problems)
0x00000002	SAP (ingress) receives fault.
0x00000004	SAP (egress) transmits fault.
0x00000008	SDP-binding (ingress) receives fault (SDP failure).
0x00000010	SDP-binding (egress) transmits fault (SDP failure).
0x00000020	Pseudowire forwarding standby (used for dual-homing MTU to indicate backup PW)

Figure 10.8 Service Disabled with Pseudowire Status Notification

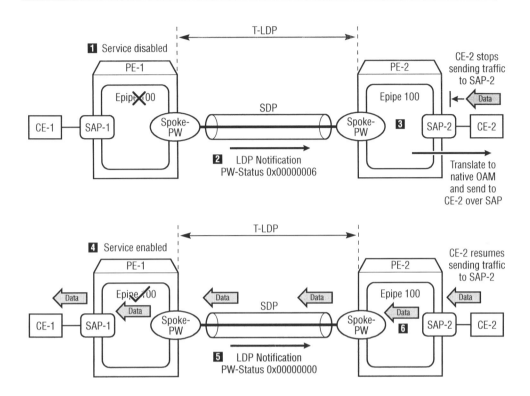

If there is more than one service object failure, all the failures are presented in the error code when the remote PE router sends the corresponding bits. For example, the following error codes are sent for the respective type of failure:

- **SAP Failure** — 0x00000006 = 0x000002 (SAP-ingress fault) + 0x00000004 (SAP-egress fault).
- **Pseudowire Failure** — 0x00000018 = 0x00000008 (PW-ingress fault) + 0x00000010 (PW-egress fault).

Tear Down the Pseudowire

When a pseudowire in a VLL service instance is administratively shut down, the PE router sends an LDP *Label Withdraw* message to the remote PE router indicating that it should withdraw the pre-signaled vc-label. The remote PE router responds with an LDP *Label Release* message that confirms the label removal. Figure 10.9 illustrates this behavior.

Figure 10.9 Signaling Process for Tearing Down the Pseudowire

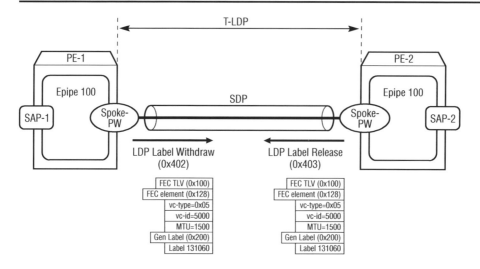

1 IN PE-1, the pseudowire is administratively disabled by a shutdown command. A Label Withdraw message is sent to the remote PE to tear down the pseudowire.

2 When PE-2 receives the Label Withdraw message, it responds with a Label Release to confirm the teardown of the pseudowire.

The remote PE router also sends the local PE router a Label Withdraw message to withdraw the vc-label. This vc-label Withdraw message specifies that the PE router should tear down the pseudowire in the reverse direction (this message is not shown in Figure 10.9). The local PE router sends the Label Release message to confirm the label removal. The two pseudowires are then torn down from the network.

10.3 Pseudowire Switching for VLL Services

In the VLL services, there are only two data-forwarding components. For regular VLL service, these are the local SAP and the spoke-pseudowire to the far-end PE. The configuration does not allow more than one pseudowire defined in a point-to-point service instance. With VLL, the services ingress native traffic from the SAP, perform service encapsulation, and send the traffic to the pseudowire. In the reverse direction, the services de-encapsulate the traffic received from the pseudowire and send it out through SAP-egress. Only the PE router is service-aware. Therefore, a full mesh of pseudowires is required if there are many VLL services that need to be deployed in a scaled network. This may cause scaling issues in the scenarios described in the following bullets.

However, there are some cases (primarily in interconnected networks designed or owned by different parties) in which one service tunnel cannot carry the traffic from the local PE to the remote PE on the other side of the network. The following possible scenarios exist:

- **RSVP-TE LSP Must Be Used in a Network with Hierarchical IGP Design** — If OSPF areas or IS-IS levels are deployed in the network, the TE database of IGP is limited to a single area. Therefore, the RSVP-TE using CSPF cannot be established across multiple IGP areas, and the LSP used by the service tunnel cannot reach the remote router in another area.

- **RSVP-TE LSP Must Be Used Between Different Routing Domains** — In certain scenarios, the provider may have a backbone network with multiple routing domains. For example, the backbone network may contain one OSPF domain and one IS-IS domain. Alternatively, the backbone network may use routing protocols in the network core and static routing at the network edge.

- **Two Parts of the Network Use Different Tunneling Methods** — If part of the network uses an LDP-created LSP as a service tunnel and another part uses RSVP-TE, a single LSP cannot be built from one part of the network to another.

- **MPLS-Capable Network Interconnecting with an IP-Only Network** — If one end of the VLL service is located in an MPLS network but the remote end of the service resides in a pure IP network, a single service tunnel using an MPLS service tunnel cannot connect these two service endpoints.

- **Service Topology Is Designed in a Hierarchical Manner to Scale Up the Number of Services in a Large Network** — When a network requires many VLL services among many PE routers, it may be desirable to avoid a full mesh of T-LDP sessions and service tunnels and not configure all service terminating PE routers to peer with each other. The operator can reduce the peering overhead of the network and increase the scalability by designating some core PE routers as pseudowire hubs. This can aggregate the service peering and relay the traffic among edge PE routers. Figure 10.10 illustrates how to use pseudowire switching to build a hierarchical service network.

- **In a Scaled Network, Building a Full Mesh of Service Transport Tunnels (MPLS LSPs) and a Full Mesh of T-LDP Sessions among All PE Routers Is Not Optimal** — Operators may not want to manage a significant amount of LSPs.

Figure 10.10 Using Pseudowire Switching to Build a Hierarchical Network

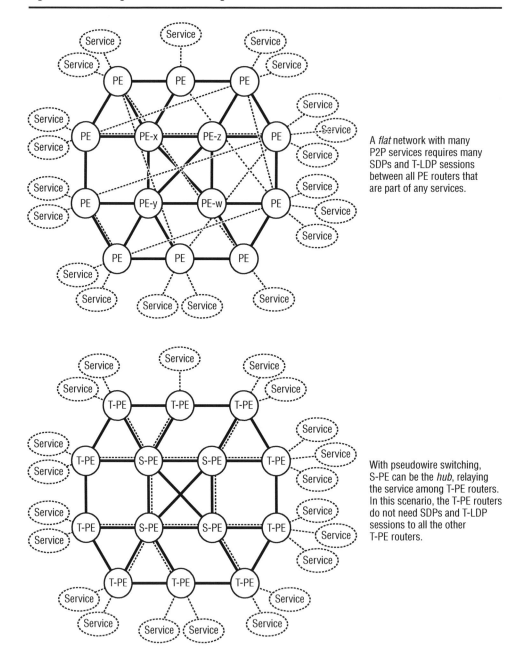

A *flat* network with many P2P services requires many SDPs and T-LDP sessions between all PE routers that are part of any services.

With pseudowire switching, S-PE can be the *hub*, relaying the service among T-PE routers. In this scenario, the T-PE routers do not need SDPs and T-LDP sessions to all the other T-PE routers.

In Figure 10.10's scenarios, the network contains many service routers and the operator needs to deploy VLL services to many customers. Each dotted line represents one service needing deployment. Because the services are widely spread over the network, deploying end-to-end VLL services requires the creation of many SDPs and many pseudowires in the network. It also requires the establishment of many T-LDP sessions among these PE routers. To make the network design more scalable, VLL services are extended to allow switching traffic between two pseudowire segments, thus creating a multi-segment pseudowire (MS-PW). Segmenting the pseudowires is also referred to as *pseudowire switching*. The following occurs in a pseudowire-switching VLL service that is defined when the service is created:

1. The service receives vc-encapsulated traffic from one pseudowire segment.

2. The service performs a de-encapsulation, followed by another vc-encapsulation.

3. The service sends the traffic out over another pseudowire segment.

In this scenario, the `vc-label` has been swapped, and traffic is switched from one pseudowire segment to another.

Figure 10.11 illustrates the logical representation of the pseudowire switching that relays Epipe services from one zone to another.

In Figure 10.11, the backbone network is divided into two domains (or parts) because it uses different routing and MPLS protocols. End-to-end service across the entire network is still desired. The problem of connecting different network domains to provide end-to-end services is solved by creating a pseudowire-switching VLL service in the PE router located in the boundary of the two networks (or network zones). The switching service relays service traffic from the source PE to the remote destination PE, and from the remote PE to the source PE.

In Figure 10.11, terminating PE (T-PE) routers remain in different areas of the network and use different IGP and MPLS protocols. To fulfill the end-to-end service requirement, the operator creates a pseudowire-switching service at the boundary of the two zones to connect the two pseudowire segments. This allows traffic to move across different domains using two different pseudowires to reach its destination. The PE-2 router is referred to as a *switching PE* (S-PE). If there are several different sections of a network requiring different service tunnels, the operator can place several S-PEs in the boundaries to relay the traffic to its destination.

Figure 10.11 Pseudowire-Switching Service Relaying Service from One Domain to Another

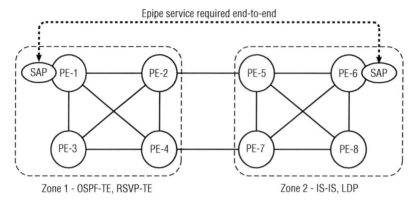

Ethernet VLL (Epipe) is required between PE-1 and PE-6. Because the network's Zone 1 and Zone 2 use different types of MPLS LSPs, the SDP cannot be built end-to-end.

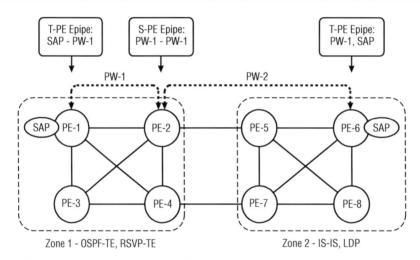

With pseudowire switching service in PE-2, two pseudowires are connected together to form an end-to-end service tunnel. There can be an unlimited number of PW-switching PE routers in the middle of the end-to-end VLL service.

When a vc-switching service is used in the S-PE router to stitch two pseudowire segments together, the ALRSP allows the two pseudowires to use SDPs with different tunnel types. This improves the flexibility of the pseudowire-switching solution. For example, a vc-switching service instance can have one pseudowire bound to an SDP using GRE tunneling and have another pseudowire bound to an SDP using RSVP-TE LSP tunneling. The service instance switches traffic between these two pseudowires without problems.

Signaling Multi-Segment Pseudowire

The purpose of the pseudowire-switching service is to connect or stitch two pseudowire segments together. The label distribution processes of the vc-switching service instances in the S-PE routers are passive, meaning that they're relaying the Label Mapping message between T-PE routers. The relationship between T-PE routers and S-PE router(s) is a master/slave-type relationship, in which the T-PE router is the master, and the S-PE router is the slave. The vc-switching service instance can only relay the Label Mapping (control plane) and the traffic (date plane) from one T-PE or S-PE router to another T-PE or S-PE router. Therefore, the vc-switching service instance in the S-PE router does not bring its pseudowires operationally up until the S-PE router ensures that both service terminating points (T-PE router's service instances and their pseudowires) are present. When the S-PE receives a service label-mapping from one T-PE router, it forwards it to the next S-PE or T-PE router but does not reply to the sender until it receives another label-mapping from the next-hop T-PE router in the other side of the network (or the next-hop S-PE router waiting for its next-hop T-PE router to send a service label-mapping).

Figure 10.12 illustrates the signaling process for signaling an end-to-end Epipe service with multiple vc-switching PE routers to relay the service.

Figure 10.12   T-PE and S-PE Router Label Distribution in Master/Slave Style

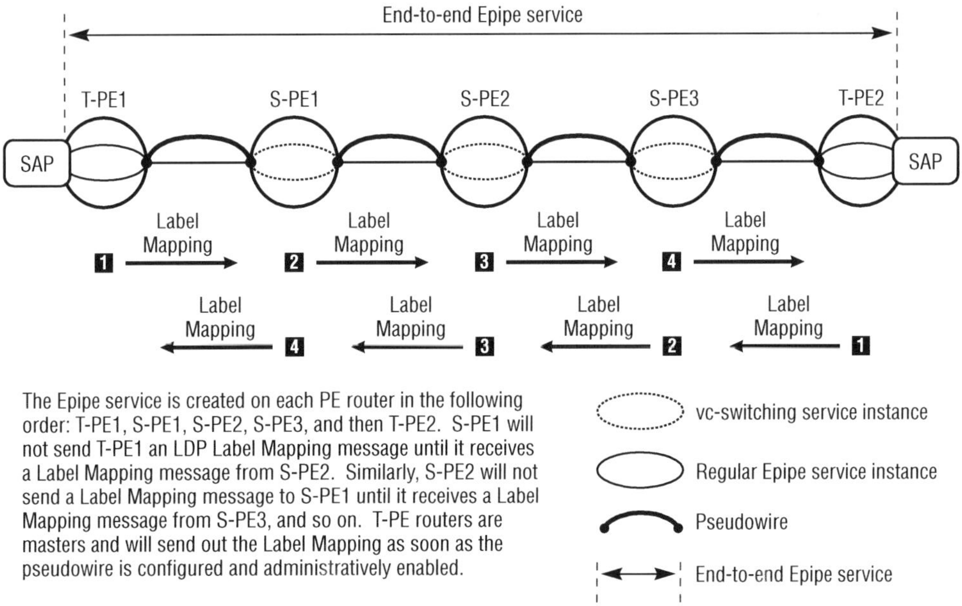

The Epipe service is created on each PE router in the following order: T-PE1, S-PE1, S-PE2, S-PE3, and then T-PE2. S-PE1 will not send T-PE1 an LDP Label Mapping message until it receives a Label Mapping message from S-PE2. Similarly, S-PE2 will not send a Label Mapping message to S-PE1 until it receives a Label Mapping message from S-PE3, and so on. T-PE routers are masters and will send out the Label Mapping as soon as the pseudowire is configured and administratively enabled.

Figure 10.12 illustrates a more complicated scenario, where there are several S-PE routers between the two T-PE routers. This scenario requires three pseudowire-switching hops for the two PE routers to reach each other. In this case, the S-PE1 does not send the Label Mapping message to the T-PE1 router until S-PE2 sends a label-mapping to S-PE3. After S-PE2 sends a label-mapping to S-PE3, S-PE3 sends a label-mapping to S-PE2, and S-PE2 sends a label-mapping to S-PE1.

This is similar to the *ordered control* principle used by RSVP-TE: A router will not send an upstream router a label-mapping until it receives a label-mapping from the downstream routers. This scenario shown in Figure 10.12 differs slightly from this principle, in that the S-PE that previously assigned a service label locally for the T-PE will not send the Label Mapping message out until it receives a label from the next hop. Also, when the S-PE loses the label-binding to one T-PE router, it withdraws the label-binding from the other T-PE router or next-hop S-PE router as well. Because the sole purpose of the pseudowire-switching service is to relay traffic from one pseudowire segment to another, it makes sense that it does not assign a binding to another pseudowire if it does not have a binding from one pseudowire.

In Figure 10.12, the network requires an end-to-end Epipe service between the two SAPs located in T-PE1 and T-PE2. The service is segmented by three S-PE routers in the middle of the network. Therefore, to achieve the end-to-end Epipe service, three vc-switching Epipe service instances are created (one at each router) to stitch the pseudowires together. When provisioning the service, the service instances are created in the following order as indicated by the numbers in Figure 10.12: T-PE1, S-PE1, S-PE2, S-PE3, and then T-PE2. When T-PE1 has the Epipe service instance provisioned and the pseudowire to S-PE1 configured, it immediately sends the Label Mapping message to S-PE1. When S-PE1 has the Epipe vc-switching service instance provisioned and the pseudowires created, it handles the two pseudowires in the following manner:

- After the configuration of the pseudowire from S-PE2, S-PE1 immediately sends the Label Mapping message to S-PE2. Because S-PE1 has already received the Label Mapping from the downstream router T-PE1 (master), it can distribute the label for the master's upstream PE router (T-PE or S-PE) to establish the pseudowire (see Step 2 in Figure 10.12).

- After the configuration of the pseudowire to S-PE1, S-PE2 does not send a Label Mapping message to S-PE1 (even if T-PE1 has sent a Label Mapping message to itself). This is because, as a slave, S-PE2 cannot send the Label Mapping to an upstream router (T-PE or S-PE) until it receives the Label Mapping from the downstream T-PE or S-PE router.

In this example, the service instances must be created in all PE routers, and the label distribution must be sent from T-PE2 to S-PE3, then from S-PE3 to S-PE2 and then from S-PE2 to S-PE1. At that stage, the S-PE1 sends the Label Mapping to T-PE1.

Figure 10.13 illustrates an example of a pseudowire-switching service connecting the Epipe service between two PE routers. Both configurations and LDP signaling messages are provided in this figure.

Routers T-PE1 and T-PE2 have an Epipe service that needs to be connected. Router S-PE uses a vc-switching Epipe service to switch the traffic between the two pseudowires and connect the Epipe service between these two T-PE routers. The service is configured in the following order:

1. **Configure the Epipe Service in T-PE1** (`10.0.0.165`) — After the creation of the service, a `no shutdown` command is entered immediately. A SAP is created, and then the spoke-pseudowire to the S-PE router is created. At this point, the T-PE1 router sends a Label Mapping message to S-PE and distributes a service egress label `131055` for the S-PE.

2. **Configure Epipe vc-switching Service in S-PE** (`10.0.0.164`) — The service is created, a `no shutdown` command is entered, and the pseudowire pointing to T-PE1 is created. Although the pseudowire between S-PE and T-PE1 is configured on both routers, S-PE does not allocate and distribute a `vc-label` to T-PE immediately because the S-PE has only one pseudowire in a vc-switched service. The S-PE router is assigned a label locally for T-PE1 after the pseudowire to T-PE1 is configured, but the S-PE router does not distribute the label to T-PE1 at this stage. After the pseudowire pointing to T-PE2 (`10.0.0.163`) is created, a Label Mapping message is sent from S-PE to T-PE2, assigning service-egress label `131053` to T-PE2. The S-PE does not distribute a label to T-PE1 at this stage because the S-PE has not yet received a label from T-PE2 to use as a service egress label.

3. **Configure Epipe Service in T-PE2** (`10.0.0.163`) — After the creation and `no shutdown` of the service and local SAP, the pseudowire pointing to S-PE is created. When this pseudowire is created and comes operationally up, the router T-PE2 distributes the service egress label (`131053`) to the S-PE.

4. **After S-PE Receives the Label from the T-PE2 Router, It Distributes the Service-Ingress Label (131044) to the T-PE1** — At this stage, all three routers have their ingress and egress labels, and the Epipe service is operationally up and ready to carry data traffic.

In the router S-PE, if one of the pseudowires is brought down (manually or due to network failure), the S-PE withdraws the labels assigned for the other T-PE router.

Figure 10.13 Signaling VC-Switched Pseudowires

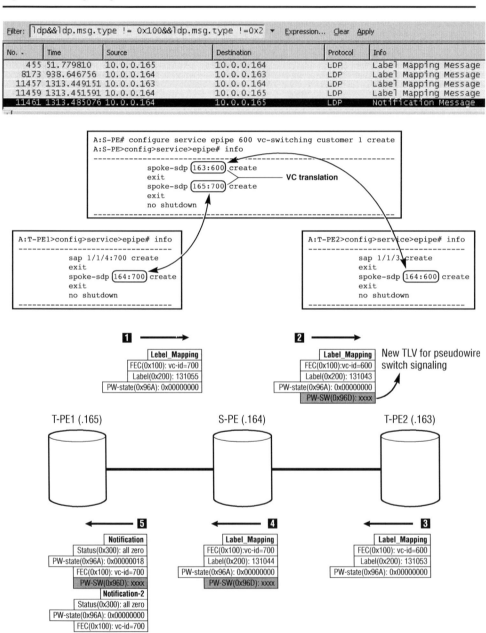

Note: When the no shutdown command is entered, it means that when the router signals the pseudowire for the VPLS, it will attach the PW-Status TLV with clear flags. This eliminates the need for the router to send another LDP Notification message (#5 in Figure 10.13) to the peer to signal the VPLS service status. This reduces the number of LDP messages to be sniffed and displayed.

Figure 10.13 illustrates the LDP messages that establish the pseudowires between the two T-PE routers and the S-PE router. The packet sniffer is configured to eliminate the LDP hello <0x0100> and keep alive <0x0201> from the packet analyzer, so it displays only relevant LDP messages. When the S-PE signals the pseudowires to the T-PE routers, it appends a pseudowire switching TLV (0x96D) to the end of the message (both the LDP Notification and Label Mapping messages have this TLV appended). Figure 10.14 illustrates the format of the pseudowire-switching TLV.

Figure 10.14 PW-Switching TLV

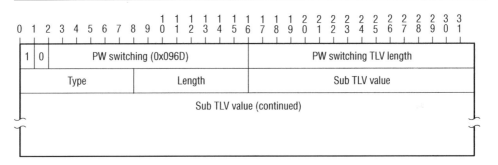

In the PW switching TLV (0x096D), two sub-TLVs are present — the value of the previous switching segment's pseudowire vc-id and the current switching hop's system-id.

Generation and/or Propagation of LDP Notification Messages in S-PE

As previously discussed, an S-PE router with pseudowire-switching service can only relay the traffic from one terminating PE to another. In a point-to-point VLL service solution with pseudowire-switching services present, the VLL service itself is no longer end-to-end. In addition to the encapsulated data traffic that must be relayed by the pseudowire-switching services, service control plane signaling (T-LDP) messages must also be generated and/or propagated by the S-PE routers to the T-PE routers.

Previous sections have explained how the S-PE router relays the Label Mapping message from T-PE routers as slave(s). In VLL services, LDP Notification messages are used to indicate the pseudowire status. When PW-switching in S-PE router(s) is used to connect two T-PE routers, the S-PE router(s) must also process and propagate the LDP Notification message from one T-PE router to another T-PE router. Also, if the status of the S-PE router's vc-switching service instance has changed, it generates LDP Notification messages to notify the PW-Status change to all other S-PE and T-PE routers. There are different scenarios where the LDP Notification message must be sent to the S-PE router:

- **When the S-PE Router's Local Components in the Service Instance Are All Operationally Up** — Upon receipt of any LDP Notification message, the S-PE router propagates the message to the next-hop PE router (S-PE or T-PE). If the received message contains `PW-switching` TLV (which means the message is generated by an S-PE router rather than a T-PE router), the S-PE router appends the `PW-switching` TLV to the message before relaying the message. When an S-PE router receives an LDP Notification message, it sets the corresponding `Peer PW bits` in the pseudowire where the message is received.

- **When the S-PE Router Has a Local Failure** — (One of the pseudowires is **down** or the service instance is **down**), it always generates an LDP Notification message with `PW-Status` TLV with pseudowire down bits. This is true regardless of whether the received status bits from the remote router indicated SAP up/down or pseudowire up/down. In addition, the S-PE router appends the `PW Switching` TLV to the message.

- **The S-PE Performs a Logical OR** — Between the local status and the status received from the peer T-PE or S-PE to decide the local status of the pseudowire.

Can Pseudowire Switching Be Used to Relay VPLS Services Traffic?

Yes, it is possible to use pseudowire switching to relay traffic for VPLS services. A VPLS service can have a pseudowire connected to a PW-switching service in an S-PE router. The PW-switching service still relays the traffic from one pseudowire to another. However, the PW-switching service will *not* pass a VPLS signaling message, such as the MAC-flush (LDP Address Withdraw message), from one T-PE router to another T-PE router. It discards the message upon receipt because it does not understand the LDP signaling message.

10.4 VLL Example: Epipe — Ethernet P2P VPN

The Ethernet point-to-point pseudowire (Epipe) connects two customer Ethernet interfaces. In an Epipe, the customer native frames are tagged or untagged Ethernet frames. Customer routers or switches connected to the Epipe service send traffic over the point-to-point wire-like connection and appear to be in the same LAN segment (same broadcast domain). Figure 10.15 illustrates the configuration of an Epipe between PE1 and PE2 routers.

Figure 10.15   Epipe Configuration Example

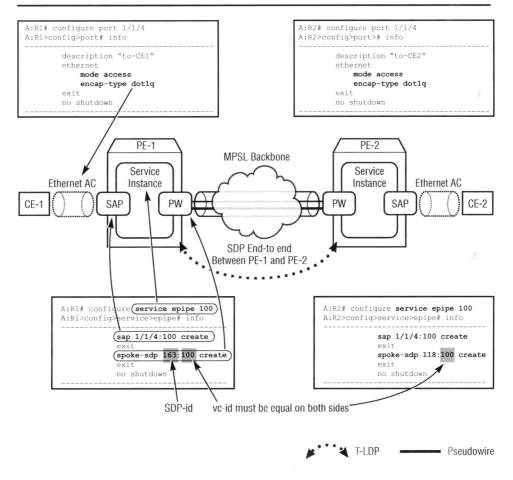

Epipe Service Access Point (SAP)

An Epipe service provides a point-to-point Ethernet bridging service. The SAPs of the Epipe services ingress and egress the native customer Ethernet frames from and to the CE devices. Before a SAP can be configured on a port, the port must be configured to use **access** mode. The port must also have a supported encapsulation type defined. After those requirements are met, the operator can define the SAP on that port in the Epipe service instance. SAPs are identified by the port or channel-id, plus the encapsulation type and value. Table 10.4 lists and defines the supported card access port encapsulation types for Epipe SAPs.

Table 10.4   Epipe Supported SAP Encapsulations

Port Type	Encapsulation	Definition
Ethernet	Null (encap-id=0; for example, 1/1/1)	Supports untagged Ethernet frames. Also supports frames containing non-service-delimiting customer VLAN tags, which are ignored by the service and carried over the SP core transparently. One service per port.
Ethernet	Dot1q (for example, 1/1/1:100)	Supports 802.1q-tagged Ethernet frames. The tag is service-delimiting and is used by the service provider to distinguish customer traffic streams sharing the same physical port. Multiple services per port.
Ethernet	Q-in-Q (for example, 1/1/1:100.200)	Supports double 802.1q-tagged Ethernet frames. Both tags are used by the service provider to distinguish the customer traffic streams sharing the same physical port. Multiple services per port.
SONET/ SDH	IPCP (for example, 1/2/1)	Supports a single IP service on a SONET/SDH port or a single service per channel (if the interface is channelized). This is typically used for router interconnection using point-to-point protocol (PPP).
SONET/ SDH	BCP-null (for example, 1/2/1)	Supports bridged services on SONET/SDH ports/ channels. It is typically used by two devices with the PPP protocol. One service per port.
SONET/ SDH	BCP-dot1q (for example, 1/2/1:200)	Supports bridged services on SONET/SDH ports/ channels. It uses the 802.1q tag to multiplex customer traffic. It is typically used by two devices with multiple bridges service. Multiple services per port.
SONET/ SDH ATM	ATM (for example, 2/1/1:10/100)	RFC 2684 Ethernet bridged encapsulation. The SAP encapsulation value is <port-id>:<vpi>/<vci>.

Port Type	Encapsulation	Definition
SONET/ SDH FR	Frame-Relay (for example, 2/2/1:300)	RFC 2427 Ethernet bridged encapsulation. The SAP encapsulation value is <port-id>:<dlci>.

Two SAPs of the same Epipe service can have different port types, encapsulation types, and values, depending on their attachment circuit type. For example, ATM or Frame-Relay to Ethernet interworking can be achieved by creating an Epipe service (local or distributed) with an ATM/FR SAP and an Ethernet SAP. In the ATM/FR SAP, the traffic is identified by the ATM VPI/VCI or Frame-Relay DLCI, and the payload is RFC 2684 or RFC 2427 Ethernet bridged frames.

Traffic flow on the SAP is in two directions:

- **SAP-ingress** — The traffic flow from the customer site into the PE router. In the SAP-ingress direction, the traffic's encapsulation type and value are verified. If the traffic's encapsulation type or value does not match the SAP's configured encapsulation type or value, the traffic is discarded at SAP-ingress. For example, if a SAP is configured with a vlan-tag value of 100, any ingress traffic from the customer site will be dropped except that traffic tagged with vlan-id 100. In the SAP ingress direction, the SAP's encapsulation type/value decides if the ingress traffic is legitimate and if it should be forwarded.

- **SAP-egress** — The traffic flow from the PE router to the customer site. In the SAP-egress direction, the SAP's encapsulation type and value decide how the traffic is encapsulated before it is sent to the customer site.

Customer Ethernet frames can be untagged, single-VLAN-tagged (dot1q), or double-tagged (Q-in-Q). When configuring SAPs in the Epipe service, the operator must use the correct encapsulation type (tagging type) and encapsulation value (VLAN-tag value). Otherwise, traffic may be discarded at the SAP-ingress or sent to the customer site with the wrong tagging value. From the SAP configuration and the VLAN-tagging behavior's perspective, the SAPs of an Epipe service are the same as the SAPs of VPLS service. The Epipe's SAP VLAN-tagging configuration options and their tagging behavior are introduced in Chapter 11. An Epipe performs VLAN-translation in the same manner as the VPLS service. Therefore, the two customer sites connected by the Epipe service are in same broadcast domain. The details regarding the VLAN-translation are introduced in Chapter 11.

Epipe service is point-to-point between two SAPs connecting two customer sites. The customer traffic arriving at one SAP can only be sent out to the peering PE routers over the pseudowire. When the remote PE router receives the traffic from the pseudowire, it can only send it to the remote customer sites through its SAP. No forwarding decisions are required. Therefore, Epipe service instances do not need to learn any MAC addresses from customer frames or build a forwarding database (FDB).

Epipe Pseudowire (SDP-Binding) Signaling

As mentioned previously, MPLS pseudowires are used to connect PE routers participating in the same end-to-end service. For distributed Epipe services, each of the two PE routers participating in the service requires one established pseudowire to reach the far-end router. The two PE routers use T-LDP to signal the pseudowire. The LDP Label Mapping message establishes the pseudowire used by the Epipe. A local PE router sends the Label Mapping message to the remote PE router with the following three TLVs in the message:

- FEC TLV — The FEC TLV indicates the purpose of the pseudowire (for example, the forwarding equivalent class that uses this pseudowire). For Epipe, the FEC TLV uses the vc-id FEC element (type 0x128), with the following information:

  - C-flag — The *control word* flag. A control word is not required for pseudowires in the Epipe service instance.

  - vc-id — The virtual circuit ID for the pseudowire. It is specified when configuring the SDP-binding in the Epipe configuration.

  - vc-type — The pseudowire type. In Epipe and VPLS services, the pseudowire circuit type can be either VLAN (0x04) or Ether (0x05, default). The details regarding vc-type are discussed in Chapter 11.

  - Interface Parameter sub-TLV — Contains the following additional information:

    - The MTU sub-TLV contains the virtual circuit MTU (vc-MTU), which is the MTU allowed for Layer 3 traffic. In Epipe and VPLS service, the vc-MTU is the service MTU minus the L2 Ethernet overhead (value of 14).

    - The VCCV sub-TLV is used to negotiate Virtual Circuit Connectivity Verification (VCCV; RFC 5085) capability. The sub-TLV indicates the method used, MPLS router alert (Label 1), or PWE3 control word. It also indicates the ping method supported, ICMP or LSP-ping.

- `Generic Label TLV` — Contains the label distributed to the peering PE router. The label is used by the local PE router as the ingress label for the pseudowire's ingress traffic from the remote PE router. The label is used by the remote PE router as an egress label for the VPN traffic encapsulation and to egress the traffic over the pseudowire.

- `Pseudowire Status TLV` — Indicates the status of the service instance and pseudowire with the status code. The remote PE router tracks the status of the pseudowire by storing the received status code.

Figure 10.16 illustrates a packet capture of the LDP Label Mapping message for a signaling pseudowire for an Epipe service.

Figure 10.16 Epipe Pseudowire Establishment: LDP Label Mapping Message

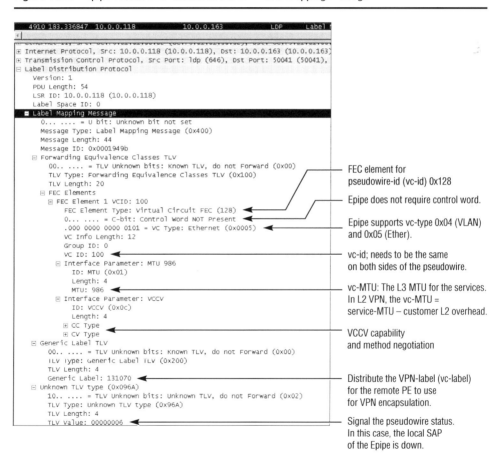

After the pseudowire is established between both PE routers and the status codes of the pseudowires are both clear (all zero), the service is ready to forward the traffic. Where there is a status change in a PE router's service instance (SAP down, or service instance down), the PE router sends LDP Notification messages to notify the far-end router of the failure. The far-end router sets the Peer PW Bits flag in the pseudowire and stops sending traffic over the pseudowire until the failure is removed.

When the pseudowire is administratively disabled (shutdown command executed in the pseudowire configuration in the service instance), the local PE router uses the LDP Label Withdraw message to remove the label-mapping; the remote PE router confirms this by sending the LDP Label Release message. The detailed procedures for pseudowire establishment and tearing down procedures are provided in Chapter 9.

Epipe Data Encapsulation

The Epipe service is ready to forward customer data frames between the two customer sites when these conditions are met:

- Both PE routers participating in the same Epipe service have configured service instances with SAPs.

- The pseudowire connecting the two PE routers' service instances is configured and operationally up.

When a PE router receives the traffic, it must decide whether to accept the traffic for forwarding. The following three criteria must be matched before the PE service instance accepts the traffic:

- **Traffic Identification Validation** — This validation compares the tagging value of the received customer traffic with the SAP's encapsulation type/value configuration at the SAP ingress.

- **Access Control Policing** — If there is a filtering policy deployed in the SAP-ingress, the filter is applied to the ingress customer frames and the frames that are rejected by the filter are discarded.

- **QoS Policy** — A SAP-ingress QoS policy may be deployed in the SAP-ingress direction to perform classification marking and policing/shaping. The ingress customer traffic may be dropped or buffered for rate-limiting reasons.

If the customer frame passes these three checks in the SAP-ingress, the Epipe service pseudowire performs VPN-encapsulation using the vc-label on the customer frame and then sends the frame to the SDP. The SDP carrying the pseudowire performs transport-tunnel encapsulation using the transport-label on the customer frame and then sends the frame to the far-end PE router. The customer frame now has two MPLS labels and travels across the provider backbone network to the remote PE router. When the remote PE router receives the traffic, it removes the transport-label and uses the vc-label as a demux to identify the traffic's service instance. The vc-label is then removed, and the customer frame arrives at the service instance. When the remote PE router's SAP forwards the traffic to the customer site, the router considers the following:

- **Access Control Policing** — If there is any filtering policy deployed in the SAP-egress, the filter is applied to the customer frames to be egressed to the customer site. Any frames rejected by the filter are discarded.

- **QoS Policy** — A SAP-ingress QoS policy may be deployed in the SAP-ingress direction to perform classification marking and policing/shaping. The ingress customer traffic may be dropped or buffered for rate-limiting reasons.

- **Encapsulation Type/Value** — After the frame is granted passage by the Security and QoS policies, it is ready to be forwarded to the customer site. The SAP applies the configured encapsulation type and value to the customer traffic before it egresses the traffic to the customer site. Encapsulation is done regardless of how the customer frame is tagged when it is received from the pseudowire. The SAP egress appends its own tagging value to the customer frame without changing the existing tagging on the frame.

Figure 10.17 illustrates the packet walk-through in the Epipe service in one direction. The traffic in the reverse direction is processed in the same manner.

An Ethernet pseudowire does not require a control word in the VPN encapsulation. In this case, the pseudowire attaches only the MPLS label stack with two labels (inner vc-label and outer transport label) to the customer frames before the PE router places the VPN-encapsulated traffic on the pseudowire toward the remote PE router.

Figure 10.17 Epipe Service Data Frame Walk-Through

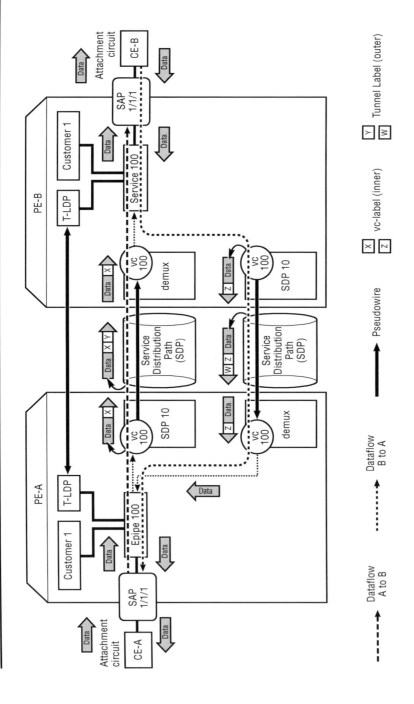

10.5 VLL Connection Admission Control

When a service sends traffic over the backbone network, it uses SDP to carry the traffic over the transport tunnel. Bandwidth (BW) is consumed by the service traffic on the SDP's network port. The VLL Connection Admission Control (CAC) requests the service to book bandwidth on the SDP on which it binds the pseudowire. This request is done prior to sending the traffic. This section discusses the functionality and the configuration of VLL CAC.

VLL CAC Architecture

When services are deployed in the network, operators may want to monitor the bandwidth booking of the transport tunnel. In addition, the operator may want to control the bandwidth used by VLL services on an SDP or LSP. This can be achieved by deploying VLL CAC in the network. When using VLL CAC, it is recommended, but not mandatory, that RSVP-TE LSPs are used as transport tunnels by the SDP. If the SDP uses the GRE tunnel or LDP-LSP as service transport tunnel, no CAC is performed and spoke-pseudowire is always accepted into the SDP. The RSVP-TE LSP tunnel is capable of reserving network BW in the control plane. Once this BW is reserved, the system performs CAC when establishing the LSP.

The strategy of using VLL CAC is simple. When a VLL service needs to establish a pseudowire to a remote PE router, the BW requirement can be explicitly specified in the pseudowire configuration. Every pseudowire is associated (bound) with an SDP. When the system attempts to establish the pseudowire over the SDP it is bound to, it verifies the SDP's available BW against the CAC criteria. If the SDP has enough available BW for the pseudowire, the pseudowire can then be established and used to forward traffic over that SDP. The SDP's available BW is derived from the bandwidth of its LSPs. Figure 10.18 illustrates a sample network with VLL CAC enabled.

In Figure 10.18, four Epipe services must be connected to PE-B over the SDP. The SDP has three RSVP-TE LSPs inside. The SDP's maximum BW is the sum of the BW of all the operationally **up** LSPs multiplied by the SDP's booking factor. In the example, the SDP has a booking factor of 150 percent, and the total BW of all LSPs is 700 Mbps. Therefore, the SDP has a maximum BW of 1,050 Mbps. There are four VLL services that need to use this SDP. They all book bandwidth from the SDP for their pseudowires, and VLL CAC checks the available bandwidth before establishing each pseudowire. The VLL CAC subtracts the booked BW when the CAC grants the BW requirement and the pseudowire is connected. In this example, the

SDP has available BW (not booked) of 200 Mbps. If there is a fifth VLL, with BW higher than 200 Mbps, requiring the use of the same SDP to establish a pseudowire, the VLL CAC will fail, and the pseudowire will not forward traffic over the SDP.

Figure 10.18 VLL CAC in a Service Network

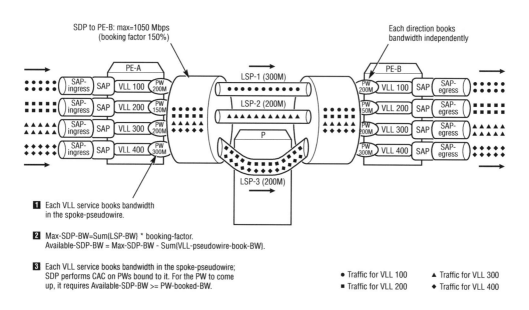

Note: The VLL CAC is a control plane function only, similar to the CAC performed by RSVP-TE on establishing LSPs. It does not force the data plane to forward traffic only at the rate under the booked value. Without using a QoS policy to rate-limit the traffic flow on the data plane, VLL CAC may not reflect the actual traffic distribution correctly. Without a QoS policy, a VLL can still book 100 Mbps BW from the SDP but send 200 Mbps of traffic on the data path.

The best practice is to configure the VLL CAC BW booking values as accurately as possible to the predicted BW requirement. In addition, use QoS policies to ensure that the VLL or SDP only forwards traffic on the rate configured in the control plane.

When deploying VLL CAC in the network, the following configuration options are highly recommended:

- Use RSVP-TE LSPs in the SDP. When configuring LSPs, apply bandwidth values to the LSP for RSVP-TE to perform CAC and bandwidth reservation. SDP uses the BW values of LSPs with a booking factor to perform CAC.

- When configuring VLL service pseudowires, configure the pseudowire's BW value as accurately as possible to the actual traffic volume expectation. Thus, when SDP performs CAC on the pseudowires to grant or deny traffic forwarding, it uses relatively accurate information.

- For accurate VLL CAC performance, if the network is combined with VLL services and other services (VPLS, VPRN), only use an SDP overlay (and an LSP overlay used by the SDPs) for VLL services requiring CAC. Use another set of SDPs for other services. This setup is required because the SDP CAC is in the control plane only. If a service sends traffic without booking the BW from the control plane or if booking is not supported, the SDP is not aware of these hidden BW requirements and cannot take them into consideration for CAC.

- Use a single RSVP-TE LS in the SDP as the service transport tunnel to ensure that the bandwidth calculation and accounting are more accurate.

Pseudowire Signaling with VLL CAC

As mentioned previously, when a VLL service instance is provisioned on the PE router, the operator must provision and establish a pseudowire with the remote PE router. When the pseudowire is provisioned in the local service instance and administratively enabled, the system tries to establish the pseudowire with the remote PE router through the SDP it is bound to. With VLL CAC, there are several additional processes that must occur before the system can signal the pseudowire:

- When provisioning the pseudowire using the `spoke-sdp <sdp-id>:<vc-id>` command, the required BW must be specified in the configuration.

- Before the system starts to signal the pseudowire, it must verify that there is enough available BW for the local SDP that the pseudowire binds to. This is done by comparing the available (not booked) BW of the SDP with the bandwidth specified in the pseudowire configuration. If the SDP does not have enough available BW (CAC failure), the pseudowire is still signaled. However, the pseudowire is placed in an operationally **down** status locally, and a LDP

Label Mapping message is sent to the remote PE router with the `PW-Status TLV` flag set to `0x1: PW-not-forwarding`.

- If the BW requirement from the pseudowire is granted by the SDP's CAC (it has enough available BW), the pseudowire is placed in an operationally **up** status, and the SDP reduces its available-BW value by subtracting the amount booked by the new pseudowire.

When there is a CAC failure on a pseudowire of a VLL service, the pseudowire is still established between two PE routers. However, the pseudowire is flagged as `pseudowire not forwarding (PW-Status code 0x01)`. Note that two PE routers establish a pseudowire using LDP Label Mapping messages over the T-LDP session between them. When using signaling VLL services spoke-pseudowire, the LDP Label Mapping message contains the `PW-Status-TLV (0x96A)`. If the VLL CAC fails on a pseudowire for a VLL service, the local PE router uses the `PW-Status-TLV 0x01` to notify the far-end PE router. As discussed previously, the traffic in the VLL service drops at the PE that detected the failure, which is the CAC failure in this case. The remote PE may translate this pseudowire status into a native OAM message over the SAP to the remote CE device. When the CAC admission fails on a pseudowire, the pseudowire remains in the `PW not forwarding` state until one of the following occurs:

- The pseudowire's bandwidth is reconfigured to a lower value to pass the bandwidth check.
- The pseudowire is administratively disabled and re-enabled after the SDP has more available bandwidth.

Bandwidth Calculation in VLL CAC

The VLL CAC decides if the pseudowire is granted or denied to pass traffic by comparing the available bandwidth of an SDP with the bandwidth requested by the VLL service's pseudowire. The SDP's bandwidth is calculated by the following formulas:

SDP-Max-Bandwidth = Sum{LSP-bandwidth} × booking-factor

SDP-Available-Bandwidth = SDP-Max-Bandwidth − Sum{bandwidth-used-by-pseudowire}

CAC grants the pseudowire BW requirement when `SDP-Available-Bandwidth` is greater than or equal to the BW required by the pseudowire.

Each time a new pseudowire must be established over an SDP, the bandwidth check is performed. Pseudowires failing the bandwidth check are flagged to `pseudowire not forwarding (0x01)` during the T-LDP signaling and are not used to forward traffic.

One SDP can have more than one LSP in it. The SDP's maximum bandwidth is the sum of all operationally **up** LSPs. Recall that one LSP can have multiple LSP-Paths (one primary and up to seven secondary LSP-Paths), and all these LSP-Paths can have their own reserved bandwidth. In this case, the reserved bandwidth of the *active forwarding path* is the LSP's bandwidth. If the LSPs bandwidth reservation changes (owing to an active forwarding path change or a bandwidth configuration change), the SDP's maximum and available BW also changes immediately. Similarly, if LSPs are added or removed from an SDP, the BW change is reflected in the SDP BW immediately. However, if the change actually reduces the bandwidth and causes overbooking, the pseudowires for the VLL services remain operationally **up**. The system generates warnings and traps to notify the system and/or the network management devices of the CAC failure, but this does not affect the established pseudowires.

Conversely, one LSP can be used by multiple SDPs. In this case, the LSP's BW reservation is taken into account by all the SDPs using it. For example, consider the scenario where there is one LSP with a 100-Mbps BW reservation that is used by three different SDPs. When VLL CAC is performed, these three SDPs count this single LSP's 100 Mbps as part of their BW. Because VLL CAC is a control plane booking function and does not track the BW consumption in the data plane, all three SDPs consider that the LSP's bandwidth is their own, as if there are three 100-Mbps LSPs.

SDP can also use LDP-LSPs or GRE tunnels as transport tunnels. LDP-LSPs and GRE tunnels do not have tunnel bandwidth reservation capability. Therefore, an SDP using GRE or LDP tunneling has zero available bandwidth from VLL CAC's perspective. However, if a VLL pseudowire with bandwidth booking is established over (bound to) an SDP using GRE or LDP tunneling, the pseudowire will come operationally **up**. This is because the system is aware that the SDP is LDP- or GRE-tunneled even though the CAC fails. The system then generates warnings and traps to notify the system of the CAC failure. Static-LSP can also be added into RSVP-TE LSP-tunneled SDPs. Note that static-LSP has no BW reservation and its addition into an SDP does not increase the SDP's maximum or available BW. If VLL CAC is performed on an SDP with all static-LSPs, the VLL CAC will fail, and the pseudowire is flagged as `pseudowire not forwarding`.

SDP Traffic Forwarding with VLL CAC

VLL CAC is a control-plane BW booking function. The bandwidth reservations are based on the control plane configuration of LSPs and pseudowire bandwidth and may not reflect the actual bandwidth consumption in the data paths. In addition, the VLL CAC does not affect the traffic forwarding decision of the SDP unless a pseudowire encounters a CAC failure during establishment (in this case, the pseudowire is flagged as PW not forwarding and cannot pass traffic). The SDP's traffic forwarding decision (for example, determination of which LSP of the SDP is used to forward the traffic for each service traffic flow) is independent of the VLL CAC result.

Where an SDP has more than one RSVP-TE LSP to forward traffic, it must decide which LSPs will forward traffic with each new traffic flow. Recall that there are two traffic distribution methods for an SDP with multiple LSPs: ECMP or CoS-based LSP forwarding.

> **Note:** For VLL services, if shared queuing is not used, the SDP performs ECMP traffic distribution based on the service-id even if CoS-based forwarding is configured.

With ECMP, the SDP performs a load-balancing hashing algorithm to decide the combination of traffic flow and LSPs. With CoS-based LSP forwarding, the SDP selects the LSP based on the traffic flow's forwarding class (FC) mapping. It also selects the corresponding LSP (or default LSP if there is no match) to forward the traffic flow. *Note that the SDP's selection of LSP is not affected by the VLL CAC.* The VLL CAC only grants or denies a pseudowire's request to book bandwidth over an SDP. If there is enough available SDP BW that the VLL CAC can succeed, the pseudowire can forward traffic using the SDP. The SDP's traffic distribution among LSPs of all traffic, belonging to all pseudowires bound to the SDP, is based solely on either the ECMP hashing result or the CoS-based LSP forwarding mapping. Also, if CoS-based LSP forwarding is used, the SDP counts the bandwidth of all the LSPs when performing VLL CAC, regardless of which FC the LSP is mapped to. However, the SDP will forward traffic based on the FC-LSP mapping without considering the LSP bandwidth configuration. The VLL CAC works the best with SDPs that have single RSVP-LSPs as service transport tunnels.

Configuring VLL CAC

Figure 10.19 illustrates an example of CLI configuration of VLL CAC in a network with an Epipe service booking 25 Mbps of bandwidth over an SDP.

Figure 10.19 VLL CAC Configuration Example

```
A:PE2# configure router mpls
A:PE2>config>router>mpls# info
------------------------------
[1]      lsp "163-164-30M"
             to 10.0.0.164
             cspf
             primary "loose"
                 bandwidth 30
             exit
             no shutdown
         exit
         lsp "163-164-2-20M"
             to 10.0.0.164
             cspf
             primary "loose"
                 bandwidth 20
             exit
             no shutdown
         exit
         lsp "163-164-3-15M"
             to 10.0.0.164
             cspf
             primary "164"
                 bandwidth 15
             exit
             no shutdown
         exit
         no shutdown
------------------------------
```

```
A:PE2# configure service sdp 164
A:PE2>config>service>sdp# info
------------------------------------
[2]      far-end 10.0.0.164
         lsp "163-164-30M"
         lsp "163-164-20M"
         lsp "163-164-15M"
         keep-alive
             shutdown
         exit
         booking-factor 200
         no shutdown
------------------------------------
```

```
A:PE2# configure service epipe 1000
A:PE2>config>service>epipe# info
------------------------------------
[3]      sap 1/1/4:1000 create
         exit
         spoke-sdp 164:1000 create
             bandwidth 25
         exit
         no shutdown
------------------------------------
```

```
A:PE2#   show service sdp 164 detail                          [4]
===============================================================================
Service Destination Point (Sdp Id : 164) Details
===============================================================================
-------------------------------------------------------------------------------
 Sdp Id 164  -(10.0.0.164)
-------------------------------------------------------------------------------
SDP Id               : 164              SDP Source        : manual
Admin Path MTU       : 0                Oper Path MTU     : 1492
Far End              : 10.0.0.164       Delivery          : MPLS
Admin State          : Up               Oper State        : Up
Signaling            : TLDP             Metric            : 0
Acct. Pol            : None             Collect Stats     : Disabled
Last Status Change   : 05/03/2004 19:09:41  Adv. MTU Over. : No
Last Mgmt Change     : 05/03/2004 19:09:41  VLAN VC Etype  : 0x8100
Bw BookingFactor     : 200              PBB Etype         : 0x88e7
Oper Max BW(Kbps)    : 65000            Avail BW(Kbps)    : 129975
Flags                : None
--- Output Omitted ---
```

The configuration of VLL CAC is a three-step procedure:

1. The LSPs are configured with bandwidth reservation so the SDP can use the bandwidth reservation to calculate its maximum and available bandwidth.

2. The SDP using VLL CAC is normally an RSVP-TE LSP-tunneled SDP. The SDP adds LSPs and optionally configures the booking-factor (the default value is 100%).

3. The VLL service's spoke-pseudowire configuration books the bandwidth from the SDP it binds to so the VLL CAC can perform a bandwidth check against it.

The SDP's current bandwidth booking status can be checked by viewing the SDP details (see Step 4 in Figure 10.19).

Before configuring the VLL CAC, carefully study the bandwidth allocation of the network and the traffic expectation of the VLL services. Because the VLL CAC does not actually check the data plane bandwidth consumption, the bandwidth values in the configuration are based on the operator's prediction of the traffic pattern and are manually specified. Therefore, it is beneficial to specify the traffic volume prediction as close as possible to actual values. It is also recommended that operators use QoS policies to reinforce the traffic volume in the data plane so that the volume corresponds to the bandwidth allocation in VLL CAC. For example, the Epipe in Figure 10.19 is requesting 25 Mbps of bandwidth for VLL CAC. A SAP-ingress QoS policy should be applied in the Epipe's SAP to shape or police the customer ingress traffic rate to remain under 25 Mbps so that the service will not actually send traffic over the pseudowire at a higher rate. To achieve the best effect, network designs should specify that a QoS design always accompany a control plane BW booking (VLL CAC, RSVP-TE LSP BW reservation).

VLL CAC with PW-Redundancy and PW-Switching

When VLL CAC is used in a VLL service with pseudowire redundancy, each spoke-pseudowire can have its own bandwidth checked against the SDP it binds to. The bandwidth check result is reflected by the pseudowire's state. If VLL CAC fails in a pseudowire, the pseudowire is flagged as `PW not forwarding (0x01)`. The pseudowire's state affects its eligibility and priority when the endpoint performs the *active forwarding object election*. Details regarding pseudowire redundancy for VLL services are discussed in Chapter 14.

When VLL CAC is used in a VLL service with vc-switching enabled, each spoke-pseudowire with bandwidth reservation is verified against each SDP in the same manner as in a regular VLL service. If the VLL CAC fails, the pseudowire is flagged as `PW not forwarding` to notify the far-end router.

Summary

VLL services are point-to-point VPN services that carry customer native traffic from one site to another site over the IP/MPLS VPN-based core. The VLL service involves two PE routers; each PE router has one service instance created with one SAP and one pseudowire connected to the remote PE router. VLL service PE routers process the customer native traffic received from SAP-ingress and perform VPN-encapsulation before sending the traffic to the remote PE router.

VLL services use MPLS pseudowires to connect two PE router service instances. T-LDP is used to perform the pseudowire establishment signaling, the tearing down of the pseudowire, and the notification of the pseudowire status change.

The normal VLL service involves only two PE routers end-to-end. In certain situations, the end-to-end VLL service provisioning is not desired or is not possible. For example, when the IP/MPLS network contains two different traffic engineering domains, the end-to-end service transport tunnel cannot be established. In this scenario, a VLL service instance with two pseudowires and no SAP can be created to perform Pseudowire Switching to relay the VLL traffic from one service-terminating PE router (T-PE) router to another T-PE router. The Switching PE (S-PE) router(s) between the two T-PE routers relay the LDP Label Mapping messages to establish the pseudowires. The S-PE router also propagates and generates the LDP Notification messages.

VLL Connection Admission Control can be used to monitor the bandwidth reservation and the LSP traffic booking in the control plane. With VLL CAC, the SDP sums all the reserved bandwidth from its LSPs, and the pseudowire for the VLL service books the bandwidth from the SDP it binds to. If the SDP does not have enough available bandwidth for a pseudowire, the pseudowire is flagged as `pseudowire not forwarding` and cannot forward traffic for its service.

Virtual Private LAN Service

11

Virtual Private LAN Service (VPLS) is a multipoint to multipoint Ethernet Layer 2 VPN service. VPLS provides transparent bridging services between all customer sites connected to it. This chapter introduces the architecture of the VPLS services.

Chapter Objectives

- Introduce VPLS and its advantages over traditional Ethernet services

- Present the VPLS architecture

- Discuss the mesh-pseudowires that are used to connect VPLS member PE routers

- Discuss the VPLS Service Access Points (SAPs)

- Explain how to manage the VPLS forwarding database (FDB)

This chapter introduces the Virtual Private LAN Service (VPLS). VPLS is widely deployed to provide private Ethernet bridging services over geographically separated locations. VPLS is a multipoint Layer 2 VPN over an IP/MPLS backbone. VPLS takes full advantage of the resiliency, flexibility, scalability, and reliability of IP/MPLS VPN service architecture. VPLS services are deployed by carriers, service providers, and large enterprises that require highly available Ethernet services with high performance and guaranteed Quality of Service (QoS).

11.1 VPLS Service Overview

Virtual Private LAN Service (VPLS) is a multipoint-to-multipoint Ethernet bridging service over an IP/MPLS backbone. VPLS connects multiple geographically separated customer sites by emulating a bridging domain. All customer sites connected to the same VPLS service appear to be in the same Local Area Network (LAN) segment. VPLS is also referred to as *Transparent LAN Service* (TLS).

Historically, Ethernet technology was used only in LANs because of its broadcast nature. Ethernet switches are usually located in office LANs to switch local traffic and provide access to routers. Today, with the development of high-speed Ethernet, more and more service providers and large enterprises are using Ethernet in their backbone networks as a Wide Area Network (WAN) technology. Point-to-point high-speed Ethernet links (Gigabit, 10 GB, or higher speeds) are replacing the ATM and TDM links in backbone networks.

VPLS enhances the service offering for service providers who have already deployed an MPLS backbone complementing the Layer 3 Virtual Private Routed Network (VPRN) services. VPLS has been widely deployed in the networks of service providers and enterprises because of its advantages:

- **High Bandwidth Throughput** — Ethernet can provide Gigabit, 10 GB, or higher bandwidth.

- **Plug and Play** — Ethernet switching techniques (for example, MAC switching and Learning, VLAN usage, STP) are mature and well-known. Therefore, Ethernet has lower maintenance costs and provides higher bandwidth throughput than legacy carrier technologies such as ATM, TDM, and Frame-Relay.

- **Service Peering Simplicity** — Service providers provide only Layer 2 bridging services to the customers. Customers do not have to consider the routing peering policy, requirements, and limitations from service providers. The service boundary is clearer: The service provider provides Layer 2 bandwidth; customers take care of their own Layer 3 routing. Customers have the liberty of designing their own IP addressing plans and routing architectures.

- **Ability to Carry Non-IP Traffic** — VPLS provides bridged Ethernet services, so it transports any data traffic that has Ethernet encapsulation, not just IP traffic.
- **Ability to Take Full Advantage of MPLS** — VPLS is usually delivered over an MPLS backbone network. Therefore, VPLS can take full advantage of MPLS resiliency and flexibility, including:
  - Using MPLS Fast Reroute (FRR) or secondary LSP to protect the service transport tunnel, achieving tens of milliseconds failover performance
  - Manipulating the forwarding path in the MPLS domain using traffic engineering (TE)

VPLS was enhanced with features destined to address the Carrier ETH requirements in different market segments. VPLS is used as an end-to-end Ethernet service or as an aggregation to IP VPN PE for the business services market, as DSLAM/PON aggregation and video distribution media for Triple Play, or as Mobile Backhaul aggregation for wireless solutions. VPLS service also inherits all the benefits brought by the MPLS infrastructure, such as traffic engineering on the service transport tunnels, rich tunnel resiliency features, and converged backbone for deploying multiple services. Service policies such as QoS, security, and accounting are deployed on the individual SAPs of service instances and can be different for the ingress direction and the egress direction. These benefits are strong market drivers for VPLS, increasing its popularity among service providers and enterprises.

VPLS has many advantages over the traditional Ethernet bridging service. Figure 11.1 illustrates an example of an IP/MPLS backbone network (with PE and P routers) that provides VPLS service to two customers. Both customers have sites in different geographical locations.

If the services are provided using a legacy Ethernet bridging solution such as Q-in-Q (see [IEEE 802.1ad]) and the P/PE routers are regular Ethernet switches, the service provider must use VLANs to separate the two customers and configure VLAN trunking in all backbone switches end-to-end. When using Ethernet technologies, service providers are limited to a few thousand services (maximum 4K). If redundant forwarding paths exist in the network, the Spanning Tree Protocol (STP) must be used to prevent forwarding loops, providing for minimal traffic engineering capabilities.

Figure 11.1 Example of a VPLS Service Network

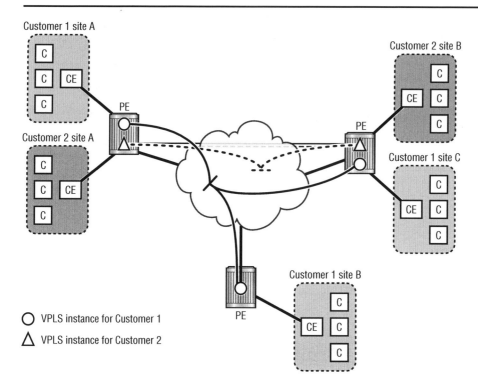

The service provider can take advantage of VPLS to simplify this scenario, as follows:

- Only PE routers have VPLS service instances provisioned. Pseudowires are used to connect the service instances on different PE routers. The P routers are not aware of the VPLS service instances; therefore, VPLS service configuration on the P routers is not required.

- Inside the service provider's core network, the traffic flows of different customers are isolated by the VPLS service instances and pseudowires — VLANs are not required for traffic isolation purposes. In a single PE router, many customers can use the same vlan-id, as long as the customers do not share the same access port.

- VPLS makes VLAN translation between customer sites effortless. In VPLS, the vlan-id is significant only in the local SAP. The vlan-id is stripped off when the traffic enters the service provider's network and is inserted back into the traffic when the traffic leaves the service provider's network. There is no correlation between the ingress vlan-id and the egress vlan-id. Therefore, VLAN translation is a natural characteristic of VPLS.

- VPLS has its own loop prevention mechanism (details are presented in Chapter 15). The backbone network carrying VPLS traffic is an IP/MPLS network; therefore, there is no need to run STP in the backbone network.

- Customers can use STP in their own network. If they do, VPLS can be configured either to participate in STP with the customer as part of their network topology or to transparently pass through the customer's bridged protocol data units (BPDUs). STP interworking is described in Chapter 15.

11.2 VPLS Architecture

VPLS is a pseudowire-based Layer 2 VPN service based on IP/MPLS. The VPLS solutions are defined in RFC 4761 and RFC 4762. VPLS service can be local or distributed over multiple PE routers. In a *local VPLS*, all customer sites are connected to one PE router. Only one PE router participates in the VPLS service. That PE router has one VPLS service instance defined. The PE router's VPLS service instance has at least two SAPs assigned to it. Because no pseudowire is involved, there is no VPN or MPLS encapsulation added to customer traffic.

In a *distributed VPLS*, customer sites are connected to more than one PE router. A PE router participating in a VPLS service is referred to as a *member PE* of that VPLS. Every PE router participating in the VPLS service has a service instance defined on it. The service instance contains at least one SAP and one or more pseudowires to connect to other PE routers participating in the same VPLS. A distributed VPLS requires a pseudowire infrastructure among the participating PE routers.

VPN encapsulation is required when PE routers participating in the same VPLS exchange traffic over the provider backbone network. VPLS encapsulation uses a service-label to differentiate the VPLS traffic belonging to different customers. The PE routers use the label signaling protocol to exchange the service-label (and other pseudowire-related) information. The VPLS service model has two different implementations using two different label-signaling protocols:

- **BGP-VPLS (RFC 4761)** — This implementation uses the Multi-Protocol Border Gateway Protocol (MP-BGP) to signal the service-labels for each VPLS instance. The MP-BGP is also the only option used to signal VPLS membership information. Each PE router uses MP-BGP to exchange l2vpn family prefixes, where the

BGP advertisement contains the VPLS instances provisioned in the PE router, and the service-label information. BGP-VPLS is beyond the scope of this book.

- **LDP-VPLS (RFC 4762, Pseudowire)** — This implementation uses Targeted LDP (T-LDP) to signal the service-labels among PE routers within the same VPLS service. The VPLS members (the PE routers that are part of the same VPLS) may be specified manually or through different auto-discovery procedures — Radius, MP-BGP, or Network Management System (NMS)–based.

The ALSRP VPLS solution currently uses the LDP-VPLS implementation. Targeted LDP sessions among the PE routers are a prerequisite for VPLS service deployment. Figure 11.2 illustrates a distributed VPLS service.

Figure 11.2   VPLS Service Components, Pseudowire Mesh Example

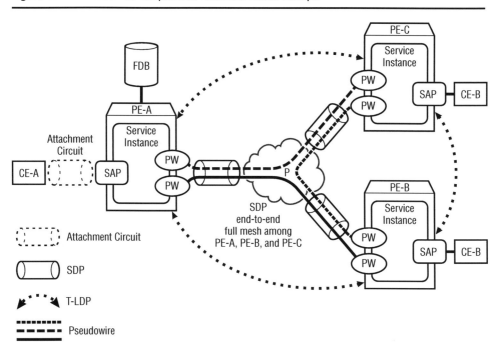

In Figure 11.2, the customer has three sites that need to be connected by the VPLS service. Three PE routers are participating in the VPLS service, each of which has a VPLS service instance created. In the VPLS mesh case, member PE routers must maintain a full mesh of the pseudowires in the service instance to connect to other member PE routers. The fully meshed pseudowires in the VPLS network obey the *split-horizon rule: They do not exchange traffic between each other, but only*

with SAPs. Therefore, forwarding loops are eliminated from the core of the VPLS network. There is no need to deploy the Spanning Tree Protocol (STP) in the VPLS core with pseudowire full mesh. The service instance in each PE router is also referred to as a Virtual Switching Instance (VSI). It performs Ethernet bridging and builds its own forwarding database (FDB). An FDB is also referred to as a *MAC table.* Details of the pseudowire topology within the VPLS instances and forwarding behaviors are discussed in later sections of this chapter. Table 11.1 lists the components required to build a VPLS service instance.

Table 11.1 VPLS Service Components

Component	Description
Customer	The VPLS service instance must be associated with a customer when it is created.
Service Instance	The VPLS's implementation in each member PE router is a service instance. The procedures of VSI for handling traffic are based on Ethernet transparent bridging.
SAP	The customer-facing endpoint of the VPLS, which is connected to CE devices over a native Ethernet attachment circuit (AC). In a VPLS mesh each VPLS service instance must have at least one SAP.
SDP	The Service Destination Point (SDP) represents the tunnel connectivity between two PEs. It is built around one or more backbone tunnels. SDP can be shared by multiple VSIs and by all types of services; it is not exclusive to VPLS. Among all the PE routers participating in the same VPLS, an SDP full mesh is required to provide VPLS infrastructure.
Pseudowire	The connection between related VSIs in all member PE routers of a VPLS. A pseudowire connects two VPLS service instances in the two PE routers and provides appropriate encapsulation and de-encapsulation for the customer Ethernet frames. Pseudowires bind to the SDP to carry traffic over the provider's backbone network.
Forwarding database	The MAC table built by performing MAC learning on the Ethernet traffic. Every service instance has its own FDB.
STP state machine	VPLS is capable of participating in STP with the customer devices, or it can transparently bypass (flood) BPDUs to customer sites without processing them.
T-LDP	Pseudowire signaling requires Targeted LDP sessions among VPLS member PE routers.

Among these required components, T-LDP and SDP are discussed in detail in Chapter 9. STP in the VPLS service is explained in Chapter 13. VPLS SAP, pseudowire, and FDB are discussed in later sections of this chapter.

Ethernet Transparent Bridging

VPLS provides Ethernet bridging services to the customer. Therefore, understanding Ethernet bridging behavior is key to understanding VPLS learning and forwarding behavior. The basic function provided by standard Layer 2 Ethernet switches is called *transparent bridging*, defined by IEEE 802.1d.

Transparent bridging consists of the following five basic processes:

- **Learning** — The switch learns the source MAC address of the frame upon receiving it. If the MAC entry already exists, it is refreshed. *Learning* is the process of recording the frame's MAC address, the ID of the service entity (SAP or pseudowire) where the frame is received, and, optionally, the ID of the VLAN to which the bridge port belongs. This information is used to build the FDB of the switch. The FDB can learn only unicast MAC addresses.

- **Forwarding** — The switch forwards frames to the destination if the destination MAC address of the frame is a unicast MAC address, and a matching entry is found in the FDB.

- **Filtering** — When a switch receives a frame, it performs FDB lookup on the frame's destination MAC address to make a forwarding decision. If a matching entry is found in the FDB and it is associated with the SAP or pseudowire where the frame is received, the switch ignores the forwarding request and discards the frame. This is referred to as *filtering*.

- **Flooding** — If the switch receives a frame that has an unknown unicast MAC address or is a multicast or broadcast frame, the switch replicates the frame and floods it to all bridge ports with split-horizon rules assumed. These three types of traffic are sometimes referred to as BUM traffic — Broadcast, unknown Unicast, and Multicast.

- **Aging** — The MAC entries stored in the FDB are refreshed by ingress traffic with the same source MAC address. If traffic with a matching *source* MAC address does not arrive within a certain amount of time, the MAC entry expires from the FDB. If later traffic with the same MAC address as *destination* arrives, the switch floods the frames to prevent traffic loss from a potential network failure.

VPLS performs the same transparent bridging function for the customer's switches. From the customer's point of view, the VPLS core behaves exactly like an Ethernet switch, and all CE devices appear to be connected to one LAN.

VPLS Virtual Switching Instance (VSI)

A VPLS service instance contains SAPs and pseudowires. SAPs connect the VPLS PE routers to customer devices. Pseudowires connect member PE routers that participate in the same VPLS. In a PE router, the VPLS service instance provides Ethernet bridging services to the SAPs and pseudowires. A PE router can participate in more than one VPLS service for more than one customer; therefore, a PE router may have more than one VPLS service instance. SAPs and pseudowires that belong to different service instances are *isolated* by the service instances and never exchange traffic. In the case of Layer 3 VPRN, as per RFC 4364 (formerly RFC 2547bis), each participating PE router has a *Virtual Routing Forwarder* (VRF) that acts as a virtual router to a particular customer. Similarly, in VPLS, a service instance is a *Virtual Switching Instance* (VSI). A VSI performs the same Ethernet bridging functions as an Ethernet bridge, but only among the SAPs and pseudowires that belong to the same VPLS service instance. VSIs are isolated from each other by the PE router. Each customer can see only its own VSIs.

An Ethernet bridge has bridge ports and an FDB (MAC table). It forwards traffic among the bridge ports according to the FDB. So does the VPLS Virtual Switching Instance. Every VPLS service instance has its own FDB. FDBs belonging to different VPLS services are isolated. The difference is that the VSI is *virtual*: It is created by the VPLS service instance in the PE router's hardware. VSIs perform full Ethernet bridging services.

A VSI has the following features and capabilities:

- Bridge ports; in a VPLS service instance, the VSI's bridge ports are either SAPs or the pseudowires that connect to the remote PE router.

- Builds a forwarding database (MAC table); in a VPLS service instance, the VSI learns the traffic's unicast source MAC addresses and builds the FDB.

- Performs transparent bridging among bridge ports (details of transparent bridging are reviewed in the next section).

- Recognizes VLANs and is capable of VLAN trunking and translation.

- Can participate in STP and processing the BPDUs or transparently bypassing the BPDUs.

- Can participate in other Ethernet protocols or transparently bypass them, depending on the SAP type and the VPLS service configuration, for example, EFM OAM (802.3ah), CFM (802.1ag), and Link Aggregation (LACP or static).
- Supports multicast features such as IGMP snooping and PIM snooping. (Multicast features in VPLS are beyond the scope of this book.)

As an advanced Ethernet bridging service, the VPLS VSI has some enhanced functions. Table 11.2 lists the five *transparent bridging processes*, comparing legacy Ethernet bridging with the VPLS bridging.

Table 11.2 Comparison of Ethernet Bridging and VPLS VSI Bridging

Process	Ethernet Bridging	Virtual Switching Instance (VSI)
Learning	Learns the traffic source unicast MAC addresses and adds them to FDB, or refreshes existing entries.	Same as Ethernet bridging. A VSI learns the MAC addresses from both SAPs and pseudowires. Learning can be disabled in a VSI.
Forwarding	Forwards known unicast traffic to the destination bridge port. When the switch receives traffic, it performs an FDB lookup to find the proper bridge port to send the traffic out.	Same as Ethernet bridging. If the destination point is a remote PE, traffic is encapsulated and sent over a pseudowire. VSI supports policy-based forwarding, directing traffic to the target bridge port, overriding the FDB lookup result.
Flooding	Floods BUM traffic to all other bridge ports, respecting the split-horizon rule.	Same as Ethernet bridging. In addition, VSI can be configured to discard rather than flood unknown unicast traffic. BUM traffic can be treated separately by QoS.
Filtering	Discards traffic destined to a port where it is received.	Same as Ethernet bridging
Aging	Removes a MAC entry from the FDB if it is not refreshed by incoming traffic for a period longer than the MaxAgeOut timer.	Same as Ethernet bridging. In VPLS, the default age for SAP-learned MAC entries is 300 seconds. The default age for pseudowire-learned MAC entries is 900 seconds.

More details about the learning and forwarding behavior of VPLS are presented in later sections.

VPLS Forwarding Decisions

VPLS forwards customer Ethernet frames to their destinations the same way an Ethernet bridge does. When VPLS service is provisioned in the service provider's network, the service is ready to accept customer frames and forward them to the correct destinations. A VPLS service instance can receive traffic from either a customer SAP or from a pseudowire from the remote PE router. In both cases, the VPLS service instance first validates the traffic and then, if the traffic is legitimate, performs learning and forwarding.

> **Note:** The Quality of Service (QoS) process is also involved in the VPLS service instance's forwarding decision. QoS may decide to buffer or drop a legitimate frame to meet the service quality requirement. Because QoS is beyond the scope of this book, any discussions on forwarding assume that QoS approves all frames for forwarding

When a customer frame arrives at an access port on a PE router with VPLS SAPs defined, the PE router performs several actions, as follows:

1. **Filtering** — The PE router must decide if the frame received is legitimate or not. If not, the frame is discarded. If it is legitimate, one of the VPLS SAPs accepts the frame and starts the learning and forwarding process. If there is any filter configured in the SAP-ingress residing on the frame receiving port, the frame is examined against the filter. The filter can have matching criteria (for Layer 2, Layer 3, or Layer 4) as conditions. If the frame is accepted by the filters, it will be further handled by the VSI. Otherwise, the frame is discarded.

2. **Classifying and Mapping** — Next, the PE router decides which service the frame belongs to (classify) and lets the corresponding VSI further handle the traffic (map). All SAPs residing on the frame receiving port compare the tagging values in the received frame to the tagging configuration of the SAPs to determine if they should accept the traffic. SAPs with different encapsulation types and values accept different frames. Details regarding SAPs with different encapsulation values and which types of frames are accepted are discussed in the "VPLS Service Access Point" section of this chapter.

3. **Learning** — If the frame is accepted by the SAP in the ingress point, the VSI learns the frame's source MAC address (also referred to as the *customer*

source address or C-SA) and adds it to the FDB. The C-SA is associated with the SAP that accepts the frame. Details are discussed in later sections.

4. **Encapsulation and Forwarding** — After learning the frame's C-SA, the VSI compares the destination MAC address of the customer frame (also referred to as the *customer destination address* or C-DA) to the FDB entries:

    - If a matching entry is found, the traffic is forwarded to the port associated with that entry. If not, traffic is categorized as BUM traffic and processed accordingly (either flooded or discarded, based on the configuration of the VPLS service instance).

    - If the destination of the frame is another SAP local to the PE router, the frame is sent to the egress direction of the target SAP. The SAP may perform VLAN tagging on the frame depending on the SAP's configured VLAN encapsulation type and value (this is discussed in detail in the "VPLS Service Access Points" section). The frame is then sent to the SAP-egress point and then to the customer site.

    - If the destination of the frame is a remote PE router, the PE router must send the traffic through a pseudowire to reach the remote PE router. The pseudowire performs VPN encapsulation on the frame by inserting the vc-label in the frame. Then, the SDP associated with the pseudowire performs tunnel encapsulation on the frame by inserting the transport-label or GRE header in the frame. The double-encapsulated traffic is then sent to the remote PE router across the backbone network. Details of pseudowire encapsulation are discussed in the "VPLS Mesh Pseudowire" section of this chapter.

When a customer frame arrives at the SDP from a remote PE router, it is a double-encapsulated packet, and the following process is used:

1. The SDP validates the tunnel encapsulation (GRE header or MPLS tunnel-label). If the validation succeeds, the SDP removes the tunnel encapsulation and exposes the vc-label (VPN encapsulation). The de-multiplexer (demux) in the SDP uses the service-label to determine which pseudowire owns the traffic. Then the service-label is removed, and the frame is sent to the pseudowire.

2. When the pseudowire receives the de-encapsulated frame, the VSI learns (or refreshes) the C-SA address in the FDB and associates the C-SA with the pseudowire. The VSI then performs an FDB lookup against the traffic frame's

C-DA to determine the destination. If a matching entry is found, the VSI forwards the frame to its destination.

3. If the destination is a SAP local to the PE router, the frame is sent to the egress direction of the target SAP. The SAP may perform VLAN tagging on the frame depending on the VLAN encapsulation type and value of the SAP (this is discussed in detail in the "VPLS Service Access Point" section). The frame is then sent through the SAP-egress direction to the customer site.

4. Under certain conditions, the result of the FDB lookup may be that the destination is another pseudowire. These conditions (H-VPLS, PW-switching, or PBB-VPLS) are discussed in detail in other chapters.

VPLS Data Frame Encapsulation

When a VPLS service instance receives a data frame from a customer's network, it performs a lookup in its FDB to determine where to forward or flood the traffic. If the traffic destination is one of the remote member PE routers, the frame is sent to the pseudowire connected to that PE. VPLS uses Ethernet pseudowire encapsulation to encapsulate traffic as per RFC 4448. Figure 11.3 illustrates a frame walk-through in a VPLS service.

Figure 11.3 VPLS Traffic Packet Walk-Through

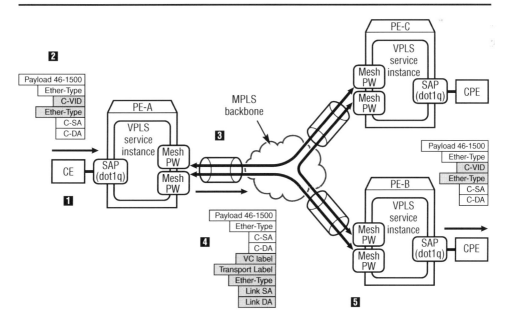

Figure 11.3 is an overview of a typical traffic flow from one CE device to another across an MPLS backbone network. The actual frame format along the path varies depending on the configuration of the SAP and the pseudowire. The forwarding behavior of each service entity is covered in detail in later chapters.

The details for the packet walk-through begin when the customer's frame arrives at the SAP-ingress in PE-A's VPLS service instance. The numbered steps in the figure indicate the following tasks:

1.   The SAP in PE-A strips off the VLAN tag(s) used for service delimitation in the SAP-ingress direction. The VSI updates the FDB with the C-SA (associated with the SAP where the traffic is received) or refreshes the existing entry.

2.   The service instance then performs FDB lookup on the C-DA and determines that the traffic must be forwarded to PE-B. Since PE-B is remote, the pseudowire to PE-B is used to transport the traffic.

3.   The pseudowire performs Ethernet pseudowire encapsulation by adding a vc-label to the customer frame and then passes the traffic to the SDP it is bound to. The SDP then performs tunnel encapsulation by adding a transport-label. The traffic travels across the MPLS backbone to PE-B.

4.   PE-B receives the double-encapsulated frame and first strips the transport-label. Then, it uses the vc-label to identify the service instance to which the frame belongs. In the example, the result indicates that the frame belongs to the VPLS instance.

5.   The VSI receives the traffic and learns the C-SA (associated with the pseudowire on which the traffic is received) or refreshes the existing entry. The FDB lookup on C-DA determines that the traffic should be sent from the SAP to the CE device. The service-delimiting VLAN tags on the egress SAP are added before the packet is sent out on the egress SAP. Now frame forwarding in this VPLS is complete.

11.3 VPLS Mesh-Pseudowires

The basic concept of pseudowires was presented in Chapter 9. This section describes:

- How pseudowires are used in a VPLS service to connect VPLS member PE routers
- VPLS service topology variations and different types of pseudowires in VPLS
- The T-LDP signaling process used to signal the mesh-pseudowires between VPLS member PE routers

- The learning and forwarding behavior of VPLS mesh-pseudowires
- An example of a distributed VPLS service configuration

Pseudowires are bidirectional. A pseudowire carries VPLS traffic between two PE routers. In the ALSRP VPLS solution, pseudowires are referred to as *SDP-bindings*. In this book, the terms *SDP-binding* and *pseudowire* are interchangeable.

A distributed VPLS service requires more than one PE router to participate in the service. All PE routers involved in a VPLS service are *members* of that VPLS. Pseudowires connect the service instances in all member PE routers. When provisioning a VPLS service instance in a member PE router, pseudowires are configured to connect the service instances in all remote member PE routers.

There are two prerequisites for establishing the pseudowires:

- SDPs among all member PE routers are required. The SDPs perform tunnel encapsulation on the Ethernet pseudowire-encapsulated VPLS traffic and carry it over the provider backbone to the remote member PE router. A pseudowire must be bound to an SDP that terminates at the correct far-end PE router.
- T-LDP sessions are required among all member PE routers. The T-LDP sessions signal the vc-label for the pseudowire.

VPLS Mesh-Pseudowire Learning and Forwarding Behavior

In a VPLS mesh, a member PE router is connected to every other remote member PE by a pseudowire resulting in a mesh infrastructure. In ALRSP terminology, these pseudowires are referred to as *mesh-pseudowires*. Any two peering PE routers have a direct pseudowire between them. VPLS is a Layer 2 VPN service. Each PE router has a VPLS service instance for the end-to-end VPLS service. Each service instance has a VSI that performs transparent bridging among the bridge ports — pseudowires and SAPs. (SAPs are discussed in detail in the next section.) In a fully meshed network, the traffic forwarding behavior of the pseudowire must be regulated to prevent forwarding loops.

VPLS provides loop avoidance for the mesh using the following *split-horizon rule: When a PE router receives VPLS traffic from a mesh-pseudowire, it can only forward or flood the traffic to SAPs in the VPLS service instance.* Exchanging traffic between mesh-pseudowires is not allowed, to prevent forwarding loops from being formed by mesh-pseudowires in the VPLS core network. This eliminates the need for STP in the VPLS core network.

A pseudowire connects the service instances of two PE routers participating in the same VPLS service. The pseudowire uses service-labels to perform traffic encapsulation and sends traffic through the SDP to the far-end PE router. *Mesh attribute* refers to the rule of traffic forwarding defined by the VPLS service instance (the VSI); it is *not* a characteristic of the pseudowire. Mesh and spoke are alternative ways to use the pseudowires to forward traffic. It is the decision of the local VPLS service instance whether or not to prevent the pseudowires from exchanging traffic with each other. When the service instances of two PE routers set up the pseudowire, the mesh characteristic is not exchanged in the pseudowire signaling.

Provisioning mesh-pseudowire is a two-step process:

1.	First, the PE router creates a pseudowire.

2.	Then, if the configuration specifies the mesh type, the VSI adds the pseudowire to the *mesh bridge group*.

All pseudowires created in the PE router with `mesh` specified cannot exchange traffic between themselves.

If the member PE routers in a VPLS service are connected in a mesh topology and a mesh-pseudowire fails, the connection between the PE routers at each end of the pseudowire is lost.

The pseudowire resides on the SDP, and the SDP usually contains one or a group of MPLS tunnels. As a result, all pseudowires that share the same SDP take advantage of these redundancy mechanisms associated with the MPLS tunnels — for example, Fast Reroute (FRR).

This section explains only mesh-pseudowire forwarding. The term *pseudowire ingress* describes the direction of the traffic from a far-end PE router to the local service instance through the SDP. The term *pseudowire egress* describes the direction of the traffic from the local service instance to a far-end PE router through the SDP.

Figure 11.4 illustrates the basic forwarding behavior of a mesh-pseudowire in a VPLS instance.

The forwarding behaviors of mesh-pseudowires are as follows:

•	When a mesh-pseudowire receives unicast traffic with a known destination from a far-end PE router, it forwards the traffic to the destination SAP according to the result of the FDB lookup.

•	The mesh-pseudowire is not supposed to receive unicast traffic that has a destination of another PE router connected to another mesh-pseudowire. If this happens, it means that the VPLS service is incorrectly configured; and the mesh-pseudowire discards the traffic (shown by the black X in the left diagram in Figure 11.4).

- If the mesh-pseudowire receives broadcast, unknown unicast and multicast (BUM) traffic from the customer site, it replicates the traffic and floods it to all SAPs. It does not replicate BUM traffic to other mesh-pseudowires (shown by the black X in the right diagram in Figure 11.4).

- If another SAP receives ingress BUM traffic, the bridge port floods the traffic to all mesh-pseudowires and to the other SAPs. The mesh-pseudowires then encapsulate the traffic and send it to the far-end PE routers.

Figure 11.4   VPLS Mesh-Pseudowire Forwarding Behavior

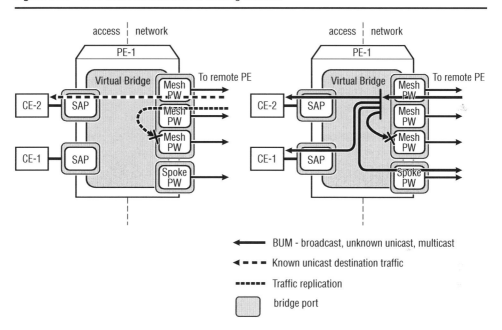

VPLS Mesh-Pseudowire Signaling Process

T-LDP is used to signal the pseudowires for the VPLS service as per RFC 4762. T-LDP signals the service-label, which is used by the receiving router as the service de-multiplexer.

After a VPLS service instance is provisioned on a PE router, pseudowires must be locally defined. For every pseudowire defined, the PE router locally assigns a value for the vc-label. This label is the *ingress vc-label* for the local router because it is used for de-encapsulating the ingress traffic. The same vc-label must be distributed to the remote PE routers to be used for VPLS encapsulation before the remote PE router sends the traffic to the local PE router. The PE router then sends an LDP *label-*

mapping message, which distributes the vc-label to the remote PE router. The far-end PE router performs the same action — it also generates and distributes a vc-label to the local PE router. The local PE router uses this service-label to perform VPLS encapsulation before it sends traffic to the far-end PE router. The local PE router considers the vc-label distributed by the far-end PE router as the egress service-label because it is used for encapsulating the egress traffic.

Figure 11.5 illustrates the processes of setting up the mesh-pseudowire (Steps 1 and 2) and tearing it down (Steps 3 and 4).

Figure 11.5 Setting Up and Tearing Down the Mesh-Pseudowire

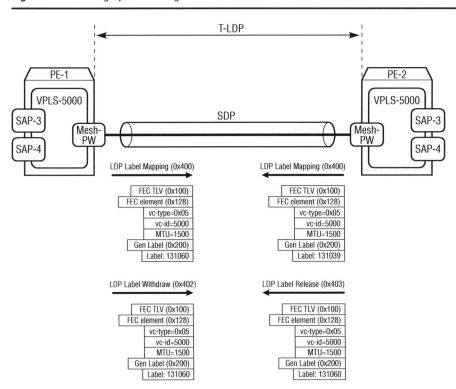

1 VPLS 5000 is configured and enabled in PE-1. The mesh-pseudowire is then configured. PE-1 assigns an ingress-vc-label (131060) and distributes it to PE-2.

2 VPLS 5000 is configured and enabled in PE-2. The mesh-pseudowire is then configured. PE-2 assigns an ingress-vc-label (131039) and distributes it to PE-1.

3 VPLS 5000 is `shutdown`. The PE withdraws the vc-label from the remote PE-router.

4 PE-2 removes the vc-label (131060) from the label database. PE-2 then responds to the Label Withdraw with a Label Release to confirm the removal of the vc-label.

PE routers use four T-LDP messages for mesh-pseudowire signaling with a remote PE router:

- **Label Mapping** — Establishes the mesh-pseudowire. A Label Mapping message contains a Forwarding Equivalent Class (FEC) type–length value (TLV) with the following pseudowire identification information: vc-type, vc-id, and interface parameters. The interface parameter sub-TLV contains the vc-mtu. There is also a General Label TLV that contains a service-label. The PE router uses the Label Mapping message to establish the pseudowire and distributes the service-label to the peering remote PE router.

- **Label Withdraw and Label Release** — The local PE router sends a label withdraw message to tear down the mesh-pseudowire. The remote PE router sends a label release message to confirm the removal of the label. Both messages contain an FEC TLV with the following pseudowire identification information: vc-type, vc-id, and interface-parameter. There is also a General Label TLV that contains the service-label being withdrawn.

- **Address Withdraw** — An address withdraw message notifies the peering PE router that it should flush the MAC address. This is part of the MAC-flush operation, which is explained later in this book.

Mesh-Pseudowire Configuration Example

Figure 11.6 illustrates a sample configuration for PE-1 participating in VPLS 5000 and the SDP configuration from PE-1 to reach PE-2.

The SDP connected to the far-end router must be created before the pseudowire is created. The SDP configuration on the left in Figure 11.6 contains the far-end PE router's router-id. In the ALSRP VPLS implementation, the creation of mesh-pseudowire is a *binding* process, binding the vc-id with an SDP using the `mesh-sdp <sdp-id>:<vc-id>` command in the VPLS service configuration context. The command uniquely defines a pseudowire for its VPLS service instance:

- The `mesh-sdp` command creates the mesh-pseudowire. Both `mesh-sdp` commands create the pseudowire and *bind* the pseudowire to an SDP. The binding process associates the pseudowire with an SDP. The pseudowire uses the service transport tunnels contained in the SDP to carry the traffic.

- The `sdp-id` parameter specifies the ID of the SDP that the pseudowire is to be bound to. The SDP is provisioned prior to the creation of the pseudowire. Each

SDP is configured to connect to a specific far-end PE router, defined in the SDP configuration using the **far-end** command.

- The **vc-id** parameter specifies the pseudowire's identification used by the T-LDP as a value for Layer 2 FEC (0x128) to signal the pseudowire. A vc-id is a manually specified value that has a range from 1 to 4,294,967,295. It is *point-to-point significant*, meaning that the same vc-id value must be used in the pseudowire creation command on both sides of the PE router. *The vc-id is not the same as the vc-label:* The vc-id is the circuit-identifier used to identify the pseudowire. The service-label is an MPLS label that the pseudowire uses to encapsulate VPN traffic. The label value is automatically assigned by the local PE router from the router's label space and is distributed to the far-end PE router.

Figure 11.6 VPLS Mesh-Pseudowire Configuration Example

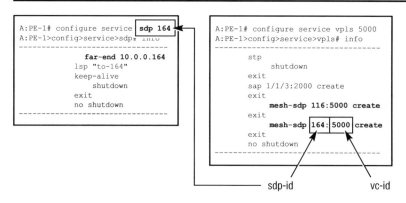

VPLS Static Mesh-Pseudowire

It is also possible to create a static mesh-pseudowire. When creating s static mesh-pseudowire, the vc-labels used by the pseudowire are manually configured in the PE routers. T-LDP signaling is not required to establish the static pseudowire. The operator statically specifies the ingress and egress vc-labels in the pseudowire configuration on PE routers on both sides of the pseudowire. The command of mesh-sdp <sdp-id>:<vc-id> is also used to configure the static mesh-pseudowire. The pseudowire is bound to the SDP specified in the command. However, the vc-id is not used because there is no T-LDP pseudowire signaling. Figure 11.7 illustrates an example of configuring static vc-labels in a mesh-pseudowire configuration.

Figure 11.7 VPLS Static Mesh-Pseudowire Configuration Example

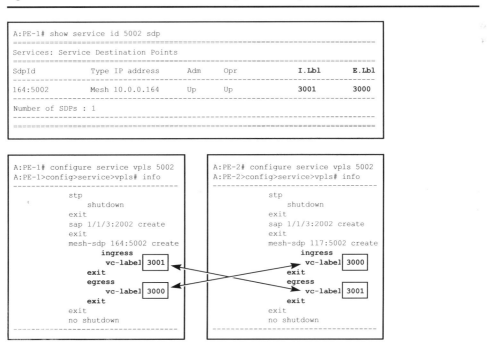

In both PE-1 and PE-2, the ingress and egress service-labels are statically configured under the mesh-pseudowire configuration. PE-1's ingress vc-label (3001) is PE-2's egress vc-label, and vice versa. The static pseudowire is operationally up as long as the SDP carrying it is operationally up. The VPLS service instance between two PE routers uses the static mesh-pseudowire to carry traffic the same way as if the pseudowire were dynamically signaled.

Static vc-label mapping is not scalable and should be used only in rare conditions, for example, if the peering PE device is a third-party device that is not compatible with T-LDP pseudowire signaling. It is strongly recommended that the operator accurately document the label mappings and VPLS service instances when using static label mapping.

Data Traffic Format on the Pseudowire: vc-type

Once the pseudowire is established and operationally up, it is ready to forward traffic to the far-end PE router over the SDP. When a VPLS service instance receives customer frames from the SAP, it determines whether the frames should be forwarded to the remote PE router through a pseudowire. If the customer frames are VLAN-tagged, the service instance must determine whether the VLAN tag should be forwarded with the traffic or stripped off. The next part of the discussion focuses on the customer data format in the pseudowire; in particular, how the service instance handles the traffic's VLAN tag when using pseudowires to carry the traffic.

When a customer frame enters the VPLS service instance from the SAP-ingress, it may be tagged with a vlan-id. From the perspective of the VPLS service provider, the vlan-id can be:

- **Non-Service-Delimiting** — The vlan-id is only used by the customer. It is not meaningful to the service provider at all. The service provider does not care about the existence or the value of the VLAN tag on the customer frames. When a customer asks the service provider to trunk all of their VLANs transparently, this means that the vlan-id is non-service-delimiting.

- **Service-Delimiting** — The service provider understands the vlan-id and uses it to distinguish the traffic flows from different customers. For example, Customers A and B have different VPLS services purchased for their networks. The two customers may share the same access port in the PE router to connect their sites to the provider's network. In order to distinguish the two customers, the service provider has an agreement with the two customers that Customer A uses vlan-id 100 to tag traffic sent to the VPLS network, and Customer B uses vlan-id 200 to tag its traffic. Therefore, the service provider can deploy two *dot1q*-type SAPs, one with vlan-id 100 and the other with vlan-id 200, to distinguish the traffic flows of the two customers. The vlan-ids are meaningful to the service provider because the service provider uses the vlan-ids as service delimiters.

If the VLAN tags are non-service-delimiting, the VPLS service's SAPs are configured to ignore the VLAN tags at the SAP-ingress (for example, `null SAP` or `dot-1q default SAP`). The provider does not need to know the value of the VLAN tags. The VPLS service then treats the VLAN tag as part of the customer data and sends it to the remote customer site. Because the VPLS service treats non-service-delimiting VLAN tags as part of the customer traffic, the VLAN tags of the customer remain in the frame, treated as part of the customer data frame, and are carried by the pseudowire to the far-end PE router.

If the VLAN tags are service-delimiting, the SAPs in the VPLS service are configured with a specific VLAN-tag value. The provider configures the tag to identify which customer owns the traffic. The SAPs accept only traffic with matching vlan-ids. This type of tag is called a *service-delimiting VLAN-tag*. When the received customer frames have service-delimiting VLAN-tags, the type (or mode) of the pseudowire determines whether or not the pseudowire carries the VLAN-tag.

As mentioned in Chapter 8, VPLS uses Ethernet pseudowire encapsulation defined in RFC 4448 and PW signaling procedures defined in RFC 4447. These RFCs specify two types of Ethernet pseudowires: *tagged* mode represented in T-LDP signaling as `vc-type vlan` (0x0004), and *raw* mode represented in T-LDP signaling as `vc-type Ethernet` (0x0005). The two modes differ as to whether or not they add a service-delimiting tag to the packet sent on the pseudowire:

- In tagged mode (vc-type vlan) a service-delimiting tag is added to the VPLS-encapsulated Ethernet frame traveling through the pseudowire. The tag value is signaled through T-LDP by the remote PE using the Requested vlan-id field from the Interface parameter sub-TLV. The remote PE will strip the service delimiting tag received on the pseudowire.

- In raw mode (vc-type ether) there is no service-delimiting VLAN tag added to the packet sent on the pseudowire. This is the default mode for VPLS pseudowires.

Note: A vc-type VLAN adds more encapsulation overhead, especially if the customer traffic is tagged or double-tagged when it is received from the SAP-ingress. This may cause the MPLS-encapsulated traffic packet size to exceed the SDP's packet size limit (MTU). If the SDP path MTU value is close to the service MTU value and the network port MTU value, use a vc-type VLAN with caution.

To maintain service integrity, the vc-type must be the same on both ends of the pseudowire. The vc-type is configured in the pseudowire configuration in the VPLS service instance on a per pseudowire basis. A pseudowire does not become operationally up if the LDP label-mapping messages sent by the PE routers on the two sides of the pseudowire have different vc-type values.

The vc-type vlan (0x0004) was designed to accommodate older PE implementations requiring a service-delimiting tag in the frame to distinguish the destination VSI. Although it supports both Ethernet PW vc-types, ALSRP VPLS does not require this service-delimiting tag. The PW vc-label is used to identify the VSI.

For the VLAN vc-type, the VLAN tag may be different for each pseudowire. If that's the case, the vlan-vc-tag command can be used in the pseudowire configuration to specify the required vlan-id to be used to tag the traffic. Figure 11.8 illustrates a pseudowire with a service-delimiting VLAN tag and vlan-vc-tag configured. The sample configuration shows a pseudowire between PE-1 and PE-2. The PE-1 router expects to receive the traffic from the pseudowire with a service-delimiting tag value of 2,000, and the PE-2 router expects to receive the traffic from the pseudowire with a service-delimiting tag value of 3,000.

Figure 11.8   Pseudowire vc-type Configuration and vc-vlan Translation

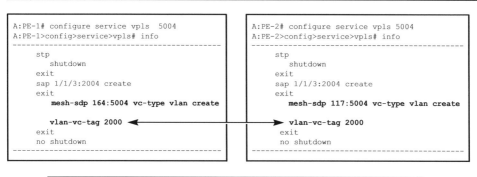

```
A:PE-1# configure service vpls  5004
A:PE-1>config>service>vpls# info
-------------------------------------------------
    stp
        shutdown
    exit
    sap 1/1/3:2004 create
    exit
        mesh-sdp 164:5004 vc-type vlan create

        vlan-vc-tag 2000 ◄
    exit
    no shutdown
-------------------------------------------------
```

```
A:PE-2# configure service vpls 5004
A:PE-2>config>service>vpls# info
-------------------------------------------------
    stp
        shutdown
    exit
    sap 1/1/3:2004 create
    exit
        mesh-sdp 117:5004 vc-type vlan create

     ► vlan-vc-tag 2000
     exit
     no shutdown
-------------------------------------------------
```

```
A:PE-2# show service id 5004 sdp detail
===============================================================
Services: Service Destination Points Details
===============================================================
---------------------------------------------------------------
  Sdp Id 117:5004  -(10.0.0.117)
---------------------------------------------------------------
SDP Id            : 117:5004            Type            : Mesh
VC Type           : VLAN                VC Tag          : 2000
Admin Path MTU    : 0                   Oper Path MTU   : 9190
Far End           : 10.0.0.117          Delivery        : MPLS
Admin State       : Up                  Oper State      : Up
Acct. Pol         : None                Collect Stats   : Disabled
Ingress Label     : 131045              Egress Label    : 131036
Ing mac Fltr      : n/a                 Egr mac Fltr    : n/a
--- output omitted ---
```

The vc-type and vlan-vc tag translation affects only the tagging format of the frames on the pseudowire. Service-delimiting VLAN tags do not affect forwarding decisions, and do not impact the frame's tagging value when the frame is sent to customer sites. The SAP encapsulation type/value configuration determines the tagging of the customer frames sent to a customer site.

11.4 VPLS Service Access Points

VPLS provides Layer 2 Ethernet bridging services to customers. Customer sites are connected to the VPLS through Ethernet Service Access Points (SAPs) over attachment circuits. Traffic enters into and is sent out of the SAP in a format native to the customer network. The SAP is the customer traffic's entrance point to and exit point from the service provider's network.

The SAP exchanges traffic with customer sites in two directions: SAP-ingress and SAP-egress. From the SAP's perspective, the *ingress* direction is from the CE to the provider's network, and the *egress* direction is from the provider's network to the CE devices. Each direction can be configured with different QoS, security, and accounting policies to provide service quality differentiation, protection, and statistics. The SAP is a logical service entity and is associated with physical ports to forward traffic. The SAP can be associated only with ports that are in *access mode*. If an access port is configured with a certain encapsulation type (dot1q or qinq), multiple SAPs (belonging to the same or different VPLS service instances) can share the same access port by using different VLAN tag values. The encapsulation value is used as the de-multiplexer to differentiate the SAPs. One typical example is where several SAPs (belonging to the same VPLS or different VPLS services) use different vlan-ids to share the same physical port and access circuit. Figure 11.9 illustrates the direction of traffic in a VPLS service instance.

The SAPs and pseudowires are connected through the local VSI. From a packet forwarding perspective, the SAPs and pseudowires within the same VSI are connected through the *switching fabric*. The *switching fabric* is the data path engine of the service router and switches data packets from one bridge port to another. This is a logical view of switching fabric — a hardware discussion is beyond the scope of this book. Figure 11.10 illustrates the forwarding behavior of VPLS SAPs.

Figure 11.9 VPLS Traffic Direction

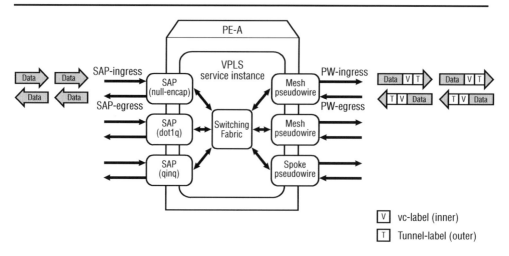

Figure 11.10 VPLS SAP Forwarding Behavior

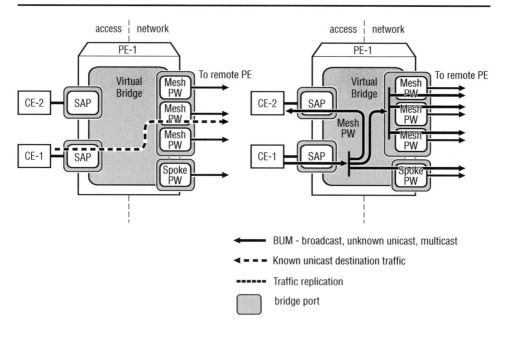

The VSI in the VPLS service instance considers each SAP to be a single bridge port. The forwarding behaviors of a VPLS SAP are as follows:

- When the SAP receives unicast traffic with a known destination MAC address from the customer site, it forwards the traffic to the destination according to the result of the FDB lookup.
- When the SAP receives BUM traffic from the customer site, it replicates the traffic and floods it to all other SAPs and pseudowires.
- When other bridge ports receive ingress BUM traffic, they flood the traffic to the local SAPs (except the one where the traffic is received). The local SAP forwards the traffic to the customer site.

Note: This description of forwarding behavior considers only the bridge port to which the traffic is sent — the frame's VLAN tagging is not discussed.

SAP Types Supported by VPLS

Different types of VPN services support different types of physical interfaces. VPLS accepts Ethernet and SONET/SDH interfaces. Table 11..3 lists the supported types of SAP encapsulation and sample encapsulation-ids.

Table 11.3 SAP Encapsulation Supported by VPLS

Port Type	Encapsulation	Definition
Ethernet	Null (encap-id=0, for example, 1/1/1)	Supports untagged Ethernet frames (or frames that contain non-service-delimiting customer VLAN tags that are ignored by the service and carried over the SP core transparently). One service per port.
Ethernet	dot1q (for example, 1/1/1 :100)	Supports 802.1q-tagged Ethernet frames. The service provider uses the service-delimiting tag to differentiate customer traffic streams that share the same physical port. Multiple services per port.

(continued)

Table 11.3 SAP Encapsulation Supported by VPLS *(continued)*

Port Type	Encapsulation	Definition
Ethernet	Q-in-Q (for example, 1/1/1 :100.200)	Supports double-802.1q-tagged Ethernet frames. The service provider uses both tags to differentiate customer traffic streams that share the same physical port. Multiple services per port.
SONET/SDH TDM	BCP-null (for example, 1/2/1)	Supports bridged services on a SONET/SDH port/channel. Typically used by two devices with point-to-point protocol (PPP). One service per port.
SONET/SDH TDM	BCP-dot1q (for example, 1/2/1:200)	Supports bridged services on a SONET/SDH port/channel. Uses an 802.1q tag to multiplex customer traffic. Typically used by two devices that have multiple bridged service. Multiple services per port.
SONET/SDH ATM	ATM (for example, 2/1/1:10/100)	Supports RFC 2684, Ethernet bridged encapsulation. The SAP encapsulation value is <port-id>:<vpi>/<vci>.
SONET/SDH FR	Frame-Relay (for example, 2/2/1:300)	Supports RFC 2427, Ethernet bridged encapsulation. The SAP encapsulation value is <port-id>:<dlci>.

The SAP forwarding behaviors discussed previously apply to all VPLS SAPs, regardless of access port type (for example, Ethernet or ATM) or encapsulation type and value. For the ease of discussion, Ethernet ports are used to discuss VPLS SAP. There are three types of encapsulation for Ethernet frames: untagged, 802.1q tagging, and Q-in-Q double tagging. Different SAP types are designed to forward these different types of traffic. The SAP in the VPLS service instance must be configured to the correct encapsulation type and value so it can correctly forward the Ethernet frames. If the SAP's type or value does not match the data traffic's type or value, the Ethernet frames are discarded. Therefore, the operator must understand the forwarding behavior of each SAP type. VPLS SAP supports Ethernet Link Aggregation Groups (LAGs). A LAG group must be set to access mode before it can be used by any SAP.

SAP Encapsulation Type and Value

VPLS performs transparent bridging for the data traffic in the service instance just like a legacy Ethernet bridge. However, VPLS is significantly more flexible in handling VLAN-tagged (or double-tagged) traffic.

Consider the following items when a VPLS SAP receives or sends Ethernet frames:

- **Ingress Behavior** — When the SAP receives traffic from a customer site, the service instance must determine:
  - Should the frame should be accepted or discarded?
  - If it is accepted, what is the destination of the frame?

- **Egress Behavior** — When the SAP sends traffic to a customer site, the service instance must determine:
  - Should the VLAN tag(s) be added?
  - What is the value of the VLAN tag?

The VPLS service instance (VSI) performs an FDB lookup of the destination MAC address in the customer frame and determines the outgoing port. If the FDB lookup fails, the traffic is flooded to all bridge ports, respecting the split-horizon rule. This answers the second question, "If it is accepted, what is the destination of the frame?" The other questions are answered by comparing the SAP's encapsulation type and value with the traffic's encapsulation type and value.

Ethernet ports (access or network ports) have three configurable encapsulation types: null, dot1q, and qinq. When the SAP is associated with an access port, it inherits the port's encapsulation type. Therefore, VPLS Ethernet SAPs have the same three encapsulation types. A *null encapsulated* access port can be used by only one SAP (the null-SAP). Dot1q- or qinq-encapsulated SAPs can share the same physical access port, if the access port is dot1q- or qinq-encapsulated, and if the vlan-ids used by these SAPs are not duplicated. The SAP encapsulation value is specified when the SAP is created in the VPLS service instance. In the ALSRP VPLS solution, the vlan-id is port-significant — the value of the vlan-id needs to be unique only within a port. The same vlan-id in different ports can be used by different SAPs that belong to the same or different services.

Note: In the VPLS implementations of some vendors, especially in some MTU devices, the vlan-id is globally significant. Therefore, a vlan-id can be used for only one VPLS instance. For example, if VPLS 100 is using SAP 1/1/1:100, no other VPLS can use vlan-id 100, even if the other VPLS's SAP is associated with a different port.

In a VPLS solution, when a customer uses VLAN tags to differentiate the different flows from its own network, the VLAN tags are meaningful only to the customer switches. Therefore, the VPLS's local SAP should ignore the VLAN tags in the ingress traffic and pass them through to the remote customer site. In this case, the VLAN tags are considered as part of the traffic and are carried over the backbone network.

Because the ignored VLAN tag is treated as data in the VPLS service instance, the service-MTU value of the VPLS service may need to be increased. For example, if the VPLS service provider needs to configure a VPLS service to ignore the vlan-ids in the customer's single-tagged traffic, the service-MTU of the VPLS service should be increased from 1,514 bytes to 1,518 bytes to ensure that the space used by the vlan-id is counted along the forwarding path.

Null-Encapsulated SAP

Null-SAP is associated with null-encapsulated access ports. A provider uses null-SAP in a VPLS to ignore all VLAN tags in the customer frames coming from the associated port. In the null-SAP ingress direction, any untagged, tagged, or double-tagged customer traffic is accepted by the VPLS. The VSI learns the C-SA MAC addresses and then forwards the traffic to its destination. In the null-SAP egress direction, the SAP sends traffic to the customer network without adding extra VLAN tagging (the traffic is unchanged).

Dot1q-Encapsulated SAP

Dot1q-SAPs associate with the dot1q-encapsulated access port. A dot1q-SAP must have a vlan-id value associated with it. The SAP format is `<port-id>: vlan-id`. A provider uses a dot1q-SAP in a VPLS when at least one VLAN tag is a service delimiter and needs to be matched by the SAP. There three subtypes of dot1q-SAP:

- **dot1q-SAP** — A dot1q-SAP with a regular VLAN tag value, for example, 1/1/1:100. The 100 is the part of the VLAN tag that is meaningful to the service provider. Dot1q-SAP forwarding behavior is:
  - **SAP-ingress** — The SAP accepts only customer ingress traffic tagged with a value of 100, or double-tagged with an outer tag value of 100. All other ingress traffic (untagged, or not tagged with a value of 100) is rejected. When the traffic is accepted, the SAP strips off the VLAN tag at the ingress point before forwarding the frame to its destination.
  - **SAP-egress** — The SAP adds a VLAN tag value specified in the SAP to all egress traffic frames.

- **dot1q-null-SAP** — A dot1q-SAP that has a 0 encapsulation value, for example, 1/1/1:0. Null-SAP forwarding behavior is:
    - **SAP-ingress** — Null-SAP accepts only untagged ingress customer frames. All tagged customer frames are rejected.
    - **SAP-egress** — The SAP sends the data to the customer site as is, without adding any new tags.
- **dot1q-default-SAP** — A dot1q-SAP with a wildcard encapsulation value, for example, 1/1/1:*. When a default dot1q-SAP is defined in an access port, it accepts all frames that other SAPs in the same port rejected. Default-SAP forwarding behavior is:
    - **SAP-ingress** — The default-SAP accepts any traffic (untagged, tagged, or double-tagged) with any vlan-id, if there are no SAPs with more specific encapsulation values. The SAP ignores any tags and treats them as part of the customer data.
    - **SAP-egress** — The SAP sends the data to the customer site as is, without adding or removing tags.

A SAP is a logical entity. Many SAPs can share the same physical port unless the port is null-encapsulated. A SAP can reject traffic, but the rejected traffic is not necessarily discarded by the port — traffic rejected by one SAP can be accepted by another SAP that shares the same port. For example, an ingress customer frame with a vlan-id of 200 is rejected by SAP 1/1/1:100 in VPLS 1. However, it is accepted by SAP 1/1/1:200, in the same VPLS or a different VPLS. If all SAPs in the same port (from all services) reject the traffic, it is discarded by the port because no SAP in the port accepts it.

One VPLS can have many SAPs. These SAPs can reside in the same VPLS service instance in one PE router, or in different service instances in different PE routers. A VPLS has no limit on which types of SAP and encapsulation-ids can coexist. The only exception is that dot1q null-SAP (for example, 1/1/1:0) and dot1q default-SAP (for example, 1/1/1:*) cannot reside in the same physical access port, regardless of whether the two SAPs belong to the same service. This is because the two SAPs have overlapping VLAN acceptance — both accept untagged frames. For example, if an access port has one null-SAP and one default-SAP, when an untagged frame arrives at the port, the system is confused and cannot decide which SAP should accept the frame.

Because dot1q default-SAP x-x-x:* has the same forwarding behavior as a SAP in a null-encapsulated port, why use it? If the VPLS customer wants the provider to trunk all of its traffic, regardless of the VLAN tagging, the null-encapsulated port can be used with one SAP for that customer. If a customer wants a trunking service but some VLANs (for example, vlan-500) must be forwarded differently, using a dot1q access port with dot1q-SAPs can provide the required flexibility. The provider can provide two SAPs to the customer site: 1/2/1:500 and 1/2/1:*. In this case, the customer traffic from VLAN 500 is accepted by SAP 1/2/1:500. All other flows are handled by SAP 1/2/1:*. When multiple SAPs share the same physical access port, the SAP with the more specific encapsulation value picks up the matching traffic first, whether or not the SAPs belong to the same VPLS. This is similar to the rule: *the route with the longest (most specific) match forwards traffic in the routed IP network.*

Qinq-Encapsulated SAP

qinq SAPs are associated with qinq-encapsulated access ports. Qinq-SAPs must have two encapsulation values: the outer (or top) vlan-id and the inner (or bottom) vlan-id. The qinq-SAP format is <port-id>:top-vlan-id.bottom-vlan-id. Qinq-SAPs are used if the service provider expects customer frames to be double-tagged and wants to examine the values of both tags. Both tags are service delimiters and are meaningful to the provider.

There are four subtypes of qinq-SAPs:

- **qinq-SAP** — A qinq-SAP that has both VLAN tag values explicitly specified: for example, 1/1/1:100.200. 100 is the top (outer) VLAN tag, and 200 is the bottom (inner) VLAN tag. The service provider examines both tags. qinq-SAP forwarding behavior is:

  - **SAP-ingress** — The SAP accepts only customer traffic that has both tags, and the values of both tags match the vlan-ids configured in the SAP. Untagged frames and single-tagged frames, or double-tagged frames that have different tag values, are rejected by the SAP. When a frame is accepted, the SAP strips off both tags at the ingress point before forwarding the frame to its destination.

  - **SAP-egress** — The SAP double-tags the frame with the provisioned tag values before it sends the frame to the customer site.

- **qinq-null-bottom-SAP** — A qinq-SAP with a *null (0)* bottom encapsulation value, for example, 1/1/1:100.0. This SAP is used when a qinq-SAP is required (because the port using the SAP is qinq-typed), but single-tagged traffic is expected. The only tag in the traffic should be the service delimiter. Null-bottom-SAP forwarding behavior is:

- **SAP-ingress** — The SAP accepts only the single-tagged frames that have a matching tag value (vlan-id). Other frames are rejected. When the frame is accepted, the SAP strips the VLAN tag at the ingress point before forwarding the frame to its destination.

- **SAP-egress** — The SAP adds the specified top tag value to each frame before it sends the frame to the customer.

- **qinq-wildcard-SAP** — A qinq-SAP that has a wildcard (*) bottom encapsulation value, for example, `1/1/1:100.*`. This SAP is used if the provider expects doubled-tagged frames but is interested only in the value of the top tag (service-delimiter). Wildcard-SAP forwarding behavior is:

  - **SAP-ingress** — The wildcard-SAP accepts any frames that match the specified top tag value, whether the frame is single-tagged or double-tagged with a tag value that matches the top tag value specified in the SAP. Other frames (untagged, tagged, or double-tagged with a mismatched top tag value) are rejected by the SAP. The SAP strips the matching tag before forwarding the frame to its destination. If the ingress frame is double-tagged and the top tag matches the SAP's configured top tag value, the bottom tag is ignored and treated as part of the customer data frame.

  - **SAP-egress** — The SAP adds the tag with the configured top tag value in the SAP to each frame before it sends the frame to the customer.

- **qinq-null-SAP** — A qinq-SAP that has a null (0) top tag and a wildcard (*) bottom tag as encapsulation values, for example, `1/1/1:0.*`. The qinq-SAP that has an encapsulation value of `0.*` accepts only untagged frames. Default-SAP forwarding behavior is:

  - **SAP-ingress** — The default-SAP accepts only untagged frames.

  - **SAP-egress** — The SAP sends the data to the customer as is, just like a null-encapsulated SAP.

A qinq-null-bottom-SAP and a qinq-wildcard-SAP cannot coexist on the same access port, whether or not the two SAPs belong to the same service, because both these SAPs accept untagged traffic (the same reason that a dot1q null-SAP and a dot1q default-SAP cannot coexist in the same access port). If the system allows both these SAPs to be associated with the same qinq access port and the access port receives untagged traffic, the system is confused and cannot decide which SAP should accept the traffic.

Similar to what happens when dot1q-SAPs share a dot1q-encapsulated access port, when qinq SAPs share a qinq-encapsulated access port, the SAP with the more specific encapsulation value picks up the traffic first. This happens whether or not the SAPs belong to the same VPLS.

For example, assume that the following four SAPs are associated with qinq port 1/1/1: 1/1/1:100.200, 1/1/1:100.0, 1/1/1:100.*, and 1/1/1:0.*.

- If the customer ingress traffic from port 1/1/1 is tagged with 100.200, the first SAP (1/1/1:100.200) accepts the traffic because both tag values match. SAP 1/1/1:100.200 is more specific.

- If the customer ingress traffic is tagged with 100.300, SAP 1/1/1:100.* accepts the traffic. SAP 1/1/1:100.200 rejects the traffic because the bottom tag value does not match. Because 1/1/1:100.* has a top tag match, it accepts the traffic.

- If the customer ingress traffic is tagged with 200.300, the frame is rejected by all SAPs because no SAP has a tag value that matches the frame's tag values.

SAP Tagging Summary

The SAP's encapsulation type and value determine whether or not a SAP accepts customer ingress frames. Furthermore, along with the pseudowire's vc-type, the SAP's encapsulation type and value determine the frame tagging format for the VPN-encapsulated frames traveling in the backbone network. Table 11.4 summarizes all SAP encapsulation types and values and the corresponding ingress and egress behavior.

Table 11.4 VPLS Ethernet SAP Encapsulation Type and Value and Forwarding Behavior

Type	Ingress Behavior	Egress Behavior
null-SAP (1/1/1)	Accepts all frames from the customer. If a VLAN tag exists, it is ignored and treated as part of the customer data.	Does not add a VLAN tag to the frames sent to the customer.
dot1q-SAP (1/1/1:100)	Accepts only single-tagged frames that have a matching VLAN tag value. Rejects all other frames.	Adds the configured tag to the egress traffic.
dot1q-null-SAP (1/1/1:0)	Accepts only untagged frames sent from the customer.	Does not add a VLAN tag to the frames sent to the customer.

Type	Ingress Behavior	Egress Behavior
dot1q-default-SAP (1/1/1:*)	Accepts all frames from the customer. If a VLAN tag exists, it is ignored and treated as part of the customer data.	Does not add a VLAN tag to the frames sent to the customer.
qinq-SAP (1/1/1:100.200)	Accepts double-tagged frames that have both VLAN tag values matching.	Adds both configured VLAN tags to the egress traffic.
qinq null-bottom SAP (1/1/1:100.0)	Accepts single-tagged frames that have a matching VLAN tag value.	Adds the configured top VLAN tag to the egress traffic.
qinq wildcard-SAP (1/1/1:100.*)	Accepts single-tagged frames that have a matching VLAN tag value, and double-tagged frames that match the top tag value.	Adds the configured top VLAN tag to the egress traffic.
qinq null-SAP (1/1/1:0.*)	Accepts untagged customer frames.	Does not add a VLAN tag to the frames sent to the customer.

The discussion of SAP encapsulation type and value and VLAN processing of ingress and egress frames shows the flexibility of VPLS with respect to processing VLAN tags. The VSI determines the traffic destination solely by performing the FDB lookup. The traffic's VLAN tagging information determines only whether the SAP accepts the frame, and how to VLAN-tag the frame sent to the customer — it has no impact on where the traffic is forwarded to:

- When a customer frame enters the provider network through a SAP-ingress point, the VSI's FDB lookup of the frame's C-DA determines whether to forward the traffic to a local SAP or to a pseudowire connected to a remote PE.

- When an encapsulated frame enters the PE router from the backbone over the pseudowire, the VSI's FDB lookup of the frame's C-DA determines whether to forward the traffic to a local SAP or to another pseudowire.

- If the traffic destination is a local SAP connected to the customer site, the SAP-egress point may or may not add VLAN tags to the frames before sending them to the customer, depending on configuration of the SAP encapsulation type and value.

If SAPs within the same VPLS have different VLAN encapsulation types and values, the VPLS forwards traffic among these SAPs. If one of these SAPs receives a BUM frame, the frame is flooded to all other SAPs where the required tags are added as configured. This behavior causes VPLS to automatically perform VLAN translation.

VLAN Translation

In a legacy Ethernet bridged network, VLAN is used to create different broadcast domains and isolate the traffic among them. In an Ethernet bridge, only the bridge ports that belong to the same VLAN exchange traffic. An Ethernet bridge is a single broadcast domain, and it performs learning and forwarding in all of its bridge ports. In a large Ethernet network, there are many ports in one bridge, and many bridges are connected together. In such a network, having one broadcast domain that contains all the ports becomes inefficient in bandwidth usage and not secure. A VLAN separates these ports to create separate broadcast domains. Figure 11.11 illustrates examples of using VLAN to divide an Ethernet network.

Figure 11.11 VLAN and VLAN Trunking in an Ethernet Network

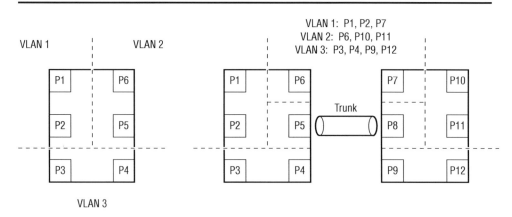

In the left diagram, one switch has six ports, and three VLANs are created in the bridge. VLAN 1 contains P1 and P2, VLAN 2 contains P5 and P6, and VLAN 3 contains P3 and P4. Each VLAN is a single-broadcast domain, and only ports belonging to the same VLAN exchange traffic. The bridge records the VLAN membership of each port and forbids traffic exchange between two ports that are members of different VLANs. No extra configuration or operation is required — the switch isolates the traffic belonging to different VLANs.

In the right diagram, two six-port switches are connected by P5 and P8. All three VLANs are extended to include two switches and have member ports in both switches. As the only connection between the two bridges, the trunk between P5 and P8 must carry traffic for all three VLANs. The challenge is how to transport the traffic that belongs to three VLANs over one shared single port and still maintain the VLAN isolation.

VLAN tagging and trunking solve this problem. The VLAN trunking port and VLAN tagging are used to determine which VLAN the traffic belongs to and forward it to the correct VLAN. P5 and P8 are configured as *trunk ports*. If a trunk port sends a frame to another switch, the VLAN membership is *tagged* into the frame using a VLAN-tag. The identification of the VLAN (vlan-id) is encoded in the VLAN-tag. When a trunk port receives a tagged frame from the peering port, it checks the VLAN-tag value to determine the VLAN to which the traffic belongs. The trunk port then removes the tag and forwards the frame to the VLAN member ports. P5 and P8 are *VLAN trunking ports* and can tag frames and remove tags. The other ports are *access ports* and can send and receive only untagged Ethernet frames.

Each VLAN is a broadcast domain. Different VLANs cannot exchange traffic through a switch. Two approaches can be used to exchange traffic among VLANs. One method is to use a router to route traffic among VLANs. The second method is to use *VLAN translation*. Figure 11.12 illustrates an example of Ethernet VLAN translation.

Figure 11.12   Ethernet VLAN Translation

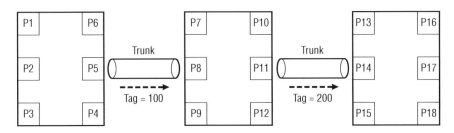

In Figure 11.12, the bridge in the middle has two trunking ports — P8 connects to the bridge on the left, and P11 connects to the bridge on the right. The left bridge uses VLAN 100, and the right bridge uses VLAN 200, and they want to exchange traffic. By default, traffic exchange between two VLANs is not allowed; the bridge in the middle is configured with VLAN translation. Traffic from P8 that has a tag of 100 is bridged to P11 and tagged with a vlan-id of 200. VLAN 100 and VLAN 200 are merged to create one VLAN and are now in one broadcast domain and can exchange traffic.

In summary, in legacy Ethernet bridging, traffic exchange is restricted within VLANs. When VLAN-translation is configured, VLANs can exchange traffic. VLAN membership affects the forwarding decision. A frame that has a particular VLAN tag can be forwarded or flooded only to the same VLAN, or to a VLAN that is on the translation list.

VPLS forwards a frame based solely on the FDB lookup of its C-DA. Because VLAN tagging is performed at the SAP-egress point when the frame leaves the VPLS, VLANs in different SAPs in the VPLS are automatically subject to translation and can exchange traffic. This makes the end-to-end VPLS service a single broadcast domain with VLAN translation. Separate VPLS services must be created for other broadcast domains — one VPLS service should be deployed for each customer broadcast domain.

The Effect of VLAN Translation on Multicast-Based Protocols

When multiple SAPs have different vlan-id values configured (globally, not only the same service instance), VLAN translation is automatic. In this case, there are two options for VPLS design:

- Allocate multiple customer VLANs to one VPLS service. VLAN translation is automatically performed based on the SAP's VLAN tagging configuration. The operator must carefully review the VLAN mapping.

- Use one VLAN per VPLS service, or use several VPLS services to isolate the traffic from different VLANs. Different VPLS services do not exchange traffic with each other, even if they have SAPs sharing the same access port in the same PE router. ALSRP service routers support many VPLS service instances per PE router. Using different VPLS services to perform traffic isolation can be a good choice for many customers.

If the operator wants to put multiple customer VLANs into one VPLS service, the automatic VLAN-translation based on SAP configuration must be seriously considered because it can affect the behaviors of some protocols running in the customer's networks. Pay extra attention if customers use multicast-based or broadcast-based protocols. Here are some examples:

- **Spanning-Tree Protocol** — STP BPDUs are multicast Ethernet frames. When connecting multiple VLANs using a single VPLS service, the BPDUs may be flooded to all customer VLANs. This may not be desired by customers.

- **OSPF** — OSPF uses multicast IP addresses as the protocol data packet's destination: for example, 224.0.0.5 (all OSPF routers), 224.0.0.6 (OSPF-DR: Designated Router). If several of the customer's routers' IP interfaces that have OSPF running are directly attached to the VPLS, VLAN translation may bridge all OSPF packets to all VLANs in that customer's network. This may not be the customer's intention. RIP may have a similar issue with VLAN translation.

- **Virtual Router Redundancy Protocol (VRRP)** — VRRP routers use the multicast IP address 224.0.0.18 to communicate with each other. VLAN translation may leak the packets to all equipment connected to the same VPLS.

Other broadcast-based or multicast-based protocols such as DHCP, ARP, and NTP can also have this issue. When designing a VPLS service for customers, the operator must clearly understand the VLAN architecture of the original customer's network and the customer's plan. In many cases, customers use different VLANs to isolate certain protocol instances or services. In such scenarios, one VLAN per VPLS or one VPLS per customer isolation domain is the best approach.

Case Study: VLAN Design and VLAN Translation in VPLS

The number of SAPs and the SAP encapsulation type and value depend on the requirements from the VPLS customer. Figure 11.13 illustrates an example of designing VPLS services to fit a customer's requirement of having different traffic flows with different VLAN tags.

Figure 11.13 Case Study: Customer with Multiple VLANs

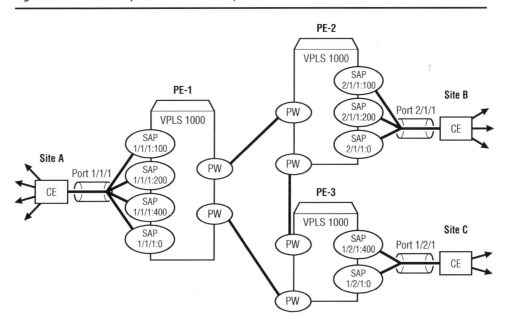

The customer purchases VPLS service from the provider. The customer has three sites in different locations: A, B, and C. The customer is an enterprise business with three departments:

- Department 1 uses VLAN 100 and 200 and is located at sites A and B.
- Department 2 uses VLAN 400 and is located at sites A, B, and C.
- Department 3 belongs to IT, requires access to all sites, and has untagged traffic.

Each site has one CE device to aggregate the traffic and send it to the service provider.

The service provider for this customer uses dot1q-SAPs to differentiate traffic flows. All three departments have a presence at Site A, so four SAPs are deployed at Site A: 1/1/1:100 and 1/1/1:200 for Department 1, 1/1/:400 for Department 2, and 1/1/1:0 for Department 3. At Site B, only three SAPs with corresponding vlan-ids are deployed. At Site C, two SAPs are provisioned for Departments 1 and 3.

Policy-Based Forwarding in VPLS

With the introduction of Layer 2 firewall and DPI (Deep Packet Inspection) equipment, VPLS is enhanced with *forwarding policy* support to provide more flexibility in controlling the traffic forwarding path. If the forwarding policy is deployed in the SAP or pseudowires, forwarding decisions made by FDB lookup can be overridden and the customer traffic can be directed to a particular destination.

The matching criteria of the forwarding policy can be either Layer 2 information (for example, source MAC or destination MAC) or Layer 3 or Layer 4 information (for example, source IP, destination IP, source port, or destination port). The policy can be deployed in any direction (ingress/egress) on a SAP or a pseudowire. The forwarding policies are effective only on Layer 2 services. If applied to Layer 3 services, the traffic matching the policy entries are dropped. Figure 11.14 illustrates the VPLS policy forwarding behavior.

In Figure 11.14, the default VSI forwarding decision-making process is overriden by the forwarding policy as follows:

1. SAP-1 uses the ingress policy to force the incoming traffic to be forwarded to SAP-2, which is connected to the DPI or firewall devices. If no policy is

in effect, the traffic is directly forwarded to the pseudowire based on the FDB forwarding decision, and then enters the remote VPLS network.

2. Traffic received by SAP-2 travels through the DPI/Firewall device and exits from SAP-3.

3. SAP-3 forwards the traffic from the DPI/firewall based on the SDP's FDB, which forwards the traffic to the VPLS network.

4. The forwarding policy forces the traffic traveling from the VPLS network to the local VPLS instance to SAP-3. If no policy is in effect, the traffic is directly forwarded to SAP-1 and exits the VPLS.

5. The traffic exiting from SAP-3 from the SDP travels through the DPI/firewall to SAP-2.

6. The traffic exits from the DPI firewall and enters SAP-2, and is then forwarded to SAP-1, based on the FDB decision.

Figure 11.14　VPLS SAP/Pseudowire Forwarding Policy Traffic Flow

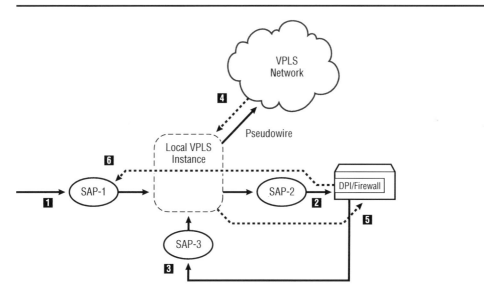

Note that in the diagram, the DPI or firewall device is a Layer 2 device. It filters traffic but does not rewrite the packets. The MAC address for the traffic exiting the

DPI/firewall device does not change. MAC address learning should be disabled on SAP-2 and SAP-3 because they are connected to the DPI/Firewall. Otherwise, the VPLS FDB learns the same MAC address from both SAP-1 and SAP-3 for the traffic entering the VPLS, and the same MAC address from the SDP and SAP-2 for the traffic from remote VPLS networks.

Figure 11.15 illustrates an example of configuring policy-based forwarding and deploying the policy to a VPLS SAP in the ingress direction.

Figure 11.15 VPLS Policy-Based Forwarding Configuration Example

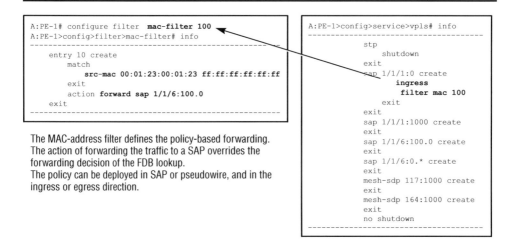

11.5 VPLS Forwarding Database Management

A VPLS service instance in a PE router creates a VSI. The VSI performs transparent bridging between SAPs and pseudowires in the same VPLS service instance. When bridging the traffic, the VSI builds the FDB by learning the customer source MAC addresses (C-SA) of all frames associated with the source-port-id. The source-port-id is the identifier of the SAP or pseudowire from which the MAC is learned. Figure 11.16 illustrates an FDB from a VPLS service instance. The output at the top of the diagram is the FDB's administrative status and configuration. The output at the bottom of the diagram is a display of the content of the FDB.

Figure 11.16 VPLS FDB Status and Content

```
A:PE-3#    show service id 1000 fdb
=================================================================
Forwarding Database, Service 1000
=================================================================
Service Id        : 1000         Mac Move          : Disabled
Primary Factor    : 3            Secondary Factor  : 2
Mac Move Rate     : 2            Mac Move Timeout  : 10
Table Size        : 250          Total Count       : 8
Learned Count     : 8            Static Count      : 0
OAM-learned Count : 0            DHCP-learned Count: 0
Host-learned Count: 0
Remote Age        : 900          Local Age         : 300
High WaterMark    : 95%          Low Watermark     : 90%
Mac Learning      : Enabl        Discard Unknown   : Dsabl
Mac Aging         : Enabl        Relearn Only      : False
=================================================================
```

```
A:PE-3#    show service id 1000 fdb detail
=================================================================
Forwarding Database, Service 1000
=================================================================
ServId    MAC                Source-Identifier   Type/Age  Last Change
-----------------------------------------------------------------
1000      00:00:00:00:01:16  sdp:116:1000        L/0       01/17/2004  12:15:37

1000      00:00:00:00:01:17  sdp:117:1000        L/0       01/17/2004  12:15:48

1000      00:00:00:00:01:18  sdp:117:1000        L/0       01/17/2004  12:15:55

1000      00:00:00:00:01:63  sap:1/1/3:1000      L/0       01/17/2004  09:37:31

1000      00:00:00:00:01:65  sdp:116:1000        L/0       01/17/2004  12:15:38

1000      8e:74:ff:00:00:00  sdp:116:1000        L/4       01/17/2004  12:42:58

1000      8e:75:ff:00:00:00  sdp:117:1000        L/9       01/17/2004  12:42:53

1000      8e:a3:01:01:00:02  sap:1/1/3:1000      L/0       01/17/2004  09:37:32

-----------------------------------------------------------------
No. of MAC Entries: 8
=================================================================
```

Table 11.5 gives a brief description of some important database parameters.

Table 11.5 FBD Parameters

Item	Description
FDB size	The number of entries a VSI's FDB can contain. When the size limit of the FDB is reached, MAC learning stops. This may cause more flooding in the VPLS. The default FDB size is 250. The FDB is configurable on a per-VPLS-service-instance basis and per-SAP basis.
Learned count	The number of MAC addresses that are learned and have not yet expired. The learned count is not configurable.

(continued)

Table 11.5 FBD Parameters *(continued)*

Item	Description
Remote age	The age of the entries learned from a pseudowire. (The source-id is the pseudowire-id.) The default value is 900 seconds. The remote age is configurable on a per-service-instance basis.
Local age	The age of the entries learned from the SAP. (The source-id is the SAP-id.) The default value is 300 seconds. Local age is configurable on a per-VPLS-service-instance basis.
Disable learning	Learning is enabled by default. When learning is disabled, the VSI does not learn the traffic source. Disable learning is configurable on a per-VPLS-service-instance and on a per-SAP or per-spoke-pseudowire basis. Using the disable learning feature can cause traffic flooding.
Disable aging	Aging is enabled by default. When aging is disabled, the MAC addresses in the FDB do not expire. The learned MAC addresses can still be flushed or cleared. Disable aging is configurable on a per-VPLS-service-instance basis and on a per-SAP and per-spoke-pseudowire basis.
Discard unknown	The default behavior is to flood unknown unicast traffic. When discard unknown is enabled, unknown unicast frames are discarded instead of flooded. Discard unknown is configurable on a per-VPLS-service-instance basis.

For detailed information about FDB management features, refer to the ALSRP service routing product manuals.

Summary

VPLS is an MPLS pseudowire-based Layer 2 Ethernet bridging VPN service provided to the customer to connect a geographically separated Ethernet network. All customer sites connected to the same VPLS service network appear to be in the same LAN. The end-to-end VPLS performs Ethernet learning and forwarding with STP support similar to a regular Ethernet switch.

In a VPLS network, all PE routers participating in the same VPLS service are member PEs of that VPLS service. Each member PE has a VPLS service instance provisioned on it. The service instance is a VSI that contains an FDB and bridge ports. The VPLS service instance has SAPs that connect to the customer sites and pseudowires connected to other VPLS member PE routers. VPLS performs learning and forwarding based on the customer traffic's source and destination MAC addresses.

VPLS is an Ethernet bridging service. To ensure that the VPLS service's internal forwarding infrastructure is loop-free and optimal, a fully meshed pseudowire deployment with local split-horizon rule is required:

- Each PE router must have one pseudowire for each peering member PE router — a fully meshed forwarding topology must be deployed.
- In the PE router, all pseudowires belong to a single split-horizon group, which means they do not exchange traffic among each other.

This method of deploying pseudowires is called *mesh-pseudowire*. Similar to an iBGP full mesh, it ensures an optimal forwarding path between any two PE routers and eliminates the possibility of looping the traffic back.

The fully meshed rule can be violated, with the introduction of H-VPLS with spoke-pseudowires used to forward traffic among PE routers. H-VPLS and spoke-pseudowire are introduced in Chapter 12.

The SAP of VPLS must have the encapsulation type and value defined. VPLS SAP supports three types of Ethernet encapsulation: null, dot1q, and qinq. The SAP and access port encapsulation type and value must be configured correctly for different service requirements.

Hierarchical VPLS

12

Hierarchical VPLS allows the operator to use spoke-pseudowires to connect VPLS meshes. H-VPLS provides a more flexible and scalable solution to the operator. H-VPLS also provides a more efficient multicast forwarding mechanism.

Chapter Objectives

- Provide an overview of H-VPLS services

- Review typical network topologies where H-VPLS can be used to build a more efficient forwarding infrastructure

- Discuss the forwarding behavior of the spoke-pseudowires used by H-VPLS

- Present a case study of the deployment of several H-VPLS services

The previous chapter introduced the basic concepts and components of the Virtual Private LAN Service (VPLS). VPLS requires fully meshed pseudowires among all member PE routers. In a large scaled network, this may create issues for both the data plane and the control plane. There may be a large number of packets to replicate (especially for the case of using VPLS to carry multicast traffic) and a large number of pseudowires to maintain. Hierarchical VPLS (H-VPLS) enhances the scalability of the VPLS solution by allowing a large meshed VPLS network to be divided into several smaller meshes connected with *spoke-pseudowires*. H-VPLS also allows VPLS to be built using hub-spoke topology, by retaining mesh-pseudowires only in the core and by using spoke-pseudowires to connect to the PE routers closest to the Customer Edge.

Spoke-pseudowires have different forwarding behavior from mesh-pseudowires. Relaying traffic between spoke-pseudowires is allowed, and it is also possible to pass traffic between mesh-pseudowires and spoke-pseudowires.

New service topologies can be implemented by using spoke-pseudowires in the VPLS service: Point-to-point Ethernet pipe (Epipe) can now use spoke-pseudowire to connect to a VPLS mesh, and VPLS can also use spoke-pseudowire to connect to Layer 3 services [either Internet Enhanced Service in the routed core or Virtual Private Routed Network (VPRN) service]. Thus, VPLS services can also have Layer 3 connectivity. Layer 3 service is beyond the scope of this book.

12.1 Hierarchical-VPLS Overview

The VPLS mesh introduced in Chapter 10 defines the basic VPLS infrastructure: a fully meshed mesh-pseudowire connecting all member PE routers. This is the most basic VPLS topology. However, in some cases, there may be too many member PE routers for a fully meshed topology to be practical. Sometimes provisioning fully meshed pseudowires is not the most efficient network design. This chapter discusses a new type of VPLS architecture — H-VPLS. H-VPLS is based on the *spoke-pseudowire* concept. Unlike mesh-pseudowires, spoke-pseudowires can exchange traffic with other pseudowires (mesh and spoke), so they can relay traffic between PE routers. A more flexible, scalable, and optimal network design can be achieved by using a combination of spoke-pseudowire and mesh-pseudowire. There are two major reasons for a provider to deploy H-VPLS instead of a single VPLS mesh:

- In a large network where the number of pseudowires required for a full mesh is not desired or beyond the scalability of the service instances

- In a network with physical topology or connectivity requirements where pseudowire full mesh is not efficient, especially for a VPLS service mainly used to distribute multicast traffic

The split-horizon rule *"Do not relay traffic among mesh-pseudowires"* is used to prevent forwarding loops in VPLS networks. All mesh-pseudowires are put into one Bridge Port in the Virtual Switching Instance (VSI) so they do not exchange traffic. If this rule is not used, the VPLS core may no longer be loop-free. The spoke-psuedowires do not obey the split-horizon rule. Therefore, any VPLS network with spoke-pseudowires must be carefully designed. Several loop-prevention mechanisms are available to prevent forwarding loops. Even if the service provider's VPLS core is designed to be loop-free, the customer's network may have potential forwarding loops. VPLS services should be able to resolve this issue. Loop-prevention in a VPLS network is discussed in detail in Chapter 15.

Using Spoke-Pseudowires to Improve Scalability and Efficiency

Regular VPLS services using fully meshed mesh-pseudowire to connect member PE routers are discussed in Chapter 11. For each VPLS, if there are n member PE routers participating in the service, $n(n-1)/2$ mesh-pseudowires are required. Realistically, the number of PE routers in the same VPLS must stay within a reasonable level. Because the mesh-pseudowires are not allowed to relay traffic with each other, all member PE routers must have one mesh-pseudowire connected to each peering member PE router. Reducing the number of mesh-pseudowires causes loss of connectivity. The problem, therefore, is to reduce the pseudowires while maintaining full connectivity.

The solution for the VPLS pseudowire scaling problem is to introduce a different type of pseudowire to reduce the number of pseudowires required to maintain full service connectivity. A *spoke-pseudowire*, does not obey the rule of *no relay of traffic among pseudowires*. Two VPLS member PE routers can use the third PE router to relay the VPLS traffic using the spoke-pseudowire. The full mesh of pseudowire in the VPLS network can be removed by using spoke-pseudowires and by designing the network properly.

In VPLS, member PE routers are connected by the pseudowires provisioned in the VPLS service instance. In each member PE router, all other member PE routers are specified by creating a pseudowire connecting to these member PE routers. This is because the pseudowire is bound to a Service Distribution Path (SDP), and the SDP specifies the router-id of the remote PE router it connected to. If the VPLS is fully meshed, each member PE is aware of the existence of all other member PEs. This is because every PE router has SDPs and pseudowires configured, which connect to all other member PE routers. This type of VPLS network is called a *flat* VPLS network.

When spoke-pseudowires are added to a VPLS network, the VPLS network is no longer fully meshed. A member PE router can see only a subset of the PE routers — the ones to which it has pseudowires connected. But each member still has full connectivity to all other PE routers. A PE router may communicate to some PE routers indirectly by using the spoke-pseudowire to relay the traffic to them. The existence of these indirect member PE routers is hidden by the spoke-pseudowires. This type of VPLS network is called a *hierarchical* VPLS (H-VPLS) network. H-VPLS is a hierarchical infrastructure in which elements may reach each other through transiting elements.

Figure 12.1 illustrates the three typical VPLS topologies:

- **Fully Meshed VPLS Service Implementation** — The diagram on the left shows a fully meshed VPLS topology, which is a basic form of VPLS implementation. Each member PE router has one pseudowire directly connected to every other member PE router. This basic VPLS form is often referred to as *VPLS mesh*. In the VPLS mesh of n member PE routers, $n(n-1)/2$ pseudowires are required. The optical forwarding path is guaranteed. Because each PE router is connected to every other member in the VPLS by pseudowires, it is aware of all other member PE routers participating in the same VPLS service. Pseudowire used by the VPLS mesh to forward traffic is referred to as *mesh-pseudowire*.

- **Meshed Core, Spoke Edge VPLS Service Implementation** — The diagram on the bottom represents another common VPLS network design. The PE routers in the core are connected in a fully meshed manner with mesh-pseudowires to ensure optimal forwarding and redundancy in the core. The PE routers close to the edge connect to the PE routers closer to the core in a hub-spoke manner, so they do not have to peer with every member PE in the VPLS service. This topology reduces the number of pseudowires required in the VPLS service. Pseudowire used to connect the spoke-PE and the hub-PE is referred to as *spoke-pseudowire*. It also provides for efficient handling of broadcast, unknown-unicast and multicast (BUM) traffic by replicating the traffic closer to the destination PEs and leaves. Each hub router can also see that the two spoke-PE routers are connected to pseudowires. However, each hub-PE cannot see the spoke-PE routers behind the other three hub routers. The network is divided into two tiers: the meshed core tier and the spoke edge tier.

- **VPLS Meshes Connected by Spoke-Pseudowire** — The diagram on the right shows a topology in which two VPLS meshes are connected by two spoke-pseudowires. In such a network, the traffic within each VPLS mesh is forwarded on an optimal path. Traffic between the two meshes travels through the spoke-pseudowire. (For loop prevention, only one spoke-pseudowire is active and forwarding traffic at any time. The details regarding loop prevention in a VPLS service are discussed in Chapter 15.)

The latter two H-VPLS topologies are discussed in detail in later sections.

Figure 12.1 Typical VPLS Service Network Topologies

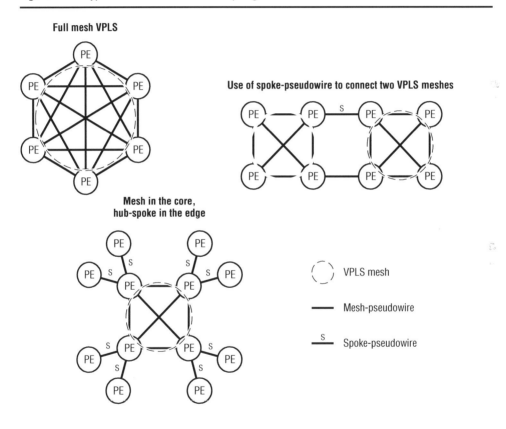

The H-VPLS network design reduces the number of pseudowires and T-LDP sessions required for the spoke-PE routers in the edge, because they need to only connect to the closest core hub-PE routers. This makes it possible to use downscaled routers in the edge of the VPLS network to reduce the cost of building the VPLS network. H-VPLS also helps to reduce the operational cost as new services need to be provisioned only on the spoke-PE and on the local hub-PE. Growth of services requires psuedowire scaling just on the local spoke and hub-PEs without affecting the rest of the PEs. This significantly reduces the cost for the service providers to expand their networks. H-VPLS also allows flexible service options where bandwidth in one domain (metro) might be different than the bandwidth offered over the long haul/wide area network. Clear delimitation between the two domains can be easily enforced on one spoke-pseudowire rather than a set of meshed pseudowires exit points from the metro domain.

The diagram on the right is another typical H-VPLS network. Two VPLS meshes are connected by the spoke-pseudowire in the middle. In this network, 10 pseudowires connect eight PE routers, while full connectivity is maintained. This is typical when large operators want to connect several of their metro-Ethernet networks (with existing VPLS services) together. Large operators often have several networks that need to be connected together (merging). These networks may be built of different vendors' equipment and may have inter-operatability issues. Also, because these networks may be geographically separated, it does not make sense to deploy full mesh among all routers. H-VPLS design is then used to connect these networks with spoke-pseudowires. H-VPLS topologies are discussed in detail later in this chapter.

With the use of spoke-pseudowires, a large VPLS service network can be divided into several smaller *meshes* and still maintain full connectivity. H-VPLS adds to the operator's toolset, allowing more flexibility in addressing different service models and topology requirements through a combination of mesh-pseudowires and spoke-pseudowires to connect member PE routers.

Another significant benefit for operators to deploy H-VPLS rather than flat VPLS is to improve the data plane efficiency when carrying multicast traffic. As discussed in Chapter 11, in a VPLS mesh, when a PE router receives multicast traffic from a SAP, it must replicate one copy of the traffic for each pseudowire connected to the remote member PE router. Therefore, for a VPLS mesh with n member PE routers, the multicast traffic must be replicated $(n - 1)$ times. In certain topologies, using VPLS mesh to forward multicast traffic is not bandwidth-efficient. Because H-VPLS uses spoke-pseudowires to reduce the number of pseudowires required to maintain the full connectivity, the multicast traffic distribution in H-VPLS is more efficient. Figure 12.2 illustrates the use of H-VPLS network design with spoke-pseudowires to reduce the replication of multicast traffic.

Figure 12.2 Using Spoke-Pseudowires to Improve Multicast Replication Efficiency in VPLS

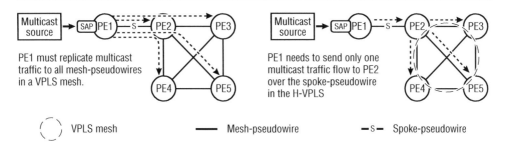

In Figure 12.2, the network contains five PE routers and requires VPLS service to provide full connectivity for the customer devices connected to these PE routers (not shown in the diagram). The physical topology of the network is as presented in both diagrams. There are fully meshed physical links among routers PE2, PE3, PE4, and PE5. PE1 is connected with PE2 over a single physical link.

The diagram on the left shows the multicast traffic packet replication scenario if a fully meshed VPLS service is deployed. When PE1 needs to distribute the multicast traffic received from its SAP to other PE routers, it must send four multicast streams individually to the four PE routers over four mesh-pseudowires. The link between PE1 and PE2 may become a congestion point because it carries four streams of the same traffic. Obviously, this is not an optimal network design.

The diagram on the right shows an improved H-VPLS design. In the H-VPLS, routers PE2, PE3, PE4, and PE5 remain fully meshed. There is a *physical* link mesh among these four routers, so having a VPLS mesh takes advantage of the physical topology and is efficient. PE1 has only one spoke-pseudowire, connected to PE2 In such a topology, including PE1 into the VPLS mesh does not improve the network resiliency, but increases the number of pseudowires. With the H-VPLS design, when PE1 needs to distribute the multicast traffic received from its SAP to the VPLS member PE routers, it needs to distribute only one multicast stream to router PE2 over the spoke-pseudowire. With H-VPLS design, the same service connectivity is maintained when the extra pseudowires (PE1 to PE3, PE4, and PE5) are removed from the topology. More efficient network design and traffic distribution are achieved by using spoke-pseudowires to build H-VPLS.

VPLS Network Topology: Mesh versus Hub and Spoke

Pseudowires connect the service instances of multiple member PE routers in the same VPLS service to transport encapsulated VPLS traffic. When many network elements must be connected with an any-to-any communication requirement, there are three options: mesh, partial-mesh, and hub-spoke. Each topology has its pros and cons. *Partial-mesh* is a combination of mesh and hub-spoke and therefore is not discussed in this book as an individual topology type. Figure 12.3 illustrates examples of each topology.

Figure 12.3 ▪ Possible Network Topologies

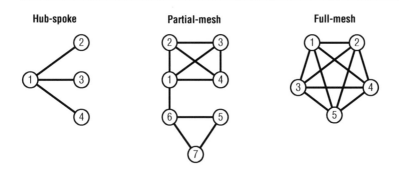

The hub-spoke topology requires the fewest connections. For an *n* node network, only (*n* – 1) connections are required to provide full connectivity. The *hub* is the node that peers with every other node. It has one connection to every spoke node. The other nodes are *spoke nodes* — each with only one connection, peering with the hub node. The spoke nodes cannot exchange traffic directly with each other; they must use the hub node to transit or relay their traffic. The hub-spoke topology is the most scalable topology because it provides full connectivity with the fewest number of connections. However, hub-spoke topology has the following drawbacks:

- **Single Point of Failure** — If the hub node fails, all connections in the network are lost. Also, if the connection from a spoke node to the hub is broken, the spoke node loses its connectivity to all other nodes in the network.

- **Suboptimal Forwarding** — The hub node can reach any spoke node through a direct connection. However, traffic from a spoke node must pass through the hub before it can reach another spoke node. Because traffic from one spoke node to another spoke node does not take the shortest possible path, traffic forwarding between the spoke nodes is suboptimal.

- **Bandwidth and FDB Scaling Challenge** — As the transiting point of the entire network, the hub router must build a forwarding table that contains all the possible destinations in the network. Also, the volume of traffic going through the hub node is the aggregation of all spoke nodes. Maintaining a large forwarding database (FDB) and providing high bandwidth for all spoke nodes can be a challenge in a scaled network.

Full-mesh topology is the opposite of spoke topology. It requires the highest number of connections to implement full connectivity. For an n node network, $n(n-1)/2$ connections are required to connect all the nodes. Each node has one connection to every other node. Mesh topology cannot be used when the number n becomes large — too many connections are required. However, mesh topology is the most traffic- and bandwidth-efficient. Mesh topology has the following benefits:

- **Optimal Forwarding** — Each node has one dedicated connection to every other node. Therefore, traffic between any two nodes is forwarded through a direct connection. All traffic in the network uses the best path, as long as there is no failure.

- **Redundant Design** — In a full-mesh topology, there is no single point of failure. A node or link failure affects only the traffic between the two nodes involved. If relaying traffic between nodes is allowed, link failure does not cause connectivity loss.

Chapter 11 discussed fully meshed VPLS (or VPLS mesh) as a basic form of the VPLS service implementation. This chapter discusses hierarchical VPLS and spoke-pseudowires.

12.2 Spoke-Pseudowire Details

First, as mentioned in Chapter 11, a pseudowire is just a pseudowire. *Mesh* and *spoke* are forwarding behavior regulations controlled by the VSI that is local to the service instance. The types of mesh or spoke are meaningful only locally to the service instance where the pseudowires are configured, and are *not* signaled to the far-end PE router in the pseudowire signaling process as one of the pseudowire characteristics. Therefore, the remote PE router is not aware of whether the pseudowire is used as mesh or spoke type pseudowire on the local PE router. If a pseudowire is defined as a mesh-pseudowire, it is put into the *mesh Bridge Port* to which all mesh-pseudowires belong so that they do not exchange traffic with each other. The VSI creates a separate Bridge Port for each pseudowire defined as a spoke-pseudowire. Just like any SAP, each spoke-pseudowire has its own Bridge Port. Spoke-pseudowire is actually a new way for a VSI to use pseudowires to forward traffic locally, not a new type of pseudowire. Table 12.1 lists the differences between mesh-pseudowire and spoke-pseudowire.

Table 12.1 Pseudowire Types: Spoke-Pseudowire versus Mesh-Pseudowire

Binding	Mesh-Pseudowire	Spoke-Pseudowire
PW usage	VPLS core	VPWS, H-VPLS, VPLS termination to L3 service (VPRN or IES)
Definition	Mesh-pseudowire is a type of pseudowire that cannot exchange traffic with other mesh-pseudowires. All mesh-pseudowires belong to one Bridge Port in the VSI. When a mesh-pseudowire receives encapsulated traffic from a remote member PE, it can forward the traffic only to spoke-pseudowires and SAPs. When using only this type of pseudowire in the VPLS network, full-mesh deployment among all member PEs is required; there-fore, it is called *mesh-pseudowire*.	A spoke-pseudowire is a type of pseudowire that can exchange traffic with any other forwarding entities (mesh-pseudowires, other spoke-pseudowires, SAPs). Spoke-pseudowires are used in H-VPLS networks to relay traffic between VPLS meshes or to connect spoke sites to hub sites.
Forwarding behavior	Assuming a split-horizon group, traffic received from one mesh-pseudowire is not relayed to another mesh-pseudowire. All mesh-pseudowires in the same service instance belong to one Bridge Port. Within one service mesh, all PE routers need to have a full mesh of SDPs and a full mesh of mesh-pseudowires con-nected to each other to achieve full service reachability.	No default split-horizon group. Traffic received from spoke-pseudowires may be forwarded to any Bridge Port (mesh-pseudowires, other spoke-pseudowires, or SAPs).
vc-id used for binding	All mesh-pseudowires in one VPLS service instance must share the same vc-id locally. By default, the vc-id is the same as the ser-vice-id (configurable). Both sides of the mesh-pseudowire must use the same vc-id for the pseudowire to come up.	Spoke-pseudowires can use any vc-id value. As long as both sides of the spoke-pseudowire use the same vc-id value, the pseudowire comes up. There is no default vc-id for spoke-pseudowires — the vc-id value must be explicitly specified when creating the pseudowire.

Binding	Mesh-Pseudowire	Spoke-Pseudowire
Forwarding loop	A VPLS mesh using only fully meshed mesh-pseudowire is loop-free inside the core. Mesh-pseudowire does not relay traffic to PE routers. Therefore, there is only one forwarding path between any two PE routers — the directly connected mesh-pseudowire.	Spoke-pseudowire can relay traffic between PE routers. Inappropriate VPLS network design may cause forwarding loops in the VPLS service core. When designing VPLS networks using spoke-pseudowires, consideration needs to be given to avoid forwarding loops, just as when designing a bridged Ethernet network.

Note: VPRN and IES services are beyond the scope of this book. They are mentioned in Table 12.1 only to ensure the accuracy of the description of pseudowires.

Other than the local forwarding behavior, all other aspects of the spoke-pseudowires are exactly the same as mesh-pseudowires, as follows:

- They both use T-LDP to signal the pseudowire to the far-end PE router and to exchange vc-labels.
- They both require SDPs to which to bind.
- Their vc-ids are both point-to-point significant; otherwise, the pseudowire does not come up.
- They both support static vc-label mapping without T-LDP signaling.
- They both support the vc-types `vlan (0x0004)` and `ether (0x0005)`.

VPLS Spoke-Pseudowire Learning and Forwarding Behavior

The learning and forwarding behavior of mesh-pseudowire was explained in Chapter 11. In H-VPLS, a new type of pseudowire usage in VPLS is introduced: the spoke-pseudowire. In most cases, the H-VPLS solution is a combined deployment of both mesh-pseudowires and spoke-pseudowires. Figure 12.4 illustrates the learning and forwarding behavior of a VPLS spoke-pseudowire.

Figure 12.4 VPLS Spoke-Pseudowire Learning and Forwarding Behavior

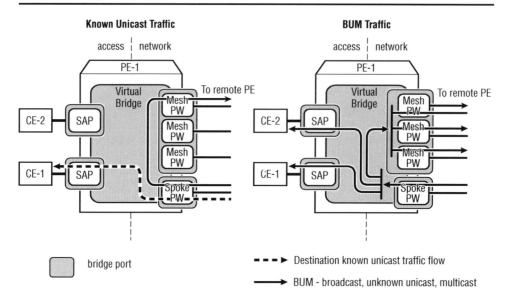

The term *pseudowire ingress* denotes the direction going from the far-end PE router into the local service instance through the SDP. The term *pseudowire egress* denotes the direction going from the local service instance to the far-end PE router through the SDP. H-VPLS uses spoke-pseudowires and mesh-pseudowires to connect members. The VSI in the VPLS service instance considers each spoke-pseudowire as an individual Bridge Port. The forwarding behaviors of spoke-pseudowires are:

- When a spoke-pseudowire receives unicast traffic with a known destination from the far-end PE router, it forwards the traffic to the destination SAP, mesh-pseudowire, or another spoke-pseudowire according to the FDB lookup result.

- When a spoke-pseudowire receives BUM (broadcast, unknown unicast, multicast) traffic from the customer site, it replicates the traffic and floods it to all SAPs, all mesh-pseudowires, and all other spoke-pseudowires.

- When other Bridge Ports receive ingress BUM traffic, it is flooded to all spoke-pseudowires. The traffic is then encapsulated by the spoke-pseudowires and sent to the far-end PE routers.

VPLS Spoke-Pseudowire Signaling Process

Targeted LDP (T-LDP) is used to signal the spoke-pseudowires as per RFC 4762. The purpose of T-LDP signaling is to signal the vc-label as the service de-multiplexer.

The basic signaling process for establishing spoke-pseudowires between two PE routers is similar to the mesh-pseudowire signaling process. After VPLS service instances are provisioned on a PE router, pseudowires need to be locally defined. For every pseudowire defined, the PE router locally assigns a value for vc-label. This locally assigned label is the *ingress vc-label* for the local router, since it is used for de-encapsulating the ingress traffic. The ingress vc-label should be distributed to the remote PE routers to use in VPLS encapsulation before they send the traffic to this local PE router. The PE router sends an LDP Label Mapping message to distribute the vc-label to the remote PE router.

The PE router also expects the peering far-end PE router to perform the same action — to generate and distribute its vc-label to the local PE router. The local PE router can then use this vc-label to perform VPLS encapsulation before it sends traffic to the far-end PE router. The local PE router considers the vc-label distributed by the far-end PE router as the *egress vc-label*, since it is used for encapsulating the egress traffic. This vc-label generation and distribution is the same for both mesh-pseudowires and spoke-pseudowires. The difference is that in the spoke-pseudowire signaling process, the PW-Status TLV is appended to the LDP Label Mapping message.

Figure 12.5 illustrates the process of setting up the spoke-pseudowire (1 and 2) and the service instance being administratively enabled (3 and 4).

Spoke-pseudowire setup signaling differs from mesh-pseudowire setup signaling as follows:

- The Label Mapping message contains the PW-Status (0x96A) TLV to signal the status of the service instance's entities.

- Even if the service instance is administratively disabled, the spoke-pseudowire is still signaled. However, the spoke-pseudowire is operationally **down**, and the PE router signals the PW-Status TLV indicating that the service instance is down to the remote PE router.

- When the service instance is administratively enabled, the LDP Notification message is sent to the far-end PE to clear the error flag on the spoke-pseudowire. The spoke-pseudowire is then ready to forward traffic.

Figure 12.5 Establishing a Spoke-Pseudowire Using T-LDP Messages

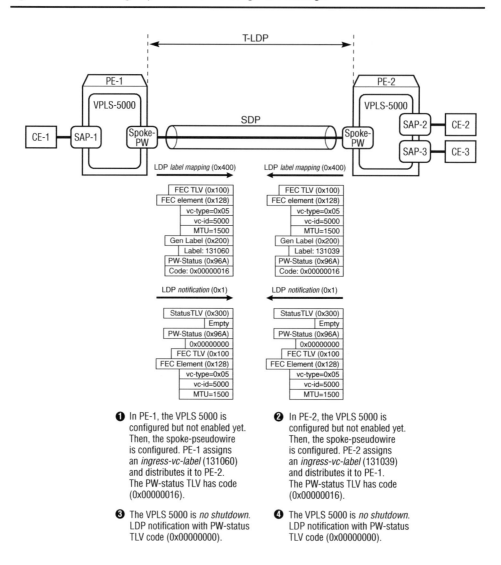

When the spoke-pseudowire is administratively disabled, the pseudowire is torn down. The process of tearing down a spoke-pseudowire and the message content of tearing down a spoke-pseudowire are the same as tearing down a mesh-pseudowire — the local PE sends a Label Withdraw message to withdraw the vc-label, and the far-end PE confirms with a Label Release message.

Spoke-Pseudowire Configuration Example

Figure 12.6 illustrates a configuration example for PE1 in VPLS service 5000. The SDP configuration to PE2 is also included. Figure 12.6 also includes the status display of a VPLS service with spoke-pseudowire.

Figure 12.6   VPLS Spoke-Pseudowire Configuration Example

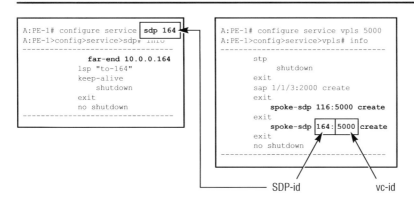

```
A:PE-1# configure service  sdp 164
A:PE-1>config>service>sdp# info
-------------------------------
            far-end 10.0.0.164
            lsp "to-164"
            keep-alive
                shutdown
            exit
            no shutdown
-------------------------------
```

```
A:PE-1# configure service vpls 5000
A:PE-1>config>service>vpls# info
-------------------------------
        stp
            shutdown
        exit
        sap 1/1/3:2000 create
        exit
            spoke-sdp 116:5000 create
        exit
            spoke-sdp 164:5000 create
        exit
        no shutdown
-------------------------------
```

```
A:PE-1#   show service id 5000 base
===============================================================================
Service Basic Information
===============================================================================
Service Id         : 5000            Vpn Id             : 0
Service Type       : VPLS
Customer Id        : 1
Last Status Change: 08/08/2003 21:00:32
Last Mgmt Change  : 08/08/2003 22:12:18
Admin State        : Up              Oper State         : Up
MTU                : 1514            Def. Mesh VC Id    : 5000
SAP Count          : 1               SDP Bind Count     : 2
Snd Flush on Fail : Disabled         Host Conn Verify   : Disabled
Propagate MacFlush: Disabled
Def. Gateway IP    : None
Def. Gateway MAC   : None
-------------------------------------------------------------------------------
Service Access & Destination Points
-------------------------------------------------------------------------------
Identifier                          Type      AdmMTU  OprMTU  Adm  Opr
-------------------------------------------------------------------------------
sap:1/1/3:2000                      q-tag     1518    1518    Up   Up
sdp:116:5000 S(10.0.0.116)          n/a       0       9190    Up   Up
sdp:164:5000 S(10.0.0.164)          n/a       0       9190    Up   Up
===============================================================================
```

The SDP configuration on the top left of the figure contains the far-end PE router's router-id. When creating a pseudowire in a VPLS service instance, the SDP-id is quoted to create the pseudowire that points to the far-end router with the same IP address. In the ALSRP VPLS solution, the creation of spoke-pseudowire is a *binding* process — binding the vc-id with an SDP using the `spoke-sdp <sdp-id>:<vc-id>` command under the VPLS service context. The command uniquely defines a pseudowire for its VPLS service instance:

- The SDP-id specifies the ID of the pre-provisioned SDP. Each SDP is configured to connect to a specific far-end PE router, defined in the SDP configuration using the `far-end` command.

- Binding the vc-id to an SDP specifies the SDP to be used by the pseudowire and inherits the IP address of the far-end PE router from the SDP. Implicitly, it also tells the service instance that this far-end PE router is a VPLS member. The vc-id is a manually specified value and is point-to-point significant, meaning that the same value should be used in the binding command on both sides of the pseudowire. (The vc-id is the circuit-identifier used to identify the pseudowire, not the vc-label.) The local PE router automatically generates the vc-label value and distributes it to the far-end PE router.

- The `spoke` specifies that this pseudowire is to be used as a spoke-pseudowire in this service instance. As explained previously, each spoke-pseudowire is assigned to its own Bridge Port by the VSI.

Static Spoke-Pseudowire Configuration and Inter-AS VPLS

Spoke-pseudowire also supports static vc-label configuration without T-LDP signaling. The configuration process is exactly the same as static mesh-pseudowire, except that the static-vc is defined under the spoke-pseudowire of the VPLS configuration. Refer to Chapter 11 for a configuration example of static mesh-pseudowire. As mentioned in Chapter 11, static-vc configuration should be used only in rare cases because the static vc-label configuration is not scalable or manageable. However, one typical application for static spoke-pseudowire is the interconnection of two VPLS service networks belonging to different operators. That is the case because some service providers prefer a static provisioning method to running a full control plane with a third-party PE.

It makes sense from an ease of provisioning perspective to use a dynamic provisioning method. In the static PW case a pair of vc-labels must be configured for every VPLS service required to be connected between the two operator domains. If many inter-provider services are required, the provisioning scale can get out of control. Also, it is difficult to track the many manual vc-label pairs and to troubleshoot such a network.

Split-Horizon Group for Spoke-Pseudowire

As mentioned in previous sections, the VSI of a VPLS service instance considers every spoke-pseudowire as an individual Bridge Port. A spoke-pseudowire can forward traffic to any other pseudowire (mesh or spoke) and to SAPs in the local VPLS service instance. In some cases, operators may want to regulate the forwarding scope of spoke-pseudowire. For example, in a Triple Play network, the service provider may want to prevent the customers aggregated by the same VPLS services from using spoke-pseudowires to communicate with each other, bypassing the Layer 3 service gateway in Layer 3. (Triple Play service is beyond the scope of this book.) This can be done by using *split-horizon* groups.

First, a split-horizon group is defined in the VPLS service instance in PE router. Next, all spoke-pseudowires that should not exchange traffic with each other are associated to the split-horizon group. SAPs can also be added to a split-horizon group. Mesh-pseudowires cannot be added to the split-horizon group. The association of the spoke-pseudowires to the split-horizon group must be performed during the creation of the spoke-pseudowires and SAPs. Figure 12.7 illustrates an example of using split-horizon groups to prevent communications between certain network elements.

Figure 12.7 Split-Horizon Group Topology Example

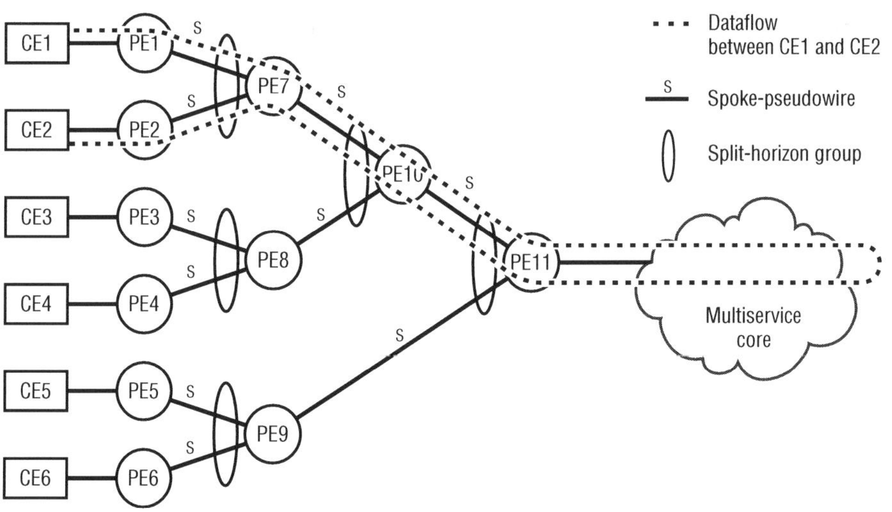

The dotted line represents the traffic flow between CE1 and CE2. PE1 is connected to CE1 with a local SAP, and PE2 is connected to CE2 with a local SAP. All *aggregating* PE routers (PE7, PE8, PE9, PE10, and PE11) have their downstream (closer to CE) spoke-pseudowires associated with the split-horizon group. Assume that CE1 wants to communicate with CE2.

The path PE-1 → PE-7 → PE-2 does not work because the two downstream spoke-pseudowires are in the same split-horizon group. The traffic from CE1 must go up to PE10, then to PE11 to reach the router, and back down to CE2. Therefore, all CE routers must communicate through the Multi-service core. (This is a typical requirement of access service providers, where direct Layer 2 access between customers is prohibited. Network access is beyond the scope of this book.) Figure 12.8 demonstrates the creation of a split-horizon group and the association of the split-horizon group to spoke-pseudowires.

Figure 12.8 Associating Spoke-Pseudowires with a Split-Horizon Group

```
A:PE-2# configure service vpls 5005
A:PE-2>config>service>vpls# info
----------------------------------------------------------------
            split-horizon-group "group1" create
        exit
        stp
            shutdown
        exit
        sap 1/1/3:2005 split-horizon-group "group1" create
        exit
        spoke-sdp 116:5005 split-horizon-group "group1" create
        exit
        spoke-sdp 164:5005 create
        exit
        spoke-sdp 165:5005 split-horizon-group "group1" create
        exit
        no shutdown
----------------------------------------------------------------
```

```
A:PE-2#  show service id 5005 sdp detail
===============================================================
Services: Service Destination Points Details
===============================================================
---------------------------------------------------------------
 Sdp Id 116:5005  -(10.0.0.116)
---------------------------------------------------------------
SDP Id           : 116:5005      Type           : Spoke
Split Horiz Grp  : group1
VC Type          : Ether         VC Tag         : n/a
Admin Path MTU   : 0             Oper Path MTU  : 9190
Far End          : 10.0.0.116    Delivery       : LDP
Admin State      : Up            Oper State     : Up
Acct. Pol        : None              Collect Stats   : Disabled
--- output omitted ---
```

With the addition of split-horizon groups, spoke-pseudowires can also change when required to emulate the mesh-pseudowire behavior. Actually, the mesh-pseudowires are equivalent of spoke-pseudowires belonging to the same split-horizon group.

12.3 H-VPLS Topologies

As mentioned in the "Hierarchical-VPLS Overview" section, there are two typical H-VPLS deployment topologies. The first topology uses spoke-pseudowires to connect several VPLS meshes. The optimal forwarding path within each mesh is maintained, and the total number of pseudowires required is reduced. The second topology is the hub-spoke topology, wherein the hub-PE router is connected to multiple spoke-PE routers by spoke-pseudowires. The hub-PE router aggregates the traffic from the spoke-PE routers and sends it to the VPLS mesh in the core. Therefore, the spoke-PE router does not have to peer with every other PE router. In this section, both typical topologies are analyzed in detail to familiarize the reader with the differences in behavior between H-VPLS and VPLS mesh. A variety of other topologies can be provided through a combination of these two models.

H-VPLS: Connecting VPLS Meshes with Spoke-Pseudowires

The first typical H-VPLS topology presented here is the breaking up of a VPLS mesh. The original VPLS mesh is broken into several VPLS meshes that are connected by spoke-pseudowires. This topology is similar to the method of breaking one internal BGP (iBGP) mesh into several smaller iBGP meshes and using *confederation* eBGP to connect them. Figure 12.9 illustrates the use of spoke-pseudowires to connect two VPLS meshes.

Figure 12.9   H-VPLS: Using Spoke-Pseudowires to Connect VPLS Meshes

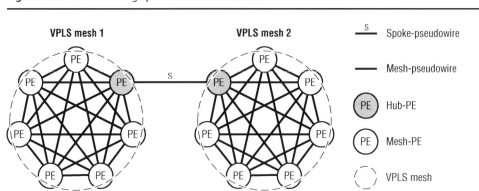

The spoke-pseudowire that connects the two hub-PE routers hides the detailed topology information behind the connected PE sites. This is different from a mesh topology, in which all nodes are fully aware of the topology of the entire network. For all mesh PE routers in VPLS mesh 1, all customer traffic from VPLS mesh 2 reaches the PE routers in VPLS mesh 1 through the spoke-pseudowire between the two hub-PE routers. Therefore, all MAC addresses belonging to customers that are attached to VPLS mesh 2 are learned through the hub-PE. The same thing happens in VPLS mesh 2. Mesh-PE routers learn the MAC addresses of customers in VPLS mesh 1 through the hub-PE.

Designing a scaled VPLS service network topology can be complicated. The operator must decide whether or not to use spoke-pseudowires to break the VPLS mesh, and where to break the mesh. There is no answer that is applicable to all scenarios. The network architecture must be decided case-by-case using *best practice* guidelines. *The choice between mesh-pseudowires and spoke-pseudowire H-VPLS is a balance between optimal data forwarding paths and control plane complexity (quantity of pseudowires).*

The network design may be different for different VPLS service requirements and different traffic types. For example, in a VPLS service used for network management purposes, the volume of traffic is low. A network management service usually requires *any-to-any* connectivity in the VPLS provisioned for management services, which means that all PE routers in the network participate in the service. This scenario creates low traffic volume but with a large number of member PE routers involved in the service. Hub-spoke H-VPLS is a better choice. For services that consume a large amount of bandwidth, the forwarding path should be as optimal as possible, with less concern about the number of pseudowires in the network.

H-VPLS: Connecting Spoke Sites with Spoke-Pseudowire

The second type of H-VPLS topology is to keep the VPLS mesh in the core of the network and to use spoke-pseudowires to connect the remote PE routers. The core network aggregates the traffic among the remote edge PE routers, so the core network should be fully meshed to ensure optimal forwarding paths. There are more PE routers in the edge of the provider networks than in the core of a provider network. The spoke-pseudowires (not mesh-pseudowires) connect the spoke-PE routers to the hub-PE routers, so the total number of pseudowires in the network is significantly reduced. Figure 12.10 illustrates a case in which PE routers use mesh-pseudowires to connect to each other and spoke-pseudowires to connect to their edge PE routers or Multi Tenant Units (MTUs).

Figure 12.10 H-VPLS: PE Spoke to Remote MTU

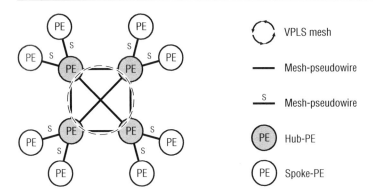

In a network with a physical layout like this, even if the number of pseudowires required for full-mesh service topology is not a concern, using the spoke-edge, mesh-core design is still more efficient. Assuming that a fully meshed VPLS service is built, all traffic among the PE routers at the edge still travels through the four hub-PE routers. The data-forwarding path in a fully meshed logical service topology is less optimal than the hub-spoke design. Networks should always be designed case-by-case, and the physical layout of the network should be used as a starting point, along with the consideration of the service topology requirements.

This type of hub-spoke design is also typically used when Multi Tenant Unit (MTU) devices are on the edge of the service network. MTUs are usually customer-facing devices on the edge of the service provider network. In most cases, the MTU is physically located close to the last mile, frequently in the cable dwelling of multi-tenant residential high-rise buildings. From the provider's perspective, an MTU is a lower-cost extension of a PE router into a customer location.

MTU devices are service-aware and IP/MPLS-capable, but have a lower scale limit. An MTU is a down-sized service router and is mostly used in the PE role in a service network at the location closest to the customers' sites. The name *MTU* is a description of a device's location and functions. A regular carrier-level service router can also be used as an MTU. In a network that uses MTU devices to extend its services, PE routers are used as hubs, connecting multiple MTUs with spoke-pseudowires. Customer traffic enters the provider's network and is VPN-encapsulated by MTU. The traffic then travels through the hub-PE routers toward the core network.

The *single point of failure* needs to be considered when designing a network with hub-spoke topology. A fully meshed service topology has more redundancy; therefore, it is more robust. In a fully meshed network, loss of a single mesh-pseudowire affects only the traffic between two PE routers. In a hub-spoke topology, the uplink from an MTU, a spoke-PE connected to the hub, and the hub-PE itself can all become a single point of failure. If a hub-PE router fails, all spoke-PE and MTU devices connected to it lose connectivity to the core network. To enhance the resiliency of hub-spoke design, the spoke device (an MTU or a PE router in the customer-facing edge) is often dual-homed to more than one hub PE router. When using a dual-homed network design for VPLS services, a loop-prevention mechanism must be used to ensure that only one Head-End hub device is actively forwarding traffic for the spoke devices at any time. The dual-homing network design and loop prevention is introduced in Chapter 15.

The fully meshed VPLS and the H-VPLS each has its own pros and cons. When choosing one type of VPLS to deploy, the forwarding behavior of the solution must be researched carefully, and the benefits and drawbacks of the solution must be considered thoroughly. Compared to fully meshed VPLS, the H-VPLS has the following benefits:

- **Accommodates existing (administrative) domain boundaries** — Large operators may have several network domains (administratively separated) to merge. The operator can use spoke-pseudowire to connect several domains to form a large H-VPLS network.

- **Replication efficiency** — This is especially important for the network carrying multicast traffic. As discussed previously, H-VPLS solution reduces the number of pseudowires required in the network to achieve full connectivity. The multicast traffic replication is therefore reduced.

- **Provides support for flexible service models** — H-VPLS gives the operator the flexibility to design their service topology:
  - It allows enforcement of tiered rates. For example, the operator can rate control different spoke-pseudowires in different portions of the network — allowing 100Mbps in the Metro links, and allowing 10Mbps in the WAN links at the entrance/exit boundary spoke-pseudowires.
  - The operator can deploy different service topologies: any-to-any, hub-spoke, or ring-based service topologies.

- **Provides a manageable, low-cost operational model important for a large VPLS deployment:**
  - The service growth in one metro region impacts only the local spoke PE routers and hub PE routers.
  - Provisioning of new sites only requires configuration on local hub PE routers, which achieves the domain separation.

- **Allows for low cost spoke-PE** — In the H-VPLS network, the spoke sites require just one or two pseudowires per service and one or two T-LDP sessions per node. Therefore, the low cost PE devices (such as MTU) can be used on the spoke sites.

  The H-VPLS also has the following cons which operators must be aware of:

- **Complicates the service topology by introducing a new switching element** — The forwarding behavior of the spoke-pseudowire is different than the mesh-pseudowire. When deploying H-VPLS, you must take care to ensure forwarding loops are not introduced.

- **Requires a resiliency scheme to be implemented to avoid single point of failure at the hub PE router** — The hub PE router either aggregates traffic from many spoke PE routers, or carrys traffics among different meshed VPLS networks. It is crucial to protect the hub PE router with resiliency.

- **Increased scalability requirements into the hub-PE router** — The hub-PE router must peer with many spoke PE routers in a hub-spoke VPLS topology. Therefore, the number of service transport tunnels, T-LDP sessions, and pseudowires for the hub-PE router to maintain can be high. The hub-PE router must have strong scalability.

12.4 H-VPLS Design Case Study — Where to Break the Mesh?

VPLS network design in a scaled service provider network can be challenging. The large number of PE routers means a full-mesh service tunnel may not be possible, and packet replication for flooded traffic can cause core congestion. If improperly designed, the spoke-pseudowire solution may cause suboptimal forwarding, a bandwidth bottleneck, and forwarding loops. The network design must have a balance of scalability, configuration complexity, and service performance. In most cases, the following factors need to be considered:

- **Administrative domain/bandwidth cost boundaries** — Large operators often have several administratively separated VPLS networks. H-VPLS is usually used in this case to define subnetwork boundaries for cost and management reasons.

- **Physical network topology: many alternate paths or simple hub and spoke topology** — The operator may want to design the VPLS service topology to fit the physical topology to take advantage of the physical redundancy.

- Size of the network and available capital expenditure/business model:

  - **How much for a network element** — With a hub and spoke topology, the low cost MTUs can be deployed in the spoke locations to reduce the overall network cost.

  - **Geographical location** — In a metro network, the operators may want to deploy a meshed VPLS network with a few hundred PE routers. However, the same network distributed over three continents might be better off with an H-VPLS design with different meshes connected by spoke pseudowires.

  - **Service scale** — For a WAN network that requires thousands of PE routers, the H-VPLS solution should be seriously considered.

Table 12.2 compares the characteristics of mesh-pseudowire and spoke-pseudowire in network design.

Table 12-2 Network Design: Mesh-Pseudowire versus Spoke-Pseudowire

PW Type	Pros	Cons
Mesh-pseudowire	• Optimal Forwarding — Each PE router has a direct forwarding path to any peering PE router (if the physical layout is also meshed). • Loop-Free Core Network — Mesh-pseudowires do not exchange traffic with each other. All mesh-pseudowires from one PE node belong to one Bridge Port and therefore do not cause forwarding loops.	• In a network with n PE routers, $n * (n-1)/2$ mesh-pseudowires are required for full connectivity. • Requires configuration changes in *all* PE nodes when adding sites. • Flooding traffic requires packet replication for each mesh service tunnel. • The number of LSPs requires processing power to maintain an RSVP session state.
Spoke-pseudowire	• Requires less service tunnel (LSP) configuration, fewer SDPs, and fewer pseudowires to signal within the service. • Adding sites requires configuration changes in only one PE node.	• Can cause forwarding loops inside the VPLS instance. • Single point of failure. • Redundancy requires running STP in the service provider's core network (separate from CE STP). • More FDB lookups end-to-end.

Note that in this case study, it is assumed that the operator is deploying new VPLS services. The operator does have the option to design the service topology as optimally as possible. In many large operators' networks, this may not be a typical case. The operator may already have several smaller networks, and some of them may have VPLS services deployed with a certain design already. In such cases, the operator must first consider the network device compatibility, the current service requirement and topology, and the migration path before the optimal VPLS network design can be started.

Figure 12.11 illustrates a topology where the design of the network makes it difficult to balance between scalability and traffic optimization. Many regional service providers have a topology like the one in Figure 12.11: High-speed SONET/SDH rings connect most PE routers located in geographically separated sites. Because the cost of installing the fiber over large areas is significant, ring topology is often used instead of physical mesh topology. The ideal topology (fully meshed core and spoke ring sites) is not practical for typical regional SP networks.

In the scenario represented by Figure 12.11, three customers are requesting VPLS services from the provider:

- Customer 1's connectivity requirement is represented by the triangles in the diagram. All sites belonging to Customer 1 require full connectivity to each other; therefore, 20 sites need to be connected by VPLS. The bandwidth requirement for Customer 1 is relatively low, and the traffic is relatively evenly distributed among all sites.

- Customer 2's connectivity requirement is represented by the hexagons in the diagram. The traffic volume of Customer 2 is high; therefore, the most efficient forwarding paths are desired.

- Customer 3's connectivity requirement is represented by the squares in the diagram. Customer 3 has 11 stub sites (represented by the empty squares), and all are required to be connected to the center site router (represented by the square marked with R). The stub sites do not exchange traffic with each other, and all use the center site router as the Internet gateway.

Figure 12.11 SP Network Example: Geographically Distributed Network

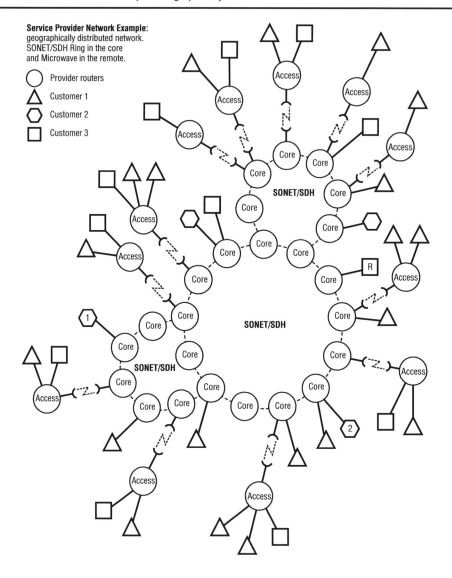

The service provider needs to consider many factors when designing the VPLS service topology for these three customers. The network designer tries to find an *optimized* approach in which the service implementation is efficient, reliable, manageable, and expandable. Following are a few questions to consider:

- How many sites require connectivity from each customer?
- What is the expected traffic pattern and volume?

- Will the customers expand their networks to have more sites in the future?

- Will the traffic volume from the customers increase in the future?

- Will the network design have a clear and trackable structure that can be easily documented?

- Is the network design easy to troubleshoot?

Because of the differences in each customer's connectivity and traffic volume requirements, a different type of VPLS service topology should be used to service the needs of each of the three customers in the example. In the following case study, recommended VPLS topologies are presented for each customer.

VPLS Design for Customer 1: Many Sites Requiring Any-to-Any Connectivity

Customer 1 requires any-to-any Ethernet connectivity for each of its 20 sites. One possible approach is to create VPLS service instances on every provider router where there is a site for Customer 1, and create a VPLS full mesh. Every PE router containing a VPLS service instance for Customer 1 has one mesh-pseudowire connected to every other VPLS member PE router. However, the single full VPLS mesh approach in this case requires the deployment of a significant number of pseudowires (and the supporting SDP, LSP, etc.), leading to high management overhead. Using H-VPLS with spoke-pseudowires can reduce the configuration overhead. As mentioned previously, using H-VPLS may lead to suboptimal forwarding paths. Because Customer 1's traffic volume is low, this should not be a significant issue. Figure 12.12 illustrates the recommended VPLS topology design for Customer 1.

The VPLS service designed for Customer 1 uses the hub-spoke approach. The basic idea is to break the VPLS full-mesh design into a hub-spoke design to reduce the number of pseudowires in the network. The VPLS service for Customer 1 uses a two-tier hierarchical design:

- The PE routers that have local customer sites attached to them are spoke-PE routers. The spoke-PE routers accept customer traffic from their SAPs and forward the traffic to the core of the provider's network.

- Several routers in the core are chosen to be hub-PE routers. A hub-PE router aggregates the traffic from the spoke-PE routers located close to it. The hub-PE routers are connected to each other using mesh pseudowires to ensure optimal forwarding in the core of the network.

Figure 12.12 VPLS Design for Customer 1: Hub-Spoke VPLS Topology

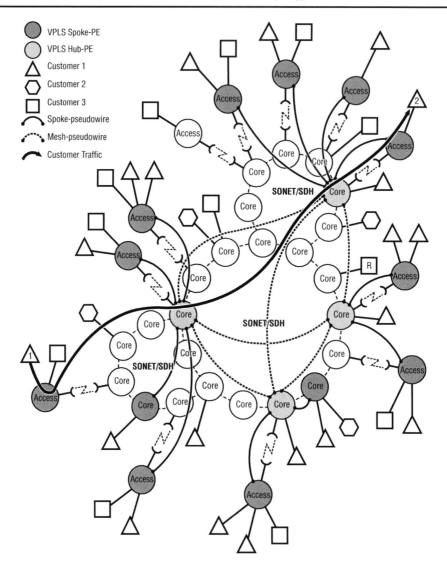

Therefore, the provider does not need to deploy a full VPLS mesh among all PE routers that are connected to local customer sites. Because the hub-PE routers are fully meshed with each other, the aggregated traffic in the core network is forwarded along the optimal path.

Figure 12.12 illustrates four hub-PE routers (represented by the light gray Core circles) located in the center of a SONET ring. The spoke-PE routers are located at the edge of the network where local customer sites are attached. Each spoke-PE router has one service instance that has one or more SAPs attached to the customer site, and to a spoke-pseudowire connected to the closest hub-PE router. There are four hub-PE routers in the core of the network. Each hub-PE router has many spoke-pseudowires connected to adjacent spoke-PE routers, and three mesh-pseudowires connected to the other three hub-PE routers. All other routers in the service provider's network act as P routers and have no visibility of the VPLS service for Customer 1.

In this network, Customer 1's traffic from one site travels through a spoke-PE router, hub-PE routers, and another spoke-PE router to reach the far-end site. As an example, the traffic from Site 1 (the leftmost triangle in the figure, marked with a *1*) travels through four VPLS PE routers (represented by the solid black line) to Site 2 (the rightmost triangle in the figure, marked with a *2*):

1. Customer traffic from local Site 1 enters the provider network through the SAP of the local spoke-PE router.

2. The local spoke-PE router forwards the traffic to the closest hub-PE router.

3. The closest hub-PE router forwards the traffic to the hub-PE router closest to the remote spoke-PE router.

4. The remote spoke-PE router forwards the traffic to remote customer Site 2 through its SAP.

If Customer 1 wants to add new sites in new locations in the future, the service provider needs to add only one new spoke-PE router and a spoke-pseudowire to the hub-PE router that is located closest to the new customer site. The configuration modification requirements for adding, deleting, and moving customer sites are minimized.

VPLS Design for Customer 2: Fully Meshed VPLS for Optimal Forwarding

Customer 2 requires any-to-any Ethernet connectivity with high-bandwidth throughput for its four sites. Because Customer 2 requires high bandwidth for its dataflow, the most optimal forwarding path is desired. In this case, the VPLS full mesh is used to ensure that the traffic between any two sites takes the shortest possible path. Each router connected to a site of Customer 2 acts as a PE router. The VPLS service instance in each PE router contains SAPs to the local site(s) and mesh-pseudowires to all other PE routers. Figure 12.13 illustrates a recommended VPLS topology design for Customer 2.

Figure 12.13 VPLS Design for Customer 2: Fully Meshed VPLS for Optimal Forwarding

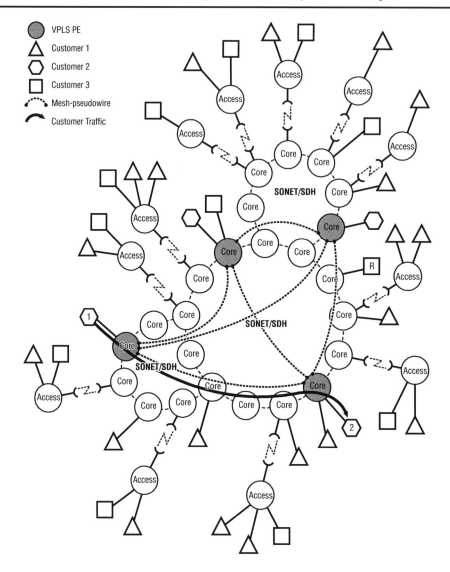

The VPLS service designed for Customer 2 uses the fully meshed VPLS approach. Four PE routers (represented by the shaded circles in the figure) have fully meshed mesh-pseudowires connected among them. Each PE router also has SAP(s) connected to the customer site(s). The data-forwarding path within the VPLS mesh is optimal.

In this network, Customer 2's traffic from one site travels through two PE routers, then to a remote router site. As an example, the traffic from Site 1 (the leftmost hexagon in the figure, marked with a *1*) travels through two VPLS PE routers to Site 2 (the rightmost hexagon in the figure, marked with a *2*):

1. Customer traffic from local Site 1 enters the provider network through the SAP of the local PE router.

2. The local PE router forwards the traffic to the closest remote PE router.

3. The remote PE router forwards the traffic to the remote customer Site 2 through its SAP.

If Customer 2 wants to add new sites in new locations in the future, the service provider needs to add a new PE router and mesh-pseudowires to all existing PE routers. The VPLS mesh for Customer 2 can be expanded but should retain the fully meshed topology to ensure optimal forwarding.

VPLS Design for Customer 3: Hub-Spoke Topology with Split-Horizon Group

Customer 3 requires all stub sites to be connected to the central router site (represented in the diagrams by the square marked with an *R*). All stub sites use the router site as an Internet gateway, and direct traffic exchange among stub sites without going through the gateway is not allowed. For Customer 3, hub-spoke VPLS topology is the best VPLS service design. Figure 12.14 illustrates the recommended VPLS topology design for Customer 3.

The VPLS service designed for Customer 3 uses the hub-spoke VPLS approach. The PE router connected to the router site (represented by the lighter gray Core circle in the diagram) is the hub-PE router. All other routers connected to Customer 3's sites are spoke-PE routers. The VPLS service instance for Customer 3 on the hub-PE router contains one SAP connected to the customer router site and many spoke-pseudowires connected to all of the spoke-PE routers. The VPLS service in each spoke-PE router has one spoke-pseudowire connected to the hub-PE router and SAP(s) connected to the locally attached customer site(s).

In this network, Customer 3's traffic from one site travels through two PE routers, first the spoke-PE router, then the hub-PE router. As an example, the traffic from Site 1 (the leftmost left square in the figure, marked with a *1*) travels through two VPLS PE routers to the router site (the rightmost square, marked with an *R*):

1. Customer traffic from local Site 1 enters the provider network through the SAP of the local spoke-PE router.

2. The local PE router forwards the traffic to the hub-PE router.

3. The remote PE router forwards the traffic to the customer's router site through its SAP.

Figure 12.14 VPLS Design for Customer 3: Hub-Spoke Topology with a Split-Horizon Group

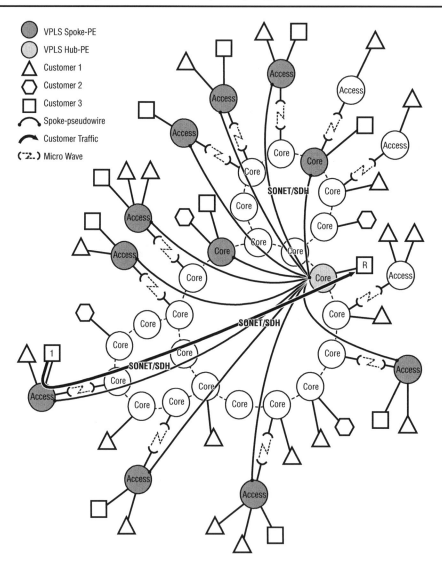

If Customer 3 wants to add new sites in new locations in the future, the service provider needs to add only one new PE router and spoke-pseudowires connected to the hub-PE router.

Summary

Hierarchical VPLS (H-VPLS) is a variation of VPLS service deployment. Regular VPLS uses a fully meshed mesh pseudowire set to connect all member PE routers. In certain scenarios, a full mesh of pseudowires among PE routers may be inefficient or impossible because of scale limitations. H-VPLS can be deployed in these scenarios to reduce the number of pseudowires required to provide full connectivity.

H-VPLS introduces *spoke-pseudowire* into the VPLS network. In a VPLS service instance, each spoke-pseudowire belongs to a single Bridge Port. Therefore, spoke-pseudowire can exchange traffic with any SAPs, mesh-pseudowires, or other spoke-pseudowires.

There are two typical scenarios in which H-VPLS is used. The first scenario is a hub-spoke topology in which several *central PE routers* have stub PE routers spread around them. The central PE routers can be deployed with regular fully meshed mesh-pseudowires to form a VPLS full mesh. The stub PE routers use spoke-pseudowire to connect to the closest central PE router. The second scenario is when two VPLS networks need to be connected. A spoke-pseudowire can be configured between two PE routers in the boundary to connect the two VPLS meshes.

13

High Availability in an IP/MPLS VPN Network

This chapter discusses several mechanisms that can improve network robustness and speed up the performance of network convergence after failures.

Chapter Objectives

- Explain Bidirectional Forwarding Detection (BFD)

- Introduce Ethernet Link Aggregation Groups (LAGs)

- Explain Multi Chassis LAG (MC-LAG)

- Describe traffic load balancing in LAGs for IP/MPLS VPN networks

High Availability (HA), robustness, and quick convergence are crucial for today's network operators and for the IT departments of large enterprises. Service providers need their networks to achieve minimal downtime so they can fulfill their five-nine Service Level Agreements (SLAs) with their customers. Large enterprises are very sensitive to service outages in their networks. To build a network with HA, redundant equipment and links should be used to remove any single points of failure, and the network should use any available technology to ensure that it can achieve fast convergence and restore services as quickly as possible. Several components need to be considered to achieve fast convergence:

- Quickly detect the failure.
- If necessary, quickly propagate the failure (horizontally to other peering network elements, or vertically to the upper-layer protocol engine).
- React quickly to work around the failure.
- Optionally, when the failure is recovered, restore the network to its original status, with minimum or no impact to the services.

13.1 Building a Network with High Availability

Service providers always want to build highly reliable networks. HA is a measure of the uptime of the network over a long period of time and is generally measured using Mean Time Between Failures (MTBF) and Mean Time To Repair (MTTR). When deploying multiple services in a converged IP/MPLS VPN network, many resiliency mechanisms can be used to improve network robustness and reliability and therefore make the network highly available.

Resiliency and HA features can be categorized as follows:

- **Nodal (System) Resiliency** — The ability of the router to protect the service from hardware or software failures, such as routing instance failure, control card failure, switching fabric failure, and so on
- **Service and Network Backbone Resiliency** — The ability of the router to protect the service from network failures, such as a link failure, a failure of the peering router, and so on

An IP/MPLS VPN service network has many resiliency features and mechanisms to protect the routing and services from different types of failures. To design a network with HA, the operator must understand how each mechanism works and which types of failure each mechanism can protect against.

Nodal Resiliency

To provide nodal resiliency, the routers should have redundant hardware and software components, such as a redundant control plane, redundant switching fabric, redundant line cards, a redundant power supply, and so on. The redundant components make the router capable of:

- **Non-Stop Routing (NSR)** — Redundant routing instances running in the standby control plane protect the routing protocol from control plane failure.

- **Non-Stop Forwarding (NSF)** — The ability to continue forwarding traffic using the forwarding information kept in the data plane if the control plane fails

- **Non-Stop Signaling** — Redundant signaling protocol instances running in the standby control plane maintain the signaling processes required by MPLS and the services if the signaling protocol on the active control plane fails.

- **Non-Stop Service (NSS)** — The full state and information for the services are maintained in the standby control card, so that if the control plane fails, the standby control card immediately takes over the service instances, resulting in zero downtime for the services.

NSR is achieved by running separate routing protocol instances in the active and standby control planes and by keeping the state machines synchronized. NSR protects routing protocols such as OSPF, ISIS, and BGP. If the routing process on the active control card fails, the standby control card immediately takes over the routing process (hot standby) and stores all state machine and routing information. The peering router is not aware of the local control plane switchover.

NSF is achieved by separating the control plane and the data plane. The system keeps the content of the Forwarding Information Base (FIB) in the data plane so that if the routing process in the control plane fails, traffic can still be forwarded to the destination. It can reduce the service outage during a control plane failure that affects the routing protocol and the routing table. The drawback of NSF is that during a routing protocol failure in the control plane, the Routing Information Base (RIB) is affected by the failure and may be out of synchronization with the FIB because NSR maintains the content of the FIB during the failure. The router may send traffic to an incorrect destination because the FIB content may no longer be correct.

Similar to NSF, Non-Stop Signaling is achieved by running redundant signaling protocol instances in the active and standby control planes and keeping them synchronized. An IP/MPLS VPN network requires the LDP and RSVP-TE signaling protocols to build service transport tunnels to carry service traffic. Non-Stop

Signaling protects the MPLS LSPs and keeps them operational during an active control card failure, or a failure of the signaling protocol instance in the active control card.

NSS is achieved by maintaining all service entities and related components on the active and standby control planes. Therefore, if the active control plane fails, the standby control plane keeps the state of the service instances operational. For example, if the active control card in a VPLS PE router fails, the router switches over to the VPLS service instance in the standby control card. The service in the standby control card maintains all information (pseudowires, forwarding databases, and so on) so that the VPLS service has zero downtime.

Service and Network Resiliency

Service and network (backbone) resiliency is the ability of the service router to protect the system from a network component failure. A network always has cases in which a link is down or a peering router is out of service. If the network is deployed with service and network resiliency features, the service can be protected from these network component failures as follows:

- **Network Resiliency** — Protects the network infrastructure that is shared by all services deployed in the network.

- **Service Resiliency** — Protects each service from failures that affect that particular service.

Network resiliency protects the service backbone infrastructure. In an IP/MPLS VPN network, many services share the same infrastructure, for example, the common physical links connected to the remote provider (P) or Provider Edge (PE) routers, the service transport tunnels established to the remote PE routers to carry service traffic, and so on. During a network failure, many features protect the infrastructure; therefore, services that share the infrastructure are also protected. Network resiliency includes:

- **MPLS Resiliency** — When MPLS LSPs are used as transport tunnels, the MPLS resiliency features, such as RSVP-TE Secondary LSP (discussed in Chapter 6) and RSVP-TE LSP Fast Reroute (discussed in Chapter 7), protect the transport tunnels from link or nodal failures. If LDP-LSP is used, Equal Cost Multi-Path (ECMP) provides MPLS transport tunnel redundancy (discussed in Chapter 8).

- **Link Resiliency** — Link Aggregation Groups (LAGs) can be used to group several Ethernet links together between two routers, so that if a link fails, other links in the same LAG can protect the connectivity between the two routers. Features like Bidirectional Forwarding Detection (BFD) and EFM OAM (802.3ah) can also be used to improve the speed of failure detection to minimize traffic outage during a failure.

Service resiliency protects each individual service. Network failures may affect a particular service, such as a router failure in a service's member PE, if a link connected to a SAP of a service fails, or if a pseudowire used by one service fails. Service resiliency mechanisms are as follows:

- **SAP Protection (Access Resiliency)** — To protect the SAP from a link failure, LAG and MC-LAG (discussed later in this chapter) can be deployed on the SAP connected to the CE devices. If a link between the PE and the CE routers fails, other available links take over the traffic. For ATM VLL services, Automatic Protection System (APS) or MC-APS can be used to protect against link failure on the SAP. Furthermore, in VLL solutions or VPLS residential context, Multi Chassis Ring (MC-Ring) can also be deployed to provide SAP protection. MC-Ring is beyond the scope of this book. Please refer to ALSRP product manuals for details regarding MC-Ring.

- **Pseudowire Redundancy** — The service can be deployed with redundant pseudowires (*multi-homing*). By defining service endpoints and grouping redundant pseudowires into the endpoints, if one pseudowire fails, the service can use other pseudowires in the same endpoint to the remote PE router. Both VLL and VPLS services can use pseudowire redundancy to improve service robustness (discussed in Chapters 14 and 15).

- **VPLS Redundancy with Spanning Tree Protocol** — VPLS services can also be deployed with redundant SAPs and/or pseudowires with STP enabled to prevent forwarding loops. This is a less preferred network design than pseudowire redundancy in VPLS because of the slow convergence performance of STP.

When designing a network with HA, it is important to consider using as many as possible multiple resiliency features to protect the network and the services. When multiple resiliency features are deployed in a network, it is also important to understand the failover behavior during different failure scenarios. A network with multiple services deployed may encounter a link failure between two routers; the operator must understand which resiliency feature protects against such a failure and be able to predict the network behavior. Both FRR and pseudowire redundancy can protect a service from a core link failure, but FRR protects the transport tunnels, so all services using that transport tunnel are protected. On the other hand, pseudowire redundancy can only provide protection on a per-service basis.

VLL services and VPLS services provide different connectivity. Therefore, the pseudowire resiliency features available for the two types of services are deployed differently and behave differently. The next two chapters discuss the service resiliency of VLL (Chapter 14) and VPLS (Chapter 15) in detail. The remaining portion of this chapter discusses more common resiliency features applicable to all services and the network, such as BFD and LAG.

13.2 Bidirectional Forwarding Detection

Bidirectional Forwarding Detection (BFD) is not a routing protocol. The purpose of BFD is to speed up network failure detection using a lightweight Hello protocol as a *heartbeat*. If a system stops receiving the heartbeat from its BFD peer, it assumes that there is a network failure in between it and its peer and notifies the upper-layer protocol(s) (for example, IGP and MPLS) so the protocol(s) can react accordingly. From the perspective of a network device, there can be two types of failure: local and remote. Figure 13.1 illustrates local failure and remote failure scenarios.

Figure 13.1   Local versus Remote Network Failure

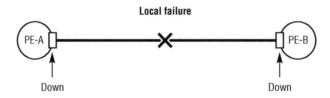

1 PE-A will detect local cable failure immediately because the port status will be down when it happens.

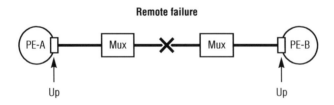

2 If the link failure is in between the two muxes, and if the mux will keep the local port to PE-A and PE-B up (active mux, or microwave Hut equipment), the time consumed for the PE routers to detect the link failure is much longer. In most cases, it relies on protocol timeout (OSPF hello time-out, or STP BPDU age-out), which is significantly longer than local failure response time.

A *local failure* is a failure that affects the physical state of the ports of a device. In the top example in Figure 13.1, the link failure brings down both ports in PE-A and PE-B. PE-A and PE-B immediately notice the port status change and react accordingly by withdrawing link advertisements, clearing RSVP-TE sessions, raising alarms, and so on.

A *remote failure* is a failure that does *not* affect the physical state of the port(s) of the device. In the bottom example in Figure 13.1, the link between two optical multiplexers (muxes) goes down, but the physical links between each optical multiplexer and the peering PE router are still up. This is a typical topology in the network of a large service provider in which routers located in different cities are connected through multiple hops of optical switching devices. Because the physical ports in PE-A and PE-B are still operationally up, they do not detect the failure until the protocols running between them experience a time-out. Depending on the type of protocol running between PE-A and PE-B, it may take some time before the two routers detect a network failure between them. For example, if OSPF is running between PE-A and PE-B with a default dead interval of 40 seconds, the failure is not detected and propagated to the rest of the network until 40 seconds later. Most IGPs have a granularity of only 1 second in their Hello intervals; with the help of BFD, the convergence performance can be reduced to milliseconds.

In this case, the failure detection time depends on the Hello timer of the protocol. Shortening the protocol Hello interval makes the IGP respond more quickly to the remote failure, but it also adds an extra processing load to the system. Most IGP routing protocols support only the minimum Hello timer value of several seconds, which may not be enough because most service providers require the failover time to be within 1 second, and some require tens of milliseconds. BFD can help speed up failure detection and failover in this type of scenario. The BFD Hello interval can be set to less than 1 second, so it can rapidly notify the upper-layer protocol of the network failure. Because BFD is a lightweight protocol, the effect on router performance of implementing BFD is minimal.

BFD notification of network failure to the IGP (or to another upper-layer protocol) is a two-step process. First, the routers connected by intermediate transmission equipment must have BFD adjacency between them. By exchanging Hello packets, BFD monitors the health of the connection. If a failure occurs between the BFD peering devices, the BFD session times out, indicating a transmission problem. Second, BFD reports the network failure to the upper-layer protocol(s), and the protocol using BFD reacts accordingly.

The configuration of BFD also requires two steps: configuring the BFD session with peering attributes and configuring the upper-layer protocol to use BFD to detect failure. Similarly, when a network failure recovers, BFD detects the restoration of the session and reports it to the upper-layer protocol. The upper-layer protocol then puts the interface back to a functional state and notifies the neighbors. Table 13.1 lists the protocols that support BFD failure detection.

Note: BFD supports two types of adjacencies. One type allows only single BFD sessions; the other allows multiple sessions between two peering devices. Both types are explained in detail later in this chapter.

Table 13.1 BFD Support of Other Protocols

Protocol	BFD Support	Reaction to BFD Failure Report
RIP	Not supported	Not applicable. (RIP is a distance vector protocol, which is not recommended in the core of a provider network because of its slow convergence and scale limitations.)
OSPF	Yes	When a BFD session is declared down, the associated OSPF interface is brought down and the corresponding LSA is withdrawn.
IS-IS	Yes	When a BFD session is declared down, the associated IS-IS interface is brought down and the corresponding LSP is withdrawn.
Static route	Yes	When a particular static route is enabled with BFD, the route is withdrawn if the corresponding BFD session goes down.
BGP	Yes	Supports both loopback-sourced BGP and interface-sourced BGP sessions. When a BFD session is declared down, the associated BGP sessions are also cleared.
RSVP-TE	Yes	When a BFD session is declared down, the associated RSVP interface is brought down and all RSVP-TE sessions over that interface are cleared. A BFD session time-out triggers FRR if it is enabled.

Protocol	BFD Support	Reaction to BFD Failure Report
LDP	No direct support	LDP convergence is based on IGP. As long as IGP is using BFD, the LDP convergence time is also shortened. No configuration is required for LDP to take advantage of BFD over IGP.
PIM	Yes	When a BFD session is declared down, the associated PIM interface is brought down and is removed from the multicast distribution tree.
GRE	No direct support	GRE service tunnel convergence is based on IGP. As long as IGP is using BFD, GRE convergence time is also shortened. No configuration is required for GRE to take advantage of BFD over IGP.

BFD has three modes of operation: asynchronous, demand, and echo. In *asynchronous mode*, the system uses periodic BFD packets to constantly test the link. In *demand mode*, the BFD packets are sent only when the remote-end system thinks there may be a problem and requires a continuity check. In *echo mode*, one system sends a series of BFD packets, and the peer loops them back to the originator. If the originator does not see several BFD packets return, it considers the BFD session to be down.

BFD Control Packets and Session Parameters

Devices that are configured with BFD peering exchange BFD control packets among each other. BFD control packets are IP packets that have a UDP destination port of 3784 (the source port must be within the range from 49,152 to 65,535). All protocol modes and related parameters (Tx/Rx interval, protocol mode, discriminator for the session de-multiplexer, and so on) are encapsulated in the BFD control packets. All BFD packets have an IP TTL of 255. Figure 13.2 illustrates the format of the BFD packets with a live packet capture example.

The BFD control packets contain all required BFD session parameters: modes of operation, requirement of authentication, BFD packet intervals, local and peer discriminators, and so on.

Figure 13.2   BFD Control Packet Format

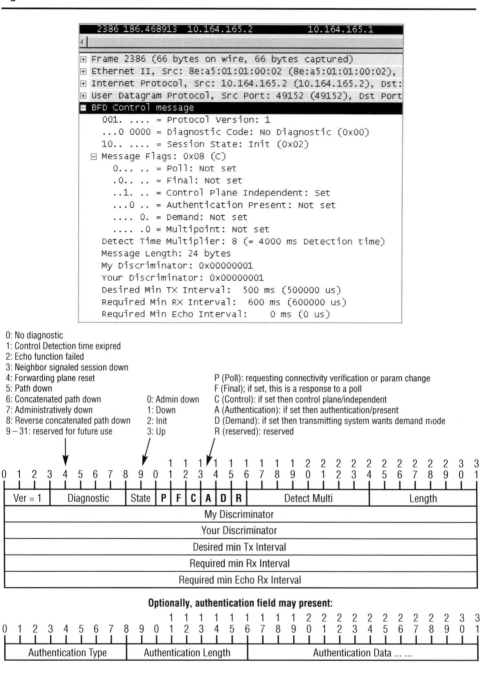

BFD Session Establishment and Operation

BFD adjacency is established on a per-link basis. Two BFD devices form a *session* over one physical link by exchanging BFD control packets, using the discriminator field in the packet to identify each session. As illustrated in Figure 13.3, before receiving a BFD packet from a neighbor, the BFD device sets its own discriminator value in the My discriminator field and sets a value of 0x00 in the Your discriminator field. After the BFD interface receives the incoming BFD packet, it copies the value in the My discriminator field of the incoming packet to the Your discriminator field of the next BFD packet to be sent to the peer. Two-way adjacency is established when both routers see their own discriminator value in the Your discriminator field of the peer.

This is similar to the way the OSPF protocol forms a two-way adjacency between two routers: when a BFD device sees its own discriminator value in a packet from a peer, it knows there is a common agreement to build a session. After two-way communication is established, the BFD considers the path to be operationally up. If there are several links between two systems that require BFD, multiple BFD sessions are created and maintained. In this case, the systems use the discriminator value as a de-multiplexer to identify different BFD sessions. Figure 13.3 illustrates the establishment of a BFD session between two routers.

Figure 13.3   BFD Session Establishment

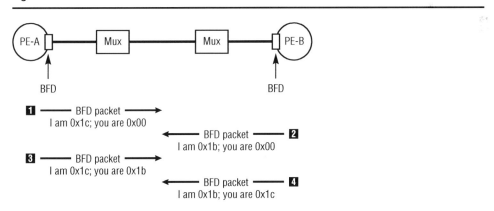

In asynchronous mode, after two systems establish one BFD session over one path, they periodically send BFD packets to each other to monitor the health of the path. The session peers negotiate the rate of the BFD packets traveling over the path between them. The rate is determined by comparing the values of the trip-let {Desired Min Tx Interval | Required Min Rx Interval | Detect-time Multiplexer} (the unit used for the interval configuration is milliseconds) from the configured local session and from the BFD packet received from the session peer. Each system performs value comparison on a per-session basis and determines the BFD packet sending rate and the rate of expected incoming BFD packets:

1. The maximum numerical local value [Desired Min Tx Interval] and received value [Required Min Rx Interval] is used as the interval for the system to send out BFD packets.

2. The maximum numerical local value [Required Min Rx Interval] and received value [Desired Min Tx Interval] is used as the interval for the system to expect incoming BFD packets.

3. The system considers the BFD session to be operationally **down** if a BFD packet is not received in the interface after a time longer than the local value [Detect-time-multiplexer] multiplexes the *ingress BFD packet expecting interval* (determined by the previous step).

For example, suppose a BFD session in a system is configured with {1000 | 5000 | 3} and receives {2000 | 3000 | 4} from the peer's BFD packet. The system chooses 3 seconds as the BFD packet-sending interval and expects an incoming BFD packet every 5 seconds. If the system does not receive BFD packets from the peer for more than $3 \times 5 = 15$ seconds, the BFD session is declared **down**. On the other hand, if the peer chooses 5 seconds as the packet-sending interval and expects incoming BFD packets every 3 seconds, the system declares the session **down** if it does not receive BFD packets for more than $4 \times 3 = 12$ seconds. The rule can be summarized as follows: *Tell me how fast you want to send, and I will tell you how fast I want to receive. We will agree on the* slower *rate.*

BFD Protocol Dependency

In the ALSRP, the BFD session's initial state is dependent on the upper-layer protocol(s) it serves. The BFD session comes up only if an upper-layer protocol is asso-ciated with it and the upper-layer protocol is operationally **up**. For example, if BFD is used to speed up OSPF convergence, two configuration steps are required — config-uring the logical OSPF interface facing the remote peer to use BFD detection, and configuring BFD parameters in the physical interface. The BFD session does not come up until the upper-layer protocol comes up. In this example, OSPF discovers its neighbor and forms the adjacency. The BFD session comes up and starts monitoring the path only after OSPF peering with a Full state to the neighbor is established.

If a physical layer failure occurs, BFD rapidly detects the failure and reports it to the protected protocol (OSPF). OSPF then considers the neighbor to be in the **down** state and starts to send Hello packets to rebuild the adjacency. When the failure is recovered, the BFD session state does not revert to **up** until OSPF adjacency is re-established and is in the Full state. When multiple protocols are served by BFD, only a single session exists between two BFD peering routers.

Note: When BFD serves multiple protocols simultaneously, the vendor must decide whether to use one shared BFD session for all upper-layer protocols or to maintain a separate BFD session for each upper-layer protocol. In Alcatel-Lucent SR/ESS family service routers, one BFD session between two routers is shared by all user protocols.

Configuring and Monitoring BFD

BFD is a lightweight protocol, and its configuration is straightforward. As previously discussed, deploying BFD is a two-step process: configuring BFD parameters in the interface(s) that requires BFD; then configuring the upper-layer protocol(s) to use it. Because BFD serves Layer 3 protocols, it can be enabled only in Layer 3 interfaces, including router interfaces, IES interfaces, and VPRN interfaces. Remember that the BFD session does not come up right after it is enabled on both sides of the path. The upper-layer protocol adjacency between the two systems needs to come up first, with BFD enabled under the protocol interface. In the case in which several protocols share the same BFD session, only one protocol needs to bring up the adjacency so that the BFD session can come up. Figure 13.4 illustrates a configuration example of BFD and the association of OSPF and RSVP-TE.

Ethernet in the First Mile (EFM) OAM

Another way of rapidly detecting Ethernet link failure is 802.3ah EFM OAM. EFM OAM is a standard Ethernet link-level OAM. Network operators can use it to monitor the health of the Ethernet link and to detect link failures or fault conditions. EFM OAM can detect and report link failures in a subsecond time frame. The details regarding EFM OAM are presented in Chapter 18.

When quick failure detection is required on Ethernet links (access or the core network), both BFD and EFM OAM can be used (together or alone). EFM does have some advantage over BFD because it works at a lower layer than BFD, and it shuts down the physical interface when failure is detected, so the upper layer protocols are disconnected right away, without involvement of the control plane. Compare this to BFD, which has to notify the control plane of the failure and let the control plane disable the routing or signaling protocols. As a general recommendation, when possible, use EFM OAM because it requires less control plane overhead. Figure 13.4 presents a configuration example of BFD.

Figure 13.4 BFD Configuration Example

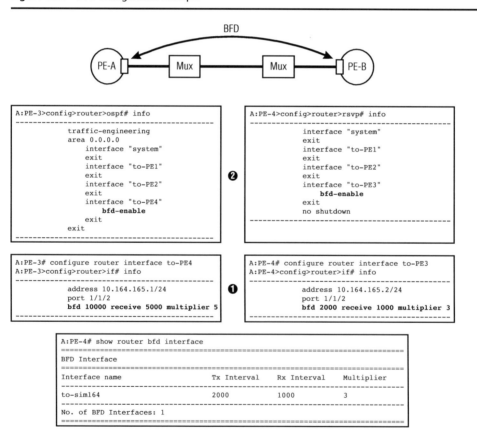

Figure 13.4 *(continued)*

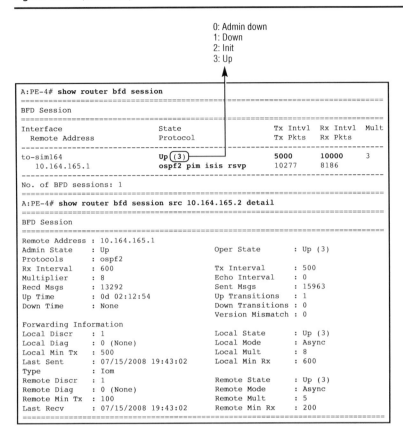

```
                                              0: Admin down
                                              1: Down
                                              2: Init
                                              3: Up

A:PE-4# show router bfd session
===================================================================================
BFD Session
===================================================================================
Interface                    State                    Tx Intvl  Rx Intvl  Mult
   Remote Address            Protocol                 Tx Pkts   Rx Pkts
-----------------------------------------------------------------------------------
to-sim164                    Up (3)                   5000      10000     3
   10.164.165.1              ospf2 pim isis rsvp      10277     8186
-----------------------------------------------------------------------------------
No. of BFD sessions: 1
===================================================================================
A:PE-4# show router bfd session src 10.164.165.2 detail
===================================================================================
BFD Session
===================================================================================
Remote Address : 10.164.165.1
Admin State    : Up                   Oper State        : Up (3)
Protocols      : ospf2
Rx Interval    : 600                  Tx Interval       : 500
Multiplier     : 8                    Echo Interval     : 0
Recd Msgs      : 13292                Sent Msgs         : 15963
Up Time        : 0d 02:12:54          Up Transitions    : 1
Down Time      : None                 Down Transitions  : 0
                                      Version Mismatch  : 0

Forwarding Information
Local Discr    : 1                    Local State       : Up (3)
Local Diag     : 0 (None)             Local Mode        : Async
Local Min Tx   : 500                  Local Mult        : 8
Last Sent      : 07/15/2008 19:43:02  Local Min Rx      : 600
Type           : Iom
Remote Discr   : 1                    Remote State      : Up (3)
Remote Diag    : 0 (None)             Remote Mode       : Async
Remote Min Tx  : 100                  Remote Mult       : 5
Last Recv      : 07/15/2008 19:43:02  Remote Min Rx     : 200
===================================================================================
```

13.3 Link Aggregation Group Overview

Link Aggregation Group (LAG) is a well-known mechanism used to group multiple Ethernet links in one logical link to provide more bandwidth and link redundancy. Because most readers know LAG well from legacy Ethernet switching and many well-written publications introduce LAG and Link Aggregation Control Protocol (LACP) in great detail, this book does not discuss Ethernet LAG in depth. This section reviews the basic concepts and components of LAG, as preparation for the introduction of Multi Chassis LAG (MC-LAG), which is an ALSRP-proprietary implementation.

Bandwidth Requirements

Today's service provider networks require higher and higher bandwidth. This is especially true when service providers turn to advanced IP/MPLS applications that involve high-bandwidth consumption services like Triple-Play or Quad-Play networks, which involve IPTV delivery constantly requiring large amounts of bandwidth in the core of the network. A typical high-definition channel requires 10 to 20 Mbps of bandwidth, and the service provider may have more than 100 such channels available to their subscribers at all times. To ensure a cable-TV-like user experience to the IPTV subscriber, most service providers choose to push all of the IPTV content as close as possible to the subscribers (usually in the aggregation zone, sometimes in the access zones). It is a big challenge for the core networks to provide such high bandwidth.

Note: Triple-Play networks provide IPTV, VoIP, and Internet services; in addition, Quad-Play networks provide high-bandwidth wireless services. The details regarding the design and implementation of Triple-Play, Quad-Play, and IPTV networks are beyond the scope of this book.

Ethernet LAG provides a solution to the high-bandwidth requirement by aggregating multiple (up to eight links per group) Ethernet links to appear as one logical link with higher bandwidth. Hashing algorithms are used to spread traffic flows among the member physical links to share the bandwidth and maintain the packet sequence. Grouping multiple physical links to a logical LAG also improves reliability. If some of the group member links fail, the traffic is moved to the available links in the same group with minimal packet loss. Table 13.2 lists the characteristics of LAG.

Table 13.2 Basic LAG Characteristics

Characteristic	Description
Protocol	Static configuration or LACP. (LACP is described later in this chapter.)
Threshold	The number of ports that need to stay up to keep the LAG status operational. When the number of ports that are up is fewer than the threshold number, the router can either bring down the entire LAG or keep the group up but reduce the advertising bandwidth over the routing protocols. This is defined by the action {dynamic-cost | down}.
Dynamic cost	If the number of active ports in the group changes, with dynamic cost enabled, the LAG can change the bandwidth value in the routing advertisement in real time to reflect the available bandwidth.

Characteristic	Description
Port parameters	Operational mode {`network` | `access`}, encapsulation {`null` | `dot1q` | `qinq`}. These are the characteristics of a physical port. When several ports are grouped into a LAG, these parameters are defined under the LAG.

Active links that belong to the LAG can be manually specified by configuration (static) or dynamically negotiated using a control protocol (LACP). Figure 13.5 illustrates the LACP partnership status of a LAG.

Note: Link aggregation requires that all physical links being aggregated operate with the same duplex settings and link speed. To ensure this, the auto-negotiation mode in the member port must be set to *limited* (only sends out negotiation parameters but does not listen to the received parameters) or *disabled* (no `auto-negotiation`) before the port can be added to the LAG.

What Is LACP and How Does It Work?

Link Aggregation Control Protocol (defined in IEEE 802.3ad) automatically detects multiple Ethernet links between two switches/routers and configures them to use as much available bandwidth between them as possible. By sending and receiving LACP Data Units (LACPDUs) between the Actor (self) and the Partner (the other end of the link), each side of the link detects the availability of the remote side. LACPDUs use the protocol broadcast MAC address of `01:80:c2:00:00:02` as the packet destination MAC address, and can be sent every 1 or 30 seconds. A port participating in LACP may be in either active or passive mode. Active ports send out LACPDUs to seek partners immediately after the physical layer comes up, and passive ports send out LACPDUs only in response to the reception of an LACPDU from the other side.

During LACP negotiation, the triplet of {`LACP-key` \| `system-id` \| `system-priority`} identifies one LAG instance. When the ports in LAG are detecting partners to aggregate, they can peer with only one LAG instance in the remote device; therefore, all port partners must have the same value for {`LACP-key` \| `system-id` \| `system-priority`} in the LACPDU so that the ports can be aggregated to a particular LAG running LACP.

Figure 13.5 LAG Using LACP to Detect a Partner

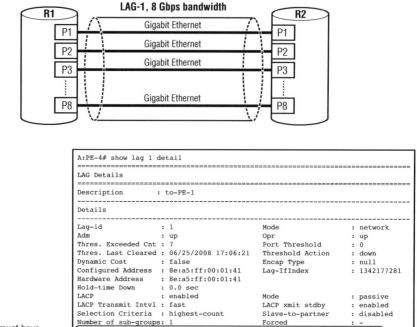

All partner ports must have the same value of {key | sys-id | sys-priority} to be accepted in the single LAG group.

Exp – Expired
Def – Defaulted
Dist – Distribute (sending)
Col – Collect (receiving)
Syn – Synchronized
Aggr – Aggregatable

LAG Subgroups

By default, as long as a port that is a member of the LAG is **up** and detects the eligible partner (all partner ports have the same {key | sys-id| sys-priority}), the port is considered active in the LAG, and the system load-balances the traffic among all active ports. However, in some circumstances, this behavior is not desired. The operator may want to allow only certain ports to be active in a LAG and to keep other ports in standby status so that they become active and forward traffic only if a failure occurs in the active ports. To achieve this, LAG allows the definition of *subgroups*. Up to eight subgroups are allowed in one LAG, and LACP allows only one subgroup to be active at any time. Dynamic LACP negotiation is required in order to make use of subgroups. Subgroups can be defined but have no effect on static LAGs. All eligible ports that have not failed are active, regardless of subgroup configuration.

> ### Best Practice—Configure Subgroups Only on One Side of the LAG Device
>
> To maintain consistency in configuration, it is highly recommended that a LAG subgroup be configured only on one side of a LAG device. This is sufficient for the two LAG devices to negotiate the number of active links: Only one subgroup can come up on the side on which the subgroup is configured; the port(s) that belongs to the other subgroup(s) remains down so that the far-side LACP device does not also bring the corresponding port up.
>
> If a subgroup is configured on each LACP device, there may be a chance that each side selects a different subgroup to be active, which causes a mismatch, and therefore no port can come up.

When multiple subgroups are defined in one LAG, only one subgroup can stay in the active state and send and receive traffic. The selection criteria for the active subgroup are as follows:

1. First, the subgroup with the maximum number of eligible members is selected (highest count).
2. Second, if there is a tie, the subgroup with highest weight (lowest numerical value for priority in the LAG port configuration) is selected.
3. If there is still a tie, the subgroup with the numerically lower port-id wins the selection.

Also, in the subgroup configuration, a subgroup can rely on its partner (peering port in the remote router) to decide which subgroup is active by using the command slave-to-partner. When this command is used, the first decision criterion is based on the out-of-sync bit sent by the partner.

Figure 13.6 illustrates a LAG with two subgroups.

Figure 13.6 LAG Subgroups

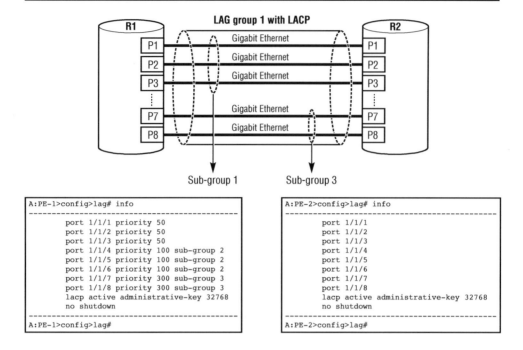

```
A:PE-1>config>lag# info
-------------------------------------------------
        port 1/1/1 priority 50
        port 1/1/2 priority 50
        port 1/1/3 priority 50
        port 1/1/4 priority 100 sub-group 2
        port 1/1/5 priority 100 sub-group 2
        port 1/1/6 priority 100 sub-group 2
        port 1/1/7 priority 300 sub-group 3
        port 1/1/8 priority 300 sub-group 3
        lacp active administrative-key 32768
        no shutdown
-------------------------------------------------
A:PE-1>config>lag#
```

```
A:PE-2>config>lag# info
-------------------------------------------------
        port 1/1/1
        port 1/1/2
        port 1/1/3
        port 1/1/4
        port 1/1/5
        port 1/1/6
        port 1/1/7
        port 1/1/8
        lacp active administrative-key 32768
        no shutdown
-------------------------------------------------
A:PE-2>config>lag#
```

In the ALSRP, a subgroup can also be defined by the location of the ports. For example, all ports in the same LAG that belong to the same Input/Output Module (IOM) or Media Device Adapter (MDA) are grouped into the same subgroup. Therefore, if the IOM or MDA fails, the LAG switches to the standby subgroup to forward the traffic. This can be done using the `auto-iom` or `auto-mda` option when defining port subgroup membership in the LAG configuration.

LAG Configuration Example

In the ALSRP, Ethernet LAG can be configured on all types of Ethernet ports: 10/100 Fast Ethernet, 1 Gigabit Ethernet, or 10 Gigabit Ethernet. When configuring LAG, the following regulations apply to all member ports:

- To be a member of any LAG, a port must have auto-negotiation disabled or set to limited mode.
- A port must have the same operation mode (access or network) as the LAG of which it is a member.
- A port must have the same Ethernet encapsulation type (null/dot1q/qinq) as the LAG of which it is a member.

An Ethernet LAG can be used in both network mode and access mode.

Figure 13.7 illustrates an example of configuring LAG 10 in access mode on router R1, to be used for the SAP in VPLS service 260.

Figure 13.7 LAG Configuration Example: LAG in Access Mode for Service SAPs

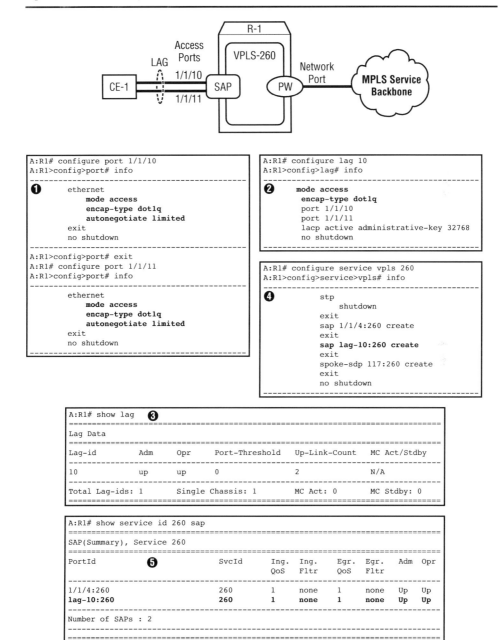

```
A:R1# configure port 1/1/10
A:R1>config>port# info
-----------------------------------------
❶      ethernet
           mode access
           encap-type dot1q
           autonegotiate limited
       exit
       no shutdown
-----------------------------------------
A:R1>config>port# exit
A:R1# configure port 1/1/11
A:R1>config>port# info
-----------------------------------------
       ethernet
           mode access
           encap-type dot1q
           autonegotiate limited
       exit
       no shutdown
-----------------------------------------
```

```
A:R1# configure lag 10
A:R1>config>lag# info
-----------------------------------------
❷      mode access
       encap-type dot1q
       port 1/1/10
       port 1/1/11
       lacp active administrative-key 32768
       no shutdown
-----------------------------------------
```

```
A:R1# configure service vpls 260
A:R1>config>service>vpls# info
-----------------------------------------
❹      stp
           shutdown
       exit
       sap 1/1/4:260 create
       exit
       sap lag-10:260 create
       exit
       spoke-sdp 117:260 create
       exit
       no shutdown
-----------------------------------------
```

```
A:R1# show lag   ❸
===============================================================================
Lag Data
===============================================================================
Lag-id      Adm    Opr    Port-Threshold    Up-Link-Count    MC Act/Stdby
-------------------------------------------------------------------------------
10          up     up     0                 2                N/A
-------------------------------------------------------------------------------
Total Lag-ids: 1     Single Chassis: 1     MC Act: 0     MC Stdby: 0
===============================================================================
```

```
A:R1# show service id 260 sap
===============================================================================
SAP(Summary), Service 260
===============================================================================
PortId          ❺           SvcId    Ing.   Ing.   Egr.   Egr.   Adm  Opr
                                      QoS    Fltr   QoS    Fltr
-------------------------------------------------------------------------------
1/1/4:260                    260      1      none   1      none   Up   Up
lag-10:260                   260      1      none   1      none   Up   Up
-------------------------------------------------------------------------------
Number of SAPs : 2
-------------------------------------------------------------------------------
===============================================================================
```

The steps in the following list correspond to the circled numbers in Figure 13.7.

1. The member ports are configured with the correct parameters: access mode, auto-negotiation limited, and dot1q encapsulation.

2. The LAG is created with access mode and dot1q encapsulation, and the two member ports are added to the group.

3. The status of the LAG may be checked before adding the LAG to the service.

4. Access mode LAG 10 is used by one SAP that belongs to VPLS service 260.

5. The SAP status of the VPLS service should then be checked.

Figure 13.8 illustrates an example of configuring LAG 10 in network mode to be used as the router interface for router R1. The steps in the following list correspond to the circled numbers in Figure 13.8.

1. The member ports are configured with the correct parameters: network mode (default port mode, not shown in the `info` command) with auto-negotiation limited.

2. The LAG is created and the member ports are added to the group.

3. The status of the LAG may be checked before adding the LAG to the router interface.

4. The router interface `to core 1` is created and assigned IP addresses, with the LAG added in as a network port.

5. The status of the router interface should then be checked.

The status of a LAG can be manually forced to test the network failover or to control the forwarding path while performing maintenance operation on particular links. Figure 13.9 illustrates a CLI example of forcing the LAG to be in a particular state. The forced state can also be cleared from the same context.

In Figure 13.9, the `force all-mc` and `force peer-mc` commands are used to force the MC-LAG to change its state.

Figure 13.8 LAG Configuration Example: LAG in Network Mode for Router Interface

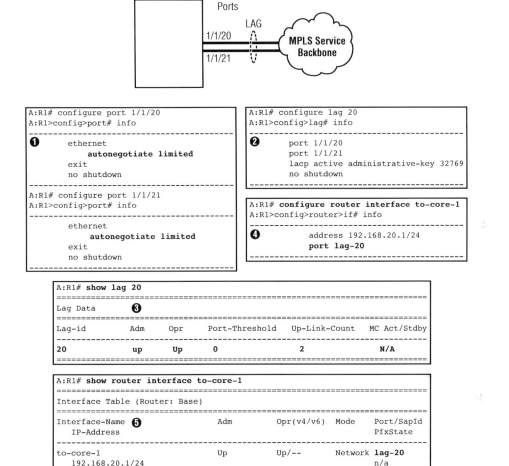

```
A:R1# configure port 1/1/20
A:R1>config>port# info
----------------------------------------
❶        ethernet
             autonegotiate limited
         exit
         no shutdown
----------------------------------------
A:R1# configure port 1/1/21
A:R1>config>port# info
----------------------------------------
         ethernet
             autonegotiate limited
         exit
         no shutdown
----------------------------------------
```

```
A:R1# configure lag 20
A:R1>config>lag# info
-----------------------------------------------
❷            port 1/1/20
             port 1/1/21
             lacp active administrative-key 32769
             no shutdown
-----------------------------------------------
```

```
A:R1# configure router interface to-core-1
A:R1>config>router>if# info
-----------------------------------------------
❹            address 192.168.20.1/24
             port lag-20
-----------------------------------------------
```

```
A:R1# show lag 20
===============================================================
Lag Data        ❸
===============================================================
Lag-id      Adm     Opr    Port-Threshold  Up-Link-Count  MC Act/Stdby
---------------------------------------------------------------
20          up      Up     0               2              N/A
===============================================================
```

```
A:R1# show router interface to-core-1
===============================================================
Interface Table (Router: Base)
===============================================================
Interface-Name ❺           Adm     Opr(v4/v6)  Mode     Port/SapId
   IP-Address                                            PfxState
---------------------------------------------------------------
to-core-1                   Up      Up/--       Network  lag-20
   192.168.20.1/24                                       n/a
---------------------------------------------------------------
Interfaces : 1
===============================================================
```

Figure 13.9 Forcing the LAG State: CLI Example

```
A:PE1# tools perform lag force
  - force all-mc {active|standby}
  - force lag-id <lag-id> [sub-group <sub-group-id>] {active|standby}
  - force peer-mc <peer-ip-address> {active|standby}

<lag-id>          : [1..200]
 <sub-group-id>   : [1..16]
 <all-mc>         : keyword
 <peer-ip-address> : a.b.c.d
 <active|standby> : keywords
```

13.4 Multi Chassis Link Aggregation Group

Regular Ethernet link aggregation provides physical link bandwidth aggregation and redundancy, but cannot provide node redundancy. In many networks, implementing node redundancy by dual-homing the customer-facing devices is desired: One MTU/CE device connects to more than one upstream PE router. There are several ways of doing this:

- **Dual-Home the Service** — The MTU device is connected to two PE routers with IP/MPLS interfaces, and two pseudowires are used to ensure that the service is dual-homed to both PE routers. This requires the MTU device to be a service router that fully supports MPLS and service implementation.
- **Dual-Home the Layer 2 Interface** — The CE device is connected to two PE routers by access ports through SAPs with Layer 2 interfaces, and STP runs in the service (if it is VPLS) to ensure that forwarding loops do not occur. The CE device does not have to be service-aware or MPLS-capable. The device relies on STP to perform failover and recovery; therefore, convergence performance time is several seconds shorter.

However, there is a method of providing CE dual-home redundancy without the service/MPLS requirement for the CE device, and to eliminate STP to achieve a faster convergence time. Although currently no IEEE standards define such a solution, several vendors have created proprietary solutions. The ALSRP implementation is referred to as *Multi Chassis LAG* (MC-LAG).

MC-LAG is an ALSRP-proprietary solution that provides link and nodal redundancy with the use of Ethernet LAG. The MC-LAG solution is transparent to the CE devices: From the perspective of the CE device, one Ethernet LAG with several links is connected to the service provider's network, exactly the same way it normally is. The CE device is not aware that these Ethernet links that belong to the same LAG are actually connected to two PE routers instead of one. The LAG has some links that are active and other links that are standby, as if the subgroup is locally configured. On the other side of the MC-LAG, two PE routers each have one LAG connected to the same CE device; they exchange MC-LAG control protocol information to perform active/standby selection, ensuring that only one PE router's LAG ports are active and carrying the traffic, and perform switchover when failure is detected in the active links.

Compared to other dual-homing techniques, MC-LAG has the following benefits:

- **Transparent to the Customer** — The MC-LAG peering configuration and MC-LAG protocol are deployed only in the PE routers, so customer-facing CE devices are not aware of MC-LAG. From the perspective of the CE device, only one LAG is connected to the service provider network. Therefore, no function or configuration changes are required on the customer side to deploy MC-LAG, making deployment and migration much easier.

- **No MPLS or Service Support Is Required in the CE Devices** — MC-LAG uses Ethernet links to connect to the CE device, and it is deployed on the PE router side on the access port that has the SAPs. Therefore, the CE device is not required to be aware of MPLS and services. This can make the customer-access portion of the network more cost-effective because the CE device can consist of any equipment as long as it has Ethernet ports, and supports link aggregation and LACP.

- **STP and mVPLS Are Not Required in the Service** — With MC-LAG, both redundancy and loop prevention are achieved without using STP. Some customers and service providers prefer not to interoperate STP for many reasons (for example, convergence issues, vendor equipment compatibility issues, and so on). The use of MC-LAG eliminates these issues. Compared to STP, MC-LAG has quicker convergence during network failure and recovery.

Figure 13.10 illustrates an example of two PE routers connected to a CE device with multiple Ethernet links using MC-LAG.

From the perspective of the MTU, four ports belonging to one LAG are connected to the service provider network. All of these ports are active, but only two are operationally up at any one time; the other two ports are in the down state. On the side of the PE routers, two types of configuration are required: regular LAG configuration, to define the ports facing the CE devices; and MC-LAG configuration, to define the MC-LAG peer and the LACP parameters.

In order for the two PE routers to synchronize all the ports that belong to the same MC-LAG (port 1/1/1 and 1/1/2 from both routers), they must appear to be links that belong to the same LACP instance when sending the LACPDU to the connected CE device. Therefore, the {key | sys-id | priority} triplet in the message must be consistent (in Figure 13.10, the circled portions of the MC-LAG configuration must match, as indicated by the double-arrowed lines).

Figure 13.10 MC-LAG Configuration Example

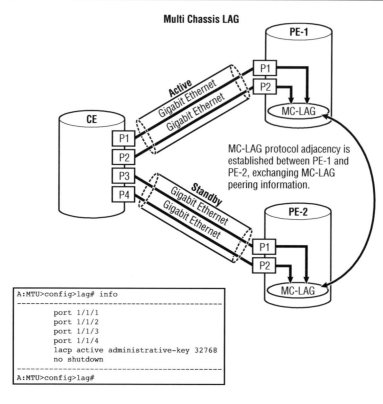

```
A:MTU>config>lag# info
----------------------------------------------------
        port 1/1/1
        port 1/1/2
        port 1/1/3
        port 1/1/4
        lacp active administrative-key 32768
        no shutdown
----------------------------------------------------
A:MTU>config>lag#
```

The CE device has no idea MC-LAG is
running. From its perspective, it seems like
all the LAG ports have been divided into two
sub-groups; only one is active at any time.

```
A:MTU# show lag 1 detail
===================================================================================
LAG Details
===================================================================================
-----------------------------------------------------------------------------------
Details
-----------------------------------------------------------------------------------
Lag-id          : 1               Mode          : network
Adm             : up              Opr           : up
--- output omitted ---
-----------------------------------------------------------------------------------
Port-id     Adm      Act/Stdby Opr    Primary  Sub-group   Forced   Prio
-----------------------------------------------------------------------------------
1/1/1       up       active    up     yes      1           -        32768
1/1/2       up       active    up              1           -        32768
1/1/3       up       active    down            1           -        32768
1/1/4       up       active    down            1           -        32768
-----------------------------------------------------------------------------------
--- output omitted ---
```

Figure 13.10   *(continued)*

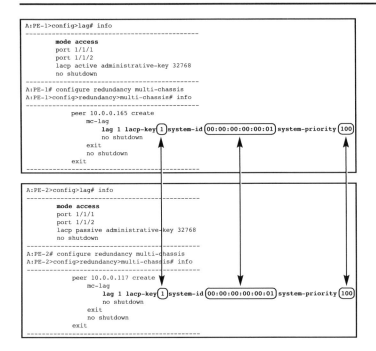

```
A:PE-1>config>lag# info
----------------------------------------------
        mode access
        port 1/1/1
        port 1/1/2
        lacp active administrative-key 32768
        no shutdown
----------------------------------------------
A:PE-1# configure redundancy multi-chassis
A:PE-1>config>redundancy>multi-chassis# info
----------------------------------------------
            peer 10.0.0.165 create
                mc-lag
                    lag 1 lacp-key 1 system-id 00:00:00:00:00:01 system-priority 100
                    no shutdown
                exit
                no shutdown
            exit
----------------------------------------------
```

```
A:PE-2>config>lag# info
----------------------------------------------
        mode access
        port 1/1/1
        port 1/1/2
        lacp passive administrative-key 32768
        no shutdown
----------------------------------------------
A:PE-2# configure redundancy multi-chassis
A:PE-2>config>redundancy>multi-chassis# info
----------------------------------------------
            peer 10.0.0.117 create
                mc-lag
                    lag 1 lacp-key 1 system-id 00:00:00:00:00:01 system-priority 100
                    no shutdown
                exit
                no shutdown
            exit
----------------------------------------------
```

Figure 13.11 illustrates a view of all LAG ports from the perspectives of both the MTU device and the PE router, in which the CE device has one LAG containing four Ethernet links that connect to the service provider.

Figure 13.11 MC-LAG Port Status from MTU and PE Router

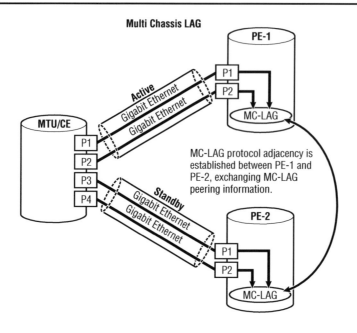

```
A:PE-1# show redundancy multi-chassis all
===============================================================================
Multi-Chassis Peers
===============================================================================
Peer IP         Src IP          Auth         Peer Admin      MC-Ring Oper
  MCS Admin       MCS Oper        MCS State    MC-LAG Admin    MC-LAG Oper
-------------------------------------------------------------------------------
10.0.0.165      10.0.0.117      None         Enabled         unknown
  --              --              --           Enabled         Enabled
===============================================================================
A:PE-1# show redundancy multi-chassis mc-lag peer 10.0.0.165
===============================================================================
Multi-Chassis MC-Lag Peer 10.0.0.165
===============================================================================
Last State chg  : 07/08/2003 11:37:59
Admin State     : Up             Oper State         : Up
KeepAlive       : 10 deci-seconds   Hold On Ngbr Failure : 3
-------------------------------------------------------------------------------
Lag Id Lacp Key Remote Lag Id System Id       Sys Prio Last State Changed
-------------------------------------------------------------------------------
1      1    1              00:00:00:00:00:01  100      07/08/2003 11:38:08
-------------------------------------------------------------------------------
Number of LAGs : 1
===============================================================================
```

Figure 13.11 *(continued)*

```
A:MTU# show lag 1 detail
===================================================================
LAG Details
===================================================================
-------------------------------------------------------------------
Details
-------------------------------------------------------------------
Lag-id             : 1                  Mode               : network
Adm                : up                 Opr                : up
Thres. Exceeded Cnt : 8                 Port Threshold     : 0
Thres. Last Cleared : 07/08/2003 11:31:09   Threshold Action : down
Dynamic Cost       : false              Encap Type         : null
Configured Address : 8e:74:ff:00:01:41  Lag-IfIndex        : 1342177281
Hardware Address   : 8e:74:ff:00:01:41
Hold-time Down     : 0.0 sec
LACP               : enabled            Mode               : active
LACP Transmit Intvl : fast              LACP xmit stdby    : enabled
Selection Criteria : highest-count      Slave-to-partner   : disabled
Number of sub-groups: 1                 Forced             : -
System Id          : 8e:74:ff:00:00:00  System Priority    : 32768
Admin Key          : 32768              Oper Key           : 32768
Prtr System Id     : 00:00:00:00:00:01  Prtr System Priority : 100
Prtr Oper Key      : 1
-------------------------------------------------------------------
Port
-id      Adm    Act/Stdby Opr    Primary  Sub-group  Forced  Prio
-------------------------------------------------------------------
1/1/1         up     active   up      yes      1          -       32768
1/1/2         up     active   up               1          -       32768
1/1/3         up     active   down             1          -       32768
1/1/4         up     active   down             1          -       32768
-------------------------------------------------------------------
--- output omitted ---
```

```
A:PE-1# show lag 1 detail
===================================================================
LAG Details
===================================================================
-------------------------------------------------------------------
Details
-------------------------------------------------------------------
Lag-id             : 1                  Mode               : access
Adm                : up                 Opr                : up
Thres. Exceeded Cnt : 2                 Port Threshold     : 0
Thres. Last Cleared : 07/08/2003 11:39:02   Threshold Action : down
Dynamic Cost       : false              Encap Type         : null
Configured Address : 8e:75:ff:00:01:41  Lag-IfIndex        : 1342177281
Hardware Address   : 8e:75:ff:00:01:41  Adapt Qos          : distribute
Hold-time Down     : 0.0 sec
LACP               : enabled            Mode               : active
LACP Transmit Intvl : fast              LACP xmit stdby    : enabled
Selection Criteria : highest-count      Slave-to-partner   : disabled
Number of sub-groups: 1                 Forced             : -
System Id          : 8e:75:ff:00:00:00  System Priority    : 32768
Admin Key          : 32768              Oper Key           : 1
Prtr System Id     : 8e:74:ff:00:00:00  Prtr System Priority : 32768
Prtr Oper Key      : 32768
MC Peer Address
 : 10.0.0.165        MC Peer Lag-id      : 1
MC System Id       : 00:00:00:00:00:01  MC System Priority  : 100
MC Admin Key       : 1                  MC Active/Standby   : active
MC Lacp ID in use  : true               MC extended timeout : false
MC Selection Logic : local master decided
MC Config Mismatch : no mismatch
-------------------------------------------------------------------
Port
-id      Adm    Act/Stdby Opr    Primary  Sub-group  Forced  Prio
-------------------------------------------------------------------
1/1/1         up     active   up      yes      1          -       32768
1/1/2         up     active   up               1          -       32768
-------------------------------------------------------------------
--- output omitted ---
```

Figure 13.11 *(continued)*

```
A:PE-2# show redundancy multi-chassis all
===============================================================================
Multi-Chassis Peers
===============================================================================
Peer IP         Src IP          Auth          Peer Admin      MC-Ring Oper
   MCS Admin       MCS Oper        MCS State     MC-LAG Admin    MC-LAG Oper
-------------------------------------------------------------------------------
10.0.0.117      10.0.0.165      None          Enabled         unknown
   --              --              --            Enabled         Enabled
===============================================================================
A:PE-2# show redundancy multi-chassis mc-lag peer 10.0.0.117
===============================================================================
Multi-Chassis MC-Lag Peer 10.0.0.117
===============================================================================
Last State chg  : 06/27/2008 10:17:01
Admin State     : Up             Oper State          : Up
KeepAlive       : 10 deci-seconds   Hold On Ngbr Failure : 3
-------------------------------------------------------------------------------
Lag Id Lacp Key Remote Lag Id System Id         Sys Prio Last State Changed
-------------------------------------------------------------------------------
1      1        1            00:00:00:00:00:01  100      06/26/2008 16:08:12
-------------------------------------------------------------------------------
Number of LAGs : 1
===============================================================================
```

```
A:PE-2# show lag 1 detail
===============================================================================
LAG Details
===============================================================================
-------------------------------------------------------------------------------
Details
-------------------------------------------------------------------------------
Lag-id              : 1                Mode                : access
Adm                 : up               Opr                 : down
Thres. Exceeded Cnt : 9                Port Threshold      : 0
Thres. Last Cleared : 06/27/2008 10:17:04   Threshold Action    : down
Dynamic Cost        : false            Encap Type          : null
Configured Address  : 8e:a5:ff:00:01:41   Lag-IfIndex         : 1342177281
Hardware Address    : 8e:a5:ff:00:01:41   Adapt Qos           : distribute
Hold-time Down      : 0.0 sec
LACP                : enabled          Mode                : passive
LACP Transmit Intvl : fast             LACP xmit stdby     : enabled
Selection Criteria  : highest-count    Slave-to-partner    : disabled
Number of sub-groups: 1                Forced              : -
System Id           : 8e:a5:ff:00:00:00   System Priority     : 32768
Admin Key           : 32768            Oper Key            : 1
Prtr System Id      : 8e:74:ff:00:00:00   Prtr System Priority : 32768
Prtr Oper Key       : 32768
MC Peer Address
: 10.0.0.117            MC Peer Lag-id     : 1
MC System Id        : 00:00:00:00:00:01   MC System Priority  : 100
MC Admin Key        : 1                MC Active/Standby   : standby
MC Lacp ID in use   : true             MC extended timeout : false
MC Selection Logic  : peer decided
MC Config Mismatch  : no mismatch
-------------------------------------------------------------------------------
Port
-id        Adm    Act/Stdby Opr    Primary  Sub-group   Forced   Prio
-------------------------------------------------------------------------------
1/1/1      up     standby   down   yes      1           -        32768
1/1/4      up     standby   down            1           -        32768
-------------------------------------------------------------------------------
--- output omitted ---
```

From the perspective of the CE device, all four links belong to the same LAG, and they are all connected to one peering LACP device, because all four links are receiving the LACPDU that contains the values {key = 1 | sys-id = 00:00:00:00:00:01 | sys-priority = 100}. The MTU node sees that only two links are operationally up and carrying traffic at any time. The CE device has no knowledge that the four links are physically connected to two PE routers inside the service provider network using the MC-LAG protocol to provide redundancy.

The two PE routers have two sets of configurations for the LAG — the regular LAG configuration and the MC-LAG definition. The show command on the right side of Figure 13.11 illustrates that the regular LAG is defined containing the physical peering links, and the LACP parameters of the MC-LAG ({ key | sys-id | sys-priority }) are actually used to detect the partner and to negotiate with the CE device. Comparing the LAG status output from Routers PE-1 and PE-2 shows the difference in the *MC Selection Logic*: PE-1 wins the selection (local master decided); therefore, the links in PE-1 that face the CE device are active and operationally up. PE-2 loses the selection (peer decided); therefore, the links in PE-2 that face the CE device are standby and operationally down. On the CE side, only the links facing the PE router that contains active links are operationally up and carrying traffic.

Prerequisite for Using MC-LAG

A regular LAG must be configured with LACP enabled, and the ports used for MC-LAG must be members of that LAG. In the ALSRP, MC-LAG is available only to access ports; therefore, LAGs must be configured in access mode (which can only be used by SAP) before they can be part of an MC-LAG.

- The peering PE routers must be Alcatel-Lucent SR/ESS platform service routers to be able to provide MC-LAG redundancy to the CE device, because the MC-LAG configuration and protocol are proprietary.

- The MC-LAG control protocol is an extension of LACP. Therefore, both the CE device and the PE redundancy pair must use LACP to communicate the formation of a LAG (no static LAG definition).

The MC-LAG control protocol works in a similar way to the Virtual Router Redundancy Protocol (VRRP), in which two routers connected to a common LAN segment can provide *virtual Layer 3 peering* to the hosts to provide routing gateway services (transparent to the user of the services). The two VRRP peering routers perform master selection to determine the active and standby roles and to monitor the health of the peer. If the active router fails, the standby router takes over and continues to provide routing services. MC-LAG provides similar functionality in the Ethernet layer with link aggregation, where the peering router pair uses the MC-LAG control protocol to communicate with each other.

MC-LAG Control Protocol Overview

The previous two figures illustrated configuration examples and the state display of a MC-LAG peered network. The MC-LAG solution is transparent to the dual-homed CE devices; all intelligence and multi-chassis awareness resides in the two PE routers. Therefore, the PE routers are responsible for maintaining the consistency, transparency, and integrity of the MC-LAG. To achieve this, the two routers containing the primary/standby MC-LAG peering run the MG-LAG control protocol between them. The MC-LAG control protocol is an extension of the LACP protocol, with the function of exchanging information between MC-LAG peering routers. It has the following major functionality:

- The protocol supports adjacency over IP addresses, so the two routers participating in the same MC-LAG do not have to be directly connected to each other by physical links. Neighbor relationship authentication is also provided as an option for enhanced security.

- While forming the adjacency, the protocol maintains the integrity of the MC-LAG by checking the consistency of the LACP instance parameters (the value of the { key | sys-id | sys-priority } triplets). If the values do not match, the MC-LAG is put into the standby state, so it does not use inconsistent LACPDU content to communicate with the CE device on the other side of the Ethernet link.

- The protocol provides a heartbeat monitoring mechanism (keep-alive) so that each router can monitor the health of its MC-LAG peer. This enhances the network robustness, so that if one router fails, the MC-LAG peer can detect the remote failure and take over the active role.

- The protocol also supports the signaling of an operational switchover. At any time, the operator can force a switchover from active to standby and later clear the forced switchover.

> **Warning:** *Do not filter UDP port 1025 when using MC-LAG in PE routers.* The MC-LAG control protocol uses UDP port 1025 as the source and destination port to exchange protocol data. For two PE routers to form MC-LAG peering adjacency, UDP [port 1025] must *not* be filtered by any security filters. Otherwise, the communication between the peering PE routers is broken; both PE routers may consider that the MC-LAG peer is down, so they may become active at the same time. Because MC-LAG is transparent to the CE device, this causes the CE device to bring up the links connected to both PE routers and to balance the load of the traffic over these links to two different PE routers.

MC-LAG Adjacency: Peer Definition, Authentication, and Timers

The MC-LAG solution has its own characteristics: For each MC-LAG, only two regular LAGs are involved in two PE routers; any PE router can have multiple LAGs running the MC-LAG protocol to another PE router, or to different PE routers. Therefore, the MC-LAG peering adjacency is always point-to-point between two PE routers, and more than one MC-LAG can appear under the same pair of peering routers. Therefore, MC-LAG configuration is hierarchical:

1. Define the peering router first with the characteristics of adjacency: the keep-alive interval (how frequently the heartbeat is sent and expected to be received), the hold-down count (bringing down the adjacency after missing a certain number of heartbeats), and optionally, the MD5 authentication key. In MC-LAG, the values of the keep-alive timer and the hold-down count do not need to match between peers, although it is always a best practice to minimize the variation of configuration among the network elements.

2. After the adjacency is defined, all MC-LAGs (instances) that belong to the same peering router are created under the same peer. They all share the adjacency. For example, if the peer is determined to be in the down state, the local router sets all MC-LAGs under that peer to the active state; if multiple MC-LAGs belong to the same peer router, the remote lag ID needs to be provided so that the remote router can understand which MC-LAGs belong to which peer.

Figure 13.12 illustrates an example of Router PE-1 with two MC-LAG peers and two MC-LAG instances with peer 10.0.0.164.

Figure 13.12 MC-LAG Peering Configuration Example

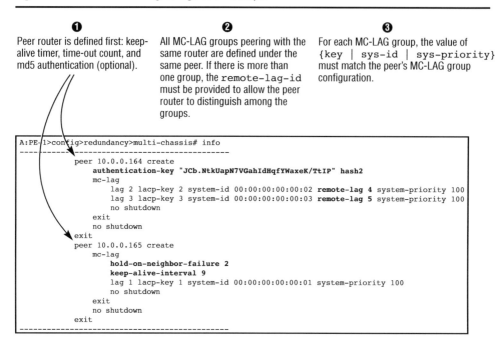

❶ Peer router is defined first: keep-alive timer, time-out count, and md5 authentication (optional).

❷ All MC-LAG groups peering with the same router are defined under the same peer. If there is more than one group, the `remote-lag-id` must be provided to allow the peer router to distinguish among the groups.

❸ For each MC-LAG group, the value of {`key` | `sys-id` | `sys-priority`} must match the peer's MC-LAG group configuration.

```
A:PE-1>config>redundancy>multi-chassis# info
----------------------------------------
            peer 10.0.0.164 create
                authentication-key "JCb.NtkUapN7VGahIdHqfYWaxeK/TtIP" hash2
                mc-lag
                    lag 2 lacp-key 2 system-id 00:00:00:00:00:02 remote-lag 4 system-priority 100
                    lag 3 lacp-key 3 system-id 00:00:00:00:00:03 remote-lag 5 system-priority 100
                    no shutdown
                exit
                no shutdown
            exit
            peer 10.0.0.165 create
                mc-lag
                    hold-on-neighbor-failure 2
                    keep-alive-interval 9
                    lag 1 lacp-key 1 system-id 00:00:00:00:00:01 system-priority 100
                    no shutdown
                exit
                no shutdown
            exit
----------------------------------------
```

When designing or deploying a network with MC-LAG to provide dual-home access to the customer (CE) device, the impacts on legacy LAG features, such as dynamic cost, threshold, and so on need to be considered. Although MC-LAG is transparent to the customer access equipment, the customer needs to be aware that the network is designed in a redundant fashion, so that only some of the member links are active at any time. This is usually not an issue because in most cases using redundant access links is required by the customer, so they should be not only aware of, but also desire, the active/standby behavior.

Two factors need to be considered regarding the impact of LAG behavior:

- **Dynamic Cost** — From the perspective of the CE, only some of the members in the LAG stay **up**. If the customer wants to advertise the bandwidth of the LAG to the network Layer 3 peer, the expected cost should not count in the redundant standby links.

- **Port Threshold** — For the same reason, the port threshold value in the CE device cannot be set to equal the total number of member ports in the LAG. It should be no more than the number of links connected to the intentional primary PE router.

MC-LAG with Pseudowire Redundancy in a VPLS Network

This chapter has introduced many HA techniques that use different mechanisms to provide redundancy at different layers (services, MPLS, IP, Ethernet, and so on). The following case study discusses in detail a network design with multiple HA functions so that readers can understand how these features interact and how they improve network performance and reliability. HA network design not only makes the network more robust against various types of failures, but also makes it possible to have a smooth (in some cases, even lossless) service migration or network upgrade. Figure 13.13 illustrates a network designed with MC-LAG redundancy and pseudowire redundancy.

Figure 13.13 A VPLS Network Designed Using MC-LAG and Pseudowire Redundancy

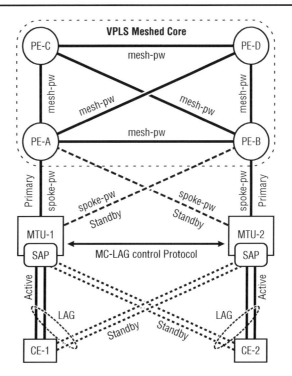

VPLS Core Network
The PE routers are connected with pseudowire full mesh. MPLS FRR and secondary LSP can also be used to protect the core network.

Aggregation Network
MTU routers aggregate traffic from customers to the core network. They can be dual-homed with pseudowire redundancy.

Access Network
CE routers/switches in the Customer Edge of the network use MC-LAG to access the PE/MTU devices for connection robustness.

In this network design example, redundancy is implemented from the core to the edge, as follows:

- The VPLS core network (where the PE routers reside) uses fully meshed pseudowire to connect all the PE routers, to ensure an optimal forwarding path and maximum robustness. If RSVP-TE LSPs are used as transport tunnels to carry all traffic from the pseudowires, RSVP-TE MPLS LSP resiliency features such as Fast Reroute (FRR) and secondary LSP can significantly improve the failure convergence performance.

- In the aggregation layer (where the MTU routers reside), MTU routers are dual-homed to the upstream PE routers by redundant primary/standby spoke-pseudowires. MPLS FRR and secondary LSPs can also be deployed in this layer.

- In the edge (where the CE equipment resides), the CE switches/routers are dual-homed to the MTU routers using MC-LAG. If the MTU fails, or if the physical links to one MTU fail, the standby LAG ports transport the traffic to the other MTU routers.

This type of network has no single point of failure because both the CE equipment and the MTU routers are dual-homed. Because pseudowire redundancy and MC-LAG are used in the dual-homing scenarios, STP is not required to prevent forwarding loops anywhere in the network. Also, with this type of hierarchical and redundant network design, the service provider can balance the load of traffic from different services among the redundant links by setting different redundancy preferences for different service instances. This example assumes that both CE devices belong to the same customer and that one common VPLS service instance is deployed across the entire network. On both MTU routers, the MC-LAG ports are used as SAPs for the VPLS service instance.

MC-LAG Switchover: flush-all-from-me

Suppose there is a link failure between MTU-1 and CE-1 in the network described previously. CE-1 is dual-homed to both MTU-1 and MTU-2 with one LAG; MTU-1 and MTU-2 are configured as MC-LAG peers, and exchange the Inter-Chassis Control Protocol to constantly monitor the health of the node and the LAG links. If the Ethernet link between MTU-1 and CE-1 fails, the original standby router (MTU-2) takes over the active role of the MC-LAG and starts to pass traffic for CE-1 through the CE-1–to–MTU-2 LAG. This is the expected behavior of an MC-LAG.

When this happens, regardless of whether the `send-flush-on-failure` is configured in the VPLS instances of both MTU routers, when an MC-LAG switchover occurs, the MTU router that has the failure will notify the upstream PE routers (PE-A and PE-B in this example) with an LDP `flush-all-from-me` message so that they can unlearn all CE-1 MAC addresses (learned from MTU-1).

When the failure is cleared, the MC-LAG reroutes the traffic back to the original CE-1–to–MTU-1 link. This switchover causes the CE-1-facing LAG of MTU-2 to go to standby status. Similarly, regardless whether `send-flush-on-failure` is enabled or not in MTU-2, the MC-LAG switchover triggers an LDP `flush-all-from-me` message from MTU-2; therefore, the upstream PE routers again unlearn the CE-1 MAC addresses (learned this time from MTU-2).

In the case of MC-LAG or MC-Ring switchover, the system will always generate a `flush-all-from-me` MAC-Flush message to the peering member PE routers.

13.5 Traffic Load Balancing in Link Aggregation Groups

The previous three sections introduced LAG and MC-LAG. The use of LAG to group multiple Ethernet links has two main purposes:

- **To Improve Link Reliability** — If one link in a LAG goes down, the entire LAG can still be operationally up (depending on its configuration). Therefore, configuring Layer 3 interfaces in LAGs instead of in individual links makes the Layer 3 interface more stable. Also, adding more links to the existing LAG does not cause service outages on the Layer 3 interface defined on the LAG.

- **To Expand the Bandwidth** — In a LAG, the available bandwidth is the sum of the bandwidth of all member links. The LAG balances the load of the traffic among all active member links. Therefore, more bandwidth can be assigned to a single Layer 3 interface defined in the LAG.

This section discusses the traffic load-balancing function performed by a LAG and ways to improve the efficiency of bandwidth usage.

Note: The discussion in this section regarding LAG load balancing is focused on unicast traffic. Multicast traffic is beyond the scope of this book.

Load Balancing and Hashing Algorithms

When LAG is used for bandwidth expansion, the efficiency of the load balancing performed by the LAG needs to be seriously considered. To fully use the aggregated bandwidth from a LAG, the LAG load-balancing function must efficiently distribute the traffic among all member links. If the load-balancing function pulls all traffic into only one of the member links, the maximum bandwidth that can be used is the bandwidth of that link only.

Load balancing means to spread out the traffic carried in the logical link (a LAG) into different physical links when transmitting the traffic. For a system to perform load balancing among different links, several factors must be considered. The load balancing should:

- Not disrupt the order of the packets.
- Not duplicate packets.
- Be able to adjust the number of links to which the traffic is distributed based dynamically in real time if the number of active links in the group changes.
- Be able to distribute the traffic as evenly as possible among all available links.

The system that is performing the load balancing uses certain algorithms to decide which physical link the packet(s) should be sent to. One typical example is Inverse Multiplexing Access (IMA) in an ATM network. When connecting two ATM switches with multiple links, the links can be grouped into IMA groups. Eight T1 (1.5-Mbps) links can be grouped into one IMA group to provide 12 Mbps of bandwidth. IMA uses a *cell-based round robin* load-balancing algorithm to ensure that the bandwidth utilization is maximized and that the order of the cells is not disrupted. Each cell is sent through a different physical link to the peer in a round-robin fashion. Therefore, the traffic is distributed evenly to all functioning member links. However, this per-packet-based round robin is an expensive operation, so it can be used only in low-speed links (in most cases, T1/E1 speed) and use the relatively expensive ATM technology. Figure 13.14 demonstrates the packet-based round-robin behavior of ATM IMA.

Figure 13.14 ATM IMA Load Balancing: Per-Packet Round Robin

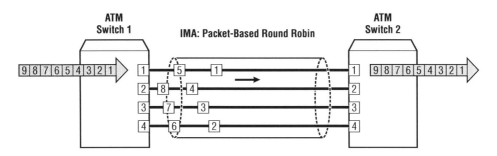

Unlike ATM, Ethernet technology provides high bandwidth with low cost. As one of its legacy functions, load balancing in LAG uses a relatively inexpensive *per-flow-based hashing algorithm*:

- It is per-flow-based, so the risk of disrupting the order of the packets is low. The criteria for defining flow are discussed later in this section.

- It uses a hashing algorithm. In general, *hashing* is the operation of transforming an input (for example, a string of characters or a series of numbers) into a fixed length value or key. In Ethernet LAG load balancing, the characteristics of the flow (for example, the source and destination MAC addresses) are used as the hash input, and the hash result is the id of the egress port to which the flow is sent.

Figure 13.15 illustrates the flow-based hashing behavior of Ethernet LAG.

Figure 13.15 Ethernet LAG Load Balancing: Per-Flow Hashing

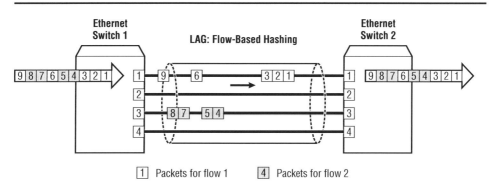

Ethernet LAG hashing for load balancing always occurs in the traffic egress direction for the traffic being sent to the peer router. Ethernet LAG hashing is flow-based, not frame (packet)–based. In general, the more flows a network has to spread out among the LAG members, the more efficient the LAG load balancing is. In Figure 13.15, only two flows in the traffic need to be forwarded over the LAG between Switch 1 and Switch 2. The hashing algorithm sends the traffic over two links, maintaining the packet order within the flow and sending the traffic to the far-end switch.

When a LAG performs load balancing, the hashing is based on the number of *flows* in the data traffic. It is important to understand which criteria the hashing algorithm uses to determine whether the stream of data is a flow. The hashing algorithm balances the load of different flows over different available physical links only if it considers that the data belongs to different flows. The criteria differ depending on the different types of data and on the different types of networks. The criteria come from the header information in the data. Figure 13.16 illustrates five different types of data packets and their headers.

Figure 13.16 Different Types of Traffic over Ethernet Links

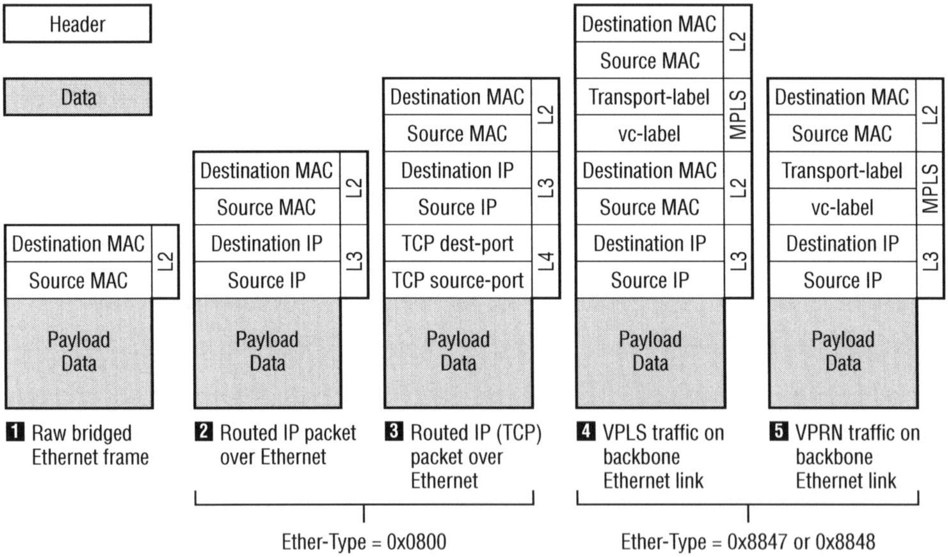

Ethernet frame Types 1, 2, and 3 appear in a regular Ethernet bridged network or in a routed IP network that has Ethernet links (2 and 3). Ethernet frame Types 4 and 5 are IP/MPLS VPN traffic traveling over the Ethernet backbone links. When

a LAG is used to bundle Ethernet links to carry these different types of traffic, the hashing algorithm balances the load differently. All hashing is performed using the header of the packets.

Two important perspectives about hashing need to be emphasized:

- Hashing is a many-to-few mapping exercise. Hashing in a LAG does not guarantee that different links are assigned to the different flows every time, especially if there are very few flows. For example, if a LAG contains eight member links and the traffic contains only eight flows, LAG hashing cannot guarantee that the eight flows are each assigned one physical link. In the best-case scenario, the eight flows are distributed over eight links (one flow for each link). In the worst-case scenario, the eight flows may all be put onto one physical link, and the other seven links may carry no traffic. Other results are also possible, with the traffic distributed over two to seven links. The hashing result is determined by the header information as the flow-defining criteria (the numerical values of the addresses of the packets), and the particular hashing algorithm.

- It is always true that the more flows the traffic contains, the better the load-balancing result the hashing algorithm will achieve (the traffic is distributed almost evenly among all member Ethernet links). In other words, if the hashing algorithm has more input to deal with, the more variety the hashing result can have. If there are 1,000 flows in the aforementioned eight-link LAG, it is more likely that the traffic is distributed almost evenly among all physical links.

Ethernet LAG Load Balancing in Ethernet Bridged and IP Routed Networks

In legacy Ethernet-based switched or routed IP networks, LAGs are used to carry regular Ethernet frames that contain mostly IP traffic (Ethernet payload type 0x0800). When multiple Ethernet links are grouped into a LAG in a legacy Ethernet bridged or IP routed network, the hashing for LAG load balancing is performed on the Ethernet header information (Layer 2 header) and sometimes on the upper-layer header information (for example, the IP header or IPX header).

Take routed IP packets over Ethernet links as an example. The hashing algorithm considers all IP packets that have the same addressing in the IP header (Layer 3 header) ({source IP address, destination IP address} pair) in the headers as a single flow. Therefore, if the traffic over a LAG has many different source IP addresses and destination IP addresses, the hashing algorithm sees many flows and spreads them over different physical member Ethernet links. This is the default LAG hashing criteria for the ALSRP to hash pure IP traffic over Ethernet LAGs.

As previously mentioned, the more flows the traffic has, the better the load-balancing result the hashing algorithm will achieve. To improve the hashing result variety, Layer 4 header information (for example, TCP port number or UDP port number) can be added to the hashing algorithm criteria. This is achieved by configuring the Ethernet port to consider the Layer 4 header when performing LAG load balancing. Figure 13.17 illustrates a CLI configuration example.

Figure 13.17   Enabling LAG Hashing on Layer 4 Header Information

```
A:R1# configure port 1/1/1
A:R1>config>port# ethernet load-balancing-algorithm
  - load-balancing-algorithm <option>
  - no load-balancing-algorithm

<option>                 : include-l4|exclude-l4

A:R1>config>port# ethernet load-balancing-algorithm include-l4
```

```
    A:R1# show system load-balancing-alg detail
    ==============================================================
    System wide load balancing algorithm : exclude-L4
    ==============================================================
    PortId            Algorithm
    --------------------------------------------------------------
    1/1/1             : include-L4
    1/1/10            : include-L4
    1/1/11            : include-L4
    lag-10            : include-L4
    ==============================================================
```

When an Ethernet port is configured to perform LAG hashing that includes IP Layer 4 header information, the TCP/UDP port number (source port and destination port) is considered as part of the hashing input. The hashing still includes IP Layer 3 header information (source and destination IP addresses) as the hashing input. With more input, the LAG hashing returns more possible output results.

Ethernet LAG was originally designed for bandwidth expansion in a bridged or routed network. It works well in a network with many IP or TCP *microflows*.

Ethernet LAG Load Balancing in IP/MPLS VPN Networks

Today, Ethernet is more and more popular for provider backbone networks because of its plug-and-play nature and its ability to provide large bandwidth at low cost. Providers also use LAGs to group Ethernet links in the backbone to gain more bandwidth. Typically, a provider may think that 1 Gbps is not enough for backbone links and that

10 Gbps is too much. The provider may want to group four 1-Gbps Ethernet links in one LAG with 4 GB of bandwidth. In some cases, providers even group multiple 10Gbps Ethernet links together to acquire more bandwidth. Furthermore, the provider using LAGs in the backbone network may use the LAGs to carry IP/MPLS VPN traffic. It is important to understand how LAGs perform load balancing for MPLS traffic, so that the LAGs can distribute the traffic to different member links as evenly as possible to take advantage of the available bandwidth provided by the LAGs. Figure 13.18 illustrates a network in which the MPLS backbone is composed of four 1-Gbps LAGs.

Figure 13.18 LAGs in an IP/MPLS VPN Backbone Network

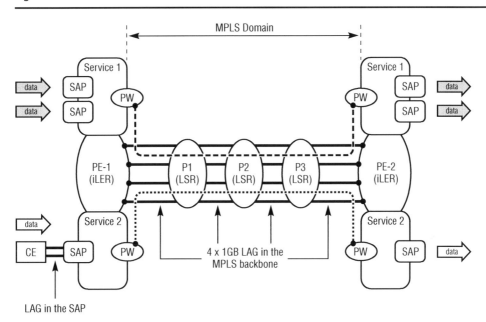

Chapter 9 describes the details of each component of an IP/MPLS VPN service network. Service instances are configured in the PE routers at the edge of the IP/MPLS VPN service network. The PE routers are connected by P routers in the backbone of the service network. Ethernet LAGs can be deployed in two locations:

- **SAPs** — The Ethernet ports in access mode can be grouped into LAGs and deployed in the SAPs so that the service instances can connect to the customer LAG. LAGs in SAPs carry regular Ethernet/IP traffic.

- **Layer 3 Interfaces (Network Ports)** — The Ethernet ports in network mode can be grouped into LAGs and deployed in the Layer 3 interfaces connected in the backbone to other adjacent P or PE routers. LAGs in Layer 3 interfaces carry IP/MPLS VPN–encapsulated traffic. They can also carry pure IP-routed traffic for internal routing or IES services.

In the case of LAGs in Layer 3 interfaces (network ports) that carry pure IP traffic, the LAG hashing behavior is the same as it is in legacy IP networks:

- By default, when sending traffic over LAGs, hashing is based on the IP header (source and destination IP addresses) to distribute traffic over multiple physical links.

- The command `ethernet load-balancing-algorithm include-l4` can be configured on the member ports to add TCP/UDP headers (source and destination ports) to the hashing inputs to create more variety.

In the IP/MPLS VPN PE router, when a LAG is configured in access mode and used by the service SAP, the load-balancing hashing algorithm balances the service traffic in the SAP egress direction to the customer equipment. The load balancing in the SAP egress direction to the customer behaves similarly to the LAGs in a legacy Ethernet network because this traffic is native Ethernet-format traffic:

- If the SAP egress traffic is non-IP traffic (from an Epipe or a VPLS service), the hashing is based on the source and destination MAC addresses of the frame (Layer 2 header). All frames that have the same {`source MAC address, destination MAC address`} pair are considered as one flow. The hashing algorithm distributes different flows to different LAG member ports according to the hash output.

- If the SAP egress traffic is IP traffic (from an Epipe or a VPLS service), the hashing is based on the source and destination IP addresses of the frame (Layer 3 header). All frames that have the same {`source IP, destination IP`} pair are considered as one flow. The hashing algorithm distributes different flows to different LAG member ports according to the hash output. Furthermore, the LAG can also be configured to use the Layer 4 header (TCP/UDP ports) as hashing input to load-balance the traffic.

When a LAG is used as the network port in an IP/MPLS VPN backbone network, it carries VPN-encapsulated traffic. An IP/MPLS VPN network has two types of routers: service-aware PE routers and service-transparent P routers. The LAGs on these two types of routers behave differently.

A PE router is service-aware. PE routers are the LERs where the customer traffic enters and exits the MPLS domain. They receive native customer traffic from the SAPs of all the different services and put the traffic on the network port to the MPLS backbone network. If the network port is actually a LAG, hashing is performed to balance the traffic load among member links, as follows:

- For Epipe and VPLS non-IP traffic, the source and destination MAC address pair (Layer 2 header) of the customer traffic is used as the hash input.

- For Epipe and VPLS IP traffic, the source and destination IP address pair (Layer 3 header) of the customer traffic is used as the hash input. Optionally, if the LAG member ports are configured with an Ethernet load-balancing algorithm, the hashing includes the TCP/UDP port number (Layer 4 header) as input.

P routers are not service-aware. In the IP/MPLS VPN architecture, the P routers are LSRs and are used to transparently carry traffic from PE routers and send it to remote PE routers. P routers provide VPN traffic aggregation and transportation. Therefore, P routers receive and send only VPN-encapsulated MPLS traffic, without looking at the actual encapsulated customer packets (frames). When P routers perform MPLS switching, they do not check the customer MAC or IP addresses because they are irrelevant. Therefore, if there are LAGs in the P routers, from a load-balancing perspective, *P routers cannot hash based on customer addresses (Layer 2, Layer 3, or Layer 4) to distribute traffic because the P router does not check the headers of the customer traffic.* The P router can perform LAG load-balancing hashing based only on:

- The system IP address of the traffic sender

- The traffic ingress physical port number (a port index value assigned by the system)

- The entire MPLS label stack (up to five labels in depth). All VPN traffic in MPLS backbone has at least two labels — the outer transport label and the inner vc-label.

Because the P router is not service-aware, LAG hashing on the P router has much less input. As previously mentioned, the less input the hashing has, the less the hashing output varies. Therefore, even if there are many flows in the customer traffic for a service, because the P router cannot see these flows, it uses only the MPLS encapsulation header and the traffic ingress port as hashing input to balance the traffic among the LAG member ports.

If there is only one service (one vc-label) traveling over one SDP (one transport label), all customer traffic for that service is sent to one physical member port in the LAG in the LSR. This scenario may cause issues for a provider that has Ethernet LAGs in the MPLS backbone network, especially if the Ethernet LAGs are used to connect multiple P routers (LSR) in the core. Because of the service blindness, the load-balancing ability of the P routers (LSR) is weaker than the PE routers and may cause *traffic aggregation*. Figure 13.19 illustrates the scenario of LAG traffic aggregation in the LSR.

Figure 13.19   LAG Traffic Aggregation Caused by P Routers (LSRs)

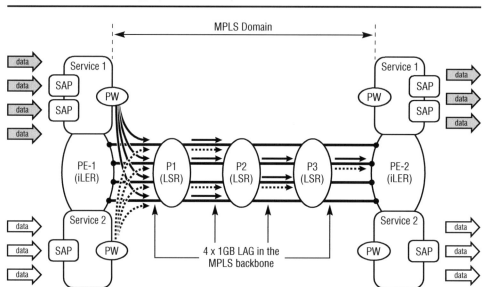

In Figure 13.19, both services between the two PE routers connected by three P routers in the MPLS domain are VPLS services. Assume that both customers of the services have many flows in their native traffic. When the traffic from both services travels into Router PE-1 through the SAPs, Router PE-1 performs LAG hashing on the traffic of each service before sending the VPN-encapsulated traffic to the LAG network port. Because both services have many flows, the hashing of PE-1 is efficient, and the traffic from both services is distributed across all four member ports.

However, when the traffic arrives in P1, P1 needs to perform LAG hashing on the VPN traffic traveling to the LAG connected to P2. Because P1 is an LSR, it can hash based only on the ingress port indexes of the received traffic and the MPLS label stack. The traffic is from two different VPN services, so the vc-labels are different. The traffic is coming in from four different physical ports; therefore, four ingress-port indexes can be used as hash input. All traffic is coming from the same SDP, so the transport label is the same. Based on the different vc-labels and ingress-port indexes, the hashing algorithm balances the egress traffic sent to P2. In the example, the hashing algorithm generates three outputs, so traffic is sent to three of the four LAG Ethernet links.

Similar behavior is repeated in P2 and P3. When P2 performs hashing, there are only three ingress port indexes and two vc-labels to be used as hash input. The hashing result of P2 sends the traffic to two of the four LAG ports. Similarly, P3 uses the two ingress port indexes and two vc-labels as hashing input. This time, the hashing result sends all traffic to one physical link. Customer VPN traffic is *aggregated* hop-by-hop on the LAGs by the LSRs that connect the two PE routers.

This example is a conceptual explanation only. The reality may be better than presented in the example; not every LSR hop aggregates the traffic (depending on the result of the hashing output). But this example illustrates the issue of using LAG in the MPLS backbone to carry VPN traffic: *because P routers (LSRs) are not service-aware, they cannot use customer traffic headers to perform LAG hashing; therefore, the variety of hashing output may be lost when sending traffic over LAG ports.* The more LSR hops there are between two PE routers participating in the same service, the higher the risk of traffic aggregation.

To solve this problem, the network designer needs to consider how to minimize the aggregating effects of the LSRs on the service traffic when it is sent over the core LAG links. Of course, the most ideal solution is to remove the LAG in the core and replace the links with 10-GB Ethernet links. However, this may not be cost-efficient. If Ethernet LAGs are required in the backbone of an MPLS service network, several methods can improve the efficiency of LAG load balancing. These methods are discussed in the next section.

Improving Load Balancing in LAGs Carrying IP/MPLS VPN Traffic on LSRs

The previous section explained how the hashing algorithm for LAG load balancing works and the hashing criteria used by the system for different types of traffic. The problem is that LSRs perform hashing only on the ingress port indexes and the MPLS label stack so the variety of hashing output may be lost and traffic may be aggregated. This section discusses methods to improve the variety of LSR hashing input so that the traffic is balanced over more LAG member ports. There are two main approaches:

- Adding more values as hash input so that LSR hashing can have more output variety

- Reducing the number of LSR hops that the VPN traffic has to travel across the backbone

The basic idea to improve hashing variety in LSRs is to add more possible values as hash input. The fact that LSRs cannot use the customer traffic header underneath the VPN encapsulation cannot be changed. Three criteria are used by LSR to hash the traffic flows:

- The system IP address of the LSR
- The traffic ingress port indexes
- The MPLS label stack of the traffic

The purpose of including the system IP address of the LSR is to make the hashing output more random. Because each LSR has only one system IP address, changing it does not make the load balancing more efficient.

The ingress port index, which is also hard to manipulate, represents the port from which the encapsulated VPN traffic enters the LSR. Changing the numerical value of the ingress port may change the hash output result. The system automatically assigns the port index, and therefore it is not a configurable parameter. Assigning a different physical port as a member of the LAG may improve the load balancing, but this method is not guaranteed and can be attempted in a live network only by replacing actual traffic-barring ports. Figure 13.20 illustrates that when P2 moves one of the ingress ports, the downstream hashing result is better.

Again, this is an example to demonstrate the theory. Changing the ports does not guarantee a better hashing result. This is more like a work-around than a solution.

> **Note:** When changing ports to improve LAG hashing, the *ingress* port (in the example, P2 port facing P1) for the traffic needs to be balanced (in the example, traffic PE1 → P1 → P2 → P3 → PE2) and should be changed. The purpose is to balance the traffic when it *egresses* downstream. If the reverse direction also needs improvement, the other side of the port in the LAG (in our example, P-2 facing P-3) needs to be moved to another location.

The best option is to add more values to the MPLS label stack for the VPN-encapsulated traffic. In normal circumstances, VPN-encapsulated traffic has a two-label MPLS stack that contains a vc-label (inner) and a transport label (outer). Each vc-label represents a service instance for a service in one PE router. Each transport label represents an LSP that connects one PE router to another PE router.

Figure 13.20   Changing the Location of the Ingress Physical Port

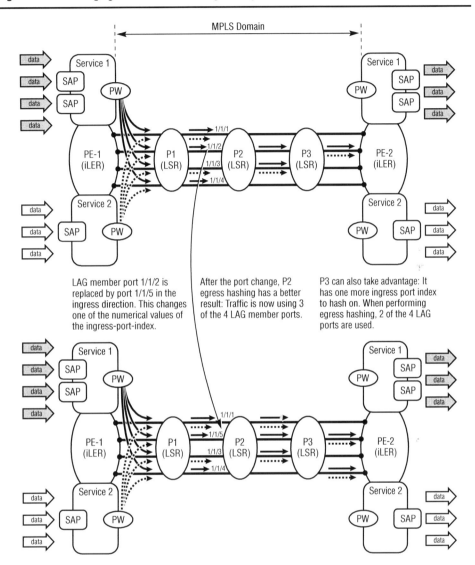

LAG member port 1/1/2 is replaced by port 1/1/5 in the ingress direction. This changes one of the numerical values of the ingress-port-index.

After the port change, P2 egress hashing has a better result: Traffic is now using 3 of the 4 LAG member ports.

P3 can also take advantage: It has one more ingress port index to hash on. When performing egress hashing, 2 of the 4 LAG ports are used.

All traffic from one PE router that belongs to one service instance uses one vc-label to reach another remote PE router. In the example topology, all traffic that belongs to Service 1 in PE-1 uses the same vc-label to reach Service 1 in PE-2. Allowing more vc-labels for the traffic requires the creation of more service instances for the same customer and the splitting of customer traffic into different services. This may or may not be possible depending on the connectivity requirements of the customer.

For example, assume that Service 1 is a service for a VPLS customer. If the customer actually has two VLANs that require VPLS services and the two VLANs do not exchange traffic, the provider can create two VPLS services to carry the traffic, one for each VLAN. Therefore, the traffic has two vc-labels and can be more efficiently balanced by the transiting LSRs. But if the two VLANs exchange traffic, they must remain in the same VPLS service because different VPLS service instances do not exchange traffic. Therefore, *if the customer traffic can be divided into different domains and the different domains do not exchange traffic, multiple services can be created serving the single customer to allow better LAG load balancing.*

The transport label of the VPN traffic is assigned by the system from the SDP from which the pseudowire is established. As mentioned in Chapter 9, an SDP can have up to 16 LSPs and can perform ECMP among all available LSPs. Therefore, more LSPs can be added to the SDP to add varieties to the transport label so that the transiting LSRs can perform more efficient LAG hashing. Figure 13.21 illustrates that when more LSPs are added to the SDP in PE-1 that carries the VPN traffic between PE-1 and PE-2, the transiting LSRs perform more efficient load balancing among the LAG member ports.

In Figure 13.21, six LSPs are associated with the SDP that connects PE-1 to PE-2. This gives the traffic six transport labels for variety. All VPN traffic from PE-1 to PE-2 that uses this SDP is first load-balanced by the SDP using ECMP, so traffic belonging to the same service from PE-1 can have six different transport labels when it travels across the backbone to PE-2. The transiting LSRs then have more values as hashing input and generate more hashing output values, improving LAG load balancing in the backbone LAGs. This configuration benefits only the traffic in the PE-1 to PE-2 direction. If the traffic in the reverse direction needs to be balanced, more LSPs must be added to the SDP in PE-2 that points to PE-1. Up to 16 LSPs can be added to one SDP.

Figure 13.21 Adding More LSPs to SDP to Improve LAG Hashing in Transiting LSRs

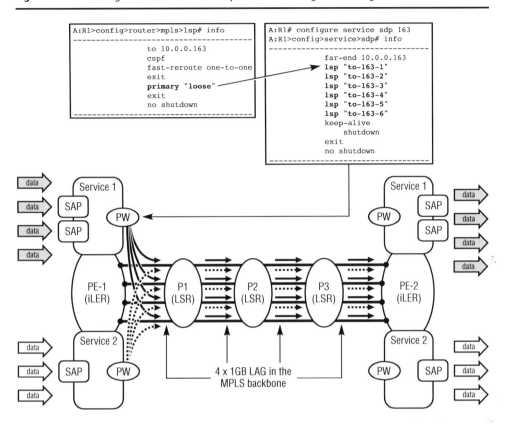

In some cases, many services exist in the provider's network, and only some services with significant traffic require more efficient load balancing. The operator may want to create a different SDP overlay with multiple LSPs in these SDPs. Then these SDPs can be used exclusively for the services that require more variable hashing output. Having a separate set of SDPs with multiple LSPs for the services requires more efficient load balancing while keeping other services in single LSP SDPs helps to reduce the total number of LSPs in the network. LSPs are created only in the locations for services that require them. Also, most customer traffic flows are asymmetric, so the multiple LSP SDP solution may be deployed only unidirectionally. The balance between increasing LSPs to improve LAG hashing and controlling the number of LSPs and the network management complexity needs to be studied on a case-by-case basis.

Again, hashing algorithms for load balancing take all different values from the traffic as input, and generate output. The result is sensitive to numerical values. All these aforementioned methods can improve the hashing on the LAG, but there is no guarantee that the LAG will use the bandwidth from all member links equally.

Because PE routers have service awareness, they can perform better load-balance hashing than P routers. It is also possible to reduce the number of LSRs between PE routers to lower the chance of P routers aggregating traffic. Sometimes a provider has a few customers with heavy traffic and wants to improve hashing for these customers. In the example, assume that the customer that has Service 2 has a large volume of traffic to balance, and therefore the provider wants to improve the load balancing for Service 2. One possible method is to create a service instance in P2, so that P2 acts as a transiting PE router for Service 2. The service instance in P2 has only two pseudowires, one connected to PE-1 and one connected to PE-2. Therefore, P2 now has service awareness for Service 2 and can hash the traffic for Service 2 based on customer MAC or IP addresses. If this approach is used, the forwarding infrastructure and loop prevention for Service 2 must be carefully researched to ensure that the customer connectivity is not changed. Figure 13.22 illustrates a scenario in which the transiting PE router (P2) has been added to the end-to-end service (Service 2) so that it balances the traffic load using customer MAC or IP addresses over the LAG.

Figure 13.22 Reducing LSR Hops: Adding Transiting PE Routers to Rehash the Traffic

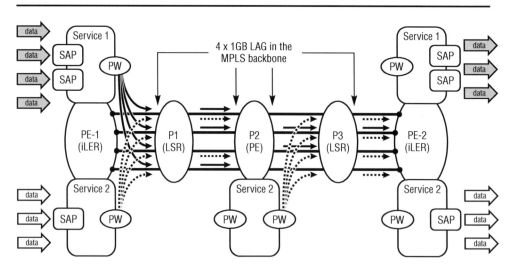

Adding a service instance to Router P-2 benefits the traffic for Service 2 in both directions. Router P-2 becomes a PE router. P-2 rehashes the traffic based on the customer Layer 2/Layer 3 header (MAC/IP addresses), and there is only one LSR between the two PE routers for Service 2. Therefore, the traffic is efficiently distributed over more member links.

Each time a PE is added along the route of the end-to-end VPLS service, the service router needs to have a service instance created, and an FDB is therefore generated to learn all customer MAC addresses. The PE router must perform an FDB lookup to forward the traffic. This adds control plane overhead for the service router whose role in the service is changed from a P to a PE router. Also, adding PE routers in a VPLS service requires forwarding path analysis to ensure that forwarding loops are not formed when the PE router is added; otherwise, a loop-prevention configuration must be in place.

For Epipe service, adding a PE router along the path is not as costly as VPLS. Adding a PE router along the end-to-end service path of Epipe is actually the deployment of *pseudowire switching*. The transiting PE in the Epipe service has a *vc-switching* service instance that contains two spoke-pseudowires and no SAP. Because the Epipe service instance does not learn customer MAC addresses and has no FDB, the control plane overhead is low. Also, because Epipe service is point-to-point, designing a loop-free Epipe service with pseudowire-switching PE router(s) is much easier.

Summary

Resiliency and fast failover are desired by both service providers and customers. The IP/MPLS VPN network has many HA features that service providers can use to build robust networks that can quickly react to failures and protect services for customers.

BFD is a lightweight protocol that detects a failure on a link that connects two routers. By setting up BFD adjacency on a common link, two routers exchange BFD packets periodically to monitor the availability of the link. BFD uses a smaller packet interval so that it can detect failure more quickly than the Hello mechanisms used by routing protocols. If BFD detects a failure, it reports the failure to the upper-layer protocols such as OSPF or RSVP-TE, so they can react accordingly.

If the link that requires rapid failure detection is an Ethernet link, EFM OAM can also be deployed. Compared to BFD, EFM OAM works at a lower layer and results in less control plane overhead. Details of EFM OAM are discussed in Chapter 18.

Grouping Ethernet links into a LAG can improve link stability and expand bandwidth. By extending the LAG to MC-LAG, CE devices can connect to links that belong to two PE routers so that if one PE router fails, the other PE router picks up the traffic. In MC-LAG, two PE routers exchange MC control protocol packets to elect the master role and monitor the availability of the MC-LAG peer. If the peer goes down, the local router assumes the active role and brings up the Ethernet ports on the CE device.

LAGs use a hashing algorithm to spread traffic among available member Ethernet ports on a per-flow basis. When a LAG is used in the MPLS backbone, the P routers may not spread the traffic among links efficiently because P routers are not service-aware and therefore have less hashing input. In such a network, adding more LSPs to the SDPs used by the services, or segmenting the service by adding service instances in the core network, improves the efficiency of the LAG hashing.

VLL Service Resiliency

Multi-homing the customer-facing Provider Edge (PE) router is widely recognized as a mature service redundancy scheme. In the point-to-point Virtual Leased Line (VLL) service, the PE router can have more than one spoke-pseudowire to aggregate traffic from customer locations and to connect to the core tier of the service network.

Chapter Objectives

- Provide an overview pseudowire redundancy — the use of active and standby pseudowires to provide PE router resiliency

- Discuss the use of pseudowire redundancy in VLL

- Discuss the use of LAG and MC-LAG to protect attachment circuits in VLL

This chapter introduces the VLL resiliency solution: the use of redundant spoke-pseudowires in VLL services, where one PE router can have more than one pseudowire connected to one or more PE routers. One pseudowire is in the active state, forwarding traffic, and other pseudowires are put in standby state and only forward traffic when the primary pseudowire fails.

Note: VLL service is also referred to as *Virtual Private Wire Service* (VPWS). In this book, the terms *VLL* and *VPWS* are interchangeable.

Pseudowire redundancy is currently in the process of being standardized. There are two drafts in the Internet Engineering Task Force (IETF):

- **Draft-muley-pwe3-redundancy** — Describes the basic framework and architecture of pseudowire redundancy.
- **Draft-ietf-pwe3-redundancy-bit** — Describes a mechanism for standby status signaling used by pseudowire redundancy.

14.1 VLL Service Resiliency Overview

As described in Chapter 9, a *pseudowire* is a bidirectional, point-to-point, end-to-end Multi Protocol Label Switching (MPLS) connection between two service instances in two service routers. Pseudowires use MPLS labels (vc-label for Layer 2 VPN, vpn-label for Layer 3 VPN) to perform VPN encapsulation of customer packets and deliver them to the far-end PE router. All distributed IP/MPLS VPN services use pseudowires to connect the service instances in each member PE router across the backbone network.

An IP/MPLS VPN service network is highly reliable. Many resiliency features can be deployed in the network to improve its robustness, as follows:

- Layer 1 and Layer 2 network failure quick detection with Bidirectional Forwarding Detection (BFD) or an Ethernet OAM mechanism (EFM OAM–802.3ah, CFM–802.1ag) detects remote failures and rapidly propagates them to the upper-layer protocols (for example, OSPF and RSVP).
- MPLS resiliency features such as secondary LSP or Fast Reroute (FRR) allow the MPLS service transport tunnel using RSVP-TE to quickly detour the traffic to alternative paths if the primary LSP-Path fails.

- IGP and/or Label Distribution Protocol (LDP) with Equal Cost Multi-Paths (ECMP) allow traffic of a failed path to be re-distributed across remaining available paths.

These resiliency features provide a reliable way to carry traffic through the backbone network and have the best failover performance. The resiliency features protect the transport tunnel in the backbone network. Therefore, these features can be categorized as network resiliency or backbone resiliency features. All services using the backbone network to transport traffic can take advantage of the enhanced robustness of the network. However, these features protect the services only from the failures along the service transport tunnel [the provider (P) routers and the links in the backbone]. Another possibility to consider is what happens if the service instance in a PE router fails, a pseudowire connecting two service instances fails, or if a PE router with many service instances fails. These failure scenarios are specific to the services; therefore, the backbone resiliency cannot protect the service against these failures.

As discussed in Chapter 9, each VLL service has two member PE routers, and each member PE router has one Service Access Point (SAP) and one pseudowire. Each SAP connects one Customer Edge (CE) device. The entire VLL service provides a point-to-point Layer 2 connectivity between two customer sites. To improve the service resiliency, various redundancy mechanisms can be deployed in the network:

- Using Link Aggregation Group (LAG) to protect the attachment circuits on the SAP
- Using pseudowire redundancy to protect the service from a pseudowire failure
- Using Multi Chassis LAG (MC-LAG) with pseudowire redundancy to protect the SAP and the PE router failures

Depending on the resiliency requirement for the services, network resources availability, and the network topology, the operator can choose from the above options to deploy VLL service resiliency.

Using LAG to Protect Attachment Circuit Failures

The most efficient way of protecting against Ethernet attachment circuit failure on an Epipe service is to deploy more than one physical link between the PE and CE devices with Link Aggregation Group (LAG). With LAG, all physical links appear like one logical link to the SAP. Figure 14.1 illustrates the use of LAG in the Epipe service SAPs.

Figure 14.1 Using LAG to Protect Epipe SAPs

With LAG deployed in the SAP (or in both SAPs), the point-to-point nature of the Epipe service is maintained, and there is no service behavior modification. The only difference is that the SAP is defined on the LAG including more than one access port. The LAG used to protect the SAP must be configured as **access mode**.

Similarly, if the VLL service is ATM type (Apipe), Automatic Protection System (APS) can be used to protect the ATM SAPs. The Apipe SAP can be defined on the APS group, instead of a LAG group. The APS and ATM VCC resiliency is beyond the scope of this book.

Both LAG and APS can only provide protection against link failures between the PE and the CE device. If the PE router fails, the service is corrupted. To protect the VLL service against PE router failures, pseudowire redundancy must be deployed in conjunction with LAG or APS.

Using Pseudowire Redundancy to Protect PE Router Failures

In a distributed VLL service, two member PE routers participate in the service by each having a service instance configured on it. A pseudowire connects the service instances of the routers. If the pseudowire fails, or one of the PE routers fail, the VLL service is interrupted and cannot process traffic for customers anymore. To protect the VLL service from pseudowire failure, pseudowire redundancy must be deployed. When pseudowire redundancy and Multi Chassis LAG (MC-LAG) are deployed together in the VLL service, the PE router failure protection is provided. MC-LAG is discussed in detail in Chapter 13.

Pseudowire redundancy allows the service instance of a PE router to be connected to the service instances of a group of remote PE routers. Among the group of pseudowires, only one, the *active* pseudowire, forwards traffic. The other pseudowires are in the standby state and do not forward traffic.

Figure 14.2 illustrates a case of using pseudowire redundancy in an Epipe service to protect it from PE router failure. In the diagram, the Epipe service instance in PE-1 uses two pseudowires connected to two PE routers for Epipe services. In a regular Epipe configuration, only one SAP and one pseudowire are allowed because Epipe is a point-to-point service. When pseudowire redundancy is configured in PE-1, the system understands that the multiple pseudowires work in a primary/backup manner. At any time, only one pseudowire is active and forwarding traffic. If router PE-2 fails, PE-1 uses the backup pseudowire to forward traffic to PE-3; therefore, the service is protected against member PE router failure. Pseudowire redundancy is discussed in detail later in this chapter.

Figure 14.2 Pseudowire Redundancy in VLL Service

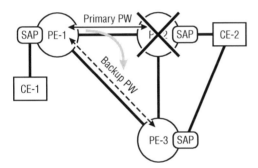

Combining MC-LAG with Pseudowire Redundancy

To achieve maximum resiliency in service access and service backbone, MC-LAG and pseudowire redundancy can be used together to provide end-to-end protection on the VLL services.

Figure 14.3 demonstrates the use of pseudowire redundancy in both PE routers of an Epipe service, with MC-LAG deployed in the SAP. This solution provides full protection from all possible failures in the service network. As indicated in the diagram, pseudowire redundancy can find a forwarding path for the service traffic even if there are failed routers on both sides of the service. MC-LAG with pseudowire redundancy is discussed in detail later in this chapter.

Figure 14.3 MC-LAG with Pseudowire Redundancy in Epipe Service

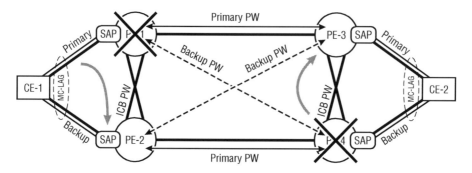

The following sections discuss in detail all pseudowire redundancy solutions with forwarding behaviors in both VPLS and VLL services.

> ## Terminology—Primary/Backup and Active/Standby
>
> It is important to clarify the terminology regarding resiliency to prevent confusion during the in-depth discussion of pseudowire redundancy. In this book, the terms *primary* and *backup* indicate the preference of the pseudowire—they are configuration characteristics of the pseudowire. The *primary pseudowire* has the highest preference and carries service traffic. The *backup pseudowire* protects the primary pseudowire and carries service traffic only when the primary pseudowire is not available. There can be only one single primary pseudowire. There can be more than one backup pseudowire to protect a primary pseudowire.
>
> The terms *active* and *standby* indicate the state of the pseudowire, which can change over the lifetime of the pseudowire. When a pseudowire is in the *active* state, it is the *active forwarding pseudowire* that forwards the traffic between two PE routers. Once created, the pseudowire is either primary or backup, regardless of its current operational state. The pseudowire's state (active or standby) depends on the pseudowire's operational status (local and remote operational status) and the preference defined. Only the pseudowire with the best status and the highest preference can be active and forwarding traffic. All other pseudowires are in the standby state. Pseudowire in the standby status can still accept packets in its ingress direction.

14.2 VLL Service Resiliency Using Pseudowire Redundancy

It is important to protect the pseudowires that connect the two PE routers in order to provide service robustness for VLL services. For example, if a network core uses MPLS technology, FRR or secondary LSP can be used to protect LSP service transport tunnels from link failure or LSR router failure. (P routers, which transport VPN encapsulated traffic using the tunnel label, have no service awareness.) Therefore, if a network failure is on the path of an SDP that carries the pseudowire, the path is protected by the MPLS resiliency features or IGP convergence. However, if the failure is not in the transport link but in the PE router itself or on the pseudowire connecting the service instances, MPLS resiliency cannot protect the services. Also, if the pseudowire is segmented, MPLS resiliency cannot protect the service from the failure of the pseudowire switching PE (S-PE) router failure.

Using Pseudowire Redundancy to Protect a Service from PE Router Failure

The best method of providing protection to a VLL PE router is to add a backup remote PE router as a member of the service. This is also referred to as *multi-homing* the service. The backup remote PE router has all the VLL service components: a service instance, a local SAP, and a spoke-pseudowire connected to the local PE router. Therefore, if one remote PE router fails, the backup remote PE router that has the VLL service instance picks up the traffic and sends it to the remote customer site. It will also forward traffic from the customer site to the core network in the reverse direction. In the case of pseudowire switching, extra S-PE routers with spoke-pseudowires connected to terminating PE (T-PE) routers provide PE resiliency. The method of adding backup PE routers to VLL services with extra pseudowires to protect the service is called *pseudowire redundancy*. Figure 14.4 illustrates two typical scenarios of deploying pseudowire redundancy.

There are three basic scenarios of deploying pseudowire redundancy to improve service resiliency:

- **Customer Site Access Redundancy** — The service provider may want to dual-home the point-to-point service by adding a redundant backup service-terminating PE router (the top portion of the diagram). If router PE-2 fails (that is, the primary pseudowire is down) or the primary SAP in PE-2 fails, the backup service endpoint in router PE-2 becomes active and provides the termination of the point-to-point service. From the customer's perspective (CE-1 to CE-2), the service is still end-to-end and point-to-point. Note that in this topology, customer device CE-2 has more than one attachment circuit (AC) connected to the provider's network. If the CE-2 device is a Layer 2 Ethernet switch, a loop-prevention mechanism must be deployed to prevent forwarding loops. For example, if device CE-2 is a Broadband Remote Access Server (BRAS), it does not send traffic to both SAPs at the same time. If only customer attachment circuit protection is desired, the operator can use multiple Ethernet links to form LAG in the service SAP.

Figure 14.4   Dual-Homing a VLL Service with a Pseudowire-Switching PE

Dual-home point-to-point services

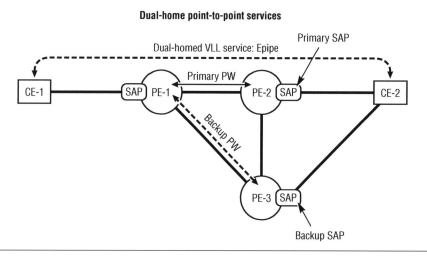

Dual-home pseudowire-switching PE router

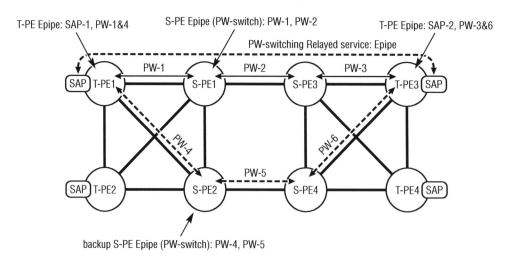

- **Using Redundancy Pseudowires to Protect Switching PE Router Failure** — Pseudowire switching (introduced in Chapter 10) is used in large-scale networks to relay the point-to-point services from one service area to another to reduce T-LDP sessions and service tunnels required for service deployment. One S-PE router may be a hub router and switch many pseudowires for different services. The S-PE router can be a single point of failure affecting many services if it fails. Having a backup S-PE router(s) with backup pseudowires significantly improves the robustness of the network. (In this case, the T-PE router has multiple redundant pseudowires configured. Pseudowire redundancy configuration in vc-switching pseudowire services in an S-PE router is not allowed.)
- **Using Pseudowire Redundancy with MC-LAG** — Use pseudowire redundancy with MC-LAG to provide end-to-end VLL service protection. The use of MC-LAG with pseudowire redundancy is discussed in detail later in this chapter. This protects the service from both the AC failure and the PE router failure.

VLL service is always point-to-point. An end-to-end VLL service involves two PE routers, each with one service instance containing one pseudowire and one SAP. Simply adding a third PE router with another service instance, SAP, and pseudowire to improve the resiliency does not work. The VLL service configuration allows VLL service to be configured in only two cases:

1. If the router is a T-PE router for a VLL service, the service instance can have one SAP and one pseudowire.

2. If the router is an S-PE router for a VLL service, the service instance can have two pseudowires and no SAP.

A third backup PE cannot simply be added into the service, because it breaks the point-to-point characteristic of the VLL service. A mechanism must be implemented to ensure that the extra pseudowire(s) in the PE router are configured in a primary/backup manner. At any time, only one *active forwarding object* is allowed in each direction so that the VLL service in the PE router maintains point-to-point forwarding behavior. Adding an *endpoint* to the VLL service instance fulfills this requirement.

Endpoints in a VLL Service Instance

The services protected by pseudowire redundancy are still point-to-point. This means at any time, there should be only one active forwarding path from one service termination point to another service termination point. When traffic ingresses from the SAP of a PE router, it should only have one choice of egress direction — only one pseudowire to send traffic to one remote PE router.

Pseudowire redundancy allows more than one spoke-pseudowire to be defined in the same service instance in the PE router. To ensure that these redundant pseudowires do not break the point-to-point nature of the service, the concept of *endpoint* is introduced to regulate the forwarding behavior of these pseudowires.

Figure 14.5 shows an endpoint in a VLL T-PE router. A VLL service instance in a PE router has two endpoints:

- If the service instance is a regular VLL (non-vc-switching VLL service) service instance, one endpoint contains all pseudowires (for redundancy) and may have one Inter-Chassis Backup (ICB) pseudowire; the other endpoint contains a SAP. If MC-LAG is used, the endpoint containing the SAP may also have an ICB pseudowire. MC-LAG and ICB-PW are introduced later in this chapter.

- If the service instance is a VLL vc-switching service instance, both endpoints contain only pseudowires. Furthermore, only one pseudowire is allowed in each endpoint for vc-switching services. Pseudowire redundancy is supported only in the terminating PE (T-PE) router, not the switching PE (S-PE) router.

Figure 14.5 ■ An Endpoint in a VLL Service

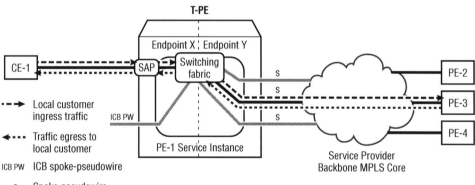

Regardless of the type of VLL service instance, the regulations for endpoints passing traffic are as follows:

1. Traffic coming into one endpoint can be forwarded through the switching fabric only to another endpoint. Two *objects* in the same endpoint cannot exchange traffic.

2. An endpoint can have only one *active forwarding object* carrying traffic. Other objects are put in *standby* mode and do not forward traffic to the remote

PE router (in the pseudowire egress direction). If the standby pseudowire receives traffic from the remote PE router (in the pseudowire ingress direction), it will forward the traffic to the switching fabric.

> **Note:** The behavior of standby pseudowire in VLL service instances is different from that in VPLS service instances. When using pseudowire redundancy in VLL, only the egress (Tx) of the standby pseudowire is blocked. The ingress (Rx) of the pseudowire can still receive traffic. Compare this to pseudowire redundancy in VPLS, in which both the Tx and Rx of the standby pseudowire are blocked. Pseudowire redundancy in VPLS service is discussed in Chapter 15.

3. Any SAP or pseudowire must belong to only one endpoint, defined during the creation of the SAP or the pseudowire. One endpoint can contain only a certain combination of objects, as follows:

   - If an endpoint has a SAP, only one ICB pseudowire (used by MC-LAG) can be added to the endpoint. (ICB and MC-LAG are discussed later in this chapter.)

   - If an endpoint does not have a SAP, it can contain up to four spoke-pseudowires. The spoke-pseudowires can consist of one primary pseudowire, one or many backup pseudowire(s), and one ICB pseudowire if required.

4. The implicit rule — *Traffic can go only from one endpoint to another, never within the same endpoint* — applies for all endpoints, with any combination of objects.

Therefore, multiple pseudowires can be placed into one endpoint, and only one active pseudowire forwards the traffic. Multiple remote PE routers provide pseudowire redundancy. The VLL service is multi-homed to more than one remote PE router and maintains a point-to-point active forwarding topology.

When defining endpoints in the VLL service, a *precedence* value can be specified for each pseudowire. All pseudowires that reside in the same endpoint use the precedence value to determine the active forwarding object. The available pseudowire with the lowest numerical precedence value is chosen as the active forwarding object. The precedence value ranges from 0 to 4, with 0 as the highest preference (Primary). Zero (0) is not configurable; when the pseudowire is configured as `primary` in the endpoint, the precedence value of that pseudowire is set to 0. Values 1–4 are configurable to the backup pseudowire. The precedence value of a pseudowire can be changed on the fly, and it is preemptive.

Figure 14.6 demonstrates how pseudowire redundancy protects a point-to-point service. The example discussed is an Epipe service, but pseudowire redundancy is applicable to all point-to-point VLL services: Epipe, Cpipe, Apipe, Fpipe, and Ipipe.

Figure 14.6 PW Redundancy Example: Peering with Four Remote PE Routers

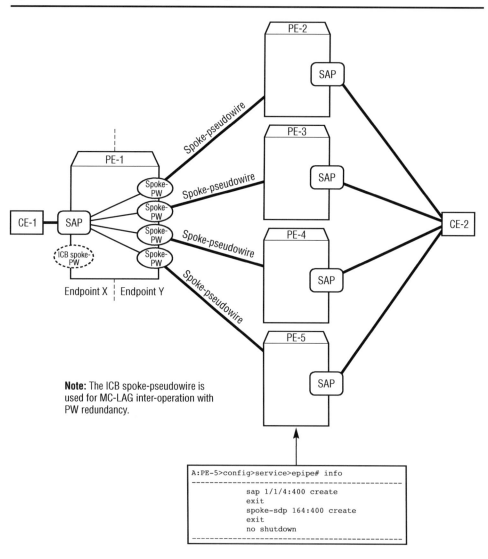

Figure 14.6 *(continued)*

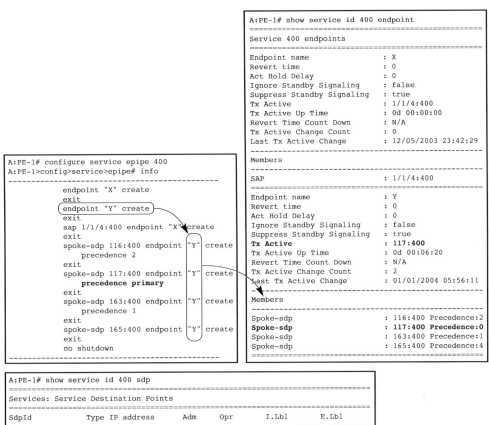

```
A:PE-1# show service id 400 endpoint
=======================================================
Service 400 endpoints
=======================================================
Endpoint name                : X
Revert time                  : 0
Act Hold Delay               : 0
Ignore Standby Signaling     : false
Suppress Standby Signaling   : true
Tx Active                    : 1/1/4:400
Tx Active Up Time            : 0d 00:00:00
Revert Time Count Down        : N/A
Tx Active Change Count       : 0
Last Tx Active Change        : 12/05/2003 23:42:29
-------------------------------------------------------
Members
-------------------------------------------------------
SAP                          : 1/1/4:400
=======================================================
Endpoint name                : Y
Revert time                  : 0
Act Hold Delay               : 0
Ignore Standby Signaling     : false
Suppress Standby Signaling   : true
Tx Active                    : 117:400
Tx Active Up Time            : 0d 00:06:20
Revert Time Count Down        : N/A
Tx Active Change Count       : 2
Last Tx Active Change        : 01/01/2004 05:56:11
-------------------------------------------------------
Members
-------------------------------------------------------
Spoke-sdp                    : 116:400 Precedence:2
Spoke-sdp                    : 117:400 Precedence:0
Spoke-sdp                    : 163:400 Precedence:1
Spoke-sdp                    : 165:400 Precedence:4
=======================================================
```

```
A:PE-1# configure service epipe 400
A:PE-1>config>service>epipe# info
-----------------------------------------------
        endpoint "X" create
        exit
        endpoint "Y" create
        exit
        sap 1/1/4:400 endpoint "X" create
        exit
        spoke-sdp 116:400 endpoint "Y" create
            precedence 2
        exit
        spoke-sdp 117:400 endpoint "Y" create
            precedence primary
        exit
        spoke-sdp 163:400 endpoint "Y" create
            precedence 1
        exit
        spoke-sdp 165:400 endpoint "Y" create
        exit
        no shutdown
-----------------------------------------------
```

```
A:PE-1# show service id 400 sdp
=================================================================
Services: Service Destination Points
=================================================================
SdpId          Type IP address    Adm    Opr    I.Lbl    E.Lbl
-----------------------------------------------------------------
116:400        Spok 10.0.0.116    Up     Up     131034   131068
117:400        Spok 10.0.0.117    Up     Up     131038   131050
163:400        Spok 10.0.0.163    Up     Up     131032   131050
165:400        Spok 10.0.0.165    Up     Up     131031   131049
-----------------------------------------------------------------
Number of SDPs : 4
-----------------------------------------------------------------
=================================================================
```

The example in this figure uses four redundant pseudowires in Router PE-1 to protect the Epipe service with an ID of 400. The remote multi-homing PE routers (PE-2, PE-3, PE-4, and PE-5) are configured as regular Epipe services with no redundancy. Two explicit endpoints (X and Y) are created under the service context.

The configuration example in Figure 14.6 shows four spoke-pseudowires defined with precedence values in endpoint Y. At any time, only one pseudowire is in the

Tx Active state, forwarding the traffic to the remote PE router. In the remote PE router, the service instance is defined as a regular VLL service without any changes. One SAP and one SDP are defined under the service instance, and the PE router cannot tell whether its peer is using multi-homing backup pseudowires. The *intelligence* of the pseudowire redundancy resides in the PE router in which the endpoints are defined, with multiple spoke-pseudowires under the same endpoint. When the router determines that a pseudowire is in the standby state, it does not send any traffic over that pseudowire.

There may be more than one object in each endpoint. For example, multiple pseudowires can be associated with one endpoint, but there can be only one active forwarding object that can send out traffic in any endpoint. The active pseudowire selection is discussed later in this section. If more than one object resides in an endpoint, the router elects one object to be the active forwarding object, and therefore the other objects are in the standby state. In a service with pseudowire redundancy configured, multiple pseudowires are associated with one endpoint, and only one pseudowire is elected as the Tx Active pseudowire and forwards traffic to the remote PE router. The winner is listed in the Tx Active state in the CLI output of the show command. Every endpoint that is operationally up has one Tx Active object (but that does not necessarily mean that the object is currently carrying data traffic). Note that when pseudowire redundancy is used in VLL service, only the egress of the standby pseudowire is blocked. In comparison, when pseudowire redundancy is used in VPLS service, both the ingress and the egress of the standby pseudowire are blocked. VPLS resiliency is discussed in Chapter 15.

Pseudowire Status Bit

As discussed previously, the Targeted LDP (T-LDP) message uses PW-Status TLV to indicate the forwarding status of a pseudowire. The PW-Status TLV is carried either by the Label Mapping message (during the pseudowire setup) or the Notification message (after the pseudowire has been established).

The LDP status bits in the PW-Status TLV can be categorized to two different types. One type is the *operational status bits*, which the local PE uses to convey to remote PEs the following events:

- SAP receive/transmit fault (0x00000002, 0x00000004)
- Pseudowire receive/transmit fault (0x00000008, 0x00000010)

- Pseudowire not forwarding (0x00000001)

Another type is the *preferential forwarding bit*, which can have a value of active (default) or standby:

- Pseudowire forwarding (0x00000000)
- Pseudowire forwarding standby (0x00000020)

When multiple pseudowires are grouped under the same endpoint for redundancy purposes, the local PE router needs to perform active forwarding object selection to select one pseudowire to forward traffic to the remote PE routers. The selection algorithm takes into account the *local* operational state of the pseudowires and their *remote* operational state as signaled by the remote PEs in the status TLV. It also takes into account the *remote* forwarding status bit (active/standby) in the selection criteria.

Meanwhile, the local PE router also needs to set the pseudowire status bit in the PW-Status TLV to notify the remote PE routers about the forwarding states of the pseudowires within the endpoints.

In a VLL service, the pseudowire status bit set by the local PE router *reflects the forwarding state of the local SAP*. If the SAP is dual-homed and enters the standby state, then the local PE sets this bit to standby (this is the case when using MC-LAG with pseudowire redundancy, which is discussed in detail later). If the SAP is not dual-homed, the local PE router never sets the pseudowire to standby state. The pseudowire forwarding status bit is left to the default value of active (all zeros).

Upon receiving the pseudowire status bit, the remote PE does not block traffic forwarding over a pseudowire that signaled standby if this is the only pseudowire that is available. This was done to allow additional resilience through the ICB pseudowire (ICB-PW), which may be configured in the remote PE (in the case in which MC-LAG is deployed). However, such a pseudowire will not be selected for traffic forwarding if there exists another PW that signaled active and that is operationally **up** locally and remotely. Also, the local PE *will forward* a data packet *received* on a PW that is currently signaling standby to the local SAP or ICB-PW. The complete active pseudowire selection criteria are discussed next.

Pseudowire Redundancy: Selection of the Active Forwarding Object

When a service configured with pseudowire redundancy comes **up**, the PE router signals all peering PE routers with a T-LDP Label Mapping message that contains a 0x00000000 (clear) flag in the PW status TLV to establish all pseudowires. [This is different from when pseudowire redundancy is used in VPLS, where the value 0x00000020 (pseudowire standby) is set in the PW status TLV in the Label Mapping message.] From all pseudowires associated with the same endpoint, the router selects one of the established pseudowires as the *active pseudowire* and uses only that pseudowire to send traffic, based on the following selection criteria:

- The *healthiest* pseudowire is selected to be the active pseudowire. The health status is based on the pseudowire status reported from both locally (SAP status) and the remote peering router. If one pseudowire has all zeros (clear flag) and other pseudowires have some status bits set (for example, 0x00000006 indicating a local SAP failure), the pseudowire with the clear flag is selected.

- If the pseudowire status is tied, the pseudowire with the lowest numerical precedence value is selected. The pseudowire with a precedence value of 0 is the *primary pseudowire*. Pseudowires with other precedence values are *secondary pseudowires*. Only one primary pseudowire is allowed in each endpoint, and it is possible for an endpoint to have no primary pseudowires and several secondary pseudowires.

- In the case of a tie, the pseudowire that has the lowest `vc-id` wins the selection.

- When MC-LAG is used together with pseudowire redundancy, the pseudowires are all secondary type and there is no primary pseudowire. The system will select the pseudowire to forward traffic based on the local and remote SAP status, which is based on the MC-LAG status. Details regarding the pseudowire status with MC-LAG are discussed later in this chapter.

After the initial selection, the router sends traffic to the corresponding remote PE router only over the selected active pseudowire. When a network event occurs, a pseudowire switchover may be triggered, causing the router to use another pseudowire and remote PE router to send traffic. The switchover activity is local to the PE router that has the redundant pseudowire configured and is invisible to the remote peering routers (other than the fact that the router stops sending traffic to the remote PE). Events that may trigger a switchover are:

- **Manual Modification of the Pseudowire Precedence Value** — An active pseudowire may be exempt if other pseudowire(s) in the same endpoint are configured with a lower precedence value. In other words, the precedence of the pseudowires is preemptive.

- **The Health Status of the Pseudowire Changes** — For example, the router may receive an LDP Notification message including the PW-Status TLV from the current active peer, indicating a local SAP failure or a pseudowire failure. Upon receiving such a message, the router switches to a healthier pseudowire if one is available.

- **The Active Pseudowire Goes Down** — This may be triggered if the T-LDP session connected to the peer goes down or if the remote PE withdraws the label owing to a manual shutdown of a session or a network failure.

When the event that caused the switchover is cleared, the PE router configured with local pseudowire redundancy may or may not revert back to using the original active pseudowire. Several factors determine whether it reverts back:

- The system reverts back to the primary pseudowire from a secondary pseudowire (when the event that caused the switchover is cleared).

- The system does not revert to a secondary pseudowire after the cause of the switchover is cleared.

- If the default value of the revert-time configuration in the endpoint is 0, the system reverts to the primary pseudowire as soon as possible. If the value is set to `infinite`, the system does not revert back to the primary pseudowire.

Table 14.1 lists the criteria for the selection of the active forwarding object. Information regarding ICB pseudowires is listed for the completeness of the table, but this topic is not discussed in this chapter.

Table 14.1 Electing the Best Possible Pseudowires to Forward Traffic

Priority	Peer PW-Status TLV Flag	Description
0	—	Only pseudowires that are local and operationally up are eligible for the election.
1	0x00000000	The remote pseudowire is active, and the remote SAP and pseudowire endpoint are operationally up.
2	0x00000020	The remote pseudowire is in the standby state, and the remote SAP and pseudowire endpoint are operationally up.

(continued)

Table 14.1 Electing the Best Possible Pseudowires to Forward Traffic *(continued)*

Priority	Peer PW-Status TLV Flag	Description
3	0x00000006	The remote pseudowire is active, the remote SAP is down, and the remote pseudowire endpoint is operationally up.
4	0x00000026	The remote pseudowire is in the standby state, the remote SAP is down, and the remote pseudowire endpoint is operationally up.
5	0x00000001	The remote pseudowire is active, and the remote pseudowire is not forwarding.
6	0x00000021	The remote pseudowire is in the standby state, and the remote pseudowire is not forwarding.
7	0x00000018	The remote pseudowire is active, and the remote pseudowire is operationally down.
8	0x00000038	The remote pseudowire is in the standby state, and the remote pseudowire is operationally down.
9	—	If there is a tie after going through priorities 1–8, choose the lowest local precedence value as the tiebreaker. If it is still tied, the lower PW-id is the next tiebreaker.
10	—	If the active pseudowire selected after going through priorities 0–9 has a peering flag other than 0x00000000 or 0x00000006, use the ICB-PW to forward traffic, providing the ICB-PW does not receive a *pseudowire down* or *pseudowire not forwarding* status TLV.
11	—	If no active pseudowire is found after going through priorities 0–10, use the ICB-PW to forward the traffic, providing the ICB-PW does not receive a *pseudowire down* or *pseudowire not forwarding* status TLV.
12	—	If the election process ends up with the ICB-PW as the active forwarding object on both endpoints of the service instance, the traffic is discarded. A router never forwards traffic between two ICB-PWs, even if they belong to different endpoints and are both the best current choice for traffic forwarding.

14.3 VLL Network Design Using MC-LAG with Pseudowire Redundancy

A High Availability (HA) design of a VPLS network using MC-LAG, pseudowire redundancy, and a fully meshed core with FRR protection was discussed earlier. This section gives an example of implementing a similar network with VLL point-to-point services and the highest level of redundancy and protection, along with an in-depth analysis of the signaling and forwarding behavior.

Figure 14.7 presents a configuration example of the use of MC-LAG in a network containing an Epipe service with pseudowire redundancy. The service network uses multiple redundancy mechanisms to protect the Ethernet point-to-point service, as follows:

1. Customer equipment devices CE-1 and CE-2 are connected by an Epipe service with a service-id of 800. Routers PE-1 and PE-2 are both connected to device CE-1, running the MC-LAG control protocol to ensure that only one active LAG is forwarding traffic to and from the CE-1 device at any time. Both PE-1 and PE-2 have Epipe 800 configured, with the LAG ports in the MC-LAG group as service SAP ports. If any access link failures occur between one CE router and the PE router, the MC-LAG protocol switches the traffic to a healthy link.

2. In the service provider's network, to achieve maximum service redundancy, four PE routers are involved with Epipe 800, with pseudowire redundancy configured. Both PE-1 and PE-2 are dual-homed to the far end of the service (Routers PE-3 and PE-4). Multiple pseudowires with different precedence values are configured in the PE routers to ensure that only one active pseudowire is forwarding traffic to one remote PE router.

3. In the core of the service provider's network, MPLS with FRR is enabled to ensure that the service tunnels are protected (not shown in Figure 14.7).

4. An ICB-PW is configured between the PE routers with the MC-LAG SAP pair.

In this VLL service network design, the two pseudowires marked as *ICB-PW* connect the MC-LAG peering routers (PE-1/PE-2 and PE-3/PE-4). This type of pseudowire is used exclusively between two MC-LAG peering PE routers with VLL service configured using pseudowire redundancy.

Note: ICB pseudowires can also be used with non-Ethernet L2VPN services. As a prerequisite, MC-redundant SAPs must be supported in the services. For example, Apipe services with MC APS SAP can take advantage of ICB pseudowires for extra protection. A detailed discussion of MC features for non-Ethernet services is beyond the scope of this book.

Figure 14.7 MC-LAG with Pseudowire Redundancy for VLL Services — Topology

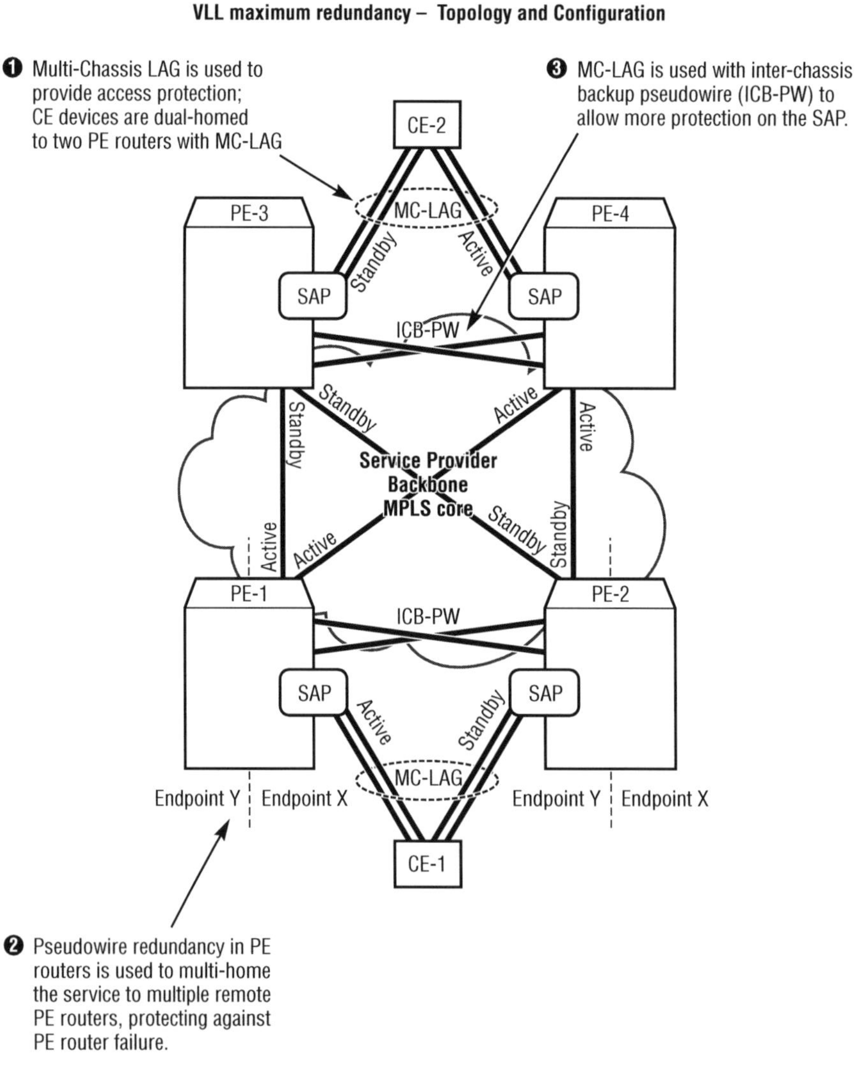

VLL maximum redundancy – Topology and Configuration
❶ Multi-Chassis LAG is used to provide access protection; CE devices are dual-homed to two PE routers with MC-LAG
❸ MC-LAG is used with inter-chassis backup pseudowire (ICB-PW) to allow more protection on the SAP.
CE-2
MC-LAG
PE-3
PE-4
Standby
Active
SAP
SAP
ICB-PW
Standby
Active
Standby
Active
Service Provider Backbone MPLS core
Active
Active
Standby
Standby
PE-1
PE-2
ICB-PW
SAP
SAP
Active
Standby
MC-LAG
Endpoint Y
Endpoint X
Endpoint Y
Endpoint X
CE-1
❷ Pseudowire redundancy in PE routers is used to multi-home the service to multiple remote PE routers, protecting against PE router failure.

Figure 14.7 *(continued)*

```
A:PE-1# configure service epipe 800
A:PE-1>config>service>epipe# info
----------------------------------------------
            endpoint "X" create
            exit
            endpoint "Y" create
            exit
            sap lag-1:800 endpoint "X" create
            exit
            spoke-sdp 164:800 endpoint "Y" create
                precedence primary
            exit
            spoke-sdp 165:800 endpoint "Y" create
                precedence 2
            exit
            spoke-sdp 117:800 endpoint "X" icb create
            exit
            spoke-sdp 117:801 endpoint "Y" icb create
            exit
            no shutdown
----------------------------------------------
```

```
A:PE-1>config>lag# info
----------------------------------------------
        mode access
        encap-type dot1q
        port 1/1/3
        lacp active administrative-key 32768
        no shutdown
----------------------------------------------
A:PE-1# configure redundancy multi-chassis
A:PE-1>config>redundancy>multi-chassis# info
----------------------------------------------
            peer 10.0.0.117 create
                mc-lag
                    lag 1 lacp-key 1 system-id 00:00:00:00:00:01 system-
priority 100
                    no shutdown
                exit
                no shutdown
            exit
----------------------------------------------
```

```
A:CE-1# show lag 1 detail
===============================================================================
LAG Details
==== Omitted ===
-------------------------------------------------------------------------------
Port-id     Adm    Act/Stdby Opr     Primary  Sub-group     Forced  Prio
-------------------------------------------------------------------------------
1/1/1       up     active    up      yes      1             -       32768
1/1/2       up     active    down             1             -       32768
-------------------------------------------------------------------------------
Port-id     Role     Exp  Def  Dist Col  Syn  Aggr Timeout Activity
-------------------------------------------------------------------------------
1/1/1       actor    No   No   Yes  Yes  Yes  Yes  Yes     Yes
1/1/1       partner  No   No   Yes  Yes  Yes  Yes  Yes     Yes
1/1/2       actor    No   No   No   No   Yes  Yes  Yes     Yes
1/1/2       partner  No   No   No   No   No   Yes  Yes     Yes
===============================================================================
```

Inter-Chassis Backup Pseudowire

The sample network in Figure 14.7 has a special type of pseudowire between two PE routers with an MC-LAG peering relationship, called an *Inter-Chassis Backup (ICB)* pseudowire. When two PE routers have MC-LAG SAPs facing the same CE device, an ICB-PW can be defined in the service instance in the two PE routers to provide another layer of protection. ICB-PWs should be deployed only between two PE routers with MC-LAG SAPs, and which are dual-homed to the same CE device. In other words, ICB-PWs should be configured only on the *same side* of the backbone network, on the pairs of PE routers that are connected to the same CE device.

ICB pseudowires act as backup resources for the object in the same endpoint: When an ICB-PW is configured in the endpoint that has an MC-LAG SAP, the ICB-PW backs up the SAP; when an ICB-PW is configured in the endpoint that has spoke-pseudowire(s), the ICB-PW backs up the active pseudowire. Figure 14.8 illustrates two examples of the use of ICB pseudowires to protect an Epipe service.

Figure 14.8 ICB Pseudowires Protecting an Epipe Service with MC-LAG

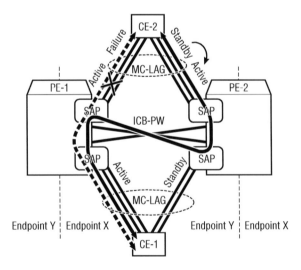

ICB-PW protection example I

ICB-PW protecting local service. In a failure of PE-1 to CE-2 link, the SAP facing CE-2 goes down. In PE-1 router's endpoint Y, the ICB-PW becomes the active forwarding object, passing traffic from PE-1 to PE-2, so PE-2 can receive the traffic from CE-1 over PE-1, then relay it to CE-2.

Figure 14.8 *(continued)*

ICB-PW protection example II

ICB-PW protecting distributed service. PE-1
has active MC-LAG SAP, but experiences
the double failure in both pseudowires to
remote PE routers. In endpoint "Y", ICB-PW
will kick in as a last resort, redirect traffic from
PE-1 to PE-2, then over to the other side
(CE-2 side) of the network.

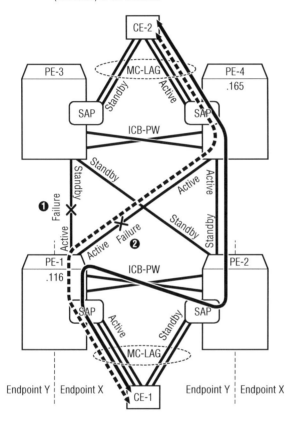

In the first diagram, a *local* Epipe service with MC-LAG protection is configured between CE-1 and CE-2. The initial stable network uses both SAPs in Router PE-1 to forward traffic between CE-1 and CE-2. If a link or port fails in the links between PE-1 and CE-2, the MC-LAG SAP in PE-2 becomes active and ready to forward traffic to and from CE-2, but CE-1 still forwards traffic to PE-1, since the links of PE-1 that face CE-1 are still functioning. In this scenario, the ICB-PW connecting endpoint Y in PE-1 with endpoint X in PE-2 forwards the traffic from CE-1 to PE-2, then PE-2 can relay the traffic to CE-2 over the SAP in endpoint Y.

The second diagram illustrates a distributed Epipe service that is experiencing a double failure, protected by pseudowire redundancy. Because both pseudowires in Router PE-1 connected to the far-end routers (PE-3 and PE-4) failed but the MC-LAG SAP in PE-1 is still active, the ICB-PW connecting endpoint Y in PE-1 to endpoint X in PE-2 forwards the traffic to PE-2, which can then forward traffic to CE-2 over its healthy pseudowires to either PE-3 or PE-4. Figure 14.9 illustrates the concept of endpoints in pseudowire redundancy and in an ICB-PW.

Figure 14.9   ICB-PW with a Service Endpoint

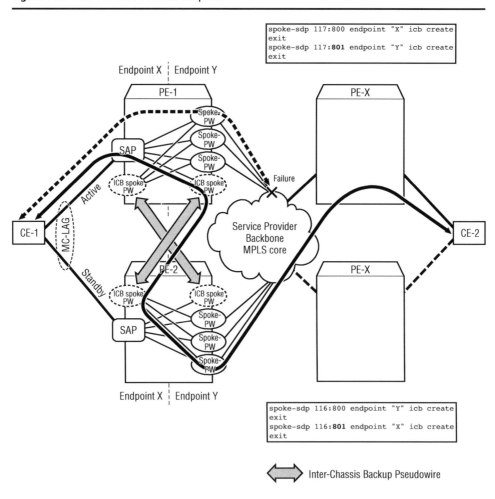

The concept of the endpoint is crucial to understanding how ICB-PW works. For any VLL point-to-point services, the router handles the traffic forwarding with an internal logical endpoint in the PE router where the service instance resides. Each service has two endpoints (in this discussion, they are referred to as *endpoint X* and *endpoint Y*). In the example, endpoint X on each router is associated with the SAP, and endpoint Y on each router is associated with pseudowires connected to the remote PE routers. In a local VLL service, two SAPs are each associated with one endpoint; in a distributed VPLS service, one endpoint must contain a SAP, and the other endpoint must contain a regular (non-ICB) spoke-pseudowire.

The router forwards traffic from one endpoint to another and vice versa, and never forwards traffic within the same endpoint. The relationship between two endpoints in a service instance is similar to the cross-connect concept in an ATM switch: Traffic received from one endpoint can be sent only to another endpoint. In a regular VLL service (non–vc-switching), the endpoint is implicitly associated with the SAP or the pseudowire without any configuration. In a VLL service with pseudowire redundancy, the endpoint must be explicitly defined in the service context and manually associated with the SAP or pseudowire(s). The rule that traffic can travel only from one endpoint to another still applies, and spoke-pseudowires belonging to the same endpoint cannot send or receive traffic among each other.

ICB-PW is a special type of pseudowire. It can be used in the VLL service only when MC-LAG SAP is used and the service is deployed with pseudowire redundancy. Therefore, it is mandatory to associate ICB pseudowires with endpoints in the service instance. The rules of assigning objects (SAP, pseudowire, or ICB pseudowire) are:

1. An ICB-PW can be associated only with an endpoint that is already associated with a spoke-pseudowire or an MC-LAG SAP port. In other words, the ICB-PW cannot be the first object added to the endpoint.

2. If an endpoint already contains an MC-LAG SAP, it can only have one ICB-PW associated with it, and no more objects can be added to the endpoint.

3. If an endpoint is associated with a spoke-pseudowire (but not associated with a SAP), it can have up to four spoke-pseudowires, only one of which can be an ICB-PW.

The ICB-PW is always used as the *last resort of traffic forwarding*, which means that the service instance uses ICB pseudowire to forward traffic only when no other object (SAP or spoke-pseudowire) is available. ICB pseudowire has the lowest preference among all the objects in the endpoint.

Figure 14.9 illustrates an example of ICB pseudowires in Router PE-1 and Router PE-2. In each PE router, each endpoint has an ICB-PW connected to the MC-LAG peer. The two gray arrows in the center of the diagram indicate the ICB pseudowires configured between the two PE routers: Endpoint X (SAP endpoint) in PE-1 is connected to endpoint Y (pseudowire endpoint) in PE-2, and vice versa. This pair of cross-connected ICB pseudowires protects the service from the following two types of failure scenarios:

- **ICB-PW Protecting Spoke-Pseudowires** — In a failure scenario where no spoke-pseudowires connected to the far-end PE routers (endpoint Y) are available, as a last resort, the ICB-PW in endpoint Y forwards traffic to the far-end PE router of the ICB-PW (endpoint X in PE-2). When the ICB-PW in endpoint X of Router PE-2 receives the traffic, according to the rule of forwarding from one endpoint to another, it forwards the traffic to the active spoke-pseudowire in endpoint Y. The traffic then reaches the remote router PE-X, which has a local SAP connected to CE-2. (If no spoke-pseudowires to PE-X from PE-1 are available, one spoke-pseudowire from PE-2 to PE-X becomes active.)

- **ICB-PW Protecting SAP Failure** — In the other direction, when PE-2 receives traffic from PE-X from the active spoke-pseudowire in endpoint Y, it forwards the traffic to endpoint X; because the SAP in endpoint X is not available (whether or not the SAP has a link failure, or MC-LAG control protocol decides it is in the standby state), as the last resort in endpoint X, the ICB-PW forwards the traffic to its far-end ICB-PW (the ICB-PW in endpoint Y of PE-1). PE-1 then forwards the traffic from endpoint Y to endpoint X and uses the available SAP to forward the traffic to CE-1.

> **Note:** Although the ICB-PW resides in endpoint X and endpoint Y, traffic is never forwarded from one ICB-PW to another. Traffic received from the ICB-PW in the endpoint that has the SAP can egress only over the spoke-pseudowire in the other endpoint. Traffic received from the ICB-PW in the endpoint that has the spoke-pseudowire can egress only over the SAP in the other endpoint. This behavior prevents forwarding loops and is not configurable.

It has been mentioned several times that the ICB pseudowire is a last resort — it can forward traffic only when no other objects in the same endpoint are available. When are other forwarding objects unavailable, so that the ICB-PW forwards the traffic?

If an endpoint contains one MC-LAG SAP and one ICB-PW, when the MC-LAG SAP is operationally **down** or in the standby state, the system switches to the ICB-PW in the same endpoint to forward traffic (providing it is healthy and does not receive *pseudowire down* or *pseudowire not forwarding* status bits in the PW-Status TLV from the peer). When the endpoint contains multiple spoke-pseudowires connected to the far-end PE router and one ICB-PW, if the active pseudowire goes down or no pseudowires can take the active role (because they are either down or have received pwForwardingStandby bits in the PW-Status TLV from the peer), the system switches to the ICB-PW to forward traffic.

The rules of electing an active forwarding object from endpoints containing multiple spoke-pseudowires and an ICB-PW are listed in Table 14.2.

Table 14.2 Electing the Best Possible Pseudowires with MC-LAG to Forward Traffic

Priority	Peer PW-Status Flag	Description
0	—	Only pseudowires that are local operationally up are eligible for the election.
1	0x00000000	The remote pseudowire is active; the remote SAP and pseudowire endpoint are okay.
2	0x00000020	The remote pseudowire is standby; the remote SAP and pseudowire endpoint are okay.
3	0x00000006	The remote pseudowire is active; the remote SAP is down, and the remote pseudowire endpoint is okay.
4	0x00000026	The remote pseudowire is standby; the remote SAP is down, and the remote pseudowire endpoint is okay.
5	0x00000001	The remote pseudowire is active; the remote pseudowire is "not forwarding."

(continued)

Table 14.2 Electing the Best Possible Pseudowires with MC-LAG to Forward Traffic *(continued)*

Priority	Peer PW-Status Flag	Description
6	0x00000021	The remote pseudowire is standby; the remote pseudowire is "not forwarding."
7	0x00000018	The remote pseudowire is active; the remote pseudowire is operationally down.
8	0x00000038	The remote pseudowire is standby; the remote pseudowire is operationally down.
9	—	If there is a tie after priority 1–8, choose the lowest local precedence value as the tiebreaker; if it still ties, use pseudowire-id (lower) as the next tiebreaker
10	—	If the "active pseudowire" selected through steps 0–9 has a peering flag other than (0x00000000) or (0x00000006), use ICB pseudowires to forward traffic. Providing the ICB-PW does not receive "pseudowire down" or "pseudowire not forwarding" status.
11	—	If there is no "active pseudowire" found from setup 0–9, use the ICB-PW to forward the traffic. Providing the ICB-PW does not receive "pseudowire down" or "pseudowire not forwarding" status.
12	—	If the election process ends up with the ICB-PW being the "active forwarding object" on both endpoints of the service instance, the traffic will be discarded. A router will *never* forward traffic between two ICB pseudowires, even if they belong to different endpoints and are both the best current choice of traffic forwarding.

The ICB-PW must be configured in an *endpoint crossover* manner between two PE routers with MC-LAG SAP peering. This means that the two MC-LAG peers should have a pair of ICB spoke-pseudowires, one on each router. The ICB spoke-pseudowire should reside on the same endpoint in each router as the MC-LAG SAP and should be connected to the MC-LAG peering router. Using the network illustrated in Figure 14.9 as an example, in Router PE-1, the two ICB pseudowires are configured as follows: 117:800 from PE-1 endpoint X to PE-2 endpoint Y, and 117:801 from PE-1 endpoint Y to PE-2 endpoint X. Router PE2 also has two ICB pseudowires configured as follows: 116:800 from PE-2 endpoint Y to PE-1 endpoint X, and 116:801 from PE-2 endpoint X to PE-1 endpoint Y.

Depending on the number of PE routers a service may have and which portion of the service the operator wants to protect with ICB-PW, the numbers and locations of ICB pseudowires may vary. Some typical topologies and design examples are presented later in this chapter. The general guideline is that to protect an object in one endpoint in one PE router, an ICB-PW should be added to the same endpoint, and the ICB-PW should be connected to the *opposite* endpoint of the MC-LAG peering router (the endpoint that contains the spoke-pseudowire, not the endpoint that contains the SAP). For example, if PE-1 and PE-2 have MC-LAG peering SAPs, to protect the SAP of PE-1 in its endpoint X, an ICB-PW is configured in the same endpoint, connected to endpoint Y in PE-2, which contains spoke-pseudowires connected to the far-end PE router(s).

Initial Stage: Determining the Best Active Forwarding Topology

Because VLL service is always point-to-point, there should be only one active forwarding path at any time. In the example illustrated in Figure 14.10, both the SAP ports and the pseudowires have redundancy, and the service terminates in more than one remote PE router. After the service is deployed in the network, how do the routers communicate with each other to reach an agreement on which active SAP, PE routers, and pseudowire to use? Figure 14.10 illustrates the selection of the MC-LAG active forwarding path.

These redundancy mechanisms are visible only to the PE routers, and transparent to the CE devices. Routers PE-1 and PE-2 first determine the active LAG in the MC-LAG group facing CE-1. If PE-1 wins, its LAG port(s) assumes the active role in the MC-LAG group. The LAG ports in PE-2 then become standby; and the result is signaled through Link Aggregation Control Protocol (LACP) to the LAG of CE-1. From the perspective of Router CE-1, ports connected to PE-1 are operationally up, and ports connected to PE-2 are operationally **down**. CE-1 does not know it is connected to two PE routers; it knows only that it has several ports connected to the provider's network and that some of them are operationally **up**.

Figure 14.10   Selecting the MC-LAG Active Forwarding Path

❸ Same MC-LAG process performed between PE-3 and PE-4. In this example, PE-4 wins the MC-LAG selection and its LAG is active. Because PE-3's SAP is the standby LAG, it will signal its pseudowires to PE-1 and PE-2 with the pwForwardingStandby bit set, just like PE-2 did.

❹ When selecting the active forwarding pseudowire, the pseudowire with both local status and peering PW status active is chosen to be the forwarding path. In this case: CE-1 -> PE-1 -> PE-4 -> CE-2.

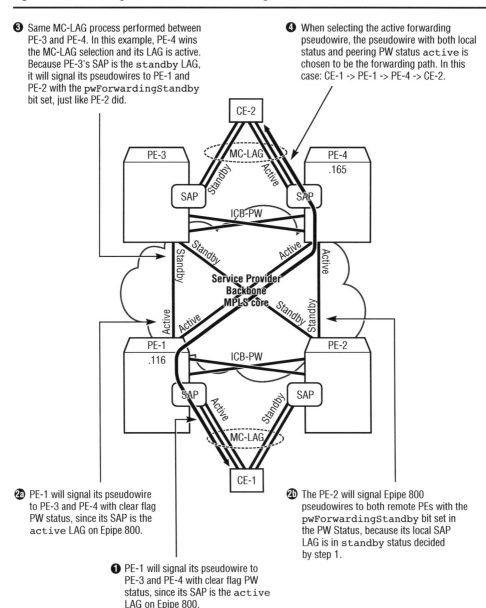

❷ⓐ PE-1 will signal its pseudowire to PE-3 and PE-4 with clear flag PW status, since its SAP is the active LAG on Epipe 800.

❷ⓑ The PE-2 will signal Epipe 800 pseudowires to both remote PEs with the pwForwardingStandby bit set in the PW Status, because its local SAP LAG is in standby status decided by step 1.

❶ PE-1 will signal its pseudowire to PE-3 and PE-4 with clear flag PW status, since its SAP is the active LAG on Epipe 800.

Figure 14.10 *(continued)*

```
A:PE-1# show service id 800 endpoint
=====================================================
Service 800 endpoints
--- details for endpoint "X" ommited ---
=====================================================
Endpoint name                 : Y
Revert time                   : 0
Act Hold Delay                : 0
Ignore Standby Signaling      : false
Suppress Standby Signaling    : true
Tx Active                     : 165:800
Tx Active Up Time             : 0d 04:12:15
Revert Time Count Down         : N/A
Tx Active Change Count        : 4
Last Tx Active Change         : 07/24/2003 12:23:24
-----------------------------------------------------
Members
-----------------------------------------------------
Spoke-sdp                     : 164:800 Precedence:0
Spoke-sdp                     : 165:800 Precedence:2
=====================================================
```

```
A:PE-4# show service id 800 sdp detail
==========================================================================
Services: Service Destination Points Details
==========================================================================
--------------------------------------------------------------------------
 Sdp Id 116:800  -(10.0.0.116)
--- omitted ---
Admin State       : Up              Oper State       : Up
Peer Pw Bits      : None
Peer Fault Ip     : None
--- omitted ---
--------------------------------------------------------------------------
 Sdp Id 117:800  -(10.0.0.117)
--------------------------------------------------------------------------
Admin State       : Up              Oper State       : Up
Peer Pw Bits      : pwFwdingStandby
Peer Fault Ip     : None
--- omitted ---
```

After PE-1 and PE-2 determine the active and standby roles in MC-LAG peering, the PE router that has the standby MC-LAG group as its local SAP sets the pwForwardingStandby bit (**0x00000020**) in the PW-Status TLV when signaling pseudowires to remote PE router(s) (Step 2b in Figure 14.10). This is because with VLL resiliency, the status of the pseudowire is the reflection of the local SAP. When the PE router's local SAP is in `standby` status, the pseudowire signal to the remote peering PE shows `standby` status as well. The winner (PE-1) signals a clear status flag for the pseudowire to PE-3 and PE-4 because its SAP is the active MC-LAG member. The same process occurs between the PE-3 and PE-4 routers — the active and standby roles are determined in the MC-LAG, and the standby MC-LAG router signals pseudowires with the pwForwardingStandby bit set.

After all four routers complete the MC-LAG role decision and the signaling of the pseudowires among each other, the active forwarding path is determined. The SAP of PE-1 is active because it resides in the active MC-LAG group. The pseudowire connecting PE-1 to PE-4 is active because its pseudowire forwarding flag is set to clear (**0x00000000**), and the pseudowire connecting PE-1 to PE-3 has a pseudowire status of pwForwardingStandby (set by PE-3 because it lost the MC-LAG election). The same result occurs in the far end between PE-3 and PE-4. The SAP of PE-4 is active, and the pseudowire connecting PE-4 to PE-1 is active. Therefore, the active forwarding path is: CE-1 ⟷ PE-1 ⟷ PE-4 ⟷ CE-2 (indicated in Figure 14.10 by the bold line between CE-1 and CE-2). After the selection process, the point-to-point service active forwarding path is determined, and all redundant ports and pseudowires are in the standby state, and therefore eliminated from the active forwarding topology.

Failover and Restoration

After the initial establishment of service, the forwarding path is determined, and customer traffic starts flowing between the two CE devices. If a network failure occurs in different locations, the network converges to a different forwarding topology by using the redundant elements.

The first network failure scenario is an access link failure between CE-1 and PE-1 (see Figure 14.11). As soon as the ports on PE-1's SAP go down, several things occur:

1. The MC-LAG group of PE-2 takes over the active role and brings up the ports facing CE-1.

2. PE-1 sends LDP Notification messages over all pseudowires (including the ICB pseudowire) with the pwForwardingStandby bit (**0x00000020**) set, since the SAP of PE-1 is no longer the active MC-LAG group.

3. PE2 sends LDP Notification messages to all peering PE routers over all pseudowires with the PW-Forwarding flag (**0x00000000**) set, since its SAP ports are now active and operationally **up**.

4. PE-3 and PE-4 receive the LDP Notification messages and start again to select the active forwarding path. (The new states for the pseudowires in PE-1 and PE-2 are noted in bold font in Figure 14.11.)

5. This time, PE-4 has a pseudowire connected to PE-2 with both local and remote active, so it becomes the new forwarding path.

6. After the failure, the traffic travels through CE-1 ⟷ PE-2 ⟷ PE-4 ⟷ CE-2.

Figure 14.11 illustrates an access link failure in a network with MC-LAG and pseudowire redundancy.

Figure 14.11   MC-LAG with Pseudowire Redundancy: Access Link Failure

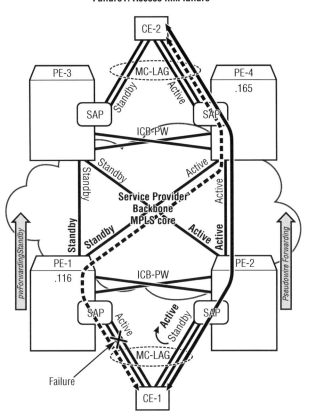

Failure1: Access link failure

The process shown in the diagram is as follows:

1.   When the failure is removed from the network, PE-1 may or may not win the active MC-LAG role back, depending on the MC-LAG group configuration.

2.   If PE-1 wins the active role back, PE-2's MC-LAG SAP ports are in the standby state and are operationally **down**.

3.   Next, PE-1 sends an LDP Notification message with a pseudowire status of 0x00000000 over the pseudowires connected to PE-3 and PE-4, and PE-2 sends a pseudowire status of 0x00000020 to PE-3 and PE-4.

4.   After the pseudowire status message is processed by PE-3 and PE-4, the forwarding path is restored to the original CE-1 ←→ PE-1 ←→ PE-4 ←→ CE-2 (the dotted line in Figure 14.11).

Figure 14.12 illustrates a pseudowire failure scenario in a network with MC-LAG and pseudowire redundancy. In this scenario, both pseudowires in Router PE-1 connected to the remote peers PE-3 and PE-4 have failed:

1. Because PE-1 still has the active MC-LAG SAP, the ICB-PW in endpoint Y of PE-1 is used as the last resort to forward traffic to PE-2.

2. In PE-3 and PE-4, the pseudowires pointing to PE-1 go down, which triggers a new election in endpoint Y of both routers.

3. In PE-4, because the pseudowire connected to PE-1 is down, two pseudowires are now eligible in endpoint Y — the ICB-PW connected to PE-3 and the spoke-pseudowire connected to PE-2 with the pwForwardingStandby bit set.

4. According to the election rule, the pseudowire connected to PE2 wins the election and becomes `Tx Active`.

5. The new traffic flow is CE-1 $\longleftrightarrow$ PE-1 $\longleftrightarrow$ ICB-PW $\longleftrightarrow$ PE-2 $\longleftrightarrow$ PE-4 $\longleftrightarrow$ CE-2.

6. When the two pseudowires in PE-1 come back up, the pseudowires connected to PE-3 and PE-4 become operationally **up**, triggering a new active forwarding object election on endpoint Y of PE-3 and PE-4.

7. This time, the PE-1 $\longleftrightarrow$ PE-4 pseudowire wins the election and becomes `Tx Active` on both routers, and the traffic flow reverts to the original path.

Deploying MC-LAG Epipe Service Redundancy with ICB-PW

Several possible network topologies can be used to deploy an Epipe service with MC-LAG and ICB-PW. In each topology, ICB-PW can protect certain portions of the network to improve its robustness.

Figure 14.13 illustrates four possible network topologies with MC-LAG SAP in the Epipe services, and ICB-PWs configured to protect the endpoints and provide more robustness, as follows:

- **Case 1** — Two PE routers in the network, with one CE device dual-homed to both of them. In this topology, CE-1 is dual-homed to PE-1 and PE-2 with MC-LAG running between the two PE routers. This is a *local* Epipe service: CE-1 and CE-2 are both connected to PE-1 with local SAPs, and no pseudowire is required. In this topology, only endpoint X in router PE1 can be protected by having an ICB-PW connected to endpoint Y of PE-2. If the link between the SAP of PE-1 and CE-1 fails, the traffic from CE-1 to CE-2 travels through the SAP of PE2, then over the ICB-PW, and reaches endpoint X in PE-1. PE-1 then forwards the traffic to endpoint Y and sends it to CE-2 over the SAP.

Figure 14.12 MC-LAG with Pseudowire Redundancy: Pseudowire Failure

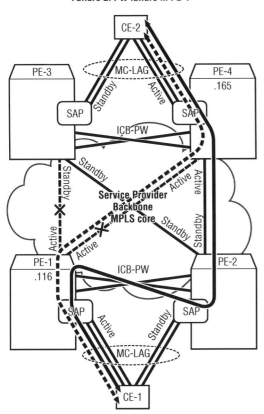

Failure 2: PW failure in PE-1

- **Case 2** — Three PE routers in the network, with one CE device dual-homed. The difference between Case 1 and Case 2 is that the Epipe service is distributed, and both PE-1 and PE-2 have a regular pseudowire in endpoint Y, connected to the remote PE-3 router. A pair of ICB-PWs is configured in PE-1 and PE-2, protecting both SAPs and pseudowires.

- **Case 3** — Three PE routers in the network, with both CE devices dual-homed. PE-1 and PE-2 use MC-LAG to protect CE-1. PE-2 and PE-3 use MC-LAG to protect CE-2. PE-1 and PE-3 are connected by a pseudowire in the Epipe service instance. If both SAPs in PE-2 are active, the service is *local*; otherwise, the service is *distributed*. Two pairs of ICB pseudowires are deployed to protect the four SAPs and the pseudowire between PE-1 and PE-3.

- **Case 4** — Four PE routers in the network, with both CE devices dual-homed. This topology is highly likely to be used in large provider networks. Similar to

Case 3, two pairs of ICB-PWs are provisioned to protect all four SAPs and four pseudowires. This is the most reliable service implementation, and all devices and entities (SAPs, pseudowires, and PE routers) are protected by MC-LAG and ICB-PWs.

Figure 14.13 Topology Examples: MC-LAG with ICB-PW Redundancy

Case 1 - 2*PEs, 1 dual-home CE

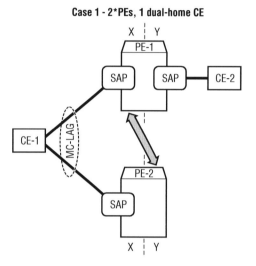

Case 2 - 3*PEs, 1 dual-home CE

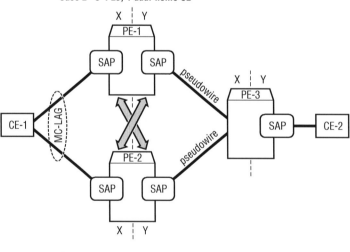

Inter-Chassis
Backup Pseudowire

Figure 14.13 *(continued)*

Case 3 - 3*PEs, 2 dual-home CEs

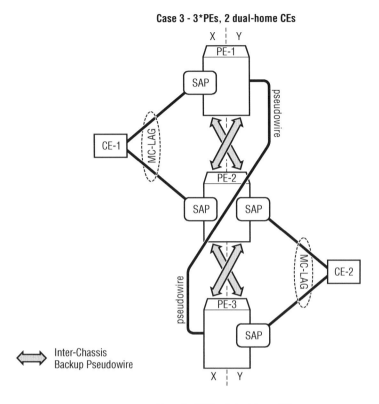

Case 4 - 4*PEs, 2 dual-home CEs

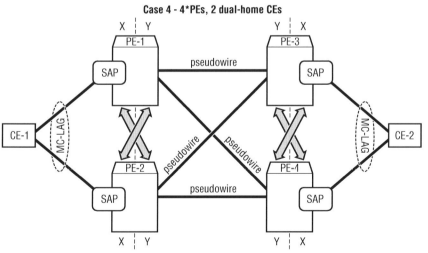

Summary

Service providers desire maximum service redundancy. VLL service uses LAG or MC-LAG to achieve access resiliency, and it uses pseudowire redundancy to achieve service backbone resiliency. When using pseudowire redundancy in VLL, the active/standby pseudowires are grouped in the same endpoint in the PE router. At any time, there is only one active forwarding object in an endpoint. This guarantees that the active/standby pseudowires do not forward traffic together and cause forwarding loops. All active/standby spoke-pseudowires have their own preference values to determine the priority of being selected as the active forwarding object. When using pseudowire resiliency along with MC-LAG, maximum resiliency can be achieved in the VLL service.

VPLS Service Resiliency

15

VPLS service supports resiliency features that can protect the service from all kinds of network failures. The resiliency features add redundant forwarding paths into the VPLS service, so loop prevention is essential. There are two methods to provide resiliency in VPLS service — pseudowire redundancy and adding redundant forwarding paths with Spanning Tree Protocol (STP) loop prevention.

Chapter Objectives

- Introduce VPLS resiliency
- Discuss VPLS access resiliency features: LAG, MC-LAG, mVPLS, mac-move, and others
- Discuss H-VPLS backbone resiliency: active/standby pseudowire
- Explain MAC-flush signaling to avoid traffic blackholes

This chapter introduces resiliency features in Virtual Private LAN Service (VPLS), where redundant forwarding paths are introduced to the VPLS service to provide service-level protection. The redundant forwarding paths can be deployed in a primary/backup manner (pseudowire redundancy) to ensure that there is only one active pseudowire carrying traffic between two Provider Edge (PE) routers. Alternatively, STP can be deployed in a VPLS network to prevent forwarding loops introduced by adding redundant forwarding paths in the service.

15.1 Introduction to VPLS Service Resiliency

VPLS provides multipoint Ethernet bridging service for the customer's sites located in different geographical locations. As discussed in Chapter 11, the basic form of VPLS is the *full mesh*. In a full-mesh VPLS network, all member PE routers participating in the same VPLS service are connected by fully meshed pseudowires. As discussed in Chapter 12, the H-VPLS solution with spoke-pseudowire is used most often in large service provider networks in which many customer sites need to be connected. An H-VPLS network is broken into two *tiers*, as follows:

- **Edge Tier** — The edge tier is composed of the MTU/PE devices that are directly connected to the customer equipment through attachment circuits (Service Access Point, or SAPs). The MTU/PE equipment aggregates customer traffic from one or several sites and sends it to the core tier. To reduce the overall number of pseudowires in the solution, spoke-pseudowires (not mesh-pseudowires) are usually used to connect the edge tier with the core tier.

- **Core Tier** — The core tier contains PE routers and provider (P) routers, which transport the aggregated traffic across the network between the closest customer location and its destination. Because the traffic is aggregated in the core network, the optimal packet forwarding is much more important, and therefore mesh-pseudowires are usually used to connect PE routers in the core tier to reduce the number of hops the traffic needs to travel.

> **Note:** The term Multi Tenant Unit (MTU) is used in this chapter as a logical functional representation of a router. Physically, MTUs can also be Alcatel-Lucent Service Router Portfolio (ALSRP) service routers, just like the routers in the core network.

VPLS services are deployed in an IP/MPLS VPN infrastructure; therefore, all IP/MPLS resiliency features deployed in the network infrastructure are inherited by the VPLS services, such as MPLS Fast Reroute (FRR) or Link Aggregation Group (LAG).

IP/MPLS resiliency features only protect the backbone network (the Service Distribution Path or SDP, and the service transport tunnel used by the SDP), but not the service entities belonging to a specific VPLS service, such as a pseudowire failure or a SAP failure. To achieve maximum resiliency, the VPLS service resiliency must be deployed to provide the following protection:

- The VPLS SAP should be protected against the attachment circuit failure.
- The pseudowires connecting member PE routers in the backbone network should be protected against the pseudowire failure.
- The end-to-end VPLS service should be protected against PE router failure.

15.2 Access Resiliency

Access resiliency provides protection on the VPLS service against failures on the attachment circuits between the PE router's SAPs, and the CE device's port facing the provider's networks. The VPLS SAP sends and receives Ethernet traffic with customer devices through the attachment circuits (ACs). There are several methods to protect the attachment circuits:

- Using LAG to protect the attachment circuits on the SAP
- Using Multi Chassis LAG (MC-LAG) to protect the attachment circuits and the CE devices on the SAPs
- Using multiple attachment circuits to connect the CE device to multiple SAPs in different PE routers. This requires the use of STP to prevent forwarding loops.

Using LAG to Protect Attachment Circuits

Customers access the VPLS networks through the attachment circuit between the CE devices and the PE router's SAPs. LAG can be deployed between the customer sites and the PE routers to protect the attachment circuits. Figure 15.1 illustrates the use of LAG in the VPLS service to protect the PE-CE connections.

Figure 15.1 Using LAG to Protect VPLS PE-CE Attachment Circuits

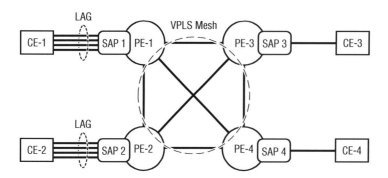

In Figure 15.1, the VPLS service has four member PE routers, connected by the mesh-pseudowire. Each PE router has one SAP connected to the customer sites. LAG is deployed between CE-1 and PE-1, and between CE-2 and PE-2. Because all Ethernet links within a LAG behave like a part of a single link, the use of LAG does not introduce forwarding loops into the VPLS service. The only configuration difference is that instead of defining the SAP over a single access port, the SAP is defined over a LAG. The encapsulation type (`null/dot1q/qinq`) and vlan tagging configuration in the SAP remain the same. All member ports of the LAG must have the same encapsulation type, and both the member ports and the LAG group must be configured to access mode.

Using MC-LAG to Protect Attachment Circuits

Multi Chassis LAG (MC-LAG) is introduced in Chapter 13. The use of the MC-LAG allows the operator to use two PE routers to connect to a single CE device over multiple Ethernet attachment circuits. The MC-LAG is transparent to the CE device connected to it. From the perspective of the CE device, there are several Ethernet links that belong to the same LAG connected to the provider's network, and only a subset of the links are active at any time. Figure 15.2 illustrates the use of MC-LAG in the VPLS service to protect the PE–CE connections.

In Figure 15.2, the CE-1 device has eight Ethernet links connected to the provider's VPLS network. The VPLS service in the provider's network is a fully meshed VPLS with four member PE routers, and PE-1 and PE-2 have MC-LAG deployed on their SAPs connected to CE-1. The Multi Chassis protocol is running between Routers PE-1 and PE-2 to ensure that only one LAG group (either in PE-1 or PE-2) is active. From CE-1's perspective, all eight Ethernet links belong to a single LAG, and only some of them are active. With MC-LAG, the PE router is protected against SAP failure. MC-LAG is discussed in detail in Chapter 13.

Figure 15.2 Using MC-LAG to Protect VPLS PE–CE Attachment Circuits

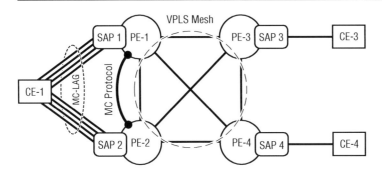

Using Multiple Attachment Circuits with STP

It is also possible to multi-home the CE devices using multiple attachment circuits to connect to multiple PE routers' SAPs. However, having redundant attachment circuits connecting to the CE device requires the use of STP to prevent forwarding loops. Similar to the legacy-bridged Ethernet network, STP blocks the redundant forwarding paths to create a loop-free forwarding infrastructure. When using STP in a VPLS network, there are two options:

- Enable STP within the VPLS service instance.
- Use management VPLS (mVPLS) with STP enabled to manage other user VPLS (uVPLS) services in the network.

  Details regarding the use of STP and mVPLS are discussed in Appendix A.

Using Other Loop-Avoidance Mechanisms on Attachment Circuits

If STP is not desired or the customer does not want STP in the network, the end-to-end VPLS service solution may contain forwarding loops. The ALSRP provides a MAC *learning rate control* as an alternative method of preventing broadcast storms in case of forwarding loops. A symptom of a broadcast storm is that the same MAC address appears to *move* frequently among several SAPs or pseudowires. This symptom is usually caused by traffic cycling around the network. When the MAC learning rate control is configured (the mac-move option in the VPLS instance), if the same MAC address is learned more than a certain number of times within a certain time period, the service router prevents a broadcast storm by disabling the SAP or the pseudowires from which the MAC address was last learned. The learning frequency can be defined by fine-tuning the mac-move configuration. SAPs or pseudowires can be configured as *non-blockable*, so that only other SAPs or pseudowires are disabled when frequent MAC moves occur. The mac-move option can be configured in conjunction with STP and/or mVPLS.

The mac-move option prevents broadcast storms, and it may eliminate forwarding loops. If a broadcast storm forms, the MAC address quickly moves among bridge ports in the fowarding database (FDB). If mac-move blocks a bridge port, it is highly likely that there is a forwarding loop in the network. mac-move temporarily disables the affected SAPs or pseudowires. When this happens, a detailed network forwarding topology review should be performed to find out where and why the forwarding loops occur. Then use a loop-prevention mechanism or modify the network design to eliminate the forwarding loop.

The mac-move option allows the operator to group VPLS-ports (SAPs and spoke-pseudowires) and to define the order in which they should be blocked. "Primary" and "secondary" ports are defined in the context of the mac-move CLI tree. By default all VPLS-ports are considered as "tertiary" ports unless they have been explicitly declared as primary or secondary. The order of blocking will always follow strict order starting from "tertiary", then secondary, and at last primary.

Furthermore, as discussed in Chapter 12, split-horizon groups can also be used on the SAPs to regulate their forwarding behavior. When adding multiple SAPs to the split-horizon group, these SAPs cannot exchange traffic between each other.

> **Note:** When SAPs or pseudowires are blocked by mac-move, begin the investigation into the location and reason for the forwarding loop. mac-move can only disable the SAPs and pseudowires affected by the broadcast storm, and this action may not eliminate the forwarding loop. Even if it does, such a forwarding infrastructure is not optimal or desired. The design of the network must be reviewed and corrected accordingly.

15.3 H-VPLS Backbone Resiliency

H-VPLS backbone resiliency is about protecting the VPLS service infrastructure. It is essential to protect the service connectivity from PE router failures and/or pseudowire failures.

H-VPLS uses spoke-pseudowires to connect PE routers. As discussed in Chapter 12, in most cases, the spoke-pseudowires are used either to connect the spoke-PE routers in the edge to the hub-PE routers in the core, or to connect multiple VPLS meshes. To provide resiliency on pseudowires, multiple spoke-pseudowires may be deployed between two VPLS member PE routers. Because spoke-pseudowires do not obey the Split-Horizon rule, having multiple spoke-pseudowires may cause forwarding loops in the VPLS service infrastructure. There are three methods to prevent the formation of forwarding loops when using redundant spoke-pseudowires:

- Use active/standby pseudowires to connect one spoke-PE router to two hub-PE routers. This feature is called *pseudowire resiliency*. When using pseudowire resiliency, the two pseudowires originating from the same spoke-PE router cannot pass traffic at the same time. Only the active spoke-pseudowire will forward the traffic.

- Use Multi Chassis End Point (MC-EP) with multiple pseudowires to protect the H-VPLS from not only the pseudowire failure, but also the gateway (hub) PE router failure.

- Use STP within the VPLS or mVPLS with STP enabled to manage the VPLS with redundant pseudowires deployed.

If applicable, it is highly recommended to use either active/standby pseudowire redundancy or MC-EP to provide H-VPLS backbone resiliency, rather than use STP to block redundant pseudowires. Pseudowire redundancy has much better convergence performance than Rapid STP (RSTP), and it is always preferable to avoid using RSTP in the core of the VPLS network.

Using Pseudowire Redundancy to Protect PE Router Failure

As discussed in Chapter 12, operators deploy H-VPLS with spoke-pseudowires in their networks for many reasons (scaling, optimizing multicast traffic forwarding, and so on). Also discussed in Chapter 12, one drawback of the H-VPLS is that a hub-PE router with many spoke-PE routers connected can be a single point of failure. In many discussions, the spoke-PE router is also referred to as a *Multi Tenant Unit* (MTU). If one hub PE router fails, all spoke-PE routers behind the hub-PE router will lose connectivity to the rest of the VPLS network.

Pseudowire redundancy can be used in H-VPLS to provide resiliency on the hub-PE router. The spoke-PE routers can peer with two hub-PE routers using pseudowire redundancy. Therefore, if one hub-PE router fails, the other hub-PE router can provide the connectivity. Having one spoke-PE router to peer with two hub-PE routers is frequently referred to as *dual-homing*. Figure 15.3 illustrates a network with a dual-homed spoke-PE router. From the perspective of the spoke-PE router, node redundancy to the VPLS service is achieved.

Figure 15.3 H-VPLS Design with Dual-Homed Spoke-PE Router

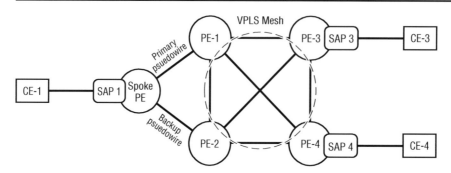

In Figure 15.3, the spoke-PE is dual-homed to PE-1 and PE-2 with two spoke-pseudowires. As discussed in Chapter 11, in normal cases, when using spoke-pseudowires, one PE router should peer with only one remote PE router at any time. Otherwise, certain loop-prevention mechanisms must be deployed to ensure that there is no forwarding loop in the VPLS forwarding topology.

Pseudowire redundancy has its built-in loop prevention mechanism. Therefore, using pseudowire redundancy allows service resiliency and eliminates the use of STP at the same time. In Figure 15.3, from the spoke PE router's perspective, the two spoke-pseudowires work in a *primary/backup* manner. When configuring the pseudowires in the spoke PE router, both spoke-pseudowires are configured within the same endpoint. At any time, only one pseudowire within the same endpoint is selected to be *active* and forward traffic. The other pseudowires within the same endpoint are in *standby* state and do not forward traffic. The pseudowire redundancy configuration and the primary/backup mechanism are discussed in detail in this chapter.

Using Multi Chassis End Point to Protect the Gateway PE

As discussed in Chapter 12, the most scalable and efficient way of connecting two VPLS meshes is to use H-VPLS. By using spoke-pseudowires to connect the PE routers on the boundary of the two VPLS meshes, the two VPLS meshes form a Hierarchical VPLS (H-VPLS) network. In such a network, the PE routers with spoke-pseudowires connecting two VPLS meshes need to be protected. The *Multi Chassis End Point* (MC-EP) is an extension of pseudowire redundancy to maximize the protection of the H-VPLS gateway PE routers. Figure 15.4 illustrates an H-VPLS network with MC-EP deployed on the four gateway PE routers.

Figure 15.4 H-VPLS Network

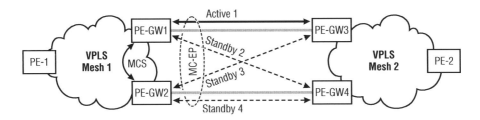

In the diagram, VPLS Mesh 1 and VPLS Mesh 2 are connected by gateway PE routers to form an H-VPLS. To achieve maximum resiliency, four gateway PE routers are deployed with MC-EP configured. The connection between VPLS Mesh 1 and VPLS Mesh 2 is protected against both pseudowire failures and PE router failures. Redundant spoke-pseudowires are configured in each gateway PE router, and the Multi Chassis Protocol (MCP) is configured to ensure that the peering gateway PE routers are in sync and to decide the mast slave status of the gateway PE routers. As indicated in the diagram, the pseudowire between PE-GW1 and PE-GW3 is active and forwarding traffic, and the other three pseudowires are in standby status. T-LDP uses pseudowire status code (0x20) to signal the standby status to PE-GW3 and PE-GW4.

Details regarding MC-EP are beyond the scope of this book. Please refer to the ALSRP product manuals for details on MC-EP.

Using mVPLS/STP in MTU Dual-Homing

In certain circumstances, using redundant pseudowires to provide service protection is desired, but the *pseudowire redundancy* feature is either not applicable or not suitable. In these scenarios, the operator can still deploy multiple pseudowires between the spoke-PE router and the hub-PE router. In such a network, STP must be deployed to preventing forwarding loops. There are two options regarding STP deployment in VPLS: either enable STP inside the VPLS service instance(s), or use management VPLS (mVPLS) with the same forwarding infrastructure to prune redundant spoke-pseudowires. However, an STP solution may not suit the requirements of some scenarios, as follows:

- A solution that relies on STP to maintain a loop-free forwarding environment can converge only in a time frame of seconds. Using the fastest Rapid STP (RSTP), a 3–5-second failover time is normal. This may not meet the customer's requirements for minimizing the network outage during failover.

- mVPLS can be used to manage multiple VPLS service instances using the same forwarding infrastructure to achieve load balancing while maintaining a loop-free topology. mVPLS requires multiple SDPs to be provisioned in the network facing the same far-end PE router to achieve load balancing. Having multiple SDPs increases the complexity of the network.

- For a network with many VPLS instances sharing the same MPLS infrastructure but with different forwarding topology requirements, multiple STP instances or mVPLS instances may need to be provisioned to eliminate loops for each forwarding topology. Designing, tracking, and managing such a network may be complicated.

Therefore, the use of STP with redundant pseudowires to provide VPLS resiliency should be the last resort. When possible, the operator should always consider using pseudowire redundancy rather than using STP solutions to achieve service resiliency. The use of STP in VPLS is discussed in Appendix A.

Chapter 14 discusses the use of pseudowire redundancy in Virtual Leased Line (VLL) services. The concepts of endpoint, the primary/backup pseudowire, and the active and standby states used for pseudowire redundancy in VPLS are exactly the same as in VLL. Therefore, the basic pseudowire redundancy concepts are not repeated in this chapter. This section focuses on the use of pseudowire redundancy in VPLS.

Primary/Backup Pseudowire Peering in PE/MTU Dual-Homing

A pair of primary/backup spoke-pseudowires can be provisioned in the VPLS instance of a customer-facing (spoke) PE router that is acting as the MTU, to connect to two aggregate (hub) PE routers in the core network. To ensure that only one pseudowire of the pair is actively forwarding traffic at any time, the two redundant pseudowires are grouped under the same *endpoint* in the VPLS instance of the spoke-PE router. The two spoke-pseudowires belong to the same endpoint with a predefined precedence in the VPLS service instance: One pseudowire is selected to carry the VPLS traffic, and the other pseudowire is standing by in a blocked (or pruned) state.

Note: When using pseudowire redundancy in VPLS, both the pseudowire-ingress (Rx) and the pseudowire-egress (Tx) directions of the standby pseudowire are blocked. This is different from using the pseudowire redundancy in VLL, where only the pseudowire's egress (Tx) is blocked.

Note that when pseudowire redundancy is used in VPLS, only two pseudowires are allowed in each endpoint. This means that the configuration allows only one primary spoke-pseudowire and one backup spoke-pseudowire for one VPLS service instance. This is different from the case of using pseudowire redundancy in the VLL service, in which more than one backup pseudowire is allowed in the same endpoint.

The endpoint configuration in the VPLS service instance of the spoke PE also contains optional configurations regarding the characteristics of the pseudowire pair that belongs to the same endpoint. The most important of these is the no suppress-standby-signaling configuration of the endpoint, which makes the spoke PE signal the standby status of the pseudowire (which loses the precedence comparison) to the peering PE router using the LDP signaling process. (The process of the LDP signaling of the primary/backup pseudowire is described later in this chapter). Figure 15.5 illustrates an example of configuring redundant pseudowires in a VPLS service.

The basic rules of the provisioning of the primary/backup pseudowires in VPLS service are as follows:

- The endpoint and the redundant pseudowires and their precedence are defined in the spoke-PE router on a per-VPLS-instance basis. Multiple VPLS instances in the same spoke PE can have different precedences set for their primary/backup pseudowire configurations while sharing the same SDP. Therefore, load balancing with redundancy among VPLS services using multiple SDPs can be achieved.

- The pseudowire with the lower numeric precedence value acts as the primary pseudowire, which is part of the active forwarding topology, unless its corresponding SDP fails. If this happens, the standby pseudowire takes over. When the failure recovers, the system may or may not revert back to the primary pseudowire, depending on the configuration.

- The configuration of the precedence value is preemptive — a value change in the pseudowire configuration takes effect immediately, and the new winner takes over the primary role in real time.

- Only two pseudowires can belong to the same endpoint in the same VPLS instance. Only one of the two pseudowires can have a precedence value of 0.

When configuring the primary pseudowire from CLI, the value 0 cannot be assigned through the CLI, and the keyword `primary` is used to configure the primary pseudowire, which will automatically set the pseudowire's precedence value of 0. It is not mandatory to have a pseudowire with a precedence value of 0; the two pseudowires can have different values ranging from 1 through 4. If both pseudowires have the save value, the one provisioned first is the most preferred forwarding path.

Figure 15.5 Spoke-PE Router Dual-Homing Configuration Example

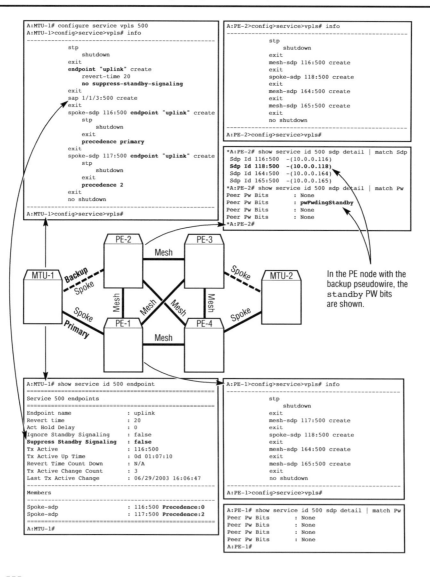

Pseudowire Status Bit

In Chapter 14, the pseudowire signaling status bits are discussed in the case of pseudowire redundancy used in VLL service. When using pseudowire redundancy in VPLS service, the pseudowire status bits — pseudowire forwarding standby — are also used to signal the active/standby status of the redundant pseudowire to the remote PE router. The meaning of the PW status bits values remains the same. Also, during the active forwarding object selection, both the case of VLL and the case of VPLS, the selection takes into account the local operational state of the pseudowires and the remote operational state of the pseudowires as signaled by the remote PE in the status TLV. It also takes into account the remote forwarding status bit (active/standby) in the selection criteria. This part is the same in both VPLS and VLL. *What is different between the use of PW status bits in these two scenarios (VLL and VPLS) is the condition that causes the local PE to set the forwarding status bit to standby value, and the behavior of the remote PE routers upon receiving the standby status bit.*

As mentioned previously, in a VLL service, the (local) pseudowire status bit reflects the forwarding state of the SAP. If the SAP is dual-homed and enters the standby state, then the local PE sets this bit to standby. If the SAP is not dual-homed, it will never enter the standby state, and the forwarding status bit is left to the default value of active. *The remote PE will not block forwarding over a PW that signaled standby if this is the only PW that is available.* This is to allow additional resilience through the Inter-Chassis Backup (ICB) pseudowire that may be configured in the remote PE. However, such a pseudowire will not be selected for forwarding if there is another PW that signaled active and that is operationally **up** locally and remotely. Also, the local PE will forward a packet received on a PW that is currently signaling standby to the local SAP or ICB PW.

In a VPLS service, the PW status bit reflects the forwarding state of the pseudowires themselves as per the result of the transmit PW selection algorithm. The SAP state has no impact on the state of the pseudowire because the use of pseudowire redundancy is meant for MTU dual-homing. In this case, the MTU node sets the forwarding status bit to standby to let the remote PE know which pseudowires are blocked locally. *The MTU node will always discard a packet received on the standby pseudowire.* However, the remote PE has a configuration option to select whether to flood packets over a PW that signaled standby. If the PE is configured to block flooding, then the PW that signaled standby will be put in the **down** state locally. This option provides the local PE with a trade-off between saving bandwidth and improving time to activate the standby PW when the MTU activates it at a later time.

Standby PW Signaling — PW-Forwarding-Standby

The dual-homed spoke-PE router is aware of the primary/backup pseudowire because of the manual configuration: The two pseudowires belonging to the same endpoint are the primary/backup pair, and based on the precedence rule, only one of these pseudowires can be active at any time. If the primary pseudowire fails or the precedence is bumped by configuration changes, a *switchover* is triggered, and the original backup pseudowire in standby state becomes active. Switching over or reverting back to a redundant pseudowire is a forwarding infrastructure change, which must be signaled to the peering PE routers. Figure 15.6 illustrates the process of switching over to redundant pseudowires.

Figure 15.6 Signaling the Pseudowire Standby Status for a Pseudowire Switchover

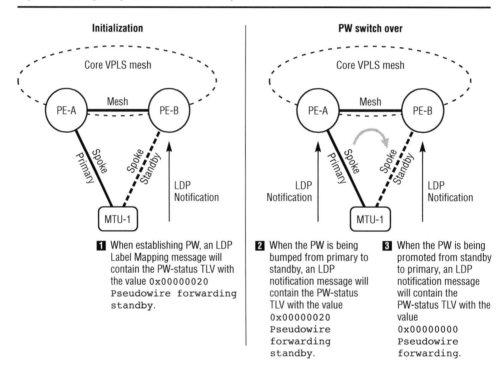

The far-end PE router (spoke) must be able to notify the *home* PE (hub) routers (the PE routers in the core tier) about the change in the status of the pseudowire

(from active to standby or vice versa). This requirement is achieved by introducing a new pseudowire status code of 0x00000020, which means "Pseudowire Forwarding Standby" in the PW-Status TLV in the LDP signaling messages. When a standby pseudowire is initially configured as standby (less preferred), and signaled from the MTU to the home PE router, the T-LDP Label Mapping message carries the PW-Status TLV with the standby flag set. If a pseudowire becomes standby because it is bumped by a more preferred pseudowire, the standby flag within the PW-Status TLV is signaled to the peering home PE router by an LDP Notification message. Upon receiving the PW-Status TLV from the MTU with the standby flag set, the PE router understands that this pseudowire should not be included in the active forwarding topology (in the same way it is blocked by STP). Then, by default, it does not forward traffic over the pseudowire, since it is not necessary.

Note: In some vendor implementations, the PE router puts the pseudowire into the operational down state upon receiving the PW-Forwarding-Standby flag. The ALSRP router implementation keeps the pseudowire operationally up, with the pseudowire status flag set, so the VPLS instance does not forward traffic over the pseudowire.

Ignoring Standby Pseudowire Signaling

The PE's behavior of excluding the standby pseudowire from the active forwarding topology and not sending the traffic over it can be modified by explicitly configuring Ignore-Standby-Signaling in the pseudowire facing the dual-homed MTU router. With this configuration, the hub PE router ignores the standby status signaled in the LDP messages, treats the standby pseudowire as a regular pseudowire in the active forwarding topology, and sends traffic over the standby pseudowire to the dual-homed MTU router. Figure 15.7 illustrates a configuration example and the use of the Ignore-Standby-Signaling.

As mentioned previously, the PW-Forwarding-Standby flag in the PW-Status TLV is used to let the peering PE router know that this pseudowire is a standby pseudowire which is not in the active forwarding topology, so that potential forwarding loops can be eliminated. However, if the receiving PE router ignores the PW-Forwarding-Standby flag, forwarding loops are *not* created. This configuration does not cause a forwarding loop. Although the PE router can be configured to ignore the standby status of a particular pseudowire, the peering dual-homed MTU router still understands that this is a standby pseudowire and discards the traffic at the ingress of the pseudowire. Provided that the MTU understands that the two pseudowires belong to the same endpoint and accept and forward traffic only over one pseudowire at a time, no forwarding loop is formed. Also, the MTU router does not learn any MAC addresses from the standby pseudowire because the standby pseudowire is eliminated from the active forwarding topology.

Figure 15.7 Ignore-Standby-Signaling in Home PE Router(s)

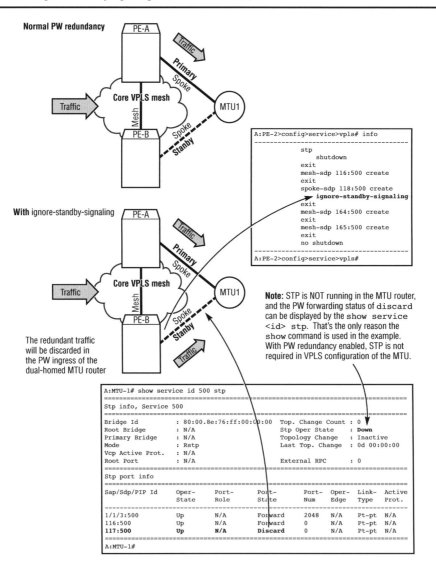

This discussion leads to the question, "When would we be willing to waste bandwidth by sending traffic to the peer and then discarding it?" The answer is, "when very quick traffic convergence is required during a switchover." Consider a switchover scenario in which the MTU router starts to use the original standby pseudowire to forward traffic. If the traffic is present in the ingress of the MTU's standby pseudowire and was discarded before the switchover, the MTU router needs to stop discarding the frames; this can happen instantly after the switchover. Otherwise (without the `Ignore-Standby-Signal` configuration), the PE router that has the newly active pseudowire starts to send traffic after the LDP signaling process clears the standby process; it may take longer for the MTU to receive the traffic.

This is particularly important in networks providing Broadcast Television (BTV) services using VPLS. In most BTV networks, significantly improving the traffic convergence with the price of wasting bandwidth by sending traffic to redundant links is acceptable, and often highly desirable. In order to provide cable TV or air-broadcast TV user experiences like instant channel changing, compromising bandwidth efficiency to gain convergence speed is necessary.

15.4 Using MAC-Flush to Avoid Blackholes

The previous section introduced the basic architecture of pseudowire redundancy in VPLS services. Chapter 14 introduced the pseudowire redundancy implementation on all point-to-point services. Point-to-point service has only one forwarding path for a customer data flow — from one site to another. No address learning or forwarding decisions need to be made. As a multipoint-to-multipoint Layer 2 bridging service, the VPLS service instance learns customer MAC addresses and makes forwarding decisions based on the FDB. Therefore, when using pseudowire redundancy in VPLS services, the impact on the learning and forwarding activities of VPLS must be considered.

Understanding MAC-Flush

VPLS provides transparent bridging services. From the end-user perspective, networks that provide VPLS services are like Ethernet switches, forwarding bridged Ethernet frames between geographically separated sites. Ethernet transparent bridging is performed in the Virtual Switching Instance (VSI) of each VPLS PE router, just like an Ethernet switch performs bridging among its bridge ports, as follows:

1. Learn the source MAC address of the customer frame, and add it to the FDB of the VSI (or refresh the entry).

2. Forward the frame based on the destination MAC address by finding matching entries in the FDB.

3. Flood broadcast, unknown unicast, and multicast (BUM) traffic to all Bridge Ports outside the split-horizon group.

The data frame forwarding decision (to which pseudowire or SAP, unicast; or replicate and multicast/flood) is made by searching for matching entries in the FDB. The content of the FDB is built by learning the traffic source MAC addresses. Each entry contains a MAC address associated with the Bridge Port where it was learned. (VLAN information may also be present in the FDB, but it is not relevant for this discussion.) Each entry in the FDB has an age timer. If the entry is not refreshed by receiving frames with the same source MAC address from the same source Bridge Port (in VPLS, the same SAP or pseudowire), the MAC address in the FDB is removed (or *flushed*), and the traffic is flooded as unknown destination traffic. If traffic with the same MAC address appears from a different Bridge Port (the source of the traffic moved from one location to another), the entry is overwritten by associating the new location (Bridge Port) with the MAC address. This is one of the interesting characteristics of a basic Ethernet bridging network: *The information required to decide where to forward a traffic flow is provided by learning the source MAC address of the returning traffic.*

For a traffic flow from logical point A to logical point B, all frames have a source MAC address of A and a destination MAC address of B. The destination address B must be present in the FDB so that the bridge (Ethernet switch, or VSI — a VPLS instance) can forward (unicast) the traffic to its destination (otherwise the traffic is flooded). Therefore, point B must send traffic to point A, because that is the only way the bridge learns the location of point B. If the traffic flow between points A and B is consistent and the network is stable (no failures, no location moves), there are no problems. The bridge always knows where A is located by the traffic flow A → B and always knows where B is located by the returning traffic flow B → A; therefore, the VSI forwards the bidirectional traffic between A and B to its correct destinations. If there are changes in a network, for example, the location of one end of the traffic moves or the link connecting the switches fails, the FDB content may no longer be correct from the perspective of each VSI. Figure 15.8 illustrates a scenario in which customer traffic is blackholed (discarded in the service network) because the FDB of the service instance is not up-to-date.

Figure 15.8 Traffic Blackhole Due to Out-of-Date FDB Content

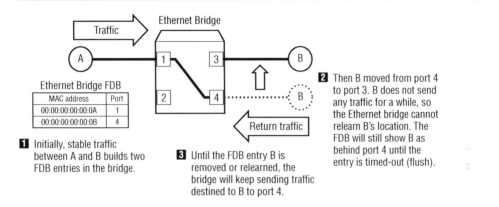

1 Initially, stable traffic between A and B builds two FDB entries in the bridge.

2 Then B moved from port 4 to port 3. B does not send any traffic for a while, so the Ethernet bridge cannot relearn B's location. The FDB will still show B as behind port 4 until the entry is timed-out (flush).

3 Until the FDB entry B is removed or relearned, the bridge will keep sending traffic destined to B to port 4.

For topology changes like the one presented in Figure 15.8, the traffic pattern between points A and B affects the network convergence:

- If the traffic is multicast, the multicast MAC addresses never appear in the FDB because no Ethernet frames have multicast MAC addresses as the source MAC addresses. The switch floods the traffic to all ports. Therefore, the service outage for multicast traffic in the VPLS service due to the topology change is minimal.

- If the traffic is unicast and symmetric (both A and B send traffic to each other constantly), the switch quickly relearns B's MAC address from the returning traffic and therefore sends the traffic flow A → B to the new location of B as soon as B's MAC address is relearned.

- If the traffic is unicast but asymmetric (A constantly sends traffic to B, but B does not send much traffic to A), provided B is not sending traffic, the FDB of the bridge is not updated. Therefore, traffic from A to B does not reach the correct new destination until the original FDB entry times out, and the traffic destined to B is flooded to all bridge ports. This can take a significant amount of time. During this time, the traffic from A to B is blackholed, causing a service outage, and the bandwidth is wasted.

Figure 15.8 illustrates only a small network with one bridge and four ports, which is a simple logical representation of what may happen in a bridged Ethernet network. Imagine that A and B are two geographically separated LAN switches belonging to a large corporation, and the Ethernet bridge is actually a VPLS service provided by a global service provider. It is quite possible that some of the customer traffic flows are asymmetric and could have longer outages during a network forwarding topology change.

If relearning a MAC address takes too long owing to the lack of returning traffic, it is beneficial to speed up the MAC unlearning process instead of waiting for the returning frames or for the MAC entry to time out. Any kind of MAC-flush mechanism can improve the convergence of unicast traffic in a network topology change, especially if the traffic pattern is asymmetric.

To reduce the traffic outage, FDB entry B must be flushed sooner. One way to do this is to shorten the age of the entries in the FDB — the sooner the MAC entry times out, the faster the bridge starts to flood the traffic to all ports so that site B receives traffic sooner in its new location. However, this solution causes more frequent flooding in the network, which is not suitable for a scaled network. This is because more intermittent traffic is flooded instead of forwarded to its destination. A more efficient mechanism is desired so that a MAC-flush is triggered immediately after a forwarding topology change is detected.

In STP, the Topology Change Notification (TCN) is such a mechanism: As soon as a topology change is detected by a switch participating in STP, the switch propagates the TCN to other switches by flooding BPDUs. This ensures that the entire network is aware of the topology change, and therefore all FDBs are flushed sooner than the age timer for the entries. (Appendix A contains a detailed discussion of TCN propagation.)

In a VPLS solution, a similar mechanism propagates topology change information and flushes the FDB of each PE router in the corresponding VSI. Instead of propagating STP BPDUs, an LDP Address Withdraw message is used. The origination and propagation of the different types of MAC-flush messages and the applicable scenarios are presented in detail in the following sections.

LDP Address Withdraw Messages — The MAC-Flush of VPLS

In a VPLS network, the PE routers use T-LDP to signal pseudowire-related information. In particular, the LDP Address Withdraw message signals MAC-flush messages among the PE routers participating in VPLS to flush the FDBs of the VPLS instance(s) when necessary. It works in a similar (but not exactly the same) manner as the use of TCNs in STP to flush the FDBs of Ethernet switches. The purpose of using an LDP Address Withdraw message to initiate the MAC-flush action in the VPLS instance(s) for forwarding topology changes is to improve the convergence time and to reduce the amount of traffic being blackholed.

The VPLS service is used mostly by service providers and large enterprise users to deploy scaled, geographically separated Layer 2 Ethernet bridged networks. The FDB of a VSI can be significantly larger than the MAC table of a regular Ethernet switch, although they perform a similar bridging function: Each Bridge Port in the VSI (SAP, spoke-pseudowire, or group of mesh-pseudowires) may be associated with hundreds, thousands, or more customer MAC addresses. Therefore, it is important to implement a fault-triggered MAC-flush mechanism for all possible failure scenarios, to minimize the amount of blackholed traffic and to improve convergence performance. The MAC-flush options in VPLS are more complicated than in a regular bridged Ethernet LAN, in which only the TCN is sent when a topology change affects the active forwarding infrastructure.

There are basically two types of MAC-flushes in a VPLS network: `flush-all-from-me` and `flush-all-but-me`. They are each triggered by different forwarding topology change events, and they are also propagated differently through the core VPLS network. Briefly, a `flush-all-from-me` message should be used to indicate a local failure (a SAP or spoke-pseudowire is down, similar to an `edge port down` in an Ethernet network). The sending router uses this message to tell peering PE routers to unlearn the MAC addresses from the sending router, so that they do not blackhole the traffic with destination MAC addresses learned behind the failed Bridge Port.

On the other hand, `flush-all-but-me` is much like the TCN in STP: The newly active core-facing Bridge Port uses it to announce a forwarding infrastructure change. A typical scenario is that when a spoke-pseudowire formally blocked by the STP is put into the forwarding state (or unblocked), a `flush-all-but-me` message is sent to the peering PE router to which the pseudowire is connected.

Table 15.1 compares the two different types of MAC-flush.

Table 15.1 flush-all-from-me versus flush-all-but-me

	flush-all-from-me	flush-all-but-me
Trigger scenario	An edge-facing Bridge Port goes down (failure).	A core-facing Bridge Port changes to the actively forwarding state.
LDP message and TLV	An Address Withdraw message (0x301) containing a vendor-specific TLV (0x3E00) (Alcatel-Lucent proprietary).	An Address Withdraw message (0x301) containing a MAC-list TLV (0x404) (RFC compliant).
Configuration	The VPLS instance requires explicit configuration of `send-flush-on-failure` for a normal SAP/PW to trigger the MAC-flush when it goes down. When the SAP is part of MC-LAG or MAC-Ring and goes to standby, it triggers the MAC-flush regardless of the `send-flush-on-failure` configuration.	No explicit configuration. If STP is used (with mVPLS or within the VPLS), or if pseudowire redundancy is configured, a flush is sent when a spoke-pseudowire is unblocked.
Flush action upon receipt of the message	The receiving router unlearns all MAC addresses learned from the originating router in the VSI.	The receiving router unlearns all MAC addresses *except* the ones learned from the originating router in the VSI.
Propagation	When `propagate-mac-flush` is configured in the VSI, the receiving router propagates the message to other peering routers participating in the same VPLS.	When `propagate-mac-flush` is configured in the VSI, the receiving router propagates the message to other peering routers participating in the same VPLS.

Note: Both `flush-all-from-me` and `flush-all-but-me` messages trigger a flush of only the dynamically learned MAC addresses. Static MAC addresses defined under a pseudowire (spoke or mesh) and OAM-populated MAC addresses are not flushed by MAC-flush messages.

Figure 15.9 illustrates the content of the two types of MAC-flush messages.

Figure 15.9   LDP Address Withdraw Message with an Address-List TLV

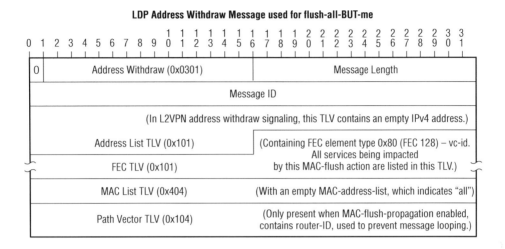

LDP Address Withdraw Message used for flush-all-BUT-me

LDP Address Withdraw Message used for flush-all-FROM-me

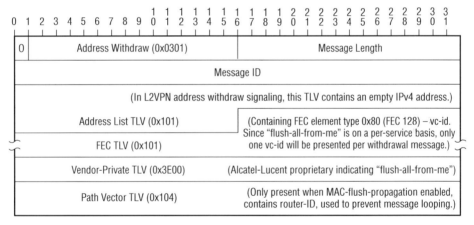

Note: Although an RFC-defined LDP Address Withdraw message allows the MAC-list TLV to contain an explicit list of MAC addresses, most vendors (including Alcatel-Lucent) choose to use an *empty list* in the MAC-flush message. The main reason for this is to reduce the size of the LDP MAC-flush message. Otherwise, in a scaled network (where VPLS is usually used), the MAC-list TLV may contain thousands or more MAC addresses. Composing, sending, processing, and propagating such messages consumes a lot of resources (for example, CPU, memory, and bandwidth). It is more efficient to use an empty list representing `flush-all`.

flush-all-from-me

If a PE router has a local SAP failure (a port goes down or the SAP is administratively shut down) or a spoke-pseudowire failure (the SDP is down, the pseudowire is disabled, or a signaling failure puts the pseudowire administratively down), and `send-flush-on-failure` is explicitly enabled (or the SAP is part of the MC-LAG) in the VPLS instance, the router sends out a `flush-all-from-me` LDP Address Withdraw message through the pseudowires to all peering PE routers in that VPLS. When the peering routers receive this message, they immediately unlearn all MAC addresses associated with the pseudowire from which the MAC-flush is received. [The vc-id is listed in the FEC element (0x80) of the FEC-TLV.]

> **Warning:** `flush-all-from-me` is an Alcatel-Lucent proprietary feature because it uses a vendor-specific TLV (0x3E00). Routers that do not recognize this message ignore its content upon receiving it and do not flush the MAC addresses learned from the originator.

Figure 15.10 demonstrates the configuration of `flush-all-from-me` and the scenarios in which a MAC-flush is sent.

When `send-flush-on-failure` is enabled in a VSI of a router, LDP Address Withdraw messages containing `flush-all-from-me` are triggered by any of the following events:

- **Local SAP Failure** — The SAP is administratively shut down or operationally down owing to a physical failure. The router sends a `flush-all-from-me` message to all peering PE routers through the pseudowires (spoke and mesh).

- **Spoke-Pseudowire Failure** — If a router detects a spoke-pseudowire failure (the pseudowire goes down for any reason), it sends a `flush-all-from-me` message to all peering routers through the pseudowires, including the far-end PE router of the failed spoke-pseudowire (providing the T-LDP session to that router is still operationally up).

- **MAC-Flush Propagation** — If a router has `propagate-mac-flush` enabled in its VSI and receives a `flush-all-from-me` message from one of the pseudowires, it propagates the MAC-flush to other pseudowires, respecting the Split-Horizon rule. (Propagation is discussed later in this chapter.)

Figure 15.10 flush-all-from-me — send-flush-on-failure

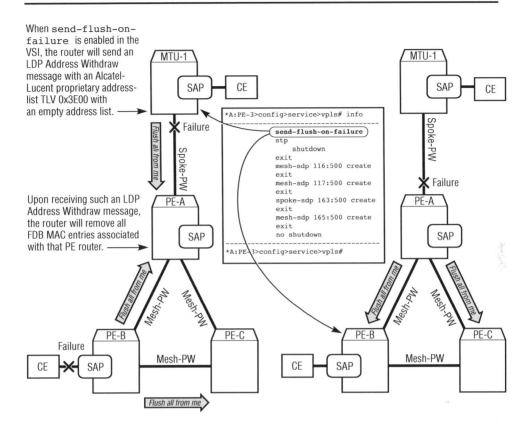

When `send-flush-on-failure` is enabled in the VSI, the router will send an LDP Address Withdraw message with an Alcatel-Lucent proprietary address-list TLV 0x3E00 with an empty address list. →

Upon receiving such an LDP Address Withdraw message, the router will remove all FDB MAC entries associated with that PE router. →

```
*A:PE-3>config>service>vpls# info
----------------------------------------
        send-flush-on-failure
        stp
                shutdown
        exit
        mesh-sdp 116:500 create
        exit
        mesh-sdp 117:500 create
        exit
        spoke-sdp 163:500 create
        exit
        mesh-sdp 165:500 create
        exit
        no shutdown
----------------------------------------
*A:PE-3>config>service>vpls#
```

flush-all-but-me

A VPLS network is often deployed in a hierarchical fashion with the use of spoke-pseudowires: either connecting the remote site MTU routers to the PE routers in the VPLS mesh or connecting several VPLS meshes. Because spoke-pseudowires do not obey the Split-Horizon rule and relay traffic among each other, redundant spoke-pseudowires connected to the same VPLS mesh may cause forwarding loops. (Refer to Chapter 12 for a detailed discussion regarding H-VPLS and spoke-pseudowire.)

If peering redundancy (spoke-pseudowire) is desired, a loop-prevention mechanism must be deployed to protect the forwarding infrastructure. Two loop-prevention mechanisms can be used in VPLS: primary/backup pseudowire redundancy or STP. Both methods block redundant forwarding path(s) to ensure that only one forwarding path between any two points of a network is active.

If a failure or a manual switchover occurs in the current active forwarding path, the blocked redundant forwarding path is unblocked and takes over the forwarding role. This switchover changes the forwarding infrastructure of the entire VPLS network, and the FDBs of other routers may no longer be correct. Therefore, the router to which the newly active spoke-pseudowire belongs sends a `flush-all-but-me` message to its peering router, to flush the FDB of the peering router. After the forwarding topology change, the only valid entries are the ones learned from the newly active pseudowire; therefore the MAC-flush used here is `flush-all-but-me`. Upon receiving this MAC-flush message, the router unlearns all MAC entries in the corresponding VSI, except the ones associated with the newly active spoke-pseudowire from which the MAC-flush message is received. This is very similar to the scenario in which the STP unblocks a switch port because of a network failure, which triggers a TCN flood through the entire network.

When a new forwarding object joins the active forwarding topology, the current forwarding infrastructure is no longer valid, so a MAC-flush must occur so that traffic is flooded and the MAC addresses are relearned. In a VPLS network, this happens through the `flush-all-but-me` LDP Address Withdraw message. Figure 15.11 illustrates the two scenarios in which a `flush-all-but-me` message should be sent because of changes to the forwarding infrastructure.

LDP Address Withdraw messages containing `flush-all-but-me` are triggered by any of the following events:

- **Pseudowire Redundancy Switchover** — The router sends a `flush-all-but-me` message to the peering router through the newly active spoke-pseudowire.

- **Spoke-Pseudowire Unblocked by STP** — If the mVPLS or the STP instances in the VSI decide to add a previously blocked spoke-pseudowire to the active forwarding topology (transition from the blocked state to the forwarding state), the router that makes the transition sends a `flush-all-but-me` message to the peering router over the newly active spoke-pseudowire.

- **MAC-Flush Propagation** — When a router has `propagate-mac-flush` enabled in its VSI and receives a `flush-all-but-me` message from one of the pseudowires, it propagates the MAC-flush to other pseudowires, respecting the Split-Horizon rule.

Figure 15.11 flush-all-but-me — Forwarding Infrastructure Changes

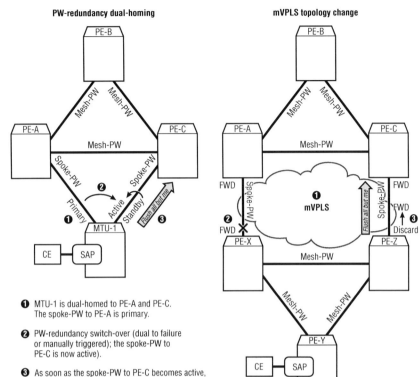

PW-redundancy dual-homing

mVPLS topology change

❶ MTU-1 is dual-homed to PE-A and PE-C. The spoke-PW to PE-A is primary.

❷ PW-redundancy switch-over (dual to failure or manually triggered); the spoke-PW to PE-C is now active).

❸ As soon as the spoke-PW to PE-C becomes active, the MTU-1 will send the flush-all-but-me over the new active PW to PE-C.

❶ mVPLS is configured to manage the redundant spoke-PW between VPLS mesh ABC and XYZ. After initial STP convergence, the spoke-PW in PE-Z to PE-C is blocked.

❷ For some reason, the spoke-PW between PE-X and PE-A fails (or preference is lowered manually); it's in down or discard status.

❸ The mVPLS will now unblock the spoke-PW in PE-Z facing PE-C, and change the port to active. Meanwhile, PE-Z is sending the flush-all-but-me to PE-C to flush its FDB.

No configuration is required for flush-all-but-me. Providing that STP is enabled (with mVPLS, or internal to the VSI) or pseudowire redundancy is configured, if a newly active spoke-pseudowire is added to the active forwarding topology, a flush-all-but-me message is sent through the pseudowire to the peering router.

The flush-all-but-me LDP message uses an RFC-defined MAC-List TLV (type 0x404), which means that it is possible to interoperate this feature with the VPLS solutions of multiple vendors, providing that MAC-flush with an LDP Address Withdraw message is supported.

Propagating a MAC-Flush Message

The previous section introduced two types of LDP MAC-flush messages used to notify the peering PE router to unlearn the corresponding MAC addresses in the VSI FDB. Certain events (for example, SAP failure, STP unblocking a spoke-pseudowire) trigger certain MAC-flush messages to be sent to the peering PE router. The receiving router flushes certain FDB entries accordingly. The next question is whether or not the PE router should let adjacent routers know about the forwarding topology changes. In other words, should the receiving router not only process the MAC-flush message, but also propagate it further to other PE routers in the network? The answer is not simply yes or no. It depends on the types of MAC-flush, the topology of the network, and the network design decisions. That is why, in the ALSRP, MAC-flush propagation is configurable on a per-VPLS instance basis.

Once propagate-mac-flush is enabled in a VPLS instance, the router performs the following tasks upon receiving a MAC-flush message from a peering router:

1. It flushes the VSI's FDB according to the type of MAC-flush (*all-from-sender* or *all-except-sender*).

2. It propagates the MAC-flush message over all pseudowires to other PE routers, respecting the Split-Horizon rule. (A MAC-flush message received from one mesh-pseudowire is not propagated over other mesh-pseudowires. A MAC-flush message received from one spoke-pseudowire is not propagated over other spoke-pseudowires belonging to the same split-horizon group.)

3. When propagate-mac-flush is enabled in a VSI on a router, any LDP MAC-flush message generated for the VSI from that router has a Path Vector TLV object appended to the message, regardless of whether the message is a triggered MAC-flush (originated locally in the router) or a propagation of a received message (originated by other routers, and propagated).

> ### Are Pseudowires in the Standby or Discard States Involved in MAC-Flush Propagation?
>
> Yes. LDP MAC-flush is a control signaling process. When a pseudowire is put into the standby state by the pseudowire redundancy configuration or when a pseudowire is blocked by STP and stays in the discard state, if it is eligible for MAC-flush propagation (but not in the same split-horizon group with the pseudowire from which the MAC-flush is received), the MAC-flush is propagated over the pseudowire. If a router receives a MAC-flush from a peering PE router over a pseudowire that is in the standby or discard state, it still flushes the FDB in its VSI accordingly.

Path Vector TLV (0x104)

The Path Vector TLV (0x104) was originally used along with the Hop Count TLV (0x103) in the LDP Label Request and Label Mapping messages to prevent loops in MPLS cell mode networks. The Path Vector TLV works in a manner similar to the use of the AS_PATH attributes that BGP uses to prevent routing loops. If an MPLS router receives an LDP message containing a Path Vector TLV, it appends its MPLS router-id to the path-vector list of the TLV before it forwards it to other routers. If an MPLS router receives a message with its own router-id present in the path-vector list, it considers that there is a loop in the message forwarding path, discards the message, and sends an LDP notification message indicating loop detected back to the source of the message.

The Path Vector TLV is also used (but not with the Hop Count TLV) in the same manner in the LDP Address Withdraw message for VPLS MAC-flush signaling: It checks its own router-id in the ingress message (if present, it claims a loop is detected) and appends its router-id to the path-vector list of the outgoing messages.

Scenario A: Propagation of flush-all-from-me Messages

When a SAP or spoke-pseudowire locally connected to a router fails, the router uses the flush-all-from-me LDP message to tell other peer routers that it has located a failure and that the MAC addresses behind it are no longer valid, so they should be discarded. Since the flush is *all-from-me*, the receiving routers unlearn all MAC addresses associated with the pseudowire that receives the message. Each time a flush-all-from-me message is propagated from one router to another, the concept of *me* changes — the receiving routers consider the *me* to be the propagator, not the original generator. Therefore, it is important to control the scope of the propagation. Figure 15.12 illustrates `flush-all-from-me` propagation behavior in a VPLS network.

Figure 15.12 flush-all-from-me Propagation Example

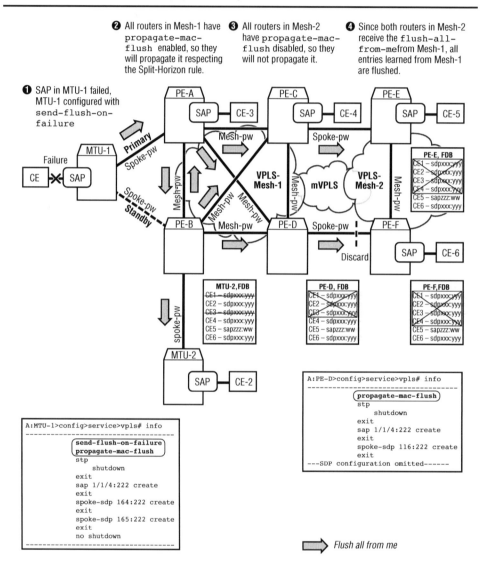

Figure 15.12 illustrates an example of a hierarchical VPLS network: Two VPLS meshes are connected by a pair of spoke-pseudowires, and mVPLS is used with RSTP to ensure that only one spoke-pseudowire is in the forwarding state at any

time. MTU-1 is dual-homed with PE-A and PE-B using pseudowire redundancy. This H-VPLS network is used as a typical topology in all of the scenarios for the MAC-flush propagation discussions in this book.

The first scenario has `propagate-mac-flush` enabled in MTU-1 and in all PE routers in VPLS Mesh 1, but not in VPLS Mesh 2. MTU-1 also has `send-flush-on-failure` enabled in the VPLS, so if the SAP connected to the CE1 fails, MTU-1 generates a `flush-all-from-me` message and sends it over the active spoke-pseudowire to notify the remote PE routers (in this case, PE-A) to unlearn all the MAC addresses from MTU-1 (or CE-1). As the MAC-flush is propagated, you can see the following:

1. Upon receiving the `flush-all-from-me` message from MTU-1, Router PE-A flushes all FDB entries learned from MTU-1 and propagates the MAC-flush to all mesh-pseudowires. PE-A propagates the MAC-flush to PE-B, PE-C, and PE-D. Then PE-B, PE-C, and PE-D propagate the MAC-flush further to the core network. Upon receiving the MAC-flush from PE-B, MTU-2 flushes FDB entries learned from PE-B (CE-1 and CE-3). Because MTU-1 learned CE-2 from the local SAP and learned CE-4, CE-5, and CE-6 from PE-C, these entries are not flushed. Because PE-A also receives the propagated flush from PE-B, it also removes entries learned from PE-B, and PE-B performs a similar action. The result is that PE-A unlearns CE-1 and CE-2, and PE-B unlearns CE-1 and CE-3.

2. Next, Router PE-D receives a `flush-all-from-me` message from both PE-A and PE-B, so it flushes FDB entries learned from both routers (CE-1, CE-2, and CE-3). PE-C behaves similarly, flushing all entries learned from PE-A and PE-B. After the flush, PE-C and PE-D propagate the flush to VPLS Mesh 2.

3. Routers PE-E and PE-F both receive `flush-all-from-me` messages from peering routers in VPLS Mesh 1. The result is that all MAC entries learned from VPLS Mesh 1 (CE-1, CE-2, CE-3, and CE-4) are removed from the FDB of both routers. Because VPLS Mesh 2 does not have propagation enabled in its VPLS, no further propagation is performed.

The conclusion to draw from the propagation sequences is that *the further the* `flush-all-from-me` *message propagates, the more MAC addresses are flushed.* This is especially important in an H-VPLS design where many MAC addresses are learned from spoke-pseudowires (the pseudowire between Mesh 1 and Mesh 2 in Figure 15.12). The propagation of `flush-all-from-me` signifies the range of MAC addresses involved. When MTU-1 sends the flush, it means *flush everything learned from MTU-1*, but once the flush is propagated to VPLS Mesh 2, it means *flush everything learned from VPLS Mesh 1.* The more MAC addresses that are flushed, the more traffic is flooded into the network as unknown unicast traffic.

Is the benefit of speeding up the convergence of asymmetric unicast traffic by using end-to-end propagation of `flush-all-from-me` messages worth the price of causing significant traffic flooding in all other routers in the network? This is a network design issue that depends on many perspectives, as follows:

- **Traffic Distribution** — How much traffic (bandwidth or percentage) is behind MTU-1? If the entire service is widely distributed, the convergence gained from propagating a SAP failure in MTU-1 is not very significant. `flush-all-from-me` should be enabled without propagation, so that PE-A or PE-B can quickly unlearn CE-1. It is appropriate to enable `flush-all-from-me` with a very limited scope of propagation. If the CE-1 behind MTU-1 is actually the hub-site of a company's headquarters, which concentrates 80 percent of the traffic and MAC addresses, propagating a `flush-all-from-me` message end-to-end may greatly improve the network convergence after a topology change.

- **Nature of the Traffic** — Is most of the traffic in the service multicast or unicast? Symmetric or asymmetric? The MAC-flush mechanism benefits only unicast traffic, and asymmetric unicast traffic the most. If the VPLS customer traffic flows are mostly symmetric or multicast, turning MAC-flush on or enabling flush propagation still causes flooding, and does not provide much benefit.

- **Performance Requirement versus Cost** — Does the customer pay more attention to the network convergence speed or to the stability of the network and economical use of bandwidth? If the customer is more concerned with bandwidth consumption, features such as MAC-flush or flush propagation may cause flooding and therefore should not be used in the service.

- **Network Management Trackability** — The need to know what is configured where all the time. As a general best practice, it is beneficial to keep the network configuration as consistent as possible, particularly in a scaled network with many network elements. From that standpoint, if there is no significant performance gain, the scope of MAC-flush propagation should be as limited as possible. This is because MAC-flush requires explicit configuration, and it is much harder to remember things like "In the network, 23 routers are participating in VPLS 100, and 14 of them have `propagate-mac-flush` enabled, and they are: ...," than "In the network, `propagate-mac-flush` is configured only on PE routers that are dual-homed by MTUs."

Scenario B: Propagation of flush-all-but-me Messages

A `flush-all-but-me` message indicates a network forwarding infrastructure change (most likely in the core). Based on its nature, the generation of `flush-all-but-me` messages cannot be disabled in the VPLS configuration. However, whether or not to propagate the flush can be controlled. Figure 15.13 illustrates the behavior of `flush-all-but-me` propagation in a VPLS network.

Figure 15.13   flush-all-but-me Propagation Example

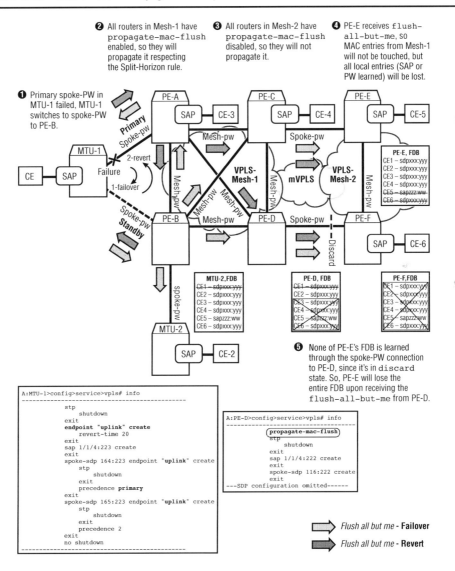

Figure 15.13 uses the same network topology as the one used in Figure 15.12. Propagate-mac-flush is enabled in all PE routers in VPLS Mesh 1, but not in any routers in VPLS Mesh 2. The difference is that in Figure 15.13, the MTU-1 switches over from the primary to the standby spoke-pseudowire. As soon as the switchover occurs, an LDP flush-all-but-me message is sent over the newly active spoke-pseudowire to PE-B. Following is a description of how this MAC-flush is propagated and its effect on each router along the propagation path:

1. First, MTU-1 switches over to the standby pseudowire, which means that the primary pseudowire has failed; therefore, all MAC entries learned from the primary pseudowire are removed.

2. The MAC-flush generated by MTU-1 is sent only to Router PE-B, because the MAC-flush is sent only over the newly active forwarding pseudowire. Because the pseudowire has just come up, nothing is learned from it. When the flush-all-but-me message arrives, Router PE-B flushes all entries from its FDB. Then PE-B propagates the MAC-flush to Routers PE-A, PE-C, and PE-D and to MTU-2.

3. When MTU-2 receives a flush-all-but-me message from PE-B over the spoke-pseudowire, MTU-2 clears all entries not learned from PE-B (CE-2). MTU-2 will likely quickly relearn CE-2 by receiving ingress traffic. When a flush-all-but-me message arrives from PE-B, Routers PE-A, PE-C, and PE-D keep only the entries learned from PE-B (CE-2) and flush all other entries (CE-1, CE-3, CE-4, CE-5, and CE-6). PE-C and PE-D then propagate the flush-all-but-me message to VPLS Mesh 2 over the redundant spoke-pseudowire.

4. In VPLS Mesh 2, when Router PE-E receives the MAC-flush, it clears entries CE-5 and CE-6, which are not learned from PE-C, and keeps all MAC addresses learned from VPLS Mesh 1. In Router PE-F, because the spoke-pseudowire to PE-D is blocked by STP, nothing can be learned from that pseudowire. When the flush-all-but-me message arrives from that pseudowire, all FDB entries in this VPLS are removed.

5. Because MTU-1 has a 20-second revert time configured, when the failure is removed from the network, another switchover occurs 20 seconds after the restore, the newly active (original primary) pseudowire immediately sends a flush-all-but-me message to PE-A, and the message is propagated through VPLS Mesh 1 to VPLS Mesh 2. (The MAC-flush generation and

propagation caused by the revert-back process are represented by the darker arrows in Figure 15.13.)

MAC-Flush and Propagation Recommendations

This section provides recommendations on when to use which type of MAC-flush and whether or not the MAC-flush should be propagated to the service backbone network.

First, we should reiterate that the purpose of enabling MAC-flush and/or MAC-flush propagation is to improve VPLS service convergence for unicast traffic. When a forwarding infrastructure change (such as SAP failure or STP convergence) occurs in VPLS, the FDB in the VPLS service may be affected and may contain incorrect entries. These incorrect entries may cause some unicast traffic to be blackholed in the VPLS service. A MAC-flush clears part (or all) of the FDB in a VPLS service instance so that these incorrect entries are removed. This triggers the VPLS service instance to flood the unicast traffic (because it becomes unknown unicast traffic) and to rebuild the FDB from the current valid forwarding infrastructure. Without a MAC-flush, the VPLS service instance must wait for the incorrect entries to time out or to be overwritten by the new correct entries, which may take significantly longer depending on the nature of the customer traffic.

MAC-flush and propagation do not benefit broadcast- or multicast-based applications such as IPTV, since BUM traffic is always flooded and is not affected by incorrect entries in the FDB. Therefore, enabling MAC-flush or MAC-flush propagation does not benefit the VPLS services if:

- They are used to distribute multicast traffic such as IPTV.

- `discard-unknown` is enabled in the VPLS service.

Under these two conditions, convergence performance is not improved by enabling MAC-flush or MAC-flush propagation (but they do not make the convergence worse).

When deploying a VPLS service network, there are three facts to consider regarding MAC-flush:

- `flush-all-but-me` is not a configurable option. It is part of the built-in VPLS process, and each time an STP convergence occurs in the VPLS service, the corresponding router generates a `flush-all-but-me` message.

- `flush-all-from-me` is a configurable option on a per-VPLS service instance basis. Each PE router participating in the VPLS service can have `send-flush-on-failure` enabled or disabled. By default, it is disabled.

- MAC-flush propagation is a configurable option on a per-VPLS service instance basis, and it is disabled by default. When propagation is enabled in the VPLS service instance of a PE router, the router propagates all MAC-flush messages it receives.

There is no single rule of thumb for MAC-flush and propagation design. Whether to enable or disable `flush-all-from-me` and MAC-flush propagation should be addressed on a case-by-case basis, taking the following factors into consideration:

- The VPLS service topology: flat VPLS full mesh or H-VPLS topology
- The STP configuration and expected behavior
- The requirements for convergence and the characteristics of the customer data traffic
- The distribution of the service entities within each VPLS service instance in each PE router (the VPLS service forwarding topology)

Figure 15.14 illustrates an example of a network in which MAC-flush and MAC-flush propagation are enabled in some of the PE routers.

Figure 15.14   Enabling flush-all-from-me and Mac-flush Propagation

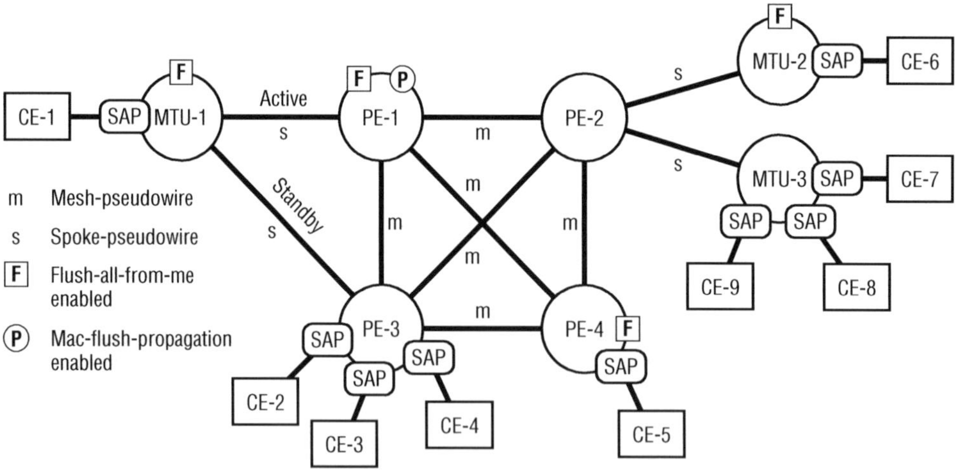

In Figure 15.14, `flush-all-from-me` and MAC-flush propagation are enabled in several VPLS PE and/or MTU routers. Table 15.2 lists the configuration of all PE and MTU routers regarding MAC-flush and its associated considerations. This is a MAC-flush design recommendation only.

Table 15.2 Network Design Recommendation: Enabling or Disabling MAC-Flush and MAC-Flush Propagation

Router	flush-all-from-me	MAC-Flush Propagation
MTU-1, MTU-2	Enabled. Because MTU-1 has only one SAP, enabling flush-all-from-me triggers PE-1 to flush the FDB entries associated with MTU-1 (CE-1) so that traffic behind CE-1 is not blackholed. The same reason applies to MTU-2.	Disabled. MTU-1 does not need to propagate a MAC-flush. If the pseudowire to PE-1 or PE-3 fails, the MTU has no other peering PE router to which to propagate the MAC-flush. The same reason applies to MTU-2.
MTU-3	Disabled. MTU-3 has three SAPs. If flush-all-from-me is enabled, any SAP failure causes MTU-3 to trigger PE-2 to flush its FDB of MAC entries associated with MTU-3, which includes traffic destined to all three CE devices. If traffic flooding is not a concern, this function can be enabled on MTU-3.	Disabled. The same reason as MTU-1 and MTU-2.
PE-1	Enabled. PE-1 has a spoke-pseudowire connected to MTU-1. If the pseudowire fails, PE-1 should ask all other PE routers to flush their FDBs so they flood the traffic for MTU-1 instead of trying to send the traffic to MTU-1 through PE-1.	Enabled. PE-1 may receive a flush-all-from-me message from MTU-1 if MTU-1's SAP fails. PE-1 may also receive a flush-all-but-me message from MTU-1 when the spoke-pseudowire becomes active. Propagating the MAC-flush to other PEs improves the convergence of traffic targeted behind MTU-1.
PE-4	Enabled. Because PE-4 has only one SAP, enabling flush-all-from-me triggers PE-1, PE-2, and PE-3 to flush the FDB entries associated with PE-4's SAP, so that traffic behind PE-4 is not blackholed.	Disabled. PE-4 does not need to propagate a MAC-flush. If PE-1, PE-2, or PE-3 sends a MAC-flush, PE-4 does not need to propagate it because there are no peering PE routers to propagate the MAC-flush further.
PE-2	Disabled. PE-2 has two spoke-pseudowires. flush-all-from-me is disabled for the same reason as MTU-3.	Disabled. If enabled, if the SAP of MTU-2 connected to CE-6 fails and PE-2 propagates the flush-all-from-me message received from MTU-2 to the entire network, all traffic for CE-6, CE-7, CE-8, and CE-9 is flooded. This wastes lots of bandwidth.

(continued)

Table 15.2 Network Design Recommendation: Enabling or Disabling MAC-Flush and MAC-Flush Propagation *(continued)*

Router	flush-all-from-me	MAC-Flush Propagation
PE-3	Disabled. PE-3 has three SAPs. flush-all-from-me is disabled for the same reason as MTU-3.	Disabled. See the explanation for PE-4.

These network design practices are general recommendations. Operators and network designers can create different network designs for different reasons. For example, if the volume of VPLS service traffic is low or if fast convergence is a much bigger concern than reducing unnecessary flooding, both flush-all-from-me and MAC-flush propagation can be enabled in every MTU and PE router to achieve this goal.

Using Block-on-Mesh-Failure to Avoid Blackholes

Block-on-mesh-failure (BOMF) can be used together with pseudowire redundancy in VPLS to avoid traffic blackholes. Consider an H-VPLS network with spoke-MTUs and hub-PE routers with active/standby pseudowires between them. In the case where the hub-PE router with the active spoke-pseudowire lost all its mesh-pseudowires to the VPLS core, the traffic being received from the spoke-MTU device is blackholed. With BOMF, the hub-PE router with the active spoke-pseudowire will bring down the spoke-pseudowire and send an LDP Notification message with pseudowire status code of 0x01 (pseudowire not forwarding) to the spoke-MTU. Therefore, the spoke-MTU will switch to the backup spoke-pseudowire, and the traffic will not be blackholed anymore. Figure 15.15 illustrates how BOMF works.

In the illustration, the MTU-s is dual-homed to PE-rs1 and PE-rs2, and the spoke-pseudowire to PE-rs1 is preferred and active. During a failure, the following events happen (the list numbers correspond to the steps in the figure):

1. There is a failure in PE-rs1, which causes all mesh-pseudowires of VPLS 1 in PE-rs1 to become down.

2. Because PE-rs1 has BOMF enabled in VPLS 1, it brings down the spoke-pseudowire to the MTU-s and then sends an LDP Notification message with pseudowire status 0x01 - pseudowire not forwarding.

3. After MTU-s receives the LDP Notification message, it performs a pseudowire switchover. It blocks the spoke-pseudowire to PE-rs1 and then changes the spoke-pseudowire to PE-rs2 from standby to active. The traffic will take the spoke-pseudowire to PE-rs2 from that on and will not be blackholed.

Figure 15.15   Block-On-Mesh Failure Applicable Scenario

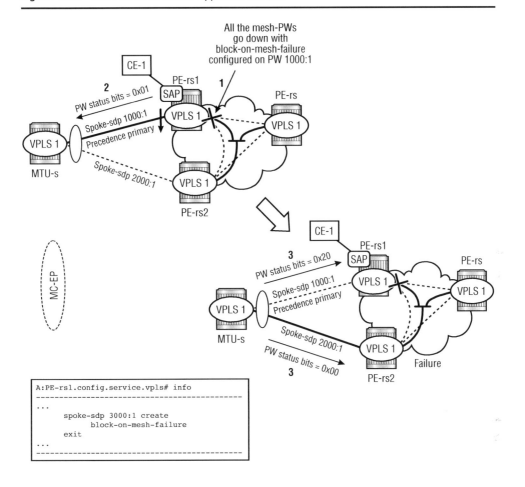

```
A:PE-rsl.config.service.vpls# info
-----------------------------------------------
...
    spoke-sdp 3000:1 create
        block-on-mesh-failure
    exit
...
-----------------------------------------------
```

Summary

Service providers desire maximum service redundancy. For VPLS services in MPLS, the MPLS FRR or secondary LSP can protect the services from failures in a link or a transiting LSR node. However, the end-to-end VPLS service may be affected if a PE router with a service instance fails. This is especially important in an H-VPLS with a hub–spoke topology. If the aggregating hub-PE router fails, all S-PE routers lose their access to the backbone network. Therefore, dual-homing is desired to allow the S-PE router to connect to more than one hub-PE router in an active/standby manner. This provides service redundancy without causing forwarding loops. This is the use of pseudowire redundancy in VPLS services.

When using pseudowire redundancy, the active/standby pseudowires are grouped in the same endpoint in the S-PE router. At any time, there is only one active forwarding object in an endpoint. This guarantees that the active/standby pseudowires do not forward traffic concurrently and cause forwarding loops. Each active/standby spoke-pseudowire has its own preference value to determine the priority of being selected as the active forwarding object.

Each time a network failure causes a switchover among active/standby spoke-pseudowires, the forwarding infrastructure changes and the previously learned MAC addresses in the FDB become invalid. In a bridged Ethernet network, this triggers a TCN to be flooded into the network to speed up the MAC address age-out in the FDB. In the case of VPLS, the role of the TCN is taken by the MAC-flush messaging in LDP. LDP uses an Address Withdraw message containing a MAC-list TLV to notify the peering PE about the forwarding topology change and to request the flush of certain entries in the FDB. There are two types of MAC-flush:

- `flush-all-from-me` — When this option is enabled, every time a PE router has a local SAP or spoke-pseudowire failure, it sends a `flush-all-from-me` message to all other peering PE routers to request the peer to remove all MAC entries associated with this PE router from their FDBs. `flush-all-from-me` is by default disabled, and it is an ALSRP proprietary message.

- `flush-all-but-me` — Each time a PE router with a spoke-pseudowire changes to the active forwarding state (by STP or by pseudowire redundancy election), it sends a `flush-all-but-me` message to the peering PE router over the newly active pseudowire.

Optionally, a MAC-flush message can be propagated by PE routers in the VPLS network. When propagation is enabled in a VPLS service, the PE router propagates received MAC-flush messages over pseudowires to all remote PE routers, obeying the Split-Horizon rule.

Advanced Ethernet VPN Topics

IV

The final section presents advanced Ethernet Layer 2 VPN topics: BGP-AD, PBB, and OAM. BGP auto-discovery simplifies the VPLS service deployment model by automatically discovering member PE routers and establishing pseudowires. Provider Backbone Bridging (PBB) VPLS significantly improves the scalability of VPLS service in extremely large networks. MPLS OAM and VPLS allow operators to monitor the health of the network and locate faults.

VPLS BGP Auto-Discovery

16

BGP-AD for LDP VPLS is a framework for automatically discovering the location of the related service instances in a VPLS, offering an operational model similar to that of an IP VPN.

Chapter Objectives

- Introduce BGP-AD in the VPLS network

- Present BGP-AD architecture and a sample configuration in an LDP-VPLS network

- Discuss the dynamic creation of Service Distribution Paths (SDPs) and pseudowires in a VPLS service using BGP-AD

- Describe a VPLS service with BGP-AD using existing (pre-provisioned) SDPs

- Explain BGP-AD import and export policies and VPLS topology control

There are two implementations of VPLS service: LDP-VPLS (defined in RFC 4762) and BGP-VPLS (defined in RFC 4761). This chapter introduces the Border Gateway Protocol Auto-Discovery (BGP-AD) mechanism used in a Label Distribution Protocol–VPLS (LDP-VPLS) implementation. This mechanism allows carriers to leverage existing network elements and functions, including but not limited to, route reflectors (RR) and BGP policies to control the VPLS topology. BGP-AD automates VPLS membership identification and pseudowire establishment, providing one-touch provisioning for LDP-VPLS. This chapter describes the BGP-AD mechanism in LDP-VPLS in detail.

16.1 VPLS BGP-AD Overview

BGP-AD is an excellent complement to an already established and well deployed LDP VPLS toolset. LDP-VPLS uses Targeted LDP (T-LDP) to signal the pseudowire (mesh or spoke) infrastructure between member PE routers. In the initial LDP-VPLS implementations, the membership information was manually configured for each VPLS Virtual Switching Instance (VSI), in each PE router. There is no need for the PE routers to track the VPLS membership of the neighbor PE routers. The addition of a new VPLS instance in a PE must be reflected in all the PE routers participating in the same VPLS service. Also, the new PE must be configured with the list of participating PEs. Similarly, removal of a member PE router from a VPLS service requires the removal of the related membership information from every related PE. In a scaled network, all these operations can be a burden for the operator. BGP-AD reduces all these provisioning steps for a new VPLS instance to one VPLS membership configured on the local PE. BGP-AD will advertise the membership information between all the participating PEs, automatically saving all the configuration steps. Moreover the use of BGP-AD ensures the reuse of the MP-BGP toolset, already operationalized for IP VPN Services.

16.2 BGP Auto-Discovery for LDP-VPLS

The VPLS control plane must complete several major tasks:

- Automatically discover the VPLS membership (the PE devices) participating in the VPLS service.
- Signal pseudowire infrastructure by setting up and tearing down the pseudowires used for the VSI, indicating status changes for existing pseudowires, and so on.

- Signal MAC-flush information to remote PE routers, similar to sending Topology Change Notifications (TCNs) to other switches in Spanning Tree Protocol (STP).

In the LDP-VPLS solution with BGP-AD, MP-BGP performs only the first task — distributing VPLS membership information across the network, so that PE routers are aware of the other active member PE routers for a VPLS service in which they are participating. The remaining tasks are performed by T-LDP.

MP-BGP Update for VPLS Membership Auto-Discovery

MP-BGP is used for VPLS membership auto-discovery. Before VPLS PE members can be discovered, the BGP connectivity (full mesh or RR equivalent) must be configured in the core network among all PE routers. VPLS membership information is then propagated through the network by routers sending/receiving MP-BGP updates. In order to propagate VPLS membership information, in MP-BGP, a new address family is defined: L2VPN [Address Family Indicator (AFI) = 65], with a Sub Address Family Indicator (SAFI) for VPLS membership information (SAFI = 25). Routers running MP-BPG must support the capabilities of AFI 65 and SAFI 25 in order to exchange VPLS membership information.

> **Note:** BGP-VPLS and LDP-VPLS with BGP-AD are different types of VPLS implementations and cannot be connected to each other. However, they do share the same Address Family and Sub Address Family in the MP-BGP update.

As soon as the MP-BGP sessions are established with appropriate capability support, the discovery process begins immediately after a new VPLS service is provisioned on the PE router. In the BGP update, the information required for VPLS membership identification includes two components: which VPLS service this PE router participates in and which Virtual Switching Instance (VSI, the VPLS switching instance in a member PE router) it is. Therefore, there are two VPLS identifiers used to indicate the VPLS membership and the individual VPLS service instance in the PE router:

- **VPLS-id** — It uniquely identifies one end-to-end VPLS service for the entire network. A VPLS-id should be globally significant in a network. All VSIs belonging to the same VPLS service share the same VPLS-id.

- **VSI-id** — It uniquely identifies an individual VSI on a PE router and in the context of a VPLS.

When every PE router exchanges these two identifiers through the MP-BGP updates, all VPLS services and their member PE routers' VSIs are discovered. In MP-BGP, the L2VPN address family update for VPLS membership information contains the following information:

- **VPLS-id** — The 8-byte value uniquely defines one VPLS service for the entire network. The VPLS-id is an *extended community*, and there are two possible formats, illustrated in Figure 16.1.

Figure 16.1 VPLS-id Format in BGP-AD for VPLS

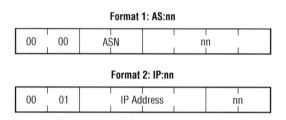

The router automatically sets the first 2-octet value of **0x0** or **0x1**, as soon as the operator configures the VPLS-id with a specific format (format 1 or 2). Only the six least significant octets are configurable by the operator, and they are the value of the VPLS-id. For example, the VPLS-id can be **65100:100**. The value of the VPLS-id must be configured manually in each VSI in each PE router.

- **VSI-id** — The identification of the VSI in the context of a VPLS. The VSI-id is encoded as *VPLS Network Layer Reachability Information (NLRI)*, built by a Router Distinguisher (RD) followed by a 4-byte identifier (usually the system-IP of the VPLS member PE router). The address family of AFI 65 (L2VPN) and SAFI 25 (BGP-VPLS) is used. Figure 16.2 illustrates the VPLS NLRI format used for BGP-AD on LDP-VPLS.

If no explicit value is configured, the VPLS-id value is used for the RD by default. The following 4-byte identifier uniquely identifies a VSI in the VPLS context. This is the key information of the MP-BGP update on VPLS. By receiving this information (for example, **65100:100:10.0.0.1**), the PE router knows that a new member PE (VSI-id) is added to the VPLS identified by the

VPLS-id, and therefore memberships are discovered. An example of VSI-id is
`65100:100:10.0.0.1`.

Figure 16.2 VPLS NLRI Format for BGP-AD

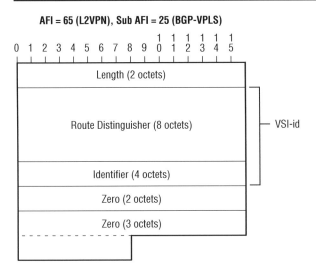

It is important to understand that the VSI-id is used only to identify the VSI in a member PE router. It does not contain any routing information. It claims a VSI of a VPLS but does not indicate the location of the VSI. Routing information is contained in the next-hop field in the MP-BGP update.

- **Next-hop** — The IP address of the next-hop router indicates the location of the VSI. The next hop indicates how to reach the VSI. The IP address in the next-hop field is also used to decide which signaling session (T-LDP peer) will be used to establish the pseudowires to connect to that VSI.

- **Route Target (RT)** — The *extended community* used for MP-BGP to control the logical topology. By manipulating the value of the RT in different routers and by deploying different import and export policies in each VSI of each PE router, the VPLS topology can be determined (fully meshed, or H-VPLS). Examples of controlling import and export policies to build overlapping VPLSs are provided later in this chapter. Two formats of AS:nn or IP:nn can be used. By default, if there is no explicit configuration, the VPLS-id is used as the RT. Figure 16-3 illustrates the CLI output of MP-BGP routes for Layer 2 VPN.

Figure 16.3 MP-BGP Routes for L2VPN

```
A:BC-PE163# show router bgp routes l2-vpn 65200:111:10.0.0.117/32
===============================================================================
  BGP Router ID : 10.0.0.163        AS : 65100    Local AS : 65100
===============================================================================
  Legend -
  Status codes  : u - used, s - suppressed, h - history, d - decayed, * - valid
  Origin codes  : i - IGP, e - EGP, ? - incomplete, > - best
===============================================================================
BGP L
2VPN-AD Routes
===============================================================================
  Network          : 10.0.0.117/32
  Nexthop          : 10.0.0.117
  Route Dist.      : 65200:111
  From             : 10.0.0.118
  Res. Nexthop     : 0.0.0.0
  Local Pref.      : None              Interface Name : NotAvailable
  Aggregator AS    : None              Aggregator     : None
  Atomic Aggr.     : Not Atomic        MED            : None
  Community        : target:65200:111  l2-vpn:65200:111
  Cluster          : No Cluster Members
  Originator Id    : None              Peer Router Id : 10.0.0.118
  Flags            : Used  Valid  Best  IGP
  AS-Path          : 65200
-------------------------------------------------------------------------------
  Routes : 1
===============================================================================
A:BC-PE163#
```

When MP-BGP sessions are established among all PE routers with L2VPN address family capability, the network is ready for the auto-discovery of LDP-VPLS membership. Each time a PE router receives a BGP update containing an L2VPN family NLRI, it checks the import policy against the carried RT value to see if that update should be accepted. If the result is positive, the router then checks whether or not it has the same VPLS service configured, comparing the local and received VPLS-id values. If it does, the router automatically triggers the T-LDP process to signal the pseudowire to the remote router from which this update is received.

> **Note:** As mentioned in the previous section, BGP-AD is only in charge of discovering the VSI in member PE routers of the VPLS service. When a member is found and accepted, it is still the task of T-LDP to exchange the vc-label and to establish the pseudowire(s).

Creating or Selecting SDPs for Pseudowires

After VSIs with BGP-AD enabled discover other VSIs in other member PE routers participating in the same VPLS service, the pseudowire infrastructure needs to be built to connect these VSIs. T-LDP is still responsible for establishing the pseudowires. Chapter 9 describes each necessary component of a service. A pseudowire is a bidirectional point-to-point connection over a pair of SDPs (one in each direction) between two PE routers participating in the same VPLS. To establish a pseudowire, an SDP must be available to carry the pseudowire, either pre-provisioned or automatically created. In a regular LDP-VPLS implementation, both the SDP and the pseudowire are manually configured. In LDP-VPLS with BGP-AD, the operator has the choice of either establishing the pseudowires over the existing pre-provisioned SDPs or allowing the router to automatically create new SDPs where necessary. If dynamic SDP creation is selected, all SDPs automatically created by the router have the signaling method set to T-LDP, and these SDPs are later used to carry the pseudowires for the VPLS services. The parameters required for the auto-discovered pseudowires and SDPs can be specified in BGP-AD templates selectable on a per-domain basis, through the use of import RT values.

SDP Selection Criteria in BGP-AD LDP-VPLS

When BGP-AD is used in LDP-VPLS and automatic pseudowire setup is configured to use the existing SDPs, the system must choose the best SDP to use from the available SDPs. Following are the *SDP selection criteria*:

1. First, the SDP must be valid. That is, the *far end* of the SDP must match the *next hop* in the BGP update. This guarantees that the SDP to be selected connects to the correct PE router.

2. Next, the validated SDP with the lowest SDP metric is selected.

3. In the case of a tie, the SDP with an operational state of up is selected.

4. If more than one SDP is operationally up, the one with the highest numerical sdp-id is selected.

Figure 16.4 illustrates an example of a dynamic SDP (id=17407).

After the SDP and the transport tunnels within the SDP are created or selected (either a new dynamic transport tunnel is created by LDP automatically or a preconfigured one is selected for the pseudowire to use), the next step is for T-LDP to establish the pseudowire over the transport tunnel.

Figure 16.4 Automatically Creating SDPs When Using BGP-AD in VPLS

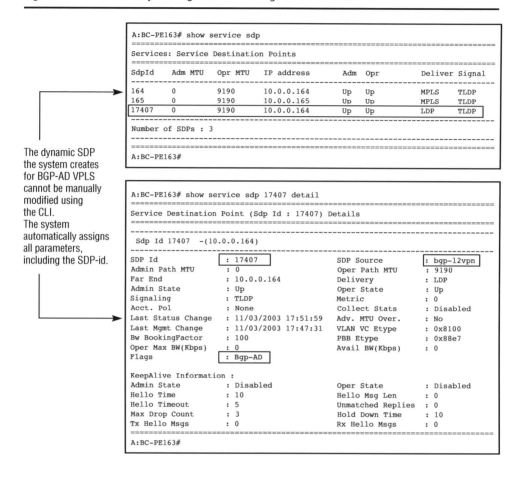

The dynamic SDP the system creates for BGP-AD VPLS cannot be manually modified using the CLI.
The system automatically assigns all parameters, including the SDP-id.

```
A:BC-PE163# show service sdp
===============================================================================
Services: Service Destination Points
===============================================================================
SdpId    Adm MTU   Opr MTU   IP address      Adm   Opr      Deliver Signal
-------------------------------------------------------------------------------
164      0         9190      10.0.0.164      Up    Up       MPLS    TLDP
165      0         9190      10.0.0.165      Up    Up       MPLS    TLDP
17407    0         9190      10.0.0.164      Up    Up       LDP     TLDP
-------------------------------------------------------------------------------
Number of SDPs : 3
-------------------------------------------------------------------------------
===============================================================================
A:BC-PE163#
```

```
A:BC-PE163# show service sdp 17407 detail
===============================================================================
Service Destination Point (Sdp Id : 17407) Details
===============================================================================
-------------------------------------------------------------------------------
 Sdp Id 17407  -(10.0.0.164)
-------------------------------------------------------------------------------
SDP Id             : 17407              SDP Source        : bgp-l2vpn
Admin Path MTU     : 0                  Oper Path MTU     : 9190
Far End            : 10.0.0.164         Delivery          : LDP
Admin State        : Up                 Oper State        : Up
Signaling          : TLDP               Metric            : 0
Acct. Pol          : None               Collect Stats     : Disabled
Last Status Change : 11/03/2003 17:51:59 Adv. MTU Over.    : No
Last Mgmt Change   : 11/03/2003 17:47:31 VLAN VC Etype     : 0x8100
Bw BookingFactor   : 100                PBB Etype         : 0x88e7
Oper Max BW(Kbps)  : 0                  Avail BW(Kbps)    : 0
Flags              : Bgp-AD

KeepAlive Information :
Admin State        : Disabled           Oper State        : Disabled
Hello Time         : 10                 Hello Msg Len     : 0
Hello Timeout      : 5                  Unmatched Replies : 0
Max Drop Count     : 3                  Hold Down Time    : 10
Tx Hello Msgs      : 0                  Rx Hello Msgs     : 0
===============================================================================
A:BC-PE163#
```

Pseudowire Endpoint Identification: FEC Element PW-id and G-PW-id

After the SDP is selected or created, the pseudowire can be established to connect to the remote VSI. As mentioned in Chapter 8, LDP establishes pseudowires using a Label Mapping message containing a Label type–length value (TLV), and a Forwarding Equivalent Class (FEC) TLV with other possible TLVs. The FEC TLV contains an FEC element (defined in RFC 4447), which describes the addressing assigned for the pseudowire endpoint.

Two LDP FEC elements are defined in RFC 4447 (PW Setup and Maintenance Using LDP). The original PW-id FEC element 128 (0x80) employs a 32-bit field to identify the virtual circuit ID and it was used extensively in the initial VLL and

VPLS deployments. The simple format is easy to understand but it does not provide the required information model for the BGP auto-discovery function. In order to support BGP AD and other new applications, a new Layer 2 FEC element, the Generalized FEC (0x81), is required.

The Generalized PW-id (G-PW-id) FEC element was designed for auto-discovery applications. It provides a field, the Address Group Identifier (AGI), which can be used to signal the membership information from the VPLS-id. Separate address fields are provided for the source and target address associated with the VPLS endpoints, called respectively the Source Attachment Individual Identifier (SAII) and Target Attachment Individual Identifier (TAII). These fields carry the VSI-id values for the two instances that are supposed to be connected through the signaled PW. The detailed format for FEC 129 is depicted in Figure 16.6.

Figure 16.5 illustrates CLI output that shows the LDP service label bindings for FEC-128 (regular LDP-VPLS) and FEC-129 (LDP-VPLS with BGP-AD).

Figure 16.5   LDP FEC TLV 128 versus 129

```
A:BC-PE163# show router ldp bindings
--- output omitted ---
==============================================================================
LDP Service FEC 128 Bindings
==============================================================================
Type   VCId    SvcId     SDPId  Peer          IngLbl  EgrLbl LMTU  RMTU
------------------------------------------------------------------------------
V-Eth  1000    1000      164    10.0.0.164    131070U 131067 1522  1522
V-Eth  1000    1000      165    10.0.0.165    131068U 131065 1522  1522
V-Eth  3000    3000      164    10.0.0.164    131069U 131065 1522  1522
V-Eth  3000    3000      165    10.0.0.165    131067U 131064 1522  1522
------------------------------------------------------------------------------
No. of VC Labels: 4
==============================================================================
LDP Service FEC 129 Bindings
==============================================================================
AGI                         SAII            TAII
Type           SvcId  SDPId Peer            IngLbl  EgrLbl LMTU  RMTU
------------------------------------------------------------------------------
65100:111                   10.0.0.163      10.0.0.164
V-Eth          111    17407 10.0.0.164      131064U 131064S 1500  1500
------------------------------------------------------------------------------
No. of FEC 129s: 1
==============================================================================
A:BC-PE163#
```

A pseudowire is a bidirectional connection between two VSIs in different PE routers. It forwards traffic between the VSIs. A pseudowire must connect the endpoints located in the two PE routers, which are referred to as *forwarders* in RFC 4447. The VSI in each PE router contains a forwarder. A forwarder is identified by an Attachment Identifier (AI). In a PW-id (**0x80**) FEC element used in a regular

LDP-VPLS implementation, the PW-id value is used as the AI. To establish a pseudowire successfully, the PW-id and PW-type must match in both PE routers. Because the PW-id is used for setting up manually configured pseudowires, the value of PW-id is preset and cannot be changed.

In LDP-VPLS with BGP-AD, because a G-PW-id (**0x81**) is used for automatic pseudowire setup, the value of the AI may be automatically assigned by the system for each router. Therefore, the value of the AI may not (and likely does not) match on both sides. However, the two endpoints must be associated with a common service to forward traffic.

In the G-PW-id, the AI is divided into two parts:

- **Attachment Group Identifier (AGI, type 1)** — The AGI describes the common service that all forwarders (or pseudowire endpoints) are servicing (for example, a distributed VPLS service). The value of the AGI is globally significant, and must match on both sides of the pseudowire.

- **Attachment Individual Identifier (AII, type 1)** — The AII uniquely identifies one endpoint (forwarder) in one router for one service. The AII value is locally significant to the PE router and thus does not need to match on both sides of the pseudowire.

Together, the AGI and AII uniquely identify one forwarder (endpoint) in one PE router for one service. Since each pseudowire has two endpoints serving the same service, one at each PE router, the AGI of the source and destination endpoints must be the same, while the AII can be different. Therefore, the content of the G-PW-id is an AGI, a source AII, and a target (destination) AII. The PW-id and Group-id fields in the PW-id (**0x80**) are not present in the G-PW-id FEC element. Figure 16.6 illustrates the content of a G-PW-id.

As shown in Figure 16.6, each of the FEC fields is designed as a sub-TLV equipped with its own type and length providing support for new applications. To accommodate the BGP-AD information model, the following FEC formats are used:

- AGI (type 1) is identical in format and content to the BGP Extended Community attribute and is used to carry the VPLS-id value.

- Source AII (type 1) is a 4-byte value destined to carry the local VSI-id (outgoing NLRI minus the RD).

- Target AII (type 1) is a 4-byte value destined to carry the remote VSI-id (incoming NLRI minus the RD).

Figure 16.6 Generalized PW-id FEC Element (0x81)

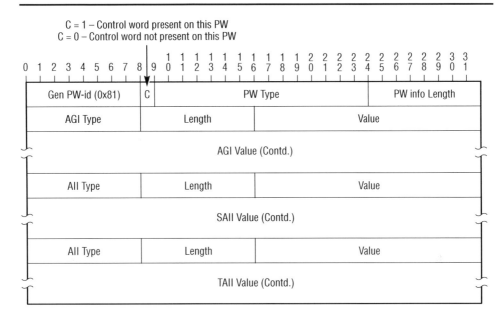

Automatically Signaling Pseudowires: Pseudowire Establishment

After the VSI is provisioned in a PE router, BGP-AD needs to be enabled in that VSI. As soon as BGP-AD is enabled in the VSI of a PE, the router uses BGP to advertise its membership in this VPLS service to all existing member PE routers of this VPLS service, and the router accepts the updates received from other PE routers containing the membership information of the same VPLS service (identified by the VPLS-id and the VSI-id).

The router uses the VPLS-id in the BGP update from member PE routers to discover other VSIs. After the remote VSI is discovered and accepted (by the import policy as well), T-LDP is used to establish the pseudowire with the newly discovered neighboring VSI.

Note: The implementation of LDP-VPLS with BGP-AD in the ALSRP takes a controlled approach: The BGP-AD must be configured and enabled on a per-VSI basis. This is beneficial when a mix of auto-discovered VSI and manually configured VSI coexist in a network. Only the specific VPLSs where BGP-AD is desired are advertised and discovered. By default, BGP-AD is not enabled in the VSI, so the VPLS membership information for that VSI is not advertised, and the BGP updates regarding the same VPLS-id are not accepted.

The following sequence of events needs to be completed when setting up a pseudowire to connect to an auto-discovered remote VPLS member:

1. The local PE router starts by sending an LDP Label Mapping message containing an FEC TLV (containing the 0x81 G-PW-id), a Generic Label TLV (containing the label value being distributed to the traffic ingress router), and other TLVs if necessary.

2. When it receives the Label Mapping message, the remote PE router validates the AGI and Target Attachment Interface (TAI) in the G-PW-id. If the TAI in the message cannot be mapped to one of the local AIs (the ID of the forwarder) of the remote PE router, it rejects the message by responding with a Label Release message containing the status error code Unassigned/ Unrecognized TAI. If the value matches one of the local AIs (AGI+AII), the remote PE router accepts the Label Mapping message and stores the label to encapsulate the ingress traffic before the VPLS traffic is sent to the pseudowire.

3. If the remote PE router accepts the Label Mapping message, it also ensures that the pseudowire's return path is created before declaring the pseudowire up. If not, the remote PE router sends a Label Mapping message to the local PE router to set up the return path of the pseudowire. In the message, the FEC element G-PW-id contains the same AGI value, and the Source Attachment Interface (SAI) and Target Attachment Interface (TAI) are the exact reverse of the G-PW-id in the received Label Mapping message. (Therefore, the SAI of the receiving message is the TAI in the sending message, and vice versa.)

4. After the local PE router validates and accepts the Label Mapping message from the remote PE router, the automatic pseudowire set-up process is complete.

At this point, the pseudowires for the newly discovered VSIs are created. These pseudowires may not be operationally up. For example, if a VSI in a certain router is discovered but is not administratively enabled, the associated pseudowire will be kept operationally down.

Automatically Signaling Pseudowires: Pseudowire Status Notification

When a spoke-pseudowire is established, T-LDP messages can be used to signal the status of the pseudowire. There are two ways of signaling the pseudowire status: using a Label Withdraw message, or using a pseudowire status TLV (0x096A) in the

LDP Notification message. The peering PE routers on both sides of the pseudowire negotiate to determine which method to use to signal the status of that pseudowire. BGP-AD pseudowire status signaling in an LDP-VPLS uses the same procedure as regular LDP-VPLS (with manual pseudowire configuration) for pseudowire status notification method negotiation. The only difference is that the PW-id in the FEC TLV is replaced by the G-PW-id FEC TLV.

Automatically Signaling Pseudowires: Tearing Down Pseudowires

When BGP-AD is enabled in a VSI in a PE router and member PE routers are discovered, pseudowires are automatically created to build the VPLS mesh. Once these dynamic pseudowires are created, they are not removed from the router as long as the far-end PE router is a member of the VPLS service (which means that MP-BGP updates from the router with the same VPLS-id are constantly received from the far-end router). If the status of the VSI changes (for example, if it is administratively disabled in one of the member PE routers) or the status of the MPLS transport tunnel changes (for example, a link failure occurs along the tunnel's path), the LDP Notification message signals the pseudowire to change to a different status. As long as the remote PE router is still participating in the VPLS service, the pseudowire connected to that peer is not removed.

The pseudowire connected to the remote PE router is removed only when the PE router considers that the remote PE router is no longer participating in the VPLS service. Possible scenarios are if the BGP-AD is disabled in that PE router for that VSI, or if the VSI is deleted from the remote PE. The local PE router in such a case uses a Label Withdraw message to withdraw the label binding assigned to that pseudowire, and the remote PE router responds with a Label Release message to confirm the removal of the label.

Case Study: LDP-VPLS with BGP-AD

Now that the BGP-AD process and the pseudowire auto-creation process have been introduced, this case study presents an example of BGP-AD in LDP-VPLS. Two PE routers (PE-163 and PE-164) are participating in VPLS service 111 and have BGP-AD enabled. MP-BGP and LDP are enabled in the network, and router P-165 acts as an MPLS LSR and is not involved in the VPLS service. Figure 16.7 illustrates an example of automatically establishing a pseudowire using BGP-AD, and the use of pseudowire status notification during the establishment and maintenance of this BGP-AD auto-created pseudowire.

Figure 16.7 Case Study: Setting Up, Maintaining, and Tearing Down a BGP-AD Pseudowire

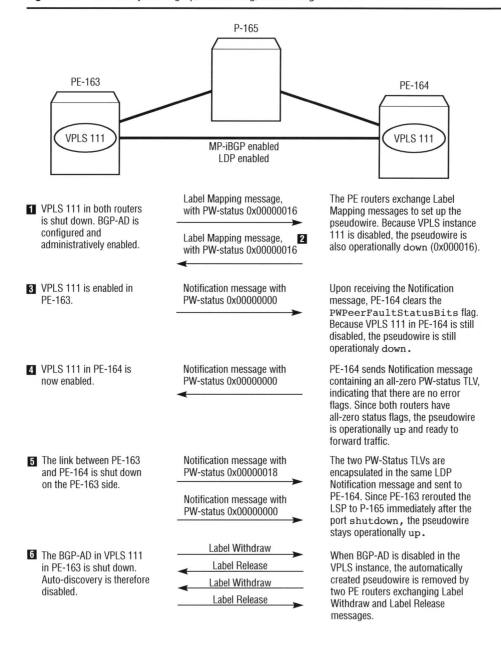

1 VPLS 111 in both routers is shut down. BGP-AD is configured and administratively enabled.

Label Mapping message, with PW-status 0x00000016

Label Mapping message, 2 with PW-status 0x00000016

The PE routers exchange Label Mapping messages to set up the pseudowire. Because VPLS instance 111 is disabled, the pseudowire is also operationally down (0x000016).

3 VPLS 111 is enabled in PE-163.

Notification message with PW-status 0x00000000

Upon receiving the Notification message, PE-164 clears the PWPeerFaultStatusBits flag. Because VPLS 111 in PE-164 is still disabled, the pseudowire is still operationaly down.

4 VPLS 111 in PE-164 is now enabled.

Notification message with PW-status 0x00000000

PE-164 sends Notification message containing an all-zero PW-status TLV, indicating that there are no error flags. Since both routers have all-zero status flags, the pseudowire is operationally up and ready to forward traffic.

5 The link between PE-163 and PE-164 is shut down on the PE-163 side.

Notification message with PW-status 0x00000018

Notification message with PW-status 0x00000000

The two PW-Status TLVs are encapsulated in the same LDP Notification message and sent to PE-164. Since PE-163 rerouted the LSP to P-165 immediately after the port shutdown, the pseudowire stays operationally up.

6 The BGP-AD in VPLS 111 in PE-163 is shut down. Auto-discovery is therefore disabled.

Label Withdraw
Label Release
Label Withdraw
Label Release

When BGP-AD is disabled in the VPLS instance, the automatically created pseudowire is removed by two PE routers exchanging Label Withdraw and Label Release messages.

Figure 16.7 (continued)

```
A:BC-PE163# show service id 111 sdp detail
===============================================================================
-------------------------------------------------------------------------------
 Sdp Id 17407:4294967295  -(10.0.0.164)
-------------------------------------------------------------------------------
--- omitted ---
Class Fwding State : Down
Flags              : SvcAdminDown
                     PWPeerFaultStatusBits
Time to RetryReset : never                  Retries Left     : 3
--- omitted ---
===============================================================================
```

```
A:BC-PE163# show service id 111 sdp detail
===============================================================================
-------------------------------------------------------------------------------
 Sdp Id 17407:4294967295  -(10.0.0.164)
-------------------------------------------------------------------------------
--- omitted ---
Class Fwding State : Down
Flags              : SvcAdminDown
                     PWPeerFaultStatusBits
Time to RetryReset : never                  Retries Left     : 3
--- omitted ---
===============================================================================
```

```
A:IB-PE-164# show service id 111 sdp
===============================================================================
Services: Service Destination Points
===============================================================================
SdpId            Type IP address     Adm     Opr     I.Lbl      E.Lbl
-------------------------------------------------------------------------------
17407:4294967295 Bgp* 10.0.0.163     Up      Up      131065     131062
-------------------------------------------------------------------------------
Number of SDPs : 1
-------------------------------------------------------------------------------
===============================================================================
```

No. ▾	Time	Source	Destination	Protocol	Info
2652168	1373.095126	10.0.0.163	10.0.0.164	LDP	Notification Message

☐ Frame 2652168 (310 bytes on wire, 310 bytes captured)
⊞ Ethernet II, Src: 8e:a5:01:01:00:02 (8e:a5:01:01:00:02), Dst: 8e:a4:01:01:00:02 (8e:a4:01:01
⊞ Internet Protocol, Src: 10.0.0.163 (10.0.0.163), Dst: 10.0.0.164 (10.0.0.164)
⊞ Transmission Control Protocol, Src Port: ldp (646), Dst Port: 51069 (51069), Seq: 2869, Ack:
⊞ Label Distribution Protocol
⊞ Label Distribution Protocol
⊞ Label Distribution Protocol
⊟ Label Distribution Protocol

In this example, the VPLS service instance is administratively enabled *after* the BGP-AD is enabled. It is also possible to administratively enable the VPLS service prior to the configuration of BGP-AD, in which case steps 3 and 4 are skipped.

1. Routers PE-163 and PE-164 have one VPLS configured with BGP-AD enabled. Router P-165 connects both routers and provides an alternate link.

2. The moment that BGP-AD is activated (by executing **no shut** on the **bgp-ad** configuration in the VPLS service instance configuration context), VPLS is administratively disabled (by default, operationally **down**). As soon as BGP-AD updates are exchanged, the pseudowire is signaled and established. Therefore, the auto-created pseudowire is also operationally **down**.

3, 4. After the pseudowire is established, the VPLS is administratively enabled, and the pseudowire changes to the operationally **up** state after receiving the LDP Notification message containing all zero flags from the remote PE router.

5. One MPLS interface is shut down (PE-163 to PE-164); however, router PE-163 reroutes the SDP through router P-165. Another LDP Notification message is sent to PE-164, containing two messages notifying PE-164 of the failure and the recovery. The pseudowire remains operationally **up** because the failure was recovered.

6. When BGP-AD is disabled in the VSI, the local PE router uses BGP to withdraw the VPLS membership, and the remote PE router uses an LDP Label Withdraw message to clear the pseudowire from the system.

In Step 5, if the effort to reroute around the link failure fails, the local PE router keeps sending LDP Notification messages containing the pseudowire status code 0x00000018. This pseudowire status message keeps the pseudowire operationally **down** in the remote PE router until the failure is removed or the rerouting succeeds. The local PE router then sends an LDP Notification message containing the pseudowire status code 0x00000000 to the remote PE router, which puts the pseudowire back to the operationally **up** state.

16.3 SDPs, Transport Tunnels, and Pseudowires Created Using BGP-AD

In the VPLS service instance of the local PE router, after BGP-AD discovers the remote member PE routers participating in the same VPLS service, the pseudowires are automatically created to connect to the VPLS service instances of these remote member PE routers. This is the most significant change BGP-AD brings to LDP-VPLS: automatic VPLS membership discovery and the auto-creation of the pseudowires connected to the member PE routers.

In regular LDP-VPLS, many pseudowire-related parameters can be defined during the manual configuration of a pseudowire. When a pseudowire is automatically created after BGP-AD discovers the remote member PE router, how are these parameters defined and modified? When there is no applicable SDP or the use of an applicable SDP is not desired, which parameters do the auto-created SDPs have? The ALSRP BGP-AD implementation provides *pseudowire templates* to allow the operator to flexibly define the pseudowire and SDP parameters for individual use cases or domains. Figure 16.8 illustrates an example of pseudowire template configuration (covered in the following section).

Figure 16.8   Pseudowire Template and Automatic SDP Parameters

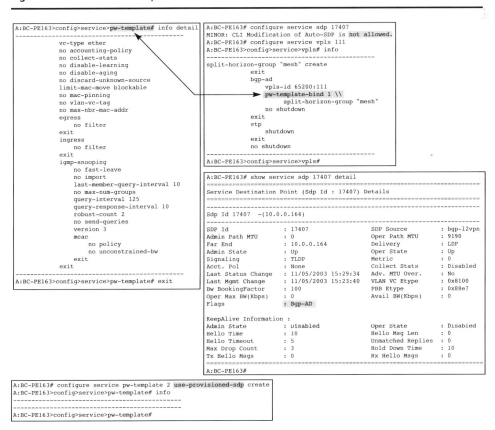

One or more `pw-templates` can be defined at the system level to define different attributes to be used for the automatic creation of PWs and related SDPs by BGP-AD. These pw-templates can be referenced from under the `bgp-ad` configuration context defined under VPLS instance. A VSI can use only one pw-template (the usual case for a VPLS mesh) or multiple pw-templates (the case when an H-VPLS is used and the individual hub and spoke domains have different needs. This is achieved by associating the pw-template with different import routing or policies related to an individual domain, for example metro versus WAN.

The ALSRP implementation allows the operator to choose to reuse a manually provisioned SDP infrastructure already in place for existing Layer 2 services. This could also be the case if the operator wants to have better control over how the SDPs are created and which paths are used. To use an existing SDP infrastructure, the pw-template is created using the `use-provisioned-sdp` option.

Automatically Created SDPs

As discussed in Chapter 9, there are three types of SDPs:

- MPLS SDPs that use RSVP-TE Label Switched Paths (LSPs) as transport tunnels
- MPLS SDPs that use LDP-LSPs
- Generic Routing Encapsulation (GRE) SDPs that use GRE tunnels

In the initial BGP-AD implementation, auto-created SDPs must use MPLS transport tunnels with LDP-LSP. If RSVP-TE LSP or GRE tunnel encapsulation is desired for the SDP, the preconfigured SDP must be used to establish the auto-created pseudowire. The attributes for auto-created SDPs are contained inside the pw-template. When the first pseudowire between two PEs must be established, the auto-created SDP gets the parameters from the related pw-template. Subsequently the SDP attributes can be changed only through the related pseudowire template. The changes can be edited and applied in a controlled fashion. Most of the parameters can be modified without affecting the service. When an attribute change does have a service impact, a warning is given, allowing the operator the option to cancel the change.

The output of the `show service sdp 17047 detail` command in Figure 16.8 shows all the default parameters used by all auto-created SDP tunnels.

Auto-Created Pseudowires

Before enabling BGP-AD in a VPLS, a pseudowire template needs to be defined, with all parameters (for example, security, multicast awareness, split-horizon groups) configured as desired. Then, when the BGP-AD is being configured in the VSI context, the pseudowire template is referred to so that the BGP-AD creates pseudowires with the desired parameters.

If the pseudowires are established over auto-created SDPs, all pseudowires connected to the same remote PE router (for different VPLS services discovered by BGP-AD) use the same auto-created SDP. Therefore, between any two PE routers in a network, BGP-AD can use only one pair of auto-created SDPs (one on each direction) to establish VSI adjacency. Figure 16.9 uses CLI output to illustrate an example of an auto-created SDP and auto-created pseudowires.

Figure 16.9 An Auto-Created SDP Shared by Two VPLS Services Using BGP-AD

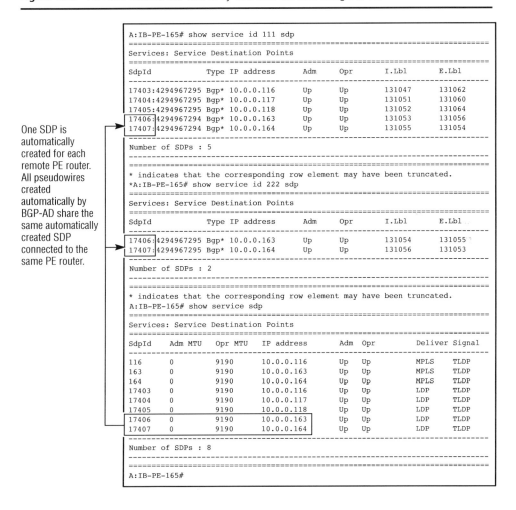

One SDP is automatically created for each remote PE router. All pseudowires created automatically by BGP-AD share the same automatically created SDP connected to the same PE router.

```
A:IB-PE-165# show service id 111 sdp
===============================================================================
Services: Service Destination Points
===============================================================================
SdpId              Type IP address      Adm   Opr    I.Lbl     E.Lbl
-------------------------------------------------------------------------------
17403:4294967295 Bgp* 10.0.0.116        Up    Up     131047    131062
17404:4294967295 Bgp* 10.0.0.117        Up    Up     131051    131060
17405:4294967295 Bgp* 10.0.0.118        Up    Up     131052    131064
17406:4294967294 Bgp* 10.0.0.163        Up    Up     131053    131056
17407:4294967294 Bgp* 10.0.0.164        Up    Up     131055    131054
-------------------------------------------------------------------------------
Number of SDPs : 5
-------------------------------------------------------------------------------
===============================================================================
* indicates that the corresponding row element may have been truncated.
*A:IB-PE-165# show service id 222 sdp
===============================================================================
Services: Service Destination Points
===============================================================================
SdpId              Type IP address      Adm   Opr    I.Lbl     E.Lbl
-------------------------------------------------------------------------------
17406:4294967295 Bgp* 10.0.0.163        Up    Up     131054    131055
17407:4294967295 Bgp* 10.0.0.164        Up    Up     131056    131053
-------------------------------------------------------------------------------
Number of SDPs : 2
-------------------------------------------------------------------------------
===============================================================================
* indicates that the corresponding row element may have been truncated.
A:IB-PE-165# show service sdp
===============================================================================
Services: Service Destination Points
===============================================================================
SdpId    Adm MTU  Opr MTU   IP address      Adm  Opr     Deliver Signal
-------------------------------------------------------------------------------
116      0        9190      10.0.0.116      Up   Up      MPLS    TLDP
163      0        9190      10.0.0.163      Up   Up      MPLS    TLDP
164      0        9190      10.0.0.164      Up   Up      MPLS    TLDP
17403    0        9190      10.0.0.116      Up   Up      LDP     TLDP
17404    0        9190      10.0.0.117      Up   Up      LDP     TLDP
17405    0        9190      10.0.0.118      Up   Up      LDP     TLDP
17406    0        9190      10.0.0.163      Up   Up      LDP     TLDP
17407    0        9190      10.0.0.164      Up   Up      LDP     TLDP
-------------------------------------------------------------------------------
Number of SDPs : 8
-------------------------------------------------------------------------------
===============================================================================
A:IB-PE-165#
```

Pseudowires automatically created by BGP-AD are of spoke type only. If a fully meshed forwarding topology is desired in BGP-AD VPLS, a split-horizon group *must* be used in the VSI of all PE routers to prevent forwarding loops. Figure 16.10 illustrates the association of a split-horizon group with a pseudowire template. In this example, all auto-created pseudowires belong to the same split-horizon group (named mesh), and traffic received from one auto-created pseudowire is not forwarded to any other auto-created pseudowires. For more details regarding the use of a split-horizon group in pseudowire binding, refer to Chapter 12.

Figure 16.10   Assigning a Split-Horizon Group in Pseudowire Automatically Created by BGP-AD

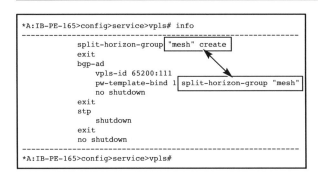

As discussed in Chapter 12, a fully meshed spoke-pseudowire topology with all pseudowires in the same split-horizon group is equivalent to a fully meshed mesh-pseudowire topology. A *mesh* in BGP-AD VPLS actually means a fully meshed spoke-pseudowire-connected forwarding topology, where all pseudowires in member PE routers are in a split-horizon group (so they cannot relay traffic among each other, which achieves the mesh-pseudowire behavior).

Because BGP-AD requires all member PE routers to identify themselves and establishes pseudowires to the VSIs of all accepted member PE routers, building a hierarchical forwarding topology (H-VPLS) using BGP-AD is possible with the help of the import and export policies/route targets.

In VSI with BGP-AD, the pseudowire's split-horizon group membership can be configured in two different CLI contexts:

- Within the `pw-template` configuration context
- In the `pw-template-bind` command within the VSI's `bgp-ad` configuration context

In the case that both configuration contexts have the split-horizon group association, the `pw-template-bind` configuration in the VSI's BGP-AD configuration overrides the split-horizon group `pw-template` configuration.

Combining Manually Provisioned PWs with BGP-AD PWs

It is possible to have manually provisioned and auto-created pseudowires coexist in the same VSI. One benefit of this is that the operators with LDP-VPLS already deployed in the field have a smoother migration path when introducing BGP-AD to their network. Note that FEC 128 and 129 have different content formats; between any two VSIs, only one FEC type can be used. Also, for certain topologies, it is more efficient to have BGP-AD enabled in the VSIs requiring a large number of pseudowires and to manually configure some pseudowires to the VSIs in some minor locations. Figure 16.11 illustrates an example of VPLS services with BGP-AD created pseudowires and manually created pseudowires.

Figure 16.11 Case Study: A VPLS Network with Mixed Pseudowire Types (BGP-AD Created and Manually Created)

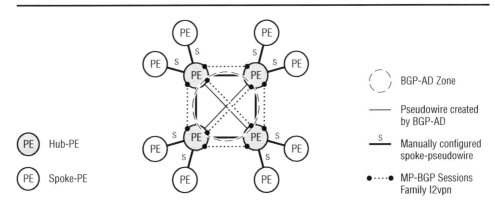

The VPLS service shown in Figure 16.11 involves several hub-PE routers and several spoke-PE routers. All the hub-PE routers have iBGP sessions with each other with the L2VPN Address Family enabled. BGP-AD is used between hub-PE routers to discover the VPLS PE membership, and it automatically establishes the required pseudowires. BGP-AD is disabled in all the spoke-PE routers, so the pseudowires between the spoke-PE routers and the hub-PE routers require manual configuration.

16.4 Using Pre-Provisioned SDPs

BGP-AD for LDP-VPLS supports the automatic creation of SDPs; however, BGP-AD can also use pre-provisioned SDPs to establish pseudowires. The use of pre-provisioned SDPs provides more flexibility in BGP-AD VPLS deployment, as follows:

- BGP-AD for VPLS can use existing RSVP-TE LSPs to take advantage of already deployed LSP resiliency (for example, secondary LSP, Fast Reroute).
- BGP-AD for VPLS can use GRE IP tunnels so that transporting traffic over a non-MPLS link or secure traffic is possible when part of the network does not support MPLS.
- Using the pre-provisioned SDP may be desirable to reduce the number of LSPs deployed in the core and to simplify the infrastructure.

SDP Selection Criteria

To route VPLS traffic, when multiple SDPs can reach the same remote PE node, the local router performs *SDP selection* based on certain criteria to choose the best SDP to carry the traffic. SDP uses three types of transport tunnels:

- **GRE Transport Tunnel** — Uses IP encapsulation. Also referred to as *IP over IP*.
- **MPLS Transport Tunnel with LDP-LSP** — Uses MPLS encapsulation, and the LSP is signaled by LDP. The tunnel's path always follows the IGP routing topology.
- **MPLS Transport Tunnel with RSVP-TE LSP** — Uses MPLS encapsulation, and the LSP is signaled by RSVP-TE. The tunnel's path can follow the IGP topology or the traffic engineering topology, or it can be manually defined (explicit strict hop LSP) when configuring the LSP. It can benefit from the resiliency features in RSVP-TE LSP (for example, Fast Reroute, secondary LSP, RSVP Hello protocol).

The eligible candidate SDPs must have the same termination point (far-end system-IP address) as the remote peering PE of the VSI. When selecting pre-provisioned SDPs, the following criteria are considered in the order they are listed (remember that only manually provisioned SDPs are qualified to be selected; auto-created SDPs cannot be candidates):

1. **The SDP with the Lowest Metric Value** — The best metric is always the first choice, even if the SDP with the best metric value (lowest numeric value) is operationally or administratively **down**. The SDP metric value by default is zero (0 is the best), regardless of the type of the tunnel (GRE, LDP, or RSVP-TE). Therefore, the operator can manually set the metric to control the SDP selection to override any other criteria.

2. **The SDP Operational Status** — If the SDP metric comparison results in a tie, the operational status of the SDP is considered, and the SDP with an operational status of **up** is preferred.

3. **The SDP with the Highest Numeric sdp-id Value** — If the SDP operational status also results in a tie, the SDP with the higher numerical sdp-id value wins the election.

If there is no eligible SDP (meaning that no pre-provisioned SDPs can reach the far-end router), whether or not the router switches to the automatic creation of SDPs depends on the vendor's implementation. In ALSRP, whether the PE router automatically creates SDPs or chooses from existing SDPs connected to the far-end PE router is decided by the pseudowire template used by the VPLS service instance. If `use-provisioned-sdp` is configured in the pseudowire template used by the VSI, the VSI does *not* automatically create any SDPs. If `use-provisioned-sdp` is not configured in the pseudowire template used by the VSI, the VPLS does not use existing SDPs but automatically creates SDPs.

16.5 Using BGP-AD Import and Export Policies to Control the Forwarding Topology of VPLS

Readers familiar with Layer 3 VPRN (RFC 4364, or formal RFC 2547biz) know that different VPRN topologies (for example, hub-spoke VPN, overlapping VPN, extranet, intranet) can be achieved by deploying different import and export Route

Target (RT) policies in the VPRN service instance in each router. In Layer 2 VPN, particularly in LDP-VPLS with BGP-AD, MP-BGP import and export policies based on RTs can also be used to control the distribution of Layer 2 VPN routes, thus controlling the topology of the BGP-AD VPLS. One of the advantages of BGP-AD in VPLS is the re-use of BGP policies to control the VPLS network overlay.

Differences between Route Distinguisher and Route Target

The *Route Distinguisher* (RD) and *Route Target* concepts can be confusing — they look similar, they are both included in the BGP update, and in some cases, they share the same format, and even the same configured numerical values. Operators who are not Layer 3 VPRN experts may need to review the comparison of RD and RT presented in Table 16.1 before continuing with this section because they are the basic building concepts of BGP policy control in VPN topologies.

Table 16.1   Route Distinguisher versus Route Target

Comparison	Route Distinguisher	Route Target
Purpose	A 64-bit value (includes a 16-bit type field and a 48-bit configurable value field) that is prepended to the prefix to ensure that the prefix is globally unique. The only function of an RD is to prevent address overlapping between VPN networks. Adding an RD to all routes from all VPNs makes all routes unique, so they can share the MP-BGP update and still be distinguished from other routes.	A 64-bit value (includes an 8-bit type-high field, an 8-bit type-low field, and a 48-bit configurable value field). RT is an extended BGP community, which is a type of route attribute. BGP attaches these attributes when it sends out updates (export), so that the receiver can decide whether to accept or reject the routes when receiving them (import).
Format	Type 0x00: AS:nn Type 0x01: IP:nn	High priority: Type 0x00 or 0x02: AS:nn Type 0x01: IP:nn Low-priority bits should always be 0x01.
In BGP update	The RD is part of the NLRI (routes) in a BGP update.	The RT is an extended community. It is one of the BGP route attributes attached with the NLRI when BGP sends out an update.

Comparison	Route Distinguisher	Route Target
Usage	Used only by BGP to distinguish the overlapped routes from different customer networks	BGP sets and reads RT values to determine whether to accept or reject NLRIs in the BGP update in different PE routers, to achieve different connectivity requirements.

When a particular connectivity topology is desired (for example, a typical hub-and-spoke topology, such as Sites A and B should both see Site C, but not each other, while Site C should be able to reach both Sites A and B), the RT should be used to manipulate the BGP import and export policies to achieve the requirement.

Deploying Fully Meshed VPLS Connectivity with BGP-AD

To achieve a fully-meshed VPLS topology, each PE router has to create the equivalent of a mesh-pseudowire that connects to every other member PE router. There is no need to deploy special MP-BGP RT import and export policies in the BGP-AD configuration in VSI to achieve this topology. Only one RT is used by the VPLS service, and all member PE routers must be configured to use the default policy of exporting the same RT when sending updates and accepting the same RT when receiving updates. A split-horizon group must be defined to ensure a loop-free pseudowire mesh in the VPLS core network, just as in the case of manually configured mesh-pseudowires.

Hub-Spoke VPLS

Another typical example of a VPLS forwarding topology is a hub-spoke topology, in which the spoke sites cannot directly pass traffic to each other but must communicate through the hub site. Such a topology can be implemented using manually created spoke-pseudowire, but an alternative implementation is to use BGP-AD with RT policies.

Figure 16.12 illustrates a hub-spoke topology with BGP-AD configured (the configuration of Router PE3 is similar to the configuration of Routers PE2 and PE1 and is omitted from the figure). A hub-spoke topology has the following two connectivity requirements:

Figure 16.12 Hub-Spoke VPLS with BGP-AD RT Policies

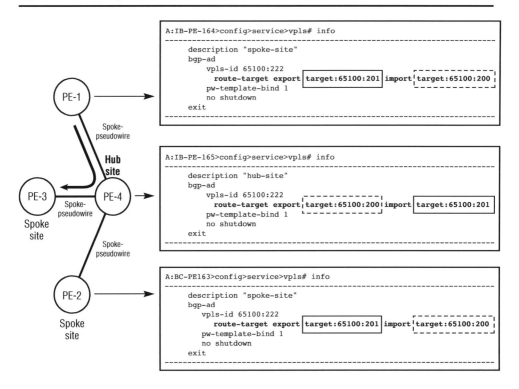

- The hub-PE router needs to have connectivity to all spoke routers.
- Spoke-PE routers need connectivity only to the hub PE router.

Two RT values are assigned, one for each connectivity requirement: `target:65100:201` and `target:65100:200`. Although the MP-BGP updates are distributed among all the PE routers, by manipulating the import and export policies in the BGP-AD of the VSI, the auto-discovery PE process becomes selective: The hub-PE router accepts L2VPN routes from all spoke-PE routers (importing RT `target:65100:201`), and each spoke-PE router accepts only L2VPN routes from the hub-PE router.

With this configuration, hub-PE router PE4 sees PE Routers PE1, PE2, and PE3 as members of VPLS 222 and establishes pseudowires to them. Spoke-PE Routers PE1, PE2, and PE3 see only hub-PE router PE4, and each spoke-PE router is connected to PE4 by only one pseudowire. If more spoke-PE routers are desired to expand the network, the operator copies the BGP-AD configuration of any spoke-PE router to the newly added PE. The connectivity topology is maintained by using the same RT import and export policies to control BGP updates.

Hierarchical VPLS

The previous two examples are typical VPLS forwarding topologies: VPLS mesh and hub-spoke. By manipulating RT values and BGP import/export policy, a combination of the two VPLS topologies can be built automatically. Figure 16.13 illustrates such an H-VPLS network, which is deployed with BGP-AD.

Figure 16.13   A Hierarchical VPLS Network Deployed with BGP-AD

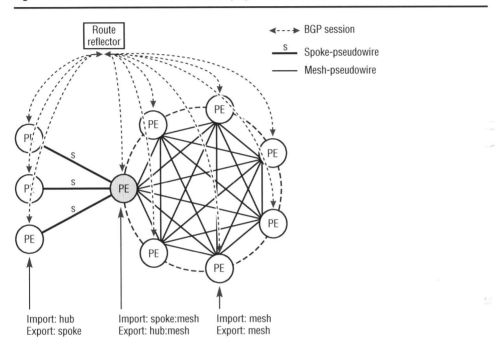

In Figure 16.13, the VPLS network is a combination of hub-spoke and mesh. The three PE routers on the left of the diagram require only spoke-pseudowires to the hub-PE router in the center. The hub-PE router and other PE routers on the right of the diagram require a full mesh of pseudowire. The hub-PE router will relay the VPLS traffic between the three PE routers on the left and the six PE routers on the right. A BGP Route Reflector (RR) is positioned in the network to reduce the number of BGP sessions required in the network. To achieve the connectivity requirement of the VPLS service, more complicated RT configurations and BGP import/ export policies must be deployed. Table 16.2 lists the MP-BGP polices required.

Table 16.2 BGP RT and Policy Configuration

Router	Import Policy	Export Policy
Spoke-PE routers	65100:200 (hub)	65100:100 (spoke)
Hub-PE router	65100:100 (spoke) 65100:300 (mesh)	65100:200 (hub) 65100:300 (mesh)
Mesh-PE routers (other than Hub-PE)	65100:300 (mesh)	65100:300 (mesh)

Each of the three spoke-PE routers exports 65100:100 (spoke) and imports only 65100:200 (hub). Therefore, each spoke-PE router has only one pseudowire established to the hub-PE router. Each of the six mesh-PE routers exports and imports 65100:300 (mesh). As a result, each mesh-PE router has pseudowires to all other mesh-PE routers (associated with a predefined split-horizon group). The hub-PE router in the center requires pseudowires connected to all other PE routers. Therefore, it exports both 65100:200 (hub) and 65100:300 (mesh). It also imports both 65100:100 (spoke) and 65100:300 (mesh). The flexibility of defining RT and BGP import/export policies makes it possible to define complex VPLS forwarding topologies using BGP-AD.

Summary

The ALSRP LDP-VPLS implementation can use BGP-AD to reduce the pseudowire configuration overhead and to simplify service management. Using BGP-AD, the PE router can broadcast its VPLS membership information to other PE routers. T-LDP is still used to signal the pseudowire, but the VPLS membership is automatically discovered by checking the MP-BGP update.

The following requirements must be fulfilled when deploying LDP-VPLS with BGP-AD:

- MP-BGP with the L2VPN Address Family capability must be enabled in all PE routers involved.

- T-LDP sessions are still required to set up the pseudowires.

- A pseudowire template needs to be provisioned in the PE router for the VPLS to use to instantiate the required pseudowires. All pseudowires that belong to one VPLS service in the PE router share the same set of parameters defined in the template.

The PE router discovers the member remote PE routers by receiving an MP-BGP update, and then uses T-LDP to set up the pseudowires. When the BGP-AD VPLS creates the pseudowire(s), the SDP associated with the pseudowires can be pre-provisioned (by manual explicit configuration) or automatically created during the pseudowire set-up process.

VPLS connectivity can be controlled by configuring different MP-BGP import and export policies. In the PE router, for every VPLS service instance, the pseudowires automatically created by BGP-AD can coexist with manually configured pseudowires, providing for easy migration and interoperability with deployed VPLS services.

PBB-VPLS

17

Provider Backbone Bridging (PBB) provides extremely scalable solutions for Ethernet transportation services. PBB is introduced in Virtual Private LAN Service (VPLS) service to enhance the scalability of VPLS solutions.

Chapter Objectives

- Provide an overview of VPLS scalability in extremely large networks

- Introduce PBB architecture

- Introduce PBB-VPLS infrastructure

- Discuss PBB-VPLS forwarding behavior

- Discuss the flooding control in PBB backbone — 802.1ak MRP protocol

- Discuss PBB-VPLS resiliency

- Discuss the use of PBB with Ethernet VLL

The VPLS solution is widely deployed in large-scale service provider networks. Hierarchical VPLS (H-VPLS) with a hub-spoke design is often implemented in this type of network to improve multicast efficiency and scalability and to allow for domain separation. H-VPLS network design removes the requirement of pseudowire full mesh for Provider Edge (PE) router peering, thereby reducing the number of Label Switched Paths (LSPs), Service Distribution Paths (SDPs), and pseudowires (PWs) each PE router must maintain.

However, both VPLS and H-VPLS solutions still make traffic forwarding decisions based on *customer MAC (C-MAC) addresses*. In very large networks, the number of customer addresses a VPLS PE router must maintain in the forwarding database (FDB) can become a concern. This is especially true in the case of a hub-spoke H-VPLS network design: Because the hub-PE router aggregates the traffic from multiple spoke-PE routers, it must maintain a much larger FDB. The central location of the hub-PE means that it must handle more customer forwarding information, increased service awareness, and related pseudowires.

To solve this problem, Provider Backbone Bridging (PBB), defined by IEEE 802.1ah, is integrated into the VPLS solution. This chapter discusses how PBB and VPLS can be combined to achieve a better service architecture and describes the end-to-end learning and forwarding behavior of the resulting PBB-VPLS solution.

In PBB, the end-to-end solution is built around two components: the backbone component (*B-component*) operating in the backbone domain (B-domain) and the customer component (also referred to as the *I-component*) operating in the customer addressing space. For PBB-VPLS, the I-component is represented by the customer-facing VPLS service instances, which are referred to as *I-VPLS*. An I-VPLS service instance still performs learning and forwarding based on C-MAC addresses and CVLANs and/ or SVLANs, just like regular VPLS service instances. An I-VPLS can also send traffic to the associated B-VPLS across the B-domain if necessary. When the I-VPLS service instance sends traffic to the Backbone VPLS (B-VPLS) service instance, the customer MAC addressing is encapsulated with another pair of MAC addresses — the backbone source and destination MAC (B-MAC) addresses. Traffic in the B-domain, B-VPLS, uses the source B-MAC for learning and bases its forwarding decisions on the destination B-MAC. The C-MAC addresses are hidden from the B-VPLS service instances.

17.1 Provider Backbone Bridge Overview

This section introduces the potential *MAC explosion* challenge that an operator may encounter when deploying a very large-scale VPLS solution. Next, the common IEEE

802.1ah PBB architecture in an Ethernet bridged network is presented. Readers who are already familiar with MAC explosion scenarios in VPLS or who already understand the common IEEE 802.1ah PBB architecture may wish to skip this section.

Potential VPLS Scaling Issue — MAC Explosion

Because of its many benefits, the VPLS service has been accepted as the de facto Layer 2 multipoint service delivery model by service providers of all sizes. Service providers deploying the technology range from those with limited local footprints to those with national or international presence supporting the largest customers. The wide acceptance and rapid expansion of VPLS networks in terms of geography, increased numbers of PE routers, numbers of services and subscribers, and more customer awareness challenge the scale limit of the VPLS solution from the following three perspectives:

- **VPLS FDB Size** — When the VPLS service is deployed in a scaled network in which many customer MAC addresses are presented to the provider's service-aware network elements, the number of entries in the VPLS FDB can be significant. This consumes a significant amount of system resources, and may affect the convergence of the service during times of flux.

- **PE Peering** — PE routers must peer with all other PE members in the same VPLS. Every peering relationship in every PE router requires at least one LSP as a transport tunnel, an SDP, and one Targeted Label Distribution Protocol (T-LDP) session. One router can handle only a certain number of T-LDP sessions and maintain a certain number of LSPs and pseudowires.

- **Data Plan Replication for Multipoint Traffic** — When a PE router receives customer multipoint traffic ("Broadcast, Unknown unicast, Multicast" or *BUM* traffic), it must replicate it to other PEs. Replicating traffic to a large number of receivers may be inefficient and may cause unexpected traffic congestion.

As mentioned in Chapter 12, the H-VPLS evolution significantly improves the scalability of the VPLS solution. H-VPLS can be used to break the flat full-mesh network into several meshes and connect them with spoke-pseudowires. This could be used to create interdomain solutions or simply introduce a hierarchy for an intradomain solution. Both solutions contain the mesh-pseudowires close to the core and connect PE routers close to the customer or at the border sites with spoke-pseudowires.

In a hub-spoke H-VPLS network, the customer-facing spoke-PE routers in the edge are also referred to as *user PEs* (uPEs), and the aggregating hub-PE routers close to the core are also referred to as *network PEs* (nPEs). Several uPEs are connected to one nPE by spoke-pseudowires. An nPE aggregates and facilitates the forwarding of traffic between uPEs and between uPEs and other nPE nodes. The nPE nodes are typically, but not always, connected using mostly mesh-pseudowires.

H-VPLS reduces the number of SDP, LSP, and T-LDP sessions required in the network by removing the requirement for a full mesh between all PE nodes. However, the H-VPLS solution does not reduce the number of MAC addresses the VPLS PEs need to learn. Traffic forwarding in H-VPLS is still based on the learning of the C-MAC addresses. In H-VPLS, the nPE contains a context for all services it aggregates from the multiple uPEs. Since the nPE is located deeper in the service provider network, the nPE needs to learn many more MAC addresses than the uPE does. This potential problem is referred to as *MAC explosion*. Figure 17.1 demonstrates the MAC explosion problem in an H-VPLS network that contains a large number of customer MAC addresses.

Figure 17.1   MAC Explosion in an H-VPLS Network with Many C-MAC Addresses

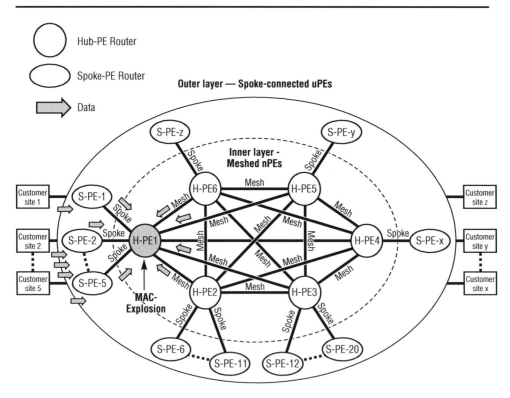

When it becomes operationally challenging to maintain the full mesh of peering sessions in a full-mesh VPLS solution, or the number of peering PE routers and associated pseudowires consumes more and more network resources, H-VPLS is introduced as an evolution of VPLS to solve the problem. When the H-VPLS solution encounters scaling issues like customer MAC explosion, PBB is introduced as the second evolution.

Provider Backbone Bridging

The official definition of PBB by IEEE 802.1ah Task Group is:

> To allow scaling for provider networks to at least 2^{24} service Virtual LANs, this standard further specifies the operation of Provider Backbone Bridges (PBBs) by means of an architecture and bridge protocols compatible and interoperable with Provider Bridged Network protocols and equipment, allowing interconnection of multiple Provider Bridged Networks.

This defines the IEEE model of the PBB: The intention is to interconnect Provider Bridged Networks (PBNs), defined by IEEE 802.1ad (Q-in-Q), with Backbone Edge Bridges (BEB) and a PBB Network (PBBN) core. In the PBB solution, the BEB adds another layer of Ethernet encapsulation to the customer Ethernet frames, referred to as a *backbone header*. The backbone header contains a B-MAC address, which is meaningful only to the BEB and backbone bridges within the PBBN core. The bridges in the PBBN core use the B-MAC address to forward traffic. The backbone VLAN-ID (B-VID) can also be used to define the backbone broadcast domain (VLAN).

Table 17.1 lists the scaling techniques available in legacy bridged Ethernet networks.

Table 17.1 Ethernet Scaling Mechanisms

Technique	Description	Frame Format
Legacy Ethernet	Customer frames use only MAC addresses in the Ethernet frames; all equipment is in the same broadcast domain. With more hosts in the network, service providers face scalability and security issues.	D-MAC+S-MAC+ E-Type+Payload

(continued)

Table 17.1   Ethernet Scaling Mechanisms *(continued)*

Technique	Description	Frame Format
VLAN	VLAN adds a vlan-id tag into the Ethernet frame to create separate broadcast domains. Only frames with the same vlan-id are switched with a VLAN. Because the vlan-id range is 0 through 4,095, service providers have a scaling limitation of 4,000 VLANs per network.	D-MAC+S-MAC+ E-Type+V-id+ E-Type+Payload
Q-in-Q (802.1ad)	To transport more than 4,000 customer VLANs through the network, an extra vlan-id is inserted by the service provider: s-vid. The provider uses the s-vid to switch within the core network. Multiple VLANs from the same customer share the same s-vid; therefore, the total number of VLANs the network can carry increases to 16 million (4,000 × 4,000). Q-in-Q still requires the service provider network to learn and forward based on the customer MAC.	D-MAC+S-MAC+ E-Type+S-Vid+ E-Type+C-Vid+ E-Type+Payload
PBB (802.1ah)	To provide a clean separation of customer and carrier forwarding information, PBB encapsulates the payload in an extra MAC address pair (source/destination). Therefore, the service provider equipment switches traffic based on the B-MAC addresses. Since all C-MAC addresses are hidden by the B-MAC addresses, the service provider's network only maintains the service provider's MACs, except on the edge BEB nodes, where a mapping of customer MACs to backbone MACs is maintained. Also, a B-VID is added to create a broadcast domain, and an I-tag is added to associate with the concept of service instance.	D-BMAC+S-BMAC+ E-Type+B-Vid+ Ethertype+I-tag+ D-CMAC+S-CMAC+ E-Type+S-Vid+ E-Type+C-Vid+ E-Type+Payload

In the past, service providers had deployed Q-in-Q encapsulation to offer Layer 2 switched services. By using Q-in-Q, the provider can define service VLAN tags (s-vid) and perform traffic bridging based on these tags while hiding the customer VLAN tags (c-vid) underneath. Although this solves the 4,000-only VLAN tag limitation as a result of the 12-bit length of the vlan-id, it does not reduce the number of C-MAC addresses that need to be kept in the FDBs of the Ethernet switches. The core switches aggregate the customer traffic flows and must learn the customer source and destination. This means that there is poor separation between the customer and carrier forwarding space and a very large increase in system resource consumption. Resource consumption is more dramatic on nodes that are deepest in the network and less dramatic on edge nodes because of distribution. The introduction of PBB into the network can overcome the challenges faced in Q-in-Q deployments.

The BEB appends backbone destination MAC (B-DMAC) addresses and backbone source MAC (B-SMAC) addresses to the customer frames, along with a B-VID and an Instance Tag (I-TAG), before it forwards the frames into the PBBN core. All PBB switches inside the PBBN learn addresses and forward traffic based only on the B-MAC address, B-VID, and I-TAG, ignoring all C-VIDs and C-MAC addresses. This significantly reduces the size of the FDB in the PBBN core switches. When the traffic reaches the remote edge switch of the PBBN, the B-MAC address, B-VID, and I-TAG are removed before the remote edge bridge forwards the frame outside the PBBN.

Note: The I-TAG is only significant to the BEB nodes and not to PBB core nodes.

PBB encapsulation has 22 bytes of overhead. This overhead is prepended to the customer Ethernet frames and contains the following three major sections:

- **I-TAG** — A 4-byte tag is placed in front of the customer MAC addressing. It contains an Interface Service Instance Indicator (I-SID), which allows each BEB to support multiple backbone service instances. The I-SID unambiguously identifies up to 2^{24} backbone service instances. (In the PBB-VPLS solution, I-SID is used as a de-multiplexer, similar to the service-label used in IP/MPLS VPN encapsulation.) Note that in PBB encapsulation, the customer source and destination MAC addresses (C-DA and C-SA) are also considered part of the I-TAG, even though PBB switches do not change customer addresses.

- **B-VID** — The vlan-id used by the PBBN backbone to define the broadcast domain.

- **B-SA and B-DA** — Backbone source and destination MAC addresses, used by PBBN backbone switches to learn and forward PBB-encapsulated traffic.

Figure 17.2 illustrates the format of the PBB header and a PBB-encapsulated Ethernet frame.

Figure 17.2 PBB Encapsulation of Customer Frames

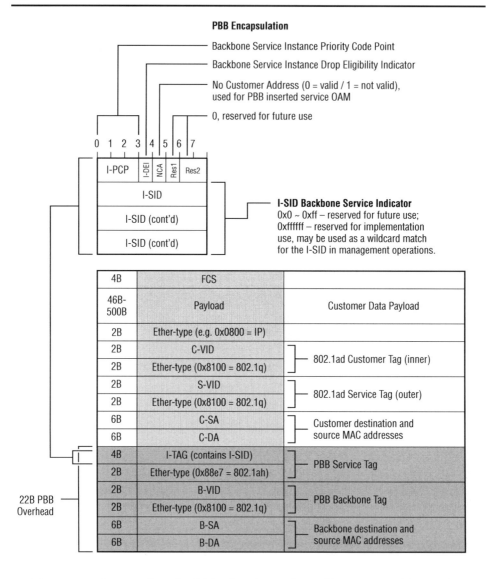

The action of prepending the PBBN header performed by PBB-capable switches is transparent to the legacy Ethernet networks connected by PBBN. The transparent bridging behavior maintained in the PBBN network and the multiple versions of STP is still supported. The broadcast domains defined by the vlan-ids are also maintained.

With the PBBN encapsulation mechanism, the C-MAC addresses are learned only by the customer-facing port of the BEB. The BEB maps the C-MAC to the appropriate B-DMAC and then forwards the frame to the PBBN core. The nodes in the PBBN core are aware of B-MAC addresses only and perform learning and forwarding based on B-MAC addresses. The broadcast domain within the PBBN is defined by the B-VID. This significantly improves the scalability of the PBBN solution.

Because the standard IEEE PBBN is an Ethernet bridged environment, Spanning Tree Protocol (STP) is required to prevent forwarding loops in the PBBN backbone network. The STP variation used in the PBBN is referred to as a *Provider Multiple Spanning Tree* (PMSTP). Figure 17.3 illustrates the PBB network architecture. In the PBB architecture, the regular Ethernet networks in the edge (PBN, dot1q-tagged networks, or networks with no VLAN tagging) are connected by a PBBN backbone network. The BEB switches perform PBB encapsulation and de-encapsulation.

Figure 17.3 Provider Backbone Bridging Network Architecture

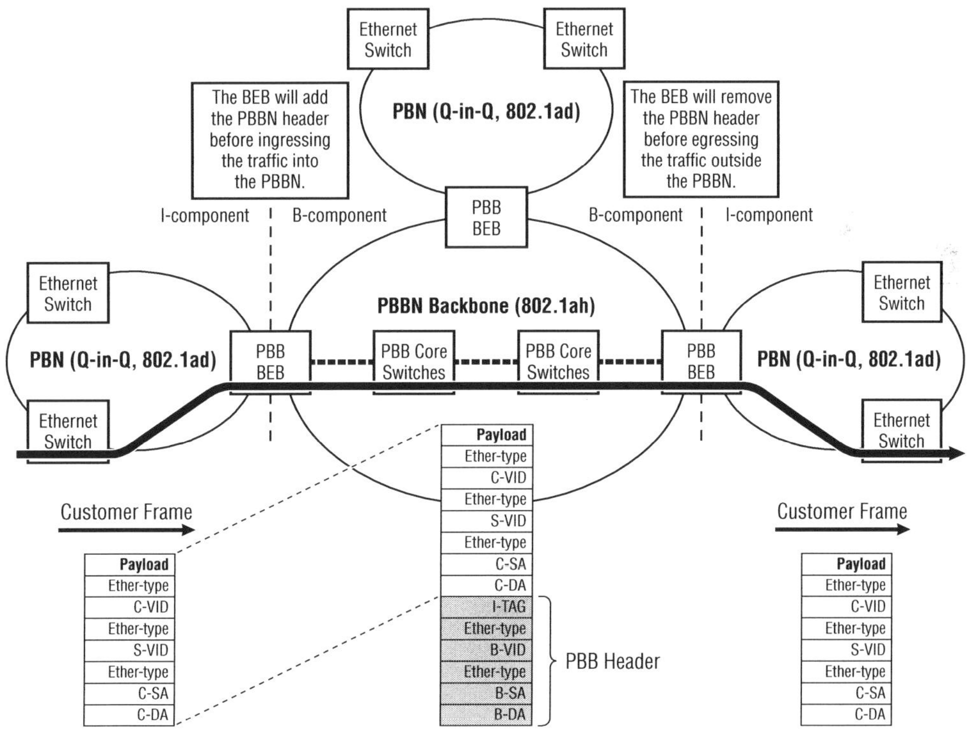

Figure 17.3 shows BEBs as the switches connecting the PBB network and the 802.1ad Q-in-Q networks. The BEB switch adds the PBB headers to the frames when customer traffic comes into the PBB network and removes the PBB headers from the frames before the traffic leaves the PBB network. The BEB can be treated as a combination of two components:

- **B-Component** — Faces the PBB backbone. The B-component learns and forwards the PBB-encapsulated frames over the PBB network to other BEBs, and runs PMSTP if necessary to maintain a loop-free forwarding infrastructure.

- **I-Component** — Faces the customer 802.1ad Q-in-Q network. The I-component adds the PBB header to the ingress customer traffic and maintains the mapping of C-MAC addresses and C-VIDs to the B-MAC addresses, and/or B-VIDs.

This section provides only an overview of IEEE-PBB architecture and PBB data frame encapsulation as a foundation for understanding PBB-VPLS. Details regarding the Ethernet PBB solution can be found in IEEE standard 802.1ah. In an IEEE-PBB solution, each customer Ethernet frame (which already has a pair of DA/SA C-MAC addresses) is appended to another MAC address pair (the B-DA/B-SA) prepended by the BEB when encapsulating the frame.

17.2 PBB-VPLS Architecture

The previous section introduced the potential risk of MAC explosion in a large-scale H-VPLS network with many customer switches and end-users presenting large numbers of MAC addresses. The mechanisms available to deal with those issues were discussed in the IEEE 802.1ah PBB solution. This section describes the adoption of PBB into the VPLS implementation — PBB-VPLS.

PBB provides exactly what is required to solve the VPLS FDB scaling problem — adding a pair of source/destination B-MAC addresses to each customer Ethernet frame. PBB allows the backbone switches to perform traffic forwarding based on the B-MAC addresses, which are much fewer in number than C-MAC addresses. When adopting PBB into VPLS, the end-to-end VPLS solution is divided into two parts: one backbone domain, and one or many edge domains. The resulting PBB-VPLS solution changes the VPLS network design from the following perspectives:

- The B-domain contains PE routers that are responsible for forwarding on information specific to the backbone. These nodes are not concerned with the encapsulated customer information. The role of these nodes is to move traffic across the backbone. These routers now have a new type of VPLS service called *Backbone VPLS* (B-VPLS) configured instead of the regular VPLS.

- The edge domain contains the PE routers that participate in customer-facing VPLS (I-VPLS) service instances and perform learning and forwarding based on C-MAC addresses. The edge domain is also called the *interface domain* (I-domain).

- The boundary between the B-domain and the I-domain exists on a PE router, which contains both I-VPLS and B-VPLS; therefore, it is referred to as the *IB-PE router*. In the boundary router, two types of VPLS are provisioned for the PBB-VPLS solution:

    - B-VPLS is configured and connected by pseudowires to other PE routers in the B-domain.

    - I-VPLS is configured and connected to other PE routers in the I-domain that are running regular VPLS.

- The IB-PE router has an *internal link* between the I-VPLS and the B-VPLS referred to as the *Provider Internal Port* (PIP). The I-VPLS is in charge of associating itself with a B-VPLS. When it receives regular VPLS traffic from the edge domain, it performs PBB encapsulation and forwards the traffic to the B-VPLS toward the B-domain. When the associated B-VPLS receives the PBB-encapsulated traffic from the backbone network, it forwards the traffic to the correct I-VPLS, and the I-VPLS then performs PBB de-encapsulation and forwards the traffic to the correct destination based on the customer information.

Figure 17.4 illustrates the basic PBB-VPLS architecture. The end-to-end VPLS network is divided into a backbone domain and several edge domains. Being the boundary, the IB-PE routers connect the two domains. In the IB-PE router, the B-VPLS and the I-VPLS service instance(s) are associated explicitly with the configuration under the I-VPLS service instance. The PIP link carries the traffic between the I-VPLS and its associated B-VPLS. As indicated in the diagram, the IB-PE router has both I-VPLS Virtual Switching Instance (VSI) and B-VPLS VSI defined within it. The I-SAP, B-SAP, I-pseudowire, and the B-pseudowire reside in the same router — the IB-PE router.

Each B-VPLS service instance in an IB-PE router or a Backbone Provider Edge (B-PE) router uses one of its MAC addresses as a B-MAC address; a B-MAC may also be configured manually. The B-MAC addresses must be globally unique for each B-VPLS instance in each PE router because each B-MAC address uniquely identifies a backbone VPLS VSI. The B-MAC address arbitrarily identifies one B-VPLS service instance in one PE router (B or IB-PE router).

Figure 17.4 PBB-VPLS Architecture

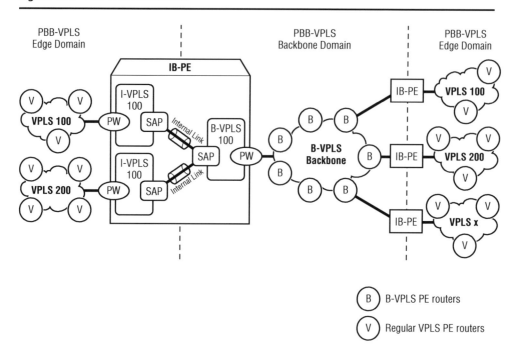

The B-VPLS service instance in the backbone PE routers performs learning and forwarding of the B-MAC addresses defined in the B-VPLS, instead of learning the C-MAC addresses. The B-MAC address can be learned from the B-SAP or the B-VPLS pseudowires. In PBB-VPLS architecture, the PE routers in the backbone domain (previously defined as nPE or hub-PE) perform forwarding based on B-MAC addresses, and uPE (or spoke-PE) routers in the edge domain continue to use C-MAC addresses to make forwarding decisions. In the backbone of the B-domain, MPLS pseudowires are used to transport the PBB-VPLS traffic between B-VPLS PE routers.

PBB-VPLS has the following advantages over the IEEE-PBB implementation in a legacy bridged Ethernet network:

- Takes full advantage of the VPLS solution by using an MPLS backbone to replace the Ethernet switched backbone:
  - MPLS resiliency
  - A full set of traffic engineering tools when the transport tunnel is RSVP based
    - Path placement
    - Fast reroute for rapid convergence

- Scalable loop-free backbone VPLS (fully meshed mesh-pseudowire) eliminating the need for MSTP in the core
    - Significantly better convergence performance from the MPLS/VPLS service than from an Ethernet bridged network with MSTP convergence
  - Operation simplification by leveraging large scale MPLS networks that are already deployed
- A common operational model supporting both multipoint services (VPLS) and point-to-point services (Epipe), all based on IP/MPLS VPN technology
- Supports native PBBN (802.1ah) interoperation — can interconnect PBN the same way IEEE PBBN functions, with MSTP maintaining a loop-free forwarding topology with the benefits of having an MPLS/VPLS core.

PBB-VPLS Building Blocks

In a PBB-VPLS architecture, the entire VPLS network is divided into two domains: the B-domain (containing B-VPLS) and the I-domain (containing I-VPLS and regular VPLS). The two domains need to communicate with each other and pass traffic through to provide end-to-end services. There are two different models for the B-domain and I-domain: the *co-located* model and the *distributed model*. In the co-located model, the I-component and the B-component both reside in the IB-PE router. The IB-PE router is the boundary router that connects the B-domain and the I-domain. Inside the IB-PE router, both I-VPLS service instances and B-VPLS service instances are created. The I-VPLS and B-VPLS communicate and exchange traffic through an internal link. In the distributed model, all B-components are configured in the B-PE router, and all I-components are configured in the customer-facing Provider Edge (I-PE) router. The B-PE and I-PE routers are connected by pseudowires in the same way as two PE routers are connected in a regular VPLS network. Figure 17.5 illustrates co-located and distributed models for a PBB-VPLS network.

Each I-VPLS can have its own B-VPLS connected to the B-domain (1:1 mode), or multiple I-VPLS instances can share a common B-VPLS connected to the B-domain (*N*:1 mode). The ALSRP implementation supports both modes, so whether to use 1:1 or *N*:1 mode is a network design choice.

Figure 17.5 PBB-VPLS Reference Model — IB-PE Router

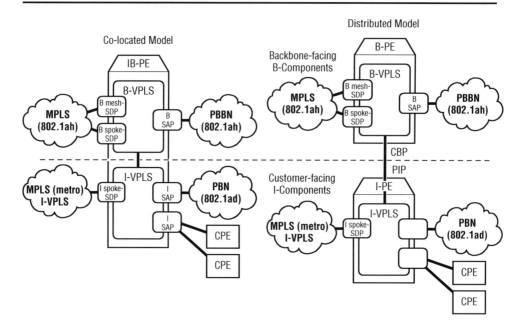

Three types of VPLS service instances can coexist in a router in a PBB-VPLS network — B-VPLS, I-VPLS, and regular VPLS. The entire IP/MPLS VPN network infrastructure can be shared by many VPLS services for many customers. It is possible and quite common that within the same network, some VPLS instances are created in some PE routers for regular VPLS or H-VPLS services for some customers, while the B-VPLS and I-VPLS service instances are created to provide PBB-VPLS service to another customer. From the customer perspective, the internal service implementation type of VPLS is transparent and irrelevant. The PBB-VPLS, H-VPLS, or regular VPLS service all provide Ethernet bridging services among different customer sites. The IB-PE router can act as a gateway router connecting PBB-VPLS to the native PBB services using B-SAPs, and native Ethernet access services using I-SAPs. Table 17.2 compares these three types of VPLS service instances.

Table 17.2 Comparison of I-VPLS, B-VPLS, and Regular VPLS Service Instances

Component	I-VPLS Service Instance	B-VPLS Service Instance	Regular VPLS Service Instance
Location	In the I-domain of a PBB-VPLS network, directly connected to the customer VPLS service, connected to one B-VPLS VSI to the B-domain through an internal link (inside the IB-PE router).	In the B-domain of a PBB-VPLS network, carries traffic over the network, provides backbone tunneling for one (1:1 mode) or many (N:1 mode) I-VPLS instances through an internal link (inside the IB-PE router).	In a regular VPLS or H-VPLS network, or in the I-domain of a PBB-VPLS.
Pseudowire support	I-VPLS uses spoke-pseudowires to communicate with regular VPLS service instances in the I-domain and uses an internal link to communicate with B-VPLS in the same IB-PE router.	Within the B-domain, B-VPLS PE routers can connect to each other through both spoke- and mesh-pseudowires; therefore, the B-VPLS service can be regular or hierarchical. B-VPLS communicates with I-VPLS(s) in the same IB-PE router through an internal link.	Regular VPLS service instances can connect to each other through both mesh- and spoke-pseudowire. Regular VPLS can use spoke-pseudowires to connect to I-VPLS in a PBB-VPLS solution.
SAP support	I-VPLS supports regular Ethernet SAP encapsulation types (null, dot1q, Q-in-Q).	B-VPLS can have only PBB (802.1ah) encapsulated SAPs to connect to the PBBN network.	Supports regular SAP Ethernet encapsulation types (null, dot1q, Q-in-Q).
FDB	Learns C-MAC addresses and forwards data traffic accordingly. Also learns B-MAC address and maps the B-VPLS to the I-VPLS.	Learns B-MAC addresses and forwards traffic accordingly.	Learns C-MAC addresses and forwards data traffic accordingly.

(continued)

Table 17.2 Comparison of I-VPLS, B-VPLS, and Regular VPLS Service Instances *(continued)*

Component	I-VPLS Service Instance	B-VPLS Service Instance	Regular VPLS Service Instance
Loop prevention	The VPLS fully meshed topology is loop-free. H-VPLS with spoke-bindings using active and redundant PW. May also be configured to support. Can interoperate STP with customers or transparently flood BPDUs.	VPLS fully meshed loop-free topology. Since the B-VPLS uses the same constructs as an I-VPLS, the techniques for ensuring a loop-free topology will include the same functions: fully meshed PW, H-VPLS spokes using active and redundant PW. Optionally by configuration, B-VPLS can also flood BPDU for I-VPLS services associated with it.	The VPLS fully meshed topology is loop-free. H-VPLS with spoke-bindings using active and redundant PW may also be configured. Can interoperate STP with customers or transparently flood BPDUs.
Traffic de-multiplexer	In the spoke-pseudowire of the I-VPLS, the service-label is used to de-multiplex the traffic just as in regular VPLS. For traffic going to the B-domain, the I-SID in the PBB header is used as a de-multiplexer.	PE routers use service-labels to identify the B-VPLS service instance. Then, B-VPLS uses the I-SID in the PBB header to identify the corresponding I-VPLS.	PE routers use the service-label as a de-multiplexer when receiving regular VPLS traffic from a pseudowire.
Inter-connectivity with pseudo-wires	I-VPLS can connect to B-VPLS to perform PBB encapsulation and send traffic to the backbone. I-VPLS can connect to regular VPLS through spoke-pseudowires. I-VPLS can connect to other I-VPLSs through regular pseudowires.	B-VPLS can connect to I-VPLS (1:1 or N:1) to carry traffic from the customer domain through the backbone domain. B-VPLS can connect to B-VPLS in other PE routers in the backbone through mesh- or spoke-pseudowire. B-VPLS cannot connect directly to regular VPLS.	A regular VPLS can connect to another regular VPLS through mesh- or spoke-pseudowire. Regular VPLS can connect to I-VPLS through spoke-pseudowire, thus sending the traffic through the backbone.

The detailed interoperation behaviors are discussed later in this chapter. As mentioned previously, the PBB-VPLS solution is transparent to customers. The customer traffic still travels into the VPLS service network from the SAP ingress of the local VPLS service instance of the local PE router and reaches the remote site through the SAP egress of the remote VPLS service instance of a remote PE router. Figure 17.6 illustrates the end-to-end customer flow of frames and the use of B-MAC addresses in a PBB-VPLS network.

Figure 17.6 PBB-VPLS Using B-MAC Addresses in the B-Domain

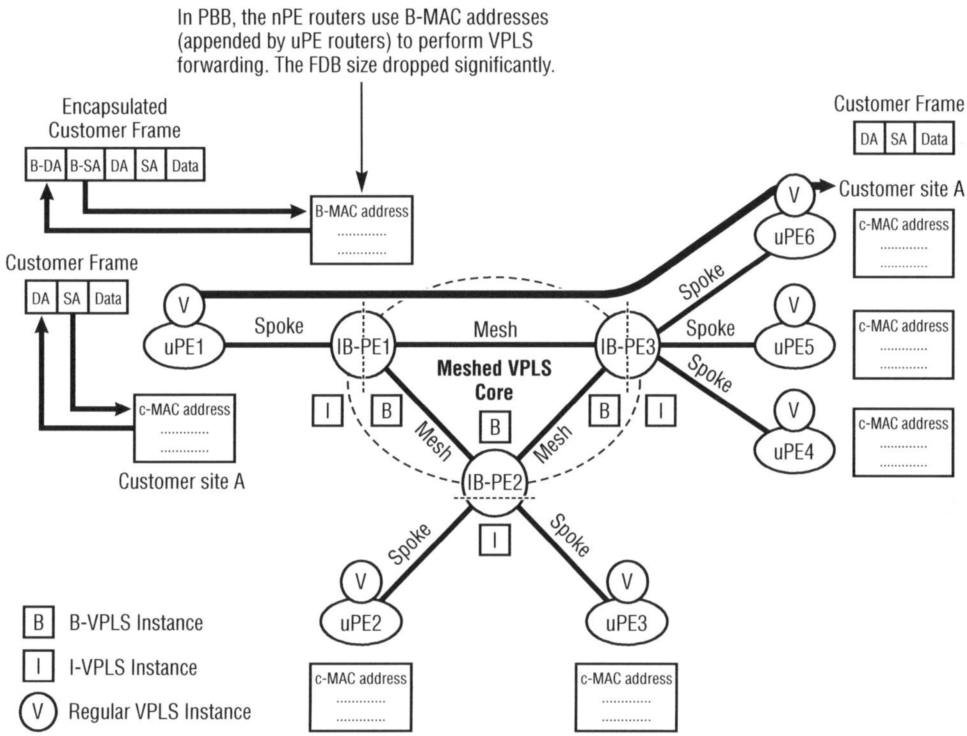

In the IB-PE router, one B-VPLS service instance is associated with each I-VPLS. The I-VPLS prepends each customer frame with an extra PBB header before it forwards the traffic to the B-VPLS and across the PBB backbone (B-domain).

Figure 17.6 illustrates a precise packet walk-through of a PBB-VPLS network (indicated by the thick line with the arrowhead on the right end):

1. The customer traffic enters the network through the SAP instance of the user VPLS service instance of Router uPE 1.

2. The user VPLS then performs VPLS traffic encapsulation on the traffic and sends it through the spoke-pseudowire to the VPLS instance of router IB-PE 1.

3. In the IB-PE 1 router, the I-VPLS service instance de-encapsulates the traffic, then performs PBB encapsulation and sends it through the internal link to the B-VPLS service instance.

4. The B-VPLS service instance in the IB-PE 1 router then performs VPLS encapsulation on the PBB-encapsulated traffic and sends it to the IB-PE 3 router through the core mesh-pseudowire.

5. The B-VPLS of IB-PE 3 receives traffic, then removes the VPLS encapsulation, exposing the PBB-encapsulated traffic.

6. Next, the B-VPLS uses the I-TAG information in the PBB header to identify to which I-VPLS service instance the traffic should be sent, and sends the traffic through the internal link to that I-VPLS.

7. The I-VPLS service instance of IB-PE 3 then removes the PBB encapsulation, performs VPLS encapsulation again, and sends the traffic to uPE 6 through the spoke-pseudowire.

8. uPE 6 then performs de-encapsulation and sends the native customer traffic to the remote customer site.

The discussion above is a brief description of the PBB-VPLS traffic forwarding process. Details regarding the encapsulation format and forwarding decisions are introduced later in this chapter.

The IB-PE routers are the key element of the PBB-VPLS solution. As the boundary between the I-domain and the B-domain, all PBB intelligence is in the IB-PE router. Two types of VPLS service instance coexist in the IB-PE router and are associated with each other — the I-VPLS service instance and the B-VPLS service instance. The I-VPLS service instance connects the regular VPLS PE routers in the I-domain and

exchanges regular VPLS traffic. The B-VPLS service instance connects the B-VPLS
PE routers in the B-domain and exchanges backbone VPLS traffic.

I-VPLS

The I-VPLS service instance in an IB-PE router is in charge of connecting the
regular user VPLS from the I-domain to the backbone VPLS in the B-domain. An
I-VPLS service instance receives its definition of the I-VPLS type upon the creation
of the service instance in the IB-PE router. As a VPLS service instance, the I-VPLS
is also a Virtual Bridge (VB) that contains bridge ports and an FDB. The I-VPLS
virtual bridge may contain the following three types of bridge ports:

- An internal link to the associated B-VPLS. The internal link is created when
  the association between the I-VPLS and the B-VPLS is created in the I-VPLS
  configuration. The I-VPLS performs PBB encapsulation on the traffic when
  sending the traffic over the internal link to the B-VPLS and performs PBB de-
  encapsulation on the traffic when receiving the traffic from the B-VPLS through
  the internal link.

- The spoke-pseudowire(s) connected to the regular user VPLS in the I-domain.
  This spoke-pseudowire sends and receives VPLS-encapsulated traffic with regular VPLS member PE routers in the I-domain of the network.

- The SAP(s) connected to the local customer site. Similar to the regular VPLS
  service instance, the I-VPLS can also have SAPs with attachment circuits to
  the VPLS customer's site(s).

Figure 17.7 illustrates an example of PBB-VPLS network architecture. The example presents the configuration of both the uPE router and the IB-PE router.

The I-VPLS service instance configuration in IB-PE 1 is shown in the top
right corner of the diagram. The configuration in the diagram illustrates that
the I-VPLS has *connections* to both the user VPLS in the I-domain (through the
spoke-pseudowire configuration) and to the backbone VPLS in the B-domain
(through the b-vpls association). Therefore, the I-VPLS VB is able to forward traffic between the I-domain and the B-domain and perform correct encapsulation and
de-encapsulation.

Figure 17.7 PBB-VPLS Network Configuration Example

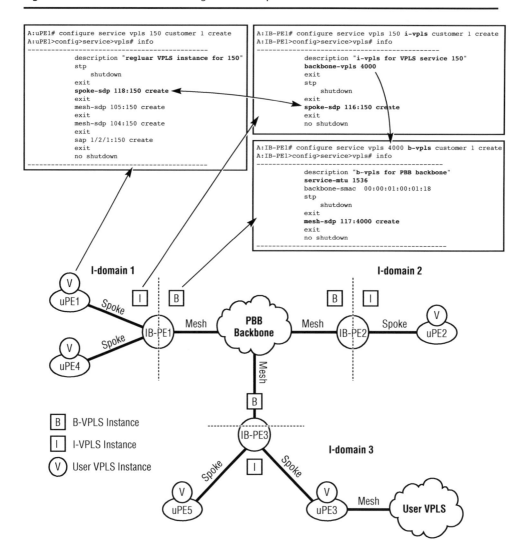

Figure 17.8 uses the I-VPLS status CLI output to illustrate the B-VPLS association.

The bottom part of Figure 17.8 presents an optional configuration of I-SID (I-VPLS service ID). One B-VPLS service instance can be associated with multiple I-VPLS service instances. When the B-VPLS receives the PBB-encapsulated traffic from remote B-VPLS PE routers, the B-VPLS uses the I-SID to identify to which I-VPLS service instance the traffic belongs. I-SID is the *I-VPLS service de-multiplexer*. Each I-VPLS service instance has its own I-SID. By default, the I-SID uses the numerical value of the service-id of the I-VPLS service instance. However, the value range of the service-id is 1–2,147,483,647, but the I-SID has a value range of only 0–16,777,215, with 0-FF and FFFFFF reserved by the standard. If the I-VPLS service has a service-id value that exceeds the I-SID value, a legitimate I-SID value must be specified explicitly when associating the I-VPLS with the B-VPLS in the I-VPLS configuration.

Figure 17.8 I-VPLS Status Output: Association with B-VPLS

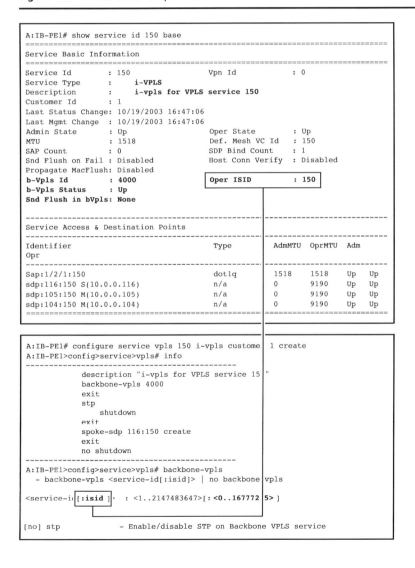

B-VPLS

The B-VPLS service instance in an IB-PE router is in charge of connecting other member PE routers participating in the B-VPLS in the backbone network. The B-VPLS service performs learning and forwarding based on the B-MAC addresses. As a VPLS service instance, the B-VPLS is also a VB that contains bridge ports and FDBs. The B-VPLS VB may contain three types of bridge ports:

- The internal link(s) to the associated I-VPLS(s). B-VPLS sends and receives traffic from I-VPLS service instances over the internal links. One B-VPLS may be associated with more than one I-VPLS service instance. The B-VPLS uses the I-SID in the PBB header as an *I-VPLS de-multiplexer* to distinguish traffic belonging to different I-VPLSs.

- The mesh- or spoke-pseudowire(s) connected to the other B-VPLS PE routers in the PBB backbone network. These pseudowires send and receive PBB-encapsulated VPLS traffic.

- The PBB SAP(s) connecting the Ethernet PBB type of customer sites. PBB-VPLS is not only capable of improving the scalability of the regular VPLS solution, it is also capable of performing PBB bridging with IEEE 802.1ah PBB-capable devices. The B-VPLS can perform PBB Ethernet bridging among these devices if a customer needs to connect native PBBN devices.

Figure 17.9 illustrates an example of B-VPLS configuration. The bottom part of Figure 17.9 presents the configuration of the service MTU of the B-VPLS. Because B-VPLS forwards PBB-encapsulated traffic with PBB headers (18-byte overhead), the B-VPLS must have a service MTU that is 18 bytes greater than any of the I-VPLSs or Epipes it services. In the example, the I-VPLS service uses the default VPLS service MTU value of 1,518. Therefore, the associated B-VPLS must have a minimum service MTU of 1,536 to be able to carry traffic for the I-VPLS.

> **Note:** The PBB encapsulation header is 18 to 22 bytes long (a 4-byte B-VID field may or may not be present depending on the vc-vlan type of the B-VPLS); therefore, the B-VPLS in the backbone network must have its MTU set to at least 18 to 22 bytes larger than the I-VPLS with which it is associated.

Figure 17.9 B-VPLS Status Output: Service MTU

```
A:IB-PE1# show service id 4000 base
=================================================================
Service Basic Information
=================================================================
Service Id        : 4000          Vpn Id            : 0
Service Type      : b-VPLS
Description       : b-vpls for PBB backbone
Customer Id       : 1
Last Status Change: 10/19/2003 16:21:04
Last Mgmt Change  : 10/19/2003 16:20:26
Admin State       : Up            Oper State        : Up
MTU               : 1536                Def. Mesh VC Id  : 4000
SAP Count         : 0             SDP Bind Count    : 1
Snd Flush on Fail : Disabled      Host Conn Verify  : Disabled
Propagate MacFlush: Disabled
Oper Backbone Src : 00:00:01:00:01:18
i-Vpls Count      : 1
Epipe Count       : 0

-----------------------------------------------------------------
Service Access & Destination Points
-----------------------------------------------------------------
Identifier                        Type     AdmMTU  OprMTU  Adm  Opr
-----------------------------------------------------------------
sdp:117:4000 M(10.0.0.117)        n/a      0       9190    Up   Up
=================================================================
```

```
A:IB-PE1# configure service vpls 4000 b-vpls customer 1 create
A:IB-PE1>config>service>vpls# info
-------------------------------------------------------
          description "b-vpls for PBB backbone "        The backbone VPLS must have
    service-mtu 1536                                     a service-MTU at least 18 bytes
          backbone-smac  00:00:01:00:01:18              bigger than the I-VPLSs it
          stp                                           serves. This is because the
               shutdown                                 traffic in the PBB-VPLS
          exit                                          backbone has an extra PBB
          mesh-sdp 117:4000 create                      encapsulation header of 18
          exit                                          bytes.
          no shutdown
-------------------------------------------------------
```

The B-VPLS service instance performs VPLS encapsulation and de-encapsulation on the traffic at the pseudowires connected to other PBB PE routers in the B-domain (remember that the I-VPLS performs PBB encapsulation). The B-VPLS service instance also performs PBB encapsulation and de-encapsulation on PBB SAPs. B-VPLS uses B-MAC addresses to perform learning and forwarding, and it is not aware of C-MAC addresses.

Each B-VPLS service instance in a PE router is explicitly configured with a B-MAC address using the command backbone-smac xx:xx:xx:xx:xx:xx in the VPLS configuration context. This MAC address uniquely identifies the B-VPLS service instance in the PE router. All I-VPLS service instances locally associated with this B-VPLS use this MAC address as the source B-MAC address when performing PBB encapsulation. When the B-VPLS service instance receives traffic from other B-VPLS PE routers, it learns the source B-MAC address and adds it to its FDB. PBB encapsulation and the formation of the B-VPLS FDB are introduced in detail in Section 17.3.

PBB-VPLS Traffic Encapsulation

In an IB-PE router in the PBB-VPLS solution, after the I-VPLS receives traffic from its SAP or I-domain-facing pseudowires, the I-VPLS performs PBB encapsulation before it forwards customer traffic to the B-VPLS. Then the B-VPLS performs VPLS encapsulation on the PBB frame before it sends the traffic to the backbone network. In the B-domain, the PBB-VPLS traffic has both VPLS pseudowire encapsulation and PBB encapsulation. Figure 17.10 illustrates the encapsulation content for this traffic.

When the I-VPLS performs PBB encapsulation, three pieces of information are required to compose the traffic's PBB header:

- **I-SID** — The I-SID is the I-VPLS service identifier used for the remote B-VPLS as an I-VPLS de-multiplexer to identify which I-VPLS service associated with it should receive the traffic. All I-VPLS instances belonging to the same service across a PBBN core must use the same I-SID value and must be associated with the same B-VPLS service in order to exchange traffic through the B-domain.

- **Source B-MAC Address** — As mentioned previously, the B-VPLS service instances in the B-domain use the B-MAC address to perform learning and forwarding. Each B-VPLS service instance has its own globally unique B-MAC address defined in the B-VPLS configuration. The I-VPLS uses the B-MAC defined in the B-VPLS instance with which it is associated as the source B-MAC address in the PBB header.

- **Destination B-MAC Address** — The destination B-MAC address is learned by receiving PBB-encapsulated traffic from other B-VPLS PE routers. When the local B-VPLS service instance receives traffic from another B-VPLS PE router, it first uses the I-SID in the PBB header to identify the correct receiving I-VPLS. Next, the traffic is sent to the I-VPLS with the PBB header. When the I-VPLS receives PBB-encapsulated traffic, it performs the following operations:

  1. It first learns the B-MAC in the PBB header and adds it to I-VPLS FDB.

  2. It then removes the PBB header and exposes the VPLS traffic, and learns the traffic's C-MAC address and adds it to its FDB.

  3. It associates this C-MAC with the B-MAC in the FDB learned from the PBB header.

4. Then, it forwards the traffic to the correct spoke-pseudowire or SAP according to the result in the FDB, based on the destination C-MAC lookup.

Figure 17.10 PBB-VPLS Encapsulation Format

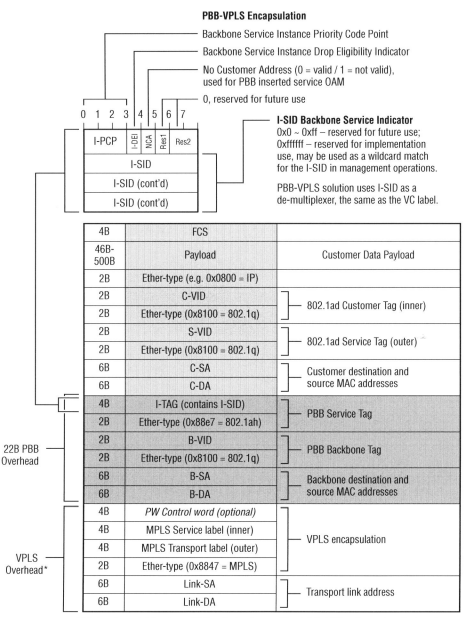

* This format example is based on an MPLS service tunnel over an Ethernet Link. A GRE service tunnel can also be used, and other interfaces can be used for transportation (e.g. POS).

Each time the I-VPLS receives traffic from the I-domain destined to a remote I-domain, it consults the PBB-related section of the FDB to find the correct B-MAC address to use as the destination B-MAC address for the PBB encapsulation. If there is no matching value, the I-VPLS uses a *group B-MAC address* as the destination B-MAC address to perform the PBB encapsulation. Group B-MAC address is a multicast MAC address used by PBB-VPLS to carry BUM traffic. The group B-MAC address is a multicast MAC address of `00:01:8e:xy;zw;rp`.

After the B-MAC address is acquired and the I-VPLS receives traffic from the I-domain, the I-VPLS performs PBB encapsulation before sending the traffic to the corresponding B-VPLS. Figure 17.10 illustrates the frame format after PBB encapsulation.

PBB encapsulation is performed in the I-VPLS instance in the IB-PE router before the traffic is sent to the associated B-VPLS. If I-VPLS determines that the ingress traffic should be forwarded to the backbone or should be flooded (including to the B-VPLS), PBB encapsulation is performed before the traffic travels to the B-VPLS VSI.

The process of PBB encapsulation is as follows:

1. Insert the B-MAC (source and destination). The B-DA should be found in the FDB mapping of the I-VPLS VSI when it receives traffic from the B-VPLS. For BUM traffic, the B-DA is a special backbone group MAC address: `01-1E-83-`*nn-nn-nn* (multicast bit set, which is discussed later in this chapter).

2. Insert the I-TAG. The I-TAG contains the I-VPLS service identifier (I-SID). The I-SID is used as a de-multiplexer for the receiving B-VPLS VSI to identify to which I-VPLS the traffic belongs.

3. Insert the B-VID. The B-VID field may or may not exist in the PBB encapsulation, depending on the types of SAPs and pseudowires configured.

In the other direction, when the B-VPLS instance of the IB-PE receives PBB-VPLS traffic from the B-VPLS of another IB-PE router in the B-domain, it removes the pseudowire encapsulation and checks the B-DA of the frame. If the B-DA matches its own B-MAC address, or the B-DA is a backbone group MAC address (`01-1E-83-`*nn*-nn-nn), the traffic is meant to be forwarded to the local I-VPLS VSI. Otherwise the traffic is dropped. Then, it performs an *I-SID lookup* to identify to which I-VPLS this traffic belongs, before if forwards the traffic to the corresponding

I-VPLS VSI. (In 1:1 mode, this is not necessary, because one B-VPLS VSI is associated with only one I-VPLS VSI. In N:1 mode, the I-SID is used as the de-multiplexer to identify which I-VPLS should receive the traffic.) Upon receiving the traffic from the B-VPLS, the I-VPLS VSI de-encapsulates the PBB frame (it becomes a regular customer Ethernet frame), then forwards or floods it to the SAP or SDP port according to the FDB lookup result.

> **Note:** Currently, I-SID translation is not mentioned in the PBB-VPLS draft or IEEE 802.1ah standard. When the two PBB-VPLS backbones are connected (inter-AS PBB-VPLS), there is a chance that the I-SID needs to be changed because the two I-VPLSs must use different I-SIDs. In this case, the I-SID must be modified when the traffic travels through the interconnecting link to enter another B-domain. This is called *I-SID translation*.

17.3 PBB-VPLS Learning and Forwarding

A PBB-VPLS network contains B-VPLSs and I-VPLSs. Each type of VPLS contains its own pseudowires to provide connectivity with other I-VPLSs or B-VPLSs or to interconnect the two. Different SAPs (I-SAP and B-SAP) may exist in the PBB-VPLS network as well, and they forward different types of traffic based on different MAC addresses. This section discusses the details regarding all possible data ingress and egress paths in the PBB-VPLS solution and the formation of the FDB in both types of VPLS service instances.

Control Plane: Learning MAC Addresses

In a PBB-VPLS network, both the I-VPLS and the B-VPLS need to perform MAC learning to build their FDBs. As mentioned in previous sections, the B-VPLS and I-VPLS perform learning and forwarding based on different MAC addresses. The I-VPLS performs PBB encapsulation on received frames that have a remote destination across the backbone.

Figure 17.11 illustrates an example of two PCs connected to the PBB-VPLS network to demonstrate all the necessary steps the routers (IB-PEs) perform in a PBB-based VPLS solution.

Figure 17.11 PBB-VPLS Forwarding Behavior Illustration

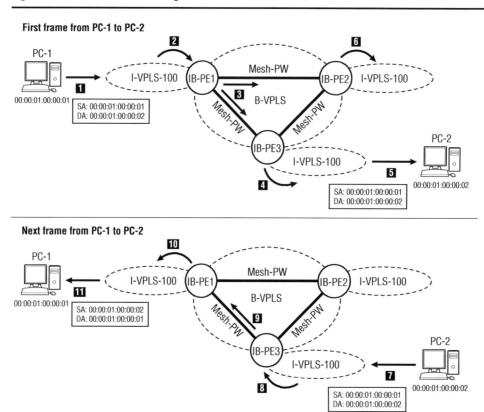

In Figure 17.11, PC-1 is connected to I-VPLS-100 via a SAP (on the left side of the network) and is trying to send an Ethernet frame to PC-2 connected to the I-VPLS-100 (on the right side of the network) (Steps 1–6). The MAC address of PC-1 is 00:00:01:00:00:01, and the MAC address of PC-2 is 00:00:01:00:00:02. After PC-2 receives the frame, it sends a frame back to PC-1 (Steps 7–11). A similar frame walk-through was illustrated in Chapter 11 regarding the learning and forwarding behavior of regular VPLS. The frame walk-through in Figure 17.11 demonstrates how PBB-VPLS components perform learning and forwarding.

The backbone network in Figure 17.11 is simplified because the existence of Backbone Core (BC)-PE routers (the PE routers only have the B-VPLS instance defined) and P routers is irrelevant to the present discussion. In most cases, service providers using a PBB-VPLS solution have a large-scale backbone network and more than one large Customer Edge network. Also, to simplify the description, the example uses an IB-PE implementation, where the I-VPLS and B-VPLS are co-located in the same router, and pass traffic through an internal link. A non-co-located implementation is similar. Figure 17.11 illustrates PBB-VPLS forwarding behavior with a series of procedures for a PBB-VPLS solution to forward traffic end-to-end.

An end-to-end data frame walk-through on a customer Ethernet frame is the best way to describe how PBB-VPLS forwards customer traffic:

1. When PC-1 sends out a frame that has its own MAC address as SA and the MAC address of PC-2 as DA, the VSI of the I-VPLS in IB-PE 1 receives the customer frame. The I-VPLS learns the SA address and associates it with the local SAP from which the traffic was received. Next, the I-VPLS looks up the DA of the frame in the FDB, but finds no matching entries. Therefore, the frame of PC-1 is treated as an unknown unicast frame, and the I-VPLS VSI in PE-1 floods it to all of its SAPs, mesh-pseudowires, and spoke-pseudowires (applying the Split-Horizon rule), including the internal link connected to the B-VPLS VSI in PE-1.

2. Before the I-VPLS VSI sends traffic to the B-VPLS, it must perform PBB encapsulation on the frame. The PBB header includes B-DA, B-SA, B-VID (optional), and I-SID. The I-VPLS needs to set the values for these fields for the encapsulation, as follows:

   • Since PC-2 has never before sent out traffic, its MAC address is unknown. For BUM traffic, the B-DA is a special backbone group MAC address: 01-1E-83-*00-00-64*, where *64* is the hex value of the I-SID (100 in decimal) of the I-VPLS VSI.

   • The B-SA is a configured value that, depending on the solution being used, could be locally configured in the I-VPLS, as in the case of dual-homing, or configured in the B-VPLS context of the PE router.

   • The I-SID is a value configured in the I-VPLS instances. By default, it uses the I-SID of the I-VPLS VSI, in this case, that would equate to a value of 100 in decimal or 0x64 (hex).

These values are inserted into the PBB header and encapsulated into the frame before it is forwarded to the B-VPLS.

3. When the B-VPLS in PE-1 receives the PBB-encapsulated Ethernet frame, it learns the B-SA with the correct association (internal link from the I-VPLS), and then forwards the frame based on the B-DA set by the I-VPLS. Because this frame has a backbone group MAC address, the I-VPLS replicates the packet and floods it to all ports in the bridge group (SAPs and SDPs), respecting the Split-Horizon rule. Therefore, all B-PE routers participating in the same B-VPLS (in this case, PE-2 and PE-3) receive the frame from PE-1.

4. When the B-VPLS VSI in PE-3 receives the frame, it removes the MPLS header of the frame and then learns the B-SA. When the PE-3 checks the B-DA of the frame, it finds that the destination is a backbone group MAC address. Therefore, it floods the packet to all ports in the bridge group, including the I-VPLS VSI attached to it, *which has an I-SID value that matches the frame's PBB header.*

5. The I-VPLS VSI in PE-3 receives the frame, removes the PBB header, and learns the B-SA and the C-SA. The VSI then performs an FDB lookup *for the C-DA MAC address.* Because no matching entry is found, it floods the frame to all ports in the bridge group (again, obeying the Split-Horizon rule, in this case, the VSI does not send the frame back to the B-VPLS from which the frame was received). Because PC-2 is attached to one SAP of the I-VPLS VSI in PE-2, it receives the frame.

6. The B-VPLS VSI in Router PE-2 also receives the frame with PBB and MPLS encapsulation. It removes the MPLS encapsulation and learns the B-SA. Then, the B-VPLS VSI floods the frame to all ports in the same bridge group because the B-DA of the frame is a backbone group MAC address.

So far, all PBB VPLS instances have been flooded with the first frame from PC-1. In the customer domain, all I-VPLS-100 members have learned the MAC address 00:00:01:00:00:01 (the mapping could be to a SAP port, an I-VPLS spoke-pseudowire, or B-VPLS links). In the B-domain, all members of the B-VPLS associated with I-VPLS-100 have learned the B-SA of the frame as well (it may be associated with an I-VPLS link or pseudowires connected to other B-VPLS PE routers).

7. PC-2 responds to PC-1 by sending a frame with a source MAC address of 00:00:01:00:00:02 and a destination MAC address of 00:00:01:00:00:01 to the SAP of the I-VPLS VSI in PE-3. When the I-VPLS-100 of PE-3

receives the frame from PC-2, it learns the SA of PC-2, associating it with the local SAP.

8. When the I-VPLS-100 VSI in PE-3 performs an FDB lookup for the frame's DA, it finds a matching entry, learned previously (Step 5), and mapped to the B-VPLS VSI with a B-MAC address. Therefore, the I-VPLS-100 knows the destination is behind the B-VPLS through the B-domain. It performs PBB encapsulation using the specific destination B-MAC contained in the mapping of C-MAC to B-MAC and sends it to the associated B-VPLS. This time, the frame is unicast to the B-VPLS because the I-VPLS in PE-3 already knows where to send it.

9. When the B-VPLS in PE-3 receives the frame, it learns the B-SA of the frame set by I-VPLS, then forwards the frame to PE-1, because the B-DA of this frame is known in the FDB (learned in Step 4). VPLS encapsulation for the frame is performed before the frame is sent.

10. When the B-VPLS in PE-1 receives the frame, it removes the pseudowire encapsulation and learns the B-SA. When the B-VPLS finds that the B-DA matches its own B-MAC address, it checks the PBB header to determine whether the I-SID matches one of its local I-TAGs. In this case, the B-VPLS finds a match of the I-SID of I-VPLS-100. Therefore, the B-VPLS forwards the frame to the VSI of I-VPLS-100.

11. When the I-VPLS-100 in PE-1 receives the frame from the B-VPLS, it removes the PBB header, learns the C-SA address of the frame, and then performs an FDB lookup on the C-DA. Because the C-DA of this frame was learned in Step 1, it unicasts the frame through the local SAP to PC-1.

From now on, all flows between PC-1 and PC-2 are unicast to each other because all involved components know the location of both MAC addresses.

> **Note:** In this example, Router IB-PE-2 and the VPLS VSI connected to it still have no knowledge of the location of PC-2 (i.e. behind which SAPs or pseudowires). This is because the flow from PC-2 to PC-1 is switched instead of flooded to all IB-PE routers.

Data Plane: Forwarding Encapsulation and De-Encapsulation

Table 17.3 lists the frame forwarding behavior of B-VPLS and I-VPLS. The ingress column lists where the frames come from, and the egress column lists the forwarding or discarding action based on the destination MAC addresses. Both I-VPLS and B-VPLS make forwarding decisions based on the destination MAC address of a frame. The differences are:

- All frames received by the B-VPLS from any of its SAPs or pseudowires or internal links (from the I-VPLS) are PBB-encapsulated; therefore, the SA and DA of the frame are always B-MAC addresses.

- The I-VPLS may receive either regular Ethernet traffic from the VPLS SAP, VPLS-encapsulated traffic from the I-domain's pseudowires, or PBB-encapsulated traffic from the internal link connected to the B-VPLS. The I-VPLS is in charge of applying the PBB encapsulation and maintaining the C-MAC to B-MAC mapping table; it needs to learn both the C-MAC and the B-MAC addresses and perform the corresponding forwarding and encapsulation and de-encapsulation functions when necessary.

Table 17.3 PBB-VPLS Traffic Forwarding Information

Ingress	Egress
I-VPLS SAP/ pseudowire	The I-VPLS learns the C-SA from its ingress. Forwarding occurs as follows: • If the C-DA is known and the next-hop is local to the I-VPLS, the I-VPLS forwards the frame to the correct pseudowire or SAP in the I-VPLS. • If the C-DA is known and the destination is a remote B-DA, the I-VPLS performs PBB encapsulation. If the B-DA is known, the I-VPLS forwards the frame to the associated B-VPLS. The B-DA should always be known (C-MAC and B-MAC address mapping ages out as soon as the B-MAC/src-id mapping ages out); therefore, it is not possible for a known C-MAC address to have no B-MAC address mapped to it. • If the C-DA is BUM, the I-VPLS floods it to all other I-VPLS SAPs and pseudowires, and to B-VPLS after performing PBB encapsulation (B-DA = I-SID group multicast address).

Ingress	Egress
B-VPLS SAP/SDP	If the B-DA and I-SID are local: • The B-VPLS learns the B-SA for the B-VPLS and the C-SA from the I-VPLS. • If the C-DA is known unicast, the B-VPLS forwards it if the next-hop is an I-VPLS SAP or SDP, and discards it if the next-hop is a B-DA (B-SAP/B-SDP). Respecting the Split-Horizon rule, the B-VPLS does not send traffic back through the internal link to the B-VPLS. • If the C-DA is BUM, the B-VPLS floods it only within the I-VPLS, respecting the Split-Horizon rule. If B-DA is local and not 802.1ah (only when PBB OAM): • The B-VPLS learns the B-SA. • If the B-DA appears in the FDB, the B-VPLS sends it to the control plane for further processing; otherwise, the B-VPLS floods it to all bridge groups in the B-VPLS(B-SAP and B-SDP) respecting the Split-Horizon rule. If the B-DA is known/unknown unicast: • The B-VPLS learns the B-SA within the B-VPLS. • If the B-DA is remote known unicast, the B-VPLS forwards it to the next-hop B-VPLS. • If the B-DA is unknown, the B-VPLS floods it to the backbone group (B-SAP and B-SDP), respecting the Split-Horizon rule. If the B-DA is a group MAC address (multicast/broadcast) with a local I-SID: • The B-VPLS learns the B-SA within the B-VPLS. • If the C-DA is known unicast and the next-hop is a local I-group, the B-VPLS forwards it to the local next-hop. If the C-DA is known unicast and the next-hop is a specific B-DA, the B-VPLS keeps flooding it to the backbone group, respecting the Split-Horizon rule. • If the C-DA is unknown unicast/broadcast, the B-VPLS floods it to both the I-group and the backbone group (respecting the Split-Horizon rule). • If the C-DA is multicast, the B-VPLS floods it to both the I-group and the backbone group (respecting the Split-Horizon rule). IGMP snooping may be supported in the future. If the B-DA is a group address (multicast/broadcast) and the I-SID is not local, the B-VPLS discards the traffic.

The forwarding behavior of PBB-VPLS components is not as complicated as it appears in Table 17.3. From the perspective of the I-VPLS, the internal link to its corresponding B-VPLS is just another bridge port in the VB. As a member of the same bridge group, the internal link is flooded with BUM traffic, and frames that have a destination behind the internal link (a matching entry from the FDB of the I-VPLS) are sent over it. Similarly, from the perspective of the B-VPLS, the PIP link to one of its corresponding I-VPLSs is like another SAP. When the I-VPLS determines that the frame has a remote destination over the backbone, it performs the corresponding PBB encapsulation and sends the frame to the B-VPLS to which it is connected.

When the frames in a PBB-VPLS network are forwarded from one location to another, the packet encapsulation may change. Figure 17.12 illustrates frame encapsulation in different components. In the B-domain, PBB encapsulation is always required, and in the I-VPLS domain, regular VPLS encapsulation is used.

Figure 17.12 Frames with Different Encapsulation in a PBB-VPLS Network

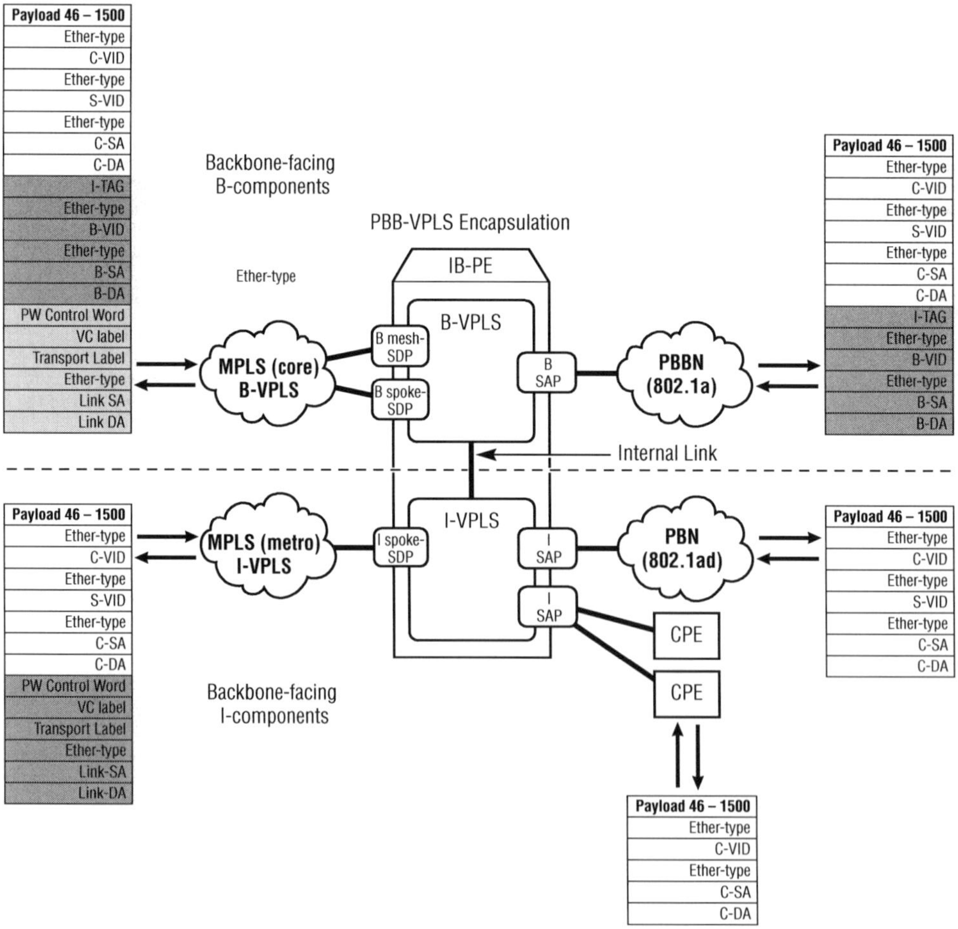

17.4 Controlling Flooding in PBB-VPLS

There are two ways of mapping I-VPLS to B-VPLS. One method is to create one B-VPLS instance for every I-VPLS, which is referred to as *1:1 mode*. In 1:1 mode, each I-VPLS representing that service connects to its own B-VPLS, and that B-VPLS connects only to the IB-PE routers that have that I-VPLS service instance configured. Therefore, multiple B-VPLSs may have different overlays serving different I-VPLSs.

On the other hand, multiple I-VPLSs can share the same B-VPLS instance, referred to as *N:1 mode*. A common B-VPLS can be created in the B-domain, and all IB-PE routers participate in that common B-VPLS. Different I-VPLS instances in different PE routers share the common B-VPLS. When the IB-PE router receives traffic from the B-VPLS, it needs to identify (using I-SID) the I-VPLS to which the traffic belongs, before it can forward it to the correct I-VPLS.

The carrier is free to choose a combination of both models if it so desires. Some services can use the 1:1 model, and others can be mapped to the *N*:1 model. Services may also be split up to use different B-VPLS *N*:1 backbones for load distribution or some logical separation. An IB-PE node can participate in many B-VPLS instances.

As mentioned previously, the ALSRP allows both 1:1 mode and *N*:1 mode; therefore, this is a network design choice. Figure 17.13 illustrates the 1:1 mode and *N*:1 mode of the PBB-VPLS infrastructure.

One issue with *N*:1 mode is that different I-VPLSs sharing the same B-VPLS may require different network overlays. For example, in the topology presented in Figure 17.14, I-VPLS-100 connects only to PE-1 and PE-4, and I-VPLS-200 connects only to PE-1 and PE-3. In such a topology, not all members of the common B-VPLS share the same IB-PE nodes. When BUM traffic arrives from an I-VPLS (in the example, I-VPLS-200), it is propagated to all IB-PE nodes connecting to that B-VPLS regardless of whether that service exists on every remote IB-PE or not. The flooding to the core may cause suboptimal bandwidth utilization. This section discusses how to control flooding in the backbone in a PBB-VPLS network. Figure 17.14 illustrates an example of several I-VPLS services sharing one backbone B-VPLS.

Figure 17.13 PBB-VPLS Mapping Mode: 1:1 versus *N*:1

1:1 Mode

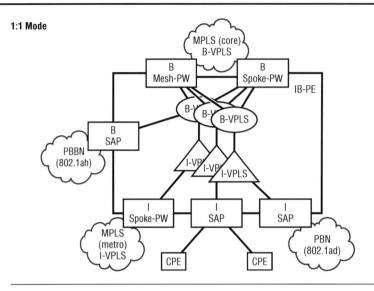

N:1 Mode

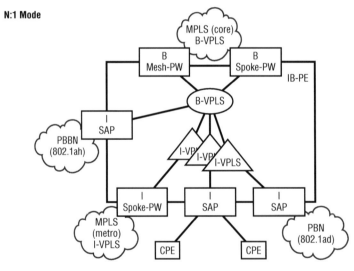

Figure 17.14 BUM Traffic Flooding in a B-VPLS Backbone

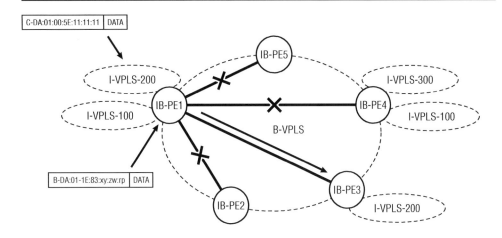

Suboptimal Flooding Behavior of PBB-VPLS

PBB-VPLS networks have a two-tier hierarchical network architecture. All I-VPLS components may share one or several B-VPLSs in the backbone network. In the backbone network, although all B-PE routers and IB-PE routers may be participating in the same B-VPLS (especially in N:1 mode), not all IB-PE routers are connected to all I-VPLS instances. If one I-VPLS instance needs to flood BUM traffic, the traffic is flooded to all ports in the bridge group (always respecting the Split-Horizon rule), including to the internal port of the backbone B-VPLS. When the backbone PBB-PE router receives this multipoint traffic from the internal port of the I-VPLS, how it handles the traffic is important from the perspective of efficiency of network bandwidth utilization.

   With no restrictions on the B-VPLS instance, any BUM traffic from the I-VPLS instances bound to that B-VPLS is flooded to all other B-PE routers participating in the same B-VPLS. The BUM traffic is then flooded through the entire backbone network, because the B-VPLS in the backbone network may be (and in fact is highly likely to be) fully meshed in the backbone network. If the I-VPLS that generates the BUM traffic is bound only to the B-VPLS in a few locations in the network, this flooding behavior in the backbone network is not efficient.

When the BUM traffic enters the B-VPLS, its B-DA is mapped to a backbone group MAC address. Therefore, each I-VPLS VSI in the IB-PE router has its own B-DA for BUM traffic; and this B-DA is never duplicated because the I-SID is globally unique in the PBB-VPLS network.

> **Note:** At the time of writing, the standards-based OUI for backbone multicasting is not finalized. The current ALSRP uses a newly assigned vendor OUI of 00-1c-8e with the group bit set to 1 as the B-DA of the BUM traffic from the I-VPLS.

Figure 17.14 shows that I-VPLS-200 VSI in the IB-PE-1 router is receiving a customer multicast frame (MAC address 01:00:5E:11:11:11); when mapping this frame to the B-VPLS in the backbone domain, the backbone group MAC address 01:1E:83:00:00:c8 is used (c8 is hex for 200, which is I-SID for VPLS 200). When IB-PE-1 floods the frame into the B-domain, only IB-PE-3 (which also has I-VPLS-200 VSI locally bound to the B-VPLS) requires the traffic. Other IB-PE routers (2, 4, and 5) discard the frame after receiving it because there is no corresponding I-VPLS (identified by the backbone group MAC address) locally bound to the B-VPLS. If the BUM traffic volume is high, a significant amount of backbone bandwidth is wasted.

In order to solve this problem, a mechanism is required to *track the membership* of the IB-PE routers in each I-VPLS instance. When one I-VPLS sends BUM traffic to the B-VPLS in the IB-PE router, the B-VPLS VSI in that router floods only (selectively, more like multicast) to the IB-PE peers that are associated with the same I-VPLS. The flooding decision in the B-VPLS is based not only on the backbone group MAC address, but also on the I-SID, which uniquely identifies the I-VPLS instance requiring the traffic to be flooded. Therefore, in the same B-VPLS, the flooding infrastructure for each I-VPLS can be different, just like in a multicast network: The Multicast Distribution Tree (MDT) can be different for different multicast groups. The Multiple Registration Protocol (MRP; defined in IEEE 802.1ak) can be used to optimize this behavior by building an MRP flooding tree for each I-VPLS service (per I-SID), and flooding the BUM frames from certain I-VPLSs only to the remote IB-PE routers that are members of the tree.

802.1ak Multiple Registration Protocol

The IEEE 802.1ak Multiple Registration Protocol (MRP) is a distributed protocol that allows attribute registration and declaration by multiple participants in a bridged LAN environment. Two applications of MRP are most frequently used — Multiple MAC Registration Protocol (MMRP) and Multiple VLAN Registration Protocol (MVRP). In a PBB-VPLS network, MMRP is used to optimize the traffic flooding in the backbone domain. In MMRP, the attribute handled by MRP is the MAC address, and in the case of PBB-VPLS, the backbone group MAC address. With MMRP, multiple virtual switching instances (participants) can declare (or withdraw) the registration of a MAC address, based on whether or not they want to receive frames from such an address. If a MAC address is registered on a bridge port, the virtual switch knows that the frames for that address should be transported to that bridge port. The MRP is a distributed multipoint-to-multipoint protocol, which means that any participant can use it to declare attributes for (or withdraw attributes from) any participants.

At a very high level, the 802.1ak application MMRP works in a way similar to the way the IGMP protocol works in a routed IP network. By explicitly tracking the *interested* members dynamically, MMRP maintains a *filter database*. Received traffic that has a backbone group MAC address that does not belong to the filter database is *filtered* (not transported) from the bridge port where there are no *interested* members. In order to maintain its registration state and receive traffic, a bridge port must declare interests (register) periodically. In a PBB-VPLS network, every backbone PBB-PE router participating in the backbone B-VPLS (shared by multiple I-VPLS instances) maintains a filtering database, and floods packets that have backbone group MAC addresses only to listed interested members. Table 17.4 reviews the terminology used in the discussion of the MMRP.

Table 17.4 MMRP Terminology

Terminology	Description
Participant	The party that is participating in the MMRP protocol. In the PBB-VPLS solution, each backbone PE router in the B-VPLS is one participant. A *full participant* has a complete applicant state machine and registrar state machine for each attribute backbone group MAC address. A full participant also has a single instance of *LeaveAll state machine* and a single instance of *PeriodicTransmission state machine*.

(continued)

Table 17.4   MMRP Terminology *(continued)*

Terminology	Description
Attribute	The information the MRP tracks. In the case of MMRP, the attribute is the MAC address; more specifically, in a PBB-VPLS network, the attribute is the backbone group MAC address. An applicant reports the existence of the attribute; then the registrar registers it into the filtering database. This forms the *I-SID group distribution tree* in the B-VPLS infrastructure.
Applicant	The element that announces its interest, ensuring that the declaration of the participant is registered by the registrars of the other participants and prompts other participants to re-register after one withdraws a declaration. In PBB-VPLS, each backbone PE router in the B-VPLS has one applicant for each I-VPLS instance. The applicant is the speaker of the protocol; it announces the backbone group MAC address and triggers Multiple Registration PDU (MRPDU) propagation.
Registrar	The element that records the declaration from the applicant made by other participants on the LAN. The registrar receives only MRPDUs; it never sends out any protocol messages. In PBB-VPLS, each backbone PE router in the B-VPLS has one registrar for each I-VPLS instance. The registrar is the listener of the protocol and accepts the MRPDU and registers the applicants into the state machine.
Declaration	The announcement made by the applicant of its interest in a MAC address by triggering the MRPDU. The declaration of a local applicant triggers MRPDU propagation and causes the corresponding registrars of the other participants to register the attributes. An IB-PE router declares a backbone group MAC address in a B-VPLS address under only two conditions: when it has a local I-VPLS instance associated with that B-VPLS, or when it has received a registration from another connected IB-PE router (respecting the Split-Horizon rule).
Registration	Registration occurs when, upon receiving an MRPDU, the registrar enables the state machine for the attributes and lists the originator of the MRPDU as an interested member. For any IB-PE router, receiving the registration of any backbone group MAC address in the B-VPLS means that there are remote IB-PE routers (behind certain pseudowires) participating in an I-VPLS.
Filtering database	The filtering database contains Group Registration Entries — a list of applicants that are currently registered in the registrar state machine. B-VPLS flooding behavior is controlled by the filtering database in each PE router.
Propagation	When an applicant in one participant declares a membership, it triggers the router to flood the MRPDU to all other participants. *The propagation (or flooding of MRPDU) always follows the active topology of the STP.*

In the MMRP for PBB-VPLS, the attribute registered is the backbone group MAC address — a unique MAC address which is reserved for each I-VPLS instance. The OUI for the backbone group MAC address is set to 01:1E:83, and the last 3 bytes of the backbone group MAC address is the hex value of the I-SID of the I-VPLS. Because the I-SID for an individual I-VPLS is globally unique in a PBB-VPLS network, each I-VPLS has its own backbone group MAC address, which is formatted as 01:1E:83:*nn:nn:nn*. Figure 17.15 illustrates the MMRP protocol operating in the B-domain of a PBB-VPLS network.

Figure 17.15   MMRP in PBB-VPLS B-Domain

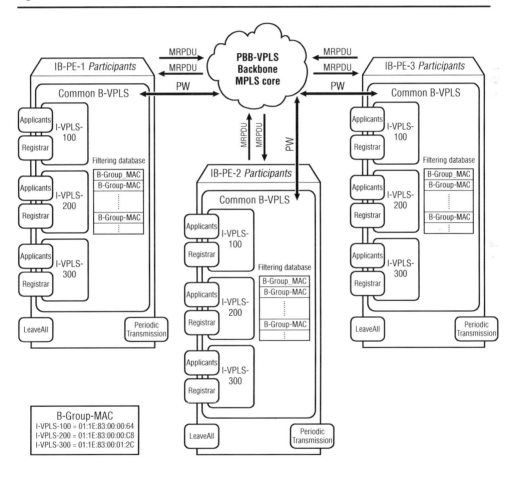

Each time a new I-VPLS instance is associated with the B-VPLS instance in an IB-PE router, the *applicant state machine* and the *registrar state machine* for the backbone group MAC address associated with the I-VPLS (01:1E:83:*nn:nn:nn*) are created in the B-VPLS instance. Next, the MMRP applicant in that I-VPLS declares the backbone group MAC address and triggers MRPDU propagation through the B-VPLS to register the backbone group MAC address with the other IB-PE routers (participants). The process of declaration propagation begins. By flooding MRPDUs through the backbone to all IB-PE routers participating in the B-VPLS, the existence of the I-VPLS association with the B-VPLS is propagated to all IB-PE members.

The *rules for a MMRP information exchange* are as follows (in all rules below, the bridge port means SAP and/or pseudowire in the B-VPLS):

- **Rule 1** — In any IB-PE router, the association of an I-VPLS VSI with a B-VPLS VSI triggers a declaration of the backbone group MAC address for that I-SID, putting the bridge port in the D (Declared) state, and flooding the information to the entire backbone network.

- **Rule 2** — In any IB-PE router, a declaration of one bridge port for a particular backbone group MAC address, triggers MRPDU generation from that bridge port to the remote peer.

- **Rule 3** — In any IB-PE router, receiving a MRPDU from one bridge port puts that port into the R (Registered) state (the MRPDU triggers registration).

- **Rule 4** — In any IB-PE router, a registration for a backbone group MAC address on a bridge port, causes the router to put all other bridge ports in the same bridge group into the D state for the same backbone group MAC address, and triggers MRPDU generation on the ports, respecting the Split-Horizon rule. This means:

  - Registration on one bridge port (receiving a MRPDU from that port) triggers the generation and flooding of the MRPDU to all other bridge ports.

  - MRPDU flooding obeys the Split-Horizon rule: If a bridge port receives an MRPDU from a port, it does not flood the MRPDU back to that port. Furthermore, if a mesh-pseudowire receives the MRPDU and therefore changes to the R state, it does *not* put other mesh-pseudowires into the D state and generate MRPDUs; only other spoke-pseudowires are set to the D state and generate MRPDUs.

- **Rule 5** — Should STP be used, the propagation of MRPDUs always follows the active STP forwarding topology. This means that if STP prunes a bridge port, the MRPDU is not propagated to that port, even if the port is operationally up.
- **Rule 6** — Only the port that is in both the D state and the R state is added to the backbone group MAC address flooding tree in the B-VPLS for that backbone group MAC address.

Table 17.5 lists all possible states for a bridge port (SAP or pseudowire) in the B-VPLS when MMRP is enabled to build the backbone group MAC address flooding tree.

Table 17.5 Building the MMRP Tree

Entry Status		Add to Tree	Description
Declared	Registered		
No	No	No	Both statuses are No, which means that the local I-VPLS that has the backbone group MAC address is not operationally up, and no remote IB-PE routers are registering the same I-VPLS. Therefore, there is no need to add the entry to the backbone group MAC address flooding tree for this group.
No	Yes	No	This combination means that remote IB-PE router(s) are member(s) of the corresponding I-VPLS, but the I-VPLS has no local instances for the router. Therefore, there is no need to join the backbone group MAC address flooding tree to receive the BUM traffic belonging to this I-VPLS.
Yes	No	No	This combination means that the IB-PE router has a local I-VPLS instance, but no remote member is participating in the same I-VPLS. Therefore, there is no need to send traffic to the backbone. The entry is not added to the backbone group MAC address flooding tree.
Yes	Yes	Yes	Both states are Yes, which means that the corresponding I-VPLS is locally active and has remote peering IB-PE routers. In this case, the BUM traffic needs to be flooded to remote member IB-PE router(s). Therefore, the entry is added to the backbone group MAC address flooding tree.

How Does MMRP Build the Flooding Tree?

Figures 17.17 and 17.18 illustrate how MMRP builds the backbone group MAC address flooding tree. The network shown in Figure 17.16 has one station in point A and one station in point B. (This is a LAN abstraction of VPLS, where the end station is similar to the I-VPLS in the IB-PE router, and the B-VPLS is represented by the switched core. The point is to find which bridge ports in the network should be involved in the flooding tree.) In such a topology, the most efficient flooding mechanism from point A to point B is a single path involving only the necessary bridge ports (follow the direction of the dashed arrow in the middle of the network). MMRP can compose this type of flooding tree between points A and B by declaring and registering attributes.

Figure 17.16 MRP: Declaration and Propagation — Stage 1 — Station in Point A (illustration from IEEE 802.1ak)

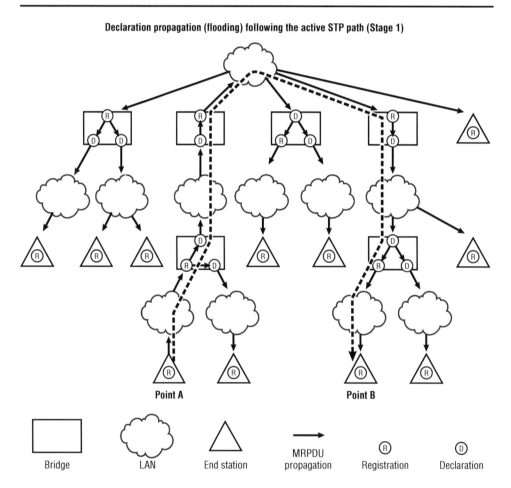

At the beginning, the end station in point A declares an attribute. This is equivalent to when an I-VPLS is associated with a B-VPLS in an IB-PE router, where the attribute is the backbone group MAC address of that I-VPLS. After the declaration from point A, the MRPDU is flooded to the entire network. The dashed line in the middle of the diagram shows a single propagation path. All other bridge ports in the active STP topology are either declaring the attribute or being registered during the MRPDU flooding. Figure 17.16 illustrates the MVR state of all bridge ports during the MRPDU flooding caused by the declaration at the end station in point A.

Next, assume the end station in point B declares the same attribute. This triggers another round of flooding of the same MRPDU, caused by different bridge ports. The dashed line in Figure 17.17 illustrates the MRPDU propagation path from point B to point A. Both processes obey the six MRP declaration propagation rules listed earlier in this chapter.

After both declaration processes are completed, all active bridge ports are in the D state, the R state, or both states. Remember that the only purpose of declaration, registration, and MRPDU flooding is to build the backbone group MAC address flooding tree. The rule of thumb is that *only the bridge port(s) that are in both the D and R states are added into the backbone group MAC address flooding tree.*

Figure 17.17 illustrates that, in this case, only the bridge ports along the dashed line are qualified to be in the flooding tree. These bridge ports form the necessary and most efficient forwarding path for the point A station and point B station to communicate. When using this mechanism for MMRP in B-VPLS, the backbone group MAC address flooding tree is formed. Only the ports along the dashed line are flooded by traffic destined to the backbone group MAC address. No other bridges (the backbone VSI in the case of PBB-VPLS) in the network receive flooded traffic. Figure 17.17 illustrates the MVR state of all bridge ports during the MRPDU flooding caused by the declaration at the end station in point B.

MMRP provides a mechanism for the IB-PE routers to exchange I-VPLS membership information. After the information is propagated throughout the B-domain, there is a filtering database for every backbone group MAC address (representing the existence of one I-VPLS service with a particular I-SID) in every IB-PE router. All known backbone group MAC addresses (by local I-VPLS association or remote MMRP registration) are stored as entries in the database. The MRP database stores the SAP/SDP number, the backbone group MAC address, and the registration/declaration status.

Figure 17.17 MRP: Declaration and Propagation — Stage 2 — Station in Point B
(illustration from IEEE 802.1ak)

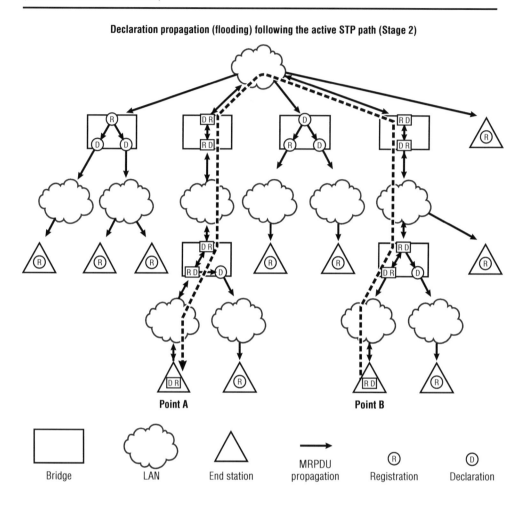

Declaration propagation (flooding) following the active STP path (Stage 2)

Point A

Point B

Bridge   LAN   End station   MRPDU propagation   (R) Registration   (D) Declaration

The registration (receiving MRPDU) creates an entry in a router's MRP data-base. The existence of the entry does not guarantee that traffic is present in the data plane. In the example illustrated in Figure 17.18, the bridge ports of all routers in the R state have an MRP entry for the received MRPDU, but only the IB-PE router with ports included in the backbone group MAC address flooding tree actually receives data traffic.

Figure 17.18 B-VPLS MRP Database

```
A:PE-165# show service id 1 mrp

---------------------------------------------------------------
MRP Information
---------------------------------------------------------------
Admin State       : Up          Failed Register Cnt: 0
Max Attributes    : 2048        Attribute Count    : 4
Attr High Watermark: 95%        Attr Low Watermark : 90%
Flood Time        : Off
---------------------------------------------------------------
A:PE-165# show service id 1 mmrp mac
---------------------------------------------------------------
SAP/SDP           MAC Address       Registered  Declared
---------------------------------------------------------------
sdp:163:1         01:1e:83:00:01:F5 Yes         Yes
sdp:163:1         01:1e:83:00:01:F6 Yes         No
sdp:163:1         01:1e:83:00:01:F7 Yes         Yes
---------------------------------------------------------------
```

If the MRP database exceeds its size limit (the number of entries exceeds the maximum allowed), the further registration to the router will fail. No traffic can be flooded for a backbone group MAC address that cannot be registered.

In the B-VPLS of each IB-PE router, the backbone group MAC address flooding tree is built based on the MRP database for that VPLS, using the principles presented in Table 17.5. Using the flooding tree, the IB-PE router floods the BUM traffic from the local I-VPLS VSI to the pseudowires listed in the tree, accepts the BUM traffic from these pseudowires, and then transports the traffic to the local I-VPLS VSI.

MRP Convergence and B-VPLS Flooding Switchover

When MRP is enabled in the backbone for a B-VPLS, flooding within the B-VPLS is limited to the registered/declared members of the flooding tree. As mentioned in the description of the MMRP registration process, when STP is enabled, MRP follows the active STP forwarding topology to build the flooding tree. This means that MRP relies on STP to provide a loop-free active forwarding topology in the VPLS.

During a network failure, the topology of the B-VPLS instance may be changed (for example, a new pseudowire is active and ready to replace a broken pseudowire to forward traffic, or a redundant SAP may be unblocked by STP). The convergence time for the B-VPLS to restore the traffic flow depends on the following:

- **xSTP Convergence** — xSTP needs to build a new active forwarding topology (whether the xSTP is enabled within the B-VPLS instances or an mVPLS B-VPLS is used to manage the forwarding topology of multiple B-VPLS) before any service can be restored. It may take several seconds for xSTP to propagate the topology change to the entire network.

- **MRP Convergence** — After xSTP builds the new active forwarding path, MRP needs time to complete the registration process and to build the flooding tree for the B-VPLS.

If desired, the carrier may configure the ability for the B-VPLS to revert to the flood to everyone behavior temporarily to speed up the convergence time during a network failure. This allows for network convergence and MRP time to build the flooding tree in the background for a predetermined amount of time, based on configuration. After this time, the B-VPLS switches to the MRP flooding behavior of flood to members only. Therefore, by paying the small price of short-term flooding in the backbone, the overall traffic outage time for the PBB-VPLS service may be shortened. Figure 17.19 illustrates a CLI configuration option of an MRP flooding revert timer.

Figure 17.19 MRP Flooding Revert Timer

```
A:IB-PE-165# configure service vpls 1000 mrp flood-time
  - no flood-time
  - flood-time <flood-time>

<flood-time>         : [3..600] secs

A:IB-PE-165#
```

When the flood-time is configured, the B-VPLS reverts to full flooding behavior under certain conditions, until the timer expires. These conditions include:

- **xSTP Events** — If STP is used to maintain the active forwarding path, any received Topology Change Notifications (TCNs) or local triggering of generation of TCNs triggers the B-VPLS to switch to full flooding.

- **B-SAP Status Change** — If the operational status of a B-SAP changes (from up to down or vice versa), the B-VPLS switches to full flooding.

- **B-SDP Status Change** — If the operational status of a pseudowire changes (from up to down or vice versa), the B-VPLS switches to full flooding.
- **Pseudowire Activation** — If the B-VPLS is using H-VPLS resiliency, the active/standby status of the pseudowire changes (when the standby pseudowire becomes active), triggering the B-VPLS to switch to full flooding.

17.5 FDB Management in I-VPLS and B-VPLS

In the PBB-VPLS solution, I-VPLS and B-VPLS are associated with each other to provide end-to-end packet forwarding. Therefore, the FDB in the PBB-VPLS must contain information about the association between the I-VPLS and the B-VPLS. Compared to the FDB of regular VPLS, more information must be stored. This section provides an analysis of the content of the FDB in PBB-VPLS, using a database output example from an IB-PE router.

FDB Content: I-VPLS versus B-VPLS

As previously discussed, the B-VPLS and I-VPLS perform learning and forwarding based on different information. Therefore, their database structures are also different. The I-VPLS FDB contains C-MAC addresses and the mapping of B-VPLS instances. Figure 17.20 illustrates the CLI output of the FDBs from I-VPLS and B-VPLS service instances.

Figure 17.20 illustrates an example of the FDBs of the I-VPLS and B-VPLS instances in the IB-PE routers. I-VPLS 100 is associated with B-VPLS 1000 in router IB-PE-165. Each VSI contains two FDBs — the FDB and the PBB FDB. In the example, a regular VPLS in the FDB of the customer domain PE router (C-PE-116) is displayed for comparison. This VPLS is connected to the I-VPLS in IB-PE-165 by a spoke-pseudowire.

The I-VPLS VSI is aware of both C-MAC and B-MAC addresses, and the pseudowire connected to the B-VPLS instance of the remote IB-PE router (b-sdp:166:1000 in the source identifier field). There are three entries in the first I-VPLS FDB display: The first one is a C-MAC address learned from a local SAP, and the last one is a C-MAC address learned from a spoke-pseudowire connected to a regular VPLS.

Figure 17.20 I-VPLS and B-VPLS FDB Example

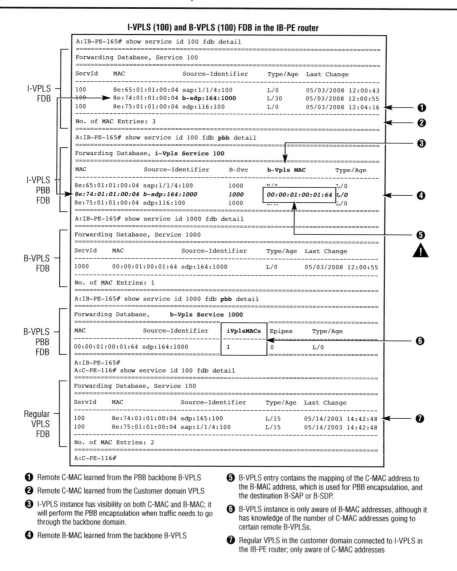

I-VPLS (100) and B-VPLS (100) FDB in the IB-PE router

❶ Remote C-MAC learned from the PBB backbone B-VPLS

❷ Remote C-MAC learned from the Customer domain VPLS

❸ I-VPLS instance has visibility on both C-MAC and B-MAC; it will perform the PBB encapsulation when traffic needs to go through the backbone domain.

❹ Remote B-MAC learned from the backbone B-VPLS

❺ B-VPLS entry contains the mapping of the C-MAC address to the B-MAC address, which is used for PBB encapsulation, and the destination B-SAP or B-SDP.

❻ B-VPLS instance is only aware of B-MAC addresses, although it has knowledge of the number of C-MAC addresses going to certain remote B-VPLSs.

❼ Regular VPLS in the customer domain connected to I-VPLS in the IB-PE router; only aware of C-MAC addresses

The second entry (the bold italic line), also referred to as the *B-VPLS entry*, contains the mapping of a C-MAC address and a B-MAC address learned from a PBB SAP or from a pseudowire connected to an associated B-VPLS. The I-VPLS instance uses this mapping to set the B-DA value when forwarding the traffic to the associated B-VPLS to the B-domain. When a packet in I-VPLS 100 has a destination

C-MAC that matches a B-VPLS-destined entry, PBB encapsulation is performed on the traffic, then the traffic is sent to the associated B-VPLS instance. In the I-VPLS FDB, the B-VPLS entry is treated differently from regular FDB management behavior, as follows:

- The `mac-move` feature (a passive loop-prevention mechanism) does not affect the B-VPLS entry.

- When a particular B-MAC address is aged out from the B-VPLS FDB, all corresponding B-VPLS entries in the I-VPLS FDB (C-MAC addresses mapped to the same B-MAC address) are automatically aged out. Traffic destined to these C-MAC addresses is treated as unknown unicast traffic after the age-out.

The B-VPLS has visibility of only B-MAC addresses. It may contain PBB entries learned from a PBB SAP (not shown in this example) and remote B-MAC addresses learned from a pseudowire. The PBB-FDB also contains information regarding the number of I-VPLS C-MAC addresses and the number of Epipes associated with the pseudowire. B-VPLS instances may also have an MRP database containing information that controls the flooding of BUM traffic in the backbone. In Router C-PE-116, the output shows the FDB of a regular VPLS instance for comparison. The B-VPLS FDB behaves differently from the FDBs of I-VPLS and regular VPLS, as follows:

- The aging-out of a B-MAC must provoke automatic aging of the related C-MAC addresses in the I-VPLS FDB. Sequential traffic uses backbone group MAC addresses as B-DA. By default, both I-VPLS and B-VPLS FDBs age out local entries after 300 seconds (5 minutes) and age out remote entries after 900 seconds (15 minutes), but they can be configured with different values. A remote entry is a MAC learned over a pseudowire.

Discard Unknown: I-VPLS versus B-VPLS

VPLS provides transparent Layer 2 bridging service to the customer traffic. If the destination MAC address is not in the FDB, by default, the traffic is flooded to the VSIs of all member PE routers. To conserve network bandwidth, this behavior can be modified by enabling the `discard unknown` feature in the VPLS. In the case of PBB-VPLS, the `discard unknown` feature can also be configured in both B-VPLS and I-VPLS instances, however, since the two types of VPLS use different MAC addresses to perform data forwarding, the meaning of *unknown* and the behavior of `discard unknown` is different.

I-VPLS instances forward traffic based on C-MAC addresses, so the term *unknown* is meaningful only for the C-DA address of the frames. When enabling the `discard unknown` feature in an I-VPLS instance:

- If the C-DA unknown traffic is received from the I-SAP or the I-SDP (not from the B-VPLS), the traffic is dropped in the same way that regular VPLS performs `discard unknown`.

- If the C-DA unknown traffic is received from the B-VPLS (B-SAP or B-SDP) and the I-SID is already validated by the ingress B-VPLS (the B-VPLS determines that the traffic belongs to the I-VPLS), it is dropped within the I-VPLS instance, and no I-SAP or I-SDP receives the traffic. However, if the B-DA of the traffic is a backbone group MAC address, the B-VPLS instance still floods the traffic to other B-SAPs and B-SDPs (respecting the Split-Horizon rule). The scope of the flooding may be limited by the MRP protocol.

B-VPLS instances forward traffic based on B-MAC addresses; therefore, `discard unknown` prohibits traffic with an unknown B-DA. When enabling the `discard unknown` feature in B-VPLS instances:

- If the B-DA unknown traffic is received from the B-SAP/B-SDP, the traffic is dropped in the same way that regular VPLS performs `discard unknown`.

- If the traffic is received from the locally associated I-VPLS, it is not possible to have unknown B-DA traffic for the frame. This is because the local I-VPLS sends traffic to the B-VPLS only under the following two conditions:

    - The I-VPLS has C-MAC or B-MAC mapping in its FDB, which means the B-DA is known.

    - The I-VPLS decides to flood the traffic to all bridge ports including the B-VPLS ports (BUM traffic). It uses the backbone group MAC address as the B-DA, which is always known (defined by the PBB protocol). The local I-VPLS VSI never sends a PBB frame to its associated B-VPLS with a B-DA that is unknown to the B-VPLS.

17.6 OAM in a PBB-VPLS Network

This section discusses OAM functionality in the PBB-VPLS solution. From a customer's perspective, the internal infrastructure of the VPLS service is transparent. As long as the VPLS service can provide the required connectivity, capacity, reliability, and quality, the customer does not care whether VPLS, H-VPLS, or PBB-VPLS is used to provide the service. From the perspective of OAM, a PBB-VPLS network behaves in the same way as a regular VPLS network. The VPLS solution behaves like a single-hop switch — it transparently carries the OAM traffic to other customer sites. 802.3ah EFM OAM can be configured at the port level when link level support is required. IEEE 802.3ah monitors single-link connectivity, and the service level abstraction is not visible.

From the provider's perspective, PBB-VPLS has a two-tier hierarchical architecture. The backbone is the B-VPLS domain, and the edge is the I-VPLS domain. From the operator's OAM perspective, the I-VPLS and the B-VPLS behave like two different entities. When there is OAM traffic in the I-VPLS, the B-VPLS transparently carries the traffic to other I-VPLS domains without processing it. The B-VPLS behaves like a switch connecting all I-VPLS domains, hiding its internal topology. When there are OAM activities in the B-VPLS, the scope of the OAM is limited to within the B-VPLS; therefore, the I-VPLS domains are not aware of the OAM in B-VPLS. Figure 17.21 illustrates the result of an OAM MAC-trace performed in the I-VPLS (service 200).

Figure 17.21   OAM MAC-Trace Output from an I-VPLS Service Instance

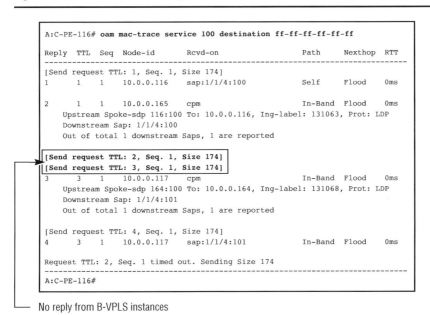

```
A:C-PE-116# oam mac-trace service 100 destination ff-ff-ff-ff-ff-ff

Reply  TTL  Seq  Node-id      Rcvd-on              Path      Nexthop  RTT
----------------------------------------------------------------------------
[Send request TTL: 1, Seq. 1, Size 174]
1     1    1    10.0.0.116    sap:1/1/4:100        Self      Flood    0ms

2     1    1    10.0.0.165    cpm                  In-Band   Flood    0ms
      Upstream Spoke-sdp 116:100 To: 10.0.0.116, Ing-label: 131063, Prot: LDP
      Downstream Sap: 1/1/4:100
      Out of total 1 downstream Saps, 1 are reported

[Send request TTL: 2, Seq. 1, Size 174]
[Send request TTL: 3, Seq. 1, Size 174]
3     3    1    10.0.0.117    cpm                  In-Band   Flood    0ms
      Upstream Spoke-sdp 164:100 To: 10.0.0.164, Ing-label: 131068, Prot: LDP
      Downstream Sap: 1/1/4:101
      Out of total 1 downstream Saps, 1 are reported

[Send request TTL: 4, Seq. 1, Size 174]
4     3    1    10.0.0.117    sap:1/1/4:101        In-Band   Flood    0ms

Request TTL: 2, Seq. 1 timed out. Sending Size 174
----------------------------------------------------------------------------
A:C-PE-116#
```

— No reply from B-VPLS instances

When using ff-ff-ff-ff-ff-ff as a destination MAC address for MAC-trace, all member PE routers of the VPLS (I-VPLS) respond. The internal topology of the VPLS is tracked. In this case, all I-VPLS components respond to the OAM MAC-trace, but the B-VPLS service instances do not respond, as noted in Figure 17.21.

Other OAM functions behave the same way in the PBB-VPLS: for example, SVC-ping, MAC-ping, MAC-trace, MAC-populate, MAC-purge, CPE-ping, IEEE 802.1ag CFM, ITU-T Y.1731, and so on. They can be executed separately in either the I-VPLS or the B-VPLS. If the OAM function is activated in the I-VPLS, the associated B-VPLS transparently passes the OAM traffic through.

17.7 Service Resiliency in PBB-VPLS Networks

Just as with regular VPLS or H-VPLS, resilience and redundancy are also desired in a PBB-VPLS network to protect the service against network failures. As a Layer 2 bridging service, loop prevention must be considered thoroughly in such a network to achieve optimal forwarding and to eliminate broadcast storms. This section discusses resiliency and loop prevention in a PBB-VPLS network. Figure 17.22 illustrates a typical PBB-network topology with multiple resiliency designs.

Figure 17.22   PBB-VPLS Network Infrastructure

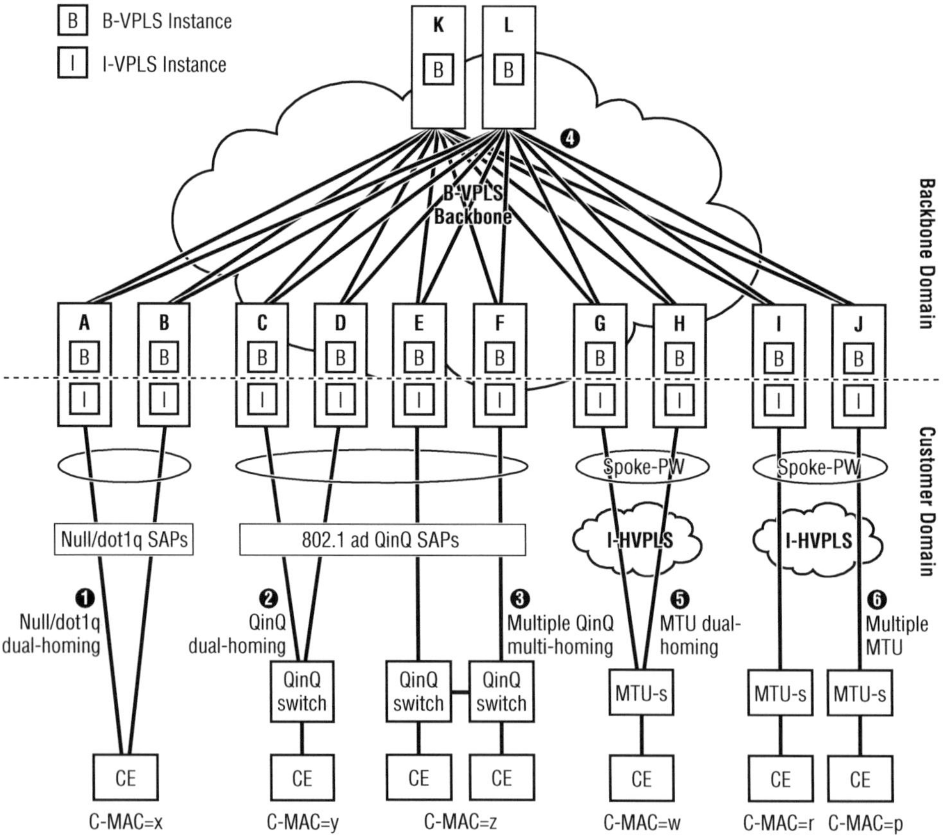

The network is divided into different tiers:

- **BC-PE Tier** — The BC-PE tier contains only BC-PE routers participating in B-VPLS instances.

- **Aggregation Switch Tier** — The aggregation switch tier contains IB-PE routers participating in both the B-VPLS and the I-VPLS. (The boundary between the backbone domain and the customer domain is located in these IB-PE routers.)

- **Edge Switch Tier** — The edge switch tier is in the customer domain and contains Q-in-Q switches (native PBN 802.1ad network), regular Ethernet (null/dot1q) switches, and MTUs connecting CE to IB-PE routers with spoke-pseudowire within the I-VPLS instance.

> **Note:** The PBB-encapsulated SAP (also referred to as *B-SAP*) in the core B-VPLS is not shown in this topology and is discussed elsewhere in this chapter.

Resilience is implemented in several locations in this type of network, for both the access and the core.

In the access side, the following cases are possible:

- **Case 1** — A single CE device can be dual-homed to the IB-PE routers (A and B). In this case, Multi Chassis Link Aggregation Group (MC-LAG) can be deployed to allow resiliency without causing forwarding loops. Less preferably, STP can also be enabled on the I-VPLS SAPs or mVPLS can be used to prevent forwarding loops.

- **Case 2** — A single Q-in-Q switch can be dual-homed to the IB-PE routers (C and D). Similar to Case 1, MC-LAG should be used to prevent forwarding loops. Less preferably, STP can be deployed.

- **Case 3** — Multiple Q-in-Q switches can be used to connect two different IB-PE routers (E and F) in the same I-VPLS to provide edge switch redundancy. In this case, STP is required to prevent forwarding loops.

In the core side:

- **Case 4** — The backbone is fully protected by a full mesh of pseudowires (naturally loop-free) connected to the PBB-PE routers (K and L), and MPLS resiliency can also be provided to the backbone network. A fully meshed PBB-VPLS backbone is loop-free.

- **Case 5** — A single MTU device may be used with the primary and backup spoke-pseudowire in the I-H-VPLS to connect to the IB-PE routers (G and H).

In this case, active/standby pseudowires on the MTU devices ensure that only one pseudowire is active at any time, to prevent forwarding loops. Less preferably, STP can be deployed.

- **Case 6** — Multiple MTU devices may be connected between the I-HVPLS and the IB-PE routers (I and J). In this case, STP is required to prevent forwarding loops.

Since multiple possible forwarding paths exist in this network in all the tiers, loop prevention must be provisioned to prevent forwarding loops in any of the domains. From a resiliency and loop-prevention perspective, deploying MC-LAG and active standby pseudowires in a PBB-VPLS network is no different from deploying them in a regular VPLS network. Deploying STP in PBB-VPLS is less preferred in all cases and requires extra care. In most cases, networks using PBB-VPLS are carrier-grade, very large scaled networks, and STP's slow convergence is not suitable for these kinds of networks.

In certain circumstances, P-MSTP can be deployed in the B-VPLS for native PBBN's (B-SAP) loop prevention. P-MSTP is a variation of MSTP that is exclusively used by B-VPLS to prevent forwarding loops caused by redundant connections between PBB SAPs. This means that when the PBB-VPLS is connected to a native PBBN network through B-SAPs with potential forwarding loops, PMSTP can be used in PBB-VPLS VSI to prevent these forwarding loops within the PBBN network. The PMSTP BPDU has the same format as a regular MSTP BPDU except that it uses a destination MAC address of 01-80-c2-00-00-08 (a regular BPDU for any type of STP uses 01-80-c2-00-00-00).

17.8 MAC-Flush in PBB-VPLS

As introduced in Chapter 15, MAC-flush is used to indicate invalid FDB entries and trigger the flush of these entries. After a flush of invalid entries, the VPLS service instance floods more unknown unicast traffic and begins relearning the MAC addresses. Therefore, the incidence of service outages caused by blackholing traffic before invalid FDB entries age out is reduced.

Quick Review of MAC-Flush

There are two types of MAC-flush:

- flush-all-but-me — This approach is considered a positive flush mechanism. In this case, the newly activated link, either via STP or standby PW transitioning to active, will generate the message. This type of MAC-flush is generated by the xSTP instance when there is a topology change or a switchover of an active/standby pseudowire. It requires the receiver of the `flush-all-but-me` message to clear all FDB entries in the VPLS, except the entries associated with the bridge port from which the MAC-flush is received. Generation of the `flush-all-but-me` MAC-flush is the default for xSTP and LDP.

- `flush-all-from-me` — This is considered a negative approach to flushing. Simply, when a failure occurs, the affected node will send the flush message. This type of MAC-flush is generated when a local SAP or spoke-pseudowire goes out of service or an MC-LAG group port fails. It requires the receiver of the message to clear all FDB entries in the VPLS that are associated with the bridge port from which the MAC-flush is received. Generation of the `flush-all-from-me` MAC-flush is disabled by default and must be enabled explicitly by the `send-flush-on-failure` command during VPLS service instance configuration. This MAC-flush message uses ALSRP vendor-specific type–length values (TLVs) in the LDP message.

Also, each VPLS service instance can be configured to propagate or not propagate (default) received MAC-flush messages over the pseudowires to other member PE routers. This can be enabled by the `mac-flush-propagate` command during the configuration of the VPLS service instance. When the flush propagation is enabled, both types of received MAC-flush messages are propagated.

In PBB-VPLS, the B-VPLS domain and the associated I-VPLS domains can support both types of MAC-flush message and the propagation of MAC-flush. Both the B-VPLS service instance and the I-VPLS service instance can be configured to generate or not generate `flush-all-from-me` messages and to propagate or not propagate MAC-flush messages. The scope of message generation and propagation configuration is limited to the I-VPLS domains or the B-VPLS domain. This means that the MAC-flush generated by the B-VPLS is not propagated to the I-VPLS service instances, and vice versa.

send-bvpls-flush — Propagating MAC-Flush from I-VPLS to B-VPLS

A local connectivity change in the I-VPLS may trigger a MAC-flush message to be sent to other I-VPLS member PE routers. Examples of a local connectivity change are as follows:

- A local SAP goes down.

- A local spoke-pseudowire connected to other member PE routers in the I-VPLS domain goes down.
- A redundant pseudowire switches over from active to standby within the I-VPLS domain.
- A Multi Chassis Link Aggregation Group (MC-LAG) switches over (from up to down).

It may be desired that the I-VPLS service instance propagates the `flush-all-from-me` message to other member PE routers. Within the I-VPLS domain, this can be enabled by the `send-flush-on-failure` command during I-VPLS service configuration. It may also be useful for the I-VPLS to propagate this information to the associated B-VPLS. This is done by using the `send-bpvls-flush all-from-me` command during the configuration of the I-VPLS service instance. This enables the IB-PE router to translate the MAC-flush from the I-VPLS service instance to the B-VPLS service instance. Figure 17.23 illustrates a CLI configuration example of enabling MAC-flush propagation from an I-VPLS to its associated B-VPLS.

Figure 17.23   Enabling I-VPLS Generation of flush-all-from-me to B-VPLS

```
A:R1# configure service vpls 260 i-vpls
A:R1>config>service>vpls# info
----------------------------------------------
          description "i-VPLS"
          send-bvpls-flush all-from-me
          backbone-vpls 250
              stp
          exit
          stp
              no shutdown
          exit
          sap 1/1/4:260 create
          exit
          spoke-sdp 117:260 create
          exit
          no shutdown
----------------------------------------------
```

When this configuration is enabled, the I-VPLS sends the `flush-all-from-me` message to the associated B-VPLS service instance whenever any of the listed three events happens in the I-VPLS service instance, even without `send-flush-on-failure` enabled in the service instance.

If the IB-PE router has all the following configurations, the `flush-all-from-me` message is generated by the I-VPLS VSI when there is a SAP or spoke-pseudowire failure, and the message is propagated to the entire PBB-VPLS network:

- The I-VPLS service instance has `send-flush-on-failure` enabled.

- The I-VPLS service instance has `send-bvpls-flush all-from-me` enabled.
- The associated B-VPLS service instance has `mac-flush-propagate` enabled.

Figure 17.24 illustrates two scenarios in which the end-to-end MAC-flush across a PBB-VPLS benefits the network.

Figure 17.24   MAC-Flush Propagation from I-VPLS to B-VPLS in an IB-PE Router

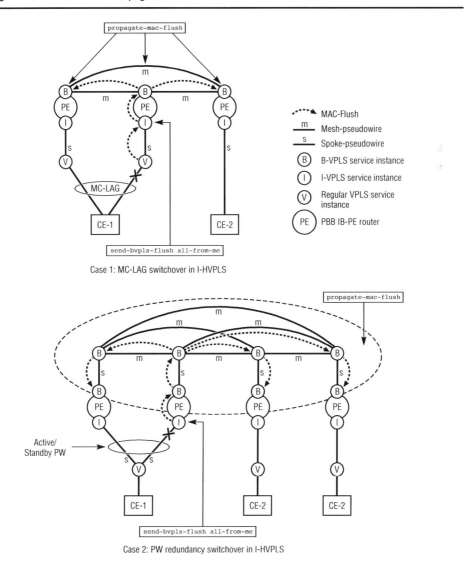

Case 1: MC-LAG switchover in I-HVPLS

Case 2: PW redundancy switchover in I-HVPLS

Case 1 is an MC-LAG switchover in the I-VPLS. The propagation of `flush-all-from-me` messages from the I-VPLS to the B-VPLS triggers all IB-PE routers to clear the C-MAC to B-MAC associations in their FDBs and to begin to relearn the MAC addresses and their associations with CE-1.

Case 2 is a pseudowire redundancy switchover. Similarly, propagation of flush-all-from-me messages from the I-VPLS to the B-VPLS triggers all IB-PE routers to flush the old B-MAC to C-MAC mapping and relearn the location of CE-1. This MAC-flush message is transparently passed through all PE routers in the core that have only a B-VPLS service instance but not a corresponding I-VPLS instance.

In both cases, when an IB-PE router receives a MAC-flush message from a remote IB-PE router, it:

1. Withdraws the corresponding B-MAC addresses from the FDB of the B-VPLS.

2. Clears the C-MAC addresses associated with the B-MAC addresses in the FDB of the local I-VPLS service instance.

17.9 PBB Epipe

The *VPLS service* is a multipoint-to-multipoint Ethernet bridging service that forwards traffic based on MAC addresses. *Epipe* is a point-to-point Ethernet bridging service that forwards traffic from one customer site to another and vice versa. When point-to-point Ethernet service is required between two locations, only one pseudowire connecting two PE routers with one SAP on each PE is required. Because the connection requirement is point-to-point and the requirement is to forward traffic received from one router's SAP to the remote router's SAP or vice versa, there is no need for the Epipe to learn any MAC addresses. Because Epipe service does not need to learn any MAC addresses, there is no FDB, and therefore there is no database scaling issue or MAC explosion. The nature of a simple cross-connect function used by Epipes, one in and one out, means that a higher scale of these service instances can be achieved as compared to more complex services like VPLS.

Why should PBB be used to support Epipe service? There are at least two good answers for this question:

- In a scaled network, it may be operationally beneficial to use a uniform provisioning model for different services, that is, to have as many services as possible that share a common infrastructure. Therefore, the operator can use a higher-level provisioning tool to speed up the service deployment process and can more easily perform tasks related to service management. If PBB-VPLS is deployed in a network, the network already has a B-domain and one or more I-domains with a B-VPLS and I-VPLS infrastructure. In this type of network, if Epipe service is also required end-to-end, using PBB-Epipe service in the customer domain connected by PBB B-VPLS to the backbone domain maintains the network infrastructure, rather than having a separate Epipe service overlay.

- If the N:1 model is used, one B-VPLS can concentrate traffic from many Epipe services in the customer domain. Also, using B-VPLS to aggregate Epipe services in the I-domain can significantly reduce the number of pseudowires deployed in the backbone network. Many Epipes in the I-domain can all be associated with the same B-VPLS and transported across the B-domain.

How Does PBB-Epipe Work?

Just like the PBB-VPLS solution, the PBB-Epipe solution divides the service provider's network into two domains — a backbone domain with B-VPLS instances and a customer domain with Epipe services. The only difference is that the I-component is a point-to-point Epipe that does not require MAC learning before it forwards the traffic. In point-to-point service, flooding is equivalent to unicasting. The only thing that needs to happen is that the Epipe in the customer domain needs to know where to forward the traffic: In the case of PBB-Epipe, the B-DA is configured during the creation of the PBB-Epipe.

The implementation of PBB-Epipe can be 1:1 mode (one B-VPLS instance per Epipe service) or N:1 mode (many Epipe services share one or several B-VPLS instances).

A basic Epipe service is a point-to-point service that connects two customer sites with the following components: One PE router has a local SAP facing one customer site, a bidirectional service tunnel connects the two PE routers, and another customer-site-facing SAP is in the remote PE router. The only difference between PBB-Epipe and a regular Epipe service is that in PBB-Epipe, the SDP used by the regular Epipe (MPLS- or GRE-encapsulated) is replaced by a B-VPLS service. Figure 17.25 illustrates a configuration example of the Epipe service 111 using PBB B-VPLS 1000 to carry its traffic across the PBB B-domain.

The forwarding behavior of PBB-Epipe is straightforward, as follows:

1. When the Epipe in the customer domain receives traffic from the local SAP, it immediately performs PBB encapsulation because the B-DA is always known in a PBB-Epipe (by configuration in the Epipe service); then the Epipe forwards the traffic to the PBB tunnel, which is a local B-VPLS instance.

2. Next, the local B-VPLS instances perform learning and forwarding based on the traffic's B-DA. If the B-DA is known to the FDB, the traffic is unicast

through the backbone to the B-VPLS instance of the target remote IB-PE router. If the B-DA is not known (the local-PE did not previously receive traffic from the B-VPLS instance of the remote IB-PE router), the traffic is flooded through the backbone to all IB-PE routers participating in the same B-VPLS.

3. When the target IB-PE router receives traffic, it performs the B-MAC learning, and I-SID lookup. Using the matching I-SID in the B-VPLS VSI, the traffic is de-encapsulated and sent to the SAP of the local Epipe.

4. When routers that are not the target of the Epipe receive traffic, the I-SID lookup in the B-VPLS instance fails and the traffic is discarded.

Figure 17.25 PBB-Epipe Configuration Example (MPLS Backbone)

PBB-Epipe between two IB-PE-routers

The pbb-tunnel in the Epipe configuration
specifies the destination B-MAC of the
B-VPLS instance in the remote IB-PE
router where the service terminates.

```
A:IB-PE-164# configure service epipe 111
A:IB-PE-164>config>service>epipe# info
----------------------------------------------
            description "ePipe"
            pbb-tunnel 1000 backbone-dest-mac
00:00:01:00:01:65 isid 111
            sap 1/1/4:111 create
            exit
            no shutdown
----------------------------------------------
A:IB-PE-164>config>service>epipe# exit
A:IB-PE-164# configure service vpls 1000
A:IB-PE-164>config>service>vpls# info
----------------------------------------------
            description "b-vpls"
            service-mtu 1536
            backbone-smac  00:00:01:00:01:64
            stp
                shutdown
            exit
            mesh-sdp 163:1000 create
            exit
            mesh-sdp 165:1000 create
            exit
            no shutdown
----------------------------------------------
A:IB-PE-164>config>service>vpls# exit
A:IB-PE-164#
```

```
A:IB-PE-165>config>service>epipe# info
----------------------------------------------
            description "ePipe"
            pbb-tunnel 1000 backbone-dest-mac
00:00:01:00:01:64 isid 111
            sap 1/1/4:111 create
            exit
            no shutdown
----------------------------------------------
A:IB-PE-165>config>service>epipe# exit
A:IB-PE-165# configure service vpls 1000
A:IB-PE-165>config>service>vpls# info
----------------------------------------------
            description "b-vpls"
            service-mtu 1536
            backbone-smac  00:00:01:00:01:65
            stp
                shutdown
            exit
            mesh-sdp 163:1000 create
            exit
            mesh-sdp 164:1000 create
            exit
            no shutdown
----------------------------------------------
A:IB-PE-165>config>service>vpls# exit
A:IB-PE-165#
```

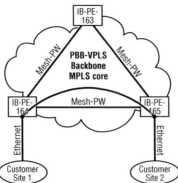

Preventing Flooding Epipe Traffic in the B-Domain

Limiting the scope of traffic flooding to the backbone is crucial for PBB-Epipe services. The issue is how to limit flooding in PBB-Epipe. The previous section discussed using MRP to build a backbone group MAC address flooding tree for each B-VPLS for each I-SID to limit the scope of flooding. The same mechanism does not apply to PBB-Epipe. MRP can register only the backbone group MAC address to build the backbone group flooding tree. Epipe that has a PBB tunnel configured never uses the backbone group MAC address to perform PBB encapsulation on the traffic before sending the traffic to the associated B-VPLS. The Epipe encapsulates traffic only with a preconfigured unicast B-MAC address. This type of traffic is unknown unicast traffic to the B-VPLS, not group multicast traffic; therefore, no backbone group MAC address flooding tree is built to control the flooding of this traffic for any PBB-Epipe service.

Therefore, one accepted method to eliminate unknown unicast flooding caused by the PBB-Epipe in the backbone is to ensure that the B-VPLS of the IB-PE router learns the B-DA. This can be achieved by using the 802.1ag Continuity Check Message (CCM) in the PBB-Epipe service. Figure 17.26 illustrates an example configuration that uses CCM to prevent unnecessary traffic flooding caused by the Epipe using B-VPLS. Details about 802.1ag CCM are discussed in Chapter 18.

When configuring PBB-Epipe in the IB-PE routers (both sides of the service), the tunneling B-VPLS can be configured with CCM enabled, and with the B-DA of the Epipe (the B-MAC address of the B-VPLS of the remote IB-PE) statically defined. Therefore, the B-DA entry is permanently in the FDB of the B-VPLS. Because the B-DA is always known, there is no flooding to the backbone network

There are also dual-homing strategies that allow the B-MAC to be shared between more than one IB-PE node in an active standby mode. Should the active node be removed from service, the backup will transition to active and perform the forwarding functions for that B-MAC. This, combined with the use of the CCM message, allows a PBB-Epipe service to successfully converge on one of the two nodes that are responsible for the destination B-MAC.

Figure 17.26 Using 802.1ag CCM in B-VPLS to Prevent Flooding

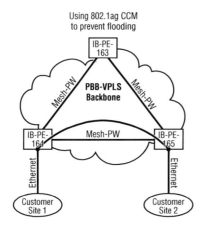

```
Using 802.1ag CCM
to prevent flooding
```

```
A:IB-PE-165# configure service epipe 111
A:IB-PE-165>config>service>epipe# info
-----------------------------------------------------------
    description "ePipe"
    pbb-tunnel 1000 backbone-dest-mac 00:00:01:00:01:64 isid 111
    sap 1/1/4:111 create
    exit
    no shutdown
-----------------------------------------------------------
A:IB-PE-165>config>service>epipe#
```

```
A:IB-PE-165>config>service>vpls# info
-----------------------------------------------------------
    description "b-vpls"
    service-mtu 1536
    backbone-smac  00:00:01:00:01:65
    stp
        shutdown
    exit
    sap 1/1/4:164 create
        shutdown
        description "dot1ag for pbb epipe"
        dot1ag
            mep 164 domain 1 association 1 direction up
                ccm-enable
                mac-address 00:00:01:00:01:64
                no shutdown
            exit
        exit
    exit
    mesh-sdp 163:1000 create
    exit
    mesh-sdp 164:1000 create
    exit
    no shutdown
-----------------------------------------------------------
A:IB-PE-165>config>service>vpls#
```

```
A:IB-PE-165# configure dot1ag
A:IB-PE-165>config>dot1ag# info
-----------------------------------------------------------
    domain 1 name "PBB_ePipes" level 5
        association 1 format string name "backbone_1000"
            bridge-identifier 1000
            exit
            ccm-interval 60
            remote-mepid 164
        exit
    exit
-----------------------------------------------------------
A:IB-PE-165>config>dot1ag#
```

Summary

VPLS/H-VPLS service provides Ethernet bridging services among customer sites. It performs learning and forwarding based on the MAC addresses of the customer's traffic. When VPLS or H-VPLS is deployed in a very large-scale network with a large amount of customer equipment in the network, MAC address scaling may become a concern. This challenges the database capacity of the PE router and affects its performance during times of fluctuations in the network. This is a problem particularly with large-scale networks that use an H-VPLS network design; the traffic-aggregating hub-PE router may have too many MAC addresses to learn. To solve this problem, the 802.1ah PBB is incorporated into the VPLS implementation.

The PBB-VPLS solution divides the entire VPLS network into two portions — the customer facing I-domain and the backbone B-domain. The VPLS in the B-domain (B-VPLS) uses B-MAC addresses to perform learning and forwarding, reducing the number of MAC addresses the B-VPLS service instance must track, while maintaining full VPLS connectivity.

The PBB solution uses I-VPLS to connect the I-domain VPLS services, and B-VPLS to connect the B-domain member PE routers. In the IB-PE router that has the I-VPLS associated with the B-VPLS, the I-VPLS tracks the mapping of C-MAC addresses to B-MAC addresses. When I-VPLS decides to send traffic to the B-VPLS in the backbone, it performs PBB encapsulation using the backbone MAC addresses so that the B-VPLS in the backbone needs to perform bridging based only on the B-MAC addresses.

A B-VPLS may carry traffic for more than one I-VPLS. By default, the BUM traffic from one associated local I-VPLS is flooded to all B-VPLS member-PE routers in the backbone. This may not be efficient because the I-VPLS may use only part of the B-VPLS in the backbone. MRP is introduced to the PBB-VPLS solution to improve the forwarding efficiency of the BUM traffic. With MRP enabled in the B-VPLS, the B-VPLS PE router exchanges MRPDUs to form a backbone group MAC address flooding tree for every I-VPLS with which it is associated. Only the active port in the MRP tree for a particular I-VPLS is flooded with BUM traffic that belongs to that I-VPLS. Therefore, BUM traffic flooding to non-I-VPLS member IB-PE routers from the backbone is prevented.

Loop prevention also needs to be addressed in the PBB-VPLS solution. Loop prevention for the B-VPLS in the backbone is handled separately from the loop prevention of the I-VPLS(s) associated with it. To prevent B-VPLS forwarding loops, a VPLS service using full-mesh PW can be deployed, or in the case of native PBB deployments, MC-LAG or PMSTP can be used, or STP can be enabled in the B-VPLS service. Each I-VPLS-connected I-domain can use several loop-prevention strategies, including VPLS, active and standby PW, or STP. I-VPLS can optionally enable STP BPDU flooding to the B-VPLS through the internal port. In this case, the B-VPLS can transparently flood the BPDU to all other I-domains that are members of the same VPLS. The recommendation to use VPLS resiliency (active/standby pseudowire, LAG, MC-LAG, etc.) whenever possible rather than STP in the VPLS solution remains true.

B-VPLS can also be used to carry Epipe traffic across the B-domain. Because Epipe service is always point-to-point, flooding PBB-encapsulated Epipe traffic to the B-VPLS backbone is not necessary. When configuring the Epipe to use the B-VPLS as a tunnel, 802.1ag CCM can be used in the B-VPLS to prevent the B-VPLS from flooding traffic to all B-VPLS member PE routers in the core network.

By leveraging the best of each technology, VPLS and PBB, carriers can realize much greater scaling than just deploying one over the other. With the integration of VPLS and PBB on the same IB-PE node, PBB-VPLS, a carrier can further reduce the amount of equipment required to deliver today's advanced Layer 2 services.

OAM in a VPLS Service Network

18

Operation, Administration, and Maintenance (OAM) functions are used by operators to monitor the health of the network and troubleshoot failures. This chapter discusses the use of OAM in a VPLS service network.

Chapter Objectives

- Provide an overview end-to-end OAM in a VPLS service network

- Explain Ethernet for the First Mile (EFM) OAM, defined by IEEE 802.3ah

- Explain Ethernet Connectivity Fault Management (CFM), defined by IEEE 802.1ag

- Describe OAM functions in an IP/MPLS backbone network

- Describe OAM functions in VPLS services

This chapter describes the Ethernet Operation, Administration, and Maintenance feature in the Virtual Private LAN Service (VPLS) service. Both VPLS providers and their customers must be able to monitor the health of a network and to diagnose its failures. The support of Ethernet OAM in VPLS service allows operators to have end-to-end visibility of the health of their networks.

18.1 OAM Functional Overview

Operations, Administration, and Management (OAM) refers to the tools that are used to perform monitoring and troubleshooting in a network. In general, OAM has several goals: continuity verification, performance monitoring, fault detection and localization. The purpose of continuity verification is to validate the health of a link or a service and to quickly detect and report a loss of connectivity. Ethernet for the First Mile OAM (EFM OAM) and Ethernet Connectivity Fault Management (CFM) belong to the continuity verification category.

The purpose of performance monitoring is to measure the quality of the connectivity over a link or a service — for example, jitter, delay, or loss — and to use the result to reinforce the Service Level Agreements (SLAs). Performance monitoring is not standardized and is beyond the scope of this book. Service providers use MPLS OAM and VPLS OAM tools to provide OAM functions in the core. Also, Ethernet OAM is added to troubleshoot the Ethernet parts towards the customer and to perform other functions such as continuity verification and performance monitoring across multiple network domains of the end-user and the operator.

Carriers are increasingly providing Ethernet services to their customers and deploying Ethernet into their backbone networks. VPLS and Ethernet pseudowire are used in the carrier backbone networks to provide Layer 2 VPN services. Both customers and providers require powerful monitoring and troubleshooting of the network. Therefore, Ethernet OAM is becoming more important. OAM functions in higher-level protocols can also be used to monitor and troubleshoot a Layer 2 VPN network. However, in an Ethernet Layer 2 VPN network, only Ethernet OAM has the granularity and compatibility required. It can locate a fault on a single Ethernet link, and it can allow the customer to use a single OAM tool to perform end-to-end OAM across the service network. Figure 18.1 illustrates a network with an end-to-end OAM requirement.

Figure 18.1 OAM in a VPLS Metro-Ethernet Network

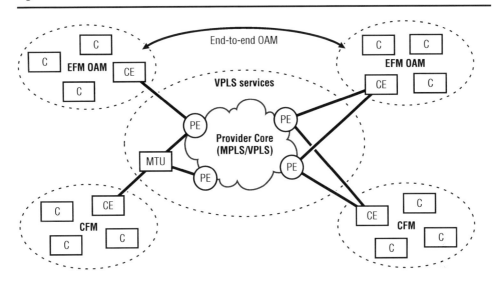

Both service providers and customers require OAM capability in their networks. The following two OAM tools are illustrated in the diagram:

- **EFM OAM (802.3ah)** — An Ethernet point-to-point link health-monitoring OAM tool

- **CFM (802.1ag)** — An end-to-end Ethernet network service health-monitoring OAM tool

Table 18.1 compares EFM OAM and CFM.

Table 18.1 Comparing EFM OAM (802.3ah) and CFM (802.1ag)

OAM Tool	Location	Functionality and Operation
EFM OAM (802.3ah)	Link layer	Monitoring and troubleshooting any point-to-point Ethernet link. Customers can use it to test the links in their own networks or test the connectivity between two sites connected by an Ethernet VLL (Epipe).
CFM (802.1ag)	Plain Ethernet, end-to-end	Monitoring and troubleshooting all endpoints in a range of networks by associating them with different levels (domains). Customers and providers can define their own OAM range over the same network without interfering with each other. End-to-end OAM can be achieved using CFM.

18.2 Ethernet in the First Mile (EFM) OAM (802.3ah)

This section introduces 802.3ah EFM OAM. EFM OAM is a standard Ethernet link-level OAM. Network operators can use it to monitor the health of the Ethernet link and to detect link failures or fault conditions. EFM OAM can detect and report link failures in a subsecond time frame. EFM OAM operates in the OAM *sublayer* under the data link layer in the OSI reference model, as illustrated in Figure 18.2.

Figure 18.2 OAM Sublayer in the OSI Model

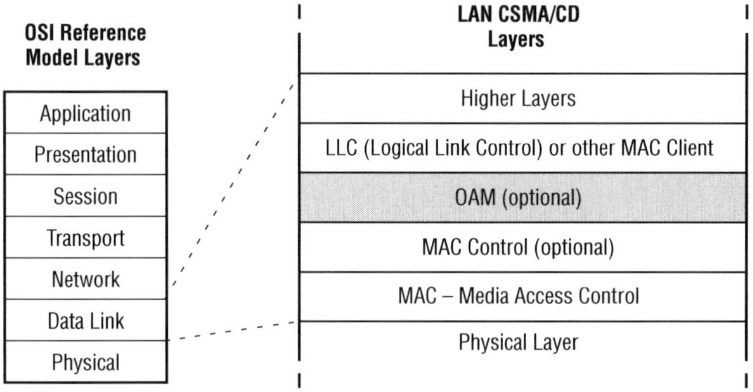

Interfaces with EFM OAM enabled monitor link health by sending each other Hello packets (OAM PDUs). If the OAM PDU from a peering device is not received by a second device within a certain amount of time, EFM OAM considers there to be a fault in the link and puts the local port into the **down** state. This is especially useful for detecting link failures that are not local (when traffic cannot reach the far-end device, but the port is still in the **up** state).

EFM OAM PDUs

All EFM OAM information exchanged between two peering devices is contained in EFM OAM Protocol Data Units (PDUs). EFM OAM PDUs are Ethernet frames with slow protocols (protocol type **0x8809**) with a subtype of **0x03** (OAM). The destination MAC address of an OAM PDU is always the protocol broadcast MAC address: **01-80-c2-00-00-02**. All EFM OAM PDUs must be untagged. Figure 18.3 shows the packet format for an EFM OAM PDU.

Figure 18.3 EFM OAM PDU Packet Format

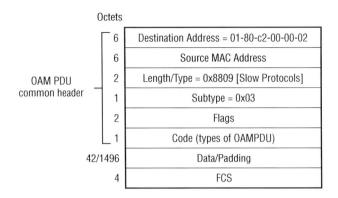

Octets	
6	Destination Address = 01-80-c2-00-00-02
6	Source MAC Address
2	Length/Type = 0x8809 [Slow Protocols]
1	Subtype = 0x03
2	Flags
1	Code (types of OAMPDU)
42/1496	Data/Padding
4	FCS

OAM PDU common header

Flag

Bit	Flag
0	Link Fault
1	Dying Gasp
2	Critical Event
3	Local Evaluating
4	Local Stable
5	Remote Evaluating
6	Remote Stable
7-15	Reserved

Code

Code	OAMPDU
0x00	Informational
0x01	Event Notification
0x02	Variable Request
0x03	Variable Response
0x04	Loopback Control
0x05-0xFD	Reserved
0xFE	Organization Specific
0xFF	Reserved

EFM OAM defines several events that may affect link operation. Three *critical events* are required to be signaled in the *Flag* field in an OAM PDU:

- **Link Fault (bit 0)** — The system determines that there is a fault in the receive direction of a local device.
- **Dying Gasp** — An unrecoverable local failure condition has occurred.
- **Critical Event** — An unspecified critical event has occurred.

Other link events defined by 802.3ah should be signaled to the EFM OAM peer using the type–length value (TLV) in the OAM PDUs. The code field in the OAM PDU indicates the types. The informational OAM PDU (**0x00**) is used in the discovery process, and as the Hello packet to monitor the link health. The event notification OAM PDU (**0x01**) is used to signal link events (other than the three critical events represented in the flag bits).

EFM OAM Discovery Process

When two devices want to use EFM OAM to monitor the health of the Ethernet link between them, they first need to form EFM OAM adjacency. EFM OAM uses a discovery process to form adjacency between two ports over an Ethernet link. The discovery process is performed by two ports exchanging informational (code 0x0) OAM PDUs that contain local and remote information. Figure 18.4 demonstrates the two-way EFM OAM discovery process.

Figure 18.4 Establishing EFM OAM Adjacency

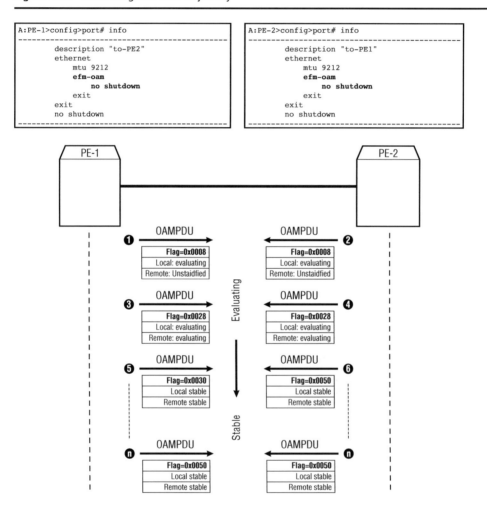

Figure 18.4   *(continued)*

```
A:PE-3# show port 1/1/1 ethernet efm-oam
===============================================
Ethernet Oam
(802.3ah)
===============================================
Admin State        : up
Oper State         : operational
Mode               : active
Pdu Size           : 2047
Config Revision    : 0
Function Support   : LB
Transmit Interval  : 1000 ms
Multiplier         : 5
Tunneling          : false
Loop Detected      : false
Peer Mac Address
: 8e:75:01:01:00:01
Peer Vendor OUI    : 00:16:4d
Peer Vendor Info   : 00:00:00:00
Peer Mode          : active
Peer Pdu Size      : 2047
Peer Cfg Revision  : 0
Peer Support       : LB
Loopback State
: None
Loopback Ignore Rx : Ignore
===============================================================================
Ethernet Oam Statistics
===============================================================================

Input              Output
-------------------------------------------------------------------------------
Information                              443                    444
Loopback Control                           0                      0
Unsupported Codes                          0                      0
Frames Lost                                                       0
===============================================================================
```

As soon as EFM OAM is enabled in a port, it sends an informational OAM PDU.

1.   The port sets the local evaluating flag bit in the outgoing OAM PDU to 1 with a Local Information TLV (`type = 0x1`).

2.   If the port on the other side of the link has EFM OAM enabled as well, it also sends an informational OAM PDU with the local evaluating flag in its Local Information TLV.

3.   When a port receives a valid OAM PDU from the peer port, it then sets the remote evaluating flag in the outgoing OAM PDUs. It also appends the Remote Information TLV (type `0x02`).

4.   The peering port performs the same action. Both ports validate the received OAM PDU with information TLVs.

5, 6. Next, both ports clear the local evaluating and remote evaluating flag bits, and set the local stable and remote stable flag bits in the outgoing OAM PDU. From this moment, the EFM OAM discovery process is completed. The two ports keep exchanging OAM PDUs with the flag set to 0x0050 (local and remote stable) as Hello packets to monitor the health of the link between them.

> **Warning:** Enabling EFM OAM in a port may temporarily bring the port down. When enabling EFM OAM in a port for the first time, the port automatically begins the discovery process. This may bring down the port if the peering device does not have EFM OAM support, or if it has not yet been enabled. The port comes operationally back up after the discovery process successfully finishes. In a live network, EFM OAM should be enabled on the two peering devices at the same time. A possible service disruption should be taken into consideration, and the traffic should be temporarily moved away from the link under the EFM OAM configuration if possible.

When two ports perform the discovery process, EFM OAM configuration information is exchanged in the Information TLV. OAM configuration includes:

- **OAM Mode** — Determines whether the device is running EMF OAM in active mode or passive mode. A device in EFM OAM passive mode does not initiate the OAM discovery process. A device in EFM OAM passive mode cannot send loopback control OAM PDUs, but it can react to received loopback control OAM PDUs. (EFM OAM loopback is explained in a later section.)
- **Unidirectional Support** — Determines whether the device sends OAM PDUs when the receive path is down
- **Loopback Support** — Determines whether the device supports OAM remote loopback mode
- **Link Events Support** — Determines whether the device can interpret link events
- **Variable Retrieval** — Determines whether the device can send variable responses

The Local Information TLV contains the configuration of the local device. The Remote Information TLV contains the OAM configuration of the remote device.

Detecting Failures

EFM OAM detects failures of a link between two devices. When two ports connected by a single link have EFM OAM enabled, they exchange OAM PDUs at a pre-negotiated time interval. The OAM PDU interval value is not exchanged between two peering devices; therefore, the operator must ensure that the interval values in the two peering devices are equal. Otherwise, the EFM OAM may periodically time-out the peering relationships, and the Ethernet link being monitored will bounce frequently. Figure 18.5 illustrates a fault in between the transmission devices that connect two PE routers.

This type of connection is quite common in operator backbone and access networks. The two transmission devices may be, for example, microwave huts or optical multiplexers. During a failure, a physical fault between the transmission devices may not be propagated to the PE routers, if the transmission devices do not have failure propagation functions such as port state dependency or the ability to raise a Remote Defect Indication (RDI) alarm.

Without EFM OAM, this failure is not detected by the physical layers of the two PE routers. The two Ethernet ports in the PE routers stay up. The two PE routers keep sending traffic to each other over this link, until the upper layer protocol (for example, OSPF) times out. Then the traffic is detoured to other links. It may take several seconds or longer for the upper-layer protocol to detect the fault and reroute the traffic.

Note: In this failure scenario, Bidirectional Forwarding Detection (BFD) may speed up the convergence to subseconds. However, BFD does not bring down the port when it detects a failure; it only notifies the upper-layer protocol. BFD cannot be enabled if the connection is a pure Layer 2 connection (for example, a link between the access port of a PE router and the Ethernet port of a CE switch).

Figure 18.5 EFM OAM Detecting a Remote Failure — Bidirectional

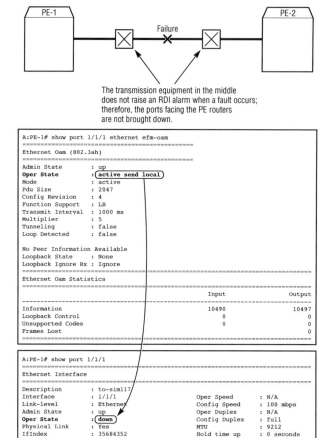

The transmission equipment in the middle
does not raise an RDI alarm when a fault occurs;
therefore, the ports facing the PE routers
are not brought down.

```
A:PE-1# show port 1/1/1 ethernet efm-oam
===============================================
Ethernet Oam (802.3ah)
===============================================
Admin State        : up
Oper State         : active send local
Mode               : active
Pdu Size           : 2047
Config Revision    : 4
Function Support   : LB
Transmit Interval  : 1000 ms
Multiplier         : 5
Tunneling          : false
Loop Detected      : false

No Peer Information Available
Loopback State     : None
Loopback Ignore Rx : Ignore
===============================================
Ethernet Oam Statistics
===============================================
                               Input          Output
-----------------------------------------------
Information                    10490           10497
Loopback Control               0               0
Unsupported Codes              0               0
Frames Lost                    0               0
===============================================
```

```
A:PE-1# show port 1/1/1
===============================================
Ethernet Interface
===============================================
Description     : to-sim117
Interface       : 1/1/1             Oper Speed    : N/A
Link-level      : Ethernet          Config Speed  : 100 mbps
Admin State     : up                Oper Duplex   : N/A
Oper State      : down              Config Duplex : full
Physical Link   : Yes               MTU           : 9212
IfIndex         : 35684352          Hold time up  : 0 seconds
Last State Change : 12/16/2003 22:13:40   Hold time down : 0 seconds
Last Cleared Time : N/A
Last Cleared Time : N/A
--- output omitted ---
```

EFM OAM can no longer receive OAMPDUs because it detects a problem.
EFM OAM reverts the state to active send local (initiating the
discovery process again) and brings down the Ethernet port.

When EFM OAM is configured on the ports of both PE routers, a failure is rap-
idly detected by both ports. Immediately after the failure, neither port can receive
OAM PDUs from the other port. EFM OAM requires the device to expect the
OAM PDU within a configurable time interval. When a certain number of OAM
PDUs are missed (the multiplexer), EMF OAM adjacency is terminated. EFM OAM
brings the Ethernet port down, and restarts the discovery process. As soon as the

failure is removed, the EFM OAM discovery process succeeds. Then, the EFM OAM puts the corresponding Ethernet port back into operation. With a short packet interval and low multiplexer configuration, the failure detection time can be a fraction of a second. Figure 18.6 illustrates a unidirectional failure between the two transmission devices.

Figure 18.6 EFM OAM Detecting a Remote Failure — Unidirectional

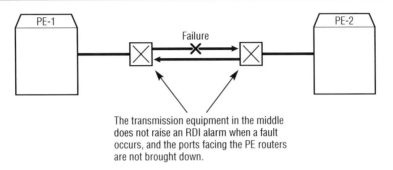

```
show port 1/1/1 ethernet efm-oam
=================================================
Ethernet Oam (802.3ah)
=================================================
Admin State        : up
Oper State         : send local and remote ok
Mode               : active
Pdu Size           : 1600
Config Revision    : 29
Function Support   : LB
Transmit Interval  : 100 ms
Multiplier         : 2
Tunneling          : false
Peer Mac Address
: 1e:66:01:01:00:01
Peer Vendor OUI    : 00:16:4d
Peer Vendor Info   : 00:00:00:00
Peer Mode          : active
Peer Pdu Size      : 1600
Peer Cfg Revision  : 42
Peer Support       : LB
Loopback State
: None
Loopback Ignore Rx : Ignore
--- output omitted ---
```

```
show port 1/1/1 ethernet efm-oam
=================================================
Ethernet Oam (802.3ah)
=================================================
Admin State        : up
Oper State         : active send local
Mode               : active
Pdu Size           : 1600
Config Revision    : 42
Function Support   : LB
Transmit Interval  : 100 ms
Multiplier         : 2
Tunneling          : false
No Peer Information Available

Loopback State
: None
Loopback Ignore Rx : Ignore
--- output omitted ---
```

In this scenario, only the link from PE-1 toward PE-2 failed. PE-1 can still receive traffic from PE-2. With EFM OAM, both PE routers still rapidly detect the failure and bring down the Ethernet ports. After the failure occurs, PE-2 can no longer receive OAM PDUs from PE-1. PE-2 restarts the discovery process and brings the Ethernet port down, similar to the example in Figure 18.5. PE-1 can still receive

OAM PDUs from PE-2, but it recognizes that the content of the OAM PDU has changed after the failure. The flag from the OAM PDU received from PE-2 is 0x0008 (local evaluation, remote unsatisfied). Because the received OAM PDU no longer contains a remote TLV, PE-1 knows that PE-2 cannot see the OAM PDUs sent from itself. PE-1 sets the EFM OAM state to `send local and remote OK` and then brings down the Ethernet port. EFM OAM detects unidirectional failures just as efficiently as it detects bidirectional failures.

EFM OAM can also be used to detect physical loops in the network. When a port with EFM OAM receives its own OAM PDU, it considers that the port is looped, and therefore the system puts the port into the `link up` state. The port's EFM OAM operational state is `active-send-local`. In this state, the port continues to send OAM PDUs, so that when the loop is removed, it can complete the discovery process. Detecting loops is a built-in function of the EFM OAM protocol. No extra configuration, beyond enabling the EFM OAM on the port, is required.

Remote Loopback

EFM OAM provides a link-layer frame loopback mode, which can be remotely controlled. The EFM OAM loopback test function can be performed locally or remotely.

Initiate and stop the local EFM OAM loopback test by executing the command `oam efm <port-id> local-loopback {start | stop}`. No extra OAM messaging is required. Figure 18.7 illustrates an example of performing an EFM OAM loopback test.

To perform the remote loopback OAM test, the `accept-remote-loopback` function must be explicitly enabled in the remote device. When performing a remote loopback test, the local device sends a loopback control OAM PDU (code 0x04). The OAM PDU contains the `enable remote loopback` command. Figure 18.7 illustrates a frame capture of the loopback control OAM PDU. To stop a remote loopback OAM test, the local device sends another loopback control OAM PDU to the remote device, containing the `disable remote loopback` command. Upon receiving this PDU, the remote device exits loopback mode. During the remote loopback test, the local port sends and receives only EFM OAM PDUs. All other frames, including the PDUs from all other protocols, are discarded in the local port of this device. All frames except the OAM PDUs in the remote port are looped back, which may cause other protocols to reset their state machines.

Figure 18.7 EFM OAM Local and Remote Loopback

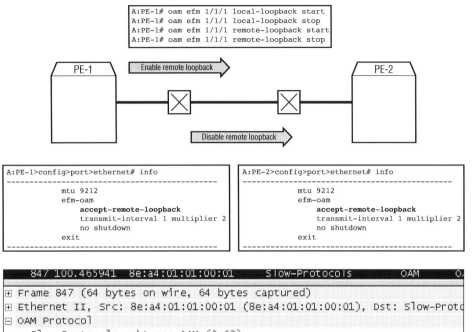

```
A:PE-1# oam efm 1/1/1 local-loopback start
A:PE-1# oam efm 1/1/1 local-loopback stop
A:PE-1# oam efm 1/1/1 remote-loopback start
A:PE-1# oam efm 1/1/1 remote-loopback stop
```

PE-1   Enable remote loopback   PE-2

Disable remote loopback

```
A:PE-1>config>port>ethernet# info
-------------------------------------------------
        mtu 9212
        efm-oam
            accept-remote-loopback
            transmit-interval 1 multiplier 2
            no shutdown
        exit
-------------------------------------------------
```

```
A:PE-2>config>port>ethernet# info
-------------------------------------------------
        mtu 9212
        efm-oam
            accept-remote-loopback
            transmit-interval 1 multiplier 2
            no shutdown
        exit
-------------------------------------------------
```

```
    847 100.465941  8e:a4:01:01:00:01      Slow-Protocols      OAM       O.
⊞ Frame 847 (64 bytes on wire, 64 bytes captured)
⊞ Ethernet II, Src: 8e:a4:01:01:00:01 (8e:a4:01:01:00:01), Dst: Slow-Proto
⊟ OAM Protocol
    Slow Protocols subtype: OAM (0x03)
    ⊟ Flags: 0x0050 (local: Discovery complete, remote: Discovery complete)
        .... ...0 = Link Fault: False
        .... ..0. = Dying Gasp: False
        .... .0.. = Critical Event: False
        .... 0... = Local Evaluating: False
        ...1 .... = Local Stable: True
        ..0. .... = Remote Evaluating: False
        .1.. .... = Remote Stable: True
    OAMPDU code: Loopback Control (0x04)
    ⊟ Commands: 0x01 (Enable Remote Loopack)
        .... ...1 = Enable Remote Loopback: True
        .... ..0. = Disable Remote Loopback: False
```

Tunneling 802.3ah EFM OAM PDU in an Epipe Service

EFM OAM is a standardized Ethernet OAM mechanism. Customers who purchase Epipe services may request the ability to perform EFM OAM between two CE devices at each end of the Epipe service. Therefore, Epipe should be able to tunnel the OAM PDUs between the two CE devices.

Epipe service is a point-to-point Ethernet service that forwards Ethernet frames from one customer to another. The service is completely transparent to the customer devices. By default, EFM OAM is disabled on all ports, so when an Epipe service receives an OAM PDU, the PDU is discarded. If the SAP of the Epipe service resides in a port that has EFM OAM enabled, it can participate in EFM OAM peering with the CE device. The SAP sends and receives OAM PDUs and discovers the CE port. Because EFM OAM is not VLAN-aware, only an Epipe SAP with null encapsulation can generate and process received OAM PDUs. Figure 18.8 illustrates a configuration example of enabling EFM OAM tunneling in an access port. All SAPs that reside on these ports tunnel EFM OAM PDUs to the service instances to which they belong.

Figure 18.8 Epipe Tunneling OAM PDUs between Customer Sites

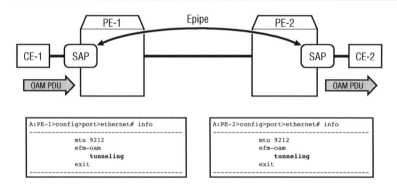

If the customer requires the Epipe to tunnel the OAM PDUs between two CE sites, the SAP ports need to have tunneling explicitly enabled under the port's `efm oam` configuration. Also, the SAP needs to be a null encapsulated SAP.

To sum up, an Ethernet port can have three EFM OAM operational modes:

- **Shutdown (Default Mode)** — The port discards all OAM PDUs received and does not establish EFM OAM peering with the remote port.
- **No Shutdown** — The port participates in EFM OAM with a remote port and generates and accepts OAM PDUs.
- **Tunneling** — The port tunnels OAM PDUs if it is configured with an Epipe null SAP, and the OAM PDUs are tunneled transparently by the SAPs of the Epipe services that reside on the port.

18.3 Ethernet Connectivity Fault Management

The previous section introduced EFM OAM as a connectivity checking mechanism to monitor the health of a point-to-point link. The purpose of having Ethernet CFM is to achieve end-to-end Ethernet OAM that can cross multiple domains to monitor the health of the entire service instance (or more than one service instance). IEEE standard 802.1ag defines Ethernet CFM. As indicated by its name, CFM is a connectivity checking mechanism that uses its own Ethernet frames (its own Ether-type value and MAC addresses) to validate the health of the Ethernet Virtual Circuit (EVC). If desired, Ethernet CFM can be deployed in a broadband access network (service edge and customer domain) to detect customer network or attachment circuit failures.

> **Note:** In this chapter's discussion, the term *service instance* can represent a native Ethernet VLAN, a concatenation of VLANs, or a VPLS instance.

CFM Terminology

Figure 18.9 illustrates the basic architecture of CFM in a bridged Ethernet network. CFM has the following components:

- **Maintenance Association (MA)** — A set of Maintenance endpoints (MEPs) that have the same MA identifier (MAID) and maintenance domain (MD) level within one service instance to verify the integrity of the service. Figure 18.9 shows two MAs: One is represented by the solid line; the other is represented by the dotted line.

- **Maintenance Domain (MD)** — An MD contains one or more MAs that have the same MD level. For example, a customer may subscribe to a service that connects several sites, and the service provider may purchase bandwidth from one or more operators to extend its coverage to serve this customer. This type of network has three types of domains: customer domain, provider domain, and operator domain. Each domain can be an OAM MD and can have one or more MAs.

- **MA Endpoint (MEP)** — MEPs initiate and terminate CFM messages, and are the origination and termination points of the CFM operations.

- **MD Intermediate Point (MIP)** — MIPs receive CFM messages and respond to the originating MEP. A MIP never initiates messages and does not expect any messages. MIPs respond to loopback and link trace messages.

- **MIP Half-Function (MHF)** — MHFs generate CFM PDUs only as a response to received CFM PDUs.
- **Maintenance Entity (ME)** — A point-to-point relationship between a pair of MEPs within a single MA.

Figure 18.9 Logical View of MEP, MIP, and MA

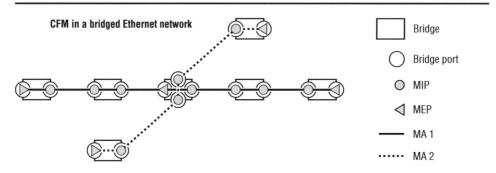

MD level is an important CFM concept. Figure 18.10 (from IEEE 802.1ag) illustrates an example of a network that has multiple MAs in different MD levels. Eight MD levels (0–7) are defined in CFM. Level 0 is the lowest level; Level 7 is the highest level. An MD level is a boundary of responsibilities. Entities at different levels have different tasks. IEEE 802.1ag defines Level 7 for ETH (Ethernet) section monitoring, Levels 6 through 1 are for Ethernet Virtual Circuit (EVC) segments, and Level 0 is for the EVC path. The MD level is encoded in each CFM message header. The MD level is also a characteristic of MEP and MIP. If a CFM message with a particular MD level reaches a MEP or MIP, the following rules apply:

1. If the MD level of the CFM message is *higher* than the MD level of the MEP/MIP, the MEP/MIP transparently *passes* the CFM message.

2. If the MD level of the CFM message is *lower* than the MD level of the MEP/MIP, the MEP/MIP *discards* the CFM message.

3. If the MD level of the CFM message is *equal* to the MD level of the MEP/MIP, the MEP/MIP *processes* the CFM message. Depending on the message type and content, the MEP/MIP responds to, transports, or accepts the message. (Different message types and the processing of messages are discussed later in this chapter.)

A MEP/MIP with a particular MD level generates CFM messages only at that level. CFM messages with a higher MD level are transparently transported over the MEPs/MIPs. Therefore, these messages travel further in the network. However, the

CFM message does not detect the lower-level MEPs/MIPs. An OAM entity (MA) with higher MD-level MEPs/MIPs covers a wider network range, but with fewer details. An MA with lower MD-level MEPs/MIPs cannot send CFM messages across higher MD-level MEPs/MIPs, but the MEPs/MIPs at the same MD level process the messages. Therefore, MAs that have a lower MD level have smaller network coverage, but with more details. Figure 18.10 illustrates a network that has multiple parties and multiple CFM MD levels.

Figure 18.10   MAs, MEPs, MIPs, and MD Levels (from IEEE 802.1ag)

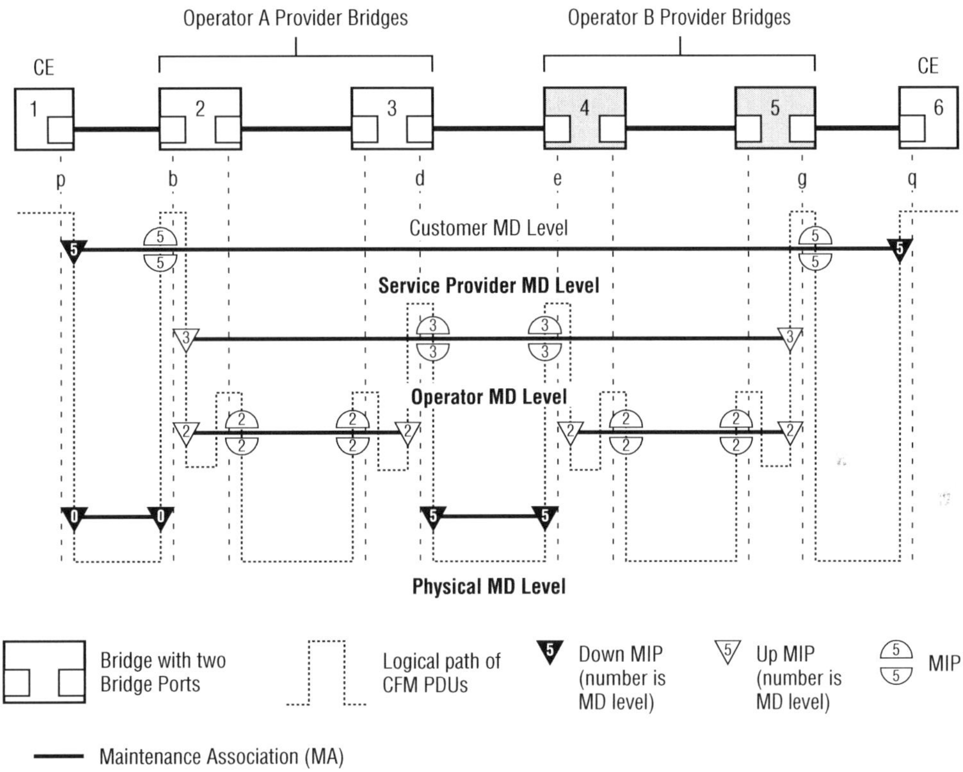

The customer purchases services from a service provider. The service provider uses two network operator networks to transport its services. There are three CFM maintenance domains — the customer domain with MD Level 5, the service provider domain with MD Level 3, and the operator domain with MD Level 2:

- The customer is interested only in the health of the end-to-end connection. Therefore, the customer MA has a high MD level (Level 5). The MEPs/MIPs in the provider and operator network transparently pass the customer's CFM messages. The customer CFM monitors only points p, b, g, and q (as illustrated in Figure 18.10). Details of the service provider and operator network are ignored.

- The service provider is interested in the health of the service it provides. Therefore, the service provider MA has a lower MD level (Level 3). The MEPs/MIPs in the operator's network transparently pass the service provider's CFM messages. The service provider CFM monitors points b, d, e, and g. Details of the operator network are ignored.

- The network provider is interested only in the health of its own network. Therefore, the network provider MA has the lowest MD level (Level 2). The CFM messages travel only within the network provider's network.

With this CFM design, each part of the network performs its own OAM tasks. The MAs are separated by the MD level. Customers can monitor the service between two CE devices. Service provider and network operator networks are not exposed to the customer(s) networks.

CFM Messages

CFM has its own frame formats. All CFM messages are Ethernet frames with protocol type 0x8902 (CFM). After the MAC header, each CFM message contains a common CFM header. The CFM *OpCode* field in the CFM common header indicates the type of the CFM messages. Different types of CFM message contain different CFM PDUs in the message body. Figure 18.11 illustrates the CFM message header.

Figure 18.11　CFM Message Header

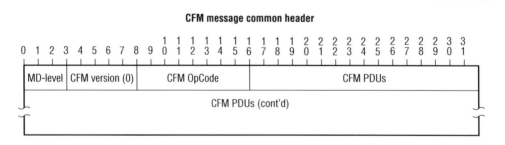

There are five CFM message types. Each type is associated with a different PDU. Each PDU contains one or more informational TLVs. All CFM messages end with an empty *End TLV*. CFM message types are listed in Table 18.2.

Table 18.2   802.1ag CFM Message Types

OpCode	Type	PDUs in the Message	Function
1	Continuity Check Message (CCM)	CCM PDU contains flag, MAID, MEP-id, and status counters defined by ITU-T Y.1731. Contains CFM TLV: port status TLV, interface status TLV.	A MEP generates CCM messages to announce its local port and interface status. If the CCM is enabled, an MA tracks CCM messages from all MEPs. If an MA finds a CCM message missing or receives unexpected CCM messages, it sets corresponding error flags. CCM messages always use a protocol multicast MAC address as the destination MAC address. The CCM protocol multicast MAC address has a format of 01–80–c2–00–00–3<x> (explained later in this chapter).
2	Loopback Reply (LBR)	CFM LBR PDU with 8-bit flags, contains an End TLV.	A MEP/MIP responds with a CFM LBR message when it receives an LBM destined to its own MAC address. The packet destination MAC address is the source MAC address of the LBM.
3	Loopback Message (LBM)	CFM LBM PDU with 8-bit flags, contains an End TLV.	A MEP generates a CFM LBM when the CFM loopback test is performed. The packet is destined to the MAC address the loopback test intends to reach.
4	Link Trace Reply (LTR)	CFM LTR PDU, contains an LTR Egress Identifier TLV, a Reply Egress TLV, an LTM Egress Identifier TLV, and an End TLV.	A MEP responds with a CFM LTR message when it receives a Link Trace Message (LTM) destined to its own MAC address. The packet destination MAC address is the source MAC address of the LTM.
5	Link Trace Message (LTM)	CFM LTM PDU, contains an LTM Egress Identifier TLV and an End TLV.	A MEP generates a CFM LTM message when the CFM link trace test is performed. The packet is destined to the protocol multicast MAC address of 01–80–c2–00–00–3<y> (explained later in this chapter).

Different types of CFM messages have different destination MAC addresses. The CCM and LTM messages intend to reach all MEPs within the same MA; they use protocol multicast MAC addresses. Different CFM entities in the same network may belong to different MAs that have different MD levels. To distinguish among messages with different MD levels, the level value is encoded in the destination multicast MAC addresses. Table 18.3 lists the MAC addresses used by CCM and LTM messages as destination MAC addresses.

Table 18.3 CCM and LTM Group Destination MAC Addresses (IEEE 802.3ah)

CCM destination 01-80-2c-00-00-3x		LTM destination 01-80-2c-00-00-3y	
MD level of CCM	Last 4 bits (x)	MD level of LTM	Last 4 bits (y)
7	7	7	F
6	6	6	E
5	5	5	D
4	4	4	C
3	3	3	B
2	2	2	A
1	1	1	9
0	0	0	8

CFM Configuration Example

When defining an MD in a system, the level of the MD must be specified. One MD can contain one or more MAs. All MAs that belong to the same MD have the same MD level. Each MA may have many MEPs/MIPs.

Figure 18.12 illustrates an example of CFM in customer and provider network domains. The service provider's network contains three PE routers: PE-1, PE-2, and PE-3. VPLS service instance 1000 is deployed in all three PE routers. In each router, under service VPLS-1000, one SAP is created and connected to the corresponding CE devices. In this network, both customer and service provider want to deploy 802.1ag CFM. In this example, the customer uses the CFM MD name customer domain with an MD level of 5; the service provider uses the CFM MD name provider domain with an MD level of 3. The customer and provider each have their own MAs. Each MA contains three MEPs. With this configuration, the customer's MD level is higher than the provider's, therefore the VPLS service will transparently bypass the customer's CFM PDU. If the customer wants to see the service details (the PE routers) in the provider's network, the customer can set the MD level equal to the provider's MD level of 3. Then the VPLS SAPs are visible to the customer's CFM.

Two steps are required to configure the CFM in a VPLS network: The MD and MA need to be created first, then the MEP/MIP can be created in the VPLS service instance and added to the defined MD and MA.

Figure 18.12 802.1ag CFM Example: Customer Domain versus Provider Domain

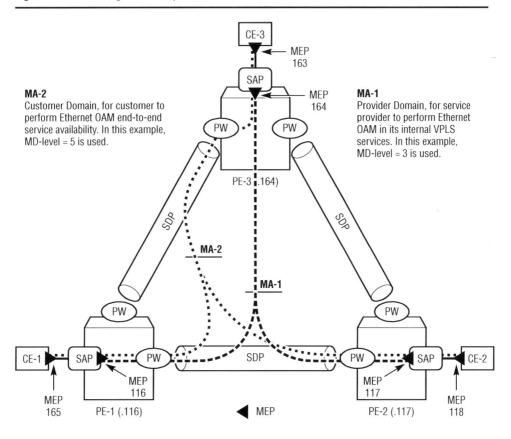

When deploying MEPs in a VPLS service, the *direction of flow* must be specified. In each PE router, a VPLS service instance contains SAPs and pseudowires. SAPs connect the PE routers with CE devices through an attachment circuit (AC). Pseudowires connect the PE routers with other PE routers in the same VPLS through the MPLS core network. When traffic comes in through the SAP ingress, it goes to the switching fabric, then reaches the pseudowire. From the pseudowire, the traffic is sent over to the far-end PE routers using IP/MPLS VPN encapsulation. When the traffic arrives at the far-end PE router, it is de-encapsulated and sent to the switching fabric. Then the traffic is sent through the SAP egress to reach the other CE device.

From the perspective of a SAP, the *up* direction means that the traffic is traveling from the SAP towards the switching fabric; the *down* direction means that the traffic is exiting the system from the SAP. From the perspective of a pseudowire, the *up* direction means that the traffic is traveling from the pseudowire towards the switching fabric; the *down* direction means that the traffic is exiting the system into the pseudowire.

Figure 18.13 illustrates an example of enabling CFM OAM with CCM in a VPLS network. The CFM is enabled by the service provider to monitor the health of the VPLS service.

The first step in enabling CFM is to create the MD. An operator may want to enable CFM for its own OAM purposes. At the same time, the downstream providers or customers need to cooperate with the operator if they want to perform end-to-end CFM. Therefore, there may be multiple CFM requirements with different MD levels, and multiple MDs are created to differentiate them. Each MD created in the system has an index, a name, and an MD level. Many MAs can be defined under the same MD.

After the MD is created, the MA can be created under the MD. Three items must be explicitly configured in the MA definition:

- **MA Name** — The MAID is formed by the MA name and the MD level.
- **Bridge Identification** — The identification of the service in which the MA is deployed
- **Remote MEP-id** — The list of IDs for all remote MEPs that belong to this MA. In this example, three MEPs are in the service provider domain: MEP-116, MPE-117, and ME-164.

Figure 18.13 CFM Example 1 — Deploying CFM in a Service Provider Network

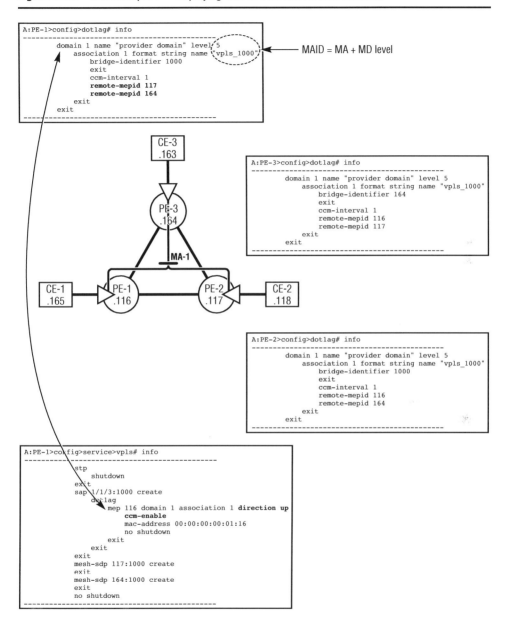

```
A:PE-1>config>dot1ag# info
-----------------------------------------------
    domain 1 name "provider domain" level 5
        association 1 format string name "vpls_1000"
            bridge-identifier 1000
            exit
            ccm-interval 1
            remote-mepid 117
            remote-mepid 164
        exit
    exit
-----------------------------------------------
```

MAID = MA + MD level

CE-3
.163

PE-3
.164

```
A:PE-3>config>dot1ag# info
-----------------------------------------------
        domain 1 name "provider domain" level 5
            association 1 format string name "vpls_1000"
                bridge-identifier 164
                exit
                ccm-interval 1
                remote-mepid 116
                remote-mepid 117
            exit
        exit
-----------------------------------------------
```

MA-1

CE-1
.165

PE-1
.116

PE-2
.117

CE-2
.118

```
A:PE-2>config>dot1ag# info
-----------------------------------------------
        domain 1 name "provider domain" level 5
            association 1 format string name "vpls_1000"
                bridge-identifier 1000
                exit
                ccm-interval 1
                remote-mepid 116
                remote-mepid 164
            exit
        exit
-----------------------------------------------
```

```
A:PE-1>config>service>vpls# info
-----------------------------------------------
            stp
                shutdown
            exit
            sap 1/1/3:1000 create
                dot1ag
                    mep 116 domain 1 association 1 direction up
                        ccm-enable
                        mac-address 00:00:00:00:01:16
                        no shutdown
                    exit
                exit
            exit
            mesh-sdp 117:1000 create
            exit
            mesh-sdp 164:1000 create
            exit
            no shutdown
-----------------------------------------------
```

After the MD and MAs are created, the MEP can be created under the SAP in the VPLS or Epipe service instances. When creating the MEP, MDs and MAs are associated. The following parameters are required:

- **MEP-id** — The ID value used to identify the MEP in the MA. This ID value must be listed in the remote-MPE-id list in the MA configuration of the other PE router.

  Correlate the MEP with the correct MD and MA. When configuring the correlation, the index value is used instead of the name of the MD and MA. All MEPs that belong to the same MA must have the same MA name and MD level.

- **Direction** — The CFM message flow direction. In the example, the CFM message should travel from the SAP to the fabric, then over the pseudowires to reach the far-end SAPs where the other MEPs are configured. Therefore, the direction is up. The CFM messages are sent from the SAP up to the fabric.

- **CCM Message Generation (Optional)** — When enabled, the MEP generates CCM messages and performs continuity checks.

- **MAC Address (Optional)** — The source MAC address of the CFM messages can be defined in the MEP. By default, the *system MAC address* is used as the source MAC address for all CFM messages. For ease of troubleshooting and management, specific MAC addresses can be used for CFM messages. Administratively enable the MEP using the `no shut` command. In Figure 18.13, the last octet of the system IP address is embedded in the CFM source MAC address.

Each MA defined in an MD has a complete view of all of its MEPs. All remote MEPs have their IDs listed under the MA configuration. The local MEP is associated with the MA under the configuration of the VPLS SAP, allowing the MA to be aware of all member MEPs in its MEP mesh. Figure 18.14 illustrates the CLI output that results from checking the CFM status.

Figure 18.14 Checking CFM Status

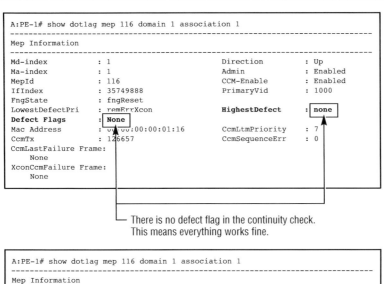

```
A:PE-1# show dot1ag mep 116 domain 1 association 1
-------------------------------------------------------------------------------
Mep Information
-------------------------------------------------------------------------------
Md-index        : 1                      Direction       : Up
Ma-index        : 1                      Admin           : Enabled
MepId           : 116                    CCM-Enable      : Enabled
IfIndex         : 35749888               PrimaryVid      : 1000
FngState        : fngReset
LowestDefectPri : remErrXcon             HighestDefect   : none
Defect Flags    : None
Mac Address      : 00:00:00:00:01:16     CcmLtmPriority  : 7
CcmTx           : 126657                 CcmSequenceErr  : 0
CcmLastFailure Frame:
    None
XconCcmFailure Frame:
    None
```

There is no defect flag in the continuity check.
This means everything works fine.

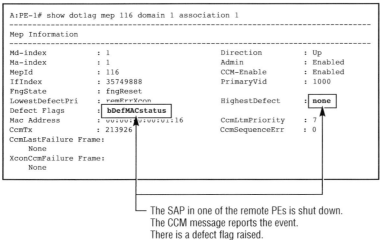

```
A:PE-1# show dot1ag mep 116 domain 1 association 1
-------------------------------------------------------------------------------
Mep Information
-------------------------------------------------------------------------------
Md-index        : 1                      Direction       : Up
Ma-index        : 1                      Admin           : Enabled
MepId           : 116                    CCM-Enable      : Enabled
IfIndex         : 35749888               PrimaryVid      : 1000
FngState        : fngReset
LowestDefectPri : remErrXcon             HighestDefect   : none
Defect Flags    : bDefMACstatus
Mac Address      : 00:00:00:00:01:16     CcmLtmPriority  : 7
CcmTx           : 213926                 CcmSequenceErr  : 0
CcmLastFailure Frame:
    None
XconCcmFailure Frame:
    None
```

The SAP in one of the remote PEs is shut down.
The CCM message reports the event.
There is a defect flag raised.

Figure 18.14 includes two examples. The output of the **show** command in the top example shows a clear CCM check result. The output of the **show** command in the bottom example shows a CCM check that has a failure. The SAP in one of the remote MEPs in the same MA failed, so a defect flag is raised.

MIPs in CFM

MIPs are intermediate points in the CFM architecture. MIPs do not initiate or consume CCMs and are therefore completely transparent for continuity checks. A MIP responds to an LBM with an LBR message if its own MAC address is the destination MAC address of the LBM. When a MIP in a router receives an LTM message generated by a MEP for a link trace test, the router performs a forwarding database (FDB) lookup in the service instance. If the FDB contains the MAC address being traced, the MIP forwards the LTM message and responds with an LTR message. A MIP half-function (MHF) is used when deploying CFM in VPLS services. Figure 18.15 illustrates a configuration example of adding an MIP to the CFM in a VPLS.

A MIP cannot exist alone in the CFM of a VPLS and is always automatically created with a MEP. Figure 18.15 illustrates the creation of a MIP. To create a MIP, an MA with a *higher* MD level than the MEP must be created. Using the `mhf-creation explicit` command during the bridge-identifier association enables the automatic creation of the MIP when a MEP is created in the same service instance. The CFM database display on the bottom of the diagram shows that a MIP is created (bold line), triggered by the creation of MEP 116 in the VPLS service.

CFM supports three basic functions — a loopback test (also referred to as a *ping*), a link trace test, and a Continuity Check test. CFM allows the system to perform end-to-end fault management both proactively (by performing a loopback or using the link trace function to locate the failure point) and reactively (by tracking and validating CCMs to detect failures).

Loopback Test

CFM supports a loopback test to verify the availability of a MAC address destination. This is similar to the IP-ping test. When a loopback test is performed, the MEP launches an LBM to another MEP or MIP along the MA to check whether there is a failure in between the two points, and the location of the failure. If there is a fault along the path, the MIP in front of the fault responds with an LBR, but the MIP/MEP that is behind the fault does not. In order to perform a loopback test, the MAC address of the destination MIP/MEP must be known, either by manual configuration, or by auto-discovery. Figure 18.16 illustrates an example of a CFM loopback test.

Figure 18.15 Adding an MIP to the CFM in a VPLS

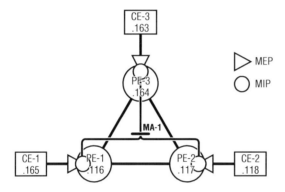

```
A:PE-1>config>dot1ag# info
--------------------------------------------------
        domain 1 name "provider domain" level 5
            association 1 format string name "vpls_1000"
                bridge-identifier 1000
                exit
                ccm-interval 1
                remote-mepid 117
                remote-mepid 164
            exit
        exit
        domain 10 name "formip" level 7
            association 10 format string name "mip"
                bridge-identifier 1000
                    mhf-creation explicit
                exit
            exit
        exit
--------------------------------------------------
```

```
A:PE-1# show dot1ag cfm-stack-table
===============================================================================
Dot1ag CFM SAP Stack Table
===============================================================================
Sap              Level Dir  Md-index   Ma-index   Mep-id Mac-address
-------------------------------------------------------------------------------
1/1/3:1000       5     Up   1          1          116    00:00:00:00:01:16
1/1/3:1000       7     Both 10         10         MIP    8e:74:01:01:00:03
===============================================================================
===============================================================================
Dot1ag CFM SDP Stack Table
===============================================================================
Sdp              Level Dir  Md-index   Ma-index   Mep id Mac address
-------------------------------------------------------------------------------
No Matching Entries
===============================================================================
```

Figure 18.16 CFM Loopback Test

```
A:PE-1# show dotlag mep 116 domain 1 association 1 loopback
-----------------------------------------------------------------------------
Mep Information
-----------------------------------------------------------------------------
Md-index          : 1                Direction        : Up
Ma-index          : 1                Admin            : Enabled
MepId             : 116              CCM-Enable       : Enabled
IfIndex           : 35749888         PrimaryVid       : 1000
FngState          : fngReset
LowestDefectPri   : remErrXcon       HighestDefect    : none
Defect Flags      : None
Mac Address       : 00:00:00:00:01:16  CcmLtmPriority  : 7
CcmTx             : 318226           CcmSequenceErr   : 0
CcmLastFailure Frame:
     None
XconCcmFailure Frame:
     None
-----------------------------------------------------------------------------
Mep Loopback Information
-----------------------------------------------------------------------------
LbRxReply         : 6                LbRxBadOrder     : 0
LbRxBadMsdu       : 0                LbTxReply        : 6
LbSequence        : 7                LbNextSequence   : 8
LbStatus          : False            LbResultOk       : True
DestIsMepId       : False            DestMepId        : 0
DestMac           : 00:00:00:00:00:00  SendCount      : 0
VlanDropEnable    : True             VlanPriority     : 7
Data TLV:
     None
```

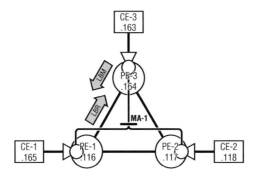

```
A:PE-3# oam dotlag loopback 00:00:00:00:01:16 mep 164 domain 1 association 1 send-count 5
Dotlag Loopback Test Initiated: Mac-Address: 00:00:00:00:01:16, out sap: 1/1/3:1000
Sent 5 packets, received 5 packets [0 out-of-order, 0 Bad Msdu] -- OK
A:PE-3#
```

```
A:PE-1# oam dotlag loopback 00:00:00:00:01:64 mep 116 domain 1 association 1
Dotlag Loopback Test Initiated: Mac-Address: 00:00:00:00:01:64, out sap: 1/1/3:1000
Sent 1 packets, received 0 packets [0 out-of-order, 0 Bad Msdu] -- FAILED
A:PE-1#
```

Link Trace Test

CFM also supports the link trace test to retrieve information about the forwarding path to a MAC destination. When a link trace test is performed, the MEP launches an LTM to the destination MAC address of the CFM link trace group. The MIPs/

MEPs along the path respond with LTR messages. If there is a fault along the path, the MIP in front of the fault responds with an LBR, but the MIP/MEP that is behind the fault does not. In order to perform a link trace test, the MAC address of the destination MIP/MEP must be known, either by manual configuration or by auto-discovery. Figure 18.17 presents an example of a CFM link trace test.

Figure 18.17 CFM Link Trace Test

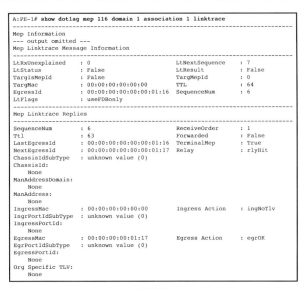

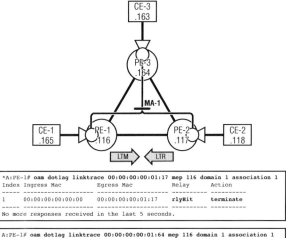

Continuity Check Test

As previously mentioned, the MA knows all MEPs in its MEP mesh. When a CC test is enabled, each MEP generates a CCM in the predefined direction (up or down). CCMs use the group destination MAC address as the message destination MAC address. All MEPs in the same MA can receive CCMs from other MEPs. It is considered a fault if the CCM of a MEP cannot be seen by other MEPs in the same MA. Therefore, certain flags are set by the MA. Figure 18.18 illustrates an example of a CC test. All three PE routers have a similar configuration with an MD, MA, and MEP. The example presents the configuration of PE-1.

MEPs with CC enabled constantly send out CCMs to all other MEPs at each ccm-interval. The MA that contains these MEPs (local and remote) keeps track of the reception of these messages. By checking the received CCMs, the MA can detect network failures or incorrect configuration scenarios, as follows:

- **Loss of Connectivity** — The MA considers that there is a loss of connectivity from a MEP if a CCM from a particular MEP was not received in a predefined time interval. The MA knows how many CCMs it should receive because it has a list of remote-MEP-ids in its configuration.

- **Incorrect Configuration of Service (Merging of Services)** — The MA considers that a service is *incorrectly configured* if it receives an unexpected CCM from a MEP, that is, if the received CCM is from a MEP that:

    - Is in the same MA, but its ID is not in the remote-MEP-id list.

    - Is not in the same MA (determined by comparing the MAID field in the message).

    - Has a lower MD level.

- **Forwarding Loops** — The MA considers that there is a forwarding loop if it receives a CCM that contains the MEP-id of its local MPE.

- **Unidirectional Failure** — The MA considers that there is a unidirectional failure if it receives a CCM with the RDI flag set in the PDU flag field of its CCM. Table 18.4 lists the error flags that can be reported by the CFM CCM function.

Figure 18.18 CFM Continuity Check

```
A:PE-1# show dot1ag mep 116 domain 1 association 1
--------------------------------------------------------------------------------
Mep Information
--------------------------------------------------------------------------------
Md-index            : 1                    Direction        : Up
Ma-index            : 1                    Admin            : Enabled
MepId               : 116                  CCM-Enable       : Enabled
IfIndex             : 35749888             PrimaryVid       : 1000
FngState            : fngReset
LowestDefectPri     : remErrXcon           HighestDefect    : none
Defect Flags        : None
Mac Address         : 00:00:00:00:01:16    CcmLtmPriority   : 7
CcmTx               : 321120               CcmSequenceErr   : 0
CcmLastFailure Frame:
    None
XconCcmFailure Frame:
    None
A:PE-1#
```

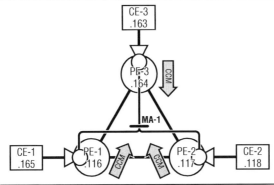

```
A:PE-1>config>service>vpls# info
----------------------------------------------
            stp
                shutdown
            exit
            sap 1/1/3:1000 create
                dot1ag
                    mep 116 domain 1 association 1 direction up
                    ccm-enable
                        mac-address 00:00:00:00:01:16
                        no shutdown
                    exit
                exit
            exit
            mesh-sdp 117:1000 create
            exit
            mesh-sdp 164:1000 create
            exit
            no shutdown
----------------------------------------------
```

```
A:PE-1>config>dot1ag# info
----------------------------------------------
        domain 1 name "provider domain" level 5
            association 1 format string name "vpls_1000"
                bridge-identifier 1000
                exit
                ccm-interval 1
                remote-mepid 117
                remote-mepid 164
            exit
        exit
----------------------------------------------
```

Table 18.4 CFM CCM Error Flags

Error	Priority	Description
None	0	No defect reported.
defRDICCM	1	The last CCM received by this MEP from a remote MEP contained a Remote Defect Indication (RDI) bit.
defMACstatus	2	The last CCM received by this MEP from a remote MEP indicated that the MAC address associated with the transmitting MEP is reporting an error status via the Port Status TLV or Interface Status TLV.
defRemoteCCM	3	This MEP is not receiving CCMs from other MEPs in its configured list (remote-MEP-id list).
defErrorCCM	4	This MEP is receiving invalid CCMs.
defXconCCM	5	This MEP is receiving CCMs that belong to some other MA.

CFM in PBB-VPLS

In a PBB-VPLS network, the operations of CFM in B-VPLS and I-VPLS instances are independent and therefore transparent to each other. Each B-VPLS instance or I-VPLS instance has its own MAs and MDs. The CFM messages from I-VPLS instances travel across the corresponding B-VPLS instances transparently, as if the B-VPLS does not exist.

18.4 OAM in an IP/MPLS VPN Service Network

OAM monitors the network health and proactively checks network connectivity. In an IP/MPLS VPN service network, all services share the IP/MPLS infrastructure. Various OAM tools are available to test different objects in this type of multi-layered network. This section introduces the OAM tools used to test the IP/MPLS infrastructure and the OAM tools used for basic service connectivity. The next section introduces OAM tools for the VPLS service.

OAM Tools

The IP/MPLS VPN backbone network consists of a routed IP core, MPLS tunnels, and a Service Distribution Path (SDP) overlay. Details regarding the IP/MPLS VPN backbone network infrastructure are introduced in Chapter 9. Each layer of the IP/MPLS VPN network has its own OAM tools, as follows:

- IP-ping and trace-route are used to test the reachability of the IP core.

- Label Switched Path (LSP) ping and trace are used to test the connectivity of MPLS service transport tunnels.
- SDP-ping and SDP-trace are used to test the connectivity of the SDP transport tunnel between a pair of PE routers. These tools can be used for both MPLS and GRE tunnels.
- Service Ping is used to test the service reachability and attributes between PE routers.
- Virtual Circuit Connectivity Verification (VCCV) and Service Ping are used to test connectivity of the pseudowire for Virtual Leased Line (VLL) services.
- CPE Ping and host connectivity tools are used for service reachability tests.

Table 18.5 lists the OAM tools used in the IP/MPLS VPN backbone network.

Table 18.5   OAM Tools in IP/MPLS VPN Networks

Function	Description
IP-ping	Used to test the router's IP connectivity using ICMP Echo Request/Reply packets
IP-trace-route	Used to locate the failure in IP routing or to discover the forwarding path to a particular IP prefix
LSP-ping	Used to test the connectivity of the LSP (created by RSVP-TE or LDP) using MPLS Echo Request/Reply packets
LSP-trace	Used to locate a failure of an LSP or to discover the path of an LSP
SDP-mtu	Used to discover the SDP path MTU supported on an SDP. By specifying a *start octet*, an *end octet*, and a *step*, the SDP-mtu function finds the largest path MTU the SDP can support, and the operator can use the value accordingly. SDP-mtu is described in Chapter 9 (Alcatel-Lucent proprietary)
SDP-ping	Used to test the service reachability of the SDP from one PE router to another. The SDP-ping packet is always sent through the data plane using the SDP's tunnel encapsulation with an MPLS RA (1) label. The reply packet can come from the control plane or the data plane depending on the request specified in the SDP-ping packet (Alcatel-Lucent proprietary)
VCCV-ping	Defined by RFC 5085. Used to test the connectivity of the pseudowire for the VLL service
VCCV-trace	Used to detect a pseudowire failure or to discover the forwarding path of a pseudowire
CPE-ping	Used to locate a PE router that is locally attached to a particular customer IP station (IP address) (Alcatel-Lucent proprietary)
SVC-ping	Used to test the connectivity and attributes of VPN services (Alcatel-Lucent proprietary)

The OAM tools in Table 18.5 are described in greater detail in the following sections.

Checking LSP Connectivity and Paths

As per RFC 4379, *Detecting Multi-Protocol Label Switched (MPLS) Data Plane Failures,* the purpose of LSP-ping and LSP-trace is to provide a series of messages and a mechanism to test the health of an MPLS LSP. The basic idea is to introduce the request-reply mechanism into the MPLS LSP so a router can launch MPLS Echo Request packet(s) to test or trace an LSP by expecting MPLS Echo Reply packet(s). The echo request and reply messages used are IP packets using UDP as the transport layer protocol. UDP port 3503 is reserved for the LSP-ping application. Figure 18.19 illustrates the format of the packet defined in RFC4379 for MPLS Echo Request/Reply packets.

Figure 18.19   MPLS Echo Request/Reply Packet Format

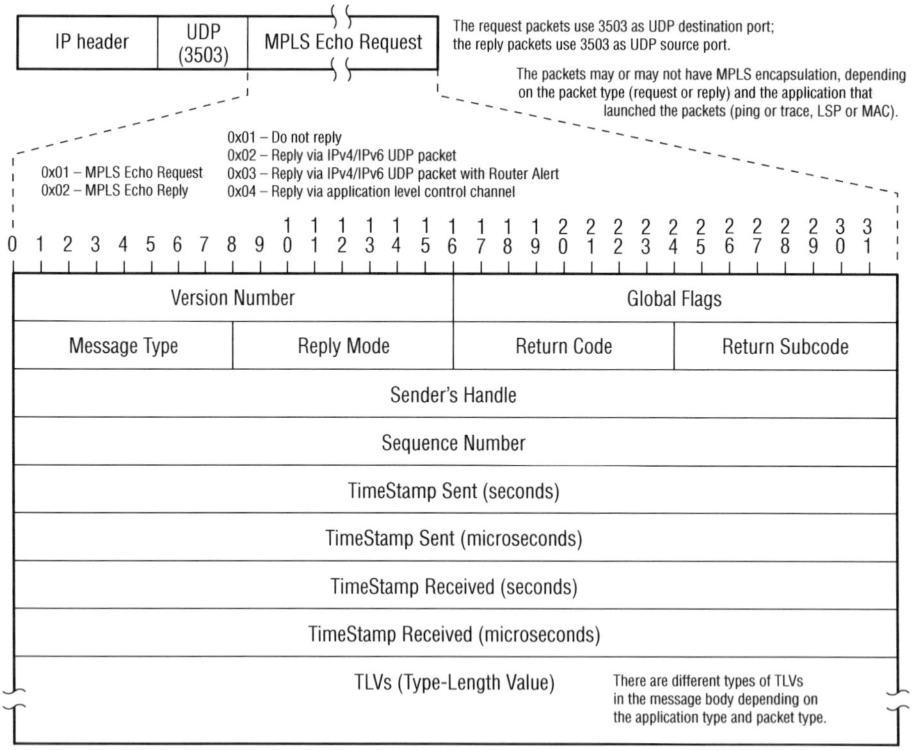

The actual MPLS Echo information is contained in the TLV. Refer to RFC 4379 for details of the TLVs used in the message, their formats, and meanings.

MPLS OAM tools have two different functions: LSP-ping and LSP-trace:

- **LSP-ping** tests the health of an MPLS LSP from the perspective of the data plane. An LSP forwards traffic that belongs to the same Forwarding Equivalent Class (FEC). The purpose of the LSP-ping is to ensure that in the data plane, the terminating router (egress LER or eLER) of the LSP *is* the egress router of the FEC. When LSP-ping is launched in a particular MPLS Label Switch Router (LSR) for an FEC, the router sends an MPLS Echo Request packet encapsulated in the same way in which the data traffic is encapsulated and forwards the packet to the destination of the FEC. The destination of the FEC is the end of the LSP, which should also be the eLER router of the FEC. The eLER router of the LSP responds to the LSP-ping by sending an MPLS Echo Reply packet. Only the end of the LSP (eLER) of the FEC being pinged should respond to the LSP-ping. All routers along the path of the LSP relay only the ping and reply packets.

- **LSP-trace** can detect failure (when the LSP-ping to the FEC fails) or determine the actual path of the LSP (when the LSP-ping to the FEC succeeds). When LSP-trace is launched in a router for a particular FEC, the router also sends the MPLS Echo Request packets to the downstream router. The difference is that the router keeps sending out the request packets with an incremental time-to-live (TTL) value in the transport label the packet uses, starting from 1. Each router along the LSP's path responds to the trace type MPLS Echo Request packet by sending back an MPLS Echo Reply packet. The Reply packet indicates whether or not the router that sent the packet is a transit hop (LSR) or the last hop (eLER) of the LSP. It also provides information about the downstream interface for the LSP. The source router of the trace keeps sending requests, increasing the TTL value until a response from the eLER router is received, or until an error code is received from a router. Refer to RFC 4379 for details of the message format and the ping and trace mechanisms.

LSP-ping

LSP-ping works in a similar manner to IP-ping. The originating router sends an MPLS Echo Request packet, and the receiving router responds with an MPLS Echo Reply packet. LSPs are always unidirectional. The MPLS Echo Request packet used by the pinging router is an MPLS-encapsulated IP-UDP packet with a destination UDP port of 3503. The MPLS Echo Reply packet is a regular IP-UDP packet. The MPLS Echo Request uses the internal host loopback IP address of 127/8 as the IP destination address of the packet, so that the receiving router must process the packet in its control plane. This packet will never be routed natively after leaving the MPLS network. Figure 18.20 illustrates the CLI options and the result of an LSP-ping.

Figure 18.20 LSP-ping CLI Example

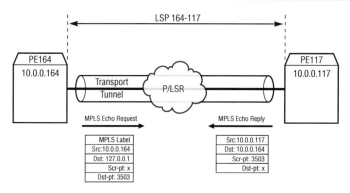

```
A:PE-164# oam lsp-ping
  - lsp-ping {{<lsp-name> [path <path-name>]}|{prefix <ip-prefix/mask>}} [fc
<fc-name> [profile {in|out}]] [size
     <octets>] [ttl <label-ttl>] [send-count <send-count>] [timeout <timeout>]
[interval <interval>] [path-destination
     <ip-address>[interface <if-name>|next-hop <ip-address>]] [detail]

<lsp-name>          : [32 chars max]
<octets>            : [80|85..9198] - Prefix specified ping  - Default 80
                      [92|97..9198] - LSP name specified ping - Default 92
<label-ttl>         : [1..255]
<timeout>           : [1..10]
<interval>          : [1..10]
<fc-name>           : be|l2|af|l1|h2|ef|h1|nc - Default: be
<in|out>            : keywords - Default: out
<send-count>        : [1..100]
<path-name>         : [32 chars max]
<ip-prefix/mask>    : ip-prefix a.b.c.d
                      mask [value MUST be 32]
<detail>            : keyword - displays detailed information
<ip-address>        : ipv4 address    a.b.c.d
<if-name>           : [32 chars max]
```

```
A:PE-164# oam lsp-ping 164-116                      ❶
LSP-PING 164-116: 92 bytes MPLS payload
Seq=1, send from intf to-117, reply from 10.0.0.116
       udp-data-len=32 ttl=255 rtt<10ms rc=3 (EgressRtr)
----
 LSP 164-116 PING Statistics ----
1 packets sent, 1 packets received, 0.00% packet loss
round-trip min < 10ms, avg < 10ms, max < 10ms, stddev < 10ms
A:PE-164#
A
:PE-164# oam lsp-ping prefix 10.0.0.116/32           ❷
LSP-PING 10.0.0.116/32: 80 bytes MPLS payload
Seq=1, send from intf to-117, reply from 10.0.0.116
       udp-data-len=32 ttl=255 rtt<10ms rc=3 (EgressRtr)
----
 LSP 10.0.0.116/32 PING Statistics ----
1 packets sent, 1 packets received, 0.00% packet loss
round-trip min < 10ms, avg < 10ms, max < 10ms, stddev < 10ms
A:PE-164#
```

Figure 18.20 shows two successful LSP-ping commands in the bottom textbox. The first example (1) is an LSP-ping for an RSVP-TE LSP. The second example (2) is an LSP-ping for an LDP-LSP. LDP does not require the explicit configuration of the LSP; instead, it distributes labels to establish automatic LSPs based on the FEC-Label mapping. To test an LDP-LSP using LSP-ping, the FEC must be specified instead of the name of the LSP. Prefix 10.0.0.116/32 is an FEC that represents the LDP-LSP from the local router (10.0.0.164) to the router (10.0.0.116).

An RSVP-TE LSP can contain multiple LSP-Paths, but there is only one active forwarding LSP-Path in an LSP at any time. The LSP-ping is always testing the active forwarding LSP-Path of an LSP for an RSVP-TE LSP. LDP-LSP can also have more than one path (active label bindings) to an FEC (prefix) if Equal Cost Multi-Path (ECMP) is enabled and there are multiple IGP paths to the destination. The LSP-ping *randomly picks one path randomly (active egress label binding) to send the echo request*. Also, for LDP-LSP, if LDP over RSVP tunneling is preferred, the LSP-ping packet is also tunneled by RSVP-TE LSP; therefore, the MPLS Echo Request packet is double-stacked (outer RSVP-TE tunnel label, inner LDP label).

LSP-trace

LSP-trace works in a similar manner to the IP-trace route. It also uses the MPLS Echo Request/Reply packets to communicate with MPLS routers. The only difference between LSP-ping and LSP-trace is that LSP-trace sends multiple Echo Request packets with incremental MPLS label (transport label) TTL values. The packet's TTL starts with a 1, and keeps increasing the TTL by 1 each time a new Echo Request is sent, until the trace reaches the destination router (the eLER of the LSP being traced). Figure 18.21 demonstrates the CLI options and the result of an LSP-trace.

Figure 18.21 shows two LSP-trace outputs in the lower textbox. The first example (1) is an LSP-trace for an RSVP-TE LSP. The second example (2) is an LSP-trace for an LDP-LSP. Similar to the LSP-ping, in order to trace an LDP-LSP using LSP-trace, the FEC must be specified instead of the name of the LSP. Prefix 10.0.0.116/32 is an FEC that represents the LDP-LSP from the local router (10.0.0.164) to the router (10.0.0.116).

An RSVP-TE LSP can contain multiple LSP-Paths, but there is only one active forwarding LSP-Path in an LSP at any time. The LSP-trace is always testing the active forwarding LSP-Path of an LSP for an RSVP-TE LSP. LDP-LSP can also have more than one path (active label bindings) to an FEC (prefix) if ECMP is enabled and there are multiple IGP paths to the destination. The LSP-trace *randomly picks one path randomly (active egress label binding) to send the echo request.* Also, for LDP-LSP, if LDPoRSVP tunneling is preferred, the LSP-trace packet is also transparently tunneled by RSVP-TE LSP. The RSVP-TE LSP used to tunnel the LDP-LSP in LDPoRSVP is not traced as a hop.

Figure 18.21 LSP-trace CLI Example

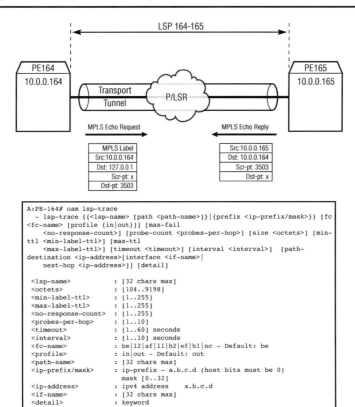

SDP-ping

SDP is unidirectional and it connects two PE routers using transport tunnel(s) to carry traffic from one PE router to another over the backbone network. SDP-ping tests the SDP tunnel connectivity. When SDP-ping is launched from a PE router over a specific SDP, the PE router generates a packet to the far-end PE router using the encapsulation of the SDP's transport tunnel. The ping packet travels the same path as the VPN data traffic (the exception is that when there is ECMP or LAG, it is possible that SDP-ping chooses a different path than the actual VPN packet). Regardless of the transport tunnel encapsulation type of the SDP (GRE or MPLS), the packet always has an MPLS label of Router Alert (1), with the TTL set to 1. Therefore, when the far-end PE router receives the packet and removes the transport label, it has to send the packet to the control plane for processing. When the PE router receives an SDP-ping packet, it has the following two options for replying (the reply method is specified in the SDP-ping packet):

- **Reply from the Control Plane** — The PE router can use a GRE packet with an MPLS Router Alert (1) label to respond to the SDP-ping. In this case, the returning packet is a GRE-encapsulated IP packet and travels as a regular IP packet to the PE router that originated the SDP-ping through the IGP-directed path.

- **Reply from the Data Plane** — The PE router uses the SDP in the reverse direction specified by the ping to respond. It uses the SDP to perform transport tunnel encapsulation and sends the reply from the data plane. The response packet follows the exact path the VPN traffic uses when traveling over the returning SDP.

Figure 18.22 demonstrates the SDP-ping CLI command options and the SDP-ping results.

Figure 18.22 shows two SDP-pings performed from Router PE-164 to Router PE-117. The first SDP-ping (the middle CLI box) does not specify the returning SDP for the remote router to use. In this case, Router PE-117 sends a reply back from the control plane and uses GRE encapsulation. The second SDP-ping (the bottom CLI box) specifies the responding SDP. Therefore, PE-117 uses SDP 164 to send the reply over the data plane with proper transport tunnel encapsulation.

If the SDP uses RSVP-TE LSPs as transport tunnels, and more than one LSP in the SDP is available to carry traffic, the SDP *randomly picks one LSP to send the*

SDP-ping packet based on the ECMP hashing algorithm. The ECMP hashing algorithm relies on multiple inputs to generate various output results, but because the SDP-ping packet is from the control plane and has no ingress MPLS label stack or service-id, the hashing algorithm always picks the same LSP to send the ping packet.

Figure 18.22   SDP-ping CLI Example

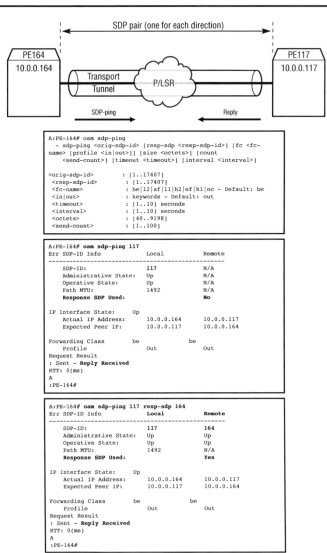

Service Ping

The Service Ping (`svc-ping`) provides an end-to-end round-trip service connectivity test on a point-to-point basis. The Service Ping works on a higher level than the SDP-ping. SDP-ping tests the service reach of an SDP between two PE routers that can be shared by many services. The Service Ping tests only the connectivity of a particular service. More specifically, each `svc-ping` command tests connectivity and service attributes over the pseudowire between the local PE router and a remote member PE router. Therefore, a Service Ping is more like a *Pseudowire Ping*, except that it provides other service attributes such as service ID, IP interface used, etc. A Service Ping is always point-to-point, and for multiple services like VPLS, the Service Ping must be launched separately for each far-end PE router to test connectivity for that PE router.

The Service Ping verifies the connectivity between two PE routers on a particular service specified in the CLI command. No customer devices are involved in the test. When performing a Service Ping, the IP address of the far-end PE router (`router-id`) and the `service-id` must be specified. Figure 18.23 illustrates an example of an `svc-ping` between two VPLS member PE routers.

Figure 18.23 illustrates a successfully executed Service Ping from PE-164 to test pseudowire connectivity to router PE-117 for VPLS service 200. Similar to other ping functions, a Service Ping can be executed on either the control plane or the data plane, depending on the command execution optional parameters. In Figure 18.23, the `local-sdp` and `remote-sdp` options are included; therefore, the Service Ping is performed on the data plane. When the Service Ping is executed on the data plane, the ping packet is triple-MPLS-labeled with a transport label, a vc-label, and a router-alert label. The MPLS-labeled Service Ping traffic follows the exact path of the MPLS-encapsulated data traffic to reach the remote PE router. The Ping Reply packet does the same. When the Service Ping is executed on the control plane, the ping packet and the reply packet are GRE-encapsulated with a router-alert label underneath the GRE header. GRE encapsulations use the router-id of the remote PE router being pinged as the destination IP of the packet, and the router-id of the local router as the source IP address. The GRE-encapsulated Service Ping packet is routed through the backbone network by the IGP routing table, just as regular IP traffic is routed in the backbone.

Figure 18.23 Service Ping Example

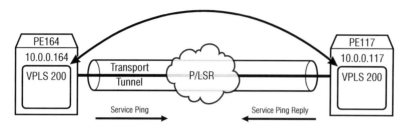

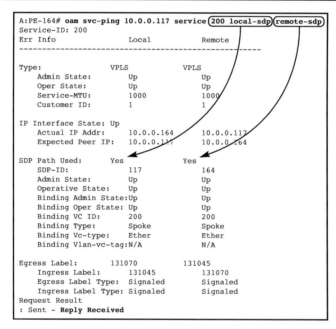

Virtual Circuit Connectivity Verification (VCCV)

VCCV is defined by RFC 5085, *Pseudowire Virtual Circuit Connectivity Verification (VCCV): A Control Plane for Pseudowire*. VCCV is an end-to-end fault-detection tool that tests pseudowires. VCCV functions in the same way as Service Ping. The difference between the two is that Service Ping is Alcatel-Lucent proprietary while VCCV is defined by an RFC standard, and it provides additional service attributes information which is not provided by VCCV-ping. Also, Service Ping can test pseudowires for all types of Layer 2 VPN services, while VCCV can test only point-to-point Layer 2 VPN services (VLL). VCCV tests a pseudowire by sending test packets that use the same pseudowire encapsulation and collect reply information. There are two types of VCCV tools: VCCV-ping and VCCV-trace. VCCV can be seen as a *pseudowire ping/trace*.

VCCV is a standards-based pseudowire connectivity check OAM tool; therefore, VCCV interoperation between different vendors is possible. VCCV uses capability advertisement to *negotiate* the possibility of interoperation. To ensure that both sides of the pseudowire (the local PE and the remote PE) support VCCV before using it to test the pseudowire, the two PE routers need to establish a VCCV capability agreement. When two PE routers signal a pseudowire, the LDP Label Mapping message (`type 0x400`) is used. VCCV capability is advertised by including a VCCV sub-TLV in the FEC element TLV in the LDP Label Mapping message. Figure 18.24 illustrates a VCCV sub-TLV format and a packet capture of an LDP Label Mapping message that has VCCV capability.

A PE router sends an LDP Label Mapping message containing a VCCV sub-TLV to indicate that the router is capable of performing a VCCV test. If the remote PE router also supports VCCV, it responds with a Label Mapping message containing a VCCV sub-TLV. If the responding Label Mapping message does not contain a VCCV sub-TLV, the local PE router understands that the remote PE router does not support VCCV and does not allow a VCCV test to be performed on that pseudowire. During VCCV capability negotiation, both PE routers need to agree upon two things:

- **Control Channel (CC) Type** — This defines the method of VCCV packet encapsulation. The system requires certain methods to distinguish the VCCV traffic from regular customer data traffic when receiving it from a pseudowire.

VCCV identification can be accomplished by using pseudowire control words in the pseudowire encapsulation, by inserting a router-alert label in the bottom of the MPLS stack, or by setting the vc-label's TTL to 1.

- **Connectivity Verification (CV) Type** — This defines which types of message the VCCV uses to test the connectivity. There are two options: using the LSP-ping method (MPLS Echo Request/Reply) or using the ICMP-ping method (ICMP Echo Request/Reply).

In Figure 18.24, the negotiation result is that both sides support VCCV. They agree to use an MPLS router-alert label as the control channel method (CC type) and to use LSP-ping as the connectivity verification mechanism (CV type).

If the negotiation is successful, VCCV-ping and VCCV-trace can be executed at any time to verify the connectivity of the pseudowire. Figure 18.25 illustrates an example of VCCV-ping and VCCV-trace between two PE routers on Epipe service 1000.

Figure 18.24 VCCV Capability Negotiation during Pseudowire Establishment

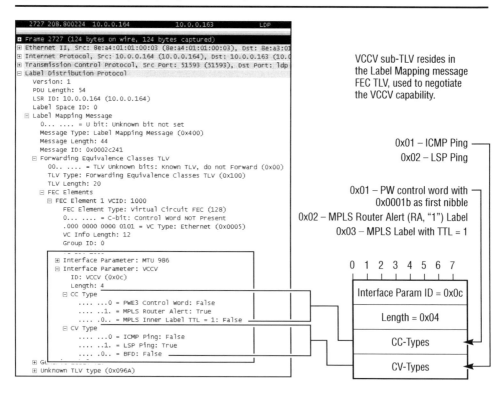

Figure 18.25 VCCV Ping/Trace on an Epipe (Ethernet VLL) Service

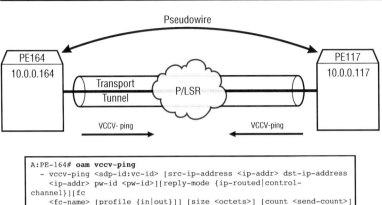

```
A:PE-164# oam vccv-ping
  - vccv-ping <sdp-id:vc-id> [src-ip-address <ip-addr> dst-ip-address
    <ip-addr> pw-id <pw-id>][reply-mode {ip-routed|control-
channel}][fc
    <fc-name> [profile {in|out}]] [size <octets>] [count <send-count>]
    [timeout <timeout>] [interval <interval>]|[ttl <vc-label-ttl>]

<sdp-id:vc-id>       : sdp-id - [1..17407]
                       vc-id  - [1..4294967295]
 <ip-routed|control*> : keywords - specify reply mode
                       Default: control-channel
<fc-name>            : be|l2|af|l1|h2|ef|h1|nc - Default: be
<in|out>             : keywords - Default: out
<octets>             : [88..9198] octets - Default: 88
<send-count>         : [1..100] - Default: 1
<timeout>            : [1..10] seconds - Default: 5
<interval>           : [1..10] seconds - Default 1
<ip-addr>            : a.b.c.d
<vc-label-ttl>       : [1..255]
<pw-id>              : [1..4294967295]
```

```
A:PE-164# oam vccv-ping 163:1000
VCCV-PING 163:1000 88 bytes MPLS payload
Seq=1, reply from 10.0.0.163 via Control Channel
        udp-data-len=32 rtt<10ms rc=3 (EgressRtr)
----
 VCCV PING 163:1000 Statistics ----
1 packets sent, 1 packets received, 0.00% packet loss
round-trip min < 10ms, avg < 10ms, max < 10ms, stddev
< 10ms
A:PE-164#
```

```
A:PE-164# oam vccv-trace 163:1000
VCCV-TRACE 163:1000  with 88 bytes of MPLS payload
1  10.0.0.163  rtt<10ms rc=3(EgressRtr)
A:PE-164#
```

In Figure 18.25, the VCCV-ping on pseudowire **163:1000** is executed from Router PE-164 to Router PE-117. The packet is sent using the same pseudowire encapsulation as the user packets, and a Router Alert Label is added to the label stack. By default, the response from PE-117 also travels using the reverse path of the pseudowire (using an MPLS-encapsulated control channel). If the command is executed using the optional parameter `reply-mode ip-routed`, the response uses regular IP/UDP packets. Although VCCV-ping performs a similar function to Service Ping, it has a slightly different MPLS label stack. Figure 18.26 compares the two types of ping packets.

Figure 18.26 MPLS Label Stacks in VCCV-ping and Service Ping Packets

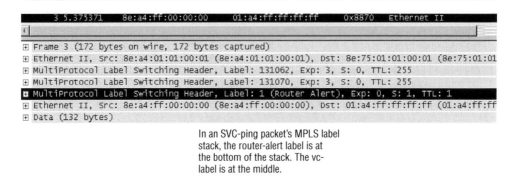

```
   3 5.375371     8e:a4:ff:00:00:00     01:a4:ff:ff:ff:ff     0x8870   Ethernet II

⊞ Frame 3 (172 bytes on wire, 172 bytes captured)
⊞ Ethernet II, Src: 8e:a4:01:01:00:01 (8e:a4:01:01:00:01), Dst: 8e:75:01:01:00:01 (8e:75:01:01
⊞ MultiProtocol Label Switching Header, Label: 131062, Exp: 3, S: 0, TTL: 255
⊞ MultiProtocol Label Switching Header, Label: 131070, Exp: 3, S: 0, TTL: 255
⊞ MultiProtocol Label Switching Header, Label: 1 (Router Alert), Exp: 0, S: 1, TTL: 1
⊞ Ethernet II, Src: 8e:a4:ff:00:00:00 (8e:a4:ff:00:00:00), Dst: 01:a4:ff:ff:ff:ff (01:a4:ff:ff
⊞ Data (132 bytes)
```

In an SVC-ping packet's MPLS label stack, the router-alert label is at the bottom of the stack. The vc-label is at the middle.

```
   59 4.160329     10.0.0.164             127.0.0.1               MPLS ECH MPLS Echo Req

⊞ Frame 59 (114 bytes on wire, 114 bytes captured)
⊞ Ethernet II, Src: 8e:a4:01:01:00:03 (8e:a4:01:01:00:03), Dst: 8e:a3:01:01:00:02 (8e:
⊞ MultiProtocol Label Switching Header, Label: 131061, Exp: 0, S: 0, TTL: 255
⊞ MultiProtocol Label Switching Header, Label: 1 (Router Alert), Exp: 0, S: 0, TTL:255
⊞ MultiProtocol Label Switching Header, Label: 131062, Exp: 0, S: 1, TTL: 1
⊞ Internet Protocol, Src: 10.0.0.164 (10.0.0.164), Dst: 127.0.0.1 (127.0.0.1)
⊞ User Datagram Protocol, Src Port: 49303 (49303), Dst Port: lsp-ping (3503)
⊟ Multiprotocol Label Switching Echo
```

In a VCCV-ping packet's MPLS label stack, the router-alter label is at the middle of the label stack, and the vc-label is at the bottom.

18.5 OAM in VPLS Services

The first two sections of this chapter introduced EFM OAM and CFM. These two Ethernet OAM tools can be used to test the health of the data-forwarding path of the ACs and the pseudowires. The previous section introduced LSP-ping, SDP-ping, Service Ping, and VCCV-ping. These OAM functions provide the ability to test the service infrastructure. However, these OAM tools do not test some of the most important capabilities of VPLS — learning MAC addresses and building the forwarding database (FDB), and making forwarding decisions based on the FDB. This section introduces the OAM tools used to test the VPLS FDB infrastructure on a per-VPLS service basis. The ALSRP implementation of these tools is based on the IETF document *draft-stokes-vkompella-ppvpn-hvpls-oam-xx.txt, Testing Hierarchical Virtual Private LAN Services.*

VPLS FDB OAM Overview

The purpose of VPLS FDB OAM tools is to test the health of the FDB and to verify the forwarding behavior of the VPLS services. As discussed in Chapter 11, each VPLS service instance in a member PE router is a Virtual Switching Instance (VSI). Similar to a regular Ethernet bridge, the VSI contains bridge ports and a MAC address table. The MAC address table is the FDB of the VPLS service instance. The VPLS service performs transparent Ethernet bridging on customer switches, and it performs the following operations in the FDB:

1. Every time the VSI receives an Ethernet frame, it checks the source MAC address of the frame. If the address does not exist in the current MAC table, a new MAC entry is created. If the address does exist in the current MAC table, the corresponding MAC entry is refreshed.

2. The service instance checks the destination MAC address of the received Ethernet frame to make a forwarding decision for the frame.

3. If a MAC entry in the table is not refreshed by receiving a frame with the same source MAC address after the age-out timer expires, the entry is removed from the MAC address table.

4. If a MAC-flush message is received from a pseudowire, its corresponding entry is removed from the FDB, as follows:

   4a. If a `flush-all-from-me` message is received from a pseudowire, the VSI removes all MAC entries in the FDB learned from that pseudowire.

   4b. If a `flush-all-but-me` message is received from a pseudowire, the VSI removes all MAC entries in the FDB except the entries learned from that pseudowire.

5. If the Spanning Tree Protocol (STP) is used for loop prevention in the VPLS (either enabled within the VPLS or mVPLS is used to manage the VPLS) and a particular topology change bridged protocol data unit (BPDU) is received, the VSI performs FDB flush or age-out in the same way a regular Ethernet bridge handles a topology change. For example, if the VPLS running the Rapid Spanning Tree Protocol (RSTP) receives a BPDU with the TCN flag set, it flushes all MAC entries from its FDB except the entries learned from the Bridge Port where the TCN BPDU is received.

When a VPLS customer begins passing data traffic through the service network, all member PE routers start to perform learning and forwarding. VPLS FDB OAM tools are used to ensure that the VPLS service performs learning and forwarding correctly. Table 18.6 lists the available VPLS FDB OAM tools.

Table 18.6 VPLS FDB OAM Tools

Function	Description
MAC-ping	Used to find the egress PE router (the router that has a local SAP) for a particular customer MAC address
MAC-trace	Used to find the VPLS forwarding path to the egress PE router to a particular customer MAC address
MAC Populate	Used to add MAC addresses to the FDB of a VSI for OAM purposes
MAC Purge	Used to remove MAC addresses from the FDB of a VSI
CPE-ping	Used to locate a PE router that is locally attached to a particular customer IP station (IP address)

All of the VPLS FDB OAM tools listed in Table 18.6 are proprietary implementations of the ALSRP.

MAC-ping

In a legacy routed IP network, a ping is used to determine whether or not a router or host knows where a certain IP address is located. Similarly, MAC-ping is used in a VPLS PE to determine whether or not the service instance knows where a particular MAC address is. MAC-ping and MAC-trace (introduced in the next subsection) are extensions of the LSP-ping and LSP-trace mechanisms.

MAC-ping is a VPLS OAM tool. It is not visible to the customer, and the ping packet is not sent to customer sites. Only the PE routers send MAC-ping packets to remote PE routers through the backbone network. Only a PE router that has a *matching MAC address* associated with a *local SAP* in the VPLS service responds to a MAC-ping.

Figure 18.27 illustrates a VPLS service involving four PE routers (fully meshed with mesh pseudowires) with a MAC-ping testing the learning and forwarding function in the VPLS. The curved lines with an arrow at one end indicate that no response is received (Case 1), and the curved lines with arrows at both ends indicate that a response is received (Cases 2 and 3).

Figure 18.27 MAC-ping Example Topology

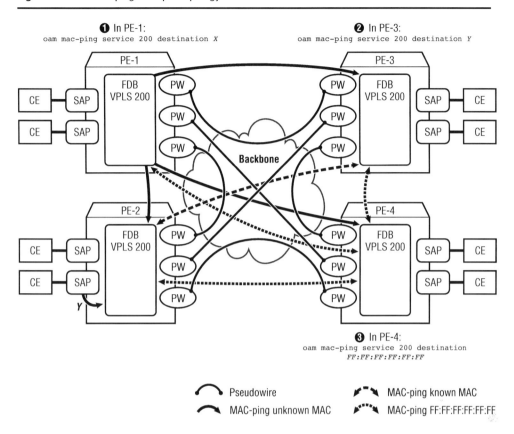

When a MAC-ping to a VPLS service is launched from a PE router, the VSI of the local router looks in its FDB for the MAC address being pinged, as if it needs to forward customer data traffic. There are several possible results:

- If the destination MAC address is known to the FDB and is associated with a local SAP or control plane address, no packet is sent (not shown in Figure 18.27). Instead, the MAC-ping launched from that router receives a CLI response indicating that the destination MAC address is either locally associated with a SAP or with the Control Processing Module (CPM).

- If the destination MAC address is known to the FDB and is associated with a pseudowire connected to a remote member PE router, a MAC-ping packet is sent to that remote PE router (Case 2). In the example, PE-2 has a destination

MAC address of Y in the FDB that is associated with the local SAP. Therefore, PE-2 responds to the MAC-ping.

- If the destination MAC address is unknown to the FDB, the PE router floods the packets to all remote PE routers over all pseudowires. Only a remote PE that has a matching MAC address in its FDB responds. If none of the remote PEs has a matching MAC address, none respond (Case 1).

- If the destination MAC address is the Ethernet broadcast MAC address of FF:FF:FF:FF:FF:FF, the packet is flooded to all remote PE routers, and all PE routers respond upon receiving the ping (Case 3).

A MAC-ping packet is *never* forwarded to a customer network. In Figure 18.27, the VPLS service is fully meshed. In this type of network, when a PE router receives a MAC-ping packet, it either responds to it (if it is a known MAC address associated with a local SAP or it is a broadcast MAC address) or does not respond to it (if it is an unknown MAC address). If the VPLS service is hierarchical, the *intermediate* PE router may forward or flood the MAC-ping to other member PE routers in the network. Figure 18.28 illustrates a case of MAC-ping in a Hierarchical VPLS (H-VPLS) network.

Figure 18.28 MAC-ping in an H-VPLS Network

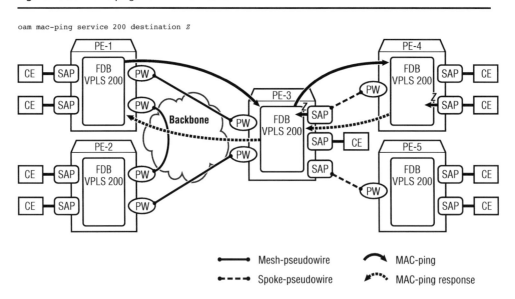

In an H-VPLS network, when a PE router receives a MAC-ping packet from a pseudowire, it may perform one of the following operations based on the FDB lookup result of the destination MAC address:

- If the FDB has a matching MAC address entry that is associated with a local SAP, the PE router responds to it (indicated by the action of PE-4 in Figure 18.28).

- If the FDB has a matching MAC address entry that is associated with another pseudowire, the PE router forwards the ping over that pseudowire instead of responding to it (indicated by the action of PE-3 in Figure 18.28).

- If the FDB has no matching MAC address entry, the PE router does not respond to the ping, but floods the ping packet to all pseudowires, respecting the Split-Horizon rule.

- If the destination MAC address is the Ethernet broadcast address of FF:FF:FF:FF:FF:FF, the PE router floods the MAC-ping to all pseudowires, respecting the Split-Horizon rule. If the VSI of a PE router has a local SAP, the PE router responds to the MAC-ping.

Figure 18.29 illustrates CLI outputs for three different MAC-ping results on the VPLS 200 service.

Figure 18.29 MAC-ping CLI Examples

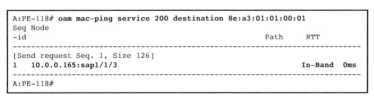

```
A:PE-118# oam mac-ping service 200 destination 8e:a3:01:01:00:01
Seq Node
-id                                              Path      RTT
-----------------------------------------------------------------------
[Send request Seq. 1, Size 126]
1    10.0.0.165:sap1/1/3                                   In-Band  0ms
-----------------------------------------------------------------------
A:PE-118#


A:PE-118# oam mac-ping service 200 destination ff:ff:ff:ff:ff:ff
Seq Node
-id                                              Path      RTT
-----------------------------------------------------------------------
[Send request Seq. 1, Size 126]
1    10.0.0.164:sap1/1/3            No FIB on Egress In-Band  0ms
1    10.0.0.165:sap1/1/3            No FIB on Egress In-Band  0ms
1    10.0.0.165:sap1/1/6            No FIB on Egress In-Band  0ms
-----------------------------------------------------------------------
A:PE-118#


A:PE-164# oam mac-ping service 200 destination 8e:a4:ff:00:00:00
Seq Node
-id                                              Path      RTT
-----------------------------------------------------------------------
MAC Ping Seq. 1 is not sent because the address is on a local SAP or CPU.
-----------------------------------------------------------------------
A:PE-164#
```

Figure 18.29 illustrates the results of a MAC-ping in the PE router from which the `mac-ping` command was executed. The top CLI output shows a successful ping with a response received from a remote PE router with its SAP number reported. The middle CLI output shows a result from pinging the broadcast MAC address (`ff:ff:ff:ff:ff:ff`). Because all PE routers must respond to the broadcast MAC-ping, it can be used to find all member PE routers and their SAPs in the VPLS service. The result shows that this VPLS service has three member PE routers: PE-118 (the local PE from which the `ping` is executed), PE 10.0.0.164 with one SAP (1/1/3), and PE 10.0.0.165 with two SAPs (1/1/3 and 1/1/6). The bottom CLI output shows the result of pinging a MAC address associated with a local SAP; no packet is sent.

Just like LSP-ping and LSP-trace, MAC-ping and MAC-trace and reply packets use the same MPLS Echo Request and MPLS Echo Reply packet format. The difference is that the MAC-ping and MAC-trace messages are actually Ethernet frames instead of the IP packets used in the LSP-ping and LSP-trace. Also, MAC-ping and MAC-trace use a different FEC element in the Target FEC Stack TLV in the packets — the FEC 0x128 (pseudowire). A MAC-ping or MAC-trace message body contains Ethernet-encapsulated frames with IP headers and UDP headers (port 3503–LSP-ping). The destination MAC address of the message is the MAC address being pinged or traced. These packets ping the pseudowire and VSIs, not the MPLS LSP. Figure 18.30 illustrates a comparison of a packet capture between LSP-ping and MAC-ping.

Both the MAC-ping and the reply packet can be sent either through the control plane or the data plane. The MAC-ping CLI command execution options determine whether the packet should go through the control plane or the data plane: If the MAC-ping command is executed with a `send-control` or `return-control` optional parameter, the ping or reply packets travel through the control plane; otherwise, the ping and reply packets travel through the data plane (this is the default behavior). When the packets are going through the data plane, they are encapsulated exactly the same way as the customer traffic — MPLS-encapsulated with a three-label stack:

- The transport label (used by the SDP to tunnel the traffic to the far-end PE)
- The vc-label (used by the far-end PE router to identify the correct service instance)
- The Router-Alert (RA) label (value = 1) used to indicate that this is an OAM packet and must be sent to the control plane of the receiving PE router for processing

Figure 18.30 Packet Capture: LSP-ping and MAC-ping

MPLS Echo Request packet for LSP-ping	MPLS Echo Request packet for MAC-ping

```
1 0.000000    10.0.0.164         127.0.0.1

Frame 1 (110 bytes on wire, 110 bytes captured)
Ethernet II, Src: 8e:a4:01:01:00:01 (8e:a4:01:01:00:01), Dst
MultiProtocol Label Switching Header, Label: 131062, Exp: 0,
Internet Protocol, Src: 10.0.0.164 (10.0.0.164), Dst: 127.0.
User Datagram Protocol, Src Port: 49259 (49259), Dst Port:
Multiprotocol Label Switching Echo
  version: 1
  Global Flags: 0x0000
  Message Type: MPLS Echo Request (1)
  Reply Mode: Reply via an IPv4/IPv6 UDP packet (2)
  Return Code: No return code (0)
  Return Subcode: 0
  Sender's Handle: 0x0000c06b
  Sequence Number: 1
  Timestamp Sent: Not representable
  Timestamp Received: NULL
  Target FEC Stack
    Type: Target FEC Stack (1)
    Length: 24
    FEC Element 1: RSVP IPv4 Session Query
      Type: RSVP IPv4 Session Query (3)
      Length: 20
      IPv4 Tunnel endpoint address: 10.0.0.117 (10.0.0.117)
      Must Be Zero: 0
      Tunnel ID: 53
      Extended Tunnel ID: 0x0A0000A4 (10.0.0.164)
      IPv4 Tunnel sender address: 10.0.0.164 (10.0.0.164)
      Must Be Zero: 0
      LSP ID: 49664
```

```
1 0.000000    10.0.0.164         127.0.0.0

Frame 1 (148 bytes on wire, 148 bytes captured)
Ethernet II, Src: 8e:a4:01:01:00:01 (8e:a4:01:01:
MultiProtocol Label Switching Header, Label: 1310
MultiProtocol Label Switching Header, Label: 1310
MultiProtocol Label Switching Header, Label: 1 (R
Ethernet II, Src: 8e:a4:ff:00:00:00 (8e:a4:ff:00:
Internet Protocol, Src: 10.0.0.164 (10.0.0.164),
User Datagram Protocol, Src Port: 49251 (49251),
Multiprotocol Label Switching Echo
  version: 1
  Global Flags: 0x0000
  Message Type: MPLS Echo Request (1)
  Reply Mode: Unknown (5)
  Return Code: No return code (0)
  Return Subcode: 0
  Sender's Handle: 0x00000000
  Sequence Number: 3227713537
  Timestamp Sent: Not representable
  Timestamp Received: NULL
  vendor Enterprise Code
  Target FEC Stack
    Type: Target FEC Stack (1)
    Length: 32
    FEC Element 1: FEC 128 Pseudowire (new)
      Type: FEC 128 Pseudowire (new) (10)
      Length: 28
      Sender's PE Address: 0.0.0.0 (0.0.0.0)
      Remote PE Address: 0.0.0.0 (0.0.0.0)
      VC ID: 327696
      Encapsulation: Unknown (65535)
      MBZ: 0xffff
```

When the packets are going through the control plane, they are encapsulated as regular IP packets with a UDP destination port of 3503 (well-known port for LSP-ping) and routed in the backbone network to the far-end PE router.

MAC-trace

The purpose of MAC-trace is to show the member PE routers (the routers participating in the service, also referred to as *service hops*) along the path to a particular MAC address in the service backbone network. It has the following characteristics:

- MAC-trace exchanges information only among PE routers and *never* sends packets to customer sites. It is similar to MAC-ping, except that the MAC addresses being traced are most likely customer MAC addresses..

- Similar to LSP, MAC-trace uses the method of sending packets with an incremental TTL value to detect each hop of the PE router between the source (where the MAC-trace is launched) and the destination (the MAC address to be traced). The difference is that LSP-trace increases the transport-label TTL each time it sends a packet, while MAC-trace increases the vc-label TTL (inner label) each time it sends a packet.

- MAC-trace can be sent through both the data plane and the control plane, depending on the command launch options used.

In a flat, fully meshed VPLS service, the VSIs of all member PE routers are directly connected to the VSIs of all other member PE routers. For two customer sites in different locations to communicate, one direct pseudowire between the local PE router and the remote PE router is enough to transport the service. Therefore, all member PE routers are one *service hop* away from each other.

In an H-VPLS network, not all PE routers are directly connected by pseudowires. Sometimes, the traffic needs to travel through more than one PE router to reach a customer site. In these cases, MAC-trace can help the operator to better understand the VPLS forwarding topology by providing the exact PE hops from a PE router to a particular destination MAC address. Figure 18.31 illustrates the MAC-trace mechanism in a VPLS network and an H-VPLS network.

The top diagram in Figure 18.31 illustrates a MAC-trace executed in Router PE-1 to trace the MAC address 00:01:02:03:04:05 in VPLS 100. VPLS 100 has a fully meshed forwarding topology. According to the FDB of VPLS 100, PE-1 sends the MAC-trace packet to PE-2. The VPLS service instance 100 of PE-2 has a local SAP associated with the MAC address 00:01:02:03:04:05 in its FDB, so it responds with a MAC-trace reply. The trace result in PE-1 shows that the destination MAC address is one service hop away, in PE-2.

The bottom diagram in Figure 18.31 illustrates a MAC-trace executed in Router PE-3 to trace the MAC address 06:07:08:09:0a:0b in VPLS 200. VPLS 200 has a hierarchical forwarding topology. The destination MAC address is locally associated with the SAP in PE-6, so it is three service hops away. PE-3 sends MAC-trace packets three times, increasing the vc-label TTL value of the packet by 1 each time (starting at 1):

1. PE-3 first sends a request packet to PE-4 with the vc-label TTL value set to 1. This is because in the FDB for VPLS 200 in PE-3, the entry 06:07:08:09:0a:0b is associated with (learned from) PE-4.

2. PE-4 receives the packet, because the vc-label TTL responds with a reply to PE-3. Because the FDB of PE-4 indicates it is not the final destination (the MAC address is not associated with a local SAP), PE-4 indicates in the reply packet that it is not the destination PE router of the MAC address.

3. PE-3 receives PE-4's response and knows that PE-4 is not the destination PE. PE-3 sends a second packet to PE-4 with the vc-label TTL set to 2. Upon receiving the packet, as a PE router, PE-4 subtracts 1 from the vc-TTL

and forwards it to PE-5. PE-5 receives the packet and responds with a reply packet, also indicating that it is not the destination.

4. PE-3 receives the reply from PE-5 and sends one more packet with the vc-label TTL set to 3. This time, the packet reaches PE-6. PE-6 has a local SAP associated with the MAC address being traced in its VPLS 200 FDB; therefore, it responds indicating that it is the destination PE.

5. PE-3 receives the reply from PE-6 and stops the MAC-trace process.

Figure 18.31 MAC-Trace in VPLS and H-VPLS Networks

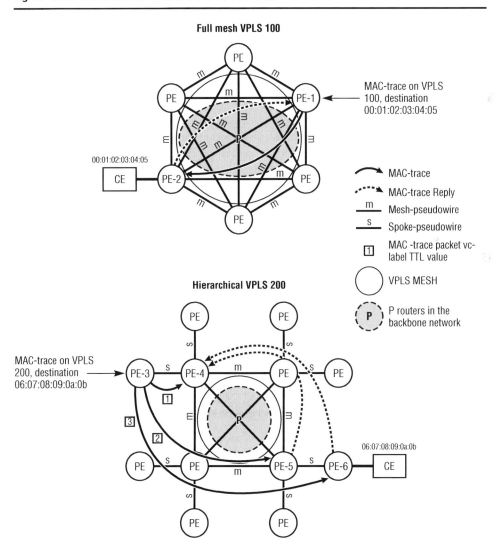

One or more P routers may be between these PE routers in the network (represented by the large shaded areas with **P** in the middle). P routers forward the traffic according to the transport tunnel label (or route the packet according to the GRE header). P routers do not care about the content of the MAC-ping or MAC-trace; therefore, the P router is invisible to the MAC-ping or MAC-trace.

If a PE router launches a MAC-trace for a local MAC address, it makes the forwarding decision as if it received a data packet with the same destination MAC address:

- If the MAC address is known to the FDB and the address is associated with a local SAP, the router does not send a packet. The CLI shows that the MAC address being traced is local.

- If the MAC address is known to the FDB and it is associated with a pseudowire to a far-end PE, the PE router sends an echo request packet starting with vc-label TTL set to 1 to the far-end PE router.

- If the MAC address is not known to the FDB, the router sends request packets, starting with the vc-label TTL set to 1 to all its pseudowires (to flood the echo request to all adjacent member PE routers).

- If the router receives a reply from the far-end PE router and the reply packet indicates that the router is not the destination, the local router sends another request with the vc-label TTL value increased by 1. The router keeps sending out request packets with increased vc-label TTL values until one of the following conditions is met:

  - It receives a reply indicating that the destination of the MAC is reached.

  - It receives a reply indicating an error.

  - The vc-label TTL value reaches 255.

When a PE router receives a MAC-trace MPLS Echo Request from another PE router, it performs the following operations:

1. The PE router removes the transport tunnel encapsulation (outer label or GRE encapsulation) to expose the vc-label. It then uses the vc-label to identify which service the packet belongs to and uses the proper service instance to process the packet.

2. Next, the system decreases the vc-label TTL value by 1. If the result is 0, it processes the packet locally. Because MAC-trace uses an MPLS Echo Request packet with a Router-Alert label in the bottom of the MPLS stack, the packet is sent to the control plane for processing. Because it is a trace request packet, the control plane sends a reply to the originating PE router with particular return codes that indicate it knows the MAC address, and whether or not it is the egress PE router of that MAC address.

3. If the vc-label TTL subtraction result is not zero, the PE router forwards the packet according to the service instance's FDB as if it is a regular VPLS-encapsulated customer packet. If the MAC address being traced is known, the PE forwards the packet to the next-hop; if the address is unknown, the packet is flooded. In either case, the new value of the vc-label TTL of the packet is decreased by 1.

Besides fault allocation and path tracing, MAC-trace can also be used to detect the forwarding topology of the VPLS service. This is accomplished by performing a MAC-trace on any member PE router of a service that uses the broadcast MAC address ff:ff:ff:ff:ff:ff as its trace destination. Figure 18.32 illustrates the result of performing a MAC-trace on the broadcast MAC address.

Figure 18.32   Using MAC-trace to Discover the VPLS Network Topology

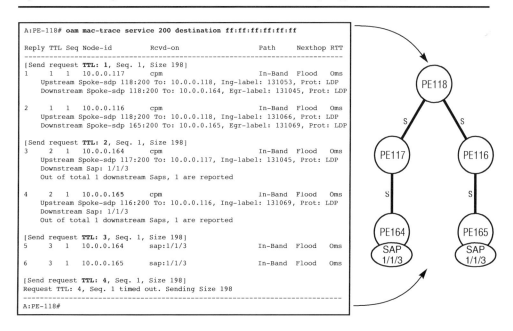

The member PEs and the forwarding infrastructure of VPLS 200 can be deduced from the MAC-trace CLI output in Figure 18.32. The MAC-trace shows that PE-117 and PE-116 are directly adjacent to PE-118 and are connected by spoke-pseudowires (spoke-sdp). The downstream (away from PE-118) next-hop router of PE-117 is PE-164; the downstream next-hop router of PE-116 is PE-165. Both PE-164 and PE-165 have local SAPs of 1/1/3, and no downstream next-hop PE routers.

> **Note:** In the previous MAC-ping and MAC-trace discussions and in the following discussion regarding MAC Populate and MAC Purge, provider (P) routers are not explicitly discussed. P routers can exist in any location in a backbone network and are transparent to pings and traces. P routers transport packets by swapping the outer transport tunnel labels and do not look into the packets for further processing.

Just like MAC-ping, MAC-trace can be launched to go though the data plane (default behavior) or the control plane (by explicitly specifying command options when launching the trace). When tracing through the data plane, the packets are encapsulated with a three-label stack (from top to bottom): transport label, vc-label, and router-alert label. When tracing through the control plane, the trace and reply packets are all regular IP UDP packets (using port 3503) routed by the core IGP routing table.

IETF draft document *draft-stokes-vkompella-ppvpn-hvpls-oam-xx.txt* specifies the extension of LSP-ping and LSP-trace (RFC 4379) to provide MAC-ping and MAC-trace capability.

CPE-ping

MAC-ping provides the ability to check inside an end-to-end VPLS service to determine which member PE router is the egress PE router for a particular customer MAC address. CPE-ping provides the ability to check inside a VPLS service to determine which PE router is attached to a particular customer's Layer 3 host (represented by the IP address). CPE-ping is a variation and extension of MAC-ping. When CPE-ping is launched on a VPLS service from a PE router, it is converted to a MAC-ping with the broadcast MAC address ff:ff:ff:ff:ff:ff. When a PE router receives this type of MAC-ping packet, it sends an Address Resolution Protocol (ARP) request to all its SAPs to see whether any customer device attached to a SAP owns the IP address, and responds to the ARP. If there is no valid response, the PE router replies to the PE router that originated the CPE-ping with a MAC-ping reply packet. Figure 18.33 illustrates an example of a successful CEP-ping in an H-VPLS service. The numbers in parentheses within the following list match the numbered steps in the figure.

Figure 18.33   Using CPE-ping to Find a Customer IP Address Location

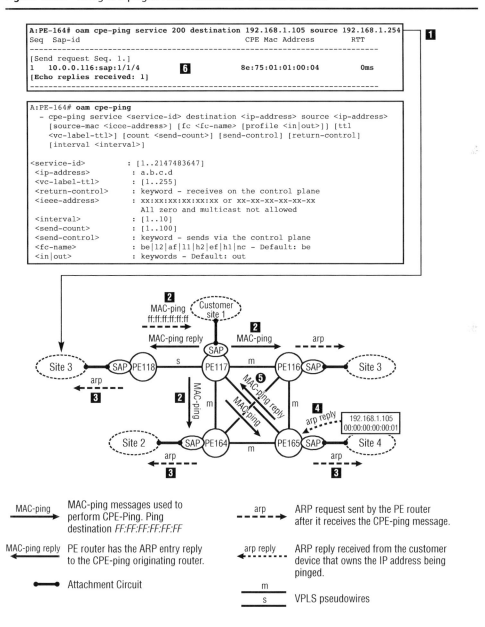

1. The `<oam cpe-ping>` command is executed from Router PE-118 on VPLS service 200 (1). The purpose is to determine which PE router is attached to the customer device that owns IP address `192.168.1.105`.

2. Router PE-118 generates a MAC-ping with a destination of `ff:ff:ff:ff:ff:ff`, so that the MAC-ping is flooded to all member PE routers for VPLS 200 (2). Also, because PE-118 has a local SAP attached to the customer network, it generates an ARP request and sends it to customer site 3 to query for the owner of IP address `192.168.1.105`. Because no devices in customer site 3 own the IP address, customer site 3 does not send an ARP reply.

3. Upon receiving the MAC-ping used for the CPE-ping, each PE router floods the MAC-ping to other PE routers (2), respecting the Split-Horizon rule. If the PE router has local SAP(s), the ARP request for the IP address being pinged is sent to all customer sites through all the SAPs (3).

4. In the example, customer site 4 attached to PE-165 has the IP address and responds to the ARP request (4).

5. Upon receiving the ARP reply from customer site 4, PE-165 learns the ARP entry and the MAC entry, then responds to PE-118 with a MAC-ping reply containing the ARP result (5).

6. PE-118 receives the MAC-ping reply and learns the ARP and MAC entry. The CPE-ping is successfully completed (6).

Just like all the other VPLS OAM tools, CPE-ping can be sent over the data plane or the control plane. By default, the CPE-ping and the possible reply are sent through the data plane in the same direction as customer traffic. The command options `send-control` and `return control` can be used to specify that the request and reply messages travel through the control plane. When using the control plane, CPE-ping messages are sent as regular IP packets to the remote member PE routers using the router-id (system IP address) as the packet source and destination addresses and are routed by the core routing table.

In the CPE-ping, the source IP address in the command *must not* be an IP address used by any VPLS customer. This is because when CPE-ping is executed on a PE router, the ping source IP address is associated with the PE router's system MAC address (chassis MAC address). This association is stored in the service instance as an ARP entry. If the CPE-ping uses a customer IP address as the ping source IP, the IP address is associated with the chassis MAC address in the ARP table. Because this ARP entry is invalid, this is called *ARP pollution*. Because polluting customer IP addresses causes an IP address to be unreachable by some remote sites, it should be avoided.

CPE-ping uses MAC-ping as the carrier for the ping request and reply to flood to all member PE routers. CPE-ping tests the PE router's knowledge regarding the Layer 3 reachability (IP address) of the customer site within the VPLS service. MAC-ping tests the PE router's knowledge regarding the Layer 2 reachability (MAC address) of the customer site within the VPLS service. MAC-ping never generates traffic to customer sites; CPE-ping generates ARP request messages to customer sites for IP/MAC mapping queries and may receive ARP reply messages. CPE-ping not only finds the PE router locally attached to a customer IP host, but also the MAC associated with it. If the forwarding path to that IP address is also desired information, a MAC-trace can be executed to find it. Therefore, there is no need for a CPE-trace.

MAC Populate

As previously discussed, VPLS FDB learns MAC addresses from customer traffic, and VPLS PE routers make forwarding decisions based on the FDB lookup result. MAC-ping and MAC-trace are used to test and find information in the FDBs of each member PE router in a VPLS service. MAC-ping and MAC-trace are executed on MAC addresses. Sometimes, MAC addresses need to be manually added to the VPLS FDB so the FDB can be tested. MAC Populate is used for this purpose. For example, if there is no customer traffic after the VPLS service is deployed, the FDBs of all VSIs are empty; therefore, there is no MAC address to ping.

MAC Populate can generate a MAC address and add it to the FDBs of all member PE routers by flooding an MPLS Echo Request message to all PE routers. The MPLS Echo Request message uses the broadcast MAC address ff:ff:ff:ff:ff:ff as the Echo Request destination and uses the address being populated as the Echo Request source. The global flag is set to do not reply. The receiving PE routers flood the message only to other PE routers, respecting the Split-Horizon rule. The receiving PE routers do not reply to the echo request. When a PE receives this type of packet, it learns the MAC address of the Echo Request source in the same way as it receives VPLS-encapsulated data traffic. The only difference is that the MPLS Echo Request message has an extra router-alert label in the bottom of the stack. When a PE router learns such a MAC address, it sets an oam flag in the FDB entry to distinguish the OAM MAC entry from the MAC entries learned from regular customer traffic. Figure 18.34 illustrates an example of using MAC Populate to add MAC addresses to a VPLS network.

Figure 18.34   MAC Populate in a VPLS Service

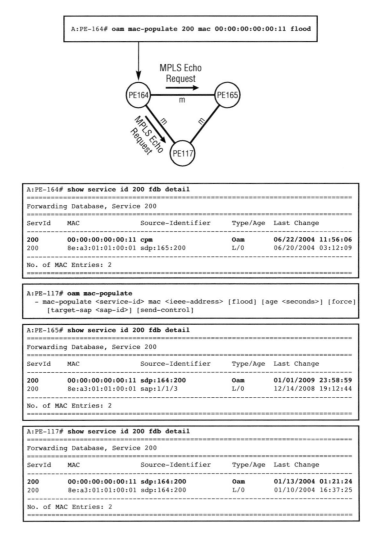

```
A:PE-164# oam mac-populate 200 mac 00:00:00:00:00:11 flood
```

```
A:PE-164# show service id 200 fdb detail
===============================================================================
Forwarding Database, Service 200
===============================================================================
ServId    MAC                   Source-Identifier       Type/Age  Last Change
-------------------------------------------------------------------------------
200       00:00:00:00:00:11 cpm                         Oam       06/22/2004 11:56:06
200       8e:a3:01:01:00:01 sdp:165:200                 L/0       06/20/2004 03:12:09
-------------------------------------------------------------------------------
No. of MAC Entries: 2
===============================================================================
```

```
A:PE-117# oam mac-populate
  - mac-populate <service-id> mac <ieee-address> [flood] [age <seconds>] [force]
    [target-sap <sap-id>] [send-control]
```

```
A:PE-165# show service id 200 fdb detail
===============================================================================
Forwarding Database, Service 200
===============================================================================
ServId    MAC                   Source-Identifier       Type/Age  Last Change
-------------------------------------------------------------------------------
200       00:00:00:00:00:11 sdp:164:200                 Oam       01/01/2009 23:58:59
200       8e:a3:01:01:00:01 sap:1/1/3                   L/0       12/14/2008 19:12:44
-------------------------------------------------------------------------------
No. of MAC Entries: 2
===============================================================================
```

```
A:PE-117# show service id 200 fdb detail
===============================================================================
Forwarding Database, Service 200
===============================================================================
ServId    MAC                   Source-Identifier       Type/Age  Last Change
-------------------------------------------------------------------------------
200       00:00:00:00:00:11 sdp:164:200                 Oam       01/13/2004 01:21:24
200       8e:a3:01:01:00:01 sdp:164:200                 L/0       01/10/2004 16:37:25
-------------------------------------------------------------------------------
No. of MAC Entries: 2
===============================================================================
```

MAC Populate can be executed to populate only the FDB of the local PE router with MAC addresses, by using the command option **target-sap <sap-id>**. In this case, the MAC address entry is created only in the FDB of the local PE router in the services on which the MAC Populate is executed. In Figure 18.34, the `populate` command is executed with the option of `flood`. This causes the PE router to populate the local database with the MAC address and to flood the MAC address to all PE routers connected by pseudowires using MPLS Echo Request messages. Figure 18.34 shows the FDBs of the three member PE routers in VPLS 200. All PE routers have an OAM-type MAC address entry of `00:00:00:00:00:11` that is flooded by PE-164.

MAC Populate flooding to remote PE routers can occur in either the control plane or the data plane. By default, the population occurs in the data plane. An MPLS Echo Request message with a three-label stack is sent: transport label, vc-label, and the router-alter label. If the command option `send-control` is used, the MPLS Echo Request messages are regular IP/UDP packets and are routed by the core routing table.

Occasionally, the MAC address being populated using the MAC Populate command can also be learned again from customer traffic, if the address being populated happens to be a duplicate of a customer MAC address. By default, when this happens, the new customer-learned MAC address entry overrides the OAM MAC address entry in the FDB. To prevent this from happening, the MAC Populate command can be executed using the `force` option so that the FDB cannot learn the same MAC address from customer traffic.

MAC Purge

As a VPLS FDB OAM tool, MAC Purge is used to make PE routers unlearn a MAC address. In other words, it is used to remove MAC entries from the FDB of a VSI. Just like MAC Populate, MAC Purge uses MPLS Echo Request messages with the `do not reply` flag set. Figure 18.35 illustrates an example of using MAC Purge to remove a MAC address entry from the FDB of a PE router.

If the command option `flood` is not used, MAC Purge can remove MAC addresses only from the FDB of a local PE router. In Figure 18.35, the `populate` command is executed with the `flood` option, causing the PE router to flood the request to purge the MAC address to the local database, and to flood the MAC Purge request using MPLS Echo Request messages to all PE routers connected by pseudowires. The diagram shows the FDBs of the three member PE routers in VPLS 200. These PE routers have 0 entries in their FDBs because the only learned entry of `00:00:00:00:01:11` is removed by the MAC Purge.

Figure 18.35 MAC Purge in a VPLS Network

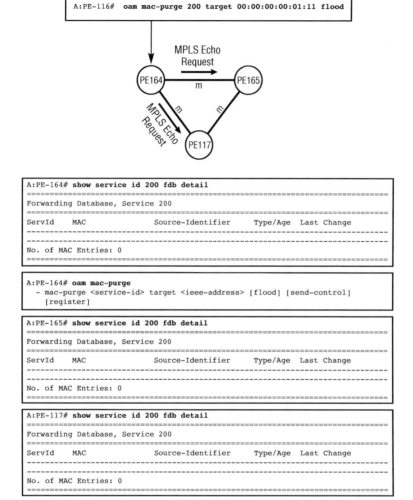

```
A:PE-116#  oam mac-purge 200 target 00:00:00:00:01:11 flood
```

```
A:PE-164# show service id 200 fdb detail
===============================================================================
Forwarding Database, Service 200
===============================================================================
ServId    MAC                Source-Identifier      Type/Age  Last Change
-------------------------------------------------------------------------------
-------------------------------------------------------------------------------
No. of MAC Entries: 0
===============================================================================
```

```
A:PE-164# oam mac-purge
 - mac-purge <service-id> target <ieee-address> [flood] [send-control]
   [register]
```

```
A:PE-165# show service id 200 fdb detail
===============================================================================
Forwarding Database, Service 200
===============================================================================
ServId    MAC                Source-Identifier      Type/Age  Last Change
-------------------------------------------------------------------------------
-------------------------------------------------------------------------------
No. of MAC Entries: 0
===============================================================================
```

```
A:PE-117# show service id 200 fdb detail
===============================================================================
Forwarding Database, Service 200
===============================================================================
ServId    MAC                Source-Identifier      Type/Age  Last Change
-------------------------------------------------------------------------------
-------------------------------------------------------------------------------
No. of MAC Entries: 0
===============================================================================
```

MAC Purges can be flooded to remote PE routers either through the control plane or the data plane. By default, MAC addresses are populated through the data plane. An MPLS Echo Request message with a three-label stack is sent: transport label, vc-label, and the router-alter label. If the command option **send-control** is used, the MPLS Echo Request messages used for address population are regular IP/ UDP packets and are routed by the core routing table.

MAC Purge can also flag a particular MAC entry in the FDB as an `oam` type, instead of removing the entry. This is done by executing the command using the `register` option. When MAC Purge is executed with the `register` option, the FDB considers the MAC entry to be an OAM-learned address, as if it were added using the MAC Populate command.

Summary

Service providers require Ethernet OAM functions in VPLS services to monitor the health of their networks and to diagnose failures. Also, service providers can use the MPLS OAM and VPLS OAM tools in the core network.

IEEE 802.3ah specifies the EFM OAM, which is a point-to-point link connectivity-monitoring protocol. EFM OAM can be enabled between directly connected Ethernet interfaces to detect physical link failure.

IEEE 802.1ag specifies the Ethernet CFM, which is an end-to-end connectivity-monitoring protocol. CFM provides end-to-end Ethernet OAM functions with different levels and domains. Both the customer and the operator can have their own CFM overlays without interfering with each other.

In an IP/MPLS network, LSP-ping and LSP-trace can be used to detect connectivity problems. SDP-ping, SDP-trace, and SDP-mtu allow the operator to test IP/MPLS connectivity in the backbone network. Service Ping and CPE-ping can be used to test the connectivity of each individual service. VCCV-ping and VCCV-trace are standardized OAM tools that test the point-to-point Layer 2 VPN services.

The VPLS service has several OAM tools to test the internal connectivity, including MAC-ping, MAC-trace, MAC Populate, and MAC Purge.

Appendix

A   Spanning Tree Protocol

Chapter 11 introduced the general behavior of *transparent bridging*. A bridge (or a Virtual Switching Instance — VSI, in the case of a VPLS service instance) *floods* all frames with unknown destination MAC addresses to all bridge ports except the one from which the frames are received. In certain network topologies, where there is more than one forwarding path to reach the same destination, this flooding behavior may cause issues.

Redundancy is generally built into a network's design to protect the traffic from network element failures. To provide redundancy, the network design should include an alternative forwarding path to forward the traffic if the primary forwarding path fails. In a bridged Ethernet network, redundant forwarding paths cause forwarding loops. Therefore, care must be taken to prevent loops and broadcast storms when deploying data path redundancy in a bridged Ethernet network or service.

In a large-scale network with complicated topology, it is sometimes hard to identify a forwarding loop or to recognize when a traffic pattern is actually a broadcast storm. Table A.1 lists some of the typical symptoms caused by forwarding loops and broadcast storms.

Table A.1 Possible Symptoms of a Broadcast Storm

Symptoms	Description
MAC address moves among ports in the FDB	In a bridge or a VSI, whenever traffic arrives at a port, its source MAC address is learned by the FDB either as a refresh of an existing entry or as a new entry. When broadcast storms occur, because the same frame circles through the network on many paths, the same source MAC address is learned over and over again from different ports. The entries are always overwritten quickly by the next time the frame enters the switch from a different port, so the age of the MAC entry is always very young.
MAC learned from unexpected port or node	In a stable network, the forwarding behavior and traffic patterns are usually predictable. If some unusual MAC addresses appear in the FDB, or the MAC address learned is not associated with a normal forwarding port, it may be a sign of a forwarding loop.
Bandwidth congestion	Broadcast storms consume a lot of bandwidth, so link congestion can be a sign of unwanted traffic circling around the network.
High CPU usage	Broadcast storms cause the switches (or PE routers) to change FDB entries frequently, raising the CPU usage significantly.

Symptoms	Description
Loss of reachability or flapping routing table	If link congestion happens because of a broadcast storm, the routers attached to the switches may lose Layer 3 routing peers because the routing protocol times out (routing PDUs are dropped because of congestion). The routers may not able to ping the peer, and the routing adjacency may become unstable.

A.1 Spanning Tree Protocol

This section reviews STP in detail. The next section, "Spanning Tree Protocol Variations," reviews the common STP variations of Rapid Spanning Tree Protocol (RSTP), Multiple Spanning Tree Protocol (MSTP), and Per Vlan Spanning Tree (PVST) in detail. These two sections reinforce your knowledge of STP. A solid understanding of STP functionality in an Ethernet-bridged network is mandatory for designing a VPLS network with STP interoperation. If you are familiar with STP and its variations, you may choose to skip these two sections.

How Does STP Prevent Forwarding Loops?

With STP, network redundancy is achieved by having multiple ports reaching other nodes. A forwarding loop is prevented by STP keeping only one port in an active forwarding state. STP prevents forwarding loops by putting the redundant forwarding path (port) into a blocking state. This allows only one forwarding path from any node to any other node at any time in an Ethernet-bridged network. The redundant ports are blocked and will forward traffic only if the primary forwarding path fails.

Ethernet switches running STP communicate with each other by exchanging bridged protocol data units (BPDUs). By exchanging BPDUs, switches form common agreements on the roles and states of all ports. Therefore, ports that are not required to build a loop-free forwarding infrastructure are excluded and put into the blocking state. If new elements are added to the network, or if the network fails or recovers, a Topology Change Notification (TCN) is triggered and exchanged among the switches to form a new forwarding infrastructure.

The name *spanning tree* refers to the way that STP builds a *tree* topology for data forwarding. First, the switches that are running STP locate the *root* of the tree by *Root Bridge election*. The *Root Bridge* is the center of the forwarding topology. There is only one Root Bridge for an entire bridged network. After the tree's root is located, the switches then explore the *branches* and *leaves* of the tree by calculating the distance (costs) of their ports to the root. In a switch, the port closest to the Root Bridge is the Root Port (RP). In any LAN segments, the port closest to the Root Bridge is the Designated Port (DP). After these elections and comparisons, the ports that are not elected to be either RP or DP are blocked. Therefore, the redundant forwarding path is eliminated, and the most optimal forwarding path becomes the active forwarding path that carries the traffic. The operator can control the forwarding path by manipulating the STP parameters (`Bridge Priority`, `Path Cost`, and `Port Priority`).

BPDU Content

Switches running STP communicate with each other by exchanging BPDUs. There are two types of BPDUs — configuration BPDUs and TCN BPDUs. Configuration BPDUs contain STP parameters and values from the switch. Switches generate, store, and exchange configuration BPDUs periodically to maintain the STP state. TCN BPDUs are generated and propagated only when there is a forwarding topology change event (for example, link failure, protocol time-out, or new ports added to the network). Both types of BPDUs use a destination MAC address of `01-80-c2-00-00-00`. When a switch is powered on in a network, it communicates with other switches in the network by generating, exchanging, and comparing configuration BPDUs. In this way, they build a common loop-free active forwarding topology. Figure A.1 illustrates the format of two types of BPDUs.

The four most important fields in the configuration BPDUs are `Root Identifier`, `Root Path Cost`, `Bridge Identifier`, and `Port Identifier`. The entire STP forwarding topology is based on the comparison of these four values among different BPDUs:

- `Root Identifier (root-id)` — The value of this field is not configurable. It is automatically set by the switch's STP protocol. The meaning of this field is: *Based on the information I have so far, who do I think should be the Root Bridge of this network?* The value represents the switch's *current view* of which switch is the root. When the switch has just been powered on, it places its own bridge ID into this field for all the BPDUs it generates.

- `Root Path Cost` — The value of this field represents the link speed of the port where the BPDU is received.

- `Bridge Identifier (bridge-id)` — The identifier the switch uses when sending BPDUs. The format is `Bridge Priority + switch MAC address`.

- `Port Identifier (port-id)` — The identifier of the port where the BPDU originates. The format is `Port Priority + port number`.

Figure A.1 BPDU Format for Spanning Tree Protocol

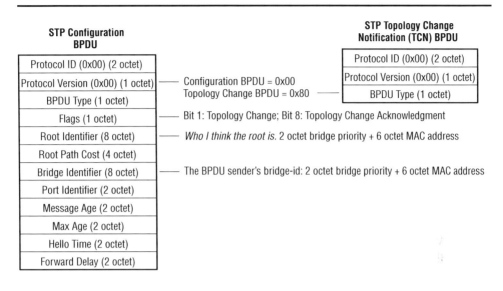

STP Configuration BPDU

Protocol ID (0x00) (2 octet)
Protocol Version (0x00) (1 octet)
BPDU Type (1 octet)
Flags (1 octet)
Root Identifier (8 octet)
Root Path Cost (4 octet)
Bridge Identifier (8 octet)
Port Identifier (2 octet)
Message Age (2 octet)
Max Age (2 octet)
Hello Time (2 octet)
Forward Delay (2 octet)

STP Topology Change Notification (TCN) BPDU

Protocol ID (0x00) (2 octet)
Protocol Version (0x00) (1 octet)
BPDU Type (1 octet)

Configuration BPDU = 0x00
Topology Change BPDU = 0x80

Bit 1: Topology Change; Bit 8: Topology Change Acknowledgment

Who I think the root is. 2 octet bridge priority + 6 octet MAC address

The BPDU sender's bridge-id: 2 octet bridge priority + 6 octet MAC address

Note: Standard STP (802.1ad) BPDU uses an STP multicast destination address of 01:80:c2:00:00:00 as the destination MAC address.

When an STP-enabled Ethernet switch boots up, it immediately composes configuration BPDUs. A race condition can occur when other switches are started at the same time. When a switch boots up, it may send a BPDU before it receives BPDUs from other adjacent switches, or it may receive BPDUs before it sends any out. This does not affect the process and result of the BPDU comparison. The switch always compares the two *versions* of BPDU — the one received from another switch from a particular port and the locally generated BPDU. The switch also starts listening to BPDUs received from adjacent switches immediately after it boots up. When composing its own BPDUs, the switch *always assumes itself as the Root Bridge* and puts its own Bridge ID into both the **root-id** and **bridge-id** fields. It also stores BPDUs received from other switches, then starts the BPDU comparison.

BPDU Storage: Local Version versus Received Version

The key to understanding how STP works to establish a loop-free active forwarding topology is to understand how BPDUs are generated, stored, compared, and changed.

Routing protocols such as OSPF use Link Status Advertisements (LSAs) to carry routing topology information. Each OSPF router generates its own LSAs and floods LSAs received from other routers without changing the LSA content. After being created, the LSAs are flooded to the entire OSPF area without being modified. Once generated, the content of the LSAs does not change. Each router receives LSAs generated from all routers in the area, stores them in the Link State Database (LSDB), and uses the Shortest Path First (SPF) algorithm to calculate the routing topology.

In contrast, STP uses BPDUs to carry switching topology information. Switches generate and exchange BPDUs to form the active forwarding topology. Each switch generates BPDUs based on both the local port status information and on the information contained in the received BPDUs. Therefore, the content of the BPDUs generated by a switch may change from time to time, especially before the STP converges in a network. *This scenario is what often causes misunderstanding of the behavior of STP.* A BPDU is a switch's current best view of the forwarding topology. By exchanging BPDUs, switches exchange their views of the forwarding topology to get more information. If a switch gets more information about the topology, it changes the content of BPDU it generates to notify other switches. When all switches exchange their information and agree on the topology, the network is converged, and the loop-free unique forwarding topology is built.

As described in the preceding section, four fields are used for BPDU comparison: `root-id`, `Root Path Cost`, `bridge-id`, and `port-id`. When a switch generates BPDUs, the `root-id` and `Root Path Cost` fields can change as a result of BPDU comparison, as follows:

- The switch always sets the `root-id` field to the best value it can see from all the BPDUs that were either locally generated or received from neighbors, into all the BPDUs it created locally. Any time the router receives a BPDU containing a *better* `root-id`, it uses that value to generate its own BPDUs.

- When a switch receives a BPDU for a port, it adds the cost (link speed) of that port to the received BPDU's `Root Path Cost` field, and then stores the BPDU and compares it with the BPDU it generated for that port. When the actual BPDU comparison is performed, the `Root Path Cost` value has already been adjusted by adding the receiving port's cost.

The BPDU generated by a switch always *represents the switch's view of the network*. The view includes the bridge that the switch considers to be the Root Bridge of the network, and the cost from the switch to the Root Bridge. As mentioned, when a switch boots up, it considers itself as the only switch in the network. Therefore, it assumes the Root Bridge role and inserts its own `bridge-id` into the `root-id` field of the BPDU it generates. After communicating with other switches, the switch may find a better Root Bridge, from a received BPDU. If this happens, *the switch's view of the network changes*, and it begins generating BPDUs with the new `root-id`.

BPDU Comparison: Four Comparison Criteria

For any port of any Ethernet switch, in the initial stage of STP convergence, it composes its own BPDUs and it may receive BPDUs from the adjacent switches. It then compares the BPDU received from the adjacent switch with its own composed BPDU. If its own BPDU is superior (decided by the BPDU comparison criteria), it discards the BPDU received and keeps sending out its own BPDUs. In contrast, if the receiving BPDU is better, the switch discards its own BPDU and stores the received BPDU for that port, and stops sending BPDUs from that port. Remember that when a switch receives a BPDU from a port, it adds the cost of that port to the BPDU's `Root Path Cost` field, and then the switch compares the BPDU with the locally generated BPDU for that port.

Four sequential criteria are used to compare BPDUs:

1. **Criterion One:** `root-id` **in the BPDUs** — The lowest numeric value takes precedence (wins); in the case of a tie, the comparison moves to Criterion Two.

2. **Criterion Two:** `Path Cost` **to Root Bridge in the BPDUs** — The lowest numeric value takes precedence (wins); in the case of a tie, the comparison moves to Criterion Three.

3. **Criterion Three: Sender's** `bridge-id` **in the BPDUs** — The lowest numeric value takes precedence (wins); in the case of a tie, the comparison moves to Criterion Four.

4. **Criterion Four: Sender** `port-id` **in BPDUs** — The lowest numeric value takes precedence (wins). It is impossible for a tie to be the result of the Criterion Four comparison. If the values of the first three criteria are identical in the BPDUs being compared, the two BPDUs must be generated by the same bridge but by different ports. Therefore, the `port-id` in the two BPDUs cannot be equal because two ports in the same switch cannot have the same `port-id`.

The comparison results in a *winning BPDU* and a *losing BPDU*. The winning BPDU is also referred to as the *superior BPDU*, and the losing BPDU as the *inferior BPDU*. If a bridge receives a superior BPDU from a port, it stops sending BPDUs from that port and stores the superior BPDU in its database. This is the most important behavior for switches running STP: *The switch keeps sending out BPDUs until it receives superior BPDUs.* Each superior BPDU stored in a switch has a maximum expiration age. If the switch does not receive the same BPDU from the other switch after the maximum age expires, the BPDU is discarded, and the switch starts sending its own BPDU.

Every port in each bridge performs the same operation and stores a copy of the *best* BPDU — either a BPDU of its own, or a superior BPDU received from a neighbor's port(s). Every time a port receives a BPDU, the BPDU comparison is performed. Only the best BPDU is stored in the switch against that port. If the superior BPDU was a received one (instead of generated by the switch), the `Path Cost` of the port that receives the BPDU is added into the `Root Path Cost` field of the BPDU when it is stored.

Building a Loop-Free Topology

The BPDU generation and comparison phase happens as soon as the switch boots up. During BPDU comparison, each port ends up with a copy of the *superior BPDU*. The switches use these BPDUs to build a loop-free topology. This three-step process is called *STP convergence*.

Step 1: Elect the Root Bridge

STP starts building the forwarding topology by determining the *root of the tree*. Using BPDU comparison, each switch stores one superior BPDU for each port. The switch then compares the `root-id` fields to determine the Root Bridge. Initially each bridge considers itself as the Root Bridge and puts its own `bridge-id` into the `root-id` field of the BPDUs it generates. The switch compares the stored BPDUs for each port to find the BPDU with the lowest `root-id` value. If it finds another BPDU with a lower `root-id` value, it changes the `root-id` field of the BPDU to that value in all BPDUs it generates or intends to generate.

> **Note:** In STP, a higher priority is actually represented by a *lower numerical value*. For example, a bridge with priority 50 is preferred over a bridge with priority 100 and becomes the Root Bridge. The lower numerical value in bridge or `Port Priority` represents a higher preference.

After each switch elects a Root Bridge, the `root-id` of every BPDU in the network is synchronized to the value of the lowest `bridge-id` in the entire network. For all non–Root Bridges, the content of the BPDUs that are generated and sent out is changed: The `root-id` fields are set to the `bridge-id` of the elected Root Bridge. When the `root-id` fields of all BPDUs are set to the elected Root Bridge's `bridge-id` (BPDUs are synchronized), the Root Bridge election is complete. Only one Root Bridge is elected in the entire bridged network.

> **Note:** During Root Bridge selection, the `root-id` field in a BPDU may change to a lower value. A port that had previously stopped sending BPDUs because it lost the BPDU comparison may win the comparison with the new `root-id` value and start sending BPDUs again, or vice versa: A port that previously won the BPDU comparison and sent BPDUs may lose the comparison after the adjacent switch changes the BPDU content with a new `root-id`. In this case, the port stops sending BPDUs and stores the BPDUs from the adjacent switch. The lowest `root-id` value gets propagated through the network.
>
> BPDU comparison in STP is preemptive. Anytime a switch receives a BPDU with better value, the comparison result is honored immediately.

After the Root Bridge is decided, the switches move on to decide their Root Port (RP).

Step 2: Elect the Root Port in Every Non–Root Switch

The RP is the one port in a switch closest to the elected Root Bridge. Any switch that is not a Root Bridge must have only one RP. (A Root Bridge has no RP.) Because the Root Bridge is decided in Step 1 (Root Bridge election), all BPDUs (received or locally generated) have the same `root-id` value. Therefore, the BPDU comparison moves to the second criterion: Compare the `Root Path Cost`.

Because the RP is the port closest to the Root Bridge, the `Root Path Cost` field is used to decide which port is the RP in a switch. In the Root Bridge, all ports send out BPDU with the cost set to 0 (because the ports are on the Root Bridge, there is no cost for them to get to the Root Bridge). All non–Root Bridges *add the cost associated with the RP to the* `Root Path Cost` *fields of the BPDUs before it sends the BPDUs.* The `Path Cost` is accumulated by each switch when the BPDUs are propagated away from the Root Bridge.

In all switches, two things happen. First, the switch performs BPDU comparison on all ports between the local BPDUs and the received BPDUs, finds the superior BPDUs, and stores them. The switch then compares the stored BPDUs from all ports and decides which port should be the RP. Because the Root Bridge election is completed, all stored BPDUs have the same `root-id` value. The BPDU comparison then uses the `Root Path Cost` values in the BPDUs to elect the RP on each switch. The port with the best BPDU among all the ports is elected as the RP of the switch. Once the RP of the switch is elected, the switch adds the `Root Path Cost` value from that port to all BPDUs it sends or intends to send.

> **Note:** Only the cost value of the link associated with the elected RP is meaningful. The switch adds the cost of the link to the BPDU when it receives any BPDU over any link. However, only one port wins the BPDU comparison and becomes the RP. A non–Root Switch adds the path cost of the RP to all BPDUs it sends; therefore, only the cost value on the elected RP affects the network forwarding topology.

Step 3: Elect the Designated Port

After an RP is elected in every non–Root Switch, the Designated Port (DP) election is performed. A DP is the port that is preferred in a common LAN segment. In any LAN segment there is only one DP.

DP election is performed in all LAN segments among the ports attached to each LAN segment. To elect a DP in a LAN segment, all ports attached to the LAN segment exchange and compare BPDUs. In a Root Bridge, all ports are DPs because the BPDUs sent from the Root Bridge have a `Root Path Cost` of 0, so they always win the BPDU comparison. In non–Root Switches, the accumulated `Root Path Cost` determines the DP of the segment: The BPDU that has the lowest `Root Path Cost` wins. In the case of a tie, the next two criteria of the BPDU comparison apply: The BPDU with the lowest sender BID wins. If there is still a tie, the BPDU with the lowest `port-id` wins.

After these three steps, all ports in all switches are assigned one of the three *roles*: RP, DP, or non-DP. Non-DPs are ports that are neither RPs nor DPs. *Only RPs and DPs forward traffic.* Non-DPs are blocked, which results in a loop-free forwarding topology.

STP Port States

This section discusses possible port states, the conditions that put a port into a certain state, and what a port can do in each state. Table A.2 lists all possible STP port states.

Table A.2 STP Port States

State	Action	Description
listening	Sends and receives BPDUs	By receiving or sending BPDUs, the listening port performs Root Bridge election, RP election, and DP election. If the election process determines that the port is a non-DP, the port transits from the listening state to the blocking state; otherwise (if the port is elected as a DP or RP), the port transits to the learning state.
learning	Receives data traffic; does not send it, and builds the forwarding table.	When the port is elected as DP or RP, it transits from the listening state to the learning state. The port starts building the FDB by learning the source MAC addresses from the received traffic. The port receives data traffic but does not forward it. It keeps receiving, processing, and sometimes generating BPDUs. The purpose of transiting a port to the learning state before it begins forwarding data traffic is to build FDBs to reduce the flooding of the unknown unicast traffic.
forwarding	Sends and receives data traffic.	A port in the forwarding state is an RP or DP that has completed the learning state. The port begins forwarding data traffic as well as processing BPDUs. Only ports in the active STP forwarding topology (loop-free) should be in this state.
blocking	Receives BPDUs.	This is the initial state when a port comes up. When a port is not elected as an RP or a DP during the listening state, it transits to the blocking state. In the blocking state, the port only receives BPDUs. The BPDUs it receives must be superior BPDUs and must arrive periodically within the BPDU age timer to keep the port in the blocking state. Otherwise, the port will move to the learning state and trigger a topology change.
disabled	Administratively down	The port has no activity. It is physically out of service or manually disabled.

Only three of these five states (blocking, forwarding, and disabled) exist in a stable, fully converged network. The listening and learning states are temporary transition states. When a port is administratively enabled and the physical link comes up, the port always starts in the blocking state. No data traffic can be sent or received, and the port only receives and sends BPDUs. The port then transits from **blocking** state to **listening** state and starts the BPDU generation, reception, and comparison. *In the* **listening** *state, the port performs BPDU comparison and receives its role (DP, RP, or neither).*

The listening phase decides the Root Bridge and the RPs and DPs. If a port is neither RP nor DP after the election is completed, it falls back to the **blocking** state and only receives BPDUs. As long as the superior BPDUs keep coming to the port before the previous BPDU ages out, the port remains in the **blocking** state.

If a port won a role of RP or DP in the election from the **listening** state, it then transits to the **learning** state. In the **learning** state, the port can receive data frames, but does not forward them. Instead, it builds the FDB by learning the source MAC addresses of the traffic. Ports remain in the **learning** state to reduce the flooding of unknown unicast frames. By putting a port in the **learning** state for a certain amount of time, the port learns more possible MAC addresses and adds them to the FDB before it starts forwarding traffic.

After the **learning** state, the port moves to the **forwarding** state. In the **forwarding** state, the port sends and receives traffic normally. A port stays in the **forwarding** state until there is a link failure (the port is *disabled*) or until the port receives a superior BPDU (the port loses its DP or RP role and moves to the **blocking** state).

Ports in the **blocking** state still participate in the STP infrastructure, and their **blocking** states are maintained because they continuously receive the superior BPDUs. This makes the switch aware of the existence of better alternative ports in the **forwarding** state. Once the superior BPDU stops arriving at a blocked port, the port assumes that the more preferred port is no longer available and tries to transit to the **forwarding** state.

Controlling the Forwarding Path in STP

The process of exchanging BPDUs and performing elections can be done automatically using default STP parameter values (**cost**, **priority**, and **timers**). When a switch is powered on, it goes through the election process and put its ports in correct states. It then starts forwarding traffic in a loop-free forwarding topology. In most cases, STP is plug-and-play in a bridged network.

However, operators may want to manually control the STP election process and results and therefore control the forwarding topology. As a Best Practice, a network's forwarding path should be predictable. Within a network, at any time, the roles and status of each network element in different scenarios (for example, with or without link failure) can be predicted. This is particularly important in scaled networks where *policy control* is desired. Therefore, it is important to understand the STP parameters and their impact on switch behavior before fine-tuning the STP configuration.

In order to make the network's switching behavior predictable, the network forwarding topology must be controlled manually by configuring STP. The operator can designate the Root Bridge, the backup Root Bridges, the primary forwarding path, and backup forwarding path(s) by using different STP parameters in different switches. Three STP parameters can be used to decide the network forwarding topology: `Bridge Priority`, `Port Cost`, and `Port Priority`. Table A.3 lists the configurable STP parameters that can impact STP network topology.

Table A.3 STP Configurable BPDU Parameters

Value	Definition	Usage
Bridge Priority	The priority to be designated as the Root Bridge	The bridge with the lowest bridge-id is elected as the Root Bridge. The bridge-id is composed of [bridge-priority (2 bytes) + bridge-MAC (6 bytes)]. Because the Bridge Priority is the most significant portion of the bridge-id, the location of the Root Bridge can be controlled by manually configuring the value of the Bridge Priority, regardless of the MAC address of the bridge.
Path Cost	Cost of the port (link speed)	The Path Cost is the cost to the adjacent bridge through a port. This value is meaningful only after the RP of a bridge is decided. Only the Path Cost value configured on the RP is added when the bridge sends out BPDUs.
Port Priority	The priority to be a DP or an RP	This value can be set manually on different ports in the same switch. In the BPDU comparison criteria, when the first three criteria tie (root-id, Root Path Cost, and Sender bridge-id), the Port Priority configuration decides which port wins the election.

The key to controlling the STP forwarding topology is the location of the Root Bridge. The location of the Root Bridge can be controlled by configuring the `Bridge Priority` values in the STP instance of each switch. The *lower* the numerical value of the `Bridge Priority`, the more likely the switch will be elected as the Root Bridge. The recommendation is to place the Root Bridge in the center of the network and to have nearby backup Root Bridges in the network. A backup Root Bridge is a Root Bridge that is less preferred than the desired Root Bridge and takes over the Root Bridge role if the current Root Bridge fails.

The Path Costs of the ports control the location of the RP and DP. *Only the configuration of* Path Cost *in the RP affects the forwarding path*, because the Path Cost of the RP is applied to the superior BPDUs after they are received from other switches. DPs receive only inferior BPDUs and send out their own BPDUs, so the Path Cost of the DP does not affect the forwarding topology. When the RP of a switch receives superior BPDUs and stores them, its Path Cost is applied. Because the RP won the election among all ports in the switch, the stored superior BPDU with Path Cost applied is propagated by all other ports in the switch to other switches. Only the Path Cost of the RP is counted and potentially affects the forwarding path. In most cases, the default Path Cost (automatically assigned to the port according to the link speed) is suitable for the network. Use caution when changing the Path Cost value of a port.

STP Timers and Convergence

The original STP is relatively slow from the perspective of convergence performance, especially with the default timers. If a port stops receiving BPDUs, it waits the Max Age time (20 seconds) before it reacts. Even if the TCN BPDU propagation time is not counted, the alternative port must take 30 seconds (15 seconds for listening, and 15 seconds for learning) before it starts forwarding traffic. Table A.4 lists all STP protocol timers.

Table A.4 STP Timers

Timer	Default Value	Definition
Hello	2 seconds	The interval between BPDUs sent out by the Root Bridge
Forward delay	15 seconds	The delay before the port is put into the forwarding state. Before the port starts forwarding traffic, it stays in the listening state for the length of time of the forward delay, and then it stays in the learning state for the length or time of the forward delay. The forward delay is the length of time the port stays in the listening or learning states.
Max Age	20 seconds	The lifetime of a BPDU

Tuning STP timers requires careful planning and testing. Consider the size of the network and how many hops a BPDU needs to be propagated across the network, as well as the timer settings.

STP Topology Changes

The initial STP convergence has been discussed. When switches boot up, they exchange configuration BPDUs to perform election. The election eliminates the redundant forwarding paths from the network.

Another aspect of STP is its reaction when there is a port state change in the network. For example, when a network has link failures, certain ports go down. Or a port previously in the **down** state returns to the normal state. These events are referred as *topology changes*. STP uses TCN BPDUs to propagate topology change information.

If there is a port or node failure, the first step is to detect the failure. After the failure is detected, the network reacts to the failure. In a bridged Ethernet network, the forwarding information is learned from the data traffic. The FDB is built by learning the source MAC address of the data traffic. When a port that was in the `forwarding` state fails, the data flow from that port stops. The MAC address associated with that port is no longer reachable through that port. In the same network, all other switches still have these MAC addresses associated with the port connected to the switch that has the port failure, so the traffic is still forwarded toward the failed port. In this scenario, the traffic is *blackholed* in the switch with the failed port. Other switches keep forwarding traffic toward the failed port until the associated MAC address entry times out in the FDB or is overwritten. It may take up to 5 minutes, based on the default MAC address aging timer. Because a 300-second traffic outage is not acceptable to most customers, STP uses TCN to propagate the topology change throughout the network quickly. TCN significantly improves the network convergence performance and reduces wasted bandwidth. Figure A.2 illustrates the scenarios of network failures without and with TCN.

In legacy STP, if a topology change occurs in a switch that is not a Root Bridge, the switch must notify the Root Bridge by generating TCN BPDUs and sending them through the RP toward the Root Bridge. The Root Bridge then propagates the topology change information to all other bridges by sending configuration BPDUs with the Topology Change (TC) flag set. The switch with the topology change generates the TCN BPDU and sends it from the RP toward the Root Bridge. It sends the TCN BPDU every `hello interval`, until it is acknowledged by an adjacent switch closer to the Root Bridge. After receiving the TCN BPDU, the adjacent switch sends a configuration BPDU with the `TCN ACK` flag set to the switch from which the TCN BPDU is received. It then sends a TCN BPDU from the RP toward the Root Bridge. Each switch along the route from the failure to the Root Bridge acknowledges the TCN and propagates the TCN toward the Root Bridge. Therefore, the TCN BPDU is propagated to the Root Bridge. After the Root Bridge receives the TCN BPDU, the Root Bridge acknowledges the TCN BPDU by sending a configuration BPDU with the TCN ACK flag set to the port from which the TCN BPDU is received. Then, the Root Bridge floods configuration BPDUs with the TCN flag set to all other ports to propagate the topology change information.

Figure A.2   How TCN BPDU Speeds Up MAC Age-Out during a Topology Change

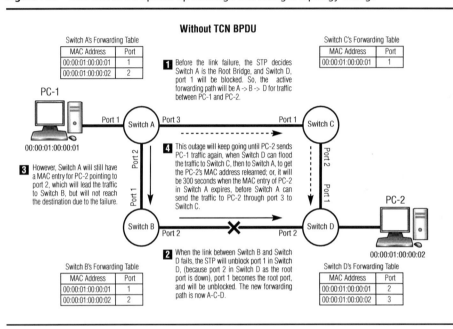

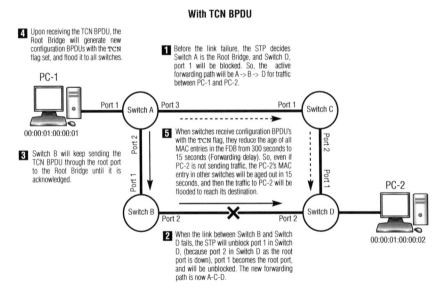

When a switch receives a BPDU with the TC flag set, it knows the current forwarding topology is changed, so the current MAC forwarding table based on the topology is no longer correct. Therefore, the switch must refresh its FDB to learn the new forwarding information. It sets all entries in the MAC table to the age of 15 seconds (forwarding delay), replacing the default value of 300 seconds (MAC entry age) to speed up the MAC aging process. If traffic flow cannot reach the switch in 15 seconds, the MAC entry is deleted. Traffic destined to that MAC address is then flooded as unknown unicast destination traffic, shortening the outage caused by the failures.

> **Note:** The forwarding behavior of a routed IP network is different from the forwarding behavior of a bridged Ethernet network. In a routed IP network, if an entry to an IP prefix is missing from the routing table and a router receives a packet destined to that entry, it discards the packets because the destination is not reachable. In a bridged Ethernet network, if an entry is missing from the MAC forwarding table and a switch receives a packet destined to that entry, it *floods* the traffic to all bridge ports. All other switches in the network then receive the traffic, and one of the switches may send the traffic to the correct destination.

The Root Bridge keeps sending a configuration BPDU with the TC flag set for a time of `BPDU Max Age` (20 seconds) + `forwarding delay` (15 seconds). Then the TCN flag is cleared.

A.2 Spanning Tree Protocol Variations

Since its introduction in the industry more than 20 years ago, STP has been implemented by many Ethernet switching equipment vendors. STP has been improved several times as well and therefore has many variations. This section introduces several common variations of STP. Originally, STP was invented to eliminate the forwarding loops in small- to mid-size bridged Ethernet networks. The major concern of the original STP was to eliminate forwarding loops from the network and to ensure that topology changes are propagated throughout the network. However, the failover convergence performance of the original STP is not very fast, and it has been modified in several ways to improve performance.

There are many variations of STP, including proprietary vendor implementations and improved open standards, such as STP, RSTP, 802.1d-2004, MSTP, PVST, PVST+. Some of these variations can coexist in the same network, and others are not compatible. All variations share the same purpose: to use BPDUs to detect and eliminate forwarding loops and to propagate topology changes. Operators must carefully consider the compatibility of different versions of STP when providing VPLS service to customers or designing a VPLS network. The network designer must ensure that the loop-prevention mechanism of the VPLS works properly.

Note: PVST and PVST+ are Cisco proprietary STP protocols. PVST uses ISL-encapsulated BPDUs, and PVST+ uses 802.1q-tagged BPDUs.

Table A.5 lists the STP variations a service provider may need to interoperate with its customers.

Table A.5   STP Variations and Compatibility

Variations	Characteristics	Compatibility with the ALSRP VPLS Solution
STP 802.1d-1998	Original version of STP	Yes. The VPLS service instance falls back to 802.1d-1998 on the port that receives the 802.1d-1998 BPDU. After the BPDU age timer expires, the switch attempts to return to 802.1d-2004 (default version) again.
MSTP 802.1s	An STP variation where one BPDU can carry information for multiple STP instances. Different VLANs can use different MSTP instances with different active forwarding topologies to achieve load sharing over the same physical link.	Yes. Only the mVPLS service instance is allowed to use MSTP. MSTP allows only untagged BPDUs; therefore, the mVPLS running MSTP must contain a null SAP or an untagged SAP.
RSTP 802.1w	Much faster convergence than the original STP, shorter timers, and a more precise converging procedure	Yes

Variations	Characteristics	Compatibility with the ALSRP VPLS Solution
STP 802.1d-2004	The most up-to-date version of RSTP	Yes. This is the default version used by the ALSRP VPLS service instances when STP is enabled.
P-MSTP 802.1ad-2005	Provider MSTP, used for Provider Backbone Bridging (PBB) or PBB-VPLS. It uses the Provider Group MAC address as the BPDU destination MAC address (01–80–2c–00–00–08).	Yes. This version is supported in PBB-VPLS service instances. Both I-VPLS and B-VPLS can use the P-MSTP both internally in the VPLS instance and interoperating with the customer's PBBN or PBN network. The PBB-VPLS and its components (I-VPLS, B-VPLS, and other terminologies) are discussed in Chapter 17.
Cisco PVST	PVST using Cisco ISL-encapsulated BPDUs. Not compatible with other vendors.	Not compatible
Cisco PVST+	Cisco proprietary version of PVST. Uses 01–00–0c–cc–cc–cd as the BPDU destination MAC address.	Yes. Supported by using BPDU tunneling or l2tp termination in a VPLS service instance.

Rapid STP (RSTP) 802.1w and 802.1d-2004

One of the most significant improved versions of the original STP is RSTP, 802.1w. The biggest disadvantage of the original STP is the slow failover performance when there is a network failure and STP must converge. It can take 50 seconds for the network to rebuild a new active forwarding topology. A 50-second failover time is not acceptable for the performance required for a network larger than a small campus LAN. RSTP was introduced in 1998 as defined by IEEE standard 802.1w. The new standard IEEE 802.1d-2004 incorporates RSTP and replaces STP. Although 802.1d-2004 incorporates RSTP, it is not exactly the same as 802.1w. The 802.1d-2004 standard has two improvements to RSTP that 802.1w does not have:

- 802.1D-2004 transitions from the discard state to the forwarding state in 4 seconds over shared media (also called *point-to-multipoint links*), whereas 802.1w transitions from the discard state to the forwarding state in 30 seconds over shared media.

- 802.1D-2004 uses the port's Designated Priority Vector (DPV), whereas 802.1w does not recognize this field and ignores it in a received BPDU.

RSTP defines a new type of BPDU — RSTP BPDU (BPDU version 0x02). RSTP BPDU is backward-compatible with STP BPDUs (BPDU version 0x01) but has the following differences:

- The protocol version field is set to 0x02, and the BPDU type field is set to 0x02, indicating that the BPDU is an RSTP BPDU.
- The Version 1 Length field is set to 0x00 at the end of the BPDU.
- The Flag field contains extra information:
    - Proposal (bit 1) and Agreement (bit 6)
    - Port Role (bit 2 & 3)
    - Learning (bit 4) and Forwarding (bit 5)
    - Topology Change (bit 0) and Topology Change ACK (bit 7) remain the same as STP BPDU for delivery of topology change information. RSTP does not use Topology Change ACK.

Figure A.3 illustrates the format of an RSTP BPDU.

Figure A.3   RSTP BPDU Format

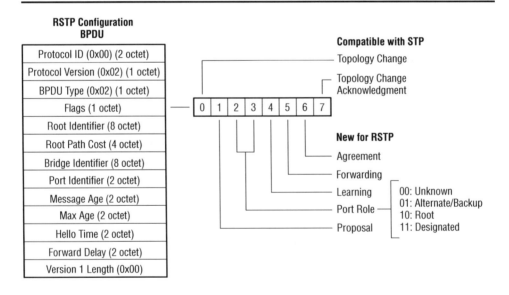

The following differences between RSTP and STP improve the convergence time of RSTP:

- After the initial STP convergence is completed, the generation of BPDUs from all non–Root Bridges is triggered by the generation of BPDUs from the Root Bridge. Non–Root Bridges send out BPDUs only when they receive BPDUs from the RP. Only the Root Bridge generates the BPDUs periodically according to the Hello interval defined for the Root Bridge. In RSTP, all switches generate and send BPDUs every Hello interval (the default is 2 seconds), regardless of whether they receive BPDUs from the RP.

- Because RSTP requires every switch to send BPDUs at every Hello interval, BPDUs are also used as Hello packets for each switch to detect if there is a failure to connect to an adjacent switch. If three consecutive BPDUs are missed (three Hello intervals) from one port, the stored BPDU expires. Therefore, BPDUs expire when they reach the lower value of the two timers: the **MaxAge** timer, or three times the Hello interval. Using BPDUs as Hello packets allows RSTP to detect non-physical link failures much faster than STP that relies on only the **MaxAge** timer.

- In STP, when a blocked port receives an inferior BPDU, it ignores the BPDU and waits for the previously received superior BPDU from the same port to expire. In RSTP, as soon as a blocked port receives an inferior BPDU, it replaces the previously received superior BPDU and sends its own BPDU to the port from which the inferior BPDU was received. This also significantly speeds up the convergence performance of RSTP. Figure A.4 illustrates this difference in RSTP.

Figure A.4   RSTP Blocked Port Accepts Inferior BPDU and Immediately Returns Its Own BPDU

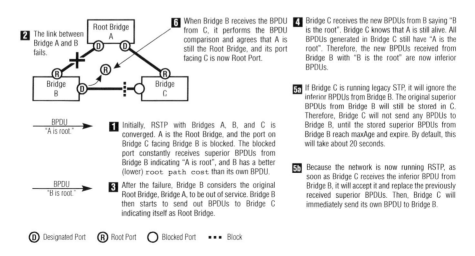

2 The link between Bridge A and B fails.

6 When Bridge B receives the BPDU from C, it performs the BPDU comparison and agrees that A is still the Root Bridge, and its port facing C is now Root Port.

4 Bridge C receives the new BPDUs from B saying "B is the root". Bridge C knows that A is still alive. All BPDUs generated in Bridge C still have "A is the root". Therefore, the new BPDUs received from Bridge B with "B is the root" are now inferior BPDUs.

1 Initially, RSTP with Bridges A, B, and C is converged. A is the Root Bridge, and the port on Bridge C facing Bridge B is blocked. The blocked port constantly receives superior BPDUs from Bridge B indicating "A is root", and B has a better (lower) `root path cost` than its own BPDU.

3 After the failure, Bridge B considers the original Root Bridge, Bridge A, to be out of service. Bridge B then starts to send out BPDUs to Bridge C indicating itself as Root Bridge.

5a If Bridge C is running legacy STP, it will ignore the inferior BPDUs from Bridge B. The original superior BPDUs from Bridge B will still be stored in C. Therefore, Bridge C will not send any BPDUs to Bridge B, until the stored superior BPDUs from Bridge B reach maxAge and expire. By default, this will take about 20 seconds.

5b Because the network is now running RSTP, as soon as Bridge C receives the inferior BPDU from Bridge B, it will accept it and replace the previously received superior BPDUs. Then, Bridge C will immediately send its own BPDU to Bridge B.

(D) Designated Port   **(R)** Root Port   **(O)** Blocked Port   **∎∎∎** Block

- RSTP introduces the concept of the *edge port*. An *edge port* is the port connected to a LAN segment to which no Bridge Ports are connected (for example, all other devices are hubs or PC hosts). Because an edge port is not connected to any bridges, it is not considered part of the active forwarding topology in a bridged Ethernet network. RSTP ignores status changes from the edge port because these status changes do not change the forwarding topology of a network. Mistakenly configuring a non-edge port as an edge port can cause forwarding loops. To prevent this, the switch monitors the edge port for incoming BPDUs. If BPDUs are received from an edge port (meaning that there are other Bridge Ports in the LAN segment to which the port is connected), the port loses its edge port status and is considered to be a regular Bridge Port.

- RSTP expedites the topology change process by allowing blocked ports to transit directly into `forwarding` states, bypassing the `listening` and `learning` states. This process is safe only if a port is an edge port or if a port is connected to a *point-to-point* link (when there are only two Bridge Ports in a LAN segment). In RSTP, as long as the port is full-duplex, it is considered a point-to-point link and transits directly from the `blocked` state to the `forwarding` state when RSTP allows it to forward traffic.

In RSTP, a Bridge Port's *state* is not connected to its *role*. The *state* of a port defines whether the port is allowed to send and receive BPDUs or data traffic. The *role* of a port defines the relevant position of the port in the network. A port receives its role during STP convergence by performing BPDU comparison. Table A.6 compares the different types of port states and roles between STP and RSTP.

Table A.6 STP versus RSTP Port States and Roles

STP State	RSTP State	STP Roles	RSTP Roles
blocking	discard	RP	RP
disabled	discard	DP	DP
listening	discard	Blocked port (not RP or DP)	Alternate Port (backup for RP)
learning	learning	Blocked port (not RP or DP)	Backup Port (backup for DP)
forwarding	forwarding	Disabled port (Administratively disabled)	Disabled port (out of service)

RSTP does not consider that there is a difference between the `learning` and `disabled` states. Neither state allows a port to send or receive traffic or to learn

MAC addresses. RSTP summarizes all non-traffic-forwarding, non-MAC-learning states into the `discard` state. The `learning` and `forwarding` states are the same in RSTP as in STP.

RSTP introduces two new roles for ports: Alternate Port and Backup Port.

- An *Alternate Port* is a port that is blocked because it constantly receives superior BPDUs from *other* switches. In a switch, the Alternate Port is the *backup* for the RP of that switch. When a switch loses its RP, it *immediately* puts the best Alternate Port into the `forwarding` state as the new RP.

- A *Backup Port* is a port that is blocked because it constantly receives superior BPDUs from the same switch. In a switch, the Backup Port is the *backup* for the DP. When a switch loses a DP on an LAN segment, it *immediately* puts the best Backup Port in that LAN segment into the `forwarding` state as the new DP.

Figure A.5 illustrates the location of the Alternate Port and the Backup Port. The network presented in the diagram is a stable network with RSTP converged.

Figure A.5 RSTP Blocked Port Roles: Alternate Port and Backup Port

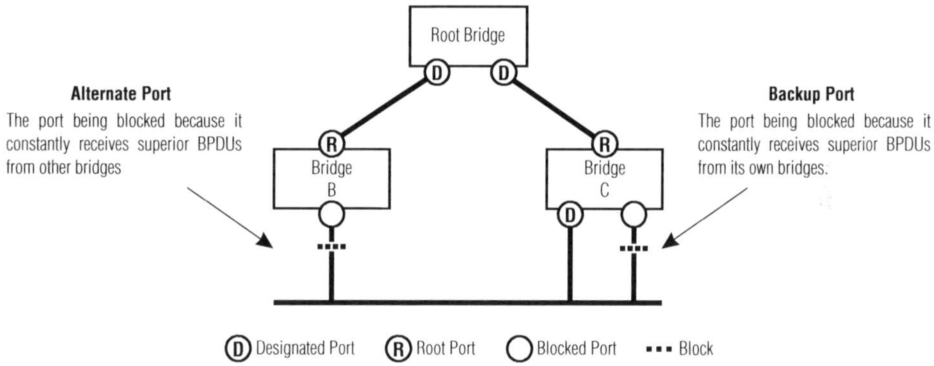

When STP encounters a topology change, the convergence is based on timers. All ports are initially in the `blocking` state and then transit to the `listening` state for the time defined by the `forward_delay_timer`. If a port is elected to be the DP or the RP, it then transits to the `learning` state for the time defined by the `forward_delay_timer`. By default, the `forward_delay_timer` is set to 15 seconds; therefore, the port cannot forward traffic until at least 30 seconds after it is elected by STP to forward traffic.

In the same situation, RSTP uses a Proposal/Agreement negotiation mechanism to speed up the convergence. Figure A.6 illustrates this mechanism in a sample network.

Figure A.6   RSTP Convergence: Proposal/Agreement and Synchronization

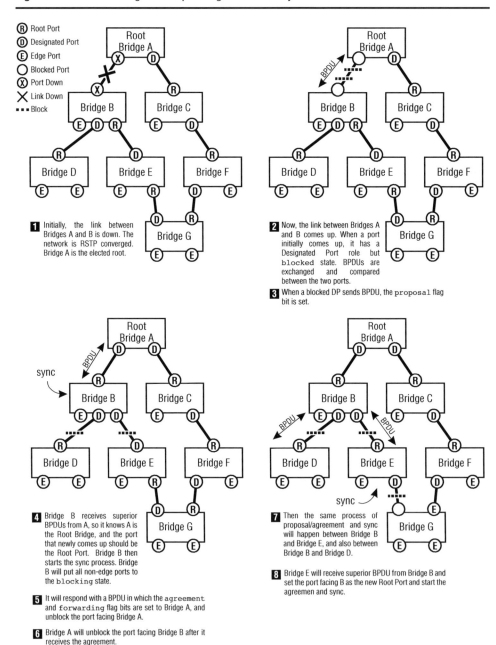

(R) Root Port
(D) Designated Port
(E) Edge Port
(O) Blocked Port
(X) Port Down
X Link Down
··· Block

1 Initially, the link between Bridges A and B is down. The network is RSTP converged. Bridge A is the elected root.

2 Now, the link between Bridges A and B comes up. When a port initially comes up, it has a Designated Port role but `blocked` state. BPDUs are exchanged and compared between the two ports.

3 When a blocked DP sends BPDU, the `proposal` flag bit is set.

4 Bridge B receives superior BPDUs from A, so it knows A is the Root Bridge, and the port that newly comes up should be the Root Port. Bridge B then starts the sync process. Bridge B will put all non-edge ports to the `blocking` state.

5 It will respond with a BPDU in which the `agreement` and `forwarding` flag bits are set to Bridge A, and unblock the port facing Bridge A.

6 Bridge A will unblock the port facing Bridge B after it receives the agreement.

7 Then the same process of proposal/agreement and sync will happen between Bridge B and Bridge E, and also between Bridge B and Bridge D.

8 Bridge E will receive superior BPDU from Bridge B and set the port facing B as the new Root Port and start the agreemen and sync.

As described in Figure A.6, every time a non-edge port initially comes up between two switches, the following sequence occurs (Point numbers match the circled steps in the figure):

- **Point 2** — The ports on both switches are set as DPs in the `discard` state and exchange BPDUs.
- **Point 3** — A DP in the `discard` state sends a BPDU with the `proposal` flag set.
- **Point 4** — The switch that receives the superior BPDU (Switch B in the example) starts the synchronization process by blocking all non-edge ports and sending out BPDUs with the `agreement` and `forwarding` flags set. This notifies the switch that is sending the superior BPDUs (Switch A in the example) to unblock its port.
- **Point 5** — After the synchronization, the switch that received the superior BPDUs unblocks the new RP. The non-edge, non-RPs are still blocked and sending BPDUs with the `proposal` flag bit set to other switches.
- **Points 6, 7, and 8** — This triggers the synchronization process in other switches that are further away from the Root Bridge. As the new BPDU propagates, the synchronization process is triggered in all switches in the forwarding topology until the convergence finishes.

Figure A.7 illustrates a newly converged network in a stable RSTP forwarding topology.

Figure A.7   Final Stable State after RSTP Convergence

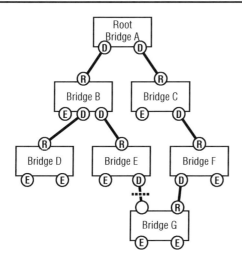

(R) Root Port   (D) Designated Port   (E) Edge Port   ···· Block

The Proposal/Agreement process used for RSTP convergence saves significant time in building the active forwarding topology. This process is triggered by sending BPDUs with `proposal` or `agreement` flag bits set. The `forward_delay timer` is not involved. As soon as the BPDU comparison and agreement is complete, ports are transited immediately to the `forwarding` state. Therefore, it requires only the time used for the BPDU propagation through the entire network.

All these changes implemented in RSTP improve convergence performance significantly. RSTP convergence time is usually within several seconds, compared to the STP convergence time of tens of seconds.

RSTP also handles the topology change differently:

- RSTP considers that there is a topology change only when a non-edge port transits to the `forwarding` state. Only then does the switch running RSTP generate TCNs. This is because only when a non-edge port transits to the `forwarding` state is a forwarding path added to the network and can cause loops. Forwarding loops can never be caused by any port moving from the **up** to the **down** state or by a state change in an edge port.

- In STP, topology changes on non–Root Bridges are reported to the Root Bridge by sending TCN BPDUs. Only the Root Bridge can propagate the topology change to other switches in the network. In RSTP, all switches are allowed to propagate a topology change:

  - When a bridge detects a local topology change, it starts a `TC_While timer` and sets the `TC bit` in all BPDUs that it sends before the timer expires. It also flushes the MAC entries in the forwarding table associated with the RP and all DPs.

  - When a bridge receives a BPDU with the `TC-bit` set, it also starts a `TC_While timer` and sets the `TC bit` in all BPDUs that it sends before the timer expires. It also flushes the MAC entries in the forwarding table associated with all RPs and DPs, except the MAC entries associated with the port that receives the BPDU with the `TC-bit` set.

- In STP, when a switch receives a topology change propagated from the Root Bridge, it does not flush the MAC entries from the forwarding table. It changes the MAC entries' age from the original `MaxAge` time (default value is 300 seconds) to `forward_delay` time (default value is 15 seconds) to speed up the aging process. In RSTP, when a switch receives a topology change, it immediately flushes the corresponding MAC entries.

Topology change propagation and MAC entry flushing in RSTP are more efficient and shorten the convergence time significantly.

Per-VLAN Spanning Tree

STP and RSTP eliminate forwarding loops from a bridged Ethernet network by blocking redundant forwarding paths. All Ethernet bridges exchange BPDUs in the network to form a loop-free common active forwarding infrastructure. Both STP and RSTP are port-based. If a port on a switch is not elected as either an RP or a DP, the port is blocked and cannot send or receive traffic and is therefore eliminated from the active forwarding topology.

Although STP and RSTP provide a loop-free forwarding topology, they do not use the network bandwidth efficiently because the blocked ports are not used to forward data traffic. If a network is designed to use VLANs to isolate different traffic flows, all VLANs use the same active forwarding topology built by STP or RSTP. In most cases, when there is link or node redundancy, load balancing is also desired. In a case in which there are two links between two switches, STP or RSTP puts all traffic on one link and blocks the other one to ensure that there is no forwarding loop. However, the operator may want some VLAN traffic to use one link and other VLAN traffic to use the other link. Load balancing cannot be achieved using regular STP or RSTP because these protocols build an active forwarding path where there is only one forwarding path between any two points of the network.

For this reason, many Ethernet switch vendors created their own implementation of Per-VLAN STP (PVSTP). These spanning tree variations allow every VLAN to have its own private spanning tree (STP or RSTP) *instance*. The BPDUs for each instance are tagged with `vlan-ids` to ensure that they are propagated only within their own VLAN. Some implementations use destination MAC addresses other than the standard STP BPDU destination MAC address of 01-80-c2-00-00-00. The STP or RSTP instance in each VLAN is configured with different `Bridge Priority` or `Port Priority` values. Therefore, different STP or RSTP instances belonging to different VLANs in the same physical network form different forwarding topologies — traffic from different VLANs is spread among different forwarding paths. Figure A.8 illustrates the port-based forwarding topologies of regular STP and Per-VLAN-based STP.

Figure A.8 Single Port-Based STP versus Per-VLAN STP

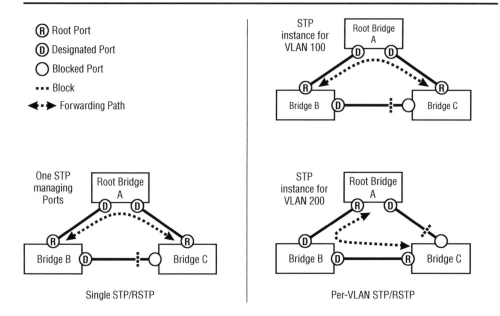

The two forwarding topologies on the right side of the figure illustrate the scenarios of VLAN 100 and VLAN 200. Each has its own spanning tree instance, and they use two different active forwarding topologies. VLAN 100 forwards traffic on the path B ⟷ A ⟷ C, while VLAN 200 forwards traffic on the path A ⟷ B ⟷ C. The traffic load for the two VLANs is balanced, forwarding loops are eliminated, and the redundancy remains.

Multiple-Instance STP (802.1s)

The drawback of PVST is scalability. If a physical network contains many VLANs, running one VPLS instance for each VLAN creates tens, hundreds, or even thousands of STP instances in every switch (one per VLAN). The control traffic overhead and BPDU processing overhead challenge the switch's hardware and software and may affect the performance of the switch. Running one STP instance for each VLAN is not efficient.

For example, the network presented in Figure A.8 has only two possible forwarding paths. If PVST is enabled and there are 100 VLANs, 50 VLANs use the top-right forwarding path, and the remaining 50 VLANs use the bottom-right forwarding path. However, since there are only two possible forwarding paths, two STP instances in the network are enough to form two forwarding paths. However, there must be a mechanism to map some VLANs to one STP instance and the rest to the other STP instance. This is the basic idea of the Multiple Spanning Tree Protocol (MSTP, 802.1s) — using multiple STP instances to build different forwarding topologies and then assigning them to different VLANs.

MSTP is a variation of RSTP. It takes advantage of the convergency speed of RSTP. Switches running MSTP can have up to 16 Multiple Spanning Tree Instances (MSTIs). MSTP configuration also contains VLAN-to-instance mapping, which allows multiple VLANs to share one MSTP instance. Compared to PVST, MSTP deployment significantly reduces the number of STP instances running in a network while still achieving load balancing among VLANs. Because MSTP can support up to 16 subinstances, it can create 16 different forwarding paths from one physical topology.

When MSTP is enabled in an Ethernet switch, there is one *common* MSTI and multiple (up to 15) subinstances. The common instance is called Common Instance Spanning Tree (CIST), which is indexed as MSTI 0. Other instances (1–15) must be created manually in the MSTP configuration. VLANs are mapped to the MSTIs so they can use the forwarding topologies built by MSTP. By default, all VLANs (1–4,094) are mapped to the CIST. If there is a VLAN-to-instance mapping, the CIST manages all VLANs that are not explicitly mapped to any MSTIs. For example, if the MSTP configuration has a VLAN-MSTI mapping of VLAN 1–100 to MSTI-1, and VLAN 300–400 to MSTI-2, the CIST manages VLANs 101–299 and 401–4,094.

Although there can be up to 16 MSTP instances, only one BPDU is sent by the CIST at any interval. The BPDU contains information for the MSTIs. MSTP BPDUs are always untagged. Figure A.9 illustrates the format of an MSTP BPDU. The RSTP BPDU format is also presented as a reference.

Within MSTP, an *MST Region* defines a domain of the network in which all Ethernet bridge switches have the same MSTP configuration, including the following values:

- **MST Region Name** — A text string of up to 32 characters for the name of the region
- **MST Revision Number** — A numerical value from 1 to 65,535
- **MST VLAN-to-MSTI Mapping** — The map of each VLAN to each MSTI

Figure A.9 MSTP Configuration BPDU Format

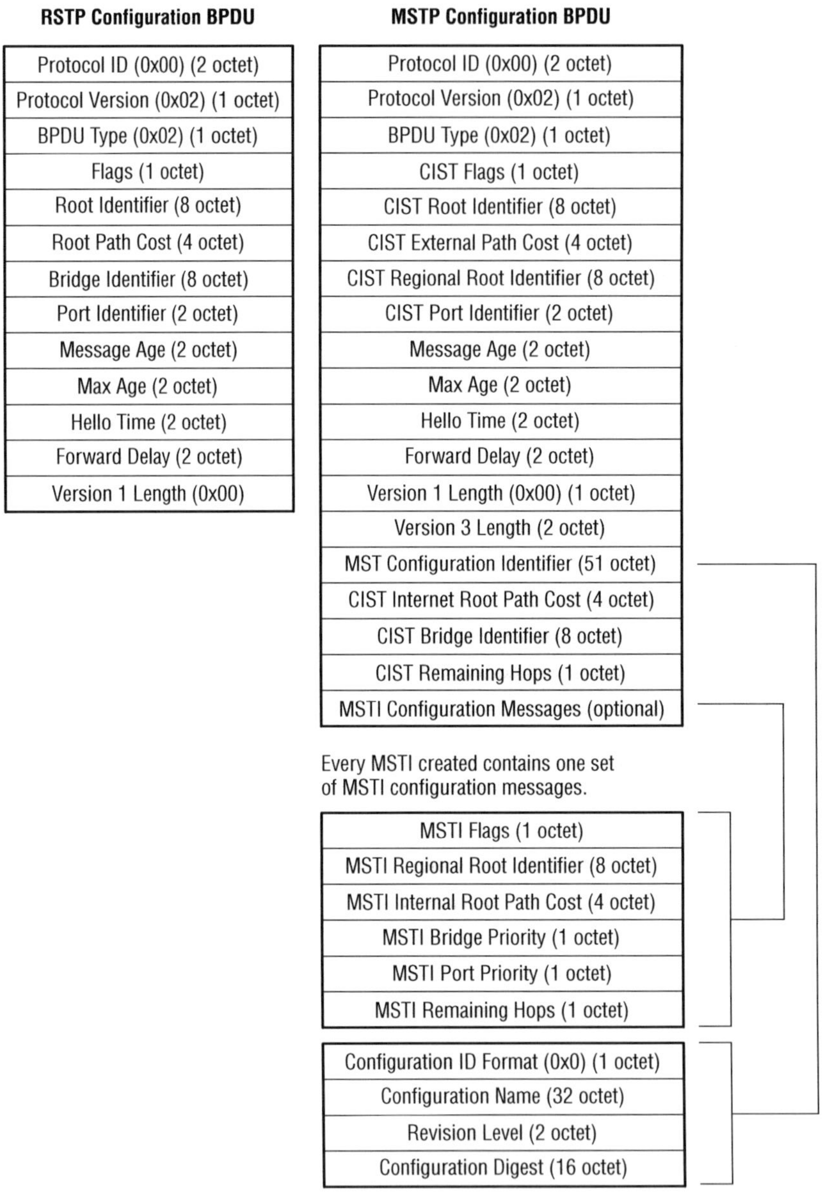

RSTP Configuration BPDU

Protocol ID (0x00) (2 octet)
Protocol Version (0x02) (1 octet)
BPDU Type (0x02) (1 octet)
Flags (1 octet)
Root Identifier (8 octet)
Root Path Cost (4 octet)
Bridge Identifier (8 octet)
Port Identifier (2 octet)
Message Age (2 octet)
Max Age (2 octet)
Hello Time (2 octet)
Forward Delay (2 octet)
Version 1 Length (0x00)

MSTP Configuration BPDU

Protocol ID (0x00) (2 octet)
Protocol Version (0x02) (1 octet)
BPDU Type (0x02) (1 octet)
CIST Flags (1 octet)
CIST Root Identifier (8 octet)
CIST External Path Cost (4 octet)
CIST Regional Root Identifier (8 octet)
CIST Port Identifier (2 octet)
Message Age (2 octet)
Max Age (2 octet)
Hello Time (2 octet)
Forward Delay (2 octet)
Version 1 Length (0x00) (1 octet)
Version 3 Length (2 octet)
MST Configuration Identifier (51 octet)
CIST Internet Root Path Cost (4 octet)
CIST Bridge Identifier (8 octet)
CIST Remaining Hops (1 octet)
MSTI Configuration Messages (optional)

Every MSTI created contains one set
of MSTI configuration messages.

MSTI Flags (1 octet)
MSTI Regional Root Identifier (8 octet)
MSTI Internal Root Path Cost (4 octet)
MSTI Bridge Priority (1 octet)
MSTI Port Priority (1 octet)
MSTI Remaining Hops (1 octet)

Configuration ID Format (0x0) (1 octet)
Configuration Name (32 octet)
Revision Level (2 octet)
Configuration Digest (16 octet)

All MSTP switches with the same MST Region configuration belong to the same MST Region. Together, the switches behave like one switch in relation to the switches outside the region. When switches on the boundaries of different MST Regions exchange BPDUs, only the CIST portion of the BPDUs is meaningful. This is because BPDUs from different Regions contain different MST information. The mismatched MST information is ignored by the boundary switches. A large network running MSTP may have more than one MST Region. The CIST of each region forms a common spanning tree. The common spanning tree elects a common Root Bridge. Within each region, a regional Root Bridge is elected. The CIST *External* Root Path Cost is the cost to the common Root Bridge. The CIST *Internal* Root Path Cost is the cost to the regional Root Bridge. The CIST External Root Path Cost is zero for the region containing the common Root Bridge. Figure A.10 illustrates a network with two MST Regions.

Figure A.10 MST Regions

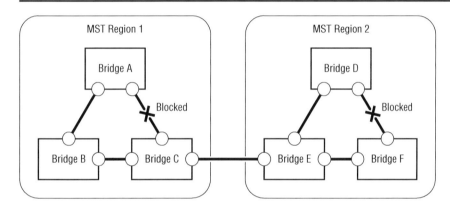

A.3 VPLS Service Loop Prevention with STP

VPLS is an Ethernet bridging service. Customer sites connected to the VPLS form a bridged Ethernet network. As with any other legacy-bridged Ethernet networks, when there are redundant forwarding paths in the network, a loop-prevention mechanism must be in place to create a loop-free forwarding environment. In a VPLS service, there are several ways of eliminating the forwarding loop:

- If the customer network has STP enabled, the service provider only needs to transparently bypass (transparently flood) the customer STP BPDUs, but does not participate in the customer's STP.

- The service provider can enable STP in the VPLS for the customer and ask the customer to bypass (flood) the BPDUs.

- The service provider and customer may both have STP enabled and interoperate with each other.

To successfully implement end-to-end loop prevention, all of the following scenarios must be considered:

- Does the VPLS service have potential forwarding loops inside the VPLS core? If the VPLS uses fully meshed topology with mesh-pseudowires, the VPLS core will be loop-free. If the VPLS uses a hierarchical design with spoke-pseudowires, the forwarding topology must be checked for forwarding loops.
- Does the customer's network have potential forwarding loops?
- When the VPLS connects several customer sites together, could there be a forwarding loop?
- When the customer currently has STP enabled in its infrastructure, should the VPLS participate in STP with the customer? Or should the VPLS transparently flood the BPDUs among the customer sites?
- On the other hand, if the provider wants to enable STP in the VPLS, should the VPLS customer devices pass the BPDU generated from the provider's VPLS through their network?
- The provider's backbone network is shared by many services for many customers. When one VPLS customer's network has a forwarding loop, how can the provider ensure that other services or customers are not affected?

When designing VPLS services, the above questions must be addressed by both the service provider and the customers. Creating a loop-free end-to-end VPLS solution is a joint effort between providers and their customers.

Potential Forwarding Loops in the VPLS Core

The first thing the VPLS service provider must ensure is that the VPLS service implemented in the backbone network is loop-free. There are two types of VPLS topology: fully meshed (discussed in Chapter 11) and hierarchical (discussed in Chapter 12). Regardless of which VPLS design is used, the provider must ensure that the VPLS core does not contain forwarding loops. Figure A.11 illustrates some basic VPLS topologies.

In Figure A.11, the topology on the top left is a fully meshed VPLS (a *flat* design) using mesh-pseudowires only. The other two topologies are Hierarchical VPLS topologies that use mesh-pseudowires and spoke-pseudowires.

Figure A.11 Basic VPLS Core Topologies

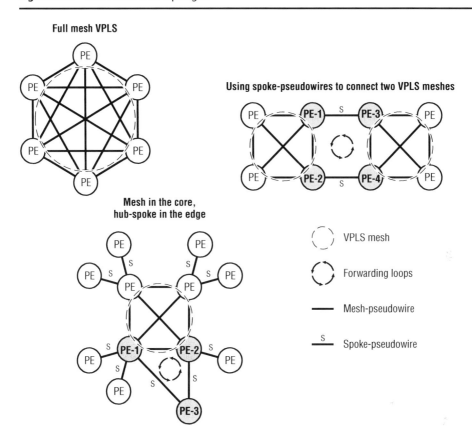

The fully meshed VPLS service is always loop-free inside the VPLS core. This is because a fully meshed VPLS network uses only mesh-pseudowires to connect member PE routers. In addition, mesh-pseudowires respect the Split-Horizon rule when forwarding traffic among member PE routers. The Split-Horizon rule prohibits traffic from forwarding among mesh-pseudowires within the same service instance. As mentioned in Chapter 11, all mesh-pseudowires in one service instance are considered as a single Bridge Port. The VSI does not allow them to exchange traffic. In a VPLS mesh, there is only one forwarding path between any two PE routers — the direct mesh-pseudowire connecting two PE routers. In Figure A.11, the fully meshed VPLS network will never have forwarding loops inside the VPLS. Also, the VPLS mesh portions of the two Hierarchical VPLS (H-VPLS) topologies will not contain forwarding loops. A VPLS mesh can be viewed as a *single Ethernet bridge*, which does not have a loop inside the mesh.

Figure A.12 illustrates the difference between mesh-pseudowire and spoke-pseudowire with respect to forwarding loops. The implementation on the top uses fully meshed mesh-pseudowire, and it is loop-free. The implementation on the bottom uses three spoke-pseudowires, and the forwarding loop is formed.

Note: This is not a design recommendation; it is an example topology for the discussion of forwarding loops.

Figure A.12 Mesh-Pseudowire and Spoke-Pseudowires: Forwarding Loop Possibilities

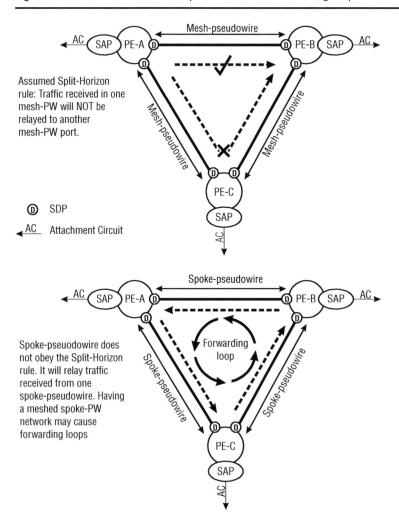

H-VPLS uses spoke-pseudowires to connect PE routers, allowing the possibility of forwarding loops inside the VPLS. This is possible because spoke-pseudowires do not obey the Split-Horizon rule. A VPLS service instance allows spoke-pseudowires to exchange traffic with other mesh-pseudowires and spoke-pseudowires, so that spoke-pseudowires can relay traffic between PE routers, which can create an alternate forwarding path. Whenever spoke-pseudowires are used in a VPLS service, the network design must be reviewed to check for potential forwarding loops inside the VPLS core.

In the three basic VPLS forwarding topologies shown in Figure A.11, the PE routers with the shadowed circles can contain forwarding loops in the VPLS services deployed on them. In the bottom topology (hub-spoke), PE-3 has two spoke-pseudowires connected to PE-2 and PE-1. If both spoke-pseudowires are actively forwarding traffic, there is a forwarding loop. Between PE-1 and PE-2, there are two forwarding paths — PE-1$\longleftrightarrow$ PE-2 (mesh-pseudowire) and PE-1 $\longleftrightarrow$ PE-3 $\longleftrightarrow$PE-2 (two spoke-pseudowires). If PE-1 needs to flood BUM traffic to PE-2 through the mesh-pseudowire, PE-2 floods the BUM traffic to PE-3 over the spoke-pseudowire between them. Then, when PE-3 receives BUM traffic from a spoke-pseudowire, it floods it to all pseudowires (mesh and spoke) except the one on which the traffic is received. Therefore, *PE-3 feeds the BUM traffic back to PE-1.* Similarly, in the third diagram, PE-1, PE-2, PE-3, and PE-4 have a forwarding loop among them if both spoke-pseudowires are actively forwarding traffic.

In the two cases where forwarding loops are possible (mesh-spoke topology, or connecting two VPLS meshes using spoke-pseudowires, indicated in Figure A.12), a loop-prevention mechanism must be implemented among the PE routers to put one spoke-pseudowire into the `blocking` state to prevent it from forwarding traffic (as indicated by the dotted spoke-pseudowire lines). There are several ways to achieve this goal:

- Enable STP within VPLS (all service instances in all member PE routers) to block the redundant spoke-pseudowire.

- Enable STP within mVPLS and use mVPLS to control the forwarding status of the Service Distribution Path (SDP) on which the redundant spoke-pseudowire resides.

- In the second hub-spoke topology, split-horizon groups can be created in PE-3 and associated with both spoke-pseudowires. Thus, the two spoke-pseudowires behave like mesh-pseudowires and do not relay traffic between PE-1 and PE-2 over PE-3.

- Also, in the second hub-spoke topology, the two spoke-pseudowires can be configured using pseudowire redundancy. Therefore, PE-3 understands that the two spoke-pseudowires are used for service dual-homing and keeps only one of them active at any time. The `standby` status of the redundant spoke-pseudowire is also signaled to the peer PE (for example, PE-1), so it does not send traffic over the standby spoke-pseudowire.

> **Note:** The discussion of forwarding loops in customer sites connected by VPLS assumes that the customer's network is Ethernet-bridged. A routed (Layer 3) customer network does not contain forwarding loops. As soon as the traffic enters the customer's network, it is routed to the customer devices. The broadcast domain stops at all attachment circuits. As long as there is no forwarding loop in the VPLS core, the entire solution is loop-free.

To eliminate possible forwarding loops from both the VPLS core and the end-to-end VPLS solution, there are two possible solutions:

- Enable STP in the VPLS core to eliminate forwarding loops inside the VPLS provider's network.
- Interoperate STP with the customer to eliminate forwarding loops formed between the VPLS core and customer sites.

These methods are discussed in detail in the following two sections.

STP in VPLS: Transparent Mode versus Participation Mode

VPLS supports STP customer interoperation using two different modes: *transparent mode* and *participation mode*. In transparent mode, STP is in a `shutdown` state in the VPLS instances in the core. VPLS floods (but does not process) the BPDUs received from customer sites in the same way it floods multicast data traffic. In contrast, in participation mode, STP protocol is enabled in the VPLS core and interoperates with the customer STP to ensure that the end-to-end bridged network is loop-free.

In transparent mode, VPLS treats STP BPDUs received from customer's networks like any other data frame. The VPLS PE does not process the BPDU content and does not distinguish a BPDU frame from other multicast frames. All customer BPDU frames use *protocol multicast group destination MAC addresses*. When the VPLS PE receives a customer BPDU from a SAP, it simply replicates the BPDU and floods the BPDU into the VPLS core to all pseudowires (mesh and spoke) and all other SAPs in the service instances, just like any other BUM traffic. When the remote member PE routers receive the BPDUs from the pseudowires, they perform the same replication and flooding action, respecting the mesh-pseudowire Split-

Horizon rule. Because BPDU content is not changed by VPLS in transparent mode, the STP topology is not aware of the existence of the VPLS service. The VPLS core acts like a transparent switch (or an Ethernet hub). Because the VPLS core does not process BPDUs in transparent mode, the STP protocol in the VPLS service instances is administratively disabled (`shutdown`). There is no STP state machine in the VSIs. Transparent mode is the default mode for all VPLS service instances.

In participation mode, VPLS actively participates in STP with the customer network. It *consumes* BPDUs and *generates* BPDUs. VPLS is involved in the STP elections for Root Bridge, RP, and DP. The STP in the customer network is aware of the VPLS core. It sees BPDUs containing the VPLS core's `bridge-id` and `port-id`. The VPLS core appears to the customer's network like a single bridge with STP enabled. When the VPLS core is in STP participation mode, the STP protocol is administratively enabled in all member PEs' service instances. The VSIs have the STP state machines created. To enable participation mode, the STP protocol must be explicitly enabled in every member PE's service instance.

Compatible STP Protocol Variations in Participation Mode

As mentioned previously, there are many variations of STP. In transparent mode, the type of STP used in a customer's network is irrelevant. Most STP variations use BPDUs with a protocol multicast group destination MAC address of `01-80-2c-xx-xx-xx`. Therefore, they are all flooded by the VPLS core as multicast traffic. Some proprietary STP implementations use other MAC addresses as BPDU destination MAC addresses. In those cases, the BPDUs are flooded by the VPLS as other Ethernet frames with unknown destination MAC addresses.

In participation mode, the type of STP running in the customer network is important, and its compatibility with the STP supported by the connected VPLS service must be checked in the network design phase. The ALSRP VPLS solution supports the following STP variations:

- IEEE 802.1D-2004 (RSTP) (default)
- Comp-dot1w
- IEEE 802.1D-1998 (STP)
- Cisco PVST+

IEEE 802.1D-2004 (new RSTP) is the default protocol running when STP is enabled in a VPLS service instance. When a SAP receives an older version of a BPDU (for example, IEEE 802.1D 1998–STP), it starts to generate the older-version

BPDUs to that SAP. This *fallback* process is on a per-SAP basis and is triggered by the reception of BPDUs. When the fallback process starts in a SAP in the PE router's VPLS service instance, two things happen:

• The PE router generates a reporting event to the system log indicating the STP fallback. If a network management or OAM system is monitoring the status of the VPLS network, it also receives a notification from the PE router.

• The PE router starts a fallback timer. Every time the SAP receives an older-version BPDU from the customer network, the timer resets, and the SAP remains in the fallback state. If the SAP stops receiving the older-version BPDUs for a period longer than the fallback timer, it reverts to the original configured STP variation.

> **Warning:** Sometimes a customer's network contains equipment with incompatible vendor-proprietary STP variations. In this case, use of the VPLS STP participation mode requires caution. If the STP topology is not designed properly, the two STP instances may not interoperate. Each STP instance operates independently, blocking different ports. This may break the end-to-end connectivity and cause service interruption.

A.4 Altered STP Behavior in the VPLS Core

The basic idea of the STP improvement is that *the fully meshed VPLS core is guaranteed to be loop-free, so STP interoperation with customers should never cause any link cuts in the VPLS mesh.* Also in VPLS, STP is deployed on a per-service basis. A provider IP/MPLS VPN backbone can contain many services for different customers. Each VPLS customer has a different service instance in every member PE. Each VPLS service instance in the PE router runs its own STP with its own state machine. In each PE router, every service instance has a VSI to isolate the learning, forwarding, and STP processing from other service instances. Within each VSI, each SAP is a Bridge Port, each spoke-pseudowire is a Bridge Port, and all mesh-pseudowires belong to one Bridge Port. Furthermore, in the VPLS core, all VSIs connected by mesh-pseudowires are one hop away from each other. The STP's behavior is altered in the VSI in the VPLS core.

The first improvement of STP implementation in the VPLS core is the concept of the *Primary Bridge*. The *Primary Bridge* is the one VSI in the VPLS core that is closest to the Root Bridge of the entire network. As in the bridged Ethernet networks, when the VPLS service participates in STP with customer switches, the Root Bridge is elected. If the elected Root Bridge is an Ethernet switch in the customer's network, the Primary Bridge is the VSI with a SAP that has the lowest `Root Path Cost` to the Root Bridge.

If the elected Root Bridge is a VSI in the VPLS core, the same VSI is the Primary Bridge. There is only one elected Root Bridge in an end-to-end VPLS-connected network, regardless of whether or not it is in the VPLS core. In the VPLS core, there is only one Primary Bridge. When the VPLS core interoperates STP with customer switches, it accepts customer BPDUs, performs BPDU comparison, and generates BPDUs if necessary. The Root Bridge for the entire network is elected by the VSIs and customer switches first. Then the Primary Bridge in the VPLS core is elected by the VSIs.

To prevent the VPLS STP participation with the customer from causing link cuts in the VPLS mesh, the *VPLS core STP automatically sets the* `Root Path Cost` *value of the Bridge Port containing all mesh-pseudowires to zero (0)*. In this way, the Bridge Port containing the mesh-pseudowires always has a lower cost than the SAPs connected to the customer and the spoke-pseudowires connected to other member PE routers. Therefore, the VSIs use the mesh-pseudowires to reach the Primary Bridge. Because of the 0 cost, the port containing the mesh-pseudowires on a VSI is always elected to be either the RP or the DP, guaranteeing that the mesh-pseudowires are never blocked by a customer STP. In each VSI, all mesh-pseudowires are all considered *Virtual Core Ports* (VCPs) by the VSI. VCPs are never blocked.

Because of the two enhancements in VPLS STP (Primary Bridge, and 0 cost VCP), each VPLS mesh behaves like a single Ethernet switch in the customer's STP topology. Obviously, there cannot be any blocked ports inside a switch's internal data path. In a VSI, only SAP ports or spoke-pseudowires can be blocked by STP. Therefore, the VPLS mesh-pseudowires are never blocked, whether or not the Root Bridge is within the provider's network. Figure A.13 illustrates the Root Bridge and Primary Bridge election in several scenarios.

Figure A.13 illustrates three examples of STP interoperation between a customer and the VPLS service for that customer.

- In the top scenario, STP is enabled only in the customer devices. The VPLS is in STP transparent mode, flooding BPDUs without processing them. After STP stabilizes, the CE-3's port on the backdoor link is blocked, and the network is loop-free.
- In the middle scenario, STP is enabled in the VPLS, so the VPLS is in participation mode. The VSIs consume and generate BPDUs. The VSI in PE-1 is elected as the Root Bridge, and, of course, it is also the Primary Bridge in

the VPLS core. After STP stabilizes, the CE-3's port on the backdoor link is blocked, and the network is loop-free.

Figure A.13   Root Bridge and Primary Bridge Election

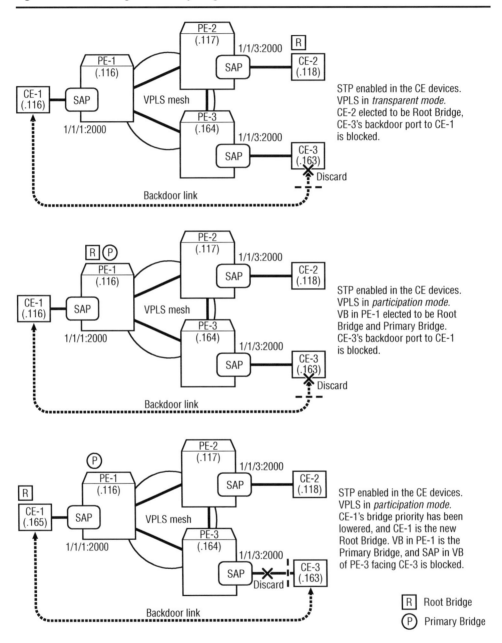

STP enabled in the CE devices. VPLS in *transparent mode.* CE-2 elected to be Root Bridge, CE-3's backdoor port to CE-1 is blocked.

STP enabled in the CE devices. VPLS in *participation mode.* VB in PE-1 elected to be Root Bridge and Primary Bridge. CE-3's backdoor port to CE-1 is blocked.

STP enabled in the CE devices. VPLS in *participation mode.* CE-1's bridge priority has been lowered, and CE-1 is the new Root Bridge. VB in PE-1 is the Primary Bridge, and SAP in VB of PE-3 facing CE-3 is blocked.

R   Root Bridge
P   Primary Bridge

- In the bottom scenario, the VPLS is also in STP participation mode, and CE-1's `Bridge Priority` has been lowered. Therefore, CE-1 becomes the Root Bridge. PE-1 becomes the Primary Bridge in the VPLS core. After STP stabilizes, the SAP in VSI of PE-3 is blocked, and the network is loop-free.

Figure A.14 uses CLI output to illustrate the STP status of a VPLS.

Figure A.14 VPLS Virtual Bridge STP State

The following displays are from the PE-1's VB.
This VB is the Primary Bridge of the service VPLS 5000.

```
A:PE-1# show service id 5000 stp
===============================================================================
Stp info, Service 5000
===============================================================================
Bridge Id           : 80:00.8e:74:ff:00:00:00  Top. Change Count : 7
Root Bridge         : 00:00.8e:a5:ff:00:00:00  Stp Oper State    : Up
Primary Bridge      : This Bridge              Topology Change   : Inactive
Mode                : Rstp                     Last Top. Change  : 0d 00:00:04
Vcp Active Prot.    : Rstp
Root Port           : 2048                     External RPC      : 10
===============================================================================
Stp port info
===============================================================================
Sap
/Sdp/PIP Id    Oper-     Port-     Port-      Port-  Oper-  Link-  Active
               State     Role      State      Num    Edge   Type
Prot.
-------------------------------------------------------------------------------
1/1/1:2000     Up        Root      Forward    2048   False  Pt-pt  Rstp
===============================================================================
```

```
A:PE-1# show service id 5000 stp detail
===============================================================================
Spanning Tree Information
===============================================================================
-------------------------------------------------------------------------------
VPLS Spanning Tree Information
-------------------------------------------------------------------------------
VPLS oper state    : Up                  Core Connectivity : Up
Stp Admin State    : Up                  Stp Oper State    : Up
Mode               : Rstp                Vcp Active Prot.  : Rstp
Bridge Id          : 80:00.8e:74:ff:00:00:00  Bridge Instance Id: 0
Bridge Priority    : 32768               Tx Hold Count     : 6
Topology Change    : Inactive            Bridge Hello Time : 2
Last Top. Change   : 0d 00:00:07         Bridge Max Age    : 20
Top. Change Count  : 7                   Bridge Fwd Delay  : 15
MST region revision: 0                   Bridge max hops   : 20
MST region name    :
Root Bridge        : 00:00.8e:a5:ff:00:00:00
Primary Bridge     : This Bridge
Root Path Cost     : 10                  Root Forward Delay: 15
Rcvd Hello Time    : 2                   Root Max Age      : 20
Root Priority      : 0                   Root Port         : 2048
-------------------------------------------------------------------------------
Spanning Tree    Virtual Core Port (VCP)    Specifics
-------------------------------------------------------------------------------
Mesh Sdp Id      Sdp          Sdp Bind     Mesh Sdp      HoldDown
Awaiting
                 Oper-state   Oper-state   Port-state    Timer
Agreement
-------------------------------------------------------------------------------
117:5000         Up           Up           Forward       Inactive   No
164:5000         Up           Up           Forward       Inactive   No
-------------------------------------------------------------------------------
--- output omitted ---
```

Figure A.14 shows the output of the STP status in the VPLS service instance in PE-1. The output shows that this VSI is the Primary Bridge, and the SAP port (1/1/2:2000) is facing the Root Bridge location. All mesh-pseudowires (VCPs) are operationally up and are forwarding traffic.

STP BPDUs flooded into the VPLS core are VPN-encapsulated, as is other customer data traffic. When the VPLS is in STP transparent mode, the customer switches generate the BPDUs. The VPLS adds the VPN encapsulation, and the SDP adds the transport tunnel encapsulation. Then the BPDUs are transparently carried over the VPLS core to other customer sites. When the VPLS is in STP participation mode, the VSI also generates the BPDUs inside the core. The `bridge-id` fields in the generated BPDUs are set to the `bridge-id` of the originator's VSI (which is the VSI's `Bridge Priority` with the PE router's chassis MAC address). The `port-id` is set to `0x8fff`, which is the VCP.

A.5 Using VPLS STP to Eliminate Customer Forwarding Loops

Figure A.15 illustrates the same VPLS topology discussed in the previous section, with an added scenario: The CE-3 is dual-homed with both PE-2 and PE-3. In this topology, although the VPLS mesh is loop-free, the customer's network contains two redundant forwarding paths, which will create forwarding loops.

Figure A.15 Using STP in a VPLS Service to Eliminate Customer Forwarding Loops

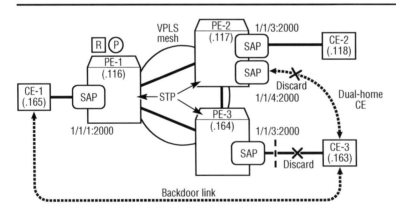

If a customer does not have STP enabled in its network, the provider can enable STP in VPLS to eliminate the forwarding loops. In this case, STP must be enabled in the VPLS core to block the SAPs connected to the customer's redundant forwarding paths. In Figure A.15, STP is enabled in the service instances of three PE routers, and the redundant SAPs in PE-2 and PE-3 are put into the discard state. When the dual-home links fail or the backdoor link fails, the redundant SAPs are put into the forwarding state to restore connectivity.

For the VPLS's STP instance to work in this topology, customer switches can either participate in the STP or transparently flood the BPDUs received from the VPLS. The configuration of the STP in the VPLS is the same as the previous section's configuration in which VPLS is participating in STP with the customer switches: The service provider should enable STP in the VPLS service instance of each PE router. If desired, configure the STP parameters to control the location of the Root Bridge. In this example, because only the VPLS core is running STP, the Root Bridge is a VSI in the VPLS core. The same VSI acts as the Primary Bridge. Figure A.16 illustrates an example of the STP configuration in such a network.

Figure A.16 illustrates the redundant SAPs blocked by the STP in the VPLS service instance, resulting in the end-to-end VPLS being loop-free. However, the solution of using only the provider's VPLS STP instance to prevent forwarding loops works only if the VPLS core is the only portion of the network that contains the redundant paths, so that VPLS STP can find the loops and remove them. If the loop is contained solely in the customer's network, VPLS STP may not eliminate it. The customer must enable STP in its network to eliminate its own loops.

Warning: To keep the VPLS core stable in this type of network, either all PE routers must have STP enabled in their service instances, or all PE routers must have STP disabled. The STP parameters (for example, timers and priorities) can be different in each VSI.

Figure A.16 VPLS Service STP Configuration Example

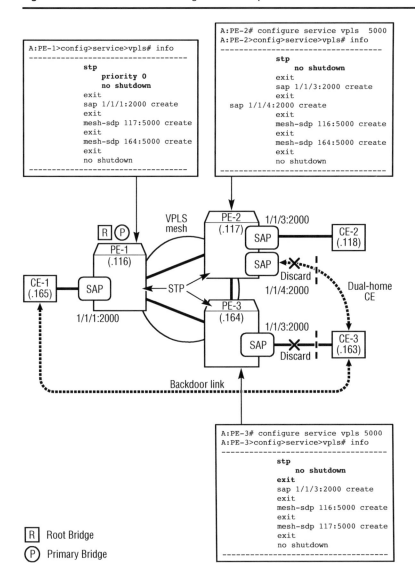

```
A:PE-2# show service id 5000 stp
================================================================================
Stp info, Service 5000
================================================================================
Bridge Id          : 80:01.8e:75:ff:00:00:00   Top. Change Count : 59
Root Bridge        : 00:00.8e:a5:ff:00:00:00   Stp Oper State    : Up
Primary Bridge     : 80:00.8e:74:ff:00:00:00   Topology Change   : Inactive
Mode               : Rstp                       Last Top. Change  : 0d 00:01:59
Vcp Active Prot.   : Rstp
Root Port          : Vcp                        External RPC      : 10
================================================================================
Stp port info
================================================================================
Sap/Sdp/PIP Id     Oper-    Port-       Port-    Port-  Oper-  Link-  Active
                   State    Role        State    Num    Edge   Type   Prot.
--------------------------------------------------------------------------------
1/1/3:2000         Up       Designated  Forward  2048   False  Pt-pt  Rstp
1/1/4:2000         Up       Alternate   Discard  2049   False  Pt-pt  Rstp
================================================================================
```

```
A:PE-3# show service id 5000 stp
================================================================================
Stp info, Service 5000
================================================================================
Bridge Id          : 80:01.8e:a4:ff:00:00:00   Top. Change Count : 48
Root Bridge        : 00:00.8e:74:ff:00:00:00   Stp Oper State    : Up
Primary Bridge     : 00:00.8e:74:ff:00:00:00   Topology Change   : Inactive
Mode               : Rstp                       Last Top. Change  : 0d 00:00:20
Vcp Active Prot.   : Rstp
Root Port          : Vcp                        External RPC      : 0
================================================================================
Stp port info
================================================================================
Sap/Sdp/PIP Id     Oper-    Port-       Port-    Port-  Oper-  Link-  Active
                   State    Role        State    Num    Edge   Type   Prot.
--------------------------------------------------------------------------------
1/1/3:2000         Up       Alternate   Discard  2048   False  Pt-pt  Rstp
================================================================================
```

A.6 Using VPLS STP to Block Redundant Spoke-Pseudowires in H-VPLS

H-VPLS connects some PE routers using spoke-pseudowires. Spoke-pseudowires aggregate the traffic from one mesh to another, or from several spoke locations to the VPLS meshed core. Redundant spoke-pseudowires can be used in either case to eliminate a single-point-of-failure. Spoke-pseudowires do not obey the Split-Horizon rule; they can relay traffic between PE routers. Therefore, redundant spoke-pseudowires in H-VPLS can cause forwarding loops. Deploying STP in the H-VPLS service eliminates forwarding loops by putting the redundant spoke-pseudowires into the discard state. The backup spoke-pseudowire transits to the forwarding state only when the active spoke-pseudowire fails.

Figure A.17 illustrates one implementation of H-VPLS. Two VPLS meshes are joined by a spoke-pseudowire between PE-1 and PE-3. A second spoke-pseudowire between PE-2 and PE-4 improves the network's reliability, but it can cause forwarding loops because there is more than one forwarding path between the four hub-PE routers. Enabling STP in the H-VPLS network blocks the redundant spoke-pseudowire.

Figure A.17 STP Manages H-VPLS Spoke-Pseudowires

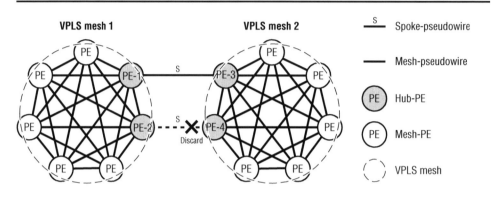

> **Note:** Primary Bridges exist only in the VPLS mesh. If a VPLS instance contains at least one operational mesh-pseudowire (VCP), the VSIs elect a Primary Bridge. VPLS instances that contain only SAP and spoke-pseudowires do not have a Primary Bridge.

A.7 LDP MAC-Flush in STP Convergence

Once the STP in the H-VPLS stabilizes, all redundant spoke-pseudowires are put into the discard state. If a topology change occurs, the active forwarding topology of the H-VPLS may change, and the STP in the H-VPLS converges. For example, in the topology illustrated in Figure A.18, if the physical link between PE-1 and PE-3 fails, STP restores connectivity by transiting the spoke-pseudowire between PE-2 and PE-4 into the forwarding state. This is a topology change (TC) in the H-VPLS. In a regular Ethernet network, a topology change causes the switches to flood TCN BPDUs to the entire network to speed up the MAC aging process. This improves network convergence and reduces the likelihood of the traffic being blackholed.

H-VPLS has a similar mechanism, but instead of sending TCNs BPDUs, the H-VPLS service instance generates LDP Address Withdraw messages with a MAC-list TLV to other PE routers. In VPLS, this message is referred to as a *MAC-flush message*, as described in Chapter 15. Every time a spoke-pseudowire transits from the `discard` state to the `forwarding` state, the local PE's service instance sends a MAC-flush to the far end of the new forwarding spoke-pseudowire. This message notifies the VPLS service instance of the receiving PE router to remove all MAC entries associated with all SAPs and pseudowires, except for the ones associated with the pseudowire from which the MAC-flush is received from its FDB. Therefore, this message is commonly referred to as `flush-all-but-me`.

This process makes sense. A spoke-pseudowire transits to the `forwarding` state, indicating a topology change in the H-VPLS core. This is similar to the case in an Ethernet network when a non-edge port transits to the forwarding state. Therefore, the original FDB of the service instance of the far-end PE router connected to the spoke-pseudowire that just transited to the `forwarding` state is no longer correct — the MAC entries may be associated with the wrong pseudowires. The pseudowire receiving the MAC-flush message is part of the new active forwarding topology; therefore, the MAC addresses associated with this pseudowire must be correct. Details about MAC-flush generation and propagation are discussed in Chapter 15.

A.8 Management VPLS

This section introduces management VPLS (mVPLS), a VPLS service that runs in the VPLS core for management purposes. mVPLS uses STP to determine the forwarding topologies for the user traffic carrying VPLS services it manages.

The previous section introduced the two conditions that require VPLS to use STP to prevent forwarding loops: a multi-homing customer site or a backdoor link, and H-VPLS with spoke-pseudowire redundancy. In both cases, STP must be activated inside the VPLS instance. When many VPLS service instances are present in a VPLS backbone network, running one STP in each of the VPLS service instances consumes a lot of resources. But as mentioned in the previous section, the STP instance can control only the forwarding topology of the VPLS service instance in which it resides. Because VPLS service instances that belong to different VPLS services are isolated by the VSIs, they cannot share the same STP instance.

STP is required when VPLS is deployed in a network that has redundant forwarding paths. If many VPLS service instances are present in the network and they all share a common topology, a mechanism is required to make STP more efficient so that many VPLS service instances can share one STP instance. This is similar to the case of using MSTP to allow multiple VLANs to share the same STP instance. More than one STP instance is required for load balancing on multiple redundant forwarding paths. However, in most cases, the number of STP instances required to build different forwarding topologies in a network is fewer than the number of VPLS service instances deployed in the network.

mVPLS significantly improves STP efficiency in a network with scaled VPLS service deployment. mVPLS does not carry any user data traffic; it only runs STP to determine loop-free forwarding topologies. Each mVPLS also has a management scope, similar to the VLAN-MSTI mapping in MSTP. Regular customer traffic carrying VPLS (also referred to as *user VPLS*, or uVPLS) in the mVPLS's management scope is managed by mVPLS and uses the active forwarding topology built by mVPLS.

The most significant benefits of mVPLS are efficiency and load balancing. Similar to MSTP in the regular Ethernet-bridged network, mVPLS uses a single STP instance running in a single VPLS to manage many customer-serving VPLSs (uVPLSs). In the most efficient network design, the number of STP instances deployed in the network should equal the number of desired forwarding topologies — not the number of VPLS services that require loop-free forwarding paths. The network design should start by determining a layout for *possible forwarding topologies*. The operator can then design the proper mVPLS services based on the available topologies. mVPLS can be deployed in the VPLS core before the uVPLS is deployed. Therefore, when provisioning customer-serving VPLS (uVPLS), the provider can choose one of the pre-controlled forwarding topologies for the uVPLS to use.

Using mVPLS to Eliminate Forwarding Loops in Customer Networks

mVPLS is a VPLS created by the provider for management purposes, and does not carry user data traffic. mVPLS is used with STP enabled from within to build a loop-free forwarding infrastructure for multiple customers serving VPLS to use. The regular VPLS (or H-VPLS) service instances created for carrying customer traffic are called *uVPLS*. mVPLS service instances may exchange or flood STP BPDUs to customer networks.

mVPLS may be deployed in either of the two following scenarios:

- When redundant forwarding paths are caused by multiple VPLS SAPs connected to the customer network. In this case, mVPLS is deployed to manage these SAPs.

- When the H-VPLS service deployed in the network uses redundant pseudowires to connect the VPLS meshes. In this case, mVPLS is deployed to manage the redundant pseudowires.

If the purpose of mVPLS is to remove loops caused by redundant SAPs, it should be deployed only where redundant SAPs are located. Figure A.18 illustrates a scenario in which mVPLS is used with configuration examples of uVPLS and mVPLS.

Figure A.18 shows CE-2 dual-homed to PE-1 and PE-2. This topology can cause forwarding loops for any VPLS using the PE-1, PE-2, CE-2 triangle. Since this triangle is the area mVPLS is managing, mVPLS only needs to be configured in PE-1 and PE-2. *The topology of the mVPLS does not have to be the same as the topologies of the uVPLS services it manages.* These topologies overlap only in the area managed by mVPLS.

Operators should use the following as the procedure to deploy mVPLS in the VPLS core:

1. Determine the area (member PE routers) to be managed by mVPLS and the VLAN range (used by the uVPLS services) on the SAPs.

2. Create the mVPLS. Specify `m-vpls` as the VPLS in the VPLS service instance creation command.

3. Create the mVPLS infrastructure, including the SAPs used by STP to send BPDUs, and create the `manage-vlan-list` in the SAPs. The `manage-vlan-list` contains the range of `vlan-id`s managed by the mVPLS. All VPLS services that have SAPs on the same access port and use the `vlan-id`s within this range are managed by this mVPLS. If mVPLS blocks this SAP, all the SAPs belonging to the uVPLS service instances that share the same access port with the `vlan-id`s in the range are blocked.

Note: The association of mVPLS and the uVPLSs it manages is not explicitly configured. All uVPLS service instances with SAPs in the same physical port that have a `vlan-id` in the management range are automatically associated with the mVPLS service instance and are therefore managed by it.

4. Enable the STP only in the mVPLS. Disable STP in the service instances of all uVPLSs being managed.

5. Create the uVPLS services (either before or after creating the mVPLS). A SAP of a uVPLS that is blocked by the mVPLS is put into a **pruned** state by the mVPLS. The **pruned** state is reflected in the uVPLS SAP port state.

Figure A.18 Using mVPLS to Manage uVPLS to Prevent Forwarding Loops

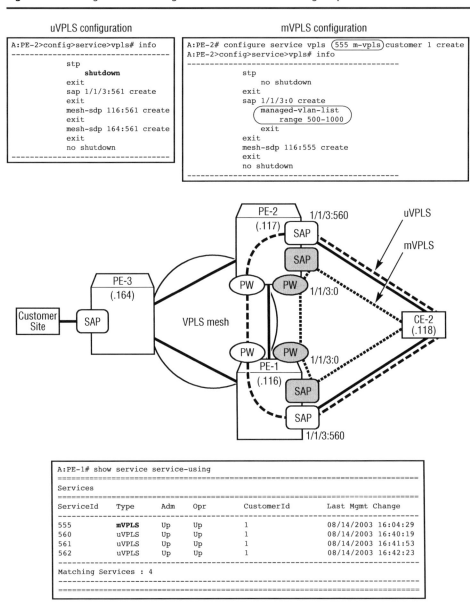

Figure A.18 *(continued)*

```
A:PE-1# configure service vpls  555 m-vpls customer 1 create
A:PE-1>config>service>vpls# info
-----------------------------------------------
                stp
                    no shutdown
                exit
                sap 1/1/3:0 create
                    managed-vlan-list
                        range 500-1000
                    exit
                exit
                mesh-sdp 117:555 create
                exit
                no shutdown
-----------------------------------------------
```

```
A:PE-2# show service id 555 stp
================================================================================
Stp info, Service 555
================================================================================
Bridge Id            : 80:01.8e:75:ff:00:00:00  Top. Change Count : 2
Root Bridge          : 80:01.8e:74:ff:00:00:00  Stp Oper State    : Up
Primary Bridge       : 80:01.8e:74:ff:00:00:00  Topology Change   : Inactive
Mode                 : Rstp                      Last Top. Change  : 0d 00:44:42
Vcp Active Prot.     : Rstp
Root Port            : Vcp                       External RPC      : 0
================================================================================
Stp port info
================================================================================
Sap/Sdp/PIP Id    Oper-     Port-      Port-      Port-  Oper- Link- Active
                  State     Role       State      Num    Edge  Type  Prot.
--------------------------------------------------------------------------------
1/1/3:0           Up        Alternate  Discard    2048   False Pt-pt Rstp
================================================================================
A:PE-2# show service id 560 stp
================================================================================
Inherited Stp State (from mVPLS), Service 560
================================================================================
Sap/Spoke Id      Oper-     Prune- Port-    Mngd by    Mngd by         Mngd by
                  State     State  State    Service    Sap/spoke       MSTI
--------------------------------------------------------------------------------
1/1/3:560         Up        Pruned Discard  555        1/1/3:0         CIST
================================================================================
A:PE-2# show service id 561 stp
================================================================================
Inherited Stp State (from mVPLS), Service 561
================================================================================
Sap/Spoke Id      Oper-     Prune- Port-    Mngd by    Mngd by         Mngd by
                  State     State  State    Service    Sap/spoke       MSTI
--------------------------------------------------------------------------------
1/1/3:561         Up        Pruned Discard  555        1/1/3:0         CIST
================================================================================
A:PE-2# show service id 562 stp
================================================================================
Inherited Stp State (from mVPLS), Service 562
================================================================================
Sap/Spoke Id      Oper-     Prune- Port-    Mngd by    Mngd by         Mngd by
                  State     State  State    Service    Sap/spoke       MSTI
--------------------------------------------------------------------------------
1/1/3:562         Up        Pruned Discard  555        1/1/3:0         CIST
================================================================================
```

The example in Figure A.18 shows an mVPLS with service instances only in PE-1 and PE-2. This is because the mVPLS is used to remove all loops in the PE-2, PE-1, CE-1 triangle for the redundant SAPs connected to CE-1. mVPLS is not implemented on PE-3. In this configuration, the mVPLS manages all uVPLS service instances with SAPs in PE-1 port 1/1/3 or PE-2 1/1/3 with a vlan-id in the range of 500 to 1,000. The SAPs in PE-2 are blocked.

If a VPLS service instance is managed by an mVPLS, it is listed as uVPLS in the show service service-using CLI output. If the VPLS is not managed by any mVPLS configured in the network, it is listed as VPLS in the show service service-using CLI output. Therefore, checking the CLI to determine whether or not a VPLS service instance is listed as uVPLS can help the operator to verify whether or not it is being managed by an mVPLS.

The VLAN range being managed must be carefully planned. For example, a VPLS service instance may have only one SAP in PE-2 1/1/3 using vlan-id 800, but no SAPs in PE-1. mVPLS still blocks the SAP because the port and vlan-id fall into its management scope. This impacts the service of that VPLS. In every PE router, for every mVPLS service instance, mVPLS considers only two things:

- Does the uVPLS have any SAPs that share access ports with the mVPLS?
- Is the vlan-id of the uVPLS's SAP within the managed-vlan-list?

If both answers are *Yes*, mVPLS is associated with that uVPLS and manages that SAP.

mVPLS is also used to balance the load of uVPLS traffic to different links. There are two approaches to achieve this:

- Create more than one mVPLS instance with a different VLAN management scope and forwarding topology.
- Use MSTP in one mVPLS to split the VLANs being managed into separate MSTP instances.

The CLI in Figure A.18 showed an example of PE-1 and PE-2 before using MSTP to load-balance the uVPLS VLANs in port 1/1/3 to two groups. Figure A.19 illustrates an example of using MSTP in mVPLS to load-balance the uVPLS traffic.

With this configuration, access port 1/1/3 in PE-1 is used by uVPLSs using VLANs 500–750. Access port 1/1/3 in PE-2 is used by uVPLSs using VLANs 751–1,000. Therefore, both redundancy and load balancing are achieved by using one mVPLS with two MSTP instances. This is an efficient network design, from both the control plane's perspective (fewer STP instances) and the data plane's perspective (customer traffic load balancing). If any of the access ports fail, both mVPLS instances send the uVPLS traffic to the operational access port.

Figure A.19 Using mVPLS with MSTP for Load Balancing

```
A:PE-1>config>service>vpls# info          A:PE-2>config>service>vpls# info
----------------------------------------  ----------------------------------------
            stp                                       stp
              mode mstp                                 mode mstp
              mst-instance 1 create                     mst-instance 1 create
                  mst-priority 0                            vlan-range 500-750
                  vlan-range 500-750                    exit
              exit                                      mst-instance 2 create
              mst-instance 2 create                         mst-priority 0
                  vlan-range 751-1000                       vlan-range 751-1000
              exit                                      exit
              no shutdown                               no shutdown
          exit                                      exit
          sap 1/1/3:0 create                        sap 1/1/3:0 create
              managed-vlan-list                         managed-vlan-list
                  range 500-1000                            range 500-1000
              exit                                      exit
          exit                                      exit
          mesh-sdp 117:555 create                   mesh-sdp 117:555 create
          exit                                      exit
          mesh-sdp 164:555 create                   mesh-sdp 164:555 create
          exit                                      exit
          no shutdown                               no shutdown
----------------------------------------  ----------------------------------------
```

Using mVPLS to Eliminate Forwarding Loops in H-VPLS with Spoke-Pseudowire Redundancy

The previous section discussed using mVPLS to block SAPs so that uVPLS prevents forwarding loops caused by redundant connections to the customer sites. When a network's backbone has a redundant topology, management H-VPLS (mHVPLS) can be deployed to control the spoke-pseudowire redundancy loop prevention and load balancing for user H-VPLS (uHVPLS) service instances. This type of mVPLS is called *mHVPLS* because it is mVPLS with a hierarchical topology.

Recall that mVPLS for SAP redundancy manages uVPLS service instances using a manage-vlan-list in its SAP configurations. If the SAP of the uVPLS uses the same access port and the vlan-id is in the range of the list, it is managed by the mVPLS.

mHVPLS uses a different approach to managing redundant pseudowires for uHVPLS. One mHVPLS manages spoke-pseudowires for many uHVPLS service instances. Spoke-pseudowires in uHVPLS share the same SDP. The mHVPLS manages the SDP shared by these spoke-pseudowires. If the spoke-pseudowires use redundant SDPs, the mHVPLS blocks the redundant SDPs and leaves only one SDP in a forwarding state. Therefore, all uVPLS service instances that have the spoke-pseudowires share the SDP that is in the discard state. Figure A.20 illustrates a typical scenario in which load balancing is achieved by having more than one mHVPLS instance in the network.

Figure A.20   mVPLS Usage: Loop Prevention and Load Balancing Using H-VPLS

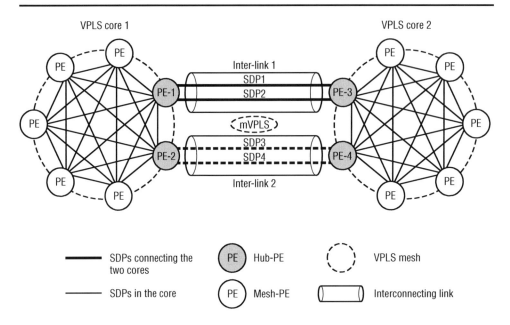

Figure A.20 shows two VPLS core networks containing meshed SDPs. They are joined by two common links, one between PE-1 and PE-3, the other between PE-2 and PE-4. This is the network's backbone infrastructure. Assume that several H-VPLS services are deployed in the network. Each H-VPLS service has two VPLS meshes in each core, and the two meshes are connected by redundant spoke-pseudowires. STP can be enabled in every H-VPLS service to prevent forwarding loops by blocking one of the spoke-pseudowires. However, this method is not efficient if there are many H-VPLS services. The backbone network in Figure A.20 can have only two *possible* forwarding topologies: two meshes connected by inter-link-1, or two meshes connected by inter-link-2. Therefore, the operator can create two mHVPLS services, each with different STP parameters, so that mHVPLS prefers to use inter-link-1, and the other mHVPLS prefers to use inter-link-2. The following list describes this approach in detail:

1.   Create two SDPs in each inter-link. When mHVPLS puts one spoke-pseudowire into the `discard` state, the entire SDP to which the spoke-pseudowire binds is in the `discard` state. No VPLS service instances can use that SDP to forward traffic until mHVPLS unblocks it. Therefore, if load balancing is desired, two separate SDPs must be created over the

same physical link. If one mVPLS blocks one SDP, the other SDP can still be used by the other mVPLS or regular VPLS services.

2. Next, create two mHVPLS service instances in every interconnecting PE router: PE-1, PE-2, PE-3, and PE-4. The mHVPLS contains only PE routers relevant to the topology it manages. mHVPLS does not require the same topology as the uHVPLS it manages. PE routers not connected to the inter-link SDPs are not involved in the mHVPLS. In the example in Figure A.20, the two mHVPLS services prefer to use different interconnecting SDP tunnels:

   2a. One mHVPLS uses the spoke-pseudowires bound to SDP-1 and SDP-3. This mHVPLS prefers SDP-1 (top) and blocks SDP-3 after its STP stabilizes. When SDP-3 is blocked by this mHVPLS, no other VPLS can use this SDP to forward traffic.

   2b. One mHVPLS uses the spoke-pseudowires bound to SDP-2 and SDP-4. This mHVPLS prefers SDP-4 (bottom) and blocks SDP-2 after its STP stabilizes. SDP-2 cannot forward VPLS traffic until the mHVPLS unblocks it.

Note: When an SDP is blocked by an mVPLS's STP, the discard state applies only to VPLS services. Other services such as Virtual Private Wire Service (VPWS) and L3 VPRN can still create spoke-pseudowires associated with this SDP and transmit traffic.

3. Deploy multiple uHVPLS services with different forwarding path preferences (now that the two mHVPLS services are provisioned and their STP instances are managing the SDPs):

   3a. Some uHPVLS services bind their spoke-pseudowires to SDP-1 and SDP-3, using the top link as the primary path, and the bottom link as a backup path.

   3b. Other uHPVLS services bind their spoke-pseudowires to SDP-2 and SDP-4, using the bottom link as the primary path, and the top link as a backup path.

Therefore, the two mHVPLS services manage multiple uHVPLS services, all of which are loop-free and have redundancy. Also, their traffic is distributed between the two inter-links. This is an optimal network design. Figure A.21 illustrates a configuration example of mHVPLS.

Figure A.21 mHVPLS Load-Balancing Configuration Example

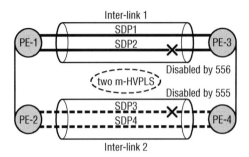

```
A:PE-1# configure service sdp 1 mpls create
A:PE-1>config>service>sdp# info
----------------------------------------------
            far-end 10.0.0.117
            lsp "to-117"
            keep-alive
                shutdown
            exit
            no shutdown
----------------------------------------------
A:PE-1# configure service sdp 2 mpls create
A:PE-1>config>service>sdp# info
----------------------------------------------
            far-end 10.0.0.117
            lsp "to-117"
            keep-alive
                shutdown
            exit
            no shutdown
----------------------------------------------
```

```
A:PE-1# configure service vpls  555 m-vpls customer 1 create
A:PE-1>config>service>vpls# info
----------------------------------------------
            stp
                priority 100
                no shutdown
            exit
            spoke-sdp 1:555 create
            exit
            mesh-sdp 100:555 create
            exit
            no shutdown
----------------------------------------------
A:PE-1# configure service vpls  556 m-vpls customer 1 create
A:PE-1>config>service>vpls# info
----------------------------------------------
            stp
                no shutdown
            exit
            spoke-sdp 2:555 create
            exit
            mesh-sdp 100:555 create
            exit
            no shutdown
----------------------------------------------
```

```
A:PE-2# configure service sdp 3 mpls create
A:PE-2>config>service>sdp# info
----------------------------------------------
            far-end 10.0.0.118
            lsp "to-118"
            keep-alive
                shutdown
            exit
            no shutdown
----------------------------------------------
A:PE-2# configure service sdp 4 mpls create
A:PE-2>config>service>sdp# info
----------------------------------------------
            far-end 10.0.0.118
            lsp "to-118"
            keep-alive
                shutdown
            exit
            no shutdown
----------------------------------------------
```

```
A:PE-2# configure service vpls  555 m-vpls customer 1 create
A:PE-2>config>service>vpls# info
----------------------------------------------
            stp
                no shutdown
            exit
            spoke-sdp 3:555 create
            exit
            mesh-sdp 100:555 create
            exit
            no shutdown
----------------------------------------------
A:PE-2# configure service vpls  556 m-vpls customer 1 create
A:PE-2>config>service>vpls# info
----------------------------------------------
            stp
                priority 100
                no shutdown
            exit
            spoke-sdp 4:555 create
            exit
            mesh-sdp 100:555 create
            exit
            no shutdown
----------------------------------------------
```

Figure A.21 is an example of configuring mHVPLS for load balancing, showing the configuration of Routers PE-1 and PE-2. PE-3 and PE-4 have similar configurations (the only difference is the value of the `stp priority` in mVPLS). In both PE routers, two SDPs are created to connect the far-end PE router. mVPLS 555 uses SDP-1 (in PE-1) and SDP-3 (in PE-2) and prefers SDP-1 (by setting the STP `Bridge Priority` of mVPLS 555 to the lower value of 100 in PE-1). mVPLS 556 uses SDP-2 and SDP-4 and prefers SDP-4 (by setting the STP `Bridge Priority` of mVPLS 556 to the lower value of 100 in PE-2).

Appendix

B

RFC and IEEE Standards

RFC 791, *Internet Protocol.*

RFC 1332, *The PPP Internet Protocol Control.*

RFC 1701, *Generic Routing Encapsulation (GRE).*

RFC 1997, *BGP Community Attributes.*

RFC 2370, *Traffic Engineering (TE) Extension to OSPF Version 2.*

RFC 2401, *Security Architecture for the Internet Protocol.*

RFC 2427, *Multiprotocol Encapsulation over Frame Relay.*

RFC 2597, *Assured Forwarding PHB Group.*

RFC 2661, *Layer Two Tunneling Protocol (L2TP).*

RFC 2684, *Multiprotocol Encapsulation over ATM Adaptation Layer 5.*

RFC 2747, *RSVP Cryptographic Authentication.*

RFC 2784, *Generic Routing Encapsulation (GRE).*

RFC 2858, *BGP-4 Multiprotocol Extensions.*

RFC 2961, *RSVP Refresh Overhead Reduction Extensions.*

RFC 3031, *Multiprotocol Label Switching Architecture.*

RFC 3032, *MPLS Label Stacking.*

RFC 3107, *Carrying Label Information in BGP-4.*

RFC 3209, *RSVP-TE: Extension to RSVP for LSP Tunnels.*

RFC 3210, *Applicability Statement for Extensions to RSVP for LSP-Tunnels.*

RFC 3446, *Anycast Rendezvous Point (RP) Mechanism Using Protocol Independent Multicast (PIM) and Multicast Source Discovery Protocol (MSDP).*

RFC 3550, *RTP: A Transport Protocol for Real-Time Applications.*

RFC 3569, *An Overview of Source Specific Multicast (SSM).*

RFC 3630, *Traffic Engineering (TE) Extensions to OSPF Version 2.*

RFC 3768, *Virtual Router Redundancy Protocol (VRRP).*

RFC 3784, *Intermediate System to Intermediate System (IS-IS) Extensions for Traffic Engineering (TE).*

RFC 3916, *Requirements for Pseudo-wire Emulation Edge-to-Edge (PWE3).*

RFC 3985, *Pseudo Wire Edge-to-Edge (PWE3) Architecture.*

RFC 4023, *Encapsulating MPLS in IP or Generic Routing Encapsulation (GRE).*

RFC 4026, *Provider Provisioned Virtual Private Network (VPN) Terminology.*

RFC 4090, *Fastreroute Extension to RSVP-TE for LSP Tunnels*.

RFC 4203, *OSPF Extension in Support of Generalized Multi-Protocol Label Switching (GMPLS)*.

RFC 4205, *ISIS Extension in Support of Generalized Multi-Protocol Label Switching (GMPLS)*.

RFC 4271, *A Border Gateway Protocol 4 (BGP-4)*.

RFC 4360, *BGP Extended Communities Attribute*.

RFC 4364 (formerly RFC 2547bis), *BGP/MPLS IP Virtual Private Network (VPNs)*.

RFC 4379, *Detecting Multi-Protocol Label Switching (MPLS) Data Plane Failures*.

RFC 4385, *Pseudowire Emulation Edge to Edge (PWE3) Control Word for Use over an MPLS PSN*.

RFC 4446, *IANA Allocations for Pseudowire Edge to Edge Emulation*.

RFC 4447, *Pseudowire Setup and Maintenance Using Label Distribution Protocol*.

RFC 4448, *Encapsulation Methods for Transport Ethernet over MPLS networks*.

RFC 4461, *Signaling Requirements for Point-to-Multipoint Traffic-Engineered MPLS Label Switched Paths (LSPs)*.

RFC 4553, *Structure-Agnostic Time Division Multiplexing (TDM) over Packet (SAToP)*.

RFC 4577, *OSPF as the Provider/Edge Protocol for BGP/MPLS IP Virtual Private Networks (VPNs)*.

RFC 4601 (formerly RFC 2362), *Protocol Independent Multicast–Sparse Mode (PIM-SM) Protocol Specification (revised)*.

RFC 4604, *Using Internet Group Management Protocol version 3 (IGMPv3) and Multicast Listener Discovery Protocol Version 2 (MLDPv2) for Source Specific Multicast*.

RFC 4605, *Internet Group Management Protocol (IGMP)/Multicast Listener Discovery (MLD)–Based Multicast Forwarding, IGMP/MLD Proxying*.

RFC 4619, *Encapsulation Methods for Transporting Frame Relay over Multiprotocol Label Switching (MPLS) Networks*.

RFC 4623, *Pseudo Wire Emulation Edge-to-Edge (PWE3) Fragmentation and Reassembly*.

RFC 4665, *Service Requirements for Layer 2 Provider Provisioned Virtual Networks*.

RFC 4684, *Constrained Route Distribution for Border Gateway Protocol/Multiprotocol Label Switching (BGP/MPLS) Internet Protocol (IP) Virtual Private Networks (VPNs)*.

RFC 4717, *Encapsulation Methods for Transporting ATM over Multiprotocol Label Switching (MPLS) Networks*.

RFC 4761, *Virtual Private LAN Services (VPLS) Using BGP for Auto-Discovery and Signaling*.

RFC 4762, *Virtual Private LAN Services (VPLS) Using Label Distribution Protocol (LDP) Signaling*.

RFC 4875, *Extension to Resource Reservation Protocol–Traffic Engineering (RSVP-TE) for Point-to-Multipoint TE label Switched Paths (LSPs)*.

RFC 5015, *Bidirectional Protocol Independent Multicast (BIDIR-PIM)*.

RFC 5085, *Pseudowire Virtual Circuit Connectivity Verification (VCCV): A Control Channel for Pseudowires*.

RFC 5086, *Structure-Aware Time Division Multiplexed (TDM) Circuit Emulation Service over Packet Switched Network (CESoPSN)*.

IEEE 802.1ad-2005, *Provider Bridges*.

IEEE 802.1ag, *Continuity Check Messages*.

IEEE 802.1ah/D4.1, *Virtual Bridged Local Area Networks–Amendment 6: Provider Backbone Bridges*.

IEEE 802.1ak/D8.0, *Virtual Bridged Local Area Networks–Amendment 7: Multiple Registration Protocol*.

IEEE 802.1d-2004, *IEEE Standard for Local and metropolitan area networks Media Access Control (MAC) Bridges*.

IEEE 802.3ah, *Ethernet in the First Mile*.

Glossary

3G *3rd Generation* The third generation of mobile communication systems.

AAA *Authentication, Authorization, and Accounting* Authentication verifies the user's identity. Authorization verifies, for example, the services that can be accessed or the levels of service quality. Accounting bills based on items such as time, data volume, and applications used.

AAL *ATM Adaptation Layer* Protocol used by ATM to segment and reassemble data for insertion into an ATM cell; also performs error checking and correction.

ABR *Area Border Router* An ABR is a router on the edge of one or more OSPF areas, and it connects the OSPF areas to the backbone network. ABRs belong to both the OSPF area and the backbone area.

AC *Attachment Circuit* The connection between the Customer Edge (CE) node and the Provider Edge (PE) node, transporting native format customer traffic.

ACL *Access Control List* An access control list, also known as a *filter policy*, is a template applied to a service or port to control ingress or egress network traffic based on IP and MAC matching criteria. Filters are applied to services to examine packets that enter or exit a SAP or network interface. An

ACL policy can be used on multiple interfaces. The same filter can apply to ingress and egress traffic.

AD *Auto Discovery* A mechanism to use BGP to discover VPLS membership information.

AF *Assured Forwarding* AF is an IP forwarding behavior that minimizes long-term local congestion events while allowing short-term burst traffic. It offers a high level of assurance that each packet will be delivered, as long as the traffic conforms to a given service profile.

AI *Attachment Identifier* The identifier used by one side of the pseudowire forwarder to identify the remote side forwarder.

AIS *Alarm Indication Signal* An AIS is a code sent downstream in a digital network to indicate that a traffic-related defect has been detected. It is also known as an *RAI* or *yellow alarm*.

Apipe *ATM pipe* A type of VLL service that provides a point-to-point ATM service between users who connect to Alcatel-Lucent 7750 SR nodes in an IP/MPLS network directly or through an ATM access network. One endpoint of an Apipe uses ATM encapsulation, and the other endpoint uses ATM or frame relay encapsulation. Also known as an ATM VLL service.

APS *Automatic Protection System* The capability of a transmission system to detect a failure on a working facility and switch to a protection facility to recover the traffic, thus increasing overall system reliability.

ARP *Address Resolution Protocol* A protocol within TCP/IP that maps IP addresses to Ethernet MAC addresses. TCP/IP requires ARP for use with Ethernet.

AS *Autonomous System* An AS is a collection of routers under one administrative entity that cooperates by using a common IGP (such as OSPF).

ASBR *Autonomous System Border Router* In OSPF, an ASBR is a router that exchanges information with devices from other ASs. ASBRs are also used to import routing information about RIP, direct, or static routes from non-OSPF attached interfaces.

ATM *Asynchronous Transfer Mode* ATM is the international standard for cell switching. It employs 53-byte cells as a basic unit of transfer. ATM networks can carry traffic for multiple service types (for example, voice, video, and data).

BA *Behavior Aggregate* A type of traffic classifier, uses a pre-marked DSCP value solely as a criterion to classify data traffic into different forwarding classes (FC).

BCP *Bridging Control Protocol* A protocol that configures, enables, and disables the bridge protocol modules on both ends of a point-to-point link.

BFD *Bidirectional Forwarding Detection* BFD is a fault diagnostic method that functions over media that normally do not support fault detection, such as Ethernet and MPLS.

BGP *Border Gateway Protocol* BGP is an IETF standard EGP used to propagate routing information between autonomous systems.

BPDU *Bridged Protocol Data Unit* BPDU is the frame that LAN bridges supporting the 802.1D spanning tree protocol use to communicate with each other.

BUM *Broadcast, Unknown unicast, Multicast* The acronym for all Layer 2 Ethernet multipoint traffic. In a standard transparent bridging system, by default, the BUM traffic will be flooded to all bridge ports in the bridge group, assuming the Split-Horizon rule.

CBP *Customer Backbone Port* In PBB-VPLS, the B-component port connecting to the I-component is called CBP.

CE *Customer Edge* A device with the functionality needed on the customer premises to access provider-provisioned services.

CES *Circuit Emulation Services* A device function that enables the encapsulation of TDM frames in protocol packets that are tunneled through a core network.

CFM *Connectivity Fault Management* CFM is an Ethernet OAM capability for testing network connectivity at Layer 2. CFM allows service providers or network operators to verify and isolate link and node faults on a bridged network. CFM is specified in the standard IEEE 802.1ag.

CIR *Committed Information Rate* The CIR is the guaranteed minimum rate of throughput between two end-user devices over a network, such as a Frame-Relay Network, under normal operating circumstances. This rate, measured in bits or kb/s, is used in congestion control procedures.

CLI *Command-Line Interface* The CLI is an interface that allows the user to interact with the operating system by typing alphanumeric commands and optional parameters at a command prompt. UNIX and DOS provide CLIs.

CoS *Class of Service* CoS is the degree of importance assigned to traffic. There are standard and premium classes of services. During queuing and forwarding, service points give preferential treatment to traffic that originates on elements configured for premium CoS.

CPE *Customer Premises Equipment* Customer-owned telecommunications equipment at customer premises used to terminate or process information from the public network.

CPM *Control Processing Module* A CPM is a module in a device such as the Alcatel-Lucent 7750 SR that uses hardware filters to perform traffic management and queuing functions that protect the control plane.

CSPF *Constrained Shortest Path First* CSPF is a component of constraint-based routing that uses a TED to find the shortest path through an MPLS domain that meets established constraints. The ingress router determines the physical path for each LSP by applying the CSPF algorithm to the TED information. Input to the CSPF algorithm includes topology link-state information learned from the IGP, LSP administrative attributes, and network resource attributes that are carried by IGP extensions and stored in the TED.

Demux Short for *de-multiplexer* The MPLS network uses a pseudowire multiplexer to aggregate multiple PW traffic into the service tunnel, then at the receiving PE, uses the de-multiplexer to spread them to different customer sites.

DLCI *Data Link Connection Identifier* A DLCI identifies a DLC. DLCIs must be unique on a frame stream but not across the network.

All frames that have the same DLCI and that are carried in the same frame stream are associated with the same logical connection.

DoS *Denial of Service* A DoS attack is an incident in which a user or organization is deprived of the services of a resource that they would normally expect to have access to.

DS *Differentiated Service* A method for providing differentiated CoS for Internet traffic. DS supports various types of IP applications.

DSCP *Differentiated Service Code Point* A 6-bit value encoded in the type-of-service field of an IP packet header. It identifies the CoS that the packet should receive.

ECMP *Equal Cost Multiple Path* A method of distributing traffic to multiple destinations over several equivalent paths.

EF *Expedited Forwarding* EF is an IP forwarding behavior that builds a low-loss, low-latency, low-jitter, assured-bandwidth, end-to-end service. EF is similar to Virtual Leased Line.

EFM *Ethernet in the First Mile* EFM is a set of copper- and fiber-based access technologies that are based on Ethernet packet transport. Refers to the collection of technologies being standardized by the IEEE to deliver Ethernet to the end user.

ET *Explicit Tracking* A feature in VPLS that is enabled when all PIM CE routers in the VPLS instance advertise Tracking support in their PIM Hello message.

FEC *Forwarding Equivalent Class* A group of packets that are forwarded in the same manner, for example, over the same path, with the same forwarding treatment.

FR *Frame-Relay* A standard for high-speed data communication that offers transmission speeds of at least 2.048 Mbps. The main application of FR is LAN interconnection.

FRR *Fast Reroute* MPLS failure protection scheme taking advantage of MPLS label stack function. Pre-signaled bypass tunnels or detour paths will protect the node/link failure in the primary path. RFC 4090.

GRE *Generic Routing Encapsulation* A protocol for the encapsulation of an arbitrary network-layer protocol over another arbitrary network-layer protocol.

HDLC *High-level Data Link Control* HDLC is an ISO standard for serial data communication. It is a family of bit-oriented protocols providing frames of information with address, control, and frame check sequence fields. It is considered a superset of several other protocols such as SDLC, LAP, LAPB, LAPD.

HQoS *Hierarchical Quality of Service* The functionality of being able to configure Quality of Service policies over a service-based hierarchical infrastructure. HQoS provides the ability to perform rate limiting across multiple queues from multiple SAPs.

IB-PE *Instance Backbone–Provider Edge* The router in the PBB network that contains both I-VPLS instances and B-VPLS instances, acting as the interconnecting point of the Backbone domain and the customer domain. The B-VPLS instance and the I-VPLS instance use an internal link to pass through traffic.

IEEE *Institute of Electrical and Electronics Engineers* The IEEE is a worldwide engineering publishing and standards-making body. It is the organization responsible for defining many of the standards used in the computer, electrical, and electronics industries.

IES *Internet Enhanced Service* IES is a routed connectivity service in which a host communicates with an IP router interface to send and receive Internet traffic. An IES has one or more logical IP router interfaces, each with a SAP that acts as the access point to the network. IES allows customer-facing IP interfaces to participate in the same routing instance that is used for core network routing. The IP addressing scheme for a customer must be unique among the provider addressing schemes in the network and possibly in the entire Internet.

IETF *Internet Engineering Task Force* The IETF is the organization that provides the coordination of standards and specification development for TCP/IP networking.

IGP *Interior Gateway Protocol* Routing protocol(s) used inside an autonomous system (AS) to exchange internal IP reachability information. The most common IGPs are OSPF, IS-IS, and RIP. Static routes are also considered an IGP type of protocol.

IMA *Inverse Multiplexing Access* IMA is an algorithm that provides modular bandwidth for user access to ATM networks over multiple links.

IP *Internet Protocol* IP is part of the TCP/IP family of protocols that describe the software that tracks the Internet address of nodes, routes outgoing messages, and recognizes messages. IP is used in gateways to connect networks at OSI network Level 3 and higher.

IPCP *IP Control Protocol* A protocol that establishes and configures IP over PPP. Elements of IPCP include packet encapsulation, code fields, and time-outs.

IPSec *IP Security* An IETF network layer security standard that is used to encrypt and authenticate IP packet data.

IPTV *IP Television* The delivery of video services over an end-to-end IP infrastructure. IPTV can include various classes of video services including video on demand, broadcast TV, video conferencing, and mobile video.

IS-IS *Intermediate System to Intermediate System* IS-IS is an ISO standard link-state routing protocol. Integrated IS-IS is an extension that allows IS-IS to be used for route determination in IP networks.

ITU *International Telecommunication Union* Standards organization that develops international telecommunications recommendations.

IWF *Inter Working Function* IWF is a translation of high-level protocols, such as Frame-Relay and ATM, between transmission media. IWF makes it possible to transmit data from one type of network to another.

L2TP *Layer 2 Tunneling Protocol* L2TP allows L2 PDUs to tunnel through a network.

LACP *Link Aggregation Control Protocol* An IEEE specification (802.3ad) that allows you to bundle several physical ports together to form a single logical channel.

LAG *Link Aggregation Group* A LAG increases the bandwidth available between two nodes by grouping up to eight ports into one logical link. The aggregation of multiple physical links allows for load sharing and offers seamless redundancy. If one of the links fails, traffic is re-distributed over the remaining links. Up to eight links can be supported in a single LAG, and up to 64 LAGs can be configured on a node.

LAN *Local Area Network* A LAN is a network that operates within a limited geographical area, usually confined to a single floor, building, or group of buildings. It connects a variety of data devices, such as PCs, servers, and printers. Communication between devices is at a very high data rate, between 1 and 100 Mbps.

LDP *Link Distribution Protocol* An MPLS dynamic signaling protocol exchanging label allocation information between MPLS routers. RFC 3036.

LER *Label Egress Router* The MPLS router located in the ingress/egress edge of the MPLS core. An LER should be capable of PUSH and POP MPLS labels.

LFI *Link Fragmentation and Interleaving* LFI interleaves high-priority traffic within a stream of fragmented lower-priority traffic. LFI helps avoid excessive delays to high-priority, delay-sensitive traffic over a low-speed link.

LOF *Loss of Frame* LOF is an alarm condition indicating that the framing of the transmission or ATM layer has been lost.

LOS *Loss of Signal* A condition at the receiver or a maintenance signal transmitted in the physical overhead, indicating that the receiving equipment has lost the received signal.

LSA *Link State Advertisement* Message of the OSPF routing protocol that informs about network topology changes.

LSP *Label Switched Path* LSPs support MPLS functionality and allow network operators to perform traffic engineering. Network operators can use the 5620 NM to configure and manage unidirectional LSPs.

LSR *Label Switch Router* An LSR is an MPLS node that runs MPLS control protocols and is capable of forwarding packets based on labels. An MPLS node may also be capable of forwarding native Layer 3 packets.

LSU *Link State Update* LSU is the type of routing information packet that the LS router uses to inform the rest of the network about its own edges.

MA *Maintenance Association* An MA is a set of MEPs, each configured with the same ID and Maintenance Domain (MD) level.

MAC *Media Access Control* The IEEE sublayer in a LAN that controls access to the shared medium by LAN-attached devices.

MAN *Metropolitan Area Network* A telecommunications network that covers a geographic area such as a city or suburb.

MD *Maintenance Domain* An MD is a network or part of a network that is managed using the CFM 802.1ag protocol. Each MD is provisioned with a set of MAs.

MEP *Maintenance association End Point* In a CFM-enabled network, MEPs can be any SAP or SDP binding in a service and associated to a MA. A set of MEPs configured with the same MA ID defines an MA. CFM tests detect connectivity failures between any pair of local and remote MEPs in a MA.

MF *Multi-Field* A type of traffic classifier; uses five-tuple (source IP address, source port number, destination IP address, destination port number, and protocol-id) as criteria to classify data traffic into different forwarding classes (FC).

MHF *MIP Half-Function* In a CFM-enabled network MIP half-function objects allow MIPs to be recognized as MIPs on one MD level and MEPs on a higher level.

MIP *Maintenance domain Intermediate Point* In a CFM-enabled network a MIP is an intermediate point between two MEPs and consists of two MHFs.

MMRP *Multiple MAC Registration Protocol* An application of MRP (Multiple Registration Protocol), which allows MAC registration.

MP-BGP *Multi-Protocol Border Gateway Protocol* The extension of the original BGP protocol to support multiple address families, to carry routing information for applications like VPRN, Multicast, and the like.

MPLS *Multi Protocol Label Switching* MPLS is a technology in which forwarding decisions are based on fixed-length labels inserted between the data link layer and network layer headers to increase forwarding performance and flexibility in path selection.

MSTP *Multiple Spanning Tree Protocol* An extension of RSTP that allows different spanning trees to coexist on the same Ethernet switched network.

MTU *Maximum Transmission Unit* The largest data packet size allowed in the path or interface.

MTU-s *Multi Tenant Unit – switch* The network element located in the edge of the service provider network, typically in a multi tenant building or residential area. The MTU-s mainly functions as switching equipment, and has a 10/100 user port facing the end customer and a GigE uplink to the service provider's core network.

Mux Short for *multiplexer* The MPLS network uses pseudowire multiplexer to aggregate multiple PW traffic into the service tunnel, then at the receiving PE, uses the de-multiplexer to spread them to different customer sites.

mVPLS *management VPLS* The VPLS instance created for a service provider to pass spanning tree information to build forwarding topology to manage multiple user VPLS instances.

MVR *Multicast VLAN Registration* MVR allows a single multicast VLAN to be shared in a network while subscriber hosts remain in separate VLANs. This mechanism allows the continuous distribution of multicast streams in the multicast VLAN and bars hosts from receiving streams to which they are not entitled. MVR and IGMP snooping are used on 7250 SAS and Telco devices to provide multicast BTV services.

NSF *Non-Stop Forwarding* A high-availability method achieved by separating the control plane and data plane. The data plane stores routing information and continuously forwards data while the control plane is down. May cause blackholes or routing loops. Notification of peering node to keep sending traffic while the control plane stops responding. Also called *graceful-restart*.

NSR *Non-Stop Routing* Non-stop routing prevents the outage of the control plane of a router due to the introduction of fault tolerance.

NTP *Network Time Protocol* NTP achieves standardized time by synchronizing the node time to servers that have access to accurate time standards, such as satellite-based GPSs or atomic clocks located on the Internet.

OAM *Operation, Administration, and Maintenance* OAM refers to a group of network management functions that provide network fault indication, performance information, and data and diagnosis functions. OAM includes network maintenance features such as connectivity verification, alarm surveillance, continuity checking, and performance monitoring.

OSPF *Open Shortest Path First* Dynamic routing protocol that responds quickly to network topology changes. As a successor to RIP, it uses an algorithm that builds and calculates the shortest path to all known destinations.

PBB *Provider Backbone Bridge* IEEE 802.1ah-2008 is a set of architecture and protocols for transporting of a customer Ethernet network over a service provider's Ethernet network while retaining the customer VLAN tagging.

PDU *Protocol Data Unit* PDU is the unit of data in the OSI model. It contains both protocol-control information and user data from the layer above and allows the two processes to coordinate interactions.

PE *Provider Edge* The name of the device or set of devices at the edge of the provider network with the functionality that is needed to interface with the customer and with the MPLS network. A PE can be a router or a switch. All the MPLS tunnels are set up and terminated in the PE. All VPN functionalities reside in the PE.

PHB *Per Hop Behavior* In the IETF Differentiated Services (DiffServ) approach to QoS differentiation, PHB is the forwarding treatment by a network router or switch applied to a group of network traffic flows for the hop to the next router or switch. Packets marked with a common service classification in the packet header are aggregated into flow bundles that are treated in the same way (for example, the packets have the same priority or the same risk of being discarded in the event of network congestion).

PHP *Penultimate Hop Popping* PHP is the removal (popping) of the top label on a packet's label stack at the penultimate node in an LSP, rather than at the egress node. PHP allows the egress node to perform one lookup before forwarding a packet, rather than the two lookups it must perform without PHP.

PIP *Provider Instance Port*   In PBB-VPLS, the I-component port connecting to the B-component is called PIP.

PIR *Peak Information Rate*   The PIR is the peak data transfer rate for a path, such as a Frame-Relay, VPC, VCC, or DE service path. The PIR is the PCR converted to kilobits per second.

PLR *Point of Local Repair*   A functional NE in a path in which a manual bypass is implemented for a defective NE in the path.

POS *Packet over SONET*   POS is a standard method of transporting native network layer packets directly on SONET interfaces using HDLC-like framing and simple link protocols like PPP. POS essentially bypasses data link layer processing by transporting network layer packets, with little modification, directly on the physical layer.

PPP *Point-to-Point Protocol*   A protocol that allows a computer to use TCP/IP with a standard telephone line and a high-speed modem to establish a link between two terminal installations.

PPPoE *Point-to-Point Protocol over Ethernet*   PPPoE is a specification for connecting multiple computer users on an Ethernet LAN to a remote site through common CPE. PPPoE allows users to share a common xDSL, cable modem, or wireless connection to the Internet. PPPoE combines the PPP protocol, commonly used in dial-up connections, with the Ethernet protocol, which supports multiple users in a LAN. The PPP protocol information is encapsulated within an Ethernet frame.

PSN *Packet Switched Network*   Generic acronym for an IP/MPLS network where data packets are switched over the network. Compare to the "circuit switched network," where data flows are transported over the network.

PVST+ *Per VLAN Spanning Tree plus*   Cisco proprietary implementation of spanning-tree protocol, using 802.1q-tagged BPDUs to maintain one STP instance per VLAN. (There are two versions of PVST: PVST using Cisco proprietary ISL-encapsulated BPDU, PVST+ using 802.1q-tagged BPDU.)

PW *Pseudowire*   A pseudowire is an emulated point-to-point connection over a packet-switched network that enables two nodes to interconnect using a Layer 2 technology. Also called *VPWS* and *VLL*.

PWE3 *Pseudowire Edge-to-Edge Emulation*   Defines encapsulation and emulation of pseudowires to transport multiple services over a Packet

Switched Network (PSN). Emulates leased lines to customers.

QoS *Quality of Service* QoS is a term for the set of parameters and their values that determine the performance of a virtual circuit.

RADIUS *Remote Authentication Dial-In User Service* RADIUS is a standardized method of information exchange between a device that provides network access to users (RADIUS client) and a device that contains authentication and profile information for the users (RADIUS server).

RD *Route Distinguisher* An 8-byte BGP field that allows an operator to create a distinct route to a common IP address prefix.

RDI *Remote Defect Indication* RDI is a signal returned to the transmitting equipment upon detection of certain defects on the incoming signal.

RFC *Request For Comment* RFC is the name of the result and the process for creating a standard on the Internet. New standards are proposed and published online, as a Request For Comments. The IETF is the consensus-building body that facilitates discussion, and eventually a new standard is established.

RIP *Routing Information Protocol* An interior gateway protocol defined by the IETF (RIPv1–RFC 1058 and RIPv2–RFC 2453) that specifies how routers exchange routing table information. RIP is a routing protocol based on the distance vector algorithm. With RIP, routers periodically exchange entire tables.

RSTP *Rapid Spanning Tree Protocol* An enhanced version of the Spanning Tree Protocol (STP). STP is used to disable a redundant forwarding path in an Ethernet switching environment to preventing forwarding loops.

RSVP-TE *Resource Reservation Protocol Traffic Engineering* The TE extension of RSVP to signal MPLS LSPs. Supports signaling of explicitly routed LSP with loose or strict hop. RFC 4090.

RT *Route Target* In BGP/MPLS VPNs, an RT is an attribute that identifies a set of sites.

RTP *Real Time Protocol* RTP provides end-to-end network transport functions for applications that transmit real-time data, such as audio, video, or simulation data, over multicast or unicast network services.

SAP *Service Access Point* The Customer Edge (CE) facing point in the service provider, providing native service to the customer through an attachment circuit.

SDH *Synchronized Digital Hierarchy* SDH is an ITU-T standard for fiber optic transmission of high-speed digital traffic. It uses a synchronous high-speed signal and provides easy access to low-speed signals by mapping low-speed signals into virtual tributaries.

SDP *Service Distribution Path* The service tunnel (MPLS or GRE encapsulated) carrying services.

SLA *Service Level Agreement* An SLA is a service contract between a network service provider and a customer that guarantees a particular QoS level. SLAs specify criteria such as network availability and data delivery reliability.

SNMP *Simple Network Management Protocol* Protocol used by network management to retrieve information about connection status, configuration, and performance.

SONET *Synchronized Optical Network* SONET is an ANSI standard for fiber optic transmission of high-speed digital traffic. SONET allows internetworking of transmission products from multiple vendors and defines a physical interface, optical line rates known as OC signals, frame format, and an OAM protocol. The base rate is 51.84 Mbps (OC-1), and higher rates are multiples of the base rate.

SP *Service Provider* Telecommunication operator who provides multiple network services over its backbone network to the customers and subscribers.

SPF *Shortest Path First* SPF is an algorithm used by IS-IS and OSPF to make routing decisions based on the state of network links.

SRLG *Shared Risk Link Group* A group of links sharing the same failure risk. One typical example is several logical links using different wavelengths sharing the same fiber. If the fiber fails, all links on that fiber will be out of service simultaneously. By defining these links to the same SRLG and requesting an MPLS resilience scheme to avoiding setting up backup paths over the same SRLG, higher availability can be achieved.

STP *Spanning Tree Protocol* A technique based on an IEEE 802.1d standard that detects and eliminates forwarding loops in a bridged network. When multiple paths exist, STP selects the most efficient path for the bridge to use. If that path fails, STP automatically reconfigures the network to activate another path. This protocol is used mostly by local bridges.

TCN *Topology Change Notification* A bridge uses TCN BPDUs to notify the root bridge about a detected topology change.

TCP *Transmission Control Protocol* An Internet transport layer protocol, TCP is a Windows-based reliable transport protocol used for many stream-related operations. TCP is the transport layer protocol for the TCP/IP protocol suite. It is often referred to in conjunction with the network layer protocol IP as TCP/IP.

TDM *Time Division Multiplexing* TDM is a process of sharing a communication channel among several users by allowing each to use the channel for a given period of time in a defined, repeated sequence.

TE *Traffic Engineering* The process of selecting the paths from one given node to another to provide efficient and reliable network operations while considering bandwidth availability and traffic characteristics in an MPLS network.

TED *Traffic Engineering Database* A TED is a database used by CSPF for storing route constraint information.

T-LDP *Targeted LDP* A specific type of LDP protocol building remote LDP sessions between explicitly specified neighbors. T-LDP is used to exchange vc-labels for L2 VPN over an MPLS core.

TLV *Type–Length Value* Traffic engineering information is carried by signaling objects, for example, LDPs. The type, length, and values of this traffic engineering information are specified in the TLV.

ToS *Type of Service* An 8-bit field in an IPv4 packet header to provide service differentiation information for QoS purposes.

TTL *Time-To-Live* A field in an IP header (or MPLS header) that specifies the maximum number of hops for a data packet before the packet expires and is discarded.

UDP *User Datagram Protocol* UDP is an IETF transport layer protocol that uses port numbers and data checksums to identify multiple applications on a machine. UDP allows applications to send messages or files to other applications with minimum protocol mechanisms; for example, there is no flow control. Because UDP is transaction-oriented rather than connection-oriented, delivery or protection against duplicate packets is not guaranteed to the application. UDP uses IP as the underlying protocol. UDP resides in the transport layer and is defined in RFC 768.

UNI *User Network Interface* UNI is an interface point between ATM end-users and a private ATM switch, or between a private ATM switch and the public carrier ATM network; defined by physical and protocol specifications per ATM Forum UNI documents. UNI is also the standard adopted by the ATM Forum to define connections between users or end stations and a local ATM network switch.

uVPLS *user VPLS* The VPLS service provisioned for a user to pass customer data.

VC *Virtual Circuit* A VC is a portion of a virtual path or virtual channel used to establish a virtual connection between two end nodes.

VCCV *Virtual Circuit Connectivity Verification* Defines a set of procedures for fault detection and diagnostics.

VLL *Virtual Leased Line* A virtual leased line is a type of VPN where IP is transported in a point-to-point manner. CPE devices are connected through nodes, and the nodes are connected to an IP tunnel.

VPLS *Virtual Private LAN Service* A VPLS is a type of VPN in which a number of sites are connected in a single bridged domain over an IP/MPLS network. Although the services may be from different locations, in a VPLS, they appear to be on the same LAN. When implemented with Layer 2 interfaces, this service is called VPLS. When implemented with Layer 3 interfaces, this service is called an IP-VPN.

VPN *Virtual Private Network* A private network that is configured within a public network (a carrier network or the Internet) in order to take advantage of the economies of scale and management facilities of large networks. VPNs are used by enterprises to create WANs that span large geographic areas to provide site-to-site connections to branch offices and to allow mobile users to dial up their company LANs.

VPRN *Virtual Private Routed Network* A network exhibiting at least some of the characteristics of a private network, even though it uses the resources of a public switched network.

VPWS *Virtual Private Wire Service* A point-to-point link connecting two CE routers. VPWS, also known as pseudowire, is a VPN service that provides a Layer 2 point-to-point service (link emulation) that connects two CE routers. The CE router in the customer network is connected to a Provider Edge in the provider network by a physical attachment or a logical circuit.

VRF *Virtual Routing Forwarder* Logically partitioned information that contains routing and forwarding information for one or more VPRNs. The information is available only to specific Layer 3 interfaces on the provider edge router that provide network connectivity for customer sites which are members of the VPRN(s).

VRRP *Virtual Router Redundancy Protocol* VRRP is a protocol to provide redundancy in statically defined routed networks, rather than in dynamically defined networks, such as RIP and OSPF. VRRP is an election protocol that dynamically assigns responsibility for one or more virtual router(s) to the VRRP router(s), allowing several routers on a multi-access link to use the same virtual IP address. A VRRP router is configured to run the VRRP protocol in conjunction with one or more other routers.

VSI *Virtual Switching Instance* Logically partitioned information that contains bridging and forwarding information for one or more VPLSs. The information is available only to specific Layer 2 interfaces on the Provider Edge router that provide network connectivity for customer sites which are members of the VPLS(s).

WAN *Wide Area Network* A WAN is a network of digital transmission equipment that provides data communications over large geographical areas.

Index

A

B

backbone component (B-component), 708, 716
Backbone Core (BC), 734
backbone destination address (B-DA)
    B-MAC, 732
    BUM, 735
    B-VPLS, 736
    unknown, 758
backbone destination MAC (B-DMAC), 730–731
    BEB, 713
    FDB, 757
backbone domain (B-domain), 708
    Epipe, 769–770
    flooding, 769–770
    I-domain, 719
    MMRP, 747
    PBB-VPLS, 723
    PE, 716
    VLAN, 711
Backbone Edge Bridges (BEB)
    B-DMAC, 713
    C-MAC, 715
    Q-in-Q, 711
backbone header, 711
backbone MAC (B-MAC), 708
    B-DA, 732
    B-PE, 717
    B-SAP, 718
    B-VPLS, 718, 729, 730
    I-VPLS, 732
    PBB, 737
    PBBN, 711
    PBB-VPLS, 723
    PE, 718
Backbone Provider Edge (B-PE), B-MAC, 717
backbone resiliency, H-VPLS, 640–641
backbone source address (B-SA)
    B-VPLS, 736
    I-VPLS, 735
Backbone VPLS (B-VPLS), 708, 716, 728–730
    ALSRP, 719
    B-DA, 736
    B-MAC, 718, 729, 730
    bridge ports, 728
    B-SA, 736
    B-SAP, 755, 761
    B-SDP, 755
    BUM, 743, 744
    discard unknown, 757–758
    encapsulation, 729
    FDB, 721, 755–758
    flooding, 753–755
    flush-all-from-me, 764
    IB-PE, 723
    internal link, 728
    I-VPLS, 719
    MAC-flush, 763–766
    mesh-pseudowire, 728
    PE, 729–730
    PW, 721, 736, 755
    SAP, 721, 728, 739
    SDP, 739
    service instance, 718, 728
    spoke-pseudowire, 728
    TCN, 754
    unknown, 757–758
    VB, 728
    VSI, 717, 736
backup pseudowire, 602. *See also* Inter-Chassis Backup pseudowire
    dual-homing, 644–646
Bandwidth, 83, 189
bandwidth (BW), 5
    active forwarding path, 457
    booking, 96, 454
    congestion, 840
    CSPF, 119
    FF, 187
    Gigabit Ethernet, 14
    hashing algorithms, 558
    IGP-TE, 158
    LAG, 557–559, 579
    MBB, 187
    PW, 453
    QoS, 384
    RSVP-TE LSP, 158, 172 173
    SDP, 453, 457
    spoke nodes, 517
    TE, 106
    10G Ethernet, 14
    unreservable, 120
    VLL CAC, 453–457
BC. *See* Backbone Core

C

Q

R

Service Routing Must Reads from Alcatel-Lucent

Alcatel-Lucent Scalable IP Networks Self-Study Guide:
Preparing for the Network Routing Specialist I (NRS I) Certification Exam (4A0-100)
ISBN 978-0-470-42906-8

A publication from the Service Routing Certification Program.

This book is your official self-study guide for the Alcatel-Lucent NRS I Certification. The certification is designed to affirm a solid foundation of knowledge in IP Service Routing, spanning the fundamentals of Layer 2 network technologies, IP addressing and routing, TCP/IP, and Carrier Ethernet services. Once completed, you will have the introductory knowledge required in an IP/MPLS and Carrier Ethernet environment that delivers consumer and business services.

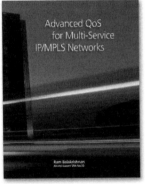

Advanced QoS for Multi-Service IP/MPLS Networks
ISBN 978-0-470-29369-0

This essential guide helps you understand the features and benefits of service-aware hierarchical Quality of Service (QoS) and how to leverage QoS in designing and implementing leading-edge IP networks.
The author's vast experience provides a solid theoretical and practical overview of how QoS can be implemented to reach the business objectives defined for an IP/MPLS network.

Designing and Implementing IP/MPLS-Based Ethernet Layer 2 VPN Services: An Advanced Guide for VPLS and VLL
ISBN 978-0-470-45656-9

This guide is a must read for any network engineer interested in IP/MPLS technologies and Carrier Ethernet Layer 2 VPN services.

Visit www.alcatel-lucent.com/srpublications to learn more about these Alcatel-Lucent books

Printed and bound by CPI Group (UK) Ltd, Croydon, CR0 4YY

28/10/2024

14581327-0001